POSTCARDS

FLORIDA

D0109994

The picturesque and aptly-named Canopy Road, located north of Tallahassee. See chapter 13.
© Robert Holmes Photography.

One of the playful residents of Sea World in Orlando. See chapter 12. © James Lemass / Sea World Florida.

Playing out of a sand trap in Tarpon Springs. See chapter 11. © M. Timothy O'Keefe Photography.

Braving the rapids at Universal's new Islands of Adventure theme park. See chapter 12. © Universal Studios Escape.

Two different views of Florida Keys "wildlife"—an ibis wading in local waters, and Sloppy Joe's Bar, a classic Key West watering hole. See chapter 6. Top photo © Stephen Frink Photography, bottom photo © Kelly / Mooney Photography.

*Every year, eager baseball fans from across the country flock to Florida for Spring Training.
See chapter 2. © M. Timothy O'Keefe Photography.*

Most everything in Miami's South Beach has an art deco feel, such as this trendy café (this page). Opposite, the stately Biltmore Hotel in Coral Gables. See chapter 4. © Opposite photo © Hollenbeck Photography, this photo © Michael Ventura Photography.

The daily motorcade along Daytona Beach. See chapter 14. © Kunio Owaki Photography.

Sea kayaking in the Lower Keys. See chapter 6. © Michael Ventura Photography.

"Houston, we have a problem . . ." —a U.S. Apollo Astronaut suit on display at the Kennedy Space Center. See chapter 14. © M. Timothy O'Keefe Photography.

The Children's Program at the South Seas Plantation Resort on Captiva Island. See chapter 10.
© M. Timothy O'Keefe Photography.

The Florida Keys offer the best scuba diving and snorkeling in Florida. See chapter 6.
© *Stephen Frink Photography.*

With every cigar he rolls, this South Beach gentleman creates a truly original work of art.
See chapter 4. © Michael Ventura Photography.

Warm weather and an abundance of marine life make Florida a year-round destination for anglers from throughout the world. © Mark Barrett / Silver Image Photography.

Visits to orange groves allow visitors the chance to send some Florida sunshine back home. © Robert Holmes Photography.

Parks and nature preserves in the Tampa Bay area are the best places to catch a glimpse of the Florida manatee. See chapter 11. © Stuart Westmorland / Tony Stone Images.

A birds-eye view of the winding channels in Everglades National Park. See chapter 7.
© David Job / Tony Stone Images.

Miles and miles of spectacular sands make Florida a beach bum's paradise. © Len Kaufman Photography.

Frommer's® 2000

Florida

**by Bill Goodwin,
Victoria Pesce Elliott
& Mary Meehan**

with Online Directory by Michael Shapiro

MACMILLAN • USA

ABOUT THE AUTHORS

Bill Goodwin began his career as an award-winning newspaper reporter before becoming legal counsel and speechwriter for two U.S. senators. He is also the author of *Frommer's South Pacific* and *Frommer's Virginia*.

Victoria Pesce Elliott is a freelance journalist who contributes to many local and national newspapers and magazines, including the *New York Times*. A native of Miami, she returned there after nearly a decade in New York City, where she graduated from the Columbia University School of Journalism.

From opening day at Universal Studios to the first plunge down the Tower of Terror, **Mary Meehan** has been on hand as travel options have exploded in Central Florida. As an Orlando-based writer, whose award-winning work appears in regional and national publications, Meehan has an insider's view of the best things to see and do in Central Florida—and the things to avoid.

MACMILLAN TRAVEL

Macmillan General Reference USA, Inc.
1633 Broadway
New York, NY 10019

Find us online at **www.frommers.com**

Copyright © 1999 by Macmillan General Reference USA, Inc.
Maps copyright © by Macmillan General Reference USA, Inc.

All rights reserved. No part of this book may be reproduced or transmitted in any form or by any means, electronic or mechanical, including photocopying, recording, or by any information storage and retrieval system, without permission in writing from the Publisher.

MACMILLAN is a registered trademark of Macmillan, Inc.
FROMMER'S is a registered trademark of Arthur Frommer. Used under license.

ISBN 0-02-863470-5
ISSN 1044-2391

Production Editor: Carol Sheehan
Photo Editor: Richard Fox
Design by Michele Laseau
Digital Cartography by John Decamillis and Roberta Stockwell

SPECIAL SALES

Bulk purchases (10+ copies) of Frommer's and selected Macmillan travel guides are available to corporations, organizations, mail-order catalogs, institutions, and charities at special discounts, and can be customized to suit individual needs. For more information write to Special Sales, Macmillan General Reference, 1633 Broadway, New York, NY 10019.

Manufactured in the United States of America

5 4 3 2 1

Contents

List of Maps

An Invitation to the Reader

In researching this book, we discovered many wonderful places—hotels, restaurants, shops, and more. We're sure you'll find others. Please tell us about them, so we can share the information with your fellow travelers in upcoming editions. If you were disappointed with a recommendation, we'd love to know that, too. Please write to:

Frommer's Florida 2000
Macmillan Travel
1633 Broadway
New York, NY 10019

An Additional Note

Please be advised that travel information is subject to change at any time—and this is especially true of prices. We therefore suggest that you write or call ahead for confirmation when making your travel plans. The authors, editors, and publisher cannot be held responsible for the experiences of readers while traveling. Your safety is important to us, however, so we encourage you to stay alert and be aware of your surroundings. Keep a close eye on cameras, purses, and wallets, all favorite targets of thieves and pickpockets.

What the Symbols Mean

✪ Frommer's Favorites

Our favorite places and experiences—outstanding for quality, value, or both.

The following abbreviations are used for credit cards:

AE	American Express	EURO	Eurocard
CB	Carte Blanche	JCB	Japan Credit Bank
DC	Diners Club	MC	MasterCard
DISC	Discover	OPT	Optima
ER	EnRoute	V	Visa

Find Frommer's Online

Arthur Frommer's Outspoken Encyclopedia of Travel (**www.frommers.com**) offers more than 6,000 pages of up-to-the-minute travel information—including the latest bargains and candid, personal articles updated daily by Arthur Frommer himself. No other Web site offers such comprehensive and timely coverage of the world of travel.

The Best of Florida

Every year, millions of visitors escape bleak northern winters to bask in Florida's warmth, lured to the Sunshine State by the promise of clear skies and 800 miles of spectacular sandy beaches. A host of kid-pleasers, from Busch Gardens to Walt Disney World, make this the country's most popular year-round family vacation destination.

Here you can choose from a wide array of accommodations, from deluxe resorts to mom-and-pop motels. You can visit remote little towns like Apalachicola or a megalopolis like Miami. Devour fresh seafood, from amberjack to oysters—and work off those calories in such outdoor pursuits as bicycling, golf, or kayaking. Despite overde-velopment in many parts of the state, Floridians have maintained thousands of acres of wilderness areas, from the little respite of Clam Pass County Park in downtown Naples to the magnificent Everglades National Park, which stretches across the state's southern tip.

Choosing the "best" of all this is a daunting task, and the selections in this chapter are only a rundown on some of the highlights. You'll find numerous other outstanding resorts, hotels, destinations, activi-ties, and attractions—all described in the pages of this book. With a bit of serendipity, you'll come up with some bests of your own.

1 The Best Beaches

- **Bill Baggs Cape Florida State Recreation Area** (Key Biscayne): At the very tip of Key Biscayne, this secluded bend of beach juts out into the Atlantic Ocean, surrounded by sand dunes, sea oats, towering palms, and palmettos. Its centerpiece is a recently restored lighthouse and small museum. Next door is an outfit that rents boating equipment and lounge chairs. And in the newly built Lighthouse Cafe (El Farito), you get good, cheap Cuban specialties. See chapter 5.
- **Crandon Park Beach** (Key Biscayne): A well-equipped, active beach, Crandon Park has 3 miles of oceanfront and nearly 500 acres of grassy grounds that sport barbecue grills, soccer and softball fields, and a public 18-hole championship golf course. Families and young soccer players scatter throughout the area on weekends, while more relaxed visitors walk along nature trails and take in the view of Miami Beach across Biscayne Bay. See chapter 5.

Florida

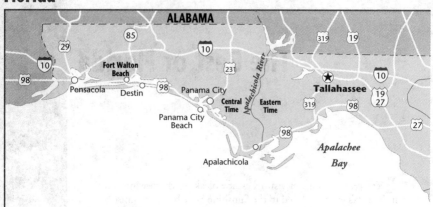

ALABAMA

85

29

10

10

231

319 19

Fort Walton
Beach

Pensacola

98

Destin

98

Panama City

Central
Time

Eastern
Time

Panama City
Beach

319

98

Tallahassee

10

19
27

98

Apalachicola

Apalachee
Bay

27

Gulf of Mexico

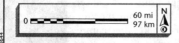

0   60 mi
         97 km

N

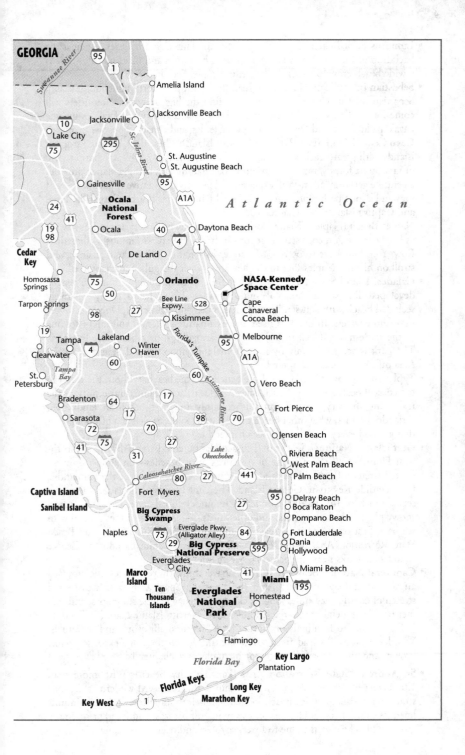

GEORGIA

95
1

St. Johns River

Suwannee River

Amelia Island

Jacksonville Beach

10 Jacksonville
Lake City
75
295

St. Augustine
St. Augustine Beach

95

Gainesville

A1A

Atlantic Ocean

Ocala
National
Forest

24
41

19
98

Ocala

40 Daytona Beach

4
1

Cedar
Key

De Land

Homosassa
Springs

75

50

Orlando

NASA-Kennedy
Space Center

Tarpon Springs

98

27

Bee Line
Expwy. 528

Kissimmee

Cape
Canaveral
Cocoa Beach

19

Tampa
Clearwater

Lakeland
4

60

Winter
Haven

95 Melbourne

A1A

St.
Petersburg

Tampa
Bay

60

Vero Beach

Bradenton

64

17

Florida's Turnpike

Kissimmee River

Sarasota

17

70

98

70

Fort Pierce

72

75

27

Jensen Beach

41

31

Lake
Okeechobee

Riviera Beach
West Palm Beach
Palm Beach

Caloosahatchee River

80

27

441

Captiva Island

95 Delray Beach
Boca Raton
Pompano Beach

Sanibel Island

Fort Myers

27

Big Cypress
Swamp

Everglade Pkwy.
(Alligator Alley)

84

Fort Lauderdale
Dania
Hollywood

Naples

75
29

Big Cypress
National Preserve

595

Everglades
City

41

Miami Beach

Marco
Island

Miami

Ten
Thousand
Islands

Everglades
National
Park

Homestead

195

1

Flamingo

Florida Bay

Key Largo

Plantation

Florida Keys

Long Key

Key West

1

Marathon Key

- **Lummus Park Beach** (South Beach, Miami): This *is* South Beach. Against the backdrop of Ocean Drive's fanciful art deco buildings and bustling cafe scene is a wide beach crowded with the beautiful people. See chapter 5.
- **Sebastian Inlet** (North Hutchinson Island): At the tip of North Hutchinson Island, Sebastian Inlet is the beach where surfers find the biggest swells. Nonsurfers will come for the flat, sandy beaches and miles of shaded walkways; facilities include kayak, paddleboat, and canoe rentals; picnic tables; and a snack shop. See chapter 9.
- **Cayo Costa Island State Park** (off Captiva Island): These days, deserted tropical islands with great beaches are scarce in Florida, but this 2,132-acre barrier strip of sand, pine forests, mangrove swamps, oak hammocks, and grasslands provides a genuine get-away-from-it-all experience. The only non-native residents are wild pigs and a lone park ranger; access is only by boat from nearby Gasparilla, Pine, and Captiva islands. See chapter 10.
- **Naples Beach** (Naples): Many Florida cities and towns have beaches, but few are as lovely as the gorgeous strip that runs in front of Naples's famous Millionaires' Row. You don't have to be rich to wander its length, peer at the mansions, and stroll on historic Naples Pier to catch a sunset over the gulf. See chapter 10.
- **Caladesi Island State Park** (Clearwater Beach): Even though it's in the heavily developed Tampa Bay area, 3½-mile Caladesi Island has a lovely, relatively secluded beach with soft sand edged in sea grass and palmettos. Dolphins cavort in offshore waters. In the park itself, there's a nature trail, and you might see one of the rattlesnakes, black racers, raccoons, armadillos, or rabbits that live here. The park is accessible only by ferry from Honeymoon Island State Recreation Area off Dunedin. See chapter 11.
- **Typhoon Lagoon** (Orlando): All the benefits of the beach, without the travel to the coast. Located within Walt Disney World, it lacks the natural beauty of the real thing, but Typhoon Lagoon is certainly the best beach in landlocked Orlando. Besides, what other beach offers a water slide, as well as a 50-foot geyser that goes off every 30 minutes? See chapter 12.
- **Gulf Islands National Seashore** (Pensacola): You could argue that all of Northwest Florida's gulf shore is one of America's great beaches—an almost uninterrupted stretch of pure white sand that runs the entire length of the Panhandle, from Perdido Key to St. George Island. The Gulf Islands National Seashore preserves much of this natural wonder in its undeveloped state. Countless terns, snowy plover, black skimmers, and other birds nest along the dunes topped with sea oats. East of the national seashore and equally beautiful are Grayton Beach State Recreation Area near Destin, and St. Joseph Peninsula and St. George Island state parks near Apalachicola. See chapter 13.
- **Canaveral National Seashore** (Cape Canaveral): Midway between the crowded attractions at Daytona Beach and the Kennedy Space Center is a protected stretch of coastline 24 miles long, backed by cabbage palms, sea grapes, and palmettos. Their neighbor is the 140,000-acre Merritt Island National Wildlife Refuge, home to hundreds of Florida birds, reptiles, alligators, and mammals. Wooden boardwalks lead from a free parking lot to the huge expanse of soft brown sand and a few well-spaced picnic tables. See chapter 14.
- **St. Andrews State Recreation Area** (Panama City Beach): With more than 1,000 acres of dazzling white sand and dunes, this preserved wilderness demonstrates what Panama City Beach looked like before motels and condominiums lined its shore. Lacy, golden sea oats sway in gulf breezes, and fragrant rosemary grows wild. The area is home to foxes, coyotes, and deer. See chapter 13.

2 The Best Snorkeling

- **John Pennekamp Coral Reef State Park** (Key Largo): This 188-square-mile park is the nation's first undersea preserve, established to protect the only living coral reef in the continental United States. The water throughout much of the park is shallow, so it's an especially great place for snorkelers to see tree-sized elkhorn coral, giant brain coral, colorful sea fans, hundreds of rainbow-colored fish, and a sunken statue, Christ of the Deep. See chapter 6.
- **Looe Key National Marine Sanctuary** (off Big Pine Key): Voted the number one dive spot in North America by *Skin Diver* magazine, Looe Key has some of the most beautiful underwater scenery in the country, including more than 150 varieties of hard and soft coral—some centuries old. Nearly all types of tropical fish, including the gold and blue parrot fish, moray eels, barracudas, French angels, and tarpon, call this dense and diverse reef home. See chapter 6.

3 The Best Fishing

- **The Keys:** The Keys boast some world-class deep-sea fishing; the prize is such big-game fish as marlin, sailfish, and tuna. There's reef fishing as well, for "eating fish" like snapper and grouper, and backcountry fishing for bonefish, tarpon, and other "stalking" fish.

  Dozens of charter-fishing boats operate from Key West marinas and less-popular Keys. Islamorada, in the Upper Keys, is the sportfishing capital of the world. Anglers, including former President Bush, compete for trophy sailfish, marlin, wahoo, and kingfish at many annual big-money tournaments. Seven-Mile Bridge, linking the Middle and Lower Keys, is known as "the longest fishing bridge in the world"; it's a favorite spot for local fishers who wait for barracuda, yellowtail, and dolphin to bite. See chapter 6.
- **Lake Okeechobee:** The second-largest freshwater lake in the country, Okeechobee covers nearly half a million acres and claims to be the "Speckled Perch Capital of the World." It's also famous for its largemouth bass and bream. Fishing tournaments go on year-round. See chapter 9.
- **Stuart:** Known as the "Sailfish Capital of the World," Stuart is an angler's haven. The fish bite all year, but peak months are December through March and June and July. Sailfishing is an art of its own—beginners need to learn to feel that exact moment to let the reel drag so the fish run with the lure. See chapter 9.
- **Boca Grande:** The deep, shadowy holes of Boca Grande Pass, between Gasparilla and Cayo Costa islands off Fort Myers, harbor the mighty tarpon, the "silver king of the seas." Teddy Roosevelt and his rich buddies used to bag tarpon in these waters, and anglers from around the globe still compete every July in the World's Richest Tarpon Tournament. See chapter 10.
- **Disney's Grand Floridian Beach Resort:** This grand resort offers fishing excursions which prove that the Disney magic extends to catching bass. Many of the Disney parks and resorts are sprinkled with lakes and connected by canals. Reel in the big ones on these artificial waterways. See chapter 12.
- **Destin:** Florida's largest charter-boat fleet, with more than 140 vessels, is based in this Panhandle town, the "World's Luckiest Fishing Village." They've landed championship catches of grouper, amberjack, snapper, mackerel, cobia, sailfish, wahoo, tuna, and blue marlin. See chapter 13.

4 The Best Golf Courses

- **Biltmore Hotel** (Miami): This rolling 18-hole course on the grounds of Miami's most historic and elegant resort was designed by Donald Ross and renovated in 1992. Despite the fancy Coral Gables backdrop, this course is open to the public and is popular with the likes of President Clinton and other world figures. See chapter 4.
- **Doral Golf Resort and Spa:** There are four championship courses here, including the famous Blue Monster, which is the site of the annual Doral-Ryder Open. The Gold Course, recently restored by golf great Raymond Floyd, has water on every hole. See chapter 4.
- **Turnberry Isle Resort and Club** (Aventura, North Miami): Unfortunately, these two Robert Trent Jones championship courses are open only to resort guests. If you like a serious challenge and want to enjoy a host of other amenities, this is a worthwhile destination. See chapter 4.
- **Crandon Park Golf Course** (Key Biscayne): Formerly known as the Links of Key Biscayne, this stunning and famous course is a stop on the Senior Men's PGA Tour. Located on a posh residential island, it's one of the few courses remaining in South Florida not surrounded by development. Golfers enjoy pristine vistas of hammocks and stretches of water, with a glimpse of Miami's dramatic skyline to the north. See chapter 5.
- **Emerald Dunes Golf Course** (West Palm Beach): This beautiful Tom Fazio championship course features 60 acres of water, including a waterfall, and great views of the Atlantic. It's pricey, but it is one of the only great courses open to the public in this area of ritzy resorts. See chapter 8.
- **PGA National Resort & Spa** (Palm Beach Gardens): The headquarters of the Professional Golfers Association of America, PGA National is the granddaddy of Florida golf venues. The five tournament courses were designed by George and Tom Fazio, Arnold Palmer, and Karl Litten. The Fazio-designed Champion was redesigned by Jack Nicklaus in 1990; his 15th, 16th, and 17th holes are called The Bear Trap to honor their 1992 induction into the "Ten Toughest Holes on the Seniors Tour." See chapter 8.
- **Mangrove Bay Golf Course** (St. Petersburg): One of the nation's top 50 municipal courses, the Mangrove Bay course hugs the inlets of Old Tampa Bay and offers 18-hole, par-72 play. Facilities include a driving range; lessons and golf-club rental are also available. See chapter 11.
- **The Westin Innisbrook Resort** (Tarpon Springs): *Golfweek* has called Innisbrook's Copperhead Course, home of the annual JCPenney Classic, number one in Florida. One thousand students a year go through Innisbrook's Golf Institute, and golfers from around the world come to play the 600 acres of courses. Saturday-morning youth clinics are complimentary. See chapter 11.
- **Bay Hill** (Orlando): Among the famous local courses is the legendary Arnold Palmer's Bay Hill Club, site of the Bay Hill Invitational. Its 18th hole, nicknamed the Devil's Bathtub, is supposed to be the toughest par-4 on the PGA tour. Open to the public. See chapter 12.
- **Hyatt Regency Grand Cypress Resort** (Orlando): Dedicated duffers will find the cost of staying at this luxury hotel worth a shot at playing on this renowned course. The 45-hole, par-72 course was designed by the Golden Bear, Jack Nicklaus, and is for guests and their guests only. The Hyatt also features a 9-hole pitch-and-putt course. See chapter 12.

- **Walt Disney World Resorts** (Orlando): Stride the same greens as some of the country's top PGA tour players at this home of the Walt Disney World Oldsmobile Golf Classic. Three courses designed by Joe Lee host the PGA players in October. The rest of the year, even amateurs whose game is not up to par can get into the swing of things. Day rates are available for those not staying in Disney hotels. See chapter 12.
- **Marriott's Bay Point Resort** (Panama City Beach): Thirty-six holes of championship golf at this Marriott include the Lagoon Legends course, one of the country's most difficult. Nearby is The Hombre, an 18-holer where O. J. Simpson played a round right after his acquittal. See chapter 13.
- **Amelia Island Plantation** (Amelia Island): This exclusive resort has three of the state's best courses. Long Point Club, designed by Tom Fazio, is the most beautiful and challenging. Pete Dye's Amelia Links is another oceanfront course. Both are open only to resort guests. See chapter 14.
- **Ladies Professional Golf Association/LPGA** (Daytona Beach): This "women friendly" course has multiple tee settings, unrestricted tee times, a great pro shop, and state-of-the-art facilities. Designed by Rees-Jones, the older of the two courses here was chosen as one of the "Top Ten You Can Play" by *Golf Magazine* and number one of "America's Most Women-Friendly Courses" by *Golf for Women*. See chapter 14.
- **Sawgrass Marriott** (Ponte Vedra Beach, near Jacksonville): With 99 holes, there's something for the scratch golfer as well as the weekend duffer. *Money* magazine has called it the number one golf-resort value in America. Pete Dye's TPC Stadium Course makes top-10 lists everywhere. The 17th hole, on a tricky island, is one of the most photographed holes in the world. See chapter 14.

5 The Best Family Attractions

- **Miami Metrozoo** (Miami): This completely cageless zoo offers such star attractions as a monorail "safari" and a petting zoo. Kids love the elephant rides. See chapter 5.
- **Miami Seaquarium** (Key Biscayne, Miami): Trained dolphins, killer whales, and frolicking sea lions are on display in this Old Florida animal park that's been popular with locals and tourists for nearly 50 years. See chapter 5.
- **Edison and Ford Winter Estates** (Fort Myers): Inventor Thomas Alva Edison and his friend, automobile magnate Henry Ford, built side-by-side winter homes on the banks of the Caloosahatchee River in Fort Myers. Today these Victorian cottages serve as memorials to the two men, and especially to Edison. The museum will show the kids how we got the light bulb, the phonograph, and hundreds of other Edison inventions. See chapter 10.
- **Busch Gardens Tampa Bay** (Tampa): Although the thrill rides, live entertainment, shops, restaurants, and games get most of the ink at this 335-acre family theme park, Busch Gardens ranks among the top zoos in the country, with several thousand animals living in naturalistic environments. If you can get them off the roller coasters, the kids can find out what all those wild beasts they've seen on the Discovery Channel look like in person. See chapter 11.
- **Medieval Times** (Kissimmee): A longtime favorite for Orlando visitors, this Kissimmee-based show is billed as "dinner and tournament." Jousting contests, armored clashes, and 80 Andalusian stallions performing with military precision are just some of the performances on display. It's all put on for you and 1,000 of

the "special" guests of the castle, who eat off heavy metal plates while watching the tournament contestants tumble about before them. The food is so-so, but it's fabulous family fun. See chapter 12.

- **Museum of Science and Industry (MOSI)** (Tampa): One of the largest educational science centers in the Southeast, MOSI has more than 450 interactive exhibits in which the kids can experience hurricane-force winds, defy the laws of gravity, cruise the mysterious world of microbes, explore the human body, and much more. They can also watch stunning movies in MOSIMAX, Florida's first IMAX dome theater. See chapter 11.

- **Orlando Science Center** (Orlando): Lift a Volkswagen to understand how pulleys work, gaze at the stars, or explore the everyday uses of math in this hands-on interactive center. A $44 million expansion completed in 1997 made the Orlando Science Center the largest center of its kind in the Southeast. Fun for inquisitive kids of all ages. Families can easily spend most of a day touring the 10 exhibit halls. See chapter 12.

- **RainForest Cafe** (Orlando): With an (almost) equal mixture of entertainment and education, the RainForest Cafe, with its indoor menagerie and wild decor, is a place where monkey business is encouraged. Located at the Disney Village Marketplace just outside Walt Disney World in Orlando, it's a themed respite from the real jungle of the theme parks. See chapter 12.

- **Universal Studios Escape** (Orlando): The "other" Orlando theme park takes itself a bit less seriously than Mickey & Co. Rides dazzle with special effects inspired by familiar Hollywood blockbusters—*Jaws, E.T.,* and *King Kong,* to name just a few—and what budding Olivier wouldn't love to be discovered during an honest-to-goodness screen test? Kids can tour the Nickelodeon studios, where, if caught unawares, they could end up getting "slimed." See chapter 12.

- **Walt Disney World, Epcot, and MGM Studios** (Orlando): The granddaddies of 'em all. It's all here: the lifelike animation, the rides both thrilling and hokey, and, yes, that song you'll *never* get out of your head ("It's a Small World"). But look past the polished Disney image and you may be surprised—by the quiet grandeur of Epcot's Temple of Heaven, in the China pavilion, for example, or the sly humor lurking in the Magic Kingdom's Haunted Mansion. So expect a crowd; take the little ones to meet Mickey, Donald, and the gang; and make sure you ride scary Space Mountain at least once. See chapter 12.

- **Daytona USA** (Daytona Beach): Opened in late 1996 on Daytona International Speedway grounds, this huge state-of-the-art interactive attraction is an exciting and fast-paced stop even for nonrace fans. Kids can see real stock cars, Go-Karts, and motorcycles, and even participate in a pit stop on a NASCAR Winston Cup race car. See chapter 14.

- **Kennedy Space Center** (Cape Canaveral): Especially since the multimillion-dollar renovation and expansion, this family destination is a must-see. There is plenty to keep kids and parents busy for at least a full day, including interactive computer games, IMAX films, and dozens of informative displays on the space program. Try to schedule a trip during a real launch; there are more than a dozen each year. See chapter 14.

6 The Best Offbeat Travel Experiences

- **Sleeping Beneath the Seas at Jules' Undersea Lodge** (Key Largo): Ever spend the night underwater? Well, this has to be the most unusual accommodation in the state. This single-room hotel offers a comfortable suite 30 feet down and is especially popular with hard-core diving honeymooners. See chapter 6.

- **Swimming with the Dolphins at the Dolphin Research Center** (Marathon): Of the four such centers in the continental United States, the Dolphin Research Center is the most organized and informative. With advanced reservations, you can swim and play with dolphins in their natural lagoon homes. There is no better way to get a feel for Florida's smartest and most loved animal. See chapter 6.

- **Houseboating** (Everglades National Park): Cruising the shallow waterways of the Everglades on your own is an exciting way to explore the region by day and by night. Available through the **Flamingo Lodge** (☎ **800/600-3813** or 941/695-3101), these spacious motorized houseboats let you get lost for days (or just overnight). You'll fall asleep to the sounds of frogs, crickets, and the lapping waves. See chapter 7.

- **Babcock Wilderness Adventures** (Fort Myers): Experienced naturalists lead "swamp buggy" tours through the Babcock Ranch, including the mysterious Telegraph Swamp, where alligators lounge in the sun. Although the Babcock Ranch is the largest cattle operation east of the Mississippi (with bison and quarter horses, too), it is a major wildlife preserve inhabited by countless birds and other creatures. See chapter 10.

- **Swimming with the Manatees** (Homosassa Springs, north of Clearwater): Some 300 manatees spend the winter in the Crystal River, and you can swim, snorkel, or scuba with them in the warm-water natural spring of Kings Bay, about 7 miles north of Homosassa Springs. It's not uncommon to be surrounded in the 72° water by 30 to 40 "sea cows," who nudge and caress you as you swim with them. See chapter 11.

- **Disney Weddings** (Orlando): Divorce court notwithstanding, this is a once-in-a-lifetime trip. Thousands of people every year forgo Elvis and Vegas in favor of Mickey and Disney, tying the knot on Disney's not-quite-hallowed ground. A special Disney department handles all arrangements; special honeymoon vacation packages are offered. From rented coachmen to topiaries in the shape of Pluto, you're limited only by your imagination and budget. They'll serve up whatever Disney reference or character you desire, even if it is Goofy. See chapter 12.

- **Sea World—Swim with the Dolphins** (Orlando): If you long to frolic with Flipper, Sea World Orlando offers a chance to get up close and personal with a porpoise. Of course, it's not cheap—a couple of hundred dollars—and it's limited to a few folks each day. Visitors climb into the water and interact under the watchful eye of the Sea World trainers. See chapter 12.

- **Learning to Surf the Big Curls at Cocoa Beach Surfing School** (Cocoa Beach): Even if you don't know how to hang ten, this school will get you riding the waves with the best of them. They offer all equipment and lessons for beginners or pros at these world-famous surf beaches. See chapter 14.

7 The Best Small Towns

- **Boca Grande** (Southwest Florida): Founded in the 1880s by the du Pont family, this little village on Gasparilla Island retains the flavor of those Victorian times. Luxurious mansions coexist with simple homes of fishermen who guide the rich folks in search of tarpon just as their ancestors did a century ago. The du Ponts, Mellons, and Astors once arrived for wintertime's "social season" at the town's railway depot, which has been restored and now houses shops and the Loose Caboose Restaurant and Ice Cream Parlor. See chapter 10.

- **Olde Naples** (Naples): Despite being founded as a real-estate development in 1886, the original part of Naples retains much of Old Florida's charm, with tree-lined streets dividing many of the original clapboard homes. With the houses on Millionaires' Row virtually hidden by dense foliage, and no high rises in sight, Naples Beach seems far removed from today's modern city. See chapter 10.
- **Tarpon Springs** (Tampa Bay Area): Tarpon Springs calls itself the "Sponge Capital of the World" because immigrants from Greece settled here in the late 1800s to harvest the sponges that grew in abundance offshore. Their descendants make Tarpon Springs a fascinating center of transplanted Greek culture. Sponges still arrive at the historic Sponge Docks, where a lively, carnival-like atmosphere and Greek cuisine prevail. Restored Victorian homes facing Spring Bayou also make this one of the most picturesque towns in the state. See chapter 11.
- **Winter Park:** This lakeside town north of downtown Orlando is a lovely place to spend the afternoon. Ladies who lunch head for the shops and restaurants that line posh Park Avenue. The city park, with its fountains, carefully tended trees, and Amtrak station, evokes some of the city's old Southern charm. The Charles Hosmer Morse Museum of American Art has an impressive collection of large-scale works in Tiffany glass. See chapter 12.
- **Apalachicola** (Northwest Florida): Located at the mouth of the Apalachicola River, this gulf-shore town was a major cotton port before the Civil War, and a later timber boom resulted in the fine Victorian homes that still grace Apalachicola's uncurbed streets. It was here that Dr. John Gorrie invented the forerunner of the air conditioner, which revolutionized Florida's tourism industry. Today, the major industry is seafood, with famous Apalachicola oysters eaten fresh off the boats (see "Aphrodisiacs from Apalachicola," below). See chapter 13.
- **Pensacola** (Northwest Florida): One of America's oldest communities, Pensacola has preserved its Spanish, French, and English heritages in the Seville Historic District and Historic Pensacola Village. Spanish-named streets are bordered both by French-style wrought-iron balconies reminiscent of New Orleans and by English colonial churches like those in Williamsburg, Virginia. See chapter 13.
- **Fernandina Beach** (Amelia Island): You can stay at two of Florida's ritziest resorts on Amelia Island, but the real charm here is in the quaint town of Fernandina Beach, where a 50-block area of Victorian and Queen Anne homes is listed on the National Register of Historic Places. See chapter 14.

8 The Best Places to Avoid the Crowds

- **Pigeon Key** (Upper Keys): At the curve of the old Seven-Mile Bridge is a tiny island that was once the camp for the crew who built "Flagler's Folly" in the early part of this century. No cars are allowed, but bikers and walkers can see for miles with sights that include bridges, many old wooden cottages, and a truly tranquil stretch of lush foliage and water. See chapter 6.
- **Cayo Costa State Park** (off Captiva Island): You can't get any more deserted than this state park, which occupies a 2,132-acre, completely unspoiled barrier island. Go for the miles of white-sand beaches, pine forests, mangrove swamps, oak-palm hammocks, and grasslands. See chapter 10.
- **Lover's Key** (Fort Myers Beach): Just south of Fort Myers Beach, the Carl E. Johnson–Lover's Key State Recreation Area provides respite from the hustle and bustle of its busy neighbor. A highway runs the length of the island, but otherwise Lover's Key is totally undeveloped. Access through a mangrove forest to a

truly fine beach is by foot or by a tractor-pulled tram driven by park rangers, who take a dim view of anyone leaving trash behind. See chapter 10.
- **Canaveral National Seashore:** See "The Best Beaches," section 1.

9 The Best Swimming Pools

- **Albion Hotel** (South Beach, Miami): An architectural masterpiece originally designed in 1939, the huge pool and artificial "beach" are fun and whimsical examples of art deco details. You can see guests swimming in the bright blue water through the portholes that line the garden walkway. See chapter 4.
- **Biltmore Hotel** (Coral Gables, Miami): This 21,000-square-foot swimming pool lays claim to the title of largest hotel pool in the country. Surrounded by dramatic, stone archways and classical sculptures, it is beautiful, too. See chapter 4.
- **The Delano** (South Beach, Miami): The large outdoor pool behind the famous Delano is designed to spill over with water like a fountain. Most of the pool is shallow, making it more appealing for waders than for swimmers. And diners can even enjoy the cool waters at the wrought-iron tables and chairs placed in the very shallowest edge. See chapter 4.
- **Venetian Pool** (Coral Gables, Miami): Built in 1924, Miami's most unusual swimming pool holds 800,000 gallons of water and is shaded by towering Spanish porticos and old stucco walls. The huge pool with dramatic fountains and waterfalls is open to the public and is a great place to spend an afternoon. See chapter 5.
- **Disney's Vero Beach Resort** (Vero Beach): This lagoon-like pool has a two-story-high winding slide that elicits squeals of delight from kids and adults alike. For younger kids, a pirate ship that squirts water is also a fun way to cool off. See chapter 9.
- **Casa Ybel Resort** (Sanibel Island): This modern condo resort is built around Thistle Lodge, a turn-of-the-century inn whose clapboard sides and steeple-like roof are dramatically mirrored in a large beachside swimming pool. See chapter 10.
- **Disney's Beach Club Resort** (Orlando): From the palm-fringed entranceway and manicured gardens to the plush, sun-dappled lobby, this Disney resort property resembles the luxury of Victorian Cape Cod. The biggest draw is Stormalong Bay, a vast free-form swimming pool/water park sprawling over 3 acres. See chapter 12.
- **Disney's Wilderness Lodge** (Orlando): In true Disney form, the "imagineers" pulled out all the stops to create this faux mountain retreat. The pool meanders through several layers and is surrounded by boulders and edged in river rock. The best part? Float amid the pool's calm, crystal waters while watching Disney's version of Old Faithful gush about 100 yards away. See chapter 12.
- **Hyatt Regency Grand Cypress Resort** (Orlando): A rope bridge spans this half-acre swimming pool, which flows through rock grottoes and includes 12 waterfalls, two steep water slides, three whirlpools, and a white-sand beach. See chapter 12.
- **Ramada Plaza Beach Resort** (Fort Walton Beach): This Panhandle resort boasts one of the most beautiful swimming-pool/patio areas anywhere. Waterfalls cascading over lofty rocks and thick tropical foliage surround a romantic grotto bar. There's even a shack that serves Southern-style barbecue. Unfortunately, it's cut off from the beach by a six-story block of hotel rooms. See chapter 13.

10 The Best Spas

- **Doral Golf Resort and Spa** (Miami; ☎ **800/22-DORAL,** 800/71-DORAL, or 305/592-2000): Voted among the top spas by Zagat and *Condé Nast Traveler,* this 650-acre resort has something for every family member. The ambience is pure luxury—marble, crystal, formal gardens, and soft-spoken white-clad therapists. The healing muds and minerals come from ancient volcanic pools. Besides the great golf, tennis, swimming, and spa services, you'll find gourmet food and newly refurbished guest rooms. Day programs are available for those wanting just a taste of the luxury. See chapter 4.
- **The Spa at Turnberry Isle Resort and Club** (Aventura, North Miami; ☎ **800/ 327-7028** or 305/932-6200): Turkish steam rooms, authentic Finnish sauna, shiatsu pressure treatments, private exercise classes, oxygenation treatments, slimming baths containing botanical extracts, and a full complement of herbal, thalassotherapy, and holistic health counseling—this spa is serious, and equally recognized for its golf, tennis, and yachting facilities. Turnberry offers a nice selection of day and half-day packages. See chapter 4.
- **PGA National Resort & Spa** (Palm Beach Gardens; ☎ **800/633-9150** or 561/627-2000): Known primarily as a golf destination, this sprawling resort also has a top-rated Mediterranean-style spa with unique offerings for pregnant guests—specialized exercise and nutrition classes, custom-designed massage tables, and more. In addition, the resort has nine pools and a private lake where you can ski or sail, as well as six restaurants and lounges (including one with a surprisingly delicious spa menu). See chapter 8.
- **Wyndham Resort and Spa** (Fort Lauderdale; ☎ **800/996-3426** or 954/ 389-3300): A $10 million renovation in 1997 has turned the former Bonaventure Resort & Spa into one of the area's premier resorts. With all the sports facilities, like tennis, golf, and lots of pools, this spa joins the ranks of Florida's other highly recommended destinations. See chapter 8.
- **Sanibel Harbour Resort & Spa** (Fort Myers; ☎ **800/767-7777** or 941/ 466-2166): Many call this high-rise resort overlooking Sanibel Island the best spa value in the country. The spa obliges your every whim. Try the amazing Betar Bed, a suspended "bed of music" that floats you to a level where stresses disappear. There are also mud, algae, seaweed, and mineral wraps; Swiss showers; paraffin facials; and more. Day packages, makeovers, and men's sports packages are popular. The fitness center is state of the art. See chapter 10.
- **Safety Harbor Resort and Spa** (Tampa Bay Area; ☎ **800/237-0155** or 813/ 726-1161): Tucked away off the beaten track amid moss-draped oaks and cobblestone streets, Safety Harbor is the oldest continually running spa in the United States, and Florida's only spa built around natural healing springs. The feeling is very European. They've recently added some spiffy, youthful programs, including the Fitness Attitude Adjustment Weekend. The Phil Green tennis school is also on the grounds, and many tennis programs are available. See chapter 11.

11 The Best Luxury Resorts

- **Biltmore Hotel** (Coral Gables, Miami; ☎ **800/727-1926** or 305/445-1926): For more than 70 years, this glorious landmark has been a centerpiece of the city. Restored to its original Mediterranean splendor, it's now one of the Miami area's most romantic and luxurious resorts. A super golf course, a huge lagoon-pool, and first-class service make it a place worth going back to. See chapter 4.

- **Grand Bay Hotel** (Coconut Grove, Miami; ☎ **800/327-2788** or 305/ 858-9600): This sleek, modern tower overlooking Biscayne Bay is especially popular with European and South American guests who appreciate the ultra-elegant details like towering vases of exotic flowers, halls of gleaming marble, and extra-courteous service that make this one of Miami's most desirable properties. See chapter 4.

- **Sonesta Beach Resort Key Biscayne** (Key Biscayne, Miami; ☎ **800/ SONESTA** or 305/361-2021): This large, luxurious beachfront resort is at the tip of an exclusive residential island and offers every imaginable amenity, from tennis to jet skiing. A great place to bring the kids—fully supervised programs keep the children as busy and happy as their parents. See chapter 4.

- **Boca Raton Resort and Club** (Boca Raton; ☎ **800/327-0101** or 561/ 395-3000): An architectural masterpiece that has kept pace with the times, this ultra-elegant resort has beaches, golf courses, tennis, and every imaginable amenity. The grounds reek of old money, but the atmosphere is casual and laid-back. See chapter 8.

- **The Breakers** (Palm Beach; ☎ **800/833-3141** or 561/655-6611): The biggest and grandest of all of Florida's resorts, this five-star historic beauty epitomizes tony Palm Beach. From the expansive manicured lawns to the elegant marble lobby, The Breakers is the place to be. Rooms may not be as huge as at some of the newer resorts, but constant retrofitting has made it as popular today as when it was first constructed, in 1926. It also boasts Florida's oldest 18-hole golf course. See chapter 8.

- **Four Seasons Resort Palm Beach** (Palm Beach; ☎ **800/332-3442** or 561/ 582-2800): With the most convenient location and modern amenities, this Four Seasons is a welcome addition to the already-superior choices on the island. First-class dining and a super-hospitable staff make it a top pick. See chapter 8.

- **Ritz-Carlton Palm Beach** (Manalpan, near Palm Beach; ☎ **800/241-3333** or 561/533-6000): As is to be expected from any member of this upscale chain, the Palm Beach Ritz-Carlton is super-luxurious. Located farther than its other five-star neighbors from Palm Beach's shopping and dining area, this resort has elegant rooms overlooking a spectacular private beach, and an incredible ambience and attention to detail. See chapter 8.

- **Naples Beach Hotel & Golf Club** (Naples; ☎ **800/237-7600** or 941/ 261-2222): A beachside setting on Millionaires' Row couldn't be better for carrying on the hallowed-but-relaxed Old Florida traditions at this family-operated hotel. The least-expensive units here, in fact, are in the Old Florida wing, a two-story relic from 1948 but recently spiffed up during a $10 million overhaul. The beachside chickee hut bar is one of Florida's best sunset venues, and the dining room serves an exceptional, reasonably priced breakfast buffet. See chapter 10.

- **Ritz-Carlton Naples** (Naples; ☎ **800/241-3333** or 941/598-3300): This opulent 14-story Mediterranean-style hotel at Vanderbilt Beach is a favorite of affluent guests who like standard Ritz-Carlton amenities such as imported marble floors, antique art, Oriental rugs, Waterford crystal chandeliers, and afternoon British-style high tea. Guests relax in high-backed rockers on the verandas or unwind by the heated swimming pool set in a landscaped terrace, but they must walk through a narrow mangrove forest to reach the beach. See chapter 10.

- **South Seas Plantation Resort & Yacht Harbour** (Captiva Island; ☎ **800/ 237-3102** or 941/472-5111): Built on what was a 330-acre copra plantation, this exclusive spot is one of the best choices in southern Florida for serious tennis buffs (22 courts with pro). Its gulfside golf course is one of the most picturesque nine-holers anywhere. There are no high-rise buildings, just an assortment of luxury homes and condos, some with private pools and their own tennis courts. With three bedrooms or more, some units are ideal for families or couples who want to share the cost of a vacation. See chapter 10.

- **Don CeSar Beach Resort and Spa** (St. Pete Beach; ☎ 800/637-7200, 800/282-1116, or 813/360-1881): Dating back to 1928 and listed on the National Register of Historic Places, this "Pink Palace" tropical getaway is so romantic you may bump into six or seven honeymooning couples in one weekend. The lobby has classic high windows and archways, crystal chandeliers, marble floors, and original artwork. Most rooms have high ceilings and offer views of the gulf or Boca Ciega Bay. See chapter 11.

- **Disney's Grand Floridian Beach Resort** (Lake Buena Vista; ☎ 407/ W-DISNEY or 407/824-3000): The Grand Floridian is magnificent, from the moment you step into its opulent five-story lobby (complete with a Chinese Chippendale aviary) under triple-domed stained-glass skylights. A pianist entertains during afternoon tea, and an orchestra plays big-band music every evening. See chapter 12.

- **Hyatt Regency Grand Cypress Resort** (Orlando; ☎ 407/239-1234): This hotel stands out among all of the many Orlando offerings. Let the numbers speak for themselves: one half-acre pool with 12 waterfalls and 3 whirlpools; 12 tennis courts; a 45-hole, 72-par Jack Nicklaus-designed golf course; and a 45-acre Audubon nature walk. It all adds up to luxury. See chapter 12.

- **Amelia Island Plantation** (Amelia Island; ☎ 800/874-6878 or 904/ 261-6161): Set amidst magnolias, oak trees, and the Atlantic Ocean, this gracious resort is straight out of the Deep South. It's more rustic than the nearby Ritz, but it has excellent hiking and biking paths, tennis, swimming, horseback riding, and boating. Golfers especially enjoy exclusive use of two of the top courses in Florida. See "The Best Golf Courses," section 4. See chapter 14.

- **Ritz-Carlton Amelia Island** (☎ 800/241-3333 or 904/277-1100): Set on 13 acres of stunning beachfront, the Ritz-Carlton is more glitzy and modern than its older neighbor, the Amelia Island Plantation. You'll find all the first-class amenities, as well as remarkable service. The Grill, the hotel's finest restaurant, is one of the island's best. See chapter 14.

12 The Best Romantic Hideaways

- **Little Palm Island** (Little Torch Key; ☎ 800/343-8567 or 305/872-2524): This former fishing camp on its own private 5-acre island is accessible only by boat and offers the ultimate escape only miles from the real world. There are no phones, faxes, or TVs in the romantic thatched-roof cottages, only lots of romantic touches and tons of luxury. See chapter 6.

- **Marquesa Hotel** (Key West; ☎ 800/869-4631 or 305/292-1919): With all the charm of a B&B but with the amenities of a large resort, the Marquesa is a well-kept secret—perfect for those who want plush, private accommodations with a fun town just out the door. See chapter 6.

- **Cabbage Key** (off Captiva Island; ☎ 941/283-2278): Sitting out in Pine Island Sound east of Fort Myers, this speck of land appears much as it did when the son of novelist Mary Roberts Rhinehart built a house on it in 1938. Today, the home serves as a casual restaurant popular with the likes of singer Jimmy Buffet. When the famous sail away at sunset, you'll have this funky Old Florida relic all to yourselves. See chapter 10.

- **Harrington House** (Holmes Beach, Bradenton; ☎ **941/778-5444**): Flowers, a private beach, and Old Florida ambience await at this B&B, built in 1925 on Anna Maria Island. Some of the eight bedrooms have four-poster or brass beds and French doors leading to balconies overlooking the gulf. Some rooms are in the adjacent Beach House, a remodeled 1920s captain's home. See chapter 11.
- **Disney's Port Orleans Resort** (Lake Buena Vista; ☎ **407/W-DISNEY** or 407/934-5000): One of Walt Disney World's more modestly priced resorts encompasses pastel buildings with shuttered windows and wrought-iron balconies that create a cozy atmosphere. The flower gardens and fountained courtyards are ideal for moonlight strolls. Bonfamille's Café offers hot Creole creations for dinner. See chapter 12.
- **Disney's Wilderness Lodge** (Lake Buena Vista; ☎ **407/W-DISNEY** or 407/824-3200): Modeled after a turn-of-the-century national park lodge, the 56-acre resort is surrounded by towering oak and pine forests; many rooms overlook 340-acre Crystal Bay. There is a secluded feeling, even though the lodge is on Disney property. A first-rate restaurant, Artist's Point, means you never have to leave this unique, romantic hideaway. See chapter 12.
- **Peabody Orlando** (Orlando; ☎ **407/345-4550**): Known for the five white ducks that serve as goodwill ambassadors, this 27-story resort offers plenty to quack about. On International Drive, this luxurious hotel steeped in sophistication feels miles away from the tourist bustle. For a romantic dinner, try Dux, the hotel's elegant signature restaurant, which has a warm, candlelit ambience. See chapter 12.
- **Seaside** (near Destin; ☎ **800/277-8696** or 904/231-1320): Ask residents of Northwest Florida where they go for romantic getaways, and they invariably will answer, "The cottages at Seaside." Built in the 1980s but evoking the 1880s, the Victorian-style village of Seaside (a short drive east of Destin) has several cozy beachfront cottages designed especially for honeymooners. See chapter 13.

13 The Best Moderately Priced Accommodations

- **Bay Harbor Inn** (Bay Harbor Island, Miami; ☎ **305/868-4141**): On an exclusive island in Miami Beach, this gem offers charm and value in an area that has precious little of either. See chapter 4.
- **Indian Creek Hotel** (Miami Beach; ☎ **800/207-2727** or 305/531-2727): It's modest but full of character, and so close to South Beach. Rooms are brightly outfitted in period furnishings, and many overlook the pretty pool and garden. For the price, there's no competition. See chapter 4.
- **Conch Key Cottages** (Marathon; ☎ **800/330-1577** or 305/289-1377): Right on the ocean, this little hideaway offers rustic but clean and well-outfitted cottages that are especially popular with families. Each has a hammock, barbecue grill, and kitchen. See chapter 6.
- **Beachcomber Apartment Motel** (Palm Beach; ☎ **800/833-7122** or 561/585-4646): This simple pink motel sits right on the ocean just a few miles from the super-high-priced accommodations that make Palm Beach, well, Palm Beach. No fancy frills here, but rooms are pleasant and clean. See chapter 8.
- **Harborfront Inn Bed & Breakfast** (Stuart; ☎ **800/294-1703** or 561/288-7289): Located on the riverfront and within walking distance of the restaurants and shops of downtown Stuart, this handsome, highly recommended B&B offers private rooms with their own entrances. See chapter 9.

- **Best Western Pink Shell Beach Resort** (Fort Myers Beach; ☎ **800/237-5786** or 941/463-6161): This popular, family-oriented spot fronting both the gulf and the bay has hotel rooms, suites, one- and two-bedroom apartments, and beach cottages. The pink-sided cottages make up for a lack of luxury with lots of 1950s-style charm. Units in two mid-rise, gulf-front buildings have lovely views of Sanibel Island from their screened balconies. See chapter 10.
- **Tides Inn of Naples** (Naples; ☎ **800/438-8763** or 941/262-6196): One of Florida's most remarkable values, this immaculate two-story motel is right on the beach and on the edge of Millionaires' Row and Olde Naples. Comfortable suites and efficiencies, all tropically furnished and decorated, have screened balconies or patios angled to face the beach across a courtyard with coconut palms and heated swimming pool. See chapter 10.
- **Island's End Resort** (St. Pete Beach; ☎ **813/360-5023**): A wonderful respite from the maddening crowd, and a great bargain to boot, this little all-cottage hideaway sits right on the southern tip of St. Pete Beach, smack-dab on Pass-a-Grille, where the Gulf of Mexico meets Tampa Bay. You can step from the six contemporary cottages right onto the beach. See chapter 11.
- **Courtyard by Marriott** (Lake Buena Vista; ☎ **800/223-9930** or 407/828-8888): The rooms are attractive, with a full-service restaurant offering American fare, a cocktail lounge, a poolside bar, and an on-site deli. Located near the shopping mecca of Disney Village Marketplace. See chapter 12.
- **Disney's Caribbean Beach Resort** (Lake Buena Vista; ☎ **407/W-DISNEY** or 407/934-3400): Five distinct Caribbean "villages" are grouped around a large duck-filled lake. In addition, each village has its own personal, smaller lake, and the 200-acre resort includes a jogging trail, a short nature trail, and a picnic area. A good value for families. See chapter 12.
- **Holiday Inn Sunspree Resort** (Lake Buena Vista; ☎ **800/FON-KIDS** or 407/239-4500): In addition to the standard amenities that make Holiday Inn a dependable choice across the country, this location has special Kids Suites. Decorated as Western fortresses or polar igloos, the suites offer separate kid-sized rooms, affording parents privacy and kids their personal space. See chapter 12.
- **Gibson Inn** (Apalachicola; ☎ **904/653-2191**): Built in 1907 as a seaman's hotel and gorgeously restored in 1985, this cupola-topped inn is such a brilliant example of Victorian architecture that it's listed on the National Register of Historic Inns. No two guest rooms are alike (some still have the original sinks in the sleeping area), but all are richly furnished with period reproductions. Grab a drink from the bar and relax in one of the high-back rockers on the old-fashioned veranda. See chapter 13.
- **Kenwood Inn** (St. Augustine; ☎ **904/824-2116**): Somewhere between a B&B and a cozy inn, the Kenwood is one of Old Town's best choices. Rooms are larger and more private than in most other B&Bs and are brimming with antiques. The large patio and outdoor swimming pool are rarities in historic downtown St. Augustine. See chapter 14.

14 The Best Seafood Restaurants

- **Fishbone Grille** (downtown Miami; ☎ **305/530-1915**): It isn't scenic and it isn't where the tourists go, but this stellar little fish restaurant has some of the area's best seafood. In addition to an excellent ceviche, the stews, crab cakes, and starters are all superb. If you like Caribbean flavor, try the daily special with jerk seasoning. See chapter 4.

- **Monty's Bayshore Restaurant** (Coconut Grove and South Beach, Miami; ☎ 305/858-1431): Forget Joe's; this multifaceted seafood restaurant serves all-you-can-eat stone crabs in season, with prices way below those of their South Beach neighbor. Other seafood specialties are available. See chapter 4.
- **Atlantic's Edge** (Islamorada; ☎ 305/664-4651): An innovative and varied menu includes some of the best fresh fish, steak, and chicken you'll find. The crab cakes are among the most delicious in the Keys; the Thai spiced fresh baby snapper is likewise spectacular. See chapter 6.
- **Marker 88** (Islamorada; ☎ 305/852-9315): A legend in the Keys, this dark, romantic restaurant has standard fare as well as a winning version of nouvelle cuisine. You'll find the area's largest selection of seafood, including lobster from the Keys, conch from the Bahamas, frog legs from the Everglades, stone crabs from the Florida Bay, and shrimp from the West Coast, among other dishes. See chapter 6.
- **Capt. Charlie's Reef Grill** (Juno Beach; ☎ 561/624-9924): The cooking is imaginative and mouthwatering. A wide range of ever-changing selections includes a Caribbean chili, a sizable tuna spring roll, and an enormous Cuban crab cake. Ask for suggestions, and enjoy this, one of the area's best-kept secrets, hidden behind a tiny strip mall. See chapter 8.
- **Channel Mark** (Fort Myers Beach; ☎ 941/463-9127): Every table looks out on a maze of channel markers on Hurricane Bay, and a dock with palms growing through it makes this a relaxing place for a waterside lunch. The atmosphere changes dramatically at night, when the relaxed tropical ambience is ideal for kindling romance. Congenial owners Mike McGuigan and Andy Welsh put a creative spin on their seafood dishes, and their delicately seasoned crab cakes are tops. See chapter 10.
- **Mad Hatter** (Sanibel Island; ☎ 941/472-0033): Brian and Jayne Baker's little gulf-front restaurant has only 12 tables, but each has a glorious water view that's best at sunset. They offer a fantasy of New American cuisines with some exotic accents. The menu changes frequently, with no dish repeated (so as not to bore their loyal local following). Whatever they serve, you'll enjoy. See chapter 10.
- **Lobster Pot** (Redington Shores, near St. Pete Beach; ☎ 813/391-8592): Owner Eugen Fuhrmann supplies the finest seafood dishes on the St. Pete and Clearwater beaches. Among his amazing variety of lobster dishes is one flambéed in brandy with garlic, and the bouillabaisse—as authentic as any you'll find in the south of France. See chapter 11.
- **Bahama Breeze** (Orlando; ☎ 407/248-2499): Traditional Caribbean foods are used to create unusual items such as "fish in a bag"—strips of mahimahi in a parchment pillow flavored with carrots, sweet peppers, mushrooms, celery, and spices. Also featured are more traditional favorites, such as paella. See chapter 12.
- **Disney's Beach Club Resort** (Lake Buena Vista; ☎ 407/W-DISNEY or 407/934-8000): The 19th-century–style clambake buffet at the Cape May Café in Disney's Beach Club Resort is a feast—seafood stews, clams, mussels, and lobster cooked in a rockwood steamer pit. It's all offered for a price that won't leave you feeling soaked. See chapter 12.
- **Back Porch** (Destin; ☎ 904/837-2022): The food isn't gourmet at this cedar-shingled shack, whose long porch offers glorious beach and gulf views, but this is where charcoal-grilled amberjack originated. Today, you'll see it on menus throughout Florida. Other fish and seafood, as well as chicken and juicy hamburgers, also come from the coals. See chapter 13.

Aphrodisiacs from Apalachicola

Seafood is a major culinary draw all across Florida. Some waterfront restaurants even operate their own fishing boats, so you're guaranteed super-fresh offerings. You'll dine on snapper, swordfish, amberjack, triggerfish, pompano, grouper, clams, gulf shrimp, blue crab, and sweet deep-sea scallops.

Some seafood specialties may be new to your palate. The clawless tropical **lobsters** are smaller and sweeter than the cold-water Maine variety, with all of their meat concentrated in the tail. You should also try **conch,** a chewy shellfish that's often served in deep-fried fritters, in chowder, or in a spicy salad marinated in lime juice. You're sure to fall in love with the taste of Florida's succulent **stone crab claws** (the crustacean is thrown back into the sea to grow another hand), and you won't soon forget the sweet, slightly briny taste of **Apalachicola oysters** (which reputedly have aphrodisiac properties).

- **Chef Eddie's Magnolia Grill** (Apalachicola; ☎ 904/653-8000): Chef Eddie Cass's pleasant restaurant occupies a small bungalow built in the 1880s and is still in possession of the original black cypress paneling in its central hallway. Nightly specials emphasize fresh local seafood and New Orleans–style sauces. He received more than 2,000 orders for his spicy seafood gumbo at a recent Florida Seafood Festival. See chapter 13.

15 The Best Local Dining Experiences

- **Bayside Seafood Restaurant and Hidden Cove Bar** (Key Biscayne; ☎ 305/361-0808): Visiting boaters and Key Biscayners call it simply "the Hut." But even those from over the bridge don't know about this laid-back bar and tiki-covered restaurant that serves good, cheap fish platters on paper plates. It's often plagued by mosquitoes, so bring protection and enjoy the rustic ambience that has become so rare in Miami. See chapter 4.
- **Caribbean Delite** (downtown Miami; ☎ 305/381-9254): Jamaicans who live in Miami frequent this little dive for authentic specialties like curried goat and oxtail stew and, for breakfast, the hard-to-find ackee and saltfish (the national dish of Jamaica). See chapter 4.
- **Versailles** (Little Havana, Miami; ☎ 305/444-0240): A tacky diner dressed up with mirrors, imitation crystal, and murals of the French countryside, this old Cuban hangout serves hearty dishes from the home country. This is the place to discover the many rich flavors of Cuban food, or at least try a *café con leche.* See chapter 4.
- **Blue Heaven** (Key West; ☎ 305/296-8666): By now everyone knows about this once-secret hideaway in Bahama Village, an area tourists are often warned not to visit (it's depressed but hardly dangerous). It's popular with bohemians and those who crave fresh homemade food, especially for breakfast. See chapter 6.
- **Coco's Kitchen** (Big Pine Key; ☎ 305/872-4495): This tiny storefront is downright cheap and has been pleasing area Cuban food fans for years. You can't go wrong with the daily special, especially if it's roasted pork or any fresh fish. It's all served with a huge portion of rice and beans or salad and crispy fries. See chapter 6.
- **Islamorada Fish Company** (Islamorada; ☎ 800/258-2559 or 305/664-9271): They've been doing it since 1948, and apparently they've been doing it right. To

accommodate the crowds, a second restaurant and an outdoor deck have opened, where tourists and locals enjoy the view and the super-rich fish sandwiches. See chapter 6.

- **Robert Is Here** (Homestead/near Everglades National Park; ☎ **305/246-1592**): Stop in for a snack or a fresh tropical fruit shake. Exotic fruits, bottled jellies, hot sauces, and salad dressings are stacked in bins throughout this local landmark farm stand. See chapter 7.

- **John G's** (Lake Worth, Palm Beach County; ☎ **561/585-9860**): This greasy spoon, right on the beach, is best known for its terrific fish-and-chips. They also serve great big breakfasts and good soups. See chapter 8.

- **Old South Barbecue Ranch** (Clewiston; ☎ **941/983-7756**): This landmark on Lake Okeechobee serves the best smoke sauce around. You can get rich and smoky barbecued pork, meat, and chicken. Try a taste of fried alligator or catfish. See chapter 9.

- **Farmers Market Restaurant** (Fort Myers; ☎ **941/334-1687**): The retail Farmers Market next door may be tiny, but the best of the cabbage, okra, green beans, and tomatoes ends up at this simple eatery, frequented by everyone from business executives to truck drivers. The specialties of the house are Southern favorites like smoked ham hocks with a bowl of black-eyed peas. See chapter 10.

- **Fourth Street Shrimp Store** (St. Petersburg; ☎ **813/822-0325**): The outside of this place looks like it's covered with graffiti, but it's actually a gigantic drawing of people eating. Inside, murals on two walls seem to look out on an early 19th-century seaport (one painted sailor permanently peers in to see what you're eating). This is the best and certainly the most-interesting bargain in St. Petersburg. See chapter 11.

- **Hopkins' Boarding House** (Pensacola; ☎ **904/438-3979**): There's a delicious peek into the past at this Victorian boardinghouse, surrounded by ancient trees and a wraparound porch with old-fashioned rocking chairs. Everyone eats family style—at your elbow could be the mayor or a mechanic, for everyone in town dines here. Platters are piled high with seasonal Southern-style vegetables from nearby farms. In true boardinghouse fashion, guests bus their own dishes. See chapter 13.

- **The Boss Oyster** (Apalachicola; ☎ **904/653-9364**): This rustic, dockside eatery is a good place to see if what they say about the aphrodisiac properties of Apalachicola oysters is true. The bivalves are served raw, steamed, or under a dozen toppings ranging from capers to crabmeat. They'll even steam three dozen of them and let you do the shucking. Dine inside or at picnic tables on a screened dockside porch. Everyone in town eats here, from bankers to watermen. See chapter 13.

- **Singleton's Seafood Shack** (Mayport/Jacksonville; ☎ **904/246-9440**): This rustic Old Florida fish camp has kept up with the times by offering fresh fish in more ways than just battered and fried. Yet they have retained the charming casualness of a riverside fish camp. Even if you don't want seafood, this spot is worth stopping in just for a feel of Old Florida. See chapter 14.

16 The Best Bars & Nightspots

- **Cafe Nostalgia** (Little Havana, Miami; ☎ **305/541-2631**): They start with films from the old country and follow up with the hot sounds of Afro-Cuban jazz. It's become popular with a few gringos and lots of sentimental exiles. See chapter 5.

- **The Clevelander** (South Beach, Miami) ☎ **305/531-3485**): On one of Ocean Drive's busiest corners, there's always a mixed crowd gathered around the large outdoor pool area drinking brightly colored concoctions from plastic cups. See chapter 5.

- **The Forge** (Miami Beach; ☎ **305/538-8533**): Step back in time at this ultra-elegant restaurant and bar, where Wednesday night is the time to hang with singles in Armani and Versace. See chapter 5.

- **Tobacco Road** (downtown Miami; ☎ **305/374-1198**): Open every day of the year since 1912, Tobacco Road is a Miami institution. No matter who is playing, this two-story dive bar is worth a visit. From homegrown blues to nationally known jazz acts to poetry readings, you'll find the best music and atmosphere at "The Road." See chapter 5.

- **Yuca** (South Beach, Miami; ☎ **305/532-9822**): One of South Beach's best restaurants also operates an expensive upstairs club on the weekends. No matter who is playing, you will appreciate the high-energy scene at this upscale Latin hot spot. See chapter 5.

- **Duval Street** (Key West): The partying-est strip this side of Bourbon Street, home to literally dozens of bars and dance spots. Explore them for yourself. See chapter 6.

- **Woody's Saloon and Restaurant** (Islamorada; ☎ **305/664-4335**): This raunchy bar has live bands almost every night, but it is the house band you want to see. Big Dick and the Extenders is headed by a 300-pound Native American who does a lewd, rude, and crude routine of jokes and songs guaranteed to offend everyone in the house. See chapter 6.

- **Clematis Street** (West Palm Beach): This newly gentrified area has some of the area's best (and only) nightlife. Just over the bridge from stodgy Palm Beach, this 5-block area, from Flagler Drive to Rosemary Avenue, has everything from late-night bookshops and wine bars to dance clubs and outdoor cafes. See chapter 8.

- **Las Olas Boulevard** (Ft. Lauderdale): This wide, scenic street, dotted with good clubs and late-night shopping, is especially popular with a more mature local crowd and European visitors. See chapter 8.

- **The Dock at Crayton Cove** (Naples; ☎ **941/263-9940**): Right on the City Dock, this lively pub is a perfect place for an open-air meal or a libation while watching the action on Naples Bay. See chapter 10.

- **Junkanoo Beach Bar** (Fort Myers Beach; ☎ **941/463-2600**): Away from the crowds of Fort Myers Beach's busy Times Square, the Junkanoo attracts a more affluent crowd for its constant Bohemian-style beach parties with live reggae and other island music. A concessionaire rents beach cabanas and water-sports toys, making it a good place for a lively day at the beach. See chapter 10.

- **Shooters Waterfront Cafe USA** (Fort Myers; ☎ **941/334-2727**): A setting right on the river makes this Fort Myers's most popular watering hole. There's music every night, and the place is absolutely packed after work on Friday and Saturday. See chapter 10.

- **Frankie's Patio Bar & Grill** (Tampa; ☎ **813/249-3337**): All you have to do is stroll along 7th Avenue East, between 15th and 20th streets, in Tampa's Ybor City to find a club or bar to your liking. Frankie's stands out for its exposed industrial pipes—a stark contrast to the Spanish-style architecture prevalent here. There's seating indoors, on a large outdoor patio, or on an open-air balcony overlooking the action on the street. Pick up a calendar at the reception desk—there's that much live jazz, blues, reggae, and rock here. See chapter 11.

- **Church Street Station** (downtown Orlando): Between Garland and Orange avenues, this renovated train depot is an architectural treat and a genuine good time. There are 20 shows nightly in this collection of bars, restaurants, and shops. Enjoy live music and bustling dance floors, or sip a cocktail while sitting along the cobblestone streets. See chapter 12.
- **CityWalk** (Orlando): The 12-acre entertainment complex, next to Universal Studios, could easily be renamed theme-restaurant heaven. It is home to not only the world's largest Hard Rock Cafe—the grande dame of them all—but also the Nascar Cafe, the Motown Cafe, and Marvel Mania, a theme homage to villains and superheroes. Along with places to dine there are places to dance to jazz, reggae, hip-hop, and pop. If you're cinematically deprived, head for the state-of-the-art Cineplex Odeon Megaplex. See chapter 12.
- **Pleasure Island** (near Disney Village, Orlando): You can two-step to Charlie Pride or groove to Charlie Parker; this all-in-one complex runs the entertainment gamut from country to jazz to modern rock to dance music. Special appearances by big-name artists on two stages are an occasional nighttime option. A nightly fireworks display ensures every evening ends with a bang. See chapter 12.
- **Flora-Bama Lounge** (Perdido Key, near Pensacola; ☎ 904/492-0611): This slapped-together gulfside pub is almost a shrine to country music, with jam sessions from noon until way past midnight on Saturday and Sunday. Flora-Bama is the prime sponsor and a key venue for the Frank Brown International Songwriters' Festival during the first week of November. Take in the great gulf views from the Deck Bar. See chapter 13.
- **Seville Quarter** (Pensacola; ☎ 904/434-6211): In Pensacola's Seville Historic District, this restored antique brick complex with New Orleans–style wrought-iron balconies contains pubs and restaurants whose names capture the ambience: Rosie O'Grady's Goodtime Emporium; Lili Marlene's Aviator's Pub; Apple Annie's Courtyard; End o' the Alley Bar; Phineas Phogg's Balloon Works (a dance hall, not a balloon shop); and Fast Eddie's Billiard Parlor (which has electronic games for kids, too). Live entertainment ranges from Dixieland jazz to country and western. See chapter 13.
- **Shuckums Oyster Pub & Seafood Grill** (Panama City Beach; ☎ 904/235-3214): "We shuck 'em, you suck 'em" is the motto of this extremely informal pub, which became famous when comedian Martin Short tried unsuccessfully to shuck oysters here during the making of an MTV spring-break special. The original bar is virtually papered over with dollar bills signed by old and young patrons who have been flocking here since 1967. See chapter 13.

2 Planning a Trip to Florida

by Bill Goodwin

In the pages that follow, you'll find everything you need to know to handle the practical details of planning your trip in advance: when to go, how to find the best airfare, and much more.

1 The Regions in Brief

The first decision you'll have to make is where to go in Florida. You'll find ample sun, sea, and sand all along the 800 miles of shoreline here, but not everywhere in the Sunshine State is warm all the time. Many Florida beaches are lined with towering hotels and condominiums, while others are pristinely preserved in their natural states. You can spend your days in busy, cosmopolitan cities, or while them away in picturesque small towns steeped in history. You can take the kids to see Mickey Mouse, or find a romantic retreat far from the maddening crowds.

Here is a brief rundown of the state's regions to help get you started. See the following chapters for details.

Miami & Miami Beach Sprawling across the southeastern corner of the state, metropolitan Miami is anything but your typical American city. Here you will hear Spanish and many other languages spoken all around you, for this cosmopolitan area is a melting pot of immigrants from Latin American and the Caribbean. Cross the causeways and you'll come to the sands of Miami Beach, long a resort mecca and home to enchanting South Beach, famous for its art deco buildings, exciting nightlife, and celebrity sightings. See chapters 4 and 5.

The Keys From the southern tip of Florida, U.S. 1 travels through a 100-mile string of islands stretching from Key Largo to famous, laid-back Key West, only 90 miles from Cuba and the southernmost point in the United States (it's always warm down here). While some of the islands are crammed with strip malls and tourist traps, most are dense with unusual species of tropical flora and fauna. The Keys don't have the best beaches in Florida, but the waters here—all in a vast marine preserve—offer the state's best scuba diving and snorkeling and some of its best deep-sea fishing. See chapter 6.

The Everglades Encompassing more than 2,000 square miles and 1.5 million acres, Everglades National Park covers the entire southern tip of Florida. The park, along with nearby Big Cypress National

Preserve, protects a unique and fragile "River of Grass" ecosystem teeming with wildlife that is best seen by canoe, by boat, or on long or short hikes. To the east of the Everglades is Biscayne National Park, preserving the northernmost living coral reefs in the continental United States. See chapter 7.

The Gold Coast   North of Miami, the Gold Coast is aptly named, for here you'll come to booming Hollywood and Ft. Lauderdale and ritzy Boca Raton and Palm Beach, famous playgrounds of the rich and famous. Beyond its dozens of gorgeous beaches, the area offers fantastic shopping, entertainment, clubbing, boating, golfing, tennis, and just plain relaxing. With some of the country's most famous golf courses and even more tennis courts, this area attracts big-name tournaments. See chapter 8.

The Treasure Coast   Despite gaining unprecedented numbers of new residents in recent years, the beach communities running from Hobe Sound north to Sebastian Inlet retain their small-town feel. In addition to a vast array of wildlife, the area has a rich and colorful history. Its name stems from a violent 1715 hurricane which sunk an entire fleet of treasure-laden Spanish ships. Excavators turned up hundreds of ancient coins in the 1950s and 1960s, and you'll still see treasure hunters prowling the beaches with metal detectors. The sea around Sebastian Inlet draws surfers to the largest swells in the state. See chapter 9.

Southwest Florida   Ever since inventor Thomas Alva Edison built a home there in 1885, some of America's wealthiest families have spent their winters along Florida's southwest coast. They are attracted by the area's subtropical climate, shell-strewn beaches, and intricate waterways winding among 10,000-plus islands. Many charming remnants of old Florida coexist with modern resorts in the sophisticated riverfront towns of Fort Myers and Naples and on islands like Gasparilla, Useppa, Sanibel, Captiva, Keewaydin, and Marco. And thanks to some timely preservation, the area has many wildlife refuges, including the "backdoor" entrance to Everglades National Park. See chapter 10.

The Tampa Bay Area   Halfway down the west coast of Florida lies Tampa Bay, home of one of America's fastest-growing metropolitan areas. A busy seaport and commercial center, the city of Tampa is home to Busch Gardens Tampa Bay, one of the state's top theme parks and one of the country's largest zoos. Boasting a unique pier and fine museums, St. Petersburg's waterfront downtown is one of Florida's most pleasant. Most visitors elect to stay near the beaches skirting the narrow barrier islands running some 20 miles between St. Pete Beach and Clearwater Beach. Across the soaring Sunshine Skyway lie Sarasota, one of Florida's prime performing-arts venues; the riverfront town of Bradenton; and another string of barrier islands with great beaches and resorts spanning every price range. See chapter 11.

Walt Disney World & Orlando   Walt Disney brought Mickey Mouse to Orlando in 1971, changing forever what was then a sleepy Southern town. In fact, Walt created a whole new world—if not universe—here in central Florida. Today, at the dawn of the millennium, it seems that at least one full-scale theme park opens every year. Walt Disney World claims four distinct parks, two entertainment districts, enough hotels to fill a small city, and several smaller attractions including water parks and miniature-golf courses. That's not even counting the rapidly expanding Universal Studios Florida and many more non-Disney attractions. Orlando is Florida's fastest-growing city, and its visitors have never had more options. See chapter 12.

Northwest Florida: The Panhandle   Historical roots run deep in Florida's narrow northwest extremity, and Pensacola's historic district, which blends Spanish, French, and British cultures, is a highlight of any visit to today's Panhandle. So, too, are the powdery, dazzlingly white beaches that stretch for more than 80 miles past the resorts of Pensacola Beach, Fort Walton Beach, Destin, and Panama City Beach. The Gulf Islands National Seashore has preserved much of this beach and its wildlife, and inland are state parks that offer some of the state's best canoeing adventures. All this makes the area a favorite summertime vacation destination for residents of neighboring Georgia and Alabama, with whom Northwest Floridians share many Deep South traditions. Sitting in a pine and oak forest just 30 miles from the Georgia line, the state capital of Tallahassee has a moss-draped, football-loving charm all its own. See chapter 13.

Northeast Florida   The northeast section of the state contains the oldest permanent settlement in America—St. Augustine, where Spanish colonists arrived and settled more than four centuries ago. Today, its history comes to life in a quaint historic district. St. Augustine is bordered to the north by Jacksonville, an up-and-coming sunbelt metropolis with miles of oceanfront beach and beautiful marine views along the St. Johns River. Just above Jacksonville, up on the Georgia border, Amelia Island has two of Florida's finest resorts and its own historic town of Fernandina Beach. To the south of St. Augustine, Daytona Beach is home of the Daytona International Speedway and is a spring-break mecca for the college crowd. Another brand of excitement is offered down at Cape Canaveral, where the Kennedy Space Center launches all manned U.S. space missions. See chapter 14.

2 Visitor Information

Your best bets for detailed information about a specific destination in Florida are the **local visitor information offices.** They're listed under "Orientation" or "Essentials" in the following chapters.

For general information about the state, contact **Visit Florida,** P.O. Box 1100, Tallahassee, FL 32302-1100 (☎ **888/7-FLA-USA;** www.flausa.com), the state's official tourism promotion agent. Ask for its annual *Visit Florida,* a comprehensive guide that lists most hotels and motels in the state; its *Planning Guide for Travelers with Disability;* its *Florida Events Calendar;* its *Florida Trails,* a booklet describing the state's many nature trails; and an official state highway map. They're all free.

Visit Florida also has offices in:

Canada: 121 Bloor St. E., Suite 1003, Toronto M4W 3M5 (☎ **416/ 928-3139;** fax 416/928-6841).

United Kingdom: Roebuck House, Palace Street, London SW1E 5BA (☎ **171/ 630-6602;** fax 171/630-7703).

Germany: Schillerstrasse 10, 60313 Frankfurt/Main (☎ **069/131-0731;** fax 069/131-0647).

Japan: Belevedere Kudan Building, no. 204, 2-15-5, Fujimi, Chiyoda-Ku, Tokyo 102 (☎ **35276-0260;** fax 35276-0264).

Visit Florida also operates **welcome centers** on I-10 west of Pensacola, I-75 north of Jennings, I-95 north of Yulee, and U.S. 231 at Campbellton. There's also a walk-in information office in the west foyer of the New Capitol Building in Tallahassee (see chapter 13).

Once you're here, you can call Visit Florida's 24-hour **tourist assistance hotline** (☎ **800/656-8777**) if you need help with lost travel documents, directions, emergencies, or references to attractions, restaurants, and shopping anywhere in the state. Hotline operators speak several languages, including Spanish, French, German, Portuguese, Japanese, and Korean.

3 When to Go

To a large extent, the timing of your visit will determine how much you'll spend—and how much company you'll have—once you get here. That's because room rates can more than double during the high seasons, when countless visitors migrate to Florida.

The weather determines the high seasons (see "Climate," below). In subtropical southern Florida, it's during the winter, from mid-December to mid-April. On the other hand, you'll be rewarded with incredible bargains if you can stand the heat and humidity of a South Florida summer between June and early September. In northern Florida, the reverse is true: Tourists flock here during the summer, from Memorial Day to Labor Day.

Presidents' Day weekend in February, Easter week, Memorial Day weekend at the end of May, the Fourth of July, Labor Day weekend at the start of September, Thanksgiving, Christmas, and New Year's are busy throughout the state, and especially at Walt Disney World and the other Orlando-area attractions, which can be packed anytime school's out (see chapter 12).

Both northern and southern Florida share the same "shoulder seasons": April and May and from September to November, when the weather is pleasant throughout Florida and hotel rates are considerably less than during the high seasons. If price is a consideration, then these months of pleasant temperatures and fewer tourists are the best times to visit.

See the accommodations sections in the chapters that follow for specifics about the local high, shoulder, and off-seasons.

CLIMATE   Northern Florida has a temperate climate, and even in the warmer southern third of the state, it's subtropical, not tropical. Accordingly, Florida sees more extremes of temperatures than, say, the Caribbean islands.

Average Temperatures in Selected Florida Cities (°F)

	Jan	Feb	Mar	Apr	May	June	July	Aug	Sept	Oct	Nov	Dec
Key West	69	72	74	77	80	82	85	85	84	80	74	72
Miami	69	70	71	74	78	81	82	84	81	78	73	70
Tampa	60	61	66	72	77	81	82	82	81	75	67	62
Orlando	60	63	66	71	78	82	82	82	81	75	67	61
Tallahassee	53	56	63	68	72	78	81	81	77	74	66	59

Spring sees warm temperatures throughout Florida, but it also brings tropical showers, and May contributes the first waves of summertime humidity.

Summer runs from May to September in Florida, when it's hot and very humid throughout the state. If you're in an inland city during these months, you may not want to do anything too taxing when the sun is at its peak. Coastal areas, however, reap the benefits of sea breezes. Severe afternoon thunderstorms are prevalent during the summer heat (there aren't professional sports teams here named Lightning and Thunder for nothing). So schedule your activities for earlier in the day, and take precautions to avoid being hit by lightning during the storms.

Fall is a great time to visit—the really hottest days are gone, and the crowds have thinned out. Unless a hurricane blows through, November usually is Florida's driest month. August through November is hurricane season here, but even if one threatens, the National Weather Service closely tracks the storms and gives ample warning if there's a need to evacuate coastal areas.

Winter can get a bit nippy throughout the state, and sometimes downright cold in northern Florida. Although snow is rare, a flake or two has been known to fall as far south as Miami. The "cold snaps" usually last only a few days in the southern half of the state, however, and daytime temperatures quickly return to the 70s.

For up-to-the minute weather info, tune in to cable TV's Weather Channel, or click on its Web site: www.weather.com.

Florida Calendar of Events

January

- **International Circus Festival and Parade,** Sarasota. Circus acts, clowns, and rides for kids honor the city's rich circus heritage. Call ☎ 941/351-8888 for schedule. Day after Christmas through January.
- **Gator Bowl,** Jacksonville. Yet two more of the country's better college football teams battle it out in Alltel Stadium. Call ☎ 904/798-1700 for information on tickets and postgame festivities. Usually January 1.
- **Outback Bowl,** Tampa. Two top college teams kick off at Houlihan's Stadium, preceded by a weeklong series of events. Call ☎ 813/874-2695 for schedule and tickets. Usually January 1.
- **Epiphany Celebration,** Tarpon Springs. After morning services at St. Nicholas Cathedral, young folks dive for the Epiphany cross in Spring Bayou. For information, call ☎ 727/937-3540. First Saturday in January.
- ✪ **Key West Literary Seminar.** This 3-day festival attracts the biggest names in literature. Some past participants included Joyce Carol Oates, Amy Tan, and Jamaica Kincaid. This event sells out months in advance. Call ☎ 888/293-9291 for details or check out the Web site at www.KeyWestLiterarySeminar.org. Early to mid-January.
- **Art Miami,** Miami. This annual fine arts fair attracts more than a hundred galleries from all over the world. International, modern, and contemporary works are featured here, attracting thousands of visitors and buyers. For information and ticket prices, call ☎ 561/220-2690. Early January.
- ✪ **Art Deco Weekend,** South Beach, Miami. Held along the beach between 5th and 15th streets, this festival—with bands, food stands, antiques vendors, artists, tours, and other festivities—celebrates the whimsical architecture that has made South Beach one of America's most unique neighborhoods. Call ☎ 305/672-2014 for details. Usually held on Martin Luther King weekend.
- ✪ **Royal Caribbean Classic,** Key Biscayne. World-renowned golfers compete for more than $1 million in prize money at Crandon Park Golf Course, formerly known as The Links. Lee Trevino has won this tournament twice. Call ☎ 305/374-6180 for more information. Late January.
- **Goodland Mullet Festival,** Marco Island. Stan Gober's Idle Hour Seafood Restaurant in Goodland is mobbed during a massive party featuring the Buzzard Lope dance and the Best Men's Legs Contest. Call ☎ 941/394-3041 for details. Sunday before Super Bowl.

February

- ✪ **Everglades Seafood Festival,** Florida City. As many as 75,000 people show up each year for this 2-day eating festival in the quaint, old town of Florida City. Florida delicacies like stone crab and gator tails are dished up from shacks and food booths on the outskirts of town. Friday night is family night where a carnival and craft fair attract the youngsters. No admission charge. Call ☎ 941/695-4100 for more details. First full weekend in February.

The Boys of Spring

Major-league baseball fans can watch the Florida Marlins in Miami and the Tampa Bay Devil Rays in St. Petersburg throughout their seasons from April through September, but the entire state is a baseball hotbed from late February through March, when many other teams tune up for the regular season with "Grapefruit League" exhibition games.

Most of Florida's spring-training stadiums are relatively small, so fans can see their favorite players up close, and maybe even get a handshake or an autograph. Also, tickets are priced from $5 to $12, a bargain when compared with regular season games. Many games sell out by early March, so don't wait until you're in Florida to buy tickets.

The teams tend to move around from season to season, but you can contact the **Florida Sports Foundation,** 2964 Wellington Circle N., Tallahassee, FL 32308 (☎ **850/488-8347;** fax 850/922-0482; www.flasports.com), or the main office of **Major League Baseball,** 350 Park Ave., New York, NY 10022 (☎ **212/339-7800;** www.majorleaguebaseball.com/springtraining), to find out the schedules and where your favorite teams will be playing.

Here's where the teams played in 1999, with their spring-training ticket-office phone numbers and their Web sites. See the outdoor activities sections in subsequent chapters for specifics.

Atlanta Braves, Lake Buena Vista, near Orlando (☎ 407/939-1500; www.atlantabraves.com); **Baltimore Orioles,** Fort Lauderdale (☎ 800/236-8908 or 954/776-1921; www.theorioles.com); **Boston Red Sox,** Fort Myers (☎ 877/733-7699 or 941/334-4799; www.redsox.com); **Cincinnati Reds,** Sarasota (☎ 941/954-4464; www.cincinnatireds.com); **Cleveland Indians,** Winter Haven (☎ 941/293-3900; www.indians.com); **Detroit Tigers,** Lakeland (☎ 941/603-6278; www.detroittigers.com); **Florida Marlins,** Melbourne (☎ 407/633-4487; www.flamarlins.com); **Houston Astros,** Kissimmee, near Orlando (☎ 407/933-5400; www.astros.com); **Kansas City Royals,** Davenport (☎ 941/424-2500; www.kcroyals.com); **Los Angeles Dodgers,** Vero Beach (☎ 407/569-6858; www.dodgers.com); **Minnesota Twins,** Fort Myers (☎ 800/338-9467 or 941/768-4200; www.mntwins.com); **Montreal Expos,** Jupiter (☎ 561/775-1818, ext. 239; www.montrealexpos.com); **New York Mets,** Port St. Lucie (☎ 561/871-2115; www.nymets.com); **New York Yankees,** Tampa (☎ 813/879-2244; www.yankees.com); **Philadelphia Phillies,** Clearwater (☎ 727/442-8496; www.phillies.com); **Pittsburgh Pirates,** Bradenton (☎ 941/748-4610; www.devilray.com); **St. Louis Cardinals,** Jupiter (☎ 561/ 775-1818, ext. 239; www.stlcardinals.com); **Tampa Bay Devil Rays,** St. Petersburg (☎ 727/825-3137; www.devilray.com); **Texas Rangers,** Port Charlotte (☎ 813/625-9500; www.texasrangers.com); and **Toronto Blue Jays,** Dunedin (☎ 813/733-0429; www.bluejays.com).

○ **Edison Pageant of Light,** Fort Myers. The spectacular Parade of Lights tops off arts-and-crafts shows, pageants, and a 5K race. Call ☎ **800/237-6444** or 941/334-2550. First 2 weeks in February.

• **Gasparilla Pirate Fest,** Tampa. Hundreds of boats and rowdy "pirates" invade the city, then parade along Bayshore Boulevard, showering crowds with beads and coins. For information, call ☎ **813/273-6495.** Early February.

- **Winter Gayla,** Ft. Lauderdale. More than 10,000 gay men and women turn out for this 10-day pride festival with parties, games, vendors and displays. Call ☎ **954/561-2020** for details. Early February.
- ✪ **Miami Film Festival,** Miami. This 10-day festival has made an impact as an important screening opportunity for Latin American cinema and American independents. It's relatively small, well-priced, and easily accessible to the general public. Contact the Film Society of Miami at ☎ **305/377-FILM.** Early February.
- ✪ **Miami International Boat Show,** Miami. This show draws almost a quarter of a million boat enthusiasts to the Miami Beach Convention Center and surrounding locations to see the mega-yachts, sailboats, dinghies, and accessories. It's the biggest anywhere. Call ☎ **305/531-8410** for more information and ticket prices. Mid-February.
- **Florida State Fair,** Tampa. Despite all its development, Florida still is a major agricultural state, a status it celebrates at this huge annual exposition. Judged competitions, botanical gardens, crafts building, carny rides, nationally known entertainers. Call ☎ **800/345-FAIR** for details. Mid-February.
- ✪ **Speedweeks,** Daytona. Nineteen days of events with a series of races that draw the top names in NASCAR stock-car racing, all culminating in the Daytona 500. All events take place at the Daytona International Speedway. Especially for the Daytona 500, tickets must be purchased even a year in advance. They go on sale January 1 of the prior year. Call ☎ **904/253-7223** for ticket information. First 3 weeks of February.

March

- **Bike Week,** Daytona Beach. An international gathering of motorcycle enthusiasts draws a crowd of more than 200,000. In addition to major races held at Daytona International Speedway (featuring the world's best road racers, motocrossers, and dirt trackers), there are motorcycle shows, beach parties, and the Annual Motorcycle Parade, with thousands of riders. Call ☎ **800/854-1234** or 904/255-0981, or get online at www.officialbikeweek.com. First week in March.
- ✪ **Sanibel Shell Fair,** Sanibel and Captiva islands. A show of shells from around the world and the sale of unusual shell art. Call ☎ **941/472-2155.** Begins first Thursday in March.
- ✪ **Calle Ocho Festival,** Miami. This salsa-filled blowout marks the end of a 10-day extravaganza called Carnival Miami. It's one of the world's biggest block parties, held along 23 blocks of Little Havana's Southwest 8th Street between 4th and 27th avenues. Call ☎ **305/644-8888** for more information. Early to mid-March.
- **Spring Break,** Daytona Beach, Miami Beach, Panama City Beach, Key West, and other beaches. College students from all over the United States and Canada flock to Florida for endless partying, wet T-shirt and bikini contests, free concerts, volleyball tournaments, and more. Tune in to MTV if you can't be here. Call the local visitor information offices. Three weeks in March.
- **Grand Prix of Miami,** Homestead. This high-purse, high-profile auto race rivals the big ones in Daytona. It attracts the top Indy car drivers and large crowds. For information and tickets, contact Homestead Motorsports Complex at ☎ **305/230-5200.** Sometime in March.
- **Blues Festival,** Coral Gables. Mozart Stub restaurateur Harald Neuweg hosts this all-day street fest featuring down-home blues tunes as well as great food and

lots of beer. Call ☎ **305/446-1600** for more details or see "Oktoberfest" listing below. Third weekend in March.

April

- **Springtime Tallahassee,** Tallahassee. One of the South's largest celebrations welcomes abundant azaleas, camellias, and other blossoms. Call ☎ **850/224-1373.** Runs 4 weeks from late March.
- **Festival of States,** St. Petersburg. Since 1921, one of the South's largest civic celebrations sees national band competition, three parades, concerts, sports, and more. Call ☎ **727/898-3654.** First full week in April.
- **Black College Reunion,** Daytona Beach. Some 75,000 students from 115 historically black universities bring an end to the spring break season. Call ☎ **800/ 854-1234** or 904/255-0415. Mid-April.
- **PGA Seniors Golf Championship,** Palm Beach Gardens. Held at the PGA National Resort & Spa, it's the oldest and most prestigious of the senior tournaments. Call ☎ **561/624-8400** for the lineup. Mid-April.
- **Sunfest,** West Palm Beach. A huge party happens on Flagler Drive in the downtown area with four stages of continuous music, a craft marketplace, a juried art show, a youth park, and fireworks. Call ☎ **561/659-5992** for details. Late April to early May.

May

- **Coconut Grove Bed Race,** downtown Coconut Grove. A colorful event in which local participants race hand-rigged beds to raise money for the Muscular Dystrophy Association. Call ☎ **305/717-9937** for details. Usually the Sunday after Mother's Day.
- **Mayfest,** Destin. Upscale arts-and-crafts festival attracts more than 20,000 people to look, buy, and sample fine cuisine at the Panhandle's ritziest resort. Call ☎ **850/837-6241.** Third full weekend in May.
- **Coconuts Dolphin Tournament,** Key Largo. This is the largest fishing tournament in the Keys, offering $5,000 and a Dodge Ram pickup truck to the person who breaks the record for the largest fish caught. The competition is fierce! Call ☎ **305/451-4107** for details. Mid-May, usually the weekend before Memorial Day.

June

- **Fiesta of Five Flags,** Pensacola. Extravaganza commemorates the Spanish conquistador Tristan de Luna's arrival in 1559. Call ☎ **850/433-6512** for information. First week in June.
- **Billy Bowlegs Festival,** Fort Walton Beach. A fleet of modern-day pirates captures the Emerald Coast in a rollicking, weeklong bash honoring notorious buccaneer William Augustus Bowles. Treasure hunt, parade, and carnival, too. Call ☎ **800/322-3319.** First week in June.
- ✪ **Coconut Grove Goombay Festival,** Miami. This bash, one of the country's largest black-heritage festivals, features a Bahamian bacchanalia with dancing in the streets of Coconut Grove and music from the Royal Bahamian Police marching band. The food and music draw thousands to an all-day celebration of Miami's Caribbean connection. It's lots of fun—if the weather isn't scorching. Call ☎ **305/372-9966** for festival details. Early June.
- **Spanish Night Watch Ceremony,** St. Augustine. Actors in period dress lead a torchlight procession through historic St. Augustine and reenact the closing of

the city gates with music and pageantry. Call ☎ **800/OLD-CITY** for details. Third Saturday in June.

July

- **Pepsi 400,** Daytona. A race marking the halfway point in the NASCAR Winston Cup Series for stock cars. Held at the Daytona International Speedway at 11am. Call ☎ **904/253-7223** for details. July 4.
- **World's Richest Tarpon Tournament,** Boca Grande. Some $175,000 is at stake in the great tarpon waters off Southwest Florida. Call the event hotline at ☎ **800/237-6444** or 941/964-2995. Second Wednesday and Thursday in July.
- ✪ **Lower Keys Underwater Music Fest,** Looe Key. At this outrageous celebration, boaters go out to the underwater reef of Looe Key Marine Sanctuary off Big Pine Key, drop speakers into the water, and pipe in music. It's entertainment for the fish and swimmers alike! A snorkeling Elvis can usually be spotted. Call ☎ **800/ 872-3722** for details. Usually second Saturday of July.
- **Space Week Celebration,** Cape Canaveral. Kennedy Space Center celebrates humans landing on the moon. Science fairs, space art, and a space-station design competition are featured. Call ☎ **407/452-2121** for details. Mid-July.
- **Blue Angels Air Show,** Pensacola. World-famous navy pilots do their aerial acrobatics just 100 yards off the beach. Call ☎ **800/874-1234** or 850/452-2583 for schedule.

August

- **Miami Reggae Festival,** Miami. Jamaica's best dance-hall and reggae artists turn out for this 2-day festival. Burning Spear, Steel Pulse, Spragga Benz, and Jigsy King have participated recently. Call Jamaica Awareness at ☎ **305/891-2944** for more details. Early August.

September

- **Labor Day Pro-Am Surfing Festival,** Cocoa Beach. One of the largest surfing events on the East Coast draws pros and amateurs from around the country. Rock-and-roll bands, swimsuit contests. Call ☎ **800/936-2326** for details. Labor Day weekend.

October

- **Destin Seafood Festival,** Destin. The "World's Luckiest Fishing Village" cooks its bountiful catch in every style of cuisine imaginable. Also offered are arts, crafts, and music. Comes right after Destin Fishing Rodeo, with 450 angler awards, giant dock parties. Call ☎ **850/837-6241.** First full weekend in October.
- ✪ **Columbus Day Regatta,** Miami. Find anything that can float—from an inner tube to a 100-foot yacht—and you'll fit right in. Yes, there actually is a race, but how can you keep track when you're partying with a bunch of semi-naked psychos in the middle of Biscayne Bay? It's free and it's wild. Rent a boat, jet ski, or sailboard to get up close. Be sure to secure a vessel early, though—everyone wants to be there. Check local newspapers for exact date and time. Columbus Day weekend.
- **Biketoberfest,** Daytona. Road-racing stars compete at the CCS Motorcycle Championship at Daytona International Speedway, plus parties, parades, concerts, and more. Call ☎ **904/253-7223** for race ticket information, ☎ **800/ 854-1235** for other activities. Mid-October.
- **Clearwater Jazz Holiday,** Clearwater. Top jazz musicians play for 4 days and nights at bayfront Coachman Park in this free musical extravaganza. Call ☎ **727/363-7866** for schedule. Mid-October.

- **Guavaween,** Tampa. Ybor City's Latin-style Halloween celebration begins with the "Mama Guava Stumble," a wacky costume parade. All-night concerts from rock to reggae. For information, call ☎ **813/248-3712.** October 31.
- ✪ **John's Pass Seafood Festival,** Madeira Beach. Tons of fish, shrimp, crab, and other seafood go down the hatch at one of Florida's largest seafood festivals. Call ☎ **813/391-7373.** Last weekend in October.
- ✪ **Jacksonville Jazz Festival.** This free weeklong, nonstop music event in Metropolitan Park features major artists. Call ☎ **904/353-7770** for details. Late October or early November.
- ✪ **Fantasy Fest,** Key West. It might feel as though the rest of the world is joining you if you're in Key West for this world-famous Halloween festival, Florida's version of Mardi Gras. Crazy costumes, wild parades, and even wilder revelers gather for an opportunity to do things Mom said not to. Definitely leave the kids at home! Call ☎ **305/296-1817.** Last week of October.

November

- **Frank Brown International Songwriters' Festival,** Pensacola. Composers gather at the infamous Flora-Bama Lounge and other beach venues to perform their country-music hits. Call ☎ **850/492-4660** for information. First week in November.
- ✪ **Florida Seafood Festival,** Apalachicola. Book a room at the Gibson Inn 5 years in advance of this huge chow-down in Florida's oystering capital. Call ☎ **850/653-9419** for details. First Saturday in November.
- **Fort Myers Beach Sand Sculpting Contest,** Fort Myers Beach. Some 50,000 people gather to sculpt or see the world's finest sand castles. Call ☎ **800/782-9283** or 941/463-6451. First weekend in November.
- **Blue Angels Homecoming Air Show,** Pensacola. World-famous navy pilots do their aerial acrobatics just 100 yards off the beach. Call ☎ **800/874-1234** or 850/452-2583 for information. Second weekend in November.
- ✪ **The Ramble,** Miami. Old-time Floridians love this yearly event at the Fairchild Tropical Gardens. Here you can buy antiques, exotic orchids, or vintage clothes. If you're not shopping, it's still worth strolling around the lush park where you can see an impressive array of botanical miracles. For more information, call ☎ **305/667-1651.** Mid-November.
- ✪ **Daytona Beach Fall Speedway Spectacular.** Featuring the Annual Turkey Rod Run, this is the Southeast's largest combined car show and swap meet, with thousands of street rods and classic vehicles on display and for sale. It takes place at the International Speedway. Call ☎ **904/255-7355** for details. Thanksgiving weekend.
- ✪ **White Party Week,** Miami. This week-long AIDS fundraiser begins with a series of events in Miami Beach nightclubs and leads up to the Sunday night gala, where more than 10,000 gay men and women from around the country come out to celebrate at Vizcaya, the Renaissance mansion. Since the gala always sells out, make sure to buy your tickets as soon as they go on sale October 1. Call ☎ **305/667-9296** for details; www.whitepartyweek.com. Thanksgiving week.

December

- **Captiva Sea Kayak Classic,** Captiva Island. Sea kayaker and surf skiers from around the nation depart from the beach in front of 'Tween Waters Inn for a series of races. Call ☎ **941/472-5161.** First weekend in December.
- ✪ **Edison/Ford Winter Homes Holiday House,** Fort Myers. Thousands of lights and Christmas music hail the holiday season. At the same time, candles create a

spectacular Luminary Trail along the full length of Sanibel Island's Periwinkle Way. Call ☎ **941/275-1088** for information. First week in December.

- **JCPenney Mixed Team Golf Classic,** Tarpon Springs. Westin Innisbrook Resort hosts mixed-gender teams of top pro golfers. Call ☎ **727/942-2000,** ext. 5393. First week in December.

○ **British Night Watch & Grand Illumination Ceremony,** St. Augustine. A torchlight procession from Government House through the Spanish Quarter. Kicks off a month of Christmas festivities: reenactments of British colonial customs, encampments, 18th-century music, crafts demonstrations, cannon firings, caroling, 18th-century bazaar, performance of Handel's *Messiah,* parade, and more. Call ☎ **800/OLD-CITY** for details. First Saturday in December.

4 Health & Insurance

STAYING HEALTHY

Florida doesn't present any unusual health hazards for most people. Folks with certain medical conditions such as liver disease, diabetes, and stomach ailments, however, should avoid eating raw oysters, which can carry a natural bacterium linked to severe diarrhea, vomiting, and even fatal blood poisoning. Cooking kills the bacteria, so if in doubt, order your oysters steamed, broiled, or fried.

Florida has millions of mosquitoes and invisible biting sand flies (known as no-see-ums), especially in the coastal and marshy areas. Fortunately, neither insect carries malaria or other diseases. Keep these pests at bay with a good insect repellent.

It's especially important to protect yourself against **sunburn.** Don't underestimate the strength of the sun's rays down there, even in the middle of winter. Limit your exposure to the sun, especially during the first few days of your trip and, thereafter, from 11am to 2pm. Use a sunscreen with a high protection factor and apply it liberally. Remember that children need more protection than adults do.

Pack any **prescription medications** you need to take in your carry-on luggage. Also bring along copies of your prescriptions in case you lose your pills or run out.

If you suffer from a chronic illness, consult your doctor before your departure. For conditions like epilepsy, diabetes, or heart problems, wear a **Medic Alert Identification Tag** (☎ **800/825-3785;** www.commedicalert.org), which will immediately alert doctors to your condition and give them access to your records through Medic Alert's 24-hour hotline. Membership is $35, plus a $15 annual fee. If you have dental problems, a nationwide referral service known as ☎ **1-800/DENTIST (336-8478)** will provide the name of a nearby dentist or clinic.

INSURANCE

Many travelers buy insurance policies providing health and accident, trip-cancellation and -interruption, and lost-luggage protection. The coverage you should consider will depend on how you're getting to Florida and how much protection is already contained in your existing health insurance or other policies. Some credit- and charge-card companies may insure you against travel accidents if you buy plane, train, or bus tickets with their cards. Before purchasing additional insurance, read your policies and agreements carefully. Call your insurers or credit/charge-card companies if you have any questions.

Among the reputable issuers of travel insurance are **Access America,** 6600 W. Broad St., Richmond, VA 23230 (☎ 800/284-8300); **Travel Guard International,** 1145 Clark St., Stevens Point, WI 54481 (☎ 800/826-1300); **Travel Insured**

International, Inc., P.O. Box 280568, East Hartford, CT 06128 (☎ 800/243-3174); **Travelex Insurance Services,** P.O. Box 9408, Garden City, NY 11530-9408 (☎ 800/228-9792); and **Worldwide Assistance,** 1133 15th St. NW, Washington, DC 20005 (☎ 800/821-2828 or 202/828-5894). Scuba divers can sign up with **Divers Alert Network (DAN)** (☎ 800/446-2671 or 919/684-2948).

5 Tips for Travelers with Special Needs

FOR TRAVELERS WITH DISABILITIES

Walt Disney World and Universal Studios do everything possible to assist guests with disabilities. Disney's many services are detailed in their *Guidebook for Guests with Disabilities.* For a free copy, contact Guest Letters, P.O. Box 10,040, Lake Buena Vista, FL 32830-0040 (☎ **407/824-4321**). For information about Universal Studios, CityWalk, and Islands of Adventure, contact **Universal Studios Florida,** 1000 Universal Studios Dr., Orlando, FL 32816 (☎ **407/393-8080**).

A free copy of the *Planning Guide for Travelers with Disability* is available from Visit Florida (see "Visitor Information," above).

Nationwide resources include **Mobility International USA,** P.O. Box 10767, Eugene, OR 97440 (☎ **541/343-1284** voice and TDD; www.miusa.org), which offers its members travel-accessibility information and has many interesting travel programs for those with disabilities. The **Moss Rehab Hospital** (☎ 215/456-9600) has been providing friendly and helpful phone advice and referrals to disabled travelers for years through its **Travel Information Service** (☎ **215/456-9603;** www. mossresourcenet.org). You can join **The Society for the Advancement of Travel for the Handicapped (SATH),** 347 Fifth Ave., Suite 610, New York, NY 10016 (☎ **212/447-7284;** fax 212/725-8253; www.sath.org), to gain access to their vast network of connections in the travel industry. They provide information sheets on travel destinations, and referrals to tour operators that specialize in traveling with disabilities. Their quarterly magazine, *Open World for Disability and Mature Travel,* is full of good information and resources. In addition, **Twin Peaks Press,** P.O. Box 129, Vancouver, WA 98666 (☎ **360/694-2462**), publishes travel-related books for people with disabilities.

Travelers with disabilities may also want to consider joining a tour that caters specifically to them. One of the best operators is **Flying Wheels Travel,** 143 W. Bridge (P.O. Box 382), Owatonna, MN 55060 (☎ **800/535-6790**). They offer various escorted tours and cruises, with an emphasis on sports, as well as private tours in minivans with lifts. Other reputable specialized tour operators include **Access Adventures** (☎ **716/889-9096**), which offers sports-related vacations; **Accessible Journeys** (☎ **800/TINGLES** or 610/521-0339), for slow walkers and wheelchair travelers; **The Guided Tour, Inc.** (☎ **215/782-1370**); **Wilderness Inquiry** (☎ **800/728-0719** or 612/379-3858); and **Directions Unlimited** (☎ **800/533-5343**).

You can obtain a copy of *Air Transportation of Handicapped Persons* by writing to Free Advisory Circular No. AC12032, Distribution Unit, U.S. Department of Transportation, Publications Division, M-4332, Washington, DC 20590.

In addition, both **Amtrak** (☎ **800/USA-RAIL;** www.amtrak.com) and **Greyhound** (☎ **800/752-4841;** www.greyhound.com) offer special fares and services for travelers with disabilities. Call at least a week in advance of your trip for details.

Avis (☎ **800/331-1212;** www.avis.com), **Hertz** (☎ **800/654-3131;** www. hertz.com), and other major car-rental companies offer hand-controlled cars for drivers with disabilities. They require reservations, so call well in advance. **Wheelchair Getaways** (☎ **800/873-4973;** www.blvd.com/wg.htm) rents specialized vans with wheelchair lifts and other disability-related features in more than 100 cities across the United States.

Vision-impaired travelers should contact the **American Foundation for the Blind,** 11 Penn Plaza, Suite 300, New York, NY 10001 (☎ **800/232-5463**), for information on traveling with Seeing Eye dogs.

FOR SENIORS

With one of the largest retired populations of any state, Florida offers a wide array of activities and benefits for senior citizens. Don't be shy about asking for discounts, but always carry some kind of identification, such as a driver's license, that shows your date of birth.

Also, mention the fact that you're a senior citizen when you first make your travel reservations. For example, both **Amtrak** (☎ **800/USA-RAIL;** www.amtrak.com) and **Greyhound** (☎ **800/752-4841;** www.greyhound.com) offer discounts to persons over 62. And many hotels offer seniors discounts, including the **Choice Hotels** (Clarion Hotels, Quality Inns, Comfort Inns, Sleep Inns, Econo Lodges, Friendship Inns, and Rodeway Inns), which give 30% off their published rates to anyone over 50, provided you book your room through their nationwide toll-free reservations numbers (that is, not directly with the hotels or through a travel agent).

Members of the **American Association of Retired Persons (AARP),** 601 E. St. NW, Washington, DC 22049 (☎ **800/424-3410** or 202/434-2277), get discounts not only on hotels but on airfares and car rentals, too.

Other helpful organizations include the **National Council of Senior Citizens,** 8403 Colesville Rd., Suite 1200, Silver Spring, MD 20910 (☎ **301/578-8800**), a nonprofit organization offering a newsletter six times a year (partly devoted to travel tips) and discounts on hotel and auto rentals. **Mature Outlook,** P.O. Box 9390, Des Moines, IA 50306 (☎ **800/336-6330**), began as a travel organization for people over 50, though it now caters to people of all ages. Members receive discounts on hotels and receive a bimonthly magazine. **Golden Companions,** P.O. Box 5249, Reno, NV 89513 (☎ **702/ 324-2227**), helps travelers 45-plus find compatible companions through a personal voice-mail service. Contact them for more information.

Companies specializing in seniors' travel include **Grand Circle Travel,** 347 Congress St., Suite 3A, Boston, MA 02210 (☎ **800/221-2610** or 617/350-7500), and **SAGA International Holidays,** 222 Berkeley St., Boston, MA 02115 (☎ **800/343-0273**).

FOR FAMILIES

Florida is a great family destination, with most of its hotels and restaurants willing and eager to cater to families traveling with children. Many hotels and motels let children 17 and under stay free in their parents' room (be sure to ask when you reserve).

At the beaches, it's the exception rather than the rule for a resort not to have a children's activities program (some will even mind the youngsters while the parents enjoy a night off!). Even if they don't have a children's program of their own, most will arrange baby-sitting services.

If you call ahead before dining out, you'll see that most restaurants have some facilities for children, such as booster chairs and low-priced kids' menus.

In Canada, **Travel CUTS,** 200 Ronson St., Suite 320, Toronto, ON M9W 5Z9 (☎ **800/667-2887** or 416/614-2887; www.travelcuts.com), offers similar services. **Campus Travel,** 52 Grosvenor Gardens, London SW1W 0AG (☎ **0171/730-3402;** www.campustravel.co.uk), opposite Victoria Station, is Britain's leading specialist in student and youth travel.

FOR GAY & LESBIAN TRAVELERS

Florida is not without its intolerant contingent, but there are active gay and lesbian contingents in most cities here. In fact, the editors of *Out and About,* a gay and lesbian newsletter, have said that Miami's **South Beach** is the "hippest, hottest, most happening gay travel destination in the world." For many years that could also be said of **Key West,** which still is one of the country's most popular destinations for gays. **Fort Lauderdale**—where gays own some 21 motels, 40 bars, and numerous other businesses—is definitely on the gay-friendly map.

The popularity of **Orlando** with gay and lesbian travelers is highlighted with Gay Weekend in early June, which draws as many as 40,000 participants and includes events at Disney World, Universal Studios, and Sea World. **Universal City Travel** (☎ 800/224-3838) offers a "Gay Weekend" tour package including tickets to Universal Studios, Sea World, and Church Street Station. For information about events for that weekend, or throughout the year, contact the **Gay & Lesbian Community Services of Central Florida,** 714 E. Colonial Dr., Orlando, FL 32804 (☎ 407/425-4527). You can get information on the World Wide Web at www.gayday.com.

Watermark, P.O. Box 533655, Orlando, FL 32853 (☎ 407/481-2243; fax 407/481-2246; www.watermarkonline.com), is a biweekly tabloid newspaper covering the gay and lesbian scene, including dining and entertainment options, in Orlando, the Tampa Bay Area, and Daytona Beach.

In addition to its editor's choices, *Out and About,* 8 W. 19th St., Suite 401, New York, NY 10011 (☎ 800/929-2268), profiles the best gay or gay-friendly hotels, gyms, clubs, and other places and destinations throughout the world. *Our World,* 1104 N. Nova Rd., Suite 251, Daytona Beach, FL 32117 (☎ 904/441-5367), is a slicker magazine devoted to options and bargains for gay and lesbian travel worldwide.

The International Gay & Lesbian Travel Association (☎ 800/448-8550 or 954/776-2626; fax 954/776-3303; www.iglta.org) links travelers up with the appropriate gay-friendly service organization or tour specialist. Members are kept informed of gay and gay-friendly hoteliers, tour operators, and airline and cruise-line representatives.

General gay and lesbian travel agencies include **Family Abroad** (☎ 800/999-5500 or 212/459-1800), gay and lesbian; **Above and Beyond Tours** (☎ 800/397-2681), mainly gay men; and **Yellowbrick Road** (☎ 800/642-2488), gay and lesbian.

6 Getting There

BY PLANE

Most major domestic airlines fly to and from many Florida cities, including **American** (☎ 800/433-7300; www.americanair.com), **Continental** (☎ 800/525-0280; www.flycontinental.com), **Delta** (☎ 800/221-1212; www.delta-air.com), **Northwest/KLM** (☎ 800/225-2525; www.nwa.com), **TWA** (☎ 800/221-2000; www.twa.com), **United** (☎ 800/241-6522; www.ual.com), and **US Airways** (☎ 800/428-4322; www.usair.com).

Of these, Delta and US Airways have the most extensive network of commuter connections within Florida (see "Getting Around," below).

Several so-called no-frills airlines—low fares but no meals or other amenities—fly to Florida. The biggest is ✪ **Southwest Airlines** (☎ 800/435-9792; www.iflyswa.com), which has flights from many U.S. cities to Fort Lauderdale, Jacksonville, Orlando, and Tampa. An arm of the popular cruise line, **Carnival Air** (☎ 800/824-7386) flies from New York and Washington, D.C., to Fort Lauderdale. **AirTran**

(☎ **800/AIR-TRAN;** www.airtran.com) flies from several Northeast, Midwest, and Southern cities to its hub in Orlando and several other Florida cities.

Others flying to Florida include **Delta Express,** a branch of Delta Airlines (☎ 800/ 325-5205); **Eastwind** (☎ 800/644-3592); **MetroJet,** an arm of US Airways (☎ 800/ 428-4322); **Midway** (☎ 800/44-MIDWAY); **Midwest Express** (☎ 800/452-2022); **Spirit** (☎ 800/722-7117); **SunJet** (☎ 800/478-6538); **Tower Air** (☎ 800/ 348-6937); and **Vanguard** (☎ 800/826-4827).

FINDING THE BEST AIRFARE

There's no shortage of **discounted and promotional fares** to Florida. November, December, and January often see fare wars that can result in savings of 50% or more. Watch for advertisements in your local newspaper and on TV, call the airlines, or check out their Web sites (see the "Cyber Deals for Net Surfers" box in this chapter).

Ask for their lowest fares, and ask if it's cheaper to book in advance, fly in midweek, or stay over a Saturday night. Don't stop at the 7-day advance purchase; ask how much the 14- and 30-day plans cost. Many of the best deals are nonrefundable.

No-frills airlines have reduced their price advantage, but some **charter flights** still go to Florida, especially during the winter season and particularly from Canada, such as **Air Transat** (☎ 800/470-1011) and **Canada 3000** (☎ 800/993-4378). They often cost less than regularly scheduled flights, but they are very complicated. It's best to go to a good travel agent and ask him or her to find a charter flight for you and to explain the disadvantages as well as the advantages.

Also known as bucket shops, **consolidators** are a good place to find low fares. Consolidators buy seats in bulk from the airlines and then sell them back to the public at prices below even the airlines' discounted rates. Their small boxed ads usually run in the Sunday travel section at the bottom of the page. Before you pay, however, ask for a confirmation number from the consolidator and then call the airline itself to confirm your seat. Be prepared to book your ticket with a different consolidator—there are many to choose from—if the airline can't confirm your reservation. Also be aware that bucket-shop tickets are usually nonrefundable or rigged with stiff cancellation penalties, often as high as 50% to 75% of the ticket price.

Among the consolidators, **Council Travel** (☎ 800/226-8624; www.counciltravel. com) and **STA Travel** (☎ 800/781-4040; www.sta.travel.com) cater especially to young travelers, but their bargain-basement prices are available to people of all ages. **Travel Bargains** (☎ 800/AIR-FARE; www.1800airfare.com) was formerly owned by TWA but now offers the deepest discounts on many other airlines, with a four-day advance purchase. Other reliable consolidators include **1-800-FLY-CHEAP** (www.1800flycheap. com); **TFI Tours International** (☎ 800/745-8000 or 212/736-1140), which serves as a clearinghouse for unused seats; or "rebaters" such as **Travel Avenue** (☎ 800/ 333-3335 or 312/876-1116) and the **Smart Traveller** (☎ 800/ 448-3338 in the U.S. or 305/448-3338), which rebate part of their commissions to you.

Another possibility is a travel club such as **Moment's Notice** (☎ 718/234-6295) and **Sears Discount Travel Club** (☎ 800/433-9383, or 800/255-1487 to join), which supply unsold tickets at discounted prices. You pay an annual membership fee to get the club's hotline number. Of course, you're limited to what's available, so you have to be flexible. You may not even have to join these clubs to get the deals, however, since some airlines now unload unsold seats directly through their Web sites (see the "Cyber Deals for Net Surfers" box in this chapter).

For tips on how to find great deals on the Internet, refer to Frommer's Online Directory a the end of the book.

If you live overseas, see "Getting to & Around the U.S.," in chapter 3.

BY CAR

Florida is reached by I-95 along the east coast, I-75 from the central states, and I-10 from the west. The Florida Turnpike, a toll road, links Orlando, West Palm Beach, Fort Lauderdale, and Miami (it's a shortcut from Wildwood on I-75 north of Orlando to Miami). I-4 cuts across the state from Cape Canaveral through Orlando to Tampa.

See "Getting Around," below, for more information about driving in Florida and the car-rental firms operating here.

If you're a member, your local branch of the **American Automobile Association (AAA)** will provide a free trip-routing plan. AAA also has nationwide emergency road service (☎ **800/AAA-HELP**).

BY TRAIN

Amtrak (☎ **800/USA-RAIL;** www.amtrak.com) offers train service to Florida from both the east and west coasts. It takes some 26 hours from New York to Miami, and 68 hours from Los Angeles to Miami, and Amtrak's fares aren't much less—if not more—than many of the airlines' lowest fares.

Amtrak's *Silver Meteor* and *Silver Star* each run twice daily between New York and either Miami or Tampa, with intermediate stops along the East Coast and in Florida. Amtrak's Thruway Bus Connections are available from the Fort Lauderdale Amtrak station and Miami International Airport to Key West, and from Tampa to St. Petersburg, Treasure Island, Clearwater, Bradenton, Sarasota, and Fort Myers. From the West Coast, the *Sunset Limited* runs three times weekly between Los Angeles and Orlando. It stops in Pensacola, Crestview (north of Fort Walton Beach and Destin), Chipley (north of Panama City Beach), and Tallahassee. Sleeping accommodations are available for an extra charge.

If you intend to stop off along the way, you can save money with Amtrak's Explore America (or All Aboard America) fares, which are based on three regions of the country.

Amtrak's Auto Train runs daily from Lorton, Virginia (12 miles south of Washington, D.C.), to Sanford, Florida (just northeast of Orlando). You ride in a coach while your car is secured in an enclosed vehicle carrier. You should make your train reservations as far in advance as possible.

7 Escorted & Package Tours

More than 120 travel agents offer hundreds of package-tour options to the Sunshine State. Quite often these deals will result in savings not just on airfares but on hotels and other activities as well. You pay one price for a package that varies from one tour operator to the next. Airfare, transfers, and accommodations are always covered, and sometimes meals and specific activities are thrown in.

Before you start your search for the lowest airfare, therefore, you may want to consider booking your flight as part of a travel package such as an escorted tour or a package tour. What you lose in adventure, you could gain in time and money saved when you book accommodations, and maybe even food and entertainment, along with your flight—but not necessarily, as I point out under "Package Tours," below.

ESCORTED TOURS

Some people love escorted tours. They let you relax and take in the sights while a bus driver fights traffic for you and a guide explains what you're seeing. They spell out your costs up front, and they take you to the maximum number of sights in the minimum

Cyber Deals for Net Surfers

It's possible to get some great deals on airfare, hotels, and car rentals via the Internet. Grab your mouse and surf before you take off—you could save a bundle on your trip. The Web sites highlighted below are worth checking out, especially since all services are free (you'll pay for the tickets, of course). Always call the airlines or a travel agent and ask the lowest published fare before you shop for flights online.

Arthur Frommer's Budget Travel (www.frommers.com)   Home of the *Encyclopedia of Travel* and *Arthur Frommer's Budget Travel* magazine and daily newsletter, this site offers detailed information on 200 cities and islands around the world, and up-to-the-minute ways to save dramatically on flights, hotels, car reservations, and cruises. Book an entire vacation online and research your destination before you leave. Consult the message board to set up "hospitality exchanges" in other countries, to talk with other travelers who have visited a hotel you're considering, or to direct travel questions to Arthur Frommer himself. The newsletter is updated daily to keep you abreast of the latest-breaking ways to save, to publicize new hot spots and best buys, and to present veteran readers with fresh, ever-changing approaches to travel.

Microsoft Expedia (www.expedia.com)   The best part of this multipurpose travel site is the "Fare Tracker." You fill out a form on the screen indicating that you're interested in cheap flights from your hometown, and, once a week, they'll e-mail you the best airfare deals on up to three destinations. The site's "Travel Agent" will steer you to bargains on hotels and car rentals, and with the help of hotel and airline-seat pinpointers, you can book everything right online. This site is even useful once you're booked. Before you depart, log on to Expedia for maps and up-to-date travel information, including weather reports and foreign exchange rates.

Travelocity (www.travelocity.com)   This is one of the best travel sites out there, especially for finding cheap airfare. In addition to its "Personal Fare Watcher," which notifies you via e-mail of the lowest airfares for up to five different destinations, Travelocity will track the three lowest fares for any routes on any dates in minutes. You can book a flight right then and there, and if you need a rental car or hotel, Travelocity will find you the best deal via the SABRE computer reservations system (another huge travel-agent database). Click on "Last Minute Deals" for the latest travel bargains, including a link to "H.O.T. Coupons" (www.hotcoupons.com), where you can print out electronic coupons for travel in the U.S. and Canada.

Trip.com (www.trip.com)   This site is really geared toward the business traveler, but vacationers-to-be can also use Trip.com's exceptionally powerful

amount of time with the least amount of hassle. If you prefer privacy, independence, and spontaneity, however, this kind fo travel just isn't for you.

In 1999, the very reputable **Tauck Tours** (☎ **800/468-2825;** fax 203/221-6828; www.tauck.com) offered an 11-day, 10-night escorted tour beginning in Miami and ending at Walt Disney World in Orlando, with at least 1 day spent in the Keys, Palm Beach, and the Kennedy Space Center along the way. It included accommodations, most meals, bus transportation between the cities, most activities, and a guide—but neither your airfare to join the tour in Miami nor that to return home from Orlando.

fare-finding engine, which will e-mail you every week with the best city-to-city airfare deals for as many as 10 routes. Trip.com uses the Internet Travel Network, another reputable travel-agent database, to book hotels and restaurants.

E-Savers Programs   Several major airlines offer a free e-mail service known as E-Savers, via which they'll send you their best bargain airfares on a regular basis. Here's how it works: Once a week (usually Wed), or whenever a sale fare comes up, subscribers receive a list of discounted flights to and from various destinations, both international and domestic. Here's the catch: These fares are usually available only if you leave the very next Saturday (or sometimes Fri night) and return on the following Monday or Tuesday. It's really a service for the spontaneously inclined and travelers looking for a quick getaway. But the fares are cheap, so it's worth taking a look. If you have a preference for certain airlines (in other words, the ones you fly most frequently), sign up with them first.

Here's a partial list of airlines and their Web sites, where you can not only get on the e-mailing lists, but also book flights directly:

- **AirTran:** www.airtran.com
- **American Airlines:** www.aa.com
- **British Airways:** www.british-airways.com
- **Canadian Airlines International:** www.cdnair.ca
- **Continental Airlines:** www.flycontinental.com
- **Delta Airlines/Delta Express:** www.delta-air.com
- **Northwest Airlines:** www.nwa.com
- **Southwest Airlines:** www.iflyswa.com
- **TWA:** www.twa.com
- **US Airways/MetroJet:** www.usairways.com
- **United Airlines:** www.ual.com
- **Virgin Airways:** www.virgin.com

One caveat: You'll get frequent-flier miles if you purchase one of these fares, but you can't use miles to buy the ticket (look for the sites' frequent flyer links, if any).

Smarter Living (www.smarterliving.com)   If the thought of all that surfing and comparison shopping gives you a headache, then head right for Smarter Living. Sign up for their newsletter service, and every week you'll get a customized e-mail summarizing the discount fares available from your departure city. Smarter Living tracks more than 15 different airlines, so it's a worthwhile time saver.

Depending on season, these "land" costs ranged from $2,575 to $2,930 per person, double occupancy ($3,515 to $4,220 if you traveled alone). The hotels were all top end, so this was a good deal, especially during the high winter season in South Florida.

If you do choose an escorted tour, you should ask a lot of questions before you buy:

What is the **cancellation policy?** Do they require a deposit? Can they cancel the trip if they don't get enough people? Do you get a refund if they cancel? If you cancel? How late can you cancel if you are unable to go? When do you pay in full?

How busy is the **schedule?** How much sightseeing do they plan each day? Do they allow ample time for relaxing by the pool, shopping, or wandering?

What is the **size** of the group? The smaller the group, the more flexible the itinerary, and the less time you'll spend waiting for people to get on and off the bus. Tour operators may be evasive about this, because they may not know the exact size of the group until everybody has made their reservations; but they should be able to give you a rough estimate. Some tours have a minimum group size and may cancel the tour if they don't book enough people.

What is included in the **price?** Don't assume anything. You may have to pay for transportation to and from the airport. A box lunch may be included in an excursion, but drinks might cost extra. Beer might be included, but wine might not. Can you opt out of certain activities, or does the bus leave once a day, with no exceptions? Are all your meals planned in advance? Can you choose your entree at dinner, or does everybody get the same chicken cutlet?

If you choose an escorted tour, think strongly about purchasing **travel insurance** from an independent agency, especially if the tour operator asks you to pay up front. See "Health & Insurance," above).

One final caveat: Because escorted tour prices are based on double occupancy, the single traveler is usually penalized (see the Tauck Tours example cited above).

PACKAGE TOURS

Package tours are not the same thing as escorted tours. They are simply a way to buy airfare and accommodations at the same time. If you plan to spend your time at one destination, such as Walt Disney World and Orlando, they are a smart way to go. In many cases, a package that includes airfare, hotel, and transportation to and from the airport will cost you less than just the hotel alone would have, had you booked it yourself. That's because packages are sold in bulk to tour operators—who resell them to the public at a cost that drastically undercuts standard rates.

In addition to these all-inclusive tours, many Florida hotels and resorts and even some motels offer **golf and tennis packages,** which bundle the cost of the room, greens and court fees, and sometimes equipment, into one price. These deals usually don't include airfare, but they do represent savings over paying for the room and golf or tennis separately. See the accommodations sections in the following chapters for hostelries offering special packages to their guests.

A few words of **caution** are in order.

First, given the propensity of discounted airfares to Florida, and the number of hotels here offering various room-and-activities packages, especially during the off-seasons, you could save just as much by making your own arrangements. This is particularly true if you're renting a car and don't need transportation from and to the airport, a cost often included in package plans.

Second, think twice before buying a package which includes meals. Many hotels include breakfasts in their rates anyway, as indicated at the top of the listings in this book. Also, Florida has a multitude of good restaurants in all price ranges, and prepaying for a dinner package could mean shelling out twice if you decide to dine out.

Third, the least-expensive tours may put you up at a bottom-end hotel. And since the lower costs depend on volume, some more-expensive tours could send you to a large, impersonal property. And since the tour prices are based on double occupancy, the single traveler is almost invariably penalized.

Fourth, ask the same questions you would of an escorted tour operator (see above).

FINDING A PACKAGE OR ESCORTED TOUR

In Orlando, the **Walt Disney World Central Reservations Office** (☎ 407/W-DISNEY) and **Universal City Travel Co.** (☎ 800/224-3838) both have numerous packages including air, hotel, and discounted admissions.

The massive retail chain Wal-Mart has its own travel agency, **Wal-Mart Vacations** (☎ 888/252-7157), which offers cut-rate packages to Orlando. Likewise, members of the warehouse chain **Costco** can take advantage of its discount travel offerings.

Premier Cruise Lines (☎ 800/726-5678) and **Disney Cruise Line** (☎ 407/939-7787) offer 3- and 4-night luxury ocean cruises to the Bahamas in conjunction with 3- or 4-day Orlando theme-park package vacations. Cruises depart from and return to Port Canaveral, 45 minutes east of Walt Disney World.

The major airlines package their flights to Florida together with accommodations. These include **America West Vacations** (☎ 800/356-6611; fax 602/3505), **American Airlines Vacations** (☎ 800/321-2121; fax 800/472-2987; www.americanair.com), **Continental Airlines Vacations** (☎ 800/634-5555; fax 954/357-4661; www.flycontinental.com), **Delta Vacations** (☎ 800/367-9112; fax 954/468-4765; www.deltavacations.com), **Midwest Express Vacations** (☎ 800/444-4479; fax 414/351-5256), **Northwest WorldVacations** (☎ 800/727-1111; fax 800/655-7890; www.nwa.com), **Southwest Airlines Vacations** (☎ 800/524-6442; fax 407/857-0232; www.iflyswa.com), and **US Airways Vacations** (☎ 800/455-0123).

Another option is the old, reliable **American Express Vacations** (☎ 800/241-1700; fax 954/357-4682; www.leisureweb.com). Check out its **Last Minute Travel Bargains** Web site, offered in conjunction with **Continental Airlines** (www6.americanexpress.com/travel/lastminutetravel/default.asp), with deeply discounted vacation packages and reduced airline fares that differ from the E-Savers bargains that Continental e-mails weekly to subscribers. **Northwest Airlines** offers a similar service. Posted on Northwest's Web site (www.nwa.com) every Wednesday, its "Cyber Saver Bargain Alerts" offer special hotel rates, package deals, and discounted airline fares.

For one-stop shopping on the Web, go to **www.vacationpackager.com**, a search engine that will link you to many different package-tour operators offering Florida vacations.

One of the biggest packagers in the Northeast, **Liberty Travel** (☎ 888/271-1584; www.libertytravel.com) usually boasts a full-page ad in Sunday papers. You won't get much in the way of service, but you will get a good deal.

The biggest hotel chains and resorts often offer package deals. If you already know where you want to stay, call the resort itself and ask if they can offer land/air packages.

Another good place to search is the travel section of your local Sunday newspaper. Also check the ads in the back of national travel magazines like *Travel & Leisure*, *National Geographic Traveler*, and *Condé Nast Traveler*.

8 Getting Around

Having a car is the best and easiest way to see Florida's sights, or just to get to and from the beach. Public transportation is available only in the cities and larger towns, and even there it may provide infrequent or even inadequate service. When it comes to getting from one city to another, cars and planes are the ways to go.

BY PLANE

The commuter arms of **Delta** (☎ 800/221-1212; www.delta-air.com) and **US Airways** (☎ 800/428-4322; www.usair.com) provide extensive service between Florida's major cities and towns. They have several daily flights between Miami, Orlando, and Tampa, much fewer to and from the smaller cities and towns.

   Gulf Stream International (☎ 800/992-8532) has an in-state network, and **Cape Air** (☎ 800/352-0714) flies between Key West, Fort Myers, and Naples. Fares for these short hops tend to be reasonable.

BY CAR

Jacksonville is about 350 miles north of Miami and 500 miles north of Key West, so don't underestimate how long it will take you to drive all the way down the state. The speed limit is either 65 m.p.h. or 70 m.p.h. on the rural interstate highways, so you can make good time between cities. Not so on U.S. 1, U.S. 17, U.S. 19, U.S. 41, and U.S. 301; although most have four lanes, these older highways tend to be heavily congested, especially in built-up areas.

   Every major car-rental company is represented here, including **Alamo** (☎ 800/327-9633; www.goalamo.com), **Avis** (☎ 800/331-1212; www.avis.com), **Budget** (☎ 800/527-0700; www.budgetrentacar.com), **Dollar** (☎ 800/800-4000; www.dollarcar.com), **Enterprise** (☎ 800/325-8007; pickenterprise.com), **Hertz** (☎ 800/654-3131; www.hertz.com), **National** (☎ 800/227-7368; www.natoinalcar.com), **Thrifty** (☎ 800/367-2277; www.thrifty.com), and **Value** (☎ 800/GO-VALUE; www.go-value.com).

   If you decide to rent a car, shop around and ask a lot of questions. The rental firms aren't going to volunteer to save you money, but competition in their industry is fierce. Their reservations clerks are used to being asked for the lowest rate available, and most will find it in order to get your business. You may have to try different dates, different pickup and drop-off points, and different discount offers yourself to find the best deal. It changes constantly. Also, if you're a member of any organization (AARP or AAA, for example), be sure to ask if you're entitled to discounts.

   Check the rental firms' Web sites. Most will automatically bring up the lowest available rate, and there are boxes to click if you are an association member or have a discount coupon.

   State and local **taxes** will add as much as 20% to your final bill. Local sales taxes will tack on at least 6% to the total, and you'll pay an additional $2.05 per day in statewide use tax. Some airports add another 35¢ per day and as much as 10% in "recovery" fees.

   Most of the companies pad their profits by selling Loss/Damage Waiver (LDW) insurance at $15 or more per day. You may already be covered by your insurance carrier and credit- or charge-card companies, so check with them before succumbing to the hard sell.

   Also, the rental companies will offer to refill your gas tank at "competitive" prices when you return. Some of their come-ons for this service quote the "average" price of a gallon of gasoline in town. Since most of their vehicles use regular unleaded gasoline, not the more expensive higher-octane fuels, this can be downright misleading. Regular gas usually is less expensive in town.

   Most companies also require a minimum age, ranging from 19 to 25, and some also set maximum ages. Others deny cars to anyone with a bad driving record. Ask about rental requirements and restrictions when you book to avoid problems later. You must have a valid credit card to rent a vehicle.

   Many packages are available that include airfare, accommodations, and a rental car with unlimited mileage. Compare these prices with the cost of booking airline tickets and renting a car separately to see if these offers are good deals.

Florida Driving Times & Distances

Pensacola
102
2:12
194
3:52
Panama
City
98
2:05
Tallahassee
111
2:04
Lake City
65
1:15
Callahan
22
0:29
Jacksonville
43
0:55
St. Augustine
170
3:31
84
1:38
104
2:02
65
1:23
Ocala
249
5:29
78
1:38
Daytona Beach
94
109
1:46
83
2:15
85
1:23
66
1:23
Orlando
45
0:55
Cocoa
Tampa
84
1:36
55
172
3:17
82
1:43
St. Petersburg
57
1:10
22
0:28
Lake
Wales
Ft.
Pierce
22
0:36
148
2:48
Sarasota
174
3:34
197
4:07
65
1:23
79
1:33
121
2:35
West
Palm
Beach
Ft. Myers
42
0:49
78
1:38
Naples
106
2:08
Miami
156
4:19
Key West

DRIVING DISTANCES
Miles 78
Average Time (Excluding Stops) 1:38

BY TRAIN

You'll find that train travel from destination to destination isn't terribly feasible in Florida, and it's not much less expensive than flying, if at all. See "Getting There," above, for Florida towns served by **Amtrak** (☎ **800/USA-RAIL;** www.amtrak.com).

9 The Active Vacation Planner

Florida will keep active vacationers very busy. Bird watching, boating and sailing, camping, canoeing and kayaking, fishing, golfing, tennis—you name it, the Sunshine State has it. In fact, you'll find them almost everywhere you go. Of course, beach lovers and water-sports enthusiasts can indulge their passions almost anywhere along the state's lengthy coastlines. Merely head east or west, and you'll easily find plenty to do—or viewed another way, Florida's multitudinous water-sports operators will find you.

These and other activities are described in the outdoor activities sections of the following chapters, but here's a brief overview of some of the best places to move your muscles, with tips on how to get more detailed information.

The **Florida Sports Foundation,** 2964 Wellington Circle N., Tallahassee, FL 32308 (☎ **850/488-8347;** fax 850/922-0482; www.flasports.com), publishes free brochures, calendars, schedules, and guides to outdoor pursuits and spectator sports throughout Florida. I've noted some of its specific publications in the sections below.

For excellent color maps of state parks, campgrounds, canoe trails, aquatic preserves, caverns, and more, contact the **Florida Department of Environmental Protection,** Office of Communications, 3900 Commonwealth Blvd., Tallahassee, FL 32399 (☎ **850/488-6327**). Some of the department's publications are mentioned below.

ACTIVITIES A TO Z

BICYCLING & IN-LINE SKATING   Florida's relatively flat terrain makes it ideal for riding bikes and skating on blades. You can bike right into the Everglades National Park along the 38-mile Main Park Road, for example, and bike or skate from St. Petersburg to Tarpon Springs on the 47-mile converted railroad bed known as the Pinellas Trail. Many towns and cities have designated routes for cyclists, skaters, joggers, and walkers, such as the paved pathways running the length of Sanibel Island, the lovely Bayshore Boulevard in Tampa, and the bike lanes from downtown Sarasota out to St. Armands, Lido, and Longboat keys. We've detailed all the many options in the following chapters.

Florida Outback Bike & Boat Tours (☎ **888/269-1169** or 407/518-9311) has biking and kayaking excursions to the Everglades. The national companies **Vermont Bicycle Touring** (☎ **800/537-3850** or 802/453-4811) and **Backroads Bicycle Touring** (☎ **800/462-2848** or 510/527-1555; www.backroads.com) sometimes offer Florida bike tours for cyclists of all fitness levels.

BIRD-WATCHING   With hundreds of both land- and sea-based species, Florida is one of America's best places for bird-watching. We've picked the best places in chapter 1, but birds are everywhere in Florida—if you're not careful, pelicans will even steal your picnic lunch on the historic Naples Pier. The J. N. "Ding" Darling National Wildlife Refuge is great for watching, and it shares Sanibel Island with luxury resorts and fine restaurants.

The Florida Audubon Society manages four exceptional sites: Corkscrew Swamp Sanctuary near Naples, Madalyn Baldwin Center for Birds of Prey in Maitland, Turkey Creek Wildlife Sanctuary in Palm Bay, and Sabal Point Wildlife Sanctuary on the Wekiva River in Central Florida.

Many of the state's wildlife preserves have gift shops that carry books about Florida's birds, including the *Florida Wildlife Viewing Guide,* in which authors Susan Cerulean and Ann Morrow profile 96 great parks, refuges, and preserves throughout the state.

BOATING & SAILING   With some 1,350 miles of shoreline, it's not surprising that Florida is a boating and sailing mecca. In fact, you won't be anyplace near the water very long before you see flyers and other advertisements for rental boats and for cruises on sailboats. Many of them are mentioned in the following chapters.

The Moorings, the worldwide sailboat charter company, has its headquarters in Clearwater and its Florida yacht base nearby in St. Petersburg (☎ **800/437-7880** or 813/530-5424; www.moorings.com). From St. Pete, experienced sailors can take its bareboats as far as the Keys and the Dry Tortugas, out in the Gulf of Mexico.

Key West keeps gaining prominence as a world sailing capital. *Yachting* magazine sponsors the largest winter regatta in America here each January, and smaller events take place regularly.

Even if you've never hauled on a halyard, you can learn the art of sailing at Steve and Doris Colgate's Offshore Sailing School, headquartered at the South Seas

Plantation Resort & Yacht Harbour on Captiva Island, and at the prestigious Annapolis Sailing School, which has bases in St. Petersburg and on Marathon in the Keys.

If you don't want to do any real work on the water, you can rent a houseboat along the St. John's River in the northeastern part of the state; contact the **Hontoon Landing Marina,** 2317 River Ridge Rd., in Deland (☎ **904/734-2474**). In the Everglades, houseboat rentals are available through the **Flamingo Lodge** (☎ **800/ 600-3813** or 941/695-3101). You might also try **Houseboat Vacations of the Florida Keys,** MM 85.9 on Islamorada (☎ **305/664-4009**), or **Houseboat Rentals of Southwest Florida** in Naples (☎ **941/775-2003;** www.ivacation.com/ p6950.htm). Book everything well in advance.

The free *Florida Boating & Fishing* has tips about safe boating in the state, available from the Florida Sports Foundation (see the introduction to this section, above). The annual *Florida Cruising Directory* is a treasure trove of regulations, locations of marinas, hotels, and resorts, marine products and services, and more, in magazine format. You can tap into the auxiliary Web site at www.floridafishing-boating.com.

CAMPING   Florida is literally dotted with RV parks (if you own such a vehicle, it's the least expensive way to spend your winters here). But for the best tent camping, look to Florida's national preserves and 110 state parks and recreation areas. Options range from luxury sites with hot-water showers and cable TV hookups to primitive island and beach camping with no facilities whatsoever.

Primitive camping in St. Joseph Peninsula State Park near Apalachicola, in fact, is a bird-watcher's dream, and you'll be on one of the nation's most magnificent beaches. Equally great are the sands at St. Andrews State Recreation Area in Panama City Beach (with sites right beside the bay). Other top spots are Fort DeSoto Park in St. Pete Beach, the remarkably preserved Cayo Costa Island State Park between Boca Grande and Captiva Island in Southwest Florida, Canaveral National Seashore near the Kennedy Space Center, Anastasia State Recreation Area in St. Augustine, Fort Clinch State Park on Amelia Island, and Bill Baggs Cape Florida Recreation Area on Key Biscayne in Miami. Down in the Keys, the oceanside sites in Long Key State Recreation Area are about as nice it gets.

Many sites are accessible only by boat, such as the chickee huts (round, square, or rectangular thatch or tin roofs supported by poles, with open sides) on stilts in Everglades National Park and the backcountry sites in Caladesi Island State Park off Clearwater and Collier Seminole State Park near Marco Island.

These are all popular campgrounds, so reservations are essential, especially in the high seasons. All of Florida's state parks take bookings up to 11 months in advance.

The **Florida Department of Environmental Protection,** Division of Recreation and Parks, Mail Station 535, 3900 Commonwealth Blvd., Tallahassee, FL 32399-3000 (☎ **850/488-9872;** www.dep.state.fl.us/parks), publishes an annual guide of tent and RV sites in Florida's state parks and recreation areas.

Pet owners note: Although pets have not been permitted at state-park beaches, campgrounds, and food service areas, the Florida Department of Environmental Protection was conducting a trial in 1999 to determine if it would change that policy. Before bringing your animal, check with the department or with the individual parks to see if it will be allowed.

For private campgrounds, the **Florida Association of RV Parks & Campgrounds,** 1340 Vickers Dr., Tallahassee, FL 32303 (☎ **850/562-7151;** fax 850/562-7179; www.floridacamping.com), issues an annual Florida Camping Directory with locator maps and details about its member establishments throughout the state.

CANOEING & KAYAKING   From picturesque rivers to sandy coastlines to gigantic Lake Okeechobee, from the marshes of northern and Central Florida to the mangroves of the southwest, canoeists and kayakers have almost limitless options here. We've picked the best in chapter 1, which generally are exceptional trails through parks and wildlife preserves, including **Everglades National Park;** the **J. N. "Ding" Darling National Wildlife Refuge,** on Sanibel Island; and **Collier Seminole State Park** and the **Briggs Nature Center,** both on the edge of the Everglades near Marco Island.

Another local favorite is **Myakka River State Park** near Sarasota, Florida's largest state park with approximately 28,000 acres of pure backcountry.

According to the Florida state legislature, however, the state's official "Canoe Capital" is the Panhandle town of **Milton,** on U.S. 90 near Pensacola. Up there, the Blackwater River, Coldwater River, Sweetwater Creek, and Juniper Creek are perfect for tubing, rafting, and paddleboating, as well as canoeing and kayaking.

Many conservation groups throughout the state offer half-day, day, and overnight canoe trips. For example, **The Conservancy of Naples** (☎ **941/262-0304**) has a popular series of moonlight canoe trips through the mangroves, among other programs.

Based during the winter at Everglades City, on the park's western border, **North American Canoe Tours, Inc.** (☎ **941/695-4666** Nov through Apr, or 860/739-0791 May through Oct), offers 1-day, 4-day, and weeklong guided canoe expeditions through the Everglades. **Florida Outback Bike & Boat Tours** (☎ **888/269-1169** or 407/518-9311) also has kayaking excursions to the Everglades.

Thirty-six creek and river trails, covering 950 miles altogether, are itemized in the excellent free *Canoe Trails* booklet published by the **Florida Department of Environmental Protection,** Office of Communications, 3900 Commonwealth Blvd., Tallahassee, FL 32399 (☎ **850/488-6327;** www.dep.state.fl.us/parks).

Specialized guidebooks include *A Canoeing and Kayaking Guide to the Streams of Florida:* Volume 1, *North Central Florida and Panhandle,* by Elizabeth F. Carter and John L. Eearch, and Volume II, *Central and Southern Peninsula,* by Lou Glaros and Dough Sphar. Both are published by Menasha Ridge Press.

ECO-TOURS   If you don't want to do it yourself, some organizations offer excursions to observe Florida's flora and fauna and have a little adventure while you're at it.

The Florida chapter of the **Nature Conservancy** has protected 578,000 acres of natural lands in Florida and presently owns and manages 36 preserves. For a small fee, you can join one of its field trips or work parties that take place periodically throughout the year; fees vary from year to year, event to event, so call for more information. Participants get a chance to learn about and even participate in the preservation of the ecosystem. For details of all the preserves and adventures, contact the Nature Conservancy, Florida Chapter, 222 S. Westmonte Dr., Suite 300, Altamonte Springs, FL 32714 (☎ **407/682-3664**).

The **Sierra Club,** America's oldest and largest grassroots environmental organization, offers exceptional eco-adventures through its Florida chapters. You can go canoeing or kayaking through the Everglades, hiking the Florida Trail in America's southernmost national forest, camping on a barrier island, or exploring the sinkhole phenomenon in north central Florida. You do have to be a Sierra Club member, but you can join at the time of the trip. Contact the national office at Department J-319, P.O. Box 7959, San Francisco, CA 94120 (☎ **415/923-5653**), for a current outings magazine and local chapter contacts.

Soft eco-adventure experiences are available at **Silver Springs,** a 350-acre nature theme park near Ocala (☎ **800/234-7458** or 352/236-2121). It has been conducting eco-tours since before the term was invented. You can take a sunrise breakfast cruise to photograph great blue herons, white-tail deer, and other wildlife; or you can take a "Jungle Cruise" or "Jeep Safari" to get a feeling of the ecosystem without getting your feet dirty.

FISHING   In addition to the amberjack, bonito, grouper, mackerel, mahimahi, marlin, pompano, redfish, sailfish, snapper, snook, tarpon, tuna, and wahoo running offshore and in its inlets, Florida has countless miles of rivers and streams, plus about 30,000 lakes and springs stocked with more than 100 species of freshwater fish. Indeed, Floridians seem to fish everywhere: off canal banks and old bridges, from fishing piers and fishing fleets. You'll even see them standing alongside the Tamiami Trail (U.S. 41) that cuts across the Everglades—one eye on their line, the other watching for alligators.

We listed our favorite places to fish in chapter 1, but nearly every marina in Florida harbors charter boats. You don't have to pay them a small fortune to try your luck, for most ports also have "party" boats that take groups out to sea. You'll have lots of company, but their rates are reasonable, they provide the gear and bait, and you won't need a fishing license.

Anglers age 16 and older need fishing licenses for any other kind of saltwater or freshwater fishing, including lobstering and spearfishing. Licenses are sold at bait and tackle shops.

The **Florida Department of Environmental Protection,** 3900 Commonwealth Blvd., Tallahassee, FL 32399-3000 (☎ **850/488-7326;** www.dep.state.fl.us/parks), publishes the annual *Fishing Lines,* a free magazine with a wealth of information about fishing in Florida, including regulations and licensing requirements. It also distributes free brochures with annual freshwater and saltwater limits. And the **Florida Sports Foundation** (see the introduction to this section, above) publishes *Florida Fishing & Boating,* another treasure trove of information.

GOLF   Florida is the unofficial golf capital of the United States—some would say the world, since the **World Golf Hall of Fame** has moved into its new home near St. Augustine. This state-of-the-art museum and shrine is worth a brief visit even if you're not in love with the game.

One thing's for certain: Florida has more golf courses than any other state—more than 1,150 at last count and growing. We picked the best in chapter 1, but suffice it to say that you can tee off almost anytime and anywhere. The highest concentration of excellent courses is in Southwest Florida around Naples and Fort Myers (some 1,000 holes!), in the Orlando area (Disney alone has 99 holes open to the public), and in the Panhandle around Destin and Panama City Beach. And it's a rare town in Florida that doesn't have a municipal golf course—even Key West has 18 great holes.

Greens fees are usually much lower at the municipal courses than at privately owned clubs. Whether public or private, greens fees tend to vary greatly depending on the time of year. You could pay $150 or more at a private course during the high season, but less than half that when the tourists are gone. The fee structures vary so much that it's best to call ahead and ask, and always reserve a tee time as far in advance as possible.

You can learn the game or hone your strokes at one of several excellent golf schools in the state. David Ledbetter has teaching facilities in Orlando and Naples, Fred Griffin is in charge of the Grand Cypress Academy of Golf at Grand Cypress Resort in Orlando, and you'll find Jimmy Ballard's school at the Ocean Reef Club on Key Largo. The Westin Innisbrook Resort at Tarpon Springs has its Innisbrook Golf

Institute, Amelia Island near Jacksonville is home to Amelia Island Plantation Golf School, and Saddlebrook Resort north of Tampa hosts the Arnold Palmer Golf Academy.

You can get information about most Florida courses, including current greens fees, and reserve tee times through **Tee Times USA,** P.O. Box 641, Flagler Beach, FL 32136 (☎ **800/374-8633,** 888/465-3567, or 904/439-0001; fax 904/439-0099). This company also publishes a vacation guide which includes many stay-and-play golf packages.

Florida Destination Golf, published by the **Florida Sports Foundation** (see the introduction to this section, above), lists every course in Florida. *Golfer's Guide* magazine publishes monthly editions covering most regions of Florida; it is available free at all the local visitor centers and hotel lobbies, or you can contact the magazine at P.O. Box 5926, Hilton Head, SC 29938 (☎ **800/864-6101** or 803/842-7878; fax 803/842-5743; www.homes.com). Northwest Florida is covered by *Gulf Coast Tee Time,* published by Tee Time LLC, 3 W. Garden St., Pensacola, FL 32501 (☎ **888/ 520-4300** or 850/435-4858; fax 850/435-7383; www.teetimeweb.com).

You also can get more information from the **Professional Golfers' Association (PGA),** 100 Avenue of the Champions, Palm Beach Gardens, FL 33418 (☎ **407/ 624-8400**), or the **Ladies Professional Golf Association (LPGA),** 2570 Volusia Ave., Suite B, Daytona Beach, FL 32114 (☎ **904/254-8800**).

HIKING   There are thousands of beautiful hiking trails in Florida. The ideal hiking months are October through April, when the weather is cool and dry and mosquitoes are less prominent. Like anywhere else, you'll find trails that are gentle and short and others that are challenging—some trails in the Everglades require you to wade waist-deep in water!

If you're venturing into the backcountry, watch out for gators, and don't ever try to feed them (or any wild animal). You risk getting bitten (they can't tell the difference between the food and your hand). You're also upsetting the balance of nature, since animals fed by humans lose their ability to find their own food. Most Florida snakes are harmless, but because a few have deadly bites, it's a good idea to avoid them all.

The **Florida Trail Association,** P.O. Box 13708, Gainesville, FL 32604 (☎ **800/ 343-1882** or 352/378-8823), maintains a large percentage of the public trails in the state and puts out an excellent book packed with maps, details, and color photos.

For a copy of *Florida Trails,* which outlines the many options, contact Visit Florida (see "Visitor Information," above). Another resource is *A Guide to Your National Scenic Trails,* Office of Greenways and Trails, Department of Environmental Protection, 3900 Commonwealth Blvd., Tallahassee, FL 32399 (☎ **850/ 487-4784**). You can also contact the office of **National Forests in Florida,** Woodcrest Office Park, 325 John Knox Rd., Suite F-100, Tallahassee, FL 32303 (☎ **850/ 942-9300**). And *Hiking Florida,* by M. Timothy O'Keefe (Falcon Press), details 132 hikes throughout the state, with maps and photos.

The **Florida Conservation Foundation, Inc.,** 1191 Orange Ave., Winter Park, FL 32789 (☎ **407/644-5377**), publishes information about the state's ecology, including "Common Florida Natural Areas," an illustrated brochure explaining what you'll find in each ecosystem.

SCUBA DIVING & SNORKELING   Divers love the Keys, where you can see magnificent formations of tree-sized elk horn coral and giant brain coral, as well as colorful sea fans and dozens of other varieties, sharing space with 300 or more species of rainbow-hued fish. Reef diving is good all the way from Key Largo to Key West, with plenty of tour operators, outfitters, and dive shops along the way. Particularly worthy are **John Pennekamp Coral Reef State Park** in Key Largo and **Looe Key National Marine Sanctuary** off Big Pine Key. *Skin Diver* magazine picked Looe Key as the number one dive spot in North America. Also, the clearest waters in which to view some of the 4,000 sunken ships along Florida's coast are in the Middle Keys and the waters between Key West and the Dry Tortugas. Snorkeling in the Keys is particularly fine between Islamorada and Marathon.

In Northwest Florida, the 100-fathom curve draws closer to the white, sandy Panhandle beaches than to any other spot on the Gulf of Mexico. It's too far north here for coral, but you can see brilliant-colored sponges, fish, and Timber Hole, an undersea "petrified forest" of sunken planes, ships, and even a railroad car. And the battleship USS *Massachusetts* lies in 30 feet of water just 3 miles off Pensacola. Every beach town in Northwest Florida has dive shops to outfit, tour, or certify visitors.

In the Crystal River area, north of the St. Petersburg and Clearwater beaches, you can snorkel with the manatees as they bask in the warm spring waters of Kings Bay.

The "cave-diving capital of the world" can be found between High Springs and Branford in northern Florida. The two most renowned spots are in crystal-clear Ginnie Springs, on the Santa Fe River, and in Ichetucknee Springs State Park, a few miles farther north. The **Ginnie Springs Resort,** 7300 NE Ginnie Springs Rd., High Springs (☎ **800/874-8571** or 904/454-2202), is a 200-acre campsite park along the Santa Fe River with dive packages and canoe rentals. Underwater explorers have found artifacts from the native tribes that once inhabited the region around Ichetucknee, and topside explorers often sight limpkin, wood duck, otter, and beaver. This 2,241-acre state park also offers camping, nature trails, canoeing, and tubing. The **Steamboat Dive Inn,** U.S. 27 at U.S. 129, Branford, FL 32008 (☎ **904/935-DIVE**), on the Suwannee River, has its own on-site, full-service diving center with certified instructors for every level. Also in Branford, the **Branford Dive Center,** U.S. 27 and the Suwannee River, Branford, FL 32008 (☎ **904/935-1141**), offers guides, air, rentals, accessories, and instruction.

If you want to keep up with what's going on statewide, you can subscribe to *Florida Scuba News,* a monthly magazine published in Jacksonville (☎ **904/ 783-1610;** www.scubanews.com). You might also want to pick up a specialized guidebook. Some good ones include *Coral Reefs of Florida,* by Gilbert L. Voss (Pineapple Press), and *The Diver's Guide to Florida and the Florida Keys,* by Jim Stachowicz (Windward Publishing).

TENNIS   Year-round sunshine makes Florida a tennis paradise. There are some 7,700 places to play, from municipal courts to exclusive resorts. Even some of the municipal facilities—Cambier Park Tennis Center in Naples leaps to mind—are equal to those at expensive resorts, and they're either free or close to it.

If you can afford it, you can learn from the best in Florida. **Nick Bollettieri** has sports academies in Bradenton. The Saddlebrook Resort in Wesley Chapel north of Tampa is home to the **Hopman Tennis Program,** while Safety Harbor Resort and Spa near St. Petersburg hosts the **Phil Green Tennis Program.** Amateurs can hobnob with the superstars at **ATP Tour International Headquarters** in Ponte Vedra Beach, near Jacksonville. **Peter Burwash International** has a tennis program at Doral Golf Resort & Spa in Miami. And **Chris Evert, Robert Seguso,** and **Carling Basset** have their own center in Boca Raton.

Other top places to learn and play are **Amelia Island Plantation** on Amelia Island; **Colony Beach and Tennis Resort** on Longboat Key off Sarasota (which *Tennis* magazine picked as the number two tennis resort in the nation); **Sanibel Harbour Resort & Spa** in Fort Myers, whose 5,500-seat stadium has hosted Davis Cup matches;

South Seas Plantation Resort & Yacht Harbour on Captiva Island; **The Registry Resort** in Naples (it will have changed names by 1999); and **World Tennis Center Resort & Club** in Naples, where the World Tennis Academy is headed by renowned tennis psychologist and coach Roland Carlstedt.

10 Tips on Accommodations

Florida has a vast array of accommodations, from rock-bottom roadside motels to some of the nation's finest resorts. Whether you'll spend a pittance or a bundle depends on your budget and your tastes. But, to repeat a well-worn phrase, you can enjoy "champagne on a beer budget" if you plan carefully.

The annual trip-planning guide published by the state's tourism-promotion agency, **Visit Florida** (see "Visitor Information," above), lists most hotels and motels in the state. It's particularly handy if you're taking your animal along, since it tells whether they accept pets.

Inn Route, P.O. Box 6187, Palm Harbor, FL 34684 (☎ **800/524-1880;** fax 281/403-9335; www.florida-inns.com; e-mail: innroute@worldnet.att.net), publishes the *Inns of Florida,* which lists inns and bed-and-breakfasts throughout the state. Inn Route inspects each property, thus ensuring quality and cleanliness of its members.

MONEY-SAVING TIPS

The rates quoted in this book are "rack" or "published" rates—that is, the highest regular rates charged by a hotel or motel. Not long ago, the rack rate was what you paid, unless you were part of a tour group or had purchased a vacation package. Today most hotels give discounts to corporate travelers, government employees, senior citizens, automobile club members, active-duty military personnel, and others.

Most hotels usually don't advertise these discounted rates or even volunteer them at the front desk, but you can take advantage of them by asking politely if there's a special rate which applies to you. One company that does advertise a major discount is **Choice Hotels** (see "For Seniors" under "Tips for Travelers with Special Needs," above).

Computerized reservation systems also have permitted many larger properties to adjust their rates on an almost daily basis, depending on how much business they anticipate having. Even if they don't officially reduce their rates, they may drop them rather than having beds go empty. Don't hesitate to ask if a less-expensive rate is available on the days you plan on being there.

Most rack rates include commissions for travel agents, which many hotels will knock off if you make your own reservations and bargain a little.

Downtown hotels catering to business travelers during the week usually have big discounts on Friday and Saturday nights. If you're staying over a weekend in an off-beach city such as Tampa, always ask about a special rate or package deal. Weekend rates don't apply in the resort areas, nor in college towns like Tallahassee, but you should ask about weekday or weeklong vacation packages.

Many Florida hotels and motels offer weekly rates, which as a general rule will knock off the price of one night if you stay for seven.

Most also have free self-parking, but fees can run up the cost at some downtown and beachfront hotels. We've indicated in the listings if a hotel or resort charges for parking; if no charge is given, parking is free. And many hotels jack up the price of long-distance phone calls made from your room. Accordingly, always inquire about the costs of parking, and use a pay phone if the hotel tacks a hefty surcharge on calls.

You're probably better off dealing directly with a hotel, but if you don't like bargaining, check out one of the national **reservation services.** They usually work as consolidators, buying up or reserving rooms in bulk and then dealing them out to customers at a profit. Most of them offer online reservation services as well. The more reputable providers include **Accommodations Express** (☎ 800/950-4685; www. accommodationsexpress.com); **Hotel Reservations Network** (☎ 800/ 96HOTEL; www.180096HOTEL.com); **Quikbook** (☎ 800/789-9887, includes fax-on-demand service; www.quikbook.com); and **Room Exchange** (☎ 800/846-7000 in the U.S. or 800/486-7000 in Canada).

Online, try booking your hotel through **Arthur Frommer's Budget Travel** (www.frommers.com), and save up to 50% off the rack rate. **Microsoft Expedia** (www.expedia.com) features a "Travel Agent" that will also direct you to affordable lodgings. Refer to Frommer's Online Directory at the back of the book for lots of guidance on how to make the Web work for you.

CONDOS, HOMES & COTTAGES

It may seem at first impression that many Florida beaches are lined with great walls of high-rise condominium buildings. That's not much of an overstatement, for the state literally has thousands upon thousands of condo units. People actually live in many of them year-round, but others are for rent on a daily, weekly, or monthly basis. In addition, there are many private homes and cottages for rent throughout Florida.

Be aware, however, that in Florida real-estate and resort parlance, the word *villa* does not mean a luxurious house standing all by itself. Down here, *villa* means an apartment.

Some of the resorts listed in this book actually are condo complexes operated as full-service hotels, but usually you'll have to do without such hotel amenities as on-site restaurants, room service, and even daily maid service. On the other hand, almost every condo, home, and cottage has a fully equipped kitchen, and many have washers, dryers, and other such niceties of home, which means they can represent significant savings, especially if you're traveling with children or are sharing with another couple or family.

We have pointed out a few of the best condo complexes in the "Where to Stay" sections of the following chapters, and we have named some of the **reputable real-estate agencies** which have inventories of condos, private homes, and cottages to rent.

If you think a condo will meet your needs, your best bet is to contact the rental agencies well in advance and request a brochure describing all the properties they represent, and their rates.

Fast Facts: Florida

American Express   There are a number of American Express offices in Florida. Call **Cardmember Services** (☎ 800/528-4800) for the location nearest you.

Banks   Banks are usually open Monday to Friday from 9am to 3 or 4pm, and most have automated teller machines (ATMs) for 24-hour banking. You won't have a problem finding a Cirrus or PLUS machine. Of the national banks, First Union Bank and NationsBank have offices throughout Florida.

Car Rentals   See "Getting Around," earlier in this chapter.

Climate   See "When to Go," earlier in this chapter.

Currency Exchange   See "Money" under "Preparing for Your Trip," in chapter 3.

Emergencies   Call ☎ **911** anywhere in the state to summon the police, the fire department, or an ambulance.

Liquor Laws   You must be 21 to purchase or consume alcohol in Florida. This law is strictly enforced, so if you look young, carry some photo identification that gives your date of birth. Minors can usually enter bars where food is served.

Newspapers/Magazines   Most cities of any size have a local daily paper, but the well-respected *Miami Herald* is generally available all over the state, with regional editions available in many areas.

Safety   Whenever you're traveling in an unfamiliar city, stay alert. Be aware of your immediate surroundings. Always lock your car doors and the trunk when your vehicle is unattended, and don't leave any valuables in sight. See "Safety" under "Preparing for Your Trip," in chapter 3, for more information.

Taxes   The Florida state sales tax is 6%. Many municipalities add 1% or more to that, and most levy a special tax on hotel and restaurant bills. See "Where to Stay," in the following chapters, for details.

Time   The Florida peninsula observes eastern standard time, but most of the Panhandle west of the Apalachicola River is on central standard time, 1 hour behind the rest of the state.

Tourist Information   See "Visitor Information," earlier in this chapter, and "Orientation" or "Essentials" in the following chapters.

For Foreign Visitors 3

by Bill Goodwin

The pervasiveness of American culture around the world may make you feel that you know the U.S.A. pretty well, but leaving your own country still requires an additional degree of planning. This chapter will help prepare you for the more common problems that visitors may encounter.

1 Preparing for Your Trip

ENTRY REQUIREMENTS

DOCUMENT REGULATIONS   Immigration laws have been a hot political issue in the United States in recent years, so it's wise to check at any U.S. embassy or consulate for current information and requirements. You can also plug into the U.S. State Department's Internet site at **http://state.gov**.

Canadians may enter the United States without passports or visas; you need only proof of residence.

The U.S. State Department has a **Visa Waiver Program** allowing citizens of the United Kingdom, Australia, New Zealand, Japan, and most western European countries to enter the United States without a visa for stays of up to 90 days. If you're from one of these countries, you will need only a valid passport and a round-trip air or cruise ticket in your possession upon arrival. Once here, you may then visit Mexico, Canada, Bermuda, and/or the Caribbean islands and return to the United States without needing a visa. Further information is available from any U.S. embassy or consulate.

If you're from any other country, you must have (1) a valid **passport** with an expiration date at least 6 months later than the scheduled end of your visit to the United States; and (2) a **tourist visa,** which may be obtained without charge from the nearest U.S. consulate.

To obtain a tourist visa, submit a completed application form with a 1½-inch-square photo and demonstrate binding ties to your residence abroad. If you cannot go in person, contact the nearest U.S. embassy or consulate for directions on applying by mail. Your travel agent or airline office may also be able to provide you with the visa application forms and instructions. The U.S. embassy or consulate where you apply will determine whether you receive a multiple- or single-entry visa and any restrictions regarding the length of your stay. This may take a few days or even weeks, so apply well in advance.

British subjects can obtain up-to-date passport and visa information by calling the **U.S. Embassy Visa Information Line** (☎ 0891/200-290) or the **London Passport Office** (☎ 0990/210-410 for recorded information).

Foreign **driver's licenses** are recognized in Florida, but you may want to get an international driver's license if your home license is not written in English.

MEDICAL REQUIREMENTS   No inoculations are needed to enter the United States unless you are coming from, or have stopped over in, areas known to be suffering from epidemics, particularly cholera or yellow fever. Requirements for HIV-positive visitors entering the United States are somewhat vague and change frequently. For up-to-the-minute information concerning HIV-positive travelers, contact the Center for Disease Control's **National Center for HIV** (☎ 404/332-4559; www.hivatis.org) or the **Gay Men's Health Crisis** (☎ 212/367-1000; www.gmhc.org).

If you have a disease that requires treatment with narcotics or syringe-administered medications, carry a valid signed prescription from your physician to allay any suspicions that you may be smuggling narcotics (a serious offense that carries severe penalties in the U.S.).

CUSTOMS REQUIREMENTS   Every adult visitor may bring in free of duty: 1 liter of wine or hard liquor; 200 cigarettes or 100 cigars (but no cigars made in Cuba) or 3 pounds of smoking tobacco; and $100 worth of gifts. You must spend at least 72 hours in the United States and must not have claimed the exemptions within the preceding 6 months. It is altogether forbidden to bring into the country foodstuffs (particularly cheese, fruit, cooked meats, and canned goods) and plants (vegetables, seeds, tropical plants, and so on). Foreign tourists may bring in or take out up to $10,000 in U.S. or foreign currency with no formalities; larger sums must be declared to Customs upon entering or leaving.

Penalties are severe for smuggling illegal narcotics into the United States, so if you have a disease requiring treatment with medications containing narcotics or drugs (especially those administered by syringe), carry a valid signed prescription from your physician to allay any suspicions that you are smuggling drugs.

For more specific information regarding U.S. Customs, call your nearest U.S. embassy or consulate, or contact the **U.S. Customs** office at ☎ 202/927-1770; www.customs.ustreas.gov.

What You Can Bring Home   **U.K. subjects** returning from the U.S. can bring back 200 cigarettes; 50 cigars; 250g of smoking tobacco; 2 liters of still table wine; 1 liter of spirits or strong liqueurs (over 22% volume); 2 liters of fortified wine, sparkling wine, or other liqueurs; 60cc (ml) perfume; 250cc (ml) of toilet water; and £145 worth of all other goods, including gifts and souvenirs. People under 17 cannot have the tobacco or alcohol allowance. For more information, contact **HM Customs & Excise**, Passenger Enquiry Point, 2nd Floor Wayfarer House, Great South West Road, Feltham, Middlesex, TW14 8NP (☎ 0181/910-3744; from outside the U.K. 44/181-910-3744), or consult their Web site at www.open.gov.uk.

Canadians get a $500 exemption, and you're allowed to bring back duty-free 200 cigarettes, 2.2 pounds of tobacco, 40 imperial ounces of liquor, and 50 cigars. In addition, you're allowed to mail gifts to Canada from abroad at the rate of C$60 a day, provided they're unsolicited and don't contain alcohol or tobacco (write on the package "Unsolicited gift, under $60 value"). All valuables should be declared on the Y-38 form before departure from Canada, including serial numbers of valuables you already own, such as expensive foreign cameras. *Note:* The $500 exemption can be used only once a year and only after an absence of 7 days. For a summary of Canadian rules, write for the booklet *I Declare,* issued by **Revenue Canada,** 2265 St. Laurent Blvd., Ottawa K1G 4KE (☎ **613/993-0534**).

The duty-free allowance in **Australia** is A$400 or, for those under 18, A$200. Personal property mailed back from England should be marked "Australian goods returned" to avoid payment of duty. Upon returning to Australia, citizens can bring in 250 cigarettes or 250 grams of loose tobacco, and 1,125ml of alcohol. If you're returning with valuable goods you already own, such as foreign-made cameras, you should file form B263. A helpful brochure, available from Australian consulates or Customs offices, is *Know Before You Go.* For more information, contact **Australian Customs Services,** GPO Box 8, Sydney NSW 2001 (☎ **02/9213-2000**).

The duty-free allowance for **New Zealand** is NZ$700. Citizens over 17 can bring in 200 cigarettes, or 50 cigars, or 250 grams of tobacco (or a mixture of all three if their combined weight doesn't exceed 250 grams); plus 4.5 liters of wine and beer, or 1.125 liters of liquor. New Zealand currency does not carry import or export restrictions. Fill out a certificate of export, listing the valuables you are taking out of the country; that way, you can bring them back without paying duty. Most questions are answered in a free pamphlet available at New Zealand consulates and Customs offices: *New Zealand Customs Guide for Travellers, Notice no. 4.* For more information, contact New Zealand Customs, 50 Anzac Ave., P.O. Box 29, Auckland (☎ **09/359-6655**).

INSURANCE   There is no national health-care system in the United States, and the cost of medical care here is extremely high; therefore, we strongly advise that you secure health-insurance coverage before setting out. You may want to take out a comprehensive travel policy that covers sickness or injury costs (medical, surgical, and hospital), as well as loss or theft of your baggage, trip-cancellation costs, guarantee of bail in case you are arrested, and costs of accident, repatriation, or death. See "Health & Insurance," in chapter 2, for more information. Packages such as Europ Assistance in Europe are sold by automobile clubs and travel agencies at attractive rates. **Worldwide Assistance Services, Inc.** (☎ **800/821-2828** or 202/347-2025), is the agent for Europ Assistance in the United States.

Canadians should check with their provincial health-plan offices or call **Health-Canada** (☎ **613/957-3025**) to find out the extent of their coverage and what documentation and receipts they must take home in case they are treated in the United States.

In Great Britain, most big travel agents offer their own insurance, and will probably try to sell you their package when you book a holiday. Think before you sign. **Britain's Consumers' Association** recommends that you insist on seeing the policy and reading the fine print before buying travel insurance. The **Association of British Insurers** (☎ **0171/600-3333**) gives advice by phone and publishes the free *Holiday Insurance,* a guide to policy provisions and prices. You might also shop around for better deals: Try **Columbus Travel Insurance Ltd.** (☎ **0171/375-0011**) or, for students, **Campus Travel** (☎ **0171/730-2101**).

MONEY

The U.S. monetary system has a decimal base: one American dollar ($1) = 100 cents (100¢). Notes come in $1 (we call it a "buck"), $5, $10, $20, $50, and $100 denominations (the last two are not welcome when paying for small purchases and are not accepted in taxis or at subway ticket booths). There are also $2 bills, but you are unlikely to see one since Americans consider them to be unlucky. There are six denominations of coins: 1¢ (one cent, known here as "a penny"), 5¢ (five cents or "a nickel"), 10¢ (ten cents or "a dime"), 25¢ (twenty-five cents or "a quarter"), 50¢ (fifty cents or "a half dollar"), and the rare $1 piece.

Changing foreign currency in the United States is a hassle, so leave any currency other than U.S. dollars at home—it will prove more of a nuisance than it's worth. Even banks here may not want to change your home currency into U.S. dollars. The exceptions are the currency exchange desks in the Miami, Orlando, Tampa, and Fort Myers airports, and **Thomas Cook Foreign Exchange,** which changes foreign currency and sells commission-free foreign and U.S. traveler's checks, drafts, and wire transfers. Thomas Cook has offices in Miami, Fort Lauderdale, Orlando, and Fort Myers. Call ☎ **800/287-7362** for its branch locations and hours.

Traveler's checks denominated in U.S. dollars are readily accepted at most hotels, motels, restaurants, and large stores. Do not bring traveler's checks denominated in other currencies. Sometimes a passport or other photo identification is necessary. The three traveler's checks that are most widely recognized—and least likely to be denied—are **Visa, American Express,** and **Thomas Cook.** Be sure to record the numbers of the checks, and keep that information separate in case the checks get lost or stolen.

American Express, Diners Club, Discover, MasterCard (EuroCard in Europe, Access in Britain, Chargex in Canada), and Visa (BarclayCard in Britain) **credit and charge cards** are the most widely used form of payment in the United States, and you should bring at least one with you—if for no other reason than to rent a car, since all rental companies require them.

Widespread in Florida, some **automated teller machines (ATMs)** will allow you to draw U.S. currency against your bank and credit cards. When available, this is the easiest way to get U.S. dollars, and you get the bank's rate of exchange, normally better than you will receive at hotels and other businesses. Check with your bank before leaving home, and remember that you will need your personal identification number (PIN) to do so.

SAFETY

GENERAL   While tourist areas are generally safe, crime is on the increase everywhere, and U.S. urban areas tend to be less safe than those in Europe or Japan. You should always stay alert. This is particularly true of large U.S. cities. It is wise to ask your hotel front desk staff or the city's or area's tourist office if you're in doubt about which neighborhoods are safe.

Remember also that hotels are open to the public, and in a large hotel, security may not be able to screen everyone entering. Always lock your room door—don't assume that once inside your hotel you are automatically safe and no longer need to be aware of your surroundings.

DRIVING   Recently, more and more crime has involved vehicles, so safety while driving is particularly important. Question your rental agency about personal safety, or ask for a brochure of traveler safety tips when you pick up your car. Obtain written directions, or a map with the route clearly marked, from the agency, showing how to get to your destination. And, if possible, arrive and depart during daylight hours.

If you drive off a highway into a doubtful neighborhood, leave the area as quickly as possible. If you have an accident, even on the highway, stay in your car with the doors locked until you assess the situation or until the police arrive. If you are bumped from behind on the street or are involved in a minor accident with no injuries and the situation appears to be suspicious, motion to the other driver to follow you. *Never* get out of your car in such situations. You can also keep a premade sign in your car which reads: PLEASE FOLLOW THIS VEHICLE TO REPORT THE ACCIDENT. Show the sign to the other driver and go directly to the nearest police precinct, well-lighted service station, or all-night store.

Special Services for International Visitors

Once you're here, you can call Visit Florida's 24-hour **tourist assistance hotline** (☎ **800/656-8777**) if you need help with lost travel documents, directions, emergencies, or references to attractions, restaurants, and shopping anywhere in the state. Hotline operators speak several languages, including Spanish, French, German, and Portuguese.

In Orlando, **Walt Disney World** has numerous services designed to meet foreign visitors' needs. Call ☎ **407/W-DISNEY** for details. Services include:

- A special phone number (☎ **407/824-7900**) to speak with someone in French, Spanish, German, and other languages.
- Personal translator units (in French, German, and Spanish) to translate narration at some shows and attractions.
- Detailed guidebooks to the three major parks in Spanish, French, German, Portuguese, and Japanese (available at any guest-relations location).
- Currency exchange.
- World Key Terminals at Epcot that offer basic park information and assistance with dining reservations in Spanish.
- Resort phones equipped with software that expedites international calls by allowing guests to dial direct to foreign destinations.

If you see someone on the road who indicates a need for help, do *not* stop. Take note of the location, drive on to a well-lighted area, and telephone the police by dialing ☎ **911.**

Park in well-lighted, well-traveled areas if possible. Always keep your car doors locked, whether attended or unattended. Look around you before you get out of your car, and never leave any packages or valuables in sight. If someone attempts to rob you or steal your car, do *not* try to resist the thief/carjacker—report the incident to the police department immediately.

Also, make sure that you have enough gasoline in your tank to reach your intended destination so that you're not forced to look for a service station in an unfamiliar and possibly unsafe neighborhood, especially at night.

2 Getting to & Around the U.S.

A number of U.S. airlines offer service from Europe and Latin America to Florida, including American, Delta, Northwest, and United (see "Getting There," in chapter 2). Many of the major international airlines, such as **British Airways, KLM Royal Dutch Airlines,** and **Lufthansa,** also have direct flights from Europe to various Florida cities, either in their own planes or in conjunction with an American "partner" airline (KLM and Northwest, to name one partnership). You can get here from Australia and New Zealand via **Air New Zealand, Qantas,** and **United,** with a change of planes in Los Angeles. Call the airlines' local offices or contact your travel agent, and be sure to ask about promotional fares and discounts.

Canadians should check with **Air Canada** (☎ **800/776-3000**), which offers service from Toronto and Montréal to Miami, Tampa, West Palm Beach, Fort Lauderdale, and Fort Myers. Also ask your travel agent about **Air Transat** (☎ **800/470-1011**) and **Canada 3000** (☎ **800/993-4378**), which have wintertime charter flights to several Florida destinations.

From Great Britain, **Virgin Atlantic Airways** (☎ 800/662-8621 in the U.S. or 01/293-74-77-47 in the U.K.) has attractive deals on its flights from London and Manchester to Miami and Orlando. From Germany, **LTU International Airways** (☎ 800/888-0200 in the U.S. or 11/948-8466 in Germany) frequently has reduced fares to Miami, Orlando, and Fort Myers from Frankfurt, Munich, and Düsseldorf.

Whichever airline you choose, always ask about **advance purchase excursion (APEX)** fares, which represent substantial savings over regular fares. Most require tickets to be bought 21 days prior to departure.

On the World Wide Web, the European Travel Network (ETN) operates a site at **www.discount-tickets.com**, which offers cut-rate prices on international airfares to the United States, accommodations, car rentals, and tours. Another site to click for current discount fares worldwide is **www.etn.nl/discount.htm#disco**.

When you arrive in the United States, getting through immigration control may take as long as 2 hours on some days, especially summer weekends. Accordingly, you should make very generous allowances for delay in planning connections between international and domestic flights.

In contrast, travelers arriving by car or by rail from Canada will find border-crossing formalities streamlined to the vanishing point. And air travelers from Canada, Bermuda, and some places in the Caribbean can sometimes go through Customs and Immigration at the point of departure, which is much quicker.

For further information, see "Getting There," in chapter 2.

GETTING AROUND THE U.S.

BY AIR   The United States is one of the world's largest countries, with vast distances separating many of its key sights. From New York to Miami, for example, is more than 1,350 miles (2,173km) by road or train. Accordingly, flying is the quickest and most comfortable way to get around the country.

Some large airlines (for example, Northwest and Delta) offer travelers on their transatlantic or transpacific flights special discount tickets under the name **Visit USA,** allowing mostly one-way travel from one U.S. destination to another at very low prices. These discount tickets are not on sale in the United States and must be purchased abroad in conjunction with your international ticket. This system is the best, easiest, and fastest way to see the United States at low cost. You should obtain information well in advance from your travel agent or the office of the airline concerned, since the conditions attached to these discount tickets can be changed without advance notice.

BY TRAIN   Long-distance trains in the United States are operated by **Amtrak** (☎ 800/USA-RAIL; www.amtrak.com), the national passenger rail corporation. See "Getting There," in chapter 2, for information about Amtrak's services to and within Florida.

Be aware that with a few notable exceptions (for instance, the Northeast Corridor line between Boston and Washington, D.C.), intercity service is not up to European standards. Delays are common, routes are limited and often infrequently served, and fares are seldom significantly lower than discount airfares. Thus, cross-country train travel should be approached with caution.

International visitors can buy a **USA Railpass,** good for 15 or 30 days of unlimited travel on Amtrak. The pass is available through many foreign travel agents, and with a foreign passport, you can also buy them at some Amtrak offices in the United States, including Boston, Chicago, Los Angeles, Miami, New York, San Francisco, and Washington, D.C. The prices are based on a zone system: eastern, central, and western United States. Prices in 1999 for a 15-day pass are $285 off-peak, $425 peak; a 30-day pass costs $375 off-peak, $535 peak. (With a foreign passport, you can also buy passes at some Amtrak offices in the United States, including locations in San Francisco, Los Angeles, Chicago, New York, Miami, Boston, and Washington, D.C.) The highest prices are in summer and at holidays. Reservations are generally required and should be made for each part of your trip as early as possible.

If you'll be traveling in both the United States and Canada, Amtrak and VIA, the Canadian railway system, offer a joint **North American Rail Pass,** good for unlimited travel over 30 consecutive days anywhere the two systems go. One key restriction: You must travel by rail in both the United States and Canada. At press time, these cost $645 from June to mid-October, $450 the rest of the year.

BY BUS   Although it's the least expensive way to get around the country, long-distance bus service here can be both slow and uncomfortable, so it's not for everyone. **Greyhound/Trailways** (☎ 800/231-2222), the sole nationwide bus line, offers an **Ameripass** for unlimited travel for 7 days at $199, 15 days at $299, 30 days at $409, and 60 days at $599. Passes must be purchased at a Greyhound terminal. Special rates are available for senior citizens and students.

BY CAR   Traveling by car gives you the freedom to make (and alter) your itinerary to suit your own needs and interests. And especially in Florida, it offers the possibility of visiting some of the off-the-beaten-path locations, places that cannot be reached easily by public transportation. For information on renting cars in the United States, see "Getting Around," in chapter 2, and "Automobile Organizations" and "Automobile Rentals" in "Fast Facts: For the Foreign Traveler," below.

Please note that in the United States we drive on the **right side of the road** as in Europe, not on the left side as in the United Kingdom, Australia, and New Zealand.

3 Shopping Tips

The U.S. government charges very low duties when compared to the rest of the world, so you could get some excellent deals here on imported electronic goods, cameras, and clothing. Of course, it all depends on the value of your home currency versus the dollar, and how much duty you'll have to pay on your purchases when you get home.

The national "discount" chain stores consistently offer some of our best shopping deals. For televisions, VCRs, radios, camcorders, computers, and other electronic goods, go to **Best Buy, Circuit City,** and **Radio Shack.** Best Buy also has a wide selection of music. **CompUSA, Computer City,** and **Micro Center** specialize in computer hardware, accessories, and software. **Service Merchandise** is one of our best chains for cameras, and it also has electronics, jewelry, and many other items.

Many computers and other electronic equipment sold here use only 110- to 120-volt AC (60-cycle) electricity. You will need a transformer to use them at home if your power is 220 to 240 volts AC (50 cycles). Be sure to ask the salesperson if an item has a universal power adapter.

Our major department store chains are **Sears, Macy's, Saks Fifth Avenue, Lord & Taylor,** and **JC Penney.** In Florida, you'll also find **Burdines, Jordan Marsh,** and **Dillard's** anchoring many shopping malls. You get real deals in department stores only during sales, when selected merchandise is marked down 25% or more. The **Marshall's** and **TJ Maxx** chains carry name-brand clothing at department-store sale prices, but their stock tends to vary greatly.

Outlet malls are another source, in which manufacturers operate their own shops, selling directly to the consumer. Sometimes you can get very good buys at the outlets, especially when sales are going on. Most lingerie and china outlets have good prices when compared to department stores, but that's not necessarily the case with designer clothing. In addition, some manufacturers produce items of lesser quality so they can charge less at their outlets, so inspect the quality of all merchandise carefully. The main advantage to outlet malls is that if you are looking for a specific brand—Levi's jeans, for example—the company's outlet will have it.

You'll find national chain stores, department stores, and outlet malls throughout Florida; many are listed under "Shopping" in the following chapters. You can also look under their names in the white pages of the local telephone directory for addresses and phone numbers, or under subjects such as computer dealers, television and radio dealers, stereo and hi-fi dealers, department stores, and discount stores in the yellow pages directory.

Fast Facts: For the Foreign Traveler

Automobile Organizations   Auto clubs will supply maps, suggested routes, guidebooks, accident and bail-bond insurance, and emergency road service. The **American Automobile Association (AAA)** is the major auto club in the United States. If you belong to an auto club in your home country, inquire about AAA reciprocity before you leave. You may be able to join AAA even if you're not a member of a reciprocal club; to inquire, call AAA (☎ **800/222-4357**). AAA is actually an organization of regional auto clubs; in Florida, look under "AAA Automobile Club South" in the white pages of the telephone directory. AAA has a nationwide emergency road service telephone number (☎ **800/AAA-HELP**).

Automobile Rentals   See "Getting Around," in chapter 2.

Business Hours   See "Fast Facts: Florida," in chapter 2.

Currency & Currency Exchange   See "Entry Requirements" and "Money" under "Preparing for Your Trip," above.

Electricity   Like Canada, the United States uses 110 to 120 volts AC (60 cycles), compared to 220 to 240 volts AC (50 cycles) in most of Europe, Australia, and New Zealand. If your small appliances use 220 to 240 volts, you'll need a 110-volt transformer and a plug adapter with two flat parallel pins to operate them here. Downward converters that change 220 to 240 volts to 110 to 120 volts are difficult to find in the United States, so bring one with you.

Embassies & Consulates   All embassies are located in Washington, D.C. Some consulates are located in major U.S. cities, and most nations have a mission to the United Nations in New York City. Some key embassies are:

Australia: 1601 Massachusetts Ave. NW, Washington, DC 20036 (☎ **202/ 797-3000**). There are Australian consulates in New York, Honolulu, Houston, Los Angeles, and San Francisco.

Canada: 501 Pennsylvania Ave. NW, Washington, DC 20001 (☎ **202/ 682-1740**). In Florida, there's a Canadian consulate at 200 S. Biscayne Blvd., Suite 1600, Miami, FL 33131 (☎ **305/579-1600**). Other Canadian consulates are in Atlanta, Buffalo (New York), Chicago, Cleveland, Dallas, Detroit, Los Angeles, Minneapolis, New York, and Seattle.

Republic of Ireland: 2234 Massachusetts Ave. NW, Washington, DC 20008 (☎ **202/462-3939**). Irish consulates are in Boston, Chicago, New York, and San Francisco.

New Zealand: 37 Observatory Circle NW, Washington, DC 20008 (☎ **202/ 328-4800**). New Zealand consulates are in Los Angeles, Salt Lake City, San Francisco, and Seattle.

United Kingdom: 3100 Massachusetts Ave. NW, Washington, DC 20008 (☎ 202/462-1340). In Florida, there's a full-service British consulate in Miami at Suite 2800, Brickell Bay Dr. (☎ **305/374-1522**), and a vice consulate for emergency situations in Orlando at the Sun Bank Tower, Suite 2110, 200 S. Orange Ave. (☎ **407/426-7855**). Other British consulates are in Atlanta, Boston, Chicago, Cleveland, Dallas, Houston, Los Angeles, and New York.

Emergencies   Call ☎ **911** to report a fire, call the police, or get an ambulance anywhere in the United States. This is a toll-free call (no coins are required for 911 calls at public telephones).

Visit Florida, the state's tourist information agency, operates a 24-hour, multi-language **tourist assistance hotline** (☎ **800/656-8777**), which will give advice and information in case of an emergency.

If you encounter traveler's problems, check the local telephone directory to find an office of the **Traveler's Aid Society,** a nationwide, nonprofit, social-service organization geared to helping travelers in difficult straits. Their services might include reuniting families separated while traveling, providing food and/or shelter to people stranded without cash, or even emotional counseling. If you're in trouble, seek them out.

Gasoline (Petrol)   Petrol is known as gasoline (or simply "gas") in the United States, and petrol stations are known as both gas stations and service stations. Gasoline costs about half as much here as it does in Europe (about $1 per gallon at press time). One U.S. gallon equals 3.8 liters or .85 Imperial gallons. A majority of gas stations in Florida are now actually convenience grocery stores with gas pumps outside; they do not service automobiles. All but a very few stations have self-service gas pumps.

Holidays   Banks, government offices, post offices, and many stores, restaurants, and museums are closed on the following legal national holidays: January 1 (New Year's Day), the third Monday in January (Martin Luther King, Jr. Day), the third Monday in February (Presidents' Day, Washington's Birthday), the last Monday in May (Memorial Day), July 4 (Independence Day), the first Monday in September (Labor Day), the second Monday in October (Columbus Day), November 11 (Veterans' Day/Armistice Day), the last Thursday in November (Thanksgiving Day), and December 25 (Christmas). In addition, "Super Bowl Sunday"—the last Sunday in January, when our two top professional gridiron football teams play for the national championship in the Super Bowl—is tantamount to a holiday. The Tuesday following the first Monday in November is Election Day and is a federal government holiday in presidential-election years (held every four years, including 2000).

Legal Aid   The foreign tourist will probably never become involved with the American legal system. If you are "pulled over" for a minor infraction (for example, of the highway code, such as speeding), never attempt to pay the fine directly to a police officer; this could be construed as attempted bribery, a much more serious crime. Pay fines by mail, or directly into the hands of the clerk of the court. If accused of a more serious offense, say and do nothing before consulting a lawyer or your embassy or consulate. Here the government must prove a person's guilt beyond a reasonable doubt, and everyone has the right to remain silent, whether he or she is suspected of a crime or actually arrested. If arrested, a person can make one telephone call to a party of his or her choice, and foreigners have a right to call their embassies or consulates.

Mail Generally to be found at intersections, **mailboxes** are blue with a white eagle logo and carry the inscription U.S. MAIL. If your mail is addressed to a U.S. destination, don't forget to add the five-digit postal code, or zip code, after the two-letter abbreviation of the state to which the mail is addressed (FL for Florida).

Our postal service raised its rates in 1999. **Domestic postage rates** are 20¢ for a postcard and 33¢ for a letter. Airmail postcards to Canada cost 30¢, while letters are 46¢. Airmail letters to other countries are 60¢ for the first half ounce.

Safety See "Safety" in "Preparing for Your Trip," above, and in "Fast Facts: Florida," in chapter 2.

Taxes In the United States there is no value-added tax (VAT) or other indirect tax at the national level. Every state, county, and city has the right to levy its own local tax on all purchases, including hotel and restaurant checks, airline tickets, and so on. For Florida's sales taxes, see "Fast Facts: Florida," in chapter 2. Florida's hotel tax varies from county to county; we give the rates in the accommodation sections of the chapters that follow.

Telephone, Telegraph & Fax The telephone system in the United States is run by private corporations, so rates, especially for long-distance service and operator-assisted calls, can vary widely. Generally, hotel surcharges on long-distance and local calls are astronomical, so you're usually better off using a **public pay telephone,** which you'll find clearly marked in most public buildings and private establishments, as well as on the street. Convenience grocery stores and gas stations always have them. Many convenience groceries and packaging services sell **prepaid calling cards** in denominations up to $50; these can be the least expensive way to call home. Many public phones at airports now accept American Express, MasterCard, and Visa credit cards. Local calls made from public pay phones in most locales in Florida cost 35¢.

Most **long-distance and international calls** can be dialed directly from any phone. For calls within the United States and to Canada, dial 1 followed by the area code and the seven-digit number. For other international calls, dial 011 followed by the country code, the city code, and the telephone number of the person you are calling.

Calls to area codes 800, 888, and 877 are toll-free. However, calls to numbers in area codes 700 and 900 (chat lines, bulletin boards, "dating" services, and so on) can be very expensive—usually a charge of 95¢ to $3 or more per minute, and they sometimes have minimum charges that can run as high as $15 or more.

For **reversed-charge** or **collect calls,** and for **person-to-person calls,** dial 0 (zero, *not* the letter O) followed by the area code and number you want; an operator will then come on the line, and you should specify that you are calling collect, or person-to-person, or both. If your operator-assisted call is international, ask for the overseas operator.

For local **directory assistance** ("information"), dial 411; for long-distance information, dial 1, then the appropriate area code and 555-1212.

Telegraph services are provided primarily by Western Union. You can bring your telegram into the nearest Western Union office (there are hundreds across the country) or dictate it over the phone (☎ **800/325-6000**). You can also telegraph money or have it telegraphed to you very quickly over the Western Union system, but this service can cost as much as 15% to 25% of the amount sent.

Most hotels have **fax** machines available for guest use (be sure to ask about the charge to use it), and many hotel rooms are even wired for guests' fax machines.

A less expensive way to send and receive faxes may be at stores such as **Mail Boxes Etc.,** a national chain of packing service shops (look in the yellow pages directory under "Packing Services").

There are two kinds of telephone directories in the United States. The so-called **white pages** list private and business subscribers in alphabetical order. The inside front cover lists emergency numbers for police, fire, ambulance, coast guard, poison-control center, crime-victims hotline, and so on. The first few pages will tell you how to make long-distance and international calls, complete with country codes and area codes. Government numbers usually are on pages printed on blue paper. Printed on yellow paper, the so-called **yellow pages** list all local services, businesses, industries, and churches and synagogues by type of activity, with an index at the front or back. The yellow pages also include city plans or detailed area maps, often showing postal zip codes and public transportation routes.

Time   The continental United States is divided into four **time zones:** eastern standard time (EST), central standard time (CST), mountain standard time (MST), and Pacific standard time (PST). Alaska and Hawaii have their own zones. For example, noon in New York City (EST) is 11am in Chicago (CST), 10am in Denver (MST), 9am in Los Angeles (PST), 8am in Anchorage (AST), and 7am in Honolulu (HST). Most of Florida observes eastern standard time, though the Panhandle west of the Apalachicola River is on central standard time (1 hour earlier than Tallahassee, Orlando, and Miami).

Daylight saving time is in effect from 1am on the first Sunday in April through 1am the last Sunday in October. Daylight saving time moves the clock 1 hour ahead of standard time.

Tipping   Tipping is so ingrained in the American way of life that the annual income tax of tip-earning service personnel is based on how much they should have received in light of their employers' gross revenues. Accordingly, they may have to pay tax on a tip you didn't actually give them.

Here are some rules of thumb: bartenders, 10% to 15% of the check; bellhops, at least 50¢ per bag, or $2 to $3 for a lot of luggage; cab drivers, 10% of the fare; chambermaids, $1 per day; checkroom attendants, $1 per garment; hairdressers and barbers, 15% to 20% of the bill; waiters and waitresses, 15% to 20% of the check; valet parking attendants, $1 per vehicle; rest room attendants, 25¢. We do not tip theater ushers, gas station attendants, or the staff at cafeterias and fast-food restaurants.

Toilets   You won't find public toilets (euphemistically referred to here as "rest rooms") on the streets in most U.S. cities, but they can be found in hotel lobbies, bars, restaurants, museums, department stores, railway and bus stations, or service stations. Note, however, that restaurants and bars in resorts or heavily visited areas may reserve their rest rooms for the use of their patrons.

4 Settling into Miami

by Victoria Pesce Elliott

It's hard to know in which language to introduce yourself to the min-ination of Miami. When you land at Miami International Airport, the nation's second-largest hub for international travelers, you'll hear Spanish, Portuguese, Creole, French, and Italian as a matter of course. Once in Miami, you'll find a curious mix of Caribbean immigrants, orthodox Jews, retirees seeking easier winters, models, actors, artists, wealthy real-estate moguls, and movie executives, as well as an already-diverse crowd of longtime Floridians, black descendants of Bahamian railroad workers, Native Americans, and Hispanics. The city is a vir-tual mosaic of colors, sounds, and scents.

Since the Spanish first colonized the area in the 16th century, Miami has been a magnet for the masses, and it continues to grow at a rapid pace. Since 1980, Miami-Dade County's population has increased by nearly 33%. Despite the uncontrolled influx of foreigners (and partly because of it), the area has become an international tourist destination.

Through its many incarnations, two Miami characteristics have remained constant: its predictable year-round warmth and its location on a peninsula pointing emphatically toward so many other nations. Now Miami, known as "The Capital of the Americas," serves as Latin American and international headquarters for hundreds of multina-tional corporations.

Encompassing both the mainland and the barrier islands of Miami Beach, Greater Miami boasts about 2 million residents and hosts more than 9 million visitors annually. They come for different reasons. Some are drawn by the sea and surf, some for the outrageous nightlife, and others for the business opportunities; still others can't get enough of the natural wilderness right in the city's backyard.

Fortunately, the evolution of America's southernmost metropol-itan region—from a simple playground to a vibrant cosmopolitan city—has not been achieved at the expense of the area's celebrated surf and sand. Despite Miami's quick transformation, the almost-complete absence of heavy industry has left the air and water relatively unpolluted. Miami is not just a beach vacation, however—you'll also find high-quality hotels, distinctive restaurants, unusual attractions, some quality cultural offerings, incredible nightlife, and top shopping.

1 Orientation

GETTING THERE & ARRIVING

One hundred years ago, Miami, basically a swampy jungle, was a hard place to reach—but no more. Today, transportation companies, most notably airlines, fight perpetual price wars to woo tourists to the Sunshine State. In fact, airfares are so competitive that flying to Miami will almost always be your most economical option. However, take a look at your alternatives, too. An overland journey to Florida's Gold Coast is both a more scenic and a more flexible way to travel. Greyhound/Trailways offers several types of bus passes, and Amtrak offers a host of rail services to the South.

BY PLANE

More than 80 scheduled airlines serve Miami, including almost every major domestic and foreign carrier. The city is so well connected that the problem isn't getting there, but rather deciding what service and fare to select.

Major American carriers that fly into the city keep ticket offices at Miami International Airport and at some city locations listed below. They include **American,** 150 Alhambra Plaza, Coral Gables (☎ **800/433-7300** or 305/358-6800); **Continental** (☎ **800/525-0280** or 305/871-1400); **Delta,** 201 Alhambra Circle, Suite 516, Coral Gables (☎ **800/221-1212** or 305/448-7000); **Northwest/KLM** (☎ **800/447-4747**); and **United,** 178 Giralda Ave., Coral Gables (☎ **800/241-6522**).

Originally carved out of scrubland in 1928 by Pan American Airlines, **Miami International Airport (MIA)** has emerged as one of the busiest airports in the world. Unfortunately, as it undergoes major reconstruction to expand its capacity, the airport can feel like a maze with inadequate signage and surly employees.

The route down to the baggage-claim area is clearly marked. You can change money or use your Honor or Plus System ATM card at Barnett Bank of South Florida, located near the exit.

Like most good international airports, MIA has its fair share of boutiques, shops, and eateries. Unless you are starving or forgot to get a gift for the person picking you up, bypass these overpriced establishments. The airport is literally surrounded by restaurants and shops; if you can wait to get to them, you will save a lot of money. If you are exiting Miami on an international flight, don't miss the excellent duty-free selection in the departure lounge.

Visitor information is available 24 hours a day at the **Miami International Airport Main Visitor Counter,** Concourse E, 2nd level (☎ **305/876-7000**).

GETTING INTO TOWN   The airport is located about 6 miles west of Downtown and about 10 miles from the beaches, so it's likely you can get from the plane to your hotel room in less than half an hour. Of course, if you're arriving from an international destination, it will take more time to go through Customs and Immigration.

By Car   All the major car-rental firms operate off-site branches reached via shuttle from the terminals. See "Getting Around," later in this chapter, for a list of major rental companies. Signs at the airport's exit clearly point the way to various parts of the city. If you're arriving at night, I might suggest taking a taxi to your hotel and having the car-rental firm deliver a car to your hotel the next day.

By Taxi   Taxis line up in front of a dispatcher's desk outside the airport's arrivals terminals. Most cabs are metered, though some have flat rates to popular destinations. The fare should be about $12 to Coral Gables, $18 to Downtown, and $24 to South

Beach, plus tip, which should be at least 10% and more for each bag the driver handles. Depending on traffic, the ride to Coral Gables or Downtown takes about 15 to 20 minutes, and to South Beach, 20 to 25 minutes. One of the more reliable companies in the city (with an easy-to-remember number) is **Yellow Cab** (☎ 305/444-4444).

By Limo or Van   Group limousines (multipassenger vans) circle the arrivals area looking for fares. Destinations are posted on the front of each van, and a flat rate is charged for door-to-door service to the area marked.

SuperShuttle (☎ 305/871-2000) is one of the largest airport operators, charging between $10 and $20 per person for a ride within the county. Its vans operate 24 hours a day and accept American Express, MasterCard, and Visa.

Private limousine arrangements can be made in advance through your local travel agent. A one-way meet-and-greet service should cost about $50.

By Public Transportation   I do not recommend taking public transportation to get from the airport to your hotel. Buses heading Downtown leave the airport only once per hour (from the arrivals level), and connections are spotty at best. It could take about an hour and a half to get to South Beach. Journeys to Downtown and Coral Gables are more direct. The fare is $1.25, plus an additional 25¢ for a South Beach transfer.

BY CAR

No matter where you start your journey, chances are you'll reach Miami by way of I-95. This north-south interstate is the city's lifeline and an integral part of the region. The highway connects all of Miami's different neighborhoods, the airport, and the beach, and it connects all of South Florida to the rest of America. Unfortunately, many of Miami's road signs are completely confusing and notably absent when you need them. Take time out to study I-95's placement on the map. You will use it as a reference point time and again.

Other major highways to Florida include I-10, which originates in Los Angeles and terminates in Jacksonville, and I-75, which begins in North Michigan and runs through the center of Florida.

BY TRAIN

Amtrak (☎ 800/USA-RAIL) may be a good option. Two trains leave daily from New York: the Silver Meteor at 7:05pm and the Silver Star at 11:50am. They both take from 26½ to 29 hours to complete the journey to Miami. At press time, the lowest-priced round-trip ticket from New York to Miami cost $146 for a coach seat, climbing to a whopping $417 for a sleeper (based on double occupancy).

If you are planning to stay in South Florida for some time, you might consider taking your car on Amtrak's East Coast Auto Train. The 16½-hour ride, connecting Lorton, Virginia (near Washington, D.C.), with Sanford, Florida (near Orlando), has a glass-domed viewing car and includes breakfast and dinner in the ticket price. Round-trip fares are only a few dollars higher than one-way—about $170 for adults, $85 for children under 12, and $300 for your car. One-way fares are discounted as much as 50% when most traffic is going in the opposite direction.

You'll pull into Amtrak's Miami terminal at 8303 NW 37th Ave. Unfortunately, none of the major car-rental companies has an office at the train station; you'll have to go to the airport, just over 5 miles away, to rent a car.

Taxis meet each Amtrak arrival. The fare to Downtown will cost about $22; the ride takes less than 20 minutes.

VISITOR INFORMATION

The best source for any kind of specialized information about the city is the **Greater Miami Convention and Visitors Bureau,** 701 Brickell Ave., Miami, FL 33131 (☎ **800/283-2707** or 305/539-3063; www.Miamiandbeaches.com or gmcvb@aol. com). Even if you don't have a specific question, call ahead to request its free magazine, *Destination Miami,* which includes several good, easy-to-use maps and other useful contact numbers. The office is open weekdays from 9am to 5pm.

In addition to information on some of South Beach's funkier hotels, the **Miami Design Preservation League,** 1234 Washington Ave., Suite 207, Miami Beach, FL 33139 (☎ **305/672-2014**), offers an informative free guide to the Art Deco District and several books on the subject. It's open Monday through Saturday from 10am to 7pm.

Greater Miami's various chambers of commerce also send maps and information about their particular neighborhoods, including the following:

- **Coconut Grove Chamber of Commerce,** 2820 McFarlane Rd., Miami, FL 33133 (☎ **305/444-7270**).
- **Coral Gables Chamber of Commerce,** 50 Aragon Ave., Coral Gables, FL 33134 (☎ **305/446-1657**).
- **Florida Gold Coast Chamber of Commerce,** 1100 Kane Concourse (Bay Harbor Islands), Miami, FL 33154 (☎ **305/866-6020**)—this office represents Bal Harbour, Sunny Isles, Surfside, and other North Dade waterfront communities.
- **Tropical Everglades Visitor's Center,** 160 U.S. Hwy. 1, Florida City, FL 33034 (☎ **305/245-9180**); open daily 8:15am to 4:45pm.
- **Miami Beach Chamber of Commerce,** 1920 Meridian Ave., Miami Beach, FL 33139 (☎ **305/672-1270**).

The following organizations represent dues-paying hotels, restaurants, and attractions in their specific areas. These associations can provide information about accommodations and tours: **Greater Miami and the Beaches Hotel Association,** 407 Lincoln Rd., Miami Beach, FL 33139 (☎ **800/531-3553,** or 305/531-3553), and **Sunny Isles Beach Resort Association,** 17100 Collins Ave., Suite 208, Sunny Isles, FL 33160 (☎ **305/947-5826**).

CITY LAYOUT

Miami may seem confusing at first, but it quickly becomes easy to negotiate. The small cluster of buildings that make up the Downtown area is at the geographical heart of the city. You can see these sharp stalagmites from most anywhere, making them a good reference point. In relation to Downtown, the airport is northwest, the beaches are east, Coconut Grove is south, Coral Gables is west, and the rest of the country is north.

FINDING AN ADDRESS   Miami is divided into dozens of areas with official and unofficial boundaries. Street numbering in the city of Miami is fairly straightforward, but you must first be familiar with the numbering system. The mainland is divided into four sections—NE, NW, SE, and SW—by the intersection of Flagler Street and Miami Avenue. Street numbers (First St., Second St., and so forth) start from here and increase as you go farther out, as do numbers of Avenues, Places, Courts, Terraces, and Lanes. Streets in Hialeah are the exceptions to this pattern; they are listed separately in map indexes.

Numerical addresses are descriptive, with the first digits giving the cross streets. For example, 12301 Biscayne Blvd. is located at 123rd St., and 501 Ocean Dr. is at 5th

Street. It's also helpful to remember that avenues generally run north-south, while streets go east-west.

Getting around the barrier islands that make up Miami Beach is somewhat easier than moving around the mainland. Street numbering starts with First Street, near Miami Beach's southern tip, and increases to 192nd Street, in the northern part of Sunny Isles. Collins Avenue makes the entire journey from head to toe. As in the city of Miami, some streets in Miami Beach have numbers as well as names. When they are part of listings in this book, both names and numbers are given.

You should know that the numbered streets in Miami Beach are not the geographical equivalents of those on the mainland, but they are close. For example, the 79th Street Causeway runs into 71st Street on Miami Beach.

STREET MAPS   It's easy to get lost in sprawling Miami, so a reliable map is essential. If you are not planning on moving around too much, the tourist board's maps, located inside its free publication "Destination Miami," should be adequate. If you really want to get to know the city, it pays to invest in one of the large accordion-fold maps, available at most gas stations and bookstores. The Trakker Map of Miami ($2.50) is a four-color accordion map that encompasses all of Dade County.

Some maps of Miami list streets according to area, so you'll have to know which part of the city you are looking for before the street can be found. All the listings in this book include area information for just this reason.

The Neighborhoods in Brief

Much of Miami is sprawling suburbia. But every city has its charm, and aside from a fantastic tropical climate and the vast stretch of beach that lies just across its glistening Biscayne Bay, Miami's unique identity comes from extremely interesting cultural pockets within its residential communities. Here's a brief rundown of the characteristics of its diverse neighborhoods:

South Beach—The Art Deco District   In the past several years, South Beach has been the hottest area of Miami. While technically it's just 15 blocks at the southern tip of Miami Beach, South Beach has a style all its own. The thriving Art Deco District within South Beach contains the largest concentration of art deco architecture in the world.

Young investors, artists, model types, and the usual Miami smattering of Cubans, African Americans, and Caribbeans populate this vibrant community. Hip clubs and cafes are filled with vacationing Europeans, working models, photographers, musicians, and writers who enjoy the exciting and sophisticated atmosphere.

Miami Beach   To tourists in the 1950s, Miami Beach was Miami. Its huge self-contained resort hotels were vacations unto themselves, providing a full day's worth of meals, activities, and entertainment. Then, in the 1960s and 1970s, people who fell in love with Miami began to buy apartments rather than rent hotel rooms. Tourism declined, and many area hotels fell into disrepair.

However, since the late 1980s, Miami Beach has experienced a tide of revitalization. Huge beach hotels are finding their niche with new, international tourist markets and are attracting large convention crowds. The **Miami Beach Convention Center,** 1901 Convention Center Dr., Miami Beach, FL 33139 (☎ **305/673-7311**), has more than 1 million square feet of exhibition space. New generations of Americans have discovered the qualities that originally made Miami Beach so popular, and they are finding out that the sand and surf now comes with a thriving international city.

Miami at a Glance

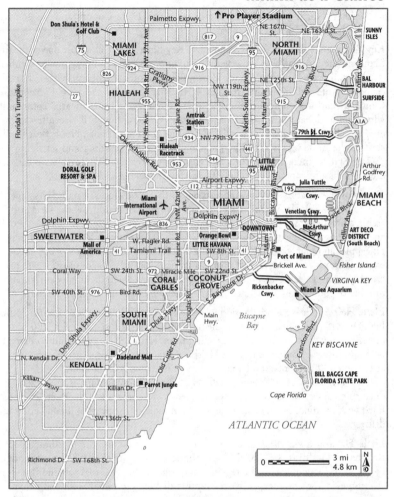

The north part of "The Beach"—Surfside, Bal Harbour, Sunny Isles, and other small neighborhoods—is, for the most part, an extension of the beach community below it. **Collins Avenue** crosses town lines with hardly a sign, while hotels, motels, restaurants, and beaches continue to line the strip. For visitors, it seems that—with some outstanding exceptions—the farther north one goes, the cheaper lodging becomes. All told, excellent prices, location, and facilities make **Surfside** and **Sunny Isles,** although a little rough around the edges, attractive places to stay. To keep up with demand for beachfront property, many of the area's moderately priced hotels have been converted to condominiums, leaving fewer and fewer kitschy and affordable places to stay.

In exclusive **Bal Harbour,** a huge alfresco mall attracts decked-out shoppers. A few elegant hotels remain amid the many beachfront condominium towers. Fancy homes, tucked away on the bay, hide behind walls, gates, and security cameras.

Note that **North Miami Beach,** a residential area near the Dade–Broward county line, is a misnomer. It is actually northwest of Miami Beach on the mainland and has no beaches. North Miami Beach is part of North Dade County and has some of Miami's better restaurants and shops.

Key Biscayne   Miami's forested and fancy Key Biscayne is technically one of the first islands in the Florida Keys. However, this luxurious island is nothing like its southern neighbors. Located south of Miami Beach, off the shores of Coconut Grove, Key Biscayne is protected from the troubles of the mainland by the long Rickenbacker Causeway and a $1 toll. Key Biscayne is largely an exclusive residential community with million-dollar homes and sweeping water views, although it also offers visitors great beaches, some top resort hotels, and several good restaurants. Hobie Beach, adjacent to the causeway, is the city's premier spot for sail-boarding and jet skiing (see "Water Sports" in chapter 5). On the island's southern tip, Bill Baggs State Park has great beaches, bike paths, and dense forests for picnicking and partying.

Downtown   Miami's downtown boasts one of the world's most beautiful cityscapes. If you do nothing else in Miami, make sure you take your time studying the area's inspired architectural designs. During the day, a vibrant community of students, businesspeople, and merchants make their way through the bustling streets. Vendors sell fresh-cut pineapples and mangos while young Latin American consumers on shopping sprees lug bags and boxes. The Downtown area has its mall (Bayside Marketplace, where many cruise passengers come to browse), its culture (Metro-Dade Cultural Center), and a number of good restaurants (listed under "Where to Dine" later in this chapter).

Little Haiti   During a brief period in the late 1970s and early 1980s, almost 35,000 Haitians arrived in Miami. Most of the new refugees settled in a decaying 200-square-block area north of Downtown. Extending from 41st to 83rd streets and bordered by I-95 and Biscayne Boulevard, Little Haiti is a relatively depressed neighborhood with at least 60,000 residents, more than half of whom were born in Haiti.

On Northeast Second Avenue, Little Haiti's main thoroughfare, is the now-closed, once-colorful Caribbean Marketplace, located at the corner of 60th Street. Previously filled with bustling shops, it stands as a sad reminder of the neighborhood's economic distress.

Little Havana   Miami's Cuban center is the city's most important ethnic enclave. Referred to locally as "Calle Ocho" (pronounced *Ka*-yey *O*-choh), SW Eighth Street, just west of Downtown, is the region's main thoroughfare. Car-repair shops, tailors, electronics stores, and inexpensive restaurants all hang signs in Spanish. Salsa rhythms thump from the radios of passersby, while old men in *guayaberas* chain-smoke cigars over their daily game of dominoes.

Coral Gables   At just over 70 years old, Coral Gables is the closest thing to "historical" that Miami has. It's also one of the prettiest parcels in the city. Created by George Merrick in the early 1920s, the Gables was one of Miami's first planned developments. The houses here were built in a Mediterranean style along lush tree-lined streets that open onto beautifully carved plazas, many with centerpiece fountains. The best architectural examples of the era have Spanish-style tiled roofs and are built from Miami oolite, a native limestone commonly called "coral rock." Coral Gables is a stunning example of "boom" architecture on a grand scale—plus it's a great area to explore. Some of the city's best restaurants are located here, as are top hotels and good shopping. See the appropriate sections below for listings.

Coconut Grove   There was a time when Coconut Grove was inhabited by artists, intellectuals, hippies, and radicals, but times have changed. Gentrification has pushed most alternative types out, leaving in their place a multitude of cafes, boutiques, and nightspots. The intersection of Grand Avenue, Main Highway, and McFarlane Road pierces the area's heart, which sizzles with dozens of interesting shops and eateries. Sidewalks here are often crowded with businesspeople, high-school students, and loads of foreign visitors—especially at night, when it becomes a great place to people-watch.

Coconut Grove's link to the Bahamas dates from before the turn of the century, when islanders came to the area to work in a newly opened hotel called the Peacock Inn. Bahamian-style wooden homes, built by these early settlers, still stand on Charles Street. Goombay, the lively annual Bahamian festival, celebrates the Grove's Caribbean link and has become one of the largest black-heritage street festivals in America.

Greater Miami South   To locals, South Miami is both a specific area, southwest of Coral Gables, and a general region that encompasses all of southern Dade County and includes Kendall, Perrine, Cutler Ridge, and Homestead. For the purposes of clarity, this book has grouped all these southern suburbs under the appellation "Greater Miami South." Similar attributes unite the communities: They are heavily residential, and all are packed with condominiums and shopping malls, as well as acres upon acres of farmland. Tourists don't stay in these parts, because there are no beaches and few cultural offerings, but Greater Miami South does contain many of the city's top attractions, making it likely you'll spend some time during the day here.

2 Getting Around

Officially, Dade County has opted for a "unified, multimodal transportation network," which basically means you can get around the city by train, bus, and taxi. However, in practice, the network doesn't work too well. In most cases, unless you are going from downtown Miami to a not-too-distant spot, you are better off in a rented car or a taxi.

With the exception of downtown Coconut Grove and South Beach, Miami is not a walker's city. Because it is so spread out, most attractions are too far apart to make walking between them feasible. In fact, most Miamians are so used to driving that they do so even when going just a few blocks.

BY PUBLIC TRANSPORTATION

BY RAIL   Two rail lines, operated by the **Metro-Dade Transit Agency** (☎ 305/ 638-6700 for information), run in concert with each other.

Metrorail, the city's modern high-speed commuter train, is a 21-mile elevated line that travels north-south, between downtown Miami and the southern suburbs. If you are staying in Coral Gables or Coconut Grove, you can park your car at a nearby station and ride the rails Downtown. Unfortunately for visitors, the line's usefulness is limited. There are plans to extend the system to service Miami International Airport, but until those tracks are built, these trains don't go most places tourists go. Metrorail operates daily from about 6am to midnight. The fare is $1.25.

Metromover, a 4.4-mile elevated line, connects with Metrorail at the Government Center stop and circles Downtown. Riding on rubber tires, the single-train car winds past many of the area's most important attractions and shopping and business districts. Metromover offers a fun, futuristic ride that you might want to take to complement your Downtown tour. You get a beautiful perspective from the towering height of the suspended rails. System hours are daily from about 6am to midnight. The fare is 25¢.

BY BUS   Miami's suburban layout is not conducive to getting around by bus. Lines operate and maps are available, but instead of getting to know the city, you'll find that relying on bus transportation will acquaint you only with how it feels to wait at bus stops. You can get a bus map by mail, either from the Greater Miami Convention and Visitors Bureau (see "Visitor Information" in chapter 2) or by writing the

Metro-Dade Transit System, 3300 NW 32nd Ave., Miami, FL 33142. In Miami, call ☎ **305/638-6700** for public-transit information. The fare is $1.25.

BY CAR

Tales circulate about vacationers who have visited Miami without a car, but they are few and far between. If you're counting on exploring the city, even to a modest degree, a car is essential. Miami's restaurants, attractions, and sights are far from one another, so any other form of transportation is impractical. You won't need a car, however, if you are spending your entire vacation at a resort, are traveling directly to the Port of Miami for a cruise, or are here for a short stay centered in one area of the city, such as South Beach.

When driving across a causeway or through Downtown, allow extra time to reach your destination because of frequent drawbridge openings. Some bridges open about every half hour for large sailing vessels that make their way through the wide bays and canals that crisscross the city, stalling traffic for several minutes. Don't get frustrated by the wait—it's all part of the easy pace of South Florida life.

RENTALS It seems as though every car-rental company, big and small, has at least one office in Miami. Consequently, the city is one of the cheapest places in the world to rent a car. Many firms regularly advertise prices in the neighborhood of $100 per week for their bottom-of-the-line tin can—not an unreasonable sum for 7 days of transportation in the land of sun and fun.

A minimum age, generally 25, is usually required of renters. Some rental agencies have also set maximum ages. A national car-rental broker, A **Car Rental Referral Service** (☎ **800/404-4482**), can often find companies willing to rent to drivers over the age of 21 and can also get discounts from major companies as well as some regional ones.

National car-rental companies with toll-free numbers include **Alamo** (☎ 800/327-9633), **Avis** (☎ 800/331-1212), **Budget** (☎ 800/527-0700), **Dollar** (☎ 800/800-4000 or 800/327-7607), **Hertz** (☎ 800/654-3131), **National** (☎ 800/328-4567), and **Thrifty** (☎ 800/367-2277). One excellent company that has offices in every conceivable part of town and offers extremely competitive rates is **Enterprise** (☎ 800/325-8007).

Many companies offer cellular phones or electronic map rental. It might be wise to opt for these additional safety features, although the cost can be exorbitant; the phone especially can come in handy if you get disoriented. There is nothing worse than being lost in a foreign city in a questionable area with no one to turn to.

Finally, think about splurging on a convertible. Few things in life can match the feeling of cruising along warm Florida highways with the sun smiling on your shoulders and the wind whipping through your hair. At most companies, the price is only about 20% more.

PARKING Always keep plenty of quarters on hand to feed hungry meters. Or, on Miami Beach, stop by the Chamber of Commerce at 1920 Meridian Ave. or any Publix grocery store to buy a magnetic parking card in denominations of $10, $20, or $25. Parking is usually plentiful (except on South Beach and Coconut Grove), but when it's not, be careful: Fines for illegal parking can be stiff, up to $18.

In addition to parking garages, valet services are commonplace and often used. Expect to pay from $3 to $10 for parking in Coconut Grove and on South Beach's Ocean Drive on busy weekend nights.

BY TAXI

If you're not planning on traveling much within the city, an occasional taxi is a good alternative to renting a car. If you plan on spending your holiday within the confines of South Beach's Art Deco District, you might also want to avoid the parking hassles that come with renting your own car. Taxi meters start at $1.50 for the first ¼ mile and 25¢ for each ⅛ mile. There are standard flat-rate charges for frequently traveled routes—for example, Miami Beach's Convention Center to Coconut Grove would cost about $16.

Major cab companies include **Metro** (☎ **305/888-8888**), **Yellow** (☎ **305/444-4444**), and, on Miami Beach, **Central** (☎ **305/532-5555**).

Fast Facts: Miami

American Express   You'll find American Express offices in downtown Miami at 330 Biscayne Blvd. (☎ **305/358-7350**); 9700 Collins Ave., Bal Harbour (☎ **305/865-5959**); and 32 Miracle Mile, Coral Gables (☎ **305/446-3381**). Offices are open weekdays from 9am to 5pm and Saturday from 10am to 4pm. The Bal Harbour office is also open on Sunday from noon to 6pm. To report lost or stolen traveler's checks, call ☎ **800/221-7282.**

Area Code   The original area code for Miami and all of Dade County was 305. That is still the code for older phone numbers, but all phone numbers assigned since July of 1998 have the area code 786 (SUN). Even though the Keys still share the Dade County area code of 305, calls to there from Miami are considered long distance and must be preceded by 1-305. Within the Keys, simply dial the seven-digit number.

Car Rentals   See "Getting Around," above.

Climate   See "When to Go," in chapter 2.

Curfew   Although not strictly enforced, there is a curfew in effect for minors after 11pm on weeknights and midnight on weekends in all of Miami-Dade County. After those hours, children under 17 cannot be out on the streets or driving unless accompanied by a parent or on their way to work.

Dentists   The East Coast District Dental Society staffs an **Emergency Dental Referral Service** (☎ **305/285-5470**). **A&E Dental,** 11400 N. Kendall Dr., Mega Bank Building (☎ **305/271-7777**), also offers round-the-clock care and accepts MasterCard and Visa.

Doctors   In an emergency, call an ambulance by dialing ☎ **911** from any phone. The Dade County Medical Association sponsors a **Physician Referral Service** (☎ **305/324-8717**) weekdays from 9am to 5pm. **Health South Doctors' Hospital,** 5000 University Dr., Coral Gables (☎ **305/666-2111**), is a 285-bed acute-care hospital with a 24-hour physician-staffed emergency department.

Drugstores   See "Pharmacies," below.

Embassies/Consulates   See chapter 3.

Emergencies   To reach the police, ambulance, or fire department, dial ☎ **911** from any phone. No coins are needed. Emergency hotlines include Crisis Intervention (☎ **305/358-HELP** or **305/358-4357**) and Poison Information Center (☎ **800/282-3171**).

Eyeglasses   **Pearle Vision Center,** 7901 Biscayne Blvd. (☎ **305/754-5144**), in Miami, can usually fill prescriptions in about an hour.

Hospitals   See "Doctors," above.

Information   See "Visitor Information," earlier in this chapter.

Laundry/Dry Cleaning   For dry cleaning, self-service machines, and a wash-and-fold service by the pound, call **All Laundry Service,** 5701 NW 7th St. (west of Downtown, ☎ **305/261-8175**); it's open daily from 7am to 10pm. **Clean Machine Laundry,** 226 12th St., South Beach (☎ **305/534-9429**), is convenient to South Beach's art deco hotels; it's open 24 hours. **Coral Gables Laundry & Dry Cleaning,** 250 Minorca Ave., Coral Gables (☎ **305/446-6458**), has been dry cleaning, altering, and laundering since 1930. It offers a lifesaving same-day service and is open weekdays from 7am to 7pm and Saturday from 8am to 3pm.

Liquor Laws   Only adults 21 or older may legally purchase or consume alcohol in the state of Florida. Minors are usually permitted in bars that serve food. Liquor laws are strictly enforced; if you look young, carry identification. Beer and wine are sold in most supermarkets and convenience stores. The city of Miami's liquor stores are closed on Sunday. Liquor stores in the city of Miami Beach are open all week.

Newspapers/Magazines   The *Miami Herald* is the city's only English-language daily. It is especially known for its Latin American coverage and its excellent Friday "Weekend" entertainment guide. There are literally dozens of specialized Miami magazines geared toward visitors and natives alike. Many are free and can be picked up at hotels, at restaurants, and in self-serve boxes all around town. The most respected alternative weekly is the giveaway tabloid called *New Times,* which contains up-to-date listings and reviews of food, films, theater, music, and whatever else is happening in town. Also free if you can find it is *Ocean Drive,* a gorgeous oversized glossy magazine, available at a number of chic South Beach boutiques and restaurants. It also sells on newsstands.

For a large selection of foreign-language newspapers and magazines, check with any of the large bookstores or try **News Cafe** at 800 Ocean Dr., South Beach (☎ **305/538-6397**), or in Coconut Grove at 2901 Florida Ave. (☎ **305/774-6397**); **Eddie's Normandy,** 1096 Normandy Dr., Miami Beach (☎ **305/866-2026**); and **Worldwide News,** 1629 NE 163rd St., North Miami Beach (☎ **305/940-4090**).

Pharmacies   The most ubiquitous drugstore is **Walgreens Pharmacy,** with dozens of locations all over town, including 8550 Coral Way (☎ **305/221-9271**), in Coral Gables; 1845 Alton Rd. (☎ **305/531-8868**), in South Beach; and 6700 Collins Ave. (☎ **305/861-6742**), in Miami Beach. The branch at 5731 Bird Rd. at SW 40th Street (☎ **305/666-0757**) is open 24 hours, as is **Eckerd Drugs,** 1825 Miami Gardens Dr. NE, at 185th Street, North Miami Beach (☎ **305/932-5740**).

Police   For emergencies, dial ☎ **911** from any phone. No coins are needed. For other matters, call ☎ **305/595-6263.**

Post Office   The **Main Post Office,** 2200 Milam Dairy Rd., Miami, FL 33152 (☎ **305/639-4280**), is located west of Miami International Airport. Conveniently located post offices include 1300 Washington Ave. (☎ **305/531-7306**), in South Beach, and 3191 Grand Ave. (☎ **305/443-0030**), in Coconut Grove.

Safety   Don't walk alone at night, and be extra wary when walking or driving though Downtown Miami and surrounding areas. It's always a good idea to stay aware of your surroundings when you're in any unfamiliar city, even in the most heavily touristed areas. Always consult a good map and know where you are going before getting in your car. Never stop on a highway—if you get a flat tire, drive to the nearest well-lighted, populated place. Keep car doors locked and stay alert.

Taxes   A 6% state sales tax (plus .5% local tax, for a total of 6.5% in Miami) is added on at the register for all goods and services purchased in Florida. In addition, most municipalities levy special taxes on restaurants and hotels. In Surfside, hotel taxes total 10.5%; in Bal Harbour, 9.5%; in Miami Beach (including South Beach), 11.5%; and in the rest of Dade County, a whopping 12.5%. In Miami Beach, Surfside, and Bal Harbour, the resort (hotel) tax also applies to hotel restaurants and restaurants with liquor licenses.

Taxis   See "Getting Around," earlier in this chapter.

Transit Information   For **Metrorail** or **Metromover** schedule information, phone ☎ **305/770-3131.**

Weather   Hurricane season runs from August through November. For an up-to-date recording of current weather conditions and forecast reports, call ☎ **305/229-4522.**

3 Accommodations

Many of the old hotels from the 1930s, 1940s, and 1950s (when most Miami resorts were constructed) have been totally overhauled, but others have survived with occasional coats of paint and new carpeting, which some owners like to call "renovation." When checking them out, be sure to ask about exactly what work has been done; especially on the ocean, sea air and years of tourist wear can result in musty, paint-peeled rooms. I've omitted the more worn hotels and tried to list only those that have been fully upgraded recently. Exceptions are noted.

If you can't get a room after inquiring at the hotels listed in this guide (an extremely unlikely prospect), look along South Beach's Collins Avenue. There are dozens of hotels and motels on this strip—in all price categories—so there's bound to be a vacancy.

SEASONS & RATES   South Florida's tourist season is well defined, beginning in mid-November and lasting until Easter. Hotel prices escalate until about March, after which they begin to decline. During the off-season, hotel rates are typically 30% to 50% lower than their winter highs.

But timing isn't everything. In many cases, rates also depend on your hotel's proximity to the beach and how much ocean you can see from your window. Small motels a block or two from the water can be up to 40% cheaper than similar properties right on the sand. When a hotel is on the beach, its oceanfront rooms are significantly more expensive than similar accommodations in the rear.

Most hotels allow one or two children to stay free when they are accompanied by their parents. Most consider children to be those under the age of 16. Others cut it off at 11 or 9. Call to check on the specific policy of the accommodation you've chosen.

Rates below have been broken down into two broad categories: winter (generally, Thanksgiving through Easter) and off-season (about mid-May through Aug). The months in between, the shoulder season, should fall somewhere in between the highs and lows. Rates always go up on holidays. Remember, too, that state and city taxes can add as much as 12.5% to your bill in some parts of Miami. Some hotels, especially those in South Beach, also tack on additional service charges. And parking is pricey.

PRICE CATEGORIES   The hotels below are divided first by area, then by price, using the following guidelines: Very Expensive, over $250; Expensive, over $180; Moderate, $90 to $180; and Inexpensive, below $90. Prices are based on published rates (or rack rates) for a standard double room during the high season. Check with

---

Be sure to find out if the hotel you're booking will be undergoing construction during your visit—there's nothing worse than the sound of jackhammers over breakfast.

---

the reservations agent since many rooms are also available above and below the category ranges listed. And always ask about packages, since it's often possible to get a better deal than these "official" rates.

LONG-TERM STAYS   If you plan to visit Miami for a month, a season, or more, think about renting a room in a long-term hotel or condominium apartment. Long-term accommodations exist in every price category, from budget to deluxe, and in general are extremely reasonable, especially during the off-season. Check with the reservation services below, or write a short note to the chamber of commerce in the area where you plan to stay. In addition, many local real-estate agents also handle short-term rentals (meaning less than a year).

RESERVATION SERVICES   Central Reservations (☎ **800/950-0232** or 305/274-6832; www.reservation-services.com; e-mail: rooms@america.com) works with many of Miami's hotels and can often secure discounts of up to 40%. It also gives advice on specific locales, especially in Miami Beach and Downtown.

The **South Florida Hotel Network** (☎ **800/538-3616** or 305/538-3616) lists more than 300 hotels throughout the area, from Palm Beach to Miami and down to the Keys.

SOUTH BEACH

Most of the art deco hotels on South Beach were built in the late 1930s, just after the Depression, in an area originally planned as an affordable destination for middle-class northeasterners. None of them were really luxurious—they just happened to be situated on one of the most beautiful strips of beach in the country. Large resorts like the Fontainebleau and Eden Roc were built later, about 20 blocks north of South Beach, to cater to celebrities and jet-setters. These were the spots where Sinatra and the rest of the Rat Pack hung out.

But after many years of transition, South Beach gained national recognition for its unique art deco architecture. The area is now South Florida's number one tourist destination and home to many of the city's best restaurants and nightclubs.

The most expensive rooms are on Ocean Drive or Collins Avenue, just across the street from the beach. Thankfully, for at least most of South Beach, new buildings cannot be built directly on the sand and cannot exceed three stories.

Unless noted otherwise, most of these hotels offer no-smoking rooms. Inquire before booking.

One of the best chain hotel options is the **Howard Johnson Tudor Hotel** (☎ **800/446-4656** or 305/534-2934) at 1111 Collins Ave., 1 block from the beach but right in the happening South Beach nightlife area. Rates are moderate, starting at $115 a night in season. Some more reasonably priced options include the **Days Inn** (☎ **800/325-2525** or 305/538-6631) at 100 21st St. (off Collins Avenue) and the **Holiday Inn** (☎ **800/HOLIDAY** or 305/534-1511) at 2201 Collins Ave. They're right on the ocean at the north edge of the historic district, within walking distance of the nightlife scene. They both play up the tropical look and offer standard chain-hotel–style rooms for under $90, even in high season. The Holiday Inn has lushly landscaped grounds, hidden behind an Eckerd's drugstore, and lots of amenities, including a private beach,

South Beach Accommodations

To Central Miami Beach
23rd St.
22nd St.
The Bass Museum of Art
Collins Park
Dade Boulevard
Miami Beach Convention Center
20th St.
19th St.
18th St.
Jackie Gleason Theater of Performing Arts
17th St.
James Ave.
Purdy Ave.
Dade Boulevard
Venetian Causeway
West Ave.
Alton Rd.
Lenox Ave.
Belle Island
Lincoln Road Mall
Lincoln Rd.
Collins Ave.
16th St.
Bay Rd.
15th St.
Española Way
14th St.
Ocean Dr.
Miami Beach Post Office
13th St.
Biscayne Bay
12th St.
Michigan Ave.
Meridian Ave.
Washington Ave.
Pennsylvania Ave.
Flamingo Park
11th St.
Beach Patrol Station
10th St.
Art Deco Welcome Center
9th St.
West Ave.
Alton Rd.
Lenox Ave.
Lummus Park
8th St.
7th St.
6th St.
Jefferson Ave.
Michigan Ave.
Atlantic Ocean
5th St.
4th St.
3rd St.
Washington Ave.
Collins Ave.
Ocean Dr.
2nd St.
1st St.
Commerce St.
Biscayne St.
South Pointe Park
Government Cut

The Albion Hotel **4**
The Avalon Hotel **18**
Banana Bungalow **1**
Casa Grande Suite Hotel **17**
Cavalier **10**
Clay Hotel & Int'l Hostel **8**
The Delano **5**
Essex House **13**
Fisher Island Club **19**
Hotel Astor **14**
Hotel Continental Riande **2**
Hotel Leon **16**
Loew's Miami Beach Hotel **7**
The Majestic Hotel **19**
Marseilles Hotel **3**
The Mermaid Guesthouse **15**
The National Hotel **6**
Park Washington Hotel **12**
The Tides **11**
Villa Paradiso **9**

0 .2 mi
0 .124 km

NA-0162

water-sports equipment rentals, and a car-rental desk. The Days Inn is on a public beach and has a car-rental deck but no water-sports equipment.

VERY EXPENSIVE

✪ **Casa Grande Suite Hotel.** 834 Ocean Dr., South Beach, FL 33139. ☎ **800/OUTPOST** or 305/672-7003. Fax 305/673-3669. www.islandlife.com. 34 units. A/C MINIBAR TV TEL. Winter $275–$450 suite; $525 two-bedroom suite; $1,500 three-bedroom suite. Off-season $225–$300 double; $345 two-bedroom suite; $750 three-bedroom suite. Additional person $15 extra. AE, CB, DC, DISC, MC, V. Valet parking $14.

Europeans and vacationing celebs looking for privacy enjoy the casual elegance and thoughtful service of this hotel right on "Deco Drive." Here you'll feel as though you're staying in a very stylish apartment, not in a cookie-cutter hotel room. Every room is outfitted in a slightly different style with fully equipped kitchenettes, beautifully tiled baths, reed rugs, mahogany beds, handmade batik prints, and antiques from all over the world, particularly Indonesia. There's no pool on the property, but considering that you can see the ocean, stock your own fridge, and veg out with a good stereo and VCR, this is one of the most desirable hotels on South Beach. Some rooms facing the ocean can be loud, especially on weekend nights.

Amenities: Room service, overnight dry cleaning and laundry, complimentary newspaper and evening turndown with chocolates, twice-daily maid service, express checkout, baby-sitting arrangements. VCRs and videos are available to rent. Full kitchens, CD/cassette stereo, conference rooms, car rental, activities desk, access to a nearby health club.

The Delano. 1685 Collins Ave., South Beach, FL 33139. ☎ **800/555-5001** or 305/672-2000. Fax 305/532-0099. 210 units, 1 penthouse. A/C MINIBAR TV TEL. Winter $310–$415 double; $475 loft; $700 suite; $800 bungalow; $1,850 two-bedroom; $2,200 penthouse. Off-season $180–$265 double (weekend rates for double same as winter rates); all other room rates same as winter rates. Additional person $35 extra. AE, DC, DISC, MC, V. Valet parking $16.

When the Delano—pronounced like FDR's middle name—opened in 1995, it made the front page of nearly every architecture and style magazine in the country for its whimsical and elegant design. Look for a huge hedge with a simple blue arched door in its center, or look up for a rocket-like fin (an original 1947 detail) sprouting from the top of the all-white building. New York's Ian Shrager, of Studio 54 fame, brought in designer Philippe Starck, who went wild with the decor, including 40-foot sheer white curtains hanging outside, mirrors everywhere, white billowing curtains, Adirondack chairs, and fur-covered beds. The guest rooms are all white; a perfectly crisp green Granny Smith apple in each one is the only dose of color. It may sound antiseptic, but it actually comes across as sexy and sophisticated. The poolside cabanas are the most desirable rooms because of their huge size, but they can be noisy since they're on an active poolside walkway.

Unfortunately, the model-gorgeous staff is often aloof or simply unavailable. But the location is ideal; it's just north of the Art Deco District strip of bars and restaurants, away from the noisy street traffic but close enough to walk to hopping Lincoln Road Mall. And, of course, it's right on the ocean with plenty of in-house activity to keep you busy.

Factoid

Remember, most of the art deco hotels are generally small, have tiny bathrooms, and few services and facilities.

Dining/Diversions: An elegant bar attracts curious and beautiful people nightly. The Blue Door (owned in part by Madonna) is known as a place to be seen and for great cuisine, but the service is full of attitude. The thatched Beach Bar restaurant serves fantastic sandwiches and salads. New in 1999 is Blue Seas, an Asian seafood restaurant with communal seating offering, among other things, sushi, stone crabs, lobster, and caviar.

Amenities: Concierge, room service, same-day dry cleaning and laundry, news-paper delivery, evening turndown, in-room massage, executive business services, express checkout. VCRs, video rentals, children's movie theater and child activity pro-grams, gorgeous large outdoor pool, wide guarded beach, business center, conference rooms, rooftop solarium, extensive water-sports recreation, funky gift shop, 24-hour state-of-the-art David Barton gym with sauna. Aqua Spa is $10 for hotel guests; open for women 9am to 7pm, men 7:30 to 11pm, and closed Tuesday night. Offers facials and a plethora of massages and water treatments.

Loews Hotel. 1601 Collins Ave., South Beach, FL 33139. ☎ **800/23LOEWS** or 305/604-1601. www.loewshotels.com. 800 units. A/C MINIBAR TV TEL. Winter from $309 double, from $600 suites; $2,500 to $5,000 for the presidential suites. Off-season from $250 double. AE, DC, DISC, MC, V. Valet parking $19.

Just opened at press time, this 800-room hotel is the first new hotel to be built in South Beach for the past 30 years. It's also the largest, which is a good thing—the Beach was sorely in need of a large hotel to accommodate business travelers who come to the nearby convention center. Accordingly, it features plenty of meeting rooms, ballrooms, a large health club, and seven restaurants and lounges. Like the Fontainebleau and Eden Roc 30 blocks north, the Loews is a full-service, beachfront resort. However, it has the advantage of being brand-new and situated right in the heart of the bustling Art Deco district.

Dining/Diversions: Six different restaurants and lounges offer American, Argen-tinean, and casual bar food. A sleek martini bar and coffee shop round out the offerings, making it possible to spend your entire time in this impressive new resort.

Amenities: 24-hour concierge service, room service, dry cleaning, laundry, news-paper delivery, in-room massage, twice-daily maid service, baby-sitting, secretarial service, express checkout. VCRs available on request, video rental, outdoor pool with jet streams, access to nearby health club, two phones in each room.

The National Hotel. 1677 Collins Ave., South Beach. ☎ **800/327-8370** or 305/532-2311. Fax 305/534-1426. www.nationalhotel.com. 154 units. A/C MINIBAR TV TEL. Winter $250–$320 room; $340–$385 room with a view and/or balcony; $580–$1,000 suites. Off-season from $240 room; $250–$320 room with a view and/or balcony; $420–$800 suite. AE, CB, DC, DISC, EC, JCB, MC, V. Valet parking $16.

This elegant newcomer has joined the ranks of South Beach's particular brand of luxury resorts. Since there is so much to offer in the neighborhood, these "resorts" tend to offer limited on-site facilities and concentrate more on style and service. The National does a super job. With its towering ceilings, sultry furnishings, and massive gilded mirrors, the elegant 1940s lobby ought to be the backdrop for a gangster flick. At 11 stories, the main building stands taller than most of its neighbors and offers grand views of the beach and ocean below. Rooms in the garden wing are slightly larger and have balconies, but all are comfortable and pretty spacious. The hotel is located a few doors down from the famed Delano, right on the ocean and just a few blocks from the best shopping and dining in town.

Dining/Diversions: The Oval Room is an elegant and formal dining room offering decent fare from an eclectic menu. Two outside dining spots overlook the pools and serve drinks, light meals, snacks, and sandwiches. There are three bars, including The Deco Lounge, which features a lively happy hour with live jazz in season.

Amenities: Concierge, room service (24 hours), dry-cleaning and laundry service, newspaper delivery, evening turndown, twice-daily maid service, baby-sitting, express checkout. Stereos and two TVs in suites, VCRs, video rental, two outdoor pools, large beach, small fitness room, small business center, water-sports concession (including scuba and sailing).

☼ **The Tides.** 1220 Ocean Dr., South Beach, FL 33139. ☎ **800/OUTPOST** or 305/604-5000. Fax 305/672-6288. www.islandlife.com. 45 units. A/C MINIBAR TV TEL. Winter $375–$450 suites; $1,000–$2,000 penthouse. Off-season $300–$375 suite; $800–$2,000 penthouse. Additional person $20 extra. Rates include continental breakfast. AE, CB, DC, JCB, MC, V. Valet parking $15.

Opened in late 1997 to rave reviews, this 12-story art deco masterpiece is one of the tallest buildings on the strip of Ocean Drive. It is the latest addition to the Island Outpost group, which includes the Cavalier, The Kent, Casa Grande (reviewed in this section), and others. Rooms are starkly white but luxurious. The welcoming staff and central location are its definite strong points. Also, all rooms are at least twice the size of a typical South Beach hotel room and have a view of the ocean. Although small, the freshwater pool on the rear mezzanine is a welcome plus for those who have had enough of the wild beach scene across the street.

Dining/Diversions: Twelve Twenty is the hotel's fine restaurant. It serves dinner nightly 6pm to midnight. The Terrace, a gorgeous outdoor cafe overlooking the ocean, does a fine job of breakfast and lunch. There's also a lobby lounge with live entertainment.

Amenities: Concierge, room service (24 hour), dry cleaning, laundry service, newspaper delivery, in-room massage, twice-daily maid service, baby-sitting, secretarial services, express check-out. Stereos with cassette and CD player and a selection of CDs in each room, VCRs, video rentals, heated outdoor pool, small health club and discount at large nearby health club, conference rooms.

EXPENSIVE

Albion Hotel. 1650 James Ave. (at Lincoln Rd.). ☎ **888/665-0008** or 305/913-1000. Fax 305/674-0507. www.rubellhotels.com. 100 units. A/C MINIBAR TV TEL. Winter $250–$325 double; $375–$700 suite. Off-season $150–$225 double; $299–$600 suite. AE, CB, DC, DISC, MC, V. Valet parking $17.

An architectural masterpiece originally designed in 1939 by internationally acclaimed architect Igor Polivitzky, this large Streamline Moderne building looks like a cruise ship with portholes, smokestack, and sleek curved lines. It was totally renovated in 1997, under the guidance of the hip New York family the Rubells. Although you have to walk a few blocks to find beach access, you may not want to. A huge pool and artificial beach are original features at this unusual and recommendable resort. Rooms are furnished with wonderful modern furnishings custom-designed for the space. The hotel is popular with those in the music and modeling industry and often serves as the backdrop for parties and shoots.

The Rubell family owns a second hotel just around the corner, The Greenview, with rates about 40 percent lower. Rooms are just as comfortable, but amenities are slightly more limited—you won't find a pool, restaurant, or bar, for example. But it's a great alternative if you want to save a little spending money for shopping on nearby Lincoln Road.

Dining: An elegant Mexican restaurant and outdoor cafe, Mayya was in the works at press time. Drinks, salads, and sandwiches are available at the pool. The Fallabella bar attracts a good-looking crowd for occasional live music and happy hours.

Amenities: Concierge, room service, dry cleaning, evening turndown, in-room massage, newspaper delivery, twice-daily maid service, baby-sitting, executive business services, valet parking, airport limo service. VCRs available on request, large outdoor heated pool with adjacent artificial-sand beach, workout room, business services on request, small conference and production rooms, stereos with CD and cassette player (but no CDs), state-of-the-art phones with data port and voice mail.

✪ **Hotel Astor.** 956 Washington Ave., South Beach, FL 33139. ☎ **800/270-4981** or 305/531-8081. Fax 305/531-3193. www.hotelastor.com. 40 units. A/C MINIBAR TV TEL. Winter $145–$200 rms; $275–$320 suites. Off-season $115–$190 rms; $245–$290 suites. Astor suite $420–$600. Additional person $30. AE, MC, V. Valet parking $14.

For the price (at least 30% less than the Delano), this is a great option for those who like intimate but terribly hip accommodations. A small but elegant and modern hotel, the Astor attracts many loyal return guests. Originally built in 1936, the renovation in 1995 greatly improved on the original design of this simple three-story gem. There are a small lap pool and a beautiful waterfall outside the sleek lobby bar area. All the details are pure luxury, like swivel stands for the large-screen TVs, Belgian linens and towels, and funky custom lighting with dimmer switches. The hotel staff is known for bending over backward. This low-profile hotel is definitely a place for those in the know. Unfortunately, the few moderately priced standard rooms are usually booked months in advance, but the more pricey ones are well worth the expense.

Dining: Astor Place is one of Miami's best restaurants. The Florida-style menu is diverse and delicious (see listing under "South Beach" in the "Where to Dine" section, below). Sunday brunch is one of the best in town.

Amenities: 24-hour concierge service, room service, dry cleaning, laundry, newspaper delivery, in-room massage, twice-daily maid service, baby-sitting, secretarial service, express checkout. VCRs available on request, video rental, outdoor pool with jet streams, access to nearby health club, two phones in suites.

MODERATE

Avalon Majestic Hotel. 700 Ocean Dr. (at 7th St.), South Beach, FL 33139. ☎ **800/ 933-3306** or 305/538-0133. Fax 305/534-0258. www.southbeachhotels.com. 103 units. A/C TV TEL. Winter $120–$210 double. Off-season $65–$175 double. Rates include continental breakfast. 10% discount for stays of 7 days or more. AE, CB, DC, DISC, MC, V. Valet parking $14.

These striking hotels offer classic art deco digs right on the beach at even more attractive prices. The simple rooms, decorated in traditional 1930s style, are nothing fancy but are comfortable if a bit on the small side. The modest lobby holds a casual restaurant, best for lunch either inside or on the breezy outdoor patio.

Room service, free coffee, refreshments, and breakfast are also available. If the Avalon is full, don't hesitate to accept a room in its companion property, the South Seas on 17th and Collins.

Cavalier. 1320 Ocean Dr., South Beach, FL 33139. ☎ **800/OUTPOST** or 305/604-5000. Fax 305/531-5543. questions@islandoutpost.com. 45 units. A/C MINIBAR TV TEL. Winter $125–$195 double; $275–$350 suite. Off-season $95–$155 double; $230–$250 suite. Additional person $15 extra. AE, DC, DISC, MC, V. Valet parking $14; self-parking $6.

The Cavalier, a hip, well-priced hotel, is kept in shape by yearly refurbishments. You can't beat its oceanfront location, adjacent to shops and restaurants. Palm trees brush the ceilings of the modest lobby, where young, trendy guests make their way to their rooms. Funky prints cover the walls, which are the colors of a tequila sunrise. A young, competent staff waits on guests and offers lots of good advice about local clubs, restaurants, and shopping. Rooms come equipped with CD players and discs. You can also use a VCR and rent videos. Despite the Ocean Drive location, most rooms are relatively quiet.

Essex House. 1001 Collins Ave., South Beach, FL 33139. ☎ **800/55-ESSEX** or 305/534-2700. Fax 305/532-3827. www.travelbase.com/destinations. 58 units. A/C TV TEL. Winter $150–$350. Off-season $109–$295. Rates include deluxe continental breakfast. Minimum stay 2 nights on weekends in season, 3 nights on holidays. AE, DC, DISC, MC, V. Valet parking $14. Nearby parking available for $4 weekdays, $6 weekends and holidays.

This art deco landmark, just a block from the ocean, is one of South Beach's architectural gems, especially since the $3 million renovation completed in 1998. The pretty Essex House is a textbook example of Streamline Moderne style, complete with large porthole windows, original etched glasswork, ziggurat arches, and detailed crown moldings. The solid-oak bedroom furnishings are also original and, like many other details in this special hotel, were carefully restored. Suites feature minibars, coffeemakers, and VCRs. Ask for a room with a refrigerator, since more than a dozen standard rooms do have them. The Essex also features 24-hour reception, a baby grand, a self-playing piano in the lobby/lounge, and a state-of-the-art security system. This hotel is spic-and-span, almost too much like a chain, but the staff is extremely pleasant and helpful.

A very small pool is just one of the many new additions here.

The Governor Hotel. 435 21st St., Miami Beach, FL 33139. ☎ **800/542-0444** or 305/532-2100. Fax 305/532-9139. 125 units. A/C TV TEL. Winter $89–$125 double. Off-season $69–$89 double. AE, DC, DISC, MC, V. Free parking.

This reasonably priced South Beach hotel frequented by conventioneers is nothing special, but the rooms are decent and the rates are pretty cheap. However, as an example of art deco architecture, this hotel is one of the most stylish in the area. It has streamlined details, from the checkerboard floor tiles to the steel marquee and looming flagstaffs, but don't expect too much inside. A recent revamping improved the slightly tacky decor and introduced some better staff. You'll want to drive to the beach since it's a few long blocks through a not-so-scenic neighborhood of mostly seedy hotels. The Governor has a medium-size pool and a small cafe and bar.

Hotel Continental Riande. 1825 Collins Ave., South Beach, FL 33139. ☎ **800/RIANDE-1** or 305/531-3503. Fax 305/531-2803. riande@iconnect.net. 251 units. A/C MINIBAR TV TEL. Winter $150–$280 double. Off-season $135–$260. Additional person $10 extra. Frommer's readers get a 20% discount. AE, DC, DISC, MC, V. Valet parking $8.

The Riande is just the ticket if you want value and convenience right on South Beach. Catering to a largely Latin and European clientele, this hotel overlooking the ocean has become quite well-known. It's just 2 blocks from The Delano and the best of South Beach. The rooms and lobby areas are clean and well maintained, but not too fussy. A large outdoor pool and sundeck are just out back. There's also a restaurant/coffee shop with both buffet and menu service. Room service is available daily for breakfast and dinner.

✪ Hotel Leon. 841 Collins Ave., South Beach, FL 33139. ☎ **305/673-3767.** Fax 305/673-5866. www.hotelleon.com. 18 units. A/C TV TEL. Winter $125 rms; $165–$215 suites; $375 penthouse. Off-season $100 rms; $135–$185 suites; $315 penthouse. $10 for an extra bed. AE, DC, MC, V. Valet parking $14.

A true value, this stylish sliver of a property has won the loyalty of fashion industrialists and romantics alike. The very central location, 1 block from the sea and in the heart of shopping and dining, means a car isn't necessary. The spacious, well-renovated rooms are sparkling clean and warmly appointed. Gleaming wood floors and simple pale furnishings are appreciated in a neighborhood where many others overdo the art deco motif. Each room has two phones, sunken oval tubs, robes, CD players, and CDs. Unfortunately, there's no pool or sundeck but the beach is only a 2-minute walk. A meeting room and business center make it a fine choice for business trips. In the standard rooms, there are no minibars or fridges, but you can order room service. In the morning, enjoy a moderately priced breakfast ($8.50) of croissants, fresh rolls, ham, cheese, and eggs cooked to order. The owners, a young German couple, have made a commitment to providing excellent service with a distinctly personal touch, and they have succeeded.

Marseilles Hotel. 1741 Collins Ave., South Beach, FL 33139. ☎ **800/327-4739** or 305/538-5711. Fax 305/673-1006. www.marseilleshotel.com. 116 units. A/C TV TEL. Winter $115–$135 double; $180 suite. Off-season $79–$99 double; $145 suites. Frommer's readers get 10% discount. AE, DC, DISC, MC, V. Self-parking $9.

With these low promotional rates, the Marseilles is one of the very best deals in this super-trendy area. It's a full-service, inexpensive, classic art deco hotel, located right on the beach and near the best of everything. The staff is pleasant, the restaurant and bar are very recommendable, and the decor is thoroughly tasteful. Still, a little worn around the edges, the property seems to improve a little bit each year. Owners Lloyd and Clara Mandell make a point of being around to see that everything runs smoothly. You may meet them in the lobby, where free refreshments are usually served.

With only about 100 rooms, the Marseilles is more intimate than the larger and similarly priced Riande, a few doors away. The suites (three of which have Jacuzzis at no extra charge) are an exceptionally good deal if you want to spend a lot of time in your room. You'll find a telescope for spying on scantily clad sunbathers below. Otherwise, standard rooms are on the small side but clean and comfortable. All have small refrigerators and bottled water upon check-in. The bar and restaurant are popular with budget-seeking locals. When the Marseilles is full, the staff may suggest putting you at the nearby Dorchester. It's cheaper and decent but not nearly as recommendable.

✪ The Mermaid Guesthouse. 909 Collins Ave., Miami Beach, FL 33140. ☎ **305/538-5324.** 8 units. A/C TEL. Winter $105–$125 single or double; $275 terraced suite. Off-season $75–$95 single or double; $175 suite. Additional person $10 extra. Discounts available for longer stays. AE, MC, V.

There's something magical about this little hideaway tucked behind tropical gardens in the very heart of South Beach. You won't find the amenities of the larger hotels here, but the charm and hospitality at this one-story guest house keeps people coming back. Plus, it's smack in the middle of the hottest part of South Beach and less than 2 blocks from the ocean.

In 1996 the new owners, Ana and Gonzalo Torres, did a thorough clean-up, adding new brightly colored fretwork around the doors and windows and installing phones in each room. Also, the wood floors have been stripped or covered in straw matting, one of the many Caribbean touches that make this place so cheery. There are no TVs, so guests tend to congregate in the lush garden in the evenings. The owners sometimes host free impromptu dinners for their guests and friends. Ask if they've scheduled any live Latin music during your stay; you won't want to miss it.

INEXPENSIVE

Banana Bungalow. 2360 Collins Ave., Miami Beach, FL 33139. ☎ **800/7-HOSTEL** or 305/538-1951. Fax 305/531-3217. www.bananabungalow.com. 90 units. A/C TV TEL. Winter $13–$16 per person in shared rms; $60–$70 single; $70–$80 double. Off-season $12–$14 per person in shared rms; $40–$50 single; $50–$60 double. MC, V. Free parking.

This youth hostel-ish hotel is a welcome addition to the South Beach budget scene. Across the street is a popular beach; the best shops, clubs, and restaurants are only 6 or 7 blocks away. A redone 1950s two-story newcomer surrounds a pool and deck complete with shuffleboard, a small alfresco cafe serving cheap meals, and a tiki bar where young European travelers hang out.

The best rooms face a narrow canal where motorboats and kayaks are available for a small charge. In general, rooms are clean and well kept, despite a few rusty faucets and chipped Formica furnishings. Guests in shared rooms need to bring their own towels. This is one of the only hotels in this price range with a private pool. Guests can also take advantage of free coffee and refreshments each morning, a communal kitchen, access to a nearby health club, a coin laundry, free movies, sightseeing tours, discounts at local clubs, and a great community spirit.

✪ **Brigham Gardens.** 1411 Collins Ave., South Beach, FL 33139. ☎ **305/531-1331.** Fax 305/538-9898. www.brighamgardens-mbch.com. 19 units. A/C TV TEL. Winter $85–$130 double. Off-season $60–$110 double. Additional person $5 extra. 10% discount on stays of 7 days or longer. Pets stay for $6 a night. AE, MC, V.

There's no pool or other niceties, but you'll find this funky place a homey and affordable oasis in the midst of high prices and commercialization. Also, the location is prime. Because most rooms have full kitchens, you'll find many people staying for longer than a weekend. You may, too. All rooms have microwaves and coffeepots, at least. You can barbecue in the garden.

When you enter the tropically landscaped garden, you'll hear macaws and parrots chirping and see cats and lizards running through the bougainvillea. The tiny but lush grounds are framed by quaint Mediterranean buildings—they're pleasant, although in need of some sprucing up. This happy spot is run by a mother and daughter who go out of their way to see that guests and their pets are well cared for. *A warning:* As with most other small properties on South Beach, parking can be a pain, though there is a city lot 1 block south.

Clay Hotel & International Hostel. 1438 Washington Ave. (at Española Way), South Beach, FL 33139. ☎ **305/534-2988.** Fax 305/673-0346. www.clayhotel.com. 350 beds in singles, doubles, and dorm rms. $40–$50 single; $45–65 double; $14–$16 dorm beds. Sheets $2 extra. During the off-season, pay for 6 nights in advance and get 7th night free. JCB, MC, V.

A member of the International Youth Hostel Federation (IYHF), the Clay occupies a beautiful 1920s-style Spanish Mediterranean building at the corner of historic Española Way. Like other IYHF members, this hostel is open to all ages and is a great place to meet people. The usual smattering of Australians, Europeans, and other budget travelers makes it Miami's best clearinghouse of "insider" travel information. Even if you don't stay here, you might want to check out the ride board or mingle with fellow travelers over a beer at the sidewalk cafe.

Although a thorough renovation in 1996 made this hostel an incredible value and a step above any others in town, don't expect nightly turndown service or chocolates. You will find a self-serve Laundromat, occasional movie nights, and a tour desk with car rental available. Reservations are essential for private rooms year-round and are recommended in season. In summer, be sure to ask for a room with air-conditioning. Don't bother with a car in this congested area.

Park Washington Hotel. 1020 Washington Ave., South Beach, FL 33139. ☎ **305/532-1930.** Fax 305/672-6706. www.parkwashingtonresort.com. 36 units. A/C TV TEL. Winter $99 double; $129 suite. Off-season $79 double; $99 suite. Rates include self-serve coffee and danish. Additional person $20 extra. AE, MC, V.

The Park Washington is a large, refurbished hotel just 2 blocks from the ocean that offers some of the best values in South Beach—good rooms at incredible prices. Designed in the 1930s by Henry Hohauser, one of the beach's most prolific architects, the Park Washington reopened in 1989. Most of the rooms have original furnishings and well-kept interiors, and some have kitchenettes. Guests also enjoy a decent-sized outdoor heated pool with a sundeck, bikes for rent, and access to a nearby health club.

The same owners run the adjacent Taft House and Kenmore hotels. All three attract a large gay clientele, and all offer privacy, lush landscaping, a great pool and sundeck, consistent quality, and a value-oriented philosophy. You can't park on the premises, but there's a public garage at 7th Street, less than 3 blocks away.

Villa Paradiso. 1415 Collins Ave., Miami Beach, FL 33139. ☎ **305/532-0616.** Fax 305/673-5874. www.sobe.com/villaparadiso. 17 units. A/C TV TEL. Winter $100–$145 apt. Off-season $69–$105 apt. Weekly rates are 10% less. Additional person $5–$10 extra. AE, DC, MC, V.

This guest house, like Brigham Gardens, is more like a cozy apartment house than a hotel. There's no elegant lobby or restaurant, but the amicable hosts, Lisa and Pascal Nicolle, are happy to give you a room key and advice on what to do. The apartments are simple but perfect for the beach, since you'll be spending most of your time outside anyway. Plus, the spacious apartments are quiet considering their location, a few blocks from Lincoln Road and all of South Beach's best clubs. Most have full kitchens or at least a fridge, and Murphy beds or foldout couches for extra friends. Bathrooms have recently been renovated with marble tile. There are also laundry facilities on the premises and free local phone service. Parking is available at a nearby city lot.

MIAMI BEACH: SURFSIDE, BAL HARBOUR & SUNNY ISLES

The area just north of South Beach encompasses Surfside, Bal Harbour, and Sunny Isles. When it was unrestricted by zoning codes throughout the 1950s, 1960s, and especially the 1970s, area developers went nuts, building ever-bigger and more brazen structures, especially north of 41st Street, which is now known as "Condo Canyon." Consequently, there's now a glut of medium-quality condos, with a few scattered holdouts of older hotels and motels casting shadows over the beach by afternoon.

Miami Beach, as described here, runs from 24th Street to 192nd Street, a long strip that varies slightly from end to end. Staying in the southern section, from 24th to 42nd streets, can be a good deal—it's still close to the South Beach scene but the rates are more affordable. Bal Harbour and Bay Harbor are at the center of Miami Beach and retain their exclusivity and character. The neighborhoods north and south of here, like Surfside and Sunny Isles, have nice beaches and some shops but are a little worn around the edges.

Just north of South Beach is the **Days Inn** (☎ **800/325-2525** or 305/673-1513) at 42nd Street and Collins Avenue. It's very well kept and right on the ocean. Rates in season start at about $99. The **Howard Johnson** (☎ **800/446-4656** or 305/ 532-4411) at 4000 Alton Rd., just off the Julia Tuttle Causeway (I-95), is a generic eight-story building on a strip of land near a busy road, but it's convenient to the beach, by car or bike. Rooms, renovated in 1995, are clean and spacious, and some have pretty views of the city and the intracoastal waterway. Winter rates start at $100.

VERY EXPENSIVE

✪ **Alexander All-Suite Luxury Hotel.** 5225 Collins Ave., Miami Beach, FL 33140. ☎ **800/327-6121** or 305/865-6500. Fax 305/341-6553. www.alexanderhotel.com. 150 units. A/C TV TEL. Winter $325 one-bedroom suite; $470 two-bedroom suite. Off-season $250 one-bedroom suite; $370 two-bedroom suite. Additional person $35 extra. Packages available. AE, CB, DC, DISC, MC, V. Valet parking $16.

This stunning hotel is a great luxury option and just a few miles to happening South Beach or ritzy Bal Harbour. It's expensive but worth it for the service and attention. The Alexander features spacious one- and two-bedroom miniapartments. Each contains a living room, a fully equipped kitchen, two bathrooms, and a balcony. The rooms are elegant without being pretentious and have every convenience you could want, including hair dryers, coffeemakers, VCRs upon request, and cable TVs. The hotel itself is well decorated, with sculptures, paintings, antiques, and tapestries, most of which were garnered from the Cornelius Vanderbilt mansion. The two oceanfront pools are surrounded by lush vegetation; one of these "lagoons" is fed by a cascading waterfall.

Dining/Diversions: A pricey steak house was opened here in 1998 by former Dolphins football coach Don Shula. A more casual garden restaurant, a piano lounge, and a pool bar are also available.

Amenities: Concierge, room service (24 hours), dry-cleaning and laundry service, newspaper delivery, evening turndown on request, in-room massage on request, twice-daily maid service, secretarial services, express checkout. Two large outdoor pools, beach, small fitness center, four Jacuzzis, sauna, business center and conference rooms, car rental through concierge, sundeck, water-sports equipment, beauty salon.

✪ **Eden Roc Resort and Spa.** 4525 Collins Ave., Miami Beach, FL 33140. ☎ **800/ 327-8337** or 305/531-0000. Fax 305/674-5568. www.edenrocresort.com. 350 units. A/C MINIBAR TV TEL. Winter $280–$350 double; $820–$1,700 suite. Off-season $185–$275 double; $620–$1,500 suite. Additional person $15 extra. Packages available. AE, CB, DC, DISC, MC, V. Valet parking $20–$25.

Just next door to the mammoth Fontainebleau, this flamboyant and large hotel, opened in 1956, seems almost intimate by comparison. The accommodations here are a bit gaudy, but this is Miami Beach, after all. The amenities by far make up for the ostentation. The huge modern spa has excellent facilities and exercise classes, including yoga. The popular pool deck overlooking the ocean is a great place to spend the afternoon.

The big, open, and airy lobby is often full of name-tagged conventioneers. The rooms, uniformly outfitted with purple and aquatic-colored interiors and retouched 1930s furnishings, are unusually spacious. Because of the hotel's size, you should be able to negotiate a good rate unless a big event is going on.

Dining/Diversions: The main restaurant serves Northern Italian cuisine. From Jimmy Johnson's, the poolside sports bar, patrons can watch swimmers through an underwater "porthole" window. A lobby lounge and bar has occasional jazz.

Amenities: Concierge, room service, dry cleaning and laundry, newspaper delivery, in-room massage, nightly turndown, baby-sitting, secretarial services, express checkout, valet parking. Kitchenettes in suites and penthouses, VCRs for rent, two outdoor pools, beach, full-service spa and health club with sauna, business center and conference rooms, car-rental desk, sundeck, squash, racquetball and basketball courts as well as a rock-climbing arena, water-sports equipment, tour desk, beauty salon, sundries shop.

Fontainebleau Hilton. 4441 Collins Ave., Miami Beach, FL 33140. ☎ **800/HILTONS** or 305/538-2000. Fax 305/674-4607. www.fontainebleau.hilton.com. 1,206 units. A/C TV TEL. Winter $280–$360 double; $550–$850 suite. Off-season $205–$310 double; $475–$675 suite. Additional person $30 extra. Packages available. AE, CB, DC, DISC, MC, V. Overnight valet parking $13.

The most famous hotel on the Beach, the Fontainebleau (pronounced "fountainblue") has built its reputation on garishness and excess. Its sheer size, with its full complement of restaurants, stores, and recreational facilities, plus over 1,100 employees, makes it a perfect place for conventioneers. Unfortunately, the same recommendation cannot be extended to individual travelers. It's easy to get lost here, both physically and personally. The lobby is terminally crowded, the staff is overworked, and lines are always long. Renovations to the rooms in 1995 and 1996 did manage to freshen up the decor with new furnishings and pastel accents.

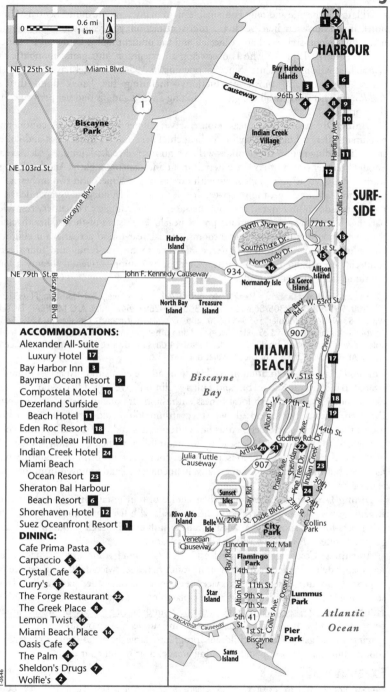

ACCOMMODATIONS:
Alexander All-Suite
  Luxury Hotel **17**
Bay Harbor Inn **3**
Baymar Ocean Resort **9**
Compostela Motel **10**
Dezerland Surfside
  Beach Hotel **11**
Eden Roc Resort **18**
Fontainebleau Hilton **19**
Indian Creek Hotel **24**
Miami Beach
  Ocean Resort **23**
Sheraton Bal Harbour
  Beach Resort **6**
Shorehaven Hotel **12**
Suez Oceanfront Resort **1**
DINING:
Cafe Prima Pasta **15**
Carpaccio **5**
Crystal Cafe **21**
Curry's **13**
The Forge Restaurant **22**
The Greek Place **8**
Lemon Twist **16**
Miami Beach Place **14**
Oasis Cafe **20**
The Palm **4**
Sheldon's Drugs **7**
Wolfie's **2**

1-0646

87

Still, this is the one and only Fontainebleau, in many ways the quintessential Miami hotel. If you don't stay here, see it as a tourist attraction; you really shouldn't miss the incredible lagoon-style pool and waterfall and the opulent lobby. Designed by famed architect Morris Lapidus, who is overseeing an expansion, this grand monolith has symbolized Miami decadence. Since its opening in 1954, the hotel has hosted presidents, pageants, and movie productions—including the James Bond thriller *Goldfinger.* This is where all the greats including Sinatra and his buddies performed in their prime.

Dining/Diversions: The Steak House serves dinner until 11pm. A continental restaurant offers a huge Sunday buffet brunch. There are five other cafes and coffee shops (including two by the pool), as well as a number of cocktail lounges, such as the Poodle Lounge, which offers live entertainment and dancing nightly. Another lounge features a Las Vegas–style floor show with dozens of performers and two orchestras.

Amenities: Concierge, room service, dry cleaning and laundry, newspaper delivery, nightly turndown on request, in-room massage, baby-sitting, secretarial services, valet parking. VCRs, two large outdoor pools, beach, large state-of-the-art health club, three whirlpool baths, sauna, game rooms, special year-round activities for children and adults, elaborate business center, conference rooms, car-rental and tour desks, sundeck, seven lighted tennis courts, water-sports equipment rental, beauty salon, boutique, large shopping arcade.

✪ **Sheraton Bal Harbour Beach Resort.** 9701 Collins Ave., Bal Harbour, FL 33154. ☎ **800/999-9898** or 305/865-7511. Fax 305/864-2601. 642 units. A/C MINIBAR TV TEL. Winter $349–$489 double; $650–$1,500 suite or villa year-round. Off-season $249–$439 double. Additional person $25 extra. Weekend and other packages and senior discounts available. Lowest rates reflect bookings made at least 14 days in advance for rooms without ocean views. AE, CB, DC, DISC, JCB, MC, V. Valet parking $12.

This hotel has the best location in Bal Harbour, on the ocean and just across from the swanky Bal Harbour Shops. Bill and Hillary Clinton have stayed here, and Bill even jogged along the beach with local fitness enthusiasts. It's one of the nicest Sheratons I've seen, with a glass-enclosed two-story atrium lobby and large, well-decorated rooms that include convenient extras like coffeemakers and hair dryers. A spectacular staircase wraps itself around a cascading fountain full of wished-on pennies. One side of the hotel caters to corporations and comes complete with ballrooms and meeting facilities, but the main sections are relatively uncongested and removed from the convention crowd.

Dining/Diversions: Guests have their choice of four restaurants and lounges. An Argentinean steak house serves good, heavy meals with live Latin music nightly. The other less-formal spots serve Mediterranean-influenced beach food, pizzas, and gourmet coffees. A lounge serves good tropical drinks.

Amenities: Concierge, room service (24 hours), laundry and dry cleaning, valet, newspaper delivery, nightly turndown, in-room massage, twice-daily maid service on request, baby-sitting, secretarial services, express checkout, valet parking. VCRs in some rooms, a full complement of aquatic playthings for rent on the beach (including sailboats and jet skis), outdoor heated pool, sundeck, large state-of-the-art fitness center and spa (with aerobics, Jacuzzi, sauna, and sundeck), two outdoor tennis courts, jogging track, games room, children's programs, large business center, conference rooms, tour desk, gift shop and shopping arcade, nearby golf course.

EXPENSIVE

Miami Beach Ocean Resort. 3025 Collins Ave., Miami Beach, FL 33140. ☎ **800/ 550-0505** or 305/534-0505. Fax 305/534-0515. www.mbo.com. 243 units. A/C TV TEL.

Winter $170–$210, 1 to 4 people; $240–$650 suite. Off-season $150–$180, 1 to 4 people; $220–$550 suite. AE, DC, MC, V. Valet parking $6.

Popular with tour groups and Europeans, this oceanfront resort is a great choice for those who want a quiet place on the ocean in close proximity to South Beach and the mainland. It's priced like many other chains on the oceanfront, but it's got more character. The vast lobby is done up in Mexican tile, wood fretwork, and attractive furnishings. Rooms are basic but very tastefully decorated with wicker and rattan furnishings and new carpeting. Rooms also include coffeemakers and hair dryers. A huge outdoor area is landscaped with palms and hibiscus and has a large heated pool as its centerpiece. It faces a popular boardwalk for runners and strollers, as well as a large beach where water-sports equipment is available.

Dining/Diversions: The recommendable restaurant serves a breakfast and dinner buffet of simple but good Caribbean and international cuisine to many who choose the meal programs. À la carte offerings and lunch are also available. A patio garden offers cake and coffee, a pool bar serves snacks and drinks, and a colorful indoor/outdoor lounge features cocktails and live music most nights.

Amenities: Concierge, room service, valet parking, laundry and dry-cleaning services, baby-sitting. Outdoor heated pool, beach, sundeck, bicycle rental, game room, self-service Laundromat, currency exchange, tour desk, conference rooms, car-rental desk, beauty salon, boutique.

MODERATE

✪ **Bay Harbor Inn.** 9660 E. Bay Harbor Dr., Bay Harbor Island, FL 33154. ☎ **305/868-4141.** Fax 305/867-9094. www.bayharborinn.com. 45 units. A/C MINIBAR TV TEL. Winter $139–$229 double; $159–$279 suite. Off-season $80–$149 double; $95–$179 suite. Additional person $25 extra. Rates include continental breakfast. AE, MC, V. Free self- or valet parking.

Under the management of Johnson & Wales University, this thoroughly renovated inn is just moments from the beach, fine restaurants, and Bal Harbour Shops, Miami's ritziest shopping mall (see "Shopping" in chapter 5). The inn comes in two parts. The more modern section sits squarely on a little river and overlooks a heated outdoor pool and a boat named *Celeste,* where guests eat a complimentary breakfast buffet. On the other side of the street, "townside" is the cozier, antique-filled portion, where glass-covered bookshelves hold good beach reading. The rooms have a hodgepodge of wood furnishings (mostly Victorian replicas). Suites boast an extra half bath. You can at times smell the aroma of cooking from the restaurant below, but you might find that this only adds to the charm of this homey inn.

Adjacent to the hotel is The Palm, a clubby steak-and-lobster house. Students from Johnson&Wales culinary institute run a superb restaurant, The Island Cafe, and bar across the street.

Baymar Ocean Resort. 9401 Collins Ave., Miami Beach, FL 33154. ☎ **800/8-BAYMAR** or 305/866-5446. Fax 305/866-8053. www.baymar.com. 96 units. A/C TV TEL. Winter $115–$125 double; $125–$135 efficiency; $150–$235 suite. Off-season $85–$95 double; $95–$105 efficiency; $125–$185 suite. Additional person $10 extra. AE, DISC, MC, V. Parking $5.

Depending on what you're looking for, this hotel could be one of the beach's best buys. It's just south of Bal Harbour, right on the ocean, with a low-key beach that attracts few other tourists. It offers all the modern conveniences, including some kitchenettes and large closets. You won't flip over the decor, but it's pleasant enough and all brand-new. A recent renovation has done wonders. The location is close enough to walk to tennis courts and some shopping and dining, and it's just a few minutes' drive to the larger attractions. It may not be worth it to pay more for the oceanfront rooms since they tend to be smaller than the others. Rooms overlooking the large pool and sundeck area can get loud on busy days. The first-floor ocean-view rooms have a nice shared balcony space. This hotel is popular with budget travelers and conservative religious groups.

A small restaurant serving basic American fare and a tiki bar are popular with guests.

Dezerland Surfside Beach Hotel. 8701 Collins Ave., Miami Beach, FL 33154. ☎ **800/ 331-9346** in the U.S., 800/331-9347 in Canada, or 305/865-6661. Fax 305/866-2630. www.travelbase.com/destinations. 227 units. A/C TV TEL. Winter $90–$135 double. Off-season $78–$125 double. Additional person $10 extra. Special packages and group rates available. AE, CB, DC, DISC, MC, V. Self-parking.

Designed by car enthusiast Michael Dezer, the Dezerland is a one-of-a-kind—part hotel and part 1950s automobile wonderland. Visitors, many of them German tourists, are welcomed by a 1959 Cadillac stationed by the front door, one of a dozen mint-condition classics around the grounds and lobby. Though not pristine, this beachfront hotel is clean and pleasant. Constant renovations improve it every year. Some rooms contain fully equipped kitchenettes. Look for the mosaic of a pink Cadillac at the bottom of its surfside pool.

Other amenities include a Jacuzzi, adjacent tennis courts and jogging track, Windsurfer and jet-ski rental, game room, laundry, car-rental and tour services desk, and an antique shop featuring 1950s memorabilia. There are also a restaurant and a lobby lounge with all-you-can-eat buffets and nightly entertainment.

✪ Indian Creek Hotel. 2727 Indian Creek Dr. (1 block west of Collins Ave.), Miami Beach, FL 33140. ☎ **800/491-2772** or 305/531-2727. Fax 305/531-5651. www.indian-creekhotelmb.com. 61 units. A/C TV TEL. Winter from $130–$160 double; from $220 suite. Off-season $90 double; $150 suite. Additional person $10 extra. Group packages available. Summer specials. 18% gratuity added to room service. AE, CB, DC, DISC, JCB, MC, V. Limited parking available on street.

Although there isn't much in the way of views or amenities, this small hotel just north of South Beach is pleasant and not too far from the action. Every detail of the 1936 building has been meticulously restored, from one of the beach's first operating elevators to the period steamer trunk in the lobby. The modest rooms are outfitted in art deco furnishings, with pretty tropical prints and all the modern amenities. They are used to hosting production crews and therefore provide things like dataports and voice mail in all rooms. Just 1 short block from a good stretch of sand, the hotel is also within walking distance to shops and inexpensive restaurants. A landscaped pool area is a great place to lounge in the sun. There are a small fitness center and conference facilities. A tiny restaurant serves continental breakfast and dinner.

INEXPENSIVE

Compostela Motel. 9040 Collins Ave., Miami Beach, FL 33154. ☎ **305/861-3083.** Fax 305/861-2996. 20 units. A/C TV TEL. Winter from $75 suite; from $65 one-bedroom apt.; $55 efficiency. Off-season from $65 suite; $55 one-bedroom apt.; $45 efficiency. Additional person $10 extra. AE, MC, V. Free parking.

At this hotel, you get a lot of space and a great location for a low price. The owners of the Compostela have recently renovated their three buildings, all within walking distance of the exclusive Bal Harbour Shops, the beaches, and many good shopping and dining areas. Although the buildings were full of run-down efficiencies for many years, the new interiors are really quite nice. All are carpeted and most have full kitchenettes. You'll find no fancy lobby, no doorman to greet you as you enter, and no amenities to speak of save an outdoor pool and laundry facilities. But you're across the street from a great beach, the area is safe, and the staff is courteous, though at some hours only Spanish speakers are available.

Shorehaven Hotel. 8505 Harding Ave. (1 block west of Collins Ave.), Miami Beach, FL 33141. ☎ **888/775-0346** or 305/867-1906. Fax 305/867-1716. info@shorehaven.com. 15 units. A/C TV TEL. Winter $89–$129. Off-season $69–$79. AE, DISC, MC, V. Rates are for up to 3 people. Additional person costs $10. Free street parking.

Located in up-and-coming North Beach, this funky one-story motel was thoroughly made over in late 1998 with style and charm by an attractive young couple, Sabrina and Scott Barnett. She is a former model who has graced the pages of major magazines, including the swimsuit edition of *Sports Illustrated,* and he is a developer. The large rooms, outfitted in bright tropical prints, offer full kitchens and spacious bathrooms. Each has its own theme, like the Lemon Twist room which has huge murals of bright yellow lemons on the walls, and wood floors painted a glossy royal blue. Other rooms have romantic canopies of mosquito netting or other creative touches. All offer a real bargain just 1 block to the beach and less than 10 minutes' drive to the hip and much pricier South Beach.

Suez Oceanfront Resort. 18215 Collins Ave., Sunny Isles Beach, FL 33160. ☎ **800/ 327-5278** or 305/932-0661. Fax 305/937-0058. www.suezresort.com. 200 units. A/C TV TEL. Winter $85–$99 double; $101–$118 suite. Off-season $65–$98 double; $83–$100 suite. Kitchenettes $10–$15 extra. AE, DC, MC, V. Free parking.

Guarded by an undersize replica of Egypt's famed Sphinx, the campy Suez offers newly renovated rooms on the beach, where most of the other old hotels have turned condo. Its Sunny Isles location is actually closer to Hallandale in Broward County than to South Beach, but the area has plenty to offer.

The strict orange-and-yellow motif makes the Suez look more like a Las Vegas attraction than anything in ancient Egypt. There are several convenient pluses, however, like a low-priced restaurant, fully equipped kitchenettes in some rooms, a large heated outdoor pool, a kiddie pool, an exercise room with saunas, lighted tennis courts, and a Laundromat. A kitschy but pleasant and inexpensive lounge reminds you that you are indeed in a tropical paradise. For the price, it's a great choice, and you can say you saw the pyramids.

KEY BISCAYNE

There are only a couple of hotels here, not counting the super-luxurious Grand Bay Resort, currently under construction. All are on the beach, and room rates are uniformly high. If you can afford it, Key Biscayne is a great place to stay. The island is far enough from the mainland to make it feel like a secluded tropical paradise, yet close enough to Downtown to take advantage of everything Miami has to offer.

Silver Sands Beach Resort. 301 Ocean Dr., Key Biscayne, FL 33149. ☎ **305/361-5441.** Fax 305/361-5477. 56 units. A/C TV TEL. Winter $149–$179 minisuite; $300 cottage; $385 oceanfront suite. Off-season $109–$129 minisuite; $200 cottage; $385 oceanfront suite. Additional person $30 extra. Weekly rates available. AE, DC, MC, V. Free parking.

If Key Biscayne is where you want to be and you don't want to pay the prices of the next-door Sonesta, consider this quaint one-story motel. Everything is crisp and clean, and the pleasant staff will help with anything you may need, including baby-sitting. But despite the name, it's certainly no resort. Except for the beach and pool, you'll have to leave the premises for almost everything, including food. The well-appointed rooms are very beachy, sporting a tropical motif and simple furnishings; extras include microwaves, refrigerators, and coffeemakers. Oceanfront suites have the added convenience of full kitchens with stoves and pantries. You'll sit poolside with an unpretentious set of Latin American families and Europeans who have come for a long and simple vacation—and get it.

Amenities: Secretarial services, twice-daily maid service. VCRs in some rooms, medium-sized outdoor pool, beach, kitchenettes, coin laundry.

✪ **Sonesta Beach Resort Key Biscayne.** 350 Ocean Dr., Key Biscayne, FL 33149. ☎ **800/ SONESTA** or 305/361-2021. Fax 305/361-3096. www.sonesta.com. 303 units. A/C MINIBAR TV TEL. Winter $295–$450 double; $600–$1,650 suite or villa. Off-season $160–$320 double; $525–$1,325 suite or villa. 15% gratuity added to food and beverage bills. Special packages available. AE, CB, DC, DISC, EC, JCB, MC, V. Valet parking $12.

One of South Florida's most private and luxurious resorts, the Sonesta is an ideal retreat. From the moment the valets, clad in tropical prints, take your car, you'll know you've entered a world of no concern. Each of the nearly 300 rooms has a private balcony or terrace. Sports, from tennis to jet skiing, are available all around you. Although you may not want to leave the lush grounds, Bill Baggs State Recreation Area and the area's best beaches are right at hand, and if you choose to venture out, you're only about 15 minutes from Miami Beach and even closer to the mainland and Coconut Grove. The vacation homes have fully equipped kitchenettes.

Dining/Diversions: The hotel has four restaurants, including Purple Dolphin, for "New World" cuisine, and Two Dragons, for Chinese. There's also an excellent seafood restaurant with a terrace, as well as several lounges and bars. The restaurants regularly draw locals, who have few dining options on "The Key."

Amenities: Concierge, room service (24 hours), dry cleaning and laundry, newspaper delivery, in-room massage, twice-daily maid service, nightly turndown, babysitting, secretarial services, express checkout, complimentary transportation to and from Miami's shopping districts. Children are well cared for, with day and night field trips and activities. Olympic-size pool, beach, large state-of-the-art fitness center, Jacuzzi, sauna, nearby jogging track, bicycle rental, access to nearby championship 18-hole golf course, game rooms, children's programs, elaborate business center, conference rooms, car-rental and tour desks, sundeck, nine tennis courts (all lighted), water-sports equipment rental, beauty salon, boutiques.

DOWNTOWN

Most Downtown hotels cater primarily to business travelers, but tourists can get well-located, good-quality accommodations, too. Although business hotels are expensive, quality and service are of a high standard. Look for discounts and packages for the weekend, when offices are closed and rooms often go empty. Downtown is closest to some of Miami's best shopping. Be warned that after dark there's virtually nothing to do outside of the hotels; the streets are often deserted and crime can be a problem.

In downtown Miami, the **Wyndham** (☎ **800/WYNDHAM** or 305/374-0000) at 1601 Biscayne Blvd., above the Omni Mall, is a good option for the thrifty business traveler. It has a full business center, as well as a heated rooftop pool. It's just a few minutes away from Bayside and Miami Beach. Rates are from $109 to $199.

VERY EXPENSIVE

✪ **Hotel Inter-Continental Miami.** 100 Chopin Plaza, Miami, FL 33131. ☎ **800/ 327-3005** or 305/577-1000. Fax 305/577-0384. www.interconti.com. 615 units. A/C MINIBAR TV TEL. Winter $209–$289 double; $325–$450 suite. Off-season $139–$259 double; $325–$450 suite. Additional person $20 extra. Weekend and other packages available. AE, CB, DC, DISC, MC, V. Valet parking $12.

Coral Gables, Coconut Grove, Downtown Miami & Key Biscayne

Especially since the $5 million renovation of all their guest rooms and some common areas, the Inter-Continental is downtown's swankiest hotel. It boasts more marble than a mausoleum (both inside and out), but it's warmed by colorful, homey touches. The five-story lobby features a marble centerpiece sculpture by Henry Moore and is topped by a pleasing skylight. Plenty of plants, palm trees, and brightly colored wicker chairs also add charm and enliven the otherwise stark space. Brilliant downtown and bay views add luster to already posh rooms, outfitted with every convenience known to hotel-dom, including VCRs. Some suites have fully equipped kitchenettes.

Dining/Diversions: Three restaurants cover all price ranges and are complemented by two full-service lounges.

Amenities: Concierge, room service, dry cleaning and laundry, newspaper delivery, twice-daily maid service, express checkout, free refreshments in lobby. Olympic-size heated outdoor pool, health spa, sundeck, jogging track, large business center, 15 conference rooms, self-service Laundromat, car-rental desk, travel-agency/tour desk, beauty salon and barbershop, shopping arcade, access to nearby golf course.

MODERATE

Everglades Hotel. 244 Biscayne Blvd., Miami, FL 33132. ☎ **800/327-5700** or 305/379-5461. Fax 305/577-8445. www.miamigate.com/everglades. 376 units. A/C TV TEL. Year-round $92 double; $125 suite. AE, CB, DC, DISC, MC, V. Parking $7.

This hotel has been around about forever on Downtown's active Biscayne Boulevard. And it shows: The lobby and rooms border on dive quality. Many traveling business types and Latin American families stay here, however, because of its convenient, safe location, low rates, and many services, which include a bank in the building. It's also one of the only Downtown properties with a pool. The hotel is near the highways and Metrorail, and there's great shopping across the street at Bayside Marketplace.

Miami River Inn. 118 SW South River Dr., Miami, FL 33130. ☎ **305/325-0045.** Fax 305/325-9227. www.travelbase.com. A/C TV TEL. 40 units. Winter $99–$145. Off-season $69–$89 double. Rates include continental breakfast. Additional person $15 extra. AE, CB, DC, DISC, MC, V. Free parking.

The Miami River is a great deal for those who want to be in a central location—close to the highway, public transportation, downtown eateries, and museums. Extras include a small outdoor pool, a Jacuzzi, and complimentary coffee and wine in the lobby. Although many predict that the riverfront will soon undergo a renaissance, for now the area is still a bit seedy. Don't venture too far out of the enclave, unless you want to see the ugly underside of Miami.

Rooms are nicely furnished with a mix of antiques from all eras and gentle wall-paper prints. In the common area is a collection of books about old Miami, with histories of this land's former owners: Julia Tuttle, William Brickell, and Henry Flagler. The low year-round rates make this hotel an attractive option for those who appreciate old things. There are a small outdoor pool on the premises and a Jacuzzi.

Riande Continental Bayside. 146 Biscayne Blvd., Miami, FL 33132. ☎ **800/RIANDE-1** or 305/358-4555. Fax 305/371-5253. 250 units. A/C MINIBAR TV TEL. Winter $115–$175 double. Off-season $85–$155 double. Frommer's readers get a 20% discount. AE, DC, MC, V. Parking $7.50.

Like its sister hotel in South Beach, this Riande caters to a Latin American crowd that descends on Downtown in droves to shop for clothes and electronics. The location is ideal, only steps away from a Bayside shopping center, many great ethnic restaurants, and a Metrorail stop. The reasonable prices and helpful staff are reason enough to consider staying here, if you want to be right in downtown Miami.

Sheraton Biscayne Bay Hotel. 495 Brickell Ave., Miami, FL 33131. ☎ **800/325-3535** or 305/373-6000. Fax 305/374-2279. www.sheraton.com. 598 units. A/C TV TEL. Winter $149–$189 double; $225–$305 suite. Off-season $99–$175 double; $200–$250 suite. Additional person $10. Senior discounts and weekend and other packages available. AE, CB, DC, DISC, MC, V. Parking $11.

This Downtown hotel's waterfront location is its greatest asset. Nestled between Brickell Park and Biscayne Bay, the Sheraton is set back from the main road and surrounded by a pleasant bayfront walkway. Since a recent $14 million renovation, this Sheraton is especially recommendable. Its identical rooms are well furnished and comfortable. There isn't much to do in the area, but you're within a short drive to anything Miami has to offer.

Dining/Diversions: The Regatta Bar and Grille serves American cuisine and a buffet with made-to-order pastas too. A huge bar has happy hours and occasional live music.

Amenities: Concierge services, room service (7am to 11:30pm), laundry and dry-cleaning services, newspaper delivery, nightly turndown, in-room massage, twice-daily maid service upon request, baby-sitting, express checkout, valet parking, free refreshments in the lobby. Large heated outdoor pool, state-of-the-art health club, access to nearby health club, sundeck, nearby golf course, game room, adequate business center, conference rooms, car-rental and tour desk, small gift shop.

WEST MIAMI/AIRPORT AREA

As Miami continues to grow at its rapid pace, expansion has begun westward, where land is plentiful. Several resorts have taken advantage of the space to build world-class tennis and golf courses. While there's no sea to swim in, a plethora of facilities makes up for the lack of an ocean view.

If you've got an early-morning flight to catch, by all means stay near the airport. If not, why not spend a few dollars to get to the beach, less than 10 miles away? You'll have a lot more options and will get a better value for your money.

If you must stay near the airport, consider any of the dozens of moderately priced chain hotels. You'll find one of the cheapest and most recommendable options at either of the **Days Inns** (☎ **305/261-4230**), at 7250 NW 11 St. (☎ **305/261-4230**) or 4767 NW 36th St. (☎ **800/446-5508** or 305/888-3661), each about 2 miles from the airport.

The larger property on 36th Street offers slightly cheaper rates with singles starting as low as $49. The 11th Street locale may charge more for weekends, but prices usually start at $70. Prices include free transportation from the airport.

A more luxurious option is the **Wyndham** at 3900 NW 21st St. (☎ **800/933-1100**), with rates from $100 to $225.

Don Shula's Hotel and Golf Club. Main St., Miami Lakes, FL 33014. ☎ **800/24-SHULA** or 305/821-1150. Fax 305/820-8190. 330 units. A/C TV TEL. Winter from $159 double; $279 suite. Off-season $99–$139 double; $189–$209 suite. Additional person $10 extra. Business packages available. AE, DC, MC, V.

Guests come to Shula's mostly for the golf, but there's plenty here to keep nongolfers busy, too. Opened in 1992 to much fanfare from the sports and business community, Shula's resort is an all-encompassing oasis in the middle of a highly planned residential neighborhood, complete with a Main Street and nearby shopping facilities—a good thing, since the site is more than a 20-minute drive on the highways from anything. The guest rooms, located in the main building or surrounding the golf course, are plain but pretty, and they come with VCRs (on request).

Dining: The award-winning Shula's Steak House and the more casual Steak House Two rank in the top 10 nationwide. They serve huge Angus beef steaks and seafood. Another restaurant on the premises serves health food.

Amenities: Concierge, room service, dry-cleaning and laundry service, newspaper delivery, in-room massage, secretarial service, express checkout, valet parking, free morning coffee in the lobby. Large outdoor swimming pool, Don Shula's state-of-the-art athletic club (with aerobics, Cybex equipment, and trainers who assist all exercisers), Jacuzzi, sauna, sundeck, 16 outdoor tennis courts, racquetball courts, two golf courses (one championship course), 22 conference and banquet rooms, beauty salon, and shopping arcade.

✪ **Doral Golf Resort and Spa.** 4400 NW 87th Ave., Miami, FL 33178. ☎ **800/ 22-DORAL,** 800/71-DORAL, or 305/592-2000. Fax 305/594-4682. www.doralgolf.com. 623 units (plus an additional 58 suites at the spa). A/C MINIBAR TV TEL. Winter $225–$315 double; $315–$945 suite; $350–$1,280 spa suite. Off-season $95–$275 double; $175–$380 golf suite; $350–$825 spa suite. Additional person $35 extra. 18% service charge added. Golf and spa packages available. AE, CB, DC, DISC, MC, V. Valet parking $8.50.

The Doral epitomizes the luxury resort in Florida. While the pamperings in the spa attract worldwide attention, the next-door golf resort hosts world-class tournaments and is home to the Blue Monster Course—rated one of the top 25 in the country. The season is booked well in advance by those who have been here before or have just read about the fantastic offerings on this 650-acre, fully self-contained resort. It's just moments from the Miami airport.

The spacious lobbies and dining areas shimmer with polished marble, mirrors, and gold. The rooms, too, are luxuriously large and tastefully decorated; big windows allow views of the tropical gardens or golf courses below. The resort is surrounded by warehouses and office buildings.

Dining/Diversions: The Spa restaurant serves delicious low-fat cuisine, including reduced-calorie desserts. Other options include a cafe with super Italian sandwiches, salads, and pasta. A sports bar at the golf club offers excellent club fare.

Amenities: Concierge, room service, laundry and dry cleaning, newspaper delivery, evening turndown, in-room massage in spa suites by appointment, baby-sitting, secretarial services, express checkout, courtesy car or limo, shuttle to the Doral Ocean Resort. Olympic-size outdoor heated pool, access to the spa ($25), small exercise room, steam room and sauna, jogging track, bicycle rentals, extensive golf facilities, game rooms, children's programs during the holidays, business center, conference wing, car-rental desk, sundeck, 15 outdoor tennis courts, tour and activities desks, beauty salon, boutiques.

Miami International Airport Hotel. P.O. Box 997510, NW 20th St. and LeJeune Rd., Airport Terminal Concourse E., Miami, FL 33299-7510. ☎ **800/327-1276** or 305/871-4100. Fax 305/871-0800. www.miahotel.com. 260 units. A/C TV TEL. Winter $159–$179 double; $275–$650 suite. Off-season $145–$165 double; $250–$270 suite. Additional person $10. AE, CB, DC, EC, JCB, MC, V. Parking $9.

If you need to be at the airport and want excellent service, this is your best bet. I don't know of a nicer airport hotel, and you can't beat the convenience—it's actually in the airport at Concourse E. You'll find every amenity of a first-class tourist hotel here, including a large rooftop pool, health club, Jacuzzi, sauna, sundeck, racquetball courts, jogging track, small business center, conference room, beauty salon, tour desk, boutiques, and several cocktail lounges and restaurants. The rooms are modern, clean, and spacious, with industrial-grade carpeting. The furnishings are nondescript but tasteful. You might think you'd be deafened by the roar of the planes, but all of the rooms have been soundproofed and actually allow very little noise. In addition, the hotel has modern security systems and is extremely safe. The restaurants are decent, but many of Miami's best are just a short cab drive away.

NORTH DADE

✪ **Turnberry Isle Resort and Club.** 19999 W. Country Club Dr., Aventura, FL 33180. ☎ **800/327-7028** or 305/932-6200. Fax 305/933-6550. www.turnberryisle.com. 340 units. A/C MINIBAR TV TEL. Winter $395–$800 resort rm or suite; $315–$500 yacht-club rm or suite. Off-season $215–$600 resort rm or suite; $170–$300 yacht-club rm or suite. AE, DC, DISC, MC, V. Valet parking $8; free self-parking.

A top-rated resort, this gorgeous 300-acre compound has every possible facility for active guests, particularly golfers. You'll pay a lot to stay here—but it's worth it. The main attractions are two newly renovated Trent Jones courses, available only to members and guests of the hotel. Impeccable service from check-in to checkout brings loyal fans back for more. The North Miami Beach location is about halfway between Fort Lauderdale and Miami, but you'll find excellent shopping and some of the best dining in Miami right in the neighborhood.

Unless you're into boating, the higher-priced resort rooms are where you'll want to stay. Here you're steps from perfect spa facilities and the renowned Veranda restaurant. The well-proportioned rooms are gorgeously tiled to match the Mediterranean-style architecture. The bathrooms even have a color TV mounted within reach of the whirlpool bathtubs. Video rental is available.

Dining/Diversions: There are six restaurants, including the Veranda, which serves healthful and tropical New World cuisine in an elegant dining room. The several bars and lounges, including a popular disco, also have enough entertainment and local flavor to keep anyone busy for weeks.

Amenities: Concierge, room service (24 hours), same-day laundry service, newspaper delivery, in-room massage, nightly turndown, twice-daily maid service, babysitting services, express checkout. Four large swimming pools, complete state-of-the-art health spa, beach, Jacuzzi, sauna, two 36-hole golf courses, nature trails, sundeck, 24 outdoor tennis courts (including 16 lighted for night play), squash/racquetball courts, water-sports equipment, 3-mile jogging course, bicycle rental, game room, children's center and programs, large business center, four large meeting and conference centers, tour desk, boutiques, limousine and car-rental desks, helipad, beauty salon.

CORAL GABLES

Coconut Grove eases into Coral Gables, which extends north toward Miami International Airport. "The Gables," as it's affectionately known, was one of Miami's original planned communities and is still among the city's prettiest neighborhoods. It's close to the shops along the Miracle Mile and the University of Miami. Two popular and well-priced chain hotels are a **Holiday Inn** (☎ 800/327-5476 or 305/667-5611), at 1350 S. Dixie Hwy. with rates between $75 and $125, and a **Howard Johnson** (☎ 800/446-4656 or 305/665-7501), at 1430 S. Dixie Hwy. Rates range from $65 to $95. Both are located directly across the street from the University of Miami and are popular with families and friends of students.

VERY EXPENSIVE

✪ **Biltmore Hotel Coral Gables.** 1200 Anastasia Ave., Coral Gables, FL 33134. ☎ **800/727-1926,** 305/445-1926, or Westin at 800/228-3000. Fax 305/442-9496. www.biltmore-hotel.com. 275 units. A/C TV TEL. Winter from $319 double; $379–$479 suite. Off-season from $239 double; $309–$389 suite. Additional person $20 extra. Special packages available. AE, CB, DC, DISC, MC, V. Valet parking $9.

The Biltmore, which was built in 1926, is the oldest Coral Gables hotel and a city landmark. It was granted national recognition as an official National Historical

Landmark in 1996—one of only two operating hotels in Florida to receive the designation. It's also one of the only four-star rated hotels in the area. Always a popular destination for golfers, including President Clinton, the Biltmore is situated on a lush, rolling ✪ **18-hole course** that is as challenging as it is beautiful. The hotel is surrounded by a pretty residential area, 5 minutes from the airport and excellent dining and shopping selections, and about 20 minutes from Miami Beach. It is a wonderful option for those seeking a luxurious getaway in a quiet setting. I especially recommend a visit to the huge, beautiful spa.

Now under the management of the Westin Hotel group, the hotel boasts large rooms decorated with tasteful period reproductions and some high-tech amenities. The enormous lobby, with its 45-foot ceilings, serves as an entry point for hundreds of weddings and business meetings each year. Rising above the Spanish-style estate is a majestic 300-foot copper-clad tower, modeled after the Giralda bell tower in Seville and visible throughout the city. Over the years, the Biltmore has passed through many incarnations (for example, it was used as a VA hospital after World War II), but it is now back to its original 1926 splendor.

Dining/Diversions: An elegant European restaurant serves excellent French/Italian cuisine nightly and champagne brunch on Sunday. An impressive wine cellar and cigar room are popular with local connoisseurs. The more casual Courtyard Café and Poolside Grille both serve three meals daily. There's also a lounge and piano bar where drinks are accompanied by live music nightly.

Amenities: Concierge, room service (24 hours), laundry and dry cleaning, newspaper delivery, nightly turndown on request, twice-daily maid service, baby-sitting, secretarial services, express checkout. Kitchenettes in tower suite, VCR and video rentals, a spectacular 21,000-square-foot swimming pool surrounded by arched walkways and classical sculptures, state-of-the-art health club, full-service spa, sauna, 18-hole golf course, elaborate business center, conference rooms, car rental through concierge, sundeck, 10 lighted tennis courts, beauty salon, boutiques.

Hyatt Regency Coral Gables. 50 Alhambra Plaza, Coral Gables, FL 33134. ☎ **800/ 233-1234** or 305/441-1234. Fax 305/441-0520. www.hyatt.com. 242 units. A/C MINIBAR TV TEL. Winter $260 double; $299–$1,800 suite. Off-season from $120 double; $175–$1,800 suite. Additional person $25. Packages and senior discounts available. AE, CB, DC, DISC, MC, V. Valet parking $10; self-parking $9.

High on style, comfort, and price, this Hyatt is part of Coral Gables's Alhambra, an office-hotel complex with a Mediterranean motif. The building itself is gorgeous, designed with pink stone, arched entrances, grand courtyards, and tile roofs. Inside you'll find overstuffed chairs on marble floors, surrounded by opulent antiques and chandeliers. The hotel opened in 1987, but like many historical buildings in the neighborhood, the Alhambra attempts to mimic something much older and much farther away.

The good-size rooms are outfitted with everything you'd expect from a top hotel—terry robes and all. Most furnishings are antique.

Dining/Diversions: A good New World cuisine restaurant serves a varied menu with many local specialties. Alcazaba is a fun Latin-style dance spot (see "Latin Clubs," in chapter 5).

Amenities: Full concierge services, room service (6am to midnight), same-day laundry and dry-cleaning services, newspaper delivery, nightly turndown on request, in-room massage, baby-sitting arrangements available, secretarial services, express checkout, valet parking. Large outdoor heated pool, health club with Nautilus equipment, Jacuzzi, two saunas, nearby golf course, basic business center, conference rooms, small gift shop.

EXPENSIVE

Hotel Place St. Michel. 162 Alcazar Ave., Coral Gables, FL 33134. ☎ **800/848-HOTEL** or 305/444-1666. Fax 305/529-0074. www.hotelplacestmichel.com. 27 units. A/C TV TEL. Winter (including continental breakfast) $165–$175 double; $200–$220 suite. Off-season $125–$140 double; $160–$180 suite. Additional person $10 extra. AE, DC, MC, V. Parking $7.

This unusual little hotel in the heart of Coral Gables is one of the city's most romantic options. The accommodations and hospitality are straight out of old-world Europe, complete with dark wood-paneled walls, cozy beds, beautiful antiques, and a quiet elegance that seems startlingly out of place in trendy Miami. Everything here is charming—from the parquet floors to the paddle fans. One-of-a-kind furnishings make each room special. Guests are treated to fresh fruit baskets upon arrival and enjoy every imaginable service throughout their stay.

Dining/Diversions: The Restaurant St. Michel is a very romantic and elegant dining choice. A lounge and deli complete the hotel options.

Amenities: Concierge, room service, laundry and dry cleaning, newspaper delivery, evening turndown, in-room massage, twice-daily maid service, complimentary continental breakfast.

The Omni Colonnade Hotel. 180 Aragon Ave. (at Ponce de Leon and Miracle Mile), Coral Gables, FL 33134. ☎ **800/THE OMNI** or 305/441-2600. Fax 305/445-3929. 157 units. A/C MINIBAR TV TEL. Winter $195–$265 double; $405 suite. Off-season $105–$225 double; $365 suite. Packages available. AE, CB, DC, DISC, MC, V. Valet parking $10.

The Colonnade occupies part of a large historic building, originally built by Coral Gables's founder George Merrick in 1926. Faithful to its original style, the hotel is a successful amalgam of new and old, with an emphasis on modern conveniences. The structure stands 14 elegant stories high, although guest rooms occupy only four floors. It's popular with business travelers.

The oversized rooms are worthy of the hotel's rates. They feature sitting areas, historic photographs, marble counters, gold-finished faucets, and solid wood furnishings. Thoughtful extras include complimentary shoe shines and champagne upon arrival.

Dining/Diversions: Doc Dammers Saloon is a good happy hour for the 30-something crowd. There's live entertainment on weekends.

Amenities: 24-hour concierge and room service, same-day laundry and dry-cleaning service, newspaper delivery, evening turndown on request, in-room massage, twice-daily maid service on request, baby-sitting, express checkout, valet parking, free morning coffee and tea in the lobby. Heated outdoor pool on rooftop, small modern rooftop fitness center, Jacuzzi, sundeck, large conference centers and meeting rooms, Laundromat, car-rental and tour desks, gift shop, and shopping arcade.

INEXPENSIVE

Riviera Court Motel. 5100 Riviera Dr. (on U.S. 1), Coral Gables, FL 33146. ☎ **800/368-8602** or 305/665-3528. 30 units. A/C TV TEL. Winter from $68 rms; $78 efficiencies. Off-season from $55 rms; $78 efficiencies. 10% discount for seniors and AAA members. AE, CB, DC, DISC, MC, V.

Besides the newly renovated Holiday Inn down the road, this family-owned motel is the best discount option in the area. The comfortable and clean two-story property, dating from 1954, has a small pool and is set back from the road, so the rooms are all relatively quiet. Vending machines are the only choice for refreshments, but guests are near many great dining spots. You can also choose to stay in one of the efficiencies, which all have fully stocked kitchens.

COCONUT GROVE

This intimate enclave hugs the shores of Biscayne Bay, just south of U.S. 1 and about 10 minutes from the beaches. The Grove is a great place to stay, offering ample nightlife, excellent restaurants, and beautiful surroundings, and the hotel rates are reflective of the high style of living found here.

VERY EXPENSIVE

◊ Grand Bay Hotel. 2669 S. Bayshore Dr., Coconut Grove, FL 33133. ☎ **800/327-2788** or 305/858-9600. Fax 305/859-2026. miami.vcn.net/grandbay. 178 units. A/C MINIBAR TV TEL. Winter from $345 double. Off-season $205 double. Year-round $350–$1,500 suite. Additional person $20 extra. Packages available. AE, CB, DC, MC, V. Valet parking $13.

The Grand Bay opened in 1983 and immediately won praise as one of the most elegant hotels in the world. This stunning pyramid-shaped hotel is a masterpiece both inside and out. The rooms are luxurious, each featuring high-quality linens, comfortable overstuffed love seats and chairs, a large writing desk, and all the amenities you'd expect in deluxe accommodations, including VCRs and video rentals. It has recently added ironing boards, irons, and voice mail to all rooms as well. Original art and armfuls of fresh flowers are generously displayed throughout.

The Grand Bay consistently attracts wealthy, high-profile people, and it basks in its image as a rendezvous for royalty, socialites, and superstars. Guests come here to be pampered and to see and be seen.

Dining/Diversions: Opened in late 1998, the hotel's main restaurant, **Bice** (pronounced Bee-chey) serves classic Northern Italian cuisine in an elegant setting. Drinks are served in the Ciga Bar, and the Lobby Lounge offers a traditional afternoon tea.

Amenities: Concierge, room service (24 hours), same-day laundry and dry cleaning, newspaper delivery, evening turndown, masseuse on call, twice-daily maid service, baby-sitting, secretarial services, express checkout, courtesy limousine service to Cocowalk, free refreshments in the lobby. Heated indoor pool, small health club, access to nearby health club, Jacuzzi, sauna, VCR and video rentals, sundeck, watersports equipment rental, bicycle rental, good-sized business center, conference rooms, car-rental and activities desks, beauty salon, gift shop, nearby golf course.

Grove Isle Club and Resort. Four Grove Isle Dr., Coconut Grove, FL 33133. ☎ **800/88-GROVE** or 305/858-8300. Fax 305/854-6702. 49 units. A/C TV TEL. Winter $245–$325 double; $475 suite. Off-season $195–$295 double; $475 suite. Rates include breakfast. Additional person $20. AE, DC, MC, V. Free valet parking.

A 1994 renovation has turned Grove Isle into one of the nicest spots to stay in Coconut Grove. Its location is stunning. From the lobby and many rooms, guests look out onto glimmering Biscayne Bay, where sailboats drift lazily about and dolphins sometimes leap circles in the clear blue water. You'd almost think the property is on an island; actually, it's only a few minutes from Coconut Grove's business district.

Grove Isle feels like a country club. Everyone dresses in white and pastels, and if they're not on their way to a set of tennis, they're not in a rush to get anywhere. Rooms are nicely furnished, as is the elegant but uncluttered lobby.

Dining/Diversions: Baleen's, an elegant continental restaurant, serves fresh seafood and other regional specialties.

Amenities: Concierge service, room service (6:30am to 10pm), laundry and dry-cleaning services, newspaper delivery, nightly turndown, in-room massage, twice-daily maid service, baby-sitting, secretarial services, express checkout, valet parking, free coffee in the lobby. VCRs, movie channels, video rental delivered to room ($5), large heated outdoor pool, deluxe fitness facilities, 12 outdoor tennis courts, water-sports equipment rental, jogging track, nature trails, conference rooms, beauty salon.

Hampton Inn. 2800 SW 28th Terrace (at U.S. 1 and SW 27 Ave.), Coconut Grove, FL 33133. ☎ **888/287-3390** or 305/448-2800. Fax 305/442-8655. www.travelbase.com/destinations. 179 units. A/C TV TEL. Winter $119–$139 double. Off-season $79–$119 single. AE, DC, DISC, MC, V. Rate includes continental breakfast buffet.

This very standard chain hotel is a welcome reprieve in an area otherwise known for having only very pricey accommodations. The rooms are nothing exciting, but the freebies, like local phone calls, parking, in-room movies, breakfast buffet, and hot drinks around the clock make this a real steal. Although there is no restaurant or bar, it is close to lots of both—only about half a mile to the heart of the Grove's shopping and retail area and about as far from Coral Gables. Rooms are brand-new and have large televisions, voice-mail phones, and refrigerators and microwaves upon request. A workout room, large outdoor pool, and Jacuzzi are added bonuses in this generic but recommendable hotel.

Mayfair House Hotel. 3000 Florida Ave., Coconut Grove, FL 33133. ☎ **800/433-4555** or 305/441-0000. Fax 305/441-1647. www.hotelbook.com/live/welcome. 179 units. A/C MINIBAR TV TEL. Winter $249–$649 suite; $450 penthouse. Off-season $220–$440 suite; $450 penthouse. Packages available. AE, DC, DISC, MC, V. Valet parking $15, self-parking $6.

If you want to be in the Grove, this hotel is a great choice. Though very expensive and more than 20 minutes from the beach, it is situated inside the posh Mayfair Shops complex. The all-suite Mayfair House is about as centrally located as you can get. Each guest unit was individually designed and renovated in 1998. All have terraces and are extremely comfortable. Some suites are downright opulent and include a private outdoor, Japanese-style hot tub. The top-floor terraces offer good views, and all are hidden from the street by leaves and latticework. Since the lobby is in a shopping mall, recreation is confined to the roof, where you'll find a small pool, sauna, and snack bar.

Dining/Diversions: The Mayfair Grill serves a varied menu with particularly good steaks and seafood. There are also a rooftop snack bar for poolside snacks and a private nightclub open late.

Amenities: Concierge and room service (24 hours), dry cleaning, newspaper delivery, nightly turndown, twice-daily maid service, secretarial services, express checkout. VCRs and video rentals, outdoor pool, access to nearby health club, Jacuzzi, elaborate business center, conference rooms.

4 Dining

Florida cooking—with its Caribbean and Asian influences, an abundance of tropical ingredients, and millions of tourists—has made a splash that has been heard around the globe. One of the area's premiere chefs, Norman van Aken of Norman's restaurant in Coral Gables, received the prestigious James Beard award as Best American Chef in the Southeast in 1997, following in the footsteps of Allen Susser of Chef Allen's, who took the award in 1994. These chefs, like so many visitors, are attracted to the energetic environment of Miami, where produce grows in backyards and fish are so fresh they're still flapping on the prep lines.

No longer do chefs get their start here with hopes of moving on to New York or Los Angeles. Quite the contrary. There are literally hundreds of successful restaurants that have opened first in the Northeast and then have opted to join the other successful outlets in sunny South Florida. They bring with them recipes and distinctive ideas about food that add even more variety to this hodgepodge of regional cuisine known as "New World."

This regional style of cooking is hard to define. It encompasses the varied tastes of the Caribbean, especially Cuba, as well as an old-Floridian and California nouvelle influence. The idea is to use locally available tropical ingredients, such as mango, papaya, avocado, jicama, coconut, snapper, lobster, and stone crab. Though at times it can be more than a bit overwhelming, in general, the results are deliciously exciting. Think of mango-infused oils over jerk tuna with jicama slaw served in a cracked coconut with yuca fries. You may need a translator. Welcome to the new world.

In addition to the exciting inventions of native chefs, you can always find the exotic foods of almost every ethnicity—from Cuban to Haitian to Jamaican to Vietnamese.

Many restaurants keep extended hours in season (roughly Dec to Apr) and may close for lunch and/or dinner on Mondays, when the traffic is slower. Call for updated schedules. If you want to picnic on the beach or pick up some dessert, check out the gourmet food shops, green markets, and bakeries listed in "Shopping," in chapter 5.

SOUTH BEACH

The renaissance of South Beach has spawned dozens of first-rate restaurants. In fact, big names from across the country have decided to capitalize on South Beach's international appeal and have begun to open branches here with great success. A few old standbys remain from the Miami Vice days, but the flock of newcomers dominates the scene, with places going in and out of style as quickly as the tides. The listings below represent the restaurants that have quickly gained national attention or should.

The Lincoln Road area is packed with places offering good food and great atmosphere. Since it's impossible to list them all, I recommend strolling and browsing. Most restaurants post a copy of their menu outside, and staff are happy to chat with curious passersby.

With very few exceptions, the places on Ocean Drive are crowded with tourists and priced accordingly. You'll do better to venture a little farther into the pedestrian-friendly streets just west of Ocean Drive.

VERY EXPENSIVE

✪ **Astor Place in the Astor Hotel.** 956 Washington Ave., South Beach. ☎ **305/ 672-7217.** Reservations recommended. Main courses $15–$30. AE, DC, MC, V. Daily 7am–2:30pm; Sun–Thurs 7–11pm; Fri–Sat 6pm–midnight. NEW FLORIDA BARBECUE.

The Astor Hotel has not only a great bar, but perhaps the very best restaurant on the beach. Favorites include corn-crusted yellowtail snapper with lemon boniato mash and roasted corn sauce or a sushi salad (a concoction of curry, fresh tuna, ginger shrimp, caviar, wasabi, and smoked salmon dressed in an orange sesame vinaigrette). All the dishes are dramatic and delicious. A stack of portobello mushrooms is served pancake style with balsamic syrup and sun-dried tomato butter. Nightly specials consistently sell out and are always worth a try. Another hot seller is the decadent lobster pot pie with shrimp and vegetables. If it's available, order it.

The sleek dining room, with low-level lighting, a glass-enclosed atrium, and marble floors, is romantic in an ultramodern way. Well-dressed hipsters flock to the restaurant, especially on weekend nights. A sophisticated family crowd shows up for the Sunday jazz brunch, which features all kinds of eggs and luscious sandwiches on crisp homemade bread. There are also Italian rice dishes, salads, and soups.

Blue Door. At the Delano Hotel, 1685 Collins Ave., South Beach. ☎ **305/674-6400.** Reservations recommended for dinner. Main courses $19–$34; soups and salads $6–$12. AE, DC, MC, V. Daily 7am–1am. AMERICAN NOUVELLE.

The Blue Door's setting—with plump circular booths, billowy white curtains, and polished oak accents—could be a backdrop for a 1930s movie. Celebrity sightings are almost guaranteed; with Madonna as a part owner, you would expect no less. The problem is that everyone, including your waiter, thinks he's the next big star. In the

South Beach Dining

To Mid Beach↗
& North Beach

Dade Boulevard

The Bass
Museum of Art

Collins
Park

Miami Beach
Convention Center

20th St.

19th St.

18th St.

Jackie Gleason Theater
of Performing Arts

17th St.

Lincoln Road Mall

Lincoln Rd.

Venetian
Causeway

Dade Boulevard

16th St.

Biscayne
Bay

15th St.

Española Way
14th Pl.

14th St.
Miami Beach
Post Office

13th St.

12th St.

Flamingo
Park

11th St.

10th St.

9th St.

8th St.

7th St.

6th St.

Beach
Patrol
Station

Art Deco
Welcome
Center

Lummus
Park

Atlantic
Ocean

5th St.

4th St.

3rd St.

2nd St.

1st St.

Commerce St.

Biscayne St.

South Pointe
Park

Government Cut

Astor Place	17
Bagel Factory	12
Balans	2
Blue Door	7
Chrysanthemum	13
Grillfish	10
Joe Allen's	1
Joe's Stone Crab	
Restaurant	25
La Sandwicherie	11
Larios on the Beach	18
L'Entrecote de Paris	22
Monty's Stone Crab/	
Seafood House	23
Mrs. Mendoza's	
Tacos al Carbon	16
Nemo's	24
News Cafe	19
Noodles of Asia	
(NOA)	4
Osteria del Teatro	8
Pacific Time	3
Puerto Sagua	20
Smith & Wollensky	26
Sport Cafe	21
Stephan's Gourmet	
Market & Cafe	9
Thai House	
South Beach	15
Toni's	14
Van Dyke Cafe	5
Yuca	6

NA-0165

.2 mi
0   .124 km

N

103

dining room, a steady stream of beautiful people parade through a center corridor on their way to the Alice-in-Wonderlandesque pool deck, where more people are posing on the luxurious furnishings. You'll want to sit on the patio if the weather is nice.

If your waiter deigns to take your order, try the delicate crab cakes, two to an order, served on a peppery fennel and tomato salad. On a recent visit, the stone crab claws were badly cracked, making the experience frustrating. The fish options, on the other hand, were fresh and prepared in a simple but elegant style. The choices include sea bass with a mashed combination of acorn squash and fennel, grilled lobster, salmon, and sautéed mahimahi in a sweet vinegar sauce.

China Grill. 404 Washington Ave. (at the corner of Fifth St.), South Beach. ☎ **305/ 534-2211.** Reservations recommended. Main courses $19–$30. AE, DC, MC, V. Mon–Fri 11:45am–5pm; Sun–Thurs 6pm–midnight; Fri–Sat 6pm–1am. NEW WORLD CUISINE/ MULTICULTURAL.

Imported from New York, like so many other Miami institutions, China Grill took Miami Beach by storm when it opened in late 1995. Unfortunately, the attitude and prices are so up there that it tends to attract mostly the aging beautiful people and a few hangers-on. It's worth going to the bar for a drink to soak up some atmosphere and to people-watch. But be warned—the food sounds better than it is in this night-club pretending to be a restaurant.

The menu and management explain that the prices are so high because the dishes are meant to be shared; however, when we tried that approach, we were left hungry. Some have complained that the service is slow and the food inconsistent. That being said, I could get addicted to the Confucius Chicken Salad, which has crispy fried noo-dles and a perfect blend of sesame and soy in the vinaigrette.

Escopazzo. 1311 Washington Ave., South Beach. ☎ **305/674-9450.** Reservations required. Pastas $12–$18; main courses $18–$28. AE, MC, V. Mon, Tues, Thurs 6pm–midnight; Fri–Sat 6pm–12:30am and Sun 6–11pm. ITALIAN.

Owned by a personable Roman called Pino Bodoni who comes from a family of restaurateurs, this South Beach gem has been a favorite of locals for years. Thankfully, the formerly tiny space doubled in size this year and can now accommodate the many who could never get in before. Once inside, you can choose from some stupendous handcrafted dishes like risotto with fresh seafood, pappardelle with wild game and mushroom ragu, and braised leg of lamb with juniper berries, rosemary, and fennel. Service and style in this romantic setting are always top-rate.

Joe's Stone Crab Restaurant. 11 Washington Ave. (at Biscayne St., just south of 1st St.), South Beach. ☎ **305/673-0365,** takeout 305/653-4611. Reservations not accepted. Market price varies but averages $42 for a serving of jumbo crab claws, $30 for large claws. AE, CB, DC, DISC, MC, V. Tues–Sat 11:30am–2pm; Sun–Thurs 5–10pm; Fri–Sat 5–11pm. Closed mid-May to mid-Oct. SEAFOOD.

Open since 1913 and steeped in tradition, this restaurant is famous in Florida and beyond, as evidenced by the ubiquitous long lines waiting to get in. A full menu is available; but to order anything but stone crabs is unthinkable, and the waiters will let you know it. Service tends to be brusque and pushy.

Even after a $5 million renovation, which more than doubled the size of the place, the lines are still ridiculously long. Too many locals claim they "know someone" at the door, which usually means they were introduced through their mutual friend, Ben Franklin. Even after heavy tipping, the wait can exceed an hour on weekend nights. If you have to say you were there, brave it and enjoy the wait in the stunning oak bar. Otherwise, try the take-out bar next door for the same price and less hassle. The claws here are the best, but also pricier than at other local restaurants. Remember, you're paying for history.

✪ **Osteria del Teatro.** 1443 Washington Ave. (at Española Way), South Beach. ☎ **305/ 538-7850.** Reservations recommended. Main courses $21–$32. AE, CB, DC, JCB, MC, V. Wed–Mon 6–11pm; Fri–Sat 6pm–midnight. Closed for 3 weeks in Sept. NORTHERN ITALIAN.

The curved entryway of this well-established enclave of reliable, if slightly overpriced, Italian cuisine is abuzz nightly. Reams of locals and tourists wait for a seat at one of the small tables. Move the fresh orchid aside to make room for a big basket of lightly toasted chunks of real Italian bread, and then wait for your very knowledgeable waiter to recommend a daily special.

Start with any of the grilled vegetables, such as portobello mushrooms with fontina or the garlic-infused peppers. All the pastas are handmade and done to perfection. The *risotto al'aragosta* is a creamy rice dish with a decadent lobster and shrimp sauce full of tasty morsels of seafood. Of the five or so entrees offered nightly, usually at least three are seafood. The tuna loin is served with a rich mushroom sauce with just a hint of rosemary. The duck breast, doused in a sweet balsamic honey sauce and fanned over a bed of wilted radicchio leaves, is rightfully very popular. Each slice of duck is perfectly seared on the outside and tender throughout without even a hint of gamy flavor.

Pacific Time and Pacific Time Next Door. 915 Lincoln Rd. (between Jefferson and Michigan aves.), South Beach. ☎ **305/534-5979.** Reservations recommended. Main courses $19.50–$29. AE, CB, DC, MC, V. Sun–Thurs 6–11pm; Fri–Sat 6pm–midnight; Next Door cafe daily 11am–midnight. PAN ASIAN.

This exciting Lincoln Road restaurant has received accolades from *The Miami Herald*, *Esquire* magazine, and *Bon Appétit*. Chef and co-owner Jonathan Eismann puts out some of the funkiest dishes ever spotted this side of the equator. One of the best for meat-eaters is the Mongolian lamb salad, which has a lightly sweet, earthy taste with a crunchy kick of onion. For a main course, the ever-changing menu offers many locally caught fish specialties, including grouper served on a bed of shredded shallots and ginger with a sweet sake-infused sauce and tempura-dunked sweet-potato slivers on the side. Under the midnight-blue sky ceiling and against the pale yellow distressed walls, you'll probably see stars. The famous chocolate bomb is every bit as decadent as they've said, with hot bittersweet chocolate bursting from the cupcake-like center. Some folks are put off by the exotic dishes, but more adventurous eaters return over and over again for a chance to experience this stunning Pacific-inspired meteor. New in 1998 was a more casual (and not as recommendable) outdoor cafe serving lunch and dinner with a more conventional menu and cheaper prices.

Smith & Wollensky. 1 Washington Ave. (in South Pointe Park), South Beach. ☎ **305/ 673-2800.** Reservations suggested. Main courses $20–$30. DC, DISC, MC, V. Daily noon–midnight. Grill open 5pm–2am. STEAK/AMERICAN.

This pricey New York import opened its doors in late 1997 and was packed from the start. The handsome clubby atmosphere is enhanced by views of the intercoastal waterway that leads to the Port of Miami. The menu, as well as the setting, is basic, almost austere, with a few chicken and fish choices and beef served about a dozen ways. The classic is the sirloin seared lightly and served naked. Also good is the thick and buttery filet mignon. Delicious side dishes such as asparagus, baked potato, onion rings, creamed spinach, and hash browns are sold à la carte. Ask for advice from the wine steward, since the vast and impressive menu can be overwhelming. Service here, unlike so many other South Beach restaurants, is usually professional and polite. Desserts are superb, too. Just hope someone else is paying.

To avoid the clanking bustle of the main dining rooms, ask for a seat upstairs or, better yet, in The Grill, where you can order from a more casual and less expensive menu. You'll find meat entrees at about 30 percent less than in the regular restaurant. Portions in here are a bit smaller, too, eliminating the need for doggie bags.

✪ **Yuca.** 501 Lincoln Rd. (corner of Drexel), South Beach. ☎ **305/532-9822.** Reservations required. Main courses $19–$32. AE, DC, DISC, MC, V. Sun–Thurs noon–4pm and 6–11pm; Fri–Sat noon–4pm and 6–midnight. Closed summer for weekday lunches. INNOVATIVE CUBAN.

This is the place to take out-of-towners you want to impress with a dose of upscale Latin culture. The menu is large and exotic. Unfortunately, it's also badly translated, so don't be shy about asking for a waiter who is proficient in English (most are) if you don't *habla español.* By the way, don't give yourself away as a gringo by pronouncing the name as "Yucka." It's "Yoo-ka," and it is a play on words, being the name of a staple root vegetable and an acronym for Young Upscale Cuban-Americans.

To enjoy your meal, insist on being seated in the front of the restaurant, facing Lincoln Road; otherwise, you'll be in the hectic path of the kitchen and too close to the very talented but loud salsa band that plays on weekends. Start with the lobster medallions with sautéed spinach and a portobello mushroom stuffed with vegetarian paella. The pieces of lobster tail are expertly grilled, with a touch of oil over just-wilted greens. The mushrooms are good, but the paella can be a bit pasty. For a main course, the pork tenderloin is a favorite—I thought it must have marinated for days, because I could cut it with a butter knife. The hearty *congri,* a mash of red beans and rice, and a green apple and mango salsa make a perfect balance. The veal loin, the menu's most expensive entree, has a rich meaty flavor but can be a bit dry. A full selection of traditional and exotic dessert choices is available, as well as some of the best coffee in town.

Go on the weekend for a late dinner and then head upstairs for live music. If Cuban diva Albita is playing, you're in for a real experience. It's pricey but well worth it.

EXPENSIVE

✪ **Monty's Stone Crab/Seafood House.** 300 Alton Rd., South Beach. ☎ **305/673-3444.** Reservations recommended. Main courses $20–$37. AE, DC, MC, V. Sun–Thurs 5:30–11pm; Fri–Sat 5:30pm–midnight. SEAFOOD.

Seafood fans have long been enamored of Monty's various menus in the Grove and in Boca. Now Monty's has moved in to South Beach, burnished the rustic oak floor, set up a raw bar outside around a large swimming pool, and opened the doors for business. The best deal in town is still the all-you-can-eat stone crabs—about $40 for the large ones and $35 for the mediums. That's about the same price that Joe's, located 2 blocks away, charges for just three or four claws. (But don't order stone crabs in summer—they're out of season.) Enjoy the incredible views and off-season fish specialties, including the Maryland she-crab soup, rich and creamy without too much thickener. Year-round, you can enjoy the saffron and tomato-based bouillabaisse, and the key lime pie is the real deal.

✪ **Nemo's.** 100 Collins Ave., South Beach. ☎ **305/532-4550.** Reservations recommended. Main courses $17–$20; sandwiches and platters $4–$12; Sun brunch $19. AE, MC, V. Mon–Sat noon–3pm and 7pm–midnight; Sun noon–3pm and 6–11pm. NEW WORLD CUISINE/ MULTICULTURAL.

This dark and super-stylish hotspot is an oasis in a hip area of South Beach below 5th Street. Here models and celebrities rub elbows—literally, since the tables are so close together. Ask to be seated in the more private back room, which has a pleasant garden and is the only place where you can hear your dining companions or your waiter. In the main dining room, the din is unbearable. The staff here is professional, personable, and efficient—the best on the beach.

The menu offers many fish dishes. One of the most popular is the charred salmon. The flash-cooking in a wok gives it a unique flavor, slightly blackened outside and tender and sweet inside. If you're in the mood for something light, try the grilled portobello mushroom appetizer, served with a rich, creamy garlic polenta. The spicy Vietnamese beef salad is indeed very spicy, but it's too small a portion. You can never go wrong choosing one of the daily specials. An exotic and delicious choice for dessert is the California figs soaked in port syrup and surrounded with balls of tamarind (said to be an aphrodisiac) ice cream.

MODERATE

Balans. 1022 Lincoln Rd. (between Lenox and Michigan), South Beach. ☎ **305/534-9191.** Reservations not accepted. Main courses $9–$17; pastas and noodles $8–$10. AE, DC, DISC, MC, V. Daily 8am–1am. INTERNATIONAL.

This well-run sidewalk cafe, a London import, is a good value, especially when the weather is right. It's a favorite hangout for the gay community and is right at home on fabulous Lincoln Road. Dinners here are a bargain, with winning entrees like a hearty lobster club sandwich served with bacon, lettuce, and tomato on toasted onion bread, and a *hoisin Port* fillet nestled over baby bok choy and crisp leek spring rolls. The tempting starters are relatively small, so you can try a few. Try Thai soup, as well as the concoction of goat, cheese, and lightly breaded fried mushrooms. A large herb salad with a mix of more than five types of baby greens is a great way to start any meal. The tahini chicken salad, however, is sadly lacking in spice. The menu, with lots of healthful salads and sandwiches, seems to please a wide audience.

✪ **Chrysanthemum.** 1256 Washington Ave., South Beach. ☎ **305/531-5656.** Main courses $11–$20. AE, CB, DC, MC, V. Tues–Thurs and Sun 6–10:30pm; Fri–Sat 6pm–midnight. SZECHUAN/PEKINESE.

At first, the unpretentious atmosphere may be a surprise in glitzy South Beach, but after you've tried the tasty dishes in Chrysanthemum, the best Chinese restaurant in Miami, you'll want to come back. Count on the service to be prompt but not solicitous. The many vegetarian specialties include spicy eggplant strips in a rich balsamic vinegar sauce and black mushrooms sautéed with tiny Shanghai lettuce hearts. Start with the Chinese salad, which comes heaped with a fresh mix of greens, vermicelli, bean sprouts, and coriander. The steamed whole fish is best with the ginger and scallions. It comes with bones, but ask the waiter to remove them; he will gladly and expertly oblige.

Grillfish. 1444 Collins Ave. (corner of Española Way), South Beach. ☎ **305/538-9908.** Reservations recommended on weekends. Main courses $8–$15. AE, DC, DISC, MC, V. In season daily 6pm–midnight; off-season daily 6–11pm. SEAFOOD.

From the beautiful Byzantine-style mural and the gleaming oak bar, you'd think you were eating in a much more expensive restaurant. Grillfish manages to pay the exorbitant South Beach rent because the restaurant has a loyal following of locals who come for fresh, simple seafood in a relaxed but upscale atmosphere. As the name implies, fish, fish, and fish is what you'll get.

The waiters are friendly and know the menu well. The barroom seafood chowder is full of chunks of shellfish, as well as some fresh white fish fillets in a tomato broth. The small ear of corn, included with each entree, is about as close as you'll get to any type of vegetable offering besides the pedestrian salad. Still, at these prices, it's worth a visit to try some local fare, including mako shark, swordfish, tuna, marlin, and wahoo (they'll either grill or sautée it). Also, I recommend the spicy red pasta sauce as a great complement to this rustic, Italian-inspired seafood fare.

Jeffrey's. 1629 Michigan Ave. (½ block south of Lincoln Rd.), South Beach. ☎ **305/ 673-0690.** Full meals $16–$21 pastas with salads $11–$17. AE, CB, DC, MC, V. Tues–Sat 6–11pm; Sun 5–10pm. AMERICAN/CONTINENTAL/BISTRO.

Jeffrey's is a real find on South Beach—the genuinely concerned and doting owner, Jeffrey Landsman, treats everyone as a regular and calls grandmothers and children alike "kids." Some say this is the most romantic restaurant on the beach, and South Beach's gay crowd certainly seems to agree. Old-fashioned lace curtains and candle-light are a welcome repast from the glitz and chrome of the rest of the island.

You can choose a succulent ¾-pound burger or try a hearty chicken breast mari-nated in a balsamic sauce served with freshly mashed sweet potatoes over spinach on white lace tablecloths. Some of the better seafood options include the conch fritters and the crab cakes. Jeffrey's is known for its perfectly dressed Caesar salad, which could use some more anchovies for my taste, but is nonetheless delicious. Most desserts are tasty, but the homemade *tarte-tartin,* a caramelly deep-dish apple tart, is superb. Go early before it sells out.

Larios on the Beach. 820 Ocean Dr., South Beach. ☎ **305/532-9577.** Reservations rec-ommended. Main courses $8–$15. AE, MC, V. Sun–Thurs 11:30am–midnight; Fri–Sat 11:30am–2am. CUBAN.

Gloria and Emilio Estefan brought their favorite chef to create this ultrastylish restaurant in the heart of the South Beach hustle. Enjoy a few appetizers at the handsome chrome and wood bar while you wait for a seat amid the sea of Spanish-speaking regulars.

Portions are large and prices are reasonable. The menu runs the gamut, from diner-style *medianoches* (Cuban sandwiches with pork and cheese) to a tangy and tender *serrucho en escabeche* (pickled kingfish) with just enough citrus to mellow the fishiness but not enough to cause a pucker. You could get away with ordering three or four *aperitivos* and *ensaladas* (appetizers and salads) for two people. If you're still hungry, try the *camarones al ajillo* (shrimp in garlic sauce), *fabada asturiana* (hearty soup of black beans and sausage), or *palomilla* (thinly sliced beef served with onions and parsley). Save room for the rich custard desserts, which include a few stunning varia-tions on the standard flan. A spoonful of pumpkin or coffee-accented custard with a cup of *cortadito* (espresso-style coffee with milk and sugar) will get you prepped for a full night of dancing.

L'Entrecote de Paris. 413 Washington Ave., South Beach. ☎ **305/673-1002.** Reserva-tions suggested on weekends. Prix fixe $14–$18 (includes potatoes and salad). DC, MC, V. Daily 6pm–1am. FRENCH BRASSERIE.

Everything in this classy little bistro is simple. For dinner, you choose between salmon and steak, and beyond a few salads, that's it—but both are great. The salmon looks like spa cuisine, served with a pile of bald steamed potatoes and a salad with pedes-trian greens and an unmatchable vinaigrette. The steak, on the other hand, is the stuff cravings are made of, even if you're not a die-hard carnivore. Its salty sharp sauce is rich but not thick, and full of the beef's natural flavor. The slices are served on top of your own little habachi, which also keeps the accompanying fries warm.

Most diners are very Euro and pack a petit attitude. Tables and booths are squeezed tight together. On the other hand, the waiters are super-quick and professional, and almost friendly in a French kind of way. The short and very French wine list includes several well-priced bottles for under $20. Even if you are on a diet or have forsaken chocolate, try the *profiteroles au chocolat,* a perfect puff pastry filled with vanilla ice cream and topped with a dark, bittersweet chocolate sauce.

✪ **Macarena.** 1334 Washington Ave., South Beach. ☎ **305/531-3440.** Reservations suggested on weekends. Tapas $3–$6; main courses $11–$18. AE, DC, MC, V. Mon–Fri noon–3pm; daily 8pm–midnight (later on Fri and Sat). SPANISH/TAPAS.

Despite its unfortunate name, this South Beach gem is a great place to eat and enjoy. It's looked after by a young crew of Spanish imports whose families own several popular restaurants in Madrid. If you're a gringo, you'll probably show up before 10pm, when you're sure to get a table. After that time, especially on weekends, it's standing room only.

The gorgeous Euro crowd shows up for foot-stomping flamenco (every Wed, Fri, and Sat) and an outrageous selection of tapas, including Miami's very best paella. Order a large portion and share it among at least four people. The garlic shrimp is tasty and aromatic, and the yellow squash stuffed with seafood and cheese is especially delicious. All the seafood, such as mussels in marinara sauce and clams in green sauce, is worth sampling. With such reasonable prices, you can taste lots of dishes and leave satisfied. Try some of the terrific sangria made with slices of fresh fruit and a subtle tinge of sweet soda.

NOA (Noodles of Asia). 801 Lincoln Rd., South Beach. ☎ **305/925-0050.** Noodles $10–$15. Sun–Thurs noon–midnight; Fri–Sat until 1am. AE, MC, V. PANASIAN/NOODLES.

Another newcomer to Lincoln Road and the latest outpost in China Grill's growing empire, this Asian-inspired noodle shop attracts a trendy, good-looking crowd that comes for a variety of noodle dishes served in a stylish but uncomfortable setting. The appetizers, especially the delicate pork dumplings and the sautéed vegetables, are first-rate. Some main courses still need fine-tuning. Prices are not outrageous, but a bit high for what you get. With some work, the place could become a favorite hangout, especially thanks to an extensive and exotic selection of drinks and outrageous desserts.

Tap Tap. 819 Fifth St. (between Jefferson and Meridian aves., next to the Shell station), South Beach. ☎ **305/672-2898.** Reservations recommended in season and for special events. Main courses $8–$15. AE, DC, MC, V. Sun–Thurs 6pm–midnight; Fri–Sat 6pm–2am. HAITIAN.

The whole place looks like an overgrown *tap tap,* a brightly painted jitney common in Haiti. Every inch of the place is painted a neon blue, pink, or purple and every color in between, and the atmosphere is always fun. It's where the Haiti-philes and Haitians, from journalists to politicians, hang out. Even Manno Charlemagne, the mayor of Port-au-Prince, shows up when he has the time to play his brand of protest music and drink some Rhum Barbancourt.

On crowded nights, the service is impossible. I recommend going for appetizers and drinks. The *Lanbi nan citron,* a tart, marinated conch salad, is perfect with a tall tropical drink and maybe some lightly grilled goat tidbits, which are served in a savory brown sauce and are less stringy than a typical goat dish. Another super-satisfying choice is the pumpkin soup, a rich brick-colored puree of subtly seasoned pumpkin with a dash of pepper. An excellent salad of avocado, mango, and watercress is a great finish. Even if you don't stay for a full meal, try the pumpkin flan with coconut caramel sauce, an ultra-Caribbean sweet treat.

✪ **Toni's.** 1208 Washington Ave., South Beach. ☎ **305/673-9368.** Reservations recommended. Main courses $11–$22; rolls $3.50–$8.50. AE, MC, V. Daily 6pm–midnight; Fri–Sat 6pm–1am. SUSHI/JAPANESE.

One of Washington Avenue's first tenants, Toni's has withstood the test of time on fickle South Beach. By serving local fish caught daily and some imports from the Pacific and beyond, Toni has created a vast menu with options from teriyaki to hand rolls. The atmosphere is comfortable and even allows for quiet conversation—a rarity in this neighborhood. The hundreds of appetizers and rolls you can order make it a fun place to go with a group.

Consider the seaweed salad, a crunchy, salty, green plant dressed with a light sesame sauce. The miso soup is hearty and a bit sweet. A good appetizer from the sushi bar is Miami Heat, which contains slabs of tuna with bits of scallion in a peppery sesame oil. I suggest skipping the entrees unless you are somehow still hungry after all the warm-ups. Many of the main dishes are good, however, like the lobster teriyaki in a dark sweet sauce over white rice.

INEXPENSIVE

✪ **La Sandwicherie.** 229 14th St. (behind the Amoco station), South Beach. ☎ **305/532-8934.** Sandwiches and salads $4.50–$7. No credit cards. Daily 9:30am–5am. Delivery 9:30am–10pm. FRENCH SNACK BAR/JUICE BAR.

For the most incredible gourmet sandwich you've ever tasted, stop by the green-and-white awning that hides this fabulously French lunch counter. Choose pâté, saucisson, salami, prosciutto, turkey, tuna, ham, roast beef, or any of the perfect cheeses (Swiss, mozzarella, cheddar, or provolone). Vegetarians can make a meal out of the optional sandwich toppings, which include black olives, cornichons, cucumbers, lettuce, onions, green or hot peppers, or tomatoes. You can have your sandwich made on delicious fresh French bread or on a relatively uninspired croissant.

If the six or so wooden stools are all taken, don't despair; you can stand and watch the tattoo artist do his work through the glass wall next door. Or douse your creation with the light tangy vinaigrette and bring lunch to the beach—that is, if you can make it 2 blocks without eating the whole thing. In addition to the cans and bottles of teas, sodas, juices, and waters, you can get coffees, fresh juices, and smoothies here.

Mrs. Mendoza's Tacos al Carbon. 1040 Alton Rd., South Beach. ☎ **305/535-0808.** Main courses $3–$5; side dishes 79¢–$3. No credit cards. Mon–Thurs 11am–10pm; Fri–Sat 11am–11pm; Sun noon–10pm. FAST FOOD/MEXICAN.

This hard-to-spot storefront is a godsend—it's the only fresh California-style Mexican place around. The steak and chicken are grilled as you wait and then stuffed into homemade flour or corn wrappings. You order at the tile counter and pick up your dish on a plastic tray in minutes. This is a popular spot for locals.

The vegetarian offerings are huge and hearty. One of my favorites is the veggie burrito, which includes rice, black beans, cheese, lettuce, and guacamole doused in tomato salsa. They offer three types of salsa, from mild to super hot. You can see the fresh-cut cilantro and taste the super-hot chilies. The chips are hand cut and flavorful, but a bit too coarse. Skip them and enjoy an order of the rich chunky guacamole with a fork.

There's another location at Doral Plaza, 9739 NW 41st St.

News Café. 800 Ocean Dr., South Beach. ☎ **305/538-6397.** Salads $4–$8; sandwiches $5–$7. AE, MC, V. Daily 24 hours. AMERICAN.

Of all the chic spots around trendy South Beach, News Café has been around the longest. Inexpensive breakfasts and cafe fare are served at about 20 perpetually congested tables. Most of the seating is outdoors, and terrace tables are most coveted. Ocean Drive's multitude of fashion photography crews and their models meet here regularly to get the international newspapers and magazines.

The food isn't remarkable, but the people-watching is. The menu is heavy on health-oriented dishes and includes yogurt with fruit salad, various green salads, imported cheese and meat sandwiches, and a choice of quiches.

Puerto Sagua. 700 Collins Ave., South Beach. ☎ **305/673-1115.** Main courses $8–$19; sandwiches and salads $3–$9. AE, DC, MC, V. Daily 7:30am–2am. SPANISH/CUBAN.

This dingy, brown-walled diner is one of the only old holdouts on South Beach. Its steady stream of regulars range from *abuelitos* (little old grandfathers) to hipsters who stop in after clubbing. It has endured because the food is good, if a little greasy. Some of the less heavy dishes are a super-chunky fish soup with pieces of whole flaky grouper, the chicken and seafood paella, and the marinated kingfish. Also good are most of the shrimp dishes, especially the shrimp in garlic sauce served with white rice and salad.

This is one of the most reasonably priced places left on the beach for simple, hearty fare. Don't be intimidated by the hunched older waiters in their white button shirts and black pants. Even if you don't speak Spanish, they're usually willing to do charades. Anyway, the extensive menu, which ranges from BLTs to grilled lobsters to yummy fried plantains, is translated into English. Hurry, before another boutique goes up in its place.

Sport Cafe. 560 Washington Ave., South Beach. ☎ **305/674-9700.** Reservations accepted for 4 or more. Main courses $8–$12; sandwiches and pizzas $4.50–$8. AE, MC, V. Daily noon–1am; sometimes earlier for coffee. ITALIAN.

Don't expect to see the latest football or baseball games at this Sports Cafe; instead you're more likely to find a soccer match or bicycle race on the television. The Sport Cafe's owners, brothers Tonino and Paolo Doino, hail from Rome. They've put together an authentic Italian menu, listing only half a dozen entrees and a few pizzas. It can be a challenge placing your order, but definitely request a plate of fresh crushed garlic when they bring your bread and oil. I recommend asking for the day's specials and ordering one of them. Always good is the perfectly al dente penne with salmon served with a pink sauce. The eggplant parmigiano, almost always available though not on the menu, is the best in the county. For dessert, try the tiramisu, which, unlike the more common cake or pudding style, is served semi-freddo, or partially frozen, like an ice cream.

The atmosphere is rustic and young and the prices so reasonable that on some nights you may have to wait for a seat, especially for sidewalk tables.

Van Dyke Cafe. 846 Lincoln Rd., South Beach. ☎ **305/534-3600.** Reservations recommended for evenings. Main courses $6–$11. AE, DC, MC, V. Daily 8am–1am; Fri–Sat 8am–3am. AMERICAN.

Owned by the same group who owns the successful News Café, the Van Dyke has used the same formula to guarantee its longevity on Lincoln Road. The smart, upscale decor inside and the European sidewalk cafe outside are always crowded because of the diner-like prices and fast, friendly service.

There is nothing too ambitious on the menu, which offers basic sandwiches, salads, and, best of all, breakfast all day long. The pastas are decent, although not too exciting. House specialties include an excellent smoked salmon on thick black bread and a smooth, lemony hummus with pita chips. Also, since you're in Miami Beach, you may want to consider a nice hot bowl of cure-all chicken soup with matzo balls. In the evenings, the sounds of a talented jazz band waft down from the dark, elegant club upstairs.

✪ World Resources. 719 Lincoln Rd., South Beach. ☎ **305/535-8987.** Main courses $6–$8; sushi hand rolls $3–$4. AE, DC, MC, V. Daily noon–midnight. SUSHI/THAI.

World Resources is an excellent little cafe and sushi bar masquerading as an Indonesian furniture and bric-a-brac store. Local hippie types and hipsters frequent this downright cheap hangout instead of cooking at home. Offerings include some of the freshest, most innovative sushi in Miami, plus many Thai specialties. The portions are generous and the cooking simple. The basil chicken, for example, is a tasty combination of white meat sautéed in a coconut sauce with subtle hints of basil and garlic. The Thai salad is heaped with fresh vegetables. Although you can get better Thai at a number of spots on the beach, you can't beat the atmosphere here, which includes dozens of outside tables surrounding a tiny pond and a stage where World Beat musicians perform nightly. From African drumming to Indian sitar playing, there is always some action at this standout on the Road. It also offers a vast selection of coffees, teas, wines, beers, and cigarettes from around the world.

MIAMI BEACH: SURFSIDE, BAL HARBOUR & SUNNY ISLES

The area north of the Art Deco District—from about 21st Street to 163rd Street—had its heyday in the 1950s when its huge hotels and gambling halls blocked the view of the ocean. Now many of the old hotels have been converted into condos or budget lodgings and the bayfront mansions renovated by and for wealthy entrepreneurs, families, and speculators. The area now has many more residents, albeit seasonal, than visitors. On the culinary front, the result is a handful of super-expensive, traditional restaurants and a number of value-oriented spots.

VERY EXPENSIVE

✪ **The Forge Restaurant.** 432 Arthur Godfrey Rd. (41st St.), Miami Beach. ☎ **305/ 538-8533.** Reservations required. Main courses $19–$30. AE, DC, MC, V. Sun–Thurs 6pm–midnight; Fri–Sat 6pm–1am. AMERICAN.

English oak paneling and Tiffany glass suggest high prices and haute cuisine, and that's exactly what you get from The Forge. Each elegant dining room possesses its own character and features high ceilings, ornate chandeliers, and high-quality European artwork. The most intimate room is the library in the back. The Forge attracts a mix of young, moneyed Miamians; well-dressed Euros; and Saudi royalty. The atmosphere is elegant but not too stuffy, especially on Wednesday nights, when the singles scene shows up for mingling at the bar and dancing next door at Jimmy's.

Like the rest of the menu, appetizers are mostly classics, from Beluga caviar to baked onion soup to shrimp cocktail and escargot. When they're in season, order the stone crabs. For the main course, all of the seafood, chicken, or veal dishes are recommendable, but The Forge is especially known for its steaks. In fact, in 1996, *Wine Spectator* magazine voted the Super Steak the "Best in America." Finally, The Forge still has one of Miami's best wine lists and an extensive cellar. Ask for a tour.

EXPENSIVE

Carpaccio. 9700 Collins Ave. (97th St., in Bal Harbour shops), Bal Harbour, ☎ **305/ 867-7777.** Reservations suggested. Main courses $15–$20; pastas $12–$15. AE, MC, V. Daily 11:30am–11pm. NORTHERN ITALIAN.

Serving up some of the best Northern Italian in Miami's ritziest shopping mall, this pricey and elegant cafe packs them in for elegant handmade pastas, pizzas, and, of course, carpaccio in a dozen variations. Service is better than at most area restaurants, though when its really busy, you'll find it hard to attract the attention of the friendly waiters who are scurrying amidst the crowds. The feel is casual though diners tend to dress in designer outfits. Some of them actually deign to wait in line on the sidewalk for a table—imagine that!

✪ **Crystal Café.** 726 41st St., Miami Beach. ☎ **305/673-8266.** Reservations recommended on weekends. Main courses $11–$25. AE, DC, DISC, MC, V. Tues–Thurs 5–10pm; Fri–Sat 5–11pm. CONTINENTAL/NEW WORLD.

The setting is sparse, with Lucite salt and pepper grinders and a bottle of wine as the only centerpiece on each of the 15 or so tables. I promise you won't need the seasoning. Chef Klime has done it all with the help of his affable wife and a superb waitstaff. Enjoy his unique sparkle at this little-known hideaway, which attracts stars like Julio Iglesias and other discriminating guests.

With approximately 30 entrees, including a few nightly specials, I can't figure out how each appears so perfectly prepared and beautifully presented. The shrimp-cake appetizer, for example, is the size of a bread plate and rests on top of a small mound of lightly sautéed watercress and mushrooms. Surrounding the delicately breaded disc are concentric circles of beautiful sauces. The veal marsala is served in a luscious brown sauce thickened not with heavy cream or flour but with delicate vegetable broth and a hearty mix of mushrooms. Most main courses come with a choice of three side dishes, such as zucchini, carrots, mashed potatoes, or pasta. The osso buco is a masterpiece.

MODERATE

Cafe Prima Pasta. 414 71st St. (½ block east of the Byron movie theater), Miami Beach. ☎ 305/867-0106. Main courses $12–$14; pastas $7–$9. No credit cards. Mon–Thurs noon–midnight; Fri noon–1am; Sat 1pm–1am. Sun 5pm–midnight. ITALIAN.

Here's another tiny pasta joint that serves phenomenal homemade noodles with good old Italian sauces, such as carbonara, dioliva, putanesca, and pomodoro. There are only 30 seats, so you might feel a bit cramped; but the crowd is generally a pleasant, young, laid-back set. The stuffed agnolotti with either tomato or pesto, spinach, and ricotta are so delicate and flavorful that you'll think you're eating dessert. Speaking of which, you'll want to try the apple tart with a pale golden caramel sauce. Ask for it à la mode and plan to come back again for more.

Cafe Ragazzi. 9500 Harding Ave. (on corner of 95th St.), Surfside. ☎ 305/866-4495. Reservations for 4 or more. Main courses $11–$15. MC, V. Mon–Fri 11:30am–3pm and 5:30–11pm; Sat–Sun 5:30–11pm. ITALIAN.

A relative newcomer in a neighborhood of old-time delis and diners, this little Italian cafe, with its rustic decor and a handsome waitstaff, enjoys great success for its tasty simple pastas. The spicy putanesca sauce with a subtle hint of fish is perfectly prepared, with just enough bits of tomato to give it some weight. Also recommended is the salmon with radicchio. You can choose from many decent salads and carpacci, too. Lunch specials are a real steal at $7, including soup, salad, and daily pasta. The mostly Italian/Argentinean staff is efficient, although sometimes limited in their ability to communicate. Expect a wait on weekend nights.

Lemon Twist. 908 71st St. (on 79th St. Causeway), Miami Beach/Normandy Isle. ☎ 305/868-2075. Reservations suggested on weekends. Main courses $8–$18; pastas $7–$9.50. AE, MC, V. In season, daily 6pm–midnight; off-season Tues–Sun 6pm–midnight. FRENCH/MEDITERRANEAN.

This hip little French bar and restaurant in a burgeoning neighborhood is certainly worth a visit. The house specialties are salads and seafood. Both are quite good, but even better is the cozy atmosphere both inside and on the outside patio. The lamb shank and the chicken with lemon and cream sauce are two of the tastier dishes, and my favorite salad here features a mound of herbed goat cheese in a puff pastry shell over a bed of fresh baby greens dressed in a delicate but spicy vinaigrette. The pastas, on the other hand, are not even worth a try—most are overcooked and others are underseasoned. An original touch: Complimentary lemon vodka shots are offered after each meal.

☉ Mama Vieja. 235-23 St. (just west of Collins Ave.), South Beach. ☎ **305/538-2400.** Reservations accepted, but not necessary. $7–$18 main courses. AE, CB, DC, DISC, MC, V. Daily noon–midnight. COLOMBIAN/INTERNATIONAL.

This funky Colombian hangout is a real find. It serves supremely fresh national specialties in a setting that might well be the backdrop for a Latin American spaghetti western. Brightly painted walls and elevated porches look out onto a large-screen TV showing music videos from the old country. The walls and ceilings are decorated with hundreds of hats that have been donated by customers and signed in exchange for a free meal. Bring in an interesting hat and mention it to the waiter or waitress before placing your order so they can bring you to the attention of the owner.

Start with an avocado salad and rich meat-filled empanadas served with spicy sauce or a creamy fish soup and green plantains stuffed with mixed seafood with large chunks of shellfish and fresh fillets. The best dishes are seafood selections—one outrageous dish is called *Pargo Rojo Estofado a la Mama Vieja,* a red snapper stuffed with a super creamy and delicate seafood sauce in a rice base. It's made for two ($29.95), but if you order the *Corvina a la Mama Vieja* for one ($12.95), you can try the same rich stuffing in a slightly smaller fish for much less money. All the dishes here are worth trying and so reasonably priced it's easy to order a lot. Try to save room for the milky sweet desserts and a good strong coffee—you'll need it if you want to dance all night. Next door is a popular disco and nightclub, Studio 23 (see "The Club & Music Scene," in chapter 5).

Wolfie Cohen's Rascal House. 17190 Collins Ave., Sunny Isles. ☎ **305/947-4581.** Omelets and sandwiches $4–$13; other dishes $5–$14. AE, MC, V. Open 24 hours. JEWISH/DELICATESSEN/BAKERY.

Open since 1954 and still going strong, this historic, nostalgic culinary extravaganza is one of Miami Beach's greatest traditions. Simple tables and booths, as well as plenty of patrons, fill the airy 425-seat dining room. The menu is as huge as the portions; try the corned beef, schmaltz herring, brisket, kreplach, chicken soup, or other authentic Jewish staples. Take-out service is available.

INEXPENSIVE

☉ The Greek Place. 233 95th St. (between Collins and Harding Aves.), Surfside. ☎ **305/866-9628.** Main courses $5–$6. No credit cards. Mon–Fri 10am–6pm. GREEK.

The only drawback of this tiny hole in the wall is that it's open only on weekdays. It's a little diner with sparkling white walls and about 10 wooden stools that serves fantastic Greek and American diner-style food. Daily specials like pastitsio, chicken alcyone, and roast turkey with all the fixings are big lunchtime draws for locals working in the area. Typical Greek dishes like shish kebab, souvlakis, and gyros are cooked to perfection as you wait. Even the hamburger, prime ground beef delicately spiced and fresh grilled, is exemplary.

Miami Beach Place. 6954 Collins Ave., Miami Beach. ☎ **305/866-8661.** Main courses (served with spaghetti, vegetables, or rice and garlic rolls) $10–$13; pizzas and pastas $7–$16. MC, V. Sun–Fri 6pm–midnight; Sat 1pm–midnight. ITALIAN/PIZZA.

This Brazilian-owned pizza parlor is full most weekends, not only because of its good inexpensive pastas and pizzas, but also because of the fun Brazilian bands that play most weekend nights after 9pm. By midnight, the place is packed with Portuguese-speaking dancers who enjoy a late-night buffet and lots of wine and beer. I think the light garlic rolls wrapped in golden twists are addictive. While the pizza tends to be too cheesy for my taste, it has fresh toppings instead of the canned variety offered at other places. If you've never tasted the ubiquitous Brazilian soda, Guaraná, I suggest trying a sip; it's like a rich ginger ale with not as much zing.

Sheldon's Drugs. 9501 Harding Ave., Surfside. ☎ **305/866-6251.** Main courses $4.50–$5; soups and sandwiches $2–$5. AE, DISC, MC, V. Mon–Sat 7am–9pm; Sun 7am–4pm. AMERICAN/DRUGSTORE.

This typical old-fashioned drugstore counter was a favorite breakfast spot of Isaac Bashevis Singer. Consider stopping into this historic site for a good piece of pie and a side of history. According to legend, he was sitting at Sheldon's, eating a bagel and eggs, when his wife got the call in 1978 that he had won the Nobel Prize for Literature. The menu hasn't changed much since then. You can get eggs and oatmeal and a good tuna melt. A blue-plate special might be generic spaghetti and meatballs or grilled frankfurters. The food is pretty basic, but you can't beat the prices.

KEY BISCAYNE

Key Biscayne has some of the world's nicest beaches, hotels, and parks, yet it's not known for great food. Most visitors eat at the island's largest hotel, where the food is reliable if not outstanding. Locals, or "Key rats" as they're known, tend to go off-island for meals or takeout, but here are some of the best on-the-island choices.

EXPENSIVE

Rusty Pelican. 3201 Rickenbacker Causeway, Key Biscayne. ☎ **305/361-3818.** Reservations recommended. Main courses $16–$20. AE, CB, DC, MC, V. Daily 11:30am–4pm; Sun–Thurs 5–11pm; Fri–Sat 5pm–midnight. CONTINENTAL.

The Pelican's private tropical walkway leads over a lush waterfall into one of the most romantic dining rooms in the city, located right on beautiful blue-green Biscayne Bay. The restaurant's windows look out over the water onto the sparkling stalagmites of Miami's magnificent downtown. Inside, quiet wicker paddle fans whirl overhead, and saltwater fish swim in pretty tableside aquariums.

The restaurant's surf-and-turf menu features conservatively prepared prime steaks, veal, shrimp, and lobster. The food is good, but the atmosphere is even better, especially at sunset, when the view over the city is magical.

Stefano's. 24 Crandon Blvd., Key Biscayne. ☎ **305/361-7007.** Reservations recommended on weekends. Main courses $15–$23; pastas $11–$15. AE, DC, MC, V. Mon–Fri 11:30am–2:30pm; Sun–Thurs 6–11pm; Fri–Sat 6pm–12:30am. Disco open later. NORTHERN ITALIAN.

For retro-elegance, Stefano's has no match. Its restaurant and disco share the same strobe-lit atmosphere. Food is traditional and reliable, if a little pricey. You'll find an older country-club crowd here in the evenings enjoying steaks and pastas and seafood. One of the best entrees is the Delfino Livornese, a dolphin (not Flipper—a type of saltwater fish) sautéed with a spicy sauce of tomato, olives, capers, and onions. Stefano's also serves some rare game, such as guinea hen in wine sauce and quail wrapped in pancetta. I recommend sticking with the pastas and fish.

After 7:30pm, the band starts playing American pop and Latin favorites. Some nights you feel as if you accidentally happened upon your long-lost cousin's wedding, as you watch the parade of taffeta dresses and tipsy uncles. Stefano's has continued to do well over time because of its dependable service and kitchen.

Sundays on the Bay. 5420 Crandon Blvd., Key Biscayne. ☎ **305/361-6777.** Reservations accepted; recommended for Sun brunch. Main courses $15–$24; Sun brunch $18.95. AE, CB, DC, MC, V. Daily 11:30am–11:45pm; Sun brunch 11am–4pm. AMERICAN.

Although its food is fine, Sundays is really a fun tropical bar that features an unbeatable view of Downtown, Coconut Grove, and the Sundays' marina. The menu features local favorites—grouper, tuna, snapper, and good shellfish in season. Competent renditions of such classic dishes as oysters Rockefeller, shrimp scampi, and lobster fra diablo are recommendable. Particularly popular is the Sunday brunch, when a buffet the size of Bimini attracts the city's in-crowd.

The lively bar stays open all week until midnight and weekends until 2am, with a deejay spinning most nights from 9pm.

INEXPENSIVE

✪ **Bayside Seafood Restaurant and Hidden Cove Bar.** 3501 Rickenbacker Causeway, Key Biscayne. ☎ **305/361-0808.** Reservations accepted only for groups of more than 15. Appetizers, salads, and sandwiches $4.50–$6; platters $7–$13. AE, MC, V. Sun–Thurs 11:30am–10:30pm; Fri–Sat 11:30am–midnight; disco on weekends ($5 cover) 11pm–4am. SEAFOOD/PASTA.

Known by locals as "the Hut," this ramshackle restaurant and bar is a laid-back outdoor tiki hut and terrace that serves pretty good sandwiches and fish platters on paper plates. A blackboard lists the latest catches, which can be prepared blackened, fried, broiled, or in a garlic sauce. I prefer the blackened, which is super-crusty, spicy, and dark. The fish dip is wonderfully smoky and moist, if a little heavy on mayonnaise. Lately, the Hut has been offering happy hours on weekday evenings with open bar and snacks for $25 per person—a great deal if you'll be having more than a couple of cocktails.

But if you come here, bring bug spray or ask the waiters for some (they usually keep packets behind the bar). For some reason, this place is plagued by mosquitoes even when the rest of town is not. Local fishermen and yacht owners share this rustic outpost with equal enthusiasm and loyalty.

✪ **La Boulangerie.** 328 Crandon Blvd. (in Eckerd's shopping mall), Key Biscayne. ☎ **305/361-0281.** Sandwiches and salads $5–$7. MC, V. Mon–Sat 7:30am–8pm; Sun 7:30am–6pm. FRENCH BAKERY.

Beware. You'll stop into this inconspicuous French bakery for a loaf of bread and find yourself walking out with an armload of the freshest sandwiches, salads, groceries, and pastries anywhere. You can also sit and enjoy a great breakfast, lunch, or early dinner with the jet-set in their designer sweat suits. There are about 15 tables inside where diners enjoy vegetarian omelets, gourmet sandwiches, and dangerous desserts. The prosciutto and goat cheese sandwich on crusty French bread is unbeatable—there must be something in the mustard.

The friendly proprietors behind the counter will no doubt talk you into a heavenly fruit tart, like the pointy-tipped apricot tart with plump fruit halves painted with a thin layer of sweet glaze. Try any of the cakes or rustic breads, too.

The Oasis. 19 Harbor Dr. (corner of Crandon), Key Biscayne. ☎ **305/361-5709.** Main courses $4–$12; sandwiches $3–$4. No credit cards. Daily 6am–9pm. CUBAN.

Everyone, from the city's mayor to the local handymen, meets for delicious paella and Cuban sandwiches at this little shack. They gather around the little window or inside at the few tables for super-powerful *cafecitos* and rich *croquetas*. It's slightly dingy, but the food is good and cheap.

DOWNTOWN

Downtown Miami is a large sprawling area divided by the Brickell bridge into two distinct areas: Brickell Avenue and the bayfront area near Biscayne Boulevard. You shouldn't walk from one to the other—it's quite a distance and unsafe at night. Convenient Metromover stops do adjoin the areas, so for a quarter, it's better to hop on the scenic sky-tram (closed after midnight).

EXPENSIVE

Hamilton's. 400 SE 2nd Ave. (in the Hyatt Regency Hotel), Miami. ☎ **305/381-6160.** Main courses $17–$28. Reservations recommended. AE, MC, V. Mon–Fri 11am–3pm and Mon–Thurs 6–11pm; Fri–Sat until midnight. CONTINENTAL/MEDITERRANEAN.

A plush dining room outfitted with mahogany and leopard prints, professional service, and elegant food raise hotel dining to a new level. Hamilton's (as in George) gives visitors everything they could ask for—at a price. From the coconut prawns with horseradish orange marmalade to the herb crusted rack of lamb and prosciutto wrapped tuna, each dish is superb. Of course, since the tan man has his own brand of cigars, you'd also expect a cigar bar—and you won't be disappointed. Nightly jazz and a great selection of martinis enhance the experience.

MODERATE

✪ **East Coast Fisheries.** 360 W. Flagler St., Downtown (south). ☎ **305/372-1300.** Reservations recommended. Main courses $9–$25. AE, MC, V. Daily 11am–10pm. From I-95 South, exit at NW 8th St. (#5A). Drive straight to NW 3rd St. and turn right. The next block is North River Dr. Turn left, and you'll see the restaurant 3 blocks down on the right side. SEAFOOD.

East Coast Fisheries is a no-nonsense retail market and restaurant offering a terrific variety of the freshest fish available. The dozen or so plain wood tables are surrounded by refrigerated glass cases filled with snapper, salmon, mahimahi, trout, tuna, crabs, oysters, lobsters, and the like. The absolutely huge menu features every fish imaginable, cooked the way you want it—grilled, fried, stuffed, Cajun-style, Florentine, hollandaise, or blackened. However, the smell of frying grease detracts from the otherwise-quaint old-Miami feel right on the riverfront. Service is fast, but good prices and good food can mean long lines on weekends.

✪ **Fishbone Grille.** 650 S. Miami Ave. (SW 7th Ave., next to Tobacco Rd.), Downtown. ☎ **305/530-1915.** Reservations recommended for parties of 6 or more. Entrees $8–$18; pizzas and pastas $9–$20. AE, CB, DC, DISC, MC, V. Mon–Thurs 11:30am–10pm; Fri 11:30am–11pm; Sat 5–11pm. SEAFOOD.

This is by far Miami's best and most reasonably priced seafood restaurant. Located in a small strip mall it shares with Tobacco Road, this sensational fish shop prepares dozens of outstanding specials daily. The atmosphere is nothing to speak of, although at one cool table you can stare into a fish tank.

Try the excellent ceviche, which has just enough spice to give it a zing yet doesn't overwhelm the fresh fish flavor. The stews, the crab cakes, and all the starters are superb. If you like a nice Caribbean flavor, try the *jerk Covina* (the Biblical fish) or one of the excellent dolphin specialties. There's another **Fishbone Grille** in Coral Gables at 1450 S. Dixie Highway (☎ **305/668-3033**).

INEXPENSIVE

✪ **Caribbean Delite.** 236 NE First Ave. (across the street from Miami Dade Community College), Downtown. ☎ **305/381-9254.** Menu items $5.50–$9; full meals $4–$7. AE, MC, V. Mon–Sat 8:30am–7pm; Sun 8:30am–4pm. JAMAICAN.

You'd never spot this tiny storefront diner if you weren't looking for it, but you might smell it from the sidewalk. The aroma of succulent jerk chicken or pork beckons regulars back over and over again. Try the Jamaican specialties, such as the oxtail stew or the curried goat, tender tasty pieces of meat on the bone in a spicy yellow sauce. The kitchen can be stingy with its spectacular sauces, leaving the dishes a bit dry; so ask for an extra helping on the side, and they are happy to oblige. Also, if you come early in the day, you can get a taste of Jamaica's national dish, salt fish and ackee (usually served for breakfast). Ask chef-owner Carol Whyte to tell you the story of the National dish of her homeland made with "brain fruit," or quiz one of the many Jamaicans who stop in while they are in port off the cruise ships a few blocks away.

La Cibeles Cafe. 105 NE 3rd Ave. (1 block west of Biscayne Blvd.), Downtown. ☎ **305/ 577-3454.** Main courses $5–$9. No credit cards. Mon–Sat 7:30am–7:30pm. CUBAN/ BRAZILIAN/SPANISH.

This typical Latin diner serves some of the best food in town. Just by looking at the line that runs out the door every afternoon between noon and 2pm, you can see that you're not the first to discover it. For about $5, you can have a huge and filling meal. Pay attention to the daily lunch specials and go with them. A pounded, tender chicken breast (*pechuga*) is smothered in sautéed onions and served with rice and beans and a salad. The trout and the roast pork are both very good. When available, try the *ropa vieja*, a shredded beef dish delicately spiced and served with peas and rice.

Perricone's Marketplace. 15 SE 10th St. (corner of S. Miami Ave.), Downtown. ☎ **305/ 374-9693.** Sandwiches $5.50–$7; pastas $10–$15. AE, MC, V. Daily 7:30am–midnightish (closing depends on customer demand). ITALIAN.

A large selection of groceries and wine, plus an outdoor porch for dining, makes this one of the most welcoming spots downtown. Sundays offer buffet brunches and all-you-can-eat dinners, too. But Perricone's is most popular weekdays at noon, when the suit types show up for delectable sandwiches, quick and delicious pastas, and hearty salads.

Raja's. 243 E. Flagler St. (in the Galeria International Mall), Downtown. ☎ **305/539-9551.** Menu items $3–$6; specials, including salad, rice, and vegetable side dishes, $5. No credit cards. Thurs–Tues 9am–6:30pm; Sun 9am–4:30pm. SOUTH INDIAN/FAST FOOD.

Nearly impossible to find, this tiny counter in the hustling Downtown food court serves some of the feistiest chicken stews and vegetarian dishes in Miami. It's surrounded by mostly Brazilian fast-food places packed with tour groups on shopping sprees.

If you like it spicy, try the rich masala spicy chili chicken. For vegetarians, the heaping platters of dahl, cauliflower, eggplant, broccoli, and chickpeas are a valuable find. For those who know to request them, there are half a dozen tasty condiments, including lemon chutney with fresh orange rinds, bright green cilantro sauce, and glistening gold mango chutney that will complement the rough stews and tasty soups. The *masala dosa* (rice crepes stuffed with vegetable mash) is a filling lunch or dinner made to order.

S & S Restaurant. 1757 NE Second Ave., Downtown. ☎ **305/373-4291.** Main courses $5–$11. No credit cards. Mon–Fri 6am–4pm; Sat–Sun 6am–2 or 2:30pm (later on Heat game nights). AMERICAN/DINER.

This tiny chrome-and-linoleum–counter restaurant in the middle of Downtown looks like a truck stop. But locals have been coming back since it opened in 1938. Expect a wait at lunchtime while the mostly male clientele, from lawyers to linemen, wait patiently for huge quantities of old-fashioned fast food.

You'll get a slice of Miami history along with your pie at S & S. Although the neighborhood has become pretty undesirable, the food—basic diner fare with some excellent stews and soups—hasn't changed in years. It's one of the only places in town I know that serves creamed chicken on toast. Also good when it's on the specials board is the stuffed cabbage roll in a pale brown sauce. In addition to cheap breakfasts, the diner serves up some of the most comfortable comfort food in Miami.

LITTLE HAVANA

The main artery of Little Havana is a busy commercial strip called Southwest 8th Street, or Calle Ocho. Auto body shops, cigar factories, and furniture stores line this street, and on every corner there seems to be a pass-through window serving super-strong Cuban coffee and snacks. In addition, many of the Cuban, Dominican, Nicaraguan, Peruvian, and Latin American immigrants have opened full-scale restaurants ranging from intimate candlelit establishments to bustling stand-up lunch counters.

VERY EXPENSIVE

Victor's Cafe. 2340 SW 32nd Ave. (1 block south of Coral Way), Little Havana. ☎ **305/445-1313.** Reservations recommended. Main courses $19–$32. AE, DC, MC, V. Sun–Thurs noon–midnight; Fri–Sat noon–1am. CUBAN.

At Victor's, you'll get good food in an upscale setting—it's a place for tourists and celebrations. Locals say it's overpriced. Strolling guitarists add an air of romance to this kitschy old Havana-style restaurant. Lively salsa music wafts through the regal dining room, where attentive waiters look after most details. Stick around for the wild cabaret most nights after 11pm. Ask to sit on El Patio, where oversized umbrellas shade you from the sun and create a private little cocoon overlooking the lush courtyard.

The cooking takes liberties with Cuban classics with generally good results. Some of the best dishes are the fish and shrimp plates, all served with rice and beans. My favorite appetizer is the snapper ceviche marinated in Cachucha pepper and lime juice. The beef dishes are also good. The *bistec alo Victor con tamal en balsa* is a tender oak-grilled top sirloin served with Cuban-style polenta.

MODERATE

✪ **Casa Juancho.** 2436 SW 8th St. (just east of SW 27 Ave.), Little Havana. ☎ **305/642-2452.** Reservations recommended, but not accepted Fri–Sat after 8pm. Tapas $6–$8; main courses $15–$34. AE, CB, DC, DISC, MC, V. Sun–Thurs noon–midnight; Fri–Sat noon–1am. SPANISH.

One of Miami's finest Hispanic restaurants, Casa Juancho offers an ambitious menu of excellently prepared main dishes and tapas. The several dining rooms are decorated with traditional Spanish furnishings and enlivened nightly by strolling Spanish musicians. Try not to be frustrated with the older staff who don't speak English or respond quickly to your subtle glance. They are used to an aggressive clientele.

I suggest ordering lots of *tapas,* small dishes of Spanish "finger food." Some of the best include mixed seafood vinaigrette, fresh shrimp in hot garlic sauce, and fried calamari rings. A few entrees stand out, like roast suckling pig, baby eels in garlic and olive oil, and Iberian-style snapper.

INEXPENSIVE

✪ **Hy-Vong.** 3458 SW 8th St. (between 34th and 35th aves.), Little Havana. ☎ **305/446-3674.** Reservations not accepted. Main courses $8–$15. No credit cards. Wed–Sun 6–11pm. Closed 2 weeks in Aug. VIETNAMESE.

Expect to wait hours for a table, and don't even think of mumbling a complaint—despite the poor service, it's worth it. Vietnamese cuisine combines the best of Asian and French cooking with spectacular results. Food at Hy-Vong is elegantly simple and super-spicy. Appetizers include small, tightly packed Vietnamese spring rolls, and kimchee, a spicy, fermented cabbage. Star entrees include pastry-enclosed chicken with watercress cream-cheese sauce, and fish in tangy mango sauce.

Enjoy the wait with a traditional Vietnamese beer and lots of company. Outside this tiny storefront restaurant, you'll meet interesting students, musicians, and foodies who come for the large delicious portions.

La Carreta. 3632 SW 8th St., Little Havana. ☎ **305/444-7501.** Main courses $4–$19. AE, CB, DC, DISC, MC, V. Daily 24 hours. CUBAN.

This cavernous family-style restaurant is filled with relics of an old farm and college kids eating *medianoches* (midnight sandwiches with ham, cheese, and pickles) after partying all night. Waitresses are brusque but efficient and will help *anglos* who may not know all the lingo. The menu is vast and very authentic. Try the *sopa de pollo,* a rich golden stock loaded with chunks of chicken and fresh vegetables, or the *ropa vieja,* a shredded beef stew in a thick brown sauce.

Because of its immense popularity and low prices, La Carreta has opened several branches throughout Miami, including a counter in the Miami airport. Check the white pages for other locations.

✪ **Versailles.** 3555 SW 8th St., Little Havana. ☎ **305/444-0240.** Soup and salad $2–$10; main courses $5–$8. DC, DISC, MC, V. Mon–Thurs 8am–2am; Fri 8am–3:30am; Sat 8am–4:30am; Sun 9am–2am. CUBAN.

Versailles is the meeting place of Miami's Cuban power brokers, who meet daily over *café con leche* to discuss the future of the exiles' fate. A glorified diner, the place sparkles with glass, chandeliers, murals, and mirrors meant to evoke the French palace. There's nothing fancy here—nothing French, either—just straightforward food from the home country. The menu is a veritable survey of Cuban cooking and includes specialties such as *Moors and Christians* (flavorful black beans with white rice), *ropa vieja,* and fried whole fish.

WEST DADE

As all of South Florida expands westward, good restaurants will follow as well. So far, however, only a few have distinguished themselves, and they are reviewed here.

VERY EXPENSIVE

Shula's Steak House. 7601 NW 154th St. (Don Shula's Golf Club off the Palmetto Expressway), Miami Lakes. ☎ **305/820-8102.** Reservations recommended. Main courses $18–$58. AE, CB, DC, MC, V. In season Mon–Fri 6:30am–2:30pm and 6–11pm; Sat–Sun 7–11am and 6pm–11pm; call for hours off-season (May–Nov). STEAK HOUSE.

This is the place to get huge slabs of red meat cooked however you like. A limited à la carte menu lists entrees by weight. You could start with the petite 12-ounce filet mignon, so tender and juicy you could almost cut it with your fork. Linebackers might consider the 48-ounce porterhouse. I haven't tried it myself, but am told it's one of the best. Potatoes and a few vegetables are available, but don't bring your vegetarian friends here—they'll go hungry.

Retired Miami Dolphins coach Don Shula is said to be spending more time around this shrine to his old team as he puts the final touches on his new location in the Alexander Hotel in Miami Beach.

MODERATE

Tony Roma's Famous For Ribs. 6728 Main St. (at Ludlum Rd.), Miami Lakes. ☎ **305/558-7427.** Main courses $9–$14; sandwiches $6. AE, CB, DC, DISC, MC, V. Mon–Thurs 11am–11pm; Fri–Sat 11am–1am. AMERICAN.

Rib lovers rave over this Miami-based chain that now has more than a dozen locations in South Florida. In Miami Lakes, the place is packed with regulars who order full slabs of thick meaty pork with the usual side dishes, such as coleslaw and a crispy onion loaf. You can't beat the prices, and the dark woody atmosphere makes you feel like you're in a much more upscale place.

Other locations include 15700 Biscayne Blvd., North Miami (☎ **305/949-2214**); 18050 Collins Ave., Miami Beach (☎ **305/932-7907**); and 2665 SW 37th Ave., Coral Gables (☎ **305/443-6626**).

NORTH DADE

Although there aren't many hotels in North Dade, the population in the winter months explodes due to the onslaught of seasonal residents from the Northeast. A number of

In case you want to see the world.

At American Express, we're here to make your journey a smooth one. So we have over 1,700 travel service locations in over 130 countries ready to help. What else would you expect from the world's largest travel agency?

do more

Travel

Call 1 800 AXP-3429 or visit
www.americanexpress.com/travel

In case you want to be welcomed there.

We're here to see that you're always welcomed at establishments everywhere. That's why millions of people carry the American Express® Card – for peace of mind, confidence, and security, around the world or just around the corner.

do more

Cards

To apply, call 1 800 THE-CARD
or visit www.americanexpress.com

In case you're running low.

We're here to help with more than 190,000 Express Cash locations around the world. In order to enroll, just call American Express at 1 800 CASH-NOW before you start your vacation.

do more **AMERICAN EXPRESS**

Express Cash

And in case you'd rather be safe than sorry.

We're here with American Express® Travelers Cheques. They're the safe way to carry money on your vacation, because if they're ever lost or stolen you can get a refund, practically anywhere or anytime. To find the nearest place to buy Travelers Cheques, call 1 800 495-1153. Another way we help you do more.

do more

Travelers Cheques

©1999 American Express

From Ceviche to Picadillo: Latin Cuisine at a Glance

In Little Havana and wondering what to eat? Many restaurants list menu items in English for the benefit of *norteamericano* diners. In case you're wondering what to eat, though, here are translations and suggestions for filling and delicious meals:

Arroz con pollo   Roast chicken served with saffron-seasoned yellow rice and diced vegetables.

Café cubano   Very strong black coffee, served in thimble-size cups with lots of sugar. It's a real eye-opener.

Camarones   Shrimp.

Ceviche   Raw fish seasoned with spice and vegetables and marinated in vinegar and citrus to "cook" it.

Croquetas   Golden-fried croquettes of ham, chicken, or fish.

Paella   A Spanish dish of chicken, sausage, seafood, and pork mixed with saffron rice and peas.

Palomilla   Thinly sliced beef, similar to American minute steak, usually served with onions, parsley, and a mountain of French fries.

Pan cubano   Long, white crusty Cuban bread. Ask for it *tostada,* toasted and flattened on a grill with lots of butter.

Picadillo   A rich stew of ground meat, brown gravy, peas, pimientos, raisins, and olives.

Plátano   A deep-fried, soft, mildly sweet banana.

Pollo asado   Roasted chicken with onions and a crispy skin.

Ropa vieja   A delicious shredded beef stew, whose name literally means "old clothes."

Sopa de pollo   Chicken soup, usually with noodles or rice.

Tapas   A general name for Spanish-style hors d'oeuvres, served in grazing-size portions.

exclusive condominiums and country clubs, including William's Island, Turnberry, and The Jockey Club, breed a demanding clientele, many of whom dine out nightly. That's good news for visitors, who can find superior service and cuisine at value prices.

VERY EXPENSIVE

✪ **Chef Allen's.** 19088 NE 29th Ave. (at Biscayne Blvd.), North Miami Beach. ☎ **305/ 935-2900.** Reservations suggested. Main courses $26–$31. AE, DC, MC, V. Sun–Thurs 6–10:30pm; Fri–Sat 6–11pm. NEW WORLD CUISINE.

For one of South Florida's finest dining experiences, Chef Allen's is a must. There simply isn't better food to be found in the county. Owner-chef Allen Susser, of New York's *Le Cirque* fame, has built a classy yet relaxed restaurant with art deco furnishings, a glass-enclosed kitchen, and a hot-pink swirl of neon surrounding the dining room's ceiling. It's more than a little kitschy, but this is Miami, after all. In a town of flash-in-the-pan restaurants, this 14-year-old spot has become an institution, helped by a young, energetic staff.

Appetizers are alluring and may include lobster-and-crab cakes served with strawberry-ginger chutneys, or baked brie with spinach, sun-dried tomatoes, and pine nuts.

Favorite main dishes include crisp roast duck with cranberry sauce, and mesquite-grilled Norwegian salmon with champagne grapes, green onions, and basil spaetzle. Local fish dishes, in various delectable guises, and homemade pastas are always on the menu. The extensive wine list is well chosen and features several good buys. Hand-made desserts are works of art and sinfully delicious.

MODERATE

The Gourmet Diner. 13951 Biscayne Blvd. (between NE 139th and 140th sts.), North Miami Beach. ☎ **305/947-2255.** Reservations not accepted. Main courses $10–$17. MC, V. Mon–Fri 11am–11pm; Sat 8am–11:30pm; Sun 8am–10:30pm. BELGIAN/FRENCH.

This retro 1950s-style diner serves plain old French fare without pretensions. The atmosphere is a bit brash, and the lines are often out the door. You'll want to get there early anyway to taste some of the house specialties, such as beef Burgundy, the trout amandine, and frog legs Provençale—these dishes tend to sell out quickly.

Check the blackboard, which—depending on where you are seated—can be hard to see. The salads and soups are all prepared to order. Even a simple hearts of palm becomes a gourmet treat under the basic, tangy vinaigrette. A well-rounded wine list with reasonable prices makes this place a standout and a great deal. The homemade pastries are also delicious.

The Lagoon. 488 Sunny Isles Blvd. (163rd St.), North Miami Beach. ☎ **305/947-6661.** Reservations accepted. Main courses $12–$22; lobster special $22.95. AE, CB, MC, V. Daily 4:30–11pm; early-bird dinner 4:30–6pm. SEAFOOD/CONTINENTAL.

This old bayfront fish house has been around since 1936. Major road construction nearby should have guaranteed its doom years ago, but the excellent view and incredible specials make it a worthwhile stop. If you can disregard the somewhat dirty bathrooms and nonchalant service, you'll find the best-priced juicy Maine lobsters around.

Yes, it's true! Lobster lovers can get two 1¼ pounders for $22.95. Try them broiled with a light buttery seasoned coating. This dish is not only inexpensive but incredibly succulent, too. Side dishes include fresh vegetables, like broccoli or asparagus, as well as a huge baked potato, stuffed or plain. The salads are good but come with too much commercial-tasting dressing. To be safe, ask for oil and vinegar on the side, or, better yet, skip all the accouterments to save room for the lobster.

P.F. Chang's China Bistro. 17455 Biscayne Blvd., Aventura/North Miami Beach. ☎ **305/957-1966.** Reservations not accepted. Main courses $8–$13; salads $5–$10. AE, MC, V. Sun–Thurs 11:30am–11pm; Fri–Sat until midnight. CHINESE/MONGOLIAN/HUNAN/SCHEZUAN.

This chain is spreading around the country and is worth a taste. An open kitchen turning out fantastically fresh cuisine and a modern, casual decor make it quite a popular place. Classic Chinese dishes from around the continent are Americanized enough to make them attractive but also authentic enough to make them interesting. In other words, you won't find chopped chicken feet, but you will find luscious warm duck salad and a variety of noodle dishes with fresh stir-fried veggies and meats. The best part is you'll find the prices moderate and the servers relatively informed. For a quick lunch or dinner, this is an excellent choice. Another **P.F. Chang's** is located in the Fall's Shopping Center at 8888 SW 136th St. ☎ **305/234-2338.**

INEXPENSIVE

Amos' Juice Bar. 18315 W. Dixie Hwy. (1 block west of Biscayne Blvd.), North Miami Beach. ☎ **305/935-9544.** Sandwiches and salads $4–$6. No credit cards. Mon–Sat 8:30am–6:30pm. HEALTH FOOD.

This brightly painted stand in the middle of a busy road attracts a varied crowd, from young pony-tailed Europeans to bikers. If you don't mind a bit of car exhaust with your snapper sandwich, consider this landmark in North Dade.

The food is made on the premises and includes one of the most unusual tuna salads I've ever run across, served in a pita with tons of crisp vegetables, including alfalfa sprouts, tomato, and lettuce. The hummus is also superb, although garlic lovers might want a hint more spark. You can also get a fresh smoothie or vegetable juice made on the spot.

Here Comes the Sun. 2188 NE 123rd St. (west of the Broad Causeway), North Miami. ☎ 305/893-5711. Reservations recommended in season. Main courses $10–$14; early-bird special $7.95; sandwiches and salads $5–$7.50. AE, DC, DISC, MC, V. Mon–Sat 11am–8:30pm. AMERICAN/HEALTH FOOD.

One of Miami's first health-food spots, this bustling grocery-store-turned-diner serves hundreds of plates a night, mostly to blue-haired locals. It's noisy and hectic but worth it. In season, all types pack the place for a $7.95 special, served between 4 and 6:30pm, which includes one of more than 20 choices of entrees, soup or salad, coffee or tea, and a small frozen yogurt. Fresh grilled fish and chicken entrees are reliable and are served with a nice array of vegetables. The miso burgers with "sun sauce" are a vegetarian's dream.

Laurenzo's Cafe. 16385 West Dixie Hwy. (at the corner of 163rd St.), North Miami Beach. ☎ 305/945-6381. Main courses $4–$12; salads $2–$5. No credit cards. Mon–Sat 11am–7pm; Sun 11am–4pm. SOUTHERN ITALIAN CAFETERIA.

This little lunch counter in the middle of a chaotic grocery store has been serving delicious buffet lunches to the *paesanos* for years. A meeting place for the growing Italian population in Miami, the store has been open for more than 40 years. Daily specials usually include a lasagna or eggplant parmigiano and two or three salad options. Also good are the rustic pizzas.

Choose a wine from the vast selection, and take your meal to go or sit in the trelliscovered seating area amid busy shoppers buying their evening's groceries. You'll get to eavesdrop on some great conversations over your plastic tray of real southern-style Italian cooking.

Tu Tu Tango. 19501 Biscayne Blvd. (in Aventura Mall), 2nd floor, Aventura. ☎ 305/932-2222. Tapas $4–$8. Sun–Thurs 11:30am–11pm; Fri–Sat 11:30am–1am. AE, MC, V. SPANISH/INTERNATIONAL.

With the same menu and setting as its Coconut Grove predecessor, this popular hangout is doomed to become a nationwide success. It attracts an attractive crowd, especially on weekdays after work. For more details, see "Coconut Grove."

CORAL GABLES & ENVIRONS
VERY EXPENSIVE

Norman's. 21 Almeria Ave. (between Douglas and Ponce de Leon), Coral Gables. ☎ 305/446-6767. Reservations highly recommended. Main courses $25–$32. Mon–Thurs noon–2pm and 6–10:30pm; Fri noon–2pm and 6–11pm; Sat 6–11pm. AE, DC, MC, V. NEW WORLD CUISINE.

Master chef Norman Van Aken, one of the originators of New World Cuisine, reemerged after a 2-year break from restauranting to open what he has called his "culmination." The result is an open kitchen, surrounded by well-dressed diners, where a handful of silent industrious chefs prepare Asian- and Caribbean-inspired dishes.

The food is the main focus of attention. Some think the exotic-sounding menu is pretentious or overwrought. I think there's plenty to enjoy, like pizzas and pastas with a good glass of wine and a hunk of bread. The fish, too, is out of this world. The Rhum-and-pepper-painted grouper on mango-Habanero Mojo is an exotic-tasting dark-fleshed fish with an explosion of sauces to complement its heavy flavor.

The staff is adoring and professional, and the atmosphere is tasteful without being too formal. The portions are realistic, but still, be careful not to overdo it. You'll want to try some of the wacky desserts, such as mango ice cream served with Asian pears and crushed red pepper (the pepper really just adds color to the plate).

EXPENSIVE

✪ **Caffe Abbracci.** 318 Aragon Ave. (between LeJeune Rd. and Miracle Mile), Coral Gables. ☎ **305/441-0700.** Reservations recommended for dinner. Main courses $16–$24; pastas $14–$20. AE, CB, DC, MC, V. Mon–Fri 11:30am–3pm; Sun–Thurs 6–11pm; Fri–Sat 6pm–midnight. NORTHERN ITALIAN.

You'll be greeted with a hug by the owner and maître d', Nino, who oversees this remarkable spot as only an Italian could. The food is remarkable, yet the restaurant is not known to many outside of the Gables. Still, it's packed on weekends by those in the know. You are guaranteed perfect service in a pretty wood and marble setting, with the only drawback being the unfortunately loud dining room.

It's hard to get beyond the appetizers here, which are all so good that you could order a few and be satisfied. My favorite is the shrimp with a bright pesto sauce that has just enough garlic to give it a kick, but not so much you won't get a kiss later. The excellent risottos are served in half portions so that you'll have room for the indescribable fish dishes.

Le Festival. 2120 Salzedo St. (5 blocks north of Miracle Mile), Coral Gables. ☎ **305/442-8545.** Reservations required for dinner. Main courses $16–$25. AE, CB, DC, DISC, MC, V. Mon–Fri 11:45am–2:30pm; Mon–Thurs 6–10:30pm; Fri–Sat 6–11pm. FRENCH.

Le Festival's contemporary pink awning hangs over one of Miami's most traditional Spanish-style buildings, hinting at the unusual combination of cuisine and decor that awaits inside. The modern dining rooms, enlivened with New French features and furnishings, belie the traditional highlights of a well-planned menu.

Shrimp and crab cocktails, fresh pâtés, and an unusual cheese soufflé are star starters. Both meat and fish are either simply seared with herbs and spices or doused in wine and cream sauces. Dessert can be a delight if you plan ahead: Grand Marnier and chocolate soufflés are individually prepared and must be ordered at the same time as the entrees. There's also a wide selection of other homemade sweets.

MODERATE

Brasserie Les Halles. 2415 Ponce de Leon Blvd. (at Miracle Mile), Coral Gables. ☎ **305/461-1099.** Reservations suggested on weekends. Main courses $14.50–$21.50. AE, DC, DISC, MC, V. Daily 11:30am–midnight. FRENCH BISTRO/STEAKS.

Known especially for its fine steaks and delicious salads, this very welcome addition to the Coral Gables dining scene became popular as soon as it opened in 1997 and has since continued to do a brisk business. The modest and moderately priced menu is particularly welcome in an area of overpriced, stuffy restaurants. For starters, try the mussels in white wine sauce and the escargot. For a main course, the duck confit is an unusual and rich choice. Pieces of duck meat wrapped in duck fat are slow-cooked and served on salad frissé and baby potatoes with garlic. Service by the young French staff is polite but a bit slow. The tables tend to be a little too close, although there is a lovely private balcony space overlooking the long thin dining room where large groups can gather.

Gables Diner. 2320 Galiano Dr. (between Ponce de Leon Blvd. and 37th Ave.), Coral Gables. ☎ **305/567-0330.** Main courses $9–$16; pasta $10–$12; burgers and sandwiches $7–$9; salads $8–$10. AE, DC, DISC, MC, V. Daily 8am–10pm; Fri–Sat until 10:30pm. AMERICAN/DINER.

This upscale diner serves an eclectic mix of comfort food and nouvelle health food. From meatloaf to Chinese chicken salad, there are moderately priced options for everyone. My favorite is the chicken pot pie, a flaky homemade crust filled with big chunks of white meat, pearl onions, peas, and mushrooms. Also good are the large burgers with every imaginable condiment. Vegetarians can find a few good choices, including pastas, bean soups, pizzas, a vegetable stir-fry, and some hearty salads. All the ingredients are fresh and crisp. No need to dress up here, although the clean, almost romantic setting is as appropriate for first dates as it is for families.

✪ **The Globe.** 377 Alhambra Circle (just off Le Jeune Rd.), Coral Gables. ☎ **305/445-3555.** Reservations only for more than 6. Main courses $9–$19; salads $4–$10; pizzas and sandwiches $7–$11. AE, DISC, MC, V. Mon–Fri 11:30am–midnight; Sat 6:30pm–2am; Sun 10:30am–10:30pm. INTERNATIONAL/CASUAL.

This funky coffee shop/travel agency is an odd and welcome addition to a neighborhood dominated by fancy eateries and hotels. Take advantage of the hip surroundings and enjoy the quite decent food. Especially good are the salads and pizzas, particularly the chicken and blue cheese pizza, my favorite. In addition to an extensive list of wines and specialty beers, there are many interesting non-alcoholic choices. More important, sample some of the excellent live music every weekend.

INEXPENSIVE

Biscayne Miracle Mile Cafeteria. 147 Miracle Mile, Coral Gables. ☎ **305/444-9005.** Main courses $3–$4. MC, V. Mon–Sat 11am–2:15pm and 4–8pm; Sun 11am–8pm. SOUTHERN.

Here you'll find no bar, no music, and no flowers on the tables—just great Southern-style cooking at unbelievably low prices. The menu changes, but roast beef, baked fish, and barbecue ribs are typical entrees, few of which exceed $5.

Food is picked up cafeteria-style and brought to one of the many unadorned Formica tables. The restaurant is always busy. The kitschy 1950s decor is an asset in this last of the old-fashioned cafeterias, where the gold-clad staff is proud and attentive. Enjoy it while it lasts.

The Daily Bread Marketplace. 2400 SW 27th St. (off U.S. 1 under the monorail), Coral Gables. ☎ **305/856-0363** or 305/856-0366. Sandwiches and salads $3–$6. Mon–Sat 8am–8pm; Sun 11am–5pm. MC, V. MIDDLE EASTERN/GREEK.

Not only is there great take-out food and homemade breads, but also backgammon and water pipes are for sale. The falafel and gyro sandwiches are large, fresh, and filling. Spinach pie for less than $1 is also recommended, though short on spinach and heavy on pastry. Salads, including luscious tabouli, hummus, and eggplant, are also worth a go. To take in or eat out, the Middle Eastern fare here is a real treat, especially in an area so filled with fancy French and Cuban fare. Plus, you can pick up hard-to-find groceries like grape leaves, fresh olives, couscous, fresh nuts, and pita bread.

Sergio's. 3252 Coral Way, Coral Gables. ☎ **305/529-0047.** Reservations not accepted. Main courses $5–$7. AE, DC, MC, V. Sun–Thurs 6am–midnight; Fri–Sat 24 hours. CUBAN/AMERICAN.

Located across from Coral Gables's Paseos Mall, Sergio's stands out like a Latin-inspired International House of Pancakes, with red-clothed tables, neon signs in the windows, and video games along the back wall. The family-style restaurant serves everything from ham-and-eggs breakfasts to grilled-steak sandwich lunches and dinners, but it specializes in native Cuban-style dishes, as well as grilled chicken, fajitas, and a variety of sandwiches. Low prices and late-night dining keep it popular with locals.

COCONUT GROVE

Coconut Grove was long known as the artists' haven of Miami, but the rush of developers trying to cash in on the laid-back charm of this old settlement has turned it into something of an overgrown mall. Still, there are several great dining spots both in and out of the confines of Mayfair or Cocowalk.

EXPENSIVE

Bocca di Rosa. 2833 Bird Ave. (between SW 27th and Virginia sts.), Coconut Grove. ☎ **305/444-4222.** Reservations suggested. Main courses $16–$24; pastas $11–$17. AE, DC, DISC, MC, V. Sun–Thurs 6–11pm; Fri–Sat 6pm–midnight. ITALIAN.

This elegant restaurant is nestled in a cozy corner of the Grove, but from the smells and tastes here you might as well be in Roma or Sicily. With dishes like *coniglio all contadina* (rabbit stew with white beans and polenta) and *penne cons salsa di sarde* (a sardine and fennel pasta), the menu touches all points on "the boot." On any day, there may be as many as 15 specials. The remarkably fresh seafood is especially recommended. My favorites are a savory bowl of steamed mussels in a white wine broth and a delicately seared swordfish. Frankly, whatever Chef Giorgio is cooking up is bound to be good.

✪ Monty's Bayshore Restaurant. 2550 S. Bayshore Dr., Coconut Grove. ☎ **305/858-1431.** Reservations recommended upstairs on weekends. Main courses $20–$37; sandwiches $6–$8; platters $7–$10. AE, CB, DC, MC, V. Daily (downstairs) 11:30am–2am. SEAFOOD.

This place comes in three parts: a lounge, a raw bar, and a restaurant. Among them, Monty's serves everything from steak and seafood to munchies such as nachos, potato skins, and Buffalo chicken wings. At the outdoor, dockside bar, there's live music nightly, as well as all day on weekends. This is a fun kind of place, usually with more revelers and drinkers than diners. Upstairs, an upscale dining room serves one of the city's best Caesar salads, fantastic she-crab soup, and respectable stone crab claws in season. Be sure, however, not to order the claws from May until October, since they'll serve you some imported version that simply doesn't compare.

MODERATE

Green Street Cafe. 3110 Commodore Plaza, Coconut Grove. ☎ **305/567-0662.** Reservations not accepted. Main courses $6–$16. AE, MC, V. Sun–Thurs 7am–11:30pm; Fri–Sat 7am–1am. CONTINENTAL.

Green Street is located at the "100% corner," the Coconut Grove intersection of Main Highway and Commodore Plaza that 100% of all tourists visit. The location and the loads of outdoor seating (great for people-watching) relieve the pressure on Green Street to turn out fine meals, but the food is still well above average. Continental-style breakfasts include fresh croissants and rolls, cinnamon toast, and cereal. Heartier American-style offerings include eggs and omelets, pancakes, waffles, and French toast. Soup, salad, and sandwich lunches are overstuffed chicken, turkey, and tuna-based meals. Dinners are more elaborate, with several decent pasta entrees, as well as fresh fish, chicken, and burgers, including one made of lamb.

Kaleidoscope. 3112 Commodore Plaza (intersects Grand Ave. and 32nd St.), Coconut Grove. ☎ **305/446-5010.** Reservations recommended. Main courses $12–$15 for pasta; $14–$20 for meat and fish. AE, CB, DC, MC, V. Mon–Fri 11:30am–3pm; Mon–Sat 6–11pm; Sun 5:30–10:30pm. NOUVELLE AMERICAN.

I'd recommend Kaleidoscope, in the heart of Coconut Grove, even if it were located somewhere less exciting. The atmosphere is relaxed, with low-key, attentive service, comfortable seating, and a terrace overlooking the busy sidewalks below. Dishes are well prepared, and pastas, topped with sauces like seafood and fresh basil or pesto with grilled yellowfin tuna, are especially tasty. The linguini with salmon and fresh dill is prepared to perfection.

Although there is no special pre-theater dinner, many locals stop into this reliable and reasonable second-floor spot for an elegant meal before a show down the street at The Coconut Grove Playhouse.

Señor Frogs. 3480 Main Hwy., Coconut Grove. ☎ **305/448-0999.** Reservations not accepted. Main courses $9–$15. AE, CB, DC, DISC, MC, V. Mon–Sat 11:30am–2am; Sun 11:30am–1am. MEXICAN.

Filled with a college-student crowd, this restaurant is known for a raucous good time, its mariachi band, and especially its powerful margaritas. The food at this rocking cantina is a bit too cheesy, but tasty, if not exactly authentic. The mole enchiladas, with 14 kinds of mild chilies mixed with chocolate, is as flavorful as any I've tasted. Almost everything is served with rice and beans in quantities so large that few diners are able to finish.

INEXPENSIVE

Cafe Tu Tu Tango. 3015 Grand Ave. (on the second floor of CocoWalk), Coconut Grove. ☎ **305/529-2222.** Reservations not accepted. Main courses $4–$8. AE, MC, V. Sun–Wed 11:30am–midnight; Thurs 11:30am–1am; Fri–Sat 11:30am–2am. SPANISH/INTERNATIONAL.

This second-floor restaurant in the bustling CocoWalk is designed to look like a disheveled artist's loft. Dozens of original paintings—some only half-finished—hang on the walls and studio easels. Seating at sturdy wooden tables and chairs is either inside, on wooden floors among the clutter, or outdoors, overlooking the Grove's main drag.

Flamenco and other Latin-inspired tunes complement a menu with a decidedly Spanish flare. Hummus spread on rosemary flat bread and baked goat cheese in marinara sauce are two good starters. Entrees include roast duck with dried cranberries, toasted pine nuts, and goat cheese, plus Cajun chicken egg rolls filled with corn, cheddar cheese, and tomato salsa. Pastas, ribs, fish, and pizzas round out the eclectic offerings, and several visits have proved each consistently good. Try the sweet, potent sangria and enjoy the warm, lively atmosphere from a seat with a view. Especially when the rest of the Grove has shut down, Tu Tu Tango is an oasis.

News Cafe in the Grove. 2901 Florida Ave. (behind Mayfair), Coconut Grove. ☎ **305/774-6397.** Main courses $6–$16. AE, DC, MC, V. Daily 24 hours. AMERICAN REGIONAL.

Like its predecessor in South Beach, this big modern diner offers everything from Caesar salads to hummus to burgers to omelets to ice-cream sundaes. The food is predictably good and the service lively and pleasant. The best part is that it's open around the clock to serve the after-movie crowd from CocoWalk and Mayfair, as well as the real late-night club-goers.

SOUTH MIAMI

This mostly residential area has some very good dining spots scattered mostly along U.S. 1.

MODERATE/INEXPENSIVE

✪ **Anacapri.** 12669 S. Dixie Hwy. (in the South Park Center at 128th St. and U.S. 1), South Miami. ☎ **305/232-8001.** Main courses $8–$16. AE, DC, DISC, MC, V. Daily 11:30am–2:30pm; Mon–Thurs 5–10:30pm; Fri–Sat 5–11:30pm; Sun 5–9pm. ITALIAN.

Neighborhood fans wait in line here happily with a glass of wine and pleasant company for somewhat heavy but flavorful Italian cuisine. Prices are reasonable and everyone is treated like a member of the family. If you're in the area, check it out. Stick with the basics, such as pastas with red sauce, which are all flavorful, although a bit heavy on the garlic and oil. An antipasto with thinly cut meats and cheeses and some good green peppers is a great start to a hearty meal.

The Crepe Maker Cafe. 8269 SW 124th St., South Miami. ☎ 305/233-4458 or 305/233-1113. Crepes $3–$7.50. No credit cards. Mon–Sat 11am–8pm; Sun noon–6pm. FRENCH/CREPES.

Create your own delicious crepes at this little French cafe. You can choose from ham, tuna, black olives, red peppers, capers, artichoke hearts, and pine nuts. Some of the best combinations include a Philly cheese steak with mushrooms and a classic Cordon Bleu. Delicious dessert crepes have ice creams, strawberries, peaches, walnuts, and pineapples. Enjoy your crepe fresh off the griddle at the counter or on a bar stool. The soups are also delicious. Kids can run around in a small play area, too.

Pollo Tropical. 18700 SW 40th St., South Miami. ☎ **305/225-7858.** Main courses $3–$6. No credit cards. Sun–Thurs 11am–10pm; Fri–Sat 11am–11pm. CUBAN/FAST FOOD.

This Miami-based chain is putting up new terra-cotta–arched fast-food places so fast you can hardly finish your meal before another one has taken root.

This is lucky for Miamians and the Southeast, where dozens of these restaurants provide hot tender chicken with a variety of healthful side dishes, such as fresh chunks of carrots, onions, zucchini, and squash on wooden skewers and a variety of salads. The chicken is marinated in a seriously secret sauce and served with well-seasoned black beans and rice. The menu, although Latin inspired, is clearly spelled out in English. Pollo Tropical is a good place to get an education in Latin *sabor* (taste).

Other locations include 1454 Alton Rd., Miami Beach (☎ **305/672-8888**), and 11806 Biscayne Blvd., North Miami (☎ **305/895-0274**). Check the phone book for others.

✪ **Shorty's.** 9200 S. Dixie Hwy. (between U.S. 1 and Dadeland Blvd.), South Miami. ☎ **305/670-7732.** Main courses $5–$9. DISC, MC, V. Mon–Thurs 11am–10pm; Fri–Sat 11am–11pm. BARBECUE.

A Miami tradition since 1951, this hokey log cabin is still serving some of the best ribs and chicken in South Florida. People line up for the smoke-flavored, slow-cooked meat that's so tender it seems to jump off the bone into your mouth. The secret, however, is to ask for your order with sweet sauce. The regular stuff tastes bland and bottled. All the side dishes, including coleslaw, corn on the cob, and baked beans, look commercial but are necessary to complete the experience. This is B-B-Q, with a neon B.

A second **Shorty's** is located in Davie at 5989 S. University Dr. (☎ **305/944-0348**).

The Tea Room. 12310 SW 224th St. (at Cauley Sq.), South Miami. ☎ **305/258-0044.** Sandwiches and salads $6–$7; soups $3–$4. AE, DISC, MC, V. Mon–Sat 11am–4pm. ENGLISH TEA.

Do stop in for a spot of tea at this recently rebuilt tea room in historic Cauley Square off U.S. 1. The little lace-curtained room is an unusual site in this heavily industrial area better known for its warehouses than its doilies.

Sample some simple sandwiches, such as the turkey club with potato salad and a small lettuce garnish or an onion soup full of rich brown broth and stringy cheese. Daily specials, like spinach-and-mushroom quiche, and delectable desserts are a must before beginning your explorations of the old antiques and art shops in this little enclave of civility down south.

Wrapido. 5812 Sunset Dr. (near 58th St.), South Miami. ☎ **305/662-7999.** Wraps and salads $5–$6. 10:30am–10pm; Sat–Sun until 11pm. AE, MC, V. WRAPS/RICE DISHES/ SMOOTHIES.

This trendy, fast-paced shop sells an impressive variety of wraps, from Thai chicken to teriyaki tofu. All ingredients are super fresh and the sauces are fantastic, too. Side choices reflect the ethnic mix of the city with choices like black beans and rice, sweet plantains, or tortillas with guacamole and salsa. More than a dozen smoothes make choosing difficult, though I like the Maui Dream with peach juice, passion fruit, strawberries, bananas, coconut, and frozen yogurt.

Another location is in Coral Gables at 2334 Ponce de Leon Blvd. (☎ **305/ 443-1884**).

5 What to See & Do in Miami

by Victoria Pesce Elliott

More and more visitors are coming to Miami each year—around 10 million in 1998—to get a taste of the incredibly diverse offerings scattered throughout this sprawling metropolis. Also, Miami's population, especially in the winter months when the "snow birds" descend, is exploding, and developers are keeping pace with the rapid growth by building ever more attractions, entertainment complexes, and shopping malls.

The best things down here are still the treasures nature put there, such as the Everglades National Park and the sea and the wide sandy beaches, but don't discount the human-made attractions altogether. The city was, and still is, designed to court visitors (and their dollars) from around the world, and many of these efforts make for fantastic entertainment. Nearly destroyed in the early 1980s by developers' wrecking balls, the Art Deco district in South Beach is now by far the area's most popular tourist site. It's here amid the cotton candy–colored architecture that locals and visitors skate, stroll, shop, play, dance, and dine beneath palm trees and neon lights.

Also worth your time are many of the city's older attractions, such as Monkey Jungle, Parrot Jungle, Coral Castle, and the Seaquarium. Historical buildings such as Villa Vizcaya, Venetian Pools, and The Spanish Monastery are also not to be missed.

Take your pick from the many suggestions below. There is plenty to keep you busy for a day or a month.

1 Hitting the Beach

Perhaps Miami's most popular attraction is its incredible stretch of beachfront, which runs more than 35 miles long from the tip of South Beach north to Sunny Isles and circles Key Biscayne and the numerous other pristine islands dotted throughout the Atlantic. The characteristics of Miami's many beaches are as varied as the city's population. Some are shaded by towering palm trees, while others are darkened by huge condominiums. Some attract families or old-timers, others a gay singles scene; but basically, there are two distinct beach alternatives: Miami Beach and Key Biscayne.

MIAMI BEACH Collins Avenue fronts more than a dozen miles of white-sand beach and blue-green waters from 1st to 192nd streets. Although most of this stretch is lined with a solid wall of hotels and condos, beach access is plentiful. There are lots of public beaches here, wide and well-maintained, complete with lifeguards, toilet facilities, concession stands, and metered parking (bring lots of quarters). Except for a thin strip close to the water, most of the sand here is hard-packed—the result of a $10 million Army Corps of Engineers Beach Rebuilding Project meant to protect buildings from the effects of eroding sand.

In general, the beaches on this barrier island become less crowded the farther north you go. A wooden boardwalk runs along the hotel side of the beach from 21st to 46th streets—about 1½ miles—offering a terrific sun-and-surf experience without getting sand in your shoes. Aside from "The Best Beaches," listed below, Miami Beach's lifeguard-protected public beaches include 21st Street, at the beginning of the boardwalk; 35th Street, popular with an older crowd; 46th Street, next to the Fontainebleau Hilton; 53rd Street, a narrower, more sedate beach; 64th Street, one of the quietest strips around; and 72nd Street, a local old-timers' spot.

KEY BISCAYNE   If Miami Beach is not private enough for you, try Virginia Key and Key Biscayne. Crossing Rickenbacker Causeway ($1 toll) is almost like crossing into the Bahamas. The 5 miles of public beach here are blessed with softer sand and are less developed and more laid-back than the hotel-laden strips to the north.

THE BEST BEACHES
Here are my picks:

- **Best Party Beach:** In Key Biscayne, ☉ **Crandon Park Beach,** on Crandon Boulevard, has 3 miles of oceanfront beach, 493 acres of park, 75 grills, three parking lots, several soccer and softball fields, and a public 18-hole championship golf course. The beach is particularly wide and the water is usually so clear you can see the bottom. Admission is $2 per vehicle. It's open daily from 8am to sunset. Many locals prefer the stretch of beach just past the toll booth under the causeway. Although the beach is narrower, admission is free and there are always salsa and merengue blaring from stereos for those who like to dance.

- **Best Beach for People-Watching:** The ultra-chic ☉ **Lummus Park Beach,** which runs along Ocean Drive from about 6th to 14th streets in South Beach, is the best place to go if you're seeking entertainment as well as a great tan. On any day of the week, you might spy models primping for a photo shoot, nearly naked sun worshippers avoiding tan lines, and the best abs anywhere.

- **Best Swimming Beach:** The **85th Street Beach,** along Collins Avenue, is the best place to swim away from the maddening crowds. It's one of Miami's only stretches of sand with no condos or hotels looming over sunbathers. Lifeguards patrol the area throughout the day.

- **Best Windsurfing Beach: Hobie Beach,** on the right side of the causeway leading to Key Biscayne, is not really a beach, but an inlet with predictable winds and a number of places where you can rent Windsurfers.

- **Best Shell-Hunting Beach:** You'll find plenty of colorful shells at **Bal Harbour Beach,** Collins Avenue at 96th Street, just a few yards north of Surfside Beach. There are also an exercise course and good shade—but no lifeguards.

- **Best (ahem) All-Around Tanning Beach:** Although the state has been trying to pass ordinances to outlaw nudity, several regional nude beaches are thriving. In Miami-Dade County, **Haulover Beach,** just north of the Bal Harbour border, attracts nudists from around the world and has created quite a boom for area businesses that cater to them.

- **Best Surfing Beach: Haulover Beach/Harbor House,** just north of Miami Beach, seems to get Miami's biggest swells. Go early to avoid the rush of young locals prepping for Maui.

2 The Art Deco District

The best single attraction in Miami is not a museum or an amusement park, but a piece of the city itself. Located in South Beach, the Art Deco District is a whole community made up of outrageous and fanciful 1920s and 1930s architecture. The district is roughly bounded by the Atlantic Ocean on the east, Alton Road on the west, 6th Street to the south, and Dade Boulevard (along the Collins Canal) to the north.

Most of the finest examples of the whimsical art deco style are concentrated along three parallel streets—Ocean Drive, Collins Avenue, and Washington Avenue—from about 6th to 23rd streets.

After years of neglect and calls for the wholesale demolition of its buildings, South Beach got a new lease on life in 1979. Under the leadership of Barbara Baer Capitman, a dedicated crusader for the art deco region and the Miami Design Preservation League, an area made up of an estimated 800 buildings was granted a listing on the National Register of Historic Places. Designers then began highlighting long-lost architectural details with soft sherbet shades of peach, periwinkle, turquoise, and purple. Developers soon moved in, and the full-scale refurbishment of the area's hotels was underway.

Today, hundreds of new hotels, restaurants, and nightclubs have been renovated or are in the process, and South Beach is on the cutting edge of Miami's cultural and nightlife scene.

EXPLORING THE AREA

If you're touring this unique neighborhood on your own, start at the **Art Deco Welcome Center,** 1001 Ocean Dr. (☎ **305/531-3484**), the only beachside building across from the Clevelander Hotel and bar. They give away lots of informational material including maps and pamphlets. Art deco books (including *The Art Deco Guide,* an informative compendium of all the buildings here), T-shirts, postcards, mugs, and other paraphernalia are for sale. It's open Monday to Saturday from 9am to 6pm, sometimes later.

Take a stroll along **Ocean Drive** for the best view of sidewalk cafes, bars, colorful hotels, and even more colorful people. Another great place for a walk is **Lincoln Road,** which is lined with galleries, cafes, and funky art and antique stores. The Community Church, at the corner of Lincoln Road and Drexel Avenue, is the neighborhood's first church and one of its oldest surviving buildings, dating from 1921.

3 Animal Parks

Kids of all ages will enjoy Miami's animal parks, which feature everything from dolphins to lions to parrots. Of course, there are plenty of alligators, too. Call to inquire about discount packages or coupons which may be offered at area retail stores or in local papers.

✪ **Miami Metrozoo.** 12400 SW 152nd St., South Miami. ☎ **305/251-0400.** Admission $8 adults, $4 children 3–12. Daily 9:30am–5:30pm (ticket booth closes at 4pm). From U.S. 1 south, turn right on SW 152nd St. and follow signs about 3 miles to the entrance.

This impressive 290-acre complex is completely cageless—animals are kept at bay by cleverly designed moats. Especially if you're with children, it's worth it. Mufasa and

Attractions in South Miami-Dade County

Coral Castle **7**
Fairchild Tropical Gardens **2**
Miami Metrozoo **4**
Monkey Jungle **5**
Parrot Jungle **1**
Preston B. Bird and Mary Heinlein Fruit and Spice Park **6**
Week's Air Museum **3**

Simba (of Disney fame) were modeled on a couple of Metrozoo's lions, still in residence. Plus, there are two rare white Bengal tigers, a Komodo dragon, rare koala bears, a monorail "safari," and a petting zoo. You can even ride an elephant. The facilities are always improving and adding new exhibits.

✪ **Miami Seaquarium.** 4400 Rickenbacker Causeway (south side), en route to Key Biscayne. ☎ **305/361-5705.** Admission $22 adults, $17 children 3–9. Daily 9:30am–6pm (ticket booth closes at 4:30pm).

You'll want to arrive early to experience this fun and educational attraction. You'll need at least 3 hours to tour the 35-acre oceanarium and see all four daily shows starring these talented ocean mammals, although you can do it in about 2 if you're on a tight schedule. Trained dolphins, killer whales, and frolicking sea lions play with trainers and visitors. New in 1999 is a program that allows visitors to touch, swim with, and even smooch dolphins. The cost is $125 per person, and the program is offered twice daily, Wednesday through Sunday. Children must be at least 52 inches tall to participate. Call ☎ **305/365-2501** in advance for reservations.

Monkey Jungle. 14805 SW 216th St., South Miami. ☎ **305/235-1611.** Admission $11.50 adults, $9.50 seniors and active-duty military, $6 children 4–12. Daily 9:30am–5pm (tickets sold until 4pm). Take U.S. 1 south to SW 216th St., or from Florida Turnpike take Exit 11 and follow the signs.

See rare Brazilian golden lion tamarins. Watch the "skin diving" Asian macaques. Yes, it's primate paradise! There are no cages to restrain the antics of the monkeys as they swing, chatter, and play their way into your heart. Screened-in trails wind through acres of "jungle," and daily shows feature the talents of the park's most progressive pupils. *Slight warning:* You've got to love primates to get over the heavy smell of the jungle; it's been here for more than 60 years.

Parrot Jungle and Gardens. 11000 SW 57th Ave., Greater Miami South. ☎ **305/ 666-7834.** Admission $13.95 adults, $12.95 seniors, $8.95 children 3–10. Daily 9:30am–6pm. Cafe opens at 8am. Take U.S. 1 south, turn left at SW 57th Ave. or exit Kendall Dr. from the Florida Turnpike and turn right on U.S. 1.

It's loud and silly, but it's fun. Not just parrots, but hundreds of magnificent macaws, peacocks, cockatoos, and flamingos occupy this 22-acre park. Continuous shows in the Parrot Bowl Theater star roller-skating cockatoos, card-playing macaws, and more stunt-happy parrots than you ever thought possible. Alligators, tortoises, and iguanas are also on exhibit. Other attractions include a wildlife show focusing on indigenous Florida animals, an area called "Primate Experience," a children's playground, and a petting zoo. It's worth the extra $3.25 to buy the jungle adventure key, which allows you access to taped trivia about the park and its inhabitants.

Important note: After more than 50 years at this location, Parrot Jungle is planning to move to its own island midway between downtown Miami and the beaches; the relocation is scheduled for the end of 2000.

4 Miami's Museum & Art Scene

Miami's museum scene has always been quirky, interesting, and inconsistent at best. Though several exhibition spaces have made forays into collecting nationally acclaimed work, limited support and political infighting have made it a difficult proposition. Recently, with the reinvention of the Wolfsonian, the reincarnation of MOCA, and the increased daring of the Miami Art Museum, the scene has improved dramatically. It's now safe to say that world-class exhibitions start here. Listed below is an excellent cross-section of the valuable treasures that have become a part of the city's cultural heritage and, as such, are as diverse as the city itself.

For gallery lovers, see "Specialized Tours," below, for scheduled gallery walks, and "Shopping" for a highlight of a few of the best.

IN SOUTH BEACH

Bass Museum of Art. 2121 Park Ave. (1 block west of Collins Ave.), South Beach. ☎ **305/ 673-7530.** Admission $5 adults, $3 students and seniors, free for children 6 and under; second and fourth Wed of the month by donation 5–9pm. Tues–Sat 10am–5pm; Sun 1–5pm (every second and fourth Wed open 1–9pm). Closed major holidays.

An important and growing visual-arts museum in Miami Beach, Bass displays European paintings, sculptures, and tapestries from the Renaissance, baroque, rococo, and modern periods as part of their small permanent collection. Temporary exhibitions alternate between traveling shows and rotations of the Bass's stock, with themes ranging from 17th-century Dutch art to contemporary architecture.

Built from coral rock in 1930, the Bass sits in the middle of more than a dozen tree-topped, landscaped acres. Under construction at press time, the museum will soon have double the gallery space.

The Wolfsonian. 1001 Washington Ave., South Beach. ☎ **305/531-1001.** Admission $5 adults; $3.50 senior citizens, students, and children 6–12; $5 tour-group members; free on Thurs evenings. Members, children under 6, and students or faculty of Florida Universities are admitted free. Mon–Tues and Fri–Sat 11am–6pm; Thurs 11am–9pm; Sun noon–5pm.

Mitchell Wolfson, Jr., an eccentric collector of late 19th- and 20th-century art and other paraphernalia, was spending so much money storing his booty that he decided to buy the warehouse that was housing it. It ultimately held more than 70,000 of his items, including glass, ceramics, sculptures, paintings, and photographs. He's given this incredibly diverse and controversial collection to Florida International University. The former storage facility has been retrofitted with such painstaking detail that it's the envy of curators around the world.

✪ **Holocaust Memorial.** 1933 Meridian Ave. (at Dade Blvd.), South Beach. ☎ **305/538-1663.** Free admission. Daily 9am–9pm.

This heart-wrenching memorial is hard to miss and would be a shame to overlook. The powerful centerpiece is a bronze statue by Kenneth Treister that depicts thousands of victims crawling into an open hand to freedom. You can walk through an open hallway lined with photographs and the names of concentration camps and their victims. From the street, you'll see the outstretched arm, but do stop and tour the sculpture at ground level—what's hidden behind the beautiful stone facade is extremely moving.

IN & NEAR DOWNTOWN

✪ **Miami Art Museum at the Miami–Dade Cultural Center.** 101 W. Flagler St., Miami. ☎ **305/375-3000.** Admission $5 adults, $2.50 seniors and students, free for children under 12, by contribution on Tues. Tues–Fri 10am–5pm; third Thurs of each month 10am–9pm; Sat–Sun noon–5pm. Closed major holidays. From I-95 south, exit at Orange Bowl–NW 8th St. and continue south to NW 2nd St.; turn left at NW 2nd St. and go 1½ blocks to NW 2nd Ave.; turn right.

The Miami Art Museum (MAM) features an eclectic mix of modern and contemporary works by such artists as Eric Fischl, Max Beckman, Jim Dine, and Stuart Davis. Rotating exhibitions span the ages and styles and often focus on Latin American or Caribbean artists. The shows are almost always superbly curated and installed, and sometimes subject to controversy from the ultrapolitical Cuban community.

The Miami–Dade Cultural Center, where the museum is housed, is an oasis for those seeking cultural enrichment during their trip to Miami. In addition to the acclaimed Miami Art Museum, the center houses the main branch of the Miami–Dade Public Library, which sometimes features art and cultural exhibits, and the Historical Museum of Southern Florida, which highlights the fascinating history of the area.

American Police Hall of Fame and Museum. 3801 Biscayne Blvd., Miami. ☎ **305/573-0070.** Admission $6 adults, $4 seniors over 61, $3 children 11 and under, $1 police officers. 50% off coupons often available from hotel racks. Daily 10am–5:30pm. Drive north on U.S. 1 from downtown until you see the building with the police car affixed to its side.

This strange museum appeals mostly to those fascinated by police and their gadgetry. Once inside, you'll find a combination of reality and fantasy that's part thoughtful tribute, part Hollywood-style drama. Just past the car featured in the motion picture *Blade Runner* is a mock prison cell, in which visitors can take pictures of themselves pretending they're doing 5 to 10. Also on hand are execution devices, including a guillotine and an electric chair. In the entry is a touching memorial to the more than 3,000 police officers who have lost their lives in the line of duty.

Miami Area Attractions & Beaches

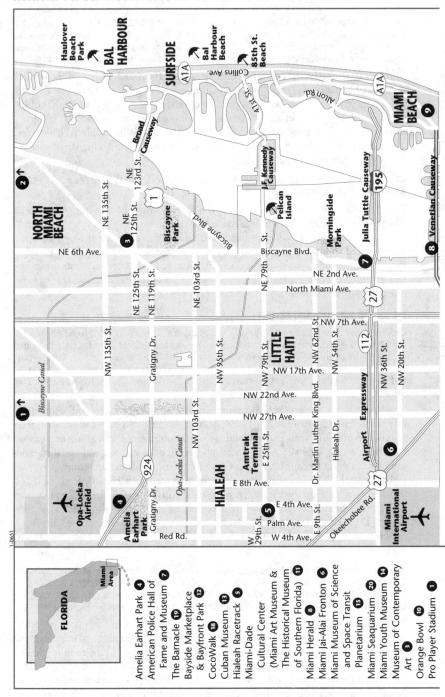

Amelia Earhart Park ❹
American Police Hall of
  Fame and Museum ❼
The Barnacle ❿
Bayside Marketplace
  & Bayfront Park ⓬
CocoWalk ⓲
Cuban Museum ⓭
Hialeah Racetrack ❺
Miami-Dade
  Cultural Center
  (Miami Art Museum &
  The Historical Museum
  of Southern Florida) ⓫
Miami Herald ❽
Miami Jai-Alai Fronton ❻
Miami Museum of Science
  and Space Transit
  Planetarium ⓯
Miami Seaquarium ⓴
Miami Youth Museum ⓮
Museum of Contemporary
  Art ❸
Orange Bowl ❿
Pro Player Stadium ❶

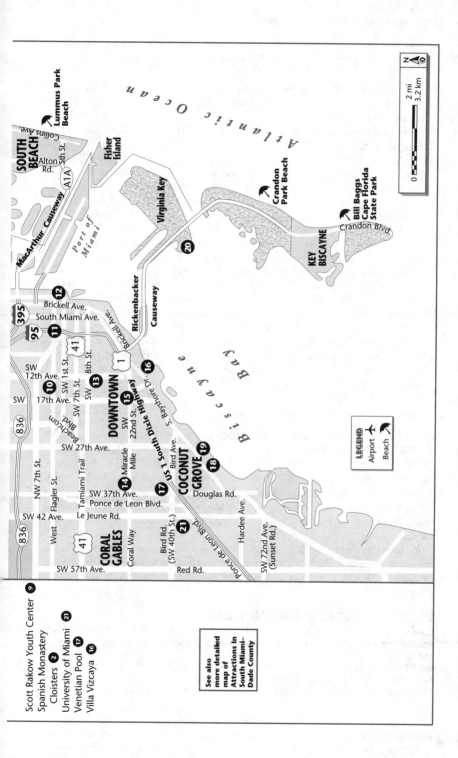

LEGEND
✈ Airport
⛱ Beach

See also
more detailed
map of
Attractions in
South Miami–
Dade County

Scott Rakow Youth Center ➒
Spanish Monastery
Cloisters ➋
University of Miami ➓
Venetian Pool ⓲
Villa Vizcaya ⓰

Atlantic Ocean

Lummus Park Beach

SOUTH BEACH
Collins Ave.
5th St.
Alton Rd.
A1A

MacArthur Causeway

Port of Miami

Fisher Island

Virginia Key

Crandon Park Beach

Bill Baggs Cape Florida State Park
Crandon Blvd.

KEY BISCAYNE

➊➋ Brickell Ave.
South Miami Ave.
395
95
⓫
41

SW 12th Ave.
SW 1st St.
SW 7th St.
8th St.
⓾
SW 17th Ave.
⓭

Rickenbacker Causeway

Brickell Ave.

⓴

➊

DOWNTOWN
⓰
⓮
SW 22nd St.
SW 27th Ave.
Beacom Blvd.

NW 7th St.
Flagler St.
Tamiami Trail
SW 37th Ave.
Ponce de Leon Blvd.
Le Jeune Rd.

Miracle Mile

US 1 South Dixie Highway
S. Bayshore Dr.
Bird Ave.

⓱ **COCONUT GROVE**
⓳
⓲
Douglas Rd.

836
SW 42 Ave.
West
41
CORAL GABLES
SW 57th Ave.
Coral Way

Bird Rd. (SW 40th St.)
Red Rd.
⓴

Ponce de Leon Blvd.
Hardee Ave.
SW 72nd Ave. (Sunset Rd.)

Biscayne Bay

N

0   2 mi
    3.2 km

A Secret Stash of Contemporary Art

Art aficionados always find their way to major art exhibitions in the cities and towns they visit, but nothing can be more exciting and more unusual than being invited to tour a private collection.

Next time you're in Miami for a weekend, consider yourself on the guest list. Your hosts are four New Yorkers, Mera and Don Rubell and their adult children, Jennifer and Jason, who together have opened two hip hotels on South Beach (The Albion and the Greenview). They have also brought with them their priceless collection of more than a thousand works of contemporary art, by the likes of Paul McCarthy, Keith Haring, Jean-Michel Basquiat, Charles Ray, and Cindy Sherman. These pieces are now on view in a former Drug Enforcement Agency warehouse in downtown Miami.

"I'm jealous," says David A. Ross, director of the San Francisco Museum of Modern Art. "There are few collections of its equal anywhere in the world."

The works, many of which are too big or too daring for your average museum, reveal the Rubells' taste for the strange, humorous, and irreverent. They include McCarthy's Cultural Gothic (1992 to 1993), a motorized sculpture of a man coaxing a young boy into an act of bestiality, and Beverly Semme's Blue Gowns (1993), three giant gowns flowing from a neck-craning height onto the floor.

If you don't know these names, you should probably skip this stop. There's no avoiding nudity, erotica, and themes some may find offensive; bring the kids at your discretion. The collection is open from 11am to 4pm Fridays through Sundays and is located at 95 NW 29th St., near the Design District (☎ **305/573-6090**).

✪ **Museum of Contemporary Art (MOCA).** 770 NE 125th St., North Miami. ☎ **305/893-6211.** Admission $4 adults, $2 seniors and students with ID, free for children 12 and under. Tues–Sat 11am–5pm; Sun noon–5pm. Closed major holidays.

MOCA recently acquired a new 23,000-square-foot space in which to display its collection of internationally acclaimed art with a local flavor. You can see works by Jasper Johns, Roy Lichtenstein, Larry Rivers, Duane Michaels, and Claes Oldenburg. Guided tours are offered in English, Spanish, French, Creole, Portuguese, German, and Italian.

An impressive screening facility allows for film presentations to complement the exhibitions. Although the $3.75 million project was built in an area otherwise avoided by tourists, MOCA is worth a drive to view important contemporary art in South Florida.

IN CORAL GABLES & COCONUT GROVE

Miami Museum of Science and Space Transit Planetarium. 3280 S. Miami Ave. (just south of the Rickenbacker Causeway), Coconut Grove. ☎ **305/854-4247** for general information, 305/854-2222 for planetarium show times. $9 adults; $7 students, seniors, and children 3–12; free for children 2 and under. Planetarium $5 adults, $2.50 children and seniors. Combination ticket $9 adults, $5.50 children and seniors. Half-price 4:30–6pm weekdays. Museum of Science daily 10am–6pm; call for planetarium show times. 25% discount for AAA members.

The Museum of Science features more than 140 hands-on exhibits that explore the mysteries of the universe. Live demonstrations and collections of rare natural history specimens make a visit here fun and informative. Two or three major traveling exhibits are usually on display as well.

The adjacent Space Transit Planetarium projects astronomy and laser shows, as well as interactive demonstrations of upcoming computer technology and cyberspace features. Plan to spend at least 3 or 4 hours exploring the fascinating exhibits and displays here.

Weeks Air Museum. 14710 SW 28th St. (south of 120th St. and west of the Florida Turnpike at the Kendall-Tamiami Airport), Miami. ☎ **305/233-5197.** Admission $6.95 adults, $5.95 seniors, $4.95 children under 12. Daily 10am–5pm.

This well-maintained museum is a must-see for aeronautic buffs, who will enjoy talking with the thoroughly dedicated staff who are always eager to answer questions from fellow enthusiasts. Exhibitions include a dramatic portrait of the Tuskegee Airmen, who tell of their experiences on video. Also on display are dozens of airplanes dating from the turn of the century and an intriguing display of planes damaged by Hurricane Andrew in 1992. Other highlights include a collection of propellers throughout the ages, a J47 jet engine, an aerobatic plane, the "Little Stinker" Soviet bombers, and lots of war memorabilia.

5 Fantastic Feats of Architecture

Not all the great buildings in Miami are in South Beach's Art Deco district. You'll also find many exciting enclaves filled with Mediterranean gems and eclectic wonders, especially in Coral Gables. Even if you aren't staying there, check out the Biltmore Hotel (see "Accommodations" in chapter 4) and the stunning Congregational Church across the street.

Villa Vizcaya. 3251 S. Miami Ave. (just south of Rickenbacker Causeway), North Coconut Grove. ☎ **305/250-9133.** Admission $10 adults, $5 children 6–12, free for children 5 and under. Villa daily 9:30am–5pm (ticket booth closes at 4:30pm); gardens daily 9:30am–5:30pm.

Sometimes referred to as the "Hearst Castle of the East," this magnificent villa is the setting for many society weddings and galas. It was built in 1916 as a winter retreat for James Deering, cofounder and former vice president of International Harvester. The industrialist was fascinated by 16th-century art and architecture, and his ornate mansion—which took 1,000 artisans 5 years to build—became a celebration of that period. Most of the original furnishings, including dishes and paintings, are still intact.

The spectacularly opulent villa wraps itself around a central courtyard. Outside, lush formal gardens, accented with statuary, balustrades, and decorative urns, front an enormous swath of Biscayne Bay, near the homes of Sylvester Stallone and Madonna.

The Barnacle State Historic Site. 3485 Main Hwy. (1 block south of Commodore Plaza), Coconut Grove. ☎ **305/448-9445.** Admission $1. Tours Fri–Sun at 10am, 11:30am, 1pm, and 2:30pm. Group tours Mon–Thurs with 2-week advance reservations. From downtown Miami, take U.S. 1 south to 27th Ave., make a left, and continue to South Bayshore Dr.; then make a right, follow to the intersection of Main Hwy., and turn left.

The former home of naval architect and early settler Ralph Middleton Munroe is now a museum in the heart of Coconut Grove. The house's quiet surroundings, wide porches, and period furnishings illustrate how Miami's privileged class lived in the days before skyscrapers and luxury hotels. Enthusiastic and knowledgeable state-park employees offer a wealth of historical information to those interested in quiet, low-tech attractions like this one. Call for details on monthly moonlight concerts, during which folk, blues, or classical music are presented. Cost is $5 for adults, free for children under 10.

Coral Castle. 28655 S. Dixie Hwy., Homestead. ☎ **305/248-6344.** Admission $7.75 adults, $6.50 seniors, $5 children 7–12. Daily 9am–6pm. Take U.S. 1 south to SW 286th St.

There's plenty of competition, but Coral Castle is probably the strangest attraction in Florida. In 1923, the story goes, a crazed Latvian, suffering from unrequited love, immigrated to South Miami and spent the next 25 years of his life carving huge boulders into a prehistoric-looking, roofless "castle." It seems impossible that one rather short man could have done all this, but there are scores of affidavits on display from neighbors who swear it happened. Apparently, experts have studied this phenomenon to help figure out how the Great Pyramids and Stonehenge were built.

Listen to the audio tour to learn about this bizarre spot, now in the National Register of Historic Places. The commentary lasts about 25 minutes and is available in four languages. Although Coral Castle is overpriced and undermaintained, it's worth a visit when you're in the area.

✪ **Spanish Monastery Cloisters.** 16711 W. Dixie Hwy. (at NE 167th St.), North Miami Beach. ☎ **305/945-1461.** Admission $4.50 adults, $2.50 seniors, $1 children 11 and under. Mon–Sat 10am–4pm; Sun noon–4pm.

Did you know that the oldest building in the Western Hemisphere dates from 1141 and is located in Miami? The Spanish Monastery Cloisters were first erected in Segovia, Spain. Centuries later, newspaper magnate William Randolph Hearst purchased and brought them to America in pieces. The carefully numbered stones were quarantined for years until they were finally reassembled on the present site in 1954. Visitors are free to explore; you'll want to spend about an hour touring the cold, ancient structure, the beautiful grounds, and the gift shop.

✪ **Venetian Pool.** 2701 DeSoto Blvd. (at Toledo St.), Coral Gables. ☎ **305/460-5356.** Admission and hours vary seasonally. Nov–Mar, $5 13 and older, $2 children under 13; Apr–Oct, $8 13 and older, $4 under 13. Children under 36 months not allowed in the facilities. Call for hours.

Miami's most beautiful and unusual swimming pool, dating from 1924, is hidden behind pastel stucco walls and is honored with a listing in the National Register of Historic Places. Underground artesian wells feed the free-form lagoon, which is shaded by three-story Spanish porticos and features both fountains and waterfalls. It can be cold in the winter months. During summer, the pool's 800,000 gallons of water are drained and refilled nightly, ensuring a cool, clean swim. Visitors are free to swim and sunbathe here, just as Esther Williams and Johnny Weissmuller did decades ago. For a modest fee, you or your children can learn to swim during special summer programs.

6 Nature Preserves, Parks & Gardens

The Miami area is a great place for outdoors-minded visitors, with beaches, parks, and gardens galore. Plus, South Florida has two national parks; see chapter 11 for coverage of the Everglades and Biscayne National Park.

BOTANICAL GARDENS & A SPICE PARK

In Miami, the **Fairchild Tropical Gardens,** 10901 Old Cutler Rd. (☎ **305/667-1651**), features a veritable rain forest of both rare and exotic plants on 83 acres. Palmettos, vine pergola, palm glades, and other unique species create a scenic, lush environment. It's well worth taking the free hourly tram to learn what you always wanted to know about the various flowers and trees during a 30-minute narrated tour. There is also a museum, cafe, and gift shop with fantastic books on gardening and cooking and edible gifts.

Admission is $8 for adults, and free for children 12 and under accompanied by an adult. Open daily from 9:30am to 4:30pm. Take I-95 south to U.S. 1, turn left onto Le Jeune Road, and follow it straight to the traffic circle; from there, take Old Cutler Road 2 miles to the park.

A testament to Miami's unusual climate, the **Preston B. Bird and Mary Heinlein Fruit and Spice Park,** 24801 SW 187th Ave., Homestead (☎ **305/247-5727**), harbors rare fruit trees that cannot survive elsewhere in the country.

Definitely ask for a guide. If a volunteer is available, you'll learn some fascinating things about this 30-acre living plant museum, where the most exotic varieties of fruits and spices, including ackee, mango, ugly fruits, carambola, and breadfruit, grow on strange-looking trees with unpronounceable names.

Admission to the spice park is $3.50 for adults and $1 for children under 12, and the park is open daily from 10am to 5pm. Closed major holidays. Tours are included in the price of admission and are offered 11am, 1pm, and 2:30pm. Take U.S. 1 south, turn right on SW 248th Street, and go straight for 5 miles to SW 187th Avenue.

MORE MIAMI PARKS

The **Amelia Earhart Park,** 401 E. 65th St., Hialeah (☎ **305/685-8389**), has five lakes stocked with bass and brim for fishing; playgrounds; picnic facilities; and a big red barn that houses cows, sheep, and goats for petting and ponies for riding. There are also a country store and dozens of old-time farm activities like horseshoeing, sugarcane processing, and more. Parking is free on weekdays and $3.50 per car on weekends. Open daily from 9am to sunset. To drive here, take I-95 north to the NW 103rd Street exit, go west to East 4th Avenue, and then turn right. Parking is 1½ miles down the street.

At the historic ✪ **Bill Baggs Cape Florida State Recreation Area,** 1200 Crandon Blvd. (☎ **305/361-5811**), at the tip of Key Biscayne, you can explore the unfettered wilds and enjoy some of the most secluded beaches in Miami. There's also a recently reopened lighthouse. A rental shack rents bikes, hydrobikes, kayaks, and many more water toys. It's a great place to picnic, and a newly constructed restaurant serves homemade Latin food, including great fish soups and sandwiches. Just be careful that the raccoons don't get your lunch, because the furry black-eyed beasts are everywhere. Admission is $4 per car with up to eight people. Open daily from 8am to sunset. Tours of the recently renovated lighthouse are available every day except Tuesday and Wednesday, at 10am and 1pm. Arrive at least half an hour early to sign up—there is room for only 10 people on each tour.

Tropical Park, 7900 SW 40th St. (☎ **305/226-8315**), has it all. Enjoy a game of tennis and racquetball for a minimal fee, or swim and sun yourself on the secluded little lake. You can use the fishing pond free, and they'll even supply you with the rods and bait. If you catch anything, however, you're on your own. Open daily from sunrise to sunset.

Named after the now-deceased champion of the Everglades, **Marjory Stoneman Douglas Biscayne Nature Center** offers hands-on marine exploration, hikes through coastal hammocks, bike trips, and beach walks. Local environmentalists and historians lead intriguing trips through the local habitat. Be sure to wear comfortable closed-toe shoes for hikes through wet or rocky terrain. The center is located in Crandon Park in Key Biscayne. Call (☎ **305/642-9600**) for tour schedules and prices.

7 Especially for Kids

The **Scott Rakow Youth Center,** 2700 Sheridan Ave. (☎ **305/673-7767**), is a hidden treasure on Miami Beach. This two-story facility boasts an ice-skating rink, bowling alleys, a basketball court, gymnasium equipment, and full-time supervision for kids. Call for a complete schedule of organized events. The only drag is that it's not open to adults (except on Sun, which is family day). Admission is $1.50 per day for visiting children 9 to 17. Open daily from 2 to 8:30pm.

The following is a roundup of other attractions kids will especially enjoy. Details on each one can be found earlier in the chapter.

AMELIA EARHART PARK *(see p. 141)*   This is the best park in Miami for kids. They'll like the petting zoos, pony rides, and private island with hidden tunnels.

MARJORY STONEMAN DOUGLAS BISCAYNE NATURE CENTER *(see p. 141)* Kids seem to enjoy touching slimy marine animals and spotting unusual creatures out at sea. This brand-new exhibit and tour center offers lots of educational and fun programs.

MIAMI METROZOO *(see p. 132)*   This completely cageless zoo offers such star attractions as a monorail "safari" and a petting zoo. Kids love the elephant rides.

MIAMI MUSEUM OF SCIENCE & SPACE TRANSIT PLANETARIUM *(see p. 138)*   At the Planetarium, kids can learn about space and science by watching entertaining films and cosmic shows. The space museum also offers child-friendly explanations for natural occurrences.

MIAMI SEAQUARIUM *(see p. 133)*   Kids can get a kiss from a dolphin and watch exciting performances.

8 Game Parks/Entertainment Centers

✪ **Game Works.** 5701 Sunset Dr., South Miami. ☎ **305/740-9091.** Mon–Fri 11am–2am, Sat 10am–2am, Sun 10am–midnight. Games 50¢–$5.

The biggest thing to hit Miami in years, Steven Spielberg's SEGA Gameworks in the Shops of Sunset Place made its debut in early 1999 and quickly became the place for young adults to play. You'll see kids, Gen-Xers, and Baby Boomers fighting off dinosaurs from Jurassic Park, racing in the Indy 500, swooshing down a snowy ski trail, throwing darts, and shooting pool in this sleek multilevel playground. The young at heart will find the perfect combination of vintage arcade games, high-tech videos, virtual-reality arenas, pool tables, food, and cocktails in this playground occupying more than 33,000 square feet.

IMAX Theatre at Sunset Place. 5701 Sunset Dr., South Miami. ☎ **305/663-4629.** Shows daily 11am–11pm. IMAX: adults $7.50, seniors and students $6.50, children under 12 $5.50. 3-D theatre: adults $9, seniors and students $8, children under 12 $7. Call for exact schedules and prices.

Utilizing high-tech film techniques, six-story-high screens, and wraparound digital sound, this unique movie experience really makes you feel like you're part of the action. At press time, the incredible story of Everest was showing. This 50-minute documentary-style film captured the terrifying experience of the mountain climbers in the Himalayas in all its frigid, blinding wonder. Also available is a 3-D theater that really tempts you to reach out and touch the images.

For other nearby arcades and game parks, see "The Gold Coast," chapter 8.

9 Sightseeing Cruises & Organized Tours

BOAT & CRUISE-SHIP TOURS

Gondola Adventures. Docked at Biscayne Bay Marina, 1633 N. Bayshore Dr. (behind the Marriott Hotel), Miami. ☎ **305/358-6400.** Rates from $5 per person (minimum 4 people).

A real gondola in Miami? Well, it may not be the canals of Venice, but with a little imagination, the Biscayne Bay will do. You can go on a simple ride around Bayside, or splurge on your own private champagne cruise for $99.

Heritage Miami II Topsail Schooner. Bayside Marketplace Marina, 401 Biscayne Blvd., Downtown. ☎ **305/442-9697.** Tickets $15 adults, $10 children 12 and under. Sept–May only. Tours leave daily at 1:30, 4, and 6:30pm, and Fri–Sun also at 9, 10, and 11pm.

More adventure than tour, this relaxing ride aboard Miami's only tall ship is a fun way to see the city. The 2-hour cruises pass by Villa Vizcaya, Coconut Grove, and Key Biscayne and put you in sight of Miami's spectacular skyline. Call to make sure the ship is running on schedule. On Friday, Saturday, and Sunday evenings, there are 1-hour tours to see the lights of the city.

A SIGHTSEEING TOUR

There are literally hundreds of tour operators in Miami and the Beaches. Check with your hotel's concierge to see which they recommend, or try the following company.

Miami Nice Excursion, Inc., Travel and Service. 18430 Collins Ave., Miami Beach. ☎ **305/949-9180.** Admission $29–$55 adults, $25 children. Daily 7am–10pm. Call ahead for directions to various pickup areas.

Pick your destination. The Miami Nice tours will take you to the Everglades, Fort Lauderdale, the Seaquarium, Key West, Cape Canaveral, or wherever you desire. Included in most Miami trips is a fairly comprehensive city tour narrated by a knowledgeable guide. The company is one of the oldest in town.

SPECIALIZED TOURS

Besides those tours listed below, a great option for seeing the city is to take a tour led by **Dr. Paul George.** Dr. George is a history teacher at Miami-Dade Community College and a historian at the Historical Museum of Southern Florida—he also happens to be "Mr. Miami." There's a set calendar of tours, but all of them are fascinating to South Florida buffs. Tours focus on neighborhoods, such as Little Havana, Brickell Avenue, or Key Biscayne, and on themes, such as Miami cemeteries. The often long-winded discussions can be a bit much for those who just want a quick look around, but Dr. George certainly knows his stuff. The cost is $15 to $25; reservations are required (☎ **305/375-1492**). Tours leave from the Historical Museum at 101 W. Flagler St., Downtown.

Miami Design Preservation League. The Art Deco Welcome Center, 1001 Ocean Dr., South Beach. ☎ **305/672-2014.** Walking tours $10 per person. Tours leave Sat at 10:30am and Thurs at 6:30pm. Self-guided audio tours also available 7 days a week for $5. Call ahead for updated schedules.

On Thursday evenings and Saturday mornings, the Design Preservation League sponsors walking tours that offer a fascinating inside look at the city's historic Art Deco District. Tourgoers meet for a 1½-hour walk through some of America's most exuberantly "architectured" buildings. The League led the fight to designate this area a National Historic District and is proud to share the splendid results with visitors.

Art Deco Cycling Tour. 601 5th St., South Beach. ☎ **305/674-0150.** $10 per person, plus $6 for bike rental. Tours depart every other Sun at 10am from the Miami Beach Bicycle Center.

If you'd rather bike or in-line skate than walk, catch this fun and interesting Sunday morning tour. The bicycle is the most efficient mode of transportation through the streets of South Beach and one of the best ways to see the historic Art Deco District. Call to reserve a spot.

Coral Gables Art and Gallery Tour. Various locations in Coral Gables. Free. For more information, call Elite Fine Art (☎ **305/448-3800**) or stop by any of the galleries in the area. First Fri of the month 7–10pm.

On this tour, art lovers are shuttled to more than 20 galleries that participate in Gables Night in the gallery section of Coral Gables. Viewers can sip wine as they gaze at American folk art; African, Native American, and Latin art; and photography. Most galleries are on Ponce de Leon Boulevard, between SW 40th and SW 24th streets. The vans run continuously from 7 to 10pm.

Lincoln Road Gallery Walk at the Art Center. 800 Lincoln Rd. (at the corner of Meridian Ave.). ☎ **305/674-8278.** Free. Tour given second Sat of every month 7–11pm.

Join a knowledgeable guide for a tour of artists' studios on the second Saturday of every month. Or feel free to wander through the more than 50 studios housed in this cooperative art complex on your own. You can also walk through the pedestrian mall to catch a look at the works on display in other galleries (if you're lucky, you'll wander into one that serves wine and appetizers).

10 Water Sports

BOATING

Private rental outfits include **Beach Boat Rentals,** 2400 Collins Ave., Miami Beach (☎ **305/534-4307**), where 50-horsepower, 18-foot powerboats rent for some of the best prices on the beach. Rates are $61.25 for an hour, $165.15 for 4 hours, and $225.70 for 8 hours. All rates include taxes and gas. A $250 cash or credit-card deposit is required. Cruising is permitted only in and around Biscayne Bay—ocean access is prohibited. Renters must be over 21. The rental office is at 23rd Street, on the inland waterway in Miami Beach. It's open from 9am to 6pm (weather permitting) during the high season and 9am to 8pm during the summer.

Club Nautico of Coconut Grove, 2560 S. Bayshore Dr., Coconut Grove (☎ **305/ 858-6258**), rents high-quality powerboats for fishing, waterskiing, diving, and cruising in the bay or ocean. All boats are Coast Guard equipped, with VHF radios and safety gear. Rates range from $199 for 4 hours and $299 for 8 hours to as much as $419 on weekends. Club Nautico is open daily from 9am to 5pm (weather permitting). Other locations include the **Crandon Park Marina,** 4000 Crandon Blvd., Key Biscayne (☎ **305/361-9217**), with the same rates and hours as the Coconut Grove location; and the **Miami Beach Marina,** Pier E, 300 Alton Rd., South Beach (☎ **305/673-2502**), where rates are $229 for 4 hours and $299 for 8 hours for a 20-foot boat; and $259 for 4 hours and $359 for 8 hours for a 24-footer. Nautico on Miami Beach is open daily from 9am to 5pm.

JET SKIS/WAVE RUNNERS

Don't miss a chance to tour the islands on the back of your own powerful watercraft. Many beachfront concessionaires rent a variety of these popular (and loud) water scooters. The latest models are fast and smooth. Try **Tony's Jet Ski Rentals,** 3601 Rickenbacker Causeway, Key Biscayne (☎ **305/361-8280**), one of the city's largest rental shops, located on a private beach in the Miami Marine Stadium lagoon. Jet skis rent for about $38 for a half hour and $64 for an hour. Wave Runners for two rent for $45 for a half hour and $70 for an hour. Tony's is open daily from 10:30am to 6:30pm.

KAYAKING

The laid-back **Urban Trails Kayak Company** rents boats at 10800 Collins Ave. (☎ 305/947-1302). It offers scenic routes through rivers with mangroves and islands as your destination. Most of the kayaks are sit-on-tops and most are plastic, although some fiberglass models are available. Rates are $8 an hour, $20 for up to 4 hours, and $25 for over 4 hours. Tandems are $12 an hour, $30 for up to 4 hours, and $35 for the day. Open daily from 9am to 5pm.

The outfitters here give interested explorers a map to take with them and quick instructions on how to work the paddles and boats. If you have at least four people, you can get a guided tour for $35 per person for half a day. This is a fun way to experience some of Miami's unspoiled wildlife, and it's good exercise, too.

SAILING

You can rent sailboats and catamarans through the beachfront concessions desk of several top resorts, such as the Doral Ocean Beach Resort, Sheraton Bal Harbour Beach Resort, and Dezerland Surfside Beach Hotel (see "Accommodations" in chapter 4).

Sailboats of **Key Biscayne Rentals and Sailing School,** in the Crandon Marina (next to Sundays on the Bay), 4000 Crandon Blvd., Key Biscayne (☎ **305/361-0328** days, 305/279-7424 evenings), can also get you out on the water. A 22-foot sailboat rents for $27 an hour, or $81 for a half day. A Cat-25 or J24 is available for $35 an hour or $110 for a half day. If you've always had a dream to win the America's Cup but can't sail, the able teachers at Sailboats will get you started. It offers a 10-hour course over 5 days for $250 for one person or $350 for you and a buddy, $50 for each additional person.

SCUBA DIVING

In 1981, the government began a wide-scale project designed to increase the number of habitats available to marine organisms. One of the program's major accomplishments has been the creation of nearby artificial reefs, which have attracted all kinds of tropical plants, fish, and animals. In addition, Biscayne National Park (see chapter 7) offers a protected marine environment just south of Downtown.

Several dive shops around the city offer organized weekend outings, either to the reefs or to one of over a dozen old shipwrecks around Miami's shores. Check "Divers" in the yellow pages for rental equipment and for a full list of undersea tour operators.

Divers Paradise of Key Biscayne, 4000 Crandon Blvd. (☎ **305/361-3483**), offers two dive expeditions daily to the more than 30 wrecks and artificial reefs off the coast of Miami Beach and Key Biscayne. You can take a 3-day certification course for $399, which includes all the dives and gear. If you already have your C-card, a dive trip costs about $90 if you need equipment and only $35 if you bring your own gear. It's open Monday to Friday from 10am to 6pm and Saturday and Sunday from 8am to 6pm. Call ahead for times and locations of dives.

WINDSURFING

Many hotels rent Windsurfers to their guests, but if yours doesn't have a water-sports concession stand, head for Key Biscayne.

Sailboards Miami, Rickenbacker Causeway, Key Biscayne (☎ **305/361-SAIL**), operates out of big yellow trucks on Hobie Beach, the most popular windsurfing spot in the city. For those who've never ridden a board but want to try it, they offer a 2-hour lesson for $39 that's guaranteed to turn you into a wave warrior or you get your money back. After that, you can rent a board for $20 an hour or $37 for 2 hours. If you want to make a day of it, a 10-hour card costs $130. Open daily from 10am to 5:30pm. Make the first right after the toll booth to find the outfitters.

11 More Ways to Play, Both Indoors & Out

BICYCLING

The cement promenade on the southern tip of the island is a great place to ride. Biking up the beach is great for surf, sun, sand, exercise, and people-watching. Most of the big beach hotels rent bicycles, as does the **Miami Beach Bicycle Center,** 601 5th St., South Beach (☎ **305/674-0150**), which charges $5 per hour or $14 per day. It's open Monday to Saturday from 10am to 7pm and Sunday from 10am to 5pm.

Bikers can also enjoy more than 130 miles of paved paths throughout Miami. The beautiful and quiet streets of Coral Gables and Coconut Grove are great for bicyclists. Old trees form canopies over wide, flat roads lined with grand homes and quaint street markers. Several bicycle trails are spread throughout these neighborhoods, including one that begins at the doorstep of **Dade Cycle,** 3216 Grand Ave., Coconut Grove (☎ **305/444-5997**); it's open Monday to Saturday from 9:30am to 5:30pm, Sunday from 10:30am to 5:30pm.

The terrain in Key Biscayne is perfect for biking, especially along the park and beach roads. If you don't mind the sound of cars whooshing by, **Rickenbacker Causeway** is also fantastic since it is one of the only bikeable inclines in Miami from which you get fantastic elevated views of the city and waterways. **Key Cycling,** 61 Harbor Dr., Key Biscayne (☎ **305/361-0061**), rents mountain bikes for $5 an hour or $15 a day. It's open Monday through Friday from 10am to 7pm, Saturday from 10am to 6pm, and Sunday from 11am to 4pm.

Intra Mark, off the Rickenbacker Bridge across from the Rusty Pelican, Hobie Beach (☎ **305/365-0502**), rents scooters for $20 an hour or $35 for 2 hours, and bicycles for $5 an hour or $10 for 4 hours. The eco-minded staff directs bikers to the best paths for nature watching.

If you want to avoid the traffic altogether, head out to **Shark Valley** in the Everglades National Park—one of South Florida's most scenic bicycle trails and a favorite haunt of city-weary locals. See chapter 7 for more details.

Biking note: Children under the age of 16 are required by Florida law to wear a helmet, which can be purchased at any bike store or retail outlet selling cycling supplies.

FISHING

Bridge fishing is popular in Miami; you'll see people with poles over almost every waterway.

Some of the best surf casting in the city can be had at **Haulover Beach Park** at Collins Avenue and 105th Street, where there's a bait-and-tackle shop right on the pier. **South Pointe Park,** at the southern tip of Miami Beach, is another popular fishing spot; it features a long pier, comfortable benches, and a great view of the ships passing through Government Cut.

You can also choose to do some deep-sea fishing. One bargain outfitter, the **Kelley Fishing Fleet,** at the Haulover Marina, 10800 Collins Ave. (at 108th Street), Miami Beach (☎ **305/945-3801**), has half-day, full-day, and night fishing aboard diesel-powered "party boats." The fleet's emphasis on drifting is geared toward trolling and bottom fishing for snapper, sailfish, and mackerel, but it also schedules 2- and 3-day trips to the Bahamas. Half-day and night fishing trips are $21 for adults and $14.50 for children; full-day trips are $33 for adults and $26.50 for children; rod and reel rental is $5. Daily departures are scheduled at 9am, 1:45pm, and 8pm; reservations are recommended.

Also at the Haulover Marina is the charter boat *Helen C,* 10800 Collins Ave., Haulover (☎ **305/947-4081**). Although there's no shortage of private charter boats here, Captain Dawn Mergelsberg is a good pick, since she puts individuals together to get a full boat. Her Helen is a twin-engine 55-footer, equipped for big-game "monster" fish like marlin, tuna, dolphin, shark, and sailfish. The cost is $70 per person. Sailings are scheduled for 8am to noon and 1 to 5pm daily; call for reservations. Private charters and transportation are also available. Children are welcome.

Key Biscayne offers deep-sea fishing to those willing to get their hands dirty and pay a bundle. The competition among the boats is fierce, but the prices are basically the same no matter which you choose. The going rate is about $400 to $450 for a half day and $600 to $700 for a full day of fishing. These rates are usually for a party of up to six, and the boats supply you with rods and bait, as well as instruction for first-timers. Some will take you out to Key Biscayne and even out to the Upper Keys if the fish aren't biting in Miami.

You might consider the following boats, all of which sail out of the Key Biscayne marina: *Sunny Boy III* (☎ **305/361-2217**), *Queen B* (☎ **305/361-2528**), and *L & H* (☎ **305/361-9318**). Call them for reservations.

GAMBLING

Although gambling is technically illegal in Miami, there are plenty of loopholes which allow all kinds of wagering. Gamblers can try their luck at off-shore casinos, bingo, jai alai, card rooms, horse tracks, and dog races.

Especially popular is the huge outpost west of Miami, **Miccosukee Indian Gaming,** 500 SW 177th Ave. (off S.R 41) (☎ **800/741-4600** or 305/222-4600). This glitzy casino isn't Vegas, but you can play slots, high-speed bingo, and even poker (with a $10 maximum pot). With more than 85,000 square feet of playing space, the complex even offers overnight accommodations for those who can't get enough of the thrill.

A newer and more elegant option is the *Casino Princesa,* which docks behind the Hard Rock Cafe in Bayside Marketplace. This 200-foot, $15 million yacht has more than 200 slot machines, 32 tables, a restaurant, and four lounges in 10,000 square feet of gaming space on two decks. Prices range from $13 to $18 and include meals. Ships sail twice daily on weekdays and three times on weekends. Call ☎ **305/379-5825** for updated schedules.

GOLF

There are more than 50 private and public golf courses in the Greater Miami area. Contact the **Greater Miami Convention and Visitors Bureau** (☎ **800/283-2707** or 305/539-3063) for a list of more courses and costs. Some of the area's best and most expensive are at the big resorts, many of which allow nonguests to play, such as the Doral Blue Course at the Doral Resort and Spa in West Miami; Don Shula's Hotel and Golf Club, also in West Miami; and the Biltmore in Coral Gables. See chapter 5 for more details.

Otherwise, the following represent some of the area's best public courses. ۞ **Crandon Park Golf Course,** formerly known as The Links, 6700 Crandon Blvd., Key Biscayne (☎ **305/361-9129**), is the number one–ranked municipal course in the state and one of the top five in the country. The park is situated on 200 bayfront acres and offers a pro shop, rentals, lessons, carts, and a lighted driving range. The course is open daily from dawn to dusk; greens fees (including cart) are $86 per person during the winter and $45 per person during the summer. Special twilight rates are available.

One of the most popular courses among real enthusiasts is the **Doral Park Golf and Country Club,** 5001 NW 104th Ave., West Miami (☎ **305/591-8800**); it's not related to the Doral Hotel or spa. Call to book in advance since this challenging

18-holer is so popular with locals. The course is open from 6:30am to 6pm during the winter and until 7pm during the summer. Cart and greens fees vary, so call ☎ 305/594-0954 for information.

Known as one of the best in the city, the **Golf Club of Miami,** 6801 Miami Gardens Dr., at NW 68th Avenue (☎ 305/829-8456), has three 18-hole courses of varying degrees of difficulty. You'll encounter lush fairways, rolling greens, and some history to boot. The west course, designed in 1961 by Robert Trent Jones and updated in the 1990s by the PGA, was where Jack Nicklaus played his first professional tournament and Lee Trevino won his first professional championship. The course is open daily from 6:30am to sunset. Cart and greens fees are $45 to $75 per person during the winter, and $20 to $34 per person during the summer. Special twilight rates are available.

Golfers looking for some cheap practice time will appreciate **Haulover Park,** 10800 Collins Ave., Miami Beach (☎ 305/940-6719), in a pretty bayside location. The longest hole on this par-27 course is 125 yards. It's open daily from 7:30am to 5:30pm during the winter, and to 7:30pm during the summer. Greens fees are $5 per person during the winter, and $4 per person during the summer. Hand carts cost $1.40.

HEALTH CLUBS

Although many of Miami's full-service hotels have fitness centers, you can't count on them in less-upscale establishments or in the small Art Deco District hotels. Several health clubs around the city will take in nonmembers on a daily basis. If you're already a member at the mega–health-club chain **Bally's Total Fitness,** dial ☎ 800/777-1117 to find the clubs in the area. There are no outlets on the beaches; most are in South Miami.

One of the most popular clubs, which welcomes walk-in guests, is **Crunch,** 1253 Washington Ave., South Beach (☎ 305/674-8222), where you might work out with Cindy Crawford, Madonna, or any of a number of supermodels when they're in town. This club offers star appeal and top-of-the-line equipment. Use of the facility is $18 daily, with discounts for guests of most area hotels. It keeps late hours, especially in season, when it's often open until midnight.

IN-LINE SKATING

Miami's consistently flat terrain makes rollerblading easy. The heavy traffic and construction, however, make it tough to find long routes. Remember to keep a pair of sandals or sneakers with you, since many area shops won't allow you inside with skates on.

Because of the popularity of blading and skateboarding, the city has passed a law prohibiting skating on the west side (the cafe-lined strip) of Ocean Drive in the evenings. In addition, the city has passed a law that all bladers must skate slowly and safely. You wouldn't want to mow down an elderly stroller. You can still have fun, though, and the following rental outfits can help chart an interesting course for you and supply you with all the necessary gear.

In Coral Gables, **Extreme Skate & Sport,** 7876 SW 40th St. (☎ 305/261-6699), is one of South Florida's largest in-line skate dealers. Even if you know nothing about the sport, they have a knowledgeable sales staff to help you.

In South Beach, **Fritz's Skate Shop,** 726 Lincoln Rd. Mall (☎ 305/532-1954), rents top-quality skates, including safety pads, for $8 per hour, $24 per day, and $34 overnight. If you're a first-time in-line skater, an instructor will hold your hand for $25 an hour. The shop also stocks lots of gear and clothing.

TENNIS

Hundreds of tennis courts in South Florida are open to the public for a minimal fee. Most courts operate on a first-come, first-served basis and are open from sunrise to sunset. For information and directions, call the **City of Miami Beach Recreation, Culture, and Parks Department** (☎ 305/673-7730), or the **City of Miami Parks and Recreation Department** (☎ 305/575-5256).

The three hard courts and seven clay courts at the **Key Biscayne Tennis Association,** 6702 Crandon Blvd. (☎ 305/361-5263), get crowded on weekends since they're some of Miami's most beautiful. You'll play on the same courts as Lendl, Graf, Evert, McEnroe, and other greats; this the venue for one of the world's biggest annual tennis events, the Lipton Championship. There's a pleasant, if limited, pro shop, plus many good pros. Only four courts are lit at night, but if you reserve at least 48 hours in advance, you can usually take your pick. They cost $5 per person per hour. The courts are open daily from 8am to 9pm.

12 Spectator Sports

Check the *Miami Herald's* sports section for a daily listing of local events and the paper's Friday "Weekend" section for comprehensive coverage and in-depth reports. For last-minute tickets, call the venue directly, since many season ticket holders sell singles and return unused tickets. Expensive tickets are available from brokers or individuals, listed in the classified sections of the local papers. Some tickets are also available through **Ticketmaster** (☎ 305/358-5885).

BASEBALL

The **Florida Marlins** shocked the sports world in 1997 when they became the youngest expansion team to win a World Series, but then floundered as their star players were sold off by former owner Wayne Huizenga. If you're interested in catching a game, be warned that the summer heat in Miami can be unbearable, even in the evenings.

Home games are held at the **Pro Player Stadium,** 2267 NW 199th St., North Miami Beach (☎ 305/626-7426). Tickets are $4 to $30. Box-office hours are Monday to Friday from 8:30am to 6pm, Saturday from 8:30am to 4pm, and prior to games; tickets are also available through Ticketmaster. The team currently holds spring training in Melbourne, Florida.

BASKETBALL

The **Miami Heat** (☎ 305/577-HEAT or 305/835-7000), now led by celebrity coach Pat Riley, made their NBA debut in November 1988, and their games remain one of Miami's hottest tickets. The season lasts from October to April, with most games beginning at 7:30pm. They'll play the 1999/2000 season in a brand-new waterfront arena downtown on Biscayne Boulevard. Tickets are $14 to $50. Box-office hours are Monday to Friday from 10am to 4pm (until 8pm on game nights); tickets are also available through Ticketmaster.

FOOTBALL

Miami's golden boys are the **Miami Dolphins,** the city's most recognizable team, followed by thousands of "dolfans." Coached by Jimmy Johnson, the team plays at least eight home games during the season, between September and December, at **Pro Player Stadium,** 2267 NW 199th St., North Miami Beach (☎ 305/620-2578). Tickets cost between $20 and $40. The box office is open Monday to Friday from 8:30am to 5:30pm; tickets are also available through **Ticketmaster** (☎ 305/350-5050).

HORSE RACING

Wrapped around an artificial lake, **Gulfstream Park,** at U.S. 1 and Hallandale Beach Boulevard, Hallandale (☎ 305/931-7223), is both pretty and popular. Large purses and important races are commonplace at this suburban course, and the track is often crowded. Call for schedules. Admission is $3 to the grandstand, and $3 to the clubhouse. Free parking. From January through March, post times are Wednesday to Monday at 1pm. Many weekends feature live concerts by well-known musicians.

You might remember the pink flamingos at **Hialeah Park,** 2200 E. 4th Ave., Hialeah (☎ 305/885-8000), from *Miami Vice.* This famous colony is the largest of its kind. The track, listed on the National Register of Historic Places, is one of the most beautiful in the world, featuring old-fashioned stands and acres of immaculately manicured grounds. Admission is $1 to the grandstand and $2 to the clubhouse on weekdays, and $2 and $4, respectively, on weekends. Children 17 and under enter free with an adult. Parking starts at $2. Races are held mid-March to mid-May, but the course is open year-round for sightseeing Monday to Saturday from 9am to 5pm. Call for post times.

ICE HOCKEY

The young **Florida Panthers** (☎ 954/835-7000) have already made history. In the 1994–1995 season, they played in the Stanley Cup finals, and they have amassed a legion of fans who love them. Much to the disappointment of Miamians, they moved to a new venue in Sunrise, the next county north of Miami-Dade. Call for directions and ticket information.

JAI ALAI

Jai alai, sort of a Spanish-style indoor lacrosse, was introduced to Miami in 1924 and is regularly played in two Miami-area frontons. Although the sport has roots stemming from ancient Egypt, the game as it's now played was invented by Basque peasants in the Pyrenees mountains during the 17th century.

Players use woven baskets, called *cestas,* to hurl balls—*pelotas*—at speeds that sometimes exceed 170 miles per hour. Spectators, who are protected behind a wall of glass, place bets on the evening's players.

The **Miami Jai Alai Fronton,** 3500 NW 37th Ave., at NW 35th Street (☎ 305/633-6400), is America's oldest fronton, dating from 1926. It schedules 13 games per night. Admission is $1 to the grandstand, $5 to the clubhouse. It's open year-round. There are games Monday and Wednesday to Saturday at 7pm, and matinees on Monday, Wednesday, and Saturday at noon.

13 Shopping

Miami has earned a worldwide reputation as a shopping capital, especially among visitors from Latin America and the Caribbean. Take a quick glance around the airport, and you'll see more than a few departing passengers lugging refrigerator-sized cardboard boxes and bulging suitcases. From exotic tropical fruits to high-tech electronics, fine art and art deco collectibles, Latin music and hand-rolled cigars, Miami has something for everyone.

And shopping is big business. According to surveys, Latin American shoppers spend more than $1 billion annually in Miami-Dade county.

To accommodate the more than 10 million visitors from all over the world who pass through Miami each year, there are strip malls and shops everywhere. The city is blanketed with strip centers, chain stores, boutiques, and malls. And there are many more in the works.

THE SHOPPING SCENE

Below I've described some of the popular retail areas, where many stores are concentrated for easy browsing.

As a general rule, shop hours are Monday through Saturday from 10am to 6pm and Sunday from noon to 5pm. Many stores stay open late (until 9pm or so) 1 night of the week (usually Thursday). Shops in trendy Coconut Grove are open until 9pm Sunday through Thursday and even later on Friday and Saturday nights. Department stores and shopping malls also keep longer hours, with most staying open from 10am to 9 or 10pm Monday to Saturday and noon to 6pm on Sunday.

The 6.5% state and local sales tax is added to the price of all nonfood purchases.

Most Miami stores can wrap your purchase and ship it anywhere in the world via United Parcel Service (UPS). If they can't, you can send it yourself, either through **UPS** (☎ 800/742-5877) or through the U.S. Mail (see "Fast Facts: Miami," in chapter 4).

SHOPPING AREAS

Most of Miami's shopping happens at its many megamalls scattered from one end of the county to the other; however, there is also some excellent boutique shopping and browsing to be done in the following areas. See "City Layout," in chapter 4, for more information about these areas.

AVENTURA   Biscayne Boulevard between Miami Gardens Drive and the county line is a 2-mile stretch of huge retail stores, including Best Buy, Borders, Circuit City, Linens 'N' Things, Marshall's, Sports Authority, and more. Also here is Loehmann's Plaza, a small one-level open shopping mall with several good shoe stores and Loehmann's, the discount clothing store (see "Fashion," below).

CALLE OCHO   For a taste of "Little Havana," take a walk down 8th Street between SW 27th Avenue and 12th Avenue, where you'll find some lively street life and many shops selling cigars, baked goods, shoes, furniture, and record stores specializing in Latin music. Be sure to take your Spanish dictionary if you need it.

COCONUT GROVE   Downtown Coconut Grove, centered on Main Highway and Grand Avenue and branching onto the adjoining streets, is one of Miami's most pedestrian-friendly zones. The Grove's wide sidewalks, lined with cafes and boutiques, provide hours of browsing pleasure. Coconut Grove is best known for its dozens of avant-garde clothing stores, funky import shops, and excellent sidewalk cafes centered around Cocowalk and The Streets of Mayfair.

CORAL GABLES—MIRACLE MILE   Actually only a half-mile long, this central shopping street was an integral part of George Merrick's original city plan. Today, the strip still enjoys popularity, especially for its bridal stores, ladies' shops, haberdashers, and gift shops. Recently, newer chain stores, like Barnes and Noble, Old Navy, and Starbucks, have been appearing on the Mile. It also features several excellent restaurants before it terminates at the City Hall rotunda (see "Dining" in chapter 4).

DOWNTOWN MIAMI   If you're looking for discounts on all types of goods—especially watches, fabric, buttons, lace, shoes, luggage, and leather—Flagler Street just west of Biscayne Boulevard is the best place to start. Be prepared for some hustling and haggling. Most signs are printed in English, Spanish, and Portuguese; however, many shopkeepers may not be entirely fluent in English.

✪ SOUTH BEACH—LINCOLN ROAD   This luxurious pedestrian mall, originally designed in 1957 by Morris Lapidus, recently underwent a multimillion-dollar renovation, restoring it to its former glory. Here shoppers can find an array of clothing and art and a menagerie of South Beach's finest sidewalk cafes flanked on one end by a multiplex movie theater and at the other by the Atlantic Ocean. Monthly gallery tours, periodic jazz concerts, and a weekly farmer's market are just a few of the offerings on "The Road."

Impressions

Someday . . . Miami will become the great center of South American trade.
—Julia Tuttle, Miami's founder, 1896

COLLINS & WASHINGTON AVENUES   For the hippest clothing boutiques, including A/X Armani, Versace, Benneton, The Gap, Todd Oldham, Kenneth Cole, and Nicole Miller, stroll along this pretty strip of the deco district (between 6th Street and 9th Street).

SHOPPING A TO Z
ANTIQUES/COLLECTIBLES

✪ **Architectural Antiques.** 2500 SW 28th Lane (just west of U.S. 1), Miami. ☎ **305/285-1330.**

A great place to browse—if you don't mind a little dust—this huge warehouse has an impressive stash of ironwork, bronzes, paintings, lamps, furniture, and sculptures, which have been salvaged from estates worldwide. Don't be surprised to find odd items too, like an old British phone booth or a pair of gargoyles off an ancient church.

Dietel's Antiques. 6572 Bird Rd., South Miami. ☎ **305/666-0724.**

An active trade business here means lots of different styles are revolving constantly. You'll find baubles of every assortment in this stocked shop located near Coral Gables's quaint antiques district.

Miami Twice. 6562 SW 40th St., South Miami. ☎ **305/666-0127.**

While they are not technically antiques yet, the Old Florida furniture and decorations from the 1930s, 1940s, and 1950s are great fun (and collectible). In addition to loads of deco memorabilia, there are vintage clothes, shoes, and jewelry.

Modernism. 1622 Ponce de Leon Blvd., Coral Gables. ☎ **305/442-8743.**

Specializing in 20th-century furnishings, this gorgeous shop has some of the most beautiful examples of deco goods from France and the United States.

ART GALLERIES

Miami's finest art galleries are located within walking distance of one another in Coral Gables along Ponce de Leon Boulevard, extending from U.S. 1 to Bird Road. Still others are clustered in Bal Harbour's ritzy shopping district. And finally, South Beach's Lincoln Road, which once had dozens of galleries, now has only a few—a result of soaring rents.

Also, check out the burgeoning art scene in the design district north of downtown just west of Biscayne Boulevard around 40th Street. Listed below is a selection of galleries both in and out of these areas.

If you happen to be in town on the first Friday of a month, you should take the free trolley tour of the Coral Gables art district. The tour runs from 7 to 10pm; meet at Elite (listed below) or any of the other participating galleries in the area.

On the second Saturday of the month, you can actually meet artists and see them working during the Lincoln Road Gallery Walk at the **Art Center,** 924 and 1035 Lincoln Rd. (☎ **305/674-8278**), from 7 to 11pm. Join a knowledgeable guide for a tour of more than 50 artists' studios.

Ambrosino Gallery. 3095 SW 39th Ave. (1 block south of Bird Rd.), Miami. ☎ **305/445-2211.**

This well-respected gallery shows works by contemporary artists and stages performance art and installations. Closed for Christmas holidays.

Elite Fine Art. 3140 Ponce de Leon Blvd., Coral Gables. ☎ **305/448-3800.**

Touted as one of the finest galleries in Miami, Elite features modern and contemporary Latin American painters and sculptors.

✪ Evelyn S. Poole Ltd. 3925 N. Miami Ave., Miami. ☎ **305/573-7463.**

Known as the most fine of the fine antiques collections, the Poole assortment of European 17th-, 18th-, and 19th-century decorative furniture and accessories is housed in 5,000 square feet of space in the newly revived Decorator's Row. Celebrity clients shop for that special "statement piece" in these vast museum-like galleries.

Meza Fine Art. 275 Giralda Ave., Coral Gables. ☎ **305/461-2723.**

This gallery specializes in Latin American artists, including Carlos Betancourt, Javier Marin, and Gloria Lorenzo.

Books

Barnes and Noble Booksellers. More than 6 locations in Miami. Check the phone book for details.

With half a dozen outlets in the area and more on the way, this huge chain offers anything readers could ask for, including a comfortable cafe, a large children's section, and tons of magazines. Plus, you'll get a 10 percent discount on all Best Sellers and incredible close-out specials. They often schedule readings with noted authors, too.

✪ Books & Books. 296 Aragon Ave., Coral Gables. ☎ **305/442-4408.** Another location at 933 Lincoln Rd., South Beach. ☎ **305/532-3222.**

Dedicated followers turn out to browse at this warm and wonderful little independent shop. Enjoy the upstairs antiquarian room, which specializes in art books and first-edition literature. If that's not enough intellectual stimulation for you, the shop hosts free lectures from noted authors and experts almost nightly.

At the Lincoln Road location, you'll rub elbows with tanned and buffed South Beach bookworms sipping cappuccinos at the Russian Bear Cafe inside the store. They stock a large selection of gay literature.

Grove Antiquarian. 3318 Virginia St., Coconut Grove. ☎ **305/444-5362.**

One of very few out-of-print bookstores in Miami, Grove Antiquarian specializes in books about Florida and the Caribbean, but it also boasts a large selection of out-of-print cookbooks, sci-fi books, and first editions.

Kafka's Cyberkafe. 1464 Washington Ave., South Beach. ☎ **305/673-9669.**

Check your e-mail and surf the Net while you sip a latte or snack on a sandwich or pastry with friendly neighborhood regulars. This popular used bookstore also stocks a wide range of foreign and domestic magazines.

Cigars & Cigarettes

Although it is illegal to bring Cuban cigars into this country, somehow Cohibas show up at every dinner party and nightclub in town. Not that I condone it, but if you hang around the cigar smokers in town, no doubt one will be able to tell you where you can get some of the highly prized contraband. Be careful, however, of counterfeits.

The stores listed below sell excellent hand-rolled cigars made with domestic and foreign-grown tobacco. Many of the *viejos* (old men) got their training in Cuba working for the government-owned factories in the heyday of Cuban cigars.

☼ La Gloria Cubana. 1106 SW 8th St., Little Havana. ☎ **305/858-4162.**

This tiny storefront shop employs about 45 veteran Cuban rollers, who sit all day rolling the very popular torpedoes and other critically acclaimed blends. They've got back orders until next Christmas, but it's worth stopping in. They will sell you a box and show you around.

Miccosukee Tobacco Shop. 850 SW 177th Ave. (Krome Ave. and Tamiami Trail), Miami. ☎ **305/226-2701.**

At this remote Native-American–owned outpost, you are spared the state cigarette tax—national brands are available for $14 a carton, generics from $8 to $13.

Mike's Cigars. 1030 Kane Concourse (at 96th St.), Bay Harbor Island. ☎ **305/866-2277.**

Mike's recently moved to this location, but it's one of the oldest smoke shops in town. Since 1950, Mike's has been selling the best from Honduras, the Dominican Republic, and Jamaica, as well as the very hot local brand La Gloria Cubana. Most say it has the best prices, too.

COSMETICS, FRAGRANCES & BEAUTY PRODUCTS

☼ Browne's & Co. 841 Lincoln Rd., South Beach. ☎ **305/532-8703.**

Designed to look like an old-fashioned apothecary, this beauty emporium combines the city's best selection of makeup and hair products—MAC, Shu Uemura, Kiehl's, Stila, and Dr. Hauschka just to name a few—with lots of delicious-smelling bath and body stuff, plus a full-service beauty salon.

Perfumania. More than a dozen locations in Miami. Check the phone book for details.

This huge chain has many popular fragrances for men and women at discount prices. They also sell makeup and skin-care products. It's a great place to pick up a gift basket.

ELECTRONICS

The Sharper Image. 401 Biscayne Blvd. (in the Bayside Marketplace). ☎ **305/374-8539.** Another location in the Dadeland Mall, at 7507 N. Kendall Dr., South Miami. ☎ **305/667-9970.**

Electronics nuts will love this store. It tends to be high-end, both in merchandise and price, but it's free just to look and touch (yes, you're allowed); so even if you're not buying, visit the store to see what's new in the high-tech world.

Sound Advice. 12200 N. Kendall Dr., Kendall. ☎ **305/273-1225.** Other locations at 17641 Biscayne Blvd., Aventura (☎ **305/933-4434**), and 1222 S. Dixie Hwy., Coral Gables (☎ **305/665-4434**).

An audio junkie's candy store, Sound Advice features the latest in high-end stereo equipment, as well as TVs, VCRs, and telephone equipment. Techno-minded, but sometimes pushy, salespeople are on hand to help.

Spy Shops International Inc. 280 NE 4th St. ☎ **305/374-4779.**

This store is perfect for James Bond wanna-be's looking to buy electronic-surveillance equipment, day and night optical devices, stun guns, minisafes, doorknob alarms, and other anticrime gadgets.

FASHION

For the best quality designer clothes, Bal Harbour shops is your best bet. See "Malls," below.

   On the other end of the spectrum, you may want to try the popular Loehmann's (see below) for designer clothing, shoes, and accessories at deeply discounted prices. Or consider hunting the thrift stores and resale shops (see below).

Island Trading. 1332 Ocean Dr., South Beach. ☎ **305/673-6300.**

One more part of music mogul Chris Blackwell's empire, Island sells everything you'll need to wear in the tropical resort town, like batik sarongs, sandals, sundresses, bathing suits, cropped tops, and more. Many of the unique styles are created on the premises by a team of young and innovative designers.

✪ **Loehmann's.** 18701 Biscayne Blvd. (Fashion Island), North Miami Beach. ☎ **305/932-4207.**

Loehmann's has added men's clothing and shoes to its huge stock of women's wear. This discount mecca is the place to find designer clothes at bargain prices. But you've got to hunt. If you don't mind communal dressing rooms and hordes of zealous shoppers, look here for great deals on everything from bathing suits to evening wear.

Men's

Brooks Brothers. 9700 Collins Ave. (in the Bal Harbour Shops), Miami Beach. ☎ **305/865-8686.** Also at 8888 Howard Dr. (in The Falls shopping complex), Kendall. ☎ **305/259-7870.**

If you need a new navy blazer or some khaki trousers to roll up for an oceanfront stroll, shop here for the classics.

Giorgio's. 208 Miracle Mile, Coral Gables. ☎ **305/448-4302.**

One of the finest custom men's stores, Giorgio's features an extensive line of Italian suits and all the latest by Canelli.

Hugo Boss. 9700 Collins Ave., Miami Beach. ☎ **305/864-7753.**

One of many men's stores in Bal Harbour, this one appeals to hipsters and businessmen alike who are willing to pay big money for the latest styles.

Women's

A B S Clothing Collection. 226 8th St., South Beach. ☎ **305/672-8887.**

This California-based chain store fits right into South Beach. You'll find both trendy and professional stuff for women here, from zebra-print minis to tailored pantsuits.

Alice's Day Off. 5900 SW 72nd St., South Miami. ☎ **305/284-0301.** Also at the Miami International Mall, 1477 NW 107th Ave., Miami. ☎ **305/477-0393.**

For beachwear, Alice's is the place. It comes out season after season with pretty and flattering floral patterns and many flashy bikinis. If an itsy-bitsy bikini is not your style, Alice's has a range of more modest cuts for those not shaped like a Baywatch babe.

Betsey Johnson. 805 Washington Ave., South Beach. ☎ **305/673-0023.**

This New York–based shop sells slightly wild, faddish clothes for the young and young at heart, made of stretchy materials, velvet, knits, and more.

Therapy. 1065 Kane Concourse, Bay Harbor Islands. ☎ **305/861-6900.**

Opened by Ellen Lansburgh, who ran successful shops in Aspen and New York which catered to a famous clientele, including Cher and Goldie Hawn, this intimate boutique has one-of-a-kind pieces. The clothes, made of the most luxurious fabrics, like silk, taffeta, and tulle, are elegant and comfortable.

LINGERIE

Belinda's. 827 Washington Ave., South Beach. ☎ **305/532-0068.**

This German designer makes some of the most beautiful and intricate teddies, nightgowns, and wedding dresses. The styles are a little too Stevie Nicks for me to actually consider wearing in public, but the creations are absolutely worth admiring. The prices are appropriately up there.

Corset Corner. 300 Miracle Mile, Coral Gables. ☎ **305/444-6643.**

As the name suggests, this little old store on Miracle Mile sells the basic, good old-fashioned gear.

La Perla. 9700 Collins Ave. (in the Bal Harbour Shops), Bal Harbour. ☎ **305/864-2070.**

This is the only store in Florida that specializes in super-luxurious Italian intimate apparel. Of course, you could fly to Milan for the price of a few bras and a nightgown, but you can't find better quality. Also in Bal Harbour, see **Flash Lingerie** (☎ **305/868-7732**), which carries a diverse selection of imports.

Victoria's Secret. 3015 Grand Ave., Coconut Grove. ☎ **305/443-2365.** Other locations at 401 Biscayne Blvd., Miami (☎ **305/374-8030**), and Aventura Mall (☎ **305/932-0150**).

You've seen the sexy catalogs—now see the goods up close. The many shops in town stock the basic undergarments in shimmery rayons and polys, as well as a few Chinese silk robes and undies. You'll find one of the largest selections of thongs anywhere.

JEWELRY

The International Jeweler's Exchange. 18861 Biscayne Blvd. (in the Fashion Island), North Miami Beach. ☎ **305/931-7032.** Closed Mon.

At least 50 jewelers hustle their wares from individual counters at one of the city's most active jewelry centers. Haggle your brains out for excellent prices on timeless antiques from Tiffany's, Cartier, or Bulgari or on unique designs you can create yourself.

The Seybold Building. 36 NE 1st St., Downtown. ☎ **305/374-7922.**

Jewelers of every assortment gather here daily to sell their diamonds and gold. The glare is blinding as you enter this multilevel retail marketplace. You'll see handsome and up-to-date designs, but note that there aren't too many bargains to be had here.

MALLS

There are so many malls in Miami and more being built that it would be impossible to mention them all. Following is a list of the biggest and most popular: **Aventura Mall** in Aventura, ☎ 305/935-1110; ○ **Bal Harbour Shops** in Bal Harbour, ☎ 305/866-0311 (one of the most prestigious fashion meccas in the country); **Bayside Marketplace,** located Downtown, ☎ 305/577-3344; ○ **Dadeland Mall** in Kendall, ☎ 305/665-6226; **Dolphin Mall** in West Miami ☎ 305/642-1643; **Miami International Mall** in Miami, ☎ 305/593-1775; **The Falls Shopping Center** in Kendall, ☎ 305/255-4570; and **The Shops of Sunset Place** in South Miami, ☎ 305/663-9110.

MUSIC & MUSICAL EQUIPMENT

Blue Note Records. 16401 NE 15th Ave., North Miami Beach. ☎ **305/940-3394.**

For more than 15 years, Blue Note has been stocking hard-to-find progressive and underground music. There are new, used, and discounted CDs, and old vinyl, too. Call to find out about performances. Some great names show up occasionally.

Casino Records Inc. 1208 SW 8th St., Little Havana. ☎ **305/856-6888.**

The young, hip salespeople speak English and tend to be music buffs themselves. Here you'll find the largest selection of Latin music in Miami, including pop icons such as Willy Chirino, Gloria Estefan, Albita, and local boy Nil Lara. Their slogan translates to "If we don't have it, forget it." Believe me, they've got it.

CD Warehouse. 13150 Biscayne Blvd., North Miami. ☎ **305/892-1048.** Also at 1590 S. Dixie Hwy., Coral Gables. ☎ **305/662-7100.**

Buy, sell, or trade your old CDs at this eclectic music hut.

Mars (Music and Recording Superstore). 12115 Biscayne Blvd., North Miami. ☎ **305/893-0191.**

You could spend a week here. With 35,000 square feet of space, Mars offers everything from musical instruments to sheet music, plus a recording studio, live stage, and repair center.

Revolution Records and CDs. 1620 Alton Rd., Miami Beach. ☎ **305/673-6464.**

Here you'll find a quaint and fairly well-organized collection of CDs, from hard-to-find jazz to original recordings of Buddie Rich. They'll search for anything and let you hear whatever you like.

Virgin Records. 5701 Sunset Place (at the Shops of Sunset), South Miami. ☎ **305/665-4445.**

Under construction at press time, this enormous music store (33,000 square feet) promises to indulge shoppers with listening booths and an "in-store radio station." They stock a huge collection of CDs, cassettes, and videos.

SEAFOOD

East Coast Fisheries. 330 W. Flagler St., Downtown. ☎ **305/577-3000.**

This retail market and restaurant (see the review in chapter 4), has sent millions of pounds of seafood worldwide from its own fishing fleet. Order 5- or 10-pound packages of stone-crab claws, Florida lobsters, Florida Bay pompano, fresh Key West shrimp, and a variety of other local delicacies to be shipped via overnight delivery.

Joe's Stone Crab. 227 Biscayne St., South Beach. ☎ **305/673-0365** or 800/780-CRAB.

If you've never tasted Florida's favorite seafood, you must. And once you do, you'll want more. Or, you may want to send some to very dear friends at home (they are pricier than lobster). Joe's, Miami's most famous restaurant (see the review in chapter 4) ships stone crabs anywhere in the country, but only during the season, which runs from mid-October through mid-May.

SPORTS EQUIPMENT

From golf to tennis, scuba to fishing, South Florida is a virtual playground. And, of course, you can find all the toys to outfit yourself nearby. One of the area's largest chains is the Sports Authority, with at least six locations throughout the county. Check the white pages for details.

Alf's Golf Shop. 524 Arthur Godfrey Rd., Miami Beach. ☎ **305/673-6568.** Also at 15369 S. Dixie Hwy., Miami. ☎ **305/378-6086.**

The best pro shop around, Alf's can sell you balls, clubs, gloves, and instructional videos. The knowledgeable staff has equipment for golfers of every level, and the neighboring golf course offers discounts to Alf's clients.

Bass Pro Shops Outdoor World. 200 Gulf Stream Way, Dania. ☎ **954/929-7710.**

Fishing enthusiasts and sports enthusiasts must head north to Broward County to see the huge retail complex that offers demonstrations in fly fishing, archery and pistol ranges, classes in marine safety, and every conceivable gadget you could ask for. (See chapter 8 for more details.)

Bird's Surf Shop. 250 Sunny Isles Blvd., North Miami Beach. ☎ **305/940-0929.**

If you're a hard-core surfer or just want to look like one, head to Bird's Surf Shop. Although Miami doesn't regularly get huge swells, if you're here during the winter and one should happen to hit, you'll be ready. The shop carries more than 150 boards. Call its **surf line** (☎ **305/947-7170**) to find the best waves from South Beach to Cape Hatteras and even the Bahamas and Florida's West Coast.

Edwin Watts Golf Shops. 15100 N. Biscayne Blvd., North Miami Beach. ☎ **305/944-2925.**

One of 30 Edwin Watts shops throughout the Southeast, this full-service golf retail shop is one of the most popular in Miami. You can find it all, including clothing, pro-line equipment, gloves, bags, balls, videos, and books. Plus, you can get coupons for discounted greens fees on many courses.

Island Water Sports. 16231 Biscayne Blvd. ☎ **305/944-0104.**

You'll find everything from booties to gloves to baggies and tanks. Check in here before you rent that Wave Runner or Windsurfer.

Nevada Bob's. 7930 NW 36th Ave. (near the airport), Miami. ☎ **305/593-2999.**

This chain store guarantees the lowest prices on golf equipment and accessories. There's more than 6,000 square feet of store here; you can even practice your swing at an indoor driving range with a radar gun to clock your speed.

X-Isle Surf Shop. 437 Washington Ave., South Beach. ☎ **305/673-5900.** Free surf report at ☎ 305/534-7873.

Prices are slightly higher at this beach location, but you'll find the hottest styles and equipment. They also offer surfboard rental.

14 Miami After Dark

Miami's nightlife is as varied as its population.

One of the most surprising aspects of the city is the recent growth of its cultural scene. While none of it would rank as world-class, Miami now has a talented symphony, a few notable fine art galleries, a decent opera company, some fine theater, a well-respected ballet company, and occasionally great concerts.

Then again, most travelers probably don't come to Miami in order to expand their cultural horizons. After the sun goes down, the club scene is Miami's biggest attraction, and most of the action can be found in South Beach.

Unfortunately, Miami seems to have trouble sustaining consistently good live music. In the past few years, Miami has watched more than a dozen music clubs shut their doors. Some blame the lack of community support; others say it's Miami's remote geographic location, too far a drive for bands to include on their circuit; still others claim promoters in town don't work hard enough to entice good musicians to venture down here. That being said, there are still some excellent venues for live music, especially popular spots for jazz and Latin music.

Cuban and Caribbean rhythms fit the bill for this sultry town. The beat makes dancing irresistible, as do some of the world's best deejays who show up during the season, like David Padilla, JoJo Odyssey, Junior Vazquez, and David Knapp.

For up-to-date entertainment listings, check *The Miami Herald's* "Weekend" section, which runs on Fridays, or the more comprehensive listings in *New Times,* Miami's free alternative weekly, available each Wednesday. This award-winning paper prints articles, reviews, and advertisements on upcoming local events. Several telephone hotlines—many operated by local radio stations—give free recorded information on

---

Impressions _____

Party in the city where the heat is on, all night on the beach til the break of dawn.
Welcome to Miami. Bienvenido a Miami.

—Will Smith, 1999

---

current events in the city. They include the **Planet Radio Stuff To Do Hotline**
(☎ 305/770-2513), the **Zeta Concert Hotline** (☎ 305/770-2515), and the **UM
Concert Hotline** (☎ 305/284-6477). Other information lines are listed under the
appropriate headings below.

Tickets for many performances are handled by **Ticketmaster;** call ☎ 305/
358-5885 to charge tickets. For hard-to-get seats, try a ticket broker. Fran at **Sold-
Out Events** (☎ 305/534-2021) can usually find what you need. Otherwise, call
Ultimate Travel & Entertainment (☎ 305/444-8499).

BARS

There are countless bars in and around Miami, with the highest concentration on
trendy South Beach. Keeping track of them all would be a full-time job. Hmmm . . .
and not a bad one at that. The selection listed below is a mere sample. Keep in mind
that many of the popular bars are in hotels. On the beach, you'd do best to walk along
Ocean Drive and Washington Avenue to see what's hot. In Coconut Grove, check out
CocoWalk and Mayfair next door. Unless listed, the bars below generally don't charge
a cover. Most require proof that you are over 21 to enter, though some allow patrons
over 18 to enter but not drink.

✪ **The Clevelander.** 1020 Ocean Dr., South Beach. ☎ **305/531-3485.** No cover.

This old standby on one of Ocean Drive's busiest and most spacious corners is always
crowded. You'll find mostly preppy types gathered around the large outdoor pool area
up until 5am. Cheap drinks in plastic cups complete the beachy atmosphere in this
casual, spring-breaky bar.

The Delano. 1685 Collins Ave., South Beach. ☎ **305/672-2000.**

I'm surprised they haven't started charging admission to this spectacular attraction.
In the lobby is the Rose Bar, one of the best spots in South Beach to see beautiful
people decked out in trendy splendor. Lounge on a cushy sofa or in any of the plump
beds casually arranged throughout the lobby and backyard, and grab an expensive
drink.

Firehouse Four. 1000 S. Miami Ave., South Beach. ☎ **305/371-3473.** Cover varies
$0–$10.

Renowned for its raucous weekday happy hours, this old favorite had closed for several years only to resurface in late 1998 to the thrill of its former downtown corporate
patrons. Well, the ties come off after 5, and nobody works as hard as the deejays, who
keep the place rocking. Each night attracts a slightly different crowd depending on the
music. Thursday night is old Havana night. Call for a schedule.

✪ **The Forge.** 432 41st St., Miami Beach. ☎ **305/538-8533.**

Step back in time at this ultraelegant restaurant and bar, where Wednesday night is the
night to hang with dolled-up Euro-singles and New Yorkers. Call well in advance if
you want to watch the parade of characters from your dinner table (see chapter 4). An
elegant nightclub called Jimmy'z, a spin-off of Regine's, is adjacent. They say it's a private club, but if you dine at the restaurant or know someone, you can get in. Rumored

to open soon is a spin-off of the popular Latin hot spot Club Nostalgia (see "Latin Clubs," below).

Howl at the Moon Saloon. 3015 Grand Ave. (CocoWalk), Coconut Grove. ☎ **305/442-8300.** Cover $5–$10.

Drink specials are a regular fixture at night throughout the week, except Monday, when the Moon is dark. On Sunday, beers are $1.75 a pop. On Thursday night, 19- and 20-year-olds are let in, and those over 21 with a college ID can skip the cover and simply enjoy cheap buckets of beer.

Mac's Club Deuce. 222 14th St., South Beach. ☎ **305/673-9537.**

Housed in a squat, neon-covered deco building, this dive is popular with bikers, barflies, and pool players who love the dark and smoky scene. It's a real local's favorite for those who like to slum it. Here you'll no doubt catch a great conversation, some old tunes on the jukebox, or a good scene out the front picture window that faces a busy all-night tattoo parlor. Mac's is open daily from 8am to 5am. Yes, that's am.

Molly Malone's. 166 Sunny Isles Blvd. (just west of Collins Ave.), Sunny Isles Beach. ☎ **305/948-3512.**

Open all day and into the next, Molly's is a divey Irish pub, popular with young and old drinkers and folk lovers alike. There are a pool table and darts, occasional Irish rock or acoustic music, and, of course, a selection of good ales and lagers.

Murphy's Law Irish Pub. 2977 McFarlane Dr., Coconut Grove. ☎ **305/446-9956.**

This wood and brass-decorated Irish pub is for those who want to escape the more antiseptic night scene at CocoWalk down the road. Weekends offer live music, Irish or otherwise. A big-screen TV shows sports events, but this place is really about sharing a pint or two at the bar with old-timers, grungers, and young professionals.

✪ Tantra. 1445 Pennsylvania Ave. (at Espa-ola Way), South Beach. ☎ **305/672-4765.**

This super-sexy restaurant/lounge continues to be the place for the beautiful-in-black crowd. It looks like some luxurious opium den in Marrakesh from the minute you step into a small entryway covered with real grass. Continue into the lounge, where you'll find a stone waterfall, huge Indian sculptures, smoky lanterns, and low curtained tables. Plus, the food (said to have aphrodisiacal properties) is excellent, if a bit overpriced. Dinner reservations are hard to get, and a spot at the bar is even tougher, especially after 11pm.

Wet Willies. 760 Ocean Dr., South Beach. ☎ **305/532-5650.**

The upstairs deck overlooking Ocean Drive is one of the prime spots for watching the hectic parade that defines South Beach craziness. From up here, you can see the ocean as well as the spectacle of folks who walk the strip night and day. After just one Wet Willie frozen concoction, you may not be able to see much of anything. Watch out: They taste like soda pop but bite like a mad dog.

There's another Wet Willie's in Coconut Grove at 3390 Mary St., ☎ **305/443-5060,** on the third level of Mayfair.

LIVE MUSIC

Despite the spotty success of local music, Latin musicians such as Cuban diva Albita, Nil Lara, Willy Chirino, and, of course, Gloria Estefan got their start here. Julio Iglesias plays occasionally and Arturo Sandoval just moved here after defecting from Cuba.

Factoid

To find out about the latest clubs on South Beach, check with the "Virtual Doorman" on Ocean Drive's Web site, www.oceandrive.com, where a clever answer to weekly quizzes could win you a free night in a hip hotel and an escort past the velvet ropes into the club of the minute.

South Florida's jazz scene is also very much alive with traditional and contemporary performers. Keep an eye out for guitarist Randy Bernsen, vibraphonist Tom Toyama, Melton Mustafah and the flutist Nestor Torres, and many young performers who lead local ensembles. Many come out of the University of Miami's well-respected jazz studies program (☎ **305/284-6477**), which often schedules low- and no-cost recitals. Additionally, many area hotels feature live music of every description. Schedules are listed in the newspaper entertainment sections.

Churchill's Hideaway. 5501 NE Second Ave., Miami. ☎ **305/757-1807.** Cover $0–$5, depending on the band.

It's a dive in a pretty rough neighborhood, but if you want to sample Miami's local music scene, Churchill's is the place to go. You might even see a fledgling band before it makes it big. At this British pub (hence the name Churchill's), you can snack on rustic shepherd's pie and good English brew. And for those homesick Brits craving a good game of rugby, Churchill's is probably the only place that broadcasts English sports via satellite. Call ahead—there has been talk of this place shutting its doors.

The Globe. 377 Alhambra Circle (at LeJeune), Coral Gables. ☎ **305/445-3555.** No cover.

This odd little cafe is attached to a travel agency. On weekends, a red curtain transforms a corner into a stage, where you'll find decent jazz and good food, too. (See "Dining" in chapter 4.)

The Hungry Sailor. 3426 Main Hwy., Coconut Grove. ☎ **305/444-9359.** Cover Fri and Sat $5–$10. Closed Mon.

This small English-style pub has Watney's, Bass, and Guinness and reggae regularly on tap, too. This place attracts an extremely mixed crowd. Sunday is dancehall reggae night and Wednesday it's ska. On other nights, you might find other live music or dance music provided by a deejay.

Luna Star Cafe. 775 NE 125th St., North Miami. ☎ **305/892-8522.**

One of the only venues for folk musicians (there is also John Martin's), this cozy little club sponsors several open mike nights. Be warned; there are a lot of uninhibited amateurs out there. But, hey, it's better than Karaoke, and occasionally you hear some fantastic stuff.

Jazid. 1342 Washington Ave., South Beach. ☎ **305/673-9372.** No cover nightly 9pm–2am.

This split-level jazz club is an unlikely spot to find on South Beach. It's warm, welcoming, cheap and even has a pool table. Music ranges from classic jazz to blues and often includes talented locals.

Power Studios. 3701 NE 2nd Ave., Miami. ☎ **305/573-8042.** Cover varies.

Opened in an up-and-coming (seedy) area just north of downtown known as the "Design District," this large warehousey club features live music on Fridays and Saturdays—mostly jazz and blues. There's plenty of room to dance.

Rose's Bar and Lounge. 754 Washington Ave., South Beach. ☎ **305/532-0228.** Cover $3–$15 Tues–Sun, depending on show.

This hip South Beach bar features local music—live rock, jazz, or whatever else strikes your fancy or theirs—almost every night on its tiny stage. Get there early to beat the crowds and claim a spot among the sparse seating. Open every night from 5pm to 5am.

Taurus. 3540 Main Hwy., Coconut Grove. ☎ **305/448-0633.** No cover.

This rustic old favorite survived the gentrification of the surrounding area and still feels like the Grove used to. It's funky and grungy and full of great characters. Hear old rock and roll and soak up some local color. Open until midnight.

○ **Tobacco Road.** 626 S. Miami Ave. (over the Miami Ave. Bridge near Brickell Ave.), Downtown. ☎ **305/374-1198.** Cover $0–$8.

This Miami institution is a must-see. It's been around since 1912 doing more in the back room than just dancing. These days, you'll find a good bar menu along with the best live music anywhere—blues, zydeco, brass, jazz, and more. Regular performers include The Dirty Dozen Brass band from New Orleans, who play a mean mix of zydeco and blues with an actual dozen brass players; Bill Warton and the Ingredients, who make a pot of gumbo while up on stage; Monkey Meet; Iko Iko; Chubby Carrier and his band; and many more. Escape the smoke and sweat in the backyard patio, where air is a welcome commodity. The downright-cheap nightly specials, such as the $10 lobster on Tuesdays, are quite good and are served until 2am. The club is open until 5am.

Van Dyke Cafe. 846 Lincoln Rd., Miami Beach. ☎ **305/534-3600.** Cover varies $3–$6.

Enjoy live jazz 7 nights a week until midnight in an elegant upstairs lounge that features the likes of Eddie Higgins, Mike Renzi, and locals such as Don Wilner, who play strictly jazz for a well-dressed crowd of enthusiasts. You can have a drink or two at the pristine oak bar or enjoy some snacks from the bustling patio seats below.

DANCE CLUBS

In addition to quiet cafes and progressive poolside bars, Miami Beach pulsates with one of the liveliest night scenes in the city. Also check out the "Latin Clubs" listings, later in this chapter, for more places to dance.

A popular trend in Miami's club scene are "one-off" nights—events organized by a promoter and held in established venues on irregular schedules. Word of mouth, local advertising, and listings in the free weekly *New Times* are the best ways to find out about these hot events. You can also try asking a cool-looking waiter or waitress at some South Beach eatery.

And just for the record: No, Madonna, the original Material Girl, does not own a nightclub in South Beach. The club that uses her name on its oversized billboard on Washington Avenue is a strip joint, one of a handful in South Beach.

Bash. 655 Washington Ave., South Beach. ☎ **305/538-2274.** BarBashClub.com. Cover $15 weeknights and $20 weekends.

This place has been around longer than most and is still pretty hot. Bash gets going late and features an eclectic mix of music, including Euro-dance, disco, and funk, as well as special events, such as occasional funky fashion shows. The crowd is incredibly Euro-hip and super trendy. On weekends the back patio is open and plays World Beat music. Open every night but Monday from 10pm to 5am.

Rock 'n' Bowl

The latest fad to hit Miami is "Rave" bowling. Cloverleaf Lanes at 17601 NW 2nd Ave., North Dade (☎ **305/652-4197**), sets up glow-in-the dark pins and turns the lights low and the music high every Friday and Saturday night from 8:30pm until 3am. Games are $4.50 each. Shoes and balls are an extra $2. It's become especially popular with teens who are too young to get into the clubs.

Bermuda Bar and Grill. 3509 NE 163rd St., North Miami. ☎ **305/945-0196.** Cover $0–$10. No cover before 9pm.

This huge suburban danceteria specializes in ladies' nights (Wed and Thurs). Plus, it hosts cash-prize contests for women who wear the skimpiest outfits. Still, everybody loves the high-energy music that packs the dance floor. Thursday is Latin night and Friday features happy hour from 5 to 8pm. Saturday is the biggest night, when all the goings-on are broadcast live on a local radio station. Good pizzas and grilled foods are available, too. It's usually open until the sun comes up. Closed Monday, Tuesday, and Sunday.

Cafe Iguana. 8505 Mills Dr. (Town & Country Mall on the corner of 88th St. and 117th Ave.), Kendall. ☎ **305/274-4948.** Cover $0–$10.

This tropical-themed bar and dance club is a bit much for low-key club-goers, but for those looking for a high-energy party, it's the place to be. Everything from male and female hot-body contests to a raging Latin night are incorporated into this nightspot.

Chaos. 743 Washington Ave., South Beach. ☎ **305/674-7350.** Cover usually $20.

Miami's club of the moment, this is where Oliver Stone, Harrison Ford, and other celebs spend their nights when on the beach. Don't expect easy entry, since the people waiting on the sidewalk often outnumber the truly fabulous inside. Music in this intimate enclave ranges from Eurohouse to retro but is always danceable. Open Wednesday to Saturday from 11pm to 5am.

Club St. Croix. 3015 Grand Ave., Coconut Grove (CocoWalk). ☎ **305/446-4999.** Cover $0–$15.

How many bodies can fit in one club? Club St. Croix has made it its mission to find out. If you're not blinded by the pulsating disco lights and shocking Caribbean decor, and you love loud dance music and scantily clad bodies, you'll enjoy this suburban bar scene. The club normally opens at 9pm and closes at 5am except on Thursday and Friday, when the party starts at 4pm for happy hour. Open Wednesday to Sunday.

821. 821 Lincoln Rd., South Beach. ☎ **305/531-1188.** No cover.

On most nights, 821 is more gay than straight. It's something between a neighborhood bar and a nightclub, with a deejay or live music every night. Thursday night is for women only and usually features a cabaret singer. Friday night is all boys, and boy, can they party. Offering a good mix of music and people, this hot spot is a Lincoln Road staple that's open daily from 3pm until 3 or 5am.

Groove Jet. 323 23rd St. (1 block west of Collins Ave.), South Beach. ☎ **305/532-5150.** Cover $10–$20.

This fantastic hidden spot north of the South Beach scene has been through many incarnations. Its most recent, Groove Jet, has three distinct areas playing totally different music. Deep house, jungle, and trance tunes are usually heard in the front

Breaking Through the Velvet Ropes

In Miami, there are certain clued-in people who seem to know everyone on the club scene—they always look fabulous and never fret when they spy a mob at the door of the hippest spot in town. You've seen them kissing each other on both cheeks. Unless you're one of them, you may want to check out these basic rules regarding club-admission etiquette:

- Never ever wear blue jeans, shorts, or sneakers. Most clubs with a discretionary door policy see only black or shades of gray—the hipper the better.
- Bring women. At the risk of sounding sexist, there is a direct mathematical relationship between the number of attractive females in your group and your likeliness of getting into a hot club. Blonde, busty babes in skimpy clothes count for two. Half a dozen guys without dates might as well look for the nearest frat party or pool hall.
- Call ahead to request a VIP table. You'll spend more than a couple of hundred dollars for overpriced bottles of Dom Perignon or Absolut, but at least you're guaranteed to get in.
- Call a day or two in advance and get phone-friendly with someone whose name you can drop at the door.
- Fax a guest list early in the day and wait for a confirmation number.
- Don't ever flash cash at a doorman. You're better off tipping the concierge at your hotel, who can make arrangements to get on a guest list.
- Check your attitude at the sidewalk. "Don't you know who I am?" doesn't work. Be polite and positive; screaming and yelling doesn't work.
- Arrive before midnight. The later it gets, the less likely you'll get in—no matter who you are. When a club gets too full, the fire marshals show up and even Donald Trump gets the cold shoulder.

Know when to give up. If you've been hanging out for more than 20 or 30 minutes and have been looked over by the dude with the clipboard, you have probably already been pegged as a "no way." There are plenty of other hot spots in town, so try elsewhere.

As a last resort, tag onto a hip crowd (this works only for one or two). When you see a good-looking crew get the nod, grab the hand of the last one in line and follow along as if you know what you're doing.

room, with more experimental music in the back rooms. A very hip young crowd hangs in this out-of-the-way scene, which doesn't really get going until after hours (usually after 2am), Thursday to Sunday 11pm to 5am.

Liquid and The Lounge. 1439 Washington Ave., South Beach. ☎ **305/532-9154** for information, 305/532-8899 for table reservations. Cover $10–$20.

Liquid is reminiscent of the 1980s New York club scene, so you can expect to wait at the ropes until a disdainful bouncer chooses you. Don't dare to wear the usual casual South Beach attire; they are looking for "casual chic." Once inside, you'll find a pulsing, cavernous space with up-to-the-minute dance music and half a dozen packed bars, VIP seating in a cozy back area, a hip-hop side room, and a downstairs lounge playing jazz and funk. Sunday night is gay. The club opens doors at 11pm but the action starts late (around 2am).

Living Room at the Strand. 671 Washington Ave., South Beach. ☎ **305/532-2340.** Cover $5–$15.

This very Euro hot spot is the place to mix and mingle with South Beach's beautiful crowd. Models and moguls alike converge here to drink and relive the art of conversation, until the music gets loud after about 10pm.

THE GAY & LESBIAN SCENE

The gay and lesbian scene in Miami is outrageous, especially on South Beach.

Much to the shock of tourists who haven't been around, gay men and women are often seen hugging, kissing, or just holding hands in clubs and bars or walking down the street. Still, most of the gay clubs welcome hetero visitors, too. And many of the normally "straight" clubs also have gay nights. Miami Beach is one of the major stops for circuit parties around the U.S.

Amnesia. 136 Collins Ave., South Beach. ☎ **305/531-5535.**

This huge indoor-outdoor favorite hosts tea dances where buffed boys parade around in minuscule outfits while dance music plays in the background.

Loading Zone. 1426 Alton Rd., Miami Beach. ☎ **305/531-5623.** No cover.

The town's only leather bar, complete with hot men, sexy videos, and, in case you forgot something, a leather shop in back.

Salvation. 1771 West Ave., Miami Beach. ☎ **305/673-6508.** Cover varies.

Probably the largest gay dance party in the state, with pumping dance music and some of South Beach's most recognized—and wildest—drag queens. It's a weekly party at a huge place and it goes on until the sun comes up.

Twist. 1057 Washington Ave., South Beach. ☎ **305/53-TWIST.** No cover.

One of the beach's most popular cruise bars, Twist attracts mostly male clientele but has an open-door policy. Open daily from 1pm to 5am.

Warsaw Ballroom. 1450 Collins Ave., South Beach. ☎ **305/531-4555.** Cover $10–$15.

One of Miami's oldest and most fun nightclubs, Warsaw hosts various theme nights (Wed is the amateur strip contest) and some of the best dance music in town. After all these years, regulars still line up out the door, waiting to get in and dance until 5am.

West End. 942 Lincoln Rd., South Beach. ☎ **305/538-9378.** No cover.

A mellow bar and pool hall on weekdays, this Lincoln Road standby gets funky on the weekends when a deejay takes over. It's a favorite hangout for women and men. Enjoy a relaxed atmosphere and a good happy hour. Open 2pm to 5am on weekdays and noon to 5am on weekends.

LATIN CLUBS

Considering that Hispanics make up the majority of Miami's population and that there's a huge influx of Spanish-speaking visitors, it's no surprise that there are some great Latin nightclubs in the city.

Plus, with the meteoric rise of the international music scene based in Miami, many international stars come through the offices of MTV Latino, SONY International, and a multitude of Latin TV studios based in Miami—and they're all looking for a good club scene on weekends. Most of the Anglo clubs reserve at least 1 night a week for Latin rhythms.

Alcazaba. 50 Alhambra Plaza (in the Hyatt Regency Coral Gables), Coral Gables. ☎ **305/441-1234.**

The Hyatt's Top-40 lounge plays an eclectic mix of music but exudes a decidedly Mediterranean atmosphere that mixes fantasy with reality. Chill out with some tropical drinks and authentic tapas between songs. Happy hour—Wednesday and Friday from 5 to 7pm and Saturday from 9 to 11pm—offers half-price beer, wine, and drinks, plus a free buffet.

✪ **Cafe Nostalgia.** 2212 SW 8th St. (Calle Ocho), Miami. ☎ **305/541-2631.** Cover $10 Thurs–Sun nights.

As the name implies, Cafe Nostalgia is dedicated to reminiscing about old Cuba. After watching a Celia Cruz film, you can dance to the hot sounds of Afro-Cuban jazz. With pictures of old and young Cuban stars smiling down on you and a live band celebrating Cuban heritage, Cafe Nostalgia sounds like a bit much; it's more than that. Be prepared—it's packed after midnight and dance space is mostly between the tables. Open Thursday to Sunday from 9pm to 4am. Films are shown from 10pm to midnight, followed by live music. Another branch is set to open on Miami Beach in late 1999.

Casa Panza. 1620 SW 8th St. (Calle Ocho), Miami. ☎ **305/643-5343.** No cover.

Clap your hands or your castanets if you have them. Every Tuesday and Thursday night, Casa Panza, in the heart of Little Havana, becomes the House of Flamenco, with shows at 8 and 11pm. You can either enjoy a flamenco show or strap on your own dancing shoes and participate in the celebration. Enjoy a fantastic Spanish meal before the show, or just have a drink or two before you start stomping.

Mango's. 900 Ocean Dr., South Beach. ☎ **305/673-4422.** Cover $6–$15; varies by performer.

If you want to dance to a funky, loud Brazilian beat till you drop, check out Mango's on the beach. It features nightly live Brazilian and other Latin music on a little patio bar. When you need refreshment, you can choose from a wildly eclectic menu of Caribbean, Mexican, vegetarian, and Cuban specialties. Open daily from 11am to 5:30am.

Studio 23. 247 23rd St. (1 block west of Collins Ave.), South Beach. ☎ **305/538-1196.** Cover $5–$10.

You've heard of son? Hear it here—along with salsa, cumbia, merengue, vallenato, and house music. This neighborhood Latin disco and nightclub gets going after hours with a wild strobe-lit atmosphere. If you don't know how to do it, just wait. You'll have plenty of willing teachers on hand. Open Friday to Sunday from 8pm to 4am.

✪ **Yuca.** 501 Lincoln Rd., South Beach. ☎ **305/532-9822.** Cover $25, plus 2-drink minimum for the Albita performance Fri–Sat nights at 11pm.

One of the city's best restaurants (see chapter 4) also serves up hot music in an upstairs club. If Albita is playing, don't miss her. The prices are ridiculous and you'll be squeezed into a table no bigger than a cocktail napkin, but it's worth it for the high-energy dance music, including traditional sol, salsa, and son from the old country. If you don't speak Spanish, sign language works here, too.

THE PERFORMING ARTS
THEATER

In Miami, an active and varied selection of dramas and musicals is presented throughout the year. Thanks to the support of many loyal theater aficionados, especially an older crowd of New York transplants, season subscriptions are common and allow the theaters to survive, even when every show is not a hit. Some traveling Broadway shows make it to town, as well as revivals by big-name playwrights, such as Tennessee Williams, David Mamet, Neil Simon, and Israel Horowitz. The best way to find out what's playing is to check the local paper or call the theaters directly.

The **Actors' Playhouse,** at the newly restored Miracle Theater in Coral Gables (☎ 305/444-9293), is a grand 1948 art deco movie palace with a 600-seat main theater, as well as a smaller theater/rehearsal hall where a number of excellent musicals for children are put on throughout the year. In addition to these two rooms, the Playhouse recently added a 300-seat children's balcony theater. Tickets run from $26 to $50.

The **Coconut Grove Playhouse,** 3500 Main Highway in Coconut Grove (☎ 305/442-4000), was also a former movie house, built in 1927 in an ornate Spanish rococo style. Today, this respected venue is known for its original and innovative staging of both international and local dramas and musicals. The house's second, more intimate Encore Room is well suited to alternative and experimental productions. Tickets run from $37 to $42.

The **Gables Stage,** on Anastasia Avenue in Coral Gables at the Biltmore Hotel (☎ 305/445-1119), stages at least one Shakespeare play, one classic, and one contemporary piece a year. This well-regarded theater usually tries to secure the rights to a national or local premiere as well. Tickets cost $22 and $28; $10 and $17 for students and seniors.

The **Jerry Herman Ring Theatre** is on the main campus of the University of Miami in Coral Gables (☎ 305/284-3355). The University's Department of Theater Arts uses this stage for advanced-student productions of comedies, dramas, and musicals. Faculty and guest actors are regularly featured, as are contemporary works by local playwrights. Performances are usually scheduled Tuesday through Saturday during the academic year. In the summer, don't miss "Summer Shorts," a selection of superb one-acts. Tickets sell for $5 to $20.

The **New Theater,** 65 Almeria Ave., in Coral Gables (☎ 305/443-5909), prides itself on showing world-renowned works from America and Europe. As the name implies, you'll find mostly contemporary plays, with a few classics thrown in for variety. Performances are staged Thursday to Sunday year-round. Tickets are $20 on weekdays and $25 weekends. If tickets are available, students pay half price.

Miami's two well-known acting companies have suffered from poor financing and real-estate woes. Luckily, both have the support of a loyal crew of theater fans who overlook budget sets, inconsistent acting, and occasional bad taste. Call for schedules and locales.

The **Acme Acting Company** (☎ 305/576-7500) performs Wednesday to Saturday at 8pm, and Sunday at 7pm. They usually present off-beat contemporary plays to critical acclaim. Tickets are $15 to $25 depending on the venue; students and seniors pay $10 to $20.

The award-winning **Area Stage Company** (☎ 305/673-8002) has won respect from local and national audiences for their dramatic work in all manner of contemporary theater.

CLASSICAL MUSIC

In addition to a number of local orchestras and operas, which regularly offer quality music and world-renowned guest artists, each year brings a slew of special events and touring artists. One of the most important and longest-running series is produced by the **Concert Association of Florida (CAF),** 555 17th St., South Beach (☎ 305/532-3491). Known for more than a quarter of a century for its high-caliber, star-packed schedules, CAF regularly arranges the best "serious" music concerts for the city. Season after season, the schedules are punctuated by world-renowned dance companies and seasoned virtuosi like Itzhak Perlman, Andre Watts, and Kathleen Battle. Since CAF does not have its own space, performances are usually scheduled in either the Dade County Auditorium or the Jackie Gleason Theater of the Performing Arts (see below). The season lasts from October through April, and ticket prices range from $20 to $70.

Florida Philharmonic Orchestra. 1243 University Dr., Miami. ☎ **800/226-1812** or 305/476-1234. Tickets $15–$60. When extra tickets are available, students are admitted free on day of performance.

South Florida's premier symphony orchestra, under the direction of James Judd, presents a full season of classical and pops programs interspersed with several children's and contemporary popular-music dates. The Philharmonic performs Downtown in the Gusman Center for the Performing Arts and at the Dade County Auditorium.

Miami Chamber Symphony. 5690 N. Kendall Dr., Kendall. ☎ **305/858-3500.** Tickets $12–$30.

This professional orchestra is an inexpensive alternative to the high-priced classical venues. Renowned international soloists perform regularly. The season runs October to May, and most concerts are held in the Gusman Concert Hall, on the University of Miami campus.

✪ **The New World Symphony.** 541 Lincoln Rd., South Beach. ☎ **305/673-3331.** www.nws.org. E-mail: ticketsnws.org. Tickets $0–$43. Student discounts available on day of show.

This organization, led by artistic director Michael Tilson Thomas, is a stepping stone for gifted young musicians seeking professional careers. The orchestra specializes in ambitious, innovative, energetic performances and often features renowned guest soloists and conductors. The symphony's season lasts from October to May, during which time there are many free concerts.

OPERA

✪ **Florida Grand Opera.** 1200 Coral Way, Miami. ☎ **800/741-1010** or 305/854-1643. Tickets $18–$100. Student discounts available.

Nearing its 60th birthday, this company regularly features singers from top houses in both America and Europe. All productions are sung in their original language and staged with projected English supertitles. Tickets become scarce when Placido Domingo or Luciano Pavarotti (who made his American debut here in 1965) comes to town. The opera's season runs roughly from November to April, with five performances each week.

DANCE

Several local dance companies train and perform in the Greater Miami area. In addition, top traveling troupes regularly stop at the venues listed above. Keep your eyes open for special events and guest artists.

✪ **Ballet Flamenco La Rosa.** ☎ **305/672-0552** or 305/757-8475. Tickets $25 at door, $20 in advance, $18 for students and seniors.

For a taste of local Latin flavor, see this lively troupe perform impressive flamenco and other styles of dance on Miami stages.

✪ **Miami City Ballet.** Lincoln Road Mall at Jefferson Ave., South Beach. ☎ **305/ 532-4880.** Box office ☎ 305/532-7713. Tickets $17–$50.

The artistically acclaimed and innovative company, directed by Edward Villella, features a repertoire of more than 60 ballets, many by George Balanchine, and more than 20 world premieres. Stop by to watch rehearsals through the large storefront window before the company moves to their new space near the Bass museum on Collins and 22nd Street. The City Ballet season runs from September to April, with performances at the Jackie Gleason Theater of the Performing Arts (see below).

MAJOR VENUES

After years of decay and a $1 million facelift, the **Colony Theater,** on Lincoln Road, South Beach (☎ 305/674-1026), has become an architectural showpiece of the Art Deco District. This multipurpose 465-seat theater stages performances by the Miami City Ballet and the Ballet Flamenco La Rosa, as well as off-Broadway shows and other special events.

At the **Dade County Auditorium,** West Flagler Street at 29th Avenue, Miami (☎ 305/547-5414), performers gripe about the lack of space, but for patrons, this 2,430-seat auditorium is comfortable and intimate. It's home to the city's Greater Miami Opera and also stages productions by the Concert Association of Florida, many Spanish programs, and a variety of other shows.

At the 1,700-seat **Gusman Center for the Performing Arts,** 174 E. Flagler St. in Downtown Miami (☎ 305/372-0925), seating is tight, and so is funding, but the sound is superb. In addition to producing a regular stage for the Philharmonic Orchestra of Florida and The Miami Film Festival, the elegant Gusman Center features pop concerts, plays, film-festival screenings, and special events. The auditorium was built as the Olympia Theater in 1926, and its ornate palace interior is typical of that era, complete with fancy columns, a huge pipe organ, and twinkling "stars" on the ceiling.

Not to be confused with the Gusman Center (above), the **Gusman Concert Hall,** 1314 Miller Dr., at 14th Street in Coral Gables (☎ 305/284-6477), is a roomy 600-seat hall that gives a stage to the Miami Chamber Symphony and a varied program of university recitals.

The elegant **Jackie Gleason Theater of the Performing Arts (TOPA),** Washington Avenue at 17th Street, South Beach (☎ 305/673-7300), is the home of the Miami City Ballet, as well as the Miami Beach Broadway Series, which recently presented Rent, Phantom of the Opera, and Les Miserables. This 2,705-seat hall also hosts other big-budget Broadway shows, classical music concerts, opera, and dance performances.

CINEMAS

In addition to the annual Miami Film Festival in February and other, smaller film events, Miami is lucky to have some wonderful art cinemas showing a range of films from *Fresa y Chocolate* to *Crumb.*

The **Alliance Cinema** (☎ 305/531-8504) is tucked behind a little tropical walkway just next to Books & Books at 927 Lincoln Rd., Suite 119, in South Beach. This old hideaway shows art films, Latin American features, and lots of gay films, too. You may want to bring a pillow; the seats are old and rickety. Tickets cost $6.

Astor Art Cinema, 4120 Laguna St. (☎ 305/443-6777), is an oasis in the midst of a desert of Cineplex Odeons and AMCs in Coral Gables. This quaint double theater hosts foreign, classic, independent, and art films and serves decent popcorn, too. Tickets are $5, $3 for seniors.

Absinthe Cinemateque, 235 Alcazar Ave., Coral Gables (☎ 305/446-7144), is a small one-screen theater, which shows good movies, often Spanish–language films, without the hustle and bustle of the crowded multiplexes. The Alcazar shows the more artsy of the major films as well as some obscure independents. Tickets are $6.

The **Bill Cosford Cinema** at the University of Miami, on the second floor of the memorial building off Campo Sano Avenue (☎ **305/284-4861**), is named after the deceased *Herald* film critic. This well-endowed little theater was recently revamped and boasts high-tech projectors, new air-conditioning, and new decor. It sponsors independent films as well as lectures by visiting filmmakers and movie stars. Andy Garcia and Antonio Banderas are a few of the big names this little theater has attracted. It also hosts the African American Film Festival and a Student Film Festival, plus collaborations with the Fort Lauderdale Festival. Admission is $5.

The Keys 6

by Victoria Pesce Elliott

The Florida Keys bring to mind the raucous streets of Key West and the mellow guitar riffs of Jimmy Buffet, but listen up—there's so much more.

The islands of the Keys are strung out across the southern waters of Florida like loose beads of an exotic coral necklace, and each of the more than 400 islands that make up this 150-mile chain has a distinctive character. While some are crammed with strip malls and tacky shell shops, most are filled with unusual species of tropical plants, birds, and reptiles. All are surrounded by calm blue waters, populated by stunning sea life, and graced by year-round warmth.

Despite the usually calm landscape, these rocky islands can be treacherous, as the series of tropical storms, hurricanes, and tornadoes reminded residents in the summer and fall of 1998 when millions of dollars of damage was inflicted. The exposed coast has always posed dangers to those on land as well as sea.

When Spanish explorers Juan Ponce de León and Antonio de Herrera sailed amid these craggy, dangerous rocks in 1513, they and their men dubbed the string of islands "Los Martires" (The Martyrs) because they thought the rocks looked like men suffering in the surf. It wasn't until the early 1800s that the larger islands were settled by rugged and ambitious pioneers, who amassed great wealth by salvaging cargo from ships sunk nearby. Actually, legend has it that these shipwrecks were sometimes caused by the "wreckers," who occasionally removed navigational markers from the shallows to lure unwitting captains aground. At the height of the salvaging mania (in the 1830s), Key West boasted the highest per capita income in the country.

However, wars, fires, hurricanes, mosquitoes, and the Depression took their toll on these resilient islands in the early part of this century, causing wild swings between fortune and poverty. In 1938, the spectacular Overseas Highway (U.S. 1) was finally completed atop the ruins of Henry Flagler's railroad, opening the region to tourists who had never before been able to drive to this seabound destination.

These days, the highway connects more than 30 of the populated islands in the Keys. The hundreds of small, undeveloped islands that surround these "mainline" keys are known locally as the "backcountry" and are home to dozens of exotic animals and plants. To get to them, you must take to the water—a vital part of any trip to the Keys. Whether you fish, snorkel, dive, or just cruise, include some time on a boat in your itinerary; otherwise, you really haven't truly seen the Keys.

The sea and the teeming life beneath it are the main attractions here. Warm, shallow waters nurture living coral that supports a complex, delicate ecosystem of plants and animals—sponges, anemones, jellyfish, crabs, rays, sharks, turtles, snails, lobsters, and thousands of types of fish. This vibrant underwater habitat thrives on one of only two living tropical reefs in the entire North American continent (the other is off the coast of Belize). As a result, anglers, divers, snorkelers, and water-sports enthusiasts of all kinds come to explore. The heavy traffic has taken its toll on this fragile eco-scape, but efforts are underway to protect it.

Although the atmosphere throughout the Keys is that of a low-key beach town, don't expect to find many impressive beaches here. Especially since the tropical storms and hurricanes in 1998, there aren't any great beaches. Beaches are mostly found in a few private resorts and some small, sandy beaches in Bahia Honda State Park and in Key West (see "The Lower Keys," below). One great exception is Sombrero Beach in Marathon (see "Beaches" in the "Upper & Middle Keys" section, below).

The Keys are divided into three sections, both geographically and in this chapter. The Upper and Middle Keys are closest to the Florida mainland, so they are popular with weekend warriors who come by boat or car to fish, drink, or relax in towns like Key Largo, Islamorada, and Marathon. Farther on, just beyond the impressive Seven-Mile Bridge (which actually measures only 6.4 miles), are the Lower Keys, a small unspoiled swath of islands teeming with wildlife. Here in the protected regions of the Lower Keys is where you're most likely to catch sight of the area's many endangered animals. With patience, you may spot the rare eagle, egret, or Key deer. Also, keep an eye out for alligators, turtles, rabbits, and a huge variety of birds.

The last section of this chapter is devoted to the renowned island called Key West, literally at the end of the road. Made famous by the Nobel Prize–winning rogue Ernest Hemingway, this tiny island is the most popular destination in the Florida Keys, overrun with cruise-ship passengers and day-trippers, as well as franchises and T-shirt shops. More than 1.6 million visitors pass through each year. Still, you'll find in this "Conch Republic" a tightly knit community of permanent residents who cling fiercely to their live-and-let-live attitude—an atmosphere that has made Key West famously popular with painters, writers, and gay and lesbian travelers.

Note: Few people know that the Keys don't officially end at Key West. About 70 miles west lies a chain of seven small islands known as the Dry Tortugas. If you're into bird watching, you might consider making a day trip. For more information on these islands, refer to *Frommer's Miami and the Keys.*

EXPLORING THE KEYS BY CAR

After you have gotten off the Florida Turnpike and landed on U.S. 1, which is also known as the Overseas Highway (see "Getting There" under "Essentials," below), you'll have no trouble negotiating these narrow islands.

The Overseas Highway is the only main road connecting the Keys. Although some find the long, straight drive from Miami to Key West tedious, it can be enjoyable if you linger and explore the diverse towns and islands along the way. If you have the time, I recommend allowing at least 3 days to work your way down to Key West and 2 or more days once there.

Most of U.S. 1 is a narrow, two-lane highway, with some wider passing zones along the way. The speed limit is usually 55 m.p.h. (35 to 45 m.p.h. on Big Pine Key and in some commercial areas). Despite the protestations of island residents, there has been talk of expanding the highway, but by publication date plans had not been finalized. Even on the narrow road, you can usually get from downtown Miami to Key Largo in just over an hour. If you're determined to drive straight through to Key West,

The Florida Keys

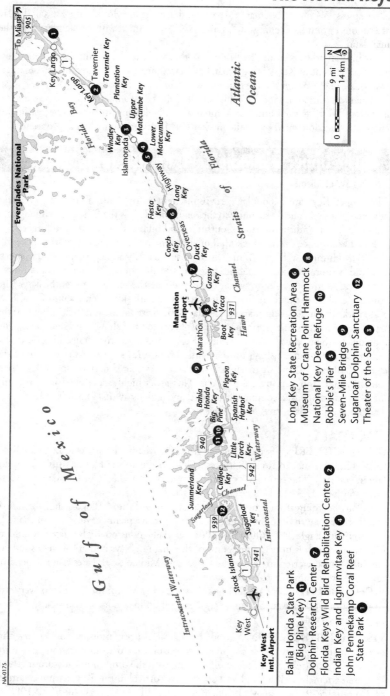

Bahia Honda State Park (Big Pine Key) **11**

Dolphin Research Center **7**

Florida Keys Wild Bird Rehabilitation Center **2**

Indian Key and Lignumvitae Key **4**

John Pennekamp Coral Reef State Park **1**

Long Key State Recreation Area **6**

Museum of Crane Point Hammock **8**

National Key Deer Refuge **10**

Robbie's Pier **5**

Seven-Mile Bridge **9**

Sugarloaf Dolphin Sanctuary **12**

Theater of the Sea **3**

allow at least 3½ hours. No matter what, avoid driving anywhere in the Keys on Friday afternoons or Sunday evenings, when the roads are jammed with weekenders from the mainland.

To find an address in the Keys, don't bother looking for building numbers; most addresses (except in Key West and parts of Marathon) are delineated by mile markers (MM), small green signs on the roadside which announce the distance from Key West. The markers start at number 127, just south of the Florida mainland. The zero marker is in Key West, at the corner of Whitehead and Fleming streets. Addresses in this chapter are accompanied by a mile marker (MM) designation when appropriate.

1 The Upper & Middle Keys: Key Largo to Marathon

58 miles SW of Miami

The Upper Keys are a popular, year-round refuge for South Floridians who take advantage of the islands' proximity to the mainland. This is the fishing and diving capital of America, and the swarms of outfitters and billboards never let you forget it.

Key Largo, once called "Rock Harbor" but renamed to capitalize on the success of the 1948 Humphrey Bogart film (which wasn't actually filmed there), is the largest Key and is more developed than its neighbors to the south. Dozens of chain hotels, restaurants, and tourist-information centers service the many water enthusiasts who come to explore the nation's first underwater state park, John Pennekamp Coral Reef State Park, and its adjacent marine sanctuary. **Islamorada,** the unofficial capital of the Upper Keys, offers the area's best atmosphere, food, fishing, entertainment, and lodging. In these "purple isles," nature lovers can enjoy nature trails, historic explorations, and big-purse fishing tournaments. **Marathon,** smack in the middle of the chain of islands, is one of the most populated Keys. It is part fishing village, part tourist center, and part nature preserve. This area's highly developed infrastructure includes resort hotels, a commercial airport, and a highway that expands to four lanes. Thankfully, high rises have yet to arrive.

ESSENTIALS

GETTING THERE   If you're coming from the Miami airport, take Le Jeune Road (NW 42nd Avenue) to Route 836 west. Follow signs to the Florida Turnpike South (about 7 miles). The turnpike extension connects with U.S. 1 in Florida City. Continue south on U.S. 1.

If you're coming from Florida's west coast, take Alligator Alley to the Miami exit and then turn south onto the turnpike extension. Have plenty of quarters for the tolls.

American Eagle (☎ 800/433-7300) has daily nonstop flights from Miami to Marathon, which is near the midpoint of the chain of Keys and at the very southern end of the area referred to here as the Upper and Middle Keys. Fares range depending on the season, from $88 to $336 round-trip.

Greyhound (☎ 800/231-2222) has buses leaving Miami for Key Largo every day. At press time, prices were $13 one-way. Seats fill up in season, so come early. It's first come, first served.

VISITOR INFORMATION   Avoid the many "Tourist Information Centers" that dot the main highway. Most are private companies hired to lure visitors to specific lodgings or outfitters. You're better off sticking with the official, not-for-profit centers that are extremely well located and staffed. In particular, the **Key Largo Chamber of Commerce** (U.S. 1 at MM 106, Key Largo, FL 33037; ☎ **800/822-1088** or 305/451-1414; fax 305/451-4726; www.floridakeys.org) runs an excellent facility, with free direct-dial phones and plenty of brochures. Now headquartered in a hand-some clapboard house, the chamber operates as an information clearinghouse for all of the Keys. It's open daily from 9am to 6pm.

The **Islamorada Chamber of Commerce,** in the Little Red Caboose (U.S. 1 at MM 82.5, P.O. Box 915, Islamorada, FL 33036; ☎ **800/322-5397** or 305/664-4503; fax 305/664-4289; e-mail: islacc@ix.netcom.com), also offers maps and literature on the Upper Keys.

You can't miss the big blue visitor center at MM 53.5, the **Greater Marathon Chamber of Commerce** (12222 Overseas Hwy., Marathon, FL 33050; ☎ **800/842-9580** or 305/743-5417; fax 305/289-0183; www.flakeys.com).

WHAT TO SEE & DO

Anne's Beach (at MM 73.5) is really more of a picnic spot than a full-fledged beach, but die-hard suntanners still congregate on this tiny strip of coarse sand, which unfortunately was damaged beyond recognition during the series of storms in 1998. There are plans to reconstruct the boardwalk and huts, but as of press time, work had not yet started.

A better choice for real beaching is **Sombrero Beach** in Marathon at the end of Sombrero Beach Road (near MM 50). This wide swath of uncluttered beachfront actually benefited from hurricane George in September of 1998 with generous deposits of extra sand and a facelift courtesy of the Monroe County Tourist Development Council. More than 90 feet of sand is dotted with stands of palms, Australian Pines, and Royal Poncianas. There are some barbecue grills and clean bathrooms. A project is currently underway to add tiki huts, a pavilion, and a pier. Admission and parking at this little-known gem are free.

Indian Key and Lignumvitae Key. Off Indian Key Fill, Overseas Hwy., MM 79. ☎ **305/664-4815.**

Named for the lignum vitae ("wood of life") trees found there, **Lignumvitae Key** supports a virgin tropical forest, the kind that once thrived on most of the Upper Keys. Over the years, human settlers have imported "exotic" plants and animals to the Keys, irrevocably changing the botanical makeup of many backcountry islands and threatening much of the indigenous wildlife. Over the past 25 years, the Department of Natural Resources has successfully removed most of the exotic vegetation, leaving this 280-acre site much as it existed in the 18th century. The island also holds a historic house built in 1919 that has survived numerous storms and major hurricanes.

Indian Key, a much smaller island on the Atlantic side of Islamorada, was occupied by Native Americans for thousands of years before European settlers arrived. The 10-acre historic site was also the original seat of Dade County before the Civil War. You can see the ruins of the previous settlement and tour the lush grounds on well-marked trails.

If you want to see both islands, plan to spend at least half a day. To get there, you can rent your own boat at **Robbie's Rent-A-Boat** (U.S. 1 at MM 77.5 on the bay side). Rates range from $60 for a 14-foot boat for half a day to $155 for an 18-foot boat for a full day. It's then a $1 admission fee to each island, which includes an informative hour-long guided tour by park rangers. This is a good option if you are a confident boater.

However, I also recommend taking Robbie's **ferry service** for $15, which includes the $1 park admission. Trips to both islands cost $25 per person. (If you are planning to visit only one island, make it Lignumvitae.) Not only is the ferry more economical, but it's easier to enjoy the natural beauty of the islands when you aren't negotiating the shallow reefs along the way. The runabouts, which carry up to six people, depart from

The Ten Keymandments

The Keys have always attracted independent spirits, from Ernest Hemingway and Tennessee Williams to Jimmy Buffett, Mel Fisher, and Zane Grey. Writers, artists, and free-thinkers have long drifted down here to escape from society's rigid demands.

Standards do seem to be different here. In 1982, for example, when drug-enforcement agents blocked off the main highway leading into Key West, residents did what they do best—they threw a party. The festivities marked the "independence" of the newly formed "Conch Republic." The distinctive flag with its conch insignia now flies throughout the island.

Although you'll generally find a very laid-back and tolerant code of behavior in the Keys, some rules do exist. Be sure to respect the Ten Keymandments while you're here, or suffer the consequences.

- Don't anchor on a reef. (Reefs are alive. Alive. A-L-I-V-E.)
- Don't feed the animals. (They'll want to follow you home, and you can't keep them.)
- Don't trash our place. (Or we'll send Bubba to trash yours.)
- Don't touch the coral. (After all, you don't even know them.)
- Don't speed. (Especially on Big Pine Key, where deer reside and tar-and-feathering is still practiced.)
- Don't catch more fish than you can eat. (Better yet, let them go. Some of them support schools.)
- Don't collect conch. (This species is protected. By Bubba.)
- Don't disturb the bird nests. (They find it very annoying.)
- Don't damage the seagrass. (And don't even think about making a skirt out of it.)
- Don't drink and drive on land or sea. (There's absolutely nothing funny about it.)

Robbie's Pier Thursday to Monday at 9am and 1pm for Indian Key, and at 10am and 2pm for Lignumvitae Key. In the busy season, you may need to book as early as 2 days before departure. Call ☎ **305/664-4815** for information from the park service or ☎ **305/664-9814** for Robbie's.

✪ **Pigeon Key.** East end of the Seven-Mile Bridge near MM 47, Marathon. ☎ **305/743-5999.** Open 9am–5pm; shuttle tours run every hour 10am–3pm. Admission $7.50; $5 for children under 13. Price includes shuttle transportation from the Visitor's Center.

Now open to the public, Pigeon Key, at the curve of the old bridge, is an intriguing historical site that has been under renovation since late 1993. This 5-mile island was once the camp for the crew who built the old railway in the early part of the century and later served as housing for the bridge builders. From here, your vista includes both bridges, many old wooden cottages, and a truly tranquil stretch of lush foliage and sea.

If you miss the shuttle tour or would rather walk or bike to the key, it's about 2.5 miles. Either way, you may want to bring a picnic to enjoy after a brief self-guided walking tour and museum visit. There is also an informative 28-minute video of the island's history offered every hour starting at 11:15am. Parking is available at the Knight's Key end of the bridge, at MM 48, or at the Visitor's Center at the old train car across the highway on the ocean side.

✪ Seven-Mile Bridge. Between MM 40 and 47 on U.S. 1. ☎ **305/289-0025.**

A stop at the Seven-Mile Bridge is a rewarding and relaxing break from the drive south. Built alongside the ruins of oil magnate Henry Flagler's incredible Overseas Railroad, the "new" bridge (between MM 40 and 47) is still considered an architectural feat. The wide arched span, completed in 1982 at a cost of more than $45 million, is impressive, its apex being the highest point in the Keys. The new bridge and especially its now-defunct neighbor provide an excellent vantage point from which to view the stunning waters of the Keys.

In the daytime, you may want to jog, walk, or bike along the scenic 4-mile stretch of old bridge, or join local fishermen, who catch barracuda, yellowtail, and dolphin on what is known as "the longest fishing pier in the world."

✪ Tropical Crane Point Hammock. 5550 Overseas Hwy. (MM 50), Marathon. ☎ **305/743-9100.** Admission $7.50 adults, $6 seniors over 64, $4 students, and free for children under 6. Mon–Sat 9am–5pm; Sun noon–5pm.

Crane Point Hammock is a little-known but very worthwhile stop, especially for those interested in the rich botanical and archaeological history of the Keys. This privately owned 64-acre nature area is considered one of the most important historical sites in the Keys. It contains what is probably the last virgin thatch palm hammock in North America. It also has an archaeological dig site with pre-Columbian and prehistoric Bahamian artifacts.

Now headquarters for the Florida Keys Land and Sea Trust, the hammock's impressive nature museum has simple, informative displays of the Keys' wildlife, including a walk-through replica of a coral-reef cave and life-size dioramas with tropical birds and Key deer. Kids can participate in art projects, see 6-foot-long iguanas, climb through a scaled-down pirate ship, and touch a variety of indigenous aquatic and land-lubbing creatures.

VISITING WITH THE ANIMALS

✪ Dolphin Research Center. U.S. 1 at MM 59 (on the bay side), Marathon. ☎ **305/289-1121.** Swim with the Dolphins, $110 per person. Call on the first day of the month to book for the following month. Educational walking tours 5 times every day: 10am, 11am, 12:30pm, 2pm, and 3:30pm. Admission $12.50 adults; $10 seniors; $7.50 children 4–12; free for children 3 and under. (Prices are scheduled to increase.) MC, V. Daily 9:30am–4pm.

Don't miss this experience. If you've always wanted to touch, swim with, or play with dolphins, this is the place to do it. Of the three such centers in the continental United States (all located in the Keys), the Dolphin Research Center is the most organized and informative.

Although some people argue that training dolphins is cruel and selfish, the knowledgeable trainers at the Dolphin Research Center will tell you that the dolphins need stimulation and enjoy human contact. They certainly seem to. They nuzzle and seem to smile and kiss the lucky few who get to swim with them in the daily program. The "family" of 15 dolphins swims in a 90,000-square-foot natural saltwater pool carved out of the shoreline. If you can't get into the swim program, you can still take a walking tour of the facilities or sign up for a class in hand signals or feed the dolphins from docks. Children must be at least 12 years old to participate.

Florida Keys Wild Bird Rehabilitation Center. U.S. 1 at MM 94, Tavernier. ☎ **305/852-4486.** Donations suggested. Daily 8:30am–6pm.

Wander through lush canopies of mangroves on narrow wooden walkways to see some of the Keys's most famous residents—the large variety of native birds, including broadwing hawks, great blue and white herons, roseate spoonbills, white ibis, cattle egrets, and a number of pelicans. This not-for-profit center operates as a hospital for the many birds who have been injured. Come at feeding time, usually about 2pm, when you can watch the dedicated staff feed the hundreds of hungry beaks.

✪ Robbie's Pier. U.S. 1 at MM 77.5, Islamorada. ☎ **305/664-9814.** Admission $1. Bucket of fish $2. Daily 8am–5pm. Look for the Hungry Tarpon restaurant sign on the right after the Indian Key channel.

One of the best and definitely one of the cheapest attractions in the Upper Keys is the famed Robbie's Pier. Here, the fierce steely tarpons, a prized catch for backcountry anglers, have been gathering for the past 20 years. You may recognize these prehistoric-looking giants that grow up to 200 pounds; many are displayed as trophies and mounted on local restaurant walls. To see them live, head to Robbie's Pier, where tens and sometimes hundreds of these behemoths circle the shallow waters waiting for you to feed them. New kayak tours promise an even closer glimpse.

Theater of the Sea. U.S. 1 at MM 84.5, Islamorada. ☎ **305/664-2431.** Fax 305/664-8162. Admission $16.25 adults; $9.75 children 3–12. Swim with the Dolphins and Trainer for a Day programs by reservation; $95 per person. Daily 9:30am–4pm.

Established in 1946, the Theater of the Sea is one of the world's oldest marine zoos. Although the facilities could use some sprucing up, the dolphin and sea-lion shows are entertaining and informative, especially for children who can also see sharks, sea turtles, and tropical fish. If you want to swim with dolphins and you haven't booked well in advance, this is the place you may be able to get in with just a few hours'—or days'—notice, as opposed to the more rigid Dolphin Research Center in Marathon (see above). A recently introduced program allows visitors to swim with the sea lions or with the stingrays for $65 per person. Cat lovers will be thrilled to learn that the facility also serves as a haven for dozens of stray cats who have free run of the grounds and gift shop.

Two Exceptional State Parks

One of the best places to discover the diverse ecosystem of the Upper Keys is in its most famous park, **✪ John Pennekamp Coral Reef State Park,** located on U.S. 1 at MM 102.5, in Key Largo (☎ **305/451-1202**). Named for a former *Miami Herald* editor and conservationist, the 188-square-mile park is the nation's first undersea preserve. It's a sanctuary for part of the only living coral reef in the continental United States. The original plans for Everglades National Park included this part of the reef within its boundaries, but opposition from local homeowners made its inclusion politically impossible.

Because the water is extremely shallow, the 40 species of corals and more than 650 species of fish here are particularly accessible to divers, snorkelers, and glass-bottom–boat passengers. You can't see the reef from the shore. To experience this park, visitors must get in the water. Your first stop should be the visitor center, which is full of educational fish tanks and a mammoth 30,000-gallon saltwater aquarium that re-creates a reef ecosystem. At the adjacent dive shop, you can rent snorkeling and diving equipment and join one of the boat trips that depart for the reef throughout the day. Visitors can also rent motorboats, sailboats, Windsurfers, and canoes. The 2-hour glass-bottom–boat tour is the best way to see the coral reefs if you refuse to get wet.

Canoeing around the park's narrow mangrove channels and tidal creeks is also popular. You can go on your own in a rented canoe, or in winter, sign up for a tour led by a local naturalist. Hikers have two short trails to choose from: a boardwalk through the mangroves and a dirt trail through a tropical hardwood hammock. Ranger-led walks are usually scheduled daily from the end of November to April. Phone for schedule information and reservations.

Park admission is $2.50 per vehicle for one occupant; $4 per vehicle for two or more, plus 50¢ per passenger; $1.50 per pedestrian or bicyclist. Call ☎ **305/451-1621** for information. On your way into the park, ask the ranger for a map. Glass-bottom–boat tours cost $13 for adults and $8.50 for children 11 and under. Snorkeling tours are $23.95 for adults and $18.95 for children 17 and under, including equipment. Sailing and snorkeling tours are $28.95 for adults, $23.95 for children 17 and under, including equipment but not tax. Canoes rent for $8 per hour or $28 for 4 hours. Reef boats (powerboats) rent for $25 to $45 per hour; call ☎ **305/451-6325.** Open daily from 8am to 5pm; phone for tour and dive times. Also, see below for more options on diving, fishing, and snorkeling these reefs.

Long Key State Recreation Area, U.S. 1 at MM 68, Long Key (☎ **305/664-4815**), is one of the best places in the Middle Keys for hiking, camping, and canoeing. This 965-acre park is situated atop the remains of an ancient coral reef. At the entrance gate, ask for a free flyer describing the local trails and wildlife.

There are two nature trails here perfect for hiking. The Golden Orb Trail is a 1-mile loop around a lagoon that attracts a large variety of birds. Rich in West Indian vegetation, this trail leads to an observation tower that offers good views of the mangroves. Layton Trail, the only part of the park that doesn't require an admission fee, is a quarter-mile shaded loop that goes through tropical hammocks before opening onto Florida Bay. The trail is well marked with interpretive signs; you can easily walk it in about 20 minutes.

The park's excellent 1½-mile canoe trail is also short and sweet, allowing visitors to loop around the mangroves in about an hour—it couldn't be easier. You can rent canoes at the trailhead for about $4 per hour. Long Key is also a great spot to stop for a picnic if you get hungry on your way to Key West.

Railroad builder Henry Flagler created the Long Key Fishing Club here in 1906, and the waters surrounding the park are still popular with game fishers. In summer, sea turtles lumber onto the protected coast to lay their eggs.

Admission is $3.25 per car plus 50¢ per person (except for the Layton Trail, which is free). Open daily from 8am to sunset.

WATER SPORTS

There are literally hundreds of outfitters in the Keys who will set up all kinds of water activities, from cave dives to parasailing. If those recommended below are booked up or unreachable, ask the local chamber of commerce for a list of qualified members.

BOATING In addition to the rental shops in the state parks, you will find dozens of outfitters along U.S. 1 offering a range of runabouts and skiffs for boaters of any experience level. **Captain Pip's,** U.S. 1 at MM 47.5, Marathon (☎ **800/707-1692** or 305/743-4403), rents 18.5- to 24-foot motorboats with 90 to 225 horsepower engines for $110 to $170 per day.

Robbie's Rent-a-Boat, U.S. 1 at MM 77.5, Islamorada (☎ **305/664-9814**), rents 14- to 27-foot motorboats with engines ranging from 15 to 200 horsepower. Boats cost $60 to $205 for a half day and $80 to $295 for a whole day.

CANOEING & KAYAKING I can think of no better way to explore the uninhabited, shallow backcountry than by kayak or canoe. You can reach places big boats just can't get to because of their large draft. Sometimes manatees will cuddle up to the boats, thinking them another friendly species.

For a more enjoyable time, ask for a sit-inside boat—you'll stay drier. Also, a fiberglass (as opposed to plastic) boat with a rudder is generally more stable and easier to maneuver. Many area hotels rent kayaks and canoes to guests, as do the outfitters listed here. **Florida Bay Outfitters,** U.S. 1 at MM 104, Key Largo (☎ **305/451-3018**), rents canoes and sea kayaks for use in and around John Pennekamp Coral Reef State Park for $20 to $30 for a half day and $35 to $50 for a whole day. Canoes cost $25 for a half day and $35 for a whole day. At **Coral Reef Park Co.,** on U.S. 1 at MM 102.5, Key Largo (☎ **305/451-1621**), you can rent canoes and kayaks for $8 per hour, $28 for a half day; most canoes are sit-on-tops.

DIVING & SNORKELING The **Florida Keys Dive Center,** on U.S. 1 at MM 90.5, Tavernier (☎ **305/852-4599;** fax 305/852-1293), takes snorkelers and divers to the reefs of **John Pennekamp Coral Reef State Park** and environs every day. PADI training courses are also available for the uninitiated. Tours leave at 8am and 12:30pm and cost $25 per person to snorkel (including mask, snorkels, and fins) and $40 per person to dive (plus an extra $30 if you need to rent all the gear).

At **Hall's Dive Center & Career Institute,** U.S. 1 at MM 48.5, Marathon (☎ **305/743-5929;** fax 305/743-8168), snorkelers and divers can choose to dive at Looe Key, Sombrero Reef, Delta Shoal, Content Key, and Coffins Patch. Tours are scheduled daily at 9am and 1pm. If you mention this guide, you will get a special discounted rate of $30 per person to snorkel (including equipment) and $40 per person to dive. Choose from a wide and impressive array of equipment. Rental is extra.

With **Snuba Tours of Key Largo** (☎ **305/451-6391**), you can dive down to 20 feet attached to a comfortable breathing apparatus that really gives you the feeling of scuba diving without having to be certified. You can tour shallow coral reefs teeming with hundreds of colorful fish and plant life, from sea turtles to moray eels. Reservations are required; call to find out where and when to meet. A 2- to 3-hour underwater tour costs $70, including all equipment. If you have never dived before, you may require a 1-hour lesson in the pool, which costs an additional $40.

FISHING For party boats or charters, see also "Robbie's Rent-a-Boat," above.

Bud n' Mary's Fishing Marina, on U.S. 1 at MM 79.8, Islamorada (☎ **800/742-7945** or 305/664-2461; fax 305/664-5592), one of the largest marinas between Miami and Key West, is packed with sailors offering guided backcountry fishing charters. This is the place to go if you want to stalk tarpon, bonefish, and snapper. If the seas are not too rough, deep-sea and coral fishing trips can be arranged. Charters cost $400 to $500 for a half day, $600 to $800 for a full day, and splits begin at $125 per person.

The Bounty Hunter, 15th Street, Marathon (☎ **305/743-2446**), offers full- and half-day outings. For years, Captain Brock Hook's huge sign has boasted no fish, no pay. You're guaranteed to catch something. Choose your prey from shark, barracuda, sailfish, or whatever else is running. Prices are $350 for a half day, $375 for three-quarters of a day, and $450 for a full day. Rates are for groups of no more than six people.

SHOPPING

On your way to the Keys, you'll find an outlet center, the **Keys Factory Shops** (☎ **305/248-4727**), at 250 E. Palm Dr. (where the Fla. Turnpike meets U.S. Hwy. 1), in Florida City. The center holds more than 60 stores, including Nike Factory Store, Bass Co. Store, Levi's, Osh Kosh, and Izod. Travelers can pick up a free discount coupon booklet called the "Come Back Pack" from the Customer Service Center. The outlet is open daily until 9pm, except Sunday, when it closes at 6pm.

The Upper and Middle Keys have no shortage of tacky tourist shops selling shells and T-shirts and other hokey souvenirs, but for real Keys-style shopping, check out the **weekend flea markets.** One of the best is held every Saturday and Sunday bayside at MM 103.5 (☎ **305/451-0677**). Dozens of vendors open their stalls from 9am until

4 or 5pm selling every imaginable sort of antiques, T-shirts, plants, shoes, books, toys, and games, as well as a hearty dose of good old-fashioned junk.

A mecca for fishing and sports enthusiasts, **The World Wide Sportsman** (☎ **305/ 664-4615**) opened in late 1997 at MM 81.5. It's not only the largest fishing store in the Keys, but also a meeting place for anglers from all over the world. Every possible gizmo and gadget, plus hundreds of T-shirts, hats, books, and gift items are displayed in its more than 25,000 square feet. The salespeople are knowledgeable and eager to help. Travel specialists can even arrange for charter trips and backcountry tours. The store is open daily from 7am until 8:30pm.

WHERE TO STAY

U.S. 1 is lined with chain hotels in all price ranges. In the Upper Keys, the best moderately priced options are the **Holiday Inn Key Largo Resort & Marina,** U.S. 1 at MM 99.7 (☎ **800/THE KEYS** or 305/451-2121), and right next door, at MM 100, the **Ramada Limited Resort & Casino** (☎ **800/THE KEYS** or 305/451-3939). Both hotels share three pools and a casino boat; however, the Ramada is cozier and offers slightly cheaper rates. Also, the **Best Western Suites at Key Largo,** 201 Ocean Dr., MM 100 (☎ **800/462-6079** or 305/451-5081), is just 3 miles from John Pennekamp Coral Reef State Park. Another good option in the Upper Keys is **Islamorada Days Inn,** U.S. 1 at MM 82.5 (☎ **800/DAYS-INN** or 305/664-3681). In the Middle Keys, the **Howard Johnson** at 13351 Overseas Hwy., MM 54 in Marathon (☎ **800/321-3496** or 305/743-8550), also offers reasonably priced oceanside rooms.

For further options, consider these recommendations, grouped first by price, and then geographically from north to south.

VERY EXPENSIVE

Cheeca Lodge. U.S. 1 at MM 82 (P.O. Box 527), Islamorada, FL 33036. ☎ **800/327-2888** or 305/664-4651. Fax 305/664-2893. 203 units. A/C MINIBAR TV TEL. Winter $295–$650 double, $400 suite; off-season $185–$430 double, $285 suite. AE, CB, DC, DISC, MC, V.

One of the better places to stay in the Upper Keys, Cheeca has been hosting celebrities, royalty, and politicians since its opening in 1949. Guests now enjoy the luxury of the Cheeca's freshly renovated and remodeled rooms. All of the 203 units offer all the amenities of a world-class resort in a very laid-back setting. You may not feel compelled to leave the sprawling grounds, but it's good to know the hotel is conveniently situated near the best restaurants and nightlife. Located on 27 acres of beachfront property, this rambling resort is known for its excellent sports facilities, including diving and snorkeling programs and one of the only golf courses in the Upper Keys.

All rooms are spacious and have small balconies. The nicer ones overlook the ocean and have large marble bathrooms.

Dining/Diversions: The Atlantic's Edge restaurant is one of the best in the Upper Keys (see "Where to Dine," below). A pool bar and comfortable lounge offer more casual options throughout the day and evening.

Amenities: Concierge, room service, dry-cleaning and laundry services, in-room massage, newspaper delivery, baby-sitting, express checkout, valet parking, free coffee and refreshments in lobby. Kitchenettes, VCRs and video rentals, three outdoor heated pools, kids' pool, five hot tubs, beach, access to nearby health club, Jacuzzi, bicycle rental, 9-hole par-3 golf course, children's nature programs, conference rooms, car-rental desk, sundeck, six lighted tennis courts, water-sports equipment rental, tour desk, nature trail, boutiques.

✪ **Hawk's Cay Resort.** U.S. 1 at MM 61, Duck Key, FL 33050. ☎ **800/432-2242** or 305/743-7000. Fax 305/743-5215. 176 units. A/C TV TEL. Winter $220–$350 double, $400–$850 suite; off-season $160–$250 double, $300–$750 suite. AE, DC, DISC, MC, V.

Located on its own 60-acre island just outside of Marathon in the Middle Keys, Hawk's Cay is a sprawling and impressive resort encompassing a marina as well as a saltwater lagoon that's home to a half-dozen dolphins. It's especially popular with families, who appreciate the many activities and reasonably priced diversions. It's also more casual than other resorts, like Cheeca Lodge, which offers many of the same amenities. The manicured grounds are dotted with handsome two- and three-story flamingo-colored buildings. The guest rooms within are all quite similar—views account for the differences in price. All are large and have walk-in closets, small refrigerators, a sliding glass door opening onto a private balcony, and Caribbean-style bamboo furnishings padded with colorful fabrics. If you want to splurge, the top-floor suites have separate seating areas with pull-out sofas and large wraparound terraces with spectacular views.

Dining/Diversions: Three good restaurants and a lounge have a wide range of food, from Italian to seafood. A well-stocked ship's store has snacks and basic groceries. A lively lounge features live music every evening and most weekend afternoons.

Amenities: Concierge, room service, overnight laundry, in-room massage, express checkout, transportation to airport and golf course, free refreshments in lobby. Outdoor heated pool, a new adults-only private pool, beach, small fitness room, Jacuzzi, nearby golf course, sundeck, eight tennis courts (two lighted), water-sports equipment, bicycle rental, game room, children's center or programs, self-service laundry, marina store and gift shop, conference rooms, car-rental desk.

EXPENSIVE

Jules' Undersea Lodge. 51 Shoreland Dr., Key Largo, FL 33037. ☎ **305/451-2353.** Fax 305/451-4789. 1 unit. A/C TV TEL. $225–$325 per person. Rates include breakfast and dinner, as well as all equipment and unlimited scuba diving in the lagoon. AE, DISC, MC, V. From U.S. 1 south, at MM 103.2, turn left onto Transylvania Ave., across from the Central Plaza shopping mall.

Originally built as a research lab in the 1970s, this small underwater compartment now operates as a single-room hotel. As expensive as it is unusual, Jules' is most popular with diving honeymooners. The lodge rests on pillars on the ocean floor. To get inside, guests swim under the structure and pop up into the unit through a 4- by 6-foot "moon pool" that gurgles soothingly all night long. The 30-foot–deep underwater suite consists of a bedroom and galley and sleeps up to six. There is a television and VCR. Also, room service will bring breakfast, lunch, and daily newspapers in waterproof containers at no extra charge. Needless to say, this novelty is not for everyone.

Marriott Key Largo Bay Beach Resort. 103800 Overseas Hwy. (MM 103.8), Key Largo, FL 33037. ☎ **800/932-9332** or 305/453-0000. Fax 305/453-0093. E-mail: baybeach@ reefnet.com. 150 units. A/C MINIBAR TV TEL. Winter $209–$269, suites $500; off-season $139–$179, $250 suites. AE, DC, DISC, MC, V.

When this mammoth chain resort was built in 1993, many thought the sleepy little island town would be forever spoiled. On the contrary, this pristine, two-story Marriott created some major competition for the area's older resorts and the run-down 1950s motels, resulting in an overall upgrade of the neighboring accommodations. While it is hardly quaint, the amenities-laden complex built on 17 acres has everything an active or resting traveler could want, including a decent-sized beach. Guests can now enjoy the new European health spa, a nine-hole mini-golf course and new tennis courts. All guests are welcome to sail free on a gambling cruise ship that anchors in international waters from 2pm until 2am daily. Rooms are decorated in a pleasant (if generic) tropical style and include extras such as coffeepots, hair dryers, and safes. Most rooms (all but 22) also offer balconies overlooking the stunning Florida bay. For real pampering, consider the enormous suites, which can easily sleep a family of five. All have large wraparound terraces and large sitting areas. With its rates being slightly cheaper than the nearby Westin and Cheeca Lodge, you'll find it a good value.

Dining/Diversions: A casual bayside grill offers casually elegant dining, and an outdoor tiki bar has snacks and cocktails throughout the afternoon and evening.

Amenities: Concierge, room service, dry-cleaning and laundry services, in-room massage, newspaper delivery, baby-sitting, express checkout. Large outdoor pool, Jacuzzi, three small beach areas, VCRs on request, gym, bicycle rental, conference rooms, sundeck, access to nearby tennis and racquetball courts, water-sports equipment rental, business center, tour desk, children's programs, game room, nature trail, boutiques.

✪ **The Moorings.** 123 Beach Rd. near MM 81.5 on the ocean side, Islamorada, FL 33036. ☎ **305/664-4708.** Fax 305/664-4242. 17 cottages. A/C TV TEL. In season, $165–$200 smaller one-bedrooms, $350 large one-bedrooms. Oceanfront two- and three-bedroom cottages $2,450–$6,300 weekly. Discounts off-season. 2-night minimum for smaller cottages; 1-week minimum for larger cottages. MC, V.

Staying at the Moorings is more like staying at your second home than at a hotel. You'll never see another soul on this 18-acre resort if you choose not to. There isn't even maid service unless you request it. The romantic whitewashed houses are spacious and modestly decorated with funky island prints, bamboo, and tropical motifs. All have full kitchens and most have washers and dryers. Some have CD players and VCRs; ask when you book. The real reason to come to this cool resort is to relax on the more than 1,000-foot beach (one of the only real beaches around). There are a simple hard tennis court and a few kayaks and Windsurfers, but absolutely no motorized water vehicles. There is no room service or restaurant. This is a place for people who like each other a lot. Leave the kids at home unless they are extremely well-behaved and not easily bored.

Amenities: Laundry and dryers, full kitchens, some VCRs, large sandy beach, sundeck, large pool, boats, jogging trails.

MODERATE

Banana Bay Resort & Marina. U.S. 1 at MM 49.5, Marathon, FL 33050. ☎ **800/ BANANA-1** or 305/743-3500. Fax 305/743-2670. 60 units. A/C TV TEL. Winter $95–$195 double; off-season $75–$150 double. Rates include continental breakfast. Weekend and 3- and 7-night packages available. AE, DC, DISC, MC, V.

It doesn't look like much from the sign-cluttered Overseas Highway, but when you enter the lush grounds of Banana Bay, you will realize you're in one of the most bucolic and best-run properties in the Upper Keys. Built in the early 1950s as a fishing camp, the resort is a maze of pink-and-white two-story buildings hidden among banyans and palms. Guest rooms are very similar, but those with better views are more expensive. The rooms are moderately sized, and many have private balconies where you can enjoy complimentary coffee and newspapers every morning.

The restaurant serves breakfast, lunch, and dinner by the pool or in a kitschy old dining room. A waterfront tiki bar offers great sunset views. Head down to the marina to sign up for charter fishing, sailing, and diving. Kids will enjoy the small game room and free use of bicycles.

✪ **Conch Key Cottages.** Near U.S. 1 at MM 62.3, Marathon, FL 33050. ☎ **800/ 330-1577** or 305/289-1377. Fax 305/743-8207. www.floridakeys.net/conchkeycottages. 12 units. A/C TV. Winter $105 efficiency, $126 one-bedroom apt, $147 one-bedroom cottage, $194–$249 two-bedroom cottage; off-season $74 efficiency, $115 one-bedroom apt, $132 one-bedroom cottage, $147–$215 two-bedroom cottage. DISC, MC, V.

Occupying its own private micro-island just off U.S. 1, Conch Key Cottages is a unique and comfortable hideaway run by live-in owners Ron Wilson and Wayne Byrnes, who are constantly fixing and adding to their unique property. This is a place to get away from it all; the cottages aren't close to much, except maybe one or two interesting eateries. The cabins, which were built at different times over the past 40 years, overlook their own stretch of natural, but very small, private beach and have screened-in porches and cozy bedrooms and bathrooms. Each has a hammock and barbecue grill. Request one of the new two-bedroom cottages, completed in 1997— especially if you are traveling with the family. They are the most spacious and well designed, practically tailor-made for couples or families. On the other side of the pool are a handful of efficiency apartments that are similarly outfitted but enjoy no beach frontage. All have fully equipped kitchens. There's also a small heated fresh-water pool.

Faro Blanco Marine Resort. 1996 Overseas Hwy., U.S. 1 at MM 48.5, Marathon, FL 33050. ☎ **800/759-3276** or 305/743-9018. Fax 305/866-5235. 123 units, 31 houseboats with 4 units each. A/C TV TEL. Winter $65–$150 cottage, $99–$200 houseboat, $185 lighthouse, $240 condo; off-season $55–$125 cottage, $79–$150 houseboat, $150 lighthouse, $210 condo. AE, DISC, MC, V.

Spanning both sides of the Overseas Highway and all on waterfront property, this huge, two-shore marina and hotel complex offers something for every taste. Free-standing, camp-style cottages with a small bedroom are the resort's least expensive accommodations but are in dire need of rehabilitation. Old appliances and a musty odor also make them the least desirable units on the property.

The houseboats are the best choice and value. Permanently tethered in a tranquil marina, these white rectangular boats look like floating mobile homes and are uniformly clean, fresh, and recommendable. They have colonial American–style furnishings, fully equipped kitchenettes, front and back porches, and water, water everywhere. The boats are so tightly moored, you hardly move at all, even in the roughest weather.

Finally, there are two unusual rental units located in a lighthouse on the pier. Circular staircases, unusually shaped rooms and showers, and nautical decor make it a unique place to stay, but some guests might find it claustrophobic. Guests in any of the accommodations can enjoy the Olympic-size pool, any of the four casual restaurants, a fully equipped dive shop, barbecue and picnic areas, and a playground.

Holiday Isle Resort. U.S. 1 at MM 84, Islamorada, FL 33036. ☎ **800/327-7070** or 305/664-2321. Fax 305/664-2703. 199 units. Winter $85–$425; off-season $65–$350. AE, CB, DISC, MC, V.

A huge resort complex encompassing five restaurants, several lounges, tiki huts, a large marina, many retail shops, and four distinct (if not distinctive) hotels, the Holiday Isle is one of the biggest resorts in the Keys. It attracts a spring-break kind of crowd year-round. Its Tiki Bar claims to have invented the rum runner drink (151-proof rum, blackberry brandy, banana liqueur, grenadine, and lime juice), and there's no reason to doubt it. Hordes of partiers are attracted to the resort's nonstop merrymaking, live music, and beachfront bars. As a result, some of the accommodations can be noisy.

Rooms can be bare-bones budget to oceanfront luxury, as the broad range of prices reflects. Even the nicest rooms could use a good cleaning. El Captain and Harbor Lights, two of the least expensive hotels on the property, are both austere. Like in the other hotels here, rooms could use a thorough rehab. Howard Johnson's, another Holiday Isle property, is a little farther from the action and a tad more civilized. If you plan to be there for a few days, choose an efficiency or suite; both have kitchenettes.

Guests can choose between two outdoor heated pools and a kids' pool. They also offer water-sports equipment rental, gift boutiques, and a shopping arcade.

✪ **Kona Kai Resort & Gallery.** 97802 Overseas Hwy. (U.S. 1 at MM 97.8), Key Largo, FL 33037. ☎ **800/365-7829** or 305/852-7200. Fax 305/852-4629. www.funandsun.com/konakai. 11 units. Winter $179–$209 rms; $211–$559 suites; off-season $96–$169 rms, $121–$315 suites. 3- to 4-night minimum stay usually required. AE, DISC, MC, V. No smoking on property.

Unique in the Upper Keys, this little haven is both casual and elegant—thanks to a total overhaul completed over 3 years under the supervision of the owners, Joe Harris and his wife, Ronnie, former executives with NBC television. The quaint, simply furnished rooms dot the lushly landscaped 2-acre property, which boasts a large variety of native vegetation like palms, bougainvillea, and ferns, plus an impressive collection of fruit-bearing trees, such as carambola, passion fruit, banana, key lime, guava, and coconut. Lounge chairs, hammocks, a Jacuzzi, and a compact artificial beach are available for those who just want to relax, while a small lighted tennis court, a heated pool, a Ping-Pong table, a volleyball court, and all kinds of water sports are available for those who are more active. For the adventurous, Joe and Ronnie will organize excursions to the Everglades, the backcountry, or wherever. No phones in the rooms and a 4-day minimum stay requirement in the winter make relaxing imperative. All the rooms are very private and simply furnished without things like blow dryers or stereos. An art gallery featuring works of local painters, photographers, and sculptors doubles as the property's office and lobby. Even if you are not staying here, stop in to see the artwork.

Lime Tree Bay Resort Motel. U.S. 1 at MM 68.5 in Layton, Long Key, FL 33001. ☎ **800/723-4519** or 305/664-4740. Fax 305/664-0750. 30 units. A/C TV TEL. $75–$110 motel rooms or efficiencies; $115–$150 cottages; $105–$125 deluxe motel rooms; $150–$180 one-bedroom suite; $155–$230 two-bedroom suites. AE, DC, DISC, MC, V.

The Lime Tree Bay Resort is the only hotel in the tiny town of Layton (pop. 183). Midway between Islamorada and Marathon, the hotel is only steps from Long Key State Recreation Area. Motel rooms and efficiencies have tiny bathrooms with standing showers, but they are clean and well maintained. The best deal is the two-bedroom bay-view apartment. The large living area with new fixtures and furnishings leads out to a large private deck, where you can enjoy a view of the gulf from your hammock. A full kitchen and two full bathrooms make it a comfortable space for six people.

This affordable little hideaway has all the amenities you could want, including shuffleboard, tennis, a small pool, water sports, and a little cafe with a small but decent menu. It's situated on a very pretty piece of waterfront graced with hundreds of mature palm trees and lots of other tropical foliage.

INEXPENSIVE

Bay Harbor Lodge. 97702 Overseas Highway, U.S. 1 at MM 97.7 (off the southbound lane of U.S. 1), Key Largo, FL 33037. ☎ **305/852-5695.** 16 units. A/C TV TEL. Season $65–$105 double; off-season $78–$98 efficiency; $85–$125 cottage. MC, V.

A small, simple retreat that's big on charm, the Bay Harbor Lodge is an extraordinarily welcoming place. The lodge is far from fancy, and the wide range of accommodations are not all created equal. The motel rooms are small and ordinary in decor, but even the least expensive is recommendable. The efficiencies are larger motel rooms with fully equipped kitchenettes. The oceanfront cottages are larger still, have full kitchens, and represent one of the best values in the Keys. The vinyl-covered furnishings and old-fashioned wallpapers won't win any design awards, but elegance isn't what the "real" Keys are about. The 1½ lush acres of grounds are planted with banana trees and have an outdoor heated pool and several small barbecue grills. Guests are free to use the rowboats, paddleboats, canoes, kayaks, and snorkeling equipment. Bring your own beach towels.

✪ **Ragged Edge Resort.** 243 Treasure Harbor Rd. (near MM 86.5), Islamorada, FL 33036. ☎ **305/852-5389.** 11 units. A/C TV TEL. Season $70–$95 motel rm/efficiency; $109 studio apt; $169 two-bedroom/two-bathroom apt. Off-season $50–$70 efficiency; $78 studio apt; $120 two-bedroom/two-bathroom apt. AE, MC, V.

This small, well-maintained property has only 11 units spread out along more than half a dozen gorgeous, grassy waterfront acres. All are immaculately clean and comfortable, and most are outfitted with full kitchens and tasteful furnishings. There's no bar, restaurant, or staff to speak of, but the retreat's affable owner, Jackie Barnes, is happy to lend you bicycles or good advice on the area's offerings. A large dock attracts boaters and a large variety of local and migratory birds.

CAMPING

John Pennekamp Coral Reef State Park. U.S. 1 at MM 102.5 (P.O. Box 487), Key Largo, FL 33037. ☎ **305/451-1202.** 47 campsites. Reservations can be made up to 11 months in advance by telephone or in person. $24–$26 per site. MC, V.

One of Florida's best parks (see above), Pennekamp offers 47 well-separated campsites, half available by advance reservation, the rest distributed on a first-come, first-served basis. The car-camping sites are small but well equipped with bathrooms and showers. A little lagoon nearby attracts many large wading birds. Reservations are held until 5pm, and the park must be notified of late arrival by phone on the check-in date. Pennekamp opens at 8am and closes around sundown. No pets.

Long Key State Recreation Area. U.S. 1 at MM 67.5 (P.O. Box 776), Long Key, FL 33001. ☎ **305/664-4815.** 60 campsites. $24–$26 per site for 1 to 4 people. MC, V.

The Upper Keys's other main state park is more secluded than its northern neighbor, and more popular. All sites are located oceanside and surrounded by narrow rows of trees and nearby toilet and bath facilities. Reserve well in advance, especially in winter.

WHERE TO DINE

Although not known as a culinary hot spot, the Upper and Middle Keys do offer some excellent restaurants, most of which specialize in seafood. Often, visitors (especially those who fish) take advantage of accommodations that have kitchen facilities and cook their own meals. Also, most restaurants will clean and cook your catch for a nominal charge.

VERY EXPENSIVE

✪ **Atlantic's Edge.** In the Cheeca Lodge, U.S. 1 at MM 82, Islamorada. ☎ **305/664-4651.** Reservations recommended. Main courses $20–$36. AE, CB, DC, DISC, MC, V. Daily 5:30–10pm. SEAFOOD/REGIONAL.

Ask for a table by the oceanfront window to feel really privileged at this, the most elegant restaurant in the Keys. Although the service and food are first-class, don't get dressed up—a sport coat will be fine but isn't necessary. You can choose from an innovative, varied menu, which offers several choices of fresh fish, steak, chicken, and pastas. The crab cakes, made with stone crab when in season, are the very best in the Keys; served on a warm salad of baby greens with a mild sauce of red peppers, they're the stuff cravings are made of. Other excellent dishes include a Thai-spiced fresh baby snapper and the vegetarian angel-hair pasta with mushrooms, asparagus, and peppers in a rich broth. Service can sometimes be less than efficient but is always courteous and professional.

EXPENSIVE

Barracuda Grill. U.S. 1 at MM 49.5 (bay side), Marathon. ☎ **305/743-3314.** Reservations not accepted. Main courses $13–$30. AE, MC, V. Open nightly 6–10pm. BISTRO/SEAFOOD.

Owned by Lance Hill and his wife, Jan (who used to be a sous chef at Little Palm Island), this casual spot serves excellent seafood, steaks, and chops. It's too bad it's open only for dinner. Some of the favorite dishes are old-fashioned meat loaf, classic beef Stroganoff, rack of lamb, and seafood stew. In addition, this small barracuda-decorated restaurant features a well-priced American wine list with a vast sampling of California vintages.

✪ **Marker 88.** U.S. 1 at MM 88 (bay side), Islamorada. ☎ **305/852-9315.** Reservations not usually required. Main courses $14–$29. AE, DC, DISC, MC, V. Tues–Sun 5–11pm. SEAFOOD/REGIONAL.

An institution in the Upper Keys, Marker 88 has been pleasing locals, visitors, and critics since it opened in the early 1970s. Chef-owner Andre Mueller has created a "gourmet" restaurant in a tropical-fish house setting. The wide range of standard fare is tinged with his take on nouvelle cuisine. Taking full advantage of his island location, Andre offers dozens of seafood selections, including Keys lobster, Bahamas conch, Everglades frogs' legs, Florida Bay stone crabs, Gulf Coast shrimp, and an impressive variety of fish from around the country. After you've figured out what kind of seafood to have, you can choose from a dozen styles of preparation. The Keys's standard is meuniere, which is a subtle, tasty sauce of lemon and parsley. Although everything looks tempting, don't over-order—portions are huge. The waitresses, who are pleasant enough, require a bit of patience, but the food is worth it.

MODERATE

Lazy Days Oceanfront Bar and Seafood Grill. U.S. 1 at MM 79.9, Islamorada. ☎ **305/664-5256.** Main courses $11–$20. AE, DISC, MC, V. Tues–Sun 11:30am–10pm. SEAFOOD/AMERICAN.

Opened in 1992, the Lazy Days quickly became one of the most popular restaurants around, mostly because of the large portions and lively atmosphere. Meals are pricier than the casual dining room would suggest, but the food is good enough and the menu varied. Steamed clams with garlic and bell peppers make a tempting appetizer. The menu focuses on—what else?—seafood, but you can also find Italian dishes. Most main courses come with baked potato, vegetables, a tossed salad, and French bread, making appetizers redundant.

✪ **Lorelei Restaurant and Cabana Bar.** U.S. 1 at MM 82, Islamorada. ☎ **305/664-4656.** Reservations not usually required. Main courses $9–$22. Daily 7am–10pm. Outside bar serves lunch menu 11am–9pm. Bar closes at midnight. SEAFOOD/BAR FOOD.

Don't resist the siren call of the enormous, sparkling, roadside mermaid—you won't be dashed into the rocks. This big old fish house and bar is a great place for a snack, a meal, or a beer. Inside, a good-value menu focuses mainly on seafood. When in season, lobsters are the way to go. For $20, you can get a good-sized tail—at least a 1-pounder—prepared any way you like. Other fare includes the standard clam chowder, fried shrimp, and doughy conch fritters. Salads and soups are hearty and satisfying. For those tired of fish, the menu also offers a few beef selections. The outside bar has live music every evening, and you can order snacks and light meals from a limited menu that is satisfying and well priced. Enjoy the live entertainment every night.

INEXPENSIVE

Calypso's. 1 Seagate Blvd. (near MM 99.5), Key Largo. Main courses $8–$16. Wed–Mon 11:30am–10pm. MC, V. SEAFOOD/PASTA.

The awning still bears the name of the former restaurant, Demar's, but the food here is all Todd Lollis's. Though he looks like he might be more comfortable at a Grateful Dead concert than in a kitchen, this inspired young chef turns out inventive seafood dishes in a casual and rustic waterside setting. If it's available, try the butter pecan sauce over whatever fish is freshest. Don't miss the white-wine sangria, full of tangy oranges and limes and topped with a dash of cinnamon. The prices are surprisingly reasonable, but the service can be a little more laid back than you're used to. The toughest part is finding the place. From south, turn right at the blinking yellow lights near MM 99.5 to Ocean Bay Drive; turn right. Look for the blue vinyl-sided building on the left.

✪ **Henry's Bakery and Gourmet Pizza Shop.** U.S. 1 at MM 82.5 (adjacent to Days Inn), 82700 Overseas Hwy., Islamorada. ☎ **305/664-4030.** Pastas $7–$9.50; pizzas $8–$18; sandwiches and salads $4.50–$8. Mon–Sat 6am–10pm (sometimes later on weekends). No credit cards. BAKERY/PIZZERIA.

This recently expanded storefront bakery serves the best pizzas and sandwiches in town. My favorite is freshly sliced turkey on homemade warm French bread, with a splash of superbly tangy vinaigrette. Most days Henry bakes fresh multigrain, semolina, and Italian bread, too. Stop by early for delicious pastries and croissants. If you want pizza, consider the decadent Sublime Pie with lobster tail, roasted bell peppers, and sun-dried tomatoes. The crust has the perfect texture—just a bit chewy, but not too doughy.

✪ **Islamorada Fish Company.** U.S. 1 at MM 81.5 (up the street from Cheeca Lodge), Islamorada. ☎ **800/258-2559** or 305/664-9271. Main courses $8–$20. DISC, MC, V. Mon–Sat 8am–9pm; Sun 9am–9pm. Also, just up the block, Islamorada Fish Company Restaurant & Bakery, MM 81.6. ☎ 305/664-8363. DISC, MC, V. Thurs–Tues 6am–9pm; Wed 6am–2pm. SEAFOOD.

The original Islamorada Fish Company has been selling seafood out of its roadside shack since 1948. It's still the best place to pick up a cooler of stone crab claws in season (mid-Oct through Apr). Also great are the fish sandwiches, served fried with melted American cheese, fried onions, and coleslaw. A few hundred yards up the road is the newer establishment, which looks like an ordinary diner but has a selection of fantastic seafood and pastas. It's also the place for breakfast. Locals gather for politics and gossip, as well as delicious grits, oatmeal, omelets, and homemade pastries.

Time Out Barbecue. U.S. 1 at MM 81.5. ☎ **305/664-8911.** Sandwiches $3.75–$4.25; rib and chicken platters to share $9–$15. Daily 11:30am–9pm (depending on football schedule). No credit cards. BARBECUE.

This roadside truck serves up hot and hearty old-fashioned barbecue that is the best I've had. The secret, they say, is in the slow-cooking—more than 10 hours for the melt-in-your-mouth soft pork sandwich. Topped off with delicious, not too-creamy coleslaw and sweet baked beans, any of the many offerings is worth a stop. You can grab a seat at the picnic table on the grassy lawn next to the Trading Post.

THE UPPER & MIDDLE KEYS AFTER DARK

Nightlife in the Upper Keys tends to start before the sun goes down, often at noon, since most people—visitors and locals alike—are on vacation. Also, many anglers and sports-minded folk go to bed early.

Opened in the early 1990s by some young locals tired of tourist traps, **Hog Heaven,** at MM 85.3 just off the main road on the ocean side in Islamorada (☎ **305/664-9669**), is a welcome respite from the neon-colored cocktail circuit. This white-washed biker bar offers a waterside view and diversions that include big-screen TVs and video games. The food isn't bad, either. The atmosphere is cliquish since most patrons are regulars, so start up a game of pool or skeet to break the ice.

No trip is complete without a stop at the **Tiki Bar at the Holiday Isle Resort,** U.S. 1 at MM 84, Islamorada (☎ **800/327-7070** or 305/664-2321). Hundreds of revelers visit this oceanside spot for drinks and dancing any time of day, but the live rock music starts at 8:30pm. (See "Where to Stay," above.)

In the afternoon and early evening (when everyone is sunburned, drunk, or just happy to be alive and dancing to live reggae), head for **Kokomo's,** just next door to the thatched-roof Tiki Bar. Kokomo's often closes at 7:30pm on weekends, so get there early. For information, call the Holiday Isle Resort.

Locals and tourists mingle at the outdoor cabana bar at **Lorelei's** (see "Where to Dine," above). Most evenings after 5pm, you'll find local bands playing on a thatched roof stage—mainly rock and roll, Caribbean, and sometimes blues.

✪ **Woody's Saloon and Restaurant,** on U.S. 1 at MM 82, Islamorada (☎ **305/664-4335**), is a lively, wacky, raunchy place serving up mediocre pizzas and live bands almost every night. The house band, Big Dick and the Extenders, showcases a 300-pound Native American who does a lewd, rude, and crude routine of jokes and songs starting at 9pm, Tuesday through Sunday. He is a legend. By the way, don't think you're lucky if you are offered the front table: It's the target seat for Big Dick's haranguing. Avoid the lame karaoke performance on Sunday and Monday evenings. There's a small cover charge most nights. Drink specials, contests, and the legendary Big Dick keep this place packed until 4am almost every night.

For a more subdued atmosphere, try the handsome wood bar at **Zane Grey's** (on the second floor of World Wide Sportsman at MM 81.5). Outside, enjoy a view of the calm waters of the bay, or inside, soak up the history of some real old anglers. You feel like a real swell in this stained-glass, mahogany-decked club. It is open from 11am to 11pm, and later on weekends. Call to find out who is playing on weekends (☎ **305/664-4244**), when there is live entertainment and no cover charge.

2 The Lower Keys: Big Pine Key to Coppitt Key

128 miles SW of Miami

Big Pine, Sugarloaf, Summerland, and the other Lower Keys are less developed and more tranquil than the Upper Keys. If you're looking for haute cuisine and a happening nightlife, look elsewhere. If you're looking to commune with nature or adventure in solitude, you've come to the right place. Unlike their neighbors to the north and south, the Lower Keys are devoid of rowdy spring-break crowds, boast few T-shirt and trinket shops, and have almost no late-night bars. What they do offer are the very best opportunities to enjoy the vast natural resources—on land and water—that make the area so rich. Stay overnight in the Lower Keys, rent a boat, and explore the reefs—it might be the most memorable part of your trip.

ESSENTIALS

GETTING THERE   See "Essentials" for the Upper and Middle Keys. Continue south on U.S. 1. The Lower Keys start at the end of the Seven-Mile Bridge.

VISITOR INFORMATION   The **Lower Keys Chamber of Commerce,** ocean side of U.S. 1 at MM 31 (P.O. Box 430511), Big Pine Key, FL 33043 (☎ **800/872-3722**

or 305/872-2411; fax 305/872-0752; e-mail: lkchamber@aol.com), is open Monday through Friday from 9am to 5pm and Saturday from 9am to 3pm. The pleasant staff will help with anything a traveler may need. Call, write, or stop in for a comprehensive, detailed information packet.

WHAT TO SEE & DO

Once the centerpiece of the Lower Keys and still a great asset is **Bahia Honda State Park,** U.S. 1 at MM 37.5, Big Pine Key (☎ **305/872-2353**), which, even after the violent storms of 1998, has one of the most beautiful coastlines in South Florida. Bahia Honda (pronounced Bah-ya) is a great place for hiking, bird watching, swimming, snorkeling, and fishing. The 524-acre park encompasses a wide variety of ecosystems, including coastal mangroves, beach dunes, and tropical hammocks. There are miles of trails packed with unusual plants and animals and a small white beach. Shaded seaside picnic areas are fitted with tables and grills. Although the beach is never wider than 5 feet even at low tide, this is the Lower Keys's best beach area.

True to its name (Spanish for "deep bay"), the park has relatively deep waters close to shore that are perfect for snorkeling and diving. Head to the stunning reefs at Looe Key, where the coral and fish are more vibrant than anywhere in the United States. **Snorkeling trips** depart daily from March through September and cost $22 for adults, $18 for youths 6 to 14, and free for children 5 and under. Call ☎ **305/872-3210** for a schedule.

Admission to the park is $4 per vehicle (plus 50¢ per person), $1.50 per pedestrian or bicyclist, free for children 5 and under. If you are alone in a car, you'll only pay $2.50. Open daily from 8am to sunset.

The most famous residents of the Lower Keys are the tiny Key deer. Of the estimated 300 existing in the world, two-thirds live on Big Pine Key's **National Key Deer Refuge.** To get your bearings, stop by the rangers' office at the Winn-Dixie Shopping Plaza near MM 30.5 off U.S. 1. They'll give you an informative brochure and map of the area. It is open Monday through Friday from 8am to 5pm.

If the office is closed, head out to the Blue Hole, a former rock quarry now filled with the fresh water that's vital to the deer's survival. To get there, turn right at Big Pine Key's only traffic light onto Key Deer Boulevard (take the left fork immediately after the turn), and continue 1½ miles to the observation site parking lot, on your left. The half-mile Watson Hammock Trail, about a third of a mile past the Blue Hole, is the refuge's only marked footpath. Try coming out here in the early morning or late evening to catch a glimpse of these gentle, dog-sized deer. Refuge lands are open daily from half an hour before sunrise to half an hour after sunset. Whatever you do, do not feed the deer—it will threaten their survival. Call the park office (☎ **305/872-2239**) to find out about the infrequent free tours of the refuge, scheduled at different times throughout the year.

The only human-made attraction in the Lower Keys is the **Sugarloaf Bat Tower,** off U.S. 1 at MM 17 (next to Sugarloaf Airport on the bay side). In a vain effort to battle the ubiquitous troublesome mosquitoes in the Lower Keys, developer Clyde Perkey built this odd structure to lure bug-eating bats. Despite his alluring design and a pungent bat aphrodisiac, his guests never showed. Since 1929, this wooden, flat-topped, 45-foot-high pyramid has stood empty and deserted, except for the occasional tourist who stops to wonder what it is. There is no sign or marker to commemorate this odd remnant of ingenuity. It's worth a 5-minute detour to see it. To get there, turn right at the Sugarloaf Airport sign, and then right again onto the dirt road that begins just before the airport gate; the tower is about 100 yards ahead.

OUTDOOR PURSUITS

BICYCLING   If you have your own bike, or your lodging offers rental (many do), the Lower Keys is a great place to get off busy U.S. 1 to explore the beautiful back roads. On Big Pine Key, cruise along Key Deer Boulevard (at MM 30). Those with fat tires can ride into the National Key Deer Refuge.

BIRD WATCHING   Bring your birding books. A stopping point for migratory birds on the Eastern Flyway, the Lower Keys are populated with many West Indian bird species, especially during spring and fall. The small vegetated islands of the Keys are the only nesting sites in the United States for the great white heron and the white-crowned pigeon. They're also some of the very few breeding places for the reddish egret, the roseate spoonbill, the mangrove cuckoo, and the black-whiskered vireo. Look for them on Bahia Honda and the many uninhabited islands nearby.

BOATING   Dozens of shops rent powerboats for fishing and reef exploring. Most also rent tackle, sell bait, and have charter captains available. **Bud Boats,** at the Old Wooden Bride Fishing Camp and Marina, MM 30 in Big Pine Key (☎ 305/872-9165), has a wide selection of well-maintained boats. Depending on the size, rentals cost between $70 and $250 for a day, between $50 and $130 for a half day. Another good option is **Jaybird's Powerboats,** U.S. 1 at MM 33, Big Pine Key (☎ 305/872-8500). They rent for full days only. Prices start at $127 for a 19-footer.

CANOEING & KAYAKING   The Overseas Highway (U.S. 1) touches on only a few dozen of the many hundreds of islands that make up the Keys. To really see the Lower Keys, rent a kayak or canoe—perfect for these shallow waters. **Reflections Kayak Nature Tours,** operating out of Parmer's Place Resort Motel, on U.S. 1 at MM 28.5, Little Torch Key (☎ 305/872-2896), offers fully outfitted backcountry wildlife tours, either on your own or with an expert. A former U.S. Forest Service guide, Mike Wedeking, keeps up an engaging discussion describing the area's fish, sponges, coral, osprey, hawks, eagles, alligators, raccoons, and deer. The 3-hour tours cost $45 per person and include spring water, fresh fruit, granola bars, and use of binoculars. Bring a towel and sea sandals or sneakers.

DIVING/FISHING   A day spent fishing, either in the shallow backcountry or in the deep sea, is a great way to ensure yourself a fresh fish dinner, or you can release your catch and just appreciate the challenge. Especially since the *Adolphus Busch* was sunk off Looe Key in 100 feet of water, the Lower Keys also offer some prime diving. Whichever you choose, **Larry Threlkeld's Strike Zone Charters,** U.S. 1 at MM 29.5, Big Pine Key (☎ 305/872-9863), is the charter service to call. Prices for fishing boats start at $250 to $400 for a half day. Especially if you have enough anglers to share the price, it isn't too steep. They may be able to match you with other interested visitors.

To get to the *Adolphus Busch Sr,* a sunken 210-foot island freighter that serves as a pretty interesting dive site, on your own boat, head to coordinates 24.31.819 N 81.27.643W between Looe Key and American Shoals. Strike Zone will take you for $50 without equipment.

HIKING   You can hike throughout the flat marshy Keys, on both marked trails and meandering coastlines. The best places to trek through nature are **Bahia Honda State Park** at MM 29.5 and **National Key Deer Refuge** at MM 30 (for more information on both, see "What to See & Do," above). Bahia Honda Park has a free brochure describing an excellent self-guided tour along the Silver Palm Nature Trail. You'll traverse hammocks, mangroves, and sand dunes and cross a lagoon. You can do the walk (which is less than a mile) in under half an hour and can explore a great cross-section of the natural habitat in the Lower Keys.

SNORKELING/DIVING Snorkelers and divers should not miss the Keys's most dramatic reefs at the ☺ **Looe Key National Marine Sanctuary.** Here you'll see more than 150 varieties of hard and soft coral, some centuries old, as well as every type of tropical fish, including the gold and blue parrot fish, moray eels, barracudas, French angels, and tarpon. **Looe Key Dive Center,** U.S. 1 at MM 27.5, Ramrod Key (☎ 305/872-2215), offers a mind-blowing 2½-hour tour aboard a 45-foot catamaran with two shallow 1-hour dives for snorkelers and scuba divers. Snorkelers pay $30, and divers with their own equipment pay $65. Good-quality rentals are available. (See "What to See & Do," above, for other diving options.)

Shopping

Certainly not known for great shopping, the Lower Keys do happen to be home to many talented visual artists, particularly those who specialize in depicting their natural surroundings. The **Artists in Paradise Gallery,** on Big Pine Key in the Winn-Dixie Shopping Plaza, near MM 30.5, 1 block north of U.S. 1 at the traffic light (☎ 305/872-1828), displays an ever-changing selection of watercolors, oils, photos, and sculptures. This cooperative gallery displays the work of more than a dozen artists who share the task of watching the store. Usually, hours are daily from 10am to 6pm. Even more impressive is the ☺ **Gallery at Kona Kai** (see "Where to Stay," below), which shows dramatic black-and-white photos, oils, watercolors, and more.

WHERE TO STAY

There are a number of cheap fish shacks along the highway for those who want bare-bones accommodations, but so far, there are no national hotel chains in the Lower Keys. For information on lodging in cabins or trailers at local campgrounds, see "Camping," below.

Very Expensive

☺ **Little Palm Island.** Launch is at the ocean side of U.S. 1 at MM 28.5, Little Torch Key, FL 33042. ☎ **800/343-8567** or 305/872-2524. Fax 305/872-4843. www.littlepalmisland.com. 28 bungalows; 2 deluxe suites. A/C MINIBAR. Winter $600–$850 per couple; off-season $350–$650 including transportation to and from the island and unlimited (nonmotorized) water sports. Meal plans include 2 meals daily for $125 per person per day. 3 meals are $140 per person. No children under 16. AE, CB, DC, DISC, MC, V.

Severely damaged in the storms of 1998, Little Palm Island was closed for reconstruction for several months. When it reopened in early 1999, it was looking even better than before. The work, at the cost of nearly $9 million, included new roofs, new furniture, a new dining room, and a thorough update of the guest rooms. Over the years this exclusive island escape—host to presidents and royalty—has not been just a place to stay while in the Lower Keys; it has been a resort destination all its own. Built on a private 5-acre island, it's accessible only by boat. Guests stay in thatched-roof duplexes amid lush foliage and flowering tropical plants. Many villas have ocean views and private sundecks with rope hammocks. Inside, the romantic suites have all the comforts and conveniences of a luxurious contemporary beach cottage, but without telephones, TVs, or alarm clocks. Note that on the breezeless south side of the island, you may get invaded by mosquitoes, even in the winter. Bring spray and lightweight long-sleeved clothing. Known for its innovative and pricey food, Little Palm also hosts visitors just for dinner or lunch. If you are staying on the island, opt for the full American plan, which includes three meals a day for about $140 per person. If you pay à la carte, you could spend that much just on dinner. At these prices, Little Palm appeals to those who aren't keeping track.

Dining/Diversions: The Little Palm Restaurant offers fine dining either indoors or alfresco at inflated prices. A pool bar offers refreshments and light snacks all day.

Amenities: Concierge, room service, dry cleaning, laundry, newspaper delivery, twice-daily maid service, in-room massage, courtesy van from Key West or Marathon airport, ferry service to and from the mainland. Outdoor pool with small waterfall, wide beach, in-room Jacuzzi tubs, sauna, sundeck, water-sports equipment, jogging trail, boutique.

MODERATE

Deer Run Bed and Breakfast. Long Beach Dr. (P.O. Box 431), Big Pine Key, FL 33043. ☎ 305/872-2015. Fax 305/872-2842. E-mail: deerrunbb@aol.com. 3 units. Winter from $110 double; off-season from $95 double. No children under 16. Rates include full American breakfast. No credit cards. From U.S. 1 south, turn left at the Big Pine Fishing Lodge (MM 33); continue for about 2 miles.

Located directly on the beach, Sue Abbott's small, homey, smoke-free B&B is a real find. One upstairs and two downstairs guest rooms are comfortably furnished with queen-size beds, good closets, and touch-sensitive lamps. Rattan and 1970s-style chairs and couches furnish the living room, along with 13 birds and three cats. Breakfast, which is served on a pretty, fenced-in porch, is cooked to order by Sue herself. The wooded area around the property is full of deer, which are often spotted on the beach as well. Ask to use one of the bikes to explore nearby nature trails. The owner prefers adults and mature children only.

INEXPENSIVE

✪ **Parmer's Place Cottages.** Barry Ave. (P.O. Box 430665), near MM 28.5, Little Torch Key, FL 33043. ☎ **305/872-2157.** Fax 305/872-2014. 41 units. In winter and during festivals from $77 double, from $93.50 efficiency; off-season $55–$65 double, from $75 efficiency. AE, DISC, MC, V. Turn right onto Barry Ave. Resort is ½ mile down on the right.

Parmer's, a fixture here for more than 20 years, is well-known for its charming hospitality and helpful staff. This downscale resort offers modest but comfortable cottages. Every unit is different. Some face the water, some are a few steps away from the water, some have small kitchenettes, and others are just a bedroom. Room 26, a one-bedroom efficiency, is especially nice, with a small sitting area that faces the water. Room 6, a small efficiency, has a little kitchenette and an especially large bathroom. The rooms all have linoleum floors, dated 1970s-style painted rattan furnishings, fake flowers, and thrift-store art. They're very clean. Many can be combined to accommodate large families. Facilities include a horseshoes court, a boat ramp, and a heated swimming pool.

CAMPING

Bahia Honda State Park (☎ 305/872-2353) offers some of the best camping in the Keys even after the devastating storms of 1998. It is as loaded with facilities and activities as it is with campers. However, don't be discouraged by its popularity—this park encompasses more than 500 acres of land. There are 80 campsites and six spacious and comfortable cabin units, though some are still under reconstruction. Cabins hold up to eight guests and come complete with linens, kitchenettes, and utensils. You'll enjoy the wraparound terrace, barbecue pit, and rocking chairs.

Camping here costs about $25 per site for one to four people without electricity and $26 with electricity. Depending on the season, cabin prices change: From December 15 to September 14, it's about $125 per cabin for one to four people; from September 15 to December 14, it's $97.30 per cabin. Additional people (over four) cost $6. MasterCard and Visa are accepted.

Another excellent value can be found at the **KOA Sugarloaf Key Resort,** near MM 20. This oceanside facility has 200 fully equipped sites that rent for about $53 a night (no-hookup sites cost about $38). Or pitch a tent on the 5 acres of lush waterfront property. The resort also rents out travel trailers. The 22-foot Dutchman sleeps six and is equipped with eating and cooking utensils. It costs about $100 a day. More luxurious trailers go for $160 a day. All major credit cards are accepted. For details, contact P.O. Box 420469, Summerland Key, FL 33042 (☎ **800/562-7731** or 305/745-3549; fax 305/745-9889; e-mail: sugarloaf@koa.net). They lost about 80 percent of their trees in the big storm of 1998 but plan to replant for next season.

WHERE TO DINE

There aren't many fine-dining options in the Lower Keys, but the following are worth a stop for those passing through.

MODERATE

✪ **Mangrove Mama's Restaurant.** U.S. 1 at MM 20, Sugarloaf Key. ☎ **305/745-3030.** Main courses $13–$19; lunch $2–$9; brunch $5–$7. MC, V. Daily 11:30am–10pm (11am in season). SEAFOOD/CARIBBEAN.

As dedicated locals who come daily for happy hour will tell you, Mangrove Mama's is a true Lower Keys institution and a dive in the best sense of the word. The restaurant is a shack that used to have a gas pump as well as a grill. Now, guests share the property with some miniature horses (out back) and stray cats. A handful of simple tables, inside and out, are shaded by banana trees and palm fronds. Fish is, not surprisingly, the menu's mainstay, although soups, salads, sandwiches, and omelets are also good. Grilled teriyaki chicken and club sandwiches are tasty alternatives to fish, as are meatless chef's salads and spicy barbecued baby back ribs.

Monte's. U.S. 1 at MM 25, Summerland Key. ☎ **305/745-3731.** Main courses $10–$14; lunch $3–$8. No credit cards. Mon–Sat 9am–10pm; Sun 11am–9pm. SEAFOOD.

Monte's has survived for more than 20 years because the food is very good and incredibly fresh. Certainly nobody goes to this restaurant/fish market for its atmosphere: Plastic place settings rest on plastic-covered picnic-style tables in a screen-enclosed dining patio. The day's catch may include shark, tuna, lobster, stone crabs, or shrimp.

INEXPENSIVE

✪ **Coco's Kitchen.** 283 Key Deer Blvd. (in the Winn-Dixie Shopping Center), Big Pine Key. ☎ **305/872-4495.** Main courses $5–$12; lunch $2–$5; breakfast $1–$4.50. No credit cards. Mon–Sat 7am–7:30pm. Turn right at the traffic light near MM 30.5. Stay in the left lane. CUBAN/NICARAGUAN.

This tiny storefront has been dishing out black beans and rice and shredded beef to Cuban-food fans for more than 10 years. The owners, who are actually from Nicaragua, cook not only superior Cuban food but also some local specialties, Italian food, and Caribbean food. The best bet is the daily special, which may be roasted pork or fresh grouper, served with rice and beans or salad and crispy fries. Top off the huge, cheap meal with a rich caramel-soaked flan.

No Name Pub. ¼ mile south of No Name Bridge on N. Watson Blvd., Big Pine Key. ☎ **305/872-9115.** Pizzas $8–$18; subs $5. MC, V. 11am–11pm. Turn right at Big Pine's only traffic light (near MM 30.5) onto Key Deer Blvd. Turn right on Watson Blvd. At stop sign, turn left. Look for a small wooden sign on the left marking the spot. PUB FOOD/PIZZA.

This funky old bar out in the boonies serves snacks and sandwiches until 11pm on most nights and drinks until midnight. Pizzas are tasty—thick-crusted and super-cheesy. Try one topped with local shrimps, or consider a bowl of chili with all the fixings—hearty and cheap. Also decent is the smoked fish dip. Everything is served on paper plates. Locals hang out at the rustic bar—one of the Florida Keys's oldest—drinking beer and listening to a jukebox heavy with 1980s selections. The decor (if you can call it that) is basic—the walls and ceilings are plastered with thousands of autographed dollar bills.

THE LOWER KEYS AFTER DARK

Although the mellow islands of the lower Keys aren't exactly known for wild nightlife, there are some friendly bars and restaurants where locals and tourists gather to hang out and drink.

One of the most scenic is **Sandbar** (☎ 305/872-9989), a wide-open breezy wooden house built on slender stilts and overlooking a wide channel on Barry Avenue (near MM 28.5). It attracts an odd mix of bikers and blue-hairs daily from 11am until 11pm. Pool tables are the main attraction, but there's also live music some nights. The drinks are reasonably priced and the food isn't too bad, either. For another fun bar scene, see **No Name Pub,** listed above in "Where to Dine."

3 Key West

159 miles SW of Miami

The locals, or "conchs" (pronounced "conks"), and the developers here have been at odds for years. This once low-key island has been thoroughly commercialized—there are a Hard Rock Cafe smack in the middle of Duval Street and thousands of cruise-ship passengers descending on Mallory Square each day. It's definitely not the seedy town Hemingway and his cronies once called their own.

Laid-back Key West still exists, but it's now found in different places: the backyard of a popular guest house, for example, or an art gallery, or a secret garden, or the hip hangouts of Bahama Village. And, of course, there are always the calm waters of the Atlantic and the Gulf of Mexico all around.

The heart of town offers party people a good time. Here you'll find good restaurants, fun bars, live music, rickshaw rides, and lots of shopping. Don't bother with a watch or tie—this is the home of the perennial vacation.

ESSENTIALS

GETTING THERE   For directions by car, see "Essentials" for the Upper and Middle Keys, above. Continue south on U.S. 1. When entering Key West, stay in the far-right lane onto North Roosevelt Boulevard, which becomes Truman Avenue in Old Town. Continue for a few blocks, and you will find yourself on Duval Street, in the heart of the city. If you stay to the left, you'll also reach the city center after passing the airport and the remnants of historic houseboat row, where a motley collection of boats once made up one of Key West's most interesting neighborhoods.

Several regional airlines fly nonstop from Miami to Key West; fares are about $120 to $300 round-trip. **American Eagle** (☎ 800/443-7300) and **US Airways Express** (☎ 800/428-4322) land at **Key West International Airport,** South Roosevelt Boulevard (☎ 305/296-5439), on the southeastern corner of the island.

Greyhound (☎ 800/231-2222) has buses leaving Miami for Key West every day. At press time, prices were $30–$32 one-way and $57–$60 round-trip. Seats fill up in season, so come early. The ride takes about 4½ hours.

VISITOR INFORMATION   The **Florida Keys and Key West Visitors Bureau,** P.O. Box 1147, Key West, FL 33041 (☎ 800/FLA-KEYS), offers a free vacation kit packed with visitor information. The **Key West Chamber of Commerce,** 402 Wall St., Key West, FL 33040 (☎ 800/527-8539 or 305/294-2587), also offers both general and specialized information. The lobby is open daily from 8:30am to 6pm; phones are answered from 8am to 8pm. The **Key West Visitors Center** also provides information on accommodations, goings-on, and restaurants; the number is ☎ **800/ LAST-KEY.** It's open weekdays from 8am to 5:30pm and weekends from 8:30am to 5pm. Gay travelers will want to call the **Key West Business Guild** (☎ **305/294-4603**), which represents more than 50 guest houses and B&Bs in town, as well as many other gay-owned businesses. Ask for its color brochure. Or try **Good Times Travel** (☎ **305/294-0980**), which will set up lodging and package tours on the island.

GETTING AROUND   With limited parking, narrow streets, and congested traffic, driving in Old Town Key West is more of a pain than a convenience. Unless you're staying in one of the more remote accommodations, consider trading in the car for a bicycle. The island is small and as flat as a board, which makes it easy to negotiate, especially away from the crowded downtown. Many tourists also choose to cruise by moped, an option that can make navigating the streets risky, especially since there are no helmet laws in Key West. Spend the extra few bucks and rent a helmet; hundreds of visitors are seriously injured each year.

Rates for simple one-speed cruisers start at about $8 per day (from $40 per week). Mopeds start at about $12 for 2 hours, $25 per day, and $100 per week. The best shops include **The Bicycle Center,** at 523 Truman Ave. (☎ **305/294-4556**); the **Moped Hospital,** at 601 Truman Ave. (☎ **305/296-3344**); and **Tropical Bicycles & Scooter Rentals,** at 1300 Duval St. (☎ **305/294-8136**). **The Bike Shop,** 1110 Truman Ave. (☎ **305/294-1073**), rents mountain bikes for $15 per day ($75 per week). Cruisers go for $8 per day and $40 per week.

PARKING   Note that parking in Key West's Old Town is particularly limited. There is a well-placed **municipal parking lot** at Simonton and Angela streets just behind the firehouse and police station. If you have brought a car, you may want to stash it here while you enjoy the very walkable downtown section of Key West.

ORIENTATION   A mere 2- by 4-mile island, Key West is simple to navigate, even though there is no real order to the arrangement of streets and avenues. As you enter town on U.S. 1 (also called Roosevelt Boulevard), you will see most of the moderately priced chain hotels and fast-food restaurants. The better restaurants, shops, and outfitters are crammed onto Duval Street, the main thoroughfare of Key West's Old Town. On surrounding streets are the many inns and lodges in picturesque Victorian/Bahamian homes. On the southern side of the island is the coral beach area and some of the larger resort hotels.

The area called Bahama Village has only recently become known to tourists. With several cool restaurants and guest houses opened over the years, this hippie-ish neighborhood, complete with street-roaming chickens and cats, is the most urban and rough you'll find in the Keys. You might see a few seedy drug dealings on street corners, but it's nothing to be overly concerned with. Resident business owners tend to keep a vigilant eye on the neighborhood. It looks worse than it is.

SEEING THE SIGHTS

Before shelling out big bucks for any of the dozens of worthwhile attractions in Key West, I recommend getting an overview on either of the two comprehensive island tours, **The Conch Train** or the **Old Town Trolley** (see "Organized Tours," below). There are simply too many attractions to list (including a Ripley's Believe it or Not! on Duval Street) and a number of historic houses. I've highlighted my favorites below but encourage you to seek out others.

✪ **Audubon House & Tropical Gardens.** 205 Whitehead St. (between Greene and Caroline sts.). ☎ **305/294-2116.** Admission $7.50 adults; $3.50 children 6–12. Daily 9:30am–5pm (last admission at 4:45pm). Discounts for students and AAA and AARP members.

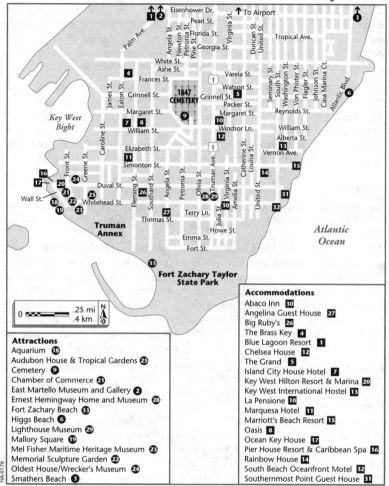

Attractions
Aquarium **18**
Audubon House & Tropical Gardens **25**
Cemetery **9**
Chamber of Commerce **21**
East Martello Museum and Gallery **2**
Ernest Hemingway Home and Museum **28**
Fort Zachary Beach **33**
Higgs Beach **6**
Lighthouse Museum **29**
Mallory Square **19**
Mel Fisher Maritime Heritage Museum **23**
Memorial Sculpture Garden **22**
Oldest House/Wrecker's Museum **24**
Smathers Beach **3**

Accommodations
Abaco Inn **30**
Angelina Guest House **27**
Big Ruby's **26**
The Brass Key **4**
Blue Lagoon Resort **1**
Chelsea House **12**
The Grand **5**
Island City House Hotel **7**
Key West Hilton Resort & Marina **20**
Key West International Hostel **13**
La Pensione **10**
Marquesa Hotel **11**
Marriott's Beach Resort **15**
Oasis **8**
Ocean Key House **17**
Pier House Resort & Caribbean Spa **16**
Rainbow House **14**
South Beach Oceanfront Motel **32**
Southernmost Point Guest House **31**

This well-preserved home dating from the early 19th century stands as a prime example of early Key West architecture. Named after the renowned painter and bird expert John James Audubon, who was said to have visited the house in 1832, the graceful two-story home is a peaceful retreat from the bustle of Old Town. Included in the price of admission is a self-guided audiotape tour that lasts about half an hour. With voices of several characters from the house's past, the tour never gets boring—although it is at times a bit hokey. See rare Audubon prints, gorgeous antiques, historical photos, and lush tropical gardens. Even if you don't want to spend the time and money to explore the grounds and home, check out the impressive gift shop, which sells a variety of fine mementos at reasonable prices.

Ernest Hemingway Home and Museum. 907 Whitehead St. (between Truman Ave. and Olivia St.). ☎ **305/294-1575** or 305/294-1136. Admission $7.50 adults; $4.50 children. Daily 9am–5pm. Free parking.

Hemingway's particularly handsome stone Spanish Colonial house, built in 1851, was one of the first on the island to be fitted with indoor plumbing and a built-in fireplace.

The author lived here from 1928 until 1940, along with about 50 six-toed cats, whose descendants still roam the premises. It was during those years that the Nobel Prize winner wrote some of his most famous works, including *For Whom the Bell Tolls, A Farewell to Arms,* and *The Snows of Kilimanjaro.* Fans may want to take the optional half-hour tour. It's interesting and included in the price of admission.

Key West Cemetery. Entrance at Margaret and Angela sts. Free admission. Daily dawn to dusk. Tours can be arranged by calling ☎ **305/294-WALK.**

This funky picturesque cemetery is the epitome of the quirky Key West image, as irreverent as it is humorous. Many tombs are stacked several high, condominium style—the rocky soil made digging 6 feet under nearly impossible for early settlers. Headstones reflect residents' lighthearted attitudes toward life and death. "I Told You I Was Sick" is one of the more famous epitaphs, as is the tongue-in-cheek widow's inscription "At Least I Know Where He's Sleeping Tonight."

East Martello Museum and Gallery. 3501 S. Roosevelt Blvd. ☎ **305/296-3913.** Admission $6 adults; $2 children 8–12; free for children 7 and under. Daily 9:30am–5pm (last admission is at 4pm).

Adjacent to the airport, the East Martello Museum is located in a Civil War–era brick fort that itself is worth a visit. The museum contains a bizarre variety of exhibits that collectively do a thorough job of interpreting the city's intriguing past. Historical artifacts include model ships, a deep-sea diver's wooden air pump, a crude raft from a Cuban "boat lift," a supposedly haunted doll, a Key West–style children's playhouse from 1918, and a horse-drawn hearse. Exhibits illustrate the Keys's history of salvaging, sponging, and cigar making. After seeing the galleries, climb a steep spiral staircase to the top of a lookout tower for good views over the island and ocean.

✪ Key West Aquarium. 1 Whitehead St. (at Mallory Sq.). ☎ **305/296-2051.** Admission $8 adults; $4 children 4–12; free for children under 4. Tickets are good for 2 consecutive days. Look for discount coupons from local hotels, at Duval St. kiosks, and from trolley and train tours. Daily 10am–6pm.

The oldest attraction on the island, the Key West Aquarium is a modest but fascinating exhibit. A long hallway of eye-level displays showcases dozens of variety of fish and crustaceans. See delicate sea horses swaying in the backlit tanks. Kids can touch sea cucumbers and sea anemones in a shallow touch tank in the entryway. If you can, catch one of the free guided tours offered daily at 11am and 1, 3, and 4pm, when you can witness the dramatic feeding frenzy of the sharks, tarpon, barracudas, stingrays, and turtles. Tickets are good for 2 consecutive days, a bonus for kids with short attention spans.

Key West's Shipwreck Historeum. 1 Whitehead St. (at Mallory Square). ☎ **305/ 292-8990.** Admission $8 adults; $4 children 4–12. Shows daily every half hour 9:45am–4:45pm.

You'll see more impressive artifacts at nearby Mel Fisher's museum, but the dramatic reenactments of the old shipwrecking days at this place are unique and entertaining. The interactive show is best for teens and adults and includes scenes starring Key West's wealthiest wrecker, Asa Tift, plus lots of intriguing video clips and stories of the area's heyday.

✪ Mel Fisher Maritime Heritage Museum. 200 Greene St. ☎ **305/294-2633.** Admission $6.50 adults; $2 children 6–12; free for children 5 and under. Open daily 9:30am–5pm.

This museum honors local hero Mel Fisher, whose death in 1998 was mourned across the country. Fisher, along with a crew of other salvagers, found a multimillion-dollar treasure trove in 1985 aboard the wreck of the Spanish galleon *Nuestra Señora de Atocha*. The admission price is somewhat steep, but if you're into diving, pirates, and the mystery of sunken treasures, check out this small informative museum, full of doubloons, pieces of eight, emeralds, and solid-gold bars. A dated but informative film provides a good background of Fisher's incredible story.

Memorial Sculpture Garden. Mallory Sq. between Whitehead and Wall sts. Free admission.

Installed in 1997, this impressive sculpture garden contains a large monument to the wreckers who made Key West rich more than a century ago. Also on display are 36 bronze busts of the island's most colorful leaders and characters. There are President Harry Truman, Henry Flagler, and, of course, Ernest Hemingway, all mounted on elegant coral columns.

Oldest House/Wrecker's Museum. 322 Duval St. ☎ **305/294-9502.** Admission $5 adults; $1 children 6–12; free for children 5 and under. Open daily 10am–4pm.

Dating back to 1829, this old New England Bahama House has survived pirates, hurricanes, fires, warfare, and economic ups and downs, and it gives witness to a slower, more easy time in the island's life. This 1½-story home was designed by a ship's carpenter and incorporates many features from maritime architecture, including portholes and a ship's hatch designed for ventilation before the advent of air-conditioning. Especially interesting is the detached kitchen building outfitted with a brick "beehive" oven and vintage cooking utensils. Though it's not a must-see on the Key West tour, history and architecture buffs will appreciate the finely preserved details.

ORGANIZED TOURS

BY TROLLEY-BUS & TRAM   Yes, it's more than a bit hokey to sit on this 60-foot tram of yellow cars, but it's worth it. The city's whole story is packed into a neat, 90-minute package on the **Conch Tour Train,** which covers the island and all its rich, raunchy history. Operating since 1958, the trains are open-air, which can make it uncomfortable in bad weather. The "train's" engine is a propane-powered jeep disguised as a locomotive. Tours depart from both Mallory Square and the Welcome Center, near where U.S. 1 becomes North Roosevelt Boulevard, on the other side of the island. For more information, contact the Conch at (☎ **305/294-5161**). The cost is $18 for adults, $9 for children 4 to 12, and free for children 3 and under. Daily departures are every half hour from 9am to 4:30pm.

The **Old Town Trolley** is the choice in bad weather or if you are staying at one of the many hotels on its route. Humorous drivers maintain a running commentary as the enclosed tram loops around the island's streets past all the major sights. Trolleys depart from Mallory Square and other points around the island, including many area hotels. For details, call (☎ **305/296-6688**). Tours are $18 for adults, $9 for children 4 to 12, and free for children 3 and under. Departures are daily every half hour (though not always on the hour or half hour) from 9am to 4:45pm. One or the other, these historic, trivia-packed tours are well worth the price of admission.

BY AIR   Proclaimed by the mayor as "the official air force of the Conch Republic," **Island Airplane Tours,** at Key West Airport, 3469 S. Roosevelt Blvd. (☎ **305/294-8687** for reservations), offers windy rides in its open-cockpit 1940 Waco biplanes over the reefs and around the islands. Thrill seekers—and they only—will also enjoy a spin in the company's S2-B aerobatics airplane that does loops, rolls, and sideways figure eights. Company owner Fred Cabanas was "decorated" in 1991, after he spotted a Cuban airman defecting to the United States in a Russian-built MiG fighter. Sightseeing flights cost $50 to $200, depending on the duration.

Going, Going, Gone . . .
Where to Catch the Famous Key West Sunset

A tradition in Key West, the Sunset Celebration can be relaxing or over-whelming, depending on your vantage point. If you're in town, you must check out this ritual at least once. Every evening, locals and visitors gather at the docks behind Mallory Square (at the westernmost end of Whitehead Street) to cele-brate the day gone by. Secure a spot on the docks early to experience the carnival of portrait artists, acrobats, food vendors, and animal acts. In season, the crowd can be overwhelming, especially when the cruise ships are in port.

Better yet, get a seat at the Hilton's **Sunset Deck** (☎ **305/294-4000**), a lux-urious bar on top of its restaurant at the intersection of Front and Greene streets. From the civilized calm of a casual bar, you can look down on the mayhem with a drink in hand.

Also near the Mallory madness is the **Ocean Key House's bar.** This long open-air pier serves up drinks and okay bar food against a dramatic pink- and yellow-streaked sky. It's located at the very tip of Duval Street (☎ **800/ 328-9815** or 305/296-7701).

For the very best potent cocktails and great bar food on an outside patio or enclosed lounge, try **Pier House's Havana Docks** at 1 Duval St. (☎ **305/ 296-4600**). There are usually live music and a lively gathering of visitors enjoying this island's bounty.

BY BOAT The Pride of Key West, **Fireball,** at Zero Duval St. (☎ **305/296-6293;** fax 305/294-8704), is a 58-foot glass-bottom catamaran that goes on both day and evening coral-reef tours and sunset cruises. Reef trips cost $20 per person; sunset cruises are $25 per person and include snacks, sodas, and a glass of champagne.

The Wolf, at Schooner Wharf, Key West Seaport (☎ **305/296-9653;** fax 305/ 294-8388), is a 44-passenger topsail schooner, equipped with a cannon, that sets sail daily for daytime and sunset cruises around the Keys. Key West Seaport is located at the end of Greene Street. Day tours cost $25 per person; sunset sails cost $30 per person and include champagne, wine, beer, soda, and live music.

OTHER TOURS For a lively look at Key West, try a 2-hour tour of the island's five **most famous pubs.** It starts daily at 2:30pm, lasts 1½ hours, costs $21, and includes four drinks. Another fun tour, for those interested in the paranormal, is the **nightly ghost tour.** Cost is $18 for adults and $10 for children. This spooky and interesting tour gives participants insight into the many old island legends. Both tours are offered by Key West Tour Association. A cemetery tour leaves daily at 10:30am (☎ **305/294 WALK**).

OUTDOOR PURSUITS

BEACHES Unlike in the rest of the Keys, you'll actually find a few small beaches here, although they don't compare to the state's wide natural wonders up the coast. Here are your options: **Smathers Beach,** off South Roosevelt Boulevard west of the airport; **Higgs Beach,** along Atlantic Boulevard between White Street and Reynolds Road; and **Fort Zachary Beach,** located off the western end of Southard Boulevard.

Although there is an entrance fee ($3.75 per car, plus more for each passenger), I recommend Fort Zachary, since it also includes a great historical fort, a Civil War museum, and a large picnic area with tables, barbecue grills, bathrooms, and showers. Plus, large trees scattered across 87 acres provide shade for those who are reluctant to bake in the sun. The vulnerable point was damaged in Hurricane Georges in 1998, but replanting of native vegetation has made it even better than before. A narrow, rocky beach is typical of the Key's beaches.

BICYCLING & MOPEDING   A popular mode of transportation for locals and visitors, bikes and mopeds are available at many rental outlets in the city (see "Getting Around," above). Escape the hectic downtown scene and explore the island's scenic side streets. Head away from Duval Street to South Roosevelt Boulevard and the beachside enclaves along the way.

DIVING   One of the area's largest scuba schools, **Dive Key West Inc.,** 3128 N. Roosevelt Blvd. (☎ **800/426-0707** or 305/296-3823; fax 305/296-0609; e-mail: divekeywest@flakeysol.com; www.divekeywest.com), offers instruction on all levels. Its dive boats take participants to scuba and snorkel sites on nearby reefs.

Wreck dives and night dives are two of the special offerings of **Lost Reef Adventures,** 261 Margaret St. (☎ **800/952-2749** or 305/296-9737). Regularly scheduled runs and private charters can be arranged. Phone for departure information.

FISHING   As any angler will tell you, there's no fishing like Keys fishing. Key West has it all: bonefish, tarpon, dolphin, tuna, grouper, cobia, and more. Sharks, too. When it comes to fishing, this is it.

Step aboard a small exposed skiff for an incredibly diverse day of fishing. In the morning, you can head offshore for sailfish or dolphin, and then by afternoon, get closer to land for a shot at tarpon, permit, grouper, or snapper. Here in Key West, you can probably pick up more cobia—one of the best fighting and eating fishes around—than anywhere else in the world. For a real fight, ask your skipper to go for the tarpon—the greatest fighting fish there is, famous for its dramatic "tail walk" on the water after it's hooked. Shark fishing is also popular.

You'll find plenty of competition among the charter fishing boats in and around Mallory Square. However, you should know that the bookers from the kiosks in town generally take 20% of a captain's fee in addition to an extra monthly fee. So you can usually save yourself money by booking directly with a captain or going straight to one of the docks. You can negotiate a good deal at **Charter Boat Row,** 1801 N. Roosevelt Ave. (across from the Shell station), home to more than 30 charter fishing and party boats. Just show up to arrange your outing, or call **Garrison Bite Marina** (☎ **305/ 292-8167**) for details.

The advantage of the smaller, more expensive charter boats is that you can call the shots. They'll take you where you want to go, to fish for what you want to catch. These "light tackles" are also easier to maneuver, which means you can go to backcountry spots for tarpon and bonefish, as well as out to the open ocean for tuna and dolphin. You'll really be able to feel the fish, and you'll get some good fights. Larger boats, for up to six or seven people, are cheaper and best for kingfish, billfish, and sailfish. Consider Jim Brienza's 27-foot *Sea Breeze,* docked at 25 Arbutus Dr. (☎ 305/294-6027), if you want a light-tackle experience. For a larger boat, try Captain Henry Otto's 44-foot *Sunday,* docked at the Hyatt in Key West (☎ **305/294-7052**).

The huge commercial party boats are more for sightseeing than serious angling, though you can get lucky and get a few bites at one of the fishing holes. One especially good deal is the *Gulfstream III* (☎ 305/296-8494), an all-day charter that goes out daily from 9:30am until 4pm. You'll pay $30, plus $3 for a rod and reel. This 65-foot party boat usually has at least 30 other anglers. Bring your own cooler or buy snacks on the boat. Beer and wine are allowed.

For the light-tackle experience of your life, call **Captain Bruce Cronin** (☎ 305/294-4929) or **Captain Kenny Harris** (☎ 305/294-8843), two of the more famous (and pricey) captains still working these docks. You'll pay from $550 for a full day, usually about 8am until 4pm, and from $400 for a half day.

GOLF   One of the area's only courses is **Key West Golf Club** (☎ 305/294-5232), an 18-hole course located just north of the island of Key West at MM 4.5 (turn onto College Road to the course entrance). Designed by Rees Jones, the course has plenty of mangroves and water hazards on its 6,526 yards. It's open to the public and has a new pro shop. Call ahead for tee-time reservations.

KAYAKING   **Mosquito Coast Outfitters,** housed in a woodsy wine bar at 1017 Duval St. (☎ 305/294-7178), operates a first-rate kayaking and snorkeling tour every day as long as the weather is mild. The tours depart at 9am sharp and cost $45 per person. Included in the price are snacks, soft drinks, and a guided tour of the mangrove-studded islands of Sugar Key or Geiger Key just north of Key West. You'll be back by about 3pm.

SHOPPING

You'll find all kinds of unique gifts and souvenirs in Key West, from coconut postcards to key lime pies. On Duval Street, T-shirt shops outnumber almost any other business. If you must get a wearable memento, be careful of unscrupulous salespeople. Despite efforts to curtail the practice, many shops have been known to rip off unwitting shoppers. It pays to check the prices and the exchange rate before signing any sales slips. You are entitled to a written estimate of any T-shirt work before you pay for it.

At Mallory Square is the **Clinton Street Market,** an over–air-conditioned mall of kiosks and stalls designed for the many cruise-ship passengers who never venture beyond this super-commercial zone. Amid the dreck are some delicious coffee and candy shops and some high-priced hats and shoes. There's also a free and clean rest room.

Once the main industry of Key West, cigar making is enjoying renewed success at the handful of factories that survived the slow years. Stroll through **"Cigar Alley,"** between Front and Greene streets, where you will find *viejitos*—little old men—rolling fat stogies just as they used to do in their homeland across the Florida Straits. Stop at the **Key West Cigar Factory,** at 308 Front St. (☎ 305/294-3470), for an excellent selection of imported and locally rolled smokes, including the famous El Hemingway. Remember, buying or selling Cuban-made cigars is illegal. Shops advertising "Cuban Cigars" are usually referring to domestic cigars made from tobacco grown from seeds that were brought from Cuba decades ago.

If you are looking for local or Caribbean art, you will find nearly a dozen galleries and shops clustered on Duval Street between Catherine and Fleming streets. You'll also find some excellent shops scattered on the side streets. One worth seeking out is the ✪ **Haitian Art Co.,** 600 Frances St. (☎ 305/296-8932), where you can browse through room upon room of original paintings from well-known and obscure Haitian artists in a range of prices from a few dollars to a few thousand. Also, check out **Cuba, Cuba!** at 814 Duval St. (☎ 305/295-9442). Here you will find paintings, sculpture, and photos by Cuban artists, and books and art from the island.

A favorite stop in the Keys is the deliciously fragrant **Key West Aloe** at 524 Front St. (between Simonton and Duval streets; ☎ 305/294-5592). Since 1971, this shop has been selling a simple line of bathroom products, including lotions, shampoos, and soothing balms for those who want a reminder of the tropical breezes once home. At the main shop (open until 8pm), you can find great gift baskets, tropical perfumes, and candies and cookies, too. In addition to frangipani, vanilla, and hibiscus scents, sample Key West for Men, a unique and alluringly musky best-seller.

Also worth checking out in the newly revitalized Bahama Village section of town are the shops along Petronia Street between Thomas and Whitehead streets. Especially interesting is **Maskerville** (☎ **305/293-6937**), which sells a variety of feather-laden artwork from masks to lamp shades. Just next door is **Hello Gorgeous,** at 315 Petronia, (☎ **305/294-1770**), which carries unique clothing, shoes, and jewelry for women and impersonators.

Off the beaten track at 814 Fleming St. (☎ **305/294-7901**) is the **Helio Gallery Store,** featuring locally made crafts and fine art.

For anything else, from bed linens to candlesticks to clothing, go to downtown's oldest and most renowned department store, **Fast Buck Freddie's,** at 500 Duval St. (☎ **305/294-2007**). For the same merchandise at reduced prices, try ✪ **Half Buck Freddie's,** 726 Caroline St. (☎ **305/294-6799**). Here you can shop for out-of-season bargains and "rejects" from the main store.

WHERE TO STAY

You'll find a wide variety of places to stay in Key West, from resorts with all the amenities to seaside motels, quaint bed-and-breakfasts, and clothing-optional guest houses. Unless you're in town during Key West's most popular holidays—Fantasy Fest (around Halloween), Hemingway Days (in July), and Christmas and New Year's—or for a big fishing tournament (many are held from Oct to Dec)—you can almost always find a place to stay at the last minute. However, you may want to book early, especially in the winter, when prime properties fill up and many require 2- or 3-night minimums. Prices at these times are also extremely high. Finding a decent room for under $100 a night is a real trick.

If all my suggestions are booked, try **Vacation Key West** (☎ **800/595-5397** or 305/295-9500; www.flakeysol.com/vkw). The phones are answered weekdays from 9am to 6pm and Saturdays from 11am to 2pm. This wholesaler offers discounts of 20 to 30 percent and can usually find last-minute deals. They represent mostly larger hotels and motels but also can place visitors in guest houses. The **Key West Innkeepers Association,** P.O. Box 6172, Key West, FL 33041 (☎ **800/492-1911** or 305/292-3600), can also help find lodging in any price range from its dozens of members and affiliates.

Most major hotel chains have at least one location in Key West; most are clustered on North Roosevelt Boulevard (U.S. 1). Moderately priced options include **Howard Johnson,** 3031 N. Roosevelt Blvd. (☎ **800/942-0913** or 305/296-6595); the **Ramada Inn,** 3420 N. Roosevelt Blvd. (☎ **800/330-5541** or 305/294-5541); the **Econo Lodge,** 3820 N. Roosevelt Blvd. (☎ **800/553-2666** or 305/294-5511); the **Holiday Inn Beachside,** 3841 N. Roosevelt Blvd. (☎ **800/292-7706** or 305/ 294-2571); and the **Quality Inn,** 3850 N. Roosevelt Blvd. (☎ **800/228-5151** or 305/294-6681). The Howard Johnson and the Holiday Inn are the only hotels with gulf-view rooms; the other hotels listed are just across the street. Duval Street is less than 5 minutes away by car or taxi.

A last resort should be **Holiday Inn La Concha Hotel** at 430 Duval St. (☎ **800/ 745-2191**). It is centrally located, but rates are high for the mediocre rooms (from $160 in season) and rude service. Do your best to avoid the **Best Western Hibiscus Hotel,** at 1313 Simonton St. The property is in bad shape, management is rude, and prices are high.

Gay travelers will want to call the **Key West Business Guild** (☎ **305/294-4603**), which represents more than 50 guest houses and B&Bs in town, as well as many other gay-owned businesses. Be advised that most gay guest houses have a clothing-optional policy. One of the most elegant and popular ones is **Big Ruby's** (☎ **800/477-7829** or 305/296-2323) at 409 Applerouth Lane (a little alley just off Duval Street). A low cluster of buildings surround a lushly landscaped courtyard, where a hearty breakfast is served each morning and wine is poured at dusk. The mostly male guests hang out by a good-sized pool tanning in the buff. Also popular is **Oasis** at 823 Fleming St. (☎ **305/296-2131**), which is super-clean and friendly, and you can enjoy the central location and a 14-seat hot tub.

Another luxurious property is **The Brass Key** at 412 Frances St. (☎ **305/296-4719**), which is more romantic and traditionally decorated and welcomes many lesbian travelers as well. Out and About gave it a five-star rating. For women only, the **Rainbow House,** 525 United St. (☎ **800/74-WOMYN** or 305/292-1450), is a large, fairly well-maintained guest house with lots of privacy and amenities, including two pools and two hot tubs. Rates in season range from $109 to $229.

VERY EXPENSIVE

✪ **Key West Hilton Resort and Marina.** 245 Front St. (at the end of Duval St.), Key West, FL 33040. ☎ **800/221-2424** or 305/294-4000. Fax 305/294-4086. 215 units. A/C MINIBAR TV TEL. Winter $259–$475 double, $325–$750 suite; off-season $169–$375 double, $250–$750 suite. 37 Sunset Key Cottages. Winter $870–$1,395; off-season $670–$925. AE, DC, DISC, MC, V.

Completed in the fall of 1996, this Hilton is a truly luxurious addition to downtown's hotel scene. Key West's only full-service AAA four-diamond resort is situated at the very end of Duval Street in the middle of all of Old Town's action. The sparkling new rooms are large and well appointed, with tropical decor and all the modern conveniences. Choose a suite in the main building if you want a large Jacuzzi in your living room. Otherwise, the marina building has great views. This giant will no doubt be very popular with corporate and convention visitors.

Amenities: Concierge, room service, laundry and dry-cleaning services, newspaper delivery, in-room massage, nightly turndown, twice-daily maid service, express checkout, valet parking, complimentary in-room coffee, secretarial services. Outdoor heated pool, offshore secluded beach, health club, Jacuzzi, sundeck, water-sports equipment, full-service marina, bicycle rental, game room, business center, self-service laundry, conference rooms, gift shops and boutiques.

Marriott's Reach Resort. 1435 Simonton St., Key West, FL 33040. ☎ **800/874-4118** or 305/296-5000. Fax 305/296-2830. 149 units. A/C MINIBAR TV TEL. Winter $309–$419 double; off-season $170–$310 double. AE, CB, DC, DISC, MC, V. Valet parking $9 per day.

The Reach is one of the few hotels on the island with its own strip of sandy beach. The location here can be either a highlight or a drawback; it's a 15-minute walk away from the center of the Duval Street action. Supported by stilts that leave the entire ground floor for car parking, the hotel offers four floors of rooms designed around atriums. The wonderful guest rooms are large and feature tile floors, sturdy wicker furnishings, and tropical colors. Each contains a small service bar with a sink, fridge, and tea/coffeemaker, and has a vanity area separate from the bathroom. The rooms are so nice you can easily forgive the small closets and diminutive dressers. All have sliding glass doors that open onto balconies, and some have ocean views.

Ample palm-planted grounds surround a small pool area. There's also a private pier for fishing and suntanning. The protected waters are tame and shallow.

Amenities: Concierge, room service, dry cleaning, newspaper delivery, in-room massage, baby-sitting, express checkout. Outdoor heated swimming pool, beach, health spa, Jacuzzi, sauna, bicycle rental, business center, tour desk, conference rooms, sailboats, Windsurfers, beauty salon.

✪ **Pier House Resort and Caribbean Spa.** 1 Duval St. (near Mallory Docks), Key West, FL 33040. ☎ **800/327-8340** or 305/296-4600. Fax 305/296-9085. 142 units. A/C MINIBAR TV TEL. Winter $280–$450 single/double, $450–$895 suite; off-season $195–$350 single/double, $325–$645 suite. AE, CB, DC, DISC, MC, V.

Pier House is one of the area's best resort choices, offering luxurious rooms, top-notch service, and even a full-service spa. Its excellent location—at the foot of Duval Street and just steps from Mallory Docks—is the envy of every hotel on the island. Set back from the busy street, on a short strip of beach, this hotel is a welcome oasis of calm. The accommodations here vary tremendously, from relatively simple business-style rooms to romantic guest quarters complete with integrated stereo systems and whirlpool tubs. Their best waterfront suites and rooms have recently been renovated. Although every accommodation has either a balcony or a patio, not all overlook the water. My favorites, in the two-story spa building, don't have any view at all. But what they lack in scenery, they make up for in opulence; each well-appointed spa room has a sitting area and a huge Jacuzzi bathroom.

Dining/Diversions: The restaurant serves very respectable meals in a dark dining room or on an umbrella-covered patio overlooking the docks. Old Havana Docks is a good waterfront bar, especially at sunset.

Amenities: Concierge, room service, laundry services, newspaper delivery, in-room massage, express checkout. Heated swimming pool, beach, health club, spa treatments, two Jacuzzis, sauna, sundeck, water-sports equipment rentals, bicycle rental, tour desk, conference rooms, beauty salon.

EXPENSIVE

Island City House Hotel. 411 William St., Key West, FL 33040. ☎ **800/634-8230** or 305/294-5702. Fax 305/294-1289. 24 units. A/C TV TEL. Winter $165 studio, $195–$225 one-bedroom suite, $255–$285 two-bedroom suite; off-season $95 studio, $125–$155 one-bedroom suite, $165–$190 two-bedroom suite. Rates include breakfast. AE, CB, DC, DISC, MC, V.

A small resort unto itself, the Island City House consists of three separate unique buildings that share a common jungle-like patio and pool. The first building, unimaginatively called the Island City House building, is a historic three-story wooden structure with wraparound verandas that allow guests to walk around the entire edifice on any floor. The warmly dressed old-fashioned interiors here include wood floors and many antique furnishings. Many rooms have full-size kitchens, queen-size beds, and sumptuous floral window treatments. The tile bathrooms could use more counter space, and the room lighting isn't always perfect, but eccentricities are part of this hotel's charm.

The unpainted wooden Cigar House has particularly large bedrooms similar in ambience to those in the Island City House. Most rooms are furnished with wicker chairs and king-size beds and have big bathrooms (although lacking in counter space). As with the Island City House, rooms facing the property's interior courtyard are best. The Arch House is the least appealing of the three buildings, but still very recommendable. Built of Dade County pine, the Arch House's cozy bedrooms are furnished in wicker and rattan and come with small kitchens and bathrooms.

Amenities: Newspaper delivery, free coffee in lobby, dry cleaning, laundry service, in-room massage, baby-sitting. Kitchenettes, VCR rental and complimentary videos, outdoor heated pool, Jacuzzi, bicycle rental, sundeck, self-service Laundromat.

✪ **Marquesa Hotel.** 600 Fleming St. (at Simonton St.), Key West, FL 33040. ☎ **800/ 869-4631** or 305/292-1919. Fax 305/294-2121. 27 units. A/C MINIBAR TV TEL. Winter $240–360; off-season $150–$255. No children under 12 allowed. AE, DC, MC, V.

One of my very favorite properties, the Marquesa offers all the charm of a small historic hotel with the amenities of a large resort. It encompasses four buildings, two adjacent swimming pools, and a three-stage waterfall that cascades into a lily pond. Two of the hotel's houses are luxuriously restored Victorian homes with rooms outfitted with extra-plush antiques and oversize contemporary furniture. The rooms in the two other, newly constructed buildings are even richer; many have four-poster wrought-iron beds with bright floral spreads. The green marble bathrooms are lush and spacious. The decor is simple, elegant, and spotless. These are the only hotel rooms I have ever seen that I would like my home to resemble.

Amenities: Concierge, valet, newspaper delivery, twice-daily maid service, valet parking. Two outdoor swimming pools (one is heated), access to nearby health club.

Ocean Key House. Zero Duval St., Key West, FL 33040. ☎ **800/328-9815** or 305/ 296-7701. Fax 305/292-7685. www.oceankeyhouse.com. 96 units. A/C MINIBAR TV TEL. Winter from $160 double, $340–$525 one-bedroom suite, $420–$700 two-bedroom suite; off-season $135 double, $225–$495 one-bedroom suite, $320–$600 two-bedroom suite. AE, CB, DC, DISC, MC, V.

You can't get much more central than this modern hotel, located across from the Pier House at the foot of Duval Street. Still, for the same price as the best rooms, you may do better at one of the more intimate accommodations, such as the Marquesa or the Pier House. Most of the guest rooms here are suites, ample-sized accommodations fitted with built-in couches. Many rooms have sliding glass doors that open onto small balconies, some of which enjoy unobstructed water views. All suites have Jacuzzi tubs in either the master bedroom or the living room. The standard guest rooms are much less desirable. They are small and dark and have no views.

Dining/Diversions: A casual dockside grill serves lunch and dinner. Breakfast is served at an indoor/outdoor cafe.

Amenities: Concierge, room service, dry-cleaning and laundry services. VCRs and video rentals, outdoor heated pool, access to nearby health club, Jacuzzi in every suite, conference rooms, sundeck, water-sports concession, tour desk.

MODERATE

Chelsea House. 707 Truman Ave., Key West, FL 33040. ☎ **800/845-8859** or 305/ 296-2211. Fax 305/296-4822. 20 units. A/C TV TEL. Winter $125–$205 double, $360 apt; off-season $75–$125 double, $250 apt. Rates include breakfast. Pets $10 extra. AE, CB, DC, DISC, MC, V.

Despite its decidedly English name, the Chelsea House is "all American," a term that in Key West isn't code for "conservative." Chelsea House caters to a mixed gay/straight clientele and displays its liberal philosophy most prominently on the clothing-optional sundeck. One of only a few guest houses in Key West that offers TVs, VCRs, private bathrooms, and kitchenettes in each guest room, Chelsea House has a large number of repeat visitors. The apartments come with full kitchens and separate living areas, as well as palm-shaded balconies in back. The bathrooms and closets could be bigger, but both are adequate and serviceable.

When weather permits, which is almost always, breakfast is served outside by the pool. There is private parking. *Important note:* children 14 and under are not accepted.

✪ **La Pensione.** 809 Truman Ave. (between Windsor and Margaret sts.), Key West, FL 33040. ☎ **800/893-1193** or 305/292-9923. Fax 305/296-6509. 9 units. A/C TEL. Winter from $158 double with Frommer's discount; summer from $98 double with Frommer's discount.

Rates include breakfast and represent a 10% discount for readers who mention this guide. AE, DC, DISC, JCB, MC, V.

This classic bed-and-breakfast in the 1891 home of a former cigar executive distinguishes itself from other similar inns by its extreme attention to details. The friendly, knowledgeable staff treat the stunning home and the guests with extraordinary care. The comfortable rooms all have air-conditioning, ceiling fans, king-size beds, and private bathrooms. Many have French doors opening onto spacious verandas. Although the rooms have no phones or televisions, the distractions of Duval Street—only steps away—should keep you adequately occupied during your visit. Breakfast, which includes made-to-order Belgian waffles, fresh fruit, and a variety of breads or muffins, can be taken on the wraparound porch or at the communal dining table. No children are allowed.

South Beach Oceanfront Motel. 508 South St. (at the Atlantic Ocean), Key West, FL 33040. ☎ **800/354-4455** or 305/296-5611. Fax 305/294-8272. 50 units. A/C TV TEL. Winter $105–$199 double; off-season $69–$140 double. AE, MC, V.

This standard two-story motel is located directly on the ocean, within walking distance of Duval Street. Because the structure is perpendicular to the water, most of the rooms overlook a pretty Olympic-size swimming pool rather than a wide swath of beach. The best—and by far most expensive—are the lucky pair of beachfront rooms on the end (numbers 115 and 215).

All rooms share similar aging decor and include standard furnishings. The smallish bathrooms could use a makeover and include showers but no tubs. A private pier, an on-site water-sports concession, and a laundry room are available for guest use. When making reservations, ask for a room that's as close to the beach (and as far from the road) as possible. If you'll be there a while, ask for one of the rooms with a kitchenette; there is no restaurant on the premises.

Southernmost Point Guest House. 1327 Duval St., Key West, FL 33040. ☎ **305/294-0715.** Fax 305/296-0641. 6 units. A/C TV TEL. Winter $95–$200 double, $150 suite; off-season $55–$135 double, $95 suite. Rates include breakfast. AE, MC, V.

One of the only inns that actually welcomes children and pets, this romantic and historic guest house is a real find. The antiseptically clean rooms are not as fancy as the house's ornate 1885 exterior. Each room has basic beds and couches and a hodgepodge of furnishings, including futon couches, high-back wicker chairs, and plenty of mismatched throw rugs. Each room is different. Room 5 is best; situated upstairs, it has a private porch, an ocean view, and windows that let in lots of light. Every room has a refrigerator and a full decanter of sherry. Mona Santiago, the hotel's kind, laid-back owner, provides chairs and towels that can be brought to the beach, which is just a block away. Plus, guests can help themselves to wine as they soak in the new 14-seat hot tub. Kids will enjoy the swings in the backyard and the pet rabbits.

INEXPENSIVE

Abaco Inn. 415 Julia St. (between Truman Ave. and Virginia St.), Key West, FL 33040. ☎ **800/358-6307** or 305/296-2212. Fax 305/295-0349. E-mail: stay@abaco-inn.com. www.abaco-inn.com. 3 units, all with bathroom (showers only). A/C TV TEL. Winter from $99 single or double. Off-season from $59 single or double. 3-day minimum stay in season. AE, DISC, MC, V. Additional person $15. No smoking on the property.

This tidy little guest house is situated on a secluded lane just off Duval Street. Though there is no pool or view, you'll find a hair dryer, an iron and ironing board, a small refrigerator, a microwave, and a coffeemaker in each of the three simple rooms. Once the home of a cigar maker, the house dates from the early 1900s. Now it is owned and operated by George Fontana, a friendly and knowledgeable tour guide and writer.

Look for his column in the *Key West Citizen* on local characters. You can't beat the price in this super-convenient location.

Angelina Guest House. 302 Angela St. (at the corner of Thomas St.), Key West, FL 33040. ☎ **888/874-7326** or 305/294-4480. Fax 305/294-0621. E-mail: info@dolphintrvl.com. 15 units, 11 with bathroom (showers only). Winter $65–$70 single or double without bathroom; $79–$150 single or double with bathroom. Suite $175 for up to 6 people. Off-season $39–$49 single or double without bathroom; $49–$79 with bathroom; $95–$125 studio with kitchenette for up to 6 people. DISC, MC, V.

This youth hostel–looking guest house is well run by a bright-eyed refugee of Chicago's cold and a longtime Key's resident, Robbie Byer. His two historic buildings in the middle of Bahama Village are about the cheapest in town and are conveniently located near a hot hippie restaurant called Blue Heaven (see "Where to Dine" below) and also in a neighborhood known for occasional drug busts. Still, it is generally safe and full of character. The rooms are all furnished differently in a modest style. There are no televisions or telephones since Robbie believes guests should be out exploring Key West, not sitting in their rooms. "I don't even put chairs in the rooms," he explained. "I've even considered confiscating cell phones and beepers." Only 6 of the 15 rooms have air-conditioning, a real consideration in the sweltering summer days. A good cross breeze and ceiling fans do cool the rooms considerably. Though sparse, the Angelina is a good place to crash if you are on the cheap.

Blue Lagoon Resort. 3101 N. Roosevelt Blvd., Key West, FL 33040-4118. ☎ **305/ 296-1043.** Fax 305/296-6499. 72 units. A/C TV TEL. Winter $80–$240; off-season $50–$110. MC, V.

More than half of the rooms at this funky oceanside resort rent for less than $100 year-round—an all-too-unusual occurrence in Key West, especially for full-service resorts. The rooms, furnished in heavy cedar wood, are basic and a bit run-down but still decent—along the lines of a Howard Johnson or another budget accommodation. Second-floor rooms are generally quieter. The pricier waterfront rooms aren't really worth the extra money (although some include a jet-ski ride). Guests tend to be young college-aged kids out for a wild time. Although pretty far from Old Town, the resort is convenient by scooter and car, and it is literally surrounded by Wave Runners, boats, parasailing, and diving fun.

✪ **The Grand.** 1116 Grinnell St. (between Virginia and Catherine sts.), Key West, FL 33040. ☎ **888/947-2630** or 305/294-0590. E-mail: thegrand@flakeysol.com. 10 units. A/C TV TEL. Winter $79–$99 rms; $121 suites. Off-season $39–$59 rms; $79 suites. AE, DISC, MC, V.

Don't expect cabbies or locals to know about this gem. Opened in 1997, this guest house wasn't even properly listed in the phone book its first or second year. Lucky for you! It's got most everything you could want, including a very moderate price tag. It's run by another one of those happy-to-be-alive Northeastern transplants, Elizabeth Rose, who goes out of her way to provide any and all services for her appreciative guests. All rooms have private bathrooms, air-conditioning, telephones, and private entrances. The floors are painted in bright colors, and beds are dressed in light tropical prints. Room number 2 on the back side of the house is the best deal; it's small, but it has a porch and the most privacy. Suites are a real steal, too. The large two-room units come with a complete kitchen. The house is in a modest residential section of Old Town, only about 5 blocks from Duval Street. This place is undoubtedly the best bargain in town.

Key West International Hostel. 718 South St., Key West, FL 33040. ☎ **800/51-HOSTEL** or 305/296-5719. Fax 305/296-0672. 100 units. A/C TV. Winter $17 for IYHF members, $20 for nonmembers dorm beds; $75–$105 motel rms. Off-season from $15 for IYHF members, from $18 for nonmembers dorm beds; $50–$85 motel rms. MC, V.

This well-run hostel is a 3-minute walk to the beach and to Old Town. It's not the Ritz but it's affordable. Very busy with European backpackers, this is a great place to meet people. The dorm rooms are dark and sparse, but clean enough. The higher-priced motel rooms are a good deal, especially those equipped with full kitchens. Facilities include a pool table under a tiki-hut roof and bicycle rentals for $6 per day. There is also cheap food available for breakfast, lunch, and dinner. As in all community living arrangements, you'll want to watch your valuables; there are minisafes in each room.

WHERE TO DINE

Key West offers a vast, tempting array of food. You'll find many ethnicities represented: Thai, Cuban, Bahamian, Japanese, and Barbecue. Plus there are the usual drive-through fast-food franchises (mostly up on Roosevelt Boulevard). Duval Street even succumbed to the lure of a Hard Rock Cafe. Wander Old Town or the newly spruced-up Bahama Village and browse menus after you have exhausted the list of my picks below.

If you don't feel like venturing out, call **We Deliver** (☎ **305/293-0078**), a service that for a small fee (between $3 and $6) will bring you anything you want from any of the area's restaurants or stores. We Deliver operates between 3 and 11pm. If you are staying in a condo or efficiency, you may want to stock your fridge with groceries, beer, wine, and snacks from the area's oldest grocer, **Fausto's Food Palace,** open since 1926. There are now two locations: 1105 White St. and 522 Fleming St. The Fleming Street location will deliver ☎ **305/294-5221** or 305/296-5663). Fausto's has a $25 minimum.

VERY EXPENSIVE

Cafe des Artistes. 1007 Simonton St. (near Truman Ave.). ☎ **305/294-7100.** Reservations recommended. Main courses $23–$39. AE, MC, V. Daily 6–11pm. FRENCH.

Open for nearly 2 decades, the Cafe des Artistes's impressive longevity is the result of its winning combination of food and atmosphere. Traditional French meals benefit from a subtle tropical twist. The food is served by uniformed waiters well versed in the virtues of fine food. Start with the duck-liver pâté made with fresh truffles and old cognac, or Maryland crabmeat served with an artichoke heart and herbed tomato confit. Nouvelle and traditional French entrees include lobster flambé with mango and basil and wine-basted lamb chops rubbed with rosemary and ginger.

Louie's Backyard. 700 Waddell Ave. ☎ **305/294-1061.** Reservations highly recommended. Main courses $25–$30; lunch $8–$15. AE, CB, DC, MC, V. Daily 11:30am–3pm and 6–10:30pm. CARIBBEAN CONTEMPORARY.

Louie's, once known as Key West's most elegant restaurant, has lost its luster. Its location, nestled amid blooming bougainvillea on a lush slice of the gulf, remains one of the most romantic on earth. Unfortunately, the gorgeous real estate doesn't improve the uneven food, sluggish service, and sometimes snooty attitude. Try the weekend brunches, which tend to be more reliable than dinners, or, to be assured of a good time, you may just want to sit at the dockside bar and enjoy a cocktail at sunset.

EXPENSIVE

Antonia's. 615 Duval St. ☎ **305/294-6565.** Reservations suggested. Main courses $17–$24; pastas $12–$15. AE, DC, MC, V. Daily 6–11pm. REGIONAL ITALIAN.

The food is great but the atmosphere a bit fussy for Key West. If you don't have a reservation in season, don't bother. Still, if you are organized and don't mind paying high prices for dishes that elsewhere go for much less, try this old favorite. From the perfectly seasoned homemade focaccia to an exemplary crème brûlée, this elegant little standout is amazingly consistent. The menu includes a small selection of classics, such as *zuppa di pesce*, rack of lamb in a rosemary sauce, and veal marsala. However, the way to go is with the nightly specials. You can't go wrong with any of the handmade pastas.

✪ **Bagatelle**. 115 Duval St. ☎ **305/296-6609**. Reservations recommended. Main courses $16–$24; lunch $5–$12. AE, DC, DISC, MC, V. Daily 11:30am–3pm and 5:30–10pm. SEAFOOD/TROPICAL.

Reserve a seat at the elegant second-floor veranda overlooking Duval Street's mayhem. From the calm above, enjoy any of the selections from a large eclectic menu. You may want to start your meal with the excellent herb-and-garlic stuffed whole artichoke or the sashimi-like seared tuna rolled in black peppercorns. Also recommended is a lightly creamy garlic-herb pasta topped with gulf shrimp, Florida lobster, and mushrooms. The best chicken and beef dishes are given a tropical treatment: grilled with papaya, ginger, and soy.

✪ **Mangoes**. 700 Duval St. (at Angela St.), Key West. ☎ **305/292-4606**. Reservations recommended for parties of 6 or more. Main courses $12–$24; pizzas $10–$12; lunch $7–$14. AE, CB, DC, DISC, MC, V. Daily 11am–midnight; pizza until 1am. AMERICAN/REGIONAL.

This restaurant's large brick patio, shaded by overgrown banyan trees, is so seductive to passersby that it's packed almost every night of the week. Appetizers include conch chowder laced with sherry, lobster dumplings with tangy key lime sauce, and grilled shrimp cocktail with spicy mango chutney. Spicy sausage with black beans and rice, crispy curried chicken, and local snapper with passion-fruit sauce are typical among the entrees, but Mangoes's outstanding individual-size designer pizzas are the best menu items by far. They're baked in a Neapolitan-style oven fired by buttonwood. Even though it is right on tourist-laden Duval Street, Mangoes enjoys a good reputation among locals.

MODERATE

✪ **Blue Heaven**. 729 Thomas St. (at the corner of Petronia St.), Key West. ☎ **305/296-8666**. Main courses $9–$24; lunch $5–$13; breakfast $3–$8.50. DISC, MC, V. Mon–Sat 8am–3pm and 6–10:30pm; Sun brunch 8am–1pm and 6–10:30pm. SEAFOOD/AMERICAN/NATURAL.

This little hippie-run gallery and restaurant has become the place to be in Key West—and with good reason. Be prepared to wait in line. The food here is some of the best in town, especially for breakfast. You can enjoy homemade granola, huge tropical-fruit pancakes, and seafood Benedict. Dinners are just as good and run the gamut from just-caught fish dishes to Jamaican-style jerk chicken, curried soups, and vegetarian stews. But if you're a neat freak, don't bother. Some people are put off by the dirt floors and roaming cats and birds. The building used to be a bordello, where Hemingway was said to hang out watching cockfights.

Mangia, Mangia. 900 Southard St. (at Margaret St.), Key West. ☎ **305/294-2469**. Reservations not accepted. Main courses $9–$15. AE, MC, V. Daily 5:30–10pm. ITALIAN/AMERICAN.

Mangia, Mangia is one of Key West's best values. Locals appreciate that they can get inexpensive good food here in a town of so many tourist traps. Off the beaten track, in a little corner storefront, this great Chicago-style pasta place serves some of the best Italian food in the Keys. The family-run restaurant offers superb homemade pastas of every description, including one of the tastiest marinaras around. The simple grilled chicken breast brushed with olive oil and sprinkled with pepper is another good choice. You wouldn't know it from the glossy glass front room, but there's a fantastic little outdoor patio dotted with twinkling pepper lights and lots of plants. You can relax out back with a glass of one of their excellent wines or homemade beer while you wait for your table.

✪ **Pepe's.** 806 Caroline St. (between Margaret and Williams sts.), Key West. ☎ **305/294-7192.** Main courses $11–$20; lunch $5–$9; breakfast $2–$9. DISC, MC, V. Daily 6:30am–10:30pm. AMERICAN.

This old dive has been serving good, basic food for nearly a century. Steaks and Apalachicola Bay oysters are the big draw for regulars, who appreciate the rustic bar-room setting and historic photos on the walls. Look for original scenes of Key West in 1909, when Pepe's first opened. If the weather is nice, choose a seat on the patio under a stunning mahogany tree. Burgers, fish sandwiches, and standard chili satisfy hearty eaters. Buttery sautéed mushrooms and rich mashed potatoes are the best comfort food in Key West. Stop by early for breakfast, when you can get old-fashioned chipped beef on toast and all the usual egg dishes. In the evening, there are reasonably priced cocktails on the deck.

Turtle Kraals Wildlife Grill. 213 Margaret St. (corner of Caroline St.), Key West. ☎ **305/294-2640.** Main courses $12–$20. DISC, MC, V. Mon–Thurs 11am–1am; Fri–Sat 11am–2am. SOUTHWESTERN/SEAFOOD.

You'll join lots of locals in this out-of-the-way converted warehouse with indoor and dockside seating that serves innovative seafood at great prices. Try the twin lobster tails stuffed with mango and crabmeat or any of the big quesadillas or fajitas. Kids will like the wildlife exhibits and the very cheesy menu. Blues bands play most nights.

INEXPENSIVE

✪ **Anthony's Cafe.** 1111 Duval St. (at Amelia St.). ☎ **305/296-8899.** Breakfast $2–$5; sandwiches and salads $4–$6; hot plates $4–$10. Cash only. Daily 8am–10pm. ITALIAN DELI/ROTISSERIE.

Though owned and operated by a Greek import, this rustic Italian-style trattoria is a welcome addition to an area crowded with more-expensive and less-delicious options. Fragrant roasted chicken and overstuffed sandwiches on fresh baked bread are the best choices. Also good are the many salads and daily specials.

The Deli. 531 Truman Ave. (corner of Truman Ave. and Simonton St.), Key West. ☎ **305/294-1464.** Full meals $5–$13; sandwiches $2–$7. DISC, MC, V. Daily 7:30am–10pm. DINER/AMERICAN.

In operation since 1950, this family owned corner eatery has kept up with the times. It's really more of a diner than a deli and has a vast menu with all kinds of hearty options, from meatloaf to yellowtail snapper. Avoid the lobster sandwich, which is fried and a bit greasy. Other seafood options are good. A daily selection of more than a dozen vegetables includes the usual diner choices of beets, corn, and coleslaw with some distinctly Caribbean additions, such as rice and beans and fried plantains. Most dinners include a choice of two vegetables and homemade biscuits or corn bread. Breakfasts are made to order and attract a loyal following of locals. The Deli also offers ice cream sundaes and gourmet coffees.

✪ **El Siboney Restaurant.** 900 Catherine St. (at Margaret St.), Key West. ☎ **305/296-4184.** Main courses $5–$13. No credit cards. Mon–Sat 11am–9pm. CUBAN.

For good, cheap Cuban food, stop at this corner dive that looks more like a gas station than a diner. Be prepared, however, to wait like the locals for succulent roast pork, Cuban sandwiches, grilled chicken, and ropa vieja, all served with heaps of rice and beans. This tiny storefront is a worthwhile, very affordable choice in a town with lots of glossy tourist traps.

PT's Late Night. 920 Caroline St. (at the corner of Margaret St.), Key West. ☎ **305/ 296-4245.** Main courses $5–$14; lunch $5–$12. DISC, MC, V. Daily 11am–4am. AMERICAN.

This place is worth knowing about not only because it's one of the only places in town serving food past 10pm, but also because it happens to serve good food at extremely reasonable prices. The sports-bar atmosphere might make you wonder, but I've never been disappointed, although service can be a bit slow and brusque. Let's say it's 1am, you're starving, and you've just parked your bike outside: You'll be ecstatic when your heaping plate of nachos arrives. Fajitas are served sizzling hot with a huge platter of fixings, including beans, rice, lettuce, jalapeños, and tomatoes. Super-fresh salads are so big they can be a meal in themselves.

KEY WEST AFTER DARK

✪ **Duval Street** is the Bourbon Street of Florida. Amid the T-shirt shops and clothing boutiques, you'll find bar after bar serving neon-colored frozen drinks to revelers who bounce from one to the next from noon till dawn. Bands and crowds vary from night to night and season to season. Your best bet is to start at Truman Avenue and head up Duval to check them out for yourself. Cover charges are rare, so stop into a dozen and see which you like.

Captain Tony's. 428 Greene St. ☎ **305/294-1838.**

Just around the corner from Duval's beaten path, this smoky old wooden bar is about as authentic as you'll find. It comes complete with old-time regulars who remember the island before cruise ships docked here; they say Hemingway drank, caroused, and even wrote here. The owner, Captain Tony Tarracino, a former controversial Key West mayor, has recently capitalized on the success of this once-quaint tavern by franchising the place.

Durty Harry's. 208 Duval St. ☎ **305/296-4890.**

This large entertainment complex features live rock bands almost every night. You can wander to one of the many outdoor bars or head up to Upstairs at Rick's, an indoor/outdoor dance club that gets going late. For the more racy singles or couples, there is the Red Garter, a pocket-size strip club popular with bachelor and divorce parties. The hawker outside reminds couples that "the family that strips together sticks together."

Jimmy Buffett's Margaritaville Cafe. 500 Duval St. ☎ **305/292-1435.**

This cafe, named after another Key West legend, is a worthwhile stop. Although Mr. Buffett moved to glitzy Palm Beach years ago, his name is still attracting large crowds. This kitschy restaurant/bar/gift shop features live bands every night—from rock to blues to reggae and everything in between. The touristy cafe is furnished with plenty of Buffett memorabilia, including gold records, photos, and drawings. The margaritas are high-priced but tasty. The cheeseburgers aren't worth singing about.

Limbo. 700 Duval St. (corner of Angela St.). ☎ **305/292-4606.**

This secret little hideaway, above the well-known restaurant Mangoes (see "Where to Dine," above), is a great bar especially for jazz lovers. Cozy individual booths allow patrons to talk while catching a great view of the eclectic patrons who sometimes dance in the small space on the outside deck.

Sloppy Joe's. 201 Duval St. ☎ **305/294-5717.**

You'll have to stop in here just to say you did. Scholars and drunks debate whether this is the same Sloppy Joe's that Hemingway wrote about, but there's no argument that this classic bar's turn-of-the-century wooden ceiling and cracked tile floors are Key West originals. There's live music most days and nights.

THE GAY SCENE

In Key West, the best music and dancing can be found at the predominantly gay clubs. While many of the area's other hot spots are geared toward tourists who like to imbibe, the gay clubs are for those who want to rave—mostly locals (or at least, recent transplants). None of the spots mentioned here discriminate—anyone open-minded and fun is welcome. Cover varies but is rarely more than $10.

A popular late-night spot is **One Saloon,** 524 Duval St. (☎ **305/296-8118**), featuring great drag and lots more disco. A mostly male clientele frequents this hot spot from 9pm until 4am. Another Duval Street favorite is **Diva's** at 711 Duval St. (☎ **305/292-8500**), where you might catch drag queens belting out torch songs or judges voting on the best package in the wet-jockey-shorts contest.

Sunday nights are fun at two local spots. **Tea by the Sea,** on the pier at the Atlantic Shores Motel, 510 South St. (☎ **305/296-2491**), attracts a faithful following of regulars and visitors alike. Show up after 7:30pm. Better known around town as La-Te-Da, **La Terraza,** at 1125 Duval St. (☎ **305/296-6706**), is a great spot to gather poolside for the best martini in town—but don't bother with the food.

7

South Florida's National Parks: The Everglades & Beyond

by Victoria Pesce Elliott

Marjory Stoneman Douglas, who fought tirelessly to save this fragile resource until her death in 1998 at the age of 108, might well be called the Mother of the Everglades. This vast and unusual ecosystem is actually a shallow, 40-mile-wide, slow-moving river. Rarely more than knee-deep, the water is the lifeblood of this wilderness. Subtle shifts in water level dictate the life cycle of plants and animals. Most folks viewed it as a worthless swamp until Ms. Douglas focused attention on the area with her moving and insightful book *The Everglades: River of Grass,* published in 1947.

It was that same year that 1.5 million acres—less than 20% of Everglades wilderness—were established as Everglades National Park. At that time few lawmakers understood how neighboring ecosystems relate to each other—you can't just chop off a chunk of a much larger wilderness and expect it to survive. The land is intertwined with its surroundings, at the butt end of every environmental insult that occurs upstream.

Recently, environmental activists have succeeded in persuading politicians to enact some legislation to clean up the pollution that has threatened this unusual ecosystem ever since the days when heavy industry—most notably the sugar industry—first moved into the area. There has been a marked decrease in the indigenous wildlife here, but it remains one of the few places where you can see dozens of endangered species in their natural habitat, including the swallowtail butterfly, American crocodile, leatherback turtle, southern bald eagle, West Indian manatee, and Florida panther.

It takes a month for 1 gallon of water to move through the park, and I recommend a similar pace for you to fully experience the Everglades's grandeur. Take your time on the trails, and a hypnotic beauty begins to unfold. Follow the rustling of a bush, and you might see a small green tree frog or tiny brown anole lizard, with its bright-red spotted throat. Crane your head around a bend and discover a delicate, brightly painted mule-ear orchid.

The slow and subtle splendor of this exotic land may not be immediately appealing to kids raised on video games and rapid-fire commercials, but they'll certainly remember the experience and no doubt thank you for it later. Meanwhile, you'll find plenty of dramatic fun around the park, like airboat rides, alligator wrestling, and biking to keep the kids satisfied for at least a day.

1 Everglades National Park

35 miles SW of Miami

In the 1800s, before the southern Everglades were designated a national park, the only inhabited piece of this wilderness was a quiet fishing village called Flamingo. Accessible only by boat and leveled every few years by hurricanes, the mosquito-infested town never grew very popular. When the 38-mile road from Florida City was completed in 1922, many of those who did live here fled to someplace either more or less remote. Today Flamingo is a center for visitor activities and the main jumping-off point for backcountry camping and exploration. Flamingo is now home to National Park Service and concessionaire employees and their families.

Some 1,400 residents still live in a small enclave in the eastern section of the park, although the local agency governing the area has recently begun a buy-out program to remove them so that the area can be returned to its original state.

Everglades National Park's northern Shark Valley entrance and the eastern approaches described in this section are the most accessible from Miami and the rest of Florida's east coast. You'll find great amenities along the way, like Indian villages, alligator farms, and boat rides. An excellent tram tour goes deep into the park along a trail that's also terrific for biking. This is also the best way to reach the park's only accommodation (and full-service outfitters), the Flamingo Lodge.

See section 3 for more information on Everglades City, the "western gateway" to Everglades National Park, and Big Cypress Preserve.

JUST THE FACTS

GETTING THERE & ACCESS POINTS   Everglades National Park has four entrances. The following three are the most popular and the ones most convenient to visitors from Florida's east coast, including Miami. No matter which part of Miami you are starting in, the drive should take no longer than an hour (unless, of course, you are traveling during rush hour, between 8 and 9:30am or from 4 to 6pm; then, the roads, especially S.R. 836, will be backed up, and your driving time could be doubled).

The main entrance, in Homestead on the park's east side, is located 10 miles southwest of Florida City. From Miami, take S.R. 836 west to the Florida Turnpike south until it ends in Florida City. Signs will point you southwest onto the road that leads into the park, S.R. 9336. The main entrance's Park Ranger Station is open 24 hours.

The Shark Valley entrance, on the park's north side, is located on the Tamiami Trail (U.S. 41), about 35 miles west of downtown Miami. From Miami, take S.R. 836 west to the Florida Turnpike south; exit on Tamiami Trail (U.S. 41), and go west for approximately 30 miles. The park will be on your left side. Shark Valley is known for its 15-mile trail loop that's used for an excellent interpretive tram tour, bicycling, and walking. This entrance is open daily from 8:30am to 5:30pm, with some seasonal variation. Call ahead.

Chekika, popular with day visitors, picnickers, and campers, is located halfway between the two entrances above in the northeast section of the park. Chekika can be reached from Miami as if you were going to Shark Valley (see above). After exiting on Tamiami Trail (Highway 41), head west 5 miles to Krome Avenue (177th Avenue); turn left, then proceed to SW 168th Street (Richmond Avenue) and head west (left) until you reach a stop sign. Turn right; the entrance will be on the left side. There are picnic facilities and a 20-site campground. You can enter Chekika from 8:30am until sundown.

Everglades National Park

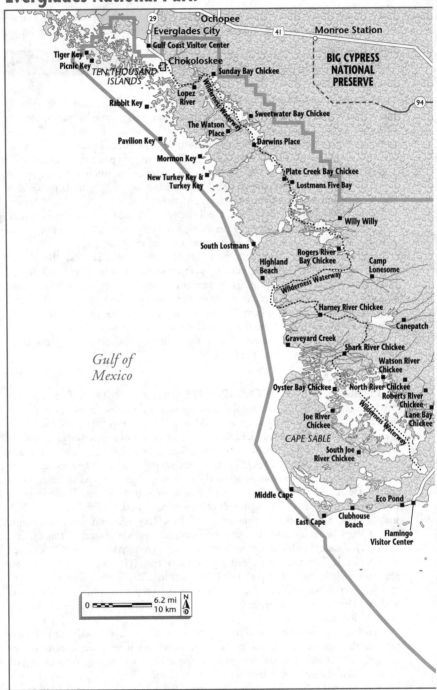

Ochopee
29
Everglades City
Gulf Coast Visitor Center
Tiger Key
Picnic Key
Chokoloskee
TEN THOUSAND ISLANDS
Sunday Bay Chickee
Lopez River
Rabbit Key
Sweetwater Bay Chickee
The Watson Place
Pavilion Key
Darwins Place
Mormon Key
Plate Creek Bay Chickee
New Turkey Key & Turkey Key
Lostmans Five Bay
Willy Willy
South Lostmans
Rogers River Bay Chickee
Camp Lonesome
Highland Beach
Wilderness Waterway
Harney River Chickee
Canepatch
Graveyard Creek
Shark River Chickee
Gulf of Mexico
Watson River Chickee
Oyster Bay Chickee
North River Chickee
Roberts River Chickee
Joe River Chickee
Lane Bay Chickee
CAPE SABLE
South Joe River Chickee
Middle Cape
Eco Pond
East Cape
Clubhouse Beach
Flamingo Visitor Center

Monroe Station
41
BIG CYPRESS NATIONAL PRESERVE
94

Wilderness Waterway

0   6.2 mi
     10 km
N

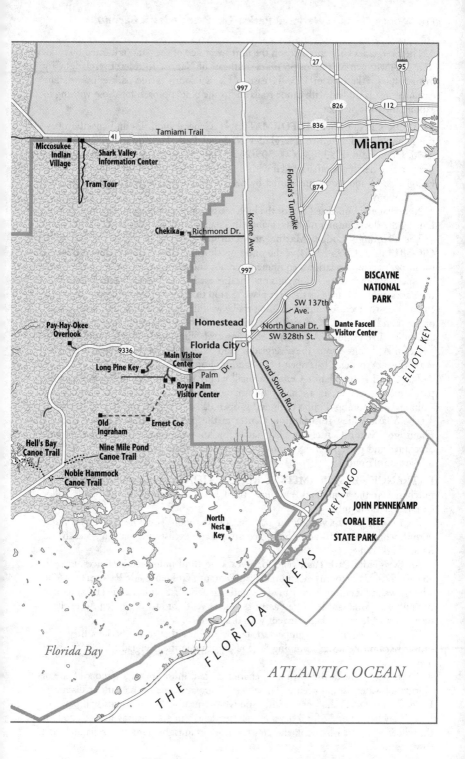

Miccosukee Indian Village

Shark Valley Information Center

Tram Tour

Tamiami Trail

Miami

Florida's Turnpike

Chekika ■ Richmond Dr.

BISCAYNE NATIONAL PARK

SW 137th Ave.

Pay-Hay-Okee Overlook

Homestead

North Canal Dr.

Dante Fascell Visitor Center

SW 328th St.

Krome Ave.

Florida City

9336

Main Visitor Center

Long Pine Key

Palm Dr.

Royal Palm Visitor Center

Card Sound Rd.

ELLIOTT KEY

Old Ingraham ■ Ernest Coe

Hell's Bay Canoe Trail

Nine Mile Pond Canoe Trail

Noble Hammock Canoe Trail

KEY LARGO

North Nest Key

JOHN PENNEKAMP CORAL REEF STATE PARK

THE FLORIDA KEYS

Florida Bay

ATLANTIC OCEAN

The Everglades City entrance, on the northwest side of the park, is located 80 miles west of downtown Miami, or 36 miles southeast of Naples. To reach Everglades City from Naples, take I-75 or U.S. 41 east to Fla. 29 south to the park entrance. The entrance area is riddled with canoe trails and is the best approach for those wishing to explore the park by boat.

VISITOR CENTERS & INFORMATION   General inquiries and specific questions should be directed to **Everglades National Park Headquarters,** 40001 S.R. 9336, Homestead, FL 33034 (☎ **305/242-7700**). Ask for a copy of *Parks and Preserves,* a free newspaper that's filled with up-to-date information on goings-on in the Everglades. Headquarters are staffed by helpful phone operators daily from 8:30am until 4:30pm.

Note that all hours listed are for the high season, generally November through May. During the slow summer months, many offices and outfitters keep abbreviated hours.

The **Flamingo Lodge, Marina and Outpost Resort,** in Flamingo (☎ **800/ 600-3813** or 941/695-3101), is the one-stop clearinghouse—and the only option— for in-park accommodations, equipment rentals, and tours.

Especially since its recent expansion, the **Ernest F. Coe Visitor Center,** located at the park's main entrance, is the best place to stop to gather information for your trip. In addition to free brochures outlining trails, wildlife and activities, and information on tours and boat rentals, you will also find state-of-the-art educational displays, films, and interactive exhibits. A gift shop sells postcards, film, unusual gift items, the best selection of books about the Everglades, and a selection of your most important gear—insect repellent. It is open from 8am until 5pm daily.

The **Royal Palm Visitor Center,** a small nature museum located 3 miles past the park's main entrance, is a smaller information center at the head of the popular Anhinga and Gumbo–Limbo trails and is open daily from 8am until 4pm.

The **Shark Valley Information Center** at the park's northern entrance and the **Flamingo Visitor Center** are also staffed by knowledgeable rangers who provide brochures and personal insight into the goings-on in the park. They are open from 8:30am until 5pm.

ENTRANCE FEES, PERMITS & REGULATIONS   Permits and passes can be purchased at the main park entrance, the Chekika entrance, or the Shark Valley entrance stations only.

Even if you are just visiting the park for an afternoon, you'll need to buy a 7-day permit, which costs $10 per vehicle. Pedestrians and cyclists are charged $5 each and $4 at Shark Valley.

An **Everglades Park Pass,** valid for a year's worth of unlimited entrances, is available for $20. U.S. citizens may purchase a 12-month **Golden Eagle Passport** for $50, which is valid for entrance into any U.S. national park. U.S. citizens aged 62 and older pay only $10 for a **Golden Age Passport**—that's valid for life. A Golden Access Passport is available free to U.S. citizens with disabilities.

Permits are required for campers to stay overnight either in the backcountry or in primitive campsites. See "Camping & Houseboating in the Everglades," in "Where to Stay" below.

Those who want to fish without a charter captain must obtain a standard State of Florida saltwater fishing license. These licenses are available in the park at Flamingo Lodge or any tackle shop or sporting-goods store nearby. Nonresidents will pay $17 for a 7-day license or $7 for 3 days. Florida residents can get a fishing license good for the whole year for $14. Snook and crawfish licenses must be purchased separately at a cost of $2.

Impressions

There are no other Everglades in the world. They are, they have always been, one of the unique regions of the earth, remote, never wholly known. Nothing anywhere else is like them: their vast glittering openness, wider than the enormous visible round of the horizon, the racing free saltiness and sweetness of their massive winds, under the dazzling blue heights of space.

—Marjory Stoneman Douglas, *The Everglades: River of Grass,* 1947

Charter captains carry vessel licenses that cover all paying passengers, but ask to be sure. Freshwater fishing licenses are available at various bait and tackle shops outside the park at the same rates. A good one nearby is **Don's Bait & Tackle** located at 30710 S. Federal Hwy. in Homestead right on U.S. 1. (☎ **305/247-6616**). Most of the area's freshwater fishing, limited to murky canals and human-made lakes near housing developments, is hardly worth the trouble when so much good saltwater fishing is available.

Firearms are not allowed anywhere in the park.

SEASONS There are two distinct seasons in the Everglades: high season and mosquito season. High season is also dry season, and lasts from late November to May. Despite the bizarre cold and wet weather patterns that El Niño brought in 1998, most winters here are warm, sunny, and breezy—a good combination to keep the bugs away. This is the best time to visit, because low water levels attract the largest variety of wading birds and their predators. As the dry season wanes, wildlife follows the receding water, and by the end of May, the only living things you are sure to spot will cause you to itch. The worst, called "no see-ums," are not even swattable. If you choose to visit during the buggy season, be sure to be vigilant in applying bug spray.

Also, realize that many establishments and operators either close or curtail offerings in the summer, so always call ahead to check schedules.

RANGER PROGRAMS More than 50 ranger programs, free with admission, are offered each month during high season and give visitors an opportunity to gain an expert's perspective. Some programs occur regularly, such as **Glade Glimpses,** a walking tour during which rangers point out flora and fauna and discuss issues affecting the Everglade's survival. These tours are scheduled at 10:15am, noon, and 3:30pm daily. The **Anhinga Ambles,** a similar program that takes place on the Anhinga Trail, starts at 10:30am, 1:30pm, and 4pm.

Park rangers tend to be helpful, well informed, good-humored, and happy to answer questions. Since times, programs, and locations vary from month to month, check a schedule, available at any of the visitor centers (see above).

SAFETY There are dangers inherent in this vast wilderness area. Always let someone know your itinerary before you set out on an extended hike. It's mandatory that you file an itinerary when camping overnight in the backcountry. When on the water, watch for weather changes; severe thunderstorms and high winds often develop very rapidly. Swimming is not recommended because of the presence of alligators, sharks, and barracudas. Watch out for the region's four indigenous poisonous snakes: diamondback and pygmy rattlesnakes, coral snakes (identifiable by their colorful rings), and water moccasins (which swim on the surface of the water). Again, bring insect repellent to ward off mosquitoes and biting flies.

First aid is available from park rangers. The nearest hospital is in Homestead, 10 miles from the park's main entrance.

SEEING THE HIGHLIGHTS

Shark Valley provides a fine introduction to the wonder of the Everglades, but don't plan on spending more than a few hours here. Bicycling or taking a guided tram tour can be a satisfying experience, but neither fully captures the wonders of the park.

If you want to see a greater array of plant and animal life, make sure that you venture into the park through the main entrance, pick up a trail map, and dedicate at least a day to exploring from there.

Stop first along the **Anhinga and Gumbo–Limbo trails,** which start right next to one another, 3 miles from the park's main entrance. These trails provide a thorough introduction to Everglades flora and fauna and are highly recommended to first-time visitors. There's more water and wildlife here than in most parts of the Everglades, especially during dry season. Alligators, turtles, river otters, herons, egrets, and other animals abound, making this one of the best trails for seeing wildlife. Arrive early to spot the widest selection of exotic birds; like the Anhinga Trail's namesake, a large black fishing bird that is so used to humans, many of these birds build their nests in plain view. Others travel deeper into the park during daylight hours. Take your time—at least an hour is recommended. If you treat the trails and modern boardwalk as pathways to get through quickly, rather than destinations to experience and savor slowly, you'll miss out on the still beauty and hidden treasures that await.

Also, it's worth climbing the observation tower at the end of the quarter-mile-long **Pa-hay-okee Trail.** The panoramic view of undulating grass and seemingly endless vistas gives the impression of a semiaquatic Serengeti. Flocks of tropical and semi-tropical birds traverse the landscape, alligators and fish stir the surface of the water, small grottoes of trees thrust up from the sea of grass marking higher ground, and the vastness of the hidden world you've entered seems unparalleled.

If you want to get closer to nature, a few hours in a canoe along any of the trails allows paddlers the chance to sense the park's fluid motion, and to become a part of the ecosphere. Visitors who choose this option end up feeling more like explorers than merely observers. (See "Sports & Active Pursuits," below.)

No matter which option you choose (and there are many), I strongly recommend staying for the 7pm program, available during high season at the **Long Pine Key Amphitheater.** This talk and slide show given by one of the park's rangers will give you a detailed overview of the park's history, natural resources, wildlife, and threats to its survival.

SPORTS & ACTIVE PURSUITS

BICYCLING   The relatively flat 38-mile paved **Main Park Road** is excellent for bicycling, as are many park trails, including **Long Pine Key.** Expect to spend 2 to 3 hours along the path.

If the park isn't flooded from excess rain (which it often is, especially in spring), **Shark Valley** in Everglades National Park is South Florida's most scenic bicycle trail. Many locals haul their bikes out to the Glades for a relaxing day of wilderness-trail riding. You can ride the 17-mile loop with no other traffic in sight. Instead, you'll share the flat paved road only with other bikers and a menagerie of wildlife. Don't be surprised to see a gator lounging in the sun or a deer munching on some grass. Otters, turtles, alligators, and snakes are common companions in the Shark Valley area.

Those who love to mountain-bike, and who prefer solitude, might check out the **Southern Glades Trail,** a 14-mile unpaved trail opened in late 1998 that is lined with native trees and teeming with wildlife like deer, alligators, and the occasional snake. The remote trail runs along the C-111 canal, off S.R. 9336 and SW 217th Street.

You can rent bikes at the **Flamingo Lodge, Marina and Outpost Resort** (see "Where to Stay," below) for $17 per 24 hours, $14 per full day, $8.50 per half day (any 4-hour period), and $3 per hour. A $50 deposit is required for each rental. Bicycles are also available from **Shark Valley Tram Tours,** at the park's Shark Valley entrance (☎ **305/221-8455**), for $3.25 per hour; rentals can be picked up any time after 8:30am and must be returned by 4pm.

BIRD-WATCHING   More than 350 species of birds make their homes in the Everglades. Tropical birds from the Caribbean and temperate species from North America can be found here, along with exotics that have blown in from more distant regions. Eco and Mrazek ponds, located near Flamingo, are two of the best places for birding, especially in early morning or late afternoon in the dry winter months. Pick up a free birding checklist from a visitor center (see "Just the Facts," above), and ask a park ranger what's been spotted in recent days.

BOATING   Motorboating around the Everglades seems like a great way to see plants and animals in remote habitats. However, environmentalists are taking stock of the damage motorboats (especially airboats) inflict on the delicate ecosystem. If you choose to motor, remember that most of the areas near land are "no wake" zones, and for the protection of nesting birds, landing is prohibited on most of the little mangrove islands. There's a long list of restrictions and restricted areas, so get a copy of the park's boating rules from National Park Headquarters before setting out (see "Just the Facts," above).

The Everglades's only marina—accommodating about 50 boats with electric and water hookups—is the **Flamingo Lodge, Marina and Outpost Resort,** located in Flamingo. The well-marked channel to Flamingo is accessible to boats with a maximum 4-foot draft and is open year-round. Reservations can be made through the marina store (☎ **941/695-3101,** ext. 304). Skiffs with 15-horsepower motors are available for rent. These low-power boats cost $90 per day, $65 per half day (any 5-hour period), and $22 per hour. A $125 deposit is required.

CANOEING   The most intimate view of the Everglades comes from the humble perspective of a simple low boat. From a canoe, you'll get a closer look into the park's shallow estuaries, where water birds, sea turtles, and endangered manatees make their homes.

Everglades National Park's longest "trails" are designed for boat and canoe travel, and many are marked as clearly as walking trails. The **Noble Hammock Trail,** a 2-mile loop, takes 1 to 2 hours and is recommended for beginning canoeists. The **Hell's Bay Trail,** a 3- to 6-mile course for hardier paddlers, takes 2 to 6 hours, depending on how far you choose to go. Park rangers can recommend other trails that best suit your abilities, time limitations, and interests.

You can rent a canoe at the Flamingo Lodge, Marina and Outpost Resort (see "Where to Stay," below) for $40 for 24 hours, $32 per full day, $22 per half day (any 4-hour period), and $8 per hour. They also have family canoes that rent for $12, $30, $40, and $50, respectively. A credit-card imprint or cash deposit ($50 or $100, depending on canoe size) is required for rental. Skiffs, kayaks, and tandem kayaks are also available. The concessionaire will shuttle your party to the trailhead of your choice and pick you up afterward. Rental facilities are open daily from 6am to 8pm.

FISHING   About one-third of Everglades National Park is open water. Freshwater fishing is popular in brackish **Nine-Mile Pond** (25 mi. from the main entrance) and other spots along the **Main Park Road,** but because of the high mercury levels found in the Everglades, freshwater fishers are warned not to eat their catch. Before casting, check in at a visitor center, because many of the park's lakes are preserved for observation only. Fishing licenses are required. See "Just the Facts," above.

Saltwater anglers will find snapper and sea trout plentiful. Charter boats and guides are available at Flamingo Lodge, Marina and Outpost Resort (see "Where to Stay," below). Phone for information and reservations.

ORGANIZED TOURS

AIRBOAT TOURS   Shallow-draft, fan-powered airboats were invented in the Everglades by frog hunters who were tired of polling through the brushes. And though they are the most efficient way to get around, airboats are not permitted in the park. Just outside the boundaries, however, you'll find a number of outfitters offering rides. These shallow-bottom runabouts tend to inflict severe damage on the animals and plants there. If you choose to ride on one, you may consider bringing earplugs; these high-speed boats are loud. Airboat rides are offered at the **Miccosukee Indian Village,** just west of the Shark Valley entrance on U.S. 41, the Tamiami Trail (☎ **305/ 223-8380**). Native American guides will take you through the reserve's rushes at high speed and stop along the way to point out alligators, native plants, and exotic birds. The price is just $7.

Also, the **Everglades Alligator Farm,** 4 miles south of Palm Drive/S.R. 9336 and on SW 192 Avenue (☎ **305/247-2628**), offers half-hour guided airboat tours from 9am until 6pm daily. The price, which includes admission to the park, is $12 for adults, $6 for children.

MOTORBOAT TOURS   Both Florida Bay and backcountry tours are offered at the **Flamingo Lodge, Marina and Outpost Resort** (see "Where to Stay," below). Both are available in 1½- and 2-hour versions that cost an average of $16 adults, $8 children, under 6 free. There are also charter-fishing and sightseeing boats that can be booked through the main reservation number (☎ **941/695-3101**). Florida Bay tours cruise nearby estuaries and sandbars, while six-passenger backcountry boats visit smaller sloughs. Tours depart throughout the day, and reservations are recommended.

TRAM TOURS   At the park's Shark Valley entrance, open-air tram buses take visitors on 2-hour naturalist-led tours that delve 7½ miles into the wilderness. At the trail's midsection, passengers can disembark and climb a 65-foot observation tower that offers good views of the Glades. The tour offers visitors considerable views that include plenty of wildlife and endless acres of sawgrass. Tours run November to April only, daily from 9am to 4pm, and are sometimes stalled by flooding or particularly heavy mosquito infestation. Reservations are recommended from December to March. The cost is $9.30 for adults, $5.15 for children 12 and under, and $8.25 for seniors. For further information, contact the **Shark Valley Tram Tours** at ☎ **305/221-8455.**

SHOPPING

You won't find big malls or lots of boutiques in this area, although there is an outlet center nearby, the **Keys Factory Shops** (☎ **305/248-4727**), at 250 E. Palm Dr. (where the Fla. Turnpike meets U.S. 1), in Florida City, with more than 60 stores including Nike Factory Store, Bass Co. Store, Levi's, Osh Kosh, and Izod. You can pick up a free coupon booklet from the Customer Service Center called the "Come Back Pack," which includes coupons good for discounts in the outlet. It's open Monday to Saturday until 9pm, Sundays until 6pm.

A necessary stop and good place for a refreshment is one of Florida's best-known fruit stands, ✪ **Robert Is Here** (☎ **305/246-1592**). Robert has been selling home-grown treats for nearly 40 years at the corner of SW 344th Street (Palm Drive) and SW 192nd Avenue. You'll find the freshest pineapples, bananas, papayas, mangos, and melons anywhere, as well as his famous shakes in unusual flavors like key lime, coconut, orange, and cantaloupe. Exotic fruits, bottled jellies, hot sauces, and salad dressings are also available. This is a great place to pick up culinary souvenirs and sample otherwise unavailable goodies. Open daily 8am until 7pm.

Along Tamiami Trail, there are several roadside shops hawking Indian handicrafts, including one at the **Miccosukee Indian Village** (☎ 305/223-8380) just west of the Shark Valley entrance. At nearly every one you'll find the same stock of feathered dreamcatchers, stuffed alligator heads and claws, turquoise jewelry, and other trinkets. *Tip:* Be sure to take note of the unique, colorful, handmade cloth Miccosukee dolls.

WHERE TO STAY

The only lodging in the park proper is the Flamingo Lodge—a fairly priced and very recommendable option. However, here are a few hotels just outside the park that are even cheaper. As of press time, there is a $45 million casino hotel under construction adjacent to the Miccosukee bingo and gaming hall on the northern edge of the park.

Though bugs can be a major nuisance, especially in the warm months, camping is really the way to go in this very primitive environment. There are dozens of campsites and chickee platforms (see below for details) for tenters.

IN & AROUND EVERGLADES NATIONAL PARK

✪ **Flamingo Lodge, Marina and Outpost Resort.** 1 Flamingo Lodge Hwy., Flamingo, FL 33034. ☎ **800/600-3813** or 941/695-3101. Fax 941/695-3921. www.flamingolodge.com. 127 units. A/C TV TEL. High season from $95 double; from $135 cottage; $135–$150 suite. Summer/fall $65–$80 double; $89–$100 cottage; $99–$110 suite. Rates for cottages or suites are for 1 to 4 people. AE, DC, DISC, MC, V. Children under 18 stay free. Take Florida Turnpike South to Florida City; exit on U.S. 1; at 4-way intersection turn right onto Palm Dr.; continue for 3 miles and turn left at Robert Is Here fruit stand; turn right at 3-way intersection. The park entrance is 3 miles ahead. Continue for about 35 more miles to reach lodge.

The Flamingo Lodge is the only lodging actually located within the boundaries of Everglades National Park. This woodsy, sprawling complex offers rooms overlooking the Florida Bay in either a two-story simple motel or the lodge. Either option feels very much like being at summer camp, with a few more amenities.

VCRs and videos are available for guests in the regular rooms or in the suite, but not in more primitively outfitted cottages. Still, the cottages are an especially good choice if you plan to stay more than a night or two since they come with small kitchens, equipped with dishes and flatware, but no television. They are also larger, more private, and almost romantic.

Facilities on the premises include a waterside bar and restaurant; a freshwater swimming pool; a convenience store, a gift shop; a coin laundry; bike, canoe, and kayak rental; and a full-service marina. The hotel is open year-round, although the restaurant (see "Where to Dine," below) closes in the summer. Reservations are accepted daily from 8am to 5pm. Guests are treated to free coffee in the lobby.

CAMPING & HOUSEBOATING IN THE EVERGLADES

Campgrounds are available in Flamingo and Long Pine Key, where there are more than 300 sites designed for tents and RVs. They have level parking pads, tables, and charcoal grills. There are no electrical hookups, and showers are cold water. Private ground fires are not permitted, but supervised campfire programs are conducted during winter months. Reservations may be made in advance through the **National Parks Reservation Service** at ☎ 800/365-CAMP or online at www.nps.gov. Campsites are $14 per night with a 14-day consecutive-stay limit, 30 days a year maximum.

Camping is also available in the backcountry year-round on a first-come, first-served basis and is accessible only by boat, foot, or bicycle. Campers must register in person or by telephone no more than 24 hours prior to the start of their trip. Permits must be obtained at ranger stations in either Flamingo or Everglades City. Campers can use only designated campsites, which are plentiful and well marked on visitor maps.

Many backcountry sites are chickees—covered wooden platforms on stilts. They're accessible only by canoe and can accommodate free-standing tents (without stakes). Ground sites are located along interior bays and rivers, and beach camping is also popular. In summer especially, mosquito repellent is necessary gear.

Houseboat rentals are one of the park's best-kept secrets. Available through the Flamingo Lodge, Marina and Outpost Resort, motorized houseboats make it possible for you to explore some of the park's more remote regions without having to worry about being back by nightfall. You can choose from two types of houseboats. The first, a 40-foot pontoon boat, sleeps six to eight people in a single large room that's separated by a central head (bathroom) and shower. There's a small galley (kitchen) that contains a stove, an oven, and a charcoal grill. Prices aren't cheap unless you are with a good-sized group. It rents for between $340 and $475 for 2 nights (there's a 2-night minimum in high season).

The newer, sleeker Gibson fiberglass boats sleep six and have a head and shower, airconditioning, and an electric stove. There's also a full rooftop sundeck. These rent for $575 for 2 nights (with a 2-night minimum). With either boat, the 7th night is free with a full-week rental.

Boating experience is helpful, but not mandatory, because the boats cruise only up to 6 miles per hour and are surprisingly easy to use. In-season reservations should be made months in advance; call ☎ **800/600-3813** or 941/695-3101.

NEARBY IN HOMESTEAD & FLORIDA CITY

Homestead and Florida City, two adjacent towns that were almost blown off the map by Hurricane Andrew in 1992, have come back better than before. Located about 10 miles from the park's main entrance, along U.S. 1, 35 miles south of Miami, these somewhat-rural towns offer several budget lodging options, including a handful of chain hotels, including a very recommendable **Days Inn** (☎ **305/245-1260**) in Homestead and a **Hampton Inn** (☎ **800/426-7866** or 305/247-8833) right off the Turnpike in Florida City. The best option is the Best Western Gateway to the Keys.

۞ Best Western Gateway to the Keys. 1 Strano Blvd. (U.S. 1), Florida City, FL 33034. ☎ **800/528-1234** or 305/246-5100. Fax 305/242-0056. 114 units, all with bathrooms (tubs only). A/C TV TEL. Winter from $89 double; from $109 suite. Off-season from $80 double; from $99 suite. AE, DC, DISC, MC, V. Rates include continental breakfast. During races and very high season, there may be a 3-night minimum.

Opened in late 1994, this two-story, pink-and-white Best Western offers contemporary style and comfort about 10 miles from the park's main entrance. A decent-sized pool and a small spa are especially attractive. Each identical standard room has bright, tropical bedspreads and oversize picture windows. The suites offer convenient extras like a microwave, a coffeemaker, an extra sink, and a small fridge. Overall, this business-oriented hotel is well priced and well maintained and is the best choice in the area. The only drawback is that in season, there is often a 3-day minimum-stay requirement. You'd do best to call the local reservation line instead of the toll-free number—on several occasions, the hotel made an exception to the rule when the central reservation line was not able to.

Everglades Motel. 605 S. Krome Ave., Homestead, FL 33030. ☎ **305/247-4117.** 14 units. AC TV TEL. Winter $43 double; off-season from $32 double. Additional person $5. AE, DISC, MC, V.

This one-story hotel is probably the cheapest option you'll find in Homestead, but certainly not the greatest. There are a small swimming pool, a coin laundry, and free coffee in the lobby. Though not thoroughly fluent in English, the East Indian staff is accommodating and friendly. Rooms are modest in size and decor but could use a good scrub. Nonetheless, the place is safe, super affordable, and perfectly fine for 1 or 2 nights. Make your local calls from here, since they are free.

WHERE TO DINE IN & AROUND THE PARK

You won't find fancy nouvelle cuisine in this suburbanized farm country, but there are plenty of fast-food chains along U.S. 1 and a few old favorites worth a taste.

Here for nearly a quarter of a century, **El Toro Taco,** at 1 S. Krome Ave. (near Mowry Drive and Campbell Drive, ☎ **305/245-8182**), opens daily at 9:30am and stays crowded until at least 9pm most days. The fresh grilled meats, tacos, burritos, salsas, guacamole, and stews are mild and delicious. No matter how big your appetite, it's hard to spend more than $12 per person at this Mexican outpost. You'll have to bring your own beer or wine.

Housed in a squat, one-story, windowless stone building that looks something like a medieval fort, the **Capri Restaurant,** 935 N. Krome Ave., Florida City (☎ **305/247-1542**), has been serving hearty Italian-American fare since 1958. Great pastas and salads complement a full menu of meat and fish dishes. Portions are big. They serve lunch and dinner every day (except Sun) until 11pm.

The **Miccosukee Restaurant** (☎ **305/223-8380**), just west of the Shark Valley entrance on the Tamiami Trail (U.S. 41), serves authentic pumpkin bread, fry bread, fish, and not-so-authentic Native American interpretations of tacos and fried chicken. This interesting spot is worth a stop for brunch, lunch, or dinner.

Once inside the Everglades, you'll want to eat at the only restaurant within the boundaries of this huge park, **The Flamingo Restaurant** (☎ **941/695-3101**). Located in the Flamingo Lodge (see "Where to Stay," above), this is a very civilized and affordable restaurant. Besides the spectacular view of Florida Bay and numerous Keys from the large, airy dining room, you'll also find fresh fish, including my very favorite, mahimahi. All fish is prepared grilled, blackened, or deep-fried; and dinner entrees come with salad or conch chowder, and steamed vegetables, black beans and rice, or baked potato. The large menu has something for everyone, including basic and very tasty sandwiches, pastas, burgers, and salads. A kids' menu offers standard choices like hot dogs, grilled cheese, and fried shrimp for less than $6. Prices are surprisingly moderate, with full meals starting at about $11 and going no higher than $22. You may need reservations for dinner, especially in season.

2 Everglades City: Western Gateway to the Everglades

The brainchild of advertising magnate Barron Collier, who funded the completion of the Tamiami Trail from Miami to Naples, Everglades City was conceived as a major center of activity on Florida's west coast.

While building the highway in the 1920s, Collier dredged a channel through the Ten Thousand Islands and created a new island with the spoil, upon which he laid out Everglades City. Although it became a popular hunting and fishing destination for the rich and famous, Everglades City never became the metropolis he hoped for. In 1947, Everglades National Park took in most of the land and bays around the town.

Everglades City is an isolated little town with one school, a post office, and a bank, as well as a dozen or so seafood restaurants, some motels and B&Bs, and a few tourist shops. It lies in the Ten Thousand Islands area, and the Wilderness Waterway twists and turns 99 miles from here all the way to Flamingo at the southwestern edge of the

Everglades. This makes the town a perfect starting point for canoe or boat explorations of the area.

ESSENTIALS

GETTING THERE   Take I-75 or U.S. 41 east to S.R. 29 and turn south to Everglades City. S.R. 29 runs through town and then over a causeway along beautiful Chokoloskee Bay to Chokoloskee Island, an old Calusa shell mound that's the highest point in the Everglades.

VISITOR CENTER & INFORMATION   The **National Park's Gulf Coast Visitor Center,** on S.R. 29 at the south end of Everglades City (☎ **941/695-3311;** fax 941/695-3621), offers information and advice to visitors during the high season from 7:30am to 5pm, and more limited hours in the summer months.

The **Everglades City Area Chamber of Commerce,** P.O. Box 130, Everglades City, FL 34139 (☎ **941/695-3941;** fax 941/695-3919), provides information on tours and outfitters operating near the park's northwestern entrance at the intersection of U.S. 41 and S.R. 29. See section 1 of this chapter for information sources within the National Park. They are there every day from 9am until 5pm.

SPORTS & ACTIVE PURSUITS

BICYCLING   In Everglades City, a 4-mile paved bike path runs from town across a picturesque causeway to Chokoloskee Island. The **Ivey House Bed & Breakfast,** 107 Camellia St., 1 block behind the Circle K store (☎ **941/695-3299**), rents bikes during the winter months for $3 per hour or $15 for the day November to May. It's open from 8:30am to 4:30pm.

BIRD WATCHING   Pick up a free brochure on area birds at the visitor center. (Also, see "Boat Tours," below.)

CANOEING   Canoes are one of the best ways to cruise through these shallow waters with gators, manatees, and dolphins. They are available at Everglades City, near the Park Ranger Station at the Everglades's western entrance, from **North American Canoe Tours,** 107 Camelia St., Everglades City, (☎ **941/695-4666** November to April, or 860/739-0791 May to October; fax 941/695-4155 November to April). The 17-foot aluminum canoes can be rented with or without camping equipment, a personal guide, or a fully outfitted tour. Canoes cost $20 per day. Canoes with camping supplies cost $50 per person per day.

For information about boat tours, hiking, canoeing, boating, fishing, and other outdoor activities in the park, see section 1 of this chapter.

SEEING THE SIGHTS BY WATER

You can wander a few trails and relax in this pristine park, and visit the simple attractions below, but most of the sights in this region are accessible only after you leave land. Try at least one of the tours below for a look at the beautiful natural wilderness.

BOAT TOURS   Flat-bottom, airplane-propeller–driven airboats can take from two people to large groups speeding across the waterways. They operate on privately owned property, since they're not allowed in the national park or other nearby federal preserves.

The most advertised—and touristy—operator is **Wooten's Everglades Adventure,** on U.S. 41, 2 miles east of S.R. 29 (☎ **800/282-2781** or 941/695-2781). This large operation has airboat and swamp-buggy rides, an alligator farm, a gift shop, and a snack bar. Buggy and boat rides cost $13.25 each. Admission to the alligator farm is $6.35 (free for children 6 and under). Combined tickets for both rides and a visit to the farm are about $30. Wooten's is open daily from 8:30am to 5pm. Discount coupons are available from the visitor center.

In town on S.R. 29, **Jungle Erv's Airboat World** (☎ **800/432-3367** or 941/ 695-2805) has a large airboat tour charging $13.95 for adults and $8 for children. Private rides in small boats cost $30 per person. A jungle tour by pontoon boat costs $13.95. With any tour you can also see the alligator park.

Tours from Everglades City are offered by **Everglades National Park Boat Tours** (☎ **800/445-7724** in Florida, or 941/695-2591). The Mangrove Wilderness Tour explores the Glades's inland rivers and creeks at high tide. White ibis, cuckoos, egrets, herons, and other animals can often be seen through the thick mangroves. The endangered manatee can often be spotted, along with dozens of species of birds, including the southern bald eagle. Tours depart daily, every half hour from 9am to 5pm (less frequently off-season); last about 90 minutes; and cost $11 for adults, $5.50 for children 6 to 12. Reservations are not accepted. Tours depart from the Park Docks, on Chokoloskee Causeway (Fla. 29), half a mile south of the traffic circle by the ranger station.

If you are up for an intriguing all-day tour, **Everglades Excursions** (☎ **800/ 592-0848** or 941/598-1050) offers full-day guided trips to Everglades City from both Naples and Marco Island, which include a nature cruise, an airboat ride, and a visit to Ted Smallwood's store (described below). The trips cost $79 for adults and $64 for children; they also stop for an Old Florida–style lunch of seafood and other fare at a neighborhood restaurant (the cost is included in the price of the trip).

One-hour boat tours leave from the dock of Ted Smallwood's Store, at the south end of Mamie Street on Chokoloskee Island. See "Seeing the Sights on Land," below. You'll see where Ed Watson, reputed murderer of the notorious female outlaw Belle Star, was gunned down. Boat tours cost $15 per person.

CANOE TOURS   David Harraden and sons Jason and Jeremy of **North American Canoe Tours** (☎ **941/695-4666** Nov to Apr or 860/739-0791 May to Oct; fax 941/ 695-4155 Nov to Apr) have been leading canoe expeditions into the Everglades every winter since 1978, offering trips ranging from a day to a week. The 1-day trips cost $40 per person.

SEEING THE SIGHTS ON LAND

For an overview of this watery region, climb the E. J. Hamilton Observation Tower, opposite the visitor center. It is not part of the national park, but for $1 you can rise above the trees and see for miles across the islands and sawgrass plains.

Plan to take at least a half-hour break at **Smallwood's Store Museum** (☎ **941/ 695-2989**), at the south end of Mamie Street on Chokoloskee Island. Looking almost exactly as it did in pioneering days, this former trading post dates back to 1906, and it operated continuously as a store, post office, and voting place until 1982. Some 90% of the stock still on its shelves was there when it closed. That stuff is not for sale but there is a well-stocked gift shop selling books, gator heads, T-shirts, and Native American dolls. The museum is open daily from 10am to 5pm during winter; hours vary the rest of the year. Admission is $2.50 for adults, $2 for seniors, and free for children 11 and under. See "Seeing the Sights by Water," above, for details on the boat tour from Smallwood's.

WHERE TO STAY

Captain's Table Lodge & Villas. 102 E. Broadway (P.O. Box 530), Everglades City, FL 34139. ☎ **800/741-6430** or 941/695-4211. Fax 941/695-2633. 26 rms, 6 suites, 24 villas. A/C TV TEL. Winter $75–$95 double. Off-season $55–$70 double. DISC, MC, V. Take I-75 to Exit 14A, which is S.R. 29, to Everglades City. Follow S.R. 29 to the front door.

Located in the heart of town, this collection of rooms, suites, and villas actually is a condo development, so the units are furnished and decorated in each owner's tastes, some with kitchens. The rooms and suites are in a main building, while the villas are built on stilts and have a cottage-like feel to them. A swimming pool sits by canal-like Lake Placid along the property's eastern flank. Bicycle rental is also available here.

Ivey House Bed & Breakfast. 107 Camellia St. (P.O. Box 5038), Everglades City, FL 34139. ☎ **941/695-3299,** or 860/739-0791 May–Oct. Fax 941/695-4155. E-mail: sandee@ iveyhouse.com. www.iveyhouse.com. 10 units with shared bathrooms. A/C. During Seafood Festival (Feb) and Christmas holidays $70 double with shared bathroom, $120 cottage. $50–$55 double, $85 cottage ($15 for each extra person up to 4). 2-night minimum during high season. Rates include continental breakfast. MC, V. Closed May–Oct.

This wooden structure was operated by a Mrs. Ivey as a boardinghouse for men working on the Tamiami Trail in the 1920s. Today it's run during the winter by canoe specialist David Harraden and clan. A center hallway separates the simple rooms. Guests share separate men's and women's bathrooms. There are two decks and a large living room for relaxation. A cottage next door has two bedrooms with baths, a screened porch, and antiques. Breakfasts and dinners are served in a spacious kitchen at the rear of the main house (dinners cost $10 to $15 per person, and outsiders are welcome by reservation). Guests have free use of bicycles but have to pay to use the coin laundry. They can smoke and drink on the decks, but not in the house. All of their bed-and-breakfast rooms have numerous 1900 to 1920 antiques—a wood washing machine and 1918 Hoosier apple-green–speckled enamelware, for example. In the plans for next year is an additional building with private baths and a hot tub. Full-day and half-day guided adventures and kayak rentals are available.

Rod & Gun Lodge. Riverside Dr. and Broadway (P.O. Box 190), Everglades City, FL 34139. ☎ **941/695-2101.** 17 units. A/C TV. Winter $90 double. Off-season $65 double. No credit cards.

This rustic, old white clapboard house has plenty of history and all kinds of activities for sports enthusiasts, including a swimming pool, bicycle rental, a tennis center, tennis courts, nearby boat rentals, and private fishing guides. This famous outpost on the banks of the sleepy Barron River was originally built as a private residence nearly 170 years ago, but Barron Collier turned it into a cozy hunting lodge in the 1920s. President Herbert Hoover vacationed here after his 1928 election victory, and President Harry S Truman flew in to sign Everglades National Park into existence in 1947. Other guests have included Richard Nixon, Burt Reynolds, and Mick Jagger. The public rooms are beautifully paneled and hung with tarpon, wild boar, deer antlers, and other trophies. Out by the swimming pool and riverbank, a screened veranda with ceiling fans offers a pleasant place for a drink. The dining room serves breakfast, lunch, and dinner.

WHERE TO DINE

Everglades City has no gourmet restaurants, but you can get your fill of fresh seafood at several local eateries. Since the town produces about two-thirds of Florida's crab catch, most have fresh-off-the-boat claws from mid-October through mid-May.

Do stop and have a chat with the friendly Joan of **Joan's Quik Stop,** at 39395 U.S. 41, in Ochopee. This pleasant little eatery serves a great breakfast from when it opens at 9am until it closes at 5pm. A favorite is the Indian breakfast of eggs on flatbread with sautéed vegetables like zucchini, eggplant, and broccoli. Lunch specials include lots of fried seafood like gator nuggets, fritters, and shrimp. Take a free postcard and send one back when you get home. It will join the hundreds of others on the walls of this quaint and inexpensive diner. Most dishes are under $7, but be sure to have cash or traveler's checks because no checks are accepted.

The Oyster House, on S.R. 29 opposite the Everglades National Park Visitor Center (☎ **941/695-2073**), also specializes in seafood. Main courses range from $12 to $17; sandwiches are $4.50 to $9.50. A narrow, screened front porch here is a fine place to sip a drink while watching the sunset over the Everglades. Open daily from 11am to 9pm. On some weekends you may find live music and dancing, too.

The down-home **Oar House Restaurant,** 305 Collier Ave. (Fla. 29), in town (☎ **941/695-3535**), offers "cooters, legs, and tails" (turtles, frog's legs, and alligator tails) as specialties. Main courses range from $8 to $16, and sandwiches and seafood baskets run $2 to $8. Open daily from 6am to 9pm.

3 Big Cypress National Preserve

50 miles W of Miami, 22 miles E of Naples

In Big Cypress, northwest of the Florida Everglades, "big" refers not to the size of the trees, but to the vastness of the stands. More than half a million acres of parkland were acquired by the National Park Service in 1974, and the Big Cypress National Preserve Addition Act of 1988 is gradually adding 146,000 acres.

The preserve is intentionally lean on visitor facilities and contains few marked trails of any kind. As a result, Big Cypress feels plenty big—and remote. If you are looking for a true wilderness experience, you'll want to spend an afternoon exploring here. Just be sure you have a full tank of gas before entering—there are no gasoline stations or food services in the preserve.

Camping is available throughout the preserve. It's free, but there are no facilities: no fresh water, no toilets, no picnic tables, no grills.

To see one artist's incredible renderings of the area, stop at **Big Cypress Gallery** (☎ **941/695-2428**) at 52388 Tamiami Trail (less than 1 mile east of the Oasis Visitor Center). This museum/gallery showcases Clyde Butcher's award-winning black-and-white photographs of his backyard—the vast expanse that is the Everglades. It's worth a drive. The gallery is open daily 9:30am to 5pm.

JUST THE FACTS

Entrance is free to Big Cypress National Preserve. Contact **Big Cypress National Preserve Headquarters,** P.O. Box 110, Ochopee, FL 33943 (☎ **941/695-4111** or 941/695-2000), for a map and specialized information on the preserve.

On-site information is dispensed at the Oasis Visitor Center, at the preserve's main entrance, on the Tamiami Trail (U.S. 41) in Ochopee, 37 miles west of Florida City and 22 miles east of Naples. During the winter months, information is also available at Preserve Headquarters, on the Tamiami Trail, about 18 miles west of Oasis. The visitor centers are staffed daily from about 8:30am to 4:30pm.

EXPLORING THE PRESERVE

The preserve is a sprawling expanse that was designated as a national preserve primarily to help protect the ecosystem of the Everglades. There's little to attract tourists except for die-hard walkers sure to enjoy over 30 miles of flat trails. Pick up a free trail map from the visitor center before heading out. Otherwise, there is nothing you will see here that you won't find in the main park area.

If you want to explore, start on the Florida Trail, the preserve's main hiking trail, that stretches northwest (with significant gaps) all the way into the Florida Panhandle. The part of the trail that's inside Big Cypress is about 30 miles long and runs north from the Oasis Visitor Center. Hikers should be prepared for wet areas ankle- to waist-deep in the rainy season. There are two primitive campsites but no potable water on the trail.

4 Biscayne National Park

35 miles S of Miami, 21 miles E of Everglades National Park

This unusual and underappreciated park celebrated its 30th birthday in 1998, when park rangers offered many free programs in order to entice more locals to visit. With only about 500,000 visitors each year (mostly boaters and divers), it is one of the least crowded parks in the country. Biscayne National Park is a little more difficult than most to access—more than 95% of its 182,00 acres are underwater.

The park's significance was first formally acknowledged in 1968, when in an unprecedented move, Pres. Lyndon Johnson signed a bill to conserve the barrier islands off South Florida's east coast as a national monument—a protected status that's a rung below national park. After being twice enlarged, once in 1974 and again in 1980, the waters surrounding the northernmost coral reef in North America became a full-fledged national park—the largest of its kind in the country.

To be fully appreciated, this should be thought of more as a preserve than a destination. I suggest using your time here to explore underwater life—but most of all, to relax.

The park's greatest dry attraction is the 29-acre island known as Boca Chita Key, once an exclusive haven for wealthy yachtsmen. It was closed for years after the devastating hurricane of 1992 wiped out much of the tiny park. Six years and nearly $2 million were spent to restore the quaint island, which is especially popular with boaters. Now, visitors can tour the island's newly restored historic buildings, including an ornamental lighthouse and a tiny chapel.

Also popular is Elliott Key, one of the park's 44 little mangrove-fringed islands, containing a visitor center, hiking trails, and a campground. It's located about 9 miles from the Dante Fascell Visitor Center.

JUST THE FACTS

GETTING THERE & ACCESS POINTS   The park's mainland entrance is Convoy Point, located 9 miles east of Homestead. To reach the park from Miami, take the Florida Turnpike to Speedway Boulevard (Exit 6). Turn left, heading south 4½ miles, then left again at North Canal Drive (SW 328th Street), and follow signs to the park. If you're coming from U.S. 1, whether you're heading north or south, turn east at North Canal Drive (SW 328th Street).

As mentioned earlier, most of Biscayne National Park is accessible only to boaters. Mooring buoys abound, since it's illegal to anchor on coral. When no buoys are available, boaters must anchor on sand or on the new docks surrounding the small harbor off Boca Chita, where boats can stay overnight for $15. Even the most experienced boaters should carry updated nautical charts of the area, which are available at the Dante Fascell Visitor's Center. The waters are often murky, making the abundant reefs and sandbars difficult to detect—and there are more interesting ways to spend a day than waiting for the tide to rise. There's a boat launch at adjacent Homestead Bayfront Park, and 66 slips on Elliott Key, available for $15 per slip per night.

For those without their own vessels, transportation to and from the visitor center costs $21 per person. Call ☎ **305/230-1100** for schedule and reservations.

VISITOR CENTERS & INFORMATION   For information on park activities and tours, contact **Biscayne National Underwater Park Inc.,** P.O. Box 1270, Homestead, FL 33030 (☎ **305/230-1100;** fax 305/230-1120; www.nps.gov/bisc). The center is open daily from 8:30am to 5pm.

The **Dante Fascell Visitor Center,** 9700 SW 328th St., at the park's main entrance (☎ **305/230-7275;** fax 305/230-1190), is the natural starting point for any venture into the park. In addition to providing comprehensive information on the park, rangers will show you a short video on request. Open daily from 8:30am to 5pm.

ENTRANCE FEES & PERMITS   Entrance is free to Biscayne National Park. There is a fee for overnight docking and camping privileges.

SEEING THE HIGHLIGHTS

Biscayne National Park is primarily underwater, but you can get a good overview of the area by touring the small museum in the visitor center. Admission is free. You can rent a speedboat in Miami and cruise south for about 1½ hours, but a better idea would be to take one of the organized tours offered every day from the main visitor center. (See "Organized Tours," below.) Beneath the surface, the aquatic universe pulses with multicolored life: Bright parrot and angelfish, gently rocking sea fans, and coral labyrinths abound. Before entering the water, be sure to apply waterproof sunblock or wear a T-shirt. Once you begin to explore, it's easy to lose track of time, and the Florida sun is brutal, even during winter.

Afterward, take a picnic out to Elliott Key and taste the crisp salt air blowing off the Atlantic. Or head to Boca Chita, an intriguing island that was once the private playground of wealthy yachtsmen.

SPORTS & ACTIVE PURSUITS

CANOEING & KAYAKING   Biscayne National Park offers excellent canoeing, either along the coast or across open water to nearby mangroves and man-made islands that dot the longest uninterrupted shoreline in the state of Florida. Since tides can be strong, only experienced canoeists should attempt to paddle far from shore. If you plan to go far, first obtain a tide table from the visitor center (see "Just the Facts," above) and paddle with the current. Free ranger-led canoe tours are scheduled for most weekend mornings; phone for information. You can rent a canoe at the park; rates are $8 an hour or $22 for 4 hours. Kayaks are also available.

FISHING   Ocean fishing is excellent year-round; many people cast their lines right from the breakwater jetty at Dante Fascell. A fishing license is required (see "Entrance Fees, Permits & Regulations," under "Just the Facts" in section 1, for complete information). Bait is not available in Biscayne but is sold in adjacent Homestead Bayfront Park. Stone crabs and Florida lobsters can be found here, but you're only allowed to catch these on the ocean side when they're in season. There are strict limitations on size, season, number, and method of take (including spear fishing) for both fresh- and saltwater fishing. The latest regulations are available at most marinas, at bait and tackle shops, and at the park's visitor centers. Or you can contact the **Florida Game and Fresh Water Fish Commission,** Bryant Building, 620 S. Meridian St., Tallahassee, FL 32399-1600 (☎ **904/488-1960**).

HIKING & EXPLORING   Since the majority of this park is underwater, hiking is not the main attraction here, but there are some interesting sights and trails. At Dante Fascell you can walk along the 370-foot boardwalk, and along the half-mile jetty that serves as a breakwater for the park's harbor. From there you can usually see brown pelicans, little blue herons, snowy egrets, and a few exotic fish.

Elliott Key is accessible only by boat, but once you're there, you have two good trail options. True to its name, the Loop Trail makes a 1½-mile circle from the bayside visitor center, through a hardwood hammock and mangroves, to an elevated oceanside boardwalk. It's likely that you'll see purple and orange land crabs scurrying around the mangrove roots.

Restored in 1998 after a devastating hurricane in 1992, Boca Chita Key is a great island to explore. Once the playground for wealthy tycoons, it still offers the peaceful beauty that attracted elite fishermen from cold climates. Many of the historical buildings are still intact, including an ornamental lighthouse which was thankfully never put into use. Since it was built on the western side of the island in the path of shallow reefs, boaters would have followed the beacon only to go aground.

Take advantage of the tours, usually led by an interpretative park ranger and available every Sunday at 1pm. Including the 45-minute boat trip and the 45-minute return, the tour will take about 3 hours. The price for adults is $19.95; for children, $9.95. However, call in advance to see if the sea is calm enough for the boat trip. Rough seas often mean no boats can reach the island safely. Also call to see if any free tours are being offered. In 1998, in order to increase awareness of this little-known destination, the park service sponsored a series of free outings.

SNORKELING & SCUBA DIVING   The clear, warm waters of Biscayne National Park are packed with colorful tropical fish that swim in the offshore reefs. If you don't have your own, or don't want to lug it to the park, you can rent or buy snorkeling and scuba gear at the full-service dive shop at Dante Fascell Visitor Center. Rates are in line with those of dive shops on the mainland.

The best way to see **Biscayne National Underwater Park Inc. (☎ 305/ 230-1100)** is to take a snorkel tour. Tours go out daily and last about 4 hours and cost $27.95 per person. The full-gear package is only $37. They also run two-tank dives for certified divers and provide instruction for beginners. The price is $35.50 per person. The shop is open daily from 8am to 5:30pm. Two-tank dives depart on Wednesday, Saturday, and Sunday at 8:30am. Make reservations a few days in advance. No matter what your choice, if you are planning to get in the water, you must know how to swim.

For a real bargain, consider a money-saving package which includes accommodations but not gear rental. A winter special in 1999 consisted of lodging for 1 night at a nearby (15-minute drive to the park) Hampton Inn and 2 days of diving for less than $100 per person, double occupancy.

SWIMMING   You can swim at the protected beaches of Elliott Key, Boca Chita Key, and adjacent Homestead Bayfront Park, but none of these beaches matches the width or softness of other South Florida beaches. Check the water conditions before heading into the sea. Strong currents that make this a popular destination for windsurfers and sailors can be dangerous even for strong swimmers.

WINDSURFING/SURFING   Strong and steady winds provide an excellent venue for windsurfers. Feel free to bring your own board or and take on some of South Florida's best waves.

ORGANIZED TOURS

The best way to see the sights without getting wet is on the glass-bottom–boat tour. **Biscayne National Underwater Park Inc. (☎ 305/230-1100)** offers daily trips to view some of the country's most beautiful coral reefs and tropical fish. Boats depart year-round from the Dante Fascell Visitor Center at 10am and stay out for about 3 hours. At $19.95 for adults, $17.95 for seniors, and $9.95 for children 12 and under, the scenic and informative tours are well worth the price. Boats carry fewer than 50 passengers; therefore, reservations are almost always necessary. The company also offers guided canoe, scuba, and snorkeling reef trips led by underwater naturalists. See above.

WHERE TO STAY

There are no facilities available for overnight guests to this watery park. Most visitors come for an afternoon on their way to the Keys and stay overnight in nearby Homestead, where there are many national chain hotels and other affordable lodgings. See "Where to Stay" in section 1 of this chapter, above.

Although you won't find hotels or lodges in Biscayne National Park, there are some of the state's most pristine campgrounds. Since they are completely inaccessible by motor vehicle, you'll be sure to avoid the mass of RVs so prevalent in so many of the state's other campgrounds. Sites are on Elliott Key and Boca Chita and can be reached only by boat. If you don't have your own, call ☎ **305/230-1100** to arrange a drop-off. Transportation to and from the visitor center costs $21 per person. The best facilities are on the northeast side of newly reopened Boca Chita, where there are brand-new showers, solar-powered rest rooms, and drinking fountains, as well as barbecue grills and picnic tables. Rates are $10 per night per site without boat dockage and $15 with dockage in the harbor. Be sure to bring plenty of bug spray.

8 The Gold Coast

by Victoria Pesce Elliott

Throughout the past decade, the cities along Florida's southeastern coast from Hallandale to the Palm Beaches have been growing at an explosive rate. Newcomers arrive by the thousands every day. While plenty have come from other countries and from the frigid cities of the Northeast, many have moved from neighboring Miami, where a number of circumstances—a huge influx of immigrants from the Caribbean, a drastic increase in violent crimes, and devastating hurricanes in 1992 and 1998—caused many old-timers to head north in the hopes of escaping the densely populated regions that they once called home.

As a result, there has been a boom in building in the existing cities and westward into the swampy areas of the Everglades. More than 20 homes per day are being built in Broward county alone. Unfortunately, the area's infrastructure isn't equipped to handle this sudden surge in popularity. Over the past decade, cow pastures have given way to strip malls, and dirt paths to traffic jams. A more positive by-product is the revitalization of several downtown areas, including Hollywood, Fort Lauderdale, and West Palm Beach. These once-desolate urban centers have been spruced up and now attract more young travelers and families than ever before. The dozens of gorgeous beaches, of course, have always drawn a steady stream of sun worshippers and water-sports enthusiasts.

Beyond the sands, the Gold Coast offers fantastic shopping, entertainment, clubbing, boating, golfing, tennis, and plain old relaxing.

Unfortunately, like its neighbors to the south, the Gold Coast can be prohibitively hot and buggy in the summer. The good news is that bargains are plentiful in the slow months (between May and Oct), when many locals take advantage of package deals and uncrowded resorts.

For the purposes of this chapter, the Gold Coast will consist of the towns of Hallandale, Hollywood, Pompano Beach, Fort Lauderdale, Dania, Deerfield, Boca Raton, Delray Beach, Boyton Beach, and the Palm Beaches.

EXPLORING THE GOLD COAST BY CAR

Like most of the rest of South Florida, the Gold Coast consists of a mainland and an adjacent strip of barrier islands. You'll have to check the maps to keep track of the many bridges that allow access to the islands, where most of the tourist activity is centered. Interstate 95, which runs north-south, is the area's main highway. Farther west is the

Florida Turnpike, a toll road that can be worth the expense since the speed limit is higher and it is often less congested than I-95. Also on the mainland is U.S. 1, which generally runs parallel to I-95 (to the east) and is a narrower thoroughfare mostly crowded with strip malls and seedy hotels.

I recommend taking Fla. A1A, a slow oceanside road that connects the long, thin islands of Florida's whole east coast. Though the road is narrow, it is the most scenic and forces you into the ultra-relaxed atmosphere of these resort towns.

1 Broward County: Hallandale & Hollywood to Fort Lauderdale

23 miles N of Miami

With more than 23 miles of beachfront and 300 miles of navigable waterways, Broward County is a great destination for outdoor lovers. Scattered amid the tacky shopping malls, gaudy condos, and glitzy tourist areas are some impressive natural wonders, including hundreds of parks, golf courses, and tennis courts, too. With year-round temperatures averaging 77° and a growing industrial base, the area attracts more than 6 million visitors each year. Some 1.5 million residents call the more than 28 cities and dozens of towns that make up Broward County home.

Like many other small American towns, the quaint city of Hollywood has been working on redeveloping its downtown area for years. Finally, in the late 1990s, the efforts seemed to start paying off. A spate of redevelopment has made the pedestrian-friendly center along Hollywood Boulevard and Harrison Street east of Dixie Highway a popular destination for travelers and locals alike. Some predict Hollywood will be South Florida's next big destination—South Beach without the attitude, traffic jams, and parking nightmares. Prices are a fraction of those at other tourist areas, and a true artsy image is apparent in the galleries, clubs, and restaurants that dot the new "strip." The town's gritty undercurrent, however, still makes it more popular with bohemians and backpackers than society-page regulars.

Fort Lauderdale and its well-known strip of beaches, restaurants, bars, and souvenir shops have also undergone a major transformation. Once especially famous (or infamous) for the annual mayhem it hosted each spring when hedonism-bent college students descended from all over the country, this area is now attracting a more affluent crowd.

In addition to beautiful wide beaches, the city includes more than 300 miles of navigable waterways and innumerable canals that permit thousands of residents to anchor boats in their backyards. Boating is not just a hobby here; it's a lifestyle. It's the reason many choose to live in this area known as the "yachting capital of the world," or the "Venice of America." Visitors can easily get on the water, too, by renting a boat, or simply by hailing a moderately priced water taxi.

Huge cruise ships also take advantage of Florida's deepest harbor, Port Everglades. It is the second-busiest cruise-ship base in Florida (after Miami) and one of the top five in the world. For further information on cruises, consult *Frommer's Caribbean Cruises and Ports of Call.*

ESSENTIALS
GETTING THERE   If you're driving up from Miami, it's a straight shot to Hollywood or Fort Lauderdale on I-95. Visitors on their way to or from Orlando should take the Florida Turnpike to Exit 53, 54, 58, or 62, depending on the location of your accommodations.

The Fort Lauderdale/Hollywood International Airport is small, easy to negotiate, and located just 15 minutes from both of the downtown areas it services.

Amtrak (☎ **800/USA-RAIL**) stations are at 200 SW 21st Terrace (Broward Boulevard and I-95), Fort Lauderdale (☎ 954/587-6692), and 3001 Hollywood Blvd., Hollywood (☎ 954/921-4517).

VISITOR INFORMATION   The **Greater Fort Lauderdale Convention & Visitors Bureau,** 1850 Eller Dr., Suite 303 (off I-95 and I-595 east), Fort Lauderdale, FL 33316 (☎ **954/765-4466;** fax 954/765-4467; www.sunny.org), is an excellent resource in Spanish, French, or English. I highly recommend calling them in advance to request a free comprehensive guide with just about everything you could want to know about events, accommodations, and sightseeing in Broward County. In addition, once you are in town, you can call an **information line** (☎ **954/527-5600**) to get easy-to-follow directions, travel advice, and assistance from multilingual operators who staff a round-the-clock help line. Also available 24 hours a day are operators who can book discount scuba, cruise, or cultural packages. Call ☎ **800/22-SUNNY** for information.

The **Greater Hollywood Chamber of Commerce,** 330 N. Federal Hwy. (on the corner of U.S. 1 and Taylor Street), Hollywood, FL 33020 (☎ **954/923-4000;** fax 954/923-8737), is open Monday through Friday from 8:30am to 5pm.

HITTING THE BEACH

The southern part of the Gold Coast, Broward County, has the region's most popular and amenities-laden beaches, which stretch for more than 23 miles. Most do not charge for access, though all are well maintained. Here's a selection of some of the county's best from south to north.

Hollywood Beach, stretching from Sheridan Street to Georgia Street, is a real carnival with an odd assortment of young hipsters, big families, and sunburned French Canadians who dodge bicyclers and skaters along the rows of tacky souvenir shops, T-shirt shops, game rooms, snack bars, beer stands, hotels, and even miniature golf courses. The 3-mile-long Hollywood Beach **Broadwalk** is notable as one of the area's only beach paths where the diversions are right on the beach separated from the sand and sea by only a thin paved strip instead of a busy highway and tall buildings. Popular with runners, skaters, and cruisers, the Broadwalk is also renowned as a hangout for thousands of retirement-age snowbirds who get together for frequent dances and shows at a faded outdoor amphitheater. Despite efforts to clear out a seedy element, the area remains a haven for drunks and scammers, so keep alert.

If you tire of the hectic diversity that defines Hollywood's Broadwalk, enjoy the natural beauty of the beach itself, which is wide and clean. There are lifeguards, showers, bathroom facilities, and public areas for picnics and parties.

The **Fort Lauderdale Beach Promenade** recently underwent a $26 million renovation, and it looks fantastic. However, note that this beach is hardly pristine; it is across the street from an uninterrupted stretch of low- and high-rise hotels, bars, and retail outlets. Also nearby is a mega-retail and dining complex, Beach Place, on Fla. A1A, midway between Las Olas and Sunrise boulevards (see "Shopping & Browsing," below).

Just across the road, on the sand, most days you will find hard-core volleyballers, who always welcome anyone with a good spike, and a calm ocean welcoming swimmers of any level. The unusually clear waters are under the careful watch of some of Florida's best-looking lifeguards. Freshen up afterward in any of the clean showers and rest rooms conveniently located along the strip.

Fort Lauderdale Area Attractions & Accommodations

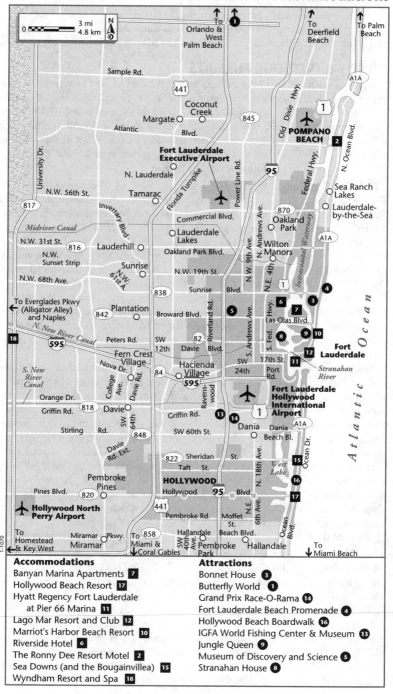

| 0 | 3 mi / 4.8 km | N |

To Orlando & West Palm Beach

To Deerfield Beach

To Palm Beach

Sample Rd.

(441)

Coconut Creek

Margate

(845)

Atlantic Blvd.

Old Dixie Hwy.

POMPANO BEACH

N. Ocean Blvd.

A1A

(1)

Fort Lauderdale Executive Airport

N. Lauderdale

Florida Turnpike

Power Line Rd.

Sea Ranch Lakes

Lauderdale-by-the-Sea

University Dr.

N.W. 56th St.

Tamarac

Inverrary Blvd.

Commercial Blvd.

N. Andrews Ave.

Oakland Park

(870)

Wilton Manors

A1A

(817)

Midriver Canal

N.W. 31st St.

(816)

Lauderhill

Oakland Park Blvd.

Lauderdale Lakes

N.W. 9th Ave.

N.E. 4th

Intracoastal Waterway

N.W. Sunset Strip

Sunrise

N.W. 19th St.

N.W. 68th Ave.

N.W. 61st A.

(838)

Sunrise Blvd.

N.E. 4th

(1)

To Everglades Pkwy (Alligator Alley) and Naples

(842)

Plantation

Broward Blvd.

Riverland Rd.

S. Andrews Ave.

S. Fed. Hwy.

Las Olas Blvd.

Atlantic Ocean

N. New River Canal

(18)

(595)

Peters Rd.

SW 12th

(82)

Davie Blvd.

Fort Lauderdale

S. New River Canal

Fern Crest Village

Nova Dr.

College Ave.

Davie Rd.

(84)

Hacienda Village

(595)

SW 24th

Ravenswood

Port Rd.

17th St.

Stranahan River

Orange Dr.

Griffin Rd.

(818)

Davie

SW 64th

Griffin Rd.

SW 60th St.

Fort Lauderdale Hollywood International Airport

(1)

Dania

Dania Beach Bl.

A1A

Stirling Rd.

Davie Rd. Ext.

(848)

(822)

Sheridan St.

Taft St.

N.E. 18th Ave.

West Lake

Ocean Dr.

Pembroke Pines

Pines Blvd.

(820)

HOLLYWOOD

Hollywood (95) Blvd.

N.E. 6th Ave.

Ocean Blvd.

Hollywood North Perry Airport

(441)

Pembroke Rd.

Moffet St.

To Homestead & Key West

Miramar Pkwy.

Miramar

To (858) Miami & Coral Gables

SW 40th Ave.

Hallandale Beach Blvd.

Pembroke Park

Hallandale

To Miami Beach

1-1070

Accommodations

Banyan Marina Apartments **7**
Hollywood Beach Resort **17**
Hyatt Regency Fort Lauderdale
   at Pier 66 Marina **11**
Lago Mar Resort and Club **12**
Marriot's Harbor Beach Resort **10**
Riverside Hotel **6**
The Ronny Dee Resort Motel **2**
Sea Downs (and the Bougainvillea) **15**
Wyndham Resort and Spa **18**

Attractions

Bonnet House **3**
Butterfly World **1**
Grand Prix Race-O-Rama **14**
Fort Lauderdale Beach Promenade **4**
Hollywood Beach Boardwalk **16**
IGFA World Fishing Center & Museum **13**
Jungle Queen **9**
Museum of Discovery and Science **5**
Stranahan House **8**

237

Especially on weekends, parking along the oceanside meters is nearly impossible to find. Try biking, skating, or hitching a ride on the water taxi instead. The strip is located on Fla. A1A, between SE 17th Street and Sunrise Boulevard.

SPORTS & OUTDOOR PURSUITS

BOATING   Known as the "yachting capital of the world," Fort Lauderdale provides ample opportunity for visitors to get on the water, either along the Intracoastal Waterway or out on the open ocean. If your hotel doesn't rent boats, try **Bill's Sunrise Watersports,** 2025 E. Sunrise Blvd., Fort Lauderdale (☎ 954/462-8962). They will outfit you with a variety of watercraft, including jet skis, Wave Runners, 13-foot Cigarettes, 15-foot jet boats, and 8-foot powerboats, year-round. Bill's is open daily from 9am to 6pm. Rates start at about $45 an hour.

CRUISES   The **Jungle Queen,** 801 Sea Breeze Blvd. (3 blocks south of Las Olas Boulevard on Fla. A1A), in the Bahia Mar Yacht Center, Fort Lauderdale (☎ 954/462-5596), a Mississippi River–style steamer, is one of Fort Lauderdale's best-known attractions cruising up and down the New River. All-you-can-eat dinner cruises and 3-hour sightseeing tours take visitors past Millionaires' Row, Old Fort Lauderdale, and the new downtown. Cruises depart nightly at 7pm and cost $24.50 for adults and $12 for children 12 and under. Sightseeing tours are scheduled daily at 10am and 2pm and cost $11.50 for adults and $8 for children 10 and under.

If you're interested in gambling, several casino-boat companies operate day cruises out of Port Everglades and offer blackjack, slots, and poker. **Discovery Cruise Lines** (☎ 800/937-4477) has daily cruises to the Bahamas, where you can gamble, eat, and party for 5 to 6 hours for about $120. The price includes breakfast, lunch, and dinner, but drinks cost extra.

Sea Escape (☎ 800/327-2005 or 954/453-3333) also launches daily casino cruises. But theirs don't travel more than a few miles offshore. These trips "to nowhere" depart every day except Monday at 10am and last until 4pm. The party cruises offer buffet meals and full casinos for about $35 a person. I'd recommend spending an additional $20 for a cabin so you can stretch out and relax in between hands. Even though the cruises don't go far from the coast, 5 or 6 hours is a long time to spend at sea, especially if the weather is rough. Evening cruises, which leave at 7:30pm and return at 12:30 or 1:30am, cost a few dollars more and offer full buffet dinners and a Las Vegas show. Port charges are included, although you must pay a $3 departure tax and $2.65 passenger charge. This is one of the best deals you'll find. Sea Escape also has a new 2- and 3-night cruise option, in which visitors can go to Nassau, the Bahamas, for as little as $199 per person with all meals included.

Also, see the box "More Than a Boat Tour," below, for details on the water taxi.

FISHING   Completed in 1999 at a cost of more than $32 million, the **IGFA World Fishing Center** at 300 Gulf Stream Way (☎ 954/922-4212) in Dania Beach is an anglers' paradise. One of the highlights of this museum, library, and park is the virtual-reality fishing simulator, which allows visitors to actually reel in their own computer-generated catch. Also included in the 3-acre park are displays of antique fishing gear, record catches, famous anglers, various vessels, and a wetlands lab. To get a list of local captains and guides, call **IGFA headquarters** and ask for the librarian (☎ 954/ 927-2628). Admission is $9 for adults, $5 for children between 3 and 12, and free for children under 3. On the grounds is also **Bass Pro Outdoor World Store,** a huge multifloor retail complex situated on a 3-acre lake.

GAME PARKS   This area seems to be the home of more mega-entertainment complexes than any other region in Southeast Florida. The **Grand Prix Race-O-Rama,** at

1801 NW 1st St., east of I-95 between Griffin and Sterling road exits, in Dania, is one of the originals and still the best for kids. With a massive video arcade, which is open 24 hours, five challenging miniature-golf greens, Go-Karts for those over 4 feet 6 inches, NASCAR racing for those over 5 feet tall, batting cages, and a huge sky coaster, this place is as exciting as it is exhausting. Plan to spend all day or night—or both. Call for prices and hours (☎ **954/921-1411**).

One of the newest additions to the scene is **Dave & Busters** at 3000 Oakwood Blvd. in Hollywood, just off the Sheridan Street exit of I-95 (☎ **954/923-5505**). This 50,000-square-foot complex caters primarily to adults; it features a full liquor bar and sit-down restaurant, as well as a more casual spot with table service. On weekends this place is packed with young adults on dates and rowdy groups of guys of all ages. An admission of $5 is charged only on Friday and Saturday after 10pm. D&B's opens weekdays at 11am, weekends at 11:30am, and usually closes by 1am.

Gameworks, the huge, high-tech creation of Hollywood movie mogul Steven Spielberg is located in the mammoth Sawgrass Mills outlet center (See "Shopping & Browsing," below.)

GOLF   More than 50 golf courses in all price ranges compete for players. Some of the best include **Emerald Hills** at 4100 North Hills Dr., Hollywood, just west of I-95 between Sterling Road and Sheridan Street. This beauty consistently lands on "best of" lists of golf writers throughout the country. The 18th hole on a two-tier green is the challenging course's signature; it's surrounded by water and is more than a bit rough. Greens fees start at $80. Call ☎ **954/961-4000** for tee times. For one of Broward's best municipal challenges, try the 18-holer at the **Orangebrook Golf Course** at 400 Entrada Dr. in Hollywood (☎ **954/967-GOLF**). Built in 1937, this is one of the state's oldest courses and one of the area's best bargains. Morning and noon rates range from $21 to $26. After 2pm, you can play for less than $20, including a cart.

SCUBA DIVING   In Broward County, the best wreck dive is the *Mercedes I,* a 197-foot freighter that washed up in the backyard of a Palm Beach socialite in 1984 and was sunk for divers the following year off Pompano Beach. The artificial reef, filled with colorful sponges, spiny lobsters, and barracudas, is located 97 feet below the surface, a mile offshore between Oakland Park and Sunrise boulevards. Dozens of reputable dive shops line the beach. Ask at your hotel for a nearby recommendation, or contact **Lauderdale Undersea Adventures,** 2150 SE 17th St., Fort Lauderdale (☎ **954/527-0187**).

SPECTATOR SPORTS   Baseball fans can get their fix at the **Fort Lauderdale Stadium,** 5301 NW 12th Ave. (☎ **954/938-4980**), where the Baltimore Orioles play exhibition games starting in early March; call ☎ **954/776-1921** for tickets. They cost $6 for general admission, $9 for a spot in the grandstand, and $12 for box seats. During the season, the Florida Marlins (World Series winners in 1997) play just south of Hallandale at the **Pro Player Stadium** near the Dade-Broward County line. Call **Ticketmaster** for tickets (☎ **305/358-5885**), which range from $2 to $40.

The **Pompano Harness Track,** 1800 SW 3rd St., Pompano Beach (☎ **954/972-2000**), the only one in Florida, features horse racing and betting from October to early August. Grandstand admission is free; clubhouse admission is $2. They, like many other pari-mutuel outlets in the area, opened poker rooms in 1997.

A sort of Spanish-style indoor lacrosse, jai-alai was introduced to Florida in 1924 and still draws big crowds who bet on the fast-paced action. Broward's only fronton, **Dania Jai-Alai,** 301 E. Dania Beach Blvd. at the intersection of Fla. A1A and U.S. 1 (☎ **954/920-1511** or 954/426-4330), is a great place to spend an afternoon or evening.

Wrapped around an artificial lake, **Gulfstream Park,** at U.S. 1 and Hallandale Beach Boulevard, Hallandale (☎ **305/931-7223**), is both pretty and popular. Large purses and important races are commonplace at this suburban course, and the track is often crowded. Call for schedules. Admission is $3 to the grandstand, and $3 to the clubhouse. Free parking. From January 3 to March 15, post times are Wednesday to Monday at 1pm. Many weekends feature live concerts by well-known musicians.

In the sport of ice hockey, the young **Florida Panthers** (☎ **954/835-7000**) have already made history. In the 1994–1995 season, they played in the Stanley Cup finals, and the fans love them. They play in Sunrise at 2555 NW 137th Way. Call for directions and ticket information.

TENNIS   There are literally hundreds of courts in Broward County, and plenty are accessible to the public. Many are at resorts and hotels. If they're not at yours, try one of these.

Famous as the spot where Chris Evert got in her early serves, **Holiday Park,** 701 NE 12th Ave. (off Sunrise Boulevard), Fort Lauderdale (☎ **954/761-5378**), has 18 clay and 3 hard courts (15 lighted). Her coach and father, James Evert, still teaches young players here, although he is very picky about who he'll accept. Non–Fort Lauderdale residents pay $3.50 to $4.50 per hour. Reservations are accepted after 2pm for the following day, but cost an extra $3. Lights are also an extra $3 per hour and are available only for the clay courts.

At the **Marina Bay Resort,** 2175 S.R. 84, west of I-95 and just behind the Ramada Inn, Fort Lauderdale (☎ **954/791-7600**), visitors can play free on any one of nine hard courts on a first-come, first-served basis. Three are lighted at night.

SEEING THE SIGHTS

For an overview of Fort Lauderdale, you may want to take an informative spin around the downtown area with **South Florida Trolley Tours** (☎ **954/946-7320**). Drivers narrate the history of the area as they loop around the city's streets past all the major (and many minor) sights. The charge for the 90-minute tour is $12 for adults, free for children 11 and under. The trolleys pick up passengers from most major hotels for six tours daily, starting at 9am. Call for current schedule.

For a tour by water, see the box below.

Museum of Discovery & Science. 401 SW 2nd St., Fort Lauderdale. ☎ **954/467-6637.** Museum admission $6 adults, $5 seniors, $5 children 3–12, free for children 2 and under; exhibit and IMAX combo prices $12.50 adults, $11.50 seniors, $10.50 children. Mon–Sat 10am–5pm, Sun noon–6pm. From I-95, exit on Broward Blvd. E.; continue to SW 5th Ave.; turn right, garage on right.

Children and teenagers especially love this interactive science museum that is a model of high-tech "infotainment." During the week, school groups meander through the cavernous two-story modern building. However, most weekend nights you'll find a diverse crowd ranging from hip high-school kids to 30-somethings enjoying a rock film in the Blockbuster IMAX 3D theater, which also shows short, science-related, super-size films daily. Out front, see the 52-foot-tall Great Gravity Clock, located in the museum's atrium, the largest kinetic-energy sculpture in the state. Exhibits vary, so call for the latest details.

Billie Swamp Safari. Big Cypress Reservation, west of Fort Lauderdale. ☎ **800/949-6101.** Free admission. Boat tours $10–$20. Daily 8am–8pm. Last airboat ride 4:30pm.

Here, you can catch a glimpse of how Florida looked before developers went wild. Skimming across the shallow swamps in an airboat with Native American guides, you

More Than a Boat Tour

Plan to spend at least an afternoon or evening cruising Fort Lauderdale's 300 miles of waterways the only way you can—by boat. **The Water Taxi of Fort Lauderdale** (☎ 954/467-6677) is one of the greatest innovations for water lovers since those cool Velcro sandals. A trusty fleet of old-port boats serves the dual purpose of transporting and entertaining visitors as they cruise through "The Venice of America."

Taxis operate on demand and also along a fairly regular route, carrying up to 48 passengers. Choose a hotel on the route so that you can take advantage of this convenient and inexpensive system. You can be picked up at your hotel, usually within 15 minutes of calling, and then be shuttled to any of the dozens of restaurants, bars, and attractions on or near the waterfront. If you aren't sure where you want to go, ask one of the personable captains who can point out historic and fun spots along the way.

For a day cruise with the kids, pack lunch, bathing suits, sunscreen, and sunglasses, and hail or call the taxi for pickup from any safe dock or seawall. Your afternoon of cruising might start with a tour of Millionaires' Row, where Lauderdale's largest yachts are dwarfed only by the homes at which they are docked. Make a stop at the Museum of Discovery and Science, where you can catch an IMAX film or just enjoy the current educational exhibits. Then, if you are up for a walk, head across the 3-mile Riverwalk, a scenic palm-lined walkway along the New River, where you can enjoy your picnic lunch, or try one of the restaurants dotting the way to Las Olas Boulevard and The Las Olas Riverfront. When you are ready for some shopping or a sit-down meal, reboard and head to Beach Place at Las Olas Boulevard and Cortez Street in the heart of Fort Lauderdale's most famous "strip." Stop for a refreshment at Casablanca Cafe and then hit the beach.

In the evening, the water taxi is ideal for bar hopping—no worrying about parking or choosing a designated driver. Make your first stop at Shooters, where professionals, boaters, and tourists share the large lively patio for a popular happy hour from 5 to 7pm on weekdays. Right next door is Bootlegger's, featuring more than 70 beers at an outside bar. You can eat at either spot or keep your eyes on the waterway for your ride (or call for a quicker pickup).

For those who enjoy jazz, you might want to debark in the downtown section of Las Olas Boulevard. O'Hara's (see "The Hollywood & Fort Lauderdale Area After Dark," below) always delivers a great mix of live jazz and blues.

Starting daily from 10am, boats usually run until midnight, and until 2am on weekends, depending on the weather. The cost is $7 per person per trip, $13 round-trip, and $15 for a full day. Children under 12 ride for half price and free on Sunday. Opt for the all-day pass; it's worth it.

may spot alligators and rare birds. Kids especially enjoy the swamp buggy rides, which leave every hour on the hour until 5pm.

Bonnet House. 900 N. Birch Rd. (1 block west of the ocean, south of Sunrise Blvd.), Fort Lauderdale. ☎ **954/563-5393.** Admission $9 adults, $8 seniors, $7 students under 18, free for children 6 and under. Tours Wed–Fri 10am–1:30pm, Sat–Sun noon–2:30pm.

This historic 35-acre plantation home and estate survives in the middle of an otherwise highly developed beachfront condominium area and is open only by guided tour.

Built in 1921, the sprawling two-story waterfront home surrounded with formal tropical gardens is really the backdrop of a love story, which the very chatty volunteer guides will share with you if you ask. Some have actually lunched with the former resident of the house, the late Evelyn Bartlett, the wife of world-acclaimed artist Frederic Clay Bartlett. If you like quirky people, whimsical artwork, lush grounds, and very interesting details of design, you'll love this tour, which takes about 1½ hours. Inquire about literary walks and science workshops offered regularly on the grounds.

Butterfly World. Tradewinds Park South, 3600 W. Sample Rd., Coconut Creek (west of the Florida Turnpike). ☎ 954/977-4400. Admission $11.95 adults, $6.95 children 4–12, free for children 3 and under. Mon–Sat 9am–5pm, Sun 1–5pm; last admission at 4pm.

One of the world's largest butterfly breeders, Butterfly World cultivates more than 150 species of these colorful and delicate insects. In the park's walk-through, screened-in aviary, visitors can see thousands of caterpillars and watch newborn butterflies emerge from their cocoons and flutter around as they learn to fly. Depending on how interested you are in these winged beauties, you may want to allow from 1 to 2 hours to tour the gardens and the well-stocked gift shop. Look for a new lorikeet aviary to open in the near future, where guests will be able to hand-feed these birds.

Stranahan House. 335 SE 6th Ave. (Las Olas Blvd. at the New River Tunnel), Fort Lauderdale. ☎ 954/524-4736. Admission $5 adults, $2 students and children. Wed–Sat 10am–4pm, Sun 1–4pm; last tour begins at 3:30pm. Also accessible by water taxi.

In a town whose history isn't even as old as many of its residents, visitors may want to take a minute to see Fort Lauderdale's very oldest standing structure and a prime example of classic "Florida Frontier" architecture. Built in 1901 by "the father of Fort Lauderdale," this house once served as a trading post for Seminole trappers who came here to sell pelts. It's been a post office, town hall, and general store and now is a worthwhile little museum of South Florida pioneer life, containing turn-of-the-century furnishings and historical photos of the area. It is also the site of occasional concerts and social functions. Call for details.

SHOPPING & BROWSING

Broward County has some of Florida's best malls and some fantastic boutique areas, too.

Dania is known for its antique district, where hundreds of shops are clustered along U.S. 1 just south of the airport. Known as **"Antique Row,"** this area has some of South Florida's best old treasures. Although many of the more upscale shops are overpriced, many of the smaller dealers offer bargains to hagglers.

Also for bargain mavens is a strip of "fashion" stores on **Hallandale Beach Boulevard's "Schmatta Row,"** east of Dixie Highway and the railroad tracks, where off-brand shoes, bags, and jewelry are sold at deep discounts. Funky Hollywood Boulevard also offers some wild shops with everything from Indonesian artifacts to used and rare books to leather bustiers to handmade hats. Dozens of shops line the pedestrian-friendly strip just west of Young Circle. The art galleries are clustered along Harrison Street just east of Dixie Highway.

The area's only beachfront mall, **Beach Place,** is in Fort Lauderdale on Fla. A1A just north of Las Olas Boulevard. Completed in 1997 at a cost of $23 million, this 100,000-square-foot giant sports the usual chains like Sunglass Hut, Limited Express, Banana Republic, and The Gap, as well as lots of popular bars and restaurants.

Other more traditional malls include the upscale **Galleria,** at Sunrise Boulevard near the Fort Lauderdale Beach, and Broward Mall, west of I-95 on Broward Boulevard, in Plantation.

If you are looking for unusual boutiques, especially art galleries, head to trendy ✪ **Las Olas Boulevard,** where there are literally hundreds of shops with alluring window decorations and intriguing merchandise. You may find kitchen utensils posing as modern art sculptures or mural-size oil paintings.

On the edge of the Arts & Science District is a new retail complex known as **Las Olas Riverfront,** with 260,000 square feet of restaurants, clothing stores, arcades, and a multiplex movie theater.

The well-known department store **Lord & Taylor** has a little-known clearance center where discounts on new clothing for women, kids, and men can be as big as 75%. If you can handle open dressing rooms, overstuffed racks, and surly sales help, it's a great find at 6820 N. University Dr. in Tamarac. You may want to call (☎ **954/ 720-1915**) to find out about specials.

The Fort Lauderdale Swap Shop, 3291 W. Sunrise Blvd. (☎ **954/791-SWAP**), is one of the world's largest flea markets. In addition to endless acres of vendors, there's a mini-amusement park, a 13-screen drive-in movie theater, weekend concerts, and even a free circus complete with elephants, horse shows, high-wire acts, and clowns.

The monster of all outlet malls is **Sawgrass Mills,** 12801 W. Sunrise Blvd., Sunrise (☎ **800/FL-MILLS** or 954/846-2350). Since the most recent expansion, completed in mid-1999, which added more than 30 new designer outlet stores, this behemoth (shaped like a Florida alligator) now holds more than 300 shops, kiosks, a 24-screen movie theater, and many restaurants and bars, including a Hard Rock Cafe. The enclosed area covers nearly 2.5 million square feet over 50 acres. There's no way to see it all in a day. Wear your most comfortable shoes or buy an extra pair while you're there. Stores include Donna Karan Company Store, Levi's Outlet, Sunglass Hut, Ann Taylor Loft, and Barney's New York, all selling goods at between 20% and 80% below retail. Label-conscious shoppers are especially impressed with Off Fifth, the Saks Fifth Avenue outlet store, and Last Call, the Neiman-Marcus clearance center. You may want to invest in a coupon booklet ($5), which entitles you to even greater discounts at many of the mall's stores and restaurants, as well as area attractions. Books are good for up to a year and can be turned in for updated books at no charge. To get there, take I-95 to I-595 west to the Flamingo Road exit, turn right, and drive 2 miles to Sunrise Boulevard; you will see the large complex on the left. From the Florida Turnpike, exit Sunrise Boulevard west. Parking is free, but don't forget where you parked; the lot holds more than 11,000 cars.

Fishing enthusiasts won't want to miss **Bass Pro Outdoor World** (☎ **954/ 929-7710**), a sprawling retail complex at Griffin Road and I-95 in Dania where you can buy anything from yachts to lures (see "Sports & Other Activities," above).

WHERE TO STAY

The Fort Lauderdale beach has a hotel or motel on nearly every block, and they range from the run-down to the luxurious. Both the **Howard Johnson** (☎ **800/327-8578** or 954/563-2451), at 700 N. Atlantic Blvd. (on Fla. A1A, south of Sunrise Blvd.), and the **Days Inn** (☎ **800/329-7466** or 954/462-0444), at 435 N. Atlantic Blvd. (Fla. A1A), offer clean oceanside rooms starting at about $150.

In Hollywood, where prices are generally cheaper, the **Holiday Inn** at 101 N. Ocean Blvd. (☎ **954/921-0990**) operates a full-service hotel right on the ocean. With prices starting at around $110 in season and discounts for AAA, it's a great deal. **Howard Johnson** (☎ **800/423-9867** or 954/925-1411) has a great location right on the beach at 2501 N. Ocean Dr. (I-95 to Sheridan Street east to Fla. A1A south).

Extended Stay America/Crossland Economy Studios has four super-clean properties in Fort Lauderdale and offers year-round rates as low as $49 a night and $159 per week. The studios are designed with business travelers in mind and include coffeemakers, irons and ironing boards, kitchens, and well-lighted desks.

Especially for rentals for a few weeks or months, call **Florida Sunbreak** (☎ **800/ SUNBREAK**). Or call the **South Florida Hotel Network** (☎ **800/538-3616**) for help finding small inns and lodges in any price range. Also, check out the annual list of small lodgings compiled by the **Ft. Lauderdale Convention & Visitors Bureau** (☎ **954/765-4466**). It is especially helpful for those looking for privately owned, charming, and affordable lodgings.

New hotels are going up all the time. One notable addition to the Hallandale area is the 1,000-room **Diplomat Resort & Country Club** on the site of the former landmark which closed in 1991. The $500 million project is due to open in the summer of 2000.

VERY EXPENSIVE

Hyatt Regency Fort Lauderdale at Pier 66 Marina. 2301 SE 17th St. Causeway, Fort Lauderdale, FL 33316. ☎ **800/233-1234** or 954/525-6666. Fax 954/728-3541. 380 units. A/C MINIBAR TV TEL. Winter $259 double. Off-season $209 double. Year-round from $1,000 suite. AE, CB, DC, DISC, MC, V.

The Pier 66 hotel and 142-slip marina has been hosting guests, especially boaters, since 1954. The luxurious resort attracts megayachts from all over the world, in addition to large groups and business travelers. Despite the emphasis on groups, for services and amenities this Hyatt is hard to beat.

The hotel's atrium-style lobby impresses with high ceilings and marble floors. The lushly landscaped grounds add to the exotic feel of this super-convenient locale, situated across from the beach, and within walking distance to the best shopping and dining. Every room has a balcony; the priciest have expansive panoramas of the marina, the beach across the street, and all of Fort Lauderdale beyond. The best part is that it is serviced by the convenient water taxi (see box, above). All rooms were renovated recently.

Dining/Diversions: Best known for its revolving rooftop lounge, the hotel also offers an American grill and a very popular waterfront cafe for dinner and lunch.

Amenities: Concierge, room service (24 hours), dry-cleaning and laundry services, newspaper delivery, twice-daily maid service, baby-sitting, secretarial services, express checkout, valet parking $8, courtesy car or limo. Spectravision movie channels, two swimming pools, beach, fully equipped spa, Jacuzzi, sauna, 40-person whirlpool, jogging track, children's center or programs, business center, conference rooms, self-service Laundromat, sundeck, two lighted clay tennis courts, water-sports equipment and boat rentals, 142-slip marina, tour desk, beauty salon, boutiques, shopping arcade.

Marriott's Harbor Beach Resort. 3030 Holiday Dr., Fort Lauderdale, FL 33316. ☎ **800/222-6543** or 954/525-4000. Fax 954/766-6193. 659 units. A/C TV TEL. Winter $349–$499 double. Off-season $169–$189 double. Year-round from $600 suite. AE, CB, DC, DISC, MC, V. From I-95, exit on I-595 east to U.S. 1 north; proceed to SE 17th St.; make a right and go over the intracoastal bridge past 3 traffic lights to Holiday Dr.; turn right.

Situated on 16 oceanfront acres just south of Fort Lauderdale's "strip" is the popular and predictable Marriott. From the spacious rooms and suites to the 8,000-square-foot swimming pool, everything in this very well run hotel is huge. All rooms open onto private balconies overlooking either the ocean or the Intracoastal Waterway. Return guests include many convention groups and families who enjoy the space to spread out. Service is more efficient than personal.

Dining: A formal restaurant serves one of Fort Lauderdale's most elegant dinners, and a less formal Japanese restaurant serves hibachi dinners that are prepared at your table. Three other casual restaurants serve breakfast, lunch, dinner, and late-night drinks.

Amenities: Concierge, room service, in-room massage, laundry services, newspaper delivery, baby-sitting, twice-daily maid service, express checkout, secretarial services, valet parking, courtesy car for shopping and golf, free coffee in lobby. Outdoor heated pool, beach, health club, Jacuzzi, sauna, sundeck, five clay tennis courts, water-sports equipment, bicycle rental, game room, children's center and programs, business center, self-service Laundromat, tour desk, boutiques, conference rooms, car-rental desk, beauty salon.

○ **Wyndham Resort and Spa.** 250 Racquet Club Rd., Fort Lauderdale, FL 33326. ☎ **800/996-3426** or 954/389-3300. Fax 954/384-6878. 500 units. A/C TV TEL. Winter from $245 double. Off-season from $175 double. Golf and spa packages (with or without meals) $65–$305 per person based on double occupancy. AE, CB, DC, DISC, MC, V. From I-95, exit at I-595 west to I-75; exit on Arvida Pkwy.; continue west to Weston Blvd.; turn right and proceed to Saddle Club Rd.; turn left to Bonaventure Blvd. Make a right to Racquet Club Rd. From Florida Turnpike, take I-595 West, take Exit 1, SW 136th Ave., S.R. 84, and proceed to Bonaventure Blvd.

Having changed hands frequently, this unusual spa and golf resort is a bit difficult to peg down. Built in 1981 on 23 acres, this active resort quickly earned a great reputation for its world-class facilities. Unfortunately, years of mismanagement resulted in its deterioration. A $10 million renovation begun in 1996 improved things, but then the resort was sold again to Wyndham resorts, which has big plans. Though it lacks any real charm, so far the overhaul looks fantastic.

The rooms, scattered throughout nine four-story buildings, have also been thoroughly gutted and reoutfitted in a bright tropical style, with conveniences like telephone voice mail and dataports, irons, ironing boards, coffeemakers, clock radios, and hair dryers. Also, suites and deluxe rooms offer wet bars and small refrigerators.

Although it is a lengthy trek to the nearest beach, this first-class property has plenty of opportunities to sun and swim—with five pools, including separate lap pools for men and women, and a private lake.

Dining/Diversions: With four restaurants, including one serving superb Tuscan food in a formal setting and another with real spa cuisine, you'll find plenty of delicious choices. You may even want to request recipes to take home. Also on the premises are four lounges for afternoon and evening entertainment and cocktails.

Amenities: Concierge, 24-hour room service, dry-cleaning and laundry service, newspaper delivery, in-room massage, twice-daily maid service, express checkout, secretarial services, valet parking, shopping transportation. Limited kitchenettes in some suites, Spectravision movie channels, five swimming pools, full-service spa, Jacuzzi, sauna, two championship golf courses, sundeck, 15 night-lit tennis courts, children's programs, business center, tour desk, boutiques, conference rooms, car-rental desk, beauty salon, and gift shop.

EXPENSIVE

○ **Lago Mar Resort and Club.** 1700 S. Ocean Lane, Fort Lauderdale, FL 33316. ☎ **800/524-6627** or 954/523-6511. Fax 954/524-6627. E-mail: reservations@lagomar. com. 212 units. A/C TV TEL. Winter $195 double; from $285 suite. Off-season $100–$135 double; from $135 suite. AE, DC, MC, V. From Federal Hwy. (U.S. 1), turn east onto SE 17th St. Causeway; turn right onto Mayan Dr.; turn right again onto S. Ocean Dr.; turn left onto Grace Dr.; then left again onto S. Ocean Lane to the hotel.

After extensive renovations, this sprawling family-owned resort is even better than before. Lago Mar, a casually elegant resort, occupies its own little island between Lake

Mayan and the Atlantic and is very family oriented, with lots of facilities and super-vised activities for children, especially during spring break and Christmas vacations. It's also good for business travelers looking for value. Unfortunately, the word has gotten out and it has become difficult to get reservations during the season.

Most accommodations here are suites, available in a variety of configurations. The smallest suites, called "executive," are decorated in contemporary prints and are simple and comfortable. The executive suites are very large, with a king-size bed, separate dressing area, pull-out sofa, and separate tub and shower in an extra-large bathroom. Each has a private balcony and full kitchen, or at least a microwave and a refrigerator. Ask for one of the newer units since they are generally larger and have more closet space. Definitely take advantage of the hotel's waterfront location to use the conve-nient water taxi (see box above).

Dining/Diversions: Three excellent restaurants and two lounges may tempt you to never leave this top-rated resort.

Amenities: Concierge, room service, dry-cleaning and laundry service, secretarial services, newspaper delivery, valet parking. Kitchenettes in most suites, outdoor pool and lagoon, beach, small fitness center, game rooms, children's playground, supervised children's programs during holiday periods, business center, conference rooms, sun-deck, four tennis courts, miniature golf course, volleyball courts, shuffleboard, water-sports concession, men's and women's apparel shops, Laundromat, tour desk.

Riverside Hotel. 620 E. Las Olas Blvd., Fort Lauderdale, FL 33301. ☎ **800/325-3280** or 954/467-0671. Fax 954/462-2148. www.riversidehotel.com. 116 units. A/C TV TEL. Winter $179–$199 double; from $249 suite. Off-season $99–$139 double; from $139 suite. AE, DC, MC, V. From I-95, exit onto Broward Blvd.; turn right onto Federal Hwy. (U.S. 1), then left onto Las Olas Blvd.

Right in the thick of Fort Lauderdale's hottest downtown area, the six-story Riverside Hotel is one of the oldest in South Florida. Built in 1936, it looks like a Wild West movie set, complete with a second-floor wooden terrace and an enormous mural on the front facade. You are in the middle of trendy Las Olas Boulevard and on the route of the popular water taxi. On weekends the hotel is often packed with wedding guests attending ceremonies that are held outside by the small heated swimming pool. A bit nicer than the public areas, which are outfitted in Mexican tile and wicker furnish-ings, the guest rooms upstairs are spacious and well maintained. Details like intri-cately tiled bathrooms and old-style furniture enhance the charm of the otherwise stark building. The best rooms face the New River, but it's hard to see the water past the parking lot and trees. The hotel does not have an abundance of services or facil-ities, but the central downtown location makes almost anything you could desire just steps away.

Dining/Diversions: Do sample Indigo, a fantastic Asian/Indonesian restaurant in the hotel lobby (see "Where to Dine" below). Also on the premises is a more standard grill restaurant and a lounge.

Amenities: Room service, dry-cleaning and laundry service, secretarial services, valet parking, gift shop. Refrigerators, outdoor pool, nearby health club, conference rooms, sundeck.

MODERATE

✪ **Banyan Marina Apartments.** 111 Isle of Venice, Fort Lauderdale, FL 33301. ☎ **954/524-4430.** Fax 954/764-4870. www.banyanmarina.com. 10 apts. A/C TV TEL. Winter $85–$190 apt. Off-season $55–$130 apt. Weekly and monthly rates available. EC, MC, V. To get there from I-95, exit Broward Blvd. E.; cross U.S. 1 and turn right on SE 15th Ave.; at the first traffic light (Las Olas Blvd.), turn left. Turn left at the third island (Isle of Venice).

One of the best accommodation values in South Florida, this hidden treasure is built around a dramatic 75-year-old banyan tree and is located directly on the active canals halfway between Fort Lauderdale's downtown and the beach. When available, you'll choose between one- and two-bedroom apartments. All are comfortable and spacious, with full kitchens and living rooms. The best part of staying here, besides your gracious and knowledgeable hosts, Peter and Dagmar Neufeldt, is that the water taxi will find you here and take you anywhere you want to be day or night. There are also a small outdoor heated pool and a marina for those with boats in tow. In 1998, the Neufeldts were honored by a local campaign to enhance the area, Broward Beautiful, winning first place in the category of small multifamily dwellings.

✪ **Hollywood Beach Resort.** 101 N. Ocean Dr. (at Fla. A1A and Hollywood Blvd.), Hollywood, FL 33019. ☎ **954/921-0990.** Fax 954/920-9480. 400 units (approximately 200 on rental program). A/C TV TEL. Winter from $109. Off-season from $68. AE, DC, DISC, MC, V.

There is nothing cozy or quaint about this sprawling 1920s beachfront hotel, but it couldn't be better located or better priced. The two best features are that all the rooms have full kitchens and the hotel is directly on the ocean. This eight-story building actually operates as a privately held condominium where owners can elect to put their units on a rental program. So there is no telling how rooms may be furnished or outfitted (management does maintain certain standards). All the units I have seen are clean and modest. Larger units and those with views are significantly more expensive than studios. If the weather is bad, consider shopping at the adjacent Ocean Walk Mall or hitting a movie at the on-site multiplex movie theater. Also on the premises is a large outdoor pool and Jacuzzi. The many conveniences of this well-situated property make it especially popular with tour groups from Europe, South America, and Canada.

INEXPENSIVE

Ronny Dee Resort Motel. 717 S. Ocean Blvd., Pompano Beach, FL 33062. ☎ **954/943-3020.** Fax 954/783-5112. 35 units. A/C TV. Winter from $65 double; from $475 efficiency. Off-season from $34 double; from $239 efficiency. AE, MC, V. From I-95, exit Atlantic Blvd. E. to Fla. A1A N.

The bad news is that this family-owned motel is located on busy Fla. A1A; the good news is that it's just 100 yards from the beach and amazingly inexpensive. Popular with European guests, this two-story yellow motel, wrapped around a central swimming pool, contains almost three dozen suburban-style wood-paneled guest rooms filled with an eclectic mix of furniture. All contain a small refrigerator, but none has a telephone; pay phones are located in a public area, near a large game room that contains a pool table, a VCR, books, and other games. Ping-Pong and shuffleboard are also available.

Sea Downs (and the Bougainvillea). 2900 N. Surf Rd., Hollywood, FL 33019. ☎ **954/923-4968.** Fax 954/923-8747. www.seadowns.com and www.bougainvilleahollywood.com. 14 units. A/C TV TEL. Winter $70–$86 efficiency; $98–$113 one-bedroom apt; $124 penthouse. Off-season $46–$62 efficiency; $60–$84 one-bedroom apt; $89–$92 penthouse. Special weekly and monthly rates also available. No credit cards. From I-95, exit Sheridan St. E. to Fla. A1A south; drive ½ mile to Coolidge St.; turn left.

This bargain accommodation is often booked months in advance by returning guests who want to be directly on the beach without paying a fortune. The hosts of this superclean 1950s motel, Claudia and Karl Herzog, live on the premises and keep things running smoothly. Renovations completed in 1997 have replaced bathroom fixtures, and many rooms have been redecorated here and at the Herzogs' other, even less expensive property next door, the Bougainvillea. Guests at either spot can use the heated pool, barbecue grills, picnic area, laundry facilities, and sundeck.

A HOSTEL

Floyd's Youth Hostel/Crew House. Please call for address and directions in Fort Lauderdale. ☎ **954/462-0631.** Fax 954/462-6881. E-mail: FECreamer@aol.com. 20-plus beds. $12.20–$13.50 per person for a dorm bed. No credit cards. Free daytime pickup.

Although a number of cheap hostels are operating near Fort Lauderdale's renowned strip, the best place to crash is Floyd's. While it is a few miles inland from the beach, this well-kept lodging offers what every backpacker and international traveler wants—safety and good, warm fellow travelers. Floyd himself takes care of the guests, many of whom have come looking for work on the area's yachts. In fact, we have agreed not to list the address since Floyd insists on interviewing each prospective guest by phone before booking. Rest assured, you've found one of the area's best and safest hostels, with extras like a cupboard full of complimentary staples, such as milk, cereal, and generic-brand mac and cheese.

WHERE TO DINE

Having hosted visitors for so long, Fort Lauderdale, and to some extent Hollywood as well, have some of South Florida's finest restaurants. Increasingly, ethnic options are joining the legions of surf-and-turf options that dominated the area for so long. **Las Olas Boulevard** has dozens of eateries (so many, in fact, that the city has disallowed any new restaurants to open on the overcrowded 2-mile street). In addition to those reviewed below, consider **Jackson's 450,** 450 E. Las Olas Blvd. (☎ **954/522-4450**), and **ZAN(Z)BAR,** a romantic South African restaurant decked out in zebra and leopard skin at 602 E. Las Olas Blvd. (☎ **954/767-3377**).

VERY EXPENSIVE

✪ **Cafe Maxx.** 2601 E. Atlantic Blvd., Pompano Beach. ☎ **954/782-0606.** Reservations recommended. Main courses $18–$32. AE, CB, DC, DISC, MC, V. Mon–Thurs 5:30–10:30pm, Fri–Sat 5:30–11pm, Sun 5:30–10pm. From I-95, exit at Atlantic Blvd. E. The restaurant is 3 lights east of Federal Hwy. INTERNATIONAL.

Every one of chef/owner Oliver Saucy's restaurants has received accolades from all who bestow them in the culinary arena. This is his best. An oak-burning grill fills the contemporary and casually formal space with enticing aromas from around the globe. The pricey à la carte offerings borrow from Italian, Asian, Creole, Cuban, and Caribbean kitchens to create exotic and delicious mixes like potato-encrusted soft-shell crab, barbecued chicken quesadilla, and pistachio-fried oysters, as well as a host of other exciting but not overwrought dishes. Reserve early on weekends, when the most coveted seats, the cozy booths, book well in advance.

EXPENSIVE

East City Grill. 505 N. Atlantic Blvd. (Fla. A1A between Las Olas and Sunrise blvds.), Fort Lauderdale. ☎ **954/565-5569.** Reservations recommended well in advance. Main courses $13–$27. AE, CB, DC, DISC, MC, V. Mon–Fri 9am–3pm and 5:30–11pm, Sat 8am–3pm and 5:30pm–midnight, Sun 8am–3pm and 5:30–10pm. ASIAN AMERICAN/SEAFOOD.

This happening spot on the beach offers an oceanside location and a killer nouvelle-style menu; it's yet another hit by the mega-Maxx group (see Cafe Maxx, above). For starters, consider steamed crab and goat-cheese dumplings, lots of innovative sushi dishes, or Jamaican beer-steamed prawns. A steamer bar allows you to create your own dinner with a choice of steaming broths, sauces, and sides. You must be creative to dine here. If you are, and you love fresh, interesting seafood, you won't mind the wait at the stunning oak bar, where you can look into the open kitchen. Otherwise, stick to the old-fashioned steak and fish houses in town.

Revolution 2029. 2029 Harrison St., Hollywood. ☎ **954/920-4748.** Reservations suggested. Main courses $13–$24. AE, DC, DISC, MC, V. Tues–Fri 11:30am–3pm, Sun–Thurs 5–10pm, Fri–Sat 5pm–midnight. MULTICULTURAL.

The first real fusion eatery in once-dowdy Hollywood, Revolution attracts upscale hipsters looking for a dining "experience." While nearby South Beach has plenty of this kind of thing, Hollywood is just catching on. The menu is as modern as the sleek decor. With the best of everything from around the world, the menu varies both nightly and seasonally. You may want to start with gorgeous green New Zealand mussels gently flavored with coriander, coconut curry broth, and chunks of crisp apple or a rich roasted corn chowder with sweet potato and spinach corn custard. For vegetarians, there are many great options like oven-roasted portobello mushrooms, crispy vegetable egg rolls, and almond-crusted goat cheese. Innovative dishes like tamarind grilled swordfish and port marinated pork chops are interesting but not overly fussy. Except on busy weekends, service is efficient and friendly.

MODERATE

Aruba Beach Cafe. 1 E. Commercial Blvd., Lauderdale-by-the-Sea. ☎ **954/776-0001.** Reservations not accepted. Main courses $9–$16. AE, DC, DISC, MC, V. Daily 11am–11pm (bar stays open later). SEAFOOD/AMERICAN.

More recommendable as a spot to drink than to eat, Aruba is popular at all hours, especially because of its very central location, directly on the beach at the end of Commercial Boulevard. The extensive menu offers salads, sandwiches, and the requisite seafood offerings. The food is fine but uninspired. Choose a few good appetizers like the creamy smoked fish dip served with seasoned flat bread, the fried calamari, or a selection from the raw bar.

✪ Casablanca Cafe. On the ocean at the corner of Fla. A1A and Alahambra St., Fort Lauderdale. ☎ **954/764-3500.** Reservations not accepted. Main courses $8–$18. AE, DC, DISC, MC, V. Daily 11:30am–11pm. CONTINENTAL/AMERICAN.

Although it may seem odd to sit next to a roaring fire while listening to live music in the warm South Florida climate, at Casablanca it's a perfect complement to the stunning architecture and stupendous cooking. Everything from the warm macadamia nut–encrusted goat-cheese salad to a filet mignon in a cognac-and-mushroom sauce served with perfectly al dente pasta is immaculately prepared and served by a friendly staff. Six or seven specials are included daily on the menu; the best are seafood creations with super-fresh local fish or lobster.

Conca D'Oro. 1833 Tyler St. (on Young Circle), Hollywood. ☎ **954/927-6704.** Reservations not accepted. Pizzas $7–$12.50. Main courses $8.95–$19.95. MC, V. Mon–Thurs 11am–11pm, Fri–Sat 11am–midnight, Sun 4–11pm. ITALIAN.

This bustling Italian restaurant is always busy. It's not that the food is so extraordinary, but that the portions are large, the service is quick, and the attitude is straight from Brooklyn. The pizzas, served Neapolitan (thin-crust) or Sicilian style, are large and topped with lots of cheese and a good tangy tomato sauce. Don't expect more than iceberg lettuce in the salads, but do take advantage of the huge heroes and tasty house wines. If you are with a group, order one or two entrees to share. You will have leftovers. Although they are not always on the menu, ask for fresh mussels if they are in season. While other appetizers are battered and fried, the young black mussels are done to perfection in a red or white sauce. Also good is the hearty lasagna that is full of chunks of garlicky meatballs and mild sausage.

✪ Indigo. In the Riverside Hotel, 620 E. Las Olas Blvd. ☎ **954/467-0671.** Reservations only for groups of 6 or more. Main courses $11–$19. AE, DC, DISC, MC, V. Daily 7am–11pm; weekends until midnight or later. SOUTHEAST ASIAN/ECLECTIC.

This not-so-traditional Southeast Asian meal begins with a basket of pappadoms, naan, and shrimp puff bread. All are delicious and easy to fill up on, especially when spread with the tangy pineapple chutney or cucumber pickle. An impressive appetizer is a lightly peppered dusted seared tuna served in a crispy basket of udon noodles. Look underneath for a hidden dab of sweet apricot puree. It's fantastically rich and a good complement to the spicy fish. A macadamia-encrusted brie is astounding, served over baby lettuce and mixed with a citrusy basil dressing. Extra-crispy crostini are scattered over the hearty dish for extra dipping advantage. Entrees run the gamut from a lean though somewhat-dry Balinese lamb to a musky smoked duckling to a rosemary skewered shrimp. As to be expected in Asian cuisine, vegetarians have plenty of choices, too. In addition to a super-rich grilled vegetable cassoulet au gratin and a fried rice dish with shallots, corn, and asparagus, there are pizzas baked on top of puffy naan bread covered with such toppings as onions, shiitake mushrooms, goat cheese, spinach, eggplant, garlic, curried tomato, and pine nuts. Particularly good is a meaty soy and portobello-mushroom combination wrapped in fluffy puff pastry served with a delicate broccoli sauce. Ask servers for suggestions, though. Even if they are a bit harried on weekends, they tend to be knowledgeable and honest.

✪ Sugar Reef. 600 N. Surf Rd. (on the Boardwalk just north of Hollywood Blvd.), Hollywood. ☎ **954/922-1119.** Reservations only for groups over 6. Main courses $12–$20; sandwiches and salads $5–$8.50. AE, DISC, MC, V. Mon 4–10:30pm, Tues–Thurs 11am–10:30pm, Fri–Sun 11am–11pm (sometimes later in winter). TROPICAL FRENCH.

A welcome addition to a strip of greasy fish joints, hot-dog stands, and bars, Sugar Reef has captured the attention of visitors and locals who appreciate superior and imaginative meals served for very reasonable prices. Chef/owner Patrick Farnault left a successful and formal restaurant in Fort Lauderdale to open this oceanside bistro. Simple offerings might include a salmon BLT with dill mayonnaise or Jamaican-style pork loin or a burger and fries. Portions are generous but not huge. Escargot in a green curry sauce with lemongrass is a delicious twist on an old favorite, evoking memories of subtle and spicy Vietnamese dishes. More than half a dozen salads, some with cheese, chicken, or fish, are a perfect meal for beachgoers looking for something light and healthful as they enjoy the view. As is fitting for a beachside eatery, service is laid-back but still professional.

Sushi Blues Cafe. 1836 S. Young Circle (east on Hollywood Blvd.), Hollywood. ☎ **954/929-9560.** Reservations recommended on weekends. Main courses $11–$20; sushi $1.75–$2.75 per piece. AE, MC, V. Mon–Thurs 6pm–midnight, Fri–Sat 6pm–2am. JAPANESE.

Live loud blues and jazz combine with pretty good sushi to make an unusual pair at this small storefront eatery located on Hollywood's largest traffic circle. There are only about 12 tables and a dozen counter stools in this relatively straightforward and unadorned sushi room. In addition to raw fish, the cafe offers some inventive specials like salmon carpaccio with caper sauce, fried soft-shell crab drizzled with a spicy sesame sauce, miso-broiled eggplant, and grilled smoked sausage with Japanese mustard. The restaurant is popular with a 20-something crowd and is packed Friday and Saturday nights, when there's live music.

Topanga! 5001 N. Federal Hwy. (at Commercial Blvd.), Fort Lauderdale. ☎ **954/ 771-8555.** Reservations for 5 or more suggested. Main courses $9–$18.95, pastas $9–$14.45. AE, DC, DISC, MC, V. Mon–Thurs 11:30am–10pm, Fri 11:30am–11pm, Sat noon–11pm, Sun noon–10pm. CALIFORNIA-STYLE GRILL AND PIZZA BISTRO.

This bright and bustling restaurant is a perfect choice for a quick, healthy lunch or dinner. Local businesspeople favor it in the afternoons since they can get in and out within 45 minutes or linger for hours in the pleasant sun-drenched eatery. There is even an outside terrace for those who don't mind the busy highway as a backdrop. With a large but not overwhelming menu featuring Italian favorites like chicken marsala, pizzas, and more than a dozen pastas, this is a place that appeals to everyone (including the kids). Salads are large (like most other entrees) and can easily be shared by three. Or ask for a half portion, which is plenty big for one or two. My favorite is a mix of fresh baby greens with large slabs of moist and spicy dolphin (mahimahi) and chunks of feta cheese, briny Greek olives, and a slightly sweet champagne vinaigrette dressing. Pizzas, too, are fresh and filling. Try the goat cheese and basil or the unusual Acapulco chicken with tequila, lime, herbs, and a side of guacamole and salsa. The daily specials, like beef and veal meat loaf, seafood quesadilla, or lemon and dill salmon, are usually a good bet. An impressive selection of wines and beers plus lots of decadent desserts makes this place a super value and a great find in the middle of a fast-food–glutted highway.

INEXPENSIVE

✪ **Deli Den.** 2889 Stirling Rd. (west of I-95), Hollywood. ☎ **954/961-4070.** Main courses $5–$11, bagel sandwiches $1–$7.50. AE, MC, V. Daily 8am–10pm. JEWISH-STYLE DELI.

Catering to Broward's New York crowd for nearly 3 decades, this warehouse-sized deli serves the area's finest cheese blintzes, red cabbage soup, and matzo balls. Breakfast selections include super-thick French toast with bacon, sausage, or ham, plus dozens of egg specialties like minced lox, eggs and onions, or corned-beef hash and eggs. All baking is done on the premises. And owners are proud to say that absolutely everything else, from coleslaw to blintzes, is also homemade. The best news is that kids under 12 eat free every Monday and Thursday.

East Coast Burrito Factory. 261 E. Commercial Blvd., Fort Lauderdale. ☎ **954/772-8007.** Tacos and burritos $3–$6; salads $4–$6. AE, CB, DC, DISC, MC, V. Mon–Sat 11am–9:45pm, Sun noon–7:45pm. FLORIDA/MEXICAN.

Just off of I-95 is an oasis. A dozen wooden benches line the counter at this super Mexican diner, which serves made-to-order soft tacos, burritos, hot dogs, and salads. For a healthier spin on a burrito, try the Florito, made with black beans instead of refried beans—a uniquely Florida invention. My favorite is the "Super Veggie," stuffed with corn, salsa, mushrooms, black olives, carrots, peppers, and hearts of palm, then doused with the restaurant's own super-hot chile pepper sauce. The guacamole and various huge salads are also fantastic, especially on a sunny day on the back patio. To finish it off, try a Latin flan or an honest slice of key lime pie.

The Floridian Restaurant. 1410 E. Las Olas Blvd., Fort Lauderdale. ☎ **954/463-4041.** Sandwiches $3–$7; breakfast combos $3.50–$8; hot platters $7–$14. AE, DC, MC, V. Daily 24 hours. AMERICAN/DINER.

A landmark on Las Olas, this popular spot turns out excellent diner fare around the clock. It's especially busy on weekend mornings, when locals and tourists come in for huge omelets, fresh oatmeal, sausage, muffins, and biscuits. Service can be a bit brusque, but it's worth it.

Thai Spice. 1514 E. Commercial Blvd. (east of I-95), Fort Lauderdale. ☎ **954/771-4535.** Reservations recommended. Main courses $9.95–$26. AE, DC, DISC, MC, V. Mon–Thurs and Sun 11am–3pm and 5–10pm, Fri–Sat 5–11pm. THAI.

The tacky and typical decor of Thai Spice belies the authentic and delicious food turned out here. Soft-shell crab in a light and subtle chile sauce and tender shrimp cakes are fantastic and frequent specials. Regular menu items include a slightly sweet and almost buttery pad Thai with a generous serving of shrimp, chicken chunks, and scallion. Lunch specials are obscenely cheap and include all the favorites.

THE HOLLYWOOD & FORT LAUDERDALE AREA AFTER DARK

The newly hip downtown area of Hollywood is centered around **Harrison Street and Young Circle** (east of Dixie Highway at Hollywood Boulevard). A funky menagerie of bookstores, coffee shops, galleries, and a couple of live-music joints are worth exploring. One of the latest and most welcome additions is **O'Hara's Pub and Jazz Cafe** at 1905 Hollywood Blvd. (☎ **954/925-2555**). Kitty Ryan, who operates another club with the same name in Fort Lauderdale, has duplicated her successes here with a smoking jazz club which attracts superior acts from all over.

A funkier set hangs out at **Warehaus 57** just across the street (☎ **954/926-6633**), where long-hairs converse over killer frozen coffee drinks or glasses of jug wine. This used bookstore, clothing store, and acoustic music venue is an inviting and happening little spot. During the week, come for a game of backgammon or a cup of joe. Folky local bands play on weekends, to the delight of an eclectic crowd that comes at the generous invitation of owner Lauren Tellman (who also designs the racy and strappy leather clothing in the back). During the week she closes at 6pm. Fridays and Saturdays, she's there until at least midnight.

Sushi Blues was one of the first spots to offer live music in this neighborhood (see "Where to Dine," above). Live bands play jazz, blues, or world music on Friday and Saturday, and if you have dinner there you can skip the cover (usually $10).

Also in Hollywood, just west of Young Circle at Federal Highway, is **Club M** (☎ **954/925-8396**), a small local blues showcase with a bit of good jazz and electric thrown in. On busy Friday and Saturday nights when live bands perform, you'll pay a small cover.

Fort Lauderdale has hundreds of bars and clubs for every taste. There are essentially four main areas that have clusters of happening scenes you can check out for yourself. To get you started, I have highlighted the best in each neighborhood. Plus, I have listed a few out-of-the-way spots for the more adventurous.

The waterfront bars and restaurants on the Intracoastal just south of Oakland Park Boulevard are especially recommendable for their outdoor-patio bar scenes at all hours. Accessible by boat or car, **Bootlegger's,** at 3003 NE 32nd Ave. (☎ **954/ 563-4337**), features more than 70 kinds of beers, with a featured draft of the day going for only $1. Here and next door at **Shooters,** 3033 NE 32nd Ave. (☎ **954/ 566-2855**), you'll find nautical types, families, and young professionals mixed in with a good dose of sunburned tourists enjoying the live reggae, jazz, or Jimmy Buffett–style tunes with the gorgeous backdrop of the bay and marinas all around. If you don't have your own boat, take the water taxi to really get the feel (see box above). Both are open until 2am.

The once-famous "Strip" on the waterfront just north of Las Olas was overrun with spring-breakers. Now it's been replaced with a mellower (and unfortunately more generic) scene. A newish shopping and entertainment complex called **Beach Place** is a sort of outdoor megamall modeled after Miami's hugely successful Bayside and Cocowalk. This block-long monster is the new home to a number of franchised bars and restaurants, like **Sloppy Joe's** (of Key West fame), **Howl at the Moon,** and **Hooters,** amid the requisite Gap and Banana Republic. The view, overlooking the ocean, makes it worth a stop for a drink.

Some of the college kids' old standbys remain in the neighborhood, including the **Elbo Room** at 241 S. Atlantic Blvd., on the corner of Las Olas Boulevard and Fla.

A1A (☎ **954/463-4615**). It has maintained its rowdy and divey reputation by serving up frequent drink specials and live bands. A dedicated beer-drinking, football-watching crowd mingles with young tourists. This area is also accessible by water taxi.

An older crowd hangs out after dark on ✪ **Las Olas Boulevard,** where there are blocks and blocks of good restaurants and music clubs. One of the most happening is **O'Hara's Pub and Jazz Cafe,** at 722 E. Las Olas Blvd. (☎ **954/524-1764**). They pack 'em in until they spill onto the sidewalk of this smoky little club. Best known for presenting original jazz performers, O'Hara's also has blues and big-band music some Sunday afternoons. Call their **jazz hotline** (☎ **954/524-2801**) to hear the lineup for this and the newer **Hollywood Cafe.**

Most of the alternative music scene is centered in the downtown area of Fort Lauderdale. One good choice is the **Chili Pepper** (☎ **954/525-0094**) at 200 W. Broward Blvd., east of I-95. With big-name concerts as well as local band showcases, this place captures the heart and soul of the young and super-charged Wednesday through Sunday.

To find the heart of Fort Lauderdale's gay scene, head to **The Copa,** at 2800 S. Federal Hwy., east on I-595, near the airport (☎ **954/463-1507**). This big 1980s-style black box has been the cornerstone of Fort Lauderdale's gay nightlife forever. Popular and updated shows are common on the many elevated stages surrounding a large and loud dance floor. **Club Cathode Ray** at 1105 E. Las Olas Blvd. (☎ **954/462-8611**) caters to a good-looking crowd and plays dance music every day from 4pm until 2am.

2 Boca Raton & Delray Beach

26 miles S of Palm Beach, 40 miles N of Miami

With its many mansions and waterfront condominiums, it is the winter home to many of society's wealthy industrialists and retirees. Increasingly, the area is also attracting young families from other areas in the state who have tired of crime, corruption, and overcrowding. This planned city, known simply as "Boca," is a bit over-manicured and glitzy for my taste, although there are certainly some great restaurants and resorts worth exploring.

Delray, named after a suburb of Detroit, grew up completely separate from its southern neighbor. This community was founded in 1894 by a Midwestern postmaster who sold off 5-acre lots through Michigan newspaper ads. Because of their close proximity, Boca and Delray can easily be explored together. Budget-conscious travelers would do well to eat and sleep in Delray and dip into Boca for sightseeing and beaching only.

ESSENTIALS

GETTING THERE   If you're driving, you'll reach the Boca Raton and Delray Beach area via I-95. Visitors en route from Orlando or Miami should take the Florida Turnpike, a toll road with a speed limit of 65 m.p.h. If you're coming from Florida's west coast, you can take either S.R. 75, which lands in Fort Lauderdale, or S.R. 80, which runs south of Lake Okeechobee to Palm Beach.

These cities are equally accessible from the Palm Beach International Airport and Fort Lauderdale airport (see "Getting There," above and below).

VISITOR INFORMATION   Before your trip, call or write the **Palm Beach County Convention and Visitors Bureau,** 1555 Palm Beach Lakes Blvd., Suite 204, West Palm Beach, FL 33401 (☎ **800/554-PALM** or 561/471-3995; fax 561/471-3990). On weekdays from 8:30am until at least 4pm, stop by the **Boca Raton**

Chamber of Commerce at 1800 N. Dixie Hwy., 4 blocks north of Glades Road (☎ **561/395-4433;** fax 561/392-3780; www.bocaratonchamber.com), Boca Raton, FL 33432, for information on attractions, accommodations, and events in the area. Also, try the **Delray Beach Chamber of Commerce** (☎ **561/278-0424;** fax 561/278-0555; e-mail: chamber@delraybeach.com), at 64 SE 5th Ave., half a block south of Atlantic Avenue on U.S. 1, Delray Beach, FL 33483.

WHERE TO PLAY, ON & OFF THE BEACH

BEACHES   Thankfully, Florida had the foresight to set aside some of its most beautiful coastal areas for the public's enjoyment. Many of the area's best beaches are located in state parks and are free to pedestrians and bikers. Most do charge for parking.

The **Delray Beach Public Beach,** on Ocean Boulevard at the east end of Atlantic Avenue, is one of the area's most popular hangouts. Weekends especially attract a young and good-looking crowd of active locals and tourists. Regular volleyball, Frisbee, and paddleball games make for good entertainment. For refreshments, a number of snack shops, bars, and restaurants are just across the street. Families enjoy the protection of lifeguards on the clean, wide beach. Gentle waters make it a good swimming beach, too. There's limited parking at meters along Ocean Boulevard.

Spanish River Park, on North Ocean Boulevard (Fla. A1A), 2 miles north of Palmetto Park Road in Boca Raton, is a huge oceanfront park with a large grassy area, making it one of the best choices for picnicking. Facilities include picnic tables, grills, rest rooms, and a bilevel 40-foot observation tower. You can walk through tunnels under the highway to nature trails that wind through fertile grasslands. Volleyball nets are oceanside and always have at least one serious game going on. The park is open from 8am until 8pm. Also, read below about Red Reef Park.

GOLF   This area has plenty of good courses. Unfortunately, most of the best are private or are in the very expensive resorts. However, from May to October or November, about a dozen private courses open their greens to visitors staying in Palm Beach County hotels. This "Golf-A-Round" program is free or severely discounted (carts are additional), and reservations can be made through most major hotels. Ask at your hotel, or contact the **Palm Beach County Convention and Visitors Bureau** (☎ **561/471-3995**) for information on which clubs are available for play.

The semiprivate, 18-hole, par-61 course at the **Boca Raton Executive Country Club,** 7601 E. Country Club Blvd. (☎ **561/997-9410**), is usually open to the public. A driving range is also on the property, as well as a pro shop and a restaurant. A PGA professional gives lessons, and rental clubs are available. From Yamato Road East, turn left onto Old Dixie Highway; after about a mile, turn left onto Hidden Valley Boulevard and continue straight to the club. Greens fees are $11 to $27.

The **Boca Raton Municipal Golf Course,** 8111 Golf Course Rd. (☎ **561/ 483-6100**), is located just north of Glades Road, half a mile west of the Florida Turnpike. This public 18-hole, par-72 course covers approximately 6,200 yards. There are a snack bar and a pro shop where clubs can be rented. Greens fees are $11 to $14 for 9 holes and $19 to $25 for 18 holes. Ask for special summer discount fees.

SCUBA DIVING & SNORKELING   **Moray Bend,** a 58-foot dive spot located about three-quarters of a mile off Boca Inlet, is the area's most popular. It's home to three moray eels that are used to being fed by scuba divers. The reef is accessible by boat from **Force E Dive Center,** 877 E. Palmetto Park Rd., Boca Raton (☎ **561/ 368-0555**). Phone for dive times. Dives cost $38 to $45 per person.

Red Reef Park, 1400 N. Ocean Park Blvd. (☎ **561/393-7974**), a fully developed 67-acre oceanfront park in Boca Raton, has year-round lifeguard protection. There's good snorkeling for beginners around the rocks and reefs that lie just off the beach in 2 to 6 feet of water. There are also good swimming and a small picnic area with grills, tables, and rest rooms. The park, located a half mile north of Palmetto Park Road, is open daily from 8am to 10pm. You pay only if you drive in. It's $8 per car during the week or $10 on weekends.

TENNIS   The snazzy **Delray Beach Tennis Center,** 201 W. Atlantic Ave. (☎ **561/ 243-7360**), has 14 lighted clay courts and 5 hard courts available by the hour. Phone for rates and reservations.

The 17 public lighted hard courts at **Patch Reef Park,** 2000 NW 51st St. (☎ **561/997-0881**), are available by reservation. The fee for nonresidents is $5.75 per person per hour. Courts are available Monday to Saturday from 7:30am to 10pm and Sunday from 7:30am to dusk; you can phone ahead to see if a court is available. To reach the park from I-95, exit at Yamato Road West and continue past Military Trail to the park.

SEEING THE SIGHTS

Boca Raton Museum of Art. 801 W. Palmetto Park Rd. (1 mile east of I-95), Boca Raton. ☎ **561/392-2500.** Admission $3 adults, $2 seniors, $1 students. Tues–Wed and Sat–Sun 10am–6pm, Thurs–Fri 10am–9pm. Closed Mon. Free admission Wed.

In addition to a relatively small but well-chosen permanent collection that's strongest in 19th-century European oils, the museum stages a wide variety of temporary exhibitions by local and international artists. Lectures and films are offered on a fairly regular basis, so call ahead for details.

Gumbo Limbo Environmental Complex. 1801 N. Ocean Blvd. (on Fla. A1A between Spanish River Blvd. and Palmetto Park), Boca Raton. ☎ **561/338-1473.** Free admission. Mon–Sat 9am–4pm, Sun noon–4pm.

Named for an indigenous hardwood tree with continuously shedding bronze bark, the 20-acre complex protects one of the few surviving coastal hammocks, or forest islands, in South Florida. Visitors can walk through the hammock, on a one-third-of-a-mile-long elevated boardwalk that ends at a 40-foot observation tower, from which you can see the Atlantic Ocean, the Intracoastal Waterway, and much of Boca Raton. From mid-April to September, sea turtles come ashore here to lay their eggs. During this time, the center conducts turtle-watching tours and sea-turtle lectures. If you haven't seen turtles doing their thing, definitely stop in for a memorable experience.

In the museum is an impressive array of local flora and fauna, including live snakes, fish, crabs, sea turtles, and scorpions. Even city kids seem to like touching all the strange creatures here.

International Museum of Cartoon Art. 201 Plaza Real at Mizner Park, Boca Raton. ☎ **561/391-2200.** Admission $6 adults, $5 seniors, $4 students, $3 children 6–12 years old, free for members and children under 5. Tue–Sat 10am–6pm, Sun noon–6pm. Closed Monday.

Reborn and hugely expanded after nearly 20 years of life in New York City, this extensive collection of cartoon art spans the decades and styles in its glitzy home in Mizner Park. In a gorgeous 52,000-square-foot gallery space, cartoon fans can see prints, frames, moving pictures, and books by some of the world's greatest cartoonists, including many by the museum's founder, Mort Walker (of *Beetle Bailey* fame). A fantastic gift shop offers posters, books, and lots of memorabilia.

✪ **Morikami Museum and Japanese Gardens.** 16869 Jog Rd., Delray Beach. ☎ **561/495-0233.** Museum $4.25 adults, $3.75 seniors, $2 children 6–18, free for children 5 and under, free for everyone Sun 10am–noon; gardens free. Museum Tues–Sun 10am–5pm; gardens Tues–Sat 10am–5pm. Closed major holidays.

Slip off your shoes and into a serene Japanese garden community that dates from 1905, when an entrepreneurial farmer, Jo Sakai, came to Boca Raton to build a tropical agricultural community. The Yamato Colony, as it was known, was short-lived; by the 1920s only one tenacious colonist remained: George Sukeji Morikami. But Morikami was quite successful, eventually holding one of the largest pineapple plantations in the area. The 200-acre Morikami Museum and Japanese Gardens, which opened to the public in 1977, was Morikami's gift to Palm Beach County and the State of Florida. The park section, dedicated to the preservation of Japanese culture, is constructed to appeal to all the senses. An artificial waterfall that cascades into a koi- and carp-filled moat, a small rock garden for meditation, and a large bonsai collection that includes miniature maple, buttonwood, juniper, and Australian pine trees are all worth contemplation—and it's free. There is also a great Asian restaurant on the premises worth checking out for lunch.

SHOPPING & BROWSING

Famous in New York City for its upscale antiques and gorgeous rugs, **ABC Carpet & Home** also has an outlet store in Delray Beach just off I-95 at 777 S. Congress (between Linton and Atlantic). Look for deep discounts (usually at least 30%) on very high-priced furnishings and flooring.

Mizner Park, on Federal Highway (between Palmetto Park and Glades roads) in Boca Raton (☎ **561/362-0606**), is the town square of this tiny enclave, complete with clothing shops, shoe stores, restaurants, live performances, and lots of beautiful landscaping. It's really an outdoor mall, with 45 specialty shops, seven good restaurants, and a multiscreen movie house. Each shop front faces a grassy island with blue and green gazebos, potted plants, and garden benches. It's extremely popular with folks who come here just to stroll, often until late in the evening.

Town Center Mall of Boca Raton has six huge department stores, including Bloomingdale's, Burdines, Lord & Taylor, and Saks Fifth Avenue. Add to that hundreds of specialty shops, an extensive food court, and a range of other restaurants, and you have the area's most comprehensive and beautiful shopping opportunity. The mall is located on the south side of Glades Road just west of I-95.

Another great area for a stroll is in the more artsy community of **Delray Beach,** known by many as Pineapple Grove. Here, along Atlantic Avenue, especially east of Swinton Avenue, you'll find a fantastic array of antique shops, clothing stores, and art galleries shaded by palm trees and colorful awnings. A lively cafe culture and many celebrations take place on this quaint old-style main street. Pick up the "Downtown Delray Beach" map and guide at almost any of the stores on this strip, or call ☎ **561/278-0424** for more information.

WHERE TO STAY

If you choose to stay in Boca or the surrounding areas, you will find some very luxurious lodgings, epitomized by the famous and often-photographed pink **Boca Raton Hotel and Country Club,** where deluxe suites have gone for up to $6,000 per night. But don't worry, there are plenty of other choices on and near the beach.

A number of national chain hotels worth considering include a moderately priced **Holiday Inn Highland Beach Oceanside** at 2809 S. Ocean Blvd., on Fla. A1A southeast of Linton Boulevard (☎ **800/234-6835** or 561/278-6241). The **Radisson**

Palm Beach & Boca Raton

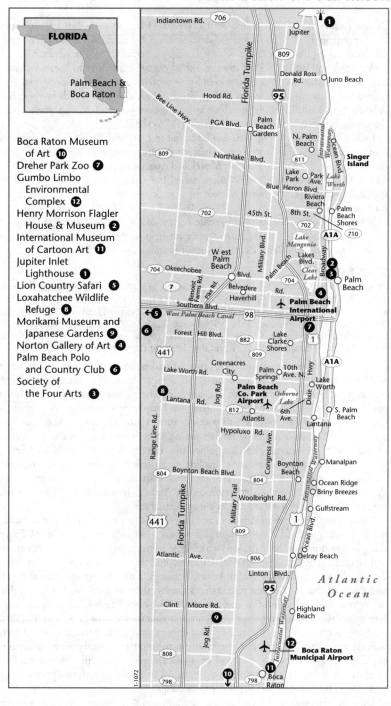

FLORIDA

Palm Beach &
Boca Raton

Boca Raton Museum
  of Art **10**
Dreher Park Zoo **7**
Gumbo Limbo
  Environmental
  Complex **12**
Henry Morrison Flagler
  House & Museum **2**
International Museum
  of Cartoon Art **11**
Jupiter Inlet
  Lighthouse **1**
Lion Country Safari **5**
Loxahatchee Wildlife
  Refuge **8**
Morikami Museum and
  Japanese Gardens **9**
Norton Gallery of Art **4**
Palm Beach Polo
  and Country Club **6**
Society of
  the Four Arts **3**

Indiantown Rd. 706
Jupiter **1**
809
Donald Ross Rd.
Juno Beach
95
811
Hood Rd.
PGA Blvd.
Palm Beach Gardens
N. Palm Beach
Singer Island
Northlake Blvd.
809
Lake Park · Park Ave.
Blue Heron Blvd.
Riviera Beach
702
45th St.
8th St.
702
Palm Beach Shores
A1A 710
Lake Mangonia
W est Palm Beach
704 Okeechobee
7
Benoist Farms Rd.
Pike Rd.
Belvedere
Haverhill
Blvd.
Clear Lake
Lakes Blvd.
704 Rd.
Palm Beach
2
3
Palm Beach
4 Palm Beach International Airport
Southern Blvd.
5 West Palm Beach Canal
98
7
1
Forest Hill Blvd.
6
882
Lake Clarke Shores
441
809
Greenacres City
Lake Worth Rd.
Jog Rd.
Palm Springs
10th Ave. N.
A1A
8
Lantana Rd.
Palm Beach Co. Park Airport
812
Atlantis
Osborne Lake
6th Ave.
Lake Worth
Dixie Hwy.
S. Palm Beach
Lantana
Hypoluxo Rd.
Range Line Rd.
Congress Ave.
Manalpan
804
Boynton Beach Blvd.
Military Trail
Boynton Beach
804
Ocean Ridge
Briny Breezes
Woolbright Rd.
809
Gulfstream
441 Florida Turnpike
1
Ocean Blvd.
Atlantic Ave.
806
Delray Beach
Linton Blvd.
95
Atlantic Ocean
Clint Moore Rd.
9
Highland Beach
Jog Rd.
808
12 Boca Raton Municipal Airport
11
10
798
Boca Raton
798

Florida Turnpike
809
Military Blvd.
Palm Beach
Lake Worth
Ocean Blvd.
Intracoastal Waterway
Bee Line Hwy.

1-1072

257

Bridge Resort at 999 E. Camino Real (☎ 800/333-3333 or 561/368-9500) operates a particularly popular and affordable resort on the Intracoastal Waterway just a few blocks from the Boca Raton Resort. Beware: It books up well in advance.

Although you won't find the rows and rows of cheap hotels as in Fort Lauderdale and Hollywood, a handful of mom-and-pop motels have survived along Fla. A1A between the towering condos of Delray Beach. Look along the beach just south of Atlantic Boulevard. Especially noteworthy is a pleasant little two-story, shingle-roofed **Bermuda Inn** at 64 S. Ocean Blvd. (☎ 561/276-5288).

Even more economical options can be found in Deerfield Beach, Boca's neighbor, south of the county line. A number of beachfront efficiencies offer great deals, even in the winter months. Try the **Panther Motel and Apartments,** at 715 S. A1A (☎ 954/ 427-0700). This clean and convenient motel has rates starting as low as $40. In season, though, you may have to book for a week at a time. Weekly rates in season start at $457.

If you are looking for something more private or for longer than just a few days, you may want to call a reservations service for help. Especially for rentals for a few weeks or months, call **Palm Beach Accommodations** (☎ 800/543-SWIM).

VERY EXPENSIVE

✪ **Boca Raton Resort and Club.** 501 E. Camino Real (P.O. Box 5025), Boca Raton, FL 33431. ☎ **800/327-0101** or 561/395-3000. Fax 561/447-3183. 1,000 units, 70 golf villa apts. A/C MINIBAR TV TEL. Winter $200–$450 double; $450 golf villa apt; $420–$6,000 suite. Off-season $135–$410 double; $375 golf villa apt; $285–$6,000 suite. Very reasonable seasonal packages available. AE, DC, DISC, MC, V. From I-95 N., exit onto Palmetto Park Rd. E.; turn right onto Federal Hwy. (U.S. 1), and then left onto Camino Real to the resort.

Boca's most historical and romantic resort straddles both sides of the Intracoastal Waterway and encompasses more than 350 acres of land, with extensive and outstanding facilities for tennis, golf, and anything else an active family or individual could want, including three fitness centers with brand-new equipment, more than 30 tennis courts, and two 18-hole golf courses. Since 1926, this palatial hotel has been hosting the most discriminating international guests. Now with a sizable population of local sports enthusiasts who have joined the country club, and lots of conferences going on, the place is still pleasing demanding visitors. Don't worry: The huge proportions of the Spanish-Moorish architecture and the sprawling grounds will ensure that you will never feel crowded or processed. And yearly renovations guarantee that you won't feel as if you are staying in a musty museum.

Compared to other destination resorts on Florida's east coast, this superior facility is a great value with all the amenities and elegance but none of the stuffiness. Everything is easy once you have decided which type of room you'll stay in. There are several options. Those in the original Cloisters building have exquisite architectural details, like arched doorways, high-beamed ceilings, a mix of reproduction antiques, and the most charm. The best part is that although they are more modest in size than newer rooms, they are also the least expensive. The Boca Beach Club building, just a 5-minute drive and accessible by free shuttle or your own car, offers spacious cabana-style rooms on the ocean with sliding glass doors that open to beach breezes. Dressed with dark woods and rich colors, the rooms in the modern 27-story tower adjacent to the Cloisters are the most formal and enjoy sweeping views of this idyllic coast. Golf villas overlook the perfectly manicured greens. All are outfitted with two phones, large bathrooms, fluffy robes, and first-class furnishings.

Dining/Diversions: There are nine restaurants and three lounges to satisfy all tastes and budgets. A formal Italian restaurant on the top floor of the main building offers extraordinary views over Boca Raton. A seafood restaurant at the Boca Beach Club is known for its excellent and diverse menu. A coffee bar in the Cloister building is particularly popular in mornings and afternoons.

Amenities: Concierge, room service (24 hours), fitness classes, evening turndown, laundry, overnight shoe shine. An impressive array of children's programs. Three fitness centers, five swimming pools, two golf courses, 34 tennis courts (9 lighted), water-sports and bicycle rentals, snorkeling and scuba instruction, croquet, volleyball, basketball court, 2-mile jogging course, business center, well-priced boutiques and gift shops, racquetball.

MODERATE

Colony Hotel & Cabana Club. 525 E. Atlantic Ave. (P.O. Box 970), Delray Beach, FL 33483. ☎ 800/552-2363 or 561/276-4123. Fax 561/276-0123. www.thecolonyhotel.com/florida/. E-mail: info-fla@thecolonyhotel.com. 66 units. A/C TV TEL. Winter $145–$190 double. Off-season $90–$140 double. AE, MC, V.

This lovely three-story hotel is located right on Delray's main commercial thoroughfare about a mile from the hotel's private beach and club. The Colony benefited from a 1996 refurbishment that brought back some of its original 1926 details, including hardwood floors and authentic furnishings. Still, the rooms are modest in size and style but comfortable and clean. The hotel is popular with families who appreciate the many planned activities at the hotel's beachfront club 1 mile away, which offers a heated saltwater swimming pool, a private beach, and putting and shuffleboard tournaments. All facilities are free for guests.

Seagate Hotel & Beach Club. 400 S. Ocean Blvd., Delray Beach, FL 33483. ☎ 800/233-3581 or 561/276-2421. Fax 561/243-4714. 70 units. A/C TV TEL. Winter $179–$299 suite; $339–$369 two-bedroom suite. Off-season $74–$105 suite; $136–$152 two-bedroom suite. AE, CB, DC, MC, V. From I-95, exit onto Atlantic Ave. E., turn right onto Ocean Blvd. (Fla. A1A), and continue ½ mile to the hotel.

This modest, well-located hotel features generously sized rooms located in two buildings directly across the street from the beach. To make your stay more affordable and convenient, the hotel furnishes coffeemakers, fully stocked kitchens or kitchenettes, irons, large closets, and safes in each room. A recent redecorating replaced the quaint Old Florida furnishings with industrial Formica, plain blond wood, and commercial-grade carpeting. Also regrettable are the tiny bathrooms with little to no counter space.

The Beach Club is located across the street, directly on the sand, where you can relax on a chaise lounge or dip into one of the heated pools. A moderately priced restaurant and bar will deliver snacks and cocktails to the beach. There's 400 feet of private beach, and special children's programs are offered during the high season. Overall, the resort is pleasant and extremely practical, especially for families. Little extras like newspapers and refreshments in the lobby make this an especially appealing option.

Spanish River Resort. 1111 E. Atlantic Ave., Delray Beach, FL 33483. ☎ 800/543-SWIM or 561/243-7946. Fax 561/276-9634. www.pbai.com. 75 units. A/C TV TEL. Winter $150–$250 studio or one-bedroom; $315–$350 two-bedroom. Off-season from $85 studio or one-bedroom; from $200 two-bedroom. DISC, MC, V. Free 6th and 7th night with weekly booking.

An especially good value for those staying longer than a few days, this pleasant family-oriented property offers fully furnished condominiums half a block from a popular beach and within walking distance to Delray's best shops, restaurants, and galleries. The 11-story Mediterranean-style building has free lighted tennis courts, a large outdoor pool, and lovely ocean-view balconies. Apartments are spacious and outfitted with fully equipped kitchens. All units also have pull-out queen-size sofa beds. The best part is there is no additional charge for extra guests. A one-bedroom unit can comfortably fit four or five people; a two-bedroom unit can easily accommodate six. Cots and rollaway beds are available at a minimum charge. Compared with many of the run-down 1950s motels in the area, this moderately priced, well-maintained tower is a real find.

INEXPENSIVE

Ocean Lodge. 531 N. Ocean Blvd. (just north of Palmetto Park Rd. on Fla. A1A), Boca Raton, FL 33432. ☎ **800/STAY-BOCA** or 561/395-7772. Fax 561/395-0554. 18 units. A/C TV TEL. Winter $95–$100 double; $105–$115 efficiency. Off-season $55–$60 double; $55–$75 efficiency. AE, MC, V.

Situated around a small heated pool and sundeck, this two-story motel is a particularly well-kept accommodation in an area of run-down or overpriced options. The large rooms offer furnishings and decor that are clean but a bit impersonal. A recent do-over that added modern Formica and floral wallpaper makes this a notch above a basic motel. Ask for a room in the back since the street noise can be a bit loud, especially in season. The bonus is that you are across the street from the ocean and in one of Florida's most upscale resort towns.

Shore Edge Motel. 425 N. Ocean Blvd. (on Fla. A1A, north of Palmetto Park Rd.), Boca Raton, FL 33432. ☎ **561/395-4491.** Fax 561/347-8759. 16 units. A/C TV TEL. Winter $75–$85 double; $95–$115 efficiency. Off-season from $45 double; from $55 efficiency. AE, MC, V.

Another relic of the 1950s recently spiffed up with new landscaping and some redecorating, this motel is a good choice, especially because of its location—across the street from a public beach, just north of downtown Boca Raton. It's the quintessential South Florida motel: a small, pink, single-story structure surrounding a modest swimming pool and courtyard. Although the rooms are a bit on the small side, they're very neat and clean. The higher-priced accommodations are larger and come with full kitchens.

WHERE TO DINE

The Boca Raton and Delray areas have more than their fair share of expensive fish and steak houses. Thankfully, too, more and more innovative and health-conscious places are moving in. Mizner Park has nearly a dozen eateries including a fantastic oyster bar, serving microbrew beers, called **Gigi's** (☎ **561/368-4488**). The area's other great options are highlighted below.

VERY EXPENSIVE

La Vieille Maison. 770 E. Palmetto Park Rd., Boca Raton. ☎ **561/391-6701** or 561/737-5677. Reservations recommended. Main courses $17–$40; fixed-price dinners $40 and $64. AE, CB, DC, DISC, MC, V. Daily 6–9:30pm (call for seating times). FRENCH.

The luxurious setting, a Mediterranean-inspired home filled with a variety of antique French furnishings and paintings, gives you the feeling of walking into a friend's country manor. Begin with lobster bisque, gratin of escargots with fennel and pistachio nuts, or pan-seared foie gras—each is equally delectable. It's difficult to choose from the many enticing entrees, which range from red snapper in black- and green-olive potato crust to medallions of beef, lamb, and venison over three sauces. You'll surely have to try at least a few of the gorgeous cheeses the server offers after your main course—the most extensive selection I've ever seen in this country. The lemon crepe soufflé with raspberry sauce is the dessert of choice—remember to order it early.

EXPENSIVE

Fifth Avenue Grill. 821 S. Federal Hwy., Delray Beach. ☎ **561/265-0122.** Additional location 4650 N. Federal Hwy., Lighthouse Point. ☎ **954/782-4433.** Reservations accepted only for large parties. Main courses $16–$29. AE, DC, MC, V. Sun–Mon 11:30am–4pm and 5–11pm. STEAK HOUSE.

The old-world Fifth Avenue Grill is very popular with well-dressed seniors who come for the superb steaks, reliable service, and classic selections—onion soup, shrimp scampi, London broil, Caesar salad, and broiled local fish. This is the kind of place where they still remember to offer a touch of sherry for your conch chowder. Every main course includes unlimited house salad and is accompanied by a cheese-stuffed baked potato, fried shoestrings, or brown rice. Add to that a huge and varied wine list, and you've got a perfect night out in Delray. Everything on the predictable menu is well prepared and presented by professional servers in a dark and woodsy dining room.

Max's Grille. 404 Plaza Real, in Mizner Park, Boca Raton. ☎ **561/368-0080.** Reservations accepted only for 6 or more. Main courses $14–$26; pastas $10.95–$16.95. AE, CB, DC, DISC, MC, V. Daily 11:30am–3pm, Mon–Thurs 5–10:30pm, Fri–Sat 5–11pm, Sun 5–10pm. AMERICAN.

One of the most popular choices in restaurant-crowded Mizner Park, Max's Grille is part of the growing chain of Unique Restaurants that have been wowing critics for years. With a large exhibition kitchen that occupies the entire back wall of the restaurant, patrons can watch as their yellowfin tuna steak or filet mignon is seared on a flaming oak grill. A large selection of chicken, meat loaf, pastas, and main-course salads provide healthful and delicious choices for sophisticated palates. A stunning bar serves trendy martinis in more than 15 varieties. For a more economical option, try Max's coffee shop next door, at 402 Plaza Real, for good old-fashioned comfort food in a real diner atmosphere.

Nick and Max's. 5050 Town Center Circle (in the Boca Center west off Palmetto Park Rd.), Boca Raton. ☎ **561/391-7177.** Reservations recommended. Main courses $16 and $30. AE, DC, DISC, MC, V. Mon–Fri 11:30am–2:30pm; Mon–Thurs 6–10:30pm; Fri–Sat until 11pm; Sun until 10pm. AMERICAN/MEDITERRANEAN.

Formerly Maxaluna, this hot spot in Boca Raton is another successful eatery in the Dennis Max empire. Serving creative Mediterranean-inspired food like oak-grilled pork chops with mushroom lasagna cherries and sage, marinated tuna with pasta, couscous paella with shrimp, calamari and pearl onions, the chef and co-owner, Nick Morfugen, lets his Greek heritage shine. A well-heeled clientele crowd the sleek, deco dining room every night and are happy to pay steep prices for food that is utterly decadent.

MODERATE

Splendid Blendeds. 432 E. Atlantic Ave., Delray. ☎ **561/265-1035.** Reservations recommended. Main courses $10.95–$19.95; sandwiches and salads $3.50–$8.95. AE, DC, MC, V. Mon–Fri 11:30am–2:30pm; Mon–Sat 5:30–10pm. Closed Sun. ECLECTIC.

Loyal regulars would like to keep this storefront bistro a secret so that the lines won't get even longer on weekends. The draw here is fresh, uncomplicated seafood and pastas that are interesting without being overly ambitious. The Southwestern-inspired chicken Santa Cruz is tender and juicy, served with a black-bean sauce and tangy pico de gallo. Many seafood specialties, like tuna, snapper, and shrimp dishes, are slight departures from classic recipes and seem to work most of the time. The drawback of this otherwise-superb spot is the staff; they're well-meaning but easily flustered.

INEXPENSIVE

The Tin Muffin Cafe. 364 E. Palmetto Park Rd. (between Federal Hwy. and the Intercoastal Bridge). ☎ **561/392-9446.** Sandwiches and salads $5.95–$8.95. No credit cards. Mon–Fri 11am–5pm, Sat 11am–4pm. BAKERY/SANDWICH SHOP.

Popular with the downtown lunch crowd, this excellent storefront bakery keeps them lining up for big fresh sandwiches on fresh bread, muffins, quiches, and good home-made soups like split pea or lentil. The curried chicken sandwich is stuffed with over-sized chunks of only white meat doused in a creamy curry dressing and fruit. There are a few cafe tables inside and even one outside on a tiny patio. Be warned, however, that service is forgivably slow and parking is a nightmare. Try parking a few blocks away at a meter on the street.

Tom's Place. 7251 N. Federal Hwy., Boca Raton. ☎ **561/997-0920.** Reservations not accepted. Main courses $8–$15; sandwiches $5–$6; early-bird special $6.95. AE, MC, V. Tues–Fri 11:30am–10pm, Sat noon–10pm. Closed Mon. BARBECUE.

There are two important factors in a successful barbecue: the cooking and the sauce. Tom and Helen Wright's no-nonsense shack wins on both counts, offering flawlessly grilled meats paired with well-spiced sauces. Beef, chicken, pork, and fish are served soul-food style, with your choice of two sides like rice with gravy, collard greens, black-eyed peas, coleslaw, or mashed potatoes. Decoration is limited to signed celebrity pho-tographs and plastic tablecloths.

BOCA RATON & DELRAY AFTER DARK
THE BAR, CLUB & MUSIC SCENE

The best variety of entertainment is offered in Delray Beach, where a younger and funkier set makes its home. Atlantic Avenue now boasts several venues for live music, including **The Back Room,** 909 W. Atlantic Ave. near the corner of Swinton Avenue (☎ **561/243-9110**). A reasonable cover, usually between $2 and $6, depends on who is playing. A funky decor, eclectic crowd, and excellent music almost every night make this old standby another good option for live music from jazz to big band to classic rock. Only beer and wine are served (in plastic glasses). It's open Tuesday to Saturday until 3am.

Boston's on the Beach, at 40 S. Ocean Blvd. (☎ **561/278-3364**), is always a good choice for happy hour, Monday to Friday from 4 to 8pm, or for live reggae on Monday. A lively bar scene and good seafood on a deck overlooking the beach keep this place packed almost every night.

Boca Raton's most famous dance spot, **Club Boca,** at 7000 W. Palmetto Park Rd. (☎ **561/368-3333**), which you'll hear advertised on obnoxious radio commercials, is a big noisy warehouse out west of the highway that attracts a range of big-haired girls and macho guys. It's a fun diversion in otherwise sterile Boca and is open Thursday to Sunday until 5am.

True to her word, Gloria Gaynor has survived, and she is in Boca at **Polly Esther's,** 99 SE 1st Ave. (☎ **561/447-8955**). She and other disco divas can be heard blasting from the enormous sound system as the mixed young and thirty-something set dances like it's Saturday night and they have the fever. Open Wednesday to Saturday. Take Palmetto Park Road East to Federal Highway; turn left onto SE 1st Avenue, where you'll see the club on the left.

THE PERFORMING ARTS

For details on upcoming events, check the Boca News, Sun-Sentinel, or call the **Palm Beach County Cultural Council** information line at ☎ **800/882-ARTS.** During business hours, a staffer can give details on current performances. After hours, a

recorded message describes the week's events. The Sun-Sentinel also hosts a comprehensive "Source Line" for information on everything from weather to garage sales.
Detailed arts information is included.

The **Florida Symphonic Pops,** a 70-piece professional orchestra, performs jazz,
swing, rock, big band, and classical music throughout Boca Raton. For nearly 50 years
this ever-growing musical force has entertained audiences of every age. Call ☎ **561/
393-7677** for a schedule of concerts.

Boca's best theater company is the **Caldwell Theatre,** and it's worth checking out.
Located in a strip shopping center at 7873 N. Federal Hwy., this equity showcase does
well-known dramas, comedies, classics, off-Broadway hits, and new works throughout
the year. Prices are reasonable (usually between $29 and $38). Full-time students will
be especially interested in the little-advertised "Student Rush." When available, tickets
are sold for $5 to those who arrive at least an hour in advance. Call ☎ **561/241-7432**
for details.

3 Palm Beach & West Palm Beach

65 miles N of Miami, 193 miles E of Tampa

Palm Beach County encompasses cities including Boca Raton in the south to Jupiter
and Tequesta in the north. But it is Palm Beach, the small island town across the
Intracoastal Waterway, that has been the traditional winter home of America's
aristocracy—the Kennedys, the Rockefellers, the Pulitzers, the Trumps, and plenty of
CEOs.

The island holds the distinction of being the only continental destination with
three resorts that have earned the prestigious AAA Five-Diamond rating. And beyond
the upscale resorts and chic boutiques, it holds some surprises, too, from a world-class
art museum to one of the top bird-watching areas in the state.

By contrast, West Palm Beach is a grittier workaday city. Recent renovations have
made the metropolitan area a lively and affordable place to dine, shop, and hang
out.

In addition to good beaching, boating, and diving, you'll find great golf and tennis
throughout the county.

Note: For a general map of Palm Beach and West Palm Beach, see the map on
page 257.

ESSENTIALS
GETTING THERE   If you're driving up or down the Florida coast, you'll probably
reach the Palm Beach area by I-95. Exit at Belvedere Road or Okeechobee Boulevard,
and head east to reach the most central part of Palm Beach.

Visitors on their way to or from Orlando or Miami should take the Florida Turnpike, a toll road with a speed limit of 65 m.p.h. If you are watching your budget, avoid
the Turnpike—tolls are high. You may pay upward of $9 from Orlando and $4 from
Miami. Finally, if you're coming from Florida's west coast, you can take either S.R. 70,
which runs north of Lake Okeechobee to Fort Pierce, or S.R. 80, which runs south of
the lake to Palm Beach.

VISITOR INFORMATION   The **Palm Beach County Convention and Visitors
Bureau,** 1555 Palm Beach Lakes Blvd., Suite 204, West Palm Beach, FL 33401
(☎ **800/554-PALM** or 561/471-3995), distributes an informative brochure and will
answer questions about visiting the Palm Beaches. Ask for a map as well as a copy of
the *Arts and Attractions Calendar,* a day-to-day guide to art, music, stage, and other
events in the county.

GETTING AROUND Although a car is almost a necessity in this area, a recently revamped public transportation system is extremely convenient for getting to some attractions. **Palm Tran** underwent a major expansion in late 1996, increasing service to 32 routes and more than 140 buses. The fare is $1 for adults, and 50¢ for children ages 3 to 18, as well as for seniors and riders with disabilities. Free route maps are available by calling ☎ **561/233-4BUS.** Information operators are available from 6am to 7pm, except Sunday.

In downtown West Palm Beach, free **shuttles** operate Monday through Friday from 9am until 4pm, with plans to expand operations to evenings and weekends, too. Look for the bubble-gum–pink minibuses throughout downtown. Call ☎ **561/833-8873** for more details.

Among the airlines serving **Palm Beach International Airport,** at Congress Avenue and Belvedere Road (☎ 561/471-7400), are **American** (☎ 800/433-7300), **Continental** (☎ 800/525-0280), **Delta** (☎ 800/221-1212), **Kiwi** (☎ 800/538-5494), **Northwest** (☎ 800/225-2525), **TWA** (☎ 800/221-2000), **United** (☎ 800/241-6522), and **US Airways** (☎ 800/428-4322).

Amtrak (☎ **800/USA-RAIL**) has a terminal in West Palm Beach, at 201 S. Tamarind Ave. (☎ 561/832-6169).

OUTDOOR PURSUITS

BEACHES Public beaches are a rare commodity here in Palm Beach. Most of the island's best beaches are fronted by private estates and inaccessible to the general public. However, there are a few notable exceptions, including the newly renourished Midtown Beach on Ocean Boulevard, between Royal Palm Way and Gulfstream Road, which boasts more than 100 feet of undeveloped beach. There are no rest rooms or concessions here, although a lifeguard is on duty until sundown. This newly widened sandy coast is now a centerpiece and a natural oasis in a town dominated by commercial glitz. Also, about 1½ miles north near Dunbar Street is a popular hangout for locals who enjoy the relaxed atmosphere. Parking is available at meters along Fla. A1A. To the south is a less popular but better equipped beach at Phipps Ocean Park. On Ocean Boulevard, between the Southern Boulevard and Lake Avenue causeways, is a large and lively public beach encompassing over 1,300 feet of groomed and guarded oceanfront. With picnic and recreation areas, as well as plenty of parking, the area is especially good for families.

BICYCLING Rent anything from an English single-speed to a full-tilt mountain bike at the **Palm Beach Bicycle Trail Shop,** 223 Sunrise Ave. (☎ **561/659-4583**). The rates—$7 an hour, $18 a half day (9am to 5pm), or $24 for 24 hours—include a basket and lock (not that it's necessary in this fortress of a town). The most scenic route is called the Lake Trail, running the length of the island along the Intracoastal Waterway. On it you'll see some of the most magnificent mansions and grounds. Enjoy the views of downtown West Palm Beach and some great wildlife.

CRUISES **Atlantic Coastal Cruises,** 900 E. Blue Heron Blvd., Singer Island (☎ 561/848-7827), runs regularly scheduled tours along the Intracoastal Waterway, offering visitors unobstructed views of the area's grand mansions. Daily sightseeing as well as lunch, dinner, and theme cruises are offered, some with live entertainment. They cost $14 to $38. Phone for more information and reservations.

The **Palm Beach Princess** (☎ **800/841-7447** or 561/845-7447), a small cruise ship (421 feet), offers reasonably priced casino gambling cruises out of the Port of Palm Beach (U.S. 1 between 45th Street and Blue Heron Boulevard) every day and evening. Evening cruises usually leave at 7pm and cost $20 to $25; they include a large buffet with ordinary food like spaghetti and meatballs, chicken, shrimp, Greek salad, and vegetables. Best is the prime rib at the carving board. Day trips cost the same and offer slightly less food. Sunday brunch trips cost $25. A popular monthly Bahamas voyage costs $95. Call during business hours for details. Choose from craps, roulette, poker, blackjack, and slots.

GOLF   There's good golfing here, but many of the private club courses are maintained exclusively for the use of their members. Ask at your hotel, or contact the **Palm Beach County Convention and Visitors Bureau** (☎ 561/471-3995) for information on which clubs are currently available for play. In the off-season, some private courses open their greens to visitors staying in a Palm Beach County hotel. This Golf-A-Round program offers free greens fees (carts are additional); reservations can be made through most major hotels.

One of the state's best courses that is open to the public is ✪ **Emerald Dunes Golf Course,** 2100 Emerald Dunes Dr. in West Palm Beach (☎ 561/687-1700). Designed by Tom Fazio, this dramatic 7,006-yard, par-72 course was voted "One of the Best 10 You Can Play" by *Golf* magazine. It is located just off the Florida Turnpike at Okeechobee Boulevard. Bookings are taken up to 30 days ahead. Fees start at $125.

The **Palm Beach Public Golf Course,** 2345 S. Ocean Blvd. (☎ 561/547-0598), a popular public 18-hole course, is a par-54 and is open at 8am; the course is run on a first-come, first-served basis. Club rentals are available. Greens fees start at $19 per person.

POLO   What's Palm Beach without polo? See the box on the next page for details.

SCUBA DIVING   Year-round warm waters, barrier reefs, and plenty of wrecks make South Florida one of the world's most popular places for diving. One of the best-known artificial reefs in this area is a vintage Rolls-Royce Silver Shadow, which was sunk offshore in 1985. Mother Nature has taken her toll, however, and divers can no longer sit in the car ravaged by time and salt water.

Call any of the following outfitters for gear and excursions: **Dixie Divers,** 1401 S. Military Trail, West Palm Beach (☎ 561/969-6688), and **Ocean Sports Scuba Center,** 1736 S. Congress Ave., West Palm Beach (☎ 561/641-1144).

TENNIS   There are literally hundreds of tennis courts in Palm Beach County. Wherever you are staying, you are bound to be within walking distance of one. In addition to the many hotel tennis courts (see "Where to Stay," below), you can play at **Currie Park,** 2400 N. Flagler Dr., West Palm Beach (☎ 561/835-7025), a public park with three lighted hard courts. They are free and available on a first-come, first-served basis.

WATERSPORTS   Call the **Seaside Activities Station** (☎ 561/835-8922) to arrange sailboat, jet-ski, bicycle, kayak, water-ski, and parasail rentals.

SEEING THE SIGHTS

Flagler Museum. 1 Whitehall Way (at Cocoanut Row), Palm Beach. ☎ 561/655-2833. Admission $7 adults, $3 children. Tues–Sat 10am–5pm, Sun noon–5pm.

Known as the "Taj Mahal of North America," this luxurious mansion was commissioned as a gift to his third wife by the renowned Henry Flagler, a cofounder of the Standard Oil Company and builder of the Florida East Coast Railroad. The classically columned Edwardian-style mansion contains 55 rooms that include a Louis XIV music room and art gallery, a Louis XV ballroom, and 14 guest suites outfitted with original antique European furnishings. Out back, climb aboard "The Rambler," Mr. Flagler's recently revamped railroad car. Allow at least 1½ hours to tour the stunning grounds and interior.

The Sport of Kings

The annual ritual of the ponies is played out each season at the posh Palm Beach Polo and Country Club. It is one of the world's premier polo grounds and hosts some of the sport's top-rated players.

Even if you're not a sports fan, you absolutely must attend a match. Although the field is actually on the mainland in an area called Wellington, rest assured the spectators, and many of the players, are pure Palm Beach. After all, a day at the pony grounds is one of the only good reasons to leave Palm Beach proper.

Don't worry, though—you need not be a Vanderbilt or a Kennedy to attend. Matches are open to the public and are surprisingly affordable.

Even if you haven't a clue how the game is played, you can spend your time people-watching. Star-gazers have spotted Prince Charles, the Duchess of York, Sylvester Stallone, and Ivana Trump in recent years, among others. Dozens of lesser-known royalty, and just plain old characters, keep box seats or chalets right on the grounds.

The general-admission seats will land you a spot on metal bleachers across the field from the boxes, where celebrity spotting during a match is a bit difficult. If you want to mingle with the elite, splurge on the more expensive boxes for a chance to overhear great tidbits, like the one I caught recently: "Oh, I know I should be rooting for the Coca-Cola team. That's how I made all my money," whined one flamboyant heiress dressed all in gold as she cheered for the opposing team. "Still, I just can't help cheering for my friends."

Good eavesdropping is possible even with a ticket from the bleachers, since you can wander the grounds and see the whole show. Between chukkers, head to the Polo Club, a covered tent where you can enjoy snacks like popcorn, hot dogs, ice cream, pretzels, and a cocktail from the full bar while listening to live music. Or on a Sunday afternoon, enjoy brunch in the Polo House or Players Club restaurant on the north end of field no. 1.

Incidentally, the point of polo is to keep the other team from getting the ball through your goal. The fast-paced game is divided into six chukkers—like an inning in baseball—each 7 minutes long. There are 3-minute breaks between chukkers except at half-time, which lasts 10 minutes. The whole thing is narrated by a British chap who sounds as though he has walked off a Monty Python set.

Oh dear, whatever will you wear? Unless it is an opening game or some other special event, dress is casual. A navy or tweed blazer over jeans or khakis is a standard for men, while neat-looking jeans or a pantsuit is the norm for ladies. On warmer days, shorts and, of course, a polo shirt are fine, too.

General admission is $6 to $10; box seats cost $10 to $36. Matches are held throughout the week. Schedules vary, but the big names usually compete on Sunday at 3:30pm from January to April.

The fields are located at 11809 Polo Club Rd., Wellington, 10 miles west of the Forest Hill Boulevard exit of I-95. Call ☎ **561/798-7000** for a detailed schedule of events.

Norton Museum of Art. 1451 S. Olive Ave., West Palm Beach. ☎ **561/832-5196.** Admission $5 adults, $2 students, free for children 12 and under. Tues–Sat 10am–5pm, Sun 1–5pm. From I-95, take Belvedere Rd. (Exit 51) east to the end; then turn left onto S. Olive Ave. to the museum.

Since a 1997 expansion doubled the Norton's space, the museum has gained even more prominence in the art world. It is world famous for its prestigious permanent collection and top temporary exhibitions. The museum's major collections are divided geographically. The American galleries contain major works by Edward Hopper, Georgia O'Keefe, and Jackson Pollack. The French collection contains Impressionist and post-Impressionist paintings by Cezanne, Degas, Gauguin, Matisse, Monet, Picasso, Pissarro, and Renoir. And the Chinese collection contains more than 200 bronzes, jades, and ceramics, as well as a collection of monumental Buddhist sculptures.

✪ **Playmobil Fun Park.** 8031 N. Military Trail, Palm Beach Gardens. ☎ **800/351-8697.** Free admission. Tues–Sun 10am–6pm. I-95 North to Palm Beach Lakes Blvd. west to Military Trail. Turn left, and the park is about a mile down on the right side.

This monstrous retail outlet and play park is one of only two such parks in the world (the other one is in Germany, the company's headquarters). Housed in a replica of a castle, this indoor fantasy world is even better than FAO Schwarz. You could spend hours here and not spend a penny. The 17,000-square-foot play floor is divided into age-specific play areas and theme areas, including a water zone for kids to play with boats, and a Victorian area with elaborately constructed doll houses.

NATURE PRESERVES & ATTRACTIONS

Lion Country Safari. Southern Blvd. W. at S.R. 80, West Palm Beach. ☎ **561/793-1084,** or 561/793-9797 for camping reservations. Admission $14.95 adults, $9.95 seniors and children 3–9, free for children under 3. Daily 9:30am–5:30pm (last vehicle admitted at 4:30pm). From I-95, exit on Southern Blvd. Go west about 18 miles.

More than 1,300 animals are divided into their indigenous regions, from the East African preserve of the Serengeti to the American West. On this 500-acre preserve you can see elephants, wildebeest, ostriches, American bison, buffalo, watusi, pink flamingos, and many other more unusual species. Even the lions and elephants roam the huge grassy landscape without a cage in sight. In fact, you're the one who's confined, in your own car without an escort (no convertibles allowed). You're given a detailed informational pamphlet with photos and descriptions and are instructed to obey the 15 m.p.h. speed limit—unless you see the rhinos charge, in which case you're encouraged to floor it. To drive the loop takes just over an hour, though you could make a day of just watching the chimpanzees play on their secluded islands. Included in the admission price is Safari World, an amusement park with paddleboats, a carousel, and a nursery for baby animals born in the preserve. Picnics are encouraged and camping is available (call for reservations). Don't miss this incredible experience.

Palm Beach Zoo at Dreher Park. 1301 Summit Blvd. (east of I-95 between Southern and Forest Hill blvds.). ☎ **561/547-WILD.** Admission $6, $5 senior citizens, $4 children 3–12, children under 3 free. Daily 9am–5pm.

Unlike big-city zoos, this intimate 23-acre park is more like a stroll in the park than an all-day excursion. It features about 500 animals representing more than 100 different species. A special monkey exhibit and petting zoo are favorites with kids. Stroller and wagon rental available.

SHOPPING & BROWSING

From thrift to jewels, Palm Beach has it all.

Known as the "Rodeo Drive of the south," Worth Avenue is a window-shopper's dream. No matter what your budget, don't miss the Worth Avenue experience. To look like you belong, you might want to dress as if you were going to an elegant luncheon, not to the mall down the street. The 4 blocks between South Ocean Boulevard and Cocoanut Row—a stretch of more than 200 boutiques, posh shops, art galleries, and upscale restaurants—are home to the stores of Armani, Louis Vuitton, Cartier, Polo Ralph Lauren, and Chanel, among like company.

Victoria's Secret, Limited Express, and several other chains have sneaked in here, too, but so have a good number of unique boutiques. Stop into **Paper Treasures,** at 217 Worth Ave.; it's an autograph gallery with a priceless collection of John Hancocks like those of Joe DiMaggio, Mickey Mantle, Andrew Jackson, Abe Lincoln, Howard Hughes, and hundreds more, all displayed in beautiful frames. At **Myer's Luggage,** 313 Worth Ave., Richard Myers is happy to demonstrate his impressive assortment of toys and gifts, including a vast collection of amusing alarm clocks, spy equipment, gorilla masks, and gag gifts, along with pricey leather bags and English picnic baskets. Just off Worth Avenue, at 374 S. County Rd., is the **Church Mouse** (☎ 561/ 659-2154), a great consignment/thrift shop with antique furnishings and tableware. Lots of good castaway clothing and shoes are reasonably priced. This shop usually closes for 2 months during the summer. Call to be sure.

The **Palm Beach Outlet Center,** at 5700 Okeechobee Blvd. (3 miles west of I-95), West Palm Beach, is the most elegant outlet mall I have ever seen. Upscale clothing, luggage, and shoes at bargain prices are offered in lushly decorated surroundings. The fully enclosed mall also sports a food court.

Downtown West Palm Beach has a number of interesting boutiques along Clematis Street. In addition to a large and well-organized bookstore, **Clematis Street Books,** at 206 Clematis (☎ **561/832-2302**), there are used-record stores, clothing shops, and a few interesting art galleries.

WHERE TO STAY

The island of Palm Beach is perhaps the most exclusive destination in the country. Royalty and celebrities come to winter here, and there are plenty of royally priced options to accommodate them. It's no accident that the only three hotels in the state to receive five stars from AAA are all located in Palm Beach County. Happily, there exist a few special little inns that offer reasonably priced rooms in elegant settings. Surrounding the island are many more modest places to lay your straw hat.

A few of the larger hotel chains operating in Palm Beach include the **Howard Johnson Palm Beach,** at 2870 S. Ocean Blvd. (☎ **800/654-2000** or 561/582-2581), which is across the street from the beach. Also beachside is the pricey **Palm Beach Hilton,** at 2842 S. Ocean Blvd. (☎ **800/433-1718** or 561/586-6542).

An excellent and affordable alternative right in the middle of Palm Beach's commercial section is a condo that operates as a hotel, too: the **Palm Beach Hotel,** at 235 Sunrise Ave. between County Road and Bradley Place, across the street from Publix (☎ **561/659-7794**). With winter prices starting at about $105, this clean and comfortable accommodation is a great option for those looking for the rarely available bargain in Palm Beach.

In West Palm Beach the chain hotels are mostly located on the main arteries close to the highways and a short drive to the activities in downtown. They include a **Best Western,** 1800 Palm Beach Lakes Blvd. (☎ **800/331-9569** or 561/683-8810), and, just down the road, a **Comfort Inn,** 1901 Palm Lakes Blvd. (☎ **800/221-2222** or 561/689-6100). Farther south is the **Parkview Motor Lodge,** 4710 S. Dixie Hwy. just south of Southern Boulevard (☎ **561/833-4644**). This 28-room, single-story motel is the best of the many motels along Dixie Highway (U.S. 1). With rates starting at $50 for a room with television, air-conditioning, and telephone, you can't ask for more.

For other options, try **Palm Beach Accommodations** (☎ **800/543-SWIM**).

VERY EXPENSIVE

☼ The Breakers. 1 S. County Rd., Palm Beach, FL 33480. ☎ **800/833-3141,** 888/BREAKERS, or 561/655-6611. Fax 561/659-8403. www.thebreakers.com. 572 units. A/C MINIBAR TV TEL. Winter $360–$675 double; $540 club double; from $600 suite. Off-season $180–$395 double; $295 club double; from $360 suite. Special packages available. AE, CB, DC, DISC, MC, V. From I-95, exit Okeechobee Blvd. E., and head east to S. County Rd.; turn left.

The biggest and grandest of all of this area's resorts, this five-star historic beauty epitomizes Palm Beach luxury. It's one of only two Florida properties to win five stars from the Mobil guide and five diamonds from AAA. From the expansive manicured lawns to the elegant marble lobby, The Breakers is the place to be in Palm Beach if you want to be on the beach but within walking distance from all the area's most exclusive shopping and dining. The lush 130-acre grounds also sport one of the island's only 18-hole golf courses.

The attentive staff is as accustomed to handling steamer trunks and fur wraps as they are to sending faxes and programming VCRs. Though this 1926 palace was built for the world's most elite, it now handles more corporate clients and families with ease. While the Gatsbyesque grounds of Palm Beach's first hotel reveal a sense of history, the newly reconstructed rooms are equipped with all the modern conveniences. A $75 million renovation completed in time for the behemoth's 100th birthday has increased the size of the smaller rooms and spruced up the fading common areas.

There are more than a dozen categories of rooms from which to choose, with the traditional and superior being the smallest and least expensive. Even these tiny rooms are luxuriously appointed and include all the amenities you could desire. Ask for one of the few corner rooms, which tend to be larger and have more windows for the same price. Oceanfront suites offer huge sitting areas, closets, and sleeping quarters.

The Breakers is great for families, though the formality of the lobbies and restaurants may put some off. Jackets are suggested (but not required) in the formal restaurants and lounge.

Dining/Diversions: Five restaurants and three bars offer a delicious range of meals and snacks from an elegant European dining room to a beach bar with burgers and fries. A romantic oceanfront bar (Palm Beach's only) is reserved for hotel guests.

Amenities: Concierge, 24-hour room service, dry-cleaning and laundry service, overnight shoe shine, newspaper delivery, in-room massage, evening turndown, twice-daily maid service, baby-sitting, secretarial services, express checkout, valet parking $15. VCR and video rentals, four outdoor pools, private beach, bicycle rental, two golf courses (one, the Ocean Course, ca. 1897, is Florida's oldest 18-hole course), putting green, game rooms, supervised children's activities, children's playground, business center, car-rental desk, 14 tennis courts (11 of which are lighted), water-sports concession (including scuba and sailing), croquet, shuffleboard, beach-volleyball courts, beauty salon, boutiques and shopping arcade, full-service spa/ fitness center.

☼ Four Seasons Resort Palm Beach. 2800 S. Ocean Blvd., Palm Beach, FL 33480. ☎ **800/332-3442** or 561/582-2800. Fax 561/547-1557. 210 units. A/C MINIBAR TV TEL. Winter $350–$625 double; from $1,200 suite. Off-season $255–$475 double; $775 suite. AE, CB, DC, DISC, EC, ER, JCB, MC, V. From I-95, take 6th Ave. exit east and turn left onto Dixie Hwy.; then, turn east onto Lake Ave. and north onto S. Ocean Blvd., and the hotel is just ahead on your right.

For over-the-top pampering in a perfect location, the Four Seasons is my favorite in an area filled with fantastic resorts. Built in 1989 at the edge of Palm Beach's downtown district, this elegant resort has quickly gained accolades from around the world.

The incredibly hospitable staff works hard to be sure this beachfront gem lives up to its reputation. The elegant marble lobby is replete with hand-carved European furnishings, grand oil paintings, tapestries, and dramatic flower arrangements.

The ambience of the common areas extends to the guest rooms as well. All are exceptionally spacious and thoughtfully appointed with extras like a small color TV in the bathroom. Club-floor rooms include access to a special lounge where continental breakfast, afternoon refreshments, and evening cocktails are served gratis. One-bedroom suites include an additional sitting room, a CD/stereo, oversize balconies, and two bathrooms.

Dining/Diversions: The main dining room for dinner serves one of the best meals in Palm Beach. An impeccable menu of Southeastern regional cuisine includes daily fish, meat, and pasta specials served in white-glove elegance. Two other less formal restaurants, including a pool bar and grill, round out the dining options. The lobby lounge is one of the best places in town for an intimate cocktail. Weekend evenings promise excellent live jazz.

Amenities: Concierge, room service (24 hours), evening turndown, dry-cleaning and laundry services, overnight shoe shine, complimentary newspaper delivery, in-room massage, twice-daily maid service, baby-sitting and a wide range of other baby and child amenities, pet amenities (including special water, biscuits, and dog walking), secretarial services, express checkout, valet parking. VCRs and complimentary video rental, movie channels and video games, outdoor heated pool, beach, whirlpool, jogging track, bicycle rentals, supervised activities for children 3 to 12, conference rooms, weekly cooking classes, sundeck, three tennis courts, water-sports rentals, beauty salon, gift shop, spa shop. The 6,000-square-foot spa contains cardiovascular equipment, free weights, and saunas and offers classes, massages, and body wraps.

✪ **Ritz-Carlton Palm Beach.** 100 S. Ocean Blvd., Manalpan, FL 33462. ☎ **800/ 241-3333** or 561/533-6000. Fax 561/540-4999. E-mail: ritzpalmbch@earthlink.net. 270 units. A/C MINIBAR TV TEL. Winter $350–$625 double; $705–$775 club-level double; from $1,095–$3,200 suite. Off-season $175–$265 double; $325–$375 club-level double; from $325–$2,700 suite. AE, CB, DISC, EC, JCB, MC, V. From I-95, take Exit 45 east; after 1 mile, turn left onto Federal Hwy. (U.S. 1), continue north for about a mile, and turn right onto Ocean Ave.; cross the Intracoastal Waterway, turn right onto Fla. A1A.

As is to be expected from any member of this upscale chain, the Palm Beach Ritz-Carlton is super-luxurious. In this case, it is on a beautiful beach in a tiny town about 8 miles from Palm Beach's shopping and dining area—a plus for those who want privacy and a drawback for those interested in the activity of "town."

The hotel's elegant and dramatic lobby is dominated by a huge, double-sided pink-marble fireplace, and French 18th- and 19th-century antique furnishings give no hint that the property is not yet 10 years old. The ambience and attention to detail here are rivaled by no other hotel in the area.

Each room has a private balcony and at least a glimpse of the ocean below. All are spacious and decorated in lush contemporary design. Thoughtful details include plush bathrobes and telephones in the large marble bathrooms. Club-level accommodations come with dedicated concierge service and a private lounge, where complimentary continental breakfasts, afternoon snacks, and evening cordials are served.

Dining/Diversions: The elegant dining room serves continental-style dinners in ornate surroundings. Other restaurants on the property include a grill, for dinner only; a casual restaurant, which serves all day; and a poolside cafe and bar. Cocktails are also served in the lobby lounge, where you can often find live entertainment. After-noon tea is served daily but is best Wednesday to Saturday when a jazz trio entertains.

Amenities: Concierge, 24-hour room service, dry-cleaning and laundry services, overnight shoe shine, newspaper delivery, in-room massage, evening turndown, twice-daily maid service, baby-sitting, secretarial services, express checkout, valet parking, airport transportation, free coffee or refreshments in lobby. VCR rentals, Spectravision movie channels, outdoor pool, beach, health club, Jacuzzi, sauna, bicycle rental, children's center and programs, business center, conference rooms, car-rental desk, seven night-lit tennis courts, scuba and snorkeling concessions, beauty salon, gift shop.

EXPENSIVE

Chesterfield Hotel. 363 Cocoanut Row, Palm Beach, FL 33480. ☎ **800/243-7871** or 561/659-5800. Fax 561/659-6707. E-mail: chesterpb@aol.com. 65 units. A/C TV TEL. Winter $269–$389 double; from $529 suite. Off-season $89–$219 double; from $219 suite. Rollaway bed $15 extra. AE, CB, DC, DISC, MC, V. From I-95, exit onto Okeechobee Blvd. E., cross the Intracoastal Waterway, and turn right onto Cocoanut Row.

With more charm than its more expensive rivals, the intimate Chesterfield, located just a block from Worth Avenue, has been popular with visitors in the know since the 1920s. Behind its light stucco facade, arched windows, and colorful flags is an overly designed interior with Laura Ashley prints battling Ralph Lauren. It all creates a wonderfully authentic country-manor feel.

Guest rooms also have formal chintz and taffeta prints. Heavy wooden furniture and plush carpets give each room a warm but dark feel. Although most rooms have no view to speak of, they are comfortable and attractive. A stunning lobby library provides a quiet nook for those who may want to read at the large oak desk or borrow a book for the beach. Afternoon tea completes the illusion of being in a well-run country inn across the Atlantic.

Dining/Diversions: The Leopard Room serves fantastic English, French, and continental favorites all day; reservations are essential for dinner and Sunday brunch. The Leopard Lounge is an area hangout in the evenings when there is usually live music and no cover charge (see "The Palm Beaches After Dark," below).

Amenities: Concierge, room service, newspaper delivery, in-room massage, dry cleaning, twice-daily maid service, baby-sitting, valet parking, secretarial services, express checkout. Swimming pool, access to nearby health club, Jacuzzi, nature trails, bicycle rental, video rentals, conference rooms, business center, car-rental desk, tour desk.

Plaza Inn. 215 Brazilian Ave., Palm Beach, FL 33480. ☎ **800/233-2632** or 561/832-8666. Fax 561/835-8776. www.plazainnpalmbeach.com. 49 units. A/C TV TEL. Winter $160–$235 double; $275 suite. Off-season $95–$145 double; $165 suite. Rates include breakfast. AE, MC, V. From I-95, exit onto Okeechobee Blvd. E., cross the Intracoastal Waterway, turn right onto Cocoanut Row, then turn left onto Brazilian Ave.

This ever-improving bed-and-breakfast–style inn is as understated and luxurious as the handsome guests it hosts. Nothing is flashy here. From the simple and elegant flower arrangements in the marble lobby to the well-worn period antiques haphazardly strewn throughout, the Plaza Inn has the look of studied nonchalance. A small staff, including owner Ajit Asrani, is remarkably hospitable and knowledgeable about the island's inner workings.

Each uniquely decorated room is dressed with quality furnishings, several with carved four-poster beds, hand-crocheted spreads, and lace curtains. The bathrooms are lovely if quite small, and the wall-mounted air conditioners can be noisy when they are needed in the warm months. Choose a corner room or one overlooking the small pool deck for the best light.

In any room, you are sure to appreciate the convenient location: less than 2 blocks from the ocean and all of the best shopping. For those who appreciate the fine hospitality of a small lodging without the sometimes-invasive feel of a bed-and-breakfast, this is the island's number one choice.

Dining/Diversions: A full cooked-to-order breakfast that includes fresh fruit, breakfast breads, and hot main dishes is served each morning in a charming English country–style dining room. The cozy Stray Fox Pub, a comfortable little bar with mahogany tables, serves cocktails throughout the evening and sometimes has live piano music on the weekends.

Amenities: Concierge, dry-cleaning and laundry services, newspaper delivery, in-room massage, baby-sitting, secretarial services. VCRs, heated outdoor pool, Jacuzzi and small workout room, access to nearby health club.

MODERATE

Heart of Palm Beach Hotel. 160 Royal Palm Way, Palm Beach, FL 33480. ☎ **800/ 523-5377** or 561/655-5600. Fax 561/832-1201. 90 units. A/C TV TEL. Winter $149–$259 double; $275 suite. Off-season $69–$149 double; $175 suite. AE, DC, MC, V. From I-95, exit onto Okeechobee Blvd. E. and continue over the Royal Palm Bridge onto Royal Palm Way.

The centrally located Heart of Palm Beach Hotel is within walking distance of Worth Avenue's shops and just half a block from the beach. Ongoing renovations since the 1990s have improved the patio space as well as the rooms in the hotel's two buildings. Most are decorated with modest but new furnishings and fittings in a colorful contemporary style. The tiled bathrooms are small, clean, and functional. Besides the great location, another plus here is that each accommodation comes with a private balcony or patio. Choose a room on a higher floor, because those on the ground floor tend to be a bit dark. The staff is particularly outgoing and will help guests plan outings and itineraries.

There are a heated swimming pool and complimentary covered parking. A clubby restaurant serves a selection of salads, sandwiches, pastas, and cocktails. Breakfast is served in a bright dining room overlooking the gardens.

Palm Beach Historic Inn. 365 S. County Rd., Palm Beach, FL 33480. ☎ **561/832-4009.** Fax 561/832-6255. 13 units. A/C TV TEL. Winter $150–$170 double; from $200 suite. Off-season $75–$95 double; from $100 suite. Rates include continental breakfast. Children stay free in parents' room. AE, CB, DC, DISC, MC, V.

Despite a rather abandoned look, this bed-and-breakfast is a cozy and comfortable place to stay in Palm Beach. Built in 1923, the Palm Beach Historic Inn is an area landmark located within walking distance of Worth Avenue, the beach, and several good restaurants. The small lobby is filled with antiques, books, magazines, and an old-fashioned umbrella stand, all of which add to the homey feel of this intimate bed-and-breakfast. All the rooms are on the second floor, and each is uniquely decorated and full of frills. Floral prints, sheer curtains, and the plethora of lace can sometimes be overwhelming, masking rather than complementing beautiful antique writing desks and dressers. Happily, there are also fluffy bathrobes, an abundance of towels, and plenty of good-smelling toiletries.

MODERATE/INEXPENSIVE

✪ **Beachcomber Apartment Motel.** 3024 S. Ocean Blvd., Palm Beach, FL 33480. ☎ **800/833-7122** or 561/585-4646. Fax 561/547-9438. 45 units. A/C TV TEL. Winter $85–$155 motel rm; from $105–$210 apt. Off-season $45–$80 motel rm; from $60–$125 apt. AE, DISC, MC, V. From I-95, exit 10th Ave. N., head east to Federal Hwy., and turn right. Continue to Lake Ave. and turn left. Go over bridge and turn right at first traffic light (S. Ocean Dr.).

It's not just the bright-pink building that makes this two-story motel stand out. For more than 35 years the Beachcomber has been bringing sanity to pricey Palm Beach by offering a good standard of accommodation at reasonable prices. Squeezed between beachfront high-rises, the motel is located oceanfront, adjacent to Lake Worth Beach and a short drive from Worth Avenue shops and local attractions. Every room has two double beds, large closets, and distinctive green-and-white tropical-style furnishings;

some have kitchenettes. The most expensive have balconies overlooking the ocean. The bathrooms are basic, and amenities are limited to towels and soap. Facilities at the motel include a coin-operated laundry, shuffleboard, a large pool, and a sundeck overlooking the Atlantic.

Hibiscus House. 501 30th St., West Palm Beach, FL 33407. ☎ **800/203-4927** or 561/863-5633. Fax 561/863-5633. www.hibiscushouse.com. 8 units. A/C TV TEL. Winter $95–$175 double. Off-season $65–$130 double. Rates include breakfast. AE, DC, MC, V. From I-95, exit onto Palm Beach Lakes Blvd. E. and continue 4 miles; turn left onto Flagler Dr., continue for about 20 blocks, then turn left onto 30th St.

Inexpensive bed-and-breakfasts are rare in Southeast Florida, making the Hibiscus House one of the area's firsts, a true find. Located a few miles from the coast in a quiet residential neighborhood, this 1920s-era B&B is filled with handsome antiques and tapestried in luxurious fabrics. Every room has its own private terrace or balcony. The backyard, a peaceful retreat, has been transformed into a tropical garden with a heated swimming pool and lounge chairs. Also, there are plenty of pretty areas for guests to enjoy inside; one little sitting room is wrapped in glass and is stocked with playing cards and board games. Beware: Breakfast portions are enormous. The gourmet creations are as filling as they are beautiful. Ask for any special requests in advance; owners Raleigh Hill and Colin Rayer will be happy to oblige.

WHERE TO DINE
Palm Beach has some of the area's finest restaurants, with many classical and elegant options, as well as a few more innovative choices. Dress here is slightly more formal than in most other areas of Florida: Men wear blazers, and women generally put on modest dresses when they dine out—even in the dog days of summer.

EXPENSIVE
Amici. 288 S. County Rd. (at Royal Palm Way), Palm Beach. ☎ **561/832-0201.** Fax 561/659-3540. Reservations strongly recommended on weekends. Main courses $18–$29; pastas and pizzas $8–$19. AE, DC, MC, V. Mon–Thurs 11:30am–3pm and 5:30–10:30pm, Fri–Sat 11:30am–3pm and 5:30–11pm, Sun 5:30–10:30pm. ITALIAN.

You'd think that there would be a dozen good Italian restaurants in Palm Beach. There are plenty of decent ones, but Amici tops them all with homemade pastas, a vast array of innovative antipasti, and a variety of lighter fare. Diners come dressed in blazers and ties at lunch, though the atmosphere here is fairly casual, with simple decor and lots of window space to let in light. The food is nothing unusual—grilled sandwiches, pastas with rustic sauces, pizzas, grilled shrimp and fish—but the execution is flawless. You could argue that the prices don't match the simple food, but where else in Palm Beach can you get *broccoli di rabe,* fresh roasted peppers loaded with garlic, and pizzas with escarole, homemade sausage, and pine nuts?

Cafe l'Europe. 331 S. County Rd. (at the corner of Brazilian Ave.), Palm Beach. ☎ **561/655-4020.** Reservations recommended. Main courses $18–$32. AE, CB, DC, DISC, MC, V. Tues–Sat noon–2:30pm and 5:45–10:30pm, Fri–Sat open until 1am. Sun 6–10:30pm. FRENCH/CONTINENTAL.

One of Palm Beach's very finest, this award-winning formal restaurant is located on the upper level of the Esplanade, a Spanish-style shopping arcade. The interior is made romantic and luxurious by the tapestried cafe chairs and linen-topped tables set with crystal and china. The enticing appetizers served by a superb staff might include Chinese spring rolls, baked goat-cheese salad with raspberry-walnut dressing, poached salmon, or chilled gazpacho with avocado. Main courses run the gamut from sautéed potato-crusted Florida snapper to lamb chops to roast Cornish game hen. Seafood dishes and steaks in sumptuous but light sauces are always exceptional.

Chuck & Harold's Cafe. 207 Royal Poinciana Way (corner of S. County Rd.), Palm Beach. ☎ 561/659-1440. Reservations recommended. Main courses $16–$33. AE, DC, DISC, MC, V. Mon–Thurs 7:30am–midnight, Fri–Sat 7:30am–1am, Sun 8am–11pm. AMERICAN.

For predictable American fare, this old standby delivers. Chuck & Harold's serves good food at inflated prices. Remember, you are paying for one of the area's best people-watching perches. Sit outside and enjoy the view. Main dishes include fresh grilled or broiled fish, boiled lobster, and a small variety of straightforward homemade pasta and chicken dishes. If you happen to visit during stone crab season, order them here. The crab claws are steamed or chilled and served with a traditional honey-mustard sauce.

MODERATE

✪ **Aquaterra.** 230 Sunrise Ave. (between Sunrise and Park aves.), Palm Beach. ☎ 561/366-4000. Reservations recommended, especially on weekends. Main courses $15–$18.50. Fixed-price menu 5–6pm $19. AE, MC, V. Tues–Sun 5–11pm. INNOVATIVE AMERICAN.

New York's Charlie Palmer, James Beard winner for best chef in 1997, has taken his spatula south and opened a stunning new lunch and dinner spot in Palm Beach. Slightly off the beaten track on Sunrise Avenue (across the street from the Palm Beach Hotel), this fantastic restaurant is bound to please even the pickiest eaters. With nearly 20 options for bar snacks and appetizers, including crispy fried oysters, beef skewers with peanut sauce, vegetable spring rolls, eggplant fritters, and rock shrimp pillows, the menu is simple yet diverse. A more limited selection of entrees, as the name suggests, is from the sea or land. The best choices are waterborne. Depending on the season there is mahimahi (dolphin), salmon, swordfish, snapper, or tuna, all of which can be prepared grilled, roasted, or sautéed with a complimentary array of herbs and seasonings. I favor the clean-tasting snapper grilled with caramelized lemon, olive oil, and fresh parsley. Likewise, you can choose how you'd like your meats or chicken cooked. A delicate filet mignon sautéed with wild mushroom ragout is memorable. Don't skip the architecturally striking and delicious desserts. Especially good are the double caramelized banana parfait and the bittersweet chocolate torte with homemade mint ice cream.

Rhythm Cafe. 3800 S. Dixie Hwy., West Palm Beach. ☎ 561/833-3406. Reservations recommended on weekends. Main courses $10–24. AE, DISC, MC, V. Tues–Sat 6–10pm; Sun 10am–2pm and 6–10pm during winter. Sometimes earlier on Sun. From I-95, exit east on Southern Blvd., 1 block north of Southern Blvd., on the right. ECLECTIC AMERICAN.

This hole-in-the-wall is where those in the know come to eat some of West Palm Beach's most laid-back gourmet food. On the handwritten, photocopied menu, you'll always find a fish specialty with a hefty dose of greens and garnishes. Also reliably outstanding is the sautéed medallion of beef tenderloin served on a bed of arugula with a tangy rosemary vinaigrette. Salads and soups are a great bargain since portions are relatively large and the display is usually spectacular. The kitschy decor of this tiny cafe comes complete with vinyl tablecloths and paintings by local amateurs. Young, handsome waiters are attentive but not solicitous. The old drugstore where the restaurant recently relocated features an original 1950s lunch counter and stools.

Taboo. 221 Worth Ave., Palm Beach. ☎ 561/835-3500. Reservations recommended. Main courses $14–$22. AE, DC, MC, V. Sun–Thurs 11:30am–11pm, Fri–Sat 11:30am–1am. AMERICAN BISTRO.

Taboo is a snazzy Worth Avenue eatery that successfully combines the classic and the trendy. Lots of greenery, a fireplace, and a contemporary Southwestern charm make it comfortable and inviting. Variety is always the chef's special, with extensive lunch and dinner offerings that are often calorie- and cholesterol-conscious. For lunch, the kitchen creates California-style individual-size pizzas topped with delicacies like barbecued chicken, goat and mozzarella cheeses, and sweet roasted red peppers. Other choices include a delicious sandwich of sweet peppers and goat cheese. The best dinner starter is fresh tuna marinated in ginger and lime. Dinner choices change nightly and may include grilled swordfish topped with olive-caper sauce or grilled veal served on the bone.

INEXPENSIVE

Green's Pharmacy. 151 N. County Rd., Palm Beach. ☎ **561/832-0304.** Breakfast $2–$5; burgers and sandwiches $3–$6. AE, MC, V. Mon–Sat 7am–6pm, Sun 7am–5pm. AMERICAN.

This neighborhood corner pharmacy offers one of the best meal deals in Palm Beach. Both breakfast and lunch are served coffee-shop style at either a Formica bar or plain tables above a black-and-white checkerboard floor. Breakfast specials include eggs and omelettes served with home fries and bacon, sausage, or corned-beef hash. At lunch the grill serves burgers and sandwiches, as well as ice-cream sodas and milkshakes, to a loyal crowd of pastel-clad Palm Beachers.

✪ **John G's.** 10 S. Ocean Blvd., Lake Worth. ☎ **561/585-9860.** Reservations not accepted. Breakfast $3–$8.50; lunch $5–$14. No credit cards. Daily 7am–3pm. Off Florida Turnpike, take the Lake Worth exit and head toward the ocean. AMERICAN.

This coffee shop is the most popular in the county. For decades, John G's has been attracting huge breakfast crowds; lines run out the door (on weekends, all the way down the block). Stop in for some good, greasy-spoon–style food served in heaping portions right on the beachfront. This place is known for fresh and tasty fish-and-chips and its selection of creative omelettes and grill specials.

TooJay's. 313 Royal Poinciana Plaza (3 miles east of I-95 off Exit 52A), Palm Beach. ☎ **561/659-7232.** Reservations not accepted. Main courses $7–$12. CB, DC, MC, V. Daily 8am–9pm. DELICATESSEN.

This simple and predictable restaurant and take-out deli is a favorite with locals and out-of-towners who want good old-fashioned deli food. So popular, in fact, that TooJay's now has more than a dozen outlets. For good cover while people-watching, choose a booth surrounded by a jungle of potted plants. The food is excellent and could hardly be fresher. All the classic sandwiches are available: hot pastrami, roast beef, turkey, chicken, chopped liver, egg salad, and more. Comfort food in the form of huge portions of stuffed cabbage, chicken pot pie, beef brisket, and sautéed onions and chicken livers is sure to satisfy.

THE PALM BEACHES AFTER DARK
THE BAR, CAFE & MUSIC SCENE: DOWNTOWN WEST PALM BEACH

A decade-old project to revitalize downtown West Palm Beach has finally become a reality, with ✪ **Clematis Street** at the heart. Artist lofts, sidewalk cafes, bars, restaurants, consignment shops, and galleries dot the street from Flagler Drive to Rosemary Avenue, creating a hot spot for a night out, especially on weekends, when yuppies mingle with stylish Euros and disheveled artists. Every Thursday night is a popular night out called *Clematis by Night.* Each week features a different rock, blues, or reggae band plus an art show. Vendors sell food and drinks, and the street's bars and restaurants are packed. It is a bit raucous at times, but fun. Note that minors unaccompanied by their guardians are not permitted in the downtown area around Clematis Street after 10pm on weeknights and after 11pm on weekend nights.

Some highlights of the Strip include **Sforza,** at 223 Clematis St.—it's the only Italian restaurant I've seen that needs a bouncer at the door. On weekends, this place draws crowds of yuppies and well-dressed Euros who wait to be picked to get in the elegant dining room to dance and sip expensive martinis (☎ **561/832-8819**).

If you are looking for a more casual scene, stop by **Ray's,** at 519 Clematis St. (☎ **561/835-1577**), on a Thursday, Friday, or Saturday for free blues and mediocre drinks. This dusty little bar hosts homegrown blues bands who give it all up for the few patrons who appreciate the rough stuff.

Across the street is a longtime favorite, **Respectable Street Café,** at 518 Clematis St. (☎ **561/832-9999**). The cafe's plain storefront exterior belies its funky, high-ceilinged interior decorated with large black booths, psychedelic wall murals, and a large checkerboard-tile dance floor, where young hipsters dance to both live and recorded alternative music.

Over the bridge in Palm Beach is **E. R. Bradley's Saloon,** at 111 Bradley Place, between Royal Poinciana Way and Sunset Avenue (☎ **561/833-3520**). Bradley's, as it is known, is about as wild as the "island" allows. Most nights a crowd of young professionals share the old wooden tavern with hard-drinking regulars in blue blazers. Check out the happy-hour buffets in the late afternoon.

A more sophisticated crowd gathers nightly at the **Leopard Lounge** in the Chesterfield Hotel (see "Where to Stay," above). Live piano music, good conversation, and a comfortable sofa make this a perfect place to spend an evening.

THE PERFORMING ARTS

With a number of dedicated patrons and enthusiastic supporters of the arts, this area happily boasts many good venues for those craving culture. Check the *Palm Beach Post* or the *Palm Beach Daily News,* known as "the shiny sheet," for up-to-date listings and reviews. Call ☎ **800/882-ARTS** for a recorded announcement of the week's events.

The **Raymond F. Kravis Center for the Performing Arts,** 701 Okeechobee Blvd., West Palm Beach (☎ **561/832-7469**), is the area's largest and most active performance space. With a huge curved-glass facade and more than 2,500 seats in two lushly decorated indoor spaces, as well as a new outdoor amphitheater, The Kravis, as it is known, stages more than 300 performances each year. Phone for a current schedule of Palm Beach's best music, dance, and theater.

4 Jupiter & Northern Palm Beach County

20 miles N of Palm Beach, 81 miles N of Miami

Northern Palm Beach County and its main town, Jupiter, are known primarily for pristine beaches and expansive tracts of land. The surrounding towns of Tequesta, Jupiter, Juno Beach, North Palm Beach, Palm Beach Gardens, and Singer Island are inviting for tourists who want to enjoy the many outdoor activities that make this area so popular with retirees, snowbirds, and families. Beaches and parks are clean, large, and easily accessible to the public.

ESSENTIALS

GETTING THERE   The quickest route from West Palm Beach to Jupiter is on the Florida Turnpike or the sometimes-congested I-95. You can also take a slower but more scenic coastal route, U.S. 1 or Fla. A1A.

Since Jupiter is so close to Palm Beach, it's easy to fly into the **Palm Beach International Airport** (☎ **561/471-7420**) and rent a car there. The drive should take less than half an hour.

VISITOR INFORMATION   A Visitor Information Center is located between I-95 and the Florida Turnpike at 8020 Indiantown Rd. in Jupiter (☎ **561/575-4636**) and is open from 9am to 6pm daily.

FUN ON & OFF THE BEACH

BASEBALL   The **Roger Dean Stadium,** 4751 Main St. (☎ **561/775-1818**), hosts spring training for both the St. Louis Cardinals and the Montreal Expos, along with minor-league action from Florida's state league, The Hammerheads. Tickets range in price from $5 to $15. Baseball aficionados should call for schedules and specific ticket information.

BEACHES   The farther north you head from populated Palm Beach, the more peaceful and pristine the coast becomes. Just a few miles north of the bustle, castles and condominiums give way to wide-open space and public parkland. There are dozens of recommendable spots. Following are a few of the best.

John D. MacArthur Beach, a state park, dominates a large portion of Singer Island, the barrier island just north of Palm Beach. Straddling the island from shore to shore, the park has lengthy frontage on both the Atlantic Ocean and Lake Worth Cove. The beach is great for hiking, swimming, and sunning. To reach the park from the mainland, cross the Intracoastal Waterway on Blue Heron Boulevard and turn north on Ocean Boulevard.

BICYCLING   Bring your own, get one from your hotel, or rent one from **Raleigh Bicycles of Jupiter,** at 103 U.S. 1, Unit F1 (☎ **561/746-0585**). Bicycle enthusiasts will enjoy exploring this flat and uncluttered area. North Palm Beach has hundreds of miles of smooth paved roads. Loggerhead Park in Juno Beach or Fla. A1A along the ocean has great trails for starters. You'll find many more scenic routes over the bridges and west of the highway.

BOATING & CANOEING   You can rent a boat at several outlets throughout northern Palm Beach County, including **Canoe Outfitters,** 8900 W. Indiantown Rd. (west of I-95), North Jupiter (☎ **561/746-7053**), which provides access to one of the area's most beautiful natural waterways. Canoeists start at Riverbend Park along an 8-mile stretch of Intracoastal Waterway, where the lush foliage supports dozens of exotic birds and reptiles. Keep your eyes open for gators, who love to sunbathe on the shallow shores of the river. You'll end up tired and thoroughly wide-eyed at Jonathan Dickinson Park about 5 or 6 hours later. Eric Bailey, a local who runs the concession, will sell the environmentally minded a pamphlet for $1 that describes local flora and fauna. Trips run Wednesday to Sunday and cost $16 per person, including park charges.

CRUISES   Several sightseeing cruises offer scenic tours of the magnificent waterways that make up northern Palm Beach County. Several water taxis conduct daily narrated tours through the scenic waters. One interesting excursion departs from Panama Hatties at PGA Boulevard and the Intracoastal Waterway. Prices are $15 per person for the 1½-hour ride. Call ☎ **561/775-2628.** The **Manatee Queen,** 1065 N. Ocean Blvd. (at the Crab House), Jupiter (☎ **561/744-2191**), a 40-foot catamaran with bench seating for up to 49 people, offers 2-hour tours of Jupiter Island departing daily at 2:30pm that pass Burt Reynolds's and Perry Como's mansions, among other historical and natural spots of interest. Reservations are highly recommended, especially in season; call for the current schedule of offerings. The cruise is wheelchair accessible. Prices start at $14 for adults and $10 for children and can range up to $15 for special tours. Bring your own lunch or purchase chips and sodas at the mini-snack bar.

FISHING   Before you leave, send for an information-packed fishing kit with details on fish camps, charters, and tournament and tide schedules, distributed by the West Palm Beach Fishing Club, c/o Fish Finder, P.O. Box 468, West Palm Beach, FL 33402. The cost is $10 and is well worth it. Allow at least 4 weeks for delivery.

Once you're in town, several outfitters along U.S. 1 and Fla. A1A have vessels and equipment for rent if your hotel doesn't. One of the most complete facilities is the **Sailfish Marina & Resort,** 98 Lake Dr. (off Blue Heron Boulevard), Palm Beach Shores (☎ **561/844-1724**). Call for equipment, bait, guided trips, or boat rentals.

GOLF   Even if you're not lucky enough to be staying at the PGA National Resort, you may still be able to play on their award-winning courses. If you or someone in your group is a member of another golf or country club, have the head pro write a note on club letterhead to Jackie Rogers at PGA (see "Where to Stay," below) or send a fax to ☎ **561/627-015** to request a play date. Be sure the pro includes his PGA number and contact information. Allow at least 2 weeks for a response. Also, ask about the Golf-A-Round program, where selected private clubs open to nonmembers for free or discounted rates. Contact the **Palm Beach County Convention and Visitors Bureau** (☎ **561/471-3995**) for details.

Plenty of other great courses dot the area, including the **Golf Club of Jupiter,** 1800 Central Blvd., Jupiter (☎ **561/747-6262**). A well-respected 18-hole, par-70 course is situated on over 6,200 yards featuring narrow fairways and fast greens. Fees are $27 to $60, depending on the season, and include a mandatory cart. The course borders I-95.

HIKING   In an area that's not particularly known for extraordinary natural diversity, **Blowing Rocks Preserve** has a terrific hiking trail along a dramatic limestone outcropping. You won't find hills or scenic vistas, but you will see Florida's unique and varied tropical ecosystem. The well-marked mile-long trail passes oceanfront dunes, coastal strands, mangrove wetlands, and a coastal hammock. The preserve, owned and managed by the Nature Conservancy, also protects an important habitat for West Indian manatees and loggerhead turtles. The preserve is located along South Beach Drive (Fla. A1A), north of the Jupiter inlet, about a 10-minute drive from Jupiter. From U.S. 1, head east on S.R. 707 and cross the Intracoastal Waterway to the park. Admission is free, but a $3-per-person donation is requested. For more information, contact the Preserve Manager, Blowing Rocks Preserve, P.O. Box 3795, Tequesta, FL 33469 (☎ **561/575-2297**).

SCUBA DIVING & SNORKELING   Year-round, warm, clear waters make northern Palm Beach County great for both diving and snorkeling. The closest coral reef is located a quarter-mile from shore and can easily be reached by boat. Three popular wrecks are clustered near each other less than a mile offshore of the Lake Worth Inlet at about 90 feet. If your hotel doesn't offer dive trips, call the **South Florida Dive Headquarters,** 23141 Lyons Rd., Boca Raton (☎ **800/771-DIVE** or 561/627-9558), or **Seafari Dive and Surf,** 75 E. Indiantown Rd., Suite 603, Jupiter (☎ **561/747-6115**).

TENNIS   In addition to using the many hotel tennis courts (see "Where to Stay," below), you can swing a racquet at a number of local clubs. The **Jupiter Bay Tennis Club,** 353 U.S. 1, Jupiter (☎ **561/744-9424**), has seven clay courts (three lighted) and charges $12 per person per day. Reservations are highly recommended.

More economical options are available at relatively well-maintained municipal courts. Call for locations and hours (☎ **561/966-6600**). Many are available free on a first-come, first-served basis.

Discovering a Remarkable Natural World

North Palm is well-known for the giant sea turtles that lay their eggs on the county's beaches from May to August. These endangered marine animals return here annually, from as far as South America, to lay their clutch of about 115 eggs each. Nurtured by the warm sand, but preyed upon by birds and other predators, only about one or two babies from each nest survive to maturity.

Many environmentalists recommend that visitors take part in an organized turtle-watching program (rather than going on their own) to minimize disturbance to the turtles. The Jupiter Beach Resort (see "Where to Stay," below) and the Marinelife Center of Juno Beach (see below) both sponsor free guided expeditions to the egg-laying sites from May to August. Phone for times and reservations.

Just south of Jupiter, in Juno Beach, is the **Marinelife Center of Juno Beach,** in Loggerhead Park, 14200 U.S. 1, Juno Beach (☎ **561/627-8280**). A small combination science museum and nature trail, the Marinelife Center is dedicated to the coastal ecology of northern Palm Beach County. Hands-on exhibits teach visitors about wetlands and beach areas, as well as offshore coral reefs and the local sea life. Visitors are encouraged to walk the center's sand-dune nature trails, all of which are marked with interpretive signs. This is one place that you're guaranteed to see live sea turtles year-round, and during high breeding season (June and July), the center conducts narrative walks along a nearby beach. Reservations are a must. The book opens on May 1 and is usually full by mid-month. Admission to the center is free, though donations are accepted. Open Tuesday to Saturday from 10am to 4pm and Sunday from noon to 3pm.

A HISTORIC LIGHTHOUSE

Jupiter Inlet Lighthouse. U.S. 1 and Alt. Fla. A1A, Jupiter. ☎ **561/747-8380**. Admission $5. Sun–Wed 10am–4pm (last tour departs at 3:15pm). Children must be 4 feet or taller to climb.

Completed in 1860, this redbrick structure is the oldest extant building in Palm Beach County. Still owned and maintained by the U.S. Coast Guard, the lighthouse is now home to a small historical museum, located at its base. The Florida History Museum sponsors tours of the lighthouse, enabling visitors to explore the cramped interior, which is filled with artifacts and photographs illustrating the rich history of the area. First, a 15-minute video explains the various shipwrecks, Indian wars, and other events that helped shape this region. Helpful volunteers are eager to tell colorful stories to highlight the 1-hour tour.

SHOPPING

Northern Palm Beach County may not have the glitzy boutiques of Worth Avenue, but it does have an impressive indoor mall, the **Gardens of the Palm Beaches,** at 3101 PGA Blvd., where you can find large department stores, including Bloomingdale's, Burdines, Macy's, and Saks Fifth Avenue, as well as more than 100 specialty shops. A large and diverse food court and fine sit-down restaurants in this 1.3 million-square-foot facility make this shopping excursion an all-day affair. Call ☎ 561/775-7750 for store information.

WHERE TO STAY

The northern part of Palm Beach County is much more laid-back and less touristy than the rest of the Gold Coast. Here there are relatively few fancy hotels or attractions. In addition to several Holiday Inns, there is a reasonably priced and recently renovated **Wellesley Inn**, at 34 Fisherman's Wharf (I-95, exit east on Indian Town Road; turn left before the bridge), in Jupiter (☎ **800/444-8888**). Suites include sofa beds, refrigerators, and microwave ovens. Though not within walking distance of the beach, the inn is located near shops and restaurants and Fla. A1A.

VERY EXPENSIVE

Jupiter Beach Resort. 5 N. Fla. A1A, Jupiter, FL 33477. ☎ **800/228-8810** or 561/746-2511. Fax 561/747-3304. 176 units. A/C MINIBAR TV TEL. Winter $200–$340 double; $310–$450 suite; $750–$1,000 penthouse. Off-season $115–$205 double; $135–$205 suite; $400–$600 penthouse. AE, DC, DISC, MC, V. From I-95, take Exit 59A east to the end of Indiantown Rd. at A1A. Jupiter Beach Resort is at this intersection on the ocean.

The only resort located directly on Jupiter's beach, this unpretentious retreat is a world away from the more luxurious resorts just a few miles to the south. The lobby and public areas have a formal Caribbean motif, accented with green marble, arched doorways, and chandeliers. The simple and elegant guest rooms are furnished in a comfortable island style, and every room has a private balcony with ocean or sunset views looking out over the uncluttered beachfront. A thorough refurbishing in the mid-1990s has made this resort very popular with conventions and large groups. In fact, it is so popular that it is being gradually converted into a timeshare property. Excursions are available to top-rated golf courses in the area.

Dining: A popular and well-run lobby restaurant serves an eclectic mix of continental, Southwestern, and Caribbean cuisine. Three other pool and beach bars serve snacks and refreshments throughout the day. The lounge features live music several nights a week.

Amenities: Concierge, room service, dry-cleaning and laundry services, overnight shoe shine, newspaper delivery, in-room massage, daily maid service, baby-sitting, express checkout, valet parking for $5, free coffee in room. Kitchenettes and VCRs in suites, VCR rentals, Spectravision movie channels, outdoor heated swimming pool, beach, exercise room, bicycle rental, supervised children's programs, conference rooms, self-service Laundromat, car-rental desk, night-lit tennis court, water-sports equipment rentals, boutique, dive shop, summer turtle-watch program.

✪ **PGA National Resort & Spa.** 400 Ave. of the Champions, Palm Beach Gardens, FL 33418. ☎ **800/633-9150** or 561/627-2000. Fax 561/622-0261. 339 units. A/C MINIBAR TV TEL. Winter $309–$369 double; from $469 suite. Off-season $119–$149 double; from $229 suite. Children 16 and under stay free in parents' room. Special packages available. AE, DC, DISC, MC, V. From I-95, take Exit 57B (PGA Blvd.) west and continue for approximately 2 miles to the resort entrance on the left.

This rambling resort, built in 1981, is known primarily as a golf destination. With five 18-hole courses on more than 2,300 acres, golfers and other sports-minded travelers will find plenty to keep them occupied—croquet, tennis, sailing, a health and fitness center, and a top-rated Mediterranean-style spa. Constant updating has kept the grounds and buildings in like-new condition. The par-72 Champion Course, redesigned in 1990 by Jack Nicklaus, is the resort's most valuable asset. More than 100 sand bunkers and plenty of water on 6,400-square-foot greens keep golfers of all levels alert. Watch out for the 16th hole.

When you are ready to rest, you will enjoy the comfortable and spacious accommodations and good food. Ample-size guest rooms are furnished with tasteful modern furnishings and tropical prints. Bathrooms are large and thoughtfully outfitted with cushy robes, good light, and magnifying mirrors. Although you are miles from the beach, the resort has nine pools and a private lake where you can ski or sail. As for views, the best you will get is the golf course or gardens.

Dining: Six restaurants and lounges include Don Shula's award-winning steak house, a poolside grill, and another with spa cuisine.

Amenities: Concierge, room service, evening turndown, overnight shoe shine, laundry, baby-sitting. This is the national headquarters of the PGA, so it's no surprise that there are five 18-hole tournament courses, plus the PGA National's Academy of Golf. There are also 19 clay tennis courts (12 lighted), nine swimming pools, a private beach on a 26-acre lake, water-sports equipment rentals, five tournament-croquet lawns, five indoor racquetball courts, a full-service Mediterranean spa, aerobics studio, salon, and car rental.

MODERATE/INEXPENSIVE

Baron's Landing Motel & Apartments. 18125 Ocean Blvd. (Fla. A1A at the corner of Love St.), Jupiter, FL 33477. ☎ **561/746-8757.** 8 units. A/C TV TEL. Winter from $90 double. Off-season from $50 double. No credit cards.

This charming family-run inn is a perfect little beach getaway. It's not elegant, but it's cozy. A single-story motel fronting the Intracoastal Waterway is often full in winter with snowbirds, who dock their boats at the hotel's marina for weeks or months at a time. Nearly all rooms, which are situated around a small pool, have small kitchenettes. Each unit has a hodgepodge of used furniture, and some have pull-out sofas. Considering that you're a few blocks from some of the most expensive real estate in the country, this is a good deal.

Cologne Motel. 220 U.S. 1, Tequesta/Jupiter, FL 33469. ☎ **561/746-0616.** 9 units. A/C TV. Winter $50–$60 double. Off-season $45 double. Weekly rates available. AE, DC, MC, V.

The pleasant Hungarian couple who run this modest roadside motel are always busy. After they finish the landscaping and pool, they hope to add more rooms to this nine-room, one-story little gem. The small rooms have just been updated with modest but bright bedspreads and curtains, and the newly retiled bathrooms are small but clean. The area is safe if not scenic and only about a 5-minute drive to the beach. A more direct route by foot gets you there in about 15 minutes.

WHERE TO DINE

In addition to all the national fast-food joints that line Indiantown Road and U.S. 1, you'll find a number of touristy fish restaurants serving battered and fried everything. There are only a few really exceptional eateries in North Palm Beach and Jupiter. Try these listed below for guaranteed good food at reasonable prices.

Athenian Cafe. In the Chasewood Shopping Center, 6350 Indiantown Rd., Suite 7, Jupiter. ☎ **561/744-8327.** Main courses $5–$16. AE, MC, V. Mon–Sat 11am–9pm. Sun 4–9pm during season. GREEK.

Peter Papadelis and his family have been running this pleasant storefront cafe for more than a decade. Tucked in the corner of a strip mall, this place is a favorite with businesspeople, who stop in for a heaping portion of rich and meaty moussaka or a flaky spinach pie made fresh by Peter himself. You could make a meal of the thick and lemony Greek soup and the large fresh antipasto. In a town replete with tourist-priced fish joints, this is a welcome alternative. Early-bird specials, served until 7pm, include many Greek favorites and broiled local fish with soup or salad, rice, vegetables, pita, dessert, and coffee or tea.

✪ **Capt. Charlie's Reef Grill.** 12846 U.S. 1 (behind O'Brian's and French Connection), Juno Beach. ☎ **561/624-9924.** Reservations not accepted. Main courses $9.95–$18.95. MC, V. Mon–Sat 11:30am–2pm, daily 5–10pm. Tapas/dessert Mon–Thurs 3–11pm, Fri–Sat 3pm–midnight. SEAFOOD/CARIBBEAN.

The trick here is to arrive early, ahead of the crowd of local foodies who come for more than a dozen daily local-catch specials prepared in dozens of styles. Imaginative appetizers include Caribbean chili, a rich, chunky stew filled with fresh seafood; or a tuna spring roll big enough for two. The enormous Cuban crab cake is moist and perfectly browned without tasting fried and is served with homemade mango chutney and black beans and rice. Sit at the bar to watch the hectic kitchen turn out perfect dishes on the 14-burner stove. Somehow the pleasant waitresses keep their cool even when the place is packed. In addition to the terrific seafood, this little dive offers an extensive, affordable wine and beer selection—more than 30 of each from around the world.

Nick's Tomato Pie. 1697 W. Indiantown Rd. (1 mile east of I-95, Exit 59A), Jupiter. ☎ **561/744-8935.** Reservations accepted only for parties of 6 or more. Main courses $11–$19; pastas $9–$14. AE, CB, DC, DISC, MC, V. Mon–Thurs 5–10pm, Fri–Sat 4:30–11pm, Sun 4:30–10pm. ITALIAN.

A Bennigan's-style family restaurant, Nick's is a popular attraction in otherwise food-poor Jupiter. With a huge menu of pastas, pizzas, fish, chicken, and beef, this cheery (and noisy) spot has something for everyone. On Saturday night you'll see lots of couples on dates and some families leaving with take-out bags left over from the impossibly generous portions. The homemade sausage is a delicious treat, served with sautéed onions and peppers. The pollo marsala, too, is good and authentic.

No Anchovies! 2650 PGA Blvd., Palm Beach Gardens. ☎ **561/622-7855.** Pizza and pasta $7–$13; main courses $10–$17. AE, DC, MC, V. Mon–Thurs 11:30am–2:30pm and 4:30–10:30pm, Fri–Sat 11:30am–2:30pm and 4:30–11pm, Sun 4:30–10:30pm. ITALIAN.

This large and colorful restaurant is popular with families who appreciate the large portions and reasonably priced children's specials. An equally colorful menu offers a large variety of pastas, pizzas, salads, and a variety of meat and fish specials. Mix and match your pasta with half a dozen sauces. My favorite is the thick and simple *fillete de tomato* over fusilli. You may also want to try some of the delicious chicken or meats prepared on the oak-burning grill.

JUPITER & NORTHERN PALM BEACH COUNTY AFTER DARK

With one notable exception, there just isn't much going on here after dark. **Club Safari,** 4000 PGA Blvd. (just east of I-95), in Palm Beach Garden's Marriott Hotel (☎ 561/622-8888), is more hip than any hotel dance club I have ever seen, although the safari theme is a bit much. The huge, sunken dance floor is surrounded by vines and lanky, potted trees. Nearby, a large Buddha statue blows steam and smoke while waving its burly arms in front of a young gyrating crowd. There are deejay music, a large video screen, and a modest cover charge on the weekends.

The Treasure Coast 9

by Victoria Pesce Elliott

Over the past few years, the Treasure Coast has been attracting unprecedented numbers of new residents. Yet this area retains its small-town feel. The growth is happening at a reasonable pace, and the influx has brought with it a renewed interest in renovating the once-abandoned downtown areas. The result is a batch of freshly spruced-up accommodations, shops, and restaurants from Stuart to Sebastian. Interspersed along the way are miles and miles of wild rivers, state parks, and of course, beaches.

In addition to a number of welcoming small communities and a vast array of wildlife, the Treasure Coast also has a history as rich and colorful as its provocative nickname.

For hundreds of years, Florida's east coast was a popular stopover for European explorers, many of whom arrived from Spain to fill coffers with gold and silver. Rough weather and poor navigation often took a toll on their ships, but in 1715, a violent hurricane stunned the northeast coast and sank an entire fleet of Spanish ships laden with gold. Though Spanish salvagers worked for years to collect the lost treasure, much of it remained buried beneath the shifting sand. Then, builders hired to excavate the area in the 1950s and 1960s discovered centuries-old coins under their tractors.

Today, on these same beaches you'll find an occasional treasure hunter trolling the sand with a metal detector, and swimmers and sunbathers who come to enjoy the stretches of beach that extend into the horizon. The sea, especially around Sebastian Inlet, is a mecca for surfers, who find some of the largest swells in the state.

The Treasure Coast, for the purposes of this chapter, runs roughly from Hobe Sound in the south to the Sebastian Inlet in the north, encompassing some of Martin, St. Lucie, and Indian River counties and all of Hutchinson Island.

Florida's largest inland lake, Lake Okeechobee, a favorite destination for anglers, lies just west of this coastal area and is covered at the end of this chapter.

TREASURE COAST ESSENTIALS
GETTING THERE
Since virtually every town described in this chapter runs along a straight route, along the Atlantic Ocean, I've given all directions below.

BY PLANE The **Palm Beach International Airport** (☎ 561/471-7420), located about 35 miles south of Stuart, is the closest gateway to this region if you're flying. See the "Getting Around" section on Palm Beach in chapter 8 for complete information. If you are traveling to the northern part of the Treasure Coast, **Melbourne International Airport,** off U.S. 1 in Melbourne (☎ 407/723-6227), is less than 25 miles north of Sebastian and about 35 miles north of Vero Beach.

BY CAR   If you're driving up or down the Florida coast, you'll probably reach the Treasure Coast via I-95. If you are heading to Stuart or Jensen Beach, take Exit 61 (Route 76/Tanner Highway) or 62 (Route 714); to Port St. Lucie or Fort Pierce, take Exit 63 or 64 (Okeechobee Road); to Vero Beach, take Exit 68 (S.R. 60); to Sebastian, take Exit 69 (County Road).

You can also take the Florida Turnpike; this toll road is the fastest (but not the most scenic) route, especially if you're coming from Orlando. If you are heading to Stuart or Jensen Beach, take Exit 133; to Fort Pierce, take Exit 152 (Okeechobee Road); to Port St. Lucie, take Exit 142 or 152; to Vero Beach, take Exit 193 (S.R. 60); to Sebastian, take Exit 193 to S.R. 60 east and connect to I-95 north.

If you are staying in Hutchinson Island, which runs almost the entire length of the Treasure Coast, you should check with your hotel, or see the listings below, to find the best route to take.

Finally, if you're coming directly from the west coast, you'll probably take S.R. 70, which runs north of Lake Okeechobee to Fort Pierce, located just up the road from Stuart.

BY RAIL   Amtrak (☎ 800/USA-RAIL) stops in West Palm Beach at 201 S. Tamarind Ave., and in Okeechobee at 801 N. Parrot Ave., off U.S. 441 north.

BY BUS   Greyhound buses (☎ 800/231-2222) service the area with terminals in Stuart, at 1308 S. Federal Hwy.; in Fort Pierce, at 7005 Okeechobee Rd. (☎ 561/461-3299); and in Vero Beach, at U.S. 1 and S.R. 60 (☎ 561/562-6588).

GETTING AROUND
A car is a necessity in this large and rural region. Although heavy traffic is not usually a problem here, on the smaller coastal roads, like Fla. A1A, expect to travel at a slow pace, usually between 25 and 40 miles an hour.

1 Hobe Sound, Stuart & Jensen Beach
130 miles SE of Orlando, 98 miles N of Miami

Once just a stretch of pineapple plantations, the towns of Martin County, which include Stuart, Jensen Beach, Port Salerno, and Hobe Sound, still retain much of their rural character. Dotted between citrus groves and mangroves are modest homes and an occasional high-rise condominium. Though the area is definitely still seasonal (with a distinct rise in street and pedestrian traffic beginning after the Christmas holidays), the atmosphere is pure small town. Even in historic downtown Stuart, the result of a successful, ongoing restoration, expect the storefronts to be dark and the streets abandoned after 10pm.

ESSENTIALS
The **Stuart/Martin County Chamber of Commerce,** 1650 S. Kanner Hwy., Stuart, FL 34994 (☎ 800/524-9704 in Florida, or 561/287-1088; fax 561/220-3437), is the region's main source for information. The **Jensen Beach Chamber of Commerce,** 1901 NE Jensen Beach Blvd., Jensen Beach, FL 34957 (☎ 561/334-3444; fax 561/334-0817), also offers visitors information about its simple beachfront town.

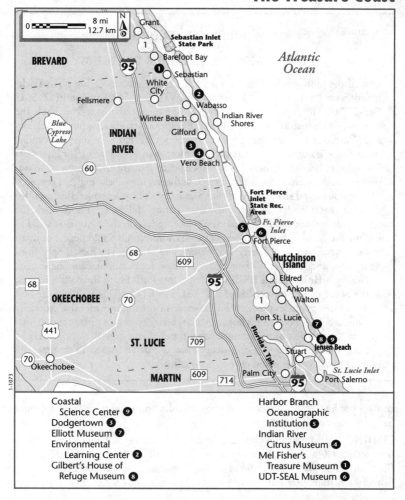

The Treasure Coast

Atlantic Ocean

Grant
Sebastian Inlet State Park
Barefoot Bay
BREVARD
95
❶ Sebastian
White City
❷ Wabasso
Fellsmere
Winter Beach
Indian River Shores
INDIAN
Gifford
RIVER
❸
❹
Vero Beach
60
Blue Cypress Lake

Fort Pierce Inlet State Rec. Area
Ft. Pierce Inlet
❺
❻
Fort Pierce
68
609
Hutchinson Island
95
Eldred
68
Ankona
OKEECHOBEE
70
Walton
1
Port St. Lucie
441
❼
ST. LUCIE
709
❽ ❾
Jensen Beach
70
Okeechobee
Stuart
St. Lucie Inlet
MARTIN
609
Palm City
714
95
Port Salerno

Coastal Science Center ❾	Harbor Branch Oceanographic Institution ❺
Dodgertown ❸	Indian River Citrus Museum ❹
Elliott Museum ❼	Mel Fisher's Treasure Museum ❶
Environmental Learning Center ❷	UDT-SEAL Museum ❻
Gilbert's House of Refuge Museum ❽	

OUTDOOR PURSUITS: THE BEACHES & BEYOND

BEACHES   Beaches are easily accessible throughout Hutchinson Island, the long, thin barrier island that stretches north and south from Stuart. Look for "coastal access" signs pointing the way to the public beach areas.

The best of them is **Bathtub Beach,** on North Hutchinson Island. Here, the calm waters are protected by coral reefs, and visitors can explore the region on dune and river trails. Pick a secluded spot on the wide stretch of beach or enjoy marked nature trails across the street. Facilities include showers and toilets open during the day. To reach the park, head east on Ocean Boulevard (Stuart Causeway) and turn right onto MacArthur Boulevard. The beach is about a mile ahead on your left, just north of the Indian River Plantation. Parking is plentiful.

CANOEING   **Jonathan Dickinson State Park** (see the "Wildlife Exploration" box) is the area's most popular for canoeing. The route winds through a variety of botanical habitats. You'll see lots of birds and, of course, the occasional manatee. Canoes

Wildlife Exploration: From Gators to Manatees to Turtles

One of the most scenic areas on this stretch of the coast is ✪ **Jonathan Dickinson State Park,** at 16450 S. Federal Hwy. (U.S. 1), Hobe Sound (☎ **561/546-2771**). The park is intentionally low managed so that it will resemble the habitat of hundreds of years ago, before Europeans started chopping, dredging, and "improving" the area. Dozens of species of Florida's unique wildlife, including alligators and manatees, live on more than 11,300 acres. Bird watchers will want to bring their books and binoculars to spot the many ospreys, woodpeckers, ibises, herons, anhingas, egrets, and even some bald eagles. Deer, reptiles, tortoises, and snakes also call this area home. There are concession areas for daytime snacks and four different scenic nature and bike trails through the scrublands and flatwoods. You can also rent canoes from the concession stand to explore the Loxahatchee River on your own. Admission is $3.25 per car of up to eight adults. Day hikers, bikers, and walkers pay $1 each. The park is open from 8am until sundown. See "Where to Stay," below for details on camping.

Nearby is **Hobe Sound Wildlife Refuge,** on North Beach Road off S.R. 708, at the north end of Jupiter Island (☎ **561/546-6141**). This is one of the best places to see sea turtles that nest on the shore in the summer months, especially in June and July. Because it's home to a large variety of other plant and animal species, the park is worth visiting at other times of year as well. Admission is $4 per car, and the preserve is open daily from sunrise to sunset. Exact times are posted at each entrance and change seasonally.

cost $6 per hour. The concession is open Monday to Friday from 9am to 5pm and Saturday and Sunday from 8am to 5pm.

FISHING　Several independent charter captains operate on Hutchinson Island and Jensen Beach. One of the largest operators is the **Sailfish Marina,** 3565 SE St. Lucie Blvd., in Stuart (☎ **561/221-9456**), which maintains half a dozen charter boats for fishing excursions year-round. Also on-site is a bait-and-tackle shop and a knowledgeable, helpful staff.

GOLF　The pricey **Indian River Plantation Beach Resort** is a terrific destination for golfers, but unless you're a guest at the resort or are playing with a member, you cannot play these courses. Instead, try the **Champions Club at Summerfield,** on U.S. 1, south of Cove Road in Stuart (☎ **561/283-1500**), a somewhat challenging championship course designed by Tom Fazio. This rural course, the best in the area, was built in 1994 and offers great glimpses of wildlife amid the wetlands. In winter, greens fees are around $60, and carts are mandatory. Reservations are a must and are taken 4 days in advance.

SCUBA DIVING & SNORKELING　Three popular artificial reefs off Hutchinson Island provide excellent scenery for both novice and experienced divers. The **USS Rankin,** sunk in 120 feet of water in 1988, lies 7 miles east-northeast of the St. Lucie Inlet. The 58-foot-deep **Donaldson Reef** consists of a cluster of plumbing fixtures sunk in 58 feet of water. It's located due east of the Gilbert's House of Refuge Museum. The **Ernst Reef,** made from old tires, is a 60-foot dive located 4½ miles east-southeast of the St. Lucie inlet.

Deep Divers Unlimited, 6083 SE Federal Hwy. (corner of Cove Road and U.S. 1), Stuart (☎ **561/286-0078**), arranges two-tank dive trips to these sites and others starting at about $37 a person. A full set of gear will cost you another $30 for the day. They can also rent gear to those wanting to explore the area's best snorkeling at Bathtub Beach (see "Beaches," above). There's a natural coral reef within swimming distance of shore.

SEEING THE SIGHTS

✪ **Coastal Science Center.** 890 NE Ocean Blvd. (across the street from the Elliott Museum), Hutchinson Island, Stuart. ☎ **561/225-0505.** Admission $3.50 adults, $2 children 3–12, free for children under 3. Mon–Sat 10am–5pm.

Opened by the South Florida Oceanographic Society in late 1994, this 44-acre site surrounded by coastal hammock and mangroves is its own little ecosystem and serves as an outdoor classroom, teaching visitors about the region's flora and fauna. The modest building houses saltwater tanks and wet and dry "discovery tables" with small indigenous animals. The incredibly eager staff of volunteers encourage visitors to wander the lush, well-marked nature trails.

✪ **Elliott Museum.** 825 NE Ocean Blvd. (north of Indian River Plantation Resort), Hutchinson Island, Stuart. ☎ **561/225-1961.** Admission $6 adults, $2 children 6–13, free for children 5 and under. Daily 10am–4pm.

A treasure trove of early Americana, the Elliott Museum is a rich tribute to inventors, sports heroes, and collectors. A series of life-size dioramas depicts an apothecary, a barbershop, a blacksmith forge, a clock and watch shop, and other old-fashioned commercial enterprises.

Sports lovers will appreciate the baseball memorabilia—a half million dollars' worth—including an autographed item from every player in the Baseball Hall of Fame.

A gallery of patents and models of machines, invented by the museum's founder, Harmon Parker Elliott, and his son, provides an intriguing glimpse into the business of tinkering. Their collection of restored antique cars is also pretty impressive. Expect to spend at least an hour seeing the highlights.

Gilbert's House of Refuge Museum. 301 SE MacArthur Blvd. (south of Indian River Plantation resort), Hutchinson Island, Stuart. ☎ **561/225-1875.** Admission $4 adults, $2 children 6–13, free for children 5 and under. Daily 10am–4pm.

Gilbert's, the oldest structure in Martin County, dates from 1875, when it functioned as one of 10 such rescue centers for shipwrecked sailors. After undergoing a thorough rehabilitation to its original condition along the rocky shores, the house now displays marine artifacts and turn-of-the-century lifesaving equipment and photographs and is worth a quick visit to get a feel for the area's early days.

A BOAT TOUR

✪ **The *Loxahatchee Queen,*** a 35-foot pontoon boat (☎ **561/746-1466**) in Jonathan Dickinson State Park in Hobe Sound, makes daily tours of the area's otherwise inaccessible backwater, where curious alligators, manatees, eagles, and tortoises often peek out to see who's in their yard. Try to catch the 2-hour tour, given Wednesday to Sunday as tide permits, when it includes a stop at Trapper Nelson's home. Known as the "Wildman of Loxahatchee," Nelson lived in primitive conditions—on a remote stretch of the water in a log cabin fashioned from his own hand—which are preserved for visitors to see. Tours leave four times daily at 9am, 11am, 1pm, and 3pm and cost $10 for adults, $5 for children 6 to 12, and free for children 5 and under. See the "Wildlife Exploration" box for more information on the park.

SHOPPING

Downtown Stuart's historic district, along Flagler Avenue between Confusion Corner and St. Lucie Avenue, offers shoppers diversity and quality in a small old-town setting. Shops offer a range of goods: antique bric-a-brac, old lamps and fixtures, books, gourmet foods, furnishings, and souvenirs.

WHERE TO STAY

Although the area boasts some beautiful beaches, the bulk of the hotel scene is downtown, where the nicer (and more reasonably priced) accommodations can be found among the shops and restaurants. There are, however, a few excellent beachfront hotels and inns. One of the bigger hotel chains in the area is the **Holiday Inn.** Its recently renovated, stunning beachfront property is at 3793 NE Ocean Blvd., on Hutchinson Island in Jensen Beach (☎ **800/992-4747** or 561/225-3000). Rates in season range from $130 to $180. Holiday Inn also has a downtown location at 1209 S. Federal Hwy. (☎ **561/287-6200**). Rates range from $99 to $140. This simple two-story building on a busy main road is kept in very good shape and is convenient to Stuart's downtown historic district.

VERY EXPENSIVE

✪ **Indian River Plantation Marriott Resort.** 555 NE Ocean Blvd., Hutchinson Island, Stuart, FL 34996. ☎ **800/775-5936** or 561/225-3700. Fax 561/225-0003. www.marriott. com/marriott/pbiir. 306 units. A/C TV TEL. Winter $179–$279 double; from $329 suite. Off-season $99–$139 double; from $149 suite. AE, CB, DC, DISC, MC, V. From downtown Stuart, take E. Ocean Blvd. over two bridges to NE Ocean Blvd.; turn right.

This sprawling 190-acre compound offers so many diversions for active (or not-so-active) vacationers that you won't want to leave. Having undergone more than $6 million worth of renovations in 1998, Indian River is now Hutchinson Island's best resort, occupying the lush grounds of a former pineapple plantation. Family-oriented activities include tennis, golfing, and boating. Sportfishing (especially for sailfish) is a big draw here, as are scuba diving and other water sports.

   The grand, white lattice-and-wicker lobby is filled with a jungle of plants, and large windows overlook the hotel's swimming pool and tiki bar. Generously sized rooms, some with fully equipped kitchens, are decorated with colorful spreads and draperies. Some rooms could use a thorough renovation, since old fixtures have suffered from years of exposure to sea air and salt.

   Be sure to sign up for a "turtle watch" in the summer months to watch the large turtles crawl onto the sand to lay their eggs.

   Dining/Diversions: Scalawags, a seafood restaurant, is the resort's top dining room and is popular with locals. A less-formal restaurant serves continental breakfast, lunch, and all-day snacks. There's live music nightly in two bars.

   Amenities: Room service, laundry and dry-cleaning services, newspaper delivery, baby-sitting, express checkout, on-property transportation, free juice in lobby. Four outdoor pools, beach, health club, Jacuzzi, 18-hole golf course, nature trails, some kitchenettes, sundeck, 13 tennis courts (5 night-lit), nearby racquetball courts, water-sports equipment, jogging track, bicycle rental, game room, children's program, Spectravision movie channels, self-service Laundromat, conference rooms, car-rental desk, boutiques.

MODERATE

✪ **Harborfront Inn Bed & Breakfast.** 310 Atlanta Ave., Stuart, FL 34994. ☎ **800/ 294-1703** or 561/288-7289. Fax 561/221-0474. www.harborfrontinn.com. 6 units. A/C TV TEL. $80–$100 double; from $135 suite, $155 suite with whirlpool and outdoor spa. Free dockage. Off-season specials. Rates include breakfast. No smoking and no children. AE, DISC, MC, V. From I-95 take Exit 61 east to U.S. 1 north; turn left on W. Ocean Blvd. and then make the first right (Atlanta Ave.).

The Harborfront Inn has the advantage of being right on the river, where you can sail, kayak, and ski. It consists of a series of little blue-trimmed shingled cottages within walking distance of the restaurants of downtown Stuart. Each room in this highly recommended B&B has its own private entrance, making it more like a rambling inn. Also, every accommodation has a sitting area and private bathroom. The two best rooms are the bright Garden Suite, which has a queen-size bed, rattan furnishings, and a deck with river and garden views; and the Guest House, which has an extra-large bathroom with two sinks and can be rented with an adjoining full kitchen.

Dining: The inn's cozy public areas are surrounded by an enclosed porch where breakfast is served. The morning meal usually includes fresh fruit from the trees that grow on the property.

Amenities: Kitchenettes in cottages, VCRs in suites, a Jacuzzi and sundeck, watersports equipment rentals.

✪ **The Home Place.** 501 Akron Ave., Stuart, FL 34994. ☎ **561/220-9148.** Fax 561/221-3265. 5 units, all with bathroom (1 with private bathroom down a hall). Year-round $85–$160. Off-season and weekday specials. Rates include full breakfast. No smoking and no children under 12. MC, V. From I-95 take Exit 61 east on S.R. 76 about 7 miles to U.S. 1. Turn left. Continue ½ mile to W. Ocean Blvd.; turn right. Turn right on Akron.

Perfect for those who like the feel of a classic B&B, Home Place is as charming as one can get. Suzanne and Michael Pescitelli are the gracious owners of this historic home, and they're just the kind of innkeepers you want in a classic little bed-and-breakfast. They offer taste, style, good conversation, superb homemade sweets, wine, an always-open fridge, and a perfectly maintained inn, which is a favorite locale for weddings. They live in the adjacent building, just a few steps from the 1913 guest house and beautifully landscaped pool and Jacuzzi area. You'll be comfortable in any of the Victorian-trimmed rooms chock-full of warm details like lace curtains, old steamer trunks, and crystal decanters. The large captain's room is a favorite for its size and big fluffy bed. While you're a few miles inland from the beach, you're only a few blocks from the quaint and rejuvenated downtown area. There isn't much in the way of grounds or amenities, but there is a medium-sized pool and sundeck with lounge chairs and cushy towels.

Hutchinson Inn. 9750 S. Ocean Dr. (Fla. A1A), Jensen Beach, FL 34957. ☎ **561/229-2000.** 21 units. A/C TV TEL. Winter from $90 double; $150–$225 efficiency or suite. Off-season $75 double; from $95–$165 efficiency or suite. Rates include continental breakfast. MC, V. From I-95 take Exit 61 east to Indian St.; turn right to St. Lucie Blvd.; turn left and continue to the bridge, where you will turn right onto E. Ocean Blvd. The inn is approximately 8 miles ahead.

It doesn't look like much from the road—only the tennis court is visible—but you'll soon happen upon striking white gazebos dotting thick green lawns. Located directly on the beach, the Hutchinson Inn is a quiet and charming two-story hideaway. Unfortunately, so many people know about it that it's usually booked a year in advance in high season.

The newly refurbished rooms have rattan furnishings; sofas convert into pull-out beds, and several rooms can be joined to accommodate large families.

Amenities: A good swimming beach, a large outdoor pool, one outdoor night-lit tennis court, water-sports equipment, bicycle rentals, a self-service Laundromat. Freshly baked cookies are offered each evening before bedtime.

CAMPING

There are comfortable campsites in **Jonathan Dickinson State Park** in Hobe Sound (see the "Wildlife Exploration" box). You can stay overnight in rustic cabins or in your tent or camper in two different sections of the park. The River Camp area offers the benefit of the nearby Loxahatchee River, while the Pine Grove site has beautiful shade trees. There are concession areas for daytime snacks and 135 campsites with showers, clean rest rooms, water, optional electricity, and an open-fire pit for cooking. Overnight rates in the winter are $18 without electricity, $20 with electricity. In the summer, rates are about $14 for four people.

For a more cushy camping experience, reserve a wood-sided cabin with a furnished kitchen, a bathroom with shower, heat and air-conditioning, and an outside grill. Bring your own linens. Cabins rent for $65 and up a night and sleep four people comfortably, six if your group is really into togetherness. Call ☎ **561/546-2771** Monday to Friday from 9am to 5pm well in advance to reserve a spot. A $50 key deposit is required.

WHERE TO DINE
EXPENSIVE

Eleven Maple Street. 11 Maple St., Jensen Beach. ☎ **561/334-7714.** Reservations recommended. Main courses $15–$25. MC, V. Wed–Sun 6–10pm. Head east on Jensen Beach Blvd. and turn right after the railroad tracks. AMERICAN.

The most highly rated restaurant in Jensen Beach, Eleven Maple Street occupies a lovely little house with a white picket fence, French doors, lace curtains, and pink-clothed tables. Dining is both indoors and out, in any one of a series of cozy dining rooms or on a covered patio surrounded by gardens. Straightforward meat and fish dishes run the gamut from local seafood to game and poultry like venison and duck. Maine lobster, filet mignon, and pastas are also available, and most everything is spiced with fresh-picked herbs from the restaurant's own organic garden.

Flagler Grill. 47 SW Flagler Ave. (just before the Roosevelt Bridge), downtown Stuart. ☎ **561/221-9517.** Reservations strongly suggested in season. Main courses $17–$25. AE, MC, V. Winter daily 5:30–10pm. Off-season Thurs–Sat 5:30–9:30pm. Lounge and bar open to 11:30pm. AMERICAN/FLORIDA REGIONAL. Note restaurant and bar are nonsmoking.

In the heart of historic downtown, this Manhattan-style bistro serves up classics with a twist. The dishes are not so unusual as to alienate the conservative pink-shirted golfers who frequent the place, yet they're fresh and light enough to quench the appetites of the more adventurous—for example, the saffron and mushroom pasta with Cajun shrimp and roasted tomatoes. The menu changes every few weeks, so see what your server recommends. It's hard to go wrong with any of the many salads, pastas, fishes, or delectable beef choices. The desserts, too, are worth the calories.

MODERATE

Black Marlin. 53 W. Osceola St., downtown Stuart. ☎ **561/286-3126.** Reservations not accepted. Salads and sandwiches $4–$8; full meals $9–$24. AE, MC, V. Mon–Thurs 5–10pm, Fri–Sat 5–11pm (the bar is open later). FLORIDA REGIONAL.

Although it sports the look and feel of an English pub, the Black Marlin offers regional flavor. The salmon BLT is typical of the dishes here—grilled salmon on a toasted bun topped with bacon, lettuce, tomato, and coleslaw. Designer pizzas are topped with shrimp, roasted red peppers, and the like; and main dishes, all of which are served with vegetables and potatoes, include lobster tail with a honey-mustard sauce, and a charcoal-grilled chicken breast served on radicchio with caramelized onions.

Conchy Joe's Seafood. 3945 NE Indian River Dr. (½ mile from the Jensen Beach Causeway), Jensen Beach. ☎ **561/334-1130.** Main courses $12–$20. AE, DISC, MC, V. Daily 11:30am–2:30pm and 5–10pm (happy hour daily 3–6pm). SEAFOOD.

Known for fresh seafood and Old Florida hospitality, Conchy Joe's enjoys an excellent reputation that's far bigger than the restaurant itself. Dining is either indoors, at red-and-white cloth-covered tables, or on a covered patio overlooking the St. Lucie River. The restaurant features a wide variety of freshly shucked shellfish and daily-catch selections that are baked, broiled, or fried. Beer is the drink of choice here, though other beverages and a full bar are available. Conchy Joe's has been the most active place in Jensen Beach since it opened in 1983. The large bar is especially popular at night and during weekday happy hours.

INEXPENSIVE

✪ **Bubba's Fish Camp.** 421 S. Federal Hwy. (at south side of Roosevelt Bridge), Stuart. ☎ **561/220-3747.** Full meals $8–$10; seafood specials $8–$12. AE, MC, V. Daily 11am–10pm and later on weekends. Call for details on weekend breakfasts. SEAFOOD/SOUTHERN.

Run by the same family who created the lovely B&B Home Place and just a stone's throw from there is an ultracasual spot designed to resemble an old-Florida fish camp. Don't miss the great crawfish gumbo, corn bread, catfish, creamy spinach, hush puppies (fried cornmeal), and fried green tomatoes, too. After 4pm, you'll find bargain deals on hearty Southern classics like meat loaf, baked Virginia ham with red-eye gravy, fried chicken, and pork chops. Each includes a choice of delicious side dishes. Fresh and crispy onion rings are actually served on tiny bathroom plunger handles. Locals and highway travelers line up outside the screen porch to get into this rustic eatery just at the base of the new Roosevelt Bridge.

✪ **Nature's Way Cafe.** 25 SW Osceola St., in the Post Office Arcade, Stuart. ☎ **561/220-7306.** Sandwiches and salads $4–$7; juices and shakes $1–$3. No credit cards. Mon–Fri 10am–4pm, Sat 11am–3pm. HEALTH FOOD.

This lovely, clean and green dining room has dozens of little tables, a few bar stools, and some sidewalk seating, too. A sort of health-food deli, Nature's Way excels in putting out quick and nutritious meals like huge salads, vegetarian sandwiches, and frozen yogurts. Try some of the homemade baked goods. Sit outside on quaint Osceola Street or ask them to pack your lunch for you to take to the beach.

STUART & JENSEN BEACH AFTER DARK

Local restaurants serve as the nightlife centers of Stuart and Jensen Beach. And "night" ends pretty early here, even on the weekends. The bar at the Black Marlin (see "Where to Dine," above) is popular with local professionals and tourists alike.

No list of Jensen nightlife would be complete without mention of Conchy Joe's Seafood (see "Where to Dine," above), one of the region's most active spots. Inside, locals chug beer and watch a large-screen TV, while outside on the waterfront patio live bands perform a few nights a week for a raucous crowd of dancers. Happy hours, weekdays from 3 to 6pm, draw large crowds with low-priced drinks and snacks. No cover.

In a strip mall just outside of downtown, you'll find pickup trucks as far as the eye can see parked outside the **Rock 'n' Horse,** 1580 S. Federal Hwy. (U.S. 1), Stuart (☎ **561/286-1281**). It's a real locals' country-and-western spot that rocks, especially on Tuesday night, when women drink all night for $5. Bring your hat and boots for line dancing, beer drinking, and a good time in one of the only real late-night spots in town. Cover varies.

The centerpiece of Stuart's slowly expanding cultural offerings is the newly restored **Lyric Theater,** at 59 SW Flagler Ave. (☎ **561/286-7827**). This beautiful 1920s-era, 600-seat theater hosts a variety of shows and films throughout the year. Programs run the gamut from amateur plays to top-name theatrical shows, poetry readings, and concerts.

2 Port St. Lucie, Fort Pierce & North Hutchinson Island

7 miles N of Stuart

Port St. Lucie and Fort Pierce, two Old Florida towns, thrive on sportfishing. A seemingly endless row of piers juts out along the Intracoastal Waterway and the Fort Pierce Inlet for both river and ocean runs. Here visitors can also dive, snorkel, beachcomb, and sunbathe in an area that hasn't been visited by the overdevelopment that has altered its neighbors to the south and north.

Most sightseeing takes place along the main beach road. Driving along Fla. A1A on Hutchinson Island, you'll discover several secluded beach clubs interspersed with 1950s-style homes, a few small inns, grungy raw bars, and a few high-rise condominiums. Much of this island is government owned and kept undeveloped for the public's enjoyment.

ESSENTIALS
The **St. Lucie County Chamber of Commerce,** 2200 Virginia Ave., Fort Pierce, FL 34982 (☎ **561/595-9999**), is the region's main source of information. Another location is at 1626 SE Port St. Lucie Blvd., in Port St. Lucie. These are open Monday through Friday from 9am to 5pm.

BEACHES & NATURE PRESERVES
North Hutchinson Island's beaches are the most pristine in this area. You won't find restaurants, hotels, or shopping; instead, spend your time swimming, surfing, fishing, and diving. Most of the beaches are private along this stretch of the Atlantic Ocean. Thankfully, the state has set aside some of the best areas for the public.

Fort Pierce Inlet State Recreation Area (☎ **561/468-3985**) is a stunning 340-acre park with almost 4,000 feet of sandy shores that was once the training ground for the original navy frogmen. A short nature trail leads through a canopy of live oaks, cabbage palms, sea grapes, and strangler figs. The western side of the area has swamps of red mangroves that are home to fiddler crabs, osprey, and a multitude of wading birds. Jack Island State Preserve, in the State Recreation Area, is popular with bird watchers and offers hiking and nature trails. Jutting out into the Indian River, the mangrove-covered peninsula contains several marked trails, varying in distance from a half mile to over 4 miles. The trails go through mangrove forests and lead to a short observation tower.

The best beach here is called Jetty Park, in the northern part of the park. Families enjoy the large picnic areas and barbecue grills. There are rest rooms and outdoor showers, and swimmers are looked after by lifeguards.

The park is located at 905 Shorewinds Dr., north of Fort Pierce Inlet. To get there from I-95, take Exit 66 east (Route 68) and turn left onto U.S. 1 north; in about 2 miles, you will see signs to Fla. A1A and the North Bridge Causeway. Turn right on A1A and cross over to North Hutchinson Island. Admission is $3.25 per vehicle, and it's open daily from 8am to sunset.

SPECTATOR SPORTS & OUTDOOR PURSUITS

BASEBALL   The **New York Mets** hold spring training in Port St. Lucie from late February through March at the **Thomas J. White Stadium,** 525 NW Peacock Blvd. (☎ **561/871-2115**). Tickets cost $9 to $12. From April through August, their farm team, the Port St. Lucie Mets, plays home games in the stadium.

FISHING   The **Fort Pierce City Marina,** 1 Avenue A, Fort Pierce (☎ **561/ 464-1245**), has more than a dozen charter captains who keep their motors running for anglers anxious to catch a few. The price starts at $150 per person for half-day tours, depending on the season. Charters are organized on an as-desired basis. In general, plan to arrive very early in the morning (by 6am) before all the other early birds.

GOLF   The most notable courses in Port St. Lucie are at the **PGA Golf Club at the Reserve** (☎ **561/467-1300**), at 1916 Perfect Dr. PGA's first public golf course opened in January 1996 and was designed by Tom Fazio. The club will soon complete its fourth 18-hole course. The South Course, a classic Old Florida–style course, is set on wetlands and offers views of native wildlife. It is the most popular. Greens fees are usually under $60.

SEEING THE SIGHTS

Harbor Branch Oceanographic Institution. 5600 U.S. 1 N., Fort Pierce. ☎ **800/ 333-4264** or 561/465-2400. Admission $6 adults, $4 children 3–13, free for children 5 and under. Mon–Sat 10am–4pm (tours scheduled at 10am, noon, and 2pm), Sun noon–5pm (tours scheduled at noon and 2pm). Arrive at least 20 min. before tour.

Harbor Branch is a working nonprofit scientific institute that studies oceanic resources and welcomes visitors on regularly scheduled tours. The first stop is the J. Seward Johnson Marine Education Center, which houses institute-built submersibles that are used to conduct marine research at depths of up to 3,000 feet. A video details current research projects, and several large aquariums simulate the environments of the Indian River Lagoon and a saltwater reef. Tourgoers are then shuttled by minibus to the Aqua-Culture Farming Center, a research facility containing shallow tanks growing seaweed and other oceanic plants. The new Lagoon Explorer Cruise, examining the Indian River Lagoon, departs at 10am, noon, and 2pm; the price is $15 adults, $12 children 3 to 13.

UDT-SEAL Museum. 3300 N. S.R. A1A, Fort Pierce. ☎ **561/595-5845.** Admission $4 adults, $1.25 children, free for children 6 and under. Mon–Sat 10am–4pm, Sun noon–4pm. Closed Mon in off-season.

Florida is full of unique museums, but none is more curious than the UDT-SEAL Museum, a most peculiar tribute to the secret forces of the U.S. Navy frogmen and their successors, the SEAL teams. Chronological displays trace the history of these clandestine divers and detail their most important achievements. The best exhibits are those of the intricately detailed equipment used by the navy's most elite members.

A BOAT TOUR

The **St. Lucie River Tours,** 500 E. Prima Vista Blvd. (☎ **561/871-2817**), offers intriguing tours of St. Lucie River twice daily (at 10:45am and again at 1pm). The 2-hour tours go through winding waterways that are home to hundreds of wading birds and reptiles. This historical and wildlife tour is well worth the $15 for adults and $7 for children under 12.

WHERE TO STAY

The Port St. Lucie mainland is pretty run-down, but there are a number of inexpensive hotel options on scenic Hutchinson Island that are both charming and well priced. Probably the best option is the **Hampton Inn** (☎ 800/426-7866 or 561/460-9855), 2831 Reynolds Dr., which is relatively new and beautifully maintained. However, if you want to be closer to the water, try the **Days Inn Hutchinson Island,** 1920 Seaway Dr. (☎ 800/325-2525 or 561/461-8737), a small motel that sits along the intracoastal inlet and is simple but very well kept.

Budget travelers will be glad to know about the **Edgewater Motel and Apartments,** 1160 Seaway Dr. (next door to and under the same ownership as the Harbor Light Inn), Fort Pierce (☎ 800/286-1745 or 561/468-3555). Motel rooms start at less than $60 in high season, and efficiencies are also available from $80. Guests can enjoy a private pool, shuffleboard courts, and a nearby fishing pier.

EXPENSIVE

Club Med—Sandpiper. 3500 SE Morningside Blvd., Port St. Lucie, FL 34952. ☎ 800/CLUB-MED or 561/335-4400. Fax 561/398-5101. www.clubmed.com. 331 units. A/C TV TEL. $170–$280 per person, based on double occupancy. Off-season $150–$275 per person, based on double occupancy. Rates include 3 meals per day. AE, MC, V. From U.S. 1 south, turn left onto Westmoreland Blvd.; turn left onto Pine Valley Rd.; the resort entrance is straight ahead.

The Sandpiper is not one of the French-owned company's flagship properties. It's a decent resort housed in buildings that could use a major overhaul. A former Hilton Hotel, the 400-acre resort was purchased by Club Med in 1985 and marketed to Europeans looking for a Florida getaway. They come in droves with all the kids and nannies for a sunny, active vacation with meals for a reasonable prepaid price. The drawback is that guests are 20 minutes to the nearest beach. On the grounds there is plenty of diversion, like golf, tennis, and waterskiing, sailing, and boating on the Indian River. There's even a circus school.

As in most other Club Meds, the rooms are sparse and small, but pleasant enough. All come with in-room safes, large closets, tiled bathrooms, and minirefrigerators.

Dining/Diversions: All-you-can-eat buffets are served in the main dining room three times a day. In addition, La Fontana serves late breakfasts and Italian cuisine at dinner, and a French restaurant is open for dinner. Excellent live entertainment is provided in bars and a showroom nightly. Another bonus is free wine and beer at lunch and dinner.

Amenities: Laundry services, massage, baby-sitting. Five outdoor heated pools, kids' pool, fitness center, three golf courses (36-hole, 18-hole, and 9-hole), 19 tennis courts (9 of which are lighted), circus workshops, Ping-Pong and billiards, children's center and programs, water-sports equipment, self-service Laundromat, tour desk, boutique, conference rooms, car-rental desk, waterskiing, volleyball courts, basketball, softball, soccer, boccie, exercise classes, in-line skating.

MODERATE

Dockside–Harbor Light Inn. 1160 Seaway Dr., Fort Pierce, Hutchinson Island, FL 34949. ☎ 800/286-1745 or 561/468-3555. 64 units. A/C MINIBAR TV TEL. Winter $50–$95 guest rooms, $67–$95 efficiencies. Off-season $43–$84 guest rooms and efficiencies. AE, CB, DC, DISC, MC, V. From I-95, exit at 66A east to U.S. 1 north to Seaway Dr.

Fronting the Intracoastal Waterway, the Harbor Light is a great choice for boating and fishing enthusiasts, offering 15 boat slips and two private fishing piers. The hotel itself carries on the nautical theme with pierlike wooden stairs and rope railings. While not exactly captain's quarters, the rooms, simply decorated with pastel colors and small wall prints, are attractive, especially since a thorough renovation completed in 1999. Higher-priced rooms have either waterfront balconies or small kitchenettes that contain a coffeemaker, a refrigerator, an oven, and a toaster. Facilities include an outdoor heated pool with a large sundeck and a self-service Laundromat.

Mellon Patch Inn. 3601 N. Fla. A1A, North Hutchinson Island, FL 34949. ☎ **800/ MLN-PTCH** or 561/461-5231. Fax 561/464-6463. www.sunet.net/mlnptch. 4 units. A/C TV TEL. $85–$120 double. Rates include breakfast. No smoking and no children. AE, DISC, MC, V.

Opened in mid-1994 by innkeepers Andrea and Arthur Mellon, the Mellon Patch offers just four bright rooms in what looks like a single-family house, each with a large bathroom and sturdy soundproof walls.

The public living room is nicer than any of the small guest rooms. It's designed with a two-story vaulted ceiling, a fireplace, and lots of windows that overlook the Indian River. A gourmet breakfast that might include waffles topped with strawberries and pecans, chocolate-chip pancakes, or spinach soufflé is served here each morning. The best part is there are a public beach and free tennis courts across the street.

○ **Villa Nina Island Beach Bed & Breakfast.** 3851 North Fla. A1A, North Hutchinson Island, FL 34949. ☎ and fax **561/467-8673.** www.gate.net/~villanin@gate.net. 4 units. Winter $115–$185. Off-season $105–$175. DISC, MC, V. No smoking.

A more private option just down the road from the Mellon Patch is Villa Nina, in another simple but brand-new home on the river's edge. Innkeepers Nina and Glenn live in the main house and have built rooms along the back, each with a private entrance and either a fully equipped kitchen or kitchenette. Enjoy breakfast delivered to your room or near the outdoor heated pool. Guests are free to use the laundry facilities, and the canoes and rowboats for river rides on this stunning 8-acre property. The nearby casino cruise ship called the *Midnight Gambler* is also available to guests (☎ **561/464-7773**), which includes a 5-hour tour with food and drink.

The honeymoon suite in the back is the largest and brightest of all the pleasant rooms. Night-lit tennis and basketball courts, a public beach, and nature trails are just across the street.

WHERE TO DINE

There are a number of good seafood restaurants in the Fort Pierce and St. Lucie area, but it's also easy to drive to Stuart for more diverse dining options. See section 1 of this chapter for recommendations in Stuart.

MODERATE

○ **Harbortown Fish House.** 1930 Harbortown Dr., Fort Pierce. ☎ **561/466-8732.** Reservations accepted. Main courses $14–$20. AE, DISC, MC, V. Sun–Thurs 11:30am–9pm, Fri–Sat 5–10pm. SEAFOOD.

You have to drive to the end of the harbor to reach this open-air waterfront fish house. It's a rustic place with outdoor tables overlooking the port, and you might be surprised to learn that it serves the area's best and freshest seafood. The menu is posted on white boards throughout the dining room and might include jumbo shrimp cocktail or New England clam chowder. The list of main courses is long and contains both fish and meat dishes. There are angel-hair pasta with scallop- and anchovy-stuffed mushrooms, roast Muscovy duck with wild-mushroom risotto, and charcoal-grilled pepper-crusted tuna served over sautéed escarole.

○ **P.V. Martin's.** 5150 N. Fla. A1A (North Hutchinson Island), Fort Pierce. ☎ **561/ 569-0700.** Reservations recommended. Main courses $9–$20. AE, MC, V. Mon–Sat 11am–3:30pm and 5–9pm, Sun 10:30am–2:30pm and 5–8:30pm. SEAFOOD/AMERICAN.

This relatively elegant eatery with an eclectic American menu is tops in Fort Pierce. The wood floors, beamed ceilings, tiled-top tables, and rattan chairs would be nice anywhere, but here they look out, through floor-to-ceiling windows, onto sweeping ocean vistas. At night, the room is warmed by a huge central stone fireplace, and on weekends there's live entertainment in the adjacent bar.

Surf-and-turf dinners run the gamut from crab-stuffed shrimp and grouper baked with bananas and almonds to Brie- and asparagus-stuffed chicken breast and barbecued baby back ribs. An excellent selection of appetizers includes escargots in mushroom caps and a succulent fried soft-shell crab (available in season).

Theo Thudpucker's Raw Bar and Seafood Restaurant. 2025 Seaway Dr., Fort Pierce. ☎ **561/465-1078.** Reservations not accepted. Main courses $8–$24. MC, V. Mon–Thurs 11:30am–9:30pm, Fri–Sat 11:30am–11pm, Sun 1–9:30pm. SEAFOOD.

Located in a little building by the beach, wallpapered with maps and newspapers, Thudpucker's is a straightforward chowder bar. There's not much more to the dining room than one long bar and a few simple tables. Prominently placed signs attest to the food's purity: Both clams and oysters are packed with ice and are not opened until you place your order. Please be patient. Chowder and stews, often made with sherry and half-and-half, make excellent starters or light meals. The most recommendable (and filling) dinner dishes are sautéed scallops, deviled crabs, and deep-fried Okeechobee catfish.

PORT ST. LUCIE/FORT PIERCE AFTER DARK

Besides a few heavy-drinking bars, waterside restaurants (see P.V. Martin's, above), and hotel lounges, the nightlife of Port St. Lucie and Fort Pierce takes place in the neighboring towns north and south of here. See sections 1 and 3 of this chapter for nightspots in Stuart, Jensen Beach, Vero Beach, and Sebastian.

3 Vero Beach & Sebastian

85 miles SE of Orlando, 130 miles N of Miami

Vero Beach and Sebastian are located at the northern tip of the Treasure Coast region in Indian River County. These two beach towns are populated with folks who knew Miami and Fort Lauderdale in the days before massive high-rises and overcrowding. They appreciate the area's small-town feel, and that's exactly the area's appeal for visitors as well: a laid-back, relaxed atmosphere, friendly people, and friendlier prices.

A crowd of well-tanned surfers from all over the state descend on the region, especially the Sebastian Inlet, to catch some of the state's biggest waves. Water-sports enthusiasts enjoy the area's fine diving, surfing, and windsurfing. Anglers are in heaven here. In spring, baseball buffs can catch some action from the L.A. Dodgers as they train in exhibition games.

ESSENTIALS

The **Indian River County Tourist Council,** 1216 21st St., Vero Beach, FL 32961 (☎ **561/567-3491;** fax 561/778-3181; www.vero-beach.fl.us/chamber), will send visitors an incredibly detailed information packet on the entire county, which includes Vero Beach and Sebastian and Fellsmere. You'll find a detailed full-color map of the area, a comprehensive listing of upcoming events, a hotel guide, and more.

BEACHES & OUTDOOR PURSUITS

BEACHES   You'll find plenty of free and open beachfront along the coast. Most beaches are uncrowded and are open from 7am until 10pm.

South Beach Park, on South Ocean Drive, at the end of Marigold Lane, is a busy, developed, lifeguarded beach with picnic tables, restrooms, and showers. It's known as one of the best swimming beaches and also attracts a young crowd that plays volley-ball and Frisbee. A well-laid-out nature walk takes you into beautiful secluded trails.

At the very north tip of the island, ✪ **Sebastian Inlet** has flat sandy beaches with lots of facilities, including kayak, paddleboat, and canoe rentals; a well-stocked surf shop; picnic tables; and a snack shop. The winds seem to stir up the surf with no jetty to stop their swells, to the delight of surfers and boarders, who get here early to catch the big waves. Campers enjoy fully equipped sites in a woody area. Admission to the Sebastian Inlet State Recreation Area, 9700 S. A1A, Melbourne, is $3.25 per car and $1 for those who walk or bike in.

FISHING   Capt. Jack Jackson works 7 days a week out of **Vero's Tackle and Sport-shop,** 57–59 Royal Palm Point (☎ 561/567-6550), taking anglers out on his 25-foot boat for private river excursions. Captain Jackson provides all the equipment. Half-day jaunts on the Indian River cost $175 for two people (the minimum required for a charter).

You can also head up to Sebastian, where **Capt. Hiram's,** 1606 Indian River Rd. (☎ 800/797-1582 or 561/589-5433), offers private sailboat charters on the Indian River. In addition, it runs a party boat, the *Capt. Kidd II,* which heads out daily for a full day of bottom fishing for grouper, snapper, and more (it's usually only a half day on Mon). The cost is $35 per person ($40 per person will get you your rod, reel, and bait). You can bring your own lunch and beer on board, and someone will be available to clean your fish for you. Call ahead to reserve your place.

Many other charters, guides, party boats, and tackle shops operate in this area. Ask at your hotel for suggestions, or call the chamber of commerce for a list of local operators.

GOLF   Hard-core golfers insist that of the dozens of courses in the area, only a handful are worth their plot of grass.

Set on rolling hills with uncluttered views of sand dunes and sky, the **Sandridge Golf Club** (☎ 561/770-5000), at 5300 73rd St., Vero Beach, offers two par-72 18-holers. The Dunes is a long course with rolling fairways, and the newer Lakes course has lots of water. Both charge less than $50, including a cart. There is a small snack bar selling beer and sandwiches. Reservations are recommended and are taken 2 days in advance.

Though less challenging, the **Sebastian Municipal Golf Course** (☎ 561/589-6800), at 1010 E. Airport Dr., is a good 18-hole par-72. It's scenic, well maintained, and a great bargain. Greens fees are $33 with a cart and about half that if you want to play 9 holes after 1:30pm.

Also, see Dodgertown, below.

SURFING   See Sebastian Inlet details under "Beaches," above. Also, consider the beach north of the Barber Bridge (S.R. 70), where waves are slightly gentler and the scene less competitive, and Wabasso Beach, Fla. A1A and County Road 510, a secluded area near Disney's resort where lots of teenage locals congregate, especially when the weather gets rough.

TENNIS   There are dozens of tennis courts around Vero Beach and Sebastian, many of which are at hotels and resorts. Check the phone book, or try **Riverside Park,** 350 Dahlia Lane, at Royal Palm Boulevard at the east end of Barber Bridge in Vero Beach (☎ 561/231-4787). This popular park has 10 hard courts (6 lighted) that can be rented for $3 per person per hour, and two racquetball courts with reasonable rates as well. Reservations are accepted up to 24 hours in advance. On the premises, you'll also find nature trails and other facilities.

SEEING THE SIGHTS

Environmental Learning Center. 255 Live Oak Dr. (just off the 510 Causeway), Wabasso Island. ☎ 561/589-5050. Free admission. Tues–Fri 10am–4pm, Sat 9am–noon, Sun 1–4pm.

The Indian River is not really a river at all, but a large brackish lagoon that's home to a greater variety of species than any other estuary in North America. The privately funded Environmental Learning Center was created to protect the local habitat and educate visitors about their environment. Situated on 51 island acres, the center features dozens of hands-on exhibits that are geared to both children and adults. There are live touch tanks, exhibits, and microscopes for viewing the smallest sea life close up. The best thing to do here is join one of the center's interpretive canoe trips, offered by reservation only. The cost for these is $10 for adults, $5 for children. Phone for details.

Indian River Citrus Museum. 2140 14th Ave., Vero Beach. ☎ 561/770-2263. Admission $1 donation. Tues–Fri 10am–4pm.

The tiny Indian River Citrus Museum exhibits artifacts relating to the history of the citrus industry, from its initial boom in the late 1800s to the present. Also, a small grove has taped information on the varieties of fruits there. The gift shop sells unique citrus-themed gift items, along with, of course, ready-to-ship fruit.

McKee Botanical Garden. 350 U.S. 1, Vero Beach. ☎ 561/794-0601.

This impressive attraction was originally opened in 1932 and featured a virtual jungle of orchids, exotic and native trees, monkeys, and birds. After years of neglect, it was placed on the National Register of Historic Places in 1998. It is currently being reconstructed and is due to reopen by the winter of 2000.

✪ **McLarty Treasure Museum.** 13180 N. A1A, Sebastian Inlet State Recreation Area, Vero Beach. ☎ 561/589-2147. Admission $1, children under 6 free. Daily 10am–4:30pm.

Erected on the actual site of a salvaging camp from a wreck in 1715, this quaint little museum is full of interesting history. It may not have the vast treasures of the nearby Fisher museum, but it does offer a very engaging 45-minute video describing the many aspects of treasure hunting. You'll also see household items salvaged from the Spanish fleet and dioramas of life in the 18th century. For the price, you can't beat it.

Mel Fisher's Treasure Museum. 1322 U.S. 1, Sebastian. ☎ 561/589-9874. Admission $5 adults, $4 seniors over 55, $1.50 children 6–12, free for children 5 and under. Mon–Sat 10am–5pm, Sun noon–5pm.

Here's where you can see millions of dollars of treasures from the fateful fleet that went down in 1715. Though not as extensive as the museum in Key West, this exhibit includes gold coins, bars, and Spanish artifacts that are worth a look. Also, the preservation lab shows how the goods are extricated, cleaned, and preserved.

DODGERTOWN

Vero is the winter home of the **Los Angeles Dodgers** (at least for the time being; there's been talk of a move), and the town hosts the team in grand style. The 450-acre compound at 3901 26th St. (☎ 561/569-4900) encompasses two golf courses, a conference center, a country club, a movie theater, and a recreation room. You can watch afternoon exhibition games during the winter (usually between mid-Feb and the end of Mar) in the comfortable 6,500-seat outdoor stadium. Even if the game sells out, you can sprawl on the lawn for just $5. The stadium has never turned away an eager fan.

Even when spring training is over, you can still catch a game; the Dodgers's farm team, the Vero Beach Dodgers, has a full season of minor-league baseball in summer.

Admission to the complex is free; tickets to games are $5 to $9. The complex is open daily from 9am to 5pm; game time is usually 1pm. From I-95 take Exit S.R. 60 east to 43rd Avenue, and turn left; continue to 26th Street, and turn right.

SHOPPING

Ocean Boulevard and Cardinal Drive are Vero's two main shopping streets. Both are near the beach and lined with specialty boutiques, including antique and home-decorating shops.

If you want to send fruit back home, the local source is **Hale Indian River Groves,** 615 Beachland Blvd. (☎ **561/231-1752**), a shipper of local citrus and jams since 1947. Note that it is closed 2 to 3 months a year, usually from summer through early fall, depending on the year's crop; the season runs generally from November through Easter. There are four locations throughout Vero Beach.

The **Horizon Outlet Center,** at S.R. 60 and I-95, Vero Beach (☎ **877/ GO-OUTLET** or 561/770-6171), contains more than 80 discount stores selling name-brand shoes, kitchenware, books, clothing, and anything else you could want. The mall is open Monday to Saturday from 9am to 8pm and Sunday from 11am to 6pm.

The **Indian River Mall** (☎ **561/770-6255**), 6200 20th St. (S.R. 60 about 5 miles east of I-95), which opened its doors in November 1996, is a big deal in Vero Beach. This monster mall has all the big national chains, like The Gap, Structure, and Victoria's Secret, as well as several large department stores, and is open Monday through Saturday from 10am to 9pm and Sunday from noon to 6pm.

WHERE TO STAY

You can choose to stay on the mainland or at the beach. Although the beaches in many areas have eroded, leaving only narrow strips of sand, most areas offer pristine beach-fronts where turtles lay eggs and sand crabs scurry around. As you might expect, the beachfront accommodations are a bit more expensive—but, I think, worth it. There are deals to be had in the chain hotels and some lovely privately owned properties, especially on weekdays and during off-season. Both **The Palm Court Inn** ☎ **800/ 245-3297** or 561/231-2800), at 3244 Ocean Dr., and the **Holiday Inn Oceanside** (☎ **800/465-4329** or 561/231-2300), at 3384 Ocean Dr., offer oceanfront rooms and suites at comparable prices (from around $80 for a standard room off-season to $185 for an oceanfront suite). The Holiday Inn may be a better choice since it offers discounts to AAA members and its restaurant and lounge directly face the ocean. The Palm Court (formerly a Days Inn) was thoroughly renovated in 1998. Also, a great spot to know, especially if you are planning to fish, is **Capt. Hiram's** (see "Fishing," above, and also "Vero Beach & Sebastian After Dark," below), where there are four clean and cozy rooms available adjacent to the restaurant and overlooking the water. Rates are between $80 and $110.

Comfortable and inexpensive chain options near the Vero Beach Outlet Center off Rte. 60 include a **Holiday Inn Express** (☎ **800/465-4329** or 561/567-2500), opened in June of 1998, and a slightly older **Hampton Inn** (☎ **800/426-7866** or 561/770-4299). Rates for both run between $70 and $80 and include breakfast and free local phone calls.

EXPENSIVE

✪ **Disney's Vero Beach Resort.** 9250 Island Grove Terrace, Vero Beach, FL 32963. ☎ **800/359-8000** or 561/234-2000. Fax 561/234-2030. 112 units, 60 cottages. A/C TV TEL. From $140 inn room (weekday rates sometimes as low as $99 per night); from $160 inn-ocean view/studio; from $220 one-bedroom villa; from $290 two-bedroom villa; from $610 three-bedroom beach cottage. AE, MC, V. From I-95 take Exit 69 (512 east); turn right onto County Rd. 510 east; turn right onto S. Fla. A1A.

This is Disney, without the rides or lines.

Situated on the tip of one of the most pristine beaches on the coast, this timeshare resort takes advantage of its setting by offering truly exciting children's programs like canoe adventures, poolside miniature golf, stories around a campfire, a trip to a working cattle ranch, and stargazing from a powerful telescope. The best part is a large lagoon-like pool with a huge winding slide that elicits squeals of delight from kids and adults alike. And also, for younger kids, a pirate ship that squirts water is a fun way to cool off.

The sprawling complex, opened in 1995, is designed to resemble a turn-of-the-century Florida beach community, complete with sand-washed buildings and faux-worn furniture. The beachside cottages are huge and tasteful. The villas have fully equipped kitchens with dishwashers and microwaves.

Dining/Diversions: The resort offers some of the best food in the region. An elegant steak house, Sonya's, serves dinner from an eclectic, Florida-inspired menu with superb steaks, pecan-crusted salmon, and salads. In addition, a casual restaurant for lunch and dinner serves interesting pizzas, sandwiches, salads, roasted vegetables, and pastas. A picturesque lounge, which overlooks the ocean and hosts live music most nights, is popular with guests and sometimes even locals. A poolside snack bar rounds out this resort's food and drink options.

Amenities: Concierge, room service, laundry services for inn rooms, dry cleaning, newspapers in lobby, express checkout, secretarial services during business hours, baby-sitting, free morning coffee in lobby. Large theme-based pool with two-story pool slide, as well as a treasure-ship pool deck, beach, health club, Jacuzzi, sauna, sundeck, nature trails, kitchenettes, VCRs, video rentals, shuffleboard, croquet lawn, two night-lit tennis courts, water-sports equipment, jogging track, tee times available at local courses, nine-hole miniature golf, basketball half-court, volleyball, tetherball, game room, extensive children's programs, conference rooms, business center, self-service Laundromat, tour desk/guest services, gift shop, general store.

Doubletree Guest Suites. 3500 Ocean Dr., Vero Beach, FL 32963. ☎ **800/841-5666** or 561/231-5666. Fax 561/234-4866. 55 units. A/C TV TEL. Winter $210–$245 one-bedroom suite; $265–$295 two-bedroom suite. Off-season $110–$150 one-bedroom suite; $165 two-bedroom suite. AE, CB, DC, DISC, MC, V.

Vero's best all-suite hotel, part of the Doubletree chain, is located directly on the beach and is close to local restaurants and shops. First-class accommodations are located in a modern four-story building. The guest rooms, which were renovated in late 1996, are unremarkable, but clean and attractive. What the nearly identical suites lack in character they make up for in content. The rooms are equipped with small refrigerators and coffeemakers, two phones, and modern baths that include hair dryers.

Dining/Diversions: The Lanai Room is open for breakfast only, daily from 7am to 10pm. The Seabreeze pool bar is open daily for lunch, dinner, and cocktails.

Amenities: Room service, dry cleaning, laundry service, newspaper delivery, express checkout. VCRs and video rentals for additional charge, outdoor heated swimming pool and kids' pool, beach, access to nearby health club, Jacuzzi, self-service Laundromat, conference rooms, sundeck.

MODERATE

Driftwood Resort. 3150 Ocean Dr., Vero Beach, FL 32963. ☎ **561/231-0550.** Fax 561/234-1981. 100 units. A/C TV TEL. Winter $99–$230 double; from $170–$230 two-bedroom suite. Off-season $60–$150 double; from $130–$150 two-bedroom suite. AE, MC, V.

Originally planned in the 1930s as a private estate by local legend Waldo Sexton, the Driftwood was opened to the public after several travelers stopped to inquire about renting a room here. Today the hotel's rooms and public areas are filled with nautical knickknacks collected by Sexton on his travels all over the world.

All the guest rooms are different. Some feature terra-cotta–tiled floors and lighter furniture, while others have a more rustic feel with hardwoods and antiques. Each accommodation has its own bath and few frills. The resort, which was recently listed on the National Register of Historic Places, offers two outdoor heated pools, a some-times-narrow beach, a bicycle trail, dry-cleaning services, and VCR and video rentals.

✪ **Islander Motel.** 3101 Ocean Dr., Vero Beach, FL 32963. ☎ **800/952-5886** or 561/ 231-4431. 16 units. A/C TV TEL. Winter $105–$125 double. Off-season $60–$90 double. Efficiencies cost $10 extra. AE, MC, V.

Resident owner Tom Collins runs one of the most comfortable and welcoming inns in the area. Well located in downtown Vero Beach, this motel is just a short walk to the beach, restaurants, and shops. Every guest room has a small refrigerator and either a king-size bed or two double beds. The accommodations are designed in a Caribbean motif with bright fabrics and white rattan furniture. There are a pool and a barbecue area in the handsomely landscaped central courtyard, along with a small walk-up cafe.

INEXPENSIVE

Davis House Inn. 607 Davis St., Sebastian, FL 32958. ☎ **561/589-4114.** Fax 561/ 589-1722. 12 units. Winter $69–$79 double. Off-season $59–$79 double. AC TV TEL. Rates include continental breakfast. Weekly and monthly rates available. AE, DISC, MC, V. From I-95, take Exit 69 east to Indian River Dr., turn left, go 1¼ mile to Davis St., turn left.

Each of the dozen rooms in this contemporary, three-story, blue-and-white bed-and-breakfast on the mainland has a private entrance and doorfront parking. The rooms are large and clean, although somewhat plain, and each has a king-size bed, a pull-out sofa, and a small kitchenette, making the rooms popular with long-term guests. The bathrooms are equally ample and have plenty of counter space. There are a large wooden deck for sunbathing, a sunny second-floor breakfast room, and a self-service Laundromat. It's a bit out of the way but is within walking distance to some nearby restaurants; the beach is a 10-minute drive.

✪ **Sea Turtle Inn & Azalea Lane Apartments.** 835 Azalea Lane, Vero Beach, FL 32963. ☎ **561/234-0788.** Fax 561/234-0717. www.vero-beach.fl.us/seaturtle@vero-beach.fl.us. 21 units. AC TV. Winter $79–$89 double. Off-season $59–$79. Weekly and monthly rates available. MC, V. From I-95, go east on Rte. 60 (about 10 mi.) to Cardinal Dr.; turn right.

This two-part property offers the very best value on the beach (just 2 blocks from the ocean). The 1950s motel and an adjacent apartment building have been fully reno-vated by Joe Police and outfitted with understated but efficient furnishings. You won't find any fancy amenities (or even a phone for that matter, unless you request one), but most units have a microwave, a coffeemaker, a toaster, cable TV, and a small refriger-ator. The properties share a small pool and sundeck. Book early. Especially in season, it fills up quickly with long-term visitors.

CAMPING

This area is popular with campers, who can choose from nearly a dozen sites throughout Vero and Sebastian. If you aren't camping at the scenic and very popular Sebastian Inlet (see "Beaches," above), then try the **Vero Beach KOA RV Park,** 8850 U.S. 1, Wabasso (☎ **561/589-5665**). This 120-site campground is 2 miles from the ocean and the Intracoastal Waterway and one quarter of a mile from the Indian River, a big draw for the crowd of regular fishing fanatics. There are running water and electricity, as well as showers, a shop, and hookups for RVs. Rates range from $20 to $24 per site, and $19 for tents. To get there, take I-95 to Exit 69 east; at U.S. 1 turn left.

WHERE TO DINE
EXPENSIVE
✪ **Chez Yannick.** 1605 S. Ocean Dr., Vero Beach. ☎ **561/234-4115.** Reservations recommended. Main courses $15–$28; fixed-price dinner $19–$21 is available in the off-season. AE, MC, V. Mon–Sat open at 6pm; closing time may vary based on last reservation. FRENCH/CONTINENTAL.

Excellent cooking, a comprehensive wine list, and white-glove service complement the crystal and gilded decor at this five-star–rated French standout. Excellent starters include a succulent sliced duckling breast, cream of lobster soup, and hearts-of-palm salad with a slightly spicy vinaigrette. Some items, like lobster and shrimp in a cognac-dill sauce, are available as either an appetizer or an entree. Other main courses include beef tenderloin stuffed with Gorgonzola cheese and sautéed soft-shell crabs. Desserts might include profiteroles with ice cream and chocolate or raspberry sauce, crème caramel, chocolate-mousse pie, or raspberry sorbet. When available, the fixed-price dinner includes soup or salad, entree, and dessert, and is a truly outstanding value.

MODERATE
✪ **Black Pearl Brasserie and Grill.** 2855 Ocean Dr., Vero Beach. ☎ **561/234-4426.** Reservations recommended. Main courses $12–$21. AE, CB, DC, DISC, MC, V. Mon–Fri 11:30am–2:30pm and 5–10pm (or later), Sat–Sun 5–10pm. Both this original unassuming restaurant and its newer counterpart, The Black Pearl Riverfront, at 4445 N. A1A (561/234-4426), serve fantastically fresh and inventive food. The riverfront location is more formal and serves only dinner from 5pm. CONTINENTAL.

The brasserie's small list of appetizers includes many salads, chilled sweet-potato Vichyssoise, crispy fried chicken fingers with mango dipping sauce, and grilled oysters with tangy barbecue sauce. Equally creative main courses are uniformly good. Don't miss their signature dish, an onion-crusted dolphin with caramel citrus glaze.

Ocean Grill. 1050 Sexton Plaza (by the ocean at the end of S.R. 60), Vero Beach. ☎ **561/231-5409.** Reservations accepted only for large parties. Main courses $11–$18. AE, DC, DISC, MC, V. Mon–Fri 11:30am–2:30pm and 5:30–10pm, Sat–Sun 5:30–10pm. AMERICAN.

Founded in 1941, the Ocean Grill is an institution that attracts tourists and locals alike with its simple but rich cooking and its stunning locale, right on the ocean's edge. For a dramatic experience, ask for a table along the wall of windows that open onto the sea. Dinners are uniformly good. Try stone crab claws when they are in season or any of the big servings of pasta or meats. This huge and handsome old-timer specializes in steaks and seafood. Try the house shrimp scampi baked in butter and herbs and served with a tangy mustard sauce. There are also a gift shop and a popular bar.

INEXPENSIVE
Beachside Restaurant. 3125 Ocean Dr., Vero Beach. ☎ **561/234-4477.** Breakfast combos $2–$5. Full dinners $7–$15. AE, DC, DISC, MC, V. Mon–Sat 6:30–9pm and Sun 6:30am–3pm. AMERICAN/DINER.

For a great big, cheap American breakfast, this is the place to go. You can get omelets, home fries, cream chipped beef, corn beef hash, pancakes, Belgian waffles, and even grits. Friendly waitresses also serve lunch and dinner in the comfy, wooden booths. The best dishes, like chili, fried chicken, and steaks, are hearty and delicious. Though it's just across the road from the beach, it attracts more locals than tourists.

Nino's Cafe. 1006 Easter Lily Lane (off Ocean Dr., next to Humiston Park), Vero Beach. ☎ **561/231-9311.** Pizzas $9–$10; subs and burgers $4.50–$5.50; pastas $7–$10. No credit cards. Mon–Thurs 11am–9pm; Fri–Sat 11am–10pm; Sun 4–9pm.

This little beachside cafe looks like your stereotypical pizza joint, complete with fake brick walls, murals of the Italian countryside, and red-and-white checked tablecloths. The atmosphere is pure cheese and so is much of the food. Pizza and parmigiana dishes are smothered in the stuff. Still, the thin crust and fresh toppings make this a step above your ordinary pizza. Entrees and pastas are tasty, especially thanks to a tangy and rich homemade sauce.

VERO BEACH & SEBASTIAN AFTER DARK

More than half the residents in this area are retirees, so it shouldn't be a surprise that even on weekends, this town retires relatively early. Still, there are a few popular spots, in addition to the many hotel lounges, that have live music and a good bar scene, especially in high season. For beachside drinks, go to the Driftwood Inn. See "Where to Stay," above.

A mostly 30-something and younger crowd goes to Vero's **Bombay Louie's,** at 398 21st St. (☎ **561/978-0209**), where a deejay spins dance music after 9pm from Wednesday to Saturday.

In Sebastian, you'll find live music every weekend (and daily in season) at **Capt. Hiram's,** 1606 N. Indian River Dr. (☎ **561/589-4345**), a salty outdoor restaurant and bar on the Intracoastal Waterway. The feel is tacky Key West, complete with a sand floor and thatched-roof bar that locals and tourists love at all hours of the day and night.

North of the inlet, head for the tried-and-true **Sebastian Beach Inn** (or SBI to locals), 7035 S. Fla. A1A (☎ **407/728-4311**), for live music on the weekends. Jazz, blues, or sometimes rock and roll starts at 9pm on Friday and Saturday. On Sunday, it's old-style reggae after 2pm. It's open daily for drinks from 11am until anywhere from midnight to 2am.

4 A Side Trip Inland: Fishing at Lake Okeechobee

60 miles SW of West Palm Beach

Many visitors to the Treasure Coast come to fish, and they certainly get their fill off the miles of Atlantic shore and on the inland rivers. But if you want to fish freshwater and nothing else, head for "The Lake"—☺ **Lake Okeechobee,** that is. The state's largest, it's chock-full of good eating fish. Only about a 1½-hour drive from the coast, it makes a great day or weekend excursion.

Two things happen in the area surrounding Lake Okeechobee: sugar production and fishing. The area, which actually encompasses five counties, is known as the bass-fishing and winter-vegetable capital of the state.

Okeechobee comes from the Seminole Indian word for "big water"—and big it is. The lake covers more than 467,000 acres; that's more than 730 square miles. At one time, the lake supported an enormous commercial fishing industry. Due to a commercial fishing-net ban, much of that industry has died off, leaving the sportfishers all the rich bounty of the lake.

As you approach the lake area, you'll notice a large levy surrounding its circumference. This was built after two major hurricanes, including one in 1947 that killed hundreds of area residents and cattle. In an effort to control future flooding, the Army Corps of Engineers, which had already built a cross-state waterway, constructed a series of locks and dams. The region is now safe from the threat of floods, but the ecological results of the flood control have not been as positive. The bird and wildlife population suffered dramatically, as did the southern portion of the Everglades, which relied on the downflow of water from the lake to replenish and clean the entire ecosystem.

Another threat to the region is posed by the area's largest employer, U.S. Sugar, which owns most of the land around Belle Glade and Clewiston, "America's Sweetest Town."

Still, the area retains its rural charm and boasts the best bass fishing in the state.

ESSENTIALS

GETTING THERE   The best route is to take I-95 south to Southern Boulevard (U.S. 98 west) in West Palm Beach, which merges with S.R. 80 and S.R. 441. Follow signs for S.R. 80 west through Belle Glade to South Bay. In South Bay, turn right onto U.S. 27 north, which leads directly to Clewiston.

VISITOR INFORMATION   Contact the **Clewiston Chamber of Commerce,** 544 W. Sugarland Hwy., Clewiston, FL 33440 (☎ **941/983-7979**), for maps, business directories, and the names of numerous fishing guides throughout the area. In addition, you might contact the **Pahokee Chamber of Commerce,** 115 E. Main St., Pahokee, FL 33476 (☎ **561/924-5579;** fax 561/924-8116); they'll send a complete package of magazines, guides, and accommodations listings.

For an excellent map and a brief history of the area, contact the **U.S. Army Corps of Engineers,** Natural Resources Office, 525 Ridgelawn Rd., Clewiston, FL 33440 (☎ **941/983-8101;** fax 941/983-8579). It is open weekdays from 8am to 4:30pm.

OUTDOOR PURSUITS

BOAT TOURS   **Captain JP's Boat Charters** (☎ **800/845-7411** or 561/924-2100) go out every day on a number of tour and dinner cruises on his 350-passenger *Viking Starliner* throughout the southern region of Lake Okeechobee. Most cruises leave from Pahokee or Moore Haven marina, though schedules change daily. Most cruises depart at 10am during the season and include breakfast and an all-you-can-eat buffet of salads, cheeses, and hot entrees. Prices start at $30. Call for seasonal schedules.

FISHING   See "Going After the Big One," box.

SKYDIVING   Besides fishing, the biggest sport in Clewiston is jumping out of planes. Because of the limited air traffic and vast areas of flat undeveloped land, this area attracts novice and expert sky divers. **Air Adventures** (☎ **800/533-6151** or 941/983-6151) operates a year-round program from the Airglades Airport. If you've never jumped before, you can go on a tandem dive, which means, as the name implies, you'll be attached to a "jumpmaster." For the first 60 seconds, the two of you free-fall, from about 12,500 feet. Then, a quick pull of the chute turns your rapid descent into a gentle, balletic cruise to the ground with time to see the whole majestic lake from a privileged perspective. Dive packages start at $150 on weekdays and $165 on weekends. Group rates are available.

WHERE TO STAY

If you aren't camping, book a room at the ✪ **Clewiston Inn,** 108 Royal Palm Ave., Clewiston (☎ **800/749-4466** or 941/983-8151). Built in 1938 by U.S. Sugar to house executives and visitors, this Southern plantation–inspired hotel is the oldest in the Lake Okeechobee region. It still hosts sugar executives and visiting sportfishers in its 52 simply decorated, nondescript, Holiday Inn–style rooms. The lounge area sports a 1945 mural depicting the animals of the region. Double rooms start at $89 a night; suites, from $109. All have air-conditioning, TVs, and telephones.

Going After the Big One

Fishing on the lake is a year-round affair, though the fish tend to bite a little better in the winter, perhaps for benefit of the many snowbirds who flock here, especially in February and March. RV camps are mobbed with fish-frenzied anglers who come down for weeks at a time for a decent catch.

You'll need a fishing license to go out with a rod and reel. It's a simple matter to apply. The chamber of commerce and most fishing shops can sign you up on the spot. The cost for non-Florida residents for 7 days is $16.50, $31.50 for the year.

You can rent, charter, or bring your own boat to Clewiston; just be sure to schedule your trip in advance. You don't want to show up during one of the frequent fishing tournaments, only to find you can't get a room, campsite, or fishing boat because hundreds of the country's most intense bass fishermen are vying for the $100,000 prizes in the Redman Competition, which happens four times a year in the spring and winter.

There are, of course, more than a few marinas where you can rent or charter boats. If it's your first time on the lake, I suggest chartering a boat with a guide who can show you the lake's most fertile spots and handle your tackle while you drink a beer and get some sun. **Roland Martin,** 920 E. Del Monte (☎ 941/ 983-3151), is the one-stop spot where you can find a guide, boat, tackle, rods, bait, coolers, picnic supplies, and choice of boats. Rates, including the boat, start at $175 for a half day. A full day costs $250 and includes all necessary equipment except bait. You'll need a license for this, too, which Roland Martin also sells. They also have boat rentals: A 16-foot john boat is $40 for half a day, $60 for a full day with a $40 deposit. A 26-foot pontoon is $125 for a full day and $85 for half a day with a $50 deposit.

Another reputable boat-rental spot is **Angler's Marina,** 910 Okeechobee Blvd. (☎ 800/741-3141 or 941/983-BASS). Rentals for a 14-footer start at $40 for a half day, with a maximum of four people. A full day is $60. I'd opt for the 22-foot pontoon, which comes with a 50-horsepower engine and fits a max of 10 people and some more space for supplies and fish. If you want a guide, rates start at $150 (for two people) for a half day, though in the summer (June to Oct), when it's slow, you can usually get a cheaper deal.

Another choice, especially if you're here to fish, is **Roland Martin,** 920 E. Del Monte (☎ 800/473-6766 or 941/983-3151), the "Disney of fishing." This RV park offers modest motel rooms, efficiencies, condominiums, apartments, or campsites, with two heated pools, gift and marina shops, and a restaurant. The modern complex, dotted with prefab buildings painted in sparse white and gray, is clean and well manicured. Rooms rent for $58 to $68 and efficiencies for $78 to $88. Condos are about $150 a night with a 3-night minimum. RV sites are about $25 with TV and cable hookup.

CAMPING

During the winter, campers own the Clewiston area. Campsites are jammed with regulars, who come year after year for the simple pleasures of the lake and, of course, the warm weather. Every manner of RV, from simple pop-top Volkswagens to Winnebagos to fully decked-out mobile homes, find their way to the many campsites along the lake. Also, see Roland Martin, above.

Okeechobee Landings, U.S. 27 east (☎ **941/983-4144**), is one of the best; it has every conceivable amenity included in the price of a site. More than 250 sites are situated around a small lake, clubhouse, snack bar, pool, Jacuzzi, horseshoe pit, shuffleboard court, and tennis court. Full hookup includes sewer, which is not the case throughout the county. RV spots are sold to regulars. But there are usually some spots available for rental to one-time visitors. Rates start at $25 a day, $235 to $305 weekly or around $350 a month, including hookup. Year-round rates for trailer rentals, which sleep two people, start at $32 from Sunday to Thursday and from $37 on Friday and Saturday.

WHERE TO DINE

If you aren't frying up your own catch for dinner, you can find a number of good eating spots in town. At the **Clewiston Inn** (see "Where to Stay," above), you can get catfish, beef Stroganoff, ham hocks, fried chicken, and liver and onions in a setting as Southern as the food. The dining room is open daily from 6am to 2pm and 5 to 9pm, and entrees cost $9 to $18.

Not to be missed is the ✪ **Old South Barbecue Ranch,** 602 E. Sugarland Hwy. (☎ **941/983-7756**). You'll see signs from miles around, imploring you to come to this Lake Okeechobee landmark. Go ahead; they're known for their barbecued pork, meat, and chicken, but the catfish isn't bad either. You can also get good fried gator. The place looks like a movie set from an old Western. It's open Sunday through Thursday from 11am to 9pm and Friday and Saturday from 11am to 10pm.

Southwest Florida   10

by Bill Goodwin

Thanks to a citizenry which has fought to protect both its history and its present-day environment, the southwest corner is one of the best parts of the state to discover remnants of Old Florida and enjoy the great outdoors.

Bordered on the east by the wild, wonderful Everglades and on the west by an intriguing, island-studded coast, Southwest Florida traces its nature-loving roots to inventor and amateur botanist Thomas A. Edison, who was so enamored of it that he spent his last 46 winters in Fort Myers. His friend Henry Ford liked it, too, and built his own winter home next door. The world's best tarpon fishing lured President Teddy Roosevelt and his buddies to Useppa, one of literally 10,000 islands dotting this coast. Some of the planet's best shelling helped entice the du Ponts of Delaware to Gasparilla Island, where they founded the Nantucket-like village of Boca Grande. The unspoiled beauty of Sanibel and Captiva so entranced Pulitzer Prize–winning political cartoonist J. N. "Ding" Darling that he campaigned to preserve much of those islands in their natural states. And the millionaires who built Naples enacted tough zoning laws that to this day make their town one of the most alluring in Florida.

Southwest Florida International Airport, on the eastern outskirts of Fort Myers, is this region's major airport (see "Essentials" in section 1, below). From here it's only 20 miles to Sanibel Island, 35 miles to Naples, or 46 miles to Marco Island. If you have a car, you can see the area's sights and participate in most of its activities easily from one base of operations.

EXCURSIONS TO THE EVERGLADES & KEY WEST You won't be in Southwest Florida for long before you see advertisements for excursions to the Everglades. Naples is only 36 miles from Everglades City, the "back door" to wild and wonderful Everglades National Park, so it's easy to combine a visit to the national park with your stay in Southwest Florida. See chapter 7 for full details about the Everglades.

During the winter season, you can also easily make a day trip to Key West from here via **Cape Air** (☎ 800/352-0714), which shuttles its small planes several times a day between Key West and both Southwest Florida International Airport and Naples Municipal Airport. The same-day round-trip is about $170. By sea, the fast catamaran *Boquebus* (☎ 877/461-0999) was slated to begin cruises between downtown Fort Myers and Key West during 1999. The trip was expected to take 3 hours each way. Call for schedules and fares.

1 Fort Myers

148 miles NW of Miami, 142 miles S of Tampa, 42 miles N of Naples

It's difficult to picture this pleasant city of broad avenues along the Caloosahatchee River as a raucous cow town, but that's exactly what Fort Myers was just a few years before inventor Thomas Alva Edison came here in 1885 to regain his health after years of incessant toil and the death of his wife. Today, the city's prime attractions are the homes Edison and Henry Ford built on the banks of the Caloosahatchee. Edison planted lush tropical gardens around the two homes and royal palms in front of the properties along McGregor Boulevard, once a cow trail leading from town to the docks at Punta Rassa. Now lining McGregor Boulevard for miles, the trees give Fort Myers its nickname: The City of Palms.

Like most visitors to the area, you'll probably opt to stay near the sands at nearby Fort Myers Beach or on Sanibel or Captiva islands (see sections 2 and 3, below), but drive into Fort Myers at least to visit the Edison and Ford homes and have a riverside lunch. You also can venture inland and observe incredible numbers of wildlife in their river and swamp habitats, including those at the Babcock Ranch, largest of the surviving cattle producers and now a major game preserve.

ESSENTIALS

GETTING THERE   This entire region is served by **Southwest Florida International Airport,** on Daniels Parkway east of I-75. You can get here on **Air Canada** (☎ 800/776-3000), **AirTran** (☎ 800/247-8726), **Air Transat** (☎ 800/470-1011), **America West** (☎ 800/235-9292), **American** (☎ 800/433-7300), **American Trans Air** (☎ 800/225-2995), **Canada 3000** (☎ 800/993-4378), **Continental** (☎ 800/525-0280), **Delta** (☎ 800/221-1212), **LTU International** (☎ 800/888-0200), **Midwest Express** (☎ 800/452-2022), **Northwest/KLM** (☎ 800/225-2525), **Royal** (☎ 800/667-7692), **Spirit** (☎ 800/772-7117), **TWA** (☎ 800/221-2000), **United** (☎ 800/241-6522), and **US Airways** (☎ 800/428-4322).

The two baggage-claim areas have information booths (with maps) and free phones to various hotels in the region.

Alamo (☎ 800/327-9633), **Avis** (☎ 800/331-1212), **Budget** (☎ 800/527-0700), **Dollar** (☎ 800/800-4000), **Enterprise** (☎ 800/325-8007), **Hertz** (☎ 800/654-3131), **National** (☎ 800/CAR-RENT), and **Thrifty** (☎ 800/367-2277) have car-rental booths at the airport.

Vans and taxis are available at a booth across the street from the baggage claim. The maximum fares for one to three passengers are $24 to downtown Fort Myers, $35 to Fort Myers Beach, $37 to $44 to Sanibel Island, $56 to Captiva Island, $38 to $56 to Naples, $70 to Marco Island, and $85 to Everglades City. Each additional passenger pays $8.

Amtrak provides bus connections between Fort Myers and its nearest station, in Tampa (☎ **800/USA-RAIL**). The Amtrak buses arrive and depart the **Greyhound/Trailways** bus station, 2275 Cleveland Ave. (☎ **800/231-2222**).

VISITOR INFORMATION   For advance information about Fort Myers, Fort Myers Beach, and Sanibel and Captiva islands, contact the **Lee Island Coast Visitor**

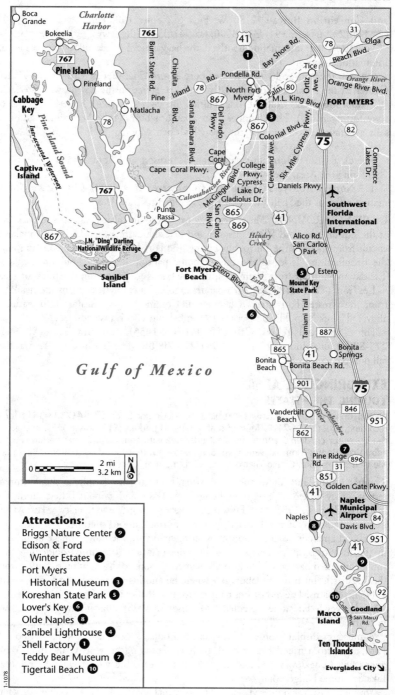

Southwest Florida

Boca Grande
Charlotte Harbor
Bokeelia
765
767
Pine Island
Pineland
41
Bay Shore Rd.
78
31
Olga
Beach Blvd.
Tice
Pondella Rd.
Orange River
Orange River Blvd.
Cabbage Key
78
North Fort Myers
Palm
80
Ortiz Ave.
FORT MYERS
Matlacha
867
Del Prado Pkwy.
2
M.L. King Blvd.
Pine Island Sound
78
867
3
82
Intracoastal Waterway
Chiquita Blvd.
Santa Barbara Blvd.
Colonial Blvd.
Cleveland Ave.
Six Mile Cypress Pkwy.
75
Commerce Lakes Dr.
Captiva Island
Cape Coral
College Pkwy.
Cypress Lake Dr.
Daniels Pkwy.
Pine Rd.
Burnt Store Rd.
Cape Coral Pkwy.
Gladiolus Dr.
McGregor Blvd.
Caloosahatchee River
767
Punta Rassa
865
San Carlos Blvd.
869
41
Hendry Creek
Alico Rd.
San Carlos Park
Southwest Florida International Airport
867
J.N. "Ding" Darling National Wildlife Refuge
4
Sanibel
Sanibel Island
Fort Myers Beach
Estero Blvd.
5
Estero
Mound Key State Park
Estero Bay
6
Tamiami Trail
887
Gulf of Mexico
865
41
Bonita Springs
Bonita Beach
Bonita Beach Rd.
901
75
846
951
Vanderbilt Beach
Cocohatchee River
862
7
Pine Ridge Rd.
896
31
851
Golden Gate Pkwy.
41
Naples Municipal Airport
Naples
84
8
Davis Blvd.
41
951
9
92
10
Goodland
San Marco Rd.
Marco Island
Collier Blvd.
Ten Thousand Islands
Everglades City ↘

0   2 mi   N
     3.2 km

Attractions:
Briggs Nature Center **9**
Edison & Ford
  Winter Estates **2**
Fort Myers
  Historical Museum **3**
Koreshan State Park **5**
Lover's Key **6**
Olde Naples **8**
Sanibel Lighthouse **4**
Shell Factory **1**
Teddy Bear Museum **7**
Tigertail Beach **10**

1-1078

and **Convention Bureau,** 2180 W. First St., Suite 100, Fort Myers, FL 33901 (☎ **800/237-6444** or 941/338-3500; fax 941/334-1106; www.leeislandcoast.com).

Volunteers staff information booths in the baggage-claim areas at Southwest Florida International Airport.

Once in town, drop by the **Greater Fort Myers Chamber of Commerce Visitor Center,** at the corner of Edwards Drive and Lee Street on the downtown waterfront (☎ **800/366-3622** from outside Florida or 941/332-3624; fax 941/332-7276; www.fortmyers.org). The chamber gives away brochures and other information and sells a detailed street map of the area. It's open Monday to Friday from 8am to 4:30pm.

There's also an information booth at the Edison and Ford Winter Estates (see "Exploring the Area," below).

The **North Fort Myers Chamber of Commerce** (☎ **941/997-9111**) has an information office at the Shell Factory, 2787 N. Tamiami Trail (U.S. 41).

GETTING AROUND   The easiest way to see the downtown sights is to park free at the Edison and Ford Winter Estates and take the narrated **trolley,** which makes a circuit from there to the Burroughs Home, the Fort Myers Historical Museum, and the Imaginarium. It leaves the Edison home parking lot every hour on the hour Tuesday to Saturday from 10am to 4pm. The fare is $3 per person regardless of age.

LeeTran (☎ **941/275-8726**) operates public buses. System maps are available from the Greater Fort Myers Chamber of Commerce (see "Visitor Information," above). There's no public bus service to Sanibel and Captiva islands.

For a taxi, call **Yellow Cab** (☎ **941/332-1055**), **Bluebird Taxi** (☎ **941/275-8294**), or **Admiralty Taxi** (☎ **941/275-7000**). Metered fares are $1.35 at flag fall plus $1.35 for each mile.

EXPLORING THE AREA
TOURING THE ESTATES

✪ Edison and Ford Winter Estates. 2350 McGregor Blvd. ☎ **941/334-3614** for a recording, or 941/334-7419. Tours of both estates $11 adults ($12 Jan–Apr), $5.50 children 6–12, free for children 5 and under. Boat rides free with admission, $3 per person without admission. Homes Mon–Sat 9am–4pm, Sun noon–4pm (last tour daily 3:30pm). Boat rides Mon–Fri 10am–4pm. Closed Thanksgiving, Christmas Eve, Christmas Day.

Thomas Edison and his second wife, Mina, brought their family to this Victorian retreat—they called it Seminole Lodge—in 1886 and wintered here until the inventor's death in 1931. Mrs. Edison gave the 14-acre estate to the city of Fort Myers in 1947, and today it stands exactly as it did during Edison's lifetime.

An avid amateur botanist, Edison experimented with the exotic foliage he planted in the lush tropical gardens surrounding the mansion (he turned goldenrod into rubber and used bamboo for light-bulb filaments). Some of his light bulbs dating from the 1920s still burn in the laboratory where he and his staff worked on some of his 1,093 inventions. The monstrous banyan tree that shades the laboratory was 4 feet tall when Harvey S. Firestone presented it to Edison in 1925; today it's the largest banyan in Florida.

A museum displays some of Edison's inventions, as well as his unique Model T Ford, a gift from friend Henry Ford. In 1916, Ford and his wife, Clara, built **Mangoes,** their bungalow-style house next door, so they could winter with the Edisons. Like Seminole Lodge, Mangoes is furnished as it appeared in the 1920s.

You must visit the homes via guided tours, which depart the visitor center every few minutes. Costumed actors portraying the Edisons, Fords, and their friends such as Harvey Firestone give "living history" accounts of how the wealthy lived in those days.

Fort Myers

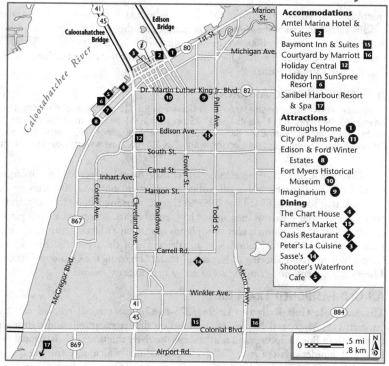

Accommodations
Amtel Marina Hotel & Suites **2**
Baymont Inn & Suites **15**
Courtyard by Marriott **16**
Holiday Central **12**
Holiday Inn SunSpree Resort **6**
Sanibel Harbour Resort & Spa **17**

Attractions
Burroughs Home **1**
City of Palms Park **11**
Edison & Ford Winter Estates **8**
Fort Myers Historical Museum **10**
Imaginarium **9**

Dining
The Chart House **4**
Farmer's Market **13**
Oasis Restaurant **7**
Peter's La Cuisine **3**
Sasse's **14**
Shooter's Waterfront Cafe **5**

A replica of Edison's electric boat *Reliance* takes guests on 30-minute scenic rides on the river weekdays (you can cruise even if you don't tour the homes).

Vendors sell snacks just outside the main entrance; you can eat them at shaded picnic tables.

OTHER DOWNTOWN ATTRACTIONS

The Georgian Revival **Burroughs Home,** 2505 1st St., at Fowler Street (☎ **941/332-6125**), was built on the banks of the Caloosahatchee River in 1901 by cattleman John Murphy and later sold to the Burroughs family. You must take a tour in order to visit the premises; they are given on the hour Tuesday to Friday from 11am to 3pm. Admission is free with Edison-Ford home tickets, or $3 for adults, $1 for children 6 to 12, free for children 5 and under. Park free in the Amtel Marina Hotel and Suites garage across the street (see "Where to Stay," below).

Housed in the restored Spanish-style depot served by the Atlantic Coast Line from 1924 to 1971, the **Fort Myers Historical Museum,** 2300 Peck St., at Jackson Street (☎ **941/332-5955**), features exhibits depicting Fort Myers's history from the ancient Calusa peoples and the Spanish conquistadors to the first settlers. A replica of an 1800s "Cracker" home stands outside, as does the Esperanza, the longest and one of the last of the plush Pullman private cars. World War II buffs can see the remains of a P-39 Aircobra, which helps explain the town's role in training fighter pilots back then. Admission is $4 for adults, $2 for children 11 and under. Open Tuesday to Saturday from 9am to 4pm.

Rather than have the kids go stir-crazy on a rainy day, head for the **Imaginarium,** 2000 Cranford Ave., at Martin Luther King Jr. Boulevard (☎ **941/337-3332**), an entertaining, hands-on museum in the old city water plant. A host of toylike exhibits explain such basic scientific principles as gravity and the weather. There are nature shows in the theater every hour on the half hour. Admission is $6 for adults, $5.50 for seniors, $3 for children 3 to 12. Open Tuesday to Saturday from 10am to 5pm. Closed Thanksgiving and Christmas.

A NEARBY HISTORIC ATTRACTION

Koreshan State Historic Site. U.S. 41 at Corkscrew Rd. (15 mi. south of downtown Fort Myers). ☎ **941/992-0311.** Admission $3.25 per vehicle, $1 pedestrians or bikers; tours $1 adults, 50¢ children. Park daily 8am–sunset; settlement buildings daily 8am–5pm; tours Sat–Sun 1–4pm. From I-75, take Corkscrew Rd. (Exit 19), go 2 miles west, cross U.S. 41 into site.

The Koreshan Unity Movement (pronounced Kor-*esh*-en), a sect led by Chicagoan Cyrus Reed Teed, established a self-sufficient settlement on these 300 acres on the narrow Estero River in 1894. They believed that humans lived *inside* the earth and—ahead of their time—that women should have equal rights. You can visit their garden and several of their buildings, plus view photos from their archives. Nature and canoe trails wind downriver to Mound Key, an islet made of the shells discarded by the Calusa Indians (see "Canoeing & Kayaking" under "Enjoying the Outdoors," below). There's also a picnic and camping area (see "Where to Stay," below).

AN OLD-FASHIONED TRAIN RIDE

The **Seminole Gulf Railway** (☎ 941/275-8487), the original railroad that ran between Fort Myers and Naples, today chugs on dinner excursions and sightseeing trips south to Bonita Springs and north across the river, and there's an occasional twilight and murder-mystery run. Call for the schedules, which vary from season to season. Reservations are required for the dinner trip. The trains depart Fort Myers from the Amtel Fleamarket Mall Station, a small blue building on the western edge of the mall's parking lot on Colonial Boulevard at Metro Parkway. The Bonita Springs station is on Old U.S. 41 at Pennsylvania Avenue.

SHOPPING

An institution for more than 50 years, **The Shell Factory,** 5 miles north of the Caloosahatchee River bridge on U.S. 41 (☎ 941/995-2141), carries one of the world's largest collections of shells, corals, sponges, and fossils. Entire sections are devoted to shell jewelry and shell lamps. Many items here cost under $10, some under $1. Open daily from 10am to 6pm.

Bargain hunters can browse more than 800 booths carrying antiques, crafts, fashions, and produce at **Fleamasters,** 4135 Dr. Martin Luther King Jr. Blvd. (Fla. 82), 1½ miles west of I-75 (☎ 941/334-7001). There are snack bars and entertainment, too. Open on Friday, Saturday, and Sunday from 8am to 4pm. You'll find more old stuff at **AMTEL Fleamarket Mall,** at the corner of Metro Parkway and Colonial Boulevard (☎ 941/939-3132), where stalls are open Wednesday to Sunday from 9am to 5pm.

Outlet shoppers will find a large Levi's store among other major-brand shops at the **Sanibel Tanger Factory Stores,** on the way to the beaches at the junction of Summerlin Road and McGregor Boulevard (☎ 888/SHOP-333 or 941/454-1616). Open Monday to Saturday from 10am to 9pm, Sunday from 11am to 6pm.

Anchored by Saks Fifth Avenue and Jacobson's, the Spanish-style **Bell Tower Shops,** Tamiami Trail (U.S. 41) at Daniels Parkway (☎ 941/489-1221), is Fort Myers's upscale mall. You'll find most of the familiar national stores at **Edison Mall,** Cleveland Avenue (U.S. 41) at Winkler Avenue (☎ 941/939-5464).

"Buggy" Rides Through a Mysterious Swamp

One of the easiest and most informative ways to see Southwest Florida's abundant wildlife is on a "swamp buggy" ride with ○ **Babcock Wilderness Adventures,** on Fla. 31 about 11 miles northeast of Fort Myers (☎ **800/500-5583** for reservations or 941/338-6367 for information). Experienced naturalists lead 90-minute tours through the Babcock Ranch, the largest contiguous cattle operation east of the Mississippi River and home to countless birds and wildlife, as well as domesticated bison and quarter horses. Alligators scurry from a bridge or lie motionless in the dark-brown waters of the mysterious Telegraph Swamp when the buggies pass overhead. Visitors dismount to visit an enclosure where southern cougars stand in for their close cousins, the rare Florida panthers (which are tan, not black).

Unlike most wildlife tours in the region, this one covers five ecosystems, from open prairie to cypress swamp. A replica of an Old Florida house built by the crew making the Sean Connery movie *Just Cause* serves as a small museum. A restaurant serves lunch (alligator bites are on the menu). Admission is $17.95 for adults, $9.95 for children 3 to 12. The tours usually leave on the hour between 9am and 3pm from November to April, from 9am to noon from May through October. Reservations are required, so call ahead.

ENJOYING THE OUTDOORS

CANOEING & KAYAKING   The area's slow-moving rivers and quiet, island-speckled inland waters offer fine canoe and kayak ventures; you'll visit birds and manatees along the way. Two popular local venues are the winding waterways around Pine Island west of town and the Estero River south of Fort Myers. The Estero River route is an official Florida canoe trail that leads 3½ miles from U.S. 41 to Estero Bay, which is itself a state aquatic preserve (see "Enjoying the Outdoors" in section 2). Near the mouth of the river lies **Mound Key State Archeological Site,** one of the largest Calusa shell middens. Scholars believe that this mostly artificial island dates back some 2,000 years and was the capital of the Calusa chief who ruled all of South Florida when the Spanish arrived. There's no park ranger on the key, but signs explain its history.

Estero River Tackle & Canoe Outfitters, 20991 S. Tamiami Trail (U.S. 41), at the Estero River Bridge (☎ 941/992-4050), has guided historic and nature tours (call for schedule and prices) and rents canoes for $22.50 to $27.50 a day, kayaks from $17.50 to $27.50. Open daily 7am to 6pm. **Koreshan State Historic Site,** half a mile south of the bridge at the intersection of U.S. 41 and Corkscrew Road (☎ 941/992-0311), rents canoes for $3 an hour, $15 per day (see "A Nearby Historical Attraction," above).

In addition to its cruises mentioned below, the *Tropic Star,* based at Knight's Landing marina, 16499 Porto Bello in Bokeelia on Pine Island (☎ 941/283-0015), rents kayaks and has guided tours over 18 miles of paddling trails. Rentals cost $35 a day for single seaters, $45 for doubles. Call for schedule and prices of guided tours. The company also has a ferry service to Cayo Costa State Park, where it rents kayaks (see "Nearby Island Hopping," in section 3, on Sanibel and Captiva islands, for information about Cayo Costa).

CRUISES   **J.C. Boat Cruises** (☎ 941/334-7474) presents a variety of year-round cruises on the Caloosahatchee River and its tributaries, including lunch and dinner voyages on the sternwheeler *Captain J.P.* The 3-hour Everglades Jungle Cruise is a good way to observe the area's wildlife, with lots of manatees to be seen from

November to April. A full-day cruise goes all the way up the Caloosahatchee to Lake Okeechobee and back. The ticket office is at the downtown Fort Myers City Yacht Basin, Edwards Drive at Lee Street, opposite the chamber of commerce. Prices range from $14 to $74 for adults. Schedules change and advance reservations are strongly recommended.

Another way to see manatees and other wildlife is with **Manatee World Boat Tours** (☎ 941/693-1434), based at the Coastal Marine Mart on Fla. 80 just east of I-75. Cruises usually depart at 10am, noon, and 2 and 4pm, but call ahead for reservations. Fares are $12.75 for adults, $6.75 for children under 12.

The *Tropic Star* (☎ 941/283-0015) leaves Knight's Landing marina, 16499 Porto Bello in Bokelia on Pine Island, daily at 9:30am on all-day nature cruises on Pine Island Sound. They include a stop at Cabbage Key and cost $25 for adults, $15 for kids under 12. The company also runs a ferry from Pine Island to Cayo Costa State Park. Call for departure times. Fares are $20 for adults, $12 for children 3 to 12. See "Nearby Island Hopping," in section 3, on Sanibel and Captiva islands, for information about Cabbage Key and Cayo Costa.

The sleek 100-foot-long yacht *Sanibel Harbour Princess* (☎ 941/644-2128) goes on dinner cruises from its base at Sanibel Harbour Resort & Spa (see "Where to Stay," below). Dinner cruises range from about $27 to $35 for adults, $13 to $16 for children, depending on the season, and include a glass of champagne, a buffet dinner, and entertainment during the winter season. A Sunday brunch cruise during winter costs $16 for adults, $10 for children. A sister pontoon boat, the *Sanibel Princess,* makes wildlife-watching cruises and picnic trips to a beach. These range from $15 to $25 for adults, $10 to $18 for children. Call ahead for departure times and reservations, which are required.

GOLF & TENNIS   For an excellent rundown of Southwest Florida golf courses, pick up a free copy of *Golfer's Guide,* available at the visitor information centers and many hotel lobbies. See "The Active Vacation Planner," in chapter 2, for information about subscribing or ordering the current edition. And don't forget that you can call **Tee Times USA** (☎ 800/374-8633 or 888/465-3356) and book starting times at Florida courses.

Although it looks like an exclusive private enclave, the **Fort Myers Country Club,** McGregor Boulevard at Hill Avenue (☎ 941/936-2457), actually is a municipal course. Designed in 1917 by Donald Ross, it's flat and uninteresting by today's standards, but it's right in town. **Smitty's,** a steak and seafood restaurant, now occupies the fine old clubhouse. The city's other municipal course is the more-challenging **Eastwood Golf Club,** on Ortiz Avenue between Colonial and Dr. Martin Luther King Jr. boulevards in the eastern suburbs (☎ 941/275-4848). Greens fees at both range from about $30 in summer to $55 during winter. Nonresidents must book tee times at least 24 hours in advance.

Other area courses open to the public include the Tom Fazio–designed **Gateway Golf & Country Club,** on Daniels Parkway east of the airport (☎ 941/561-1010); the two nationally acclaimed **Pelican's Nest** courses in Bonita Springs (☎ 941/947-4600); **Coral Oaks Golf Club** in Cape Coral (☎ 941/283-4800); **Alden Pines Country Club** on Pine Island (☎ 941/283-2179); **San Carlos Golf Club** in South Fort Myers (☎ 941/267-3131); **Bonita Springs Golf & Country Club** in Bonita Springs (☎ 941/992-2800); and **El Rio Golf Club** (☎ 941/995-2204) and **Riverbend Golf Club** (☎ 941/543-2200), both in North Fort Myers.

Tennis buffs can play at the **Fort Myers Racquet Club,** 4900 Deleon St. (☎ 941/278-7277), which has eight lighted courts. **Sanibel Harbour Resort & Spa** is well-known for its excellent tennis programs for both juniors and adults (see "Where to Stay," below).

WATCHING THE BOYS OF SPRING

While many major league baseball teams have jumped around Florida for their **spring training,** the Boston Red Sox and the Minnesota Twins have worked out in Fort Myers for years. The **Boston Red Sox** play at the 6,500-seat City of Palms Park, at Edison Avenue and Broadway (☎ **877/733-7699** or 941/334-4700). The **Minnesota Twins** work out at the 7,500-seat Lee County Sports Complex, on Six Mile Cypress Parkway between Daniels and Metro parkways (☎ **800/338-9467** or 941/768-4270).

Fort Myers is about an hour's drive south of Charlotte County Stadium (☎ **941/625-9500**), where the **Texas Rangers** hold their spring training. To get there, take I-75 north to Exit 32, then west to the end of Toledo Blade Boulevard. Turn right there onto Fla. 776. The stadium is on the left.

WHERE TO STAY

As in the rest of southern Florida, room rates here are highest, and reservations essential, during winter, from mid-December to April. Even hotels and motels removed from the beach charge premium rates then. If you can't get a room at the properties mentioned below, the **Lee Island Coast Visitor and Convention Bureau** operates a free reservation service (☎ **800/733-7935**) covering many more accommodations in Fort Myers, Fort Myers Beach, and Sanibel and Captiva islands.

Don't be misled by our categories, which are determined by high, winter-season rates. During the off-season they drop by as much as 50% or more. All hotel bills in Southwest Florida are subject to a 9% tax.

Fort Myers has almost every chain motel along Cleveland Avenue (U.S. 41), in all price ranges. Many business travelers stay at the **Holiday Inn Central,** 2431 Cleveland Ave. (☎ **800/998-0466** or 941/332-3232; fax 941/332-0590), whose location near the corner of Edison Avenue is a plus for vacationers, too; it's a 2-block walk to the Boston Red Sox training facility and a short drive to the Edison and Ford homes. There are an outdoor pool, a 24-hour Denny's restaurant, and a tavern with live entertainment. Winter rates are $129 to $139 double; off-season they drop to $59 to $85 double.

You can have more space and a kitchen at **Residence Inn by Marriott,** 2960 Colonial Blvd., at Metro Parkway (☎ **800/331-3131** or 941/936-0110; fax 941/936-4144), and at the more luxurious **Homewood Suites Hotel,** 5255 Big Pine Way (☎ **800/225-5466** or 941/275-6000; fax 941/275-6601), at the Bell Tower Shops complex. Both hotels have pools, exercise rooms, and coin laundries.

The only true campground here is at **Koreshan State Historic Site,** on U.S. 41 in Estero (☎ **941/992-0311;** fax 941/992-1607), which has 60 wooded sites for tents or RVs at $16 per night during winter, $10 a night off-season. See "Exploring the Area," above, for information about the historic site. Reservations are accepted up to 11 months in advance year-round.

Amtel Marina Hotel and Suites. 2500 Edwards Dr. (at Fowler St.), Fort Myers, FL 33901. ☎ **800/833-1620** or 941/337-0300. Fax 941/337-1530. 416 units. A/C MINIBAR TV TEL. Winter $155–$165 double; $165–$185 suite. Off-season $95–$115 double; $115–$125 suite. AE, DC, DISC, MC, V.

The former Sheraton Harbor Place, downtown Fort Myers's only large hotel, caters primarily to conventioneers and business travelers. Service is efficient, but don't expect personalized treatment if a large group such as the Boston Red Sox is in town (the big leaguers usually stay here during spring training). Most rooms in the 25-story tower have spectacular views, many over the Caloosahatchee River. Suites come equipped with kitchenettes and bookcase-like cabinets that divide the living and sleeping areas.

With a river view from the second floor, La Tiers restaurant is open for breakfast, lunch, and dinner. Entertainment is offered on Friday and Saturday evenings in the first-floor Marina Lounge, which looks out to the river. Amenities here include complimentary airport transfers, concierge, limited room service, heated outdoor swimming pool, lighted tennis court, exercise room, game room, gift shop, and guest laundry.

✪ **Baymont Inn & Suites.** 2717 Colonial Blvd., Fort Myers, FL 33907. ☎ **800/428-3438** or 941/275-3500. Fax 941/275-5426. 122 units. Winter $79–$89 double. Off-season $42–$46 double. Rates include continental breakfast. AE, DC, DISC, MC, V.

Like most members of the small but growing chain, formerly known as Budgetel Inns, this modern, four-story establishment offers exceptional value with large, well-equipped rooms. It's centrally situated near the Courtyard by Marriott and Residence Inn by Marriott (see above) and offers an outdoor swimming pool. Entered from exterior walkways, the comfortably furnished rooms have extras like coffeemakers, desks, hair dryers, irons and boards, and free local calls (I consider Baymont Inns to be the poor person's Courtyard by Marriott). An extensive continental breakfast is served in a room off the lobby.

Courtyard by Marriott. 4455 Metro Pkwy. (at the corner of Colonial Blvd.), Fort Myers, FL 33901. ☎ **800/321-2211** or 941/275-8600. Fax 941/275-7087. 149 units. A/C TV TEL. Winter $139 double. Off-season $79 double. Weekend rates available off-season. AE, DC, DISC, MC, V.

This member of the exceptionally comfortable hotel chain designed for business travelers is situated 4 miles south of downtown and 10 miles north of the beach. Surrounding a landscaped courtyard with a swimming pool, the sizable rooms all have sofas or easy chairs, rich mahogany writing tables and chests of drawers, two phones, coffeemakers, and hair dryers. The marble lobby features a fireplace and dining area serving breakfast only. Other facilities include an exercise room, an indoor spa pool, and guest laundry.

Holiday Inn SunSpree Resort. 2220 W. 1st St. (at Euclid Ave.), Fort Myers, FL 33901. ☎ **800/HOLIDAY** or 941/334-3434. Fax 941/334-3844. 146 units. A/C TV TEL. Winter $139–$189 double. Off-season $89–$139 double. AE, DC, DISC, MC, V.

This islandy riverside hotel is best known locally for the adjacent Shooters Waterfront Cafe USA, a popular restaurant and bar (see "Where to Dine," below). Some of the suites are near the outdoor bar where Shooters's bands play—which can mean a bit too much entertainment for some guests' ears (others love the constant nighttime action). Rooms at the front of the property, however, are far enough removed to render a quiet and convenient base from which to explore the nearby Edison and Ford Winter Estates and other downtown attractions. Whatever their location, the units offer coffeemakers, refrigerators, and hair dryers, and a few have big Jacuzzis a few feet from their beds.

The L-shaped building flanks a large courtyard with both adults' and children's pools surrounded by palms and a colorful patio. There's a fenced children's playground adjacent. Other facilities include a beauty salon with massage, an activities desk, a small reading room off the marble-floored lobby, and a guest laundry. Shooters opens for breakfast at 7am daily, and the Oasis Restaurant is virtually across the street (see "Where to Dine," below).

✪ **Sanibel Harbour Resort & Spa.** 17260 Harbour Pointe Rd., Fort Myers, FL 33908. ☎ **800/767-7777** or 941/466-4000. Fax 941/466-2150. www.sanibel-resort.com. 240 units, 80 two-bedroom condo apts. A/C MINIBAR TV TEL. Winter $275–$315 double; $339 suite; $339–$599 condo apt. Off-season $140–$229 double; $249 suite; $189–$455 condo apt. Packages available. AE, DC, DISC, MC, V. Valet parking $8; free self-parking. Take the last exit off Summerlin Rd. before the Sanibel Causeway toll plaza.

This secluded, sports-oriented resort overlooks San Carlos Bay and Sanibel Island from Punta Rassa, next to the Sanibel Causeway (a complimentary shuttle takes guests to the island's beaches and a bike-rental shop three times a day). A waterside cupola-topped pavilion evokes the turn-of-the-century resort that once stood on this point, but the 11-story hotel is modern and luxurious throughout. All of the hotel rooms and most of the condo apartments have wonderful water and island views from their balconies, including spectacular sunsets over Sanibel. A large, attractive pool and sunning complex area sits by the water, but don't be disappointed by the quality of the beach here—this is the bay and not the gulf, after all, so stay over on the islands if a great beach is among your top priorities. But if tennis is your game, take note: The resort has 13 lighted courts and a 5,000-seat stadium that has hosted Davis Cup matches. This large hostelry hosts many conventions and groups, although active couples make up a sizable portion of the clientele.

Dining/Diversions: The intimate Chez Le Bear leads the food outlets here, with the casual Promenade providing calorie-conscious fare for the pumping-iron set. Lounges have entertainment during the winter season, and there's a sports bar.

Amenities: Concierge, room service (6am to midnight), laundry, children's activity program. A state-of-the-art, 40,000-square-foot fitness center with spa, massage, and facials. Other sporting facilities include bayside indoor and outdoor swimming pools with hot tubs and bars; 13 lighted tennis courts; jogging, fitness, and kayak trails; a marina with boat and water-sports equipment rentals and day and sunset cruises. Except for cruises, only guests can use the facilities here, and they pay extra for most activities.

WHERE TO DINE

Some Southwest Florida restaurants adjust their hours from season to season and even from year to year, so you may want to call ahead to make sure of an establishment's business hours.

Fort Myers's main commercial strip, Cleveland Avenue (U.S. 41), has most national fast-food and family chain restaurants, especially near College Parkway. There's a branch of **Mel's Diner,** the excellent regional chain, at 4820 S. Cleveland Ave., opposite Page Field (☎ **941/275-7850**), offering inexpensive diner-style fare including breakfast served anytime.

EXPENSIVE

The Chart House. 2024 W. 1st St. (at Henley Place). ☎ **941/332-1881.** Reservations recommended. Main courses $15–$36. AE, DC, DISC, MC, V. Mon–Fri 11:30am–3pm and 5–9:30pm; Sun–Thurs 5–10pm, Fri–Sat 5–11pm. SEAFOOD/BEEF.

You can't dine outdoors here, but great views are a prime draw at this riverside member of the national chain. Seafood offerings include orange-basil salmon and charcoal-broiled fresh fish and lobster. The grill also produces fine steaks, and prime rib is a house specialty. The lengthy salad bar is one of the area's best.

✪ **Peter's La Cuisine.** 2224 Bay St. (at Bayview Court). ☎ **941/332-2228.** Reservations recommended. Main courses $26–$34; upstairs bistro $6.50–$20. AE, MC, V. Mon–Fri 11:30am–2pm and 5:30–9:30pm, Sat–Sun 5:30–9:30pm. Upstairs bistro Mon–Fri 4pm–2am, Sat–Sun 5:30pm–2am. CLASSICAL FRENCH.

Even other restaurateurs say Bavarian-born chef Peter Schmid's establishment, in downtown's second-oldest building, is their favorite place to dine. Peter's seasonally changing menu offers masterful presentations of quail, veal, steaks, racks of lamb, Dover sole, local seafood, and fresh local fruits and vegetables in the classical French style. His first-floor venue has a refined ambience, with tuxedoed waiters providing efficient and unobtrusive service, but be careful down here if you're on a budget: The dining room is strictly à la carte. Meanwhile, an elevator will take you up to his casual, lively Upstairs Bar & Bistro, where he offers lighter fare and nightly entertainment in a supper-club atmosphere. From there you can wander up to the roof and the open-air Sky Bar, whose view makes it one of the town's favorite watering holes (see "Fort Myers After Dark," below).

MODERATE

✪ **Sasse's.** 3651 Evans Ave., in Carrell Corner shopping center (between Carrell Rd. and Winkler Ave.). ☎ **941/278-5544.** Reservations not accepted. Main courses $8–$18. No credit cards. Tues–Fri 11:30am–1:15pm, Wed–Sat 5:30–8:15pm. CONTINENTAL/ITALIAN.

In a small shopping strip near the Fort Myers Recreation Center north of the Edison Mall, this popular little spot offers one of the area's most unusual and reasonably priced dining experiences. Aromas waft from the wood-fired oven in the open kitchen, from which come enormous slabs of pizzalike bread (served with seasoned olive oil for dipping) and the likes of log-roasted lemon chicken. The selections change daily, although you can usually count on braised lamb shank served over steamed vegetables and veal scallopini stuffed with prosciutto, roasted peppers, and mozzarella. It's all of a quality rarely found at these prices, and the portions are so huge that most patrons carry home doggie bags (there's a $5 fee to share a single dish). The storefront setting is too cramped for romantic dining, but it's fun and the food is certainly worth putting up with the din of busily working chefs and happily chatting diners.

✪ **Shooters Waterfront Cafe USA.** At Holiday Inn SunSpree Resort, 2220 W. First St. (at Euclid Ave.). ☎ **941/334-2727.** Reservations not accepted. Salads and sandwiches $6–$10; main courses $9–$19; Sun brunch $11. AE, DC, DISC, MC, V. Daily 7–10am and 11am–11pm (bar open later); Sun brunch 10am–2pm. AMERICAN.

Granted, this pub turns into one of Fort Myers's most popular drinking-and-meeting spots after dark on weekends. But its sliding glass walls open to a river-side deck, making this the most attractive place in town for a relaxing alfresco lunch break while seeing the sights or for watching the sun set over the Caloosahatchee. The cuisine is typically modern pub fare: a variety of pizzas, California-style pastas, grilled fish, seafood platters, steaks, and prime rib. The best bet for lunch is the reliable grouper (fried, blackened, or grilled) sandwich.

INEXPENSIVE

✪ **Farmers Market Restaurant.** 2736 Edison Ave. (at Cranford Ave.). ☎ **941/334-1687.** Breakfast $3–$5; sandwiches $3–$5.50; meals $5.50–$9. No credit cards. Mon–Sat 6am–8pm, Sun 6am–7pm. SOUTHERN.

The retail Farmers Market next door may be tiny, but the best of the cabbage, okra, green beans, and tomatoes ends up here at this plain and simple restaurant frequented by everyone from business executives to truck drivers. The specialties of the house are smoked beef, pork barbecue, and other Southern favorites like country-fried steak, fried chicken livers and gizzards, and smoked ham hocks with a bowl of black-eyed peas. Yankees can order fried chicken, roast beef, or pork chops, and they can have hash browns instead of grits with their big breakfast.

Oasis Restaurant. In Edison-Ford Sq., 2222 McGregor Blvd. (at Euclid Ave.). ☎ **941/ 334-1566.** Breakfast $2.50–$6; sandwiches, burgers, and salads $3–$5.50. No credit cards. Mon–Fri 7am–3pm, Sat–Sun 8am–2pm. AMERICAN.

Near the Edison and Ford homes, Bonnie Grunberg and Tammie Shockey work hard to make their narrow storefront establishment appeal to young professionals who don't mind sitting elbow to elbow while recovering from a night at Shooters Waterfront Cafe USA (just behind this shopping center) with a "hangover" omelette—Italian sausage and vegetables under melted cheese. Breakfast fare is served all day here, and you can take advantage of a $1.99 eye-opening special weekdays from 7 to 9:30am. Lunches provide made-to-order Reubens, Monte Cristos, and Philly cheese-steak subs, plus soups and salads.

FORT MYERS AFTER DARK

For entertainment ideas and schedules, consult the daily *News-Press,* especially Friday's "Gulf Coasting" section. Also, be on the lookout for *Happenings,* a tabloid-size entertainment guide which is distributed free at the visitor information offices and in some hotel lobbies.

The city's showcase performing-arts venue is the $7 million **Barbara B. Mann Performing Arts Hall,** 8099 College Pkwy., at Summerlin Road (☎ 941/489-3033), on the campus of Edison Community College. It features world-famous performers, Broadway plays, and wintertime concerts by the **Southwest Florida Symphony** (☎ 941/433-3040 for information, or 941/481-4849 for tickets).

Originally a downtown vaudeville playhouse, the 1908-vintage **Arcade Theater,** 2267 1st St., between Bay and Hendry streets (☎ 941/332-6688), presents a variety of performances and is home to the **Florida Repertory Theatre** (☎ 941/332-4488), which launched its inaugural season in 1998.

Leading the bar scene, ✪ **Shooters Waterfront Cafe USA,** at the Holiday Inn SunSpree Resort, 2220 W. 1st St. (☎ 941/334-2727), has live bands or a deejay spinning CDs most nights at a riverside "chickee hut," a thatched-roof bar. National musicians such as Maria Muldaur, Matt "Guitar" Murphy, Debbie Davis, and Savoy Brown often perform in the casual **Upstairs Bar & Bistro** above Peter's La Cuisine, 2224 Bay St. (☎ 941/332-2228). Peter's rooftop Sky Bar is another popular local place to meet, especially on weekends. See "Where to Dine," above for more about these establishments.

2 Fort Myers Beach

13 miles S of Fort Myers, 28 miles N of Naples, 12 miles E of Sanibel Island

Often overshadowed by trendy Sanibel and Captiva islands to the north and ritzy Naples to the south, down-to-earth Fort Myers Beach, which occupies all of skinny Estero Island, offers just as much sun and sand, and at more moderate prices, as its affluent neighbors.

Droves of both families and young singles flock to the busy intersection of San Carlos and Estero boulevards, an area so packed with bars, beach-apparel shops, restaurants, and motels that the locals call it "Times Square." The city has spiffed up Times Square by installing a pedestrian-only mall and improving traffic flow, and some of the establishments have been upgraded.

That Coney Island image certainly doesn't apply to the rest of Estero Island, where old-fashioned beach cottages, manicured condos, and quiet motels beckon couples and families in search of more sedate vacations. In fact, promoters of the southern end of the island say that they're not in Fort Myers Beach; they're on Estero

Island. It's their way of distinguishing their part of town from congested Times Square.

Narrow Matanzas Pass and broad Estero Bay separate the island from the mainland. Whereas the pass is the area's largest commercial fishing port (when they say "fresh off the boat" here, they aren't kidding), the bay is an official state aquatic preserve inhabited by a host of birds, as well as manatees, dolphins, and other sea life. Nature cruises go forth onto this lovely protected bay, which is dotted with islands.

A few miles south of Fort Myers Beach, a chain of pristine barrier islands includes unspoiled ✪ **Lover's Key,** a state park where a tractor-pulled tram runs through a mangrove forest to a lovely beach.

ESSENTIALS

GETTING THERE   See section 1 on Fort Myers, earlier in this chapter, for information about Southwest Florida International Airport, car-rental firms, Amtrak's trains, and Greyhound/Trailways bus service to the area.

VISITOR INFORMATION   The **Fort Myers Beach Chamber of Commerce,** 17200 San Carlos Blvd., Fort Myers Beach, FL 33931 (☎ **800/782-9283** or 941/454-7500; fax 941/454-7910; www.coconet.com/fmbeach), provides free information, sells a detailed street map for $2, and operates a visitor welcome center on the mainland portion of San Carlos Boulevard just south of Summerlin Road. It's open Monday to Friday from 8am to 6pm, Saturday from 10am to 6pm, and Sunday from 11am to 5pm.

GETTING AROUND   An alternative to heavy wintertime traffic and limited parking is the **Beach Connection Trolley,** which during winter operates daily from 8am to 8pm between Summerlin Square Shopping Center, at Summerlin Road and San Carlos Boulevard on the mainland, and Bonita Beach. The route takes it along the full length of Estero Boulevard, including Lover's Key. During the off-season it runs from Bowditch Regional Park at the north end of Estero Boulevard south to Lover's Key. It costs 25¢ per ride. Ask your hotel staff or call **LeeTran** (☎ **941/275-8726**) for schedules.

For a cab, call **Local Motion Taxi** (☎ **941/463-4111**).

There are no bike paths per se here, although many folks ride along the paved shoulders of Estero Boulevard. A variety of rental bikes, scooters, and in-line skates are available at **Fun Rentals,** 1901 Estero Blvd. at Ohio Avenue (☎ **941/463-8844**), and **Scooters, Inc.,** 1698 Estero Blvd. at Avenue E (☎ **941/463-1007**). Charges start at $20 a day for one-passenger scooters, $14 a day for bikes.

HITTING THE BEACH

A prime attraction for beachgoers is the gorgeous ✪ **Lover's Key State Recreation Area,** 8700 Estero Blvd. (☎ **941/463-4588**), on the totally preserved Lover's Key, south of Estero Island. Although the highway runs down the center of the island, access to this unspoiled beach from the parking lot is restricted to footpaths or a tractor-pulled tram through a bird-filled forest of mangroves and casuarinas. The beach itself is known for its multitude of shells. There are bathhouses with outdoor showers, a snack shop, and canoe and kayak rentals at the parking lot. The park is open daily from 8am to sunset. Admission is $4 per vehicle with two to eight occupants, $2 for vehicles with a single occupant, and $1 for pedestrians and bicyclists. No alcohol is allowed, nor are pets permitted on the beach or in the water (you must keep them on a leash elsewhere in the park).

On Estero Island, **Lynn Hall Memorial Park** features a fishing pier and beach in the middle of Times Square. It has changing rooms, rest rooms, and one of the few

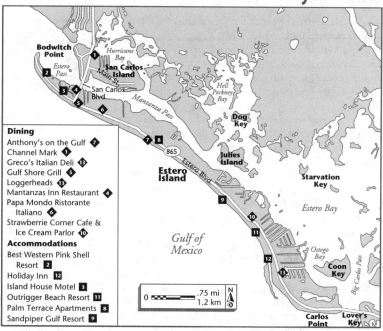

Dining
Anthony's on the Gulf **7**
Channel Mark **1**
Greco's Italian Deli **13**
Gulf Shore Grill **5**
Loggerheads **13**
Mantanzas Inn Restaurant **4**
Papa Mondo Ristorante
  Italiano **6**
Strawberrie Corner Cafe &
  Ice Cream Parlor **10**

Accommodations
Best Western Pink Shell
  Resort **2**
Holiday Inn **12**
Island House Motel **3**
Outrigger Beach Resort **11**
Palm Terrace Apartments **8**
Sandpiper Gulf Resort **9**

public parking lots in the area; the meter costs 75¢ per hour, but keep it fed—there's a $32 fine if your time runs out! At the island's north end, **Bowditch Regional Park** has picnic tables, cold-water showers, and changing rooms. It has parking only for drivers with disabled permits, but it's the turnaround point for the Beach Connection Trolley.

Several beach locations are hotbeds of parasailing, Wave Runners, sailboats, and other beach activities. **Times Square,** at the intersection of San Carlos and Estero boulevards, and the **Best Western Beach Resort,** about a quarter-mile north, are popular spots on Estero's busy north end. Another hotbed is on the beach in front of **Anthony's on the Gulf** restaurant and the **Junkanoo Beach Bar** in the middle beach area (see "Where to Dine," below). Down south, activities are centered at the **Holiday Inn** and the **Outrigger Beach Resort** (see "Where to Stay," below).

ENJOYING THE OUTDOORS

BOATING & BOAT RENTALS   Powerboats are available from the **Mid Island Marina** (☎ 941/765-4371), the **Fort Myers Beach Marina** (☎ 941/463-9552), the **Fish Tale Marina** (☎ 941/463-3600), the **Palm Grove Marina** (☎ 941/463-7333), and the **Summer Winds Marina** (☎ 941/454-6333). **Dockside Boat Rentals** (☎ 941/765-4433) rents them at the Best Western Pink Shell Resort on Estero Island's northern end.

CRUISES   Two of the most detailed nature tours in this area are with **Calusa Coast Outfitters,** 7225 Estero Blvd., at the Fish Tale Marina behind Villa Santini shopping center (☎ **941/463-4448**). Guests who go with Arden Arrington, a director of the Southwest Florida Historical Society, can listen through hydrophones as dolphins "speak" to each other, or they can go on a guided walk on historic Mound Key, the old Calusa Indian shell island at the mouth of the Estero River. Anyone can take the 3-hour dolphin tours, which cost $25 for adults, $20 for seniors, $14 for kids under 13. The Mound Key trips can be exhaustive, in both the amount of information and the physical exertion required, so are not recommended for children, adults with health problems, or anyone without a reasonably serious interest in archaeology and history. They cost $28.50 for adults. Reservations are required for all trips, so call ahead.

Another way to see the dolphins up close is on a 1½-hour Wave Runner tour with **CRS Beach Service,** which operates on the beach at the foot of Avenue C (☎ **941/463-3509**). The rides cost $75 for one person, $85 for two, and free for a third rider. Call for details and reservations.

Much easier nature excursions are on the *Island Princess* (☎ **941/765-4433,** ext. 246), a pontoon boat based at the Best Western Pink Shell Beach Resort marina on the north end of the island (see "Where to Stay," below). It usually goes on 1½-hour nature cruises Monday, Wednesday, and Friday afternoons. Prices are $12.50 for adults, $7 for children. The *Island Princess* also has bay fishing trips Monday, Wednesday, and Friday mornings ($25 adults, $22.50 children) and shelling trips on Thursday ($25 adults, $12 children). Reservations are recommended.

Docked at Snug Harbor under the Estero Island end of the Sky Bridge, the steel-hulled, 70-foot-long *Gulf Breeze* (☎ **941/572-3555** or 941/936-9300) carries up to 75 passengers on daytime and sunset nature cruises on the gulf and the backwaters. The trips depart at 10:30am and 1 hour before sunset, daily from December to April, Wednesday to Sunday off-season. Fare is $25 per person. There's a bar on board.

FISHING   Anglers can surf-cast, throw their lines off the pier at Times Square, or venture offshore on a number of charter fishing boats that dock at marinas under both ends of the Skyway Bridge. Agents at booths there will take reservations even when the boats are out, as will **Getaway Marina,** 18400 San Carlos Blvd., about half a mile north of the bridge (☎ **941/466-3600**). Expect to spend about $600 a day for a full day's fishing for up to 6 persons.

No reservations are required on "party boats" that take groups out. Operating year-round, the *Island Lady* (☎ **941/936-7470**) is docked at Fisherman's Wharf, virtually under the San Carlos Island end of the Skyway Bridge, while the **Great Getaway** and **Great Getaway II** (☎ **941/466-3600**) sail from the Getaway Marina on San Carlos Boulevard, about half a mile north of the bridge. They all depart between 8 and 9:30am; charge between $25 and $40 per person, depending on the length of the voyage; and have air-conditioned lounges with bars. Call for schedules and exact prices.

SCUBA DIVING & SNORKELING   Scuba diving is available at **Seahorse Scuba,** 17849 San Carlos Blvd. (☎ **941/454-3111**). Two-tank dives cost $55. Groups of four snorkelers can go on their own excursions for $25 each, including equipment.

The live-aboard dive boat *Ultimate Getaway,* based at Getaway Marina, 18400 San Carlos Blvd. (☎ **941/466-3600;** fax 941/644-7529), makes 4-day voyages to the Dry Tortugas. This 100-foot vessel carries a maximum of 20 divers and is equipped with a dive platform, chase boat, and TV/VCR. Trips cost $495 per person, including meals, beer, air, and weights, but bring your own regulator, mask, and fins.

WHERE TO STAY

The hostelries recommended below are removed from the crowds of Times Square, but three chain motels offer comfortable accommodations right in the center of the action: **Ramada Inn** (☎ **800/544-4592** or 941/463-6158), **Days Inn** (☎ **800/544-4592** or 941/463-9759), and **Howard Johnson's Motel** (☎ **800/544-4592** or

941/463-9231). The mid-rise **Best Western Beach Resort** (☎ **800/336-4045** or 941/463-6000) is a quarter mile north, just far enough to escape the noise but still have a lively beach.

Fort Myers Beach has a multitude of condominiums and cottages that offer good value, especially for families or groups who would like to have a kitchen and other comforts of home. The Best Western Pink Shell Beach Resort (see below) has a selection of luxurious condos and some of the most charming cottages.

Among the "condo hotels" here are **Diamond Head,** 2000 Estero Blvd., Fort Myers Beach, FL 33931 (☎ **888/765-5002** or 941/765-5002; fax 941/765-5755), a 12-story gulf-front establishment built in 1998; the 16-story **Pointe Estero Island Resort,** 6640 Estero Blvd., Fort Myers Beach, FL 33931 (☎ **800/237-5141** or 941/765-1155; fax 941/765-0657), whose 60 spacious apartments have Jacuzzi bathtubs and screened balconies with gorgeous gulf or bay views; the bayside **Santa Maria,** 7317 Estero Blvd., Fort Myers Beach, FL 33931 (☎ **800/765-6701** or 941/765-6700; fax 941/765-6909); and the **Grand View Resort,** 8701 Estero Blvd., Fort Myers Beach, FL 33931 (☎ **800/723-4944** or 941/765-4422; fax 941/765-4499), a 14-story high-rise on Lover's Key with its own palm-fringed beach and wonderful gulf, island, and bay views from balcony suites.

A number of agents offer weekly or monthly rentals, including **Hussey Real Estate** (☎ **941/463-3178;** fax 941/463-5434), and **Bluebill Properties** (☎ **800/237-2010** or 941/463-1141), which represent properties throughout Southwest Florida. The chamber of commerce (see "Essentials," above) publishes a complete list of accommodations and rental agents.

For information about rate seasons, see "Where to Stay" in section 1 on Fort Myers, earlier in this chapter.

For campers, the somewhat-cramped **Red Coconut RV Resort,** 3001 Estero Blvd. (☎ **941/463-7200;** fax 941/463-2609), has sites for RVs and tents both on the gulf side of the road and right on the beach. They cost $37 to $50 a night during winter, $24.50 to $44 off-season.

○ Best Western Pink Shell Beach Resort. 275 Estero Blvd., Fort Myers Beach, FL 33931. ☎ **800/554-5454** or 941/463-6181. Fax 941/481-4947. www.southseas.com. 208 units. A/C TV TEL. Winter $185–$259 double; $239–$395 condo or cottage. Off-season $119–$155 double; $135–$289 condo or cottage. Packages and weekly rates available. AE, DC, DISC, MC, V.

Not to be confused with the nearby Best Western Beach Resort, this popular, family-oriented establishment is quietly situated near Estero's north end; it fronts both the gulf and Matanzas Pass. It has hotel rooms, suites, one- and two-bedroom apartments, and beach cottages. Making up for a lack of luxury with lots of 1950s-style charm, the cottages are heavily booked during the winter months, so reserve early. The so-called villas here actually are spacious and luxurious, fully equipped apartments in one of two mid-rise, gulf-front buildings with lovely views of Sanibel Island from their screened balconies. The second mid-rise holds the hotel rooms and standard efficiencies, the least expensive units here.

The gulf beach side of the property has water-sports equipment to rent, three heated swimming pools, a kiddie pool, and a chickee bar serving libation and sporting entertainment at sunset. Sailboats and nature and sightseeing cruises pick up guests at the bayside marina, which rents boats and bikes. Facilities also include a coin laundry, a store for buying victuals, and lighted tennis courts. Every unit has cooking facilities, but the scenic Hungry Pelican Cafe, on a covered deck overlooking the channel, serves breakfast, lunch, and dinner.

Holiday Inn. 6890 Estero Blvd., Fort Myers Beach, FL 33931. ☎ **800/465-4329** or 941/463-5711. Fax 941/463-7038. 105 units. A/C TV TEL. Winter $179–$209 double. Off-season $89–$139 double. AE, DISC, MC, V.

Built by the shifting sands, the slowly emerging Little Estero Island (actually a peninsula) has left the surf a considerable distance from this modern, two-story motel, the center of beach activity on Estero's south end. Guests need not walk far to a courtyard swimming pool, tiki bar, and grill serving lunches and snacks. Beachfront suites are the choice accommodation here. Otherwise, you're better off paying a little more for a room facing the central courtyard rather than one looking out on the parking lots. The shops and restaurants of Villa Santini Plaza are a short walk away. With many European guests, staff members here are multilingual. The dining room serves breakfast, lunch, and dinner and has entertainment Wednesday to Sunday. Amenities include room service (7am to 9pm), free morning newspaper, outdoor heated pool, two lighted tennis courts, Wave Runners and parasailing, shuffleboard courts, valet and coin laundry, and gift shop.

Island House Motel. 701 Estero Blvd., Fort Myers Beach, FL 33931. ☎ **941/463-9282.** Fax 941/463-2080. 5 units. A/C TV TEL. Winter $99 efficiency. Off-season $55 efficiency. Weekly rates available. MC, V.

Sitting on stilts in the Old Florida fashion, but with modern furnishings, Ken and Sylvia Lachapelle's clapboard-sided establishment enjoys a quiet location along a bay-side channel, directly across the boulevard from the Best Western Beach Resort and within walking distance of busy Times Square. Four of their units have screened porches; all have kitchens and ceiling fans. Ken and Sylvia maintain an open-air lounge with a small library beneath one of the units. They also have a small heated pool, a guest laundry, beach chairs, and rental bikes. Local calls are free. Book as early as possible for February and March.

If you need a larger, two-bedroom unit, ask about the Lachapelle's **Edgewater Inn,** a short distance away at 781 Estero Blvd. (same phone and fax numbers).

✪ **Outrigger Beach Resort.** 6200 Estero Blvd. (P.O. Box 271), Fort Myers Beach, FL 33931. ☎ **800/749-3131** or 941/463-3131. Fax 941/463-6577. www.outriggerfmb.com. E-mail: rooms@outriggerfmb.com. 144 units. A/C TV TEL. Winter $115–$195 double. Off-season $85–$135 double. DISC, MC, V.

The same friendly owners have maintained this clean, pleasant gulfside motel since 1965. Their "garden efficiencies" in the original building have the feel of small cottages, with excellent ventilation through both front and rear windows and doors opening to backyard decks. Other buildings here are two-story blocks containing motel-style rooms and efficiencies. The latter have window-style air-conditioning units but also sport front and rear jalousie windows to let in natural breezes. While many rooms have views of the large parking lot, you'll quickly forget all that asphalt when you reach the beachside swimming pool, the large wooden deck for sunning, and the friendly tiki bar that dispenses libations until 8pm (it's one of the best places here for a sunset cocktail). The Deckside Cafe serves inexpensive breakfasts and is open for sandwiches and snacks until 8pm. There's a coin laundry on the premises.

Palm Terrace Apartments. 3333 Estero Blvd., Fort Myers Beach, FL 33931. ☎ **800/ 320-5783** or 941/765-5783. Fax 941/765-5783. www.all-florida.com/travel/palmterr.htm. 9 units. A/C TV TEL. Winter $82–$125 apt. Off-season $48–$79 apt. 3-day minimum stay required in winter. Weekly rates available. AE, DISC, MC, V.

Many European guests stay in these comfortable, well-maintained apartments about midway down the beach. The smaller, less-expensive units are on the ground level, with sliding glass doors opening to a grassy yard, but even they have cooking facilities including microwave ovens. Most units here are upstairs, with screened porches or decks overlooking a courtyard with a heated swimming pool, a shuffleboard court, and a gas grill for barbecuing. They all are equipped with high-quality tropical rattan and wicker furniture. Husband-and-wife owners Deborah Bowers and Peter Piazza don't provide daily maid service, but you'll have an ample supply of clean linens. There's beach access across Estero Boulevard, and Anthony's on the Gulf and the Junkanoo Beach Bar are 3 short blocks away.

Sandpiper Gulf Resort. 5550 Estero Blvd., Fort Myers Beach, FL 33931. ☎ **941/463-5721.** Fax 941/463-5721, ext. 299. 63 units. A/C TV TEL. Winter $115–$145 suite for 2. Off-season $69–$89 suite for 2. DISC, MC, V.

The units at this clean gulfside motel all have living and sleeping areas, full kitchens, convertible sofas, and sundecks overlooking either the gulf or a courtyard with a heated swimming pool and hot tub. Steps lead from the bedecked pool directly to the beach. Some suites are in two- or three-story buildings arranged in a U with the flattened ends right on the beach; others are in the Sandpiper II, a palm-fronted high-rise with its own heated pool next door. All suites are identical, but those directly facing the beach are more expensive. Facilities include a coin laundry and gift shop. Restaurants are nearby.

WHERE TO DINE

The busy area around Times Square has fast-food joints to augment several local restaurants catering to the beach crowds. The pick is the **Beach Pierside Grill,** directly on the beach at the foot of Lynn Hall Memorial Pier (☎ **941/765-7800),** a lively pub which bears the bright blond wood trim and vivid fabric colors reminiscent of establishments in Miami's South Beach. It all opens onto a large beachside patio with dining at umbrella tables, outstanding sunsets, and live bands playing at night. The reasonably priced fare is a catchall of conch fritters, shrimp and fish baskets, burgers, and seafood main courses. They take reservations—a plus in this busy area. Food is served daily from 11am to 11pm.

You'll find a row of national chain family restaurants at the Summerlin Square shopping center, on the mainland at San Carlos Boulevard and Summerlin Road. The beach trolley runs to Summerlin Square during the winter.

MODERATE

✪ **Anthony's on the Gulf.** 3040 Estero Blvd. (on the beach at Donora Blvd.). ☎ **941/463-2600.** Reservations not accepted. Pastas $9–$13; main courses $13–$17; burgers and sandwiches $5–$7. AE, DISC, MC, V. Daily 11:30am–11pm (Sun–Thurs 11:30am–10pm off-season). ITALIAN.

Right on the beach and above the constant party in the Junkanoo Beach Bar downstairs (see "Fort Myers Beach After Dark," below), this establishment has large windows with gulf views and the appropriately named Sunset Terrace, one of the better places on the island for a day-ending cocktail or an alfresco lunch or dinner. Inside, an old-fashioned, pole-driven ceiling fan reaching the full length of the dining room enhances a casual, unpretentious tropical ambience. This setting more than makes up for a somewhat less-than-inspired menu offering traditional Italian pizzas and pastas, and main courses of veal, chicken, and seafood (stick to the tomato sauces). Sandwiches and burgers are available at all hours here.

If Italian isn't your forte, the **Beach Light Grill,** on the other side of the Junkanoo Beach Bar (☎ **941/463-6139),** offers the same beachside gulf view to go with moderately priced seafood and prime beef. It's open the same hours as Anthony's.

♻ **Channel Mark.** 19001 San Carlos Blvd. (at the north end of San Carlos Island). ☎ **941/463-9127.** Reservations not accepted. Main courses $12–$25; sandwiches $6–$7. AE, DC, DISC, MC, V. Sun–Thurs 11am–10pm, Fri–Sat 11am–11pm. SEAFOOD.

Nestled by the "Little Bridge" leading onto San Carlos Island's northern end, every table here looks out on a maze of channel markers on Hurricane Bay. A dock with palms growing through it makes this a relaxing place for a waterside lunch. The atmosphere changes dramatically at night, with ceiling fans, potted plants, rattan chairs, well-spaced tables, and soft, indirect lighting creating a relaxed tropical ambience ideal for kindling romance. Congenial owner Mike McGuigan puts a creative spin on the seafood dishes, such as a rich concoction of snapper smothered in a roasted macadamia-nut sauce and topped with fresh strawberry butter. Even their fried items are more innovative than your usual fare: Their renowned, delicately seasoned crab cakes are lightly breaded with cornflakes and almonds. Calorie counters can opt for shrimp or mahimahi perfectly grilled over mesquite. The adjacent lounge offers the same menu and has live entertainment on weekends.

Gulf Shore Grill. 1270 Estero Blvd. (on the beach at Avenue A). ☎ **941/463-9951.** Reservations accepted for dinner. Breakfast $3–$9; sandwiches and burgers $6–$8.50; main courses $13–$23. AE, DISC, MC, V. Daily 8am–3pm and 5–10pm. AMERICAN.

On the southern fringes of Times Square, the old clapboard building offers splendid views of the gulf and beach. It began life in the 1920s as the Crescent Beach Casino and has seen various incarnations as bathhouse, gambling casino, dance hall, and rooming house. Now it's under command of Mark Combs and Michael Stanton, who have refurbished the interior and installed an extensive salad bar to accompany traditional Florida-style main courses, such as baked grouper imperial, grilled mahimahi, and shrimp wrapped in bacon and coated with honey. This is one of the best breakfast spots on the beach, with choices ranging from biscuits under sausage gravy to eggs served on a muffin under Alaskan crabmeat and a charon sauce.

The kitchen also provides the pub fare for **The Cottage,** an open-air drinking establishment next door (it's open daily from 11am to 2am), as well as the food for a walk-up hot-dog-and-ice-cream counter next to the beach downstairs.

Loggerheads. In Villa Santini Plaza, 7205 Estero Blvd. (at Lennel Rd.). ☎ **941/463-4644.** Reservations recommended on weekends. Sandwiches and burgers $5–$8; main courses $10–$15. AE, DISC, MC, V. Winter daily 8am–midnight. Off-season daily 11am–11pm. SEAFOOD/AMERICAN.

The motto "The Local's Nest" accurately describes this friendly storefront restaurant, where charter-boat captains congregate around a big square bar on one side of the knotty-pine–accented dining room. The menu offers a wide range of appetizers, big salads, sandwiches, burgers, and main-course options from both land and sea. Most of the main courses feature heavy cream sauces over pasta (the house specialty is scallops, spinach, artichokes, tomatoes, and bacon in a horseradish-tinged cream sauce), but you can order traditionally fried, grilled, broiled, or blackened seafood. You can order breakfast here during the winter months.

Matanzas Inn Restaurant. At Matanzas Marina, 416 Crescent St. (under the Skyway Bridge on Estero Island). ☎ **941/463-3838.** Reservations not accepted. Main courses $12–$18; sandwiches and light fare $6–$10. AE, DC, DISC, MC, V. Daily 11am–10pm. Closed Thanksgiving and Christmas. SEAFOOD.

Although it's in the busy Times Square tourist district, this casual, friendly, and consistent restaurant is popular with local residents who appreciate seafood fresh off the boats docking at Matanzas Marina. Dining is on a dock or an enclosed deck next to the marina or in a dark-paneled room hung with ceiling fans. The menu highlights fried, broiled, blackened, or charcoal-grilled seafood. A light-fare menu offers shrimp salad, fish sandwiches, and hamburgers. Up on the roof, the Upper Deck Lounge provides evening entertainment.

○ **Pappa Mondo Ristorante Italiano.** 1821 Estero Blvd. (at Ohio Ave.) ☎ **941/765-9660.** Reservations recommended. Main courses $8–$16; fixed-price menu $19. AE, MC, V. Daily noon–10pm. Closed Christmas. NORTHERN ITALIAN.

Brothers-in-law Pasquale Riso (he's the chef) and Andrea Mazzonetto hail from Italy, and the fare they present in their attractive dining room—or out on their roadside patio—is the real thing. They make everything from scratch—you can watch them producing pasta at a big machine behind a big picture window. The homemade pasta shows up in the likes of *stracci bianchi e neri ai frutti di mare,* an excellent combination of white and black pasta sautéed with fresh seafood and shaved zucchini in a white wine sauce. Ask your server to explain each evening's three pasta and three meat offerings (a special fixed-price menu features a sampling of all six).

INEXPENSIVE

○ **Greco's Italian Deli.** In Villa Santini Plaza, 7205 Estero Blvd. (at Lennel Rd.). ☎ **941/463-5634.** Subs and sandwiches $4–$5; pizzas $12–$15; ready-to-cook meals $6–$8. No credit cards. Mon–Sat 8am–9pm, Sun 9am–5pm. ITALIAN.

Wonderful aromas of baking pizzas, cannolis, breads, cookies, and fabulous calzones have been wafting from this shopping-center deli since 1958. Order at the counter over a chiller packed with fresh deli meats, Italian sausage, and cheeses, then devour your goodies at tables inside, out on the covered walkway, or at the beach for a picnic. You can also take "heat and eat" meals of spaghetti, lasagna, eggplant parmigiana, manicotti, and ravioli to your hotel or condo oven. Shelves are loaded with Italian wines, pastas, butter cookies, and anisette toast.

Strawberrie Corner Cafe & Ice Cream Parlor. 6035 Estero Blvd. (at Mound Rd.). ☎ 941/463-1155. Menu items $3–$7. No credit cards. Daily 11am–9:30pm. Closed Sept. DELI/ICE CREAM.

YOUR WILLPOWER ENDS HERE, warns a sign on the front door of this bright ice-cream parlor and deli on Estero Boulevard's only sharp curve, known as Strawberry Corner. Strawberry-print wallpaper, strawberry dolls, and photos of strawberries provide the decor, and strawberry shortcake is the house specialty. In addition, the menu offers terrific homemade soups, shrimp salads, and made-to-order deli sandwiches. Each white table here is adorned with colorful fresh flowers.

FORT MYERS BEACH AFTER DARK

For what's going while you're here, pick up copies of the *Beach Bulletin* and the *Fort Myers Beach Observer,* two local tabloid newspapers. They're available at the chamber of commerce (see "Essentials," above).

The area around Times Square is always active, every day during winter and on off-season weekends. In the very heart of Times Square at the foot of Lynn Hall Memorial Pier, the **Beach Pierside Grill,** 1000 Estero Blvd. (☎ 941/765-7800), has live entertainment on its beachside patio. Facing due west, **Jimmy's Beach Bar,** in the Days Inn at 1130 Estero Blvd. (☎ 941/463-9759), has live music nightly for the "best sunsets on the island" (actually you can say that of all the beachside establishments here). It's not directly on the beach, but locals in the know head for the rooftop bar at **The Beached Whale,** 1249 Estero Blvd. (☎ 941/463-5505). There are rock and reggae for nighttime dancing downstairs.

Away from the maddening crowds in the "middle beach" area, the ○ **Junkanoo Beach Bar,** under Anthony's on the Gulf, 3040 Estero Blvd. (☎ 941/463-2600), attracts a more affluent crowd for its Bohemian-style parties that run from 11:30am to 1:30am daily. Live bands here specialize in reggae and other island music. The menu offers inexpensive subs, sandwiches, burgers, and pizzas, and a concessionaire rents beach cabanas and water-sports toys, making it a good place for a lively day at the beach.

A few blocks north, **The Reef,** 2601 Estero Blvd. (☎ 941/463-8414), consistently has the best bands and the fewest tourists.

On the more couples- and family-oriented south end of Estero Island, the **Holiday Inn,** 6890 Estero Blvd. (☎ 941/463-5711), has live music for dancing Wednesday to Saturday and a deejay on Sunday from 9pm to 1am.

On Sunday afternoons, revelers jam the docks for the famous outdoor reggae parties at **The Bridge Waterfront Restaurant,** 708 Fisherman's Wharf (☎ 941/765-0050), which is under the Sky Bridge on San Carlos Island.

3　Sanibel & Captiva Islands

14 miles W of Fort Myers, 40 miles N of Naples

Sanibel and Captiva are unique in Florida. Here you will find none of the neon signs, amusement parks, and high-rise condos that clutter most beach resorts in the state. Indeed, Sanibel's main drag, Periwinkle Way, runs under a canopy of whispery pines and gnarled oaks so thick they almost obscure the small signs for chic shops and restaurants. This wooded ambience is the work of local voters, who have saved their trees and tropical foliage, limited the size and appearance of signs, and permitted no building higher than the tallest palm and no Wave Runner or other noisy beach toy within 300 yards of their gorgeous, shell-strewn beaches. I've been to Sanibel many times, but it was only recently that I saw an aerial photo of the island and realized its southern shore is lined with hotels and condominiums. The foliage disguises the buildings that well.

Furthermore, more than half of the two islands is preserved in its natural state as wildlife refuges. Here you can ride, walk, bike, canoe, or kayak through the J. N. (Ding) Darling National Wildlife Refuge, one of Florida's best.

Legend says that Ponce de León named the larger of these two barrier islands "San Ybel," after Queen Isabella of Spain. Another legend claims Captiva's name comes from the infamous pirate Jose Gaspar's keeping captured women here. The modern era dates from 1892, when a few farmers settled on the islands. One of them, Clarence Chadwick, started an unsuccessful key lime and copra plantation on Captiva; many of his towering coconut palms still stand, adding to that skinny island's tropical luster.

Concluding that their terrific fishing grounds could be more profitable than their sandy soil, local residents soon switched from farming to fishing camps. Affluent anglers flocked to the islands, first by private boat and then by ferry. When the Sanibel Causeway connected the islands to the mainland in 1963, the public at large began discovering their world-famous shelling beaches, wildlife, and aesthetic beauty.

ESSENTIALS

GETTING THERE　See "Getting There" in section 1 of this chapter for information about air, train, bus, and rental-car services. The Amoco station at 1015 Periwinkle Way, at Causeway Road, is the Sanibel agent for **Enterprise Rent-a-Car** (☎ 800/325-8007 or 941/395-3880).

Sanibel & Captiva Islands

Attractions:
Bailey-Matthews Shell Museum 10
J.N. (Ding) Darling National
   Wildlife Refuge 8
Sanibel Historical Village
   & Museum 14
Sanibel Lighthouse 23
Sanibel/Captiva Conservation
   Foundation 9
Tarpon Bay Recreation 11

Sanibel's Seaside Inn 24
Song of the Sea 25
South Seas Plantation Resort
   & Yacht Harbour 1
Sundial Beach Resort 32
'Tween Waters Inn 6

Accommodations:
Anchorage Inn of Sanibel 19
Beachview Cottages 34
Best Western Sanibel
   IslandBeach Resort 33
Brennen's Tarpon Tale Inn 22
Captiva Island Inn 5
Casa Ybel Resort 31
Holiday Inn Beach Resort 29
Island Inn 32
McCarthy's Marina & Cottages 5
Palm View Motel 27
Sanibel Inn 26

Dining:
Bubble Room 4
Hungry Heron 13
Jacaranda 18
Jerry's Family Restaurant 16
Lazy Flamingo 20
Lighthouse Cafe 21
Mad Hatter 7
McT's Shrimp House & Tavern 17
Morgan's Forest 28
Mucky Duck 2
R.C. Otter's Island Eats 2
Sanibel Cafe 15
Sunshine Cafe 2
Timbers 12

VISITOR INFORMATION The Sanibel-Captiva Islands Chamber of Commerce, 1159 Causeway Rd., Sanibel Island, FL 33957 (☎ 941/472-1080; fax 941/472-1070; www.sanibel-captiva.org; e-mail: island@sanibel-capitva.org), maintains a visitor center on Causeway Road as you drive onto Sanibel from Fort Myers. The chamber gives away an island guide (in English, German, and Spanish) and sells a detailed street map for $2 ($3 by mail). Other books are for sale, including comprehensive shelling guides and a helpful collection of menus from the islands' restaurants. There are phones for making hotel and condo reservations. Open Monday to Saturday from 9am to 7pm, Sunday from 10am to 5pm.

GETTING AROUND Neither Sanibel nor Capitva has public transportation. **No parking** is permitted on any street or road on Sanibel. Free beach parking is available on the Sanibel Causeway. Other municipal lots are either reserved for local residents or have a 75¢ hourly fee. Accordingly, many residents and visitors get around by bicycle (see "More Ways to Enjoy the Outdoors," below).

If you need a cab, call **Sanibel Taxi** (☎ 941/472-4160).

PARKS & NATURE PRESERVES

Named for the *Des Moines Register* cartoonist who was a frequent visitor here and who started the federal Duck Stamp program, the ✪ **J. N. (Ding) Darling National Wildlife Refuge,** on Sanibel-Captiva Road (☎ 941/472-1100), is home to alligators, raccoons, otters, and hundreds of species of birds. Occupying more than half of Sanibel Island, these 6,000-plus acres of mangrove swamps, winding waterways, and uplands have a 2-mile trail and a 5-mile, one-way **Wildlife Drive.** The visitor center shows brief videos about the refuge's inhabitants every half hour and sells a map keyed to numbered stops along the Wildlife Drive. The best times for viewing the wildlife are early morning, late afternoon, and at low tide (tables are posted at the visitor center and are available at the chamber of commerce). Mosquitoes and no-see-ums (tiny biting sand flies) are especially prevalent at dawn and dusk, so bring repellent.

Admission to the visitor center is free. The Wildlife Drive costs $5 per vehicle, $1 for hikers and bicyclists (free to holders of current federal Duck Stamps and National Park Service access passports). The visitor center is open from November to April, Saturday to Thursday from 9am to 5pm; off-season, Saturday to Thursday from 9am to 4pm. The center is open on federal holidays from January through May, closed on holidays the rest of the year. The Wildlife Drive is open all year, Saturday to Thursday from 1 hour after sunrise to 1 hour before sunset (that is, it's closed on Fri).

If you want a naturalist to explain what you're seeing, take a 2-hour narrated tram tour given by **Tarpon Bay Recreation,** at the north end of Tarpon Bay Road (☎ 941/ 472-8900). These cost $8 for adults, $4 for children 12 and under. You can board at the wildlife refuge headquarters during winter, at Tarpon Bay off-season. Schedules are seasonal, so call ahead.

Tarpon Bay Recreation also offers a variety of guided **canoe and kayak tours,** with an emphasis on the historical, cultural, and environmental aspects of the refuge (call for the schedule and reservations, which are required). It also rents canoes, kayaks, and small boats with electric trolling motors (see "More Ways to Enjoy the Outdoors," below).

Almost opposite the refuge visitor center, the nonprofit **Sanibel/Captiva Conservation Foundation,** 3333 Sanibel-Captiva Rd. (☎ 941/472-2329), maintains a nature center, a native plant nursery, and 4½ miles of nature trails on 1,100 acres of wetlands along the Sanibel River. You can learn more about the islands' unusual ecosystems through environmental workshops, guided trail walks, beach walks, and a natural-history boat cruise (call for seasonal schedules). Various items are for sale, including native plants and publications about the islands' birds and other wildlife. Admission is $3 for adults, free for children 16 and under. The nature center is open in winter Monday to Saturday from 8:30am to 4pm, off-season Monday to Friday 8:30am to 3pm.

HITTING THE BEACH: SHELLING & SEA LIFE

BEACHES   Sanibel has four public beach-access areas with metered parking: the eastern point around **Sanibel Lighthouse,** which has a fishing pier; **Gulfside City Park,** at the end of Algiers Lane, off Casa Ybel Road; **Tarpon Bay Road Beach,** at the south end of Tarpon Bay Road; and **Bowman's Beach,** off Sanibel-Captiva Road. **Turner Beach,** at Blind Pass between Sanibel and Captiva, is highly popular at sunset since it faces due west; there's a small free parking lot on the Captiva side, but parking on the Sanibel side is limited to holders of local permits. All except Tarpon Bay Road Beach have rest rooms. *Be forewarned:* Although nude bathing is illegal, the end of Bowman's Beach near Blind Pass often sees more than its share of bare straight and gay bodies.

Another popular beach on Captiva is at the end of Andy Rosse Lane in front of the Mucky Duck Restaurant. It's the one place here where you can rent motorized water-sports equipment (see "More Ways to Enjoy the Outdoors," below). There's a public beach with limited free parking just north of here, at the end of Captiva Drive (go past the entrance to South Seas Plantation Resort & Yacht Harbour to the end of the road).

SHELLING   Sanibel and Captiva are famous for their seashells, and local residents and visitors alike can be seen in the "Sanibel stoop" or the "Captiva crouch" while searching for some 200 species.

Before you start bending over, visit the impressive **Baily-Mathews Shell Museum,** 3075 Sanibel-Captiva Road (☎ **941/395-2233**), the only museum in the United States devoted solely to saltwater, freshwater, and land shells (yes, snails are included). Shells from as far away as South Africa surround a 6-foot globe in the middle of the main exhibit hall, thus showing their geographic origins. A spinning-wheel case identifies shells likely to wash up on Sanibel. Other exhibits are devoted to shells in tribal art, fossil shells found in Florida, medicinal qualities of various mollusks, the endangered Florida tree snail, and "sailor's Valentines"—shell craft made by natives of Barbados for sailors to bring home to their loved ones. The upstairs library attracts serious malacologists, and a shop purveys clever, shell-themed gifts. The museum is open Tuesday to Sunday from 10am to 4pm; admission is $5 adults, $3 children 8 to 16, free for children under 8.

February to April, or after any storm, is the best time of the year to look for whelks, olives, scallops, sand dollars, conch, and many other varieties. Low tide is the best time of day. The shells can be sharp, so wear Aqua Socks or old running shoes whenever you go walking on the beach.

With so many residents and visitors scouring Sanibel, you may have better luck on the adjacent shoals and nearby islands, such as Upper Captiva and Cayo Costa (see "Nearby Island Hopping," below). **Captiva Cruises** (☎ **941/472-5300**) has shelling trips from the South Seas Plantation Resort & Yacht Harbour on Captiva daily at 9am and 1pm. They cost $35 for adults, $17.50 for children. Reservations are required.

At least 15 charter-boat skippers also offer to take guests on shelling expeditions to these less-explored areas. Their half-day rates are about $180 for up to six people, so get up a group to go. Several operate from the **'Tween Waters Inn Marina** (☎ **941/ 472-5161**) on Captiva, including **Capt. Mike Fuery** (☎ **941/472-1015,** or 941/994-7195 on his boat). Others are based at **Jenson's Twin Palms Marina,** on Captiva (☎ **941/472-5800**), and at the **Sanibel Marina,** on North Yachtsman Drive, off Periwinkle Way east of Causeway Boulevard (☎ **941/472-2723**). They all distribute brochures at the chamber of commerce visitor center (see "Essentials," above) and are listed in the free tourist publications found there.

Caution: Florida law prohibits taking live shells from the beaches, and federal regulations prevent them from being removed from the J. N. (Ding) Darling National Wildlife Refuge.

MORE WAYS TO ENJOY THE OUTDOORS

BICYCLING, WALKING, JOGGING & IN-LINE SKATING   Paved bicycle paths follow alongside most major roads, including the entire length of Periwinkle Way and along Sanibel-Captiva Road to Blind Pass, making Sanibel a paradise for cyclists, walkers, joggers, and in-line skaters. And you can walk or bike the 5-mile, one-way nature trail through the J. N. (Ding) Darling National Wildlife Refuge.

The chamber of commerce visitor center has bike maps, as do Sanibel's rental firms: **Finnimore's Cycle Shop,** 2353 Periwinkle Way (☎ **941/472-5577**); **The Bike Rental,** 2330 Palm Ridge Rd. (☎ **941/472-2241**); **Island Moped,** 1470 Periwinkle Way (☎ **941/472-5248**); and **Tarpon Bay Recreation,** at the north end of Tarpon Bay Road (☎ **941/472-8900**). On Captiva, **Jim's Bike & Skate Rentals** on Andy Rosse Lane (☎ **941/472-1296**) rents bikes and beach equipment. Bike rates range from $5 per hour to $15 a day for basic models. Both Finnimore's and Jim's rent in-line skates.

There are no bike paths on Captiva, where trees alongside the narrow roads can make for dangerous riding.

BOATING & FISHING   On Sanibel, rental boats and charter-fishing excursions are available from **The Boat House** at the Sanibel Marina, on North Yachtsman Drive (☎ 941/472-2531), off Periwinkle Way east of Causeway Road. Tarpon Bay Recreation, at the north end of **Tarpon Bay Road** (☎ 941/472-8900), rents boats with electric trolling motors and tackle for fishing.

On Captiva, check with **Sweet Water Rentals** at the 'Tween Waters Inn Marina (☎ 941/472-6376), **Jenson's Twin Palms Marina** (☎ 941/472-5800), and **McCarthy's Marina** (☎ 941/472-5200), all on Captiva Road. Rental boats cost about $125 for half a day, $200 for a full day; that's about twice the price you'll pay elsewhere in Southwest Florida, including Naples.

Many **charter-fishing captains** are docked at these marinas. Half-day rates are about $200 for up to four people. The skippers leave free brochures at the chamber of commerce visitor center (see "Essentials," above), and they're listed in the free tourist publications found there.

CANOEING & KAYAKING   As noted under "Parks & Nature Preserves," above, **Tarpon Bay Recreation** (☎ 941/472-8900) has guided canoe and kayak trips in the J. N. (Ding) Darling National Wildlife Refuge. Do-it-yourselfers can rent canoes and kayaks here. They cost $20 for the first 2 hours, $5 for each additional hour. On Captiva, the **'Tween Waters Inn Marina** (☎ 941/472-5161) rents canoes and kayaks, as does **Captiva Kayak Co./WildSide Adventures,** based at McCarthy's Marina (☎ 941/935-2925).

Naturalist, avid environmentalist, and former Sanibel mayor **Mark "Bird" Westall** (☎ 941/472-5218; fax 941/472-6833) takes visitors on guided canoe trips through the wildlife refuge and on the Sanibel River. His excursions are timed for low tide and cost $35 for adults, $15 for children under 18. He will tailor shorter trips to accommodate children or anyone else not up to 2½ to 3 hours in a canoe. Naturalist **Brian Houston** leads kayaking trips from 'Tween Waters Inn Marina, but make your reservations at Tarpon Bay Recreation on Sanibel (☎ 941/472-8900). Brian charges $35 per person for his morning and midday trips, $25 for a shorter version leaving at 4pm. Richard Finkel of **Captiva Kayak Co./WildSide Adventures,** based at McCarthy's Marina on Captiva (☎ 941/935-2925), leads both day and night back-bay ecology trips for $35 adults, $25 for teenagers, $18 for children, plus 1-hour sunrise and sunset tours for $25 adults, $20 for teenagers, $18 for children. Richard will customize tours including camping on Cayo Costa (see "Nearby Island Hopping," below) for advanced kayakers. Reservations are essential with all these operators.

GOLF & TENNIS   Golfers may view a gallery of wild animals while playing the 5,600-yard, par-70, 18-hole course at the **Dunes Golf and Tennis Club,** 949 Sandcastle Rd., Sanibel (☎ 941/472-2535), whose back nine runs across a wildlife preserve. Call a day in advance for seasonal greens fees and a tee time. The Dunes also has seven tennis courts. The **South Seas Plantation Resort & Yacht Harbour** has tennis courts and a 9-hole golf course, but they're for guests only.

SAILING   If you want to learn how to sail, noted yachties Steve and Doris Colgate have a branch of their **Offshore Sailing School** at the South Seas Plantation Resort & Yacht Harbour (☎ 941/472-5111, ext. 7141). You can either learn to sail or polish your skills here. Half-day clinics cost $45 per person. Also ask about their popular women-only, father/son, and mother/daughter programs.

Also based on Captiva, two sailboats take guests out on the waters of Pine Island Sound: Mike McMillan's *Adventure* (☎ 941/472-7532 or 941/472-4386) and Mic

Gurley's *New Moon* (☎ **941/395-1782**). They cost $75 per hour with a 2-hour minimum. Reservations are required.

WATER SPORTS   Sanibel may prohibit motorized water-sports equipment on its beaches, but Captiva doesn't. **Yolo Watersports** (☎ **941/472-9656**) offers parasailing and Wave Runner rentals on the beach in front of the Mucky Duck Restaurant, at the gulf end of Andy Rosse Lane on Captiva.

Both scuba divers and snorkelers can go along with trips offered by the **Redfish Dive Center** (☎ 941/472-3483), the **Pieces of Eight Dive Center** (☎ 941/472-9424), and **Captiva Dive** (☎ 941/395-2000). All rent equipment and teach diving.

MORE TO SEE & DO

The **Sanibel Historical Village & Museum,** 950 Dunlop Rd. (☎ **941/472-4648**), includes the 1913-vintage Rutland home and the 1926 versions of Bailey's General Store (complete with Red Crown gasoline pumps), the post office, and Miss Charlotta's Tea Room. Displays highlight the islands' prehistoric Calusa tribal era, old photos from pioneer days, turn-of-the-century clothing, and a variety of memorabilia. Open Wednesday to Saturday from 10am to 4pm (and Sun from 1 to 4pm between mid-Dec and Easter); closed mid-August to mid-October. Admission is by $2 donation.

At the east end of Periwinkle Way, the **Sanibel Lighthouse** has marked the entrance to San Carlos Bay since 1884. The light keepers used to live in the cottages at the base of the 94-foot tower. The now-automatic lighthouse isn't open to visitors, but the grounds and beach are.

You can learn all about the islands' history on a 2-hour **Sanibel/Captiva Sights & History Trolley Tour,** staged by Adventures in Paradise (☎ **941/472-8443** or 941/437-1660). They cost $15 for adults, $10 for children, free for kids 3 and under. Call for schedule and reservations, which are required.

In addition to its island trips (see "Nearby Island Hopping," below), **Captiva Cruises** (☎ **941/472-5300**) goes out daily on dolphin-watching and sunset cruises from the South Seas Plantation Resort & Yacht Harbour on Captiva. These cost $17.50 for adults, $10 for children. Reservations are required.

SHOPPING

If you have no luck scouring the beaches for shells, several Sanibel shops sell thousands of them. **Sanibel Sea Shell Industries,** 905 Fitzhugh St. (☎ **941/472-1603**), has one of the largest collections, with more than 10,000 shells in stock. **She Sells Sea Shells** has two locations: 1157 Periwinkle Way near Causeway Road (☎ **941/472-6991**) and 2422 Periwinkle Way near the island's center (☎ **941/472-8080**). Others include **Neptune's Treasures Shell Shop,** in the Tree Tops Center, 1101 Periwinkle Way opposite the Dairy Queen (☎ **941/472-3132**), which also has a good collection of fossils.

You can burn up a rainy day and lots of credit at Sanibel's numerous upscale boutiques carrying expensive jewelry, apparel, and gifts. Many are in **Periwinkle Place** and **Tahitian Gardens,** the main shopping centers along Periwinkle Way. The larger Periwinkle Place sports mostly high-end men's and women's clothiers, while Tahitian Gardens has some excellent gift shops, including the **Audubon Nature Store** (☎ **941/395-2020**), which carries gifts and books with a wildlife theme, and **The Cheshire Cat** (☎ **941/472-3545**), offering nature toys and other unique items for kids.

More than a dozen Sanibel galleries feature original works of art; pick up a gallery guide at the chamber of commerce visitor center (see "Essentials" above). On Captiva, the tree house–like **Jungle Drums,** on Andy Rosse Lane (☎ **941/395-2266**), has the area's most unique collection of wildlife art.

Founded in 1899, **Bailey's General Store** is still going strong at the corner of Periwinkle Way and Tarpon Bay Road (☎ **941/472-1516**), with a supermarket, deli, salad bar, hardware store, beach shop, shoe repair, and Western Union all under one roof.

WHERE TO STAY

While modern resorts may try to re-create a South Seas island setting, there are still many Old Florida–style cottages on the two islands that really do look like they belong on Bora Bora. Some also represent good value if you can do without modern luxuries. The 32 pink clapboard structures at **Beachview Cottages,** 3325 W. Gulf Dr. (near Rabbit Road), Sanibel Island, FL 33957 (☎ **800/860-0532** or 941/472-1202; fax 941/472-4720), flank a narrow, unpaved lane running from the road to the beach and lined with coconut palms and colorful hibiscus. Winter rates here are $135 to $240 a day, but book well in advance because this clean, well-managed property is popular. Off-season, the cottages go for $95 to $170 a day. Also, see the introduction to Captiva Island accommodations, below, for more old-fashioned cottages.

Sanibel also has many condominium resorts; in fact, some accommodations recommended below are condo complexes operated as hotels. **1-800-SANIBEL** is a reservations service that will book you into most properties here, including condos and cottages (☎ **800/726-4235**). The largest rental agents are **Priscilla Murphy Realty,** 1177 Causeway Blvd. (P.O. Box 5), Sanibel Island, FL 33957 (☎ **800/237-6008** or 941/472-4883; fax 941/472-8995), and **VIP Vacation Rentals,** 1509 Periwinkle Way, Sanibel Island, FL 33957 (☎ **800/237-7526** or 941/472-1613; fax 941/481-8477). The chamber of commerce's island guide lists others (see "Essentials," above).

Only two chain hotels are present here. **Best Western Sanibel Island Beach Resort,** 3287 W. Gulf Dr. (at St. Kilda Road, near Rabbit Road), Sanibel Island, FL 33957 (☎ **800/645-6559** or 941/472-1700; fax 941/472-5032; www.southseas.com), has 45 spacious rooms, efficiencies, and apartments whose screened balconies face either the beach or a lawn festooned with palms, pink hibiscus, orange trees, a swimming pool, tennis courts, and white Adirondack chairs for lounging. Bicycles and beach equipment are complimentary. There's no restaurant on the premises, but you can dine at other nearby establishments. Winter rates range from $215 to $385 in a unit for two. Off-season, they cost $120 to $235.

The **Holiday Inn Beach Resort,** 1231 Middle Gulf Dr. (at the end of Donax Street), Sanibel Island, FL 33957 (☎ **800/HOLIDAY** or 941/472-4123), is on the beach, but its rooms don't have balconies or patios. It has a beachside pool and bar, a tennis court, bike rentals, a gift shop, a children's playground and activities program with an environmental emphasis, and Morgan's Forest restaurant (see "Where to Dine," below). Rates range from $200 to $350 in winter, from $145 to $168 off-season.

If you can't get into one of those, try the **West Wind Inn,** 3345 W. Gulf Dr. (☎ **800/824-0476** or 941/472-1541; fax 941/472-8134), and the **Snook Motel,** 3033 W. Gulf Dr. (☎ **800/741-6166** or 941/472-1345; fax 941/472-2148), two very comfortable, on-the-beach establishments near the Best Western Sanibel Beach Resort. The West Wind Inn has a restaurant on the premises.

In general, Sanibel and Captiva room and condo rates are highest during the shelling season, February to April. January is usually somewhat less expensive. But note that most rates fall drastically during the off-season. Don't hesitate to ask for a discount or special deal then. Since most properties on the islands are geared to 1-week vacations, you can also save by purchasing a package deal if you're staying for 7 nights or longer.

The islands' sole campground, the **Periwinkle Trailer Park,** 1119 Periwinkle Way, Sanibel Island (☎ **941/472-1433**), is so popular it doesn't even advertise. No other camping is permitted on either Sanibel or Captiva.

SANIBEL ISLAND
Very Expensive

✪ **Casa Ybel Resort.** 2255 W. Gulf Dr., Sanibel Island, FL 33957. ☎ **800/276-4753** or 941/472-3145. Fax 941/472-2109. 114 units. A/C TV TEL. Winter $375 one-bedroom suite; $430 two-bedroom suite. Off-season $195–$230 one-bedroom suite; $235–$270 two-bedroom suite. Packages and weekly rates available. AE, DISC, MC, V.

On the historic site of Sanibel's first beachfront resort, the Thistle Lodge, the present-day Casa Ybel's turn-of-the-century central building, houses a restaurant of that name, where both guests and nonguests can enjoy wonderful cuisine and magnificent gulf views. In four-story gray buildings on the beautifully landscaped grounds, the spacious one- and two-bedroom suites are bright, with tropical rattan furniture, pastel carpeting, ceramic-tile floors, and screened porches facing the gulf. Reflecting Thistle Lodge, the swimming pool here is one of Florida's most picturesque.

Amenities: Concierge, baby-sitting, adult and children's activities program, in-room massage. Whirlpool; six tennis courts with resident pro; water-sports center with sailboats, Windsurfers, and beach equipment for rent; rental bikes; children's pool and playground; golf privileges at the Dunes Golf and Tennis Club; coin laundry.

Sanibel Inn. 937 E. Gulf Dr., Sanibel Island, FL 33957. ☎ **800/554-5454** or 941/472-3181. Fax 941/472-5234. www.southseas.com. 98 units. A/C TV TEL. Winter $279–$399 double. Off-season $154–$274 double. Packages available. AE, DC, DISC, MC, V.

A back-to-nature theme prevails at this beachside inn, in both the room decor and the grounds planted with native Florida foliage specifically designed to attract butterflies and hummingbirds. The attractively furnished hotel rooms come complete with refrigerators, microwave ovens, VCRs, and coffeemakers. The fully equipped two-bedroom, two-bath condo apartments are some of Sanibel's most luxurious. All units have screened balconies.

Dining: The Portofino Restaurant offers breakfasts to guests and fine northern Italian dinners to all comers. Poolside cafe open for lunch.

Amenities: Nature-oriented children's activities program, laundry. Swimming pool in tropically landscaped area with boardwalk leading to the beach, two tennis courts with professionals available, bike and water-sports equipment rentals, gift shop; golfers can play at the Dunes Golf and Tennis Club.

Sanibel's Seaside Inn. 541 E. Gulf Dr., Sanibel Island, FL 33957. ☎ **800/831-7384** or 941/472-1400. Fax 941/472-6518. www.southseas.com. 32 units. A/C TV TEL. Winter $190–$360. Off-season $150–$205. Rates include continental breakfast. Packages available. AE, DC, DISC, MC, V.

This comfortable and friendly Key West–style establishment enjoys a tranquil location near the island's southeastern tip. All units have open-air balconies or porches. The studios have wet bars, refrigerators, microwave ovens, and coffeemakers, and all units have VCRs. The duplex, 1960s-style cottages are spacious, brightly furnished one-bedroom units, but the choice accommodations here are the beachfront efficiencies, whose screened porches face the gulf.

Amenities: Complimentary continental breakfast baskets delivered the previous afternoon. The swimming pool and suntanning patio are next to the beach. Barbecue grills, shuffleboard, guest laundry, complimentary bikes. Golfers can play at the Dunes Golf and Tennis Club.

Song of the Sea. 863 E. Gulf Dr., Sanibel Island, FL 33957. ☎ **800/231-1045** or 941/472-2220. Fax 941/472-8569. 30 units. www.southseas.com. A/C TV TEL. Winter $310–$370 double. Off-season $160–$215 double. Rates include continental breakfast. Packages available. AE, DC, DISC, MC, V.

Popular with Europeans, the rooms at this motel-like inn are warmly furnished and decorated in the continental fashion, including down pillows and comforters, duvet covers, and Thomasville pine armoires to conceal the TVs and VCRs. All units have kitchenettes, sliding glass doors opening to screened porches, dinette tables with wing chairs, and ceiling fans. The apartments have bedrooms barely large enough to hold their queen-size beds. A pathway leads next door to the Sanibel Inn (see above), where guests can use the facilities and dine at Portofino Restaurant. An extensive continental breakfast is served in the public building and eaten at umbrella tables on a brick patio.

Amenities: Valet laundry, guest Laundromat, complimentary video movies, beach umbrellas, and bicycle use. Heated swimming pool, outdoor whirlpool, shell-cleaning shack, library, bikes, coin laundry; tennis privileges at the Dunes Golf and Tennis Club.

✪ **Sundial Beach Resort.** 1451 Middle Gulf Dr., Sanibel Island, FL 33957. ☎ **800/237-4184** or 941/472-4151. Fax 941/472-8892. www.sundialresort.com. 270 units. A/C TV TEL. Winter $275–$575 condo apt. Off-season $145–$325 condo apt. Packages available. AE, DC, DISC, MC, V.

The largest resort on Sanibel, this popular family-oriented condominium complex stars an enormous, palm-studded, beachside pool and bar area. The one-, two-, and three-bedroom condominiums are housed in two- and three-story buildings (as high as they get on Sanibel) and have screened balconies overlooking the beach or tropically landscaped gardens. The condos are individually owned, so the decor varies but is always tasteful. VCRs and movies can be rented.

Dining/Diversions: There are several dining options here, including the award-winning Windows on the Water dining room, which offers glorious gulf views at breakfast, lunch, and dinner (reservations not accepted). Master chefs put on a show as they prepare delicious steak, chicken, and seafood dishes right by your table in Noopie's Japanese Seafood & Steakhouse; dinner reservations are required (☎ **941/395-6014**). The Deli offers piled-high sandwiches, snacks, pizza, and picnic foods from early morning to 11pm. Crocodial's Patio Bar and Grille offers sandwiches, hamburgers, and salads poolside. The relaxing lobby lounge is popular at sunset, and a dance band plays Top 40 hits from 7 to 11pm.

Amenities: Concierge, laundry, baby-sitting, recreation program for kids (including tours of a small ecology center with a touch tank), grocery-shopping service (stocks condos before arrival), daily adult activities program, complimentary marine biology program, in-room massage, 12 tennis courts with pro, five swimming pools, jogging trail, games area, bike and boat rentals, fitness center, coin laundry, business center; golfers get reduced greens fees at the Dunes Golf and Tennis Club.

Moderate

Brennen's Tarpon Tale Inn. 367 Periwinkle Way, Sanibel Island, FL 33957. ☎ **941/472-0939.** Fax 941/472-6202. www.tarpontale.com. 5 units. A/C TV. Winter $109–$179. Off-season $69–$139. Rates include continental breakfast. DISC, MC, V.

Self-described "reformed journalists" Terry and Carlene Brennen preside over this low-slung gray building in the "Old Sanibel" neighborhood, the island's first settlement, where the ferries from Fort Myers used to dock near the lighthouse. White walls and tile floors make their comfortable units bright, while French doors lead to gardens dense with seagrape, palm, and ficus trees, which provide privacy for a large outdoor hot tub. Three of their five units have separate bedrooms, while two other "deluxe studios" actually are two-bedroom suites. All have kitchens, and the Brennens deliver continental breakfast makings the night before. Newspapers, bicycles, and beach chairs and umbrellas (the gulf is about 150 yards away) are complimentary, and there's a social hour for guests twice a week. The rooms don't have phones (guests can hook their laptop-computer modems into a jack in the common room); but they do have TVs and VCRs, and there's a video-rental store next door. Guests can use a coin laundry.

Island Inn. 3111 W. Gulf Dr., Sanibel Island, FL 33957. ☎ **800/851-5088** or 941/472-1561. Fax 941/472-0051. 57 units. A/C TV TEL. Winter (including breakfast and dinner) $180–$290 double. Off-season (no meals) $100–$225 double. AE, DISC, MC, V.

It's difficult to get accommodations here during the peak winter season, but it's worth trying, for this classic beach resort has been in business for more than 100 years. Its original central building houses a bright, genteel dining room, a spacious lounge, and a library brightly furnished with old-style bentwood and wicker sofas and chairs. This is the kind of place where guests dress for dinner—jackets and collared shirts required, ties recommended for men at dinner—and seating is assigned (some guests have had the same table for years).

This main building looks out over a sandy, South Pacific–like yard to the gulf. Although neither charming in an Old Florida sense nor luxurious by today's standards, the cottages and motel rooms (with or without kitchens) are modern and comfortable and have screened porches or balconies. There are a small swimming pool, a tennis court, and a croquet area.

Inexpensive

Anchorage Inn of Sanibel. 1245 Periwinkle Way, Sanibel Island, FL 33957. ☎ **941/395-9688.** 9 units, 3 cottages. A/C TV. Winter $89 double; $150 cottage. Off-season $59 double; $99 cottage. AE, DISC, MC, V.

This modest establishment is well maintained by the owners of the Holiday Inn Beach Resort (guests here can use the beach and play tennis there). Standard rooms, efficiencies, and two-room units are in low-slung buildings with broad common porches facing a central courtyard with small pool. Although these units would rent for half these rates elsewhere, they are clean and a good value for Sanibel. The three cottages are A-frame contraptions with spiral staircases to a second-story sleeping loft.

✪ **Palm View Motel.** 706 Donax St., Sanibel Island, FL 33957. ☎ **941/472-1606.** Fax 941/472-1606. 8 units. A/C TV. Winter $80 double; $105–$160 efficiency and apts. Off-season $45 double; $55–$90 efficiency and apts. MC, V.

In a quiet residential area less than a block from the Holiday Inn Beach Resort, this little motel is the jewel of Sanibel's few inexpensive accommodations. It's owned and operated by the Pirate Playhouse (see "Sanibel & Captiva Islands After Dark," below), so your fellow wintertime guests could include professional actors. The traditional furnishings are from the 1970s but are nonetheless comfortable. The best choices here are the spacious, well-ventilated one- and two-bedroom apartments. All units except two motel rooms have kitchens; these two rooms interconnect and are often rented together.

CAPTIVA ISLAND

As on Sanibel, cottages offer some of the best values on Captiva. Strongly reminiscent of the genuine South Pacific is **McCarthy's Marina & Cottages,** 15041 Captiva Dr.

(P.O. Box 580), Captiva Island, FL 33924 (☎ 941/472-5200; fax 941/472-6405), where four simple houses sit in a bayside palm and orange grove. The popular beach at the end of Andy Rosse Lane is just a block away. McCarthy's cottages range from $130 to $165 a day during winter, $85 to $115 a day off-season. You'll pay about the same to rent Old Florida cottages at the nearby **Jenson's Twin Palm Cottages & Marina,** P.O. Box 191, Captiva Island, FL 33924 (☎ 941/472-5800). Over by the beach, **Jenson's On the Gulf,** P.O. Box 460, Captiva Island, FL 33924 (☎ 941/ 472-4684), has cottages as well as homes, apartments, and studios ranging from $175 to $410 in winter, $125 to $310 off-season.

Captiva Island Inn. 11509 Andy Rosse Lane (P.O. Box 1085), Captiva Island, FL 33924. ☎ 800/454-9898 or 941/395-0882 or 941/472-4104. Fax 941/472-6804. 7 units. AC TV TEL. Winter $135–$195 double. Off-season $99–$125 double. Rates include full breakfast. AE, DISC, MC, V.

Owned by Rob and Cathy DeGennaro, whose R.C. Otter's Island Eats is across the street (see "Where to Dine," below), this B&B complex sits virtually surrounded by restaurants, art galleries, and boutiques along Captiva's 1-block-long commercial street. That can make it a bit too busy for some eyes and ears, but it has its charms. Two suites in the Key West–style main building open to up- or downstairs porches overlooking the lane, while five Dutch clapboard cottages sit out back on the fringes of a gravel parking lot (you get just enough yard here for hammocks and a gas grill). One cottage once housed aviator Charles Lindbergh, in whose honor Rob and Cathy painted clouds against a blue sky on the ceiling. It and the rest of the units have ceiling fans, kitchens, large bathrooms, queen-size sofa beds in their living rooms, cool tile floors, and designer bed linens (including down comforters for the occasional chilly night). Guests get free use of bicycles, chairs for the beach (a block away), and full breakfast at R.C. Otter's Island Eats. For a fee they can go on cruises in an old stone crab boat or in Rob's 37-foot sailboat.

✪ **South Seas Plantation Resort & Yacht Harbour.** P.O. Box 194, Captiva Island, FL 33924. ☎ 800/554-5454 or 941/472-5111. Fax 941/481-4947. www.southseas.com. 600 units. A/C TV TEL. Winter $180 double; to $880 apt, cottage, town house, or private home. Off-season $110–$140 double; to $620 apt, cottage, town house, or private home. $8 per person per day gratuity added to all bills in lieu of tipping. Packages available. AE, DC, DISC, MC, V.

Formerly Clarence Chadwick's 330-acre copra plantation, this exclusive establishment is the premier property on these two islands. It's one of the best choices in southern Florida for serious tennis buffs (18 courts with pro), and its gulfside golf course is one of the most picturesque nine-holers anywhere. The resort occupies all of Captiva's northern third, making it ideal if you want to step from your luxury villa or condo right onto 2½ miles of gorgeous beach. There's no central focus here, for this really is a sprawling real-estate development. There are no high-rise buildings, but an assortment of luxury homes and condos are so spread out along the shore that a free trolley shuttles back and forth through the mangrove forests that separate them.

Most accommodations here are so-called villas (actually condo apartments), but there's a great variety of offerings, including luxury homes with private pools and their own tennis courts (many are occupied exclusively by their owners; watch for famous folks wandering about). With three bedrooms or more, some units are ideal for families or couples who want to share the cost of a vacation. The least expensive (and least inspired) units are the "Harbourside" hotel rooms at the yacht basin and marina near the island's northern tip, the jumping-off point for Captiva Cruises and Steve and Doris Colgate's Offshore Sailing School. Next up are the "Bayside Villas" and "Beachside

Villas"—condo apartments in three-story buildings near the main-gate area and its shops and restaurants. Whatever type of living space you choose, by all means inquire about package deals, which can result in significant savings for stays of 3 nights or more.

The resort's no-cash, charge-to-your-room policy prevents gate-crashers from dining or playing here.

Dining: Set in the plantation workers' waterside commissary, the upscale King's Crown serves gourmet-quality seafood dinners in a romantic setting with a bay view. Cap'n Al's Dockside Grill is a pleasant spot for alfresco breakfasts, lunches, and dinners while waiting to see the resident manatees surfacing in the yacht harbor.

Amenities: Concierge, room service (until 11pm), valet and coin-operated laundry, grocery-shopping service that stocks condos before arrival, baby-sitting and activities program for children and teenagers. 18 tennis courts (7 lighted), nine-hole golf course, 2 marinas (1 with sailing school), 18 swimming pools (many with bars), water-sports center (arranges for parasailing, windsurfing, boat rentals, scuba diving, and more), rental bikes, boutique, nature center; golfers can also play at the Dunes Golf and Tennis Club. Outside the main gate, Chadwick's Shopping Center includes high-fashion boutiques, jewelry stores, and gift shops, all open to the public.

✪ **'Tween Waters Inn.** P.O. Box 249, Captiva Island, FL 33924. ☎ **800/223-5865** or 941/472-5161. Fax 941/472-0249. 137 units. A/C TV TEL. Winter $185–$475. Off-season $110–$350. Packages available. AE, DISC, MC, V.

Wedged between the gulf beach and the bay on the narrowest part of Captiva, this venerable establishment was the regular haunt of cartoonist J. N. (Ding) Darling. Anne Morrow Lindbergh also spent a winter here, writing *A Gift from the Sea*. Just as Darling preserved the islands' wildlife, the 'Tween Waters has saved the cottages he stayed in. Situated in a sandy palm grove, these pink shiplap buildings capture Old Florida with simple white furniture and terrazzo floors. Some face the gulf; others, the bay. The hotel rooms and apartments are in three modern buildings on stilts; they all have screened balconies facing the gulf or bay.

Dining/Diversions: The Canoe Club is a bargain, with inexpensive salads, sandwiches, burgers, and pizzas; it has a bayside deck for lunches. The Old Captiva House restaurant appears very much as it did in Ding Darling's days (his cartoons adorn the walls) and offers reasonably priced breakfasts, lunches, and seafood dinners during winter (only breakfast and dinner off-season). The popular Crow's Nest Lounge has live entertainment and provides snacks and light evening meals from 9pm to 1am.

Amenities: Charter captains dock at the full-service marina (see "Hitting the Beach: Shelling & Sea Life" and "More Ways to Enjoy the Outdoors," above). Canoes, bikes, and beach cabanas can be rented. Very large swimming-pool complex, complete with wood decking and a bar, adjacent to three lighted tennis courts. Fitness center, games room, boutique.

WHERE TO DINE

Some restaurants here close or take long vacations during the off-season, so it's wise to call ahead if you're on the islands between May and November.

SANIBEL ISLAND

The lively **Cheeburger Cheeburger,** 2413 Periwinkle Way, at Palm Ridge Road (☎ **941/472-6111**), has Sanibel's biggest and best burgers.

Much of the "help" on this affluent island dines at **Jerry's Family Restaurant,** 1700 Periwinkle Way at Casa Ybel Road (☎ **941/472-9300**), which offers wholesome and inexpensive diner fare (ingredients come fresh from the adjacent Jerry's Supermarket).

Both the restaurant and the supermarket are open daily from 6am to 11pm. Breakfast is served from 6am to 4pm, and you can usually get a table quickly here (which can't be said of Sanibel's other popular breakfast spots).

Also, you'll find very reasonably priced pub fare at Sanibel's lively sports bars, such as the **Lazy Flamingo I** (see below) and the **Sanibel Grill,** 703 Tarpon Bay Rd., near Palm Ridge Road (☎ 941/472-3128), which actually serves as the bar for the Timbers, the fine seafood restaurant next door (see below). They all have reduced-price beer and munchies during televised football games.

There's no Starbucks coffee emporium here, so the local cure for caffeine withdrawal is **The Bean,** 2240 Periwinkle Way, in Sanibel Square shopping center west of Dunlop Road (☎ 941/395-1919). This little open-air spot sits next to the Pirate Playhouse, so it draws an after-theater crowd for tasty and inexpensive fare such as pannini sandwiches on foccacia bread. A peanut-butter-and-jelly on bagel sandwich should quiet the kids' hunger pangs. You also can order freshly baked muffins and scones, and there are ice cream, sodas, and shakes, too. Open daily from 7:30am to 10pm.

For picnics at Sanibel's beaches or on a canoe, the deli and bakery in **Bailey's General Store,** at Periwinkle Way and Tarpon Bay Road (☎ 941/472-1516), carries a gourmet selection of breads, cheeses, and meats. **Huxter's Deli and Market,** 1203 Periwinkle Way, east of Donax Street (☎ 941/472-6988), has sandwich fixings and "beach box" lunches to go.

Expensive

۞ Mad Hatter. 6467 Sanibel-Captiva Rd., at Blind Pass. ☎ 941/472-0033. Reservations suggested. Main courses $18–$30. AE, DISC, MC, V. Mid-Dec to Apr Tues–Sat 11:30am–2pm, daily 5–9:30pm. May to mid-Dec Mon–Sat 5–9:30pm. INNOVATIVE/NEW AMERICAN.

Brian and Jayne Baker's popular gulf-front restaurant has only 12 tables, but each has a gulf view that's perfect at sunset. Based on California, the Southwest, and the South, the food is a fantasy of New American cuisines, with some exotic accents. The menu changes frequently, with no dish repeated (so as not to bore a dedicated loyal local following). Recent offerings have included innovative treatments of grouper (topped with parmesan, bacon, green onions, and a wild-mushroom, capers, and wine sauce) and yellowfin tuna (sushi quality, coated in pistachios and lightly seared). Whatever they serve, you'll enjoy.

Moderate

Jacaranda. 1223 Periwinkle Way (east of Donax St.). ☎ 941/472-1771. Reservations recommended. Main courses $15–$22. AE, DC, DISC, MC, V. Daily 5–10pm. Lounge daily 4pm–12:30am. Closed Christmas. SEAFOOD/PASTA/STEAKS.

Named for the purple-flowered jacaranda tree, this friendly and casual restaurant features a raw bar and lounge in a screened patio. Recipient of several dining awards, it's best known for expertly prepared fish and seafood, which the chef will bake, saute, or blacken, or you can choose certified Angus steaks or prime rib. A favorite pasta dish is linguine and a dozen littleneck clams tossed in a piquant red or white clam sauce. For dessert, the gooey turtle pie—ice cream, caramel, fudge sauce, chopped nuts, and whipped cream—will send you away stuffed. With live music nightly, the Patio Lounge attracts an affluent middle-age and seniors crowd.

۞ McT's Shrimp House & Tavern. 1523 Periwinkle Way (at Fitzhugh St.). ☎ 941/472-3161. Reservations not accepted. Main courses $13–$20; early-bird specials $9. AE, DC, DISC, MC, V. Shrimp House daily 4–10pm; McT's Tavern daily 4pm–12:30am. SEAFOOD.

Shrimp reigns at this casual, Old Florida–style establishment, where you'll see a line outside at 4pm waiting for the early-bird specials served to the first 100 persons in the door. Everyone else gets to view the daily catch displayed in a chiller case, including the night's shrimp ready for the chef to prepare in one of at least a dozen ways, from steamed to fried in a coconut-and-almonds batter. There are also grouper and swordfish, plus steaks and chicken for the land-minded, but stick to the shrimp here (see below for Timbers, which does a much better job cooking fish). With a pinball machine and a huge sports TV in the rear of the building, McT's Tavern offers an extensive choice of appetizers and light dinners.

Morgan's Forest. 1231 Middle Gulf Dr., at the Holiday Inn Beach Resort. ☎ **941/472-3351.** Reservations not accepted. Main courses $14–$23. AE, DC, DISC, MC, V. Mon–Sat 7–11am and 5–10pm, Sun 9am–noon and 5–10pm. SEAFOOD.

The kids will love dining in this miniature jungle patterned after the Rainforest Cafes elsewhere. Almost hidden among all the foliage are mechanical but lifelike moving jaguars, monkeys, birds, and a huge python entangled in vines above the bar. Squawking bird sounds, strobe lightning bolts followed by claps of thunder, and an occasional faux fog rolling across the floor add to the Amazonian ambience. The owner of Fort Myers Beach's excellent Channel Mark is in charge here, which means that your taste buds will be as entertained as your eyes and ears. The fine crab cakes are the pick of a menu otherwise accented with South- and Central American seasonings. Order the shrimp Belize only if you're ready for a thick cream sauce and blazing-hot Cajun spices. Obviously there's a children's menu.

✪ **Timbers.** 703 Tarpon Bay Rd. (at Palm Ridge Rd.). ☎ **941/472-3128.** Reservations not accepted. Main courses $13–$23; early birds get $2.50 off regular price. AE, MC, V. Winter daily 4:30–10pm. Off-season daily 5–10pm. SEAFOOD/STEAK.

This casual upstairs restaurant, with bamboo railings, oversized canvas umbrellas, and paintings of tropical scenes through faux windows, consistently has the freshest fish available. You can view the catch in the fish market out front and have the chef charcoal-grill or blacken it to order. The steaks are aged and cut on the premises. You can order a drink from the adjoining Sanibel Grill sports bar and wait for a table outside on the shopping center's porch.

Inexpensive

✪ **Hungry Heron.** In Palm Ridge Place, 2330 Palm Ridge Rd. (at Periwinkle Way). ☎ **941/395-2300.** Reservations not accepted but call for preferred seating. Main courses $8–$15; sandwiches, burgers, snacks $5–$10; weekend breakfast buffet $7. AE, DISC, MC, V. Winter Mon–Fri 11am–10pm, Sat–Sun 7:30–11am and 7:30–10pm. Off-season daily 11am–8:30pm. AMERICAN.

Ted and Jim Iannelli's tropically decorated eatery is Sanibel's most popular family restaurant. There's something for everyone on their huge, tabloid-size menu—from hot and cold appetizers and overstuffed "seawiches" to pasta and steamed shellfish. And if the 250 regular items aren't enough, there's a list of nightly specials. Seafood, steaks, and stir-fries from a sizzling skillet are popular with local residents, who bring the kids here for fun and a children's menu. Cartoons run all the time, and a magician usually circulates among the tables from 5 to 9pm. An all-you-can-eat breakfast buffet on Saturday and Sunday in winter is an excellent value.

The Lazy Flamingo I. 1036 Periwinkle Way, near Causeway Blvd. ☎ **941/472-6939.** Reservations not accepted. Sandwiches and snacks $5–$9; main courses $11–$15. AE, DC, DISC, MC, V. Daily 11:30am–1am. SEAFOOD/PUB FARE.

T-shirts and shorts or jeans are the dress code at this very casual sports pub that always seems packed by the young and young-at-heart, who flock here for reasonably priced food, a wide choice of beers iced down in a huge box behind the bar, and sports TVs.

Some of that beer is used to steam shrimp and a finger-stinging collection of oysters, clams, and spices known as "The Pot." It also serves conch fritters, conch chowder, and conch salad. The flamingo-pink menu also has an array of sandwiches, burgers, fish platters, and very spicy "Dead Parrot Wings." Fillet your own catch, and the chef will cook it to order for $6. Happy-hour prices prevail whenever football games are on the TVs.

A sister institution, the **Lazy Flamingo II,** 6520-C Pine Ave., at Sanibel-Captiva Rd. one-quarter of a mile south of Blind Pass (☎ 941/472-5353), has the same menu and hours.

Lighthouse Cafe. In Seahorse Shops, 362 Periwinkle Way (at Buttonwood Lane, east of Causeway Rd.). ☎ 941/472-0303. Reservations not accepted but call ahead for preferred seating. Breakfast $3–$6; main courses $8–$14. MC, V. Daily 7am–3pm and 5–9pm. Closed for dinner Easter to mid-Dec. AMERICAN.

Decorated with photos and drawings of lighthouses, this casual storefront establishment appropriately near the Sanibel Lighthouse dishes up breakfast omelettes that are meals in themselves, especially the ocean frittata containing delicately seasoned scallops, crabmeat, shrimp, broccoli, and fresh mushrooms, and crowned by an artichoke heart and creamy Alfredo sauce. Seafood Benedict is another unusual offering. There's also an interesting sandwich menu. Reasonably priced dinners are served during winter only.

✪ **Sanibel Cafe.** In the Tahitian Gardens Shops, 2007 Periwinkle Way. ☎ 941/472-5323. Call ahead for preferred seating. Breakfast $3–$9; salads and burgers $4–$9; main courses $6–$9.50. MC, V. Daily 7am–9pm. AMERICAN.

Seashells are the theme at Lynda and Ken Boyce's pleasant cafe, whose tables are museum-like glass cases containing delicate fossilized specimens from the Miocene and Pliocene epochs. Fresh-squeezed orange and grapefruit juice, Danish Havarti omelettes, and homemade muffins and biscuits highlight the breakfast menu (eggs Benedict and fruit-filled waffles are served until closing). Lunch features specialty sandwiches; shrimp, Greek, and chicken-and-grape salads made with a very light, fat-free dressing; and a limited list of main courses such as grilled or blackened chicken breast. At dinner they add homemade meatloaf and crunchy grouper. Lynda and Ken even serve a sugar-free pancake syrup, but you can fatten up on Lynda's homemade red raspberry jam, apple or cherry crisps, and terrific key lime pie.

Captiva Island

You can't miss the **Green Flash,** 15183 Captiva Rd. (☎ 941/472-3337), which sits at the infamous "curve" where Captiva Road takes a sharp turn to the north. You won't see the green flash as the sun sets here, for this modern establishment looks eastward across Pine Island Sound. On the other hand, it makes for a nice view at lunch, and seeing the full moon turn the sound into glistening silver is worth having at least a late-evening drink here.

Just outside South Seas Plantation & Yacht Harbour, **Chadwick's Restaurant & Lounge** (☎ 941/472-1511, ext. 5181) is noted in these parts for its all-you-can-eat theme buffets at lunch Monday to Saturday ($10.50 per adult, $5.95 for kids 4 to 20, free for children under 4) and at dinner nightly ($21 to $25 adults, $11 for kids). There's also an extensive and free happy-hour munchie buffet daily from 4:30 to 7:30pm.

Big deli sandwiches and picnic fare are available at the **Captiva Island Store,** Captiva Road at Andy Rosse Lane (☎ 941/472-2374), and the gourmet-oriented **C.W.'s Market and Deli,** at the entrance to the South Seas Plantation Resort & Yacht Harbour (☎ 941/472-5111). The beach is a block from these stores.

The Bubble Room. 15001 Captiva Rd. (at Andy Rosse Lane). ☎ **941/472-5558.** Reservations not accepted. Main courses $15–$28; lunch $6–$12. AE, DC, DISC, MC, V. Daily 11:30am–2:30pm and 5:30–10pm (5–10pm Labor Day–Christmas). Closed Christmas. STEAK/SEAFOOD.

The gaudy bubble-gum pink, yellow, purple, and green exterior of this amusing restaurant is only a prelude to the 1930s, 1940s, and 1950s Hollywood motif inside. The dining rooms are adorned with a collection of puppets, statues of great movie stars, toy trains, thousands of movie stills, and antique jukeboxes that play big band–era tunes. The menu carries on the cinematic theme: prime ribs Weismuller, Eddie Fisherman fillet of fresh grouper, and Henny Young-One boneless breast of young chicken. Both adults and children (who can dine for $7 at dinner, $3.50 at lunch) are attracted to this expensive but fun establishment, where the portions are huge. For lighter appetites, the "Tiny Bubble" sampler includes a salad, a choice of appetizer, and a large slice of key lime pie.

✪ **Mucky Duck.** Andy Rosse Lane (on the gulf). ☎ **941/472-3434.** Reservations not accepted. Lunch $5–$10.50; dinner main courses $12–$19. AE, DC, DISC, MC, V. Mon–Sat 11:30am–2:30pm and 5–9:30pm. SEAFOOD/PUB FARE.

A Captiva institution since 1976, this lively, British-style pub is the one place here where you can dine right by the beach. If you don't get a real seat with this great view, the humorous staff will gladly roll a fake window over to appease you. The menu offers a selection of fresh seafood items, plus English fish-and-chips, steak-and-sausage pie, and a ploughman's lunch. There are a children's menu and a vegetarian platter. No smoking is allowed inside. You can't make a reservation, but you can order drinks, listen to live music (Mon to Sat), and bide your wait at beachside picnic tables out front (come early for sunset).

✪ **R.C. Otter's Island Eats.** 11506 Andy Rosse Lane. ☎ **941/395-1142.** Reservations not accepted. Breakfast $7–$12; salads, sandwiches, burgers $6–$9; main courses $10–$14. AE, DISC, MC, V. Daily 8am–10pm (breakfast to 11:30am). AMERICAN.

The founder of Sanibel's Hungry Heron (see above), owner Rob DeGennaro brought informality and good, inexpensive food to Captiva when he opened this fun Key West–style establishment in 1998. You can wander into this shiplap island cottage in your bare feet and not spend a fortune for an excellent breakfast, snack, lunch, or full meal. In contrast to the Captiva's 15 or so formal haute-cuisine restaurants, the tables here are covered with wrapping paper, and rolls of paper towels serve as napkins. The choice seats are under ceiling fans out on the front porch, although you can opt for the bright dining room whose walls are adorned with the works of local artists, including Rob's father, Frank, who painted the sunset scene in what once was a window. The wide-ranging menu includes salads, hot dogs, burgers, sandwiches, stir-fries, meatloaf, country fried steak, broiled fish, and soft-shell crabs, plus delicious nightly specials. The island's best breakfasts are equally varied, from bacon and eggs to house-smoked salmon. Songwriters perform their works out in the yard nightly, and you could find yourself dancing on the front porch.

Sunshine Cafe. In Captiva Village Sq., Captiva Rd. at Laika Lane. ☎ **941/472-6200.** Reservations recommended. Small platters $6–$9; large platters $19–$22; sandwiches $7–$7.50. AE, MC, V. Daily 11:30am–4pm and 5–9:30pm. ECLECTIC.

This friendly open-kitchen cafe has only 10 tables—five inside, five on the shopping center's porch—but the food is worth the close quarters. Everything except the bread is prepared on the premises. Specialties are charcoal-grilled steak and shrimp, spicy chicken breast, po-boy sandwiches, and fresh nightly pastas, but delicious daily specials usually feature fresh fish. The portions are large here, so the "small platters," such as black beans and rice, actually make a substantial meal at a reduced price. Various desserts are offered daily; the apple crisp is a winner. Anything on the menu can be ordered to carry out.

SANIBEL & CAPTIVA ISLANDS AFTER DARK

You won't find glitzy nightclubs on these family-oriented islands, but night owls have some fun places to roost at the resorts and restaurants mentioned above. Here's a brief recap:

ON SANIBEL The Sundial Beach Resort's **Lobby Lounge,** 1451 Middle Gulf Dr. (☎ 941/472-4151), features entertainers during dinner, then live bands for dancing from 9pm on. The **Patio Lounge,** in the Jacaranda, 1223 Periwinkle Way (☎ 941/ 472-1771), attracts an affluent crowd of middle-agers and seniors to its live music every evening. **McT's Tavern,** 1523 Periwinkle Way (☎ 941/472-3161), has darts, video games, and a large-screen TV for sports fans. The **Sanibel Grill,** 703 Tarpon Bay Rd. (☎ 941/472-4453), and the two **Lazy Flamingo** branches (see "Where to Dine," above) are other popular sports bars.

From December to April, professional actors perform Broadway dramas and comedies Monday to Saturday at 8pm in Sanibel's state-of-the-art, 150-seat **Pirate Playhouse,** 2200 Periwinkle Way (☎ 941/472-0006). Call for the schedule and ticket prices.

Originally a one-room school built in 1896 and later housing the Pirate Playhouse before its new facility was constructed across the road, the **Old Schoolhouse Theater,** 1905 Periwinkle Way (☎ 941/472-6862), complements its neighbor by offering Broadway musicals and revues from December to April. From May to November, the Off Beach Players perform comedies and mystery plays for all ages. Call for the current schedule and prices.

ON CAPTIVA Local songwriters perform their works nightly at **R.C. Otter's Island Eats,** 11500 Andy Rosse Lane (☎ 941/395-1142). The **Crow's Nest Lounge,** in the 'Tween Waters Inn, on Captiva Road (☎ 941/472-5161), is Captiva's top nightspot for dancing. **Chadwick's Lounge,** at the entrance to the South Seas Plantation Resort & Yacht Harbour (☎ 941/472-5111), has a large dance floor and music from 9pm on.

NEARBY ISLAND HOPPING

Sanibel and Captiva are jumping-off points for island-hopping boat trips to barrier islands and keys teeming with ancient legends and Robinson Crusoe–style beaches. You don't have to get completely lost out there, however, for several islets have comfortable inns and restaurants. The trip across shallow Pine Island Sound is itself a sightseeing adventure, with playful dolphins surfing on the boats' wakes and a variety of cormorants, egrets, frigate birds, and (in winter) rare white pelicans flying above or lounging on sandbars between meals.

Captiva Cruises (☎ 941/472-5300) has daily trips from the South Seas Plantation Resort & Yacht Harbour on Captiva. One vessel goes daily to Cabbage Key (see box) and Useppa Island, where passengers disembark for lunch. During the winter months, another goes to Boca Grande (see section 4) by way of Cayo Costa State Park. These day trips cost $27.50 per adult, $15 for children to Cabbage Key or Useppa; $35 for adults, $17.50 for children to Boca Grande or Cayo Costa. They usually leave at 10:30am. Reservations are required.

From Pine Island off Fort Myers, you can take the *Tropic Star* ferry service (☎ 941/283-0015) to Cayo Costa (see "Cruises" in section 1).

Cheeseburgers on Cabbage Key

You never know who's going to get off a boat at 100-acre Cabbage Key and walk unannounced into the funky ✪ **Cabbage Key Inn,** a rustic house built in 1938 by the son and daughter-in-law of mystery novelist Mary Roberts Rinehart. Ernest Hemingway liked to hang out here in the early days, and novelist John D. MacDonald was a frequent guest 30 years later. Today you could find yourself rubbing elbows at the bar with the likes of Walter Cronkite, Ted Koppel, Sean Connery, or Julia Roberts. Singer and avid yachtie Jimmy Buffett likes Cabbage Key so much that it inspired his hit song "Cheeseburger in Paradise."

A path leads from the tiny marina across a lawn dotted with coconut palms to this white clapboard house that sits atop an ancient Calusa shell mound. Guests dine in the comfort of two screened porches and seek libations in the Rineharts' library-turned-bar, its pine-paneled walls now plastered with dollar bills left by visitors. The straight-back chairs and painted wooden tables are showing their age, but that's part of Cabbage Key's laid-back, don't-give-a-hoot charm.

In addition to the famous thick, juicy cheeseburgers so loved by Jimmy Buffett, the house specialties are fresh broiled fish and shrimp steamed in beer. Lunches range from $4 to $9; dinners are $16 to $20.

For overnight or longer, the Cabbage Key Inn has six rooms and six cottages, all with original 1920s furnishings, private baths, and air conditioners. Four of the cottages have kitchens, and one room reputedly has its own ghost. Rates are $65 single or double for rooms, $145 to $200 for cottages. Reserve well in advance for major holidays and during the tarpon season from February to May. For information or reservations, contact **Cabbage Key Inn,** P.O. Box 200, Pineland, FL 33945 (☎ **941/283-2278;** fax 941/283-1384).

You can get to Cabbage Key from Pine Island near Fort Myers via the inn's own launch, which leaves daily from the Mattson Marine marina ($12.50 per person round-trip), or via the *Tropic Star* nature cruises (☎ **941/283-0015**), which depart Knight's Landing marina daily at 9:30am ($25 adults, $15 for children). **Captiva Cruises** (☎ **941/472-5300**) goes there daily from Captiva Island, charging $27.50 per adult, $15 for children (reservations are required).

CAYO COSTA You can't get any more deserted than at ✪ **Cayo Costa State Park** (pronounced *Kay*-oh *Cos*-tah), which occupies a 2,132-acre, completely unspoiled barrier island with miles of white-sand beaches, pine forests, mangrove swamps, oak-palm hammocks, and grasslands. Other than natural wildlife, the only permanent residents here are three park rangers.

Day-trippers can bring their own supplies and use a picnic area with pavilions. A tram carries visitors from the sound-side dock to the gulf beach (50¢ round-trip fare). The state maintains 12 very basic cabins and a primitive campground on the northern end of the island near Johnson Shoals, where the shelling is spectacular. Cabins cost $20 a day, and campsites are $13 a day all year. There's running water on the island but no electricity.

The park is open daily from 8am to sundown. There's a $1-per-person honor-system admission fee for day visitors. Overnight slips at the dock cost $13 a day. You can rent single-seat kayaks for $35 a day, $45 a day for two-seaters; for reservations, call the *Tropic Star* on Pine Island (☎ **941/283-0015**). For cabin reservations or more information about the park, contact **Cayo Costa State Park,** P.O. Box 1150,

Boca Grande, FL 33921 (☎ **941/964-0375**). Office hours are Monday to Friday from 8am to 5pm.

UPPER (NORTH) CAPTIVA   Cut off by a pass from Captiva, its northern barrier island sibling is occupied by the **North Captiva Island Club,** P.O. Box 1000, Pineland, FL 33945 (☎ **800/576-7343** or 941/395-1001; fax 941/472-5836; www.northcaptiva.com), an upscale resort. Despite the development, however, about 750 of the island's 1,000 acres are included in a state preserve. The club rents accommodations ranging from efficiencies to luxury homes. There's scheduled water-taxi service from **Jenson's Twin Palms Marina** on Captiva (☎ **941/472-5800**), or you can get here from Matson Marine on Pine Island with **Island Charters** (☎ **800/340-33321** or 941/283-1113). Both charge $25 per person round-trip.

✪ **USEPPA ISLAND**   Useppa was a refuge of President Theodore Roosevelt and his tarpon-loving industrialist friends at the turn of the century. New York advertising magnate Barron G. Collier bought the island in 1906 and built a lovely wooden home overlooking Pine Island Sound. His mansion is now the **Collier Inn,** where day-trippers and overnight guests can partake of lunches and seafood dinners in a country-club ambience. They also can visit the **Useppa Museum,** which explains the island's history and displays 4,000-year-old Calusa artifacts. Admission is by $2 donation.

The Collier Inn is the centerpiece of **the Useppa Island Club,** an exclusive development with more than 100 luxury homes, all of the clapboard-sided, tin-roofed style of Old Florida. For information, rates (all on the modified American plan), and reservations, contact **Collier Inn & Cottages,** P.O. Box 640, Bokeelia, FL 33922 (☎ **941/283-5255;** fax 941/283-0290).

4 Boca Grande

63 miles NW of Fort Myers, 105 miles NW of Naples, 50 miles SE of Sarasota

After brothers George W. Bush and Jeb Bush were elected governors of Texas and Florida, respectively, in 1998, they and the rest of the Bush clan—including their parents, former President George and First Lady Barbara—retreated to Boca Grande for a little rest and relaxation. They chose well, for this charming village on Gasparilla Island is definitely a head-of-state's kind of place. Legend says that the infamous pirate Jose Gaspar lived in style on this 7-mile-long barrier island. So did the du Pont family, which founded Boca Grande in the 1880s. They were followed by the Astors, Morgans, Vanderbilts, and other moneyed folk, who still turn the island into a Florida version of Nantucket during their winter "social season."

In addition to the warm weather, the lure was some of the ✪ **world's best tarpon fishing.** Descendants of the watermen who were here first—and who still guide the rich and famous—still work their 1920s-vintage marinas and live on streets named Dam-If-I-Know, Dam-If-I-Care, and Dam-If-I-Will. You can see their modest homes with backyards full of old sheds, boats, and fishnets, but high hedges hide the "beach-fronter" mansions around 29th Street.

ESSENTIALS

GETTING THERE   The nearest airports are in Fort Myers and Sarasota. From the north on I-75, take Exit 32 in Charlotte County, then head west to the end of Toledo Blade Boulevard. Turn right there onto Fla. 776, then left on Fla. 771 to Placida and the Boca Grande Causeway ($3.25 toll to the island, free coming back). From the south on I-75, take Exit 31 and go south on Kings Highway (Fla. 769), then an immediate right on Veterans Boulevard (Fla. 776) and left on Fla. 771 to the Boca Grande Causeway. It's about 1½ hours from Fort Myers.

Boca Grande is a popular day trip from Captiva Island during the winter months, when **Captiva Cruises** (☎ 941/472-5300) has daily trips here (see "Nearby Island Hopping," in section 3, above). The fare is $35 adults, $17.50 children, and reservations are required.

VISITOR INFORMATION   Contact the **Boca Grande Chamber of Commerce,** 5800 Gasparilla Rd. (P.O. Box 704), Boca Grande, FL 33921 (☎ 941/964-0568; fax 941/964-0620; www.charlotte-online.com/bocagrande; e-mail: bgcc@ewol.com). The office is in the Courtyard Shops, on the left as you drive onto the island, and is open Monday to Friday from 9am to 5pm. You can also find information in a rack in the Theater Mall on Park Avenue in the heart of town.

GETTING AROUND   **Boca Grande Taxi & Limousine** (☎ 800/771-7433 or 941/964-0455) will take you around in style, but many visitors choose to see this town on foot, or by bicycle or golf cart rented from **Island Bike 'n' Beach,** 333 Park Ave. (☎ 941/964-0711). Bikes range from $6 an hour to $18 a day. The company also rents baby strollers, beach chairs and umbrellas, boogie boards, tennis racquets, and other items. Now a paved, 7-mile-long **bike path,** the bed of the old Charlotte Harbor and Northern Railroad runs by the depot on its way from the island's south end all the way north to the causeway.

EXPLORING THE TOWN

The pink-brick **Railroad Depot,** at the corner of Park Avenue and 4th Street, has been restored to its turn-of-the-century grandeur when it was Boca Grande's lifeline to the world. It now houses a cluster of upscale boutiques and the Loose Caboose Restaurant and Ice Cream Parlor, where Katherine Hepburn once satiated her sweet tooth (see "Where to Dine," below).

You can stand on the railway platform and see numerous high-end **boutiques** and **art galleries** along 4th Street and Railroad and Park avenues. Across the street, **Fugate's** has been selling everything from rain slickers to wedding gowns since 1916.

Banyan Street (actually 2nd Street) is canopied with tangled banyan trees and is one of the prettiest places for a stroll. Nearby, **St. Andrew's Episcopal Church** and the **First Baptist Church,** both at Gilchrist and 4th streets, and the **United Methodist Church,** at Gilchrist and 3rd streets, all date from the town's early years.

The **Johann Fust Community Library,** at Gasparilla Road and 10th Street (☎ 941/964-2488), contains nearly 15,000 volumes and the extraordinary **Du Pont Shell Collection,** all gathered by Henry Francis du Pont during nearly 50 years of combing the island's beaches. The library has a lovely interior garden and outdoor reading room. Open December to April, Monday to Friday from 10am to noon and 4 to 6pm; the rest of the year, Monday to Friday from 4 to 6pm.

At the south end of the island, the **Boca Grande Lighthouse** began marking the pass into Charlotte Harbor in 1890 (the steel tower on Gulf Boulevard served as the light from 1966 to 1986, when the old building was restored). **Gasparilla Island State Recreation Area** around the lighthouse is open daily from 8am to sunset.

ENJOYING THE OUTDOORS

By far the biggest event here is the chamber of commerce–sponsored **World's Richest Tarpon Tournament,** usually the second week in July, when anglers try to reel in $100,000. Charter fishing is available through **Boca Grande Charter Booking Services,** located at Miller's Marina on Harbor Drive (☎ 941/964-2232). You can rent boats from **Capt. Russ's Boat Rentals,** at Whidden's Marina (☎ 941/964-0708), also on Harbor Drive. Miller's Marina (☎ 941/964-2283) has backwater nature tours and parasailing during the winter season.

Beach access is limited by the expensive homes along the gulf, but there's a **public beach** just south of town on Gulf Boulevard. **Gasparilla Island State Recreation Area** has a small beach park just south of the village and a lovely strip of sand on the island's south end. The area is open daily from 8am to sunset. Admission is $2 per vehicle.

Boca Grande Ferry Service (☎ 941/964-1100 or 941/964-2931) takes passengers out to Cayo Costa, Cabbage Key, and other islands. It departs at 10:30am daily. Fares are $20 to $25, depending on the destination. Reservations are required. See "Nearby Island Hopping," in section 3 of this chapter, on Sanibel and Captiva islands, for information about Cayo Costa and Cabbage Key.

WHERE TO STAY

The only way to stay on the beach here is to rent a condo or a house. Contact **Boca Grande Real Estate,** P.O. Box 686, Boca Grande, FL 33921 (☎ **800/881-2622** or 941/964-0338; fax 941/964-2301).

✪ **Gasparilla Inn & Cottages.** 500 Palm Ave. (P.O. Box 1088), Boca Grande, FL 33921. ☎ **941/964-2201.** Fax 941/964-2733. 150 units. A/C TV TEL. Winter $348–$554 double. Off-season $236–$310 double. Rates include all meals in winter, breakfast and dinner off-season. No credit cards. Closed June–Oct.

Opened in 1913, this architectural beauty with stately columns, Southern-style verandas, and handsome wood floors is still the winter home for affluent socialites. So exclusive is this enclave of the well-to-do that it doesn't advertise or seek publicity. So many of its regulars return from one social season to the next that it's difficult to get a room or cottage from mid-January to April. The rooms here are in the original inn, and old-fashioned but updated cottages are scattered around the grounds.

Dining: Unless you have the good fortune (literally) to stay here, forget the high-ceilinged, aristocratic dining room in which guests dress for dinner. You can have a meal in the more modern and much more relaxed Pink Elephant Restaurant, nearby at 5th Street and Bayou Avenue (☎ 941/964-0100).

Amenities: Behind the inn, guests can play tennis on private courts or golf on an excellent 18-hole course along the shores of Charlotte Harbor. At the beach, they can play with water-sports equipment at their own private club.

Innlet on the Waterfront. 12th St. (at E. Railroad Ave.; P.O. Box 248), Boca Grande, FL 33921. ☎ **941/964-2294.** Fax 941/964-0382. 32 units. A/C TV TEL. Winter $115–$140 double. Off-season $90–$120 double. MC, V.

The main building at this motel has a large veranda across the back, from which guests can view Boca Grande Bayou, the creeklike waterway forming the town's eastern boundary. The efficiencies, opening to the veranda and equipped with kitchens, are more expensive than the standard motel units, which are in a low-slung building across the parking lot. There are a swimming pool and marina on the premises, and a restaurant is in the planning stages.

WHERE TO DINE

For picnic fixings, go to the village's sole grocery, **Hudson's,** on Park Avenue between 4th and 5th streets opposite the Railroad Depot (☎ 941/964-2570). It's open Monday to Saturday from 8am to 5:30pm.

✪ **Jam's Italian Restaurant.** Railroad Ave. at 5th St. ☎ 941/964-2002. Pizzas $5–$14; pastas $5.50–$10; sandwiches $3–$6. AE, MC, V. Mon–Thurs 11am–9pm, Fri–Sat 11am–10pm, Sun noon–9pm. ITALIAN.

Although former President Bush usually hobnobs at the Gasparilla Inn when he's here, his secret-service guards make this pleasant Italian restaurant their hangout. The motto here is "More food for less lira," and you'll get excellent pizza and pasta while watching ball games on three TVs. Jam's even has a White House plaque to prove Bush's staffers were here.

Loons on a Limb. 3rd St. at Railway Ave. ☎ **941/964-0155.** Reservations recommended for dinner. Breakfast $4.50–$8; main courses $15–$22. No credit cards. Winter daily 7:30–11:30am and 6–9pm. Off-season daily 7:30–11:30am. Closed Aug, Thanksgiving, and Christmas. FRENCH/AMERICAN.

Owned and operated by Boca Grande natives, "The Loon" is famous for both eggs Benedict and grits, which speaks reams about this town's split personality. It's one of the few places on the island serving breakfast. A chalkboard dinner menu is offered from October to May, featuring seafood prepared in French and American styles. Photos and paintings of wild birds share the tongue-in-groove walls with a stuffed deer's head.

The Loose Caboose. Park Rd. at 3rd St., in the Railroad Depot. ☎ **941/964-0440.** Reservations not accepted. Salads and sandwiches $3.50–$10; main courses $6.50–$17. MC, V. Winter daily 9am–9pm. Off-season daily 9am–6pm. Closed Thanksgiving, Christmas, Super Bowl Sunday. AMERICAN.

Everyone from actress Katherine Hepburn down to local bank clerks who can't afford to live on the island flock here for good yet inexpensive fare. You can dine inside the old Railroad Depot or outside under its soaring brick arches. Tops here is the warm Oriental chicken salad, but you can order a variety of fare from New England lobster rolls to baskets of fried shrimp. A limited dinner menu is offered during the winter season.

۞ P.J.'s Seagrille. 321 Park Ave., between 3rd and 4th sts. ☎ **941/964-0806.** Reservations recommended. Main courses $15–$25. AE, MC, V. Mon–Sat 11:30am–2pm and 5:30–9:30pm. Closed Aug–Sept. FLORIDA/MEDITERRANEAN.

Chef Jimmy Turner's Gasparilla crab cakes and seafood pasta head the playbill at this 1928 movie theater turned into a minimall and fine restaurant. Nightly specials include a variety of other fresh-off-the-boat seafood, plus steaks grilled over an open flame and lamb osso buco. Dine inside or on a screened porch.

۞ South Beach. 777 Gulf Blvd. (south end of island). ☎ **941/964-0765.** Reservations recommended. Burgers, sandwiches, and baskets $9–$12; main courses $14–$22. AE, MC, V. Daily 11am–10pm. Bar open until 2am. SEAFOOD.

The only place on Gasparilla where you can dine or have a sunset cocktail by the gulf, this casual establishment has a covered patio with plastic chairs and tables right by the white sand. Patrons also have a view of the beach through the window walls of the dining room, whose solid walls bear a jungly mural and works by local artists. The regular menu features an assortment of shrimp, grouper, and broiled mahimahi, but the specials such as stone crab claws or pompano are your best bets. Wednesday usually is all-you-can-eat shrimp night ($20), while Friday offers a stuffing of fish ($18). Bands make music on the patio on weekends during the winter season.

5 Naples

42 miles S of Fort Myers, 106 miles W of Miami, 185 miles S of Tampa

Because its wealthy residents are accustomed to the very best, Naples is easily Southwest Florida's most sophisticated city. Indeed, its boutiques and galleries are at least on a par with those in Palm Beach or Beverly Hills. And yet, Naples has an easygoing friendliness to all comers, who can find some surprisingly affordable places to stay within easy reach of its long, magnificent beach and pricey resorts.

Naples was born in 1886, when a group of 12 Kentuckians and Ohioans bought 8,700 acres, laid out a town, and started selling lots. They built a pier and the 16-room Naples Hotel, whose first guest was Pres. Grover Cleveland's sister Rose. She and other notables soon built a line of beach homes known as "Millionaires' Row." Known today as Olde Naples and carefully protected by its modern residents, their original settlement still retains the air of that time a century ago.

Although high-rise buildings now line the beaches north of the old town, the newer sections of Naples still have their charm, thanks to Ohio manufacturer Henry B. Watkins, Sr. In 1946, Watkins and his partners bought the old hotel and all the town's undeveloped land and laid out the Naples Plan, which created the environmentally conscious city you see today.

About 4 miles north of Olde Naples, Vanderbilt Beach has a more traditional beach-resort character than the historic district. Lined with a mix of two-story, 1960s-style motels and high-rise hotels and condos, the main beach here sits like an island of development between two preserved areas—Delnor-Wiggins Pass State Recreation to the north, and a county reserve fronting the expensive Pelican Bay golf-course community to the south.

ESSENTIALS

GETTING THERE   Most visitors arrive at the Southwest Florida International Airport, 35 miles north of Naples (see "Getting There" under "Essentials" in section 1, on Fort Myers). **Naples Municipal Airport,** on North Road off Airport-Pulling Road (☎ **941/643-6875**), is served by **American Eagle** (☎ 800/433-7300) and **US Airways Express** (☎ 800/428-4322). Taxis await all flights outside the small terminal building, and **Avis** (☎ 800/331-1212), **Budget** (☎ 800/527-0700), **Hertz** (☎ 800/654-3131), and **National** (☎ 800/CAR-RENT) have booths at the airport.

VISITOR INFORMATION   You can contact **Visit Naples** (☎ **800/605-7878;** www.visitnaples.com) for advance information, but your best bet is the **Naples Area Chamber of Commerce,** which maintains a visitor center at 895 5th Ave. South (at U.S. 41), Naples, FL 34102 (☎ **941/262-6141;** fax 941/435-9910; www. naples-online.com). The center has a host of free information and phones for making hotel reservations, and it sells a detailed street map for $2. By mail, they will send a free list of accommodations and other basic information, or you can order a complete Naples vacation packet for $12 ($16 to Canada and other countries) and the street map for $3. The visitor center is open Monday to Friday from 9am to 5pm, Saturday from 10am to 3pm, and Sunday from December through April from 10am to 3pm.

You can get on-the-street information at kiosks in the Marketplace at Tin City on U.S. 41 at the Gordon River Bridge, and on 3rd Street South at 12 Avenue South in Olde Naples.

GETTING AROUND   You can get to the beach and most establishments in Olde Naples on foot or by bicycle. Rent a bike from **The Bike Route,** 655 N. Tamiami Trail (☎ **941/262-8373**). For scooters, call **Good Times Rental,** 1947 Davis Blvd. (☎ **941/775-7529**).

For longer distances, the **Naples Trolley** (☎ **941/262-7300**) clangs around 25 stops between the Marketplace at Tin City in Olde Naples and Vanderbilt Beach on Monday to Saturday from 8:30am to 5:15pm and on Sunday from 10:15am to

Naples

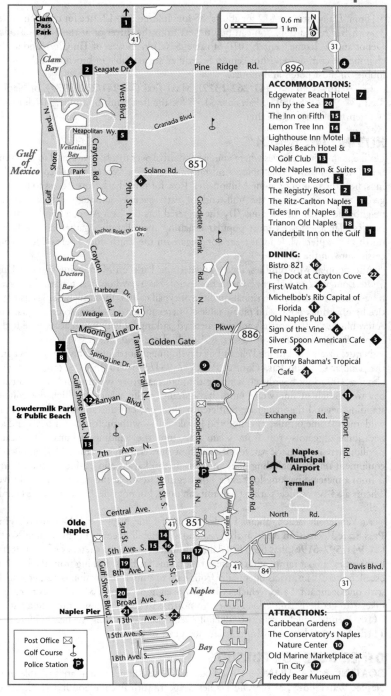

ACCOMMODATIONS:
Edgewater Beach Hotel **7**
Inn by the Sea **20**
The Inn on Fifth **15**
Lemon Tree Inn **14**
Lighthouse Inn Motel **1**
Naples Beach Hotel &
  Golf Club **13**
Olde Naples Inn & Suites **19**
Park Shore Resort **5**
The Registry Resort **2**
The Ritz-Carlton Naples **1**
Tides Inn of Naples **8**
Trianon Old Naples **18**
Vanderbilt Inn on the Gulf **1**

DINING:
Bistro 821 **16**
The Dock at Crayton Cove **22**
First Watch **12**
Michelbob's Rib Capital of
  Florida **11**
Old Naples Pub **21**
Sign of the Vine **6**
Silver Spoon American Cafe **3**
Terra **21**
Tommy Bahama's Tropical
  Cafe **21**

ATTRACTIONS:
Caribbean Gardens **9**
The Conservatory's Naples
  Nature Center **10**
Old Marine Marketplace at
  Tin City **17**
Teddy Bear Museum **4**

Post Office ✉
Golf Course ⛳
Police Station **P**

5:15pm. Daily fares are $12 for adults, $5 for children 3 to 12, free for children under 3, with free reboarding. You can buy tickets from the driver or at the Naples Trolley Depot and Welcome Center, 1010 6th Ave. S. (2 blocks west of Tin City), and at the chamber of commerce visitor center. Schedules are available in brochure racks in the lobbies of most hotels and motels.

Call **Yellow Cab** (☎ 941/262-1312), **Maxi Taxi** (☎ 941/262-8977), or **Naples Taxi** (☎ 941/775-0505). Fares are $1.75 for the first tenth of a mile, 30¢ for each two-tenths of a mile thereafter.

HITTING THE BEACH

Unlike many Florida cities where you have to drive over to a barrier island to reach the beach, it's right in Olde Naples. And rather than being fronted by tall condo buildings, here the mansions along Millionaires' Row form the backdrop. Access to the gorgeous white sand is at the gulf end of each avenue, although parking in the neighborhood can be precious. Try the metered lots on 12th Avenue South near the Naples Pier, the town's most popular beaching spot. Families gather on the beach north of the pier, while local teens congregate on the south side. There's a food concessionaire on the pier.

Also popular with families, lovely Lowdermilk Park, on Millionaires' Row at Gulf Shore Boulevard and North Banyan Boulevard, has a pavilion, rest rooms, showers, a refreshment counter, professional-quality volleyball courts (the area's best players practice here), a duck pond, and picnic tables. There's metered parking, so bring quarters. A few blocks farther north is another metered parking lot with beach access beside the Naples Beach Hotel & Golf Resort, 851 Gulf Shore Blvd. N., at Golf Drive.

Nature lovers head to the Pelican Bay development north of the historic district and the popular ✪ **Clam Pass County Park** (☎ 941/353-0404). A free tram takes you along a 3,000-foot boardwalk winding through mangrove swamps and across a back bay to a beach of fine white sand. It's a strange sight, what with high-rise condos standing beyond the mangrove-bordered backwaters, but this actually is a miniature wilderness. Some 6 miles of canoe and kayak trails—with multitudes of birds and an occasional alligator—run from Clam Pass into the winding streams. The beach pavilion here has a snack bar, rest rooms (foot showers only), picnic tables, and beach equipment rentals, including one- and two-person kayaks and 12-foot canoes. Entry is from a metered parking lot beside The Registry Resort at the end of Seagate Drive. There's a $3-per-vehicle parking fee. You can push, but not ride, bicycles on the boardwalk.

At Vanderbilt Beach, about 4 miles north of Olde Naples, the **Delnor-Wiggins Pass State Recreation Area,** at the west end of Bluebill Avenue–111th Avenue North (☎ 941/597-6196), has been listed among America's top-10 stretches of sand. It has bathhouses, a boat ramp, and the area's best picnic facilities. Fishing from the beach is excellent here. The area is open daily from 8am to sunset. Admission is $2 per vehicle with one occupant, $4 for vehicles with two to eight occupants, $1 for pedestrians and bikers. To get here from Olde Naples, go north on U.S. 41 about 4 miles to a left on 111th Avenue, which turns into Bluebill Avenue before reaching the beach. Note that 111th Avenue is known as Immokalee Road east of U.S. 41.

OTHER OUTDOOR PURSUITS

BOATING & KAYAKING   Powerboat and Wave Runner rentals are available from **Naples Watersports,** at the Old Naples Seaport, 10th Avenue South at 10th Street South in Olde Naples (☎ 941/435-9595); from **Club Nautico,** at the Boat Haven

Marina, 1484 E. Tamiami Trail (☎ 941/774-0100), on the east bank of the Gordon River behind Kelly's Fish House; and from **Port-O-Call Marina,** also behind Kelly's Fish House (☎ 941/774-0479).

Houseboat Rentals of Southwest Florida (☎ 941/775-2003; www.ivacation. com/p6950.htm) offers live-aboard boats which will sleep up to six persons. Prices start at $275 for a 2-day, 1-night rental and go up to $1,000 for a week.

You don't need experience to go paddling with **Bolster's Kayak Adventures** (☎ 941/641-1139), which offers half-day ($45 per person) and full-day ($90 per person) excursions through back bays and mangrove forests. Owner Andrew Bolster also will take you sunset or moonlight paddling. Call for schedules and reservations, which are required.

CRUISES The Gordon River and Naples Bay from the U.S. 41 bridge on 5th Avenue South to the gulf are prime territory for sightseeing, dolphin watching, and sunset cruises. The double-decked *Double Sunshine* (☎ 941/263-4949) sallies forth onto the river and bay daily from Tin City, where it has a ticket office. The 1½-hour cruises usually leave at 10am, noon, 2pm, and an hour before sunset. They cost $20 per adult, $10 for children under 12. A sister boat, the *Captain Paul,* goes on afternoon shelling and beachcombing excursions to Keewaydin Island, a private wildlife sanctuary south of Olde Naples. These cost $30 for adults, $20 for children.

The *Sweet Liberty* (☎ 941/793-3525), a 53-foot sailing catamaran, makes morning shelling cruises to Keewaydin Island. The vessel then spends the afternoon sightseeing and the evening on sunset cruises on Naples Bay before docking at Boat Haven Marina on the east side of the Gordon River Bridge. Shelling cruises cost $25 for adults, $10 for children; sightseeing and sunset cruises cost $20 for adults, $10 for children.

For a good deal more luxury, the 83-foot *Naples Princess* (☎ 800/728-2970 or 941/649-2275) has narrated breakfast, lunch, and sunset dinner cruises from Olde Naples Seaport, 10th Avenue South at 10th Street South. With extensive continental-breakfast and sandwich-lunch buffets, the two daytime cruises are excellent values at $20 and $25 per person. There's a nature cruise once a week sponsored and narrated by The Conservancy of Naples; it costs $23 and includes continental breakfast. Call for schedules and prices.

FISHING The locals like to fish from the Naples Pier (see "Exploring the Town," below). The pier has tables on which to clean your catch, but watch out for the ever-present pelicans, which are master thieves. You can buy tackle and bait from the local marinas (see "Boating & Boat Rentals," above). No fishing license is required on the pier.

The least expensive way for singles, couples, and small families to fish without paying for an entire boat is on the 45-foot *Lady Brett* (☎ 941/263-4949), which makes two daily trips from Tin City for $45 for adults, $40 for kids under 12. Rod, reel, bait, and fishing license are included, but bring your own drinks and lunch. Its sister boat, the *Captain Paul,* goes on half-day backcountry fishing trips, departing daily at 9am. These cost $35 for adults, $25 for children.

A number of charter boats are based at the marinas mentioned under "Boating & Kayaking," above; call or visit them for booking information and prices.

GOLF Most of Naples's excellent golf courses are private clubs, but the area also has a few of America's best public golf courses, including the ✪ **Lely Flamingo Island Club** and the **Lely Mustang Golf Club,** both on U.S. 41 between Naples and Marco Island (☎ 800/388-GOLF or 941/793-2223). The Lely Flamingo course was designed by Robert Trent Jones, Sr., and its hourglass fairways and fingerlike bunkers present many challenges. Designed by Lee Trevino, the new Lely Mustang course is more forgiving but still fun. Former PGA Tour player Paul Trittler has his golf school at these courses. You'll pay a price here in winter, when 18-hole fees are about $135 at Lely Flamingo and $148 at Lely Mustang, including cart and range balls, but they drop progressively after Easter to about $40 and $48, respectively, in the muggy summer months.

Boyne South, on U.S. 41 between Fla. 931 and Fla. 92 (☎ **941/732-5108**), is another winner, with lots of wildlife inhabiting its many lakes (a 16-foot alligator reportedly resides near the 17th hole). There are a driving range, practice facility, and restaurant, and instruction is available. Wintertime fees are $70, but in the off-season they drop to $35 or less. Tee times are taken up to 4 days in advance.

Another local favorite is the player-friendly **Hibiscus Golf Club,** one-half mile east of U.S. 41 off Rattlesnake Hammock Road in East Naples (☎ **941/774-0088**). A pro shop and a teaching professional are on hand. Fees are about $70 in winter, cart included, dropping to about $25 in summer.

In Olde Naples, nonguests can sign up to play at Naples Beach Hotel & Golf Club (see "Where to Stay," below).

In Golden Gate, west of I-75, the **Quality Inn Golf & Country Club,** 4100 Golden Gate Pkwy. (☎ **800/228-5151** or 941/455-1010), has an 18-hole course and 153 rooms, suites, and efficiencies.

HORSEBACK RIDING You can go on trail rides from dawn to dusk Monday to Friday at **M&H Stables,** 2750 Newman Dr. (☎ **941/455-8764**). The stables are east of C.R. 951, about a mile south of Exit 15 off I-75. Call for schedule, prices, reservations, and directions. You can also arrange hayrides here.

SCUBA DIVING The **Under Seas Dive Academy,** 998 6th Ave. S., in Olde Naples (☎ **941/262-0707**), takes divers into the gulf, teaches diver-certification courses, and rents water-sports equipment. So does Kevin Sweeney's **SCUBAdventures,** 971 Creech Rd., at Tamiami Trail (☎ **941/434-7477**), which also has a base on Marco Island (see section 6, below).

TENNIS In Olde Naples, the city's **Cambier Park Tennis Center,** 755 8th Ave. S., at 9th Street South (☎ **941/434-4694**), matches those found at luxury resorts. Play on its 12 lighted clay courts costs $6 for 90 minutes. Book at the pro shop upstairs in the modern building, which has restrooms but no showers. The courts are open Monday to Friday from 8am to 10pm, Saturday and Sunday from 8am to 5pm, but the adjacent playground with a children's area and shuffleboard and basketball courts is open 24 hours.

Nonguests can play at the **Naples Beach Hotel & Golf Club,** 851 Gulf Shore Blvd. N. (☎ **941/261-2222**), but call ahead to reserve court time.

Dedicated buffs can play to their hearts' content on the 11 clay and 5 hard courts at **World Tennis Center Resort & Club,** 4800 Airport-Pulling Rd., at Pine Ridge Road (☎ **800/292-6663** or 941/263-1900; fax 941/649-7855), but you must stay in one of the 72 two-bedroom condominiums here to use them. There are a restaurant, swimming pool, and sauna on the premises.

WATER SPORTS **Good Times Rental,** 1947 Davis Blvd. (☎ **941/775-7529**), rents Wave Runners, windsurfers, skim boards, canoes, snorkeling gear, rafts, and other beach equipment. Hobie Cats and Windsurfers can also be rented on the beach at the **Naples Beach Hotel & Golf Club,** 851 Gulf Shore Blvd. N. (☎ **941/ 261-2222**), and at **Clam Pass County Park,** at the end of Seagate Drive (☎ **941/ 353-0404**). See "Hitting the Beach," above for more about Clam Pass County Park.

EXPLORING THE TOWN

During the winter you can take evening horse-drawn carriage rides around Olde Naples with the **Naples Horse & Carriage Co.** (☎ 941/649-1210). Prices begin at $30 per person for a 30-minute ride. The carriages can hold up to four adults.

✪ OLDE NAPLES

Its history may go back only to 1886, but the beach skirting Olde Naples still has the charm of that Victorian era. The heart of the district lies below 5th Avenue South (that's where U.S. 41 takes a 45-degree turn). The town docks are on the bay side, the glorious beach along the gulf. Laid out on a grid, the tree-lined streets run between many houses, some dating from the town's beginning, and along Millionaires' Row between Gulf Shore Boulevard and the beach. With these gorgeous homes virtually hidden in the palms and casuarinas, the ✪ **Naples Beach** seems a century removed from the high-rise condos found farther north.

The Naples Pier, at the gulf end of 12th Avenue South, is a focal point of the neighborhood. Built in 1888 to let steamers land potential real-estate customers, the original 600-foot-long, T-shaped structure was destroyed by hurricanes and damaged by fire. Local residents have rebuilt it because they like strolling its length to catch fantastic gulf sunsets—and to get a glimpse of Millionaires' Row from the gulf side. The pier is now a state historic site. It's open 24 hours a day, but parking in the nearby lots is restricted between 11pm and 7am.

Nearby, **Palm Cottage,** 137 12th Ave. S., between 1st Street and Gordon Drive (☎ 941/261-8164), was built in 1885 by one of Naples's founders, *Louisville Courier-Journal* publisher Walter Haldeman, as a winter retreat for his chief editorial writer. After World War II, its socialite owners hosted many galas attended by Hollywood stars such as Hedy Lamarr, Gary Cooper, and Robert Montgomery. One of the few remaining Southwest Florida houses built of tabbie mortar (made by burning shells), Palm Cottage today is the home of the Naples Historical Society, which maintains it as a museum filled with authentic furniture, paintings, photographs, and other memorabilia. Tours are given during winter, Monday to Friday from 1 to 3:30pm. Adult admission is by $5 donation; it's free for children.

Near the Gordon River Bridge on 5th Avenue South, the old corrugated waterfront warehouses are now a shopping-and-dining complex known as the Marketplace at Tin City, which tourists throng to and local residents assiduously avoid during the winter months.

MUSEUMS & ZOOS

Caribbean Gardens. 1590 Goodlette-Frank Rd. (at Fleischmann Blvd.). ☎ 941/262-5409. Admission $13.95 adults, $8.95 children 4–15, free for children 3 and under. Daily 9:30am–5:30pm (last admission at 4:30pm). Closed Easter, Thanksgiving, and Christmas.

A family favorite formerly known as "Jungle Larry's," for noted animal trainer and owner Larry Tetzlaff, this zoo features a variety of animals and birds, including a fascinating community of primates living free on their own island. You can see them on a safari through the spectacular tropical gardens. Many visitors are captivated by the Big Cat Show, in which lions and tigers are put through their paces by Larry's son, David Tetzlaff, himself a talented trainer. Big Cat show times vary, so call for the schedule. You can also see three of the world's 40 golden tigers here. For kids, there are a Petting Farm, elephant rides, and a playground. The Canyon Cafe serves snacks, and there are picnic facilities on the premises.

✪ **Teddy Bear Museum.** 2511 Pine Ridge Rd. (at Airport-Pulling Rd.). ☎ 800/681-2327 or 941/598-2711. Admission $6 adults, $4 seniors, $2 children 4–12, free for children under

4. Mon and Wed–Sat 10am–5pm, Sun 1–5pm. Closed New Year's Day, July 4, Thanksgiving, and Christmas.

Another family favorite, this entertaining museum contains 3,000-plus examples of stuffed teddy bears from around the world. They're cleverly displayed descending from the rafters in hot-air balloons, attending board meetings, sipping afternoon tea, celebrating a wedding, even doing bear things like hibernating. There's a gift shop where you can buy your own bears.

PARKS & NATURE PRESERVES

You don't have to go far east of Naples to reach the magnificent Everglades, much of it protected by Everglades National Park and Big Cypress National Preserve. See chapter 7 for full details on activities in and near the national park. Other nearby nature preserves are described in section 6 of this chapter, on Marco Island.

One of the largest private preserves is the ✪ **Corkscrew Swamp Sanctuary** (☎ **941/348-9151**), 16 miles northeast of Naples off Immokalee Road (County Road 846). Maintained by the National Audubon Society, this 11,000-acre wilderness is home to countless wood storks that nest high in the cypress trees from November to April. Wading birds also are best seen in winter, when the swamp is likely to be dry (they don't nest when water levels are high). The birds congregate around pools near a boardwalk that leads 2 miles through the largest bald cypress forest with some of the oldest trees in the country. Ferns and orchids also flourish. Admission is $7 for adults, $5.50 for full-time college students, $3.50 for children 6 to 18, and free for children 5 and under. The sanctuary is open December to April, daily from 7am to 5pm; May to November, daily from 8am to 5pm. To reach the sanctuary, take Exit 17 off I-75 and go 15 miles east on Immokalee Road (County Road 846).

About a 30-minute drive away, the Corkscrew Marsh Trail System, on Corkscrew Road south of Fla. 82, consists of a 5-mile loop through mostly pine forests managed jointly by the **Corkscrew Regional Ecosystem Watershed Trust** (☎ **941/332-7771**) and the South Florida Water Management District. Only hikers are allowed to use these trails, which are free but have no drinking water or rest rooms.

You can also experience Southwest Florida's abundant natural life without leaving town at **The Conservancy's Naples Nature Center,** 14th Avenue North, east of Goodlette-Frank Road (☎ **941/262-0304**), one of two preserves operated by The Conservancy of Southwest Florida (see the Briggs Nature Center in section 6). There are nature trails, an aviary with bald eagles and other birds, and electric boat rides through a mangrove forest to observe wildlife (you can also rent canoes and kayaks and see it by yourself). A nature store carries interesting gift items. The trails and boat rides are free. Admission is $6 for adults, $2 for children 3 to 12, free for children under 3. Canoe and kayak rentals are $13 for 2 hours, $5 for each additional hour. The center is open year-round Monday to Saturday from 9am to 4:30pm, and also on Sunday from 1 to 5pm from January through March.

SHOPPING

Two blocks of 3rd Street South, at Broad Avenue, are the Rodeo Drive of Naples. This glitzy collection of jewelers, clothiers, and art galleries may be too rich for many wallets, but the window shopping here is unmatched. Be sure to pick up a free brochure, which lists the merchants and has a map of the area, from the chamber of commerce visitor center (see "Essentials," above).

Nearby, the 5th Avenue South shopping area, between 3rd and 9th streets south, has seen a renaissance in recent years and is now the hottest spot in town for both shopping and dining. The avenue is longer and a bit less chic than 3rd Street South, with stockbrokerages and real-estate offices thrown into the mix of boutiques and antique dealers. The most unusual stop here is **Prosperos' Gallerie Eclectic,** 659 5th Ave. S. (☎ 941/435-4517), featuring fanciful paintings and sculpture, plus fabulous, relatively inexpensive sunset shots taken by local photographer Allan Hoelzle and watercolors of Naples houses painted by artist Julie Carlson.

Also in Olde Naples, the **Old Marine Marketplace at Tin City,** 1200 5th Ave. S., at the Gordon River (☎ 941/262-4200), has 50 boutiques selling everything from souvenirs to avant-garde resort wear and imported statuary. There are more boutiques in the Dockside Boardwalk, half a block west on 6th Avenue South.

Even the malls in Naples have their charms. The **Village at Venetian Bay,** 4200 Gulf Shore Blvd., at Park Shore Drive (☎ 941/261-0030), evokes images of its Italian namesake, with 50 canal-side shops featuring high-fashion men's and women's clothiers and fine-art galleries. Ornate Mediterranean architecture and a tropical waterfall highlight the open-air **Waterside Shops at Pelican Bay,** Seagate Drive at North Tamiami Trail (U.S. 41) (☎ 941/598-1605), where the anchor stores are Saks Fifth Avenue and Jacobson's. There's a huge Barnes & Noble bookstore across Seagate Drive.

Coastland Center, on North Tamiami Trail (U.S. 41) between Fleischman Boulevard and Golden Gate Parkway (☎ 941/262-7100), is the regular mall here, but it's a monster (you'll walk nearly a mile from end to end). Burdine's, Dillards, and JCPenney anchor most of the familiar national chains.

Discount shoppers can head to **Prime Outlets Naples,** on Fla. 951 about a mile south of U.S. 41 on the way to Marco Island (☎ 888/545-7196 or 941/775-8083). You'll find the usual clothiers here, including Liz Claiborne, Jones New York, and Anne Klein, plus Mikasa, Coach Leathers, and Dansk factory stores. Shops are open 10am to 8pm Monday to Saturday, 11am to 6pm Sunday.

WHERE TO STAY

While Naples has some of the most expensive resorts in the region, it also has some surprisingly reasonable properties, particularly several older but very well-maintained "apartment hotels" in the historic district within a few blocks of the beach. The Olde Naples Inn & Suites is one of the best (see listing under "Inexpensive," below). Others include the **Beachcomber Club,** 290 5th Ave. S. (☎ 800/634-1311 or 941/262-8112); **Flamingo Apartment Motel,** 383 6th Ave. S. (☎ 941/261-7017; fax 941/261-7769); **Mahalo Apartment Motel,** 441 8th Ave. S. (☎ 941/261-6332; fax 941/263-0182); **Neptune Apartment Hotel,** 651 3rd Ave. S. (☎ 941/ 262-6126;** fax 941/263-6126); **Suntide Apartment Motel,** 649 10th Ave. S. (☎ 941/261-8131); and **Tropical Apartments,** 745 4th Ave. S. (☎ 941/ 262-1011). They are very popular from mid-December to mid-April, when many guests stay a month or more, so book as early as possible.

Most Naples establishments offer weekly and monthly rates during winter, especially the town's many condominium complexes, including the Park Shore Resort (see below). One of the biggest condo-rental agents here is **Bluebill Properties,** 26201 Hickory Blvd., Bonita Springs, FL 33923 (☎ 800/237-2010 or 941/597-1102; fax 941/597-7175).

Even the national chain motels in Naples tend to be of higher quality and better value than their counterparts elsewhere in Southwest Florida. Within walking distance of the historic district, the **Comfort Inn on the Bay,** 1221 5th Ave. S. (☎ 800/ 228-5150 or 941/649-5800), enjoys a picturesque setting on the east bank of the Gordon River. A good budget choice is the new, all-modern **Red Roof Inn,** 1925 Davis Blvd. (☎ 800/THE-ROOF or 941/774-3117), also east of the river.

I have organized the accommodations below geographically: in Olde Naples, and north of the historic district, including those in Vanderbilt Beach.

IN OLDE NAPLES
Very Expensive
Edgewater Beach Hotel. 1901 Gulf Shore Blvd. N., Naples, FL 34102. ☎ **800/821-0196** or 941/403-2000. Fax 941/403-2100. 126 suites. A/C TV TEL. Winter $270–$975. Off-season $170–$530. AE, DC, DISC, MC, V.

Situated near the northern end of Millionaires' Row, this all-suite resort attracts both couples and families. Although the Edgewater is more elegant, the ambience here is not as relaxed as at the Naples Beach Hotel & Golf Club (see below), its chief Olde Naples rival. The Edgewater doesn't have its own golf course and tennis courts, but the front desk will arrange golf, tennis, sightseeing tours, fishing excursions, and other activities. Two pastel-pink original buildings and a newer seven-story tower form a courtyard that opens to the beach. Tastefully decorated, the luxurious, oversize suites have Mexican tile floors and kitchens with microwaves and coffeemakers. The balconies are adorned with white grillwork railings.

Dining/Diversions: For guests only, the sixth-floor Club at the Edgewater offers romantic candlelight dinners and great gulf views (it's suggested that men wear jackets and ties). In winter, there's live piano music in the lobby lounge. Breakfast and lunch are served in a courtyard-level cafe, while a poolside bar serves lunch and libation.

Amenities: Concierge, valet parking, limited room service, laundry, newspaper delivery, in-room massage, baby-sitting, tour desk, health club, games room, boutiques, heated courtyard swimming pool, rental water-sports equipment, cabanas, chairs, and umbrellas. Guests have access to a nearby golf course and tennis courts.

✪ **Naples Beach Hotel & Golf Club.** 851 Gulf Shore Blvd., Naples, FL 33940. ☎ **800/237-7600** or 941/261-2222. Fax 941/261-7380. 315 units. A/C TV TEL. Winter $205–$315 double; $280–$435 suite. Off-season $95–$180 double; $155–$255 suite. Packages available. AE, DC, DISC, MC, V.

Although Henry B. Watkins Sr. bought the Naples Hotel along with the town's undeveloped land in 1946, he soon replaced that turn-of-the-century building with this charming establishment, still owned and operated by his family. The beachside setting on Millionaires' Row in Olde Naples couldn't be better for carrying on the hallowed, friendly, and relaxed Old Florida ambience Watkins installed a half century ago. The least-expensive units here, in fact, are in the Old Florida Wing, a two-story relic from 1948, but recently spiffed up during a $10 million overhaul. The old wing's comfortable rooms and suites open to long, railing-enclosed porches with views across a manicured lawn to the gulf. Other accommodations here are more modern and spacious, but all have lots of bright colors and old-style accents (the recent addition of sliding wooden louvers in the place of drapes has added a tropical touch to the deluxe units). Most suites have private balconies that look out on the beach, the gulf, and the lush gardens that contain more than 4,000 orchids.

Dining/Diversions: Since the resort predates the strict historic-district zoning laws, it has Olde Naples's only two restaurants and bars directly on the beach. HB's on the Gulf is a casual spot for an alfresco beachside lunch or dinner. Wedged between the beach and an Olympic-size pool, the Sunset Beach Bar is one of the region's most famous beachside open-air, thatch-roofed chickee bars and is always crammed as the sun sets over the gulf. It's especially active on Sunday afternoon during the winter season, when live bands perform. Facing the gulf from inside the main building, the semicircular Everglades Dining Room emphasizes traditional Florida cuisine, offers an excellent breakfast buffet to guests and nonguests alike (a genuine all-you-can-eat bargain at less than $10 a head), and has live entertainment and dancing Tuesday to Saturday night in winter. Off the lobby, the Seminole Store offers inexpensive pastries, pizzas, salads, and sandwiches, in addition to a wide range of Florida products. Complimentary afternoon tea is served in the lobby lounge.

Amenities: Concierge, valet parking, turndown, newspaper delivery, laundry, activities desk, baby-sitting and supervised children's program with its own playroom, 18-hole par-72 championship golf course, 6 tennis courts, Olympic-size heated swimming pool, sailboat and other water-sports equipment rentals at the beach, gift shop, beauty salon, car-rental desk.

Expensive

The Inn on Fifth. 699 5th Ave. S., Naples, FL 34102. ☎ **888/403-8778** or 941/403-8777. Fax 941/403-8778. www.naplesinn.com. 87 units. A/C TV TEL. Winter $175–$320 double. Off-season $75–$210 double. AE, DC, DISC, MC, V.

Built in 1998, this three-story boutique hotel with an elegant marble lobby sits in the center of the 5th Avenue South business district, with all its dining and shopping diversions just outside the door. All the reasonable, spacious guest quarters (including 11 suites) come equipped with dark wood armoires and writing tables, sofas or easy chairs, three phones (one in the bathroom), irons and boards, robes, hair dryers, French-milled soaps, thick towels, and sliding glass doors opening to standing-room-only balconies. A brick patio on the parking-lot roof is equipped with a gazebo and chairs for sunning (a pool was in the planning stages).

Dining/Diversions: The Grill on Fifth (steaks and seafood) and the lively McCabe's Irish Pub share the same kitchen.

Amenities: Complimentary valet parking, free self-parking, limited room service, daily newspaper, business facilities, fitness center, spa with massage, facials, steam room, sauna, waxing.

Trianon Old Naples. 955 7th Ave. S., Naples, FL 34102. ☎ **800/859-3939** or 941/435-9600. Fax 941/261-0025. 58 units. A/C TV TEL. Winter $165–$225. Off-season $75–$145. Rates include continental breakfast. AE, DC, DISC, MC, V.

Constructed in 1998 in a quiet residential neighborhood, this elegant Mediterranean-style building with a classical European interior offers spacious rooms quipped with Ritz-Carlton–quality furniture, including mahogany armoires, chairs, and writing desks. All have two phones, irons and boards, coffeemakers, and extra-large bathrooms equipped with hair dryers and separate tubs and showers (but no phone).

Dining: There's no restaurant here, but the staff will arrange for meals to be delivered from local restaurants, and both 5th Avenue South and Tin City are within an easy walk. Continental breakfast is served on silver in a refined lounge, where coffee and tea are available all day. Champagne and port are served at a wine bar in the evenings.

Amenities: Twice-daily beach shuttle, heated outdoor swimming pool, meeting space in a 1938 cottage restored by TV home-improvement guru Bob Vila.

Moderate

Inn by the Sea. 287 11th Ave. S., Naples, FL 34102. ☎ **941/649-4124.** 5 units (all with bathroom). A/C. Winter $149–$189 double. Off-season $94–$114 double. Rates include continental breakfast. AE, DISC, MC, V. Children 13 and under not accepted.

Listed in the National Register of Historic Places, this bed-and-breakfast 2 blocks from the beach in the heart of Olde Naples was built in 1937 as a boardinghouse by Alice Bowling, one of Naples's first schoolteachers and a grocer and entrepreneur to boot. Owned and operated by Willis and Tara Jones, the Federal-style house still has much of its original pine floors, matching pine or cypress woodwork, and exterior pinkish galvanized shingles. Comfy wicker furniture and ceiling fans add to the Old Florida ambience. Two of the five rooms have separate sitting areas. Bikes are provided, and in season, guests are served oranges from the backyard tree.

Inexpensive

Lemon Tree Inn. 250 9th St. S. (U.S. 41), Naples, FL 34102. ☎ **888/800-LEMON** or 941/262-1414. Fax 941/262-2638. 36 units. A/C TV TEL. Winter $99–$160. Off-season $50–$99. Rates include continental breakfast. AE, DISC, MC, V.

A real surprise on busy U.S. 41, this 1950s roadside motel just 3 blocks north of 5th Avenue South was completely rebuilt in 1997. Key West–style tin roofs top the two lemon-colored wings, which flank a lush tropical courtyard sporting a heated pool and a gazebo where guests congregate for complimentary continental breakfasts. The tropically accented rooms aren't spacious—their combination tub-shower bathrooms are so tiny that the wash basins are in the main living area—but they have exposed-beam ceilings hung with fans, and they are more than adequately equipped with wicker armoires serving as closets, wood dinette tables with rattan chairs, refrigerators, coffeemakers, microwave ovens, and toasters. Rooms with king beds have screened porches, while those with two double beds open to patios.

✪ **Olde Naples Inn & Suites.** 801 3rd St. S., Naples, FL 34102. ☎ **800/637-6036** or 941/262-5194. Fax 941/262-4876. www.bestof.net/naples/hotels/oldenaples inn. 60 units. A/C TV TEL. Winter $99–$179 double. Off-season $59–$119 double. Weekly rates available. Rates include continental breakfast. AE, DC, DISC, MC, V.

In the heart of Olde Naples, this dated but extraordinarily well-maintained apartment hotel is just 2 blocks from the beach and 4 blocks from the 3rd Street South and 5th Avenue South shopping areas (which more than makes up for the lack of an on-site restaurant). Its eclectic combinations of rooms, efficiencies, and one- and two-bedroom suites are in three buildings occupying about 60% of a city block, but the tropical landscaping makes it seem smaller. Most units open to two tropically landscaped courtyards with heated swimming pools. The units are comfortably furnished, immaculately maintained, and breezy. Guests can wander over to the lobby for complimentary breakfasts of pastries, juice, coffee, and tea. There are laundry facilities and off-street parking.

✪ **Tides Inn of Naples.** 1801 Gulf Shore Blvd. N., Naples, FL 34102. ☎ **800/438-8763** or 941/262-6196. Fax 941/262-3055. 35 units. A/C TV TEL. Winter $105–$235 double. Off-season $65–$130 double. AE, MC, V.

There's a very good reason why this somewhat-dated but immaculate two-story motel stays heavily booked during the winter months: It's right on the beach, just one door removed from the Edgewater Beach Hotel, and on the edge of Millionaires' Row and Olde Naples. Comfortable suites and efficiencies, all tropically furnished and decorated, have screened balconies or patios angled to face the beach across a courtyard with coconut palms and a heated swimming pool. You won't get this view in the less expensive motel rooms, which have no balcony or patio and whose windows overlook the parking lot. In winter, the suites and efficiencies must be reserved for at least a month; otherwise, reserve a room, get on the wait list, and pray for a cancellation. It's certainly worth a try, for you can't stay anywhere else on a Naples beach for these rates.

NORTH OF OLDE NAPLES

Very Expensive

The Registry Resort. 475 Seagate Dr., Naples, FL 34103. ☎ **800/247-9810** or 941/597-3232. Fax 941/597-3147. 424 units. A/C TV TEL. Winter $390–$530 double; $580–$975 suite. Off-season, $250–$330 double; $375–$650 suite. AE, DC, DISC, MC, V. From Olde Naples, go about 1½ miles north on U.S. 41; turn left on Seagate Dr. to hotel on right.

Like The Ritz-Carlton Naples (see below), its chief rival for the convention trade here, this sports-minded luxury establishment is not directly on the beach; guests must ride the free Clam Pass County Park shuttle along a 3,000-foot boardwalk through mangroves to the Gulf (see "Parks & Nature Preserves," above). Once there, they can charge lounge chairs, cabanas, and water-sports equipment rentals to their rooms. Inside its architecturally nondescript modern tower, the Registry radiates a more relaxed ambience than the traditional Ritz-Carlton.

Dining/Diversions: Dining here is at least on a par with The Ritz-Carlton, with the magnificent Lafite dining room offering some of the city's finest French cuisine (open nightly during winter, on Friday and Saturday evening off-season). Other outlets provide breakfast, lunch, and dinner, including poolside snacks, burgers, sandwiches, salads, and tropical drinks. The multilevel Club Zanzibar nightclub has dancing to deejay music in winter.

Amenities: Concierge, 24-hour room service, complimentary morning coffee, laundry, baby-sitting, children's activities program, bike rentals, games room, putting green, boutiques, hairdresser, business center, 3 heated swimming pools, whirlpools, tennis center with 15 courts (5 lighted), health club with fitness equipment, sauna, massages, facials, and body treatments. Sailboats, catamarans, aquabikes, and water-sports equipment available for rent at Clam Pass County Park.

✪ **The Ritz-Carlton Naples.** 280 Vanderbilt Beach Rd., Naples, FL 34108. ☎ **800/241-3333** or 941/598-3300. Fax 941/598-6690. 463 units. A/C TV TEL. Winter $375–$695 double; from $850 suite. Off-season $199–$425 double; from $575 suite. AE, DC, DISC, MC, V. From Olde Naples, go north 3½ miles on U.S. 41; turn left on Vanderbilt Beach Rd. (County Rd. 862), to hotel on left.

This opulent 14-story Mediterranean-style hotel at Vanderbilt Beach, 4 miles north of Olde Naples, is a favorite of affluent guests who like standard Ritz-Carlton amenities such as imported marble floors, antique art, Oriental rugs, Waterford crystal chandeliers, and British-style afternoon tea. All guest rooms overlook the gulf, but not all have balconies. The very rich book suites on the top-level Ritz-Carlton Club floor, where the rates are just as high as the rooms, but note that the cost of a standard room drops by almost half during the summer months. The staff starts fawning over you as soon as you pull up the royal palm-lined driveway, and they don't stop until you depart.

Guests can relax in high-backed rockers on the verandas or unwind by the heated swimming pool set in a landscaped terrace, but they must walk through a narrow mangrove forest to reach the beach. This stretch of sand is part of a public park, but the hotel has staff out there to answer phones, deliver drinks and snacks, and rent cabanas, boats, and other toys (only towels, chairs, and ice water are complimentary).

Dining/Diversions: The Dining Room is the hotel's signature restaurant, preparing seafood with an Asian flair. Both it and the wood-paneled Grill Room, a beef emporium reminiscent of a British private club, serve some of Naples's finest and most expensive cuisine. The casual Terrace by the pool serves breakfast, lunch, and dinner. Bands play for dancing in The Club bar each evening.

Amenities: Heated swimming pool with Jacuzzi, six lighted tennis courts, fitness center with spa treatments, golf privileges at nearby private clubs.

Expensive

Park Shore Resort. 600 Neapolitan Way, Naples, FL 34103. ☎ **800/548-2077** or 941/263-2222. Fax 941/262-0946. 156 units. A/C TV TEL. Winter $215–$245 condo. Off-season $95–$189 condo. Weekly and monthly discounts available. AE, DC, DISC, MC, V. From Olde Naples, go north on U.S. 41; turn left on Neopolitan Way, left on West Blvd. to resort.

This all-condo resort 1½ miles north of Olde Naples is a good bet if you want more space than a hotel room plus a kitchen (there's a supermarket a short walk away). The attractive one- and two-bedroom condos surround an artificial lagoon with waterfalls cascading on its own island. Guests can walk across a bridge to the artificial island, where they can swim in the heated pool, barbecue on gas grills, or order a meal from the restaurant or a drink from the bar.

Dining: The Island Club restaurant serves lunch, dinner, and Sunday brunch, and plenty of other restaurants are nearby.

Amenities: Children's activities program, daily maid service, complimentary shuttle to the beach daily at 11am, returning 2:30pm. Tennis, racquetball, volleyball, basketball, and shuffleboard courts; whirlpool; laundry room.

Vanderbilt Inn on the Gulf. 11000 Gulf Shore Dr., Naples, FL 34108. ☎ **800/643-8654** or 941/597-3151. Fax 941/597-3099. 147 units. A/C TV TEL. Winter $140–$315 double. Off-season $100–$270 double. (Highest rates for beachfront units.) Weekly rates available. AE, DC, DISC, MC, V. From Olde Naples, go 4 miles north on U.S. 41; take a left on 111th Ave. (which becomes Bluebill Ave.) to hotel on left.

Cheerful tropical decor in the accommodations and public areas sets the tempo for a casual, fun vacation at this motel. It's located 4 miles north of Olde Naples on Vanderbilt Beach, where guests can go parasailing and rent boats and water-sports equipment. About half the rooms face a beachside courtyard with a kidney-shaped, heated swimming pool surrounded by a brick terrace and tropical grounds. The other rooms face the exterior parking lots. Although the rooms are entered from exterior walkways, their big windows are darkly tinted to provide privacy. All rooms have refrigerators, and 16 also have cooking facilities.

Dining/Diversions: A thatch-roofed bar and full-service restaurant serve alfresco lunches and dinners and draw a crowd for sunset happy hour Monday to Thursday from 4:30 to 8:30pm, Friday to Sunday from 1 to 5pm. Also popular for lunch, the Seabreeze Lounge turns lively on Saturday night, when karaoke cranks up. The Jasmine Court serves breakfast and romantic candlelit dinners (early-bird specials from 5 to 7pm, and guests under 13 dine free when accompanied by adults).

Amenities: Concierge; limited room service; baby-sitting, children's program. Outdoor heated pool, kids' pool, bicycle rentals, coin laundry.

Inexpensive

Lighthouse Inn Motel. 9140 Gulf Shore Dr. N., Naples, FL 34108. ☎ **941/597-3345.** Fax 941/597-5541. 15 units. A/C TV. Winter $90 double; $95 efficiency; $105 apt. Off-season $40 double; $49 efficiency; $59 apt. MC, V. From Olde Naples, go 3½ miles north on U.S. 41, left on Vanderbilt Beach Rd. (County Rd. 862), right on Gulf Shore Dr. to hotel on right.

A relic from decades gone by, Judy and Buzz Dugan's spotlessly clean two-story motel sits across the street from other, more expensive properties on Vanderbilt Beach and within walking distance of the Ritz-Carlton Naples. The efficiencies and apartments are simple, with freshly painted cinder-block walls and small kitchens. The one kitchenless room has a small fridge and coffeemaker. Most guests take advantage of weekly and monthly rates in winter, when it's heavily booked. The Dugans also operate Buzz's Lighthouse Cafe next door, a pleasant place for an inexpensive dockside breakfast, lunch, or dinner.

WHERE TO DINE

You'll find budget-priced fast-food and family-style restaurants along U.S. 41, including a branch of **Mel's Diner,** 3650 Tamiami Trail North (☎ 941/643-9898).

Naples's beaches are ideal for picnics. In Olde Naples, you can get freshly baked breads and pastries, prepacked gourmet sandwiches, and fruit plates at **Tony's Off Third,** 1300 3rd St. S. (☎ 941/262-7999). It's also a fine place for coffee or a snack while window-shopping on 3rd Avenue South. The **Pelicatessen,** in the Waterside

Shops at Pelican Bay, Seagate Drive at North Tamiami Trail (☎ 941/597-3003), offers imported cheeses, freshly sliced meats, unusual salads, and shelves of gourmet items. Buy there and take it to Clam Pass County Park, at the end of Seagate Drive.

I have organized the restaurants below geographically: in Olde Naples, and north of the historic district.

IN OLDE NAPLES

In addition to Bistro 821 (see below), a dozen or so fine restaurants and bistros line **5th Avenue South,** Naples's "happening" venue, between 3rd and 9th streets south. They all serve fine, moderately priced fare, and they tend to be packed on weekend evenings, especially Friday, when the avenue becomes the local "meet market." My suggestion is to do as the locals do: Take a stroll and pick a place. They all post their menus out front, and you'll know the best by the number of chic customers present.

If this is your first time here, you may opt to have a lunch or dinner at the touristy Marketplace at Tin City, on the Gordon River at 5th Avenue South, where the **River-walk Fish & Ale House** (☎ 941/262-2734) and **Merriman's Wharf** (☎ 941/261-1811) specialize in moderately priced seafood and steaks. Like its sibling, The Dock at Crayton Cove (see below), the Riverwalk Fish & Ale House is a fun establishment with dockside seating.

Moderate

✪ **Bistro 821.** 821 5th Ave. S. (between 8th and 9th sts. S.). ☎ **941/261-5821.** Reservations recommended. Main courses $11–$21. AE, DC, MC, V. Sun–Thurs 5–10pm; Fri–Sat 5–10:30pm. MEDITERRANEAN.

One of several chic bistros near the eastern end of the 5th Avenue South shopping strip, this popular, noisy bistro began the trend toward Mediterranean restaurants here (see Terra, below). A bench covered in bright print fabric runs down one side of this storefront to a bar and open kitchen in the rear. Although the quarters are too close for private conversations, small spotlights hanging from the ceiling romantically illuminate each table. The house specialty is rotisserie chicken, and a daily risotto leads a menu featuring penne pasta in a vodka sauce, and a seasonal vegetable plate with herb couscous. There's sidewalk dining here, too.

Terra. 1300 3rd St. S. (actually on 13th Ave. S.). ☎ **941/262-5550.** Reservations recommended. Pizzas and sandwiches $9–$10; main courses $13.50–$27. AE, DC, DISC, MC, V. Daily 7–10:30am and 11:30am–10pm (bar until 11:30pm). MEDITERRANEAN.

This elegant yet casual restaurant in the heart of the 3rd Street South shopping district has muted lighting, a few antiques and paintings, and green-and-black woven rattan chairs at oak tables inlaid with terra-cotta tiles. A pianist lends romance as you enjoy Mediterranean dishes such as lamb shank osso buco, tasty wild mushroom lasagna, a risotto of the day, and personal-size pizzas. Sandwiches are served at both lunch and dinner, so you don't necessarily have to spend a fortune here. Breakfast features crepes, bagels, muffins, smoked salmon, and biscuits with sausage gravy.

Tommy Bahama's Tropical Cafe. 1220 3rd St. S. (at 12th Ave. S.). ☎ **941/643-6889.** Sandwiches $6–$9; main courses $14–$20. AE, DC, MC, V. Daily 11am–10pm. CARIBBEAN.

You walk through a thatch gateway into this lively, island-style pub—an incongruous sight in the middle of the staid 3rd Street South shopping enclave. Diners gather on a large front patio under shade trees or inside, where a large back-wall mural creates a Polynesian scene. There are an open kitchen and serving bar on one side of the dining room, a real bar dispensing drinks on the other. In between, round-backed cane chairs and classic ceiling fans add to the exotic mood. Although the Caribbean cuisine doesn't quite live up to the ambience, you'll have too much fun here to care if it's not gourmet. Sandwiches are served only at lunch. The restaurant is an offshoot of Tommy Bahama's tropical clothing store next door.

Inexpensive

✪ **The Dock at Crayton Cove.** 12th Ave. S. (at the City Dock in Olde Naples). ☎ **941/ 263-9940.** Reservations not accepted. Main courses $12.50–$19; sandwiches $5–$10.50. AE, DISC, MC, V. Daily 11am–midnight. SEAFOOD.

Located right on the City Dock, this lively pub is the best place in town for an open-air meal or a cool drink while watching the boats go back and forth across Naples Bay. The chow ranges from hearty chowders by the mug to seafood with a Floribbean fare, with Jamaican-style jerk shrimp thrown in for spice. On the light side, there are grilled seafood Caesar salad and a good selection of sandwiches, hot dogs, and other pub-style fare, plus a raw bar which is open daily from 9:30 to 11:30pm. Unlike its sister establishment, the tourist-frequented Riverwalk Fish House at Tin City, "The Dock" is highly popular with local residents, who regularly socialize at the bar during happy hour daily from 3 to 6pm and during "magarita madness" from 9 to 11pm. If you're here on the second Saturday in May, the "Great Dock Canoe Race" draws thousands of onlookers.

✪ **First Watch.** In Gulf Shore Sq., 1400 Gulf Shore Blvd. (at Banyan Rd.). ☎ **941/ 434-0005.** Most items $3–$6.50. AE, DISC, MC, V. Daily 7am–2:30pm. AMERICAN.

Just like its sibling in Sarasota, this corner shop with big louvered shutters to temper the morning sun is one of the locals' favorite spots for breakfast, late brunch, or a midday meal. This is anything but a diner, however. Instead you get classical music and widely spaced tables topped with pitchers of lemon-tinged ice water. A young staff provides quick and friendly service. The menu leans heavily on healthy selections, but you can get your cholesterol from a sizzling skillet of fried eggs served over layers of potatoes, vegetables, and melted cheese. Lunch features large salads, sandwiches, and quesadillas. In addition to the dining room, there's additional seating at umbrella tables in the shopping center's courtyard.

✪ **Old Naples Pub.** 255 13th Ave. S. (between 3rd and 4th sts. S., behind Thalheimer's Jewelers). ☎ **941/649-8200.** Salads, sandwiches, and burgers $5–$9; main courses $9–$13. AE, DISC, MC, V. Mon–Sat 11am–11pm, bar open until midnight; Sun noon–10pm, bar open until 11pm. AMERICAN.

You would never guess that the person sitting next to you at the bar here is very, very rich, so relaxed is this small, somewhat cramped pub in the middle of the 3rd Street South shops. Diners fortunately find more room at tables on the shopping center's patio. Inside, the pine-paneled walls are hung with trophy fish, a dart board, and old newspaper clippings about Naples. The menu features very good pub fare (and at extraordinarily inexpensive prices for Olde Naples), including homemade soups, nachos, burgers, and sandwiches ranging from charcoal-grilled bratwurst to fried grouper. Only three main courses are offered: platters with New York strip steak, grilled tuna, or fried grouper. You can catch live entertainment here Monday to Saturday evenings all year, and jazz on Sunday from 5 to 8pm during winter.

NORTH OF OLDE NAPLES

Very Expensive

✪ **Sign of the Vine.** 980 Solana Rd. (in the block east of N. Tamiami Trail/U.S. 41). ☎ **941/ 261-6745.** Reservations required. Main courses $33–$39. AE. Oct–May Mon–Sat 6–10pm; Aug–Sept Fri–Sat 6–10pm. Closed June–July. INTERNATIONAL. From Olde Naples, go north on U.S. 41, right on Solana Rd. at DeVoe Cadillac to restaurant on right.

Ever since owners/chefs Nancy and John Christiansen converted this gracious, old-fashioned house in 1985, their gourmet restaurant has been the kind of place

Neapolitans go for special celebrations when price comes second to fine cuisine and romantic ambience. Flickering candlelight, a fireplace, fresh flowers, antique dinnerware, and hand-lettered menus are perfect for such occasions. The Christiansens offer a creative international menu, including Jack's lobster hash with mushrooms and artichokes in a sassy Pernod-cream sauce accompanied by vegetable baklava. All dinners come with homemade country cheese, relish cart, salad with Nancy's own dressing, home-baked French bread, Ohio tomato pudding, corn soufflé with sweet onion cream, hot popovers with tangerine and lime butter, and fresh orange-and-ginger sorbet. Nancy specializes in grandmother-style desserts like warm bread pudding with a caramel sauce.

Moderate

Michelbob's Rib Capital of Florida. 371 Airport-Pulling Rd. (at Progress Ave.). ☎ **941/ 643-7427.** Reservations not accepted. Sandwiches $3.50–$8; platters $7–$21 (ribs $14.50–$21). AE, DC, MC, V. Mon–Fri 11am–9pm, Sat 4–9pm, Sun 9:30am–8:30pm. BAR-BECUE. From Olde Naples, go east on U.S. 41 across Gordon River, bear left on Davis Blvd. (Fla. 80), turn left on Airport-Pulling Rd. to restaurant on right.

The clientele at this casual, barnlike establishment says much about Naples's split personality, for over here east of U.S. 41 you'll see both rich and less-affluent folk chowing down on ribs which have won more than 20 national and international cook-offs. The specialties are tender baby back ribs and barbecued chicken (the sliced pork or beef platters and sandwiches are much less expensive but don't come close to matching the ribs). There are grilled chicken breast and Southern fried chicken and catfish if you're not a barbecue aficionado. All platters come with baked beans, slaw, and a choice of potato. There are a children's menu and an extensive Sunday brunch buffet. No smoking is permitted.

Inexpensive

✪ **Silver Spoon American Cafe.** In the Waterside Shops at Pelican Bay, 5395 N. Tamiami Trail (at Seagate Dr.). ☎ **941/591-2123.** Reservations not accepted, but call ahead for preferred seating. Main courses $8.50–$14; pizza and pasta $7.50–$10; soups, salads, and sandwiches $6.50–$9. AE, DC, DISC, MC, V. Sun–Thurs 11am–10pm, Fri–Sat 11am–11pm. From Olde Naples, go north on U.S. 41, left on Seagate Dr., right into shopping center, right at dead end to restaurant on left. AMERICAN/ITALIAN/SOUTHWEST.

Even though it's in the swanky Waterside Shops complex, this chic bistro is one of Naples's best dining bargains. It flaunts sophisticated black-and-white high-tech decor and has large window walls overlooking the mall action. Thick sandwiches are served with french fries, spicy pecan rice, or black beans. The tomato-basil soup is worth a try, and the brushetta appetizer—served on toasted French bread—is nearly a full meal in itself. Gourmet pizzas and pasta dishes also are popular, especially with the after-theater crowds from the nearby Philharmonic Center for the Arts, and the less-expensive main courses such as orange Dijon chicken are both tasty and an excellent value. Matron shoppers love to do lunch here, so come early or be prepared for a wait.

NAPLES AFTER DARK

For entertainment ideas, check the *Naples Daily News,* especially the "Neapolitan" section in Friday's edition.

THE PERFORMING ARTS   The impressive **Philharmonic Center for the Arts,** 5833 Pelican Bay Blvd., at West Boulevard (☎ **941/597-1900**), is the home of the Naples Philharmonic, but its year-round schedule is filled with cultural events such as performances by the Bolshoi Ballet, concerts by celebrated artists and internationally known orchestras, and Broadway plays and shows aimed at children and families. Call "The Phil" for a copy of its seasonal calendar.

A fine local theater group, the **Naples Players** hold their winter-season performances in the new Sugden Community Theatre, 701 5th Ave. S. (☎ 941/263-7990). Tickets are hard to come by, so call well in advance.

THE CLUB & BAR SCENE The restaurants and bistros along 5th Avenue South are popular watering holes, especially for singles who make this the local "meet market" on Friday nights. You can hear live music at **Hofgarten Brauhaus,** 898 5th Ave. S, at 9th St./U.S. 41 (☎ 941/263-4320); **Java Java Coffeehouse and Cybercafe,** 860 5th Ave. S. (☎ 941/435-1130); and **McCabe's Irish Pub,** in the Inn on Fifth, 699 5th Ave. S. (☎ 941/403-7170), featuring traditional Irish music Thursday to Saturday.

In the 3rd Street South shopping area, **Olde Naples Pub,** 255 13th Ave. S. (☎ 941/649-8200), has a pianist Monday to Saturday evenings year-round and jazz in the courtyard on Sunday from 5 to 8pm in winter. See "Where to Dine," above.

The **Old Marine Marketplace at Tin City,** the restored waterfront warehouses on 5th Avenue South on the west side of the Gordon River, comes alive during the winter when visitors flock to its shops and the **Riverwalk Fish & Ale House** (☎ 941/262-2734), which has live entertainment during the season.

Some of the hotels mentioned above have entertainment throughout the year. The beachside "chickee hut" bar at the **Naples Beach Hotel & Golf Club** (☎ 941/261-2222) is always popular; it has live entertainment many nights and is *the* place to go on Sunday afternoon and early evening. So is the beachside bar at the **Vanderbilt Inn on the Gulf** (☎ 941/597-3151). Club Zanzibar in the **Registry Resort** (☎ 941/597-3232) has deejay music for listening and dancing Tuesday to Saturday evenings.

6 Marco Island

15 miles SE of Naples, 53 miles S of Fort Myers, 100 miles W of Miami

Capt. William Collier would hardly recognize Marco Island if he were to come back from the grave today. No relation to Collier County founder Barron Collier, the captain settled his family on the north end of this largest of Florida's Ten Thousand Islands back in 1871. He traded pelts with the Native Americans, caught and smoked fish to sell to Key West and Cuba, and charged fishermen and other guests $2 a day for a room in his home. By 1896, he was doing such a roaring tourist business that he built a proper inn.

His Old Marco Inn still stands, along with a few other turn-of-the-century buildings. But Captain Collier would be shocked to come across the high-rise bridge to the island and see it now sliced by human-made canals and virtually covered by resorts, condos, shops, restaurants, and winter homes. These are the products of an extensive real-estate development begun in 1965, which means that Marco lacks any of the charm found in Naples and on Sanibel and Captiva islands. Much of the sales effort here was aimed at the northeastern states, so the island smacks more of New York and Massachusetts than the laid-back Midwestern style of its neighbors.

Marco's year-round population of some 10,000 swells to more than 30,000 during the winter season. Most of this multitude are retirees coming south for the winter, families on vacation, and groups convening at the island's three big resort hotels. While here, they enjoy Marco's crescent-shaped beach, the nearby waterways running through a maze of small islands, excellent boating and fishing, and the island's proximity to thousands of acres of wildlife preserves.

ESSENTIALS
GETTING THERE See the Fort Myers and Naples sections, earlier in this chapter, for information about the **Southwest Florida International Airport** and the

Naples Municipal Airport, respectively, and about Amtrak's train service and Greyhound/Trailways buses to those cities.

VISITOR INFORMATION   The **Marco Island Area Chamber of Commerce,** 1102 N. Collier Blvd., Marco Island, FL 34145 (☎ **800/788-6272** or 941/ 394-7549; fax 941/394-3061; www.marco-island-florida.com/chamber; e-mail: chamber@marco-island-florida.com), provides free information about the island. There are a message board and phone outside for making hotel reservations even when the office is closed. The chamber is open Monday to Friday from 9am to 4pm and Saturday from 10am to 3pm during winter.

GETTING AROUND   **Marco Island Trolley Tours** (☎ **941/394-1600**) makes four complete loops around the island from 10am to 3:15pm on Monday to Saturday. The conductors sell tickets and render an informative narration about the island's history. Daily fare is $10 for adults, $4 for children 11 and under, with free reboarding.

For a cab, call **A-Action Taxi** (☎ **941/394-4400**), **Classic Taxi** (☎ **941/ 394-1888**), or **A-Ok Taxi** (☎ **941/394-1113**).

Depending on the type, rental bicycles cost $5 an hour to $25 a week at **Beach Sports,** 571 S. Collier Blvd. (☎ **941/642-4282**), opposite the Hilton, and at **Scootertown,** 842 Bald Eagle Dr. (☎ **941/394-8400**), north of North Collier Boulevard near Old Marco. Scooters cost about $45 a day.

FUN ON & OFF THE BEACH

BEACHES   The sugar-white Crescent Beach curves for 3½ miles down the entire western shore of Marco Island. Its southern 2 miles are fronted by an unending row of high-rise condos and hotels, but the northern 1½ miles are preserved in **Tigertail Public Beach** (☎ **941/642-8414**). A sandbar offshore here creates a shallow lagoon safe for swimming and perfect for learning to windsurf. There are rest rooms, cold-water outdoor showers, a children's playground, and volleyball nets. Tigertail Beach Rentals gives windsurfing lessons, conducts pontoon-boat nature and shelling tours, and rents cabanas, chairs, umbrellas, sailboats, Windsurfers, kayaks, water tricycles, and other toys. A display illustrates the shells you'll find on the beach. **Todd's at Tigertail** (☎ **941/394-8828**) has a fully screened patio, where it serves inexpensive hot dogs, sandwiches, salads, and other snacks daily from 10am to 4pm. The park is at the end of Hernando Drive. It's open daily from dawn to dusk. There's no admission charge to the beach, but parking in the lot costs $3 per vehicle.

The beaches in front of the Marriott, Hilton, and Radisson resorts have parasailing, windsurfing, and other water-sports activities, all for a fee. In addition, **Beach Sports,** 571 S. Collier Blvd. (☎ **941/642-4282**), opposite the Hilton, rents Windsurfers, snorkeling gear, skim boards, fishing gear, tennis racquets, and a wide range of other equipment, including beach baby strollers. Beach Sports also has a scuba-dive operation charging $60 to $80 per dive, depending on depth, and teaches novice to advance courses.

If you're not staying at the big resorts, Collier County maintains a $3-per-vehicle parking lot and access to the developed beach on the southern end of the island, on Swallow Avenue at South Collier Boulevard.

OUTDOOR ACTIVITIES   A single source of information and the easiest way to book backcountry fishing, shelling, sightseeing, and sunset excursions through the beautiful inland waterways is through **Sea Excursions** (☎ **941/642-6400**). Per-person prices are about $20 for sightseeing, $25 for shelling, $35 for fishing, and $25 for sunset cruises. Reservations are required.

Naples's Lely and Boyne South golf courses are a short drive away (see "Other Outdoor Pursuits," in section 5, above). The closest public courses are the **Marco**

Shores Golf Club, 1450 Mainsail Dr. (☎ **941/394-2581**), and **Marriott's Golf Club at Marco** (☎ **941/353-7061**), both in the marshlands off Fla. 951 north of the island. A sign at the Marriott's course ominously warns: PLEASE DON'T DIS-TURB THE ALLIGATORS. Fees range from about $115 in winter down to $75 in summer.

PARKS & NATURE PRESERVES

Many species of birds inhabit ✪ **Collier Seminole State Park,** 20200 E. Tamiami Trail, Naples, FL 34114 (☎ **941/394-3397**), an inviting, 6,423-acre preserve on the edge of Big Cypress Swamp, 12 miles east of Marco Island on U.S. 41 (just east of Fla. 92). It offers fishing, boating, picnicking, canoeing over a 13-mile loop with a primitive campsite, observing nature along 6 miles of hiking trails (open during dry periods) and a 1-mile nature walk, and regular tent and RV camping (see "Where to Stay," below). A "walking" dredge used to build the Tamiami Trail in the 1920s sits just inside the park entrance. Housed in a replica of a Seminole Wars–era log fort, an interpretive center has information about the park, and there are ranger-led programs from December to April. Narrated boat tours wander through the winding waterways daily from 9:30am to 3:30pm. Canoes can be rented, but the park has only four camping sites along the canoe trails. Admission to the park is $3.25 per vehicle, $1 for pedestrians and bikers. The boat tours cost $8.50 for adults, $5.50 for children 6 to 12, free for children 5 and under. Canoes rent for $3 per hour, $15 a day. The park is open daily from 8am to sundown.

Operated by The Conservancy and part of the Rookery Bay National Estuarine Research Reserve, the ✪ **Briggs Nature Center,** on Shell Island Road, off Fla. 951 between U.S. 41 and Marco Island (☎ **941/775-8569**), has a half-mile boardwalk through a pristine example of Florida's disappearing scrublands, home to the threatened scrub jays and gopher tortoises. Rangers lead a variety of nature excursions (call for the seasonal schedule), and there are a self-guided canoe trail and canoes for rent during winter ($13 for the first 2 hr., $5 for each additional hr.). During winter, the Sea Queen has three nature cruises daily on the bay ($20 per person). The center is open Monday to Friday from 9am to 4:30pm year-round, Saturday from 9am to 4:30pm October to May, and Sunday from 1 to 5pm January to March. The interpretive center and a butterfly garden (27 varieties) are free. Admission to the boardwalk is $3 for adults, $1 for children 3 to 12, free for children under 3. For more information, contact **The Conservancy of Southwest Florida,** 1450 Merrihue Dr., Naples, FL 34102 (☎ **941/262-0304;** fax 941/262-0672).

WHERE TO STAY

There are no chain hotels on Marco Island other than the large Marriott, Hilton, and Radisson properties listed below, which stand in a row along Crescent Beach on the island's southwestern corner. On the other hand, Marco is loaded with condominium resorts, such as the **Paramount Suite Hotel,** 901 S. Collier Blvd., Marco Island, FL 34145 (☎ **800/323-8860** or 941/394-8860; fax 941/394-3040), on the inland side of the boulevard but near the big resorts. On the beach, **The Surf Club,** 540 S. Collier Blvd., Marco Island, FL 34145 (☎ **800/449-2837** or 941/642-5800; fax 941/ 642-7245), has 44 apartments. Rental agents representing house and condo owners include **Century 21 First Southern Trust** (☎ **800/255-9487** or 941/394-7658; fax 941/394-0004; e-mail: cent21sst@aol.com) and **Marco Beach Rentals** (☎ **800/ 423-7809** or 941/642-5400).

As elsewhere in South Florida, the high season here is from mid-December to mid-April. Rates drop precipitously in the off-season.

There's no campground in the developed part of Marco Island. **Collier Seminole State Park,** 20200 E. Tamiami Trail, Naples, FL 34114 (☎ **941/394-3397;** fax 941/394-5113), 12 miles east via Fla. 92, has 130 tent and RV sites laid out in circles and shaded by palms and live oaks. It has hot showers and a screened, open-air lounge. From December through April, sites cost $16 with electricity, $14 without. Off-season rates are $10.75 with electricity, $8.50 without. Reservations are accepted up to 11 months in advance. No pets are allowed in the campground.

✪ **Boat House Motel.** 1180 Edington Place, Marco Island, FL 34148. ☎ **941/642-2400.** Fax 941/642-2435. www.theboathousemotel.com. 25 units. A/C TV TEL. Winter $92.50–$147.50 double; $107.50–$240 apt or cottage. Off-season $57.50–$77.50 double; $75–$135 apt or cottage. MC, V.

One of the best bargains in these parts, this comfortable little motel sits beside the Marco River in Old Marco, on the island's northern end. The rooms are in a two-story, lime-green-and-white building ending at a wooden dock. Here there's a small heated swimming pool with lounge furniture, picnic tables, and barbecue grills. Two rooms on the end have their own decks, and all open to tiny courtyards. Bright paint, ceiling fans, and louvered doors add a tropical ambience throughout. The one-bedroom condos next door open to a riverside dock, upon which is built a two-bedroom cottage named "The Gazebo," whose peaked roof is supported by umbrella-like spokes from a central pole. Facilities include a guest laundry, a small library, and bicycle rentals. Olde Marco restaurants are a short stroll away.

Marco Island Hilton Beach Resort. 560 S. Collier Blvd., Marco Island, FL 34145. ☎ **800/443-4550** or 941/394-5000. Fax 941/394-8410. 298 units. A/C MINIBAR TV TEL. Winter $219–$329 double; $369 suite. Off-season $109–$209 double; $209–$249 suite. Packages available. AE, DC, DISC, MC, V.

This 11-story tower overlooks the gulf, a courtyard with a multiangled swimming pool wrapped around four coconut palms, and a shingle-roofed public building. A boardwalk leads to the beach, where a stand rents water-sports equipment. Equipped with three phones, refrigerators, coffeemakers, cherrywood armoires, writing desks, and headboards, the rooms and suites all have curved balconies angled to give water views. One-bedroom units have cooking facilities.

Dining/Diversions: One kitchen here serves two outlets: the elegant Sandcastles for dinner and the adjacent Paradise Cafe for casual breakfasts, lunches, and dinners. The Beach Club by the pool serves lunches, snacks, and drinks. Sandcastles Lounge has a piano bar with nightly entertainment.

Amenities: Concierge, room service, activities desk, baby-sitting, children's program, valet parking, laundry. Swimming pool, whirlpool spa, water-sports rentals, three lighted tennis courts, fitness center (with saunas, steam rooms, and massage therapy), gift shop, conference facilities.

✪ **Marco Island Marriott Resort & Golf Club.** 400 S. Collier Blvd., Marco Island, FL 34145. ☎ **800/438-4373** or 941/394-2511. Fax 941/642-2628. www.marcoisland-marriott.com. 786 units. A/C TV TEL. Winter $300–$360 double; from $469 suite. Off-season $129–$199 double; from $259 suite. Packages available. AE, DC, DISC, MC, V.

Often cited as one of the nation's top large resorts (it's the biggest on Florida's Gulf Coast), this deluxe establishment has two nine-story towers and two A-frame public wings forming two beachfront courtyards with swimming pools, bars, and water-sports centers. Luxuriously furnished and decorated, the spacious accommodations range from hotel rooms to two-bedroom suites. All have balconies or patios with indirect views of the gulf. Popular with couples and families as well as groups, it's the only North American resort to have won the National Parenting Center's seal of approval.

Dining/Diversions: Six restaurants offer a variety of cuisines to suit many tastes and pocketbooks, from near-gourmet northern Italian to carryout pizza. The Lobby Lounge features a large sports TV, piano music, and views of the gulf.

Amenities: Concierge, valet parking, room service, activities desk, laundry, baby-sitting, award-winning children's activities program. Golfers can play the resort's 18-hole championship golf course (on the mainland). On the premises are swimming pools, miniature golf course, lighted tennis courts and pro shop, health club, game room, boat and water-sports rental, shopping mall with chic boutiques, beauty salon, and conference facilities.

Radisson Suite Beach Resort. 600 S. Collier Blvd., Marco Island, FL 34145. ☎ **800/ 992-0651** or 941/394-4100. Fax 941/394-0419. 269 units. A/C TV TEL. Winter $259 double; $299–$509 suite. Off-season $129 double; $159–$279 suite. Packages available. Valet parking $6, free self-parking. AE, DC, DISC, MC, V.

This 11-story family-oriented resort seems like a motel with an abundance of growth hormone, since entry to the rooms and suites is from outside walkways with bright-blue railings, rather than from interior hallways. Although it lacks the quality of the Marriott and Hilton resorts, the two-bedroom suites here do directly face the gulf, which the competition's don't. Most of the 55 hotel rooms, however, look out on the Hilton next door. The building partially encloses a landscaped courtyard with a swimming pool, from which a boardwalk leads to the beach, where guests can rent umbrellas, cabanas, and water-sports equipment. The rooms have microwave ovens and coffeemakers, and the one- and two-bedroom apartments have fully equipped kitchens and dining areas (some have two baths). All units have screened balconies.

Dining/Diversions: Dining outlets here are designed to keep families fed. An indoor dining room serves moderately priced breakfasts, lunches, and dinners, while Bluebeard's Beach Club Grill offers inexpensive lunches, early dinners, snacks, and drinks by the pool. A Pizza Hut Express is on the premises, and a small store provides limited groceries, wine, and beer. There's also a poolside bar for cocktails.

Amenities: Concierge, activities desk, laundry, children's program. Heated swimming pool; whirlpool; exercise room; recreation center with programs for adults and children; shop with groceries; tennis, basketball, and volleyball courts.

WHERE TO DINE

For inexpensive fare, head for the Town Center Mall, at the corner of North Collier Boulevard and Bald Eagle Drive, where you'll find two good choices: **Susie's Diner** (☎ 941/642-6633) is popular with the locals for breakfasts and especially for Susie's inexpensive full-meal lunch specials. It's open Monday to Saturday from 6:30am to 2:30pm and Sunday from 6:30am to 1pm (for breakfast only). **Breakfast Plus** (☎ 941/642-6900) has eye-openers ranging from bacon and eggs to kippers to latkes. It's open daily from 7am to 2:30pm.

The island's popular sports bars also offer inexpensive pub fare to go with their multitudinous TVs. Most popular are **Rookie's Bar & Grill,** in Mission de San Marco Plaza at the corner of South Collier Boulevard and Winterberry Drive (☎ 941/ 394-6400), and the **Crazy Flamingo,** in the Town Center Mall, North Collier Boulevard at Bald Eagle Drive (☎ 941/642-9600).

✪ **Cafe de Marco.** 244 Palm St., Old Marco. ☎ **941/394-6262.** Reservations recommended. Main courses $15–$21; early-bird specials $11. Minimum charge $13 per adult (except early-bird specials), $4.50 per child. AE, MC, V. Winter daily 5–10pm. Off-season Mon–Sat 5–10pm. Early-bird specials 5–6pm. SEAFOOD.

Purveyor of some of the island's finest cuisine, this homelike establishment at the Marco Village shops was originally constructed as housing for maids at Capt. William Collier's Olde Marco Inn next door. The chef specializes in excellent treatments of fresh seafood, from your choice of shrimp or fresh baked fish with mushrooms, seasoned shallots, and garlic butter to his own luscious creation of seafood and vegetables combined in a lobster sauce and served over linguine. If your waist can stand it, finish with a Cafe Puff, an almond praline ice-cream ball rolled in chocolate cookie crumbs, placed in a puff pastry shell, and served with whipped cream. Early-bird specials here are a very good value.

Little Bar & Restaurant. Harbor Place (County Rd. 892), Goodland. ☎ **941/394-5663.** Reservations recommended for dinner. Main courses $13–$17; early-bird specials $8–$10. DISC, MC, V. Daily 11:30am–10pm (bar until 2am); early-bird specials 5–6pm. Closed Aug. SEAFOOD.

This very casual waterfront establishment is located in the heart of Goodland, an Old Florida fishing village on the eastern edge of Marco Island, some 7 miles (and at least 30 years) removed from the heavily developed western end of the island. One dining room here actually was the interior of the *Star of the Everglades*, a boat that took Presidents Truman and Eisenhower around and appeared in the Burl Ives movie *Winds Across the Everglades*. Other rooms possess antique bits and pieces from various buildings in the Chicago area, including an old pipe organ. A screened porch beside Goodland's fishing-boat harbor is this area's most popular spot for lunches featuring seafood and other sandwiches. Daily specials from a nightly chalkboard might include Everglades frogs' legs.

Kahuna Restaurant. 1035 N. Collier Blvd., in Town Center. ☎ **941/394-4300.** Reservations not accepted. Sandwiches and burgers $3–$7; main courses $7–$12. MC, V. Daily 11am–9pm. AMERICAN.

With a fanciful Hawaiian theme highlighted by a steaming volcano and a big mural of porpoises playing underwater on one wall, Kahuna is the most interesting and least expensive choice here. You can sit outside on the shopping center's parking lot or inside at colored booths and round tables under black ceiling fans. The burgers are some of Marco's best (there's a condiment bar with a variety of fixings). Main courses include several fried seafood selections, sautéed crab cakes, and charcoal-grilled tuna, but your best bet should be a nightly special such as salmon in a light dill sauce. Don't expect gourmet dining here, but the quality is excellent for the price.

✪ Kretch's. 527 Bald Eagle Dr. (south of N. Collier Blvd.). ☎ **941/394-3433.** Reservations recommended in winter. Main courses $13–$24. DC, MC, V. Mon–Fri 11am–3pm and 5–9pm, Sat–Sun 5–9pm. Closed Sun off-season and Easter, July 4, Thanksgiving, Christmas Eve, Christmas Day. SEAFOOD/CONTINENTAL.

Noted pastry chef Bruce Kretschmer has created a sinfully rich seafood strudel by combining shrimp, crab, scallops, cheeses, cream, and broccoli in a flaky Bavarian pastry and serving it all under a lobster sauce. Cholesterol counters can choose from broiled or charcoal-grilled fish, shrimp, Florida lobster tail, steaks, or lamb chops. Bruce's popular "Mexican Friday" lunches feature delicious tacos and other inexpensive, south-of-the-border selections. Sunday is home-cooking night during winter, with chicken and dumplings, Yankee pot roast, and braised lamb shanks.

Snook Inn. 1215 Bald Eagle Dr. (at Palm St.), Old Marco. ☎ **941/394-3313.** Reservations not accepted. Main courses $11–$19; sandwiches $8–$10. AE, DC, DISC, MC, V. Daily 11am–10pm. Closed Thanksgiving and Christmas. SEAFOOD.

The choice seats at this Old Florida establishment are in an enclosed dock right beside the scenic Marco River. Although seafood is the specialty, tasty steaks, chicken, burgers, and sandwiches are among the choices. The dockside Chickee Bar is a fun place, especially during sunset happy hour Monday to Friday from 4 to 6pm. The bar really rocks when live entertainment is featured during the winter season. Call for free shuttle service from anywhere on Marco Island.

MARCO ISLAND AFTER DARK

It's not after dark, but one of the biggest parties in Florida takes place every Sunday afternoon at ✪ **Stan's Idle Hour Seafood Restaurant,** on County Road 892 in Goodland (☎ **941/394-3041**), where owner Stan Gober—an Ernest Hemingway lookalike—plays host and fires up the barbecue grills; bands crank up country music for dancing the "Buzzard Lope"; and men compete to see who has the best legs. Stan's Goodland Mullet Festival, always the weekend before the Super Bowl, is the mother of all parties.

Over on the developed part of the island, everyone turns out for outdoor entertainment at the **Mission San Marco Plaza** shopping center, South Collier Boulevard at Winterberry Drive, every Tuesday night year-round.

The lounges in the **Marriott** and **Hilton resorts** (see "Where to Stay," above) provide pianists every evening. The schedules vary by season, so call ahead.

One of the most lively local spots is **La Casita Mexican Restaurant,** in the Shops of Marco, San Marco Road at Barfield Drive (☎ **941/642-7600**), where owners Frankie Ray and Maryellen play a variety of Mexican, Irish, popular, and traditional music Monday to Saturday. On Sunday, 1950s and 1960s dance music is highlighted.

The Tampa Bay Area 11

by Bill Goodwin

Many families visiting Orlando's theme parks eventually drive an hour west on I-4 to another major kiddie attraction, Busch Gardens Tampa Bay. But this area shouldn't be a mere side trip from Disney World, for Florida's central west coast is an exciting destination unto itself.

At the head of the bay, the city of Tampa is the commercial center of Florida's west coast—the country's 11th-busiest seaport and a center of banking, high-tech manufacturing, and cigar making (half a billion drugstore stogies a year). Downtown Tampa may roll up its sidewalks after dark, but you can come here during the day to see the sea life at the Florida Aquarium and stroll through the Henry B. Plant Museum, housed in an ornate, Moorish-style hotel built a century ago to lure tourists to Tampa. A trolley will take you on a short ride to Ybor City, the historic Cuban enclave which is now an exciting entertainment and dining venue. And out in the suburbs, Busch Gardens may be best known for its scintillating rides, but it's also one of the world's largest zoos.

Two bridges and a causeway will whisk you westward across the bay to the Pinellas Peninsula, one of Florida's most densely packed urban areas. Over here on the bay front, lovely downtown St. Petersburg is famous for wintering seniors, a shopping and dining complex built way out on a pier, and the world's largest collection of Salvador Dalí's surrealist paintings.

Keep driving west and you'll come to a line of barrier islands where St. Pete Beach, Treasure Island, Clearwater Beach, and other gulfside communities boast 28 miles of sunshine, surf, and white sand. Yes, they're lined with resorts and condos of every description and price, but parks on each end preserve two of the nation's finest beaches.

Drive north up the coast, and you'll go back in time at the old Greek sponge enclave of Tarpon Springs, one of Florida's most attractive small towns, and at Weeki Wachee Springs, a tourist attraction where "mermaids" have been entertaining underwater for half a century.

Heading south, the Sunshine Skyway will take you soaring 175 feet above the bay to Bradenton, Sarasota, and another chain of barrier islands. One of Florida's cultural centers, affluent Sarasota is the gateway to St. Armands and Longboat keys, two playgrounds of the rich and famous, and to Lido and Siesta keys, attractive to families of more modest means. Even more reasonably priced is Anna Maria Island, off the riverfront town of Bradenton. You might say the bridge from Longboat to Anna Maria goes from one price range to another.

Tampa & St. Petersburg

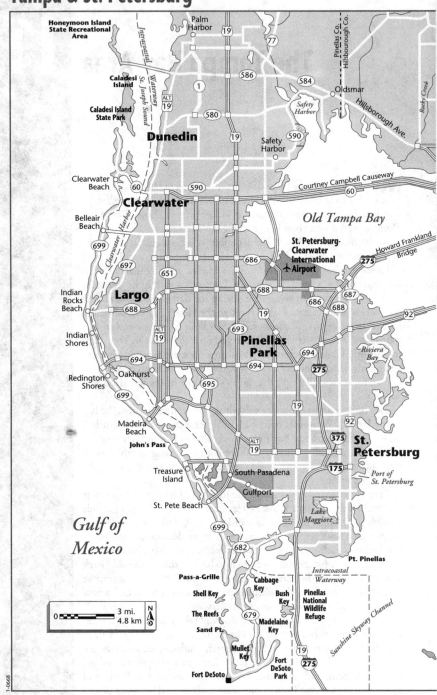

Honeymoon Island
State Recreational
Area

Palm
Harbor

Caladesi
Island

Caladesi Island
State Park

Dunedin

Clearwater
Beach

Clearwater

Belleair
Beach

Indian
Rocks
Beach

Largo

Indian
Shores

Redington
Shores

Oakhurst

Madeira
Beach

John's Pass

Treasure
Island

St. Pete Beach

*Gulf of
Mexico*

Pass-a-Grille

Shell Key

The Reefs

Sand Pt.

Mullet
Key

Fort DeSoto

Oldsmar

*Safety
Harbor*

Safety
Harbor

Old Tampa Bay

Courtney Campbell Causeway

St. Petersburg-
Clearwater
International
✈ **Airport**

Howard Frankland
Bridge

**Pinellas
Park**

*Riviera
Bay*

**St.
Petersburg**

*Port of
St. Petersburg*

South Pasadena

Gulfport

*Lake
Maggiore*

Pt. Pinellas

*Intracoastal
Waterway*

Cabbage
Key

Bush
Key

Pinellas
National
Wildlife
Refuge

Sunshine Skyway Channel

Madelaine
Key

Fort
DeSoto
Park

Pinellas Co.
Hillsborough Co.

Hillsborough Ave.

Rocky Creek

St. Joseph Sound

*Intracoastal
Waterway*

Clearwater Harbor

0   3 mi.
    4.8 km

N

1-0668

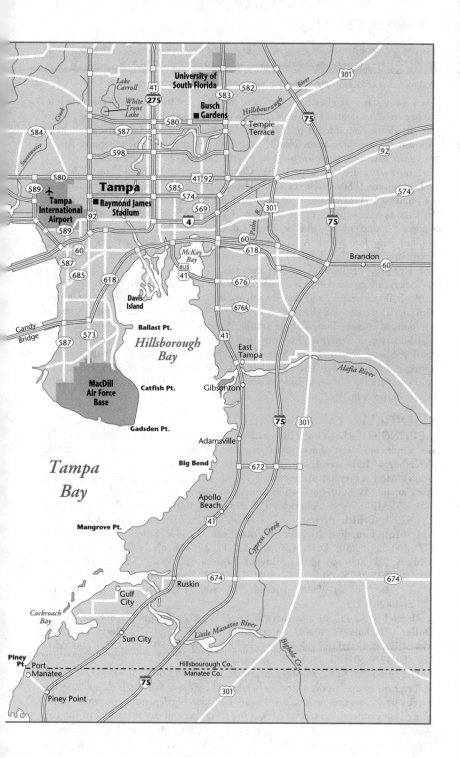

1 Tampa

200 miles SW of Jacksonville, 254 miles NW of Miami, 63 miles N of Sarasota

Even if you stay at the beaches 20 miles to the west, you should consider driving into Tampa to see its sights. If you have children in tow, they will *demand* that you go into the city so they can ride the rides and see the animals at Busch Gardens. While here, you can educate them at the Florida Aquarium and the city's fine museums. And if you don't have kids, historic Ybor City has the bay area's liveliest nightlife.

Tampa was a sleepy little port when Cuban immigrants founded Ybor City's cigar industry in the 1880s. A few years later Henry B. Plant put Tampa on the tourist map by building a railroad to town and the bulbous minarets over his garish Tampa Bay Hotel, now a museum named in his honor. During the Spanish American War, Teddy Roosevelt trained his Rough Riders here and walked the Ybor City streets with Cuban revolutionary José Marti. A land boom in the 1920s gave the city its charming, Victorian-style Hyde Park suburb, just across the Hillsborough River from downtown, now a gentrified redoubt of the baby boomers.

Today's downtown skyline is the product of the 1980s and early 1990s boom, when banks built skyscrapers and the city put up an expansive convention center, a performing-arts center, and the Ice Palace, a 20,000-seat bayfront arena that is home to professional hockey's Tampa Bay Lightning. Alongside the new Florida Aquarium, the Garrison Seaport Center is a major home port for cruise ships bound for Mexico and the Caribbean. Baseball's New York Yankees helped things along by building their spring-training complex here, including a scaled-down replica of Yankee Stadium. And the sparkling Raymond James Stadium became the home to pro football's Tampa Bay Buccaneers in 1998.

ESSENTIALS

GETTING THERE   **Tampa International Airport,** off Memorial Highway and Fla. 60, 5 miles northwest of downtown Tampa, is the major air gateway to this area (**St. Petersburg–Clearwater International Airport** has limited service; see section 2, below). Most major and many no-frills airlines serve Tampa International, including **Air Canada** (☎ 800/268-7240 in Canada or 800/776-3000 in the U.S.); **AirTran** (☎ 800/AIR-TRAN); **American** (☎ 800/433-7300); **America West** (☎ 800/235-9292); **British Airways** (☎ 800/247-9297); **Cayman Airways** (☎ 800/422-9626); **Canadian Airlines International** (☎ 800/426-7000); **Continental** (☎ 800/525-0280); **Delta** (☎ 800/221-1212); **MetroJet** (☎ 800/428-4322); **Midway** (☎ 800/446-4392); **Midwest Express** (☎ 800/452-2022); **Northwest** (☎ 800/225-2525); **Spirit** (☎ 800/722-7117); **Southwest** (☎ 800/435-9792); **TWA** (☎ 800/221-2000); **United** (☎ 800/241-6522); and **US Airways** (☎ 800/428-4322).

Alamo (☎ 800/327-9633); **Avis** (☎ 800/331-1212); **Budget** (☎ 800/527-0700); **Dollar** (☎ 800/800-4000); **Enterprise** (☎ 800/325-8007); **Hertz** (☎ 800/654-3131); **National** (☎ 800/CAR-RENT); **Thrifty** (☎ 800/367-2277); and **Value** (☎ 800/327-2501) all have rental-car operations here.

The Limo (☎ **813/396-3693** in Tampa, or 800/282-6817 or 727/572-1111 in St. Petersburg) operates van services between the airport and hotels throughout the Tampa Bay area. Fares for one person vary considerably depending on where you're going (some hotels have special rates). One passenger will pay at least $6 to Tampa's West Shore area or downtown Tampa, $13 to Busch Gardens or Clearwater Beach, and $13 to downtown St. Petersburg or to Tarpon Springs. **Taxis** are plentiful at the airport; the ride to downtown Tampa takes about 15 minutes and costs $11 to $14.

Amtrak trains arrive downtown at the **Tampa Amtrak Station,** 601 Nebraska Ave. N. (☎ **800/USA-RAIL**).

VISITOR INFORMATION   Contact the **Tampa/Hillsborough Convention and Visitors Association (THCVA)**, 400 N. Tampa St., Tampa, FL 33602-4706 (☎ **800/44-TAMPA** or 813/223-2752; fax 813/229-6616; www.thcva.com), for advance information. Once you're downtown, head to the THCVA's visitors information center at the corner of Ashley and Madison streets. It's open Monday to Saturday from 9am to 5pm.

The **Ybor City Chamber of Commerce** has a visitor center in an old cigar-roller's cottage at 1800 E. 9th Ave. (at 18th St.), Tampa, FL 33605 (☎ **877/934-3782** or 941/248-3712; fax 941/247-1764; www.ybor.org). Open Monday to Friday from 9am to 5pm.

Near Busch Gardens, the privately owned **Tampa Bay Visitor Information Center,** 3601 E. Busch Blvd., at N. Ednam Place (☎ **813/985-3601;** fax 813/985-7642), offers free brochures about attractions in Tampa and sells discounted tickets to many attractions. You may be able to both save $2 a head and avoid waiting in long ticket lines at Busch Gardens by buying here, and owner Jim Boggs worked for the park for many years and gives expert advice about how to get the most out of your visit. Open Monday to Saturday from 9am to 5:30pm, Sunday from 9am to 2pm. Operating as Swiss Chalet Tours, this same company also has organized excursions of the area (see "Organized Tours," below).

GETTING AROUND   As with most other Florida destinations, it's virtually impossible to see Tampa's major sights and enjoy the best restaurants without a car.

In the works at press time, a street car on rails was to begin hauling passengers between downtown and Ybor City in 2000, traveling by the Florida Aquarium; check with the visitor center (see above), or call the **Hillsborough Area Regional Transit/HARTline** (☎ 813/254-HART). If you're on a budget, HARTline also provides regularly scheduled bus service between downtown Tampa and the suburbs. Pick up a route map at the visitor information center (see above).

Taxis in Tampa don't normally cruise the streets for fares, but they do line up at public loading places, such as hotels, the performing-arts center, and bus and train depots. If you need a taxi, call **Tampa Bay Cab** (☎ **813/251-5555**), **Yellow Cab** (☎ **813/253-0121**), or **United Cab** (☎ **813/253-2424**). Fares are 95¢ at flag fall plus $1.50 for each mile.

EXPLORING THE THEME & ANIMAL PARKS

Adventure Island. 10001 McKinley Dr. (between Busch Blvd. and Bougainvillea Ave.). ☎ **813/987-5600.** Admission $22.95 adults, $20.95 children 3–9, plus tax. Free for children 2 and under. *Note:* Prices keep increasing, so expect to pay slightly more. Seasonal passes available. Mid-Feb to Labor Day daily 10am–5pm; Sept–Oct Fri–Sun 10am–5pm (extended hours in summer and on holidays). Closed Nov to mid-Feb. Take Exit 33 off I-275, go east on Busch Blvd. for 2 miles, turn left onto McKinley Dr. (N. 40th St.), and entry is on right.

If the summer heat gets to you before one of Tampa's famous thunderstorms brings late-afternoon relief, you can take a waterlogged break at this 25-acre outdoor water theme park near Busch Gardens Tampa Bay (see below). In fact, you can frolic here even during the cooler days of spring and fall, when the water is heated. The Key West Rapids, Tampa Typhoon, Gulf Scream, and other exciting water rides will drench the teens, while other, calmer rides are geared for kids. There are places to

Tampa Attractions

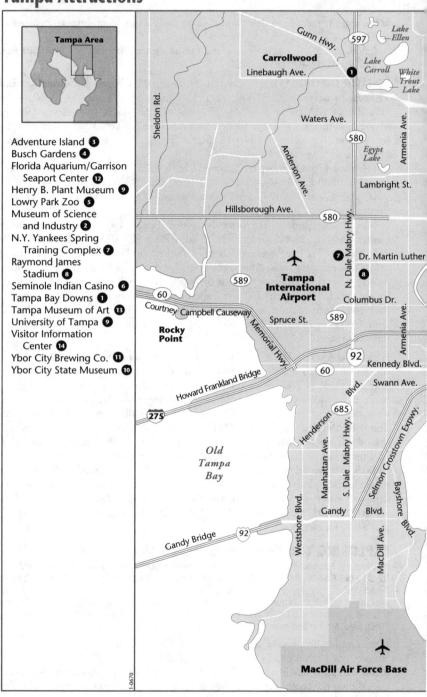

Adventure Island ❸
Busch Gardens ❹
Florida Aquarium/Garrison
    Seaport Center ⓬
Henry B. Plant Museum ❾
Lowry Park Zoo ❺
Museum of Science
    and Industry ❷
N.Y. Yankees Spring
    Training Complex ❼
Raymond James
    Stadium ❽
Seminole Indian Casino ❻
Tampa Bay Downs ❶
Tampa Museum of Art ⓭
University of Tampa ❾
Visitor Information
    Center ⓮
Ybor City Brewing Co. ⓫
Ybor City State Museum ❿

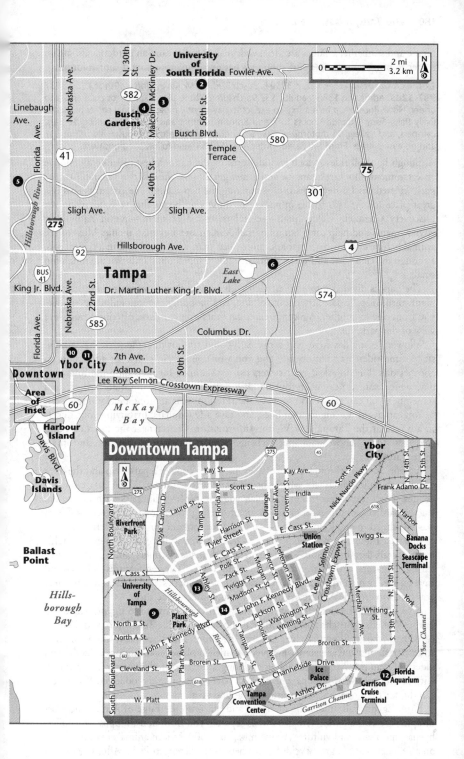

Downtown Tampa

Kay St.
Kay Ave.
Scott St.
India
Scott St.
Frank Adamo Dr.
Laurel St.
Harrison Street
Tyler Street
E. Cass St.
E. Cass St.
Union Station
Twigg St.
Banana Docks
Seascape Terminal
E. Cass St.
Polk St.
Zack St.
Twiggs St.
Madison St.
E. John F. Kennedy Blvd.
Jackson St.
Washington St.
Whiting St.
W. Cass St.
University of Tampa
Plant Park
North B St.
North A St.
W. John F. Kennedy Blvd.
Cleveland St.
W. Platt
Brorein St.
Brorein St.
Channelside Drive
Ice Palace
Tampa Convention Center
S. Ashley Dr.
Garrison Cruise Terminal
Florida Aquarium
Garrison Channel
Ybor Channel

Riverfront Park
North Boulevard
Doyle Carlton Dr.
N. Tampa St.
N. Florida Ave.
Orange
Central Ave.
Governor St.
Scott St.
Nick Nuccio Pkwy.
N. 14th St.
N. 15th St.
Harbor
Jefferson St.
Pierce St.
Morgan St.
Florida Ave.
S. Tampa Ave.
Lee Roy Selmon Crosstown Expwy.
Merdian Ave.
Whiting St.
N. 13th St.
York
South Boulevard
Hyde Park Ave.
Plant Ave.
Ashley St.

Ybor City

Hillsborough Bay

Ballast Point

picnic and sunbathe, a games arcade, a volleyball complex, and an outdoor cafe. If you forget to bring your own, a surf shop sells bathing suits, towels, and suntan lotion.

✪ **Busch Gardens Tampa Bay.** 3000 E. Busch Blvd. (at McKinley Dr./N. 40th St.). ☎ **813/987-5283.** Admission $38.95 adults, $32.95 children 3 to 9, plus tax. Free for children 2 and under. Note: Prices keep increasing, so expect to pay slightly more. Seasonal passes available. Daily 9am–6pm (extended hours to 7 and 8pm in summer and holidays). Parking $6 cars, campers, and trailers; $5 motorbikes. Take I-275 north of downtown to Busch Blvd. (Exit 33), and go east 2 miles. From I-75, take Fowler Ave. (Exit 54) and follow the signs west.

Although its thrill rides (which include some of the nation's best roller coasters), live entertainment, shops, restaurants, and games get most of the ink, this venerable theme park (it predates Disney World) ranks among the top zoos in the country. This is a great place for the kids to see in person all those wild beasts they've watched on the Discovery Channel. The animals—several thousand of them—live in naturalistic environments and help carry out an overall African and Egyptian theme. Most of the animal habitats are much bigger and more open than what you'd find in a typical zoo, although the elephants and white tigers are sadly trapped on islands that are much too small.

The park is divided into 8 areas, each with its own theme, animals, live entertainment, thrill rides, kiddie attractions, dining, and shopping. A monorail train will take you from one to another. A Skyride cable car soars over the park, offering a bird's-eye view of the park.

Allow at least a day here, and arrive early—but try not to come when it's raining, since some rides may not operate and you won't get a rain check for admission on another day (but do ask if your tickets can be stamped for admission the following day, which sometimes occurs during slow periods). Bring comfortable shoes, and remember, you can get wet on some of the rides, so wear appropriate clothing.

You can avoid waiting in long lines, and save a few dollars, by buying your tickets in advance at the **Tampa Bay Visitor Information Center** near the main entrance (see "Essentials," above). You can exchange foreign currency in the park, and interpreters are available.

As soon as you're through the turnstiles, pick up a copy of a park map and the day's activity schedule, which tells what's showing and when at the park's 14 entertainment venues. Then take a few minutes to plan your time—it's a big park with lots to do. Busch Gardens continues to grow—a set of dueling roller coasters known as Gwazi was scheduled to crank up in 1999—so be on the lookout for new attractions.

Just past the main gate you'll come to **Morocco,** a walled city with exotic architecture, craft demonstrations, a sultan's tent with snake charmers, and an exhibit featuring alligators and turtles. The Moroccan Palace Theater features "Hollywood Live on Ice," which many families consider to be the park's best entertainment. Here you can also attend "American Jukebox," a song-and-dance show.

After watching the snake charmers in Morocco, walk eastward to **Egypt,** where you can see Anheuser-Busch's fabled Clydesdale horses; visit King Tut's tomb; and listen to comedian Martin Short narrate "Akbar's Adventure Tours," a wacky simulator that "transports" one and all across Egypt via camel, biplane, and mine car. Adults and older kids can ride Montu, the tallest and longest inverted roller coaster in the world, with seven upside-down loops, one of them barely missing a crocodile pit. Youngsters can dig for their own ancient treasures in a sand area.

From Egypt, walk under the monorail and out onto the **Edge of Africa,** the most unique part of the park. Here glass walls separate you from lions, hippos, crocodiles, hyenas, meerkats, and vultures among more than 500 African animals roaming freely on an 80-acre natural grassy veldt known here as the Serengeti Plain. After you've seen them close up, the monorail will take you on "safari" out on the plain.

Next stop is **Nairobi,** where you can see gorillas and chimpanzees in the Myombe Reserve, replicating their natural tropical habitat. Nairobi also has a baby animal nursery, a petting zoo, turtle and reptile displays, an elephant exhibit (sadly much too small for these giant beasts), and Curiosity Caverns, a simulated environment that allows you to observe animals that are active in the dark.

From Nairobi, walk into **Timbuktu,** evoking an ancient desert trading center with African craftspeople at work. Here you'll find several rides, including The Sandstorm, the Phoenix, and the Scorpion, a 360-degree roller coaster. Plan to have lunch here at Das Festhaus, a 1,200-seat, air-conditioned German festival hall featuring a lively musical show "The International Celebration" (be sure to arrive at least 15 minutes before show time to get a seat). The kids will enjoy the Dolphin Theater, with performing porpoises, otters, and sea lions.

After lunch, head to **The Congo,** highlighted by rare white Bengal tigers living on Claw Island. The Congo also is home to two roller coasters: the Kumba, the largest and fastest roller coaster in the southeastern United States; and the Python, which twists and turns for 1,200 feet. You will get drenched (and refreshed on a hot day) by riding the Congo River Rapids. There are bumper cars and kiddie rides here, too.

From The Congo, walk south into **Stanleyville,** a prototype African village, with a shopping bazaar, orangutans living on an island, and the Stanleyville Theater, featuring "Stars of the Future," a show about children. Two more water rides are here: the Tanganyika Tidal Wave and Stanley Falls. Serving ribs and chicken, the Stanleyville Smokehouse has some of the best chow here. This also is a good place to board the trans-veldt railway for a sightseeing ride all the way around the park and back, since you'll avoid the crowds waiting to board elsewhere (the air-conditioned train also is a good way to cool off on a hot summer's day).

From Stanleyville, the next stop is **Land of the Dragons,** where the younger set can easily spend an entire day enjoying a variety of play elements in a fairy-tale setting, plus just-for-kids rides. The area is dominated by Dumphrey, a whimsical dragon who interacts with visitors and guides children around a three-story tree house with winding stairways, tall towers, stepping stones, illuminated water geysers, and an echo chamber.

The last stop is **Bird Gardens,** the park's original core, offering rich foliage, lagoons, and a free-flight aviary for hundreds of exotic birds, including golden and American bald eagles. Catch the Bird Show here, and be sure to see the Florida flamingos and Australian koala "bears."

You can finish your visit back at the Hospitality House, which offers piano entertainment and free samples of Anheuser-Busch's famous beers (you must be 21 to imbibe, and there's a limit of two free mugs per seating).

✪ **Florida Aquarium.** 701 Channelside Dr. ☎ **813/273-4000.** Admission $11.95 adults, $10.95 seniors, $6.95 children 3–12, free for children under 3. Parking $3. Daily 9:30am–5pm. Closed Thanksgiving and Christmas.

Visitors here are introduced to more than 5,300 aquatic animals and plants that call Florida home. Various exhibits allow you to follow the pristine springs of the Florida Wetlands Gallery, go through a mangrove forest in the Bays and Beaches Gallery, and stand amazed at the Coral Reefs. The most impressive display is a 43-foot-wide, 14-foot-tall panoramic window with schools of fish and lots of sharks and stingrays. You can watch a diver twice a day. There's a half-million-dollar "Explore a Shore" playground to educate the kids, a deep-water exhibit, and a tank housing moray eels. The Cafe Ray serves snacks and light meals.

Lowry Park Zoo. 7530 North Blvd. ☎ **813/932-0245.** Admission $8.50 adults, $7.50 seniors, $4.95 children 3–11, free for children 2 and under. Daily 9:30am–4:45pm. Closed Thanksgiving and Christmas. Take I-275 to Sligh Ave. (Exit 31) and follow the signs.

Watching the 2,000-pound manatees, the komodo dragons, and the rare red pandas makes this a worthwhile excursion after the kids have seen the plains of Africa at Busch Gardens. With lots of greenery, bubbling brooks, and cascading waterfalls, this 24-acre zoo displays animals in settings similar to their natural habitats. Other major exhibits include a Florida wildlife display, an Asian Domain, a Primate World, an Aquatic Center, a free-flight aviary with a birds-of-prey show, a children's petting zoo and hands-on Discovery Center, and an endangered-species carrousel ride. There are plenty of food outlets here, including an on-site McDonald's.

VISITING THE MUSEUMS

Henry B. Plant Museum. 401 W. Kennedy Blvd. (between Hyde Park and Magnolia aves.). ☎ 813/254-1891. Free admission; suggested donation $5 adults, $1 children 12 and under. Tues–Sat 10am–4pm, Sun noon–4pm. Take Fla. 60 west of downtown.

You can't miss the 13 silver minarets and distinctive Moorish architecture, modeled after the Alhambra in Spain, that make this National Historic Landmark a focal point of the Tampa skyline. Originally built in 1891 as the 511-room Tampa Bay Hotel by railroad tycoon Henry B. Plant, it's filled with art and furnishings from Europe and the Orient. Other exhibits focus on the history of the original railroad resort, Florida's early tourist industry, and the hotel's role as a staging point for Teddy Roosevelt's Rough Riders during the Spanish-American War.

✪ **Museum of Science and Industry (MOSI).** 4801 E. Fowler Ave. (at N. 50th St.). ☎ 813/987-6300. www.tampatrib.com/mosi. Admission $12 adults; $10 seniors, college students with identification, and children 13–18; $8 children 2–12; free for children under 2. IMAX tickets $6 adults; $5 seniors, college students, and children 3–18; $4 kids 2–12. Combination tickets available. Free parking. Daily 9am–5pm or later. From downtown, take I-275 north, then Fowler Ave. east 2 miles to museum on right.

A great place to take the kids on a rainy day, MOSI is the largest science center in the Southeast and has more than 450 interactive exhibits. Guests can step into the Gulf Hurricane and experience gale-force winds, defy the laws of gravity in the unique *Challenger* space experience, or cruise the mysterious world of microbes in LifeLab. The Amazing You allows visitors to explore the body, Our Florida focuses on environmental factors, and Our Place in the Universe introduces visitors to space, flight, and beyond. You can also watch stunning movies in Florida's first IMAX dome theater.

Tampa Museum of Art. 600 N. Ashley Dr. (at Twiggs St.), downtown. ☎ 813/274-8130. Admission $5 adults, $4 seniors and students with identification, $3 children 6–18, free for children 5 and under, by donation for everyone Wed 5–9pm and Sat 10am–noon. Mon–Tues and Thurs–Sat 10am–5pm, Wed 10am–9pm, Sun 1–5pm. Take I-275 to Exit 25 (Ashley Dr.).

Located on the east bank of the Hillsborough River next to the round NationsBank building (locals facetiously call it the "Beer Can") and just south of the Tampa Bay Performing Arts Center, this fine-arts complex offers eight galleries with changing exhibits ranging from classical antiquities to contemporary Florida art. There's also a 7-acre riverfront park and sculpture garden. Museum tours are offered on Wednesday and Saturday at 1pm and on Sunday at 2pm.

YBOR CITY

Northeast of downtown, the city's historic Latin takes its present name from Don Vicente Martinez Ybor ("*Ee*-bore," a Spanish cigar maker who arrived here in 1886 via Cuba and Key West. Soon his and other Tampa factories were producing more than 300,000 hand-rolled stogies a day.

It may not be the cigar capital of the world anymore, but Ybor is the happening part of Tampa, a cross between New Orleans's Bourbon Street, Washington's Georgetown, and New York's SoHo. By day, you can stroll past the art galleries, boutiques, and trendy new restaurants and cafes that line 7th Avenue East. At night, when good food and *loud* music dominate the scene, streets will be bustling until 4am, mostly with kids in their early 20s. Unique shops offer a wide assortment of goodies, from silk boxer shorts to unique tattoos. Dozens of outstanding nightclubs and dance clubs have waiting lines out the door. Live-music offerings run the gamut from jazz and blues to indie rock.

The area was becoming even more active with the planned opening of **Centro Ybor,** a dining-shopping-entertainment complex at 7th Avenue and 19th Street, in 2000.

Cigar smokers will enjoy a stroll through the **Ybor City State Museum,** 1818 9th Ave., between 18th and 19th streets (☎ 813/247-6323), housed in the former Ferlita Bakery (1896 to 1973). You can take a self-guided tour around the museum to see a collection of cigar labels, cigar memorabilia, and works by local artisans. Admission is $2 per person, including a 30-minute guided tour of **La Casita,** a renovated cigar worker's cottage adjacent to the museum; it's furnished as it was at the turn of the century. The museum is open daily from 9am to noon and 1 to 5pm (La Casita, from 10am to noon and 1 to 2:30pm).

Check with the museum about **walking tours** of the historic district. **Ybor City Ghost Walks** (☎ 813/242-9255) will take you to the spookier parts of the area at night. Call for reservations, schedules, and prices.

Another interesting stop here is the **Ybor City Brewing Company,** 2205 N. 20th St., facing Palm Avenue (☎ 813/242-9222). Housed in a 100-year-old, three-story former cigar factory, this microbrewery produces Ybor Gold and other brews, none with preservatives. Admission of $2 per person includes a tour of the brewery and taste of the end result. Open Tuesday to Saturday from 11am to 3pm.

ORGANIZED TOURS

Swiss Chalet Tours, 3601 E. Busch Blvd. (☎ 813/985-3601), opposite Busch Gardens in the privately run Tampa Bay Visitor Information Center (see "Essentials," above), operates guided bus tours of Tampa, Ybor City, and environs. The 4-hour tours of Tampa are given from 10am to 2pm daily, with a stop for lunch at the Columbia Restaurant in Ybor City. They cost $40 for adults and $35 for children. The 7-hour full-day tours of both Tampa and St. Petersburg cost $70 for adults and $65 for children. Reservations are required at least 24 hours in advance; passengers are picked up at major hotels and various other points in the Tampa/St. Petersburg area. Tours can also be booked to Orlando, Sarasota, Bradenton, and other regional destinations.

OUTDOOR PURSUITS & SPECTATOR SPORTS

Tampa Outdoor Adventures (☎ 800/44-TAMPA, ext. 6, or 813/223-2752) is a one-stop source of information and reservations for a variety of recreational activities in the Tampa area, from ballooning to yachting.

BICYCLING, IN-LINE SKATING & JOGGING Bayshore Boulevard, a 7-mile promenade, is famous for its sidewalk right on the shores of Hillsborough Bay. Reputed to be the world's longest continuous sidewalk, it's a favorite for runners, joggers, walkers, and in-line skaters. The route goes from the western edge of downtown in a southward direction, passing stately old homes of Hyde Park, a few high-rise condos, retirement communities, and houses of worship, ending at Ballast Point Park. The view from the promenade across the bay to the downtown skyline is unmatched here (Bayshore Boulevard also is great for a drive).

Rent bicycles and in-line skates at **Blades & Bikes,** in a pink-and-blue shop at 201-A W. Platt St., at South Parker Street (☎ 813/251-0780), a block west of the northern end of Bayshore Boulevard. Prices for both bikes and blades range from $8 for 1 hour to $20 for all day. Hours are Monday to Friday from 10am to 7pm, Saturday from 9am to 7pm, and Sunday from 10am to 5pm.

CANOEING   You can paddle downstream along a 20-mile stretch of the Hillsborough River amid 16,000 acres of rural lands in Wilderness Park, the largest regional park in Hillsborough County. **Canoe Escape,** 9335 E. Fowler Ave. (☎ **813/986-2067**), rents canoes for $14 per person. The company also has 2- to 6-hour guided trips. Open Monday to Friday from 9am to 5pm and Saturday and Sunday from 8am to 6pm.

FISHING   Pier fishing on **Hillsborough Bay** is available from **Ballast Point Park,** 5300 Interbay Blvd. (☎ 813/831-9585). Ballast Point Park is at the southern end of Bayshore Boulevard and has a terrific view back across the bay to downtown.

Light Tackle Fishing Expeditions (☎ 813/963-1930) offers sportfishing trips for tarpon, redfish, cobia, trout, and snook. Call for schedule, prices, and required reservations.

GOLF   Tampa has three municipal golf courses where you can play for $26 to $34, a relative pittance when compared to the privately owned courses here and elsewhere in Florida. The **Babe Zaharias Municipal Golf Course,** 11412 Forest Hills Dr., north of Lowry Park (☎ 813/631-4374), is an 18-hole, par-70 course with a pro shop, putting greens, and a driving range. It's the shortest of the municipal courses, but small greens and narrow fairways present ample challenges. Water presents obstacles on 12 of the 18 holes at **Rocky Point Municipal Golf Course,** 4151 Dana Shores Dr. (☎ 813/673-4316), located between the airport and the bay. It's a par-71 course with a pro shop, a practice range, and putting greens. On the Hillsborough River in north Tampa, the **Rogers Park Municipal Golf Course,** 7910 N. 30th St. (☎ **813/673-4396**), is an 18-hole, par-72 championship course with a lighted driving and practice range. They all are open daily from 7am to dusk, and lessons and club rentals are available.

Another inexpensive place to play is the **University of South Florida Golf Course,** Fletcher Avenue and 46th Street (☎ 813/632-6893), just north of the USF campus. This 18-hole, par-71 course is nicknamed "The Claw" because of its challenging layout. It offers lessons and club rentals. Greens fees range from about $19 to $25, or $25 to $35 with a cart, depending on the season and time of day. It's open daily from 7am to dusk.

Other public courses include the **Hall of Fame Golf Club,** just south of the airport at 2222 N. Westshore Blvd. (☎ 813/876-4913), an 18-hole, par-72 affair with a driving range; **Persimmon Hill Golf Club,** 5109 Hamey Rd. (☎ 813/623-6962); **Silver Dollar Trap & Golf Club,** 17000 Patterson Rd., Odessa (☎ 813/920-3884); and **Westchase Golf Club,** 1307 Radcliff Dr. (☎ 813/854-2331).

You can book starting times and get information about these and the area's other courses by calling **Tee Times USA** (☎ 800/374-8633).

If you want to do some serious work on your game, the **Arnold Palmer Golf Academy World Headquarters** is at Saddlebrook Resort, 5700 Saddlebrook Way, Wesley Chapel, 12 miles north of Tampa (☎ 800/729-8383 or 813/973-1111). Half-day and hourly instruction is available, and 2-, 3-, and 5-day programs are available for adults and juniors starting at $248 per night, double occupancy, including accommodations, breakfast, daily instruction, 18 holes of golf daily, cart and greens fees, and nightly club storage and cleaning. You have to stay at the resort or enroll in the golf program to play at Saddlebrook. See "Where to Stay," below, for more information about the resort.

SPECTATOR SPORTS   National Football League fans can catch the improving **Tampa Bay Buccaneers** at the modern, 66,321-seat Raymond James Stadium, 4201 N. Dale Mabry Hwy., at Dr. Martin Luther King Jr. Boulevard (☎ **813/879-2827**). The Bucs's season runs from September through December.

The National Hockey League's **Tampa Bay Lightning** plays in the Ice Palace, beginning in October (☎ **813/229-8800**).

New York Yankees fans can watch the Bronx Bombers during baseball spring training from mid-February through March at Legends Field (☎ **813/879-2244**), opposite Raymond James Stadium. A scaled-down replica of Yankee Stadium, it's the largest spring-training facility in Florida, with a 10,000-seat capacity. Tickets range from $6 to $10. Parking is $6. The club's minor-league team, the **Tampa Yankees** (same phone), plays at Legends Field from April to September. Tickets are $3 for adults, $2 for kids.

The only oval thoroughbred race course on Florida's west coast, ✪ **Tampa Bay Downs,** 11225 Racetrack Rd., Oldsmar (☎ **800/200-4434** in Florida, or 813/855-4401), is the home of the Tampa Bay Derby. Races are held from December to May, and the track presents simulcasts year-round. Call for post times.

TENNIS   Beginners to highly skilled players can sharpen their games at the **Hopman Tennis Program,** at the Saddlebrook Resort, 5700 Saddlebrook Way, Wesley Chapel (☎ **800/729-8383** or 813/973-1111). Packages start at $372 per person for 2 days, double occupancy, including tennis instruction, unlimited playing time, video analysis, agility exercises, fitness center, and accommodations at the Saddlebrook Resort for 5 days and 6 nights. You must be a member or a guest to play here (see "Where to Stay," below).

SHOPPING

Hyde Park and Ybor City are two areas of Tampa worth some window shopping, perhaps sandwiched around lunch at one of their fine restaurants (see "Where to Dine," below).

CIGARS   Ybor City no longer is a major producer of hand-rolled cigars, but you can watch artisans making stogies at the **Gonzales y Martinez Cigar Factory,** 2025 7th Ave., in the Columbia Restaurant building (☎ **813/247-2469**). Gonzales and Martinez are recent arrivals from Cuba and don't speak English, but the staff does at the adjoining **Columbia Cigar Store** (it's best to enter here). Rollers are on duty Monday to Saturday from 10am to 6pm.

A single roller puffs away while he makes them at **Tampa Rico Cigar Co.,** one of the stores in **Ybor Square,** 1901 13th St., at 8th Avenue (☎ **813/247-4497**), a shopping complex listed on the National Register of Historic Places. The three brick buildings date from 1886 and once composed the largest cigar factory in the world. Today it's primarily notable for several small shops selling an amazing variety of collectibles. Shops here are open Monday to Saturday 10am to 6pm, Sunday noon to 5:30pm.

You can stock up on fine domestic and imported cigars at **El Sol,** 1728 E. 7th Ave. (☎ **813/247-5554**), the city's oldest cigar store; **King Corona Cigar Factory,** 1523 E. 7th Ave. (☎ **813/241-9109**); and **Metropolitan Cigars & Wine,** 2014 E. 7th Ave. (☎ **813/248-3304**).

SHOPPING CENTERS   **Old Hyde Park Village,** 1507 W. Swann Ave., at South Dakoka Avenue (☎ **813/251-3500**), is a terrific alternative to cookie-cutter suburban malls. Walk around little shops in the sunshine and check out Hyde Park, one of the city's oldest and most historic neighborhoods at the same time. The cluster of 50 upscale shops and boutiques is set in a village layout. The selection includes Williams-Sonoma,

Pottery Barn, Banana Republic, Brooks Brothers, Crabtree & Evelyn, Godiva Chocolatier, Laura Ashley, Polo Ralph Lauren, and Talbots, to name a few. There's a free
parking garage on South Oregon Avenue behind Jacobson's department store. The
shops are open Monday to Wednesday and Saturday from 10am to 6pm, Thursday
and Friday from 10am to 9pm, and Sunday from noon to 5pm.

The main mall in the city is **West Shore Plaza,** on Kennedy Boulevard where it
turns into Memorial Highway (Fla. 60). **University Mall** is nearest Busch Gardens,
on Fowler Avenue just east of I-275. The area's largest complex is **Brandon Town-
Center,** at I-4 and Fla. 60 in the eastern suburb of Brandon, where most stores have
unusually large amounts of floor space and, hence, more merchandise from which to
choose.

WHERE TO STAY

I've organized the accommodations listings below into two geographic areas: near
Busch Gardens and downtown. If you're going to Busch Gardens, Adventure Island,
Lowry Park Zoo, and the Museum of Science and Industry (MOSI), the motels near
Busch Gardens are much more convenient than those downtown, about 7 miles to the
south. The downtown hotels are geared to business travelers, but staying there will put
you near the Florida Aquarium, the Museum of African-American Art, the Tampa
Museum of Art, the Henry B. Plant Museum, the Tampa Bay Performing Arts Center,
scenic Bayshore Boulevard, the dining and shopping opportunities in the Hyde Park
historic district, and Ybor City's restaurants and nightlife.

The Westshore area, near the bay west of downtown and south of Tampa Interna-
tional Airport, is another commercial center, with a wide range of national chain
hotels catering to business travelers and conventioneers. It's convenient to Raymond
James Stadium and the New York Yankees's spring training complex. Here you'll find
the Spanish-style **Doubletree Guest Suites,** 4400 W. Cypress St., at Manhattan
Avenue (☎ **800/222-TREE** or 813/873-8675); **Courtyard by Marriott,** 3805 W.
Cypress St., at Dale Mabrey Highway (☎ **800/321-2211** or 813/874-0555); the
Hyatt Regency Westshore, 6200 Courtney Campbell Causeway (☎ **800/233-1234**
or 813/874-1234), nestled on a 35-acre bayside nature preserve; the **Sheraton Grand
Hotel,** 4860 W. Kennedy Blvd., at Shore Boulevard (☎ **800/325-3535** or 813/
286-4400), across the street from West Shore Plaza mall and home to one of former
Miami Dolphins Coach Don Shula's steak houses; and the **Tampa Marriott West-
shore,** 1001 N. Westshore Blvd. (☎ **800/228-9290** or 813/287-2555).

The high season in Tampa generally runs from January to April, but you won't find
as large an increase here as at the beach resorts. Most hotels offer discounted package
rates in the summer and weekend specials all year, dropping their rates by as much as
50%. Hotels often combine tickets to major attractions like Busch Gardens in their
packages, so always ask about special deals.

Hillsborough River State Park, 15402 U.S. 301 North, Thonotosassa, FL 33592
(☎ **813/986-1020**), offers 118 campsites year-round, plus fishing, canoeing, and
boating.

Hillsborough County adds 12% tax to your hotel room bill.

NEAR BUSCH GARDENS

The plushest and most expensive establishment near the park is the 500-room
Embassy Suites Hotel and Conference Center, 3705 Spectrum Blvd., actually facing
Fowler Avenue (☎ **800/EMBASSY** or 813/977-7066; fax 977-7933). Almost across
the avenue stands **LaQuinta Inn & Suites,** 3701 E. Fowler Ave. (☎ **800/
NU-ROOMS** or 813/910-7500; fax 813/910-7600). There also are new, modern

editions of **AmeriSuites,** 11408 N. 30th St. (☎ **800/833-1516** or 813/979-1922; fax 813/979-1926), and **DoubleTree Guest Suites,** 11310 N. 30th St. (☎ **800/ 222-TREE** or 813/971-7690; fax 813/972-5525). They stand side-by-side just south of Fowler Avenue.

The inexpensive **Red Roof Inn,** 2307 E. Busch Blvd., between 22nd and 26th streets (☎ **800/THE-ROOF** or 813/932-0073), is a pleasant property on landscaped grounds. **Days Inn Maingate,** 2901 E. Busch Blvd., at 30th Street (☎ **800/ DAYS-INN** or 813/933-6471), is less appealing than the Baymont Inn & Suites across the street (see below), but it's convenient for families on a budget since you can walk to Busch Gardens from here. Both motels have outdoor pools.

Baymont Inn & Suites. 9202 N. 30th St. (at Busch Blvd.), Tampa, FL 33612. ☎ **800/ 428-3438** or 813/930-6900. Fax 813/930-0563. 146 units. A/C TV TEL. Winter $80 double. Off-season $57 double. Rates include continental breakfast. AE, DC, DISC, MC, V.

Fake banana trees and a parrot cage welcome guests to the terra-cotta–floored lobby of this comfortable and convenient member of the former Budgetel Inn chain of cost-conscious but amenity-rich motels. All rooms are spacious and have ceiling fans, bright wood furniture with tropical trim, desks, phones with long cords, and coffeemakers. Rooms with king beds also have recliners. Outside, a courtyard with an unheated swimming pool has plenty of space for sunning. There are a game room and coin laundry, and local telephone calls are free. There's no restaurant on the premises, but plenty are nearby.

Best Western Resort Tampa at Busch Gardens. 820 E. Busch Blvd. (at I-275), Tampa, FL 33612. ☎ **800/288-4011** or 813/933-4011. Fax 813/932-1784. 255 units. A/C TV TEL. Winter $119 double. Off-season $70–$90 double. AE, DC, DISC, MC, V.

Right at the Busch Boulevard exit off I-275, this motel is fine for families on a budget. An enclosed skylit atrium-style courtyard with fountains, streetlights, benches, and pool is a fine place for the kids when it's too hot or too cool to enjoy the outdoors. Guest rooms in the main wing open to walkways facing the indoor atrium or the parking lots. Newer units are in a four-story annex. They all have standard furnishings and coffeemakers.

The Palm Grill Restaurant off the lobby features a variety of dishes, while the Bull Pen Sports Bar offers pub fare and libation. Services include a concierge desk, secretarial services, valet laundry, limited room service, and courtesy transport to Busch Gardens. There are indoor and outdoor heated swimming pools, two whirlpools, a sauna, four lighted tennis courts, exercise and game rooms, a coin-operated laundry, and a gift shop.

✪ **Quality Suites Hotel—USF Near Busch Gardens.** 3001 University Center Dr., Tampa, FL 33612. ☎ **800/786-7446** or 813/971-8930. Fax 813/971-8935. 150 units. A/C TV TEL. Winter $99–$159 suite for 2. Off-season $89–$139 suite for 2. Rates include full breakfast buffet and evening beer-and-wine reception. AE, DC, DISC, MC, V.

Actually on North 30th Street between Busch Boulevard and Flower Avenue, this hacienda-style all-suite hotel sits about a mile from the Busch Gardens entrance. The three-story building encloses a lush tropical courtyard with heated pool, hot tub, covered games area, sun deck (with dataports in the surrounding railing), and lively tiki bar known as Ruzic's Roost (in honor of hands-on owner John Ruzic), making this the most beachlike vacation venue you'll find close to the park. The bar can get noisy before closing at 9pm, and bare-footed, wet-bathing-suited guests can leave some of the ground-level units musty; so ask for an upstairs suite away from the action. The suites' living rooms have sofa beds, La-Z-Boy recliners, dining tables, wet bars, coffeemakers,

Tampa Accommodations & Dining

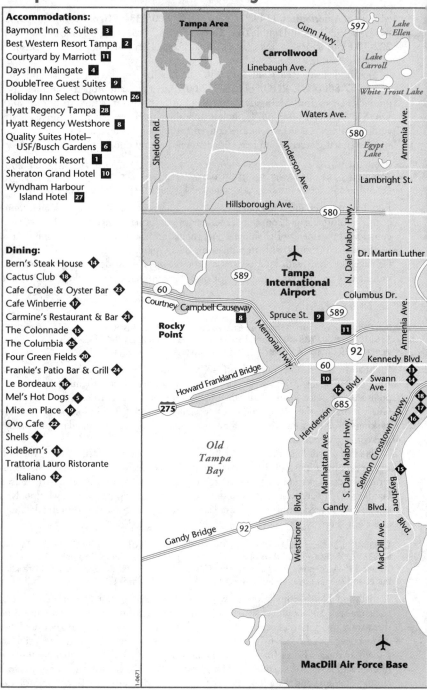

Accommodations:

Baymont Inn & Suites **3**
Best Western Resort Tampa **2**
Courtyard by Marriott **11**
Days Inn Maingate **4**
DoubleTree Guest Suites **9**
Holiday Inn Select Downtown **26**
Hyatt Regency Tampa **28**
Hyatt Regency Westshore **8**
Quality Suites Hotel–
    USF/Busch Gardens **6**
Saddlebrook Resort **1**
Sheraton Grand Hotel **10**
Wyndham Harbour
    Island Hotel **27**

Dining:

Bern's Steak House **14**
Cactus Club **18**
Cafe Creole & Oyster Bar **23**
Cafe Winberrie **17**
Carmine's Restaurant & Bar **21**
The Colonnade **15**
The Columbia **25**
Four Green Fields **20**
Frankie's Patio Bar & Grill **24**
Le Bordeaux **16**
Mel's Hot Dogs **5**
Mise en Place **19**
Ovo Cafe **22**
Shells **7**
SideBern's **13**
Trattoria Lauro Ristorante
    Italiano **12**

Tampa Area

Gunn Hwy.

597

Lake Ellen

Carrollwood

Linebaugh Ave.

Lake Carroll

White Trout Lake

Sheldon Rd.

Waters Ave.

Armenia Ave.

580

Egypt Lake

Anderson Ave.

Lambright St.

Hillsborough Ave.

580

N. Dale Mabry Hwy.

Dr. Martin Luther

589

Tampa International Airport

60

Courtney Campbell Causeway

Columbus Dr.

Spruce St. **9**

589

8

Rocky Point

Memorial Hwy.

11

92

60

Kennedy Blvd.

13

Howard Frankland Bridge

10

12

Blvd.

Swann Ave.

14

275

685

Selmon Crosstown Expwy.

18

17

16

Old Tampa Bay

Henderson

Manhattan Ave.

S. Dale Mabry Hwy.

Bayshore Blvd.

15

Blvd.

Gandy Blvd.

MacDill Ave.

Gandy Bridge

92

Westshore

1-0671

MacDill Air Force Base

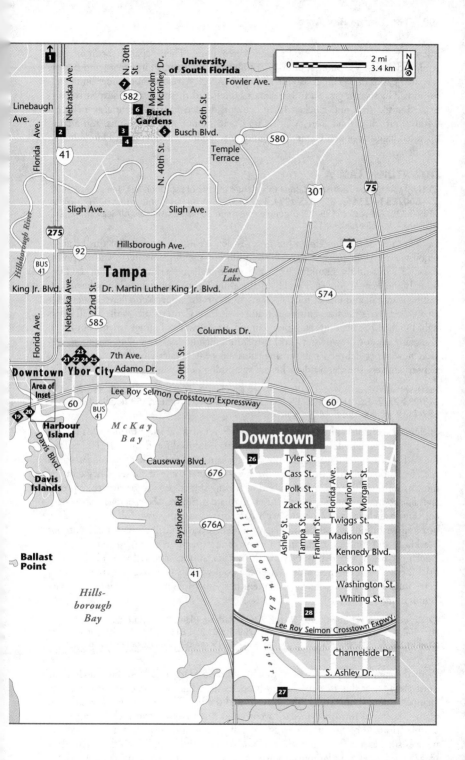

microwaves, phones, TVs, VCRs, and stereo units. Their separate bedrooms are equipped with TVs, phones, built-in armoire and mirrored vanity areas, and narrow screened patios or balconies. About 10 "family suites" have over-and-under bunk beds for kids. Guests can graze a full breakfast buffet, and the bar serves inexpensive barbecued steak, fish, and chicken for lunch and dinner. Facilities here also include a 24-hour gift shop/food store, VCR rentals, a whirlpool, meeting rooms, and a coin-operated laundry. Sports teams visiting the nearby University of South Florida like to stay here.

Downtown Tampa

✪ **Hyatt Regency Tampa.** 2 Tampa City Center (corner of E. Jackson St.), Tampa, FL 33602. ☎ **800/233-1234** or 813/225-1234. Fax 813/273-0234. 519 units. A/C TV TEL. Winter $129–$200. Off-season $99–$200 double. Weekend packages available off-season. AE, DC, DISC, MC, V. Valet parking $7.

In the center of the downtown business district, it's not surprising that this Hyatt—renovated in 1998 to the tune of $10 million—caters primarily to the corporate crowd. It's just off the Franklin Street pedestrian mall and a short walk from the Harbour Island People Mover. The Hyatt signature eight-story atrium lobby has a cascading waterfall and lots of foliage. Many units on the upper floors have bay or river views. Creative American cuisine is featured at City Center Cafe, while a deli offers light lunches. For libations with piano music, try Saltwaters Lounge (there's not much else going on downtown after dark). Amenities include concierge, 24-hour room service, newspaper delivery, baby-sitting, business center, valet laundry, guest laundry, airport courtesy shuttle, outdoor heated swimming pool, whirlpool, and health club.

Radisson Riverwalk Hotel. 200 N. Ashley Dr., Tampa, FL 33602. ☎ **800/333-3333** or 813/233-2222. Fax 813/221-5929. 284 units. A/C TV TEL. Winter $159 double. Off-season $99–$119. AE, DC, DISC, MC, V. Valet parking $5.

Sitting on the east bank of the Hillsborough River, this six-story former Quality Inn was completely remodeled and reborn as a better-equipped Radisson in 1998. Half the rooms face west and have views from their balconies of the Arabesque minarets atop the Henry B. Plant Museum across the river—quite a scene at sunset. They cost the same as units on the east, which face downtown's skyscrapers, so be sure to request a riverside room. Sporting quality Drexel Heritage furniture, the spacious rooms have coffeemakers, hair dryers, phones with dataports, and either two full beds or a king bed and writing desk. Beside the river, the Ashley Street Grill serves indoor-outdoor breakfasts and lunches, then turns to fine dinner in the evenings. Open 24 hours, Boulanger baker and deli purveys fresh pastries, soups, sandwiches, and snacks. A brick deck surrounds the outdoor riverside pool with its own bar. The Tampa Town Ferry stops at the dock, where you can rent Jets. Amenities include concierge and valet laundry service.

✪ **Wyndham Harbour Island Hotel.** 725 S. Harbour Island Blvd., Harbour Island, Tampa, FL 33602. ☎ **800/WYNDHAM** or 813/229-5000. Fax 813/229-5322. 299 units. Valet parking $6. A/C MINIBAR TV TEL. Winter $139–$219 double. Off-season $99–$169 double. AE, DC, DISC, MC, V.

With the shops closed, there's not much action on Harbour Island, but you'll enjoy quiet elegance at this 12-story luxury property. It has great views of the surrounding channels that link the Hillsborough River and the bay. The bedrooms, all with views of the water, are furnished in dark woods and floral fabrics, and each has a well-lit marble-trimmed bathroom, an executive desk, and a work area, plus in-room conveniences such as a coffeemaker, an iron, and an ironing board. Watch the yachts drift by as you dine at the Harbourview Room, or enjoy your favorite drink in the Bar, a clubby room with equally good views. Snacks and drinks are available during the day at the Pool Bar. Amenities here include concierge, limited room service, secretarial services, notary public, evening turndown, valet laundry, courtesy airport shuttle, outdoor heated swimming pool and deck, newsstand/gift shop, guest privileges at nearby health club.

A NEARBY RESORT

✪ **Saddlebrook Resort.** 5700 Saddlebrook Way, Wesley Chapel, FL 33543. ☎ **800/729-8383** or 813/973-1111. Fax 813/973-4504. 800 units. A/C TV TEL. Winter $165–$242 per person. Off-season $107–$147 per person. Rates include breakfast and dinner. AE, DC, DISC, MC, V. Valet parking $3; free self-parking. Take I-75 north to Fla. 54 (Exit 58), go 1 mile east to resort.

Set on 480 acres of natural countryside, this internationally renowned golf and tennis resort is off the beaten path (30 min. north of Tampa International Airport) but worth the trip. Join pros such as Pete Sampras at the Hopman Tennis Program, or perfect your swing at the Arnold Palmer Golf Academy (see "Outdoor Activities & Spectator Sports," above).

Dining/Diversions: The casual but elegant Cypress Restaurant consistently wins accolades. It's famous for grand holiday buffets and popular Friday-night seafood buffets. Enjoy indoor or outdoor dining at Terrace on the Green, overlooking the Cypress Lagoon and the 18th green. The Little Club offers an American menu and the popular TD's sports bar/tavern. The Poolside Cafe is great for dining in your bathing suit alfresco.

Amenities: Concierge, limited room service, newspaper delivery, in-room massage, baby-sitting, children's activities program, airport courtesy shuttle. Two 18-hole championship golf courses, 45 tennis courts, 270-foot-long half-million–gallon superpool, whirlpool, 7,000-square-foot luxury spa, fitness center, basketball and volleyball courts, softball field.

WHERE TO DINE

As with the hotels, I have organized the restaurants below by geographic area: near Busch Gardens, in or near Hyde Park (just across the Hillsborough River from downtown), and in Ybor City (on the northeastern edge of downtown).

NEAR BUSCH GARDENS

You'll find the national fast-food and family restaurants east of I-275 on Busch Boulevard and along Fowler Avenue near University Mall.

✪ **Mel's Hot Dogs.** 4136 E. Busch Blvd., at 42nd St. ☎ **813/985-8000.** Main courses $3–$6.50. No credit cards. Daily 11am–9pm. AMERICAN.

Catering to everyone from businesspeople on a lunch break to hungry families craving inexpensive all-beef hot dogs, this red-and-white cottage offers everything from "bagel-dogs" and corn dogs to a bacon/cheddar Reuben. All choices are served on a poppy-seed bun, and most come with french fries and a choice of coleslaw or baked beans. Even the decor is dedicated to wieners: The walls and windows are lined with hot-dog memorabilia. And just in case hot-dog mania hasn't won you over, there are a few alternative choices (sausages, chicken breast, and beef and veggie burgers).

Shells. 11010 N. 30th St. (between Busch Blvd. and Fowler Ave.). ☎ **813/977-8456.** Reservations not accepted. Main courses $6–$17. AE, DISC, MC, V. Mon–Thurs 11:30am–10pm, Fri–Sat 11:30am–11pm, Sun noon–10pm. SEAFOOD.

You'll see Shells restaurants in many parts of Florida, and with good reason, for this casual, award-winning chain consistently provides excellent value, especially if you have a family to feed. They all have the same menu and prices and are particularly known for their spicy Jack Daniel's buffalo shrimp and scallop appetizers. Main courses range from the usual fried seafood platters to pastas and charcoal-grilled shrimp, fish, steaks, and chicken. I counted 21 tender, bite-size shrimp in a light, garlic-tinged cream sauce served over linguine—a bargain for $9.50. Another 30 of them were perfectly charcoal-grilled on a skewer and served with saffron rice and steamed vegetables for $11. There's also a children's menu.

HYDE PARK
Expensive
Bern's Steak House. 1208 S. Howard Ave. (at Marjory Ave.). ☎ **813/251-2421.** Reservations required. Main courses $19–$35. AE, DC, DISC, MC, V. Daily 5–11pm. Closed Christmas. AMERICAN.

The exterior of this famous steak house looks like a factory built almost under the Lee Roy Selmon Crosstown Expressway. Inside, however, you'll find eight ornate dining rooms with themes like Rhône, Burgundy, and Irish Rebellion. They set an appropriately dark atmosphere for meat lovers, for here you order and pay for charcoal-grilled steaks (beef or buffalo) according to the thickness and weight. They come with onion soup, salad, baked potato, garlic toast, onion rings, and vegetables grown in Bern's own organic garden. The phone book–size wine list offers more than 7,000 selections.

The big surprise here is the dessert quarters upstairs, where 50 romantic booths paneled in aged California redwood can privately seat from 2 to 12 guests. Each of these little chambers is equipped with a phone for placing your order and a closed-circuit TV for watching and listening to a resident pianist. The dessert menu offers almost 100 delicious selections, plus some 1,400 after-dinner drinks. It's possible to reserve a booth for dessert only, but preference is given to those who dine. You can get some of the same sweet things nearby at SideBern's (see below).

Le Bordeaux. 1502 S. Howard Ave. (2 blocks north of Bayshore Blvd.). ☎ **813/254-4387.** Reservations recommended. Main courses $15–$28. AE, DC, MC, V. Mon–Thurs 5:30–10pm, Fri–Sat 5:30–11pm, Sun 5:30–9:30pm. CLASSICAL FRENCH.

This bistro's authentic French fare is some of the region's best, but keep a rein on your credit card—everything's sold à la carte, so you can ring up a hefty bill quickly. French-born chef/owner Gordon Davis offers seating in a living room–style main dining room of this converted house expanded to include a plant-filled conservatory. His classical French menu changes daily, but you can count on homemade pâtés and pastries, and occasional specials like *filet de snook a la pistache* (local snook encrusted with pistachio nuts). Part of the establishment is the lounge-style Left Bank Jazz Bistro, with live entertainment Thursday to Saturday from 9pm.

Moderate
Cafe Winberie. In Hyde Park shopping complex, 1610 Swann Ave. (at S. Dakota St.). ☎ **813/253-6500.** Reservations not accepted. Burgers and sandwiches $6.50–$7.50; main courses $6.50–$15. AE, DC, DISC, MC, V. Sun–Thurs 11am–11pm, Fri–Sat 11am–midnight. INTERNATIONAL.

With both indoor and sidewalk seating, this Parisian-style bistro at Hyde Park's main intersection makes a fine retreat on your shopping excursion for a cold latte, a snack, or a full meal. Inside, cafe curtains, dark paneling, posters, and an antique wine rack behind the bar create a chic ambience. Start with brushetta or cheese filled portobello mushrooms; then, proceed to consistently fine salmon roasted in parchment with fresh vegetables, or chicken breast sautéed in Masala wine. Several pastas include shrimp and linguini tossed with basil, garlic, and tomatoes. The least expensive main course is a fiery bowl of vegetarian chili. Godiva chocolate mousse is one of several delicious desserts.

✪ **Mise en Place.** In Grand Central Place, 442 W. Kennedy Blvd. (at S. Magnolia Ave., opposite the University of Tampa). ☎ **813/254-5373.** Reservations accepted only for parties of 6 or more. Main courses $13–$21. AE, DC, DISC, MC, V. Mon–Fri 11am–3pm, Tues–Thurs 5:30–10pm, Fri–Sat 5:30–11pm. INTERNATIONAL.

Look around at all those happy, stylish people soaking up the trendy ambience, and you'll know why chef Marty Blitz and his wife, Marianne, are the culinary darlings of Tampa. They continue to present the freshest of ingredients, with a creative international menu that changes daily. Main courses often include such choices as roast duck with Jamaica wild-strawberry sauce, grilled swordfish with three-melon mint salsa, or Ethiopian lentil stew served with steamed *injera* bread. There's valet parking at the rear of the building on Grand Central Place.

After dinner you can wander next door into **442,** an upscale bar with live jazz and blues.

✪ **Trattoria Lauro Ristorante Italiano.** 3915 Henderson Blvd. (2 blocks west of Dale Mabry Hwy., between Watrous and Neptune aves.). ☎ **813/281-2100.** Reservations recommended. Main courses $9.50–$19. AE, DC, DISC, MC, V. Mon–Fri 11:30am–2pm and 5:30–10pm, Sat 5:30–11pm, Sun 5:30–10pm. ITALIAN.

Known for extraordinary sauces and pastas, chef/owner Lauro Medeglia is a native Italian who cooks his home fare with love. Though his restaurant is off the beaten track, it's worth the detour. Classical decor and soft music have made it one of Tampa's favorite places to "pop the question," and smartly attired waiters render efficient yet friendly and unobtrusive service. Try the caprese, putanesca, gnocchi, or agnolotti.

Inexpensive

Cactus Club. In Old Hyde Park shopping complex, 1601 Snow Ave. (south of Swan St.). ☎ **813/251-4089.** Reservations not accepted. Burgers and sandwiches $6.50–$7.50; main courses $6.50–$14. AE, DC, MC, V. Mon–Thurs 11am–11pm, Fri–Sat 11am–midnight, Sun 11am–10:30pm. AMERICAN SOUTHWEST.

Watch all the shoppers go by at Old Hyde Park from this fun and casual cafe with a Southwestern accent. Dine inside or outside on tacos, enchiladas, chili, sizzling fajitas, hickory-smoked baby back ribs, Jamaican jerk chicken, burgers, fajitas, quesadillas, enchiladas (including vegetarian versions), sandwiches, smoked chicken salad, and more. It's always packed at lunchtime—get here early.

The Colonnade. 3401 Bayshore Blvd. (at W. Julia St.). ☎ **813/839-7558.** Reservations accepted only for large parties. Main courses $8–$20. AE, DC, DISC, MC, V. Sun–Thurs 11am–10pm, Fri–Sat 11am–11pm. AMERICAN/SEAFOOD.

Locals have been flocking to this rough-hewn, shiplap place since 1935, primarily for the great view of Hillsborough Bay across Bayshore Boulevard. The food is a bit on the Red Lobsterish side, but get here early or wait for a window table; the vista is worth it. Fresh seafood is the specialty: grouper prepared seven ways, crab-stuffed flounder, Maryland-style crab cakes, even wild Florida alligator as an appetizer. Prime rib, steaks, and chicken are also available.

Four Green Fields. 205 W. Platt St. (between Parker St. and Plant Ave.). ☎ **813/254-4444.** Reservations accepted. Sandwiches $6; main courses $8.50–$14. AE, MC, V. Mon–Sat 11am–2am, Sun 1pm–2am. IRISH/AMERICAN.

Just across the bridge from the downtown convention center, America's only thatched-roof Irish pub may be surrounded by palm trees instead of potato fields, but it still offers the ambience and tastes of Ireland. Staffed by genuine Irish immigrants, the large room with a square bar in the center smells of Irish ale. The Gaelic stew is predictably bland, but the salads and sandwiches are passable. The crowd usually is young, especially for live Irish music on Thursday, Friday, and Saturday nights.

SideBern's. 2208 W. Morrison Ave. (at S. Howard St.) ☎ **813/258-2233.** Reservations not accepted. Sandwiches and salads $4–$7.50; desserts $4–$5.50. AE, DC, DISC, MC, V. Sun and Tues–Thurs 6–11pm, Fri–Sat 6pm–1am. SANDWICHES/SALADS/DESSERTS.

The owners of Bern's Steakhouse (see above) opened this informal outlet to accommodate everyone who wanted to partake of their gourmet goodies but couldn't fit into the dessert rooms at the main restaurant. Their most popular desserts are offered at this sophisticated bistro, whose cathedral ceiling covers an open kitchen (wonderful aromas) and cherry-wood tables and chairs. Banana cheesecake is a consistent winner, as is the chocolate pâté served with Curaçao, raspberry, or rum sauce. Sandwiches are served on a choice of regular wheat, focaccia, or roasted-garlic potato bread. One of the best offerings is a tender, perfectly charcoal-grilled tenderloin steak accompanied by baked-potato salad, lettuce, tomato, a huge slice of onion, and shaved cucumber salad—a meal in itself. Top-notch coffees are roasted on the premises.

YBOR CITY
Moderate

✪ **Cafe Creole and Oyster Bar.** 1330 9th Ave. (at Avenida de Republica de Cuba/14th St.). ☎ **813/247-6283.** Reservations not accepted but call for preferred seating. Main courses $9–$18. AE, DC, DISC, MC, V. Mon–Thurs 11:30am–10pm, Fri 11:30am–11:30pm, Sat 5–11:30pm. CREOLE/CAJUN.

Resembling a turn-of-the-century railway station, this brick building dates from 1896 and was originally known as El Pasaje, the home of the Cherokee Club, a gentlemen's hotel and private club with a casino and a decor rich in stained-glass windows, wrought-iron balconies, Spanish murals, and marble bathrooms. Specialties include exceptionally prepared Louisiana crab cakes, oysters, blackened grouper, and jambalaya. If you're new to cuisine of the bayou, try the Creole sampler. Dine inside or out.

✪ **Columbia.** 2117 E. 7th Ave. (between 21st and 22nd sts). ☎ **813/248-4961.** Reservations recommended. Main courses $12–$23. AE, DC, DISC, MC, V. Mon–Thurs 11am–10pm, Fri–Sat 11am–11pm, Sun noon–9pm. SPANISH.

Dating from 1905, this hand-painted tile building occupies an entire city block in the heart of Ybor City. Tourists flock here to soak up the ambience and so do the locals, because it's so much fun to clap along during fire-belching floor shows in the main dining room. You can't help coming back time after time for the famous Spanish bean soup and original "1905" salad. The *paella à la valenciana* is outstanding, with more than a dozen ingredients from gulf grouper and gulf pink shrimp to calamari, mussels, clams, chicken, and pork. The decor throughout is graced with hand-painted tiles, wrought-iron chandeliers, dark woods, rich red fabrics, and stained-glass windows. You can breathe your own fumes in the Cigar Bar.

✪ **Frankie's Patio Bar & Grill.** 1905 E. 7th Ave. (between 19th and 20th sts.). ☎ **813/249-3337.** Reservations accepted only for large parties. Main courses $10–$15; sandwiches $5–$9. AE, DISC, MC, V. Mon–Tues 11am–3pm, Wed 11am–midnight, Thurs–Fri 11am–3am, Sat 5pm–3am. INTERNATIONAL.

This Ybor City attraction is known mostly as a venue for outstanding musical acts—live jazz, blues, reggae, and rock Wednesday to Saturday. With exposed industrial pipes, the large three-story restaurant stands out from the usual Spanish-themed, 19th-century architecture of Ybor City. There's seating indoors, on a large outdoor patio, or on an open-air balcony overlooking the action on the street. It's a fun atmosphere, and the food blends Cuban, American, Creole, and Italian influences. Build-your-own sandwiches are available during all hours.

Inexpensive

Carmine's Restaurant & Bar. 1802 E. 7th Ave. East (at 18th St). ☎ **813/248-3834.** Reservations not accepted. Sandwiches $4–$7; main courses $5–$15 (most $6–$9). No credit cards. Mon–Tues 11am–10pm, Wed–Thurs 11am–midnight, Fri–Sat 11am–3am, Sun 11am–6pm. CUBAN/ITALIAN/AMERICAN.

Bright blue poles hold up an ancient pressed-tin ceiling above this noisy corner cafe, one of Ybor's most popular hangouts. A great variety of loyal local patrons gather here for genuine Cuban sandwiches—smoked ham, roast pork, Genoa salami, Swiss cheese, pickles, salad dressing, mustard, lettuce, and tomato on a crispy submarine roll. There's a vegetarian version, too, and the combination half sandwich and bowl of Spanish soup made with sausages, potatoes, and garbanzo beans makes a hearty meal for just $4. Main courses are led by Cuban-style roast pork, thin-cut pork chops with mushroom sauce, spaghetti with a blue crab tomato sauce, and a few seafood and chicken platters.

✪ **Ovo Cafe.** 1901 E. 7th Ave. (at 19th St.). ☎ **813/248-6979.** Reservations not accepted. Main courses $6.50–$13.50. AE, DC, DISC, MC, V. Mon–Tues 11am–3pm, Wed–Thurs 11am–10am, Fri–Sat 11am–1am, Sun 11am–9pm. INTERNATIONAL.

This cafe, popular with the business set by day and the club crowd on weekend nights, is Tampa's answer to SoHo. The menu features a melange of sophisticated offerings. Pierogies and pasta pillows come with taste-temping sauces and fillings. The likes of tangy jerk sauce over chicken, bananas, mozzarella cheese, and roasted sweet peppers top the individual-size pizzas. Strawberries or blackberries and a splash of liqueur cover the thick waffles. And there are several creative salads. Portions are substantial, but be careful with your credit card here: Pricing is strictly à la carte. The big black bar dispenses a wide variety of Martinis, plus some unusual liqueur drinks.

TAMPA AFTER DARK

The Tampa/Hillsborough Arts Council maintains an **Artsline** (☎ 813/229-ARTS), a 24-hour information service providing the latest on current and upcoming cultural events. Racks in many restaurants and bars have copies of *Weekly Planet, Focus,* and *Accent on Tampa Bay,* three free publications detailing what's going on in the entire bay area. And you can check the "Baylife" and "Friday Extra" sections of the *Tampa Tribune* and the Friday "Weekend" section of the *St. Petersburg Times.* The visitor center usually has copies of the week's newspaper sections (see "Essentials," above). And be on the lookout for the slick bimonthly magazine *Event Guide Tampa Bay,* which gives a rundown on what's going on.

THE CLUB & MUSIC SCENE   Ybor City is Tampa's favorite nighttime venue by far. All you have to do is stroll along 7th Avenue East between 15th and 20th streets, and you'll hear music blaring out of the clubs. The avenue is packed with people, a majority of them high schoolers and early twenty-somethings, on Friday and Saturday from 9pm to 3am, but you'll also find something going on from Tuesday to Thursday and even on Sunday. You don't need addresses or phone numbers; your ears will guide you along 7th Avenue East.

Starting at 15th Street and heading east, you'll come first to **The Masquerade,** with retro and old-wave bands on Friday to Sunday. The body-pierced 20-something crowd gets primed at **Club Hedo, Atomic Age Cafe & Lounge,** and **Cherry's** before dancing at **The Rubb** across the avenue.

At 16th Street you should come to **Centro Ybor,** a dining, shopping, and entertainment complex which was under construction at press time.

Between 17th and 18th streets, you'll smell the cigar smoke coming from the sidewalk tables of the **Green Iguana Bar & Grill,** a refined establishment frequented by young professionals. The **Irish Pub** is just that, while **Fat Tuesday** has a large dance floor and long bar. Between 18th and 19th streets, you'll see **Harpo's,** which doesn't extract a cover charge. Keep going across 19th Street to one of Ybor's best clubs, **Blues Ship Café on Top,** which features live blues, jazz, and reggae. And last but not least is the warehouse-like **Frankie's Patio Bar & Grill,** known for its reasonably priced food as well as its outstanding musical acts (see "Where to Dine," above). Across the avenue, country meets city at **Spurs in Ybor,** a country-and-western joint.

Although not in the heart of Ybor's bar scene, the ✪**Jazz Cellar,** on 9th Avenue East between 13th Street and Avenida de Republica de Cuba (14th Street), features contemporary jazz, rhythm and blues, and just plain blues from 8pm to 2am Friday and Saturday. This basement establishment is on the north side of Ybor Square. Call ☎ **813/248-1862** for reservations.

Parking can be scarce during nighttime here. Play it safe and use the municipal lots behind the shops on Seventh Avenue.

Elsewhere in town, you can lose your life savings playing bingo, poker, and the video slot machines at the **Seminole Indian Casino,** 5223 N. Orient Rd., at Hillsborough Road east of the city (☎ **800/282-7016** or 813/621-1302). It's open 24 hours every day of the year.

THE PERFORMING ARTS   With a prime downtown location on 9 acres along the east bank of the Hillsborough River, the huge ✪**Tampa Bay Performing Arts Center,** 1010 N. MacInnes Place (☎ **800/955-1045** or 813/229-STAR), is the largest performing-arts venue south of the Kennedy Center in Washington, D.C. Accordingly, this four-theater complex is the focal point of Tampa's performing-arts scene, presenting a wide range of Broadway plays, classical and pop concerts, operas, cabarets, improv, and special events.

A sightseeing attraction in its own right, the restored ✪**Tampa Theatre,** 711 Franklin St. (☎ **813/223-8981**), dates from 1926 and is on the National Register of Historic Places. It presents a varied program of classic, foreign, and alternative films, as well as concerts and special events.

The 66,321-seat **Raymond James Stadium,** 4201 N. Dale Mabry Hwy. (☎ **813/673-4300**), is frequently the site of headliner concerts. The **USF Sun Dome,** 4202 E. Fowler Ave. (☎ **813/974-3111**), on the University of South Florida campus, hosts major concerts by touring pop stars, rock bands, jazz groups, and other contemporary artists.

2 St. Petersburg

20 miles SW of Tampa, 289 miles NW of Miami, 84 miles SW of Orlando

On the western shore of the bay, St. Petersburg stands in contrast to Tampa, much like San Francisco compares to Oakland in California. While Tampa is the area's business, industrial, and shipping center, St. Petersburg was conceived and built almost a century ago primarily for tourists and wintering snowbirds. Here you'll find one of the most picturesque and pleasant downtowns of any city in Florida, with a waterfront promenade and the famous pyramid-shaped Pier offering great views across the bay, plus quality museums, interesting shops, and fine restaurants.

Away from downtown, the city pretty much consists of strip malls dividing residential neighborhoods, but plan at least to have a look around the charming bayfront area. If you don't do anything else, go out on The Pier and take a pleasant stroll along Bayshore Drive.

All is not completely happy in this urban paradise, however, for St. Petersburg was rocked by riots after a white police officer shot and killed a black motorist in late 1996. Although all was calm at press time, you should avoid the area south of I-175 and east of I-275.

ESSENTIALS

GETTING THERE   **Tampa International Airport,** approximately 16 miles northeast of St. Petersburg, is the prime gateway for the area (see "Essentials" in section 1, above). **St. Petersburg–Clearwater International Airport,** on Roosevelt Boulevard (Fla. 686) about 10 miles north of downtown St. Petersburg (☎ 727/535-7600), primarily handles charter flights—the Canadian carriers **Air Transat** (☎ 800/470-1011) and **Canada 3000** (☎ 800/993-4378) fly here during the winter season—although limited regular service is provided by two commuter carriers, **American Trans Air** (☎ 800/225-2995) and **SunJet** (☎ 800/478-6538). Incidentally, the world's first scheduled carrier, the St. Petersburg–Tampa Airboat Line, took off from there in 1914.

Alamo (☎ 800/327-9633), **Avis** (☎ 800/331-1212), **Budget** (☎ 800/527-0700), **Dollar** (☎ 800/800-4000), **Enterprise** (☎ 800/325-8007), **Hertz** (☎ 800/654-3131), and **National** (☎ 800/CAR-RENT) have rental-car operations here.

Yellow Shuttle (☎ 727/525-3333) offers 24-hour van service between the airport and any St. Petersburg–area destination or hotel. The flat-rate, one-way fare is $14 to any St. Pete or gulf beach destination. **Yellow Cab Taxis** (☎ 727/799-2222) line up outside baggage-claim areas. Average taxi fare from the airport to St. Petersburg or any of the gulf beaches is about $25 to $35.

Amtrak (☎ 800/USA-RAIL for reservations) has rail service to Tampa (see "Getting There," in section 1).

VISITOR INFORMATION   For advance information about both St. Petersburg and the beaches, contact the **St. Petersburg/Clearwater Area Convention & Visitors Bureau,** 14450 46th St. N., Clearwater, FL 34622 (☎ 800/345-6710, or 727/464-7200 for advance hotel reservations; fax 727/464-7222; www.stpete-clearwater.com). The office is south of Roosevelt Boulevard (Fla. 686) opposite St. Petersburg–Clearwater International Airport.

A wealth of information is also available from the **St. Petersburg Area Chamber of Commerce,** 100 2nd Ave. N. (at 1st Street), St. Petersburg, FL 33701 (☎ 727/821-4069; fax 727/895-6326; www.stpete.com). This downtown main office and visitor center is open Monday to Friday from 8am to 5pm, Saturday 9am to 4pm, Sunday noon to 3pm. Ask for a copy of the chamber's visitor guide, which lists hotels, motels, condominiums, and other accommodations.

Also downtown, there are **walk-in information centers** on the first level of The Pier and in the lobby of the Florida International Museum (see "Seeing the Top Attractions," below).

The chamber also operates the **Suncoast Welcome Center** (☎ 727/573-1449), on Ulmerton Road at Exit 18 southbound off I-275 (there's no exit here for northbound traffic). Open daily from 9am to 5pm except New Year's Day, Easter, Thanksgiving, and Christmas.

GETTING AROUND   You can see everything on the **Looper: the Downtown Trolley** (☎ 727/571-3440), which runs out to the end of The Pier and past all of the downtown attractions every 30 minutes from 11am to 5pm daily except Thanksgiving and Christmas. Rides cost 50¢ per person.

The **Pinellas Suncoast Transit Authority/PSTA** (☎ 727/530-9911) operates regular bus service throughout Pinellas County.

If you need a cab, call **Yellow Cab** (☎ 727/821-7777) or **Independent Cab** (☎ 727/327-3444).

Pierside Rentals, on The Pier (☎ 727/822-8697), rents bicycles and in-line skates for $5 an hour, $25 a day.

SEEING THE TOP ATTRACTIONS

Florida International Museum. 100 2nd St. N. (between 1st and 2nd aves. N.). ☎ 800/777-9882 or 727/822-3693. www.floridamuseum.org. Admission $13.95 adults, $12.95 seniors, $5.95 children 6–18, free for children under 6. Sun–Fri 9am–6pm, Sat 9am–8pm (or later depending on special exhibits).

This facility attracted 600,000 visitors from around the world when it opened its first exhibition in 1995, and the success has continued (its recent exhibits on the *Titanic* and on the Incas were smash hits). Call to see what's scheduled during your visit. The museum is housed in the former Maas Brothers Department Store, long an area landmark. Tickets should be reserved and purchased in advance to be sure of a specific time. Each visitor is equipped with an audio guide as part of the admission price; allow at least 2 hours to tour a major exhibition. There's an excellent museum store here.

Museum of Fine Arts. 255 Beach Dr. NE (at 3rd Ave. N.). ☎ 727/896-2667. Admission Mon–Sat $6 adults, $5 seniors, $2 students. Free admission on Sun (donation suggested). Tues–Sat 10am–5pm, Sun 1–5pm; winter, third Thurs of each month 10am–9pm. Closed New Year's Day, Thanksgiving, and Christmas.

Resembling a Mediterranean villa on the waterfront, this museum houses a permanent collection of European, American, pre-Colombian, and Far Eastern art, with works by such artists as Fragonard, Monet, Renoir, Cézanne, and Gauguin. Other highlights include period rooms with antiques and historical furnishings, plus a gallery of Steuben crystal, a new decorative-arts gallery, and world-class rotating exhibits.

The Pier. 800 2nd Ave. NE. ☎ 727/821-6164. www.stpete-pier.com. Free admission to all the public areas and decks; donations welcome at the aquarium. Russian Submarine $8 adults, $6 seniors, $5 children. Great Explorations $5, free for children under 3. Valet parking $5, self-parking $3. Pier Mon–Thurs 10am–9pm, Fri–Sat 10am–10pm, Sun 11am–7pm. Aquarium Mon–Sat 10am–8pm, Sun noon–6pm. Russian Submarine daily 10am–7pm. Great Explorations Mon–Fri 9am–5pm. Shops and restaurant hours vary.

Walk or ride out on The Pier and enjoy this festive waterfront dining and shopping complex overlooking Tampa Bay. Originally built as a railroad pier in 1889, today it's capped by a spaceshiplike inverted pyramid offering five levels of shops and restaurants, a tourist information desk, an observation deck, catwalks for fishing, boat docks, miniature golf, boat and water-sports rentals, sightseeing boats, and a food court, plus an aquarium and a hands-on children's museum. You can rent boats and go on cruises from here (see "Outdoor Activities & Spectator Sports," below).

With a variety of hands-on exhibits, **Great Explorations Hands-On Museum** is great for a rainy day or for kids who've overdosed on the sun and need to cool off indoors. They can explore a long, dark tunnel; measure their strength, flexibility, and fitness; paint a work of art with sunlight; and play a melody with a sweep of the hand.

You can also buy tickets here to visit the 300-foot-long **Russian Submarine** (☎ 727/897-9151), actually the *U-484,* which served in the Soviet/Russian navy from the 1960s until 1994. Its retirement home was to be alongside The Pier;

Downtown St. Petersburg

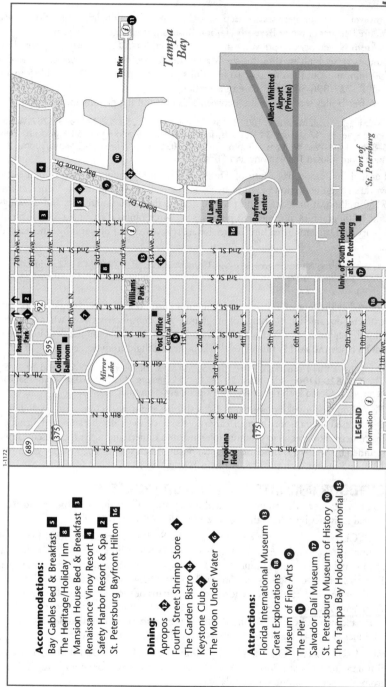

Accommodations:
Bay Gables Bed & Breakfast 5
The Heritage/Holiday Inn 8
Mansion House Bed & Breakfast 3
Renaissance Vinoy Resort 4
Safety Harbor Resort & Spa 2
St. Petersburg Bayfront Hilton 16

Dining:
Apropos 12
Fourth Street Shrimp Store 1
The Garden Bistro 14
Keystone Club 7
The Moon Under Water 6

Attractions:
Florida International Museum 13
Great Explorations 18
Museum of Fine Arts 9
The Pier 11
Salvador Dalí Museum 17
St. Petersburg Museum of History 10
The Tampa Bay Holocaust Memorial 15

however, the water here wasn't deep enough, so pending a dredging operation, it was moored at press time at Bayboro Harbor. Buses shuttle visitors to the ship.

From November to April you can climb aboard the *H.M.S. Bounty,* a replica of the famous vessel built in 1960 for the Marlon Brando version of *Mutiny on the Bounty* (30-min. tours of the ship cost $6 for adults, $5 for seniors, and $4 for kids 5 to 17; call ☎ 727/896-5668 for more information).

A free trolley service operates between The Pier and the parking lots on shore.

✪ **Salvador Dalí Museum.** 1000 3rd St. S. (near 11th Ave. S.). ☎ 727/823-3767. Admission $8 adults, $7 seniors, $4 students, free for children 9 and under. 50% discount Thurs 5–8pm. Mon–Wed 9:30am–5:30pm, Thurs 9:30am–8pm, Fri–Sat 9:30am–5:30pm, Sun noon–5pm. Closed Thanksgiving and Christmas.

Located on Tampa Bay south of The Pier, this starkly modern museum houses the world's largest collection of works by the renowned Spanish surrealist. Valued at over $150 million, it includes 94 oil paintings, more than 100 watercolors and drawings, and 1,300 graphics, plus posters, photos, sculptures, objets d'art, and a 5,000-volume library on Dalí and surrealism. There also are special exhibits of works by other famous artists.

St. Petersburg Museum of History. 335 2nd Ave. NE. ☎ 727/894-1052. Admission $5 adults, $4 seniors, $2 children 7–17, free for children 6 and under. Mon–Sat 10am–5pm, Sun 1–5pm.

Located at the foot of The Pier, this museum chronicles St. Petersburg's history with artifacts, documents, clothing, photographs, and computer stations where you can "flip through the past." Walk-through exhibits include a replica of the Benoist airboat, which made the world's first scheduled commercial flight from St. Petersburg in 1914.

The Tampa Bay Holocaust Memorial. 55 5th St. S. (between Central Ave. and 1st St. S.). ☎ 727/820-0100. Admission $6 adults, $5 seniors. Mon–Fri 10am–4pm, Sat–Sun noon–4pm. Closed Rosh Hashanah, Yom Kippur, and Christmas.

This thought-provoking museum has exhibits about the Holocaust, including a boxcar used to transport human cargo to the Auschwitz death camp in Poland. Its main focus, however, is to promote tolerance and understanding in the present. It was founded by Walter P. Loebenberg, a local businessman who escaped Nazi Germany in 1939 and fought with the U.S. Army in World War II.

OUTDOOR PURSUITS & SPECTATOR SPORTS

You can get up-to-the-minute recorded information about the city's sports and recreational activities by calling the **Leisure Line** (☎ 727/893-7500).

BICYCLING With miles of flat terrain, the St. Petersburg area is ideal for bikers, in-line skaters, and hikers. The **Pinellas Trail** is especially good, since it follows an abandoned railroad bed 47 miles from St. Petersburg north to Tarpon Springs. The St. Pete trailhead is on 34th Street South (U.S. 19) between 8th and Fairfield avenues south. It's packed on the weekends. Free strip maps of the trail are available at the St. Petersburg Area Chamber of Commerce (see "Visitor Information," above).

It's a long way from the trailhead, but you can rent bikes from **Pierside Rentals** on The Pier (see "Getting Around," above, and "Boat Rentals," below).

BOAT RENTALS On The Pier, **Pierside Rentals** (☎ 727/363-0000) rents Wave Runners and jet boats. Prices for Wave Runners begin at $45 for an hour; for jet boats, from $55 per 30 minutes. Open daily from 10am to 9pm.

CRUISES The *Caribbean Queen* (☎ 727/895-BOAT) departs from The Pier and offers 1-hour sightseeing and dolphin-watching cruises around Tampa Bay. Sailings are daily at 1, 3, and 5pm; they cost $10 for adults, $8 for seniors and juniors 12 to 17, $5 for children 3 to 11, and free for children 2 and under.

GOLF   One of the nation's top 50 municipal courses, the ✪ **Mangrove Bay Golf Course,** 875 62nd Ave. NE (☎ 727/893-7797), hugs the inlets of Old Tampa Bay and offers 18-hole, par-72 play. Facilities include a driving range; lessons and golf-club rental are also available. Fees are about $22, $32 including a cart in winter, slightly lower off-season. Open daily from 6:30am to 6pm.

The city also operates the challenging par-3 **Twin Brooks Golf Course,** 3800 22nd Ave. S. (☎ 727/893-7445).

In Largo, the **Bardmoor Golf Club,** 7919 Bardmoor Blvd. (☎ 727/397-0483), is often the venue for major tournaments. Lakes punctuate 17 of the 18 holes on this par-72 championship course. Lessons and rental clubs are available, as is a Tom Fazio–designed practice range. Call the clubhouse for seasonal greens fees. Open daily from 7am to dusk.

Adjacent to the St. Petersburg–Clearwater airport, the **Airco Flite Golf Course,** 3650 Roosevelt Blvd., Clearwater (☎ 727/573-4653), is a championship 18-hole, par-72 course with a driving range. Golf-club rentals are also available. Greens fees including cart range from $25 to $35 in winter, about $20 off-season. Open daily from 7am to 6pm.

Call **Tee Times USA** (☎ 800/374-8633) to reserve times at these and other area courses.

If you want to take up golf or sharpen your game, TV "Golf Doctor" Joe Quinzi hosts his **Quinzi Golf Academy** (☎ 727/725-1999) at the Safety Harbor Resort and Spa (see "Where to Stay," below). His school offers personalized instructions and clinics for up to six players.

SAILING   The **Annapolis Sailing School,** 6800 Sunshine Skyway Lane S. (☎ 800/638-9192 or 727/867-8102), almost at the foot of the Sunshine Skyway bridge, can teach you to sail or perfect your sailing skills. Various courses are offered at this branch of the famous Maryland-based school, lasting 2, 5, or 8 days. Call for prices and schedules.

The school is based at the **Holiday Inn SunSpree Resort,** 6800 Sunshine Skyway Lane S., St. Petersburg, FL 33711 (☎ 800/227-8045 or 727/867-1151), a recently renovated motel with an expansive bayside pool area.

SPECTATOR SPORTS   St. Petersburg has always been a baseball town, and **Tropicana Field,** a 45,000-seat domed stadium alongside I-175 between 9th and 16th streets south, is the home of the **Tampa Bay Devil Rays,** the area's expansion team which began American League play in 1998. The season runs from April through September. Call ☎ 727/898-RAYS for schedule and ticket information. The Devil Rays move outdoors to Al Lang Stadium, on 2nd Avenue South at 1st Street South (☎ 727/825-3137), for their spring-training games from mid-February through March. Tickets to the spring games range from $3 to $12.

The **Philadelphia Phillies** play their spring-training season at Jack Russell Stadium, 800 Phillies Dr., in nearby Clearwater (☎ 727/442-8496). Admission is $8 to $9. Their minor league **Clearwater Phillies** play in the stadium from April to September. The **Toronto Blue Jays** do their spring thing at Grant Field, 373 Douglas Ave. in Dunedin (☎ 727/733-0429).

SHOPPING

The Pier, at the end of 2nd Avenue NE (☎ 727/821-6164), houses more than a dozen boutiques and craft shops, but nearby Beach Drive, running along the waterfront, is one of the most fashionable downtown strolling and shopping venues. Here you'll find the **Glass Canvas Gallery,** at 4th Avenue NE (☎ 727/821-6767), featuring a dazzling array of glass sculpture, tableware, art, and craft items by 250 local, national, and international artists. Also at 4th Avenue NE, **P. Buckley Moss** (☎ 727/894-2899), a museum-grade store carrying the works of the individualistic artist best known for her portrayal of the Amish and the Mennonites. The works include paintings, graphics, figurines, and collector dolls. **Red Cloud,** between 1st and 2nd avenues (☎ 727/821-5824), is an oasis for Native American crafts, from jewelry and head-dresses to sculpture and art.

Central Avenue is another shopping area, featuring the **Gas Plant Antique Arcade,** between 12th and 13th streets (☎ 727/895-0368), the largest antique mall on Florida's west coast, with more than 100 dealers displaying their wares. The **Florida Craftsmen Gallery,** at 5th Street (☎ 727/821-7391), is a showcase for the works of more than 150 Florida artisans and craftspeople: jewelry, ceramics, woodwork, fiber works, glassware, paper creations, and metalwork.

In the suburbs, outlet shoppers can browse Corning Revere, Linens 'N' Things, BonWorth, Dress Barn, Van Heusen, Bugle Boy, L'eggs, Bass Shoes, T.J. Maxx, and more at the air-conditioned **Bay Area Outlet Mall,** at the intersection of U.S. 19 and East Bay Drive (☎ 727/535-2337), west of St. Petersburg–Clearwater International Airport.

WHERE TO STAY

Ask the **St. Petersburg Area Chamber of Commerce** (see "Essentials," above) for a copy of its visitor guide, which lists a wide range of hotels, motels, condominiums, and other accommodations.

The **St. Petersburg/Clearwater Area Convention & Visitors Bureau** (see "Essentials," above) publishes a brochure listing members of its Superior Small Lodging program; all with less than 50 rooms, they have been inspected and certified for cleanliness and value. In addition, the Bureau has a free **reservations service** (☎ 800/345-6710).

You'll find plenty of chain motels along U.S. 19.

With regard to prices, the high season is from January to April. The hotel tax rate in Pinellas County is 11%.

VERY EXPENSIVE

✪ **Renaissance Vinoy Resort.** 501 5th Ave. NE (at Beach Dr.), St. Petersburg, FL 33701. ☎ **800/HOTELS-1** or 727/894-1000. Fax 727/822-2785. 360 units. A/C MINIBAR TV TEL. Winter $269–$299 double. Off-season $149–$269 double. AE, DC, DISC, MC, V. Valet parking $12; self-parking $5.

Built as the Vinoy Park in 1925 during Florida's heyday of grand hotels, this elegant Spanish-style establishment reopened in 1992 after a total and meticulous $93 million restoration that has made it more luxurious than ever. Dominating the northern part of downtown, it overlooks Tampa Bay and is within walking distance of The Pier, Central Avenue, museums, and other attractions. All the guest rooms, many of which enjoy lovely views of the bay front, are designed to offer the utmost in comfort and include three phones, an additional TV in the bathroom, a hair dryer, bath scales, and more; some units in the new wing also have whirlpools and private patios/balconies.

Dining/Diversions: Marchand's Grille, an elegant, Mediterranean-style room overlooking the bay, serves the best steaks, seafood, and chops in town. The Terrace Room is the main dining room for breakfast, lunch, and dinner. Casual lunches and dinners are available at the indoor-outdoor Alfresco, near the pool deck, and at the Clubhouse at the golf course on Snell Isle. There are also two bar/lounges.

Amenities: Concierge, 24-hour room service, laundry service, tour desk, child care, complimentary coffee and newspaper with wake-up call. Two swimming pools (connected by a roaring waterfall), 14-court tennis complex (11 lighted), 18-hole private championship golf course on nearby Snell Isle, private 74-slip marina, two croquet courts, fitness center (with sauna, steam room, spa, massage, and exercise equipment), access to two bayside beaches, shuttle service to gulf beaches, hair salon, gift shop.

MODERATE

Bay Gables Bed & Breakfast. 136 4th Ave. NE (between Beach Dr. and 1st St. N.), St. Petersburg, FL 33701. ☎ **800/822-8803** or 727/822-8855. Fax 727/824-7223. 9 units. A/C TV TEL. Winter $85–$135 double. Off-season $65–$105 double. Rates include continental breakfast. AE, MC, V.

You can walk to The Pier from this charming B&B with wraparound porches on all three of its stories. Built in the 1930s, it overlooks a flower-filled garden with a gazebo. The guest quarters have been furnished with ceiling fans and Victorian pieces, including a canopy bed in one room. The honeymoon suite is equipped with a large double shower, Jacuzzi, and bidet; the rest have both clawfoot tubs and modern showers in their bathrooms. Half of the rooms open to the porches, while the rest have a separate sitting room and kitchenette. Continental breakfast is served in a restaurant next door. This is a professionally managed operation; the owners don't live on the premises.

⊙ **Heritage/Holiday Inn.** 234 3rd Ave. N. (between 2nd and 3rd sts.), St. Petersburg, FL 33701. ☎ **800/283-7829** or 727/822-4814. Fax 727/823-1644. 71 units. A/C TV TEL. $97–$139 double. AE, DC, DISC, MC, V.

No ordinary Holiday Inn, the Heritage dates from the early 1920s and is the closest thing to a Southern mansion you'll find in the heart of downtown. With a sweeping veranda, French doors, and a tropical courtyard, it attracts an eclectic clientele, from young families to seniors. The furnishings include period antiques. There are a heated swimming pool and a whirlpool in a small tropical courtyard between the main building and the Heritage Grill restaurant next door. Amenities include limited room service and valet laundry.

Mansion House Bed & Breakfast. 105 5th Ave. NE (at 1st St. N.), St. Petersburg, FL 33701. ☎ **800/274-7520** or 727/821-9391. Fax 727/821-9391 (same as phone). www.mansion-bandb.com. 10 units (all with bathroom). A/C TV TEL. Winter $110–$165 double. Off-season $95–$150 double. Rates include full breakfast. AE, MC, V.

Mirror images of each other, these two Arts-and-Crafts–style houses separated by a landscaped courtyard were built in 1904 and 1912 by a local doctor (one house served as his office). The comfortable living room in the main house, which has 6 of the 10 units here, opens to a sun room, off which a small screened porch provides mosquito-free lounging and the only place where guests can smoke. Both houses have upstairs front parlors with TVs, VCRs, and libraries. Tall, old-fashioned windows let lots of light into the attractive guest rooms, in which some furniture has been decorated by a local artist. The "Pembrooke" room actually is upstairs over the carriage house; it has its own refrigerator, phone, TV, and four-poster bed with mosquito net. In an unusual architectural twist, the "Harlech" room has a toilet and hand basin in one converted closet, a shower in another. Proprietors Rob and Rosie Ray serve a full breakfast in two formal dining rooms and keep fruit bowls and snacks available at all hours in both houses. There's a whirlpool bath in its own screened hut in the backyard.

St. Petersburg Bayfront Hilton. 333 1st St. S. (between 3rd and 4th aves. S., opposite Al Lang Field), St. Petersburg, FL 33701. ☎ **800/HILTONS** or 727/894-5000. Fax 727/823-4797.

333 units. A/C TV TEL. Winter $159 double. Off-season $119 double. Packages available. AE, DC, MC, V.

This 15-story convention hotel has a spacious lobby with a rich decor of marble, tile, and potted trees and plants. The bedrooms are furnished with traditional dark woods, floral fabrics, a king-size bed or two double beds, and an executive desk; many have views of the bay. Cafe 333 is a full-service restaurant specializing in continental cuisine, while the First Street Deli provides light fare and Pizza Hut pies. Brandi's Lobby Bar has piano entertainment. Facilities include an outdoor heated swimming pool, a whirlpool, a health club with a sauna, and a gift shop.

A NEARBY SPA

✪ **Safety Harbor Resort and Spa.** 105 N. Bayshore Dr., Safety Harbor, FL 34695. ☎ **888/ BEST-SPA** or 727/726-1161. Fax 727/726-4268. www.southseas.com. 193 units. Winter $169–189 double. Off-season $99–$169 double. Packages available. AE, DC, DISC, MC, V. Valet parking $4, free self-parking. Pets up to 30 pounds accepted with nonrefundable deposit.

Hernando de Soto thought he had found Ponce de Léon's fabled Fountain of Youth when he happened upon five mineral springs here on the shores of Old Tampa Bay in 1539. You won't get your youth back at this venerable spa, which has been in operation since 1926 and got a face-lift in 1998, but you are in for some serious pampering, from massages to hydrotherapy and a full menu of fitness classes from boxing to yoga. The springs enable the spa to offer acclaimed water-fitness programs. This is also a good place to work on your games at the Quinzi Golf Academy and the Phil Green Tennis Academy (see "Outdoor Pursuits & Spectator Sports," above). The sprawling complex of beige stucco buildings with Spanish tile roofs sits on 22 waterfront acres in the sleepy town of Safety Harbor, north of St. Petersburg. Moss-draped Safety Harbor has a charming, small-town ambience, with a number of shops and restaurants just outside the spa's entrance.

Dining: Nutritious menus emphasizing American fusion cuisine use lots of Florida ingredients in both the Spa Dining Room and the resort's Cafe, which is open to the public for lunch and dinner.

Amenities: Concierge, limited room service, valet laundry, guest laundry, valet parking, Clarins Skin Institute, 50,000-square-foot spa and fitness center, 3 heated pools, 9 lighted tennis courts, bike rentals, business center, beauty salon, boutiques.

WHERE TO DINE

Don't overlook the food court at **The Pier,** where the inexpensive chow is accompanied by a very rich, but quite free, view of the bay. Among The Pier's restaurants is a branch of Tampa's famous Columbia (☎ 727/822-8000; see "Where to Dine" in section 1, above).

MODERATE

Apropos. 300 2nd Ave. NE (at Bayshore Dr.). ☎ **727/823-8934.** Reservations accepted only for dinner. Breakfast $3.50–$6; lunch $5–$9; dinner main courses $14–$21. AE, DC, MC, V. Tues–Sat 7:30–10:30am and 11am–2pm; Thurs–Sun 6–10:30pm (Sun brunch 8:30am–2pm). AMERICAN.

Sitting at the foot of The Pier, Apropros is a fine place to breakfast before your tour of downtown, perhaps with a brie and bacon omelette, or a seasonal fruit plate, or just plain eggs. At lunch, the view through the masts in the adjacent marina sets the scene for the likes of shrimp and artichoke salad with a sherry mayonnaise dressing. At night the scene changes to linen table cloths, bow-tied waiters, and a menu of fine nouvelle American cuisine. You'll find as many locals here as tourists.

Garden Bistro. 217 Central Ave. (between 2nd and 3rd sts.). ☎ **727/896-3800.** Reservations recommended for dinner. Main courses $11–$17. AE, DISC, MC, V. Daily noon–2am. MEDITERRANEAN.

This lively restaurant combines European ambience with Moroccan cuisine. Choice seats are under huge shade trees in the garden, screened from the street by a trellis fence. Inside, the decor blends the American Southwest with the Mediterranean, with arches, a 19th-century tiled floor, modern local art, and lots of flowers and plants. The creative menu features couscous, a daily *tajin* (a traditional Moroccan stew), pastas such as wild mushrooms with strips of roast duck, and smoked salmon in a light cream sauce. On Friday and Saturday, live jazz adds to the ambience from 9pm to 1am.

Keystone Club. 320 4th St. N. (between 3rd and 4th aves. N.). ☎ **727/822-6600.** Reservations recommended. Main courses $11–$23; early-bird specials $7.50–$12. AE, DC, DISC, MC, V. Mon–Fri 11am–2:30pm and 5–10pm, Sat 4–10pm, Sun 4–9pm. Early-bird specials winter only, Mon–Fri 4:30–5:30pm, Sat–Sun 4–5:30pm. STEAKS/PRIME RIB.

Resembling an exclusive men's club, this cozy restaurant's forest-green walls accented by dark wood and etched glass create an atmosphere that's reminiscent of a Manhattan-style chophouse. But women are also welcome to partake of the beef, which is king here. Specialties include roast prime rib, New York strip steak, and filet mignon. Seafood also makes an appearance, with fresh lobster and grouper at market price. During winter, "sunset" early-bird specials include lunch-size portions, a beverage, and dessert.

INEXPENSIVE

✪ Fourth Street Shrimp Store. 1006 4th St. N. (at 10th Ave. N.). ☎ **727/822-0325.** Reservations not accepted. Sandwiches $2.50–$6; main courses $4–$12. MC, V. Sun–Thurs 11am–9pm, Fri–Sat 11am–10pm. SEAFOOD.

If you're anywhere in the area, don't miss at least driving by to see the colorful, cartoonlike mural on the outside of this eclectic establishment just north of downtown. On first impression it looks like graffiti, but it's actually a gigantic drawing of people eating. Inside, it gets even better, with paraphernalia and murals on two walls making the dining room seem like a warehouse with windows looking out on an early-19th-century seaport (one painted sailor permanently peers in to see what you're eating). You'll pass a seafood market counter when you enter, from which comes the fresh namesake shrimp, the star here. You can also pick from grouper, clam strips, catfish, or oysters fried, broiled, or steamed, all served in heaping portions. This is the best and certainly the most interesting bargain in town.

The Moon Under Water. 332 Beach Dr. (between 3rd and 4th sts.). ☎ **727/896-6160.** Reservations not accepted. Sandwiches and salads $6–$8; main courses $8–$16. AE, DC, DISC, MC, V. Sun–Thurs 11:30am–9:30pm, Fri–Sat 11:30am–10pm. AMERICAN/INDIAN.

The British raj rules supreme at this pub facing the bayfront park. You can choose a table on the veranda out front, or inside the darkly paneled dining room with a host of slowly twirling fans hung from the ceiling and a plethora of colonial artifacts along the walls, including obligatory pith helmets. The menu covers a number of former British outposts, including America (grilled steak and pork chops). But the emphasis here is on mild, medium, or blazing-hot Indian curries—with a recommended wine or cold Irish, British, or Australian beer to cool the taste buds. For lighter fare, consider specialty salads served in a tortilla basket, or perhaps mid-eastern taboule. Served until 5pm, lunch includes burgers, sandwiches, beef pastry turnovers, and spicy, pizza-like *bombayli*, made with Indian *nan* bread. There's entertainment Friday and Saturday evenings.

ST. PETERSBURG AFTER DARK

Good sources of nightlife information are the Friday "Weekend" section of the *St. Petersburg Times,* the "Baylife" and "Friday Extra" sections of the *Tampa Tribune,* and the *Weekly Planet,* a tabloid available at the visitor information offices and in many hotel and restaurant lobbies. The bimonthly magazine *Event Guide Tampa Bay* gives a rundown on what's going on.

THE CLUB & MUSIC SCENE A historic attraction as well as an entertainment venue, the Moorish-style **Coliseum Ballroom,** 535 4th Ave. N. (☎ **727/892-5202**), has been hosting dancing, big bands, boxing, and other events since 1924 (it even made an appearance in the 1985 movie *Cocoon*). An acquaintance of mine said it's fun to watch the town's many seniors doing the jitterbug just like it was 1945 again! Call for the schedule and prices.

A much younger set heads to the casual downtown **Big Catch,** 9 1st St. NE (☎ **727/821-6444**), featuring live and danceable rock and Top 40 hits, as well as darts, pool, and hoops. North of downtown, the **Ringside Cafe,** 2742 4th St. N. (☎ **727/894-8465**), in a renovated boxing gymnasium, is an informal neighborhood cafe with a decided sports motif. The music focuses on jazz and blues (and sometimes reggae).

PERFORMING-ARTS VENUES **Tropicana Field,** 1 Stadium Dr. (☎ **727/825-3100**), has a capacity of 50,000 for major concerts but also hosts a variety of smaller events when the Devil Rays aren't playing baseball.

The **Bayfront Center,** 400 1st St. S. (☎ **727/892-5767,** or 727/892-5700 for recorded information), houses the 8,100-seat Bayfront Arena and the 2,000-seat Mahaffey Theater. The schedule includes a variety of concerts, Broadway shows, big bands, ice shows, and circus performances.

3 The St. Pete & Clearwater Beaches

If you're looking for sun and sand, you'll find plenty of both on the 28 miles of slim barrier islands that skirt the gulf shore of the Pinellas Peninsula. With some one million visitors coming here every year, don't be surprised if you have lots of company. But you'll also discover quieter neighborhoods geared to families, and this area has some of the nation's finest beaches, which are protected from development by parks and nature preserves.

At the southern end of the strip, St. Pete Beach is the granddaddy of the area's resorts. In fact, visitors started coming here nearly a century ago, and they haven't quit. Today St. Pete Beach is heavily developed and often overcrowded during the winter season. If you like high-rises and mile-a-minute action, St. Pete Beach is for you. But even here, Pass-a-Grille, on the island's southern end, is a quiet residential enclave with eclectic shops and a fine public beach.

A more gentle lifestyle begins just to the north on 3½-mile-long Treasure Island. From there, you cross famous John's Pass to Sand Key, a 12-mile island occupied by primarily residential Madeira Beach, Redington Beach, North Redington Beach, Redington Shores, Indian Shores, Indian Rocks Beach, and Belleair Beach. Finally the road crosses a soaring bridge to Clearwater Beach, whose silky sands attract active families and couples.

If you like your great outdoors unfettered by development, the jewels here are Fort Desoto Park, down below St. Pete Beach at the mouth of Tampa Bay, and Caladesi Island State Park, north of Clearwater Beach. They are consistently rated among America's top beaches. And Sand Key Park, looking at Clearwater Beach from the southern shores of Little Pass, is one of Florida's finest local beach parks.

Accommodations:
Beach Haven **16**
Belleview Biltmore
    Resort & Spa **1**
Best Western Sea
    Stone Resort **27**
Captain's Quarters Inn **8**
Clearwater Beach Hotel **21**
Days Inn Island
    Beach Resort **11**
Don CeSar Beach
    Resort and Spa **17**
Great Heron Inn **4**
Island's End Resort **19**
Palm Pavilion Inn **20**
Pelican—East & West **2**
Radisson Suite Resort
    on Sand Key **29**
Sheraton Sand Key
    Resort **28**
Sun West Beach Motel **26**
TradeWinds Resort **15**
TradeWinds Sandpiper
    Beach Resort **13**
Travelodge St. Pete
    Beach **9**

Dining:
Bob Heilman's
    Beachcomber **23**
Bobby's Bistro
    & Wine Bar **24**
Crabby Bill's **14**
Frenchy's Cafe **22**
Guppy's **3**
Hurricane **18**
Internet Outpost **10**
Lobster Pot **6**
Seafood & Sunsets
    at Julie's **25**
Scandia **5**
Skidder's **12**
The Wine Cellar **7**

ESSENTIALS

GETTING THERE   See "Getting There" in sections 1 and 2 for information about flights to, and transportation from, Tampa International and St. Petersburg–Clearwater International airports.

VISITOR INFORMATION   See "Visitor Information" in section 2 for the St. Petersburg/Clearwater Area Convention & Visitors Bureau and the St. Petersburg Area Chamber of Commerce. You can get information specific to the beaches from the **Gulf Beaches of Tampa Bay Chamber of Commerce,** 6990 Gulf Blvd. (at 70th Avenue), St. Pete Beach, FL 33706 (☎ **800/944-1847** or 727/360-6957; fax 727/360-2233). The main office is open Monday to Friday from 9am to 5pm. The chamber also has welcome centers at 501 150th Ave. in Maderia Beach (☎ 727/391-7373); on Walsingham Road just east of Gulf Boulevard in Indian Rocks Beach (☎ 727/595-4575); and at 152 108th Ave. in Treasure Island (☎ 727/367-4529).

For advance information about Clearwater Beach, contact the **Greater Clearwater Chamber of Commerce,** 128 N. Osceola Ave. (P.O. Box 2457), Clearwater, FL 34615 (☎ **727/461-0011**). You can also walk into the beaches branch of the city-operated **Clearwater Tourist Information Center,** on Causeway Boulevard in the Clearwater Beach Marina Building lobby (☎ **727/462-6531**). It's open daily in winter from 9am to 5pm, off-season Monday to Saturday from 9am to 5pm, Sunday from 1 to 5pm.

GETTING AROUND   **BATS City Transit** (☎ 727/367-3086) offers bus service along the St. Pete Beach strip. The fare is $1.

Treasure Island Transit System (☎ 727/547-4575) runs buses along the Treasure Island strip. The fare is $1.

The **Jolley Trolley** (☎ 727/445-1200), operated in conjunction with the City of Clearwater, provides service in the Clearwater Beach area, from downtown to the beaches as far south as Sand Key. The ride costs 50¢ per person, 25¢ for seniors.

Along the beach, the major cab company is **BATS Taxi** (☎ 727/367-3702).

HITTING THE BEACH

This entire stretch of coast is one long beach, but since hotels, condominiums, and private homes occupy much of it, you may want to sun and swim at one of the area's public parks. The very best are described below, but there's also the fine **Pass-a-Grille Public Beach,** on the southern end of St. Pete Beach, where you can watch the boats going in and out of Pass-a-Grille Channel. This and all other Pinellas County public beaches have metered parking lots, so bring a supply of quarters.

Clearwater Public Beach (also known as Pier 60) has beach volleyball, water-sports rentals, lifeguards, rest rooms, showers, and concessions. The swimming is excellent, and there are a children's playground and a pier for fishing. Gated municipal parking lots here cost $1 per hour or $7 a day. The lots are right across the street from Clearwater Beach Marina, a prime base for boating, cruises, and other waterborne activities (see "Outdoor Activities," below).

✪ **CALADESI ISLAND STATE PARK**   Occupying a 3½-mile island north of Clearwater Beach, **Caladesi Island State Park** boasts one of Florida's top beaches, a lovely, relatively secluded stretch with fine soft sand edged in sea grass and palmettos. Dolphins cavort in the waters offshore. In the park itself, there's a nature trail, and you might see one of the rattlesnakes, black racers, raccoons, armadillos, or rabbits that live here. A concession stand, a ranger station, and bathhouses (with rest rooms and showers) are available. Caladesi Island is accessible only by ferry from **Honeymoon Island State Recreation Area,** which is connected by Causeway Boulevard (Fla. 586) to Dunedin, north of Clearwater. You'll first have to pay the admission to Honeymoon Island: $4 per vehicle with two to eight occupants, $2 per single-occupant vehicle, $1 for pedestrians and bicyclists. Beginning daily at 10am, the ferry departs Honeymoon Island every hour on winter weekdays, every 30 minutes on summer weekdays, and every 30 minutes on weekends year-round. Rides cost $6 for adults and $3.50 for kids. The two parks are open daily from 8am to sunset. The two islands are administered by Gulf Islands Geopark, no. 1 Causeway Blvd., Dunedin, FL 34698 (☎ 727/469-5942).

Dolphin Encounter, the concessionaire which operates the Honeymoon-Caladesi ferry (☎ 737/442-7433), also has cruises to Caladesi Island from Clearwater Beach, usually on Wednesday and Friday from 10:30am to 5:30pm. These cost $24.30 for adults, $20.55 for children, including lunch. Call for reservations.

✪ **FORT DESOTO PARK**   South of St. Pete Beach at the very mouth of Tampa Bay, this group of five connected barrier islands has been set aside by Pinellas County as a 900-acre bird, animal, and plant sanctuary. Besides the stunning white-sugar sand beach (where you can watch the manatees and dolphins play offshore), there are a Spanish-American War–era fort, great fishing from piers, large playgrounds for kids, and 4 miles of trails winding through the park for in-line skaters, bicyclists, and joggers.

Sitting on an island by themselves, the park's 230 campsites all have water and electricity hookups, but they usually are sold out, especially on weekends. Sites cost $18.75 a night. To make reservations, you must appear in person and pay for your site no more than 30 days in advance at the campground office, at 631 Chestnut St. in Clearwater, or at 150 5th St. N. in downtown St. Petersburg. You must camp here at least 2 nights, but you can stay no more than 14 nights. The park is open from 8am to dusk, although campers and persons fishing from the piers can stay later. Admission is free. To get here, take the Pinellas Byway (50¢ toll) east from St. Pete Beach, and follow Fla. 679 (35¢ toll) and the signs south to the park. For more information, contact the park at 3500 Pinellas Bayway, Tierra Verde, FL 33715 (☎ 727/582-2267).

SAND KEY PARK   This fine county park on the northern tip of Sand Key facing Clearwater Beach sports a wide beach and gentle surf and is relatively off the beaten path in this commercial area. It's great to get out of the hotel for a morning walk or jog here. Open 8am to dark. Admission is free, but the parking lot has meters. For more information, call ☎ 727/464-3347.

OUTDOOR PURSUITS

BICYCLING & IN-LINE SKATING   With miles of flat terrain and paved roads, the beach area is ideal for bikers and in-line skaters, and the 47-mile-long Pinellas Trail runs close by on the mainland (see "Outdoor Activities & Spectator Sports," in section 2, above). In St. Pete Beach, you can rent bicycles, skates, and scooters from **Beach Cyclist Sports Center,** 7517 Blind Pass Rd. (☎ 727/367-5001). In Clearwater Beach, contact **Transportation Station,** 652 Gulfview Blvd. (☎ 727/443-3188). Bikes at all three range from about $5 per hour to $20 a day; scooters, about $13 an hour to $40 per day.

BOATING, FISHING & OTHER WATER SPORTS   You can indulge in parasailing, boating, deep-sea fishing, wave running, sightseeing, dolphin watching, waterskiing, and just about any other waterborne diversion your heart could desire here. All you have to do is head to one of two beach locations: **Hubbard's Marina,** at John's Pass Village and Boardwalk (☎ 727/393-1947), in Madeira Beach on the southern tip of Sand Key; or **Clearwater Beach Marina,** at Coronado Drive and Causeway Boulevard (☎ 800/772-4479 or 727/461-3133), which is at the beach end of the causeway leading to downtown Clearwater. Agents in booths there will give you the schedules and prices, answer any questions you have, and make reservations if necessary. Go in the early morning to set up today's activities, or in the afternoon to book tomorrow's.

CRUISES   Several boats cruise from John's Pass Village and Clearwater Beach Marina to undeveloped barrier islands, with dolphin viewing on the way out and back.

The largest operator is **Hubbard's Sea Adventures,** based at John's Pass Village and Boardwalk in Madeira Beach (☎ 727/398-6577). It offers a 2-hour dolphin-watching excursion, Monday to Saturday from 10am to noon, 1 to 3pm, and 4 to 6pm (1 to 3pm on Sunday), at $15 for adults, $7.50 for kids under 12. A 6-hour trip goes to lovely **Shell Key,** one of Florida's last completely undeveloped barrier islands. Shell Key is great for bird-watchers, who could spot a remarkable 88 different species, including some of North America's rarest shorebirds. These trips usually depart at 10:30am Monday, Tuesday, and Saturday, for $25 adults, $13 kids. You can rent beach chairs, umbrellas, snorkeling gear, and other equipment once you get there. A third cruise goes to **Egmont Key State Park,** on historic Egmont Key at the mouth of Tampa Bay. This uninhabited island is the site of a lighthouse, of now-crumbling Fort Dade (built in 1900 during the Spanish-American War but abandoned long ago), and of threatened gopher tortoises. Sea turtles come ashore here to nest. You can go snorkeling and shelling here, so bring your swimsuit (snorkeling gear is available for $5 per person). This cruise leaves at 10:30am Tuesday, Friday, and Sunday and costs $30 for adults, $20 for children. A barbecue lunch on either Shell or Egmont keys costs $7 for adults, $5 for kids. Call to confirm the schedule and make reservations, which are recommended.

The **Shell Key Shuttle,** Merry Pier, on Pass-a-Grille Way at the eastern end of 8th Avenue in southern St. Pete Beach (☎ 727/360-1348), uses a 57-passenger catamaran to shuttle out to Shell Island. Boats leave daily at 10am, noon, and 2pm. Prices are $12 for adults, $6 for children 12 and under. The ride takes 15 minutes, and you can return on any shuttle you wish.

The most unusual outings here are with **Captain Memo's Pirate Cruise,** at Clearwater Beach Marina (☎ 727/446-2587), which sails the *Pirate's Ransom,* a reproduction of a pirate ship, on 2-hour daytime "pirate cruises," as well as sunset and evening champagne cruises. Cruises operate year-round, daily at 10am and 2, 4:30, and 7pm. For adults, daytime or sunset cruises cost $27, and evening cruises are $30; both daytime and evening cruises cost $20 for seniors and juniors 13 to 17, $17 for children 2 to 12, free for children under 2.

Two paddle-wheel riverboats operate here: the *Show Queen* has lunch, sunset-dinner, and Sunday-brunch cruises from Clearwater Beach Marina (☎ 727/461-3113). The *Starlite Princess* does likewise from 3400 Pasadena Ave. S. (☎ 727/462-2628), at the eastern side of the Corey Causeway linking St. Pete Beach to the mainland. Call for schedules and prices.

ATTRACTIONS ON LAND

Clearwater Marine Aquarium. 249 Windward Passage, Clearwater. ☎ **888/239-9414** or 727/447-0980. Admission $6.75 adults, $4.25 children 3–11, free for children 2 and under. Mon–Fri 9am–5pm, Sat 9am–4pm, Sun 11am–4pm. The aquarium is off the causeway between Clearwater and Clearwater Beach; follow the signs.

This little jewel of an aquarium on Clearwater Harbor is very low-key and friendly; it's dedicated to the rescue and rehabilitation of marine mammals and sea turtles. Exhibits include dolphins, otters, sea turtles, sharks, stingrays, mangroves, and sea grass.

✪ **John's Pass Village and Boardwalk.** 12901 Gulf Blvd. (at John's Pass), Madeira Beach. ☎ **800/944-1847** or 727/397-1511. Free admission. Shops and activities daily 9am–6pm or later.

Casual and charming, this Old Florida fishing village on John's Pass consists of a string of simple wooden structures topped by tin roofs and connected by a 1,000-foot boardwalk. Most of the buildings have been converted into shops, art galleries, restaurants, and saloons. The focal point is the boardwalk and marina, where many water sports are available for visitors (see "Outdoor Activities," above).

✪ **Suncoast Seabird Sanctuary.** 18328 Gulf Blvd., Indian Shores. ☎ **727/391-6211.** Free admission, donations welcome. Daily 9am–dusk. Free tours Wed and Sun 2pm.

At any one time there are usually more than 500 sea and land birds living at the sanctuary, from cormorants, white herons, and birds of prey to the ubiquitous brown pelican. The nation's largest wild-bird hospital, dedicated to the rescue, repair, recuperation, and release of sick and injured wild birds, is also here.

SHOPPING

John's Pass Village and Boardwalk, on John's Pass in Madeira Beach, just north of Treasure Island (☎ 727/391-7373), has an unremarkable collection of beach souvenir shops, but the atmosphere makes it worth a stroll. The houses of this old fishermen's village have been converted into more than 60 stores, bars, and restaurants. The pick of the lot is the **Bronze Lady** (☎ 727/398-5994), featuring the world's collection of works by the late comedian-artist Red Skelton, best known for his numerous clown paintings. The shops here are open daily from 9am to 6pm or later.

If you're in the market for some one-of-a-kind hand-hammered jewelry, try **Evander Preston Contemporary Jewelry,** 106 8th Ave., Pass-a-Grille (☎ 727/ 367-7894), a unique gallery/workshop housed in a 75-year-old building in Pass-a-Grille's 1-block-long 8th Avenue business district. Check out the golden miniature train with diamond headlight (it's not for sale). Open Monday to Saturday from 10am to 5:30pm.

Among the shops in St. Pete Beach's Corey Landings Area, the town's original business strip along 75th Street east of Gulf Boulevard, **The Shell Store** (☎ 727/ 360-0586) specializes in corals and shells, with an on-premises minimuseum illustrating how they live and grow. There are a good selection of shell home decorations, shell hobbyist supplies, shell art, planters, and jewelry. Open Monday to Saturday from 9:30am to 5pm.

On the mainland in Clearwater, the ✪ **Senior Citizen Craft Center Gift Shop,** 940 Court St. (☎ 727/442-4266), is one of the area's most unique gift shops—an outlet for the work of some 400 local senior citizens. You'll find knitwear, crochet work, woodwork, stained glass, clocks, scrimshaw, jewelry, pottery, tile work, ceramics, and hand-painted clothing. It's off the beaten tourist track but well worth a visit. It's open Monday to Friday from 10am to 4pm, but it's staffed by volunteers, so call ahead.

WHERE TO STAY

St. Pete Beach and Clearwater Beach have national chain hotels and motels of every name and description. For even more choices, the **St. Petersburg Area Chamber of Commerce** lists a wide range of hotels, motels, condominiums, and other accommodations in its annual visitor guide, and it publishes a brochure listing all members of its Superior Small Lodgings Program (see "Essentials" in section 2). You can also use the St. Petersburg/Clearwater Convention & Visitors Bureau's free **reservations service** (☎ 800/345-6710).

As is the case throughout Florida, there are at least as many rental condominiums here as there are hotel rooms. Many of them are in high-rise buildings right on the beach. Among several local rental agents, **Excell Vacation Condos,** 14955 Gulf Blvd., Madeira Beach, FL 33708 (☎ **800/733-4004** or 727/391-5512; fax 727/393-8885; www.islandtime.com/vacation), and **JC Resort Management,** 17200 Gulf Blvd., North Redington Beach, FL 33708 (☎ **800/535-7776** or 727/397-0441; fax 727/397-8894; www.jcresort.com), have many from which to choose. **Resort Rentals,** 9524 Blind Pass Rd., St. Pete Beach, FL 33707 (☎ **800/293-3979** or 727/363-3336; fax 727/360-5086; www.resort-realty.com), specializes in luxury rental homes.

With regard to prices, high season runs from January to April. Ask about special discounted packages in the summer. Any time of year, though, it's wise to make reservations early. The hotel tax in Pinellas County is 11%.

I have organized accommodations geographically, starting with the congested St. Pete Beach area on the south end of the strip, then the mostly residential Indian Rocks Beach area, then the relatively quiet but still busy Clearwater Beach at the north.

ST. PETE BEACH AREA
Very Expensive

✪ **Don CeSar Beach Resort and Spa.** 3400 Gulf Blvd. (at 34th Ave./Pinellas Byway), St. Pete Beach, FL 33706. ☎ **800/282-1116,** 800/637-7200, or 727/360-1881. Fax 727/367-6952. www.media.don-cesar.com. 345 units. A/C MINIBAR TV TEL. Winter $289–$369 double; $359–$784 suite. Off-season $184–$314 double; $244–$709 suite. Packages available. AE, DC, MC, V. Parking $10.

Dating from 1928 and listed on the National Register of Historic Places, this Moorish-style "Pink Palace" tropical getaway is so romantic you may bump into six or seven honeymooning couples in one weekend. Sitting majestically on 7½ acres of beachfront, the landmark sports a lobby of classic high windows and archways, crystal chandeliers, marble floors, and original artworks. Most rooms have high ceilings and offer views of the gulf or Boca Ciega Bay. In addition to the 275 rooms under the minarets of the original building (some of these may seem rather small by today's standards), the resort has 70 spacious luxury condos in The Don CeSar Beach House, a mid-rise building three-quarters of a mile to the north (there's complimentary transportation between the two). The service is good, although the front desk can get a bit overwhelmed when groups are checking in.

Dining/Diversions: The pricey but intimate Maritana Grille can't be beat for fresh gourmet seafood and caviar, if your budget can afford a serious splurge. Other outlets include the King Charles Restaurant (offering a sumptuous Sun brunch), the Sea Porch Cafe for indoor or outdoor dining by the pool and beach, the Lobby Bar, two beachside bars, and an ice-cream parlor.

Amenities: Concierge, 24-hour room service, valet parking, laundry, newspaper delivery, in-room massage, business services, complimentary coffee in lobby, babysitting, children's program. Beach, two outdoor heated swimming pools, whirlpool, exercise room, sauna, steam room, volleyball, gift shops, rentals for water-sports equipment, hairdresser, shopping arcade with upscale jewelers and men's and women's resort wear.

Expensive

✪ **TradeWinds Resort.** 5500 Gulf Blvd. (at 55th Ave.), St. Pete Beach, FL 33706. ☎ **800/237-0707** or 727/562-1212. Fax 727/562-1222. 577 units. A/C TV TEL. Winter $199–$309 double, $295–$569 suite. Off-season $140–$221 double, $185–$399 suite. Packages available. AE, DC, DISC, MC, V. Valet parking $3–$6; free self-parking.

Don't be dismayed by the outward appearance of this six- and seven-story, concrete-and-steel monstrosity, for underneath and beside it runs a maze of brick walkways, patios, and lily ponds connected by a quarter mile of streams. It all gives surprising charm to this employee-owned hotel. The guest units, which look out on the gulf or the 18 acres of grounds, have up-to-date kitchens or kitchenettes, contemporary furnishings, and private balconies. The children's program and summer packages are a big hit with families from around the world, attracting lots of Europeans.

Dining/Diversions: The top spot for lunch or dinner is the Palm Court, with an Italian-bistro atmosphere; for dinner, there's also Bermudas, a casual family spot. Other food outlets include the Fountain Square Deli, Pizza Hut, and Tropic Treats. Bars include Reflections piano lounge; B.R. Cuda's, with live entertainment and dancing; and the Flying Bridge, a Florida cracker-house–style beachside bar floating on one of the lily ponds.

Amenities: With the employees having a stake in the profits as well as the tips, you should get good service here. Room service, valet parking, laundry, baby-sitting, children's program. Four heated swimming pools, whirlpools, sauna, fitness center, four tennis courts, racquetball, croquet, water-sports rentals, gas grills, guest laundry, gift shops, full-service hair salon with massage and tanning.

TradeWinds Sandpiper Beach Resort. 6000 Gulf Blvd. (at 60th Ave.), St. Pete Beach, FL 33706. ☎ **800/237-0707** or 727/562-1212. Fax 727/562-1222. 159 units. A/C TV TEL. Winter $155–$207 double; $235–$299 suite. Off-season $115–$147 double; $157–$199 suite. Packages available. AE, DC, DISC, MC, V.

Right on the beach, this employee-owned sister of the TradeWinds Resort (see above) has two six-story chevron-shaped wings, both set back from the main road. The beach wing is more expensive but much more desirable. Decorated with light woods, pastel tones, and touches of rattan, most units here have coffeemakers, toasters, small refrigerators, dishwashers, and wet bars. Suites also have a living area with sofa bed. But note: None of the units here has a patio or balcony.

Dining: Piper's Patio is a casual poolside cafe with indoor/outdoor seating, and the Sand Bar offers frozen drinks, snacks, and fine sunsets by the pool.

Amenities: Concierge, room service, valet laundry, newspaper delivery, in-room massage, children's activities program, baby-sitting, beachfront heated swimming pool, another heated swimming pool in its own greenhouse, fitness center, volleyball, shuffleboard, game room, gift shop/general store.

Moderate

Days Inn Island Beach Resort. 6200 Gulf Blvd. (at 62nd Ave.), St. Pete Beach, FL 33706. ☎ **800/544-4222** or 727/367-1902. Fax 727/367-4422. 102 units. A/C TV TEL. Winter $118–$148 double. Off-season $78–$108 double. AE, DC, DISC, MC, V.

Two long, gray buildings flank a courtyard with heated swimming pool at this beachside property popular with young families. Furnished in dark woods and rich tones, most of the guest rooms have picture-window views of the courtyard. All units have refrigerators and coffeemakers, and about half have kitchenettes. Inside the building, Players Bar & Grille has sports TVs, pizzas, pub fare, and free hot snacks from noon to 7pm daily. Outside, Jimmy B.'s beach bar is a fine place for a sunset cocktail (happy hour runs from noon to 7:30pm) and evening entertainment, including beachside bonfires on Saturdays in winter. Facilities include two outdoor heated swimming pools, volleyball, horseshoes, shuffleboard, and a game room.

Travelodge St. Pete Beach. 6300 Gulf Blvd. (at 63rd Ave.), St. Pete Beach, FL 33706. ☎ **800/237-8918** or 727/367-2711. Fax 727/367-7068. 200 units. A/C TV TEL. Winter $99–$131 double. Off-season $75–$119 double. Efficiencies $10 more. AE, DC, DISC, MC, V.

Until recently the Colonial Gateway Inn, this U-shaped beachfront complex of one- and two-story units is a favorite with families. The rooms, most of which face the pool and a central landscaped courtyard, are contemporary, with light woods and beach tones. About half the units are efficiencies with kitchenettes.

On the premises is a branch of the very good Shells seafood restaurant (see "Where to Dine," in section 1). An indoor lounge and a beach bar offer light refreshments. Facilities include an outdoor heated swimming pool with an expansive concrete deck, a kiddie pool, shuffleboard, and a game room. The water-sports shack here offers para-sailing equipment rentals and also services the Days Inn Island Beach Resort next door (see below).

Inexpensive

✪ **Beach Haven.** 4980 Gulf Blvd. (at 50th Ave.), St. Pete Beach, FL 33706. ☎ **727/ 367-8642.** Fax 727/360-8202. E-mail: jzpag@aol.com. 18 units. A/C TV TEL. Winter $75–$125 double. Off-season $50–$108 double. MC, V.

Nestled on the beach between two high-rise condos, these low-slung, pink-with-white-trim structures look from the outside like the early 1950s motel they once were. But Jone and Millard Gamble (they also own the charming Island's End Resort, below) have replaced the innards and installed bright tile floors, vertical blinds, pastel tropical furniture, and many modern amenities, including TVs, VCRs, refrigerators, and coffeemakers. Five of the original quarters remain as motel rooms (with shower-only bathrooms), but the Gambles linked the others to make 12 one-bedroom units and one two-bedroom unit. The top choice is the one-bedroom unit with sliding glass doors opening to a deck shaded by a sprawling Brazilian pepper tree. There's an outdoor heated pool surrounded by a white picket fence, plus a sunning deck with lounge furniture by the beach. You don't get maid service on Sunday or holidays, and the rooms and baths are 1950s smallish; but every unit here is bright, airy, and comfortable. Complimentary coffee and tea are served to all guests 2 days a week, and guests can use barbecue grills and a coin laundry. This is the heart of the hotel district, so lots of restaurants are just steps away.

Captain's Quarters Inn. 10035 Gulf Blvd. (between 100th and 101st aves.), Treasure Island, FL 33706. ☎ **800/526-9547** or 727/360-1659. Fax 727/363-3074. 8 units, 1 cottage. A/C TV TEL. Winter $70–$100 double. Off-season $55–$75 double. Weekly rates available. MC, V. Pets accepted at extra charge.

Purchased in 1998 by Britishers Nick and Deborah Russell, this nautically themed property offers well-kept accommodations on the gulf at inland rates. All but one of the units are huddled along 100 yards of beach, an ideal vantage point for sunset watching. Six units are efficiencies (two of them on the beach) with minikitchens, including microwave oven, coffeemaker, and wet bar or sink. There's also a bayside cottage with a separate bedroom and a full kitchen. Facilities include an outdoor solar-heated freshwater swimming pool, a sundeck, guest barbecues, and a library.

✪ **Island's End Resort.** 1 Pass-a-Grille Way (at 1st Ave.), St. Pete Beach, FL 33706. ☎ **727/ 360-5023.** Fax 727/367-7890. www.stpetebeach.com/islandsend. E-mail: jzgpag@aol.com. 6 units. A/C TV TEL. Dec 15 to June 1 $82–$175 cottage. Off-season $61–$175 cottage. Weekly rates available. MC, V.

A wonderful respite from the madding crowd, and a great bargain to boot, this little all-cottage hideaway sits right on the southern tip of St. Pete Beach, smack-dab on Pass-a-Grille, where the Gulf of Mexico meets Tampa Bay. You can step from the six contemporary cottages right onto the beach. And since the island curves sharply here, nothing blocks your view of the emerald bay. Strong currents run through the pass, however, but you can safely swim in the gulf or grab a brilliant sunset at the Pass-a-Grille public beach, just one door removed. Linked to each other by boardwalks, the comfortable one- or three-bedroom cottages have dining areas, living rooms, VCRs, and kitchens; the one three-bedroom unit also has its own private beachside pool. You can meet your fellow guests at complimentary continental breakfasts served under a gazebo Tuesday, Thursday, and Saturday mornings (you can squeeze your own oranges). Facilities include a fishing dock, patios, decks, barbecues, and hammocks. Owners Jone and Millard Gamble are no fools: They live at this shady, idyllic setting.

INDIAN ROCKS BEACH AREA

Great Heron Inn. 68 Gulf Blvd. (south of 1st Ave.), Indian Rocks Beach, FL 33785. ☎ **727/ 595-2589.** Fax 727/596-7309. www.llc.net/~heroninn. E-mail: heroninn@llc.net. 16 units. A/C TV TEL. Winter $85–$88 double. Off-season $59–$63 double. Weekly and monthly rates available. DISC, MC, V. Hotel is 4 blocks south of Fla. 688.

A real heron named Harry patrols the beach at this family-oriented motel owned and operated by transplanted Michiganders Ralph and Teena Hickerson. It sits at the narrowest section of Indian Rocks Beach, facing the gulf on one side and its own Intracoastal Waterway dock on the other. The buildings flank a central courtyard, with a heated pool, which opens to the beach. The rooms offer modern furnishings and Berber carpets, and each unit has a full kitchen and dining area. Facilities include coin-operated laundry and picnic tables. There's a boat dock across the boulevard.

○ **Pelican—East & West.** 108 21st Ave. (at Gulf Blvd.), Indian Rocks Beach, FL 33785. ☎ **727/595-9741.** Fax 727/596-4170. 8 units. A/C TV. Winter $50–$75 double. Off-season $45–$65 double. Weekly rates available. MC, V.

"PDIP" (Perfect Day in Paradise) is the motto at Mike and Carol McGlaughlin's motel complex, which offers a choice of two settings. Their lowest rates are at Pelican East, in a residential setting 500 feet from the beach, where four suites each have a bedroom and a separate kitchen. You'll pay more at Pelican West, but it's directly on the beach-front. The four beachside apartments each have a living room, a bedroom, a kitchen, a patio, and unbeatable views of the gulf. You don't get phones in your rooms here or a swimming pool to splash around in, but it's clean and modern in all other respects. There's no restaurant on the premises, either, but Guppy's is 4 blocks away (see "Where to Dine," below).

CLEARWATER BEACH
Expensive

○ **Radisson Suite Resort on Sand Key.** 1201 Gulf Blvd., Clearwater Beach, FL 33767. ☎ **800/333-3333** or 727/596-1100. Fax 727/595-4292. 220 units. A/C MINIBAR TV TEL. $239–$289 suite. AE, DC, DISC, MC, V.

You'll see the beauty of Sand Key from the suites in this boomerang-shaped, 10-story hotel overlooking Clearwater Bay. The gulf is just beyond a row of high-rise condos across the street, and beautiful Sand Key Park is a few steps away. The whole family will enjoy exploring the adjacent boardwalk with 25 shops and restaurants. Each suite has a bedroom with a balcony offering water views, as well as a complete living room with a sofa bed, a wet bar, an entertainment unit, a coffeemaker, and a microwave oven. Like the Sheraton Sand Key across the boulevard (see below), this Radisson gets many European guests during the summer months, so there's negligible fluctuation in room rates during the year.

Dining/Diversions: The Harbor Grille offers fresh seafood, steaks, and grand bay views. The Harbor Lounge has live entertainment. In a clapboard, shingle-roof building out by the pool, Kokomo's serves light fare and tropical drinks.

Amenities: Room service, laundry, free trolley to the beach, year-round children's activities program at "Lisa's Klubhouse," free valet parking, masseuse. Bayside outdoor heated swimming pool with rock waterfall and bar, sundeck, sauna, exercise room, guest laundry, waterfront boardwalk with a variety of shops and restaurants.

Moderate

Best Western Sea Stone Resort. 445 Hamden Dr. (at Coronado Dr.), Clearwater Beach, FL 33767. ☎ **800/444-1919,** 800/528-1234, or 727/441-1722. Fax 727/449-1580. 106 units. A/C TV TEL. Winter $103–$201 double. Off-season $72–$140 double. AE, DC, DISC, MC, V.

Located just across the street from the beach in Clearwater's busy south end, the Sea Stone Suites is a six-story building of classic Key West–style architecture containing 43 one-bedroom suites, each with a kitchenette and a living room. Their living-room windows look across external walkways to the harbor. A few steps away, the older five-story Gulfview Wing offers 65 bedrooms. The furnishings are bright and airy, with pastel tones, light woods, and sea scenes on the walls. The on-site Marker 5 Restaurant serves breakfast only. There are valet laundry service, newspaper delivery, and complimentary coffee in the lobby. Facilities include a heated outdoor swimming pool, a whirlpool, a boat dock, a coin-operated laundry, and meeting rooms.

✪ Clearwater Beach Hotel. 500 Mandalay Ave. (at Baymont St.), Clearwater Beach, FL 33767. ☎ **800/292-2295** or 727/441-2425. Fax 727/449-2083. 157 units. A/C TV TEL. Winter $109–$249 double. Off-season $98–$118 double. AE, DC, MC, V.

Besides the great beach location, you'll enjoy easy access to many nearby shops and restaurants from this Old Florida–style hotel. It's been owned and operated by the same family for more than 40 years, and it attracts an older clientele. Directly on the gulf, the complex consists of a six-story main building and two- and three-story wings. Rooms and rates vary according to location—bay view or gulf view, poolside or beachfront. Some rooms have balconies. The dining room is romantic at sunset and offers great views of the gulf, while the nautically themed lounge has entertainment nightly. A bar provides snacks and libations beside an outdoor heated swimming pool. There are limited room service, valet laundry and parking, newspaper delivery, and in-room massage.

Palm Pavilion Inn. 18 Bay Esplanade (at Mandalay Ave.), Clearwater Beach, FL 33767. ☎ **800/433-PALM** or 727/446-6777. 28 units. A/C TV TEL. Winter $82–$117 double. Off-season $56–$81 double. AE, DISC, MC, V.

Just north of the tourist area, this three-story walk-up beachfront spot is removed from the bustle yet within easy walking distance of all the action. The three-story art deco building is artfully trimmed in peach and teal. The lobby area and guest rooms, also art deco in design, feature rounded light-wood and rattan furnishings, bright sea-toned fabrics, photographs from the 1920s to 1950s era, and vertical blinds. Entered from internal corridors (no balconies or patios here), rooms in the west side of the house face the gulf, while those in the east face the bay. Four efficiencies have kitchenettes. Facilities include a rooftop sundeck, beach access, a heated swimming pool, complimentary coffee, and beach chair and umbrella rentals. By the beach, the Palm Pavillion Grill & Bar is a fine place to catch the sunset and some live entertainment Tuesday to Sunday nights during winter, on weekends off-season. Lighted tennis courts and an athletic center are across the street.

Sheraton Sand Key Resort. 1160 Gulf Blvd., Clearwater Beach, FL 33767. ☎ **800/325-3535** or 727/595-1611. Fax 727/596-8488. 390 units. A/C TV TEL. Winter $170–$220 double. Off-season $109–$170 double. AE, DC, DISC, MC, V.

Away from the honky-tonk of Clearwater, this nine-story hotel on 10 acres next to Sand Key Park is a big favorite with water-sports enthusiasts and groups. It also gets lots of

European guests year-round. The guest rooms here all have dark-wood furniture, coffeemakers, hair dryers, and a balcony or patio with views of the gulf or the bay.

Rusty's Restaurant serves breakfast and dinner; for lighter fare, try the Island Café, the Sundeck, or Fast Johnny's Poolside Snack Bar. The Snack Store is open 24 hours.

Amenities include limited room service, newspaper delivery, in-room massage, valet parking and laundry, baby-sitting, children's program (summer only), beachside outdoor heated swimming pool, fitness center, whirlpool, three lighted tennis courts, beach volleyball, newsstand, game room, children's pool, playground, water-sports rentals, 24-hour general store.

Inexpensive

✪ **Sun West Beach Motel.** 409 Hamden Dr. (at Bayside Dr.), Clearwater Beach, FL 33767. ☎ **727/442-5008.** Fax 727/461-1395. www.clearwaterbeach.com/SUNWEST/sunwest. E-mail: sunwest@gte.net. 14 units. A/C TV TEL. $40–$61 double; $48–$79 efficiency. MC, V.

Sitting among several small motels a 2-block walk from the beach, John and Pat Joniec's one-story establishment dates from 1954, but it's well-maintained, overlooks the bay, and has a fishing/boating dock, a heated bayside pool and sundeck, a shuffleboard court, and a guest laundry. All units, which face the bay, the pool, or the sundeck, have contemporary resort-style furnishings. The four motel rooms have small refrigerators, the 10 efficiencies have kitchens, and a few units have separate bedrooms.

TWO NEARBY GOLF RESORTS

Belleview Biltmore Resort & Spa. 25 Belleview Blvd. (P.O. Box 2317), Clearwater, FL 33757. ☎ **800/237-8947** or 727/442-6171. Fax 727/441-4173 or 727/443-6361. 240 units. A/C MINIBAR TV TEL. Winter $190–$210 double; $260–$450 suite. Off-season $150–$190 double; $220–$430 suite. AE, DC, DISC, MC, V. Resort is 1 mile south of downtown on Belleview Rd., off Alt. U.S. 19.

The Gulf Coast's oldest operating luxury tourist hotel, this gabled clapboard structure was built in 1896 by Henry B. Plant as the Hotel Belleview to attract customers to his Orange Belt Railroad. On a bluff overlooking the bay, it's the largest occupied wooden structure in the world. Today it attracts mostly groups and serious golfers (guests can play at the adjoining Belleview Country Club, an 18-hole, par-72 championship course), but there's no denying its Victorian charm and old-fashioned ambience— once you get past the out-of-place, glass-and-steel foyer added by more recent owners. Historic tours are given daily at 11am ($5 for adults, $3 for children 13 to 17, free for kids under 17). The creaky hallways lead to several shops and a museum explaining the hotel's history. Large, high-ceilinged guest rooms are decorated in Queen Anne style, with dark-wood period furniture.

Dining/Diversions: The informal indoor/outdoor Terrace Café provides breakfast, lunch, or dinner. There are also a pub in the basement, a lounge, and a poolside bar.

Amenities: Room service, dry cleaning and valet laundry, nightly turndown on request, currency exchange, baby-sitting. Four red-clay tennis courts; indoor and outdoor heated swimming pools (one with a waterfall); whirlpool; spa with sauna, Swiss showers, workout gym; jogging and walking trails; bicycle rentals; yacht charters; gift shops; newsstand; golf privileges at the country club.

✪ **The Westin Innisbrook Resort.** 36750 U.S. 19 (P.O. Box 1088), Tarpon Springs, FL 34688. ☎ **800/456-2000** or 727/942-2000. Fax 727/942-5577. 900 units. Winter $260–$585 double. Off-season $190–$340 double. Golf packages available. AE, DC, DISC, MC, V.

Golf Digest, Golf magazine, and others pick this as one of the country's best places to play (provided you stay here, of course). Situated off U.S. 19 between Palm Harbor and Tarpon Springs, this 1,000-acre resort has 90 holes on championship courses that are more like the rolling links of the Carolinas than the usually flat courses found in Florida. The most famous course, the Copperhead, hosts the JCPenney Classic, a major stop on the PGA circuit, the first weekend in December. Innisbrook has the largest resort-owned and -operated golf school in North America. The resort also boasts 11 clay and 4 Laykold tennis courts. There's even a children's program to take care of the kids. The spacious quarters actually are privately owned homes and apartments spread all over the premises, so there are no focal points here except the building where you check in and the golf and tennis clubhouses.

WHERE TO DINE

St. Pete Beach and Clearwater Beach both have a wide selection of national chain fast-food and family restaurants along their main drags.

As with the accommodations above, I have grouped the restaurants by geographic area: St. Pete Beach, including Pass-a-Grille; Indian Rocks Beach, including Madeira Beach, Redington Beach, North Redington Beach, Redington Shores, and Indian Shores; and finally, Clearwater Beach.

ST. PETE BEACH AREA

✪ **Crabby Bill's.** 5100 Gulf Blvd. (at 51st Ave.), St. Pete Beach. ☎ **727/360-8858.** Reservations not accepted. Sandwiches $4–$6; main courses $6–$18. AE, MC, V. Mon–Thurs 11:30am–10pm, Fri–Sat 11:30am–11pm, Sun noon–10pm. SEAFOOD.

The least expensive gulfside dining here, this member of a small local chain sits right on the beach in the heart of the hotel district. It's a great place to bring the kids, especially after 5:30pm Tuesday, when they eat free and are entertained by games and contests. There are a rooftop tiki bar and a small alfresco area off one of the two bars here, but big glass windows enclose the large dining room. They offer fine water views from picnic tables equipped with rolls of paper towels and buckets of saltine crackers, the better to eat the Alaskan, snow, golden, and stone crabs that are the big draws here. The crustaceans fall into the moderate price category, but most other main courses, such as fried clam strips or a combo broiled fish platter, are inexpensive. The creamy smoked fish spread is a delicious appetizer, and you'll get enough to whet the appetites of at least two persons for just $4.

Hurricane. 807 Gulf Way (at 9th Ave.), Pass-a-Grille. ☎ **727/360-9558.** Reservations not accepted. Salads and sandwiches $2.50–$9; main courses $8–$16. AE, MC, V. Daily 8am–1am (breakfast Mon–Fri 8–11am, Sat–Sun 8am–noon). SEAFOOD.

A longtime institution across the street from Pass-a-Grille Public Beach, this three-level gray Victorian building with white gingerbread trim is a great place to toast the sunset, especially on the rooftop. It's more beach bar than fine restaurant, but the grouper sandwiches are a big hit, and there's always fresh fish to be broiled or fried and shrimp and crab to be steamed. Downstairs you can dine inside the knotty-pine paneled dining room or on the sidewalk terrace, where bathers from across Gulf Way are welcome (there's a walk-up bar for beach libation). The second-floor dining area also has seating on a wraparound veranda, and up on the roof, the Hurricane Watch adds great sunset views. The joint jumps at night when the second level turns into a virtual dance hall.

Internet Outpost Cafe. 7400 Gulf Blvd. (at Corey Ave./75th Ave.), St. Pete Beach. ☎ **727/360-7806.** Reservations not accepted. Coffee and pastries $1–$3; sandwiches $3.50–$5.50. AE, MC, V. Mon–Thurs 10am–10pm, Fri–Sat 10am–midnight. PASTRIES/SANDWICHES.

If you left your laptop at home and can't stand not getting your e-mail or surfing the Net any longer, head for this cozy coffee emporium with nine computer terminals, all with fast connections to the Internet ($2 for 15 minutes' access time). You can also lounge on the sofas and wing chairs while sipping your caffeine, kill a rainy afternoon playing chess, or listen to live music on Friday and Saturday evenings. In addition to coffees, teas, and pastries available all hours, the lunch fare (11am to 2pm) includes freshly made chicken salad, as well as Cuban, spicy turkey, and other sandwiches.

Skidder's Restaurant. 5799 Gulf Blvd. (at 60th Ave.), St. Pete Beach. ☎ **727/360-1029.** Reservations not accepted. Breakfast $3–$6; sandwiches and burgers $3.50–$8; pizza $5.50–$16; main courses $7.50–$15. AE, DC, DISC, MC, V. Daily 7am–11pm. ITALIAN/GREEK/AMERICAN.

A local favorite, this inexpensive family restaurant in the hotel district offers a full range of breakfast fare plus pizzas (available to eat here or carry out), burgers and sandwiches, big salads, gyro and souvlaki platters, and Italian-style veal and chicken dishes (sautéed in wine with artichokes is a house specialty). Divided by cut-glass panels, the dining room has ceiling fans rotating over gray tables and booths. A children's menu features burgers and spaghetti.

INDIAN ROCKS BEACH AREA

You'll find a bayfront edition of **Shells,** the fine and inexpensive local seafood chain, opposite the Lobster Pot on Gulf Boulevard at 178th Avenue in Redington Shores (☎ **813/393-8990**). See "Where to Dine," in section 1, for more information about Shells's menu and prices, which are the same at all branches.

✪ Guppy's. 1701 Gulf Blvd. (at 17th Ave.), Indian Rocks Beach. ☎ **813/593-2032.** Reservations not accepted. Sandwiches $5–$7; main courses $9–$20. AE, DC, DISC, MC, V. Sun–Thurs 11:30am–10:30pm; Fri–Sat 11:30am–11pm. SEAFOOD.

Locals love this small bar and grill across from Indian Rocks Public Beach because they know they'll always get terrific chow (it's associated with the excellent Lobster Pot, mentioned below). You won't soon forget the salmon coated with potatoes and lightly fried to brown, then baked with a creamy leek and garlic sauce; it's fattening, yes, but also a bargain at $9. Another good choice is lightly cooked tuna (only slightly more done than sushi) finished with a peppercorn sauce. The atmosphere is casual beach friendly, with a fun bar in the rear. Scotty's famous upside-down apple-walnut pie topped with ice cream will require a little extra work on the weights tomorrow. You can dine outside on a patio beside the main road.

✪ Lobster Pot. 17814 Gulf Blvd. (at 178th Ave.), Redington Shores. ☎ **727/391-8592.** www.beachdirectory.com. Reservations recommended. Main courses $14.50–$29.50. AE, DC, MC, V. Mon–Thurs 4:30–10pm, Fri–Sat 4:30–11pm, Sun 4–10pm. SEAFOOD.

Step into this weathered-looking, very traditional restaurant near the beach, and owner Eugen Fuhrmann will tell you to get ready to experience the finest seafood in the area. The prices are high, but the variety of lobster (of the Maine variety) dishes is amazing. The lobster américaine is flambéed in brandy with garlic, and the bouillabaisse is as authentic as any you'd find in the south of France. In addition to lobster, there's a wide selection of grouper, snapper, salmon, swordfish, shrimp, scallops, crab, and Dover sole, prepared simply or with elaborate sauces. There's no ordinary children's menu here: It features half a Maine lobster and a petite filet mignon.

Scandia. 19829 Gulf Blvd. (between 198th and 199th aves.), Indian Shores. ☎ **727/595-5525.** Reservations accepted. Main courses $6–$20. Early-bird specials $6–$8. DISC, MC, V. Tues–Sat 11:30am–9pm, Sun noon–8pm. Early-bird specials Mon–Fri 4–6pm. Closed Sept. SCANDINAVIAN.

Unique in decor and menu in these parts, this chalet-style restaurant in the northern fringes of Indian Shores brings a touch of Hans Christian Andersen to the beach strip.

The menu offers Scandinavian favorites, from smoked salmon and pickled herring to roast pork, sausages, schnitzels, and Danish lobster tails. There are also a few international dishes such as curried chicken, North Sea flounder, Canadian scallops, Boston scrod, and shrimp and grouper from gulf waters.

○ **Wine Cellar.** 17307 Gulf Blvd. (at 173rd Ave.), North Redington Beach. ☎ **727/393-3491.** Reservations recommended. Main courses $15–$26. Five-course sampler $35. AE, DC, MC, V. Tues–Sat 4:30–11pm, Sun 4–11pm. CONTINENTAL.

Every evening during the high season and on weekends all year, the cars pack the parking lot at this restaurant, which is highly popular with locals and visitors alike. You'll find an assortment of divided dining rooms with lots of wine racks and casks. The cuisine offers the best of Europe and the States. Start off with garlicky peppered shrimp in dry vermouth, move on to a fresh North Carolina rainbow trout in butter and pecans, and top it all off with chocolate velvet torte. There's music and dancing in the lounge on Thursday, Friday, and Saturday evenings, and jazz on Sunday.

CLEARWATER BEACH

○ **Bob Heilman's Beachcomber.** 447 Mandalay Ave. (at Papaya St.). ☎ **727/442-4144.** Reservations recommended. Main courses $12–$27. AE, DC, DISC, MC, V. Mon–Sat 11:30am–11pm, Sun noon–10pm. AMERICAN.

In a row of restaurants, bars, and T-shirt shops, Bob and Sherri Heilman's establishment has been popular with the locals since 1948. Each dining room here has its own special theme: large model sailing crafts making one seem nautical, a pianist making music in a second, works of art creating a gallery in a third, and booths and a fireplace making for a cozy fourth. The menu presents a variety of fresh seafood, beef, veal, and lamb selections. If you tire of fruits-of-the-sea, the "back to the farm" fried chicken—from an original 1910 Heilman family recipe—is incredible. The Beachcomber shares an extensive wine collection with Bobby's Bistro & Wine Bar (see below).

Bobby's Bistro & Wine Bar. 447 Mandalay Ave. (at Papaya St., behind Bob Heilman's Beachcomber). ☎ **727/446-9463.** Reservations not accepted. Sandwiches and pizzas $6–$10; main courses $10–$16. AE, DC, DISC, MC, V. Daily 5pm–midnight. AMERICAN.

Bob and Sherri Heilman opened this dark, very urban bistro behind their popular restaurant in 1993, and it's been a local hit ever since. The wine-cellar theme is amply justified by the real thing: a walk-in closet with several thousand bottles kept at a constant 55°F. Walk through and pick your vintage, then listen to jazz while you dine inside at tall, bar-height tables or outside on a covered patio. The chef specializes in gourmet pizzas on homemade focaccia crust (as a tasty appetizer), plus charcoal-grilled veal chops, filet mignon, fresh fish, and monstrous pork chops with caramelized Granny Smith apples and a Mount Vernon mustard sauce. Everything's served à la carte here, so watch your credit card. On the other hand, there's an affordable sandwich menu featuring the likes of bronzed grouper and chicken with a spicy Jack cheese.

Frenchy's Cafe. 41 Baymont St. ☎ **727/446-3607.** Reservations not accepted. Sandwiches and burgers $4–$7. AE, MC, V. Mon–Thurs 11:30am–11pm, Fri–Sat 11:30am–midnight, Sun noon–11pm. SEAFOOD.

Always popular with locals and visitors in the know, this casual pub makes the best grouper sandwiches in the area and has all the awards to prove it. They're fresh, thick, juicy, and delicious. The atmosphere is pure Florida casual style, and there's usually a wait during winter, on weekends all year.

For more casual fare directly on the beach, **Frenchy's Rockaway Grill,** at 7 Rockaway St. (☎ **727/446-4844**), has a wonderful outdoor setting.

⚪ **Seafood & Sunsets at Julie's.** 351 S. Gulfview Blvd. (at 5th St.), Clearwater Beach. ☎ **727/441-2548.** Reservations not accepted. Salads and sandwiches $5–$8; main courses $8–$22. AE, MC, V. Daily 11am–10pm. SEAFOOD.

A Key West–style tradition takes over Julie Nichols's place at dusk as both locals and visitors gather at sidewalk tables or in the tiny, rustic upstairs bar to toast the sunset over the beach across the street. The predominantly seafood menu features fine renditions of charcoal-broiled mahimahi with sour cream, parmesan, and herb sauce; bacon-wrapped barbecued shrimp on a skewer; broiled, fried, or blackened fresh Florida grouper; and flounder stuffed with crabmeat. Everything is cooked to order here, so come prepared to linger over a cold drink.

THE BEACHES AFTER DARK

If you haven't already found it during your sightseeing and shopping excursions, the restored fishing community of **John's Pass Village and Boardwalk,** on Gulf Boulevard at John's Pass in Madeira Beach, has plenty of restaurants, bars, and shops to keep you occupied after the sun sets. Elsewhere, the nightlife scene at the beach revolves around rocking bars that pump out the music until 2am.

Down south in Pass-a-Grille, there's the popular, always lively lounge in **Hurricane,** on Gulf Way at 9th Avenue opposite the public beach (see "Where to Dine," above).

On Treasure Island, **Beach Nutts,** on West Gulf Boulevard at 96th Avenue (☎ 727/367-7427), is perched atop a stilt foundation like a wooden beach cottage on the Gulf of Mexico. The music ranges from Top 40 to reggae and rock. **Manhattans,** Gulf Boulevard at 116th Avenue (☎ **727/363-1500**), offers a variety of live music, from country to contemporary and classic rock. Up on the northern tip of Treasure Island, **Gators on the Pass** (☎ 727/367-8951) claims to have the world's longest waterfront bar, with a huge deck overlooking the waters of John's Pass. The complex also includes a no-smoking sports bar and a three-story tower with a top-level observation deck for panoramic views of the Gulf of Mexico. There's live music, from acoustic and blues to rock, most nights.

In Clearwater Beach, the **Palm Pavilion Grill & Bar,** on the beach at 18 Bay Esplanade (☎ 727/446-6777), has live music Tuesday through Sunday nights during winter, on weekends off-season. Nearby, **Frenchy's Rockaway Grill,** at 7 Rockaway St. (☎ 727/446-4844), is another popular hangout.

If you're into laughs, **Coconuts Comedy Club,** at the Howard Johnson motel, Gulf Boulevard at 61st Avenue in St. Pete Beach (☎ 727/360-5653), has an ever-changing program of live stand-up funny men and women. Call for the schedule, performers, and prices.

For a more highbrow evening, go to the Clearwater mainland and the 2,200-seat **Ruth Eckerd Hall,** 1111 McMullen-Booth Rd. (☎ 727/791-7400), which hosts a varied program of Broadway shows, ballet, drama, symphonic works, popular music, jazz, and country music.

4 An Excursion to Tarpon Springs

30 miles N of St. Petersburg, 23 miles W of Tampa, 13 miles N of Clearwater

One of Florida's most fascinating small towns and a fine day trip from Tampa, St. Petersburg, or the beaches, Tarpon Springs calls itself the "Sponge Capital of the World." That's because Greek immigrants from the Dodecanese Islands settled here in the late 19th century to harvest sponges, which grew in abundance offshore. By the 1930s, Tarpon Springs was producing more sponges than any other place in the world. A blight ruined the business in the 1940s, but the descendants of those early immigrants stayed on. Today they compose about a third of the population, making Tarpon Springs a center of transplanted Greek culture.

Although sponges still arrive at the historic Sponge Docks on Dodecanese Boulevard, the town's mainstays today are commercial fishing and tourism. With a lively, carnival-like atmosphere, the docks are a great place to spend an afternoon or early evening, poking your head into shops selling sponges and other souvenirs while Greek music comes from the dozen or so family restaurants purveying authentic Aegean cuisine. You can also venture offshore from here, for booths on the docks hawk sightseeing and fishing cruises.

Just south of the docks, restored Victorian homes facing the winding creek known as Spring Bayou make this one of the most picturesque towns in the state.

ESSENTIALS

GETTING THERE   From Tampa or St. Petersburg, take U.S. 19 north and turn left on Tarpon Avenue (County Road 582). From Clearwater Beach, take Alt. U.S. 19 north through Dunedin. The center of the historic downtown district is at the intersection of Pinellas Avenue (Alt. U.S. 19) and Tarpon Avenue. To reach the Sponge Docks, go 10 blocks north on Pinellas Avenue and turn left at Pappas' Restaurant onto Dodecanese Boulevard.

VISITOR INFORMATION   The **Tarpon Springs Chamber of Commerce,** 11 E. Orange St., Tarpon Springs, FL 34689 (☎ **727/937-6109;** fax 727/937-6100; www.tarponsprings.com), has an information office on Dodecanese Boulevard at the Spong Docks. Open Tuesday to Saturday from 10:30am to 4:30pm, Sunday from 11am to 5pm.

EXPLORING THE TOWN

Two areas are worth visiting here. You'll first come to the **Tarpon Springs Downtown Historic District,** with its turn-of-the-century commercial buildings along Tarpon Avenue and Pinellas Avenue (Alt. U.S. 19). The **Tarpon Springs Cultural Center,** on Pinellas Avenue a block south of Tarpon Avenue, explains the town's history and has visitor information. On Tarpon Avenue west of Pinellas Avenue, you'll come to the Victorian homes overlooking **Spring Bayou.** This creekside area makes for a delightfully picturesque stroll.

The carnival-like **Sponge Docks** run alongside Dodecanese Boulevard, which is peppered with shops, restaurants, and fishing and sightseeing boats pulling at their mooring lines along the riverside boardwalk. Poke your head into the tin-roofed **Spongeorama** (☎ 727/943-9509), a museum dedicated to sponges and sponge divers. You can buy a wide variety of sponges here (they'll ship them home) and watch a 30-minute video about sponge diving several times a day. Admission is free. The Spongeorama is open daily from 10am to 5pm. In the **Coral Sea Aquarium,** at the western end of the boulevard (☎ 727/938-5378), a scuba diver feeds sharks at 11:30am and 1, 2:30, and 4pm. The aquarium is open daily from 10am to 5pm. Admission is $4.75 adults, $4 seniors, $2.75 for children 3 to 11, free for kids under 3.

You also can go on sightseeing, lunch, or sunset cruises down the Anclote River with **Island Cruises** (☎ 727/934-0606); spend 30 minutes watching the sponge divers at work with **St. Nicolas Boat Line** (☎ 727/942-6425); or try your luck in the gulf on a party boat operated by **Dolphin Deep Sea Fishing** (☎ 727/937-8257). Booths along the docks sell tickets for these and other excursions. Make your reservations as soon as you get here, and then go sightseeing ashore while you wait for the next boat to shove off.

Bikers, in-line skaters, hikers, and joggers can come right through downtown on the **Pinellas Trail,** which runs along Safford Avenue and crosses Tarpon Avenue 2 blocks east of Pinellas Avenue (see "Outdoor Activities & Spectator Sports" in section 2, above).

WHERE TO DINE

Your Tarpon Springs experience will be incomplete if you don't take a Greek meal here. In addition to Hellas Restaurant & Bakery, listed below, you'll find about a dozen other family-owned restaurants along the lively Sponge Docks, all of them clean, inviting, and serving authentic, inexpensive Greek fare.

Weight watchers should studiously avoid the **Parthenon Bakery & Pastry Shop,** 751 Dodecanese Blvd. (☎ 727/938-7709), where huge cabinets are filled with Greek and other delights, including luscious chocolate-covered baklava. Open daily 9am to 10pm.

✪ **Hellas Restaurant & Bakery.** Sponge Docks, 785 Dodecanese Blvd. ☎ **727/ 943-2400.** Reservations not accepted. Sandwiches and salads $4–$6; main courses $7.50–$14. AE, DC, DISC, MC, V. Daily 11am–10pm. GREEK.

The lovely hand-painted tile tables on the street-side patio here make fine spots from which to watch the action on the Sponge Docks while sampling authentic Aegean cuisine. If you like feta cheese, you'll enjoy the pungent Greek-style shrimp or scallops. If not, opt for the perfectly pan-fried grouper or any of the Aegean standbys: moussaka, pastisio, dolmades, or one of the largest gyro sandwiches in town (you can try a little of each on the sampler platter). The bakery supplies baklava, *galactombouriko* (egg custard), and other desserts from the old country. With Greek cuisine, Greek music, and a Greek-looking (if not Greek-accented) waiter, it's easy to imagine yourself quayside on Mykonos.

Louis Pappas' Restaurant and Riverside Cafe. Sponge Docks, 10 Dodecanese Blvd. (at Pinellas Ave./Alt. U.S. 19). ☎ **727/937-5101.** Reservations not accepted. Sandwiches and tapas $6–$8; main courses $10–$18. AE, MC, V. Sun–Thurs 11:30am–10pm, Fri–Sat 11:30am–11pm (bar closes 1 hr. later). GREEK/SEAFOOD.

The most upscale restaurant here, Pappas is famous statewide for its fresh American-style seafood—shrimp, grouper, red snapper, and even stone crab claws in season—most of it right off the boat. There are also Greek salads and other dishes with an Aegean flair, such as salmon with a Greek-seasoned stuffing. The family-run restaurant has been operating on the banks of the Anclote River since 1925, when it was founded by Louis Pappamichaelopoulus of Sparta, Greece. The bar area doubles as the Riverside Cafe, serving a light menu of sandwiches and tapas. You get nice river views from the tall windows of this modern building. Downstairs, you can poke through several shops, including one selling hand-rolled cigars.

5 Sarasota

52 miles S of Tampa, 150 miles SW of Orlando, 225 miles NW of Miami

Far enough away from Tampa Bay to have an identity very much its own, Sarasota is one of Florida's cultural centers. In fact, many retirees spend their winters here because there's so much to keep them entertained and stimulated, including the very fine Asolo Center for the Performing Arts and the Van Wezel Performing Arts Hall. Like affluent Naples down in Southwest Florida, it also has an extensive array of first-class resorts, restaurants, and upscale boutiques.

Sarasota is also known for the series of long, narrow barrier islands lying just offshore: **St. Armands Key,** with one of Florida's ritziest shopping and dining districts;

Mermaids & Manatees

Drive north of Clearwater for an hour on congested U.S. 19, and you'll come to one of Florida's original tourist attractions, the famous ✪ **Weeki Wachee Spring** (☎ **800/678-9335** or 352/596-2062). "Mermaids" have been putting on acrobatic swimming shows behind 4-inch-thick windows here every day since 1947. It's a sight to see them doing their dances in waters that come from one of America's most prolific freshwater springs, which pours some 170 million gallons of 72°F water a day into the river. The show combines elements of Hans Christian Andersen's "The Little Mermaid." Admission is $16.95 for adults, $12.95 for children 3 to 10, plus tax. Kids under 3 get in free. The spring is open daily from 10am to 4pm in winter, to 5pm the rest of the year.

There's more than mermaids at Weeki Wachee Spring, for you can take a Wilderness River Cruise across the Weeki Wachee River, take in the live Exotic Birds of Prey show, and send the kids on the flume, or float on a tube at **Buccaneer Bay** water park (☎ **352/596-2062**). Buccanner Bay is open from March to mid-autumn, daily from 10am to 5pm. Admission is $12.95 for adults, $9.95 for children 3 to 10, free for kids under 3.

If you decide to stay overnight here, there's the **Best Western Weeki Wachee Resort,** across U.S. 19 from the springs (☎ **800/528-1234** or 352/596-2007). From Weeki Wachee, travel 21 miles north to the ✪ **Homosassa Springs State Wildlife Park,** 4150 S. Suncoast Blvd. (U.S. 19) in Homosassa Springs (☎ **352/628-5343**). The highlight here is a floating observatory where visitors can "walk" underwater and watch manatees in a rehabilitation facility, as well as thousands of fresh- and saltwater fish. You'll also see deer, bear, bobcats, otters, egrets, and flamingos along unspoiled nature trails. The park is open daily from 9am to 5:30pm. Admission is $7.95 for adults and $4.95 for children 3 to 12, which includes a 30-minute narrated boat ride.

About 7 miles north of Homosassa Springs, some 300 manatees spend the winter in Crystal River, and you can swim or snorkel with them in the warm-water natural spring of Kings Bay. **American Pro Diving Center,** 821 SE Hwy. 19, Crystal River, FL 34429 (☎ **800/291-DIVE** or 352/563-0041), offers daily dive and snorkel tours. Early mornings are the best time to see the manatees, so try to take the 7am departure. The trips range from $21.50 to $50 per person. Call for the schedule and reservations.

You can stay in Crystal River at hotels that have their own dive shops and marinas, such as the 142-room **Plantation Inn and Golf Resort,** at 9301 W. Ft. Island Trail (☎ **800/632-6262** or 352/795-4211), or the 100-room **Best Western Crystal River Resort,** at 614 NW U.S. 19 (☎ **800/435-4409** or 352/795-3171).

During mid-February you can enjoy the Crystal River Chamber's **Florida Manatee Festival,** with a seafood festival, a golf tournament, an art show, concerts, and manatee displays.

For more information about the area, contact the **Nature Coast Chamber at Crystal River,** 28 NW Hwy. 19, Crystal River, FL 34425 (☎ **352/795-3149;** fax 352/795-4260). The chamber's visitor center is open Monday to Thursday from 8:30am to 5pm, Friday from 8:30am to 4pm.

Sarasota & Bradenton

Tampa Bay

Fort DeSoto
Fort DeSoto Park
679

Sunshine Skyway

Edgemont Channel

Egmont Key State Park

Southwest Channel

275
19

Gillette

41

683

Parrish

Terra Ceia
19
41
Rubonia

75

301

Anna Maria

DeSoto National Monument

Memphis

Ellenton

683

Holmes Beach

Palmetto

Manatee River

Arcadia Rd.

64

Manatee Ave.

70

Anna Maria Island
789

64

Bradenton

Cortez

Samoset

Bradenton Beach

684

Oneco

70

70

Longbeach

Bayshore Gardens

41

301

Tallevast

Braden River

Longboat Key

Sarasota Bay

Whitfield Estates

Sarasota-Bradenton Airport

MANATEE CO.

789

University Parkway

SARASOTA CO.

75

Mote Marine Aquarium

Sarasota

780

Fruitville

780

Gulf of Mexico

St. Armands Key
Lido Key

773

Siesta Key

758

Bee Ridge Road

41

Bee Ridge

72

Gulf Gate

Crescent

789

Vamo

Osprey

Casey Key

41

681

Cow Pen Slough

Laurel

Nokomis

Venice

0   3 mi.
    4.8 km

N

1-1083

Siesta Key, a quiet residential enclave popular with artisans and writers but also home to Siesta Village, this area's funky, laid-back, and often-noisy beach hangout; **Lido Key,** with a string of affordable hotels attractive to family vacationers; and **Longboat Key,** one of Florida's wealthiest islands that stretches north to Bradenton. Together, 35 miles of gloriously white beaches fringe these keys.

Legend has it that Sarasota was named after the explorer Hernando de Soto's daughter, Sara (hence, Sara-sota). In more recent times, the town's most famous resident was circus legend John Ringling, who came here in the 1920s, built a palatial bayfront mansion known as Ca'd'Zan, acquired extensive real-estate holdings, erected a magnificent museum to house his world-class collection of baroque paintings, and built the causeway out to St. Armands and Lido keys.

ESSENTIALS

GETTING THERE You may get a less expensive fare by flying into **Tampa International Airport** (see "Essentials" in section 1, above), and you could save even more since the rental-car agencies there often offer some of the best deals in Florida. If you decide to fly directly here, **Sarasota-Bradenton International Airport** (☎ **941/359-2770**), north of downtown off University Parkway between U.S. 41 and U.S. 301, is served by **American Eagle** (☎ 800/433-7300), **America Trans Air** (☎ 800/225-2995), **Canadian Airlines International** (☎ 800/426-7000), **Continental** (☎ 800/525-0280), **Delta** (☎ 800/221-1212), **Northwest/KLM** (☎ 800/225-2525), **TWA** (☎ 800/221-2000), and **US Airways** (☎ 800/428-4322).

Alamo (☎ 800/327-9633), **Avis** (☎ 800/331-1212), **Budget** (☎ 800/527-0700), **Dollar** (☎ 800/800-4000), **Hertz** (☎ 800/654-3131), and **National** (☎ 800/CAR-RENT) have car-rental booths at the airport.

Diplomat Taxi (☎ **941/355-5155**) has a monopoly on service from the airport to hotels in Sarasota and Bradenton. Look for the cabs at the west end of the terminal outside baggage claim. The fare is about $9 to downtown Sarasota, $10 to $15 to St. Armands and Lido keys, $14 to $21 to Siesta Key, and $14 to $32 to Longboat Key.

Amtrak has bus connections to its Tampa station (☎ **800/USA-RAIL**).

VISITOR INFORMATION Contact the **Sarasota Convention and Visitors Bureau,** 655 N. Tamiami Trail (U.S. 41), Sarasota, FL 34236 (☎ **800/522-9799** or 941/957-1877; fax 941/951-2956; www.sarasota/online.com). The bureau and its helpful visitor center are in a blue pagoda-shaped building on Tamiami Trail (U.S. 41) at 6th Street. They're open Monday to Saturday from 9am to 5pm.

For specific information about Siesta Key, contact the **Siesta Key Chamber of Commerce,** 5100-B Ocean Blvd., Sarasota, FL 34242 (☎ **941/349-3800;** fax 941/349-9699), and ask for a copy of its biennial visitor guide.

GETTING AROUND **Sarasota County Area Transit (SCAT)** (☎ **941/316-1234**) provides regularly scheduled bus service. The Sarasota Convention and Visitors Bureau distributes route maps (see "Visitor Information," above).

Taxi companies include **Diplomat Taxi** (☎ **941/355-5155**), **Green Cab Taxi** (☎ **941/922-6666**), and **Yellow Cab of Sarasota** (☎ **941/955-3341**).

HITTING THE BEACH

Much of the area's 35 miles of beaches are occupied by hotels and condominium complexes, but there are excellent public beaches here. The area's most popular beach is **Siesta Key Public Beach,** with a picnic area, a 700-car parking lot, crowds of families, and quartz sand reminiscent of the blazingly white beaches in Northwest Florida. There's also beach access at **Siesta Village,** which has a plethora of casual restaurants and pubs with outdoor seating (see "Where to Dine," below). More secluded and quiet is **Turtle Beach,** at Siesta Key's south end. It has shelters, boat ramps, picnic tables, and volleyball nets.

After you've driven the length of Longboat Key and admired the luxurious homes and condos blocking access to the beach, take a right off St. Armands Circle onto Lido Key and **North Lido Beach.** The south end of the island is occupied by **South Lido Beach Park,** with plenty of shade making it a good spot for picnics and walks.

OUTDOOR PURSUITS & SPECTATOR SPORTS

BICYCLING & IN-LINE SKATING   You can bike and skate from downtown to Lido and Longboat keys, since paved walkways/bike paths run alongside the John Ringling Causeway and then up Longboat. On the mainland, you can rent bikes and blades at **Sarasota Bicycle Center,** 4084 Bee Ridge Rd. just east of downtown (☎ 941/377-4505). **C.B.'s Saltwater Outfitters,** 1249 Stickney Point Rd., at the Siesta Key side of the Stickney Point Bridge (☎ 941/349-4400), rents bicycles, while **Siesta Sports Rentals,** 6551 Midnight Pass Rd. on Siesta Key (☎ 941/346-1797), has bikes of various sizes, including stroller attachments for kids, plus motor scooters. Bike rentals range from about $14 a day to $45 a week.

BOAT RENTALS   **All Watersports,** in the Boatyard Shopping Village, on the mainland end of Stickney Point Bridge (☎ 941/921-2754), rents personal watercraft such as Wave Runners, jet boats, and jet skis, as well as speedboats, runabouts, and bowriders. At the island end of the bridge, **C.B.'s Saltwater Outfitters,** 1249 Stickney Point Rd. (☎ 941/349-4400), and **Siesta Key Boat Rentals,** 1265 Old Stickney Point Rd. (☎ 941/349-8880), both rent runabouts, pontoon boats, and other craft. Bait and tackle are available at the marinas.

CRUISES   The area's best nature cruises go forth from Mote Marine Aquarium (see "Parks, Nature Preserves & Gardens," below).

From October to May, you can head over to Marina Jack, U.S. 41 at Island Park Circle, for 2-hour sightseeing and sunset cruises around Sarasota's waterways aboard the 65-foot, two-deck *Le Barge* (☎ 941/366-6116). The cruises run Tuesday to Sunday, with the sightseeing cruise leaving at 2pm. The sunset cruises with live music change with the time of sunset. The cruises cost $15 adults, $5 for kids under 13. Snacks and libation are available for an extra charge. Call for reservations.

FISHING   Charter fishing boats dock at most marinas here. The **Flying Fish Fleet,** downtown at Marina Jack's Marina, U.S. 41 at Island Park Circle (☎ 941/366-3373), offers party-boat charter-fishing excursions, with bait and tackle furnished. Prices for half-day trips are $28 adults, $23 seniors, $18 for kids 4 to 12. All-day voyages cost $40, $35, and $30, respectively. Call for the schedule. Charter boats also line up along the dock here.

GOLF   The **Bobby Jones Golf Complex,** 1000 Circus Blvd. (☎ 941/365-GOLF), is Sarasota's only municipal facility, but it has two 18-hole championship layouts—the American (par 71) and British (par 72) courses—and the 9-hole Gillespie executive course (par 30). Tee times are assigned 3 days in advance. Greens fees range from $25 to $31, including cart rental.

You can also tune your game at the public **Village Green Golf Club,** 3500 Pembroke Dr., near Bee Ridge and Beneva roads (☎ 941/925-2755), whose executive-length 18 holes can be parred in 58.

The semiprivate **Rolling Green Golf Club,** 4501 Tuttle Ave. (☎ 941/355-6620), is an 18-hole, par-72 course. Facilities include a driving range, rental clubs, and lessons. Tee times are assigned 2 days in advance. Prices, including cart, are about $40 in winter, $25 off-season.

Also semiprivate, the **Sarasota Golf Club,** 7820 N. Leewynn Dr. (☎ **941/ 371-2431**), is an 18-hole, par-72 course. Facilities include a driving range, lessons, club rentals, a restaurant, a lounge, and a golf shop. Fees, including carts, are about $42 in winter, $25 off-season.

If you have reciprocal privileges, **University Park Country Club,** west of I-75 on University Parkway (☎ **941/359-9999**), is Sarasota's only nationally ranked course.

KAYAKING **Sarasota Bay Explorers** (☎ **941/388-4200**), at Mote Marine Aquarium (see "Parks, Nature Preserves & Gardens," below), uses a 38-foot pontoon boat to ferry both novice and experienced kayakers and their craft to a marine sanctuary, where everyone paddles out to visit the creatures. Experienced naturalists serve as guides. The boat anchors off a secluded beach for swimming and snorkeling before returning to the aquarium. Wear swimsuits and tennis shoes or rubber-soled booties, and bring a towel and lunch. The 5-hour trips usually go on Tuesday and Thursday (call for departure times and reservations). They cost $65 for adults, $50 for children 5 to 17 (kids under 5 are not allowed).

Kayak Treks, 1239 Beneva Rd. S. (☎ **941/365-3892**), has escorted kayak adventures on the area's backwaters, at $30 per person for half-day trips, $45 for full-day voyages, and $35 per person for moonlight cruises on Sarasota Bay. Full-day trips include lunch, and moonlight guests get coffee and dessert. Call for schedule and reservations. The company also rents kayaks.

SAILING The 41-foot, 12-passenger sailboat *Enterprise,* docked at Marina Jack's Marina, U.S. 41 at Island Park Circle (☎ **941/951-1833**), cruises the waters of both Sarasota Bay and the Gulf of Mexico. Half-day cruises cost $35; the sunset cruise, $20. Departure times vary, and reservations are required.

Siesta Key Sailing, 1219 Southport Dr. (☎ **941/346-7245**), has half-day, full-day, and 2-day cruises, ranging from $50 to $325 per person, respectively. Reservations are essential.

SPECTATOR SPORTS **Ed Smith Stadium,** 2700 12th St., at Tuttle Avenue (☎ **941/954-4464**), is the winter home of the **Cincinnati Reds,** who hold spring training here in February and March. East of downtown, the stadium seats 7,500 fans. Admission is $5 to $10.

The **Sarasota Polo Club,** 8201 Polo Club Lane, Sarasota (☎ **941/359-0000**), midway between Sarasota and Bradenton, is the site of weekly polo matches from November through March, on Sunday afternoons. Call for the schedule of matches and admission fees.

WATER SPORTS The downtown center for jet skiing, wave running, sailing, and other water-sports activities is **O'Leary's,** in the Island Park Marina, U.S. 41 and Island Park Circle (☎ **941/953-7505**). It's open daily from 8am to 8pm.

Siesta Sports Rentals, 6551 Midnight Pass Rd. (☎ **813/346-1797**), rents kayaks and sailboats, plus beach chairs and umbrellas.

You can soar above the bay with **Siesta Parasail,** based at CB's Saltwater Outfitters at the western end of the Stickney Point Bridge (☎ **941/349-1900**).

EXPLORING THE AREA
MUSEUMS & ART GALLERIES

Museum of Cars & Music. 5500 N. Tamiami Trail (at University Pkwy.). ☎ **941/ 355-6228**. Admission $9 adults, $5 children 6–12, free for children under 6. Daily 9am–6pm. Take U.S. 41 north of downtown; museum is 2 blocks west of the airport.

View more than 80 classic and antique autos, from Rolls-Royces and Pierce Arrows to the four cars used personally by circus czar John Ringling. In addition, there are more than 1,200 antique music boxes, from tiny music boxes to a huge 30-foot Belgian organ. Check out the Penny Arcade with antique games, and grab a cone at the ice-cream and sandwich shop.

○ **Ringling Museums.** 5401 Bay Shore Rd. at N. Tamiami Trail (U.S. 41). ☎ **941/ 351-1550,** or 941/351-1660 for recorded information. Admission $9 adults, $8 seniors, free for children 12 and under. Daily 10am–5:30pm. Closed New Year's Day, Thanksgiving, Christmas. From downtown, take U.S. 41 north to University Pkwy. and follow signs to museum.

This is a huge 60-acre site—showman John Ringling collected art on a grand scale. **The John and Mable Ringling Museum of Art,** housed in a pink Italian Renaissance villa, is filled with more than 500 years of European and American art, including one of the world's most important collections of grand 17th-century baroque paintings. The old master collection also includes five world-renowned tapestry cartoons by Peter Paul Rubens and his studio. The museum houses collections of decorative arts and traveling exhibits. The Ringlings' 30-room winter residence, **Ca'd'Zan** (House of John), built in 1925 and modeled after a Venetian palace, is on display and filled with personal mementos. The grounds also include **Circus Galleries,** a building devoted to circus memorabilia including parade wagons, calliopes, costumes, and colorful posters; the historic **Asolo Theater,** a 19th-century Italian court playhouse; and a classical courtyard, a rose garden, a restaurant, and shops.

Sarasota Visual Art Center. 707 N. Tamiami Trail (at 6th St.). ☎ **941/365-2032.** Free admission ($1 donation suggested). Daily 10am–4pm.

Sarasota is home to more than 40 art galleries and exhibition spaces, all open to the public year-round. A convenient artistic starting point is this downtown community art center, next to the Sarasota Convention and Visitors Bureau. It contains three galleries and a small sculpture garden, presenting the area's largest display of art by national and local artists, from paintings and pottery to sculpture, cartoons, jewelry, and enamelware. There are also art demonstrations and special events.

PARKS, NATURE PRESERVES & GARDENS

A must-see for serious plant lovers, the peaceful ○ **Marie** is said to be the only botanical garden in the world specializing in the preservation, study, and research of epiphytic plants and bromeliads—that is, "air plants" such as orchids, pineapples, and ferns. It's home to more than 20,000 exotic plants, including more than 6,000 orchids, as well as a bamboo pavilion, a butterfly and hummingbird garden, a medicinal plant garden, a waterfall garden, a cactus and succulent garden, a fernery, a hibiscus garden, a palm grove, two tropical food gardens, and a native shore-plant community. Admission is $8 for adults, $4 for children 6 to 11, free for children 5 and under accompanied by an adult. Open daily from 10am to 5pm. Closed Christmas.

If you don't mind black Asian leopards, squirrel monkeys, and other animals being locked up in cages, the 10-acre **Sarasota Jungle Gardens,** 37–01 Bayshore Rd. (☎ **941/355-5305**), between downtown and the airport, features lush tropical vegetation, cool jungle trails, tropical plants, exotic waterfowl (there's a resident flock of pink flamingoes), and reptiles including "Roscoe," a huge Aldabra tortoise similar to those found in the Galapagos Islands. Children like the petting zoo, pony rides, and bird and reptile shows. Admission is $9 for adults, $8 for seniors, $5 for children 4 to 12, free for children 3 and under. Open daily from 9am to 5pm except Christmas. From downtown, take U.S. 41 north to Myrtle Street, turn left, and go 2 blocks.

On City Island, at the southern end of Longboat Key, kids love the ✪ **Mote Marine Aquarium,** 1600 Thompson Pkwy. (☎ **800/691-MOTE** or 941/388-4441), because they get to touch cool stuff like a stingray (minus the stinger, of course) and watch sharks in the shark tank. Part of the noted Mote Marine Laboratory complex, this facility focuses on the marine life of the Sarasota area and nearby gulf waters, including a manatee exhibit. The kids won't believe all the sea horse babies that come from the dad's pouch (one of Mother Nature's strange-but-true surprises). There are also many research-in-progress exhibits, and you can go on 1-hour, 45-minute environmental tours aboard a boat named the *Explorer* daily or on tropical sunset cruises daily (call ahead for times, reservations, and prices). Admission is $8 for adults, $6 for children 4 to 17, free for children 3 and under. Open daily from 10am to 5pm. From St. Armands Circle, go north toward Longboat Key; the aquarium is at the foot of the Lido-Longboat bridge.

Based at the aquarium, **Sarasota Bay Explorers** (☎ **727/388-4200**) has narrated sea-life encounter cruises daily at 11am, 1:30pm, and 4pm. These 90-minute narrated trips visit a deserted island, and the guides wade out with nets and bring up sea life for inspection. The trips cost $24 for adults, $20 for children 5 to 17, free for kids under 5. Or you can buy a combination ticket including both the trip and the aquarium admission for $28 adults, $22 for children. This company has unusual kayaking adventures, too (see "Outdoor Activities & Spectator Sports," above).

Next to the aquarium, **Pelican Man's Bird Sanctuary,** 1708 Thompson Pkwy. (☎ **941/388-4444**), is a sanctuary and rehabilitation center where more than 5,000 injured birds and other wildlife are treated each year. The sanctuary is home to about 30 species of birds. There's a gift shop with many bird-oriented items for sale. Admission is free, but donations are encouraged. Open daily from 10am to 5pm. From St. Armands Circle go north toward Longboat Key and follow the signs.

In the country, the **Myakka River State Park,** on Fla. 72 about 9 miles east of I-75, is one of Florida's largest, covering more than 35,000 acres of wetlands, prairies, and dense woodlands along the Myakka River. It's an outstanding wildlife sanctuary and breeding ground, home to hundreds of species of plants and animals, including alligators. Admission is $4 per car with two to eight occupants, $2 for car with driver, or $1 per pedestrian or bicyclist. **Myakka Wildlife & Nature Tours** (☎ **941/365-0100**) has nature excursions through the park by boat and tram. These cost $7 for adults, $3 for children 12 and under. Call for the schedules, which change seasonally. The park is open daily from 8am to sunset. For more information, contact the headquarters at 13207 S.R. 72, Sarasota, FL 34241 (☎ **941/361-6511**).

Near Myakka, you can see the famous **Lippizzan Stallions** do their dancing show at the Ottomar Herrmann training grounds, on Singletary Road (☎ **941/322-1501**). They perform at 3pm Thursday and Friday, at 10am Saturday from January to March. Call for ticket prices and directions.

SHOPPING

Visitors come from all over the world to shop at ✪ **St. Armands Circle,** on St. Armands Key just inside Lido Key. Wander around this outdoor circle of more than 150 international boutiques, gift shops, galleries, restaurants, and nightspots, all surrounded by lush landscaping, patios, and antiques. Pick up a map at the Sarasota Convention and Visitors Bureau (see "Essentials," above). Many shops here are comparable to those in Palm Beach and on Naples's Third Avenue South, so check your credit-card limits—or resort to some great window shopping. I love to browse through **Global Navigator** (☎ **813/388-4515**), a travel-equipment and apparel shop that reminds me of Banana Republic when it carried really cool stuff.

Parking on or near St. Armands Circle can be scarce, and on-street parking is limited to 3 hours. Your best bets are the free, unrestricted lots on Adams Drive at Monroe and Madison drives.

Downtown, the **Burns Court** and **Herald Square** historic districts, centered on Pineapple Avenue south of Ringling Boulevard, have a trove of upscale boutiques and art galleries worth exploring. You can pick from the freshest of Florida's fruits and vegetables at the downtown **farmer's market,** from 7am to noon on Saturday on Lemon Avenue between Main and 1st streets.

Sarasota Square Mall, 8201 S. Tamiami Trail, at Beneva Road (☎ 941/922-9600), south of downtown, is the area's largest enclosed mall. **Sarasota Outlet Mall,** on University Parkway just west of I-75 (☎ 941/359-2050), has about 40 of the better-known factory stores.

WHERE TO STAY

In addition to the chain hotels listed below, you'll find the **Comfort Inn** (☎ 800/228-5150 or 941/355-7091), **Days Inn Airport** (☎ 800/329-7466 or 941/355-9271), and **Hampton Inn** (☎ 800/336-9335 or 941/351-7734) standing side by side on Tamiami Trail (U.S. 41) just south of the airport and near the Ringling Museums and the Asolo Center for the Performing Arts. All are of recent vintage and thoroughly modern. A **Courtyard by Marriott** (☎ 800/321-2211 or 941/355-3337) and a **Sleep Inn** (☎ 800/627-5447 or 941/359-8558) are nearby on University Parkway opposite the airport.

Also on U.S. 41 north between downtown and the airport, the local **Knights Inn** (☎ 800/843-5644 or 941/355-8867) and **Super 8 Motel** (☎ 800/800-8000 or 941/355-9326) have been renovated and offer clean, comfortable, and inexpensive motel rooms.

With the beaches here virtually lined with condominiums, it's not surprising that the Resort at Longboat Key Club and the Colony Beach & Tennis Resort (see below) actually are all condo projects operated as hotels. The annual visitors guide published by the Sarasota Convention and Visitors Bureau (see "Essentials," above) is a good starting point in finding other options. Among the rental agencies requiring stays of less than a month are **Argus Property Management,** 1200 Siesta Bayside, Sarasota, FL 34242 (☎ 800/237-2252 or 941/346-3499; fax 941/349-6156; www.argus-mgmt.com); **Longboat Accommodations,** 4030 Gulf of Mexico Dr., Longboat Key, FL 34228 (☎ 800/237-9505 or 941/383-9505; fax 941/383-1830; www.long-boatkey.com); and **Michael Saunders & Company,** 100 S. Washington Blvd., Sarasota, FL 34236 (☎ 800/881-2222 or 941/951-6668; www.michaelsaunders.com).

The hotels below are organized by geographic region: on the mainland, on Lido Key, on Longboat Key, and on Siesta Key. Some of the Longboat Key hotels mentioned below actually are in Manatee County, about halfway between Bradenton and downtown Sarasota.

The high season here is from January to April. Rates are usually higher along the beaches at all times, so bargain hunters should stick to the downtown area and commute to the beach. The hotel tax here is 9%.

ON THE MAINLAND

Best Western Midtown. 1425 S. Tamiami Trail (U.S. 41, at Prospect St.), Sarasota, FL 34239. ☎ **800/722-8227,** 800/528-1234, or 941/955-9841. Fax 941/954-8948. 100 units. A/C TV TEL. Winter $99–$109 double. Off-season $59–$69 double. Rates include continental breakfast. AE, DC, DISC, MC, V.

Location is the buzzword here, for this modern L-shaped two- and three-story hotel is 2 miles in either direction from the main causeways leading to the keys. Although positioned next to the Midtown Plaza shopping center, it's set back from the busy U.S. 41. Tropical palms and plantings surround a heated outdoor swimming pool and sundeck. Guests can graze a buffet-style breakfast, and there's a guest laundry. The rooms are modern and cheery, with light woods and Florida pastel tones. Some of them have kitchenettes.

Hyatt Sarasota. 1000 Blvd. of the Arts, Sarasota, FL 34236. ☎ **800/233-1234** or 941/953-1234. Fax 941/952-1987. 297 units. A/C TV TEL. Winter $200–$220 double. Off-season $109–$159 double. AE, DC, DISC, MC, V.

Located beside Sarasota Bay and boasting its own marina, this 10-story tower is the downtown area's centerpiece hotel. Attracting business travelers and groups, it sits adjacent to the Civic Center, the Van Wezel Performing Arts Hall, and the Sarasota Garden Club and is within walking distance of downtown shops and restaurants. The contemporary bedrooms have balconies overlooking the marina or bay; they have coffeemakers, hair dryers, and irons and boards.

Dining/Diversions: The main dining room, Scalini, features northern Italian cuisine. Out on the docks, the publike Boathouse offers casual fare and water views of the marina. Inside, Tropics Lounge provides libations.

Amenities: Concierge, room service, valet parking and laundry, newspaper delivery, business center, airport shuttle ($3 per person), heated outdoor swimming pool, patio, health club, marina.

Wellesley Inn & Suites. 1803 N. Tamiami Trail (U.S. 41, at 18th St.), Sarasota, FL 34234. ☎ **800/444-8888** or 941/366-5128. Fax 941/953-4322. 106 units. A/C TV TEL. Winter $110 double; $140 suite. Off-season $60 double; $80 suite. Rates include continental breakfast. AE, DC, DISC, MC, V.

The closest chain motel to downtown, this four-story hotel with an impressive portico overlooks a marina and boatyard, but you won't have a balcony from which to enjoy the view. The bedrooms are spacious, with light woods, pastel tones, and coffeemakers. Suites have microwave ovens and refrigerators, which you can request for the rooms. There are laundry service, an outdoor heated swimming pool, and complimentary airport transportation.

LIDO KEY

✪ **Half Moon Beach Club.** 2050 Ben Franklin Dr. (at Taft Dr.), Sarasota, FL 34236. ☎ **800/358-3245** or 941/388-3694. Fax 941/388-1938. 85 units. A/C MINIBAR TV TEL. Winter $119–$229 double. Off-season $85–$159 double. AE, DC, DISC, MC, V.

Near the south end of Lido, this two-story art deco–style hotel is right on the beach and less than half a block from South Lido Beach Park. The front of the building forms a circle around a small but very attractive courtyard with a heated pool and sunning area. From there, guests take a hallway through a motel-style block of rooms to the beach, where they can rent cabanas and order libation to be delivered from the bar inside. The spacious guest rooms are furnished with light woods, refrigerators, and coffeemakers, and some have kitchenettes with microwave ovens. Facilities include Seagrapes, an indoor/outdoor restaurant; an outdoor heated swimming pool; volleyball; a gulf-front sundeck; a coin laundry; and bike and video rentals. Complimentary newspapers are delivered to the rooms each morning.

Holiday Inn Lido Beach. 233 Ben Franklin Dr. (at Thoreau Dr.), Sarasota, FL 34236. ☎ **800/892-9174** or 941/388-5555. Fax 941/388-4321. 140 units. A/C TV TEL. Winter $179–$269 double. Off-season $125–$185 double. AE, DC, DISC, MC, V.

Conveniently located at the north end of Lido, this modern seven-story hotel is within walking distance of St. Armands Circle. Unfortunately, the beach across the street has been heavily eroded by recent storms, losing much of the sand that once covered the rocks here. The bedrooms have balconies that face the gulf or the bay and are furnished with light woods, pastel fabrics, coffeemakers, and hair dryers.

The rooftop restaurant and lounge offers panoramic views of the Gulf of Mexico. There are also a lobby lounge and a casual pool bar. Amenities include valet laundry, coin laundry, newspaper delivery, outdoor heated swimming pool with gulf view, bicycle rentals, water-sports equipment.

LONGBOAT KEY

✪ **Colony Beach & Tennis Resort.** 1620 Gulf of Mexico Dr., Longboat Key, FL 34228. ☎ **800/4-COLONY** or 941/383-6464. Fax 941/383-7549. www.colonybeachresort.com. 235 units. Winter $300–$450 suite. Off-season $190–$350 suite. Packages available. AE, DISC, MC, V.

Sitting 3 miles north of St. Armands Circle, this beachside facility is consistently rated one of the nation's finest tennis resorts. Luxurious one- and two-bedroom apartments—complete with living rooms, dining areas, fully equipped kitchenettes, and sun balconies—are built around 21 courts, two of them lighted for night play. A staff of 10 professionals conducts highly acclaimed programs for adults and children. The beachside Colony Restaurant and swimming pool date from 1952, when this was a beach club. Next door are three private gulfside cottages right on the superb beach; they are the most expensive accommodations here. The villa suites date from 1974 but were extensively renovated and modernized in 1997.

Dining/Diversions: One of the finest dining venues here, the beachside Colony Restaurant offers continental cuisine for lunch and dinner (jackets requested for men at dinner). Sharing the old building, the informal Dining Room provides breakfast, lunch, and dinner. The poolside Colony Patio & Bar has casual dining. The lavish Sunday brunch here is popular with locals as well as out-of-towners. The Colony Lounge has nightly entertainment.

Amenities: Concierge, laundry and dry cleaning, baby-sitting, valet parking, courtesy limo, outstanding year-round supervised children's programs for ages 3 to 12, health spa, complimentary tennis, beachfront swimming pool, fitness center, golf, deep-sea fishing, water sports, aerobic classes, bicycle rental, boutiques, beauty salon.

Holiday Inn Hotel & Suites. 4949 Gulf of Mexico Dr., Longboat Key, FL 34228. ☎ **800/ HOLIDAY** or 941/383-3771. Fax 941/383-7871. 146 units. A/C TV TEL. Winter $189–$259 double; $229–$329 suite. Off-season $129–$229 double; $159–$299 suite. AE, DC, DISC, MC, V.

In Manatee County about halfway up Longboat Key, 8 miles north of St. Armands Circle, this family-oriented beachside motel is built around an indoor courtyard with a swimming pool, a whirlpool, a games area, and Longboat Key's only fast-food outlets (Pizza Hut, Nathan's Famous, Mrs. Fields Cookies, and Seattle's Best Coffee). The enclosed area makes this a good respite on rainy days or during a cool snap. The contemporary rooms and suites have patios or balconies, with the choice units facing the beach. All units have coffeemakers and refrigerators.

Dining: In addition to the fast-food outlets, there's a restaurant with adjacent clubby bar plus a beachside snack bar.

Amenities: Concierge, limited room service, laundry, indoor and outdoor pools and whirlpools, four lighted tennis courts, exercise room with sauna, gift shops, guest laundry, bicycle rental, water sports.

✪ **Longboat Key Hilton Beach Resort.** 4711 Gulf of Mexico Dr., Longboat Key, FL 34228. ☎ **800/282-3046** or 941/383-2451. Fax 941/383-7979. 102 units. A/C MINIBAR TV TEL.

Winter $195–$295 double; $275–$375 suite. Off-season $140–$200 double; $225–$315 suite. Packages available. AE, DC, MC, V.

Also in Manatee County, 7½ miles north of St. Armands Circle, this five-story concrete building is surrounded by lush foliage and gardens. A much more charming gray wooden structure to one side holds all of the public facilities and more than makes up for the blandness of the rooms' building. The bar and pool area here are pleasant areas for relaxing lunches or sunset cocktails. The bedrooms are furnished in a tropical style. All have coffeemakers and hair dryers, and most have a patio or narrow balcony. A few gulf-front rooms are the most expensive.

Dining: The main restaurant offers great views of the gulf to accompany a seafood menu, while the poolside bar serves lunch and beverages.

Amenities: Room service, valet laundry, free shuttle to St. Armands Key for shopping. Heated outdoor swimming pool, private beach, bicycle and water-sports equipment rentals, one tennis court, shuffleboard.

○ **Resort at Longboat Key Club.** 301 Gulf of Mexico Dr. (P.O. Box 15000), Longboat Key, FL 34228. ☎ **800/237-8821** or 941/383-8821. Fax 941/383-0359. www.longboatkey-club.com. 232 units. Winter $350–$975 suite. Off-season $180–$445 suite. Packages available off-season. AE, DISC, MC, V. From St. Armands Key, take Gulf of Mexico Drive north, take first left after bridge.

Part of a real-estate development on 410 acres at the southern end of Longboat Key, this award-winning condo resort pampers the country-club set with upscale restaurants and a variety of recreational activities in a lush tropical setting. The spacious and luxurious suites have private balconies overlooking the Gulf of Mexico, a lagoon, or golf-course fairways. All have custom-designed furnishings and neoclassical decor. All but 20 units have full kitchens.

Dining/Diversions: Orchid's Restaurant has the feel of an informal but elegant supper club, serving classical Italian cuisine in a romantic setting, while the adjacent Orchid's Lounge offers casual dining and live entertainment. Barefoots Bar & Grille offers relaxed poolside dining. Overlooking the Islandside Golf Course, Spike 'n Tees serves breakfast and lunch in an outdoor setting. At Harborside Marina, the Dining Room offers nightly theme buffets, while breakfast, lunch, and dinner are served at The Grille.

Amenities: Concierge, room service (7am to midnight), valet laundry, baby-sitting, supervised children's activities (in summer), in-room massage, newspaper delivery. Two golf courses (45 holes), golf school, two tennis centers (38 courts), 500 feet of beach with water sports, exercise track, steam rooms, jogging paths, nature trails, swimming pool, whirlpool, bicycle rentals, tour desk, boutiques.

SIESTA KEY

○ **Best Western Siesta Beach Resort.** 5311 Ocean Blvd. (at Calle Miramar), Sarasota, FL 34242. ☎ **800/223-5786** or 941/349-3211. Fax 941/349-7915. 53 units. A/C TV TEL. Winter $149 double; $179–$260 suite. Off-season $84 double; $104–$155 suite. Weekly rates available. AE, DC, DISC, MC, V.

In Siesta Village on the northern end of the key, this older but very well-maintained motel has two buildings across the street from each other. It offers standard hotel rooms and one- and two-bedroom suites, all decorated in pastel tones with light woods. The suites have kitchenettes. Facilities include a heated swimming pool, whirlpool, and guest laundry. Public beach access is across the street, and Siesta Key Public Beach is about half a mile away.

Captiva Beach Resort. 6772 Sara Sea Circle, Siesta Key, FL 34242. ☎ **800/349-4132** or 941/349-4131. Fax 941/349-8141. www.captivabeachresort.com. 20 units. A/C TV TEL.

Winter $110–$190. Off-season $75–$170. Weekly and monthly rates available. AE, DISC, MC, V.

On a narrow, closely packed circle populated by other small motels, Robert and Jane Ispaso's clean, well-maintained property occupies two buildings about half a block from the beach. Every unit here has some form of cooking facilities, and some have separate living rooms with sleeper sofas. Although substantially updated and quite comfortable, these are older buildings, so you'll find window air conditioners mounted through the walls, and shower-only bathrooms in some units. It's popular with longer-term guests during winter, so you'll get fresh towels daily but maid service only once a week (there is a coin laundry here). This and the circle's other motels share a common pool area. There's no restaurant on the premises, but several are a short walk away in Siesta Key's Stickney Point commercial area.

Gulf Sun Motel. 6722 Midnight Pass Rd. (at Sarasota Circle), Sarasota, FL 34242. ☎ **941/ 349-2442.** Fax 941/349-7141. 17 units. A/C TV TEL. Winter $90 double; $115–$125 efficiency. Off-season $50 double; $65–$75 efficiency. DISC, MC, V.

Also in Siesta Key's midsection business district, this one-story, 1960s motel with red Spanish tile roof is clean and within a 2-block walk of Crescent Beach. The bedrooms have standard furnishings with queen-size beds and refrigerators. All but two units here are efficiencies with kitchens. A swimming pool is set in the motel's roadside lawn.

✪ Turtle Beach Resort. 9049 Midnight Pass Rd., Sarasota, FL 34242. ☎ **941/349-4554.** Fax 941/312-9034. E-mail: grubi@ix.netcom.com. 10 units. A/C TV TEL. Winter $1,275– $1,875 per week double. Off-season $125–$225 per day double. AE, DISC, MC, V.

On Siesta Key's south end near Turtle Beach, this intimate little bayside charmer began life years ago as a traditional Old Florida fishing camp. In the early 1990s, owners Gail and Dave Rubinfeld renovated the five original clapboard cottages (still the preferable choice for charm), and in 1998 they added five units in a rustic but modern motel-style building (these are larger but lack great water views). The complex is tightly packed, and although some units are very close to a small bayside swimming pool, heavy tropical foliage provides a reasonable degree of privacy, and high wooden fences surround each unit's private whirlpool.

The cottages are done in Victorian, Southwest, Key West, Caribbean, country French, and traditional American country decor. The living room of the American country model sits, docklike, right on the bay (it's justifiably the honeymoon cottage), and the Southwest model looks across the bayside pool to the water. There's no restaurant on the grounds, but Ophelia's on the Bay seafood restaurant next door was once the old fishing camp's dining room, and two units have kitchens (all have microwave ovens and coffeemakers). Guests can use fishing poles and paddleboats. No smoking is allowed inside, but the Rubinfelds do take pets (10% extra charge). Winter rentals are by the week, but you might be able to get a few nights if there's a vacancy.

WHERE TO DINE

The restaurants below are organized geographically: on the mainland, on St. Armands Key (next to Lido Key), and on Siesta Key. On the mainland, the Tamiami Trail (U.S. 41) has most of the national chain fast-food and family restaurants, especially in the area around Sarasota Square Mall south of downtown.

ON THE MAINLAND

The local **Shells** seafood restaurant is at 7253 S. Tamiami Trail (U.S. 41) south of downtown (☎ **941/924-2568**). See "Where to Dine" in section 1, above, for details about this inexpensive chain.

Moderate

Bijou Cafe. 1287 1st St. (at Pineapple Ave.). ☎ **941/366-8111.** Reservations recommended. Main courses $17–$26. AE, DC, MC, V. Mon–Thurs 11:30am–2pm and 5–9:30pm, Fri 11:30am–2pm and 5–10:30pm, Sat 5–10:30pm, Sun 5–9:30pm. Closed Sun June–Dec. INTERNATIONAL. Free valet parking.

Locals always recommend the award-winning cuisine at this charming cafe in the heart of the theater district. Menu highlights include the likes of prime veal Louisville (with crushed pecans and bourbon-pear sauce), sautéed red snapper, New Orleans crab cakes, and rack of lamb. Watching your weight? You may request a "fit and trim" menu. The outstanding wine list has been recognized by *Wine Spectator* magazine.

Cafe of the Arts. 5230 N. Tamiami Trail (south of University Pkwy.). ☎ **941/351-4304.** Reservations recommended. Main courses $11–$20. AE, DISC, MC, V. Mon–Fri 11am–3pm and 5–9pm, Sat–Sun 9am–3pm and 5–9pm. Closed June–Sept. FRENCH.

Warm and soothing hospitality with a French flair welcomes you to Alain Taulere's cafe-bakery-wine bar, in a Spanish-style building across from the Ringling museum complex. He offers an artsy ambience in several dining rooms, one of which spans the rear of the building and enjoys a view out to a lush tropical courtyard. It's a much bigger establishment than at first meets the eye, but volume results in reasonable prices for this quality French fare. Dinner dishes range from heart-healthy vegetable platters to rack of lamb dijonnais. Don't leave until you sample the chocolate eclair or strawberry mousse. The popular Saturday and Sunday brunch features both breakfast and lunch selections.

Coasters Seafood Co. In Sarasota Boat Yard Shopping Village, 1500 Stickney Point Rd. (east end of Stickney Point Rd. Bridge). ☎ **941/925-0300.** Reservations recommended. Main courses $15–$30. AE, DC, DISC, MC, V. Sun–Thurs 11:30am–10pm, Fri–Sat 11:30am–10:30pm (bar to 1:30am). SEAFOOD.

On the bay in a quaint, New England–style shopping complex and marina across Stickney Point Bridge from Siesta Key, this casual restaurant offers great water views and fine preparations of fresh seafood selections like shrimp etoufee, Maryland-style crab cakes, and Caribbean lobster tails. The indoor brasserie-style dining room leads to a large open-air deck with ceiling fans dangling from a rustic roof (the tables out here are preferable if it's not too hot and the insects aren't on a rampage). There's entertainment Friday and Saturday evenings during winter.

Marina Jack. In Island Park, Bayfront at Central Ave. ☎ **941/365-4232.** Reservations recommended in dining room, not accepted in lounge and raw bar. Dining room main courses $13–$28. Lounge and raw bar sandwiches and salads $6–$8, main courses $9–$20. MC, V. Dining room daily noon–3pm and 5–10pm. Lounge and raw bar Mon–Sat 11:45am–3pm and 5–10pm, Sun noon–10pm. SEAFOOD/CONTINENTAL.

Overlooking the waterfront with a wraparound 270-degree view of Sarasota Bay and Siesta and Lido keys, this two-restaurants-in-one establishment has spectacular water vistas and a carefree "on vacation" attitude, especially on the open-air raw bar deck, which usually is packed all afternoon on weekends and at sunset every day. You'll have to wait for a table or bar stool down here, but be sure to make reservations if you attempt to have a meal in the upstairs dining room. The menu in both venues offers fresh native seafood, with grilled grouper your best bet upstairs. The downstairs lounge and raw bar adds sandwiches and burgers. The food is good but not the best in town, so come here for a relaxing, fun time.

If you prefer to dine on the bay rather than beside it, the paddle-wheel sightseeing boat *Marina Jack II* (☎ 941/366-9255) offers dinner cruises at $23 per person Wednesday to Sunday from October to August. Call for reservations, which are required.

✪ **Michael's on East.** 1212 East Ave. S. (between Bahia and Prospect sts.). ☎ **941/ 366-0007.** Reservations recommended. Main courses $14.50–$26. AE, DC, MC, V. Winter Mon–Fri 11:30am–2pm, daily 5:30–10pm. Off-season Mon–Fri 11:30am–2pm, Mon–Sat 6–10pm. CREATIVE INTERNATIONAL.

At the rear of the Midtown Plaza shopping center on U.S. 41 south of downtown, Michael Klauber's chic bistro is one of the top places here for fine dining, and the local's favorite after-theater haunt. Huge cut-glass walls create three intimate dining areas, one with a black marble bar for pre- or after-dinner drinks. Prepared with fresh ingredients and a creative flair, the offerings here will tempt your taste buds. A heart-of-palm salad with mangoes, stone crab meat, and a brazil-nut dressing make an exciting starter. From there, you can progress to spicy Louisiana-style crab cakes, seared Chilean sea bass with a roasted garlic and lemon sauce, or perhaps duckling served with a Bartlett-pear relish. A light-fare menu goes until midnight, and there's dancing in the lounge starting at 9:30pm.

Inexpensive

First Watch. 1395 Main St. (at Central and Pineapple aves.). Reservations not accepted. Breakfast $3–$6; sandwiches and salads, $4–$6.50. AE, DISC, MC, V. Daily 7am–2:30pm. AMERICAN.

Like its sister establishment in Naples (see section 5 in chapter 10), this bright dining room with natural-wood Windsor chairs at oak-trimmed tables is the downtown place for breakfast or lunch (it's usually packed on weekend mornings, so be prepared to wait). Traditional breakfast offerings range widely, from bacon and eggs and omelettes to a skillet layered with eggs and vegetables. There are several healthy choices, too, such as oatmeal cooked with cinnamon and apples. Lunch adds sandwiches on fresh bread and creative salads, including a tasty white-meat chicken version with raisins and crunchy water chestnuts.

If the wait's too long, walk south along Main Street to Palm Avenue; this block has several coffee houses and cafes with sidewalk seating.

Patrick's. 1400 Main St. (at Pineapple and Central aves.). ☎ **941/952-1170.** Reservations not accepted. Sandwiches and burgers $5.50–$7; main courses $11–$15. AE, MC, V. Daily 11am–midnight (Sun brunch 11am–3pm). AMERICAN.

With a semicircular facade, this informal, polished-oak and brass-rail brasserie offers wide-windowed views of downtown's main intersection. The decor also boasts hanging plants and ceiling fans, plus a unique collection of sports memorabilia. The menu offers a range of pub fare: steaks and chops, burgers, seafood, pastas, pizzas, salads, sandwiches, and omelettes; plus veal piccata, francese, or marsala; broiled salmon with dill-hollandaise sauce; and sesame chicken.

✪ **Yoder's.** 3434 Bahia Vista St. (west of Bahia Rd.). ☎ **941/955-7771.** Reservations not accepted. Breakfast $2–$6; sandwiches and burgers $3–$6; main courses $6.50–$12. AE, DC, DISC, MC, V. Mon–Sat 6am–8pm. AMISH/AMERICAN.

It's worth driving about 3 miles east of downtown to check out this good-value, award-winning eatery operated by an Amish family (both Sarasota and Bradenton have sizable Amish communities). Evoking the Pennsylvania Dutch country, the simple dining room displays handcrafts, photos, and paintings celebrating the Amish way. The menu emphasizes plain, made-from-scratch cooking such as home-style meat loaf, baked and southern fried chicken, country-smoked ham, and fried fillet of flounder. Burgers, salads, soups, and sandwiches are also available. Leave room for traditional shoo-fly pie. There's neither alcohol nor smoking here. They don't take credit cards, but there's an ATM machine near the entrance.

St. Armands Key

The evening scene here is like a fair, with locals and visitors alike strolling around St. Armands Circle, poking their heads into a few stores which stay open after dark, and window-shopping the others. It's fun and safe, so come early and plan to stay late.

Like its sibling in Naples (see "Where to Dine" in section 5 of chapter 10), the local edition of **Tommy Bahama's Tropical Cafe,** 300 John Ringling Blvd. (☎ 941/388-2888), draws a lively crowd of young professionals to its moderately priced seafood. It's upstairs over Tommy Bahama's clothing store.

Instead of ordering dessert after your meal, wander on over to **Kilwin's,** 312 John Ringling Blvd. (☎ 941/388-3200), for some gourmet chocolate, Mackinac Island fudge, or ice cream or yogurt in a homemade waffle cone. It's open Sunday to Thursday until 10:30pm, Friday and Saturday until 11pm.

See "Shopping," above, for parking tips.

Expensive

✪ **Cafe l'Europe.** 431 St. Armands Circle (at John Ringling Blvd.). ☎ **941/388-4415.** Reservations recommended. Main courses $18–$26. Pretheater dinner, $55 per couple. AE, DC, MC, V. Daily 11am–4pm and 5–10pm (pretheater dinner, daily 5–6:15pm). CONTINENTAL.

As its name implies, a European atmosphere prevails at this consistently excellent restaurant, with a decor of brick walls and arches, dark woods, brass fixtures, pink linens, and hanging plants. The menu offers selections ranging from bouillabaisse Marseilles (with lobster, snapper, shrimp, and clams) to veal and portobello napoleon with fresh tomato, garlic, and herb sauce over bow-tie pasta. A fine value, the fixed-price, pretheater dinner includes a bottle of wine.

Moderate

Charley's Crab. 420 St. Armands Circle (between John Ringling Blvd. and Blvd. of the Presidents). ☎ **941/388-3964.** Reservations recommended. Main courses $15–$25; dinner sandwiches $9–$11. AE, MC, V. Mon–Thurs 11:30am–4pm and 5–10pm, Fri–Sat 11:30am–4pm and 5–10:30pm, Sun noon–4pm and 5–10pm. SEAFOOD.

A favorite for people-watching, Charley's is popular not just for crab cakes and crab fettuccine (with mushrooms, tomatoes, and basil in a herbed shrimp sauce) but for a full range of seafood dishes. Alfresco diners fill sidewalk tables early at lunch and dinner as shoppers stroll past. A pianist adds to the lively outdoor atmosphere. Large windows in the comfortable indoor dining room give a great view of the passing parade as well.

Columbia. St. Armands Circle (between John Ringling Blvd. and John Ringling Pkwy.). ☎ **941/388-3987.** Reservations recommended. Main courses $14–$22. Early-bird specials $10–$14. AE, DC, DISC, MC, V. Mon–Sat 11am–11pm, Sun noon–10pm. Early-bird specials daily 4–6pm. SPANISH.

Like the original Columbia in Tampa's Ybor City (see "Where to Dine," in section 1, above), this one is a culinary tour de force of Spanish specialties. You can dine outside or inside, where old-world decor combines graciousness with New World efficiency and impeccable service. If you can't decide what to order, try the paella valenciana prepared with grouper, shrimp, calamari, mussels, clams, chicken, and lean pork. All main dishes include Cuban bread and rice or potato. The early-bird specials are good values for pretheater dining, and you can virtually make a meal from the tapas appetizer menu. The Patio Lounge is one of the liveliest spots here for evening entertainment from Thursday to Sunday.

Hemingway's. 325 John Ringling Blvd. (½ block off St. Armands Circle). ☎ **941/388-3948.** Reservations recommended. Main courses $12–$22; dinner sandwiches $8–$12.

AE, DC, DISC, MC, V. Sun–Thurs 11:30am–10pm, Fri–Sat 11:30am–11pm. FLORIDIAN/ CARIBBEAN.

For a casual spot with an eclectic "Floribbean" menu and a large bar with a friendly, laid-back Key West ambience, take the elevator or climb the winding stairs to this above-the-mob second-floor hideaway. Hemingway's is charming and comfortable in the best Old Florida tradition. The decor features a mix of green floral booths and tables with rattan chairs. You might start with gator bits or conch fritters, then choose from an evenly distributed mix of seafood, barbecued ribs, and other meats. Mariner's shrimp is a healthy winner: It's perfectly charcoal grilled, basted with a light teriyaki sauce, and served over rice with fresh asparagus and baby carrots.

Inexpensive

Blue Dolphin Cafe. 470 John Ringling Blvd. (1 block off St. Armand's Circle). ☎ **941/ 388-3566.** Reservations not accepted. Breakfast $4–$6.50; sandwiches, burgers, salads $4.50–$7. No credit cards. Daily 7am–3pm. AMERICAN/DINER.

On the John Ringling Boulevard spoke of St. Armands Circle, this plain, informal diner is the only inexpensive place to have breakfast or lunch in this affluent area. It offers standard breakfast and lunch choices plus chicken fajita sandwiches, homemade chili, and a wrap enclosing Thai-style stir-fried vegetables. You can order breakfast anytime.

SIESTA KEY

Ocean Boulevard, which runs through **Siesta Village,** the area's funky, laid-back beach hangout, is virtually lined with restaurants and pubs, including Blase Cafe (see below). Most have outdoor seating and bars, which attract the beach crowd during the day. At night the strip turns into a lively scene of teenagers, college students, and rock-and-roll bands.

Among the establishments here, the **Library Cafe** (☎ **941/346-1379**) is indeed library-like, but it also has a big sports TV in the cozy lounge.

✪ **Blase Cafe.** In Village Corner, 5263 Ocean Blvd. (at Calle Miramar), Siesta Village. ☎ **941/349-9822.** Reservations not accepted. Breakfast $5–$8; lunch $5–$9; main courses $9–$14. No credit cards. Daily 8:30am–10pm. Closed Mon June–Nov. INTERNATIONAL.

One of Florida's most unusual restaurants, this super-casual alfresco establishment has a few tables under cover of the Village Corner shopping center's walkway, but most guests sit at umbrella tables on a wooden deck built around a palm tree in the center's asphalt parking lot. Never mind the cars pulling in and out virtually next to your chair: the food here is so good and inexpensive that it draws droves of locals, who don't mind waiting for a table (a Chinese carryout shares the deck, so reservations are impossible). This is the key's best breakfast spot, offering Italian- and Louisiana-flavored fritattas, as well as plain old bacon and eggs. Lunch sees big salads and platters such as chicken Alfredo and Florentine crepes with shrimp. At night, chefs who've previously worked at St. Armands Circle's upscale restaurants come on duty and put forth the likes of shrimp Vera Cruz—sautéed with tomatoes, mushrooms, and artichoke hearts in a delightfully light basil cream sauce. Potato encrusted Myakka River snapper is another winner, as is pan-seared sushi quality yellowfin tuna with tangy wasabi and pickled ginger.

Turtles. 8875 Midnight Pass Rd. (at Turtle Beach Rd.). ☎ **941/346-2207.** Reservations not accepted. Salads and sandwiches $6–$9; main courses $9–$15; early-bird specials $8. AE, DC, DISC, MC, V. Winter daily 11:30am–10pm. Off-season daily 11:30am–9:30pm. Early-bird specials daily 4–6pm. AMERICAN.

With tropical overtones and breathtaking water vistas across from Turtle Beach, this informal restaurant on Little Sarasota Bay has tables both indoors and on an outside deck at which to try dishes such as snapper New Orleans, Florida-style blue crab cakes, or steak under a Jack Daniels whiskey sauce. There's a selection of pastas and platters to devour. The early-bird specials include a medium-sized fish portion.

SARASOTA AFTER DARK

The cultural capital of Florida's west coast, Sarasota is home to a host of performing arts, especially during the winter season. To get the latest update on what's happening any time of year, call the city's 24-hour **Artsline** (☎ 941/365-ARTS).

THE CLUB & MUSIC SCENE   You can find plenty of music to dance to on the mainland at **Sarasota Quay,** the downtown waterfront dining-shopping-entertainment complex on Tamiami Trail (U.S. 41) a block north of John Ringling Causeway. Just walk around this brick building and your ears will take you to the action. The laser sound-and-light crowd gathers at **In Extremis** (☎ 941/954-2008), where a high-energy deejay spins Top 40 tunes. **Downunder Jazz Bar** (☎ 941/951-2467) offers contemporary jazz. Michael's Seafood Grill turns into **Anthony's After Dark** rocking disco at 10:30pm.

And don't forget the evening entertainment at **Marina Jack** and **Michael's on East** (see "Where to Dine," above).

Over on St. Armands Circle, the **Patio Lounge** in Columbia restaurant (☎ 941/388-3987) is one of the liveliest spots along the beach strip, featuring live, high-energy dance music on Tuesday to Sunday evenings. And on Siesta Key, the pubs and restaurants along Ocean Boulevard in Siesta Village have noisy rock-and-roll bands entertaining a mostly young crowd (see "Where to Dine," above).

THE PERFORMING ARTS   Designated as the State Theater of Florida in 1965, the ✪ **Asolo Center** for the Performing Arts, 5555 N. Tamiami Trail (U.S. 41), at the Ringling museum complex (☎ 941/351-8000), is home to the Asolo Theatre Company and the Conservatory for Professional Actor Training. The main stage, the 487-seat Harold E. and Ethel M. Mertz Theatre, is an attraction in itself—the former Dumfermline Opera House, originally constructed in Scotland in 1900 and transferred piece by piece to Sarasota in 1987. In 1994 and 1995 the 161-seat Asolo Conservatory Theatre was added as a smaller venue for experimental and alternative offerings. The season runs from December to mid-June for the main stage and from November to May for the smaller theater. Ticket prices range from $5 to $39.

Free guided tours of the center are offered Wednesday to Saturday from 10 to 11:30am, except from June to August and during technical rehearsals between plays; call for tour times.

Downtown, the lavender, seashell-shaped **Van Wezel Performing Arts Hall,** 777 N. Tamiami Trail (U.S. 41), at 9th Street (☎ 941/953-3366), is visible for miles on the bayfront skyline. It offers excellent visual and acoustic conditions, with year-round programs ranging from symphony and jazz concerts, opera, musical comedy, and choral productions to ballet and international productions. It's the home of the Florida West Coast Symphony, the Jazz Club of Sarasota, the Sarasota Ballet of Florida, and the Sarasota Concert Band.

Downtown Sarasota's theater district is home to the **Florida Studio Theatre,** 1241 N. Palm Ave., at Cocoanut Avenue (☎ 941/366-9796), which has contemporary performances from December to August, including a New Play Festival in May. Built in 1926 as the Edwards Theater, **The Opera House,** 61 N. Pineapple Ave., between Main and 1st streets (☎ 941/953-7030), hosts the Sarasota Opera in February and March, while the Sarasota Ballet and other companies take the stage the rest of the year. Next door to The Opera House, the **Golden Apple Dinner Theatre,** 25 N.

Pineapple Ave. (☎ 941/366-5454), presents cocktails, dinner, and a professional Broadway-style show year-round. The professional, nonequity **Theatre Works,** 1247 1st St., at Cocoanut Ave. (☎ 941/952-9170), presents musical revues and other works all year.

6 Bradenton & Anna Maria Island

26 miles S of St. Petersburg, 41 miles SW of Tampa, 15 miles N of Sarasota

Visitors often overlook Bradenton as they speed south on their way to Sarasota and beyond. But here you can visit "Snooty" the famous manatee, and you can take an entire vacation on **Anna Maria Island,** northernmost in the chain of barrier islands stretching from Tampa Bay to Sarasota. Anna Maria claims 7½ miles of white-sand beaches—but no glitzy resorts, just casual island getaways. The island's communities—Bradenton Beach, Holmes Beach, and Anna Maria—are popular with family vacationers and seniors, offering a variety of public beaches, fishing piers, bungalows, low-rise motels, and a terrific bed-and-breakfast. You can have a very relaxing beach vacation here without the bustle and out-of-sight prices found elsewhere.

Bradenton and Manatee County also own the northern half of Longboat Key, connected by bridge to Anna Maria Island. Most of the Longboat resorts are closer to Sarasota than to Bradenton, so I have included them in section 5, above. On the northern tip of Longboat, the little fishing village of Longbeach was established in 1885 and still has some remnants of Old Florida.

ESSENTIALS

GETTING THERE   Bradenton shares **Sarasota-Bradenton International Airport** with Sarasota (see "Essentials," in section 5, above). **Diplomat Taxi** (☎ 941/355-5155) charges about $15 to downtown Bradenton, $22 to $30 to Bradenton Beach, and $35 to Anna Maria Island.

VISITOR INFORMATION   For a packet of information about Bradenton, Anna Maria Island, and surrounding Manatee County, contact the **Greater Bradenton Area Convention and Visitors Bureau,** P.O. Box 1000, Bradenton, FL 34206 (☎ 800/4-MANATEE or 941/729-9177; fax 941/729-1820; www.floridaislandbeaches.org).

For maps, brochures, and information, call or drop by the **Manatee County Tourist Information Center,** on U.S. 301 just west of Exit 43 off I-75 (☎ 941/729-7040). Open daily except holidays from 8:30am to 5:30pm, it has a volunteer staff on hand to answer your questions.

GETTING AROUND   Manatee County Area Transit, known locally as **Manatee CAT** (☎ 941/749-7116), operates scheduled public bus service throughout the area.

Taxi companies include **Bruce's Taxi** (☎ 941/755-6070), **Checker Cab** (☎ 941/751-3181), and **Yellow Cab** (☎ 941/748-4800).

HITTING THE BEACH

There are four public beaches on Anna Maria Island, all with rest rooms, picnic areas, lifeguards, and free parking. The largest and best is **Coquina Beach,** which occupies the southern mile of the island below Bradenton Beach. It has both gulf and bay sides, is sheltered by whispering Australian pines, and has large parking lots. **Cortez Beach** is in Bradenton Beach, just north of Coquina Beach. In the island's center, **Manatee County Public Beach** is at Gulf Drive. **Holmes Beach** is at the west end of Manatee Avenue (Fla. 64). **Anna Maria Bayfront Park** is on Bay Boulevard at the northwest end of the island, fronting both the bay and the Gulf of Mexico.

OUTDOOR PURSUITS & SPECTATOR SPORTS

BICYLING & IN-LINE SKATING   The flat terrain makes for good in-line skating and fine if not challenging bike riding. **Native Rentals,** in S&S Plaza, 5340 Marina Dr. in Holmes Beach (☎ **941/778-7757**), rents both, with bikes starting at $3 an hour or $9 per day, skates for $4 an hour or $15 a day. The office is opposite the BP service station in the Holmes Beach business district. Open Monday to Saturday from 7am to 7pm, Sunday from 9am to 5pm.

BOATING & FISHING   When Florida's ban on net fishing devastated its traditional business, the village of Cortez on the east side of the Cortez Bridge aimed for another catch: tourist dollars. Here you can go deep-sea fishing with the **Cortez Fleet,** 4330 127th St. W. (☎ **941/794-1223**). Party-boat deep-sea fishing voyages range from 4 hours to 9 hours, with prices starting at $25 for adults, $22 for seniors, and $12.50 for children. Call for the schedules, which can change from day to day. The rental part of the business has ski and pontoon boats, Wave Runners, and other equipment, ranging in price from about $45 an hour for Wave Runners to $155 for a day's use of a pontoon boat.

On Anna Maria Island, you can rent boats from **Bradenton Beach Marina,** 402 Church Ave. (☎ **941/778-2288**); **Captain's Marina,** 5501 Marina Dr., Holmes Beach (☎ **941/778-1977**); and **Five O'Clock Marina,** 412 Pine Ave., Anna Maria (☎ **941/778-5577**). On northern Longboat Key, **Cannons Marina,** 6040 Gulf of Mexico Dr. (☎ **941/383-1311**), also rents boats. Several deep-sea fishing charter boats are based at these marinas.

You also can fish from **Anna Maria City Pier,** on the north end of Anna Maria Island, and at the **Bradenton Beach City Pier,** at Cortez Road. Both are free of charge.

CRUISES   The *Cortez Lady* (☎ **941/794-1223**), in Cortez (☎ **941/761-9777**), makes sightseeing cruises to **Egmont Key State Park,** on historic Egmont Key 3 miles off the northern end of Anna Maria Island at the mouth of Tampa Bay, site of the crumbling Spanish-American War–era Fort Dade and home to threatened gopher tortoises. Sea turtles come ashore here to nest. You can go snorkeling and shelling here, so bring your swimsuit and gear. This cruise costs $20 for adults, $15 seniors, $10 children 14 and under. Call for schedules and reservations.

You can also get to Egmont Key on a 30-foot sloop-rigged sailboat with **Spice Sailing Charters** (☎ **941/778-3240**), based at the Galati Yacht Basin on Bay Boulevard on northern Anna Maria Island. The company also has sunset cruises. Call for schedules, prices, and reservations, which are required.

That paddle wheeler you see going up and down the bay is the ***Seafood Shack Showboat,*** operated by the Seafood Shack restaurant, 4110 127th St. W., in Cortez (☎ **800/299-5048** or 941/794-5048). It has afternoon and sunset cruises to Sarasota Bay, Tampa Bay, and as far away as the Sunshine Skyway. Prices range from $13 to $15 for adults, $11 to $13 for seniors, and $5.60 for children 4 to 11. The *Showboat* goes to a different destination each day, so call for the schedule.

Open-air, eight-passenger craft are operated by **Manatee Airboat Tours,** Perico Harbour Marina, 12310 Manatee Ave. (Fla. 64) (☎ **941/730-1011**). The ride lasts 55 minutes, with departures year-round. Rides cost $12 for adults, $10 for children. Call for schedule and reservations.

GOLF   The city and county operate several municipal courses where you can play without breaking your budget.

Locals say they prefer the county's 18-hole, par-72 **Buffalo Creek Golf Course,** on the north side of the river at 8100 Erie Rd. in Palmetto (☎ **941/776-2611**). At well over 7,000 yards, it's the longest in the area, and lots of water and alligators will keep you entertained. Wintertime greens fees are about $34 with cart, $24 without. They drop to about $18 and $16, respectively, during summer.

You'll pay the same at **Manatee County Golf Course,** 5290 66th St. W. (☎ 941/792-6773), an 18-hole, par-72 course on the southern rim of the city. Both county courses require that tee times be set up at least 2 days in advance.

Also open to the public, the city's **River Run Golf Links,** 1801 27th St. E. (☎ 941/747-6331), set beside the Braden River, is an 18-hole, par-70 course with lots of water in its layout. Winter fees here are about $26 with cart, $17 walking. They're about $16 riding, $8 walking in summer. A 2-day advance notice is required for tee times here, too.

Other courses include the **Palma Sola Golf Club,** 3807 75th St. W. (☎ 941/792-7476), just north of Fla. 684 and east of Palma Sola Bay, with an 18-hole, par-72 course and the same 2-day advance booking requirement.

Situated just off U.S. 41, the **Heather Hills Golf Club,** 101 Cortez Rd. W. (☎ 941/755-8888), operates an 18-hole, par-61 executive course on a first-come, first-served basis. There's a driving range and clubs can be rented. It's open daily from 6:30am until dark.

Bradenton also is home to the well-known **David Leadbetter Golf Academy,** 1414 69th Ave. (at U.S. 41) (☎ 800/424-3542 or 941/739-2483), a part of the Nick Bollettieri Sports Academy (see "Tennis," below). Presided over by one of golf's leading instructors, this facility offers practice tee instruction, video analysis, and scoring strategy, as well as general tuition. Prices start at $150.

KAYAKING   **Native Rentals,** in S&S Plaza, 5340 Marina Dr., opposite the BP service station in Holmes Beach (☎ 941/778-7757), rents one- and two-person kayaks and has guided tours around the mangrove islands dotting some of the bay near here. Rentals start at $8 a hour, $24 a day. Call for details about the tours.

SPECTATOR SPORTS   The **Pittsburgh Pirates** do their February-through-March spring training at 6,562-seat McKechnie Field, 9th Street West and 17th Avenue West (☎ 941/748-4610), south of downtown. Admission ranges from $5.50 to $8.50.

TENNIS   The **Nick Bollettieri Sports Academy,** 5500 34th St. W. (☎ 800/872-6425 or 941/755-1000), is one of the world's largest tennis-training facilities, with more than 70 championship courts and a pro shop. It's open year-round, and reservations are required for all activities. One-day instructional programs cost $165 for adults, $175 for juniors age 8 to 18. Overnight packages start at $278 for adults, $205 for juniors. The academy also has training courses in soccer, baseball, and golf.

EXPLORING THE AREA

On weekends, you can see the sights of rural Manatee County northwest of Bradenton on a 1¼-hour narrated sightseeing tour aboard a 1950s diesel-engine train operated by the **Florida Gulf Coast Railroad,** 83rd Street East, off U.S. 301 in Parrish (☎ 941/722-4272). The schedule and fares are seasonal, so call before driving out here.

Art League of Manatee County. 209 9th St. W. (Business U.S. 41, at 3rd Ave. W.). ☎ 941/746-2862. Free admission. Mon–Fri 9am–4:30pm.

Bradenton's downtown cultural hub, this gallery offers an ever-changing program of art exhibits, shows, courses, workshops, and craft demonstrations.

✪ **DeSoto National Memorial.** DeSoto Memorial Hwy. (north end of 75th St. W.). ☎ 941/792-0458. Free admission. Daily 9am–5pm. Take Manatee Ave. (Fla. 64) west to 75th St. W. and turn right; follow the road to its end and the entrance to the park.

Nestled on the Manatee River west of downtown, this park re-creates the look and atmosphere of when Spanish explorer Hernando de Soto landed here in 1539. It includes a restoration of de Soto's original campsite and a scenic half-mile nature trail that circles a mangrove jungle and leads to the ruins of one of the first settlements of the area. From December to March, park employees dress in 16th-century costumes and portray the way the early settlers lived, including demonstrations of cooking and musket firing.

Gamble Plantation. 3708 Patten Ave. (U.S. 301), Ellenton. ☎ **941/723-4536.** Free admission. Tours $3 adults, $1.50 children 6–12, free for children under 6. Thurs–Mon 9am–4:30pm; guided tours given at 9:30 and 10:30am, and 1, 2, 3, and 4pm. Take U.S. 301 north of downtown to Ellenton; the site is on the left just east of Ellenton-Gillette Rd. (Fla. 683).

Situated northeast of downtown Bradenton, this is the oldest structure on the southwestern coast of Florida, and a fine example of an antebellum plantation home. Built over a 6-year period in the late 1840s by Maj. Robert Gamble, it was constructed primarily of "tabby mortar" (a mixture of oyster shells, sand, molasses, and water), with 10 rooms, verandas on three sides, 18 exterior columns, and 8 fireplaces. It's maintained as a state historic site and includes a fine collection of 19th-century furnishings. Entrance to the house is by tour only, although the grounds may be explored on your own.

Manatee Village Historical Park. 6th Ave. E. and 15th St. E. ☎ **941/749-7165.** Free admission; donations welcome. Mon–Fri 9am–4:30pm. From downtown, go east on 6th Ave. E. through a merger with Manatee Ave., then right on 15th St. E.

A tree-shaded park with a courtyard of hand-laid bricks, this national historic site features restored buildings, including the Manatee County Court House, dating from 1860 and the oldest structure of its kind still standing on the south Florida mainland; a Methodist church built in 1887; a typical "Cracker Gothic" house built in 1912; and the Wiggins General Store, dating from 1903 and full of local memorabilia from swamp root and grub dust to louse powder.

☉ South Florida Museum, Bishop Planetarium, and Parker Manatee Aquarium. 201 10th St. W. (on the riverfront, at Barcarrota Blvd.). ☎ **941/746-4131.** Admission $7.50 adults, $6 seniors, $4 children 5–12, free for children 4 and under. Admission includes planetarium shows. Mon–Sat 10am–5pm, Sun noon–5pm. Closed New Year's Day, Thanksgiving, Christmas. From U.S. 41, take Manatee Ave. west to 10th St. W. and turn right.

The star at this downtown complex is "Snooty," the oldest manatee born in captivity (1948) and Manatee County's official mascot. Snooty lives in the Parker Manatee Aquarium. The South Florida Museum tells the story of Florida's history, from prehistoric times to the present, including a Native American collection with life-size dioramas and a Spanish courtyard containing replicas of 16th-century buildings. The Bishop Planetarium features a 50-foot hemispherical dome that arcs above a seating area, for laser light and educational star shows.

SHOPPING

For discount shopping, the focal point of the Bradenton area is the **Prime Outlets Ellenton,** on U.S. 301 at exit 43 off I-75 in Ellenton (☎ **941/723-1150**), about a 15-minute drive northeast of downtown (turn left at the first stoplight east of I-75). This Spanish-style outdoor center has more than 100 factory and outlet stores, including a Saks Off Fifth Avenue, Coach Leather, Liz Claiborne, Bass Shoes, Corning Revere, Jockey, Levi's, Nike, Ann Taylor, Donna Karan, Jones New York, Paul Harris, Tommy Hilfiger, Geoffrey Beene, Van Heusen, Maidenform, Royal Doulton, Mikasa, Seiko, Sony, and Bose. Shops are open Monday to Saturday from 10am to 9pm and Sunday from 11am to 6pm.

WHERE TO STAY

The Bradenton Area Convention and Visitors Bureau (see "Essentials," above) operates a free **reservation service** (☎ 800/4-MANATEE), and its annual visitor guide lists all of Manatee County's accommodations, including condominium complexes. **A Paradise Rental Management,** 5201 Gulf Dr., Holmes Beach, FL 34217 (☎ 800/237-2252 or 941/778-4800; fax 941/778-7090; www.manatee-online.com/aparadise), represents a number of condo complexes with weekly rates ranging from $500 off-season to $1,950 a week during winter.

Except for those near I-75 east of the city, Bradenton has few national chain motels. On the other hand, those on U.S. 41 and University Parkway near the Sarasota-Bradenton International Airport are about halfway between downtown and Sarasota. On Longboat Key, the Hilton and Holiday Inn are equally convenient to Anna Maria Island and Bradenton. See "Where to Stay," in section 5, above, for details about nearby Sarasota accommodations. The high season here is January to April. Hotel tax is 9% in Manatee County.

ON THE MAINLAND

Holiday Inn Riverfront. 100 Riverfront Dr. W. (at 3rd St. W.), Bradenton, FL 34205. ☎ **800/HOLIDAY** or 941/747-3727. Fax 941/746-4289. 153 units. A/C TV TEL. Winter $109–$139 double. Off-season $89–$109 double. Golf packages available. AE, DC, DISC, MC, V. From U.S. 41, go west on Manatee Ave. (Fla. 64) and turn right on 3rd St. W. to hotel on left.

This five-story Spanish hacienda–style structure overlooking the Manatee River is downtown Bradenton's only commercial hotel. The highlight is a remarkable riverside landscaped courtyard with fountains and tropical trees. Inside, the public areas reflect an Iberian ambience, with dark wood trim, tile floors, and high-beamed ceilings. The bedrooms lack this charm, with standard hotel furnishings augmented by coffeemakers, irons and boards, and hair dryers. Those above the ground floor have balconies and views of the river or the courtyard. Facilities include a restaurant, lounge, heated outdoor swimming pool, exercise room, and gift shop. There are laundry and room service and complimentary newspaper delivery.

○ **Park Inn Club and Breakfast.** 4450 47th St. W. (at 44th Ave./Cortez Rd.), Bradenton, FL 34210. ☎ **800/437-PARK** or 941/795-4633. Fax 941/795-0808. www.parkinnclub-bradenton.com. 130 units. A/C TV TEL. Winter $104–$134 double. Off-season $74–$114 double. Rates include continental breakfast and evening cocktails. Golf packages available. AE, DC, DISC, MC, V. Pets accepted with fee. From I-75, take Exit 41 and follow Fla. 70 west 6½ miles, turn right on U.S. 41 north, left on 44th Ave. W. (Fla. 684) to 47th St. W., and hotel is on left.

Families will find this Cortez Road/44th Avenue location to be busy but convenient, for there are ample chain restaurants and a multiscreen cinema in the adjacent shopping centers. And you can't get lost driving to Bradenton Beach, a straight-line, 6-mile trip west on Cortez Road. The three-story contemporary building is wrapped around a lush central courtyard with a patio and swimming pool and Jacuzzi. The guest rooms are spacious, and the suites have whirlpools. All bathrooms here have hair dryers, phones, and TV speakers. Facilities include a courtyard pool and a lounge in which guests are served breakfast and complimentary cocktails each evening. Guests get free use of Gold's Gym next door.

ANNA MARIA ISLAND

Anna Maria's lone chain motel is the moderately priced **Econo Lodge Surfside,** 2502 Gulf Dr. N. (at 25th St. N.), Bradenton Beach, FL 34217 (☎ **800/55-ECONO** or

941/778-6671; fax 941/778-0360). This clean and well-maintained beachfront facility has 18 suites and 36 spacious rooms in its main three-story building, plus 18 rooms in another one-story building on the beach and 5 more across the street (the least expensive).

The Beach Inn. 101 66th St., Holmes Beach, FL 34217. ☎ **800/823-2247** or 941/778-9597. Fax 941/778-8303. www.thebeachinn.com. 14 units. A/C TV TEL. Winter $189–$249 double. Off-season $149–$199 double. Rates include continental breakfast. MC, V.

Jo and Frank Davis, owners of the Harrington House (see below), took over this two-story beachfront motel in 1998, gave it a thorough remodeling, and turned it into a couples-oriented inn. The property has two buildings, one on the beach, the other to the rear facing a tropical courtyard. Beachfront rooms have fireplaces, raised Jacuzzi tubs, bar areas, small microwaves, king-size beds, shower-only bathrooms, and either balconies or spacious decks separated from the gulf by sea oats. The less expensive units in the rear building are less well equipped; they have two full-size beds. There's no restaurant here, but guests receive complimentary continental breakfast, and the excellent Beach Bistro (see below) is next door.

✪ **Harrington House.** 5626 Gulf Dr. (at 58th St.), Holmes Beach, FL 34217. ☎ **888/828-5566** or 941/778-5444. Fax 941/778-0527. www.harringtonhouse.com. 14 units. A/C TV. Winter $19–$249 double. Off-season $129–$179. MC, V.

Flowers will be everywhere and a private beach will be awaiting when you arrive at Jo and Frank Harris's bed-and-breakfast, the best romantic lovers' getaway hereabouts. In a tree-shaded setting on the beach overlooking the Gulf of Mexico, this three-story coquina-and-rock house was built in 1925 and exudes an Old Florida ambience. The eight bedrooms are individually decorated with antique, wicker, or rattan furnishings. Some units have four-poster or brass beds, and the higher-priced rooms have French doors leading to balconies overlooking the gulf. In addition to the bedrooms in the main house, four rooms are available in the adjacent Spangler Beach House, a remodeled 1940s captain's home, and four more in the nearby Huth House, a low-slung beachside residence (three units here open to an expansive covered lanai facing the beach through a row of Australian pines). All guests enjoy use of the high-ceilinged living room with a fireplace, a beachside pool, a patio, and complimentary use of bicycles, kayaks, and other sports equipment. No smoking inside here.

Tropic Isle Inn. 2103 Gulf Dr. N. (at 22nd St.), Bradenton Beach, FL 34217. ☎ **941/778-1237.** Fax 941/778-7821. www.annamarisland.com. 15 units. A/C TV TEL. Winter $80–$115. Off-season $55–$80. Weekly and monthly rates available. Minimum 1-week rental Feb–Apr. AE, DISC, MC, V.

Across Gulf Drive from its own narrow strip of beach, this older motel was spiffed up in 1998 and is now the inexpensive choice here. Three units are standard motel rooms, but the others have one or two bedrooms in addition to living areas with cooking facilities. You'll have to make do with small, shower-only baths, but the entire complex is clean and well maintained. There are a guest laundry and a roadside courtyard with gazebo and heated pool. Restaurants are within walking distance. This is a no-smoking establishment.

WHERE TO DINE
ON THE MAINLAND

✪ **Miller's Dutch Kitchen.** 3401 14th St. W. (U.S. 41 Business, at 34th Ave. W.). ☎ **941/746-8253.** Reservations not accepted. Sandwiches $2.50–$5; main courses $6.25–$13. MC, V. Mon–Sat 11am–8pm. Closed Christmas. AMERICAN.

There's a charming treat waiting inside this modern, nondescript brick building among the auto dealers on U.S. 41 Business, for its Pennsylvania Dutch country dining room is surrounded by a balcony, around whose edge chugs a model train. Over the balcony railing you'll see quilts and other handcrafts, all products of Bradenton's Amish community and all very much for sale. Although plain, the food here is as fresh as it gets. The regular American items such as fried shrimp, stuffed flounder, and barbecued pork ribs are augmented by daily Amish specialties such as cabbage rolls and Dutch casserole (noodles, peas, cheese, potatoes, beef, mushrooms, and chicken soup with croutons). Leave room for dessert: You can choose from 20 types of homemade pies. No smoking and no alcohol here.

Twin Dolphin Marina Grill. On The Pier, 1200 1st Ave. W. (north end of 12th St. W.). ☎ **941/748-8087.** Reservations recommended on weekends. Main courses $14–$24. AE, DC, DISC, MC, V. Sun–Thurs 11:30am–9pm, Fri–Sat 11:30am–11pm. FLORIBBEAN.

Commanding views of the Manatee River draw lunch and after-work crowds to this downtown restaurant housed in a stately Spanish-style landmark building at the foot of 12th Street (Old Main Street) on Memorial Pier. The menu offers the day's fresh catch grilled, broiled, blackened, bronzed, or jerked Jamaican-style. For starters, shrimp are fried in a light tempura sauce and served with a Floribbean dipping sauce. For a main course you can opt for fresh fish, crab cakes, or shrimp Provençal. Lighter fare is available outside at **Flipper's Dockside Patio Grill,** a tropical-style bar by the river; it has a light fare menu. There are valet parking at night and entertainment Friday to Sunday evenings.

ANNA MARIA ISLAND

The local **Shells** seafood restaurant is at 3200 East Bay Dr. in Holmes Beach (☎ **941/778-5997**). See "Where to Dine" in section 1, above.

Expensive

✪ **Beach Bistro.** 6600 Gulf Dr. N. (at 66th St.), Holmes Beach. ☎ **941/778-6444.** Reservations recommended. Main courses $22–$34. AE, DC, DISC, MC, V. Daily 5:30–10pm. INTERNATIONAL.

Winner of a Golden Spoon award as one of Florida's 20 best restaurants, this culinary oasis is Anna Maria Island's top place for fine dining. It sits right beside the beach, offering wide-windowed views of the gulf waters. A romantic ambience and overall elegance is enhanced by crisp linens, sparkling crystal, and fresh flowers on every table. Bistro bouillabaisse made with premium fish, shrimp, scallops, and squid is the signature dish here. Other regular offerings include grouper Picasso—sautéed in a coconut and cashew crust and finished with a red pepper and papaya sauce.

Moderate

The Beachhouse. 200 Gulf Dr. N. (at Cortez Rd.), Bradenton Beach. ☎ **941/779-2222.** Reservations not accepted on patio, but call for preferred seating inside. Sandwiches $7–$10; main courses $10–$20. AE, DC, DISC, MC, V. Daily 11:30am–10pm. AMERICAN.

This large, lively place sits right on Bradenton Beach with a huge open deck and a covered pavilion facing out to the gulf. Even inside, wide windows let in the view. Owned by Ed Chiles, son of the late Florida governor and U.S. senator, the Beachhouse offers daily fresh fish specials, including the signature beechnut grouper (with nutty crust in citrus-butter sauce). There's also a good variety of fare, including seafood salads and pastas, crab cakes, fish-and-chips, and broiled steaks. Local musicians play out on the patio most afternoons and evenings.

Rotten Ralph's. 902 S. Bay Blvd., Anna Maria. ☎ **941/778-3953.** Reservations not accepted. Sandwiches and burgers $4–$8; main courses $10–$17. DC, DISC, MC, V. Daily

11am–9pm. From Gulf Dr., turn toward the bay on Pine Ave., then right at a dead end to the end of Bay Blvd. SEAFOOD.

On the north end of the island overlooking Bimini Bay, this casual Old Florida–style restaurant has both indoor and outdoor seating. The menu offers many seafood choices from British-style fish-and-chips (the house specialty) to crab cakes, snow crab, oysters, and grouper. Other choices include Danish baby back ribs and Anna Maria chicken (marinated and grilled with a honey-mustard sauce).

✪ **Sandbar.** 100 Spring Ave. (east of Gulf Dr.), Anna Maria. ☎ **941/778-0444.** Reservations not accepted on deck; call for preferred seating in the main restaurant. Salads and sandwiches $6–$10; main courses $14–$20. AE, DC, DISC, MC, V. Dining room daily 11:30am–3pm and 4–10pm; deck daily 11:30am–10pm. SEAFOOD.

Sitting on the site of the former Pavilion, built in 1913 when people from Tampa and St. Pete took the ferry here, this popular restaurant is perched right on the beach overlooking the gulf. The air-conditioned, knotty-pine dining room offers several traditional as well as innovative preparations of seafood (crab cakes over a roasted pepper sauce, Southwestern-style grouper). The real action here is under the umbrellas on the lively beachside deck, where a menu of appetizers, sandwiches, salads, and platters are served all day and night. Live music makes a party on the deck Monday to Friday nights and on Saturday and Sunday from 1 to 10pm. The inside bar is one of the few I've seen in Florida with no sports TVs.

Inexpensive

✪ **Gulf Drive Café.** 900 Gulf Dr. N. (at 9th St.), Bradenton Beach. ☎ **941/778-1919.** Reservations not accepted. Breakfast $2.50–$5.50; sandwiches and burgers $4–$5.25; main courses $7–$11. DISC, MC, V. Daily 7am–9:30pm. SEAFOOD.

Locals flock to this bright gulfside cafe for the best bargains on the beach. With big windows, bentwood cafe chairs with colorful cushions, and lots of hanging plants and ceiling fans, the coral and green dining room opens to a beachside patio with tables shaded by a trellis (the wait is worth it). The breakfast fare is led by sweet Belgian waffles, which are available all day. You can also order salads, sandwiches, and burgers anytime here, with quiche du jour, Mediterranean seafood pasta, and regular seafood platters joining the show at 4pm.

Rod & Reel Pier Restaurant & Snack Bar. 875 North Shore Dr., Anna Maria. ☎ **941/ 778-1885.** Reservations not accepted. Breakfast $2.50–$5; sandwiches $3–6; main courses $6–$10. No credit cards. Daily 7am–10pm. Closed Christmas. SEAFOOD. From Gulf Dr., turn toward the bay on Pine Ave., left at a dead end onto Bay Blvd., right on Allamanda Ave. to pier.

Sitting out on the Rod & Reel Pier at the north end of the island, this little no-frills fish-camp enjoys an extraordinary view of Tampa Bay, including Egmont Key and the Skyway Bridge on the horizon. The chow is mostly fried seafood—fish, shrimp, scallops, forgettable crab cakes, and a piled-high combination platter of all of the above. On the other hand, owner Rayna Stowe's tasty Mexican-style grouper (sautéed with peppers, onions, and salsa) is her most popular and by far best dish. Rayna will cook your catch, provided you snag it from the pier.

LONGBOAT KEY

✪ **Moore's Stone Crab.** 800 Broadway (at Bayside Dr.). ☎ **941/383-1748.** Reservations not accepted. Sandwiches and salads $6–$10; main courses $10–$22. DISC, MC, V. Winter daily 11:30am–9:30pm. Off-season Mon–Fri 5–10pm, Sat–Sun 11:30am–10pm. SEAFOOD.

In Longbeach, the old fishing village on the north end of Longboat Key, this popular bayfront restaurant began in 1967 as an offshoot of a family seafood business established 40 years earlier. From the outside, in fact, it still looks a little like a packing house, but the view of the bay dotted with mangrove islands makes a fine complement to stone crabs fresh from the family's own traps from October to March. Otherwise, the menu offers every imaginable seafood, most of it fried or broiled. Sandwiches and salads are served all day.

BRADENTON AFTER DARK

Locals and visitors alike head south to neighboring Sarasota for their culture (see "Sarasota After Dark," in section 5). Meantime, the action here is at beach restaurants and pubs.

Live bands lend a party atmosphere to the gulfside deck at the **Sandbar** restaurant every night and from 1pm on weekends (see "Where to Dine," above). The **elegant Cafe Robar,** at the corner of Gulf Drive and Pine Avenue in Anna Maria (☎ **941/ 778-6969**), offers piano music and a sing-along bar on Tuesday to Sunday evenings. **D. Coy Ducks Bar & Grille,** in the Island Shopping Center at Marina Drive and 54th Street in Holmes Beach (☎ **941/778-5888**), has a varied program of live Dixieland bands, jazz pianists, and guitarists.

12 Walt Disney World & Orlando

by Mary Meehan

More than 30 years ago, while flying over 43 square miles of scrub brush and swampland just south of a sleepy Southern town, Walt Disney saw what he needed to create a whole new world. Orlando, where the biggest tourist draw before 1972 had been a downtown fountain, would never be the same. Now, with the millennium upon us, it seems that at least one full-scale theme park opens every year, and visitors have never had more options.

Especially in Orlando, with so many tourist attractions vying for your time and money, advance planning is a must. Walt's world now claims four distinct parks, two entertainment districts, enough hotels to fill a small city, and several smaller attractions, including water parks and miniature-golf courses.

Universal Studios Escape is expanding rapidly, and it added a night-time entertainment destination, CityWalk, in 1999. Universal's second park, which also opened in 1999, is called Islands of Adventure; it showcases stomach-churning thrill rides and many attractions with Baby Boomer appeal, like Cat in the Hat and Spider Man. The one-two punch of both parks could give the Mouse some serious competition and means more bargains for travelers in the form of multiday ticket packages.

Universal is also trying to lure some of the public away from Disney with the opening of its first on-property resort, Portofino Bay. This 750-room Loews hotel opened in 1999 and offers perks similar to those you'd get at a Disney resort, such as transportation to the parks and early admission. The same perks will be available at Universal's second property, the Hard Rock Hotel, which is scheduled to open late in 2000.

Sea World is also growing, although at a slower pace. A major renovation in 1997 updated its 1970s look, and additional renovations are ongoing throughout the park. The marine park also upped the thrill factor in 1998 by adding a water roller coaster called Journey to Atlantis, and new shows are being added all the time. Discovery Cove, an additional 30-acre park, will open sometime within the next few years.

And as if that weren't enough competition, after years of cowering to the Mouse, Universal and other non-Disney attractions are banding together to offer special packages and discounts. These "Flex Passes" offer visitors the choice of several parks for one flat price and is a direct assault on Disney's multiday-pass system.

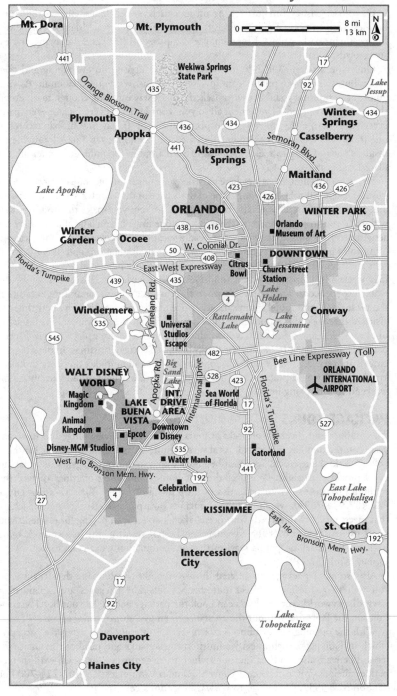

Of course, Disney isn't just resting on its laurels, either. It has entered the cruise business with two ocean-going vessels that visit their own private islands. The newest Disney theme park, Animal Kingdom, was completed in 1999 and is drawing impressive crowds.

Once you arrive in Orlando, it's easy to get the urge to do everything and then some. But, to borrow a phrase from my New York in-laws: Fuhgeddaboudit. As your guide, I can promise you that even a packed 2-week stay isn't long enough to hit everything. But don't panic—I've done it all so you won't have to. Every inch of every park, every restaurant, every hotel—I've inspected them all. (Okay, my husband checked out those theme-park men's rooms, but he assures me they're fine.) I provide an insider's view of how to make the most of your time in Orlando. It is, after all, the place I call home.

Yes, there are enough options here to make your head spin like one of those famous Disney teacups. But by following some of the advice in this chapter, you'll be prepared and informed about all your choices. My goal? To help you make the decisions that will make your trip easy and enjoyable. If I've done my job, you'll be able to enjoy the activities at such a pace that you won't need a vacation to recover from your vacation.

As you know, Orlando is essentially a theme-park destination, and its busiest seasons are whenever kids are out of school—summer (early June to about Aug 20), holiday weekends, Christmas season (mid-Dec to mid-Jan), and Easter. Obviously, the whole experience is more enjoyable when the crowds are thinnest and the weather is the most temperate (hotel rooms are also priced lower off-season). The best times to visit are the week after Labor Day until Thanksgiving, the week after Thanksgiving until mid-December, and the 6 weeks before and after school spring vacations. Packed parking lots are the norm during the weeks before and after Christmas. In the summer, crowds are very large and weather is oppressively hot and humid. I probably shouldn't say this, but I would pull the kids out of school for a few days around an off-season weekend to avoid long lines.

PACKAGE TOURS

The number and diversity of package tours to Orlando is staggering, and in recent years competition has intensified. As always, significant savings are available for those willing to do the research. Your best bet: Stop into a sizable travel agency and pick up every brochure in sight. Pore over them at home, comparing offerings to find the optimum package for your trip. Also pick up the *Walt Disney World Vacations Guide* (☎ 407/934-7639), which lists the company's own packages. Try to find a package that meets rather than exceeds your needs; there's no sense in paying for elements you won't use. Also, read over the advantages to Disney resort guests in section 3; some packages list as selling points services that are automatically available to every Walt Disney World (WDW) guest.

Also, so many packages are offered through the Disney company that it will serve you well to go online to check out the options. The packages are explained at **www.disneyworld.com,** and you can book the package and make your hotel reservations on the Web site, without the assistance of an operator or travel agent.

With the opening of Portofino Bay, Universal is offering more extensive packages, which include perks such as early admission to the parks and head-of-the-line privileges. There are also land/sea vacations which package trips to the beach with theme-park excursions. You can contact Universal Studio Vacations at ☎ 407/224-7000 or ☎ 888/322-5537. Online, go to **www.usevacations.com**.

Sea World also offers 3-night packages which include hotel accommodations at a handful of Orlando hotels, car rental, and tickets to Sea World and, in some cases,

Disney on the High Seas

The Disney empire has expanded yet again to include two state-of-the-art cruise ships, the *Disney Magic* and the *Disney Wonder*. Both ships have been applauded for their characteristically Disney attention to detail and providing a uniquely Disneyesque cruising experience. (At over 950 feet in length, the *Disney Magic* is longer than the Eiffel Tower, and its smoke stacks play that Disney favorite, "When You Wish Upon a Star.")

Each luxury liner offers a wide variety of things to occupy guests' time, including dining, nightlife, shows, and packages of activities designed specifically for adults, kids, or teens. There are numerous restaurants and clubs aboard, and extensive areas devoted to children and teenagers. There is even a company-owned island, Castaway Cay, which serves as a 1,000-acre playground port.

Seven-day cruise packages include 3 or 4 days afloat, with the rest of the week divided among the landlocked properties. Prices range from $1,295 to $4,225 per adult, depending on level of accommodations. Some of the land/sea packages include round-trip air transportation and unlimited admissions to the Disney parks, Pleasure Island, the water parks, and Disney's Wide World of Sports. Cruise-only options range from $799 to $2,789 for a 3-day cruise and $909 to $2,999 for 4 days.

Cruises depart from Port Canaveral, about an hour by car from Orlando. Book well in advance—the cruises are proving popular with the legions of true fans looking for something new. For information call ☎ **407/566-3500** or visit the Web site **www.disneycruise.com**.

other parks. You can get information at ☎ **800/423-8368** or online at **www.seaworld.com/vacation/orlando**.

Delta Dream Vacations are good examples of airline-run packages, and span several price categories. These packages include round-trip air transport, accommodations (including state and hotel-room tax and baggage gratuities), a rental car with unlimited mileage or round-trip airport transfer, a "Magic Passport" that provides unlimited admission to all Walt Disney World parks for the length of your stay, and a single choice from the nine items on Disney's Flex Feature list. Those who stay off Disney property can also gain early entrance into selected parks on certain days. In packages utilizing Walt Disney World Resorts, you get all the advantages available to guests at these properties. Three price options are available: standard, ultimate, and preferred. The prices vary widely depending on the property you choose, your departure city, and the time of year. To figure out availability and cost go to **www.deltavacations.com/disney**.

With some Delta packages, WDW tickets and resorts are optional. For details, call ☎ **800/872-7786**.

American Express Vacations (☎ **800/241-1700; www.americanexpress.com**), run by the "official card of Walt Disney World," offer discounts on merchandise, dinner shows, and selected Disney-related tours to card members who use AmEx to book reservations at Disney resorts.

Continental Airlines Vacations (☎ **800/525-0280**) offers a variety of packages including airfare, hotel stays, and car rental at numerous central Florida hotels and five moderately priced properties at Walt Disney World. This service can be applied toward the Continental's frequent-flyer program, or used just for hotel reservations without air service. Reach them online at **www.coolvacations.com**.

Marriott Villas Vacations (☎ 888/255-5338) features packages which include round-trip air reservations on Delta or Continental, accommodations, and rental car. The hotels are more upscale, condo-type accommodations. You can also use the service to make reservations without airfare. Visit them on the Web at **www. marriottvillas.com.**

SunStyle (☎ 888/786-7895) is a wholesale tour operator offering a variety of packages targeting not only Disney and Disney properties, but also Universal Studios Escape, Sea World, and properties close to those parks. You can also book airfare and car rental through this agency.

Touraine Travel (☎ 800/967-5583) also offers a wide variety of tour packages within Disney properties, Universal Studios Escape, and Sea World.

Additional airline and tour-operator sources for airfare-inclusive packages include **US Airways Vacations** (☎ 800/455-0123), **www.usairwaysvacations.com**, and **American Airlines Vacations** (☎ 800/321-2121), **www.americanair.com.**

1 Orientation

GETTING THERE

BY PLANE   Delta (☎ 800/221-1212) has the most flights into Orlando International Airport (more than 27% of airplane traffic). It offers service from 200 cities and has a Fantastic Flyer program for kids. Delta Express offers direct service from 14 cities and also has the Fantastic Flyer program for kids. Other carriers include **Air Jamaica** (☎ 800/523-5585), **America West** (☎ 800/235-9292), **American** (☎ 800/ 433-7300), **American Trans Air** (☎ 800/293-6194), **British Airways** (☎ 800/ 247-9297), **Canadian Airlines** (☎ 800/426-3838), **Continental** (☎ 800/231-0856), **Midway** (☎ 800/446-4392), **Northwest** (☎ 800/225-2525), **SunJet** (☎ 800/ 478-6738), **Southwest** (☎ 800/435-9792), **Transbrasil** (☎ 800/872-3153), **TWA** (☎ 800/221-2000), **United** (☎ 800/241-6522), **US Airways** (☎ 800/428-4322), and **Virgin Atlantic** (☎ 800/862-8621).

Orlando International Airport, which is undergoing a billion-dollar expansion, is very user-friendly, with centrally located information kiosks (see "Visitor Information," below). All major car-rental companies are located at or near the airport.

The airport is 25 miles from Walt Disney World. **Mears Transportation Group** (☎ 407/423-5566) shuttle vans ply the route from the airport (board right outside baggage claim) to all Disney resorts and official hotels, as well as most other area hostelries. Their vehicles operate around the clock, departing every 15 to 25 minutes in either direction. Rates vary with your destination. The round-trip cost for adults is $21 between the airport and downtown Orlando or International Drive, $25 for Walt Disney World/Lake Buena Vista or Kissimmee/U.S. 192. Children 4 to 11 are charged $14 and $17, respectively; and children 3 and under ride free.

BY CAR   Orlando is 436 miles from Atlanta and 230 miles from Miami.

From points north, take I-75 south to the Florida Turnpike to I-4, which runs right through the city. If you're taking I-95 south, you'll intersect with I-4 near Daytona Beach.

The **American Automobile Association (AAA)** (☎ 800/336-4357) and some other automobile-club members can call local offices for maps and optimum driving directions.

BY TRAIN   Amtrak trains (☎ 800/872-7245) pull into stations at 1400 Sligh Blvd., between Columbia and Miller streets in downtown Orlando (about 23 mi. from Walt Disney World), and at 111 Dakin Ave., at Thurman Street in Kissimmee (about 15 mi. from Walt Disney World). There is also a stop in Winter Park, about 10 miles north of Orlando, at 150 W. Morse Blvd., and in Sanford, about 23 miles northeast of Orlando. The Sanford station, located at 600 Persimmon Ave., is also the end terminal for the Auto Train.

Amtrak's Auto Train offers the convenience of having a car in Florida without having to drive it there. The Auto Train begins in Lorton, Virginia—about a 4-hour drive from New York, 2 hours from Philadelphia—and ends up at Sanford, Florida, about 23 miles northeast of Orlando. Once again, reserve early for the lowest fares. The Auto Train departs Lorton and Sanford at 4:30pm daily, arriving at its destination at 9am the next morning. *Note:* You have to arrive 1 or 2 hours before departure time so they can board your car. Call ☎ **800/872-7245** for details.

To inquire about Amtrak's money-saving packages, including hotel accommodations (some at WDW resorts), car rentals, tours, and so on, with your train fare, call ☎ **800/321-8684.**

VISITOR INFORMATION

Contact the **Orlando/Orange County Convention & Visitors Bureau,** 8723 International Dr., Suite 101, Orlando, FL 32819 (☎ **407/363-5871**). They can answer all your questions and will send you maps; brochures (including the informative *Official Visitors Guide,* the *Official Attractions Guide,* the *Official Accommodations Guide,* and the *African-American Visitors Guide*); and the "Magicard," good for discounts of 10% to 50% on accommodations, attractions, car rentals, and more. Discount tickets to attractions other than Disney parks are sold on the premises, and the multilingual staff can also make dining reservations and hotel referrals. The bureau is open daily, except Christmas, from 8am to 8pm.

For general information about Walt Disney World and a copy of the informative *Walt Disney World Vacations,* write or call the Walt Disney World Co., Box 10000, Lake Buena Vista, FL 32830-1000 (☎ **407/934-7639**). You can get information about Universal Studios Escape by writing Guest Services, 1000 Universal Studios Plaza, Orlando, FL 32819-7610.

If you're driving, you can stop at the Disney/AAA Travel Center in Ocala, Florida, at the intersection of I-75 (exit 68) and Fla. 200, about 90 miles north of Orlando (☎ **904/854-0770**). Here you can purchase tickets and Mickey ears, get help planning your park itinerary, and make hotel reservations. Hours are 9am to 6pm, until 7pm June through August.

Also contact the **Kissimmee–St. Cloud Convention & Visitors Bureau,** 1925 E. Irlo Bronson Memorial Hwy. (P.O. Box 422007), Kissimmee, FL 34742-2007 (☎ **800/327-9159** or 407/847-5000). They'll send maps, brochures, discount coupon books, and the *Kissimmee–St. Cloud Vacation Guide,* which details the area's accommodations and attractions. The state of Florida also instituted a toll-free number in 1998 (☎ **888-7-FLA-USA** [735-2872]), over which you can request a visitors guide for the state, including Orlando, in English, Spanish, German, and Portuguese.

ONLINE RESOURCES

The state information Web site is **www.flausa.com**. Visit Walt Disney World's own Web site at **www.disneyworld.com**, which has extensive, entertaining, and regularly updated information, including a live-action look from video cameras perched throughout the various parks. You can check out every resort by clicking on Resorts & Spas (not Resort Reservations). In addition, you can also book a package deal at this site, or make hotel reservations.

Beat the Traffic

There is a shuttle, the **I-Ride,** with stops about every 2 blocks along International Drive. The trolley runs from 7am to midnight and costs about 75¢ for adults and 25¢ for seniors. Children under 12 ride free when accompanied by adults. Due to a large volume of traffic, this may be the best way to get around the I-Drive area if you are staying at a hotel on the strip. It will certainly cut down on the hurry-up-and-wait frustration of bumper-to-bumper traffic.

For information about Universal Studios Escape and Sea World, visit **www. uescape.com** and **www.seaworld.com**, respectively. Both sites offer maps, a basic description of rides and shows, and ticket information. The city newspaper, the *Orlando Sentinel,* also produces Orlando Sentinel Online at **www.orlandosentinel. com**. Once there, click into Theme Park Central for a variety of information and updates on what is going on at local attractions. The Orlando/Orange County Convention & Visitors Bureau also offers a Web site at **www.goflorida.com**.

If you subscribe to AOL, type the keyword **GO2ORLANDO**. This site has regularly updated information about theme parks, accommodations, and special events. Another resource—although this one is geared more to locals and a little more difficult to use—is **www.insidecentralflorida.com**.

CITY LAYOUT

Orlando's major artery is I-4, which runs diagonally across the state from Tampa to Daytona Beach. Exits from I-4 take you to Walt Disney World, Sea World, International Drive, U.S. 192, Kissimmee, Lake Buena Vista, Church Street Station, downtown Orlando, and Winter Park. The **Florida Turnpike** crosses I-4 and links up with I-75 to the north. **U.S. 192,** a major east-west artery, stretches from Kissimmee (along a major motel strip) to **U.S. 27,** crossing I-4 near the Walt Disney World entrance road. Farther north, a toll road called the **Bee Line Expressway** (Fla. 528) goes east from I-4 past Orlando International Airport to Cape Canaveral.

Walt Disney World property is bounded roughly by I-4 and Fla. 535 to the east (the latter also north), World Drive (the entrance road) to the west, and U.S. 192 to the south. Epcot Center Drive (Fla. 536, the south end of International Drive) and Buena Vista Drive cut across the complex in a more-or-less east-west direction; the two roads cross at Bonnet Creek Parkway. Excellent highways and explicit signs make it very easy to find your way around.

Note: The Disney parks are actually much closer to Kissimmee than to downtown Orlando.

The Neighborhoods in Brief

Walt Disney World (WDW)　A city unto itself, WDW sprawls over more than 26,000 acres containing theme parks, resorts, hotels, shops, restaurants, and recreational facilities galore.

Lake Buena Vista　This area centers on a hotel village/marketplace owned and operated by Walt Disney World on the eastern edge of Disney property. However, while Disney owns all the real estate, many of the hotels, and some shops and restaurants here, are independently owned. Lake Buena Vista is a charming area of manicured lawns and verdant thoroughfares with traffic islands shaded by towering oak trees. The lovely scenery can be hard to see over the tour buses, however. This is a very busy part of town, so expect long waits at restaurants during peak season. (The RainForest Cafe, for example, can have waits up to 4 hours!)

Celebration   Can you imagine living in a Disney world? Disney tries to re-create its squeaky-clean, completely controlled magic in this town, the first residential area ever to receive the special Disney touch. Located on 4,900 acres in northwest Osceola County, Celebration will eventually have about 8,000 residents living in Disney-designed homes and attending a Disney-run school. The homes go for around $256,000, and at least two have reportedly sold for as much as $900,000. Celebration's downtown, designed mostly for tourist trade, is architecturally interesting and features some first-rate shops and restaurants.

Kissimmee   South of the Disney parks, Kissimmee centers on U.S. 192/Irlo Bronson Memorial Highway—a somewhat-tacky strip, as archetypal of American cities as Main Street. U.S. 192 is lined with budget motels, lesser attractions like Gatorland, and every fast-food restaurant you can name. Kissimmee is still, in many ways, true to its cowboy routes, and there are some wide-open spaces to explore if you are in the mood for a ride in the country.

International Drive (Fla. 536)   Can you say "tourist mecca"? This area extends 7 to 10 miles north of the Disney parks between Fla. 535 and the Florida Turnpike. From bungee jumping to ice-skating and dozens of theme restaurants and T-shirt shops, this is the tourist strip in Central Florida. It contains numerous hotels, restaurants, shopping centers, and the Orange County Convention Center, and it offers easy access to Sea World and Universal Studios Escape. The place is already packed, but somehow developers manage year after year to find space for just one more attraction. *Note:* Locally, this road is always referred to as I-Drive.

Downtown Orlando   No, Downtown Disney is not *really* Downtown, the heart of the city's business and entertainment districts. To get there you have to travel on I-4 East, reaching a burgeoning Sunbelt metropolis 17 miles northeast of Walt Disney World. It includes the entertainment/shopping complex Church Street Station and the Orlando Science Center, a recently completed multimillion-dollar complex, which is the largest in the Southeast. Hundreds of clubs, shops, and restaurants are located in the heart of the city, one of the fastest growing in the country. Dozens of antique shops line "Antique Row" on Orange Avenue near Lake Ivanhoe. The free downtown bus system, called Lymmo, makes it easy to park in one place and travel throughout downtown, including the Orlando Arena and Bob Carr Centre for the Performing Arts. Both City Hall and the courthouse offer art exhibits reflecting the diverse work of Florida artists.

Winter Park   Just north of downtown Orlando, Winter Park is the place many of central Florida's old-money families call home. As the name implies, it began as a haven for Yankees traveling away from the cold. Today, it's home to Park Avenue, a collection of upscale shops and restaurants along an original cobblestone street that is frequented by the local ladies who lunch. With the main attractions being shopping, dining, and several small museums, Winter Park is definitely a grown-up diversion.

2 Getting Around

BY CAR   Though you can get to and around Walt Disney World and other major attractions without a car, it's always handy to have one, especially if you want to see attractions beyond Disney. All major car-rental companies are represented in Orlando and maintain desks at the airport. **Value Rent-A-Car** (☎ **800/GO-VALUE**), offers excellent service and 24-hour pickup and return. Some other handy phone numbers: **Alamo** (☎ 800/327-9633), **Avis** (☎ 800/331-1212), **Budget** (☎ 800/527-0700), **Dollar** (☎ 800/800-4000), **Enterprise** (☎ 800/325-8007), **Hertz** (☎ 800/654-3131), **National Car Rental** (☎ 800/227-7368), and **Thrifty** (☎ 800/367-2277). If you are looking for something a little more upscale, say a Jaguar or a Porsche, try **Exotic Car Rentals** (☎ 407/855-6325).

BY BUS   Disney has its own internal transportation system that allows people staying at Walt Disney World (WDW) resorts to move throughout the property. This is supposed to be exclusively for Disney guests, although I've never seen anyone check for a hotel key before you board. Within WDW you can also travel via monorail, ferry, and water taxi to all three parks from 2 hours before opening until 2 hours after closing; you can also ride to Disney Village Marketplace, Typhoon Lagoon, Pleasure Island, Fort Wilderness, and other Disney resorts. During peak seasons, be prepared to stand on crowded buses.

Disney hotels offer transportation to other area attractions as well, though it's not complimentary. Almost all area hotels and motels also offer transportation to Walt Disney World and other attractions, but it can be pricey.

Mears Transportation Group (☎ 407/423-5566) operates buses to all major attractions, including Cypress Gardens, the Kennedy Space Center, Universal Studios Escape, Sea World, Busch Gardens (in Tampa), and Church Street Station, among others. Call for details.

BY TAXI   Taxis line up in front of major hotels, and at smaller hostelries the front desk will be happy to call you a cab. Or call **Yellow Cab** (☎ 407/699-9999). The charge is $2.75 for the first mile, $1.50 per mile thereafter.

Fast Facts: Walt Disney World & Orlando

American Express   There is an American Express Travel Service Office at the Epcot's main gate and in the lobby of Disney's Contemporary Resort.

Baby-sitters   Most Orlando hotels offer baby-sitting services. If yours doesn't, call **KinderCare** (☎ 407/827-5444); 24-hour advance notice is required. Several Disney resorts, including the Beach Club, the Grand Floridian, the Contemporary, and the Wilderness Lodge, offer babysitting for $4 or $5 an hour. Inquire at the front desk.

Convention Center   The Orange County Convention Center is located at 9800 International Dr. (☎ 407/345-9800).

Doctors & Dentists   Tourists have encountered ill-trained doctors making calls in hotels—so beware. You can get a reputable referral from **Ask-A-Nurse**, a free service operated by a local hospital chain. In Kissimmee call ☎ 407/870-1700; in Orlando call ☎ 407/897-1700. There are basic first-aid centers in all the major parks. Disney also offers an In-Room Health service at its resorts; call ☎ 407/238-2000.

Emergencies   Dial ☎ 911 to contact the police or fire department or to call an ambulance.

Hospitals   Sand Lake Hospital, 9400 Turkey Lake Rd., is about 2 miles south of Sand Lake Road (☎ 407/351-8550). From the WDW area, take I-4 east to Exit 29, turn left at the exit onto Sand Lake Road, and make a left onto Turkey Lake Road. The hospital is 2 miles up on your right. Celebration Health

(☎ 407/764-4000), located in the Disney-owned town of Celebration, is at 400 Celebration Place. From I-4, take exit 25a. At the first traffic light, turn right onto Celebration Avenue. At the first stop sign, take another right.

Walk-in medical clinics are available, with a visit usually costing under $50. Prescriptions are extra. **CentraCare,** operated by a locally run Florida Hospital, is a reputable medical facility with more than a dozen locations throughout the Orlando area. For information, and the nearest location, call ☎ 407/660-8118. In recent years, several freestanding medical clinics have popped up, especially in the Kissimmee area. My advice: Stick with CentraCare whenever possible.

Kennels   All the major theme parks offer animal-boarding facilities at reasonable fees. At Walt Disney World, there are kennels at Animal Kingdom, Fort Wilderness, Epcot, the Magic Kingdom, and Disney-MGM Studios. Sea World and Universal Studios Escape also have kennel facilities.

Kosher Food   It can be arranged at restaurants at Disney parks and resorts with 24-hour advance notice. Call ☎ 407/WDW-DINE (939-3463).

Liquor Laws   Minimum drinking age is 21. No liquor is served in the Magic Kingdom at Walt Disney World. However, drinks are available at the other parks and are quite evident at Universal's Mardi Gras celebration and its Halloween Horror Nights.

Lost Children   Every theme park has a designated spot for parents to meet up with lost children. Find out where it is when you enter any park. Point out the uniformed park personnel in each park, and instruct your children to ask people dressed in that uniform for help. Young children should have name tags.

Pharmacies   Walgreens drugstore, 1003 W. Vine St. (Hwy. 192), just east of Bermuda Avenue (☎ 407/847-5252), operates a 24-hour pharmacy. They can deliver to hotels for a charge ($10 from 7am to 5pm, $15 at all other times). There is an **Eckerd** drugstore at 7324 International Dr. (☎ 407/345-0491), open 24 hours a day. There is also a 24-hour Eckerd's store at 1306 Bermuda Ave. (☎ 407/847-5174). Many stores, such as Target, Wal-Mart, and Kmart, also have pharmacies.

Taxes   The hotel tax is 11% in Orlando and Kissimmee; that rate includes a state sales tax (6%) that's charged on all goods except most grocery-store items and medicines.

Tourist Information   See "Orientation," earlier in this chapter.

Weather   Call ☎ 407/851-7510 for a weather recording from the National Weather Service.

3 Accommodations

Reserve as far in advance as possible—the minute you decide on the dates of your trip. The year-round sunshine combined with the huge number of annual conventions and international visitors to Orlando virtually eliminate the concept of high and low seasons. That being said, the lowest rates are generally available in fall from September to Thanksgiving and again during January and February. The highest are during the Christmas holidays and the summer months.

Consider the cost of parking or shuttle buses to and from Disney and other theme parks when making your hotel choice—it can add up to quite a bit. Also remember to factor in the 11% hotel tax.

The rates below represent "rack rates," basic prices that should serve as a guide for comparison shopping only. Almost no one ever really pays them, so if you see a hotel that's just outside your budget, don't be deterred from trying to get a discounted rate as part of a package deal (see details earlier in this chapter) or simply by calling and asking if a discount is available.

Many hotels, especially the larger chains, offer organizational discounts. Being a member of AAA, owning a certain credit card, or being a card-carrying member of a specific credit union or fraternal organization can pay off with reduced rates.

Prices, obviously, are subject to change, but this should give you a good idea of the price range for each property.

THE PERKS OF STAYING WITH MICKEY

There are 18 Disney-owned properties (hotels, resorts, villas, wilderness homes, and campsites) and nine privately owned "official hotels," all adjacent to the Walt Disney World complex. Due to high demand, especially during summer, you often have to take what you can get. Finding a room is a little like a game of "Go Fish"—you lay down your card and hope to find a match. Keep in mind there are often reasonably priced accommodations at some of the more expensive resorts (it doesn't hurt to ask whether that $294 room at the Grand Floridian is available). So consider your priorities. The more expensive properties are closer to the theme parks. You may want to consider staying a short distance away and renting a car.

In addition to the proximity to the parks, there are a number of advantages to staying at a Disney hostelry or official hotel. At all Disney resorts and official hotels, these include:

- Unlimited complimentary transportation via bus, monorail, ferry, and/or water taxi to and from all three parks from 2 hours before opening until 2 hours after closing. Unlimited complimentary transport is also provided to and from Disney Village Marketplace, Typhoon Lagoon, Pleasure Island, Fort Wilderness, and other Disney resorts. Three hostelries—the Polynesian, Contemporary, and Grand Floridian—are stops on the monorail. This free transport can save a lot of money. It also means that you're guaranteed admission to all parks, even during peak times when the parking lots sometimes fill up.
- Free parking at WDW parking lots (other visitors pay $5 a day).
- Reduced-price children's menus in almost all restaurants, and character breakfasts and/or dinners at most resorts.
- A guest-services desk where you can purchase tickets to all WDW theme parks and attractions and obtain general information.
- Use of—and in some cases, complimentary transport to—the five Disney-owned golf courses and preferred tee times (these can be booked up to 30 days in advance).
- Access to most recreational facilities at other Disney resorts.

Additional perks at Disney-owned hotels, resorts, villas, and campgrounds (but not at "official" hotels) include charge privileges throughout Walt Disney World; early admission to Magic Kingdom, Epcot, and Disney-MGM on specific days; and the ability to make restaurant and show reservations (including Epcot restaurants) through the hotel.

WALT DISNEY WORLD CENTRAL RESERVATIONS OFFICE

To reserve a room at Disney hotels, resorts, and villas, at official hotels, and at Fort Wilderness homes and campsites, contact **Central Reservations Operations (CRO)**, P.O. Box 10100, Lake Buena Vista, FL 32830-0100 (☎ **407/W-DISNEY**

[934-7639]), open Monday to Friday from 8am to 10pm and Saturday and Sunday from 9am to 6pm. Have your dates and credit card ready when you call.

The CRO can also give you information about various park ticket options and make dinner, show, and character-breakfast reservations when you book your room.

When you call, be sure to inquire about their numerous package plans, which include meals, tickets, recreation, and other features. Be sure to ask if any special discounts are being offered at the time of your trip. All WDW properties offer some disabled/accessible accommodations and special no-smoking rooms. You can check out the various resorts at **www.disneyworld.com** (click on Resorts & Spas). In all WDW resorts, children under 17 stay free in their parents' room.

DISNEY RESORTS
VERY EXPENSIVE

✪ **Disney's Beach Club Resort.** 1800 Epcot Resorts Blvd. (off Buena Vista Dr.; P.O. Box 10000), Lake Buena Vista, FL 32830-0100. ☎ **407/W-DISNEY** (934-7639) or 407/ 934-8000. Fax 407/934-3850. 597 units. A/C MINIBAR TV TEL. $264–$535 double; $421–$1,110 suites. Prices depend on view and season. AE, MC, V. Free self- and valet parking.

From its palm-fringed entranceway and manicured gardens to its plush, sun-dappled lobby, the Beach Club resembles a luxurious Victorian Cape Cod resort. The big draw here—especially for families—is Stormalong Bay, a vast free-form swimming pool/water park that sprawls over 3 acres between the Yacht Club and Beach Club and flows into a lake; it includes a 150-foot serpentine water slide. So posh is the Beach Club—and so extensive are its sports facilities—that you might consider it for an upscale resort vacation even without the draw of the Disney parks nearby. In a similar category are its sister properties, the Yacht Club and the Grand Floridian (described below). The charming rooms, some with balconies, are furnished in bleached woods and equipped with ceiling fans, extra phones in the bathroom, and safes.

Dining: Ideal for family dining is the Cape May Café, serving character breakfasts and authentic New England clambake buffet dinners. At the adjoining Disney Yacht Club, the Yachtsman Steakhouse, open only for dinner, specializes in hearty meals such as porterhouse steak, chateaubriand, and prime rib. Other facilities here serve drinks, wine by the glass, light fare, and ice cream.

Amenities: Room service (24 hours), baby-sitting, guest-services desk, complimentary daily newspaper, boat transport to MGM theme park, large outdoor swimming pool, whirlpool, quarter-mile sand beach, boat rental, fishing, two tennis courts, state-of-the-art health club, volleyball, croquet, boccie ball courts, 2-mile jogging trail, coin-op washers/dryers, unisex hair salon, shops, business center, video-game arcade, Sandcastle Club (a counselor-supervised children's activity center).

✪ **Disney's BoardWalk.** 2101 N. Epcot Resorts Blvd. (off Buena Vista Dr.; P.O. Box 10000), Lake Buena Vista, FL 32830-1000. ☎ **407/W-DISNEY** (934-7639) or 407/939-5100 (407/939-6200 for villas). Fax 407/934-5150. 378 units, 532 villas. A/C TV TEL. $254–$580 double; $415–$1,200 suites; $590–$1,540 for villas. AE, MC, V. Free self-parking. Rates vary depending on view and season. Children 17 and under stay free in parents' room. AE, MC, V. Free self- and valet parking.

The BoardWalk—occupying 45 acres along the shores of Lake Crescent—takes its theme from the plush mid-Atlantic Victorian seaside resorts of the 1920s and 1930s. A large deck with rocking chairs overlooks a village green and the lake beyond, and the stunning 70-foot lobby has a working fireplace. With shingled rooftops surrounding private courtyards and New England–style flower gardens, the property connects to a quarter-mile boardwalk complete with shops, restaurants, and street

Walt Disney World Attractions & Accommodations

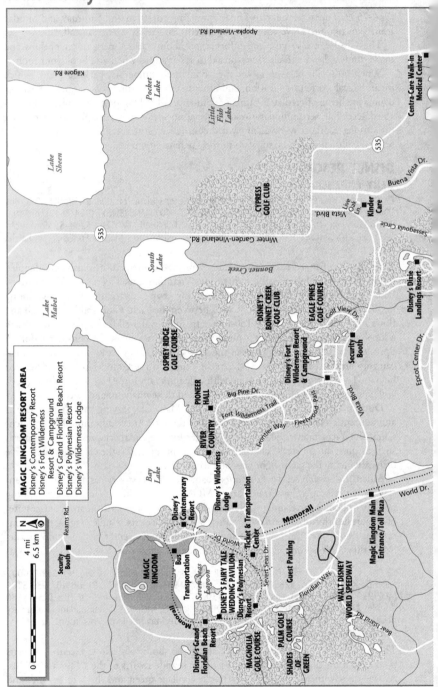

MAGIC KINGDOM RESORT AREA
Disney's Contemporary Resort
Disney's Fort Wilderness
   Resort & Campground
Disney's Grand Floridian Beach Resort
Disney's Polynesian Resort
Disney's Wilderness Lodge

N
4 mi
6.5 km
0

Apopka-Vineland Rd.
Kilgore Rd.
Pocket Lake
Little Fish Lake
Lake Sheen
535
Centra-Care Walk-In Medical Center
Buena Vista Dr.
CYPRESS GOLF CLUB
Live Oak Ln
Vista Blvd.
Kinder Care
Sassagoula Circle
Winter Garden-Vineland Rd.
535
South Lake
Bonnet Creek
Lake Mabel
DISNEY'S BONNET CREEK GOLF CLUB
EAGLE PINES GOLF COURSE
Golf View Dr.
Disney's Dixie Landings Resort
OSPREY RIDGE GOLF COURSE
Disney's Fort Wilderness Resort & Campground
Security Booth
Epcot Center Dr.
PIONEER HALL
Big Pine Dr.
Fort Wilderness Trail
Frontier Way
Fleetwood Pass
RIVER COUNTRY
Vista Blvd.
Disney's Wilderness Lodge
Bay Lake
Ticket & Transportation Center
Monorail
World Dr.
Disney's Contemporary Resort
Reams Rd.
Security Booth
Bus Transportation
MAGIC KINGDOM
Seven Seas Lagoon
World Dr.
DISNEY'S FAIRY TALE WEDDING PAVILION
Disney's Polynesian Resort
Seven Seas Dr.
Guest Parking
Floridian Way
Magic Kingdom Main Entrance/Toll Plaza
WALT DISNEY WORLD SPEEDWAY
Bear Island Rd.
Monorail
Disney's Grand Floridian Beach Resort
MAGNOLIA GOLF COURSE
PALM GOLF COURSE
SHADES OF GREEN

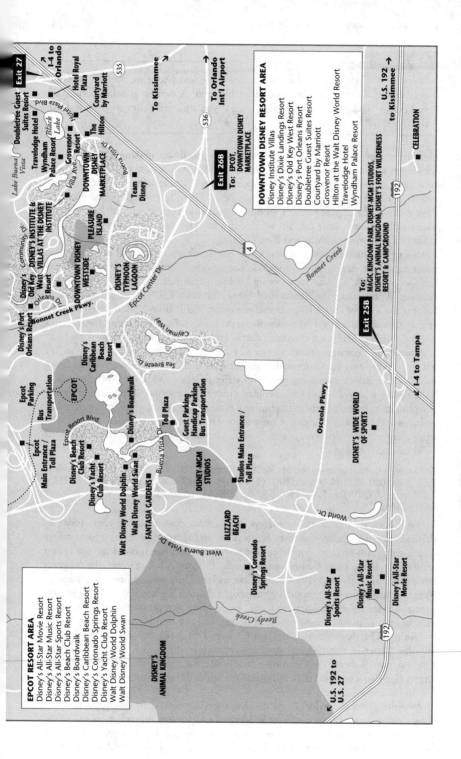

EPCOT RESORT AREA
Disney's All-Star Movie Resort
Disney's All-Star Music Resort
Disney's All-Star Sports Resort
Disney's Beach Club Resort
Disney's Boardwalk
Disney's Caribbean Beach Resort
Disney's Coronado Springs Resort
Disney's Yacht Club Resort
Walt Disney World Dolphin
Walt Disney World Swan

DOWNTOWN DISNEY RESORT AREA
Disney Institute Villas
Disney's Dixie Landings Resort
Disney's Old Key West Resort
Disney's Port Orleans Resort
Doubletree Guest Suites Resort
Courtyard by Marriott
Grosvenor Resort
Hilton at the Walt Disney World Resort
Travelodge Hotel
Wyndham Palace Resort

Exit 27
To I-4 to Orlando

Exit 26B
To: EPCOT, DOWNTOWN DISNEY MARKETPLACE

Exit 25B
To: MAGIC KINGDOM PARK, DISNEY-MGM STUDIOS, DISNEY'S ANIMAL KINGDOM, DISNEY'S FORT WILDERNESS RESORT & CAMPGROUND

To Orlando Int'l Airport

To Kissimmee

Hotel Royal Plaza

Courtyard by Marriott

Doubletree Guest Suites Resort

Travelodge Hotel

Wyndham Palace Resort

Grosvenor Resort

The Hilton

DOWNTOWN DISNEY MARKETPLACE

Team Disney

Lake Buena Vista

Black Lake

Hotel Plaza Blvd.

Villa Ave.

Buena Vista Dr.

Community of Lake Buena Vista

DISNEY'S INSTITUTE & WEST VILLAS AT THE DISNEY INSTITUTE

Disney's Old Key West Resort

DISNEY'S INSTITUTE

PLEASURE ISLAND

DOWNTOWN DISNEY WESTSIDE

DISNEY'S TYPHOON LAGOON

Orleans Dr.

Disney's Port Orleans Resort

Bonnet Creek Pkwy.

Epcot Center Dr.

Cayman Way

Sea Breeze Dr.

Disney's Caribbean Beach Resort

Epcot Parking

Bus Transportation

EPCOT

Epcot Main Entrance / Toll Plaza

Epcot Resort Blvd

Disney's Boardwalk

Disney's Beach Club Resort

Disney's Yacht Club Resort

Walt Disney World Dolphin

Walt Disney World Swan

FANTASIA GARDENS

Buena Vista Dr.

Guest Parking Handicap Parking Bus Transportation

Studios Main Entrance / Toll Plaza

DISNEY-MGM STUDIOS

BLIZZARD BEACH

West Buena Vista Dr.

Disney's Coronado Springs Resort

DISNEY'S ANIMAL KINGDOM

Reedy Creek

Disney's All-Star Sports Resort

Disney's All-Star Music Resort

Disney's All-Star Movie Resort

DISNEY'S WIDE WORLD OF SPORTS

Osceola Pkwy.

World Dr.

Bonnet Creek

I-4 to Tampa

U.S. 192 to Kissimmee

CELEBRATION

U.S. 192 to U.S. 27

535

536

4

192

Factoid

Since April of 1999, you must dial the area code and phone number for all numbers within the 407 area code covering Orlando. A rapidly growing population makes this 10-digit dialing necessary, even if you are calling somewhere just down the block.

---

performers. There's plenty to do here once the sun goes down, making it a good choice for singles and couples without children. The B&B-style accommodations are gorgeous and may include a brass or four-poster bed. All have safes, irons and ironing boards, and hair dryers; refrigerators are available. The villas, though pricey, might be a good choice for large families or groups; they offer kitchenettes or full kitchens and washers/dryers, and some contain whirlpool tubs. This hotel is within walking distance of Epcot and the Yacht and Beach Clubs.

Dining/Diversions: Situated along the boardwalk promenade to provide scenic water views, the dining facilities include the upscale Flying Fish Café for steak and seafood; Spoodle's, a casual spot serving Mediterranean fare; the Big River Grille and Brewing Works (featuring handcrafted beers and ales); ESPN Club, a sports bar; a bakery; and a coffee bar. A 10-piece orchestra plays music from 1940 through Top 40s at the Atlantic Dance, a 1920s-style dance hall. Jellyrolls, a sing-along bar, features dueling pianos. There are also several cocktail lounges and a carousel-themed pool bar.

Amenities: Concierge, room service (24 hours), baby-sitting, boat transport (to MGM, Epcot, and Epcot resorts), guest-services desk, complimentary daily newspaper, large outdoor swimming pool with water slide, two additional secluded pools, kiddie pool, whirlpool, two tennis courts, croquet, bike rental, 2-mile jogging path, playground, convention center, full business center, shops, extensively equipped health club, two video-game arcades, Community Hall (for games, crafts, recreational-equipment rentals, videotapes, and books), Harbour Club (a counselor-supervised child-care activity center).

✪ Disney's Contemporary Resort. 4600 N. World Dr. (P.O. Box 10000), Lake Buena Vista, FL 32830-1000. ☎ **407/W-DISNEY** (934-7639) or 407/824-1000. Fax 407/824-3535. 1,121 units. A/C TV TEL. $201–$460 double; $680–$1,365 suites. AE, MC, V. Free self- and valet parking.

When it opened in 1971, the Contemporary's aesthetics were cutting-edge. Today its dramatic angular planes, free-form furnishings, and abstract paintings appear rather charmingly retro-modern. However, a major renovation has spruced up the fading centerpiece of the park. Centering on a sleek, 15-story A-frame tower, the property comprises 26 acres bounded by a natural lake and the Disney-made Seven Seas Lagoon. Kids are thrilled that the monorail whizzes right through the hotel; they also enjoy on-premises character meals. Location is the biggest thing to recommend the Contemporary. Since it is literally on the monorail system, you can zip right to the parks.

Dining: The magnificent 15th-floor California Grill (see "Disney Resorts" under "Dining," later in this chapter) provides panoramic vistas of the Magic Kingdom. Other options here are the Concourse Steakhouse, the garden-themed Chef Mickey's Buffet (for character breakfasts and prime-rib buffet dinners), and several other spots for drinks and light fare.

Amenities: Room service (24 hours), guest-services desk, daily newspaper delivery, baby-sitting, boat transport (to Fort Wilderness and River Country), monorail to the Polynesian and Grand Floridian resorts, two swimming pools, kiddie pool, white-sand beach with volleyball court, shuffleboard, boat rental, unisex hair salon, six tennis courts (lessons available), shops, American Express desk, car-rental desk, coin-op washers/dryers, full business center, extensive health club, sauna/massage/tanning rooms, video-game arcade, the Mouseketeer Clubhouse (a counselor-supervised child-care/activity center).

✪ **Disney's Grand Floridian Beach Resort.** 4401 Floridian Way (P.O. Box 10000), Lake Buena Vista, FL 32830-1000. ☎ **407/W-DISNEY** (934-7639) or 407/824-3000. Fax 407/824-3186. 933 units. A/C MINIBAR TV TEL. $299–$654 double, depending on view and season; $754–$1,875 suites. AE, MC, V. Free self- and valet parking.

The Grand Floridian is truly world renowned and magnificent from the moment you step into its opulent, five-story lobby (complete with a Chinese Chippendale aviary) under triple-domed stained-glass skylights. Here a pianist entertains during afternoon tea, and an orchestra plays big-band music every evening. This could be a romantic choice for couples—even honeymooners (the Disney wedding pavilion is here, by the way). And if you're into fitness, you'll appreciate the first-rate health club. The sunny rooms—with private balconies or verandas overlooking formal gardens, the pool, or a 200-acre lagoon—have two-poster beds dressed with lovely floral-chintz spreads. In-room amenities include safes and ceiling fans; in the bathroom you'll find an extra phone, a hair dryer, and a terry robe. The great location offers quick access to parks, boating, and water activities.

Dining/Diversions: This property is the place for those who appreciate fine food. Victoria & Albert's, Orlando's finest restaurant, is described in "Disney Resorts" under "Dining," below. There is also Citricos, featuring light, flavorful French cuisine. The lovely Grand Floridian Café, overlooking formal gardens, features Southern special-ties. The exposition-themed 1900 Park Fare is the setting for character breakfasts and dinners. Flagler's offers northern Italian fare. At the gazebo-like Narcoossee's, grilled meats and seafood are prepared in an exhibition kitchen. Intimate and very Victorian, Mizner's Lounge features an international selection of ports, brandies, and appetizers. The Garden View Lounge, off the lobby, is the setting for elegant afternoon teas. Other options include the Gasparilla Grill (open 24 hr.) and a pool bar.

Amenities: On-premises monorail, boat transport to Magic Kingdom, room service (24 hr.), nightly turndown, baby-sitting, free trolley transport around the hotel grounds, shoe shine, massage, guest-services desk, complimentary daily newspaper, large outside swimming pool with poolside changing area, kiddie pool, whirlpool, two tennis courts, boat rental, waterskiing, croquet, volleyball, playground, jogging trails, fishing excursions, white-sand beach, unisex hair salon, coin-op washers/dryers, shops, car-rental desk, state-of-the-art spa, video-game arcade, organized children's activities in summer and peak seasons, the Mouseketeer Clubhouse (a counselor-supervised child-care activity center).

Disney's Old Key West Resort. 1510 N. Cove Rd. (off Community Dr.; P.O. Box 10000), Lake Buena Vista, FL 32830-1000. ☎ **407/W-DISNEY** (934-7639) or 407/827-7700. Fax 407/827-7710. 709 units. A/C TV TEL. $195–$215 deluxe rooms; $229–$1,050 villa. Range reflects high and low seasons and one-, two-, and three-bedroom villas. AE, MC, V. Free self-parking.

An understated theme (at least by Disney standards) makes the Old Key West a good choice for those seeking a quieter environment. Architecturally mirroring Key West at the turn of the century, this is a "vacation ownership" (timeshare) property that rents accommodations when they're not in use by the owners. The 156-acre complex is beautifully landscaped: Tree-lined, brick walkways are edged by white picket fences, palms sway softly in the breeze, shorebirds swoop lazily over lagoons, and the air is scented with honeysuckle. Most accommodations are gorgeous homes away from home with living rooms (equipped with large-screen TVs and VCRs, smaller sets and extra phones in the bedroom), fully equipped kitchens, furnished patios (offering water, woodland, or fairway views; the property overlooks the Buena Vista Golf Course), and laundry rooms. Many units contain whirlpool tubs in the master suite, and the Grand Villas have stereo systems.

Dining: The Key West–themed Olivia's Cafe, overlooking a canal, serves all meals. There are a few other spots for drinks and light fare.

Amenities: Guest-services desk, ferry service to Disney Village Marketplace and Downtown Disney, free bus transport around the grounds, food shopping, two tennis courts, basketball court, white-sand play area, four swimming pools, whirlpool, kiddie pool, bicycle rental, boat rental, playground, extensive health club, sauna, shuffleboard, horseshoes, volleyball, complimentary use of washers/dryers, general store, video-game arcade, video library. The Community Hall, a recreation center, shows Disney movies nightly and offers various activities.

Disney's Polynesian Resort. 1600 Seven Seas Dr. (P.O. Box 10000), Lake Buena Vista, FL 32830-1000. ☎ **407/W-DISNEY** (934-7639) or 407/824-2000. Fax 407/824-3174. 853 units. A/C TV TEL. $275–$580 double, depending on view and season; $595–$1,425 suites. AE, MC, V. Free self- and valet parking.

Just below the Magic Kingdom, the 25-acre Polynesian Resort is fronted by lush tropical foliage, waterfalls, and koi ponds. Inside, its skylit lobby is a virtual rain forest of tropical plantings—gorgeous by day but rather depressingly lit for evenings. A private white-sand beach—dotted with canvas cabanas, hammocks, and large swings—overlooks a 200-acre lagoon. Waterfalls, grottoes, and a water slide enhance an immense swimming pool. The large, beautiful rooms—most with balconies or patios—have canopied beds, bamboo and rattan furnishings, and walls hung with Gauguin prints. This is a great choice with kids, who will enjoy the Polynesian theme and child-pleasing eateries.

Dining/Diversions: 'Ohana (see "Disney Resorts" under "Dining," later in this chapter) is the setting for character breakfasts and all-you-can-eat island dinners featuring open-pit rock-grilled specialties. Luau Cove hosts Mickey's Tropical Luau and the Polynesian Luau Dinner Show. Kona Cafe, the newest restaurant on the property, specializes in gourmet coffee and Pacific-influenced New American cuisine. There are several other restaurants and bars, including a 24-hour ice-cream parlor.

Amenities: Two swimming pools, kiddie pool, boat rental, waterskiing, volleyball, playground, 1½-mile jogging trail, fishing excursions, room service, baby-sitting, on-premises monorail, boat transport (to the Magic Kingdom and the Grand Floridian Beach Resort), guest-services desk, complimentary daily newspaper, coin-op washers/dryers, shops, video-game arcade, the Neverland Club (a counselor-supervised evening activity center for children).

✪ **Disney's Yacht Club Resort.** 1700 Epcot Resorts Blvd. (off Buena Vista Dr.; P.O. Box 10000), Lake Buena Vista, FL 32830-1000. ☎ **407/W-DISNEY** (934-7639) or 407/934-7000. Fax 407/924-3450. 642 units. A/C MINIBAR TV TEL. $264–$540 double, depending on view and season; $441–$1,208 concierge-level double. AE, MC, V. Free self- and valet parking.

Though first-time visitors to Orlando—who generally spend all their time in the parks—don't require extensive recreational facilities, return visitors will appreciate the extensive sports and entertainment options here. This stunning resort—its main five-story, oyster-gray clapboard building evoking a turn-of-the-century New England yacht club—shares a 25-acre lake, facilities, and gorgeous landscaping with the adjacent Beach Club (described earlier). The nautical theme carries over to the very inviting rooms, decorated in snappy blue and white, with brass sconces, ship lights, and vintage maps on the walls. French doors open onto porches or balconies. Amenities include ceiling fans, extra phones in the bathroom, and safes. The fifth floor is a concierge level, which will especially appeal to business travelers.

Dining/Diversions: The plush Yachtsman Steakhouse grills select cuts of steak, chops, and fresh seafood over oak and hickory. The Yacht Club Galley, a comfortable family restaurant, serves American regional fare. The Crew's Cup Lounge airs sporting events and features international beers. And the cozy Ale and Compass Lounge, a lobby bar with a working fireplace, proffers specialty coffees and cocktails.

Amenities: Room service (24 hours), baby-sitting, guest-services desk, complimentary daily newspaper, boat transport to the MGM theme park, tram and boat transport to Epcot. Yacht Club facilities are identical to those of the Beach Club (described earlier).

Walt Disney World Dolphin. 1500 Epcot Resorts Blvd. (off Buena Vista Dr.; P.O. Box 22653), Lake Buena Vista, FL 32830-2653. ☎ **800/227-1500** or 407/934-4000. Fax 407/934-4884. www.swandolphin.com. 1,509 units. A/C MINIBAR TV TEL. $275–$430 double, depending on view and season; $395–$2,990 suites. Up to 2 children under 18 stay free in parents' room. Inquire about packages. AE, CB, DC, DISC, JCB, MC, V. Take I-4 east to 25B. This is the exit to Epcot/Magic Kingdom. Follow purple and red signs to the resort areas. Free self-parking; valet parking $6.

Though distinctive architecture is its keynote, sports enthusiasts will also appreciate this resort's extensive health club, boat rentals, and tennis facilities. Designed by whimsical architect Michael Graves, the property centers on a 27-story pyramid with two 11-story wings crowned by 56-foot twin dolphin sculptures. Graves dubs his more-Disneyesque-than-Disney creations "entertainment architecture." Close to a dozen cascading fountains on the property range from a seven-dolphin extravaganza at the entrance to waters rushing across rock-faced grottoes in a fiber-optic "starlit" foyer. A free-form rock-sculpted grotto—with waterfalls, a water slide, a rope bridge, and three secluded whirlpools—sprawls over 2 acres between the Dolphin and the adjoining Swan. Both properties also share a white sandy beach on Crescent Lake.

There are thousands of works of art in public areas. In the rooms, walls are hung with art prints (Picasso, Matisse, and others), and painted wood furnishings are stenciled with palm trees and pineapples. Amenities include pay movies, desk and bedside phones, safes, coffeemakers, hair dryers, and irons and ironing boards. The Dolphin Towers comprise a 77-room concierge level.

Dining/Diversions: The elegant Sum Chows serves haute-cuisine pan-Asian dinners. Juan and Only's Bar & Jail offers moderately priced Tex-Mex fare. Harry's Safari Bar & Grille, highlighting steak and seafood, is open for dinner nightly and Sunday character-brunch buffets (details in the "Dining" section). Other venues are the delightful fish-themed Coral Cafe for American fare, an ice-cream/malt shop, a 24-hour cafeteria, Copa Banana (with a deejay spinning tunes for nightly dancing plus karaoke), a lobby lounge, and a poolside bar.

Amenities: Water-launch transport to Epcot & MGM, concierge, 24-hour room service, guest-services desk (sells tickets and arranges transport to all nearby attractions), baby-sitting, Japanese tour desk, water volleyball, boat rentals, four hard-surface night-lit tennis courts, tennis pro shop, fully equipped Body by Jake health club, two beach volleyball courts, miniature golf, 3-mile jogging trail, coin-op washers/dryers, unisex hair salon, shops, full business center, Delta Airlines desk, large video-game arcade, Camp Dolphin (a counselor-supervised children's activity center, open daily).

Walt Disney World Swan. 1200 Epcot Resorts Blvd. (off Buena Vista Dr.; P.O. Box 22786), Lake Buena Vista, FL 32830-2786. ☎ **800/248-SWAN** (7926), 800/228-3000, or 407/

934-3000. www.swandolphin.com. (*Note:* You may get a lower rate by reserving through the second toll-free number for Westin hotels.) Fax 407/934-4499. 758 units. A/C MINIBAR TV TEL. $275–$435 double, depending on view and season; $330–$2,990 suites. Children under 18 stay free in parents' room. Inquire about packages. AE, CB, DC, DISC, JCB, MC, V. Free self-parking; valet parking $8.

Operated by Westin Hotels & Resorts, this 12-story hotel—its rooftop flanked by 45-foot swan statues and seashell fountains—is adjacent to the Dolphin (above) and shares with it a white-sand lakeside beach and facilities. The hotels are connected by a canopied walkway. Here Michael Graves has created a festive interior replete with swan fountains, sea horse–motif chandeliers, hallway walls painted with beach scenes, and striped room doors evocative of cabanas. The luxurious rooms, decorated in cheerful pastels, have furnishings stenciled with parrots and pineapples. Lamps decorated with swans and palm trees and, like the Dolphin, walls hung with fine-art prints carry out the theme. King-bedded rooms have pull-out sleeper sofas. The 11th and 12th floors compose the Royal Beach Club, a concierge level.

Dining/Diversions: Serving dinner only, the casually elegant Italian-modern Pail has large windows overlooking scenic canals. Strolling musicians entertain while you dine. The delightful Garden Grove Café serves steaks and prime rib, and, in the morning, a traditional Japanese breakfast is an option. Another venue is Kimono's, which serves a wide selection of sushi and becomes a karaoke bar after 8:30pm.

Amenities: Water launch to Epcot & MGM, Olympic-size lap pool, children's wading pool, fully equipped health club, full business center, children's playground, shops, video-game arcade, concierge, 24-hour room service, guest-services desk, complimentary daily newspaper, nightly turndown on request, baby-sitting. See also the earlier description of facilities at the Dolphin.

EXPENSIVE

✪ **Disney's Wilderness Lodge.** 901 W. Timberline Dr. (on the southwest shore of Bay Lake just east of the Magic Kingdom; P.O. Box 10000), Lake Buena Vista, FL 32830-1000. ☎ **407/W-DISNEY** (934-7639) or 407/824-3200. Fax 407/824-3232. 728 units. A/C TV TEL. $180–$390 double, depending on view and season; $575–$825 junior suites; $540–$665 suites. AE, MC, V. Free self- and valet parking.

The geyser out back, the bubbling creek and mammoth stone hearth in the lobby, and bunk beds for the kids are just a few reasons this is one of my favorite WDW resorts. The main dining room, with its sweeping view of 340-acre Bay Lake, might even inspire some romance. Reminiscent of rustic turn-of-the-century national park lodges, this 56-acre resort is surrounded by towering oak and pine forests. Wilderness Lodge has the advantage of feeling removed from the rest of WDW and, unfortunately, is one of the more difficult places to access via the WDW transportation system. The 5-minute geyser shows take place in the meadow periodically throughout the day, and nightly electric water pageants can be viewed from the shores of Bay Lake. A lakefront sand beach and an immense serpentine swimming pool seemingly excavated out of the rocks make up for the modest-sized rooms.

The guest rooms—with patios or balconies overlooking lake, woodlands, or meadow scenery—are furnished in Mission style and adorned with tribal friezes and landscape paintings of the Northwest. In-room safes are a plus. To get the lower room rates, ask for a "standard view."

Dining: The stunning lodgelike Artist Point, overlooking Bay Lake, is adorned with murals based on the works of Rocky Mountain School painters such as Albert Bierstadt; the menu highlights steak, seafood, and game specialties.

Amenities: Immense swimming pool (see above); kiddie pool with water slide; lakefront sand beach; spa pools; boat rental; bicycle rental; 2-mile jogging/bike trail;

video-game arcade; Cub's Den (a counselor-supervised activity center for children 4 to 12); room service; guest-services desk; baby-sitting; boat transport to the Magic Kingdom and Contemporary Resort; bus transport to MGM, Epcot, and other park areas.

MODERATE

✪ **Disney's Caribbean Beach Resort.** 900 Cayman Way (off Buena Vista Dr.; P.O. Box 10000), Lake Buena Vista, FL 32830-1000. ☎ **407/W-DISNEY** (934-7639) or 407/934-3400. Fax 407/934-3288. 2,112 units. A/C MINIBAR TV TEL. $119–$184 double. Children 16 and under stay free in parents' room. AE, MC, V. Free parking.

Though the facilities here aren't as extensive as those at some other Disney resorts, the Caribbean Beach offers especially good value for families. It occupies 200 lush, palm-fringed tropical acres, with accommodations in five distinct Caribbean "villages" grouped around a large, duck-filled lake. The main swimming pool here replicates a Spanish-style Caribbean fort, complete with water slide, kiddie pool, and whirlpool. There are other pools as well as lakefront white-sand beaches in each village. A 1.4-mile promenade—popular for jogging—circles the lake. An arched wooden bridge leads to Parrot Cay Island, where there are a short nature trail, an aviary of tropical birds, and a picnic area. The rooms are charming, with oak furnishings and chintz bedspreads. Amenities include coffeemakers and ceiling fans; refrigerators are available at $5 per night. All rooms have a veranda, many of them overlooking the lake.

Dining: Facilities include a festive food court, the nautical themed Captain's Tavern for American fare, and a pool bar.

Amenities: Seven swimming pools, room service (pizza only), guest-services desk, baby-sitting, complimentary shuttle around the grounds, video-game arcade, shops, boat rental, bicycle rental, coin-op washers/dryers, playgrounds.

Disney's Coronado Springs Resort. 1000 Buena Vista Dr., near All-Star Resorts and Blizzard Beach, Lake Buena Vista, FL 32830. ☎ **407/W-DISNEY** (934-7639), 407/934-6632, or 407/939-1000. Fax 407/939-1001. 1,967 units. A/C MINIBAR TV TEL. $119–$184 double, depending on view and season; $238–$655 suites. Children under 17 stay free in parents' room. AE, MC, V. Free parking.

Everything here is themed on the American Southwest, with lots of muted pastels, sculptured wolves, and cacti. Its four- and five-story hacienda-like buildings have terra-cotta tile roofs and palm-shaded courtyards, and the property itself also houses a major 95,000-square-foot convention center and the largest ballroom in the Southeast. The temple-inspired pool is an interesting addition to the Florida landscape. There are 99 rooms specially designed to accommodate travelers with disabilities, and nearly three-fourths of the rooms are nonsmoking (good news for the very allergic). Since the hotel is new, this means the rooms have always been smoke free.

Dining/Diversions: There is a 420-seat food court, called the Pepper Market, to satisfy the munchies with a variety of fast food. Francisco's is a sit-down, 200-seat Mexican restaurant with the feeling of an outdoor cafe. You won't find a triple-decker burrito here, but rather superbly prepared native dishes such as corn tamales in a spicy green sauce. Siestas offers snacks and light fare.

Amenities: White-sand beach, beach volleyball, boat rentals, four large outdoor swimming pools, kiddie pool, arcade, complimentary parking, boutiques, shops, access to golf course, voice-mail system, spa, coin-op laundry, room service from 6am to 11pm, nightly turndown, lounge, transportation to all WDW parks.

✪ **Disney's Dixie Landings Resort.** 1251 Dixie Dr. (off Bonnet Creek Pkwy.; P.O. Box 10000), Lake Buena Vista, FL 32830-1000. ☎ **407/W-DISNEY** (934-7639) or 407/934-6000. Fax 407/934-75777. 2,048 units. A/C TV TEL. $119–$184 room for up to 4. AE, MC, V. Free parking.

Low rates, extensive child-oriented facilities, and a food court make the Dixie Land-ings popular with families, even though the rooms are midsize and the bathrooms rather small. Adults traveling alone might prefer a more sedate setting. Nestled on the banks of the "mighty Sassagoula River" and dotted with bayous, it shares its 325-acre site with the Port Orleans Resort (described next). It includes Ol' Man Island, a woodsy 3½-acre recreation area containing an immense swimming pool with water-falls cascading from a broken bridge, as well as a water slide, playground, children's wading pool, whirlpool, and fishin' hole (rent bait and poles and angle for catfish and bass). The accommodations areas, themed after the Louisiana countryside, are divided into "parishes," with rooms housed in stately colonnaded plantation homes or rural Cajun-style dwellings fronted by brick courtyards.

Dining/Diversions: Boatwright's Dining Hall, housed in a replica of an 1800s boat-building factory, serves American/Cajun fare at breakfast and dinner. The Cotton Co-op lounge airs Monday-night football games and offers entertainment (singers and comedians) Tuesday to Saturday nights. A food court and pool bar round out the facilities.

Amenities: Six large swimming pools (one with a water slide), 1.7-mile riverfront jogging/biking path, Fulton's General Store, room service (pizza only), guest-services desk, baby-sitting, boat transport (to Port Orleans, Village Marketplace, and Down-town Disney), coin-op washers/dryers, video-game arcade, car-rental desk, bicycle and boat rental.

✪ **Disney's Port Orleans Resort.** 2201 Orleans Dr. (off Bonnet Creek Pkwy.; P.O. Box 10000), Lake Buena Vista, FL 32830-1000. ☎ **407/W-DISNEY** (934-7639) or 407/934-5000. Fax 407/934-5353. 1,008 units. A/C TV TEL. $119–$184 room for up to 4. AE, MC, V. Free parking.

This beautiful resort, themed after turn-of-the-century New Orleans, shares a site on the banks of the Sassagoula with Dixie Landings, described above. Its identical room rates and comparable facilities make it, too, a good bet for families. The midsize rooms, with small bathrooms, are housed in pastel buildings with shuttered windows and lacy wrought-iron balconies; they're fronted by lovely flower gardens opening onto fountained courtyards. Cherrywood furnishings, swagged draperies, and walls hung with botanical prints and family photographs make for pretty room interiors. And the landscaping throughout the property is especially nice, with stately oaks, formal boxwood hedges, azaleas, and fragrant jasmine.

Dining/Diversions: Bonfamille's Café is open for breakfast and dinner, the latter featuring Creole specialties. Scat Cat's Club, a cocktail lounge off the lobby, airs Monday-night football and features family-oriented live entertainment. A food court and pool bar round out the facilities.

Amenities: Room service (pizza only), guest-services desk, baby-sitting, boat trans-port (to Dixie Landings, Village Marketplace, and Downtown Disney). The larger-than-Olympic-size Doubloon Lagoon swimming pool has an enormous water slide. Whirlpool, kiddie pool, coin-op washers/dryers, video-game arcade, bicycle rental, car-rental service, boat rental, 1.7-mile riverfront jogging path, shops.

INEXPENSIVE

✪ **Disney's All-Star Movie Resort.** 1991 W. Buena Vista Dr., Lake Buena Vista, FL 32830-1000. ☎ **407/W-DISNEY** (934-7639) or 407/939-7000. Fax 407/939-7111. 1,900 units. A/C TV TEL. $74–$104 double. Children 17 and under stay free in parents' room. AE, MC, V. Free parking.

The latest of Disney's budget properties, this place features giant Dalmatians leaping from the balconies and a host of larger-than-life Disney movie characters throughout.

Like the other All-Star resorts, the rooms are on the small side but carry the lowest price in the (Walt Disney) World. And with Blizzard Beach right next door, I doubt you'll be spending too much time in the room anyway. There is a food court, movie themed of course, that serves pizza, pasta, sandwiches, and family dinner platters. There's also a full-sized pool. Babysitting and activities for children are available.

✪ **Disney's All-Star Music Resort.** 1801 W. Buena Vista Dr. (at World Dr. and Osceola Pkwy.; P.O. Box 10000), Lake Buena Vista, FL 32830-1000. ☎ **407/W-DISNEY** (934-7639) or 407/939-6000. Fax 407/939-7222. 1,920 units. A/C TV TEL. $74–$104 double. Children 17 and under stay free in parents' room. AE, MC, V. Free parking.

Though the unbeatable combination of rock-bottom rates and extensive facilities at Disney's All-Star Music and Sports resorts is very attractive to families, there is one caveat: The rooms are small (a mere 260 square feet). They're perfect for single adults or couples traveling with one child; larger families had best be into togetherness. Set amid pristine pine forests, this Disney hostelry is part of a 246-acre complex that also includes the adjacent All-Star Sports Resort (described next) and will soon include a third resort. Its 10 buildings are musically themed around country, jazz, rock, calypso, and Broadway show tunes. The calypso building, for instance, has a palm-fringed roof frieze and balconies adorned with tropical birds and musical notes, while a convoy of 18-wheelers travels around the country building, which is decorated with fiddles and banjos. Oversized icons in the public areas—such as three-story cowboy boots and a walk-through jukebox—are lit by neon and fiber optics at night. The attractive rooms have musically themed bedspreads, paintings, and wallpaper borders. In-room safes are a plus. There's a cheerful food court with an adjoining bar. Room service (pizza only), baby-sitting, guest-services desk. Two vast swimming pools, kiddie pool, playground, coin-op washers/dryers, large retail shop, car-rental desk, video-game arcade.

✪ **Disney's All-Star Sports Resort.** 1701 W. Buena Vista Dr. (at World Dr. and Osceola Pkwy.; P.O. Box 10000), Lake Buena Vista, FL 32830-1000. ☎ **407/W-DISNEY** (934-7639) or 407/939-5000. Fax 407/939-7333. 1,920 units. A/C TV TEL. $74–$104 double. Children 17 and under stay free in parents' room. AE, MC, V. Free parking.

Adjacent to the above-described All-Star Music Resort, this 82-acre hostelry is elaborately sports themed. The rooms are housed in buildings designed around football, baseball, basketball, tennis, and surfing motifs. For instance, the turquoise surf buildings have waves along their rooflines, surfboards mounted on the exterior walls, and pink fish swimming along the balcony railings. The immense public-area icons include tennis ball–can stairways and four-story football helmets and whistles. The cheerful rooms feature sports-action-motif bedspreads, paintings, and wallpaper borders; in-room safes are among your amenities. As noted above, however, the rooms here are small.

There's a brightly decorated food court with an adjoining bar. Room service (pizza only), baby-sitting, guest-services desk. Two vast outdoor swimming pools (one surfing themed with two 38-foot shark fins, the other shaped like a baseball diamond with an "outfield" sundeck), kiddie pool, playground, coin-op washers/dryers, shops, car-rental service, video-game arcade.

A DISNEY CAMPGROUND

✪ **Disney's Fort Wilderness Resort and Campground.** 3520 N. Fort Wilderness Trail (P.O. Box 10000), Lake Buena Vista, FL 32830-1000. ☎ **407/W-DISNEY** (934-7639) or 407/824-2900. Fax 407/824-3508. 784 campsites, 408 wilderness homes. A/C TV TEL (homes only). $35–$54 campsite (depending on season, location, number of people, size, and extent of hookup); $180–$235 wilderness cabins. AE, MC, V. Free self-parking.

This woodsy 780-acre camping resort—shaded by towering pines and cypress trees and crossed by fish-filled streams, lakes, and canals—is ideal for family vacations. Though it's a tad less central than other Disney hostelries, its abundance of on-premises facilities more than compensates. Secluded campsites offer 110/220-volt outlets, barbecue grills, picnic tables, and children's play areas. There are also wilderness homes—rustic, one-bedroom cabins with piney interiors that accommodate up to six people. These have cozy living rooms with Murphy beds, fully equipped eat-in kitchens, picnic tables, and barbecue grills. Guests here enjoy extensive recreational facilities ranging from a riding stable to a nightly campfire program hosted by Chip 'n' Dale.

Dining: The rustic log-beamed Trails End offers buffet meals, and the cozy Crockett's Tavern features Texan fare. During summer, guests enjoy a dazzling electrical water pageant from the beach, nightly at 9:45pm. And the rambunctious *Hoop-Dee-Doo Musical Revue* takes place in Pioneer Hall nightly (details in "Walt Disney World & Orlando After Dark," later in this chapter).

Amenities: Guest-services desk, baby-sitting, boat transport (to Downtown Disney, the Magic Kingdom, and the Contemporary Resort). Comfort station in each campground area (with rest rooms, private showers, ice machines, phones, and laundry rooms), two large swimming pools, white-sand beach, horseback riding (trail rides), petting farm, pony rides, fishing, three sand volleyball courts, ball fields, tetherball, shuffleboard, bike rentals, boat rental, 1½-mile nature trail, 2.3-mile jogging path, two tennis courts, two 18-hole championship golf courses, shops, kennel, two video-game arcades.

LAKE BUENA VISTA/OFFICIAL HOTELS

These choices, designated "official" Walt Disney World hotels, are located on and around Hotel Plaza Boulevard, and guests at these hotels enjoy many privileges (see above). The location is a big advantage—close to the Disney parks and within walking distance of Disney Village Marketplace/Downtown Disney and Crossroads shops and restaurants, as well as Pleasure Island nightlife.

One difference between "official" hotels and actual Disney resorts is that the former (with the exception of the Swan and Dolphin) generally have less relentless themes; decide for yourself if that's a plus or a minus. *Note:* You can also make reservations for all of the below-listed properties through Central Reservations Operations at ☎ **407/W-DISNEY** (934-7639); see above for details.

EXPENSIVE

Doubletree Guest Suites. 2305 Hotel Plaza Blvd. (just west of Apopka–Vineland Rd./Fla. 535), Lake Buena Vista, FL 32830. ☎ **800/222-8733** or 407/934-1000. Fax 407/934-1011. 229 units. A/C TV TEL. $164–$239 one-bedroom suites for up to 6; $375–$1,015 two-bedroom suites. Rates depend on view and season. Children 17 and under stay free in parents' room. AE, CB, DC, DISC, JCB, MC, V. From I-4, Exit 27, to Disney Village Marketplace. Left on Hotel Plaza Blvd. Free parking.

Entered via a cheerful, skylit atrium lobby with an aviary of tropical birds and theme-park murals, this seven-story all-suite hotel is a great choice for families. Children have their own check-in desk where they receive a free gift. The large one-bedroom suites—which can sleep up to six—are delightfully decorated and include full living rooms, dining areas, and separate bedrooms. Among your in-room amenities are a wet bar, a refrigerator, a coffeemaker, a microwave oven, TVs with pay-movie options in the living room and bedroom, a smaller black-and-white TV in the bathroom, two phones, and a hair dryer.

Dining/Diversions: The festive Streamers serves buffet and à la carte breakfasts and dinners featuring American fare with Southwestern specialties. A bar/lounge adjoins, as does a theater where kids can watch Disney movies while mom and dad linger over coffee. Another bar serves the pool.

Amenities: Free shuttles to WDW parks, room service, baby-sitting, guest-services desk (sells tickets and arranges transport to all nearby attractions), large swimming pool, whirlpool, kiddie pool with fountain, two tennis courts, jogging path, volleyball, playground, car-rental desk, exercise room, shops (including a grocery), coin-op washers/dryers, video-game arcade, boat rental at nearby Disney Village Marina.

✪ **Marriott Orlando World Center.** 8701 World Center Dr. (on Fla. 536 between I-4 and Fla. 535), Orlando, FL 32821. ☎ **800/621-0638** or 407/239-4200. Fax 407/238-8777. www.marriott.com. 1,599 units. A/C MINIBAR TV TEL. $224–$265 room for up to 5 people, range reflects season; $265–$2,400 suites. AE, CB, DC, DISC, JCB, MC, V. Free self-parking; valet parking $8.

Providing the only viable competition for the Grand Cypress Resort (described below), this sprawling 230-acre resort just 2 miles from WDW parks is a top convention venue that also offers recreational facilities for tourists. These include three swimming pools (one larger than Olympic size with slides and waterfalls), eight tennis courts, and an 18-hole, par-71 Joe Lee–designed championship golf course. A grand palm-lined driveway, flanked by rolling golf greens, leads to the main building—a massive 27-story tower fronted by flower beds and fountains.

Spacious guest rooms are cheerfully decorated in pastel hues with bamboo and rattan furnishings. All have patios or balconies, extensive pay-movie options, irons and ironing boards, safes, and hair dryers. Step outside the tower and you'll find magnificently landscaped grounds, punctuated by rock gardens, shaded groves of pines and magnolias, and cascading waterfalls; swans and ducks inhabit more than a dozen lakes and lagoons spanned by arched bridges.

Dining/Diversions: The luxurious Tuscany, Marriott's premier restaurant, offers northern Italian haute cuisine dinners. The Mikado Japanese Steak House is a serene setting for classic teppanyaki dinners. JW's Steakhouse serves breakfasts and lunches on a screened balcony and cozy dinners in a rustic pine interior. Allie's American Grille is a rather-elegant family restaurant. Among several smaller eateries and bars are the plush Pagoda Lounge for nightly piano-bar entertainment and Champion's, a first-rate sports bar.

Amenities: Mears transportation/sightseeing desk (sells tickets to all nearby attractions, including WDW parks; also provides transport, by reservation, to WDW, other attractions, and the airport; the round-trip fare to WDW parks is $5 per day, free for children 11 and under), concierge, room service (24 hours), baby-sitting, shoe shine, complimentary newspaper weekdays, 1-hour film developing, golf and tennis pro shops and instruction, 18-hole miniature golf course, two volleyball courts, four whirlpools, large kiddie pool, car-rental desk, unisex beauty salon, extensive business center, state-of-the-art health club, coin-op washers/dryers, shops, video-game arcade, Lollipop Lounge (a counselor-supervised child-care/activities center). Inquire as well about organized children's activities—games, movies, nature walks, and more.

Summerfield Suites Lake Buena Vista. 8751 Suiteside Dr. (off Apopka–Vineland Rd./Fla. 535), Lake Buena Vista, FL 32836. ☎ **800/830-4964** or 407/238-07777. Fax 407/238-07787. www.summerfield-orlando.com. 150 units. A/C TV TEL. $119–$249 one-bedroom suites for up to 4; $159–$319 two-bedroom suites for up to 8. Range reflects season. Rates include continental breakfast. AE, CB, DC, DISC, MC, V. Free parking.

This all-suite property, offering free transport to and from the nearby Disney parks, is an excellent choice for families. It's notable for its friendliness and immaculate accommodations—and in 1998 underwent a complete redecoration in the suites, adding brighter, livelier colors. The spacious suites—in buildings surrounding a palm-fringed brick courtyard with umbrella tables, fountains, and gazebos—have fully equipped eat-in kitchens, comfortable living rooms, and a bathroom for each bedroom. Amenities include bedroom and kitchen phones (with two lines), TVs in each bedroom and in the living room (with pay-movie options), VCRs (movies can be rented), and irons and ironing boards. There are also coffeemakers and unstocked refrigerators in all rooms.

Dining: Guests enjoy continental breakfast in the pleasant dining room or at umbrella tables in the courtyard; omelets and waffles may be purchased. An on-premises lobby deli (which sells light fare and liquor) also serves the pool area. Many local restaurants deliver to the hotel.

Amenities: Free shuttle to the Disney parks, plus a $35-per-person round-trip shuttle to the airport and other attractions. Guest-services desk (sells tickets to WDW parks and other nearby attractions, many of them discounted), free daily newspaper, complimentary grocery shopping, baby-sitting, large swimming pool, whirlpool, kiddie pool, car-rental desk, full business services, exercise room, coin-op washers/dryers, shops, video-game arcade.

Wyndham Palace Resort & Spa. 1900 Buena Vista Dr. (just north of Hotel Plaza Blvd.; P.O. Box 22206), Lake Buena Vista, FL 32830. ☎ **800/327-2990** or 407/827-2727. Fax 407/827-6034. 1,014 units. A/C MINIBAR TV TEL. $209–$278 double; $229–$529 one- and two-bedroom suites; range reflects view and season. Children 17 and under stay free in parents' room. AE, CB, DC, DISC, MC, V. Free self-parking; valet parking $7. From I-4 west, take Exit 27. At end of ramp, turn left. At first light, turn left into Walt Disney World Village. At first stoplight, turn right onto Buena Vista Dr. First hotel on the right. Free self-parking; valet parking $7.

Complete room renovations in the fall of 1997 added new luster to this already-luxurious 27-acre resort. A European-style spa, added in 1996, is just one perk, along with extensive boating and recreational facilities. The spacious rooms—most with lake-view balconies or patios—are appealingly decorated and equipped with Spectravision, safes, bedroom and bathroom phones, and ceiling fans. There are also luxurious one- and two-bedroom suites with living and dining rooms and a 10th-floor concierge level. For those with sensitive systems, or a Howard Hughes inclination toward cleanliness, there are 65 eco-friendly rooms featuring nonallergenic pillows and blankets; nondyed tissue, towels, and linens; filtered water; and extra air-cleaning systems.

Dining/Diversions: Arthur's 27 (perched on the 27th floor) offers haute cuisine and panoramic park views, as well as live jazz, piano-bar entertainment, and dancing in an adjoining lounge. In the Outback Restaurant, complete with a three-story indoor waterfall, an Australian storyteller entertains during dinner; steak and seafood are featured. Character breakfasts take place in the Watercress Cafe. Other venues include pool and snack bars, a pastry shop, and the Laughing Kookaburra Good Time Bar, which offers a selection of 99 beers and nightly hosts happy-hour buffets and live bands for dancing.

Amenities: Free shuttle serving WDW, two large swimming pools, whirlpool, kiddie pool, three tennis courts, boat rental, 2- and 3-mile jogging paths, sand volleyball court, bike rental, playground, car-rental desk, room service (24 hours), baby-sitting, guest-services desk, complimentary newspaper for crown-level guests, full business center, shops, coin-op washers/dryers, video-game arcade, counselor-supervised child-care program. The spa offers massage, herbal wraps, a fully equipped health club.

MODERATE

✪ **Courtyard by Marriott.** 1805 Hotel Plaza Blvd. (between Lake Buena Vista Dr. and Apopka–Vineland Rd./Fla. 535), Lake Buena Vista, FL 32830. ☎ **800/223-9930** or

407/828-8888. Fax 407/827-4623. www.marriott.com. 323 units. A/C TV TEL. $89–$169 double, depending on view and season. AE, CB, DC, DISC, JCB, MC, V. Free parking. From I-4, Exit 27 to Downtown Disney. Turn left on Hotel Plaza Blvd. On left. Free parking.

The Courtyard is a moderately priced link in the Marriott chain, with lower prices achieved via limited services. But don't envision a Spartan, no-frills atmosphere. This property was recently renovated to the tune of $4.5 million, and it's looking great. The attractive, standard-sized rooms—most with balconies—have in-room safes, coffeemakers, pay-movie options, and refrigerators available on request. Kids will love in-room Nintendo.

Dining/Diversions: A full-service restaurant serves American fare at all meals and provides room service. There are also a lobby cocktail lounge, a poolside bar (in season), and an on-premises deli featuring pizza and frozen yogurt.

Amenities: Free transportation to WDW parks and attractions, guest-services desk that sells tickets and arranges transport to all nearby attractions, two outdoor swimming pools, whirlpool, kiddie pool, boat rental at nearby Disney Village Marina, playground, car-rental desk, exercise room, shops, coin-op washers/dryers, and video-game arcade.

Grosvenor Resort. 1850 Hotel Plaza Blvd. (just east of Buena Vista Dr.), Lake Buena Vista, FL 32830. ☎ **800/624-4109** or 407/828-4444. Fax 407/828-8192. www.grosvenorresort. com. 626 units. A/C TV TEL. $99–$175 room for up to 4 people, depending on view and season. AE, CB, DC, DISC, JCB, MC, V. Free self-parking; valet parking $6. From I-4, take Exit 27 to Walt Disney World Village. Turn left.

In the moderately priced category, this is a comfortable choice with a British colonial theme and a few unique entertainment options. Occupying 13 lushly landscaped lakeside acres, it centers on a 19-story peach stucco building fronted by towering palms. The rooms are nicely decorated in an attractive resort motif and are equipped with VCRs (tapes can be rented), coffeemakers, safes, and minibars (stocked on request); refrigerators can be rented.

Dining/Diversions: Baskervilles Restaurant—with a Sherlock Holmes museum on the premises—hosts Saturday-night mystery dinner-theater and buffet breakfasts and dinners, some with Disney characters. Also here: a 24-hour food court, a pool bar, and a lounge where sporting events are aired on a large-screen TV.

Amenities: Free shuttle to WDW parks and attractions, guest-services desk (sells tickets and arranges transport to all nearby attractions), doctor on call, limited room service, baby-sitting for a fee, free daily newspaper, two swimming pools, whirlpool, kiddie pool, exercise room, two tennis courts, boat rental, playground, lawn games, car-rental desk, coin-op washers/dryers, shops, video-game arcade, video rentals.

Hotel Royal Plaza. 1905 Hotel Plaza Blvd. (between Buena Vista Dr. and Apopka–Vineland Rd./Fla. 535), Lake Buena Vista, FL 32830. ☎ **800/248-7890** or 407/828-2828. Fax 407/827-6338. www.royalplaza.com. 394 units. A/C MINIBAR TV TEL. $109–$229 double, depending on view and season. AE, CB, DC, DISC, JCB, MC, V. Free self- and valet parking. From I-4, take Exit 27. Turn into Walt Disney World Village. It's the tall, pink-hued building. Free self-parking. Valet parking $7 a day.

The Royal Plaza recently completed a multimillion-dollar renovation and upgrade, including the refurbishment of all accommodations and public areas. Spiffy new rooms—decorated in soft resort hues with bleached oak furnishings—are equipped with VCRs (movies are available for rental), safes, coffeemakers, and hair dryers. Both executive kings and concierge-level rooms, which are among the more expensive choices, contain Jacuzzis (the former also offer full living rooms). Every room has a patio or balcony.

Dining/Diversions: The Verandah, a full-service restaurant, specializes in foods with a hint of the islands. Plaza Diner is a full-service family restaurant featuring American foods such as burgers, meat loaf, and daily specials. Intermission, a sports bar with a handful of big-screen televisions, offers a chance to catch that big game—whether hockey, basketball, baseball, or football. A pool bar is set up during the busy season.

Amenities: Free shuttle service to Disney parks. Room service, guest-services desk (sells tickets and arranges transport to all nearby attractions), baby-sitting, foreign-currency exchange, extensive meeting facilities, large L-shaped swimming pool, whirlpool, four tennis courts, boat rental, sauna, coin-op washers/dryers, shops, video-game arcade.

Travelodge Hotel. 2000 Hotel Plaza Blvd. (between Buena Vista Dr. and Apopka–Vineland Rd./Fla. 535), Lake Buena Vista, FL 32830. ☎ **800/348-3765** or 407/828-2424. Fax 407/828-8933. www.travelodge.com. 325 units. A/C MINIBAR TV TEL. $103–$179 room for up to 4 people, depending on room size and season. Inquire about packages. AE, CB, DC, DISC, JCB, M, V. Free parking. From I-4, take Exit 27. Go to Downtown Disney/Walt Disney World Village. Turn left onto Hotel Plaza Blvd. Across from the Doubletree hotel. Free parking.

This 12-acre lakefront hostelry is spiffy and immaculate, with more upscale rooms and public areas than you might expect at a Travelodge. The rates are also higher than the Travelodge norm but represent good value for your money. The reason: This is the company's flagship hotel. Designed to resemble a Barbados plantation manor house, it has a Caribbean-resort ambience, enhanced by tropical foliage and bright floral-print fabrics. The rooms are particularly inviting, with light bleached-wood furnishings and lovely framed botanical prints and floral friezes, and extras like Spectravision movies, Nintendo, coffeemakers, safes, hair dryers, and free local phone calls. Furnished balconies overlook Lake Buena Vista.

Dining/Diversions: Traders, with a wall of windows facing a wooded area, is open for breakfast and for steak and seafood dinners. On the 18th floor, Toppers offers magnificent views of Lake Buena Vista, as well as dancing, music videos, pool tables, and dart boards; it's a great vantage point for watching the nightly laser shows and fireworks. There are also a cocktail bar and a casual self-service eatery.

Amenities: Free shuttle to the Disney parks, room service, baby-sitting, guest-services desk (sells tickets and arranges transport to all nearby attractions), free newspaper weekdays, large swimming pool, kiddie pool, boat rental, playground, car-rental desk, coin-op washers/dryers, shops, video-game arcade.

OTHER LAKE BUENA VISTA AREA HOTELS

The following hotels are all within a few minutes' drive of WDW parks. In addition to the listings below, there's a **Comfort Inn** at 8442 Palm Pkwy. (☎ **800/999-7300** or 407/239-7300), charging only $39 to $69 for up to four people in a room.

VERY EXPENSIVE

✪ **Hyatt Regency Grand Cypress Resort.** One Grand Cypress Blvd. (off State Rd. 535), Orlando, FL 32836. ☎ **800/233-1234** or 407/239-1234; **800/835-7377** or 407/239-4700 for villas. Fax 407/239-3800, or 407/239-7219 for villas. 750 units, 146 villas. A/C MINIBAR TV TEL. $205–$265 room for up to 5; $305–$410 Regency Club double; $190–$1,400 villas. AE, CB, DC, DISC, JCB, MC, V. Free self-parking; valet parking $9. I-4 Exit 27, right on County Rd. 535, left at second traffic light onto S.R. 535. Two lights on right.

Although only a mile from WDW, this 1,500-acre retreat, ablaze with bougainvillea and hibiscus, is a world away. A romantic getaway, an award-winning golf course, a top-notch equestrian center, and a major renovation in 1997 put this Hyatt resort in a class by itself. Spacious rooms are a welcome respite from the crowded parks—that's if you really find a need to leave. Topping the list of outstanding facilities is a half-acre swimming pool spanned by a rope bridge and flowing through rock grottoes (with 12 waterfalls and 2 steep water slides). Relax on the white-sand beach or play on 12 tennis courts or a Jack Nicklaus–designed golf course.

Deluxe accommodations with wicker furnishings evoke the Southern luxury of a bygone era. The Regency Club, a concierge level, comprises two floors. And especially lavish are the Mediterranean-style Villas of Grand Cypress, all with patios, kitchens, living rooms, and dining rooms; some have working fireplaces and whirlpool baths. Prices for both of these accommodations are considerably more than the $205 to $265 rate cited above. For those looking for a truly luxurious experience, some villas top $1,400 a night.

Dining/Diversions: Casual yet elegant, Hemingway's serves Florida seafood at lunch and dinner. The lodgelike Black Swan, overlooking the golf course, features haute American/continental dinners. Similar fare is offered at the plush La Coquina, where a harpist entertains at dinner and the Sunday brunches are exquisite. Other venues include the White Horse Saloon, for prime-rib dinners and country music; Trellises, a bar/lounge where a jazz ensemble entertains evenings; the lovely lake-view Cascade, serving American fare at all meals, plus Japanese breakfasts; and several pool-side snack bars.

Amenities: Free transportation around grounds and to all major attractions except for WDW; hourly shuttle to all WDW parks (round-trip fare $6 per day); concierge (sells tickets to WDW parks and other nearby attractions); room service (24 hours); baby-sitting; Mears airport shuttle; gorgeous swimming pool; renowned golf course; golf and tennis instruction and pro shops (the golf school here has been called one of the finest in the country); 45-acre Audubon nature walk; 4.7-mile jogging path; racquetball, volleyball, and shuffleboard courts; playground; car-rental desk; unisex beauty salon; full business center; state-of-the-art health club; shops; helicopter landing pad; video-game arcade; counselor-supervised child-care center/Camp Hyatt activity center.

MODERATE

✪ **Holiday Inn Sunspree Resort Lake Buena Vista.** 13351 Fla. 535 (between Fla. 536 and I-4), Lake Buena Vista, FL 32821. ☎ **800/FON-MAXX** or 407/239-4500. Fax 407/239-7713. www.kidsuites.com. e-mail: max@kidsuites.com. 507 units. A/C TV TEL. $89–$152 kidsuites available for up to 4 people, depending on season. AE, CB, DC, DISC, JCB, MC, V. Free parking.

About a mile from the Disney parks, this Holiday Inn offers the chain's "no surprises" dependability, while catering to children in a big way. Kids "check in" at their own pint-size desk; receive a free fun bag containing a video-game token coupon, a lollipop, and a small gift; and get a personal welcome from animated raccoon mascots, Max and Maxine. More than 200 of these kid suites are available.

Camp Holiday activities—magic shows, clowns, sing-alongs, arts and crafts, and much more—are available at a minimal charge for kids ages 2 to 12. And parents can arrange (by reservation) for Max to come tuck a child into bed. Pretty rooms have kitchenettes with refrigerators, microwave ovens, and coffeemakers. And if you're renting a second room for the children, "kidsuites" here—themed as igloos, space capsules, Noah's Ark, and others—sleep up to three. Amenities include VCRs (tapes can be rented), hair dryers, safes, coffeemakers and unstocked refrigerators in all rooms. Ask about special offers for grandparents traveling with grandchildren.

Dining: Maxine's serves all meals, including steak and seafood dinners. Max's Funtime Parlor offers nightly bingo and karaoke; it also airs sporting events on a large-screen

---

Believe It or Not: Orlando B&Bs

Although most of the properties in Orlando are megaresorts or standard chains, there are a few bed-and-breakfast options. These following two properties offer a nice respite from the crowded, commercial world of the theme parks and are ideal for couples traveling without children who are looking for a little quiet time.

The **Perrihouse,** in Lake Buena Vista, is an eight-bedroom, gray brick house nestled amid 6 acres of flowers and trees. Opened in 1990, it was first a rooming house for Disney employees but soon switched to a B&B. An on-site bird sanctuary is a draw for nature lovers. Each room has a private bath, and an expanded continental breakfast is offered each morning. For more information, call ☎ **407/876-4830** or go online to www.perrihouse.com. Room rates range from $99 to $129.

The **Unicorn Inn,** in Kissimmee, offers an authentic English experience in the midst of this still-rural American town. Opened in 1995, Unicorn Inn is housed in a blue-shingled house originally built in 1901. The eight rooms offer basic accommodations that are clean and cozy. For more information, call ☎ **407/846-1200.** The price is $75 a night, including a full breakfast.

TV. Kids 12 and under eat all meals free, either in a hotel restaurant with parents or in Kid's Kottage, a cheerful facility where movies and cartoons are shown and dinner includes a make-your-own sundae bar.

Amenities: Guest-services desk (sells tickets to all nearby attractions, including WDW parks), free scheduled transport to WDW parks (there's a charge for transport to other nearby attractions), large swimming pool, two whirlpools, kiddie pool, playground, fitness center, coin-op washers/dryers, shops, car rental, video arcade, Camp Holiday (a counselor-supervised child-care/activity center for ages 2 to 12), room service.

○ **Residence Inn by Marriott.** 8800 Meadow Creek Dr. (just off Fla. 535 between Fla. 536 and I-4), Orlando, FL 32821. ☎ **800/331-3131** or 407/239-7700. Fax 407/239-7605. 688 units. A/C TV TEL. $85–$135 suites; range reflects season. Rates include full breakfast. AE, CB, DC, DISC, JCB, MC, V. Free parking.

This delightful all-suite hostelry occupies 50 acres, alternating wooded grounds with neatly manicured lawns, duck-inhabited ponds, fountains, and flower beds. Guests, up to four in a single suite and up to six in a double, enjoy a serene environment offering the seclusion and safety of a private community. They can also avail themselves of the extensive facilities at the adjoining Marriott Orlando World Center (see details earlier) with room-charge privileges. The tastefully decorated accommodations—with fully equipped eat-in kitchens, private balconies or patios, and large living rooms—are equipped with Spectravision, VCRs (tapes can be rented), two phones (kitchen and bedroom), ceiling fans, and safes. The two-bedroom units have two bathrooms.

Dining: A full breakfast is available in the gatehouse each morning, a Pizza Hut is on the premises, and local restaurants deliver food.

Amenities: Guest-services desk (sells tickets and provides transport to all nearby theme parks and attractions; round-trip to WDW parks is $8), baby-sitting, complimentary daily newspaper, next-day film developing, free food-shopping service, Mears airport shuttle. Three large swimming pools, two whirlpools, sports court (basketball, badminton, volleyball, paddle tennis, shuffleboard), tennis court, playground, coin-op washers/dryers, shops, two video-game arcades.

ON U.S. 192/KISSIMMEE

This very American stretch of highway, dotted with fast-food eateries, isn't what you'd call scenic, but it does contain many inexpensive hotels and motels within 1 to 8 miles of Walt Disney World parks. Almost all provide, or can arrange, for shuttle service to WDW and other attractions. The cost usually runs from $10 to $14 per person. New to this stretch of highway are markers, about 20 feet tall, along the side of the road. Aptly tagged with the word "Marker" and a number, they are a new effort to help tourists find their way along this stretch of road.

MODERATE

Comfort Inn Maingate. 7571 W. Irlo Bronson Memorial Hwy. (U.S. 192; between Reedy Creek Blvd. and Sherbeth Rd., markers 15 and 16), Kissimmee, FL 34747. ☎ **800/221-2222** or 407/396-7500. AE, DC, DISC, MC, V. 225 units. AC TV TEL. $69–$199 double. Just 6 miles from WDW parks, and 7 miles from Universal Studios. Free self-parking.

Interiors are recently refurbished and include refrigerators, microwaves, and sleep sofas. The rooms are a bit small but large enough for a family to be comfortable.

Courtyard Marriott Maingate. 7675 Irlo Bronson Memorial Hwy., Kissimmee, FL 34747. ☎ **800/568-3352** or 407/396-4000. Fax 407/396-0714. 198 units. A/C TV TEL. $69–$135. AE, DC, DISC, MC, V. From I-4 take Exit 25B. Go west U.S. 192 about 2 miles. Near marker 5. Free parking.

The plain, brown, five-story brick building belies a pleasant, tropical theme carried throughout the lobby and rooms. All rooms have two double or one king-sized bed and a small table and chair. In-room extras include a full-length mirror, mini coffeemaker, safe, hair dryer. Kids and adults will enjoy the outside recreation area, adorned with a few palm trees, which includes a pool, a kiddie pool, a small whirlpool, and an outdoor bar.

Dining: The breakfast-only Courtyard Café serves a full buffet each morning, and for each paying adult, one child (9 years old and younger) may eat free.

Amenities: Free shuttle service to WDW parks. Transportation to other area attractions for a fee; gym, hair dryer, handicapped accessible, in-room safe, kiddie pool, video-game room.

Holiday Inn Nikki Bird Resort. 7300 Irlo Bronson Memorial Hwy., Kissimmee, FL 34747. ☎ **800/206-2747** or 407/396-7300. Fax 407/396-7555. 529 units. A/C TV TEL. $79.95–$129. AE, DC, DISC, MC, V. From I-4 exit 25B. 1.5 miles past the Disney entrance on the left, between markers 5 and 6. Free parking.

How many hotels have their own roaming mascot? Yes, Nikki Bird, who strolls the grounds giving hugs, is just one of the family-friendly perks at this property. There is a large arcade in the lobby, and each room is equipped with a refrigerator, microwave, safe, and hair dryer. Connecting rooms and roll-away beds are available. Children under 12 eat free at the full-breakfast buffet next door at Angel's Diner, and nightly entertainment, including songs, puppet shows, and games, is presented each night. Free transportation provided to WDW parks.

INEXPENSIVE

In addition to the accommodations described here, there are scores of other inexpensive but perfectly serviceable motels within a few miles of the WDW parks. All have swimming pools and arrange transportation to the Disney parks for a fee. Many sell tickets to attractions, but there have been problems with low prices truly being too good to be true. Tourists end up at the gate without a valid ticket. Stick to ordering tickets through the parks themselves.

Factoid

U.S. 192 is also known as W. Irlo Bronson Memorial Highway and eventually turns into Vine Street.

Days Inn. 4104 and 4125 W. Irlo Bronson Memorial Hwy. (U.S. 192; at Hoagland Blvd. N., markers 15 and 16), Kissimmee, FL 34741. ☎ **800/647-0010,** 800/DAYS-INN, or 407/ 846-4714. Fax 407/932-2699. 220 units. A/C TV TEL. $39–$99.95 room for up to 4, depending on season; $37–$63 efficiency; $55–$75 Jacuzzi room (for 1 or 2 people). Rates include continental breakfast. Rates may be higher during major events. AE, CB, DC, DISC, MC, V. Free parking.

Offering good value for your hotel dollar, these two Days Inns—on either side of U.S. 192—share facilities, including two swimming pools, coin-op washers and dryers, and a video-game arcade. Several restaurants (which deliver food), a large shopping mall with a 12-theater movie house, and a supermarket are within close walking distance.

The rooms at both locations are clean and attractive standard motel units. The best bets are the efficiency units with fully equipped kitchenettes at no. 4104. The Jacuzzi rooms are at no. 4125 and also include a refrigerator and a microwave oven. All accommodations offer pay-movie options and in-room safes, and both locations serve free coffee, juice, and doughnuts in their lobbies each morning. The guest services desk at no. 4104 sells tickets (many of them discounted) and arranges transport to all nearby attractions, including WDW parks. A big plus: Round-trip transport to WDW parks is free. Airport transfers can be arranged.

Days Inn Lake Buena Vista Village. 12490 Apopka Vineland Rd., Lake Buena Vista, FL 32703. ☎ **800/521-3297** or 407/239-4646. Fax 407/239-8469. A/C TV TEL. $39–$119. AE, DC, DISC, MC, V. From I-4, take Exit 27. At the bottom of the ramp turn left. Property is ½ mile on the left.

Although not far from Disney, this property is probably better suited for those planning to spend most of their time at Universal and Sea World.

This is a good option for families, with connecting rooms and cribs available, along with microwaves and refrigerators also available for an additional fee. A coin-operated laundry, a kid's eat-free program, and a kiddie pool round out the perks for tikes. For the grown-ups, there are an outdoor pool and free transportation to Disney parks, and pets are accepted.

Hampton Inn Maingate. 3104 Parkway Blvd., Kissimmee, FL 34747. ☎ **800/426-7866** or 407/396-8484. Fax 407/396-7644. www.hamptoninn.com. 164 units. A/C TV TEL. $59— $95 double. Rates include continental breakfast. AE, DC, DISC, MC, V. Take I-4 to exit 25A. At the first traffic light turn left, between markers 8 and 9. (Across the street from Celebration.) Free parking.

Sitting just a quarter mile off the road, this wooded property has a laid-back, secluded feel. The rooms here, as you might expect, are nothing fancy, but they are well-maintained and clean. You can choose from two double beds or one king-sized bed, and there is a small safe in the closet. Recreational activities are limited with only a small rectangular pool and basketball and shuffleboard courts. There is no room service, but a pretty good complimentary breakfast is served in a small dining area off the lobby. A host of restaurants are located nearby on U.S. 192.

Hampton Inn, Orlando Disney Maingate. 3000 Maingate Lane, Kissimmee, FL 34747. ☎ **800/426-7866** or 407/396-6300. Fax 407/396-8989. www.hamptoninn.com. 118 units. A/C TV TEL. $59–$99 double. AE, DISC, MC, V. From I-4 take Exit 25B to U.S. 192 west for about 2 miles. Turn right on Maingate Lane.

Since this is one of the newer low-cost hotels in the Disney World area, rooms show none of the wear of some older properties. The property is clean and nicely, if simply, landscaped. Although the rooms are only average in size, connecting rooms and cribs are available. Those, along with a coin-operated laundry, make this a good location for a larger family or several families traveling together. Other pluses are the free continental breakfast buffet, a pool, and a car rental desk.

Howard Johnson Express Inn. 4836 W. Irlo Bronson Hwy. (U.S. 192), Kissimmee, FL 34746. ☎ **800/952-5464** or 407/396-4762. Fax 407/396-4866. 131 units. A/C TV TEL. $39.95–$66 double. AE, DC, DISC, MC, V. Free parking. Take I-4 to Exit 25A, 3½ miles on right, between markers 11 and 12.

As a lakefront property, this is one of the more scenic Kissimmee offerings. You can have picnics by the lake or rent jet skis for about $60 an hour. The pink-and-blue buildings contain clean, comfortable rooms, and some of the suites contain an in-room Jacuzzi, a microwave oven, and a refrigerator. There are a large heated swimming pool and a video-game room. Another plus is a free shuttle to the WDW parks. Transportation to other attractions can be arranged for a fee.

Magic Castle. 5055 W. Irlo Bronson Memorial Hwy. (U.S. 192), Kissimmee, FL 34746. ☎ **800/446-5669** or 407/396-2212. Fax 407/396-0253. 107 units. A/C TV TEL. $35.95–$61.95 room for up to 4, depending on season. Rates include continental breakfast. AE, DC, DISC, MC, V. From I-4 take Exit 25A, near marker 11; the motel is about 3½ miles on the left, next to the Olive Garden. Free self-parking.

The owner of this property has discontinued his affiliation with Ramada Inn, but this three-story stucco building continues to provide adequate accommodations at a good price. The standard-sized rooms are equipped with cable TV (with Disney Channel and HBO movies), safes, and refrigerators.

Facilities include an outdoor swimming pool and coin-op washers/dryers. Continental breakfast is served in the lobby each morning. Shuttle service to WDW parks is available for $9 per person, round-trip. Service to other parks will cost about $12 or $14. Pets are accepted ($6 per night).

✪ Ramada Inn. 4559 W. Irlo Bronson Memorial Hwy. (U.S. 192), Kissimmee, FL 34746. ☎ **800/544-5712** or 407/396-1212. Fax 407/396-7926. 114 units. A/C TV TEL. $39.95–$59.95 for up to 4; range reflects season. AE, DC, DISC, MC, V. Free self-parking. From I-4, between markers 13 and 14, take Exit 25A; the motel is about 5 miles on left, across from Jungleland. Free self-parking.

This Ramada offers standard motel rooms, which are a little on the small side, with cable TV and safes; refrigerators and microwaves are available on request for $8 a night. Facilities include coin-op washers/dryers, a swimming pool, a children's playground, and picnic tables. The 1950s-style Hollywood Diner, which has an adjoining bar/lounge, serves American fare at all meals. Shuttle service to WDW parks is available for $10 per person, round-trip. Pets are accepted ($6 per night). Children stay and eat free.

Riu Orlando Hotel. 8688 Palm Pkwy. (between Fla. 535 and I-4), Lake Buena Vista, FL 32830. ☎ **407/239-8500.** Fax 407/239-8591. www.riuhotels.com. 167 units. A/C TV TEL. $80–$175 double, depending on season. Children 17 and under stay free in parents' room. AE, CB, DC, DISC, OPT, MC, V. Free self-parking.

Taken over by new management in 1997, this six-story property still has a location on a pleasant, tree-lined street and overlooks a lake out back—a big plus. The Crossroads Shopping Center and Walt Disney World Village Marketplace/Downtown Disney put dozens of shops, services, and restaurants within easy walking distance. There are free shuttles to all the major attractions, and the in-room coffeemakers are a nice touch and

Pillow Talk

If you're looking for a basic room, you might also try these chain hotels and motels. They are all moderate or inexpensive in price and located in the budget motel corridors of Kissimmee/U.S. 192 or International Drive, all relatively convenient to the attractions. While we can't vouch for these personally, their brand names generally mean reliability:

In Kissimmee

Best Western Eastgate, 5565 W. Irlo Bronson Memorial Hwy., Kissimmee (☎ 407/396-0707).

Best Western Kissimmee, 2261 E. Irlo Bronson Memorial Hwy., Kissimmee (☎ 407/846-2221).

Best Western Maingate, 8600 W. Irlo Bronson Memorial Hwy., Kissimmee (☎ 407/396-0100).

Budget Inn East, 307 E. Vine St., Kissimmee (☎ 407/847-8010).

Budget Inn West, 4686 W. Vine St., Kissimmee (☎ 407/846-1547).

Comfort Suites Hotel, 4018 W. Vine St., Kissimmee (☎ 407/870-2000).

Comfort Suites Maingate Hotel, 7888 W. Irlo Bronson Memorial Hwy., Kissimmee (☎ 407/390-9888).

Courtyard by Marriott, 7675 W. Irlo Bronson Memorial Hwy., Kissimmee (☎ 407/396-4000).

Days Inn East of the Magic Kingdom, 5840 W. Irlo Bronson Memorial Hwy., Kissimmee (☎ 407/396-7969).

Days Inn West-Maingate, 7980 W. Irlo Bronson Memorial Hwy., Kissimmee (☎ 407/396-1000).

Doubletree Guest Suites Resort, 4787 W. Irlo Bronson Memorial Hwy., Kissimmee (☎ 407/397-0555).

Econo Lodge Hawaiian, 7514 W. Irlo Bronson Memorial Hwy., Kissimmee (☎ 407/396-2000).

Econo Lodge Maingate Central, 4985 W. Irlo Bronson Memorial Hwy., Kissimmee (☎ 407/396-4343).

Holiday Inn Kissimmee, 2009 W. U.S. Hwy. 192, Kissimmee (☎ 407/826-2713).

---

a plus for families. The rooms have cable, Nintendo, hair dryers, irons, and ironing boards.

Dining: The Garden Café, serving American fare at breakfast and dinner, has an outdoor poolside seating area and an adjoining bar/lounge.

Amenities: Room service, baby-sitting, and a complimentary daily newspaper are available. The guest-services desk sells tickets (many of them discounted) and arranges transport to all nearby attractions. On the premises are a nice-size swimming pool and whirlpool, coin-op washers/dryers, an exercise room, a business center, and a small video-game arcade.

INTERNATIONAL DRIVE

The hotels and resorts listed here are 7 to 10 miles north of the Walt Disney World parks (a quick freeway trip) and close to Universal Studios Escape and Sea World.

Hotel & Suites Main Gate East, 5678 Irlo Bronson Memorial Hwy., Kissimmee (☎ **800/366-5437** or 407/96-4488).

Howard Johnson, 4643 W. Irlo Bronson Memorial Hwy., Kissimmee (☎ **407/396-1340**).

Motel 6, 7455 W. Irlo Bronson Memorial Hwy., Kissimmee (☎ **407/396-6422**).

Motel 6, 5731 W. Irlo Bronson Memorial Hwy., Kissimmee (☎ **407/396-6333**).

Quality Inn on Lake Cecile, 4944 W. Irlo Bronson Memorial Hwy., Kissimmee (☎ **407/396-4455**).

Quality Suites Maingate East, 5876 W. Irlo Bronson Memorial Hwy., Kissimmee (☎ **407/396-4455**).

Ramada Limited, 5055 W. Irlo Bronson Memorial Hwy. (☎ **407/396-2212**).

Ramada Plaza Hotel Gateway, 7370 W. Hwy. 192, Kissimmee (☎ **407/396-4400**).

In the International Drive Area

Best Western Plaza International, 8738 International Dr., Orlando (☎ **407/345-8195**).

Days Inn, 9990 International Dr., Orlando (☎ **407/352-8700**).

Days Inn, 7200 International Dr., Orlando (☎ **407/351-1200**).

Days Inn/East of Universal Studios, 5827 Caravan Court, Orlando (☎ **407/351-3800**).

Econo Lodge International Dr., 5859 American Way, Orlando (☎ **407/345-8880**).

Holiday Inn Express International Dr., 6323 International Dr., Orlando (☎ **407/351-4430**).

Holiday Inn International Drive Resort, 6515 International Dr., Orlando (☎ **407/351-3500**).

Ramada Hotel Resort Florida Center, 7400 International Dr., Orlando (☎ **407/351-8400**).

Roadway Inn International, 6327 International Dr., Orlando (☎ **407/351-4444**).

VERY EXPENSIVE

✪ **Peabody Orlando.** 9801 International Dr. (between the Bee Line Expwy. and Sand Lake Rd.), Orlando, FL 32819. ☎ **800/PEABODY** (732-3639) or 407/352-4000. www. peabody-orlando.com. Fax 407/351-0073. 891 units. A/C MINIBAR TV TEL. $300–$360 for up to 3 people; $495–$1,435 suites. Children 17 and under stay free in parents' room. Inquire about packages and holiday/summer discounts and senior rate for those over 50. AE, CB, DC, DISC, JCB, MC, V. Free self-parking; valet parking $7.

Okay, let's get the pun out of the way: This property is just ducky, especially those famous avian ambassadors who make their daily march of the mallards through the lobby to John Philip Sousa. There may be a little disarray until 2000, since a second 700-room tower is under construction. But that may translate into better deals. The Peabody's hallmark ambience of sophistication, which extends to its top-rated restaurants, is not found anywhere else and will surely survive the jackhammers.

The existing, already-luxurious rooms, which underwent a renovation and redecoration in 1999, have handsome bamboo and bleached-wood furnishings but still contain two phones, Spectravision, and laser-disc movie setups (there's a vast video library). The bathrooms have cosmetic lights, fine European toiletries, hair dryer, and small TV. The concierge-level Peabody Club occupies the top three floors. Seniors should note the over-50 prices, compensation for wrinkles indeed.

Dining/Diversions: Dux, the Peabody's elegant signature restaurant, and the casual 24-hour B-Line Diner are detailed in the "Beyond Disney: International Drive" section of "Dining," below. Capriccio, for sophisticated Italian fare, is open for dinner and for champagne Sunday brunches. Combos play jazz, blues, and show tunes in the atrium Lobby Bar nightly. The lobby is the setting for exquisite afternoon English teas on weekdays. Sporting events are aired in the cozy duck-themed Mallards Lounge. And alfresco jazz concerts take place on the fourth-floor recreation level in the spring and fall.

Amenities: Concierge (7am to 11pm), room service (24 hours), baby-sitting, nightly bed turndown on request, free daily newspaper, transport between the hotel and all WDW parks throughout the day (unlimited daily round-trips cost $6), Mears transportation/sightseeing desk (sells tickets to all nearby attractions, including WDW parks and dinner shows; also provides transport, by reservation, to attractions and the airport), Olympic-length swimming pool, outdoor whirlpool, kiddie pool, four tennis courts, 7-mile jogging path, car-rental desk, Delta Airlines desk, full-service unisex salon, business center, state-of-the-art health club, shops, video-game arcade, golf privileges at four nearby courses.

EXPENSIVE

Summerfield Suites. 8480 International Dr. (between the Bee Line Expwy. and Sand Lake Rd.), Orlando, FL 32819. ☎ **800/833-4353** or 407/352-2400. Fax 407/238-0778. 146 units. A/C TV TEL. $119–$211 one-bedroom suites for up to 4; $157–$319 two-bedroom suites for up to 8. Range reflects room size and season. Rates include continental breakfast. AE, CB, DC, DISC, MC, V. From I-4, take Exit 29 (Sand Lake Road) to International Dr. Turn right on International Dr. Hotel is ½ mile on right. Free parking.

This delightful hotel—with potted palms on open-air balconies creating a welcoming resort ambience—is built around a nicely landscaped central courtyard. Like its sibling property in Lake Buena Vista, it's notably friendly and well run. The spacious, neat-as-a-pin suites, very attractively decorated, contain fully equipped eat-in kitchens, comfortable living rooms, and large dressing areas. All offer irons and ironing boards, phones in each bedroom and kitchen, and satellite TVs (with pay-movie options) in each bedroom and living room (the latter with a VCR; rent movies downstairs).

Dining: An extensive continental buffet breakfast is served in a charming dining room (waffles and omelets can be purchased), and the cozy lobby bar is a popular gathering place in the evenings. Local restaurants deliver food to the premises.

Amenities: Concierge/tour desk (sells tickets to WDW parks and other nearby attractions), daily newspaper delivery, transport between the hotel and all WDW parks (round-trip fare is $7), shuttle available to the airport and nearby attractions, complimentary grocery shopping, nice-size swimming pool, whirlpool, kiddie pool, car-rental desk, business services, exercise room, coin-op washers/dryers, 24-hour shop, video-game arcade.

MODERATE

Country Hearth Inn. 9861 International Dr. (between Bee Line Expwy. and Sand Lake Rd.), Orlando, FL 32819. ☎ **800/447-1890** or 407/352-0008. Fax 407/352-5449. 150 units. A/C TV TEL. $69–$103 double, depending on view and season. Extra person $10. Children under

18 stay free in parents' room. Rates include continental breakfast. AE, CB, DC, DISC, MC, V. Free self-parking.

Though it doesn't offer much in the way of resort facilities, the Country Hearth Inn's low rates, great location, and very pretty rooms and restaurant—not to mention wine-and-cheese receptions for guests several times a week—make this an appealing choice. Centered on a white-trimmed, pale-peach octagonal building crowned by a windowed cupola, the inn evokes 19th-century Florida—the leisurely era of riverboat travel and gracious plantations. Ceiling fans whir slowly over verandas and balconies furnished with wicker rocking chairs, and an inviting landscaped courtyard with neat lawns and flower beds encompasses a large free-form swimming pool backed by verdant wood-lands and a wide canal. Charming guest rooms, furnished in handsome maple or mahogany pieces, are adorned with floral friezes and 19th-century folk art. French doors open onto patios, balconies, or courtyards, and bathrooms have art-nouveau lighting fixtures. In-room amenities include cable TVs (with HBO and Spectravision movie options), coffeemakers, phones with modem jacks, wood-bladed chandelier ceiling fans, safes, and small refrigerators. Larger deluxe rooms offer sleeper sofas, microwave ovens, and hair dryers.

Dining: The elegant Country Parlor, in the balustraded Victorian lobby, serves moderately priced American fare at all meals; a pianist entertains at Sunday cham-pagne brunches. Equally turn-of-the-century in decor is the Front Porch Lounge, a popular gathering spot for locals. It features happy-hour buffets weekdays from 5:30 to 7pm.

Amenities: Room service, guest-services desk (sells tickets, many of them dis-counted, and arranges transport to all nearby attractions, including WDW parks), baby-sitting, Mears airport shuttle. Round-trip fare to WDW parks is $10.

Radisson Barcelo Hotel. 8444 International Dr., Orlando, FL 32819. ☎ **800/333-3333** or 407/345-0505. Fax 407/352-5894. 299 units. A/C TV TEL. $99–$119. AE, DC, DISC, MC, V. From I-4, take Exit 29 (Sand Lake Rd.) Turn right on International Dr. Turn right on the *second* entrance to Jamaican Court. The hotel is on the left. Free parking.

Guests still benefit from a major room renovation that took place in 1997. All rooms have bright, tropical decor, queen-size beds, and two phones. A perk for fitness buffs is access to the adjacent YMCA.

There's also an aquatic Center, which houses two Olympic-size pools, 23 Nautilus machines, and racquetball courts. (The hotel also has its own outdoor heated pool.) Since it is in the heart of the I-Drive tourist hub, there are dozens of restaurants and shops nearby. The hotel's restaurant serves a full breakfast buffet, which is included in some room rates.

There is also a "kids eat free" program. It's just a few minutes from Universal Stu-dios and Sea World, and about 20 minutes from Walt Disney World.

Dining: Restaurant, bar.

Amenities: Coin-operated laundry, dataports in room, in-room refrigerator, gift shop, indoor and outdoor pool, gym, tennis, playground, rooms have Nintendo-equipped televisions.

Residence Inn by Marriott. 7975 Canada Ave. (just off Sand Lake Rd., a block east of Inter-national Dr.), Orlando, FL 32819. ☎ **800/227-3978** or 407/345-0117. Fax 407/352-2689. www.marriott.com. 176 units. A/C TV TEL. $85–$135 for up to 8. Rates include extended con-tinental breakfast. AE, DC, DISC, MC, V. Free parking.

Marriott's Residence Inns were designed to offer home-away-from-home comfort for traveling business people, but the concept also works well for families. The accommodations buildings are surrounded by well-tended lawns, shrubs, and beds of geraniums, and the handsomely decorated suites offer full eat-in kitchens and comfortable living-room areas. All but studio doubles have wood-burning fireplaces, and two-bedroom penthouses (great for families) have full bathrooms upstairs and down. Amenities include irons, ironing boards, and safes.

Dining: The comfortably furnished gatehouse is the setting for an extended continental breakfast daily, and complimentary beer, wine, and hors d'oeuvres Monday to Thursday from 5:30 to 7pm. Local restaurants deliver food (there are menus in each room).

Amenities: Guest-services desk (sells tickets—most of them discounted—and provides transport to all nearby theme parks and attractions), Mears airport shuttle, free shuttle to WDW parks, large swimming pool, whirlpool, basketball court, sand volleyball court, coin-op washers/dryers, food/sundries shop, picnic tables, barbecue grills; free use of nearby health club.

INEXPENSIVE

Best Western Plaza International. 8738 International Dr., Orlando, FL 32819. ☎ **800/654-7160** or 407/345-8195. Fax 407/352-8196. 672 units. A/C TV TEL. $80–$95. AE, DC, DISC, MC, V. Free parking. From I-4 take Exit 29 (Sand Lake Rd.). The first traffic light is International Dr.; the hotel is 1 mile on the right.

Although there is free transportation to WDW parks, this property, located less than 3 miles from Sea World, is a good bet for those planning to spend most of their time at that marine-life park or at Universal Studios Escape. Along with the standard features such as coin-operated laundry, connecting rooms, and cribs, fitness-conscious guests have access to a nearby, and quite large, YMCA. On the property there are a kiddie pool and an outdoor pool, plus a small game room.

Fairfield Inn by Marriott. 8342 Jamaican Court (off International Dr. between the Bee Line Expwy. and Sand Lake Rd.), Orlando, FL 32819. ☎ **800/228-2800** or 407/363-1944. Fax 407/363-1944. www.marriott.com. 134 units. A/C TV TEL. $69–$79 room for up to 4; range reflects season. Rates include continental breakfast. AE, CB, DC, DISC, JCB, MC, V. Free parking. From I-4 take Exit 29 (Sand Lake Rd.), go east 1 block, turn right on International Dr. Turn right on Jamaican Court. The hotel is on the right.

I love this inn's quiet and safe location in a secluded area off International Drive. It nestles in Jamaican Court, a neatly landscaped complex of hotels and restaurants (that means a number of places are within walking distance). The spiffy-looking rooms offer cable TV with HBO, and the phones are equipped with 25-foot cords and modem jacks. Daily newspapers and local calls are free, as is the continental breakfast served in the lobby each morning.

The guest-services desk sells tickets (most of them discounted) and can arrange transport to all nearby theme parks and attractions and the airport; round-trip to WDW parks is $10. A small outdoor swimming pool and video-game room are on the premises, and the lobby has a microwave oven for guest use.

Amenities include three swimming pools (one quite large), two kiddie pools, whirlpool, four tennis courts, sand volleyball court, playground, business center, exercise room, 1.4-mile jogging trail, coin-op washers/dryers, car-rental desk, unisex hair salon, shops, two video-game arcades.

Quality Inn Plaza. 9000 International Dr., Orlando, FL 32819. ☎ **800/999-8585** or 407/345-8585. Fax 407/996-6839. 1,020 units. A/C TV TEL. $39.95–$79.95. AE, DISC, MC, V. From I-4 take Exit 29 (Sand Lake Rd). Take a right at the bottom of ramp. Turn at the first right, International Dr. The property is 1 mile on the right, next to the Amazing Animals attraction. Free parking.

The rooms at this property are spread throughout five-, six-, and seven-story buildings which feature two double beds. Built in 1983, the property is clean but the furnishings are the bare necessities. A plus is the proximity to the nightlife, restaurants, and shops along I-Drive. The lobby includes a restaurant, bar, game room, and shop that sells snacks and premade sandwiches. Kids under 11 eat free in the hotel restaurant with a paying adult. Cribs are available, and there is an in-room safe and an outdoor pool. Pets are accepted.

BEYOND THE PARKS: ORLANDO & WINTER PARK
ORLANDO

The Courtyard at Lake Lucerne. 211 N. Lucerne Circle E., Orlando, FL 32801. ☎ **800/ 444-5289** or 407/648-5188. Fax 407/246-1368. 24 units. A/C TV TEL. $69 double; $96–$165 suites. Rates include continental breakfast. AE, DC, MC, V. Free self-parking. Take Orange Ave. south, immediately following City Hall (domed building with fountains and glass sculpture); turn left onto Anderson. After 2 lights, at Delaney Ave., turn right. Take first right onto Lucerne Circle N. (Be aware of 1-way streets.) Follow brown "historic inn" signs.

Orlando literally grew around this B&B, which now stands incongruously amid a tangle of interstate ramps. Each unit in the three distinct buildings (Phillips, Norment-Perry, Wellborn) that make up the property was designed by a different artist or decorator. With wide porches and ceiling fans, the I.W. Phillips House (1916) creates an antebellum splendor that never actually flourished this far south.

Suites at the Phillips overlook a shared courtyard insulated from the urban hum by old-growth trees. A fountain's gentle trickle is the only sound you'll hear while strolling the brick walkways. The solitude isn't as complete in the front rooms of Norment-Perry. Traffic sounds there are minimal but audible.

Since opening in 1986, the Courtyard has served mostly business VIPs and locals on weekend getaways. With few amenities, it's a place for simple, private pleasures.

Downtown's most famous entertainment district, Church Street Station, is less than 6 blocks north. Since the Courtyard is undergoing an expansion as this book goes to press, more rooms should be available soon.

Amenities: The staff fulfills most duties of a hotel concierge. Nightly turndown, coffee and refreshments in lobby, complimentary chilled wine with check-in. Suites in the Wellborn include minikitchens with refrigerators, microwaves, and coffeemakers. The Courtyard's two honeymoon suites have double whirlpool tubs. Others have clawfoot tubs and sun rooms. The single room has a basic shower and closet-sized toilet.

The Harley of Orlando. 151 E. Washington St., Orlando, FL 32801. ☎ **800/321-2323** or 407/841-3220. Fax 407/849-1839. 264 units. A/C TV TEL. $95–$150 double. AE, MC, V. Free self-parking. Take I-4 to the Anderson St. exit. Turn left on Rosalind. The hotel entrance is located on the left, directly across from the entrance to Lake Eola Park.

Just 15 minutes from the Orlando International Airport and about 25 minutes from the attractions, the Harley of Orlando is an urban alternative to the Disney resorts. Request a balcony room so you can overlook Lake Eola Park, one of the most beautiful spots in the city. The carpet in this five-story structure is a little threadbare in places, but the rooms, done in dark colors, are comfortable and clean.

Dining/Diversions: The Cafe on the Park Restaurant does a competent job on standards such as prime rib. The Sunday brunch, which is buffet style, is well worth the price. The Monkey Bar Lounge, done up in gilded chrome and leather, isn't the hippest place in town, but the drinks pack a punch and you don't have to drive to get home. The Church Street Station entertainment complex and the nightclubs and restaurants of downtown are just a short walk away. (Or catch a ride on the free city bus, Lymmo, which picks up passengers just up the block.)

Amenities: Room service, no-smoking rooms, complimentary weekday morning paper, free parking, pool, sundeck.

Universal's First Resort

The war is on. In addition to competing with Disney for theme-park visitors, Universal Studios Escape is now battling for overnight guests.

Portofino Bay Hotel is the first of five properties built by Universal Studios Escape which are designed to go head-to-head with Disney by offering on-property resorts adjacent to the theme parks. Opened in late 1999, the 750-room Portofino Bay features eight restaurants/lounges, a spa and fitness center, and a children's play area. The Loews hotel evokes a Mediterranean seaside village with a harbor setting. Boccie ball courts, in addition to two swimming pools, carry through this old-world theme. The second hotel, a 650-room Hard Rock Hotel filled with rock-and-roll memorabilia, should open by the end of 2000.

Just as at Disney, there are perks for staying at a Universal hotel. Those include:

- Free water-taxi transportation to Universal Studios Florida, Islands of Adventure, and CityWalk.
- Early theme-park admission, 1 hour before the general public.
- Front-of-the-line access to specific attractions within the theme parks during first hour park is open to general public.
- Resort ID card which can be used to purchase food, merchandise, and other items at Universal Studios Florida, Islands of Adventure, and CityWalk.
- Priority seating at restaurants.
- Length-of-stay tickets which provide park access for the duration of a visit.

For information about Portofino Bay, write 5601 Universal Blvd., Orlando, FL 32819, or call ☎ **407/503-1000.**

Packages can also be booked through **Universal Studio Vacations** at ☎ **888/ 322-5537** or 407/224-7000. Online, go to **www.usevacations.com**.

Radisson Place Hotel Orlando. 60 S. Ivanhoe Blvd., Orlando, FL 32804. ☎ **800/ 333-3333** or 407/425-4455. Fax 407/425-7440. 367 units. A/C TV TEL. $104–$129 double. AE, DISC, MC, V. Take I-4 to Princeton St. (Exit 43). Turn right at the bottom of the ramp. Turn left on Orange Ave. Go through the light, bearing to the right around the landscaping and the miniature Statue of Liberty; the hotel is on the left.

The 15-story Radisson Place Hotel, built in 1985, is really geared more toward the business traveler than the family crowd, but because it's located right off I-4, just blocks from downtown and 15 minutes from the airport, it's also a good bet for families. However, this place has a relatively stuffy air, with the gleaming brass, marble, and oversized ferns. The rooms are tastefully appointed with solid-color bedspreads and carpets. The views of downtown Orlando from the upper floors are impressive, and the suites are a cut above what you will find for the price elsewhere. The hotel is located just across from Lake Ivanhoe, which has a series of exercise stations and a well-lit path for walking or jogging. There is even a small park for the kids less than a mile away. There are some rooms on the premises designed to accommodate the physically challenged.

Dining: 'Lando Sam's Restaurant offers American cuisine in a casual, colorful setting with a piano player tinkling the ivories on a dark-wood baby grand. The decor is heavy on the shiny brass and ferns. The food isn't anything you wouldn't expect at any run-of-the-mill hotel eatery. The same goes for 'Lando Sam's Lounge. There are daily breakfast and luncheon buffets in the restaurant that are, if nothing else, solid values for the price.

Your best bet, however: Ask for a list of restaurants in nearby downtown; there are a few choice eateries within walking distance (if under a mile or so is walking distance). Try Brian's, just down the street, a nonretro diner with great breakfast food and coffee.

Amenities: Concierge, room service (including late-night room service), minibars, valet parking, transportation desk to arrange for taxi or limo service, attraction ticket information available. (Also, right next door is the Greater Orlando Chamber of Commerce, which has plenty of brochures on area attractions in the lobby.) Outdoor swimming pool, Jacuzzi, sundeck, two outdoor tennis courts, well-equipped health club, boutique.

Radisson Twin Towers Hotel. 5780 Major Blvd., Orlando, FL 32819. ☎ **800/327-2110** or 407/351-1000. Fax 407/363-0106. 761 units. A/C TV TEL. Summer $119–145 double depending on the season; $375–$900 suite year-round. AE, DC, DISC, MC, V. Located directly across from the main gate of Universal Studios. Free parking.

From your balcony you can watch the palms waving at Universal's entrance and the bungee jumpers in the parking lot next door waving on their way down. Built in the 1970s as a convention hotel, the property underwent a makeover in the 1980s as owners realized families would be flocking to Universal right across the street. The location is convenient without being amid the congestion of International Drive, and you're just minutes from WDW without being engulfed by the Mouse and the associated higher prices. The hotel still attracts a lot of convention business, but those facilities are in a building separate from the rooms. Aside from occasionally being trapped in the elevator with a herd of human Elk, you'll hardly notice. Just a side note: That red building on the property that looks like an old-fashioned schoolhouse is just that—the Little Red School House, a public school run in cooperation with the local school district for the children of Twin Towers employees.

Dining/Diversions: The Palm Court Restaurant serves three meals a day, and the Everglades Lounge has frequent entertainment and a big-screen TV. Although Palm Court does an adequate job, there are plenty of other dining options nearby. Most, like the Hard Rock Cafe, are comparable in price but more interesting. The lounge acts are best left alone, but the big-screen TV offers a great respite for sports fans who need a break from quality time with the family.

Amenities: Room service, baby-sitting, children's program, laundry, deli, pool, whirlpool, sauna, exercise room, playground, game room.

WINTER PARK

Best Western Mount Vernon Inn. 110 S. Orlando Ave., Winter Park, FL 32789 ☎ **407/647-1166.** Fax 407/647-8011. 147 units. A/C TV TEL. $78–$88 double; manager special Mar–Christmas, $51.50 double. AE, MC, V. Free self-parking. The Inn is located on U.S. Rte. 17–92 between Fairbanks Ave. and Lee Rd., across from Houston's steak house.

This is one of the best bargains in town, a place where old-money families know their guests will get comfortable accommodations at a reasonable price (look for lots of late-model Caddies in the parking lot). There are some nice views available overlooking the pool, and about a block away across the street is a city park the kiddies will love. But, overall, there is nothing too fancy about the Mount Vernon. It is, however, centrally located between the beaches and the theme parks and very close to downtown Winter Park and downtown Orlando. There is a pool, but from there you're pretty much on your own. What do you expect for $78?

The Red Fox Lounge features nightly entertainment that's generally along the lines of a guy with a hair weave and a synthesizer. Unless that sounds really hip to you, it's better to venture to downtown Winter Park or Orlando for entertainment. The Coach Dining room is open for breakfast and lunch from 6:30am to 2pm. The food is plentiful and filling, but this is a place you eat to be sated, not necessarily satisfied. There are many fine restaurants nearby.

One tip: If you make reservations significantly in advance, save yourself a late-night check-in headache by calling before you leave home to make sure you are still on the books.

✪ **Langford Resort Hotel.** 300 E. New England Ave. (at Interlachen Ave.), Winter Park, FL 32789. ☎ **407/644-3400.** Fax 407/628-1952. 220 units. A/C TV TEL. $75–$115 double; $200 suite. Children 17 and under stay free in parents' room. Rooms with kitchenettes $10 extra. AE, DC, MC, V. Free self-parking. I-4 West through downtown Orlando to Winter Park. Take Fairbanks exit, 69. Go east 2 miles to Park Ave, turn left. Go 2 blocks. Turn right on New England; 2 blocks on right.

In pre-Disney days, Winter Park was one of central Florida's most-visited resorts, and the Langford was the place to stay. Vaughn Monroe entertained in the lounge, and the guest roster listed people like Eleanor Roosevelt, Mamie Eisenhower, Lillian Gish, Vincent Price, and Dina Merrill. Ronald and Nancy Reagan celebrated their 25th wedding anniversary here. Stars and just-plain-folk alike came to gawk at the "jungle" and other theme rooms, as well as the poolside bathrooms with their wacky paintings of mermaids and mermen.

Today, while kitschy but no longer glamorous, this friendly, family-run resort offers extensive facilities at very reasonable rates. The midsize rooms show the wear of the years, but the lobby and hallways have recently been renovated. An on-site spa offers a full range of treatments: sauna, steam, massage (shiatsu, Swedish, and deep athletic), body wraps, seaweed wraps, salt glows, facials, manicures, pedicures, and beauty packages. The hotel's central location, on a lovely street shaded by tall oaks draped with Spanish moss, is another plus. Room decor varies and it is notably eclectic. Many rooms have balconies and/or fully equipped kitchenettes with two-burner stoves and small refrigerators. The little ones will love the kiddie pool and the small video-game arcade.

4 Dining

Since most visitors spend the majority of their time in the Walt Disney World area, I've focused on the best choices throughout that vast enchanted empire. Also listed are a few worthwhile choices beyond the realm.

Almost every mid- and low-priced restaurant offers a children's menu, and most provide some kind of kids' activity (mazes, coloring, paper dolls) as well. The downside of restaurants that cater to kids is that they're noisy. If that will ruin your appetite, remember this rule: The higher the prices, the fewer the children. If you're looking for a quiet meal, head for restaurants on International Drive, Downtown Disney, or downtown Orlando. Keep in mind that, especially in Downtown Disney, the waits may be considerable . . . sometimes several hours during peak season.

See also the listings for dinner shows in section 15 of this chapter.

HOW TO ARRANGE PRIORITY SEATING AT WALT DISNEY WORLD RESTAURANTS

Priority seating at Walt Disney World restaurants means you get the next available table but does not reserve a table specifically for you. That means you may still have a bit of a wait, even with a reservation. Without priority seating you may not be able to get a table at all, especially during special events or peak season. You can arrange priority seating up to 60 days in advance at almost all full-service Magic Kingdom, Epcot, Disney-MGM Studios, Animal Kingdom resort, and Disney Village restaurants—as well as character meals and shows throughout the complex—by calling ☎ **407/ WDW-DINE** (939-3463). Nighttime shows can actually be booked as far in advance as you wish. Exceptions to this format are noted in the listings below.

Since this priority-seating phone number was instituted in 1994, it has become much more difficult to obtain a table by just showing up. So I strongly advise you to avoid disappointment by calling ahead. However, if you don't reserve in advance, you can take your chances reserving in the parks themselves:

Epcot: Make reservations at the WorldKey interactive terminals at Guest Relations in Innoventions East, at Worldkey Information Service Satellites located on the main concourse to World Showcase and at Germany in World Showcase, or at the restaurants themselves.

Magic Kingdom: Reserve at the restaurants themselves.

Disney-MGM Studios: Make reservations at the Hollywood Junction Station on Sunset Boulevard or at the restaurants themselves.

Animal Kingdom: Call ☎ **407/WDW-DINE** (939-3463).

TIPS ON WALT DISNEY WORLD RESTAURANTS

- A pocket-sized guide produced by American Express, appropriately titled *Guidebook,* offers invaluable assistance in picking a restaurant. There are also pocket-sized guides to individual restaurants displayed in the lobbies of some hotels.

- All park restaurants have no-smoking interiors; you can smoke only on patios and terraces.

- All sit-down restaurants in Walt Disney World take American Express, Master-Card, Visa, and the Disney Card. The Disney Card enables WDW resort guests to charge items at WDW restaurants and shops to their rooms.

- Guests at Disney resorts and "official" hostelries can make restaurant reservations through the guest-services or concierge desks.

WALT DISNEY WORLD

The following listings encompass restaurants in the Magic Kingdom, Epcot, Disney-MGM Studios, Disney Village, and Animal Kingdom.

Note: Alcohol is not served in the Magic Kingdom, though it's available in the other Disney parks.

EPCOT

An ethnic meal at one of the World Showcase pavilions is a traditional part of the Epcot experience, but many are a bit pricey for the value. Families on a budget will probably opt to eat at the outdoor cafes near each pavilion. Check the Guidemap you receive upon entering the park for details.

Renovations are ongoing at Epcot's World Showcase restaurants, so there may be changes that were not available at press time. The general theme and price of the restaurants discussed below should, however, remain constant.

All the sit-down restaurants are expensive, except for the moderately priced Le Cellier Steakhouse in Canada, the Biergarten in Germany, and Akershus in Norway.

World Showcase

These restaurants are arranged geographically, beginning at the Canada pavilion and proceeding counterclockwise around the World Showcase Lagoon.

CANADA   This is a good choice for families. Located in the Victorian Hotel du Canada, **Le Cellier Steakhouse** has a castle-like ambience, offering seating in tapestried chairs under vaulted stone arches. Regional dishes include Cheddar-cheese soup, carved pemeal bacon (a pork loin with a light cornmeal crust), French-Canadian *tourtière,* maple-syrup pie, and Canadian beers. Lunch runs about $10 per person, dinner $20.

UNITED KINGDOM The Tudor-beamed **Rose & Crown,** entered via a cozy pub with a pungent aroma of ale, is evocative of Victorian England. The outdoor seating overlooking the lagoon is a good place to check out IllumiNations. The menu features traditional items—smoked salmon with Stilton cheese, prime rib, Yorkshire pudding, sherry trifle. Wash it all down with a pint of Irish lager beer, Bass ale, or Guinness stout. Lunch entrees are $9 to $15; dinner is $10 to $30. Traditional afternoon tea is served daily at 3:30pm; the cost is $9.95. Another option here is bar fare (sausage rolls, Cornish pasties, a Stilton cheese and fruit plate), all under $4.50. If the pub is too crowded, as it can be in peak season, grab some tasty fish-and-chips sold from the outdoor cart.

FRANCE   Chefs de France The art nouveau/*fin-de-siècle* interior is agleam with mirrors and brass candelabra chandeliers. I recommend the seafood cream soup with crab dumplings (as featured by Vergé at Moulin de Mougins). Entree selections at dinner include a superb broiled salmon in sorrel-cream sauce *à la façon de Bocuse* (it's served with ratatouille and new potatoes), and Vergé's sautéed beef tenderloin with raisins and brandy sauce. And among desserts, LeNôtre's soufflé Grand-Marnier is the standout. There is also an extensive wine list. Entrees range from $21 to $40.

MOROCCO The palatial ✪ **Restaurant Marrakesh** features exquisitely carved archways, hand-set mosaic tile work, and a beamed ceiling painted with Moorish motifs. Belly dancers perform while you dine on lamb couscous, braised tagine of chicken, or shish kebab. This exotic restaurant perhaps best captures the international-experience spirit of Epcot. Entrees range from $14.95 to $24.95 per person.

JAPAN The **Teppanyaki Dining Room** centers on a teppanyaki steak house where you'll sit at a grill table while white-hatted chefs rapidly dice, slice, stir-fry, and propel cooked food onto your plate. It's a real treat to watch the cleaver-wielding chef preparing your food. An elaborate dinner for two (of which an abbreviated version is available at lunch) includes a shrimp appetizer, salad, soup, grilled fresh vegetables with udon noodles, succulent morsels of grilled beef tenderloin and lobster, steamed rice, choice of dessert (perhaps chestnut cake), and green tea. And even à la carte entrees include plenty of extras. Lunch will run between $10 and $20 per person; the complete meal described above costs $39.50 for two at lunch, $59.90 for two at dinner.

Adjoining the teppanyaki rooms is a U-shaped **Tempura Kiku** where you can also order some sushi and sashimi items, as well as tempura-battered and fried shrimp, scallops, lobster, beef, and chicken.

Meals will cost between $10 and $20 for lunch and $21 to $40 for dinner. No reservations are required for counter seating.

For me, the gem of this complex is the peaceful, plant-filled **cocktail lounge** with large windows overlooking the lagoon—a very pleasant setting for appetizers and sake. Menu items are $3.95 to $8.25, and no reservations are required. A window seat here is another great venue to view IllumiNations.

Finally, housed in a replica of the 16th-century Katsura Imperial Villa in Kyoto is **Yakitori House,** a bamboo-roofed cafeteria serving Japanese snack-fare items, all under $9, and full children's meals for under $5. The umbrella tables on a terrace overlooking a rock waterfall are a nice touch. Serves lunch and dinner.

ITALY Patterned after Alfredo De Lelio's celebrated establishment in Rome, **L'Originale Alfredo di Roma Ristorante** suggests a seaside Roman palazzo with beautiful trompe l'oeil frescoes. The theatricality of an exhibition kitchen, charming Italian waiters, and exuberant strolling musicians create a festive ambience. If you want a quieter setting, ask for a seat on the veranda. De Lelio invented fettuccine Alfredo—and it remains an excellent entree choice here. And there's a sublime tiramisu for dessert. A special vegetarian menu is available, and the list of Italian wines is extensive. Meals will cost between $10 and $20 for lunch, $21 to $40 for dinner. Inquire about the early-bird special when making reservations.

GERMANY   Lit by street lamps, the **Biergarten** simulates a Bavarian village court-yard at Oktoberfest with autumnal trees, a working water wheel, and geranium-filled flower boxes adorning Tudor-style houses. Entertainment might be an oompah band or a strolling accordionist, and guests are encouraged to dance and sing along. All-you-can-eat buffet meals featuring traditional fare (sauerbraten, spaetzle with gravy, sauer-kraut with salads) are offered at lunch and dinner. Beverages and desserts are extra. The lunch buffet is $10.95 for adults, $5.50 for children 3 to 11; dinner is $15.75 for adults, $7 for children.

At **Sommerfest,** a cafeteria with indoor seating and courtyard tables overlooking a fountain, you can purchase bratwurst sandwiches with sauerkraut, goulash soup, and desserts such as apple strudel. All items are under $5.

CHINA   One of the most attractive of the World Showcase restaurants, ✪ **Nine Dragons,** with windows overlooking the lagoon, has intricately carved rosewood pan-eling and furnishings and a beautiful dragon-motif ceiling. Begin your meal here with a selection of dim sum. Entrees highlight dishes from four regions of China. You can order Chinese or California wines with your meal, but I especially love the fresh melon juice, either nonalcoholic or mixed with rum or vodka. Meals cost from $8.50 to $18.50 at lunch (most are under $15), $10.50 to $23.75 at dinner.

Or you can opt for egg rolls, pork fried rice, or stir-fried chicken and vegetables served over noodles at the open-air **Lotus Blossom Café,** a pleasant and inexpensive self-service eatery.

NORWAY   **Akershus** re-creates a 14th-century castle fortress that stands in Oslo's harbor. Its pristine white stone interior, with Gothic stone archways creating intimate dining niches, is softly lit by gas lamps, candelabra chandeliers, and flickering sconces. The meal is an immense smorgasbord of traditional dishes—smoked pork with honey mustard, strips of venison in cream sauce, gravlax in mustard sauce, an array of Norwegian breads and cheeses, and much more. Norwegian beer and aquavit complement a list of French and California wines. The lunch buffet costs $11.95 for adults, $5.25 for children 4 to 9, free for children 3 and under; the dinner buffet is $18.50 for adults, $7.95 for children. There are also nonsmorgasbord children's meals for $4.75.

Another facility in this pavilion, the **Kringla Bakeri og Kafe,** offers covered out-door seating and inexpensive light fare—open-face sandwiches, cheese and fruit plat-ters, waffles sprinkled with powdered sugar, and fresh-baked Norwegian pastries. No reservations are required.

MEXICO   The setting for the ✪ **San Angel Inn** is a hacienda courtyard amid dense jungle foliage in the shadow of a crumbling Yucatán pyramid. It's nighttime: The tables are candlelit (even at lunch) and the lighting is very low. The Popocatepetl vol-cano erupts in the distance, spewing molten lava, and you can hear the sounds of far-away birds. Thunder, lightning, and swiftly moving clouds add a dramatic note, but the overall ambience is soothing and, importantly, cool. Order an appetizer of *queso fundido* (melted cheese with Mexican pork sausage, served with homemade corn or flour tortillas), and follow it with an entree of *filete ranchero* (grilled tenderloin of beef served over corn tortillas with sauce ranchero, poblano pepper strips, Monterey Jack cheese, onions, and refried beans). Combination platters are also an option at both meals. They also offer a vegetarian menu, and the margaritas here are as good as they get. Meals cost $10 to $20 per person.

The **Cantina de San Angel,** a cafeteria with outdoor seating at umbrella tables overlooking the lagoon, offers affordable tacos, burritos, and combination plates, along with frozen margaritas; a complete children's meal is under $5.

Future World

At the Living Seas pavilion, dine "under the sea" at the enchanting ✪ **Coral Reef,** where all seating rings a 5.6-million-gallon coral-reef aquarium inhabited by more than 4,000 denizens of the deep. Strains of Debussy's *La Mer* and Handel's *Water Music* playing softly in the background help set the tone. Tiered seating, much of it in semicircular booths, ensures everyone a good view. The menu features (what else?) seafood—creamy lobster bisque, sautéed mahimahi in lemon-caper butter, and shrimp satay served atop red-pepper pasta. There are also steak and chicken dishes. For dessert, choose the white-chocolate-mousse cake topped with Mickey ears. Meals cost between $21 and $40 per person.

THE MAGIC KINGDOM

There are dozens of fast-food eateries throughout the Magic Kingdom. In addition to the places below, I also recommended the Diamond Horseshoe Saloon Revue in Frontierland, which combines a light meal with a 30- to 45-minute Western-themed musical revue (see section 6).

LIBERTY SQUARE The **Liberty Tree Tavern** replicates an 18th-century pub, with low-beamed ceilings and a vast brick fireplace hung with copper pots. Main courses range from New England pot roast with mashed potatoes and vegetables to a traditional roast-turkey dinner with all the trimmings, and there's apple crisp topped with vanilla ice cream for dessert. Prices range from around $9.75, for charbroiled chicken, to $14.25, for the fresh catch of the day. Open from 11am to 3pm and 4pm until park closing. See details about character dinners below.

In the mood for a light but satisfying meal? I'm partial to the baked- and sweet-potato cart in Liberty Square and the adjacent fruit stand. The turkey legs in Frontierland, although not exactly light, are tasty, easy to eat, and filling.

CINDERELLA'S CASTLE **Cinderella's Royal Table** has an imposing Gothic interior with leaded-glass windows and heraldic banners suspended from a vaulted ceiling. The sturdy oak tables are candlelit. The dainty damsel herself probably never dined on hearty cuts of steak and prime rib, but you may as well indulge in a caloric splurge. For an appetizer, I recommend the almond-breaded Brie served with wild-lingonberry relish. Cinderella often greets guests in the downstairs entrance hall. Lunch will cost between $10 and $20 per person, dinner $21 to $40 per person.

MAIN STREET Inspired by the Disney movie *Lady and the Tramp,* **Tony's Town Square Restaurant** is Victorian plush. The walls are hung with original cels from the movie. There's additional seating in a sunny plant-filled solarium. Tony's opens early for breakfast (you can eat here while waiting for the other lands to open). The rest of the day the fare is Italian—antipasto, pastas, calzones, subs, and salads—while at dinner your options range from garlicky sautéed shrimp and vegetables over linguine in a light cream sauce to a 12-ounce strip steak/sautéed lobster combination. Breakfast items cost under $10; lunch, $10 to $20; and dinner, $20 to $40.

DISNEY-MGM STUDIOS

There are more than a dozen eateries in this park, with names like the Studio Commissary and Starring Rolls Bakery. The four listed below, my favorites, are all sit-down restaurants requiring reservations. You'll find the best food at the Derby.

The **Hollywood Brown Derby,** modeled after the famed Los Angeles celebrity haunt where Louella Parsons and Hedda Hopper held court, mirrors its defunct West Coast counterpart with interior palm trees, and mahogany-wainscoted walls hung with more than 1,500 caricatures from Barbara Stanwyck to Rin Tin Tin. The Derby's signature dish is the Cobb salad, invented by owner Bob Cobb in the 1930s. You might try the champagne-flavored oyster-Brie soup, followed by baked grouper meunière served atop pasta, and a dessert of grapefruit cake with vanilla icing (another house specialty). Lunch ranges from $10 to $20 per person; dinner, $21 to $40.

The **Sci-Fi Dine-In Theater Restaurant** replicates a 1950s Hollywood drive-in movie theater. Diners sit in flashy convertible cars under a twinkling starlit sky, while friendly servers bring complimentary popcorn. The video plays (just like TV at home), with newsreels, cartoons, horror-movie clips, and coming attractions. Try a Towering Terror (barbecued pork ribs with veggies and fries) and Plucked from Deepest Space (a grilled chicken sandwich with Cajun rèmoulade sauce and fries). Finish up with the Cheesecake That Ate New York. Your bill is presented as a speeding ticket. Meals cost between $10 and $20 for lunch, $21 to $40 for dinner.

The **50s Prime Time Cafe** places diners in a time-warp/sitcom psychodrama. The eating areas look like homey 1950s kitchens, wherein black-and-white TV sets air clips of shows like *My Little Margie* and *Topper*. The service staff greets diners like family ("Hi, Sis, I'll go tell Mom you're home!") and may threaten you with no dessert if you don't eat your veggies or report you to Mom for resting your elbows on the table. The food—meat loaf with mashed potatoes, Granny's pot roast, Dad's chili, and such—isn't all that great, but the place is fun anyway. Desserts include banana splits and S'mores. Between $10 and $20 for lunch, $21 to $40 for dinner.

Toy Story Pizza Planet, located in the Muppet's Courtyard, offers what the name implies, along with salads, espresso, and cappuccino. The food is not exactly gourmet; but meals are under $10 per person, and kids of all ages love the many games and diversions. This is a boisterous family eatery.

ANIMAL KINGDOM

The **RainForest Cafe** here, just like the one in Disney Village Marketplace, is a huge draw for sit-down dining. Other options include **Tuskers House** in Africa, which serves Rotisserie, grilled and fried chicken, and salads. The **Restaurantorsaurus** (yep, you guessed it, this one is in DinoLand U.S.A.) serves hamburgers, hot dogs, and authentic McDonald's french fries and Chicken McNuggets. The meals at both restaurants will run between $10 and $20 per person.

IN THE DISNEY RESORTS & LAKE BUENA VISTA
VERY EXPENSIVE

California Grill. At Disney's Contemporary Resort, 4600 N. World Dr. ☎ **407/WDW-DINE** (939-3463) or 407/824-1576. Main courses $14.75–$27.50. AE, MC, V. Daily 5:30–10pm. CALIFORNIA.

High above the Magic Kingdom (on the resort's 15th floor), this stunning restaurant offers scenic views of the park and lagoon below. A zigzaggy Wolfgang Puckish interior incorporates art deco elements, but the central focus is a dramatic exhibition kitchen with a wood-burning oven and rotisserie.

The menu changes seasonally, but the sushi sampler always makes for a good beginning here, as does ravioli filled with goat cheese, shiitake mushrooms, and sun-dried tomatoes. The whole-wheat–crusted pizzas might compose a light entree. Heartier choices include braised lamb shank (with wild-chanterelle risotto and orange-nuanced bread topping) or grilled pork tenderloin served atop polenta with crimini mushrooms and a garnish of crispy fried sage. For dessert, it's hard to surpass the butterscotch crème brûlée with almond biscotti. If you like a close-up view of chefs at work, ask to sit at the kitchen counter. There's a good selection of California wines to complement your meal.

Hemingway's. In the Hyatt Regency Grand Cypress, 1 Grand Cypress Blvd. (off Fla. 535). ☎ **407/239-1234.** Reservations recommended. Main courses $7.50–$19.75 at lunch, $20–$28 at dinner. AE, CB, DC, DISC, JCB, MC, V. Tues–Sat 11:30am–2:30pm; daily 6–10:30pm. Free self- and validated valet parking. SEAFOOD.

Fronted by a waterfall cascading into stone-bedded streams, Hemingway's evokes Key West's famous denizen, with photographs of "Papa" and his fishing and hunting trophies adorning the walls. This casually elegant (and generally child-free) restaurant is ideal for romantic dinners. Weather permitting, you can sit on a screened wooden deck near the waterfall.

Ask not for whom the bell tolls, but rather for an appetizer of deep-fried baby squid and grilled eggplant in garlicky herb-seasoned tomato coulis. For dinner you might try the golden brown beer-battered coconut shrimp served with roasted potatoes, al dente vegetables, and orange marmalade-horseradish sauce. Also recommended are the deliciously light, moist crab cakes; ask for Cajun tartar sauce to top them. For dessert, key lime pie appropriately reaches its apogee here. The lunch menu offers similar fare, along with paella, sandwiches, and salads. In the adjoining Hurricane Lounge—a congenial setting with a beautiful oak bar—specialties include a variety of island rums and the Papa Doble, a potent tropical rum and fruit libation invented by Hemingway himself (legend has it he once drank 16 of them in one sitting!).

✪ Victoria & Albert's. In Disney's Grand Floridian Beach Resort, 4401 Floridian Way. ☎ **407/WDW-DINE** (939-3463). Reservations required. Jackets required for men. No children's menu. Children are highly discouraged. $80–$145 per person fixed price. AE, MC, V. Daily seatings 6–6:45pm and 9–9:45pm. Free self- and validated valet parking. AMERICAN REGIONAL.

It's not often that I'd describe a dining experience as flawless, but Victoria & Albert's, the World's (Walt Disney World, that is) most elite restaurant, won me over, though you certainly pay for the experience. The intimate dining room is plush; diners sink into leather-upholstered Louis XIII–style chairs at exquisitely appointed tables. A maid and butler provide deft and gracious service, and a harpist plays softly while you dine.

Dinner, a seven-course affair, changes nightly. It might include hors d'oeuvres of Florida lobster tail or vermouth-poached jumbo sea scallops served in a crisp rice-noodle basket. Entrees include delicacies such as a fan of juicy sautéed Peking duck breast with wild rice and crabapple chutney. A salad of esoteric greens in an orange-sherry vinaigrette clears the palate for the next course—English Stilton served with pine-nut bread, port wine, and a pear poached in burgundy, cognac, and cinnamon sugar. The conclusion: a sumptuous hazelnut and Frangelico soufflé, followed by coffee and chocolate truffles. There is, of course, an extensive wine list. I suggest that you opt for the Royal Wine Pairing, which offers an appropriate wine with each course.

MODERATE

Cape May Café. At Disney's Grand Floridian Beach Resort, 1800 Epcot Resorts Blvd. ☎ **407/WDW-DINE** (939-3463). Dinner $19.95 adults, $9.50 children 3–11; character breakfast $14.95 adults, $8.50 children. AE, MC, V. Daily 5:30–9:30pm. Free valet and self-parking. CLAMBAKE BUFFET.

A hearty 19th-century–style New England clambake is featured here nightly. Sand sculptures and furled striped beach umbrellas create the ambience of an upscale sea-side resort. Aromatic New England chowder, steamed clams and mussels, corn on the cob, chicken, lobster, and red-skin potatoes are cooked up in a crackling rockweed steamer pit that serves as the restaurant's centerpiece. And these traditional clambake offerings are supplemented by dozens of salads, hot dishes (barbecued pork ribs, smoked sausage, pastas), and a wide array of oven-fresh breads and desserts. There's a full bar.

'Ohana. At Disney's Polynesian Resort, 1600 Seven Seas Dr. ☎ **407/WDW-DINE** (939-3463). Family-style meal $20.95 adults, $9.95 children 3–11, free for children 3 and under. Breakfast $14.95 adults, $8.95 children 3–11. AE, MC, V. Daily 5–10pm. Transportation to WDW resorts. Free parking. PACIFIC RIM.

You'll be welcomed here with warm island hospitality by a server who'll address you as "cousin." The setting is South Seas exotic, with thatched roofing and tapa-cloth tenting overhead, carved Polynesian columns, and an open kitchen centering on a wood-burning 18-foot fire-pit grill. There's lots going on at all times. The blowing of a conch shell summons a storyteller, coconut races take place down the central aisle, couples get up and dance to island music, and people celebrating birthdays participate in hula-hoop contests as everyone sings "Happy Birthday" to them in Hawaiian. Kids especially love all the hoopla, so if you're looking for an intimate venue, this isn't it.

Soon after you're seated, a lazy Susan arrives laden with steamed dumplings in soy-sesame oil, napa cabbage slaw with honey mustard, black-bean and corn relish, and several tangy sauces. The courses tend to arrive in rapid succession, so ask your waiter to slow the pace if it's too fast. The feast includes salad; fresh-baked herbed focaccia; grilled chicken, smoky pork sausage, marinated turkey breast, mesquite-seasoned beef, teriyaki ribs, and jumbo shrimp; stir-fry noodles and vegetables; fresh pineapple with caramel sauce; soft drinks; and coffee. The passion-fruit crème brûlée is extra but worth it. A full bar offers tropical drinks, including nonalcoholic ones for kids.

DOWNTOWN DISNEY (INCLUDING DISNEY VILLAGE MARKETPLACE, PLEASURE ISLAND & DISNEY'S WEST SIDE)

"Downtown Disney" encompasses **Disney Village Marketplace, Pleasure Island,** and **Disney's West Side.** See "Walt Disney World & Orlando After Dark" for more information on the bars, clubs, and other diversions there; in addition, this being Disney, there's tons of shopping as well. Pleasure Island charges an admission fee (the others do not), but if you're going strictly to dine in one of its restaurants, you don't have to pay it.

VERY EXPENSIVE

Fulton's Crab House. Aboard the riverboat docked at Pleasure Island. ☎ **407/934-BOAT** (2628). Reservations recommended, especially during peak season. Main courses lunch $8.95–$15.95; dinner $14.95–$50. AE, MC, V. Daily 4pm–midnight. SEAFOOD/STEAKS.

Fulton's operates aboard a replica of a 19th-century Mississippi riverboat that's perma-nently moored on the shores of Lake Buena Vista. An interior decorated with nautical artifacts reflects the seafood menu. There are a deck for outdoor dining and a children's menu. The casual Stone Crab Lounge serves light fare from 11:30am to 2am.

Start with the Florida stone crab claws with mustard sauce and lime, or sample the oyster bar. For a main course, try the tuna fillet, grilled and served with lemon-grass dipping sauce. A hearty eater may want to try the steak and lobster dinner, served with asparagus and a tangy house steak sauce. For a tart taste of Florida, try the key lime cheesecake for dessert. This place boasts one of the area's better wine lists. A character breakfast, 8:30 and 10am daily, is $12.95 for adults, $7.95 for children; it features Mickey, Minnie, Pluto, and Goofy.

MODERATE

Bongo Cuban Cafe. Disney's West Side. ☎ **407/828-0999.** Reservations not accepted. Priority seating for parties of 7 or more. Main courses $8.95–$24.95. Daily 11am–2am. AE, DC, DISC, MC, V. CUBAN.

Created by Cuban-American singer Gloria Estefan and her husband, Emilio, the cafe is Disney's version of old Havana. There are leopard-spotted chairs and mosaic bar stools shaped like bongo drums. A Desi Arnaz look-alike might even show up to sing a few tunes. The upbeat salsa music makes this a noisy location, so seek out the patio or the upstairs lounge for some privacy and quiet. A Cuban sandwich, thinly toasted bread with ham and cheese, is prepared right here. (Kids also might like it.) Start with the thick, slightly spicy, black bean soup and try a dinner of arroz con pollo. Coffee lovers will love the thick, dark Cuban blend.

House of Blues. Disney's West Side, under the old-fashioned water tower. ☎ **407/934-2583.** Reservations not accepted (except for Gospel Brunch). $13.95–$18.95. AE, DISC, MC, V. MISSISSIPPI DELTA.

This place offers hearty potions of down-home food served in an atmosphere literally shaking with rock and roll. The music in the nightclub next door is as much of a draw as the food—it's incredibly packed on days of big concerts. Funky, colorful folk art covers the rustic walls from floor to ceiling. There's a nice view of the bay from tables on the back patio. But let's not forget the food. The spicy jambalaya and gumbo are good bets, and the baby back ribs with garlic mashed potatoes and turnip greens are literally finger-lickin' good. Try the bread pudding for dessert. There's a children's menu offering staples like grilled cheese and burgers. The Sunday Gospel Brunch, $24 for adults and $12 for children 4 to 12, features foot-stomping music and an awe-inspiring array of Southern fare such as cheese grits and sausage. Foreign visitors might especially enjoy this cultural immersion. Make your reservations early because this tends to sell out.

Planet Hollywood. Pleasure Island. ☎ **407/827-7827.** Reservations not accepted. Main courses $7.50–$18.95. AE, DC, MC, V. Daily 11am–2am. AMERICAN.

Planet Hollywood was born in 1994 with a lavish opening-night party hosted by Schwarzenegger, Stallone, Willis, and Moore. The excitement they generated has started to dim, and the once–hours-long lines have thinned. A fiber-optic ceiling creates a planetarium effect, and a veritable show-business museum displays more than 300 items ranging from Peter O'Toole's *Lawrence of Arabia* costume to the front end of the bus from the movie *Speed* (it's suspended from the ceiling!). Previews of soon-to-be-released movies and video montages from films and TV are aired while you dine.

The big surprise amid all the special effects is that the food is actually good. You can opt to nosh on appetizers—hickory-smoked buffalo wings, pot stickers, or nachos. There are also burgers, sandwiches, salads, pizzas, pastas, and platters of grilled steak, ribs, or pork chops. The desserts are worth saving room for. Lines can get long during special events and peak season.

Portobello Yacht Club. Pleasure Island. ☎ **407/934-8888.** Reservations strongly recommended. Main courses lunch $7.95–$8.95, dinner $14.95–$29.95; pizzas $6.95–$8.95. AE,

MC, V. Daily 11:30am–midnight (dinner served from 4pm). Valet parking $5; free self-parking. NORTHERN ITALIAN.

Occupying a gabled Bermuda-style house and having undergone extensive recent renovations, Yacht Club is casual, with an interior suggesting a luxury cruise ship. From the lively mahogany-paneled bar, you can watch oak-fired pizzas being prepared in an exhibition kitchen. Multipaned windows overlook Lake Buena Vista, as do the tables on the covered patios.

The pizzas, with crisply thin crusts and toppings such as *quattro formaggi* (four cheeses) with sun-dried tomatoes, are a tasty deal for lunch or dinner. For the evening meal try Costoletta Di MaiAle, marinated roasted pork loin with fennel, carrots, and roasted-garlic whipped potatoes. Also try the Spaghettini Alla Portobello with Alaskan crab and other seafood in a light sauce of olive oil, wine, and herbs. For dessert, I recommend the *crema bruccioto* (white-chocolate custard with a caramelized sugar glaze). The Portobello also has quite an extensive wine list.

RainForest Cafe. Disney Village Marketplace; look for the smoking volcano. ☎ **407/ 827-8500.** Reservations accepted on-site. Main courses $5.50–$17.95. AE, DISC, MC, V. Sun–Thurs 10:30am–11pm; Fri–Sat 10:30am–midnight. CALIFORNIA.

First piece of advice: Don't arrive starving. Waits of 4 hours aren't unheard of, so plan on making your reservations and then exploring the rest of the Village. (Lines may shorten as a second RainForest is added near Animal Kingdom, but don't count on it.) With its lush, dark interiors, calls of the wild, and unique animal-style bar stools, you feel far removed from the rush of the parks. Kids especially love the jungle setting—this is, after all, one place where monkey business is encouraged. The food is pretty good, too. Try unusual delicacies like Rasta Pasta, bow-tie noodles mixed with spinach, roasted red peppers, broccoli, and Parmesan cheese—the whole dish smothered in a garlic-pesto cream sauce. There is an extensive menu, including a reduced-price menu for children. Top off your meal with coconut bread pudding with dried apricots; the lavish garnish of whipped cream, toasted coconut, and chocolate shavings is almost as good as the dessert itself. There's a good selection of beer and wine. *Note:* The tables are very close together, so those with physical disabilities may find it difficult to maneuver.

Wolfgang Puck's Cafe. Disney's West Side. ☎ **407/WDW-DINE** (939-3463). Reservations recommended. $8.95–$18.95. AE, MC, V. Daily 11am–midnight. CALIFORNIA CUISINE.

Avant-garde chef Wolfgang Puck has brought his West Coast creations to the heart of Florida. You can eat gourmet pizza, with a thin crisp crust and exotic toppings, on an outdoor patio or dine inside. An appetizer of vegetable spring rolls or a sampling from the sushi bar should be followed by the fresh grilled chicken or the Chinois chicken salad.

✪ CITYWALK

Universal's answer to Pleasure Island and Disney's West Side, CityWalk opened in early 1999. This 12-acre entertainment complex could easily be renamed theme-restaurant heaven. It is home not only to the world's largest **Hard Rock Cafe**—the grande dame of all theme restaurants—but also to the **NASCAR Cafe,** the **Motown Cafe,** Jimmy Buffet's **Margaritaville,** and will welcome an NBA-themed restaurant in time for the millennium.

CityWalk also contains a hearty dose of Cajun spice with **Pat O'Brien's,** a re-creation of the joint in New Orleans, and **Emeril's of New Orleans,** featuring the Creole-based cuisine of chef Emeril Lagasse. If that's not enough to keep you busy, you can visit the Down Beat Jazz Hall of Fame in **City Jazz,** see a tribute to reggae mon

Bob Marley, or dance the night away at the **Latin Quarter or the groove.** Music fans will flock to **Hard Rock Live,** a 2200-capacity venue that features performances by well-known music artists.

Unlike Disney's Pleasure Island, which has a single admission price, CityWalk's clubs and restaurants have different hours and cover charges.

BEYOND DISNEY: INTERNATIONAL DRIVE

There are some top-notch restaurants along International Drive, located about a 10-minute drive from Walt Disney World parks.

VERY EXPENSIVE

✪ **Dux.** In the Peabody Orlando, 9801 International Dr. ☎ **407/345-4550.** Reservations recommended. Main courses $19–$45.95. AE, CB, DC, DISC, JCB, MC, V. Mon–Thurs 6–10pm, Fri–Sat 6–11pm. Closed Sun. Free self- and validated valet parking. INTERNATIONAL.

Named for the hotel's signature ducks that parade ceremoniously into the lobby each morning to Sousa's *King Cotton* march, this is one of Central Florida's most highly acclaimed restaurants. Its textured gold walls are hung with watercolors representing 72 ducks! The tables are exquisitely appointed, and a lavish dessert display table with a floral centerpiece serves as a visual focus.

The internationally nuanced menu changes seasonally. At a recent dinner, I started off with an appetizer of pot stickers stuffed with portobello mushrooms, scallions, and creamed goat cheese. The entree was grilled Florida black grouper marinated in West Indian spices, served with a plantain-yam mash and tropical chutney. And dessert was a hazelnut-meringue napoleon topped with homemade Frangelico ice cream and a dusting of Brazilian cocoa. Dux has an extensive, award-winning wine list.

MODERATE

B-Line Diner. In the Peabody Orlando, 9801 International Dr. ☎ **407/345-4460.** Reservations not accepted. Main courses $5.95–$29. AE, CB, DC, DISC, JCB, MC, V. Daily 24 hours. Free self- and validated valet parking. AMERICAN.

This popular local eatery is of the nouvelle art deco diner genre—an idealized version of America's ubiquitous roadside joints. A high-gloss peach-and-gray interior gleams with chrome edging that adorns everything from a cove ceiling to peach Formica tables, and gorgeous flower arrangements add upscale panache. A jukebox plays oldies tunes.

The seasonally varying menu offers sophisticated versions of diner food such as honey-ginger buffalo wings, a grilled pork chop with hazelnut wild rice and sun-dried cherry sauce, or a ham-and-cheese sandwich on baguette. Other items, such as a falafel sandwich on pita bread with mint-yogurt sauce, bear no relation to traditional diner fare. Portions are hearty. A glass display case here is filled with scrumptious fresh-baked desserts, and they also offer ice-cream sundaes. There's a full bar.

✪ **Cafe Tu Tu Tango.** 8625 International Dr. (just west of the Mercado). ☎ **407/248-2222.** Reservations accepted. Tapas (tasting portions) $3–$7.95. AE, DISC, MC, V. Sun–Thurs 11:30am–11pm, Fri–Sat 11:30am–1am. INTERNATIONAL TAPAS.

Though you might question the need for yet another theme experience outside the parks, this restaurant is a welcome respite from Orlando's predictable chain gang. For one thing, there's the ongoing performance-art experience taking place while you dine: One evening, an elegantly dressed couple might tango past your table. Another time, a belly dancer might perform, or a magician might demonstrate a few tricks tableside. In addition, there is a studio area in which artists are always creating pottery, paintings, and jewelry.

Tu Tu's colorful ambience is a lot of fun, but the real draw here is the food. The larger your party, the more dishes you can sample; two full plates will sate most appetites. My favorites include Cajun egg rolls (filled with blackened chicken, corn, and Cheddar and goat cheese, served with chunky tomato salsa and Creole mustard) and pepper-crusted seared-tuna sashimi with crispy rice noodles and cold spinach in a sesame-soy vinaigrette. International wines can be ordered by the glass or bottle. There are great desserts here, too, such as creamy almond/amaretto flan and rich guava cheesecake with strawberry sauce.

Ming Court. 9188 International Dr. (between Sand Lake Rd. and the Bee Line Expwy.). ☎ **407/351-9988.** Reservations recommended. Dim sum items mostly $1.95–$2.50; main courses $12.50–$19.95. AE, CB, DC, DISC, JCB, MC, V. Daily 11am–2:30pm and 4:30pm–midnight. Free self-parking. CHINESE REGIONAL.

This is sophisticated Chinese cuisine. Ming Court is fronted by a serpentine "cloud wall" crowned by engraved sea-green Chinese tiles (it's a celestial symbol; you dine above the clouds here, like the gods). Its candlelit interior is stunningly decorated in soft earth tones. The glass-walled terrace rooms overlook lotus ponds filled with koi. A musician plays classical Chinese music on a zheng (a long zither) at dinner.

The menu offers diverse specialties from throughout China. Begin by ordering a variety of appetizers such as wok-charred Mandarin pot stickers or crispy wontons stuffed with vegetables and cream cheese. Entrees will open up new culinary vistas to even the most sophisticated diners. Lightly battered deep-fried chicken breast is served with a delicate lemon-tangerine sauce. The Szechuan charcoal-grilled filet mignon is topped with a toasted onion/garlic/chile sauce and served with stir-fried julienne vegetables. And crispy stir-fried jumbo Szechuan shrimp are enhanced by a light, fresh tomato sauce. At lunch, you can order dim sum. There's an extensive wine list.

INEXPENSIVE

✪ **Bahama Breeze.** 8849 International Dr., Orlando. ☎ **407/248-2499.** Reservations not accepted. Main courses $6.95–$14.95; sandwiches and salads $5.95–$6.95. AE, MC, V. Sun–Thurs 4pm–1am, Fri–Sat 4pm–2am. CARIBBEAN.

Traditional Caribbean foods are used to create unusual items such as moist and tasty "fish in a bag"—strips of mahimahi in a parchment pillow flavored with carrots, sweet peppers, mushrooms, celery, and spices. Also try the paella, a rice dish brimming with shrimp, fish, mussels, chicken, and chunks of sausage. The coconut curry chicken is also worth a try—sautéed chunks of chicken sprinkled with fresh coconut. For dessert try the piña colada bread pudding, a cube of custard bread in a sweet coconut sauce, or the tart key lime pie. Created by Orlando-based Darden Restaurants, the same folks who brought you Red Lobster and Olive Garden, this Bahama Breeze is essentially a test kitchen for what may soon be a national chain. Unlike Darden's other creations, which serve solid but not necessarily savory offerings, Bahama Breeze is a unique dining experience that challenges the taste buds. You can even watch your entrees being prepared in the open kitchen. The drink menu includes more than 50 beers, and the expected collection of fruity, pseudo-exotic drinks such as the Very Berry Daiquiri. Happy-hour prices are featured round-the-clock.

DINING WITH DISNEY CHARACTERS

Especially for the 10-and-under set, it's a thrill to dine in a restaurant where costumed Disney characters show up to greet the customers, sign autographs, pose in family photos, and interact with little kids. Be sure to make reservations as far in advance as possible for these very popular meals. The **breakfast** prices are all around $15 for adults and $8 for children; **dinner,** $20 for adults, $9 for children 3 to 11, free for children 2 and under. Prices vary from location to location, but you will often have to take what is available, especially if you don't make reservations far in advance. It's best to make reservations when you book your hotel. Call ☎ **407/WDW-DINE** (939-3463). AE, MC, V.

Note: On selected days, Disney resort guests can arrive earlier at some of the below-listed character breakfasts.

✪ Artist Point. At Disney's Wilderness Lodge, 901 Timberline Dr. Breakfast with Winnie the Pooh, Tigger, and the other inhabitants of the Hundred Acre Woods. Daily 7:30–11am.

In a rustic lodge-like dining room with a beamed ceiling supported by tree-trunk beams and large windows providing scenic lake views, **Pooh** and **Tigger** host an all-you-can-eat buffet breakfast.

Cape May Café. At Disney's Grand Floridian Beach Resort, 1800 Epcot Resorts Blvd. Daily 7:30–11am.

The Cape May Café, a delightful New England–themed dining room, serves lavish buffet character breakfasts with Admiral Goofy and his crew as hosts, including Chip 'n' Dale and Pluto (exact characters may vary).

Chef Mickey's. At Disney's Contemporary Resort, 4600 N. World Dr. Daily 7:30–11:30am and 5–9:30pm.

The whimsical Chef Mickey's is the setting for buffet character breakfasts and dinners. Chef Mickey's ✪ **prime-rib buffet dinner,** complete with a varying cast of characters, includes a make-your-own-sundae bar.

Cinderella's Royal Table. In Cinderella Castle in the Magic Kingdom. Daily 8:30–10am.

This magnificent castle, the focal point of the park, serves up character breakfast buffets daily. Hosts vary, but Cinderella always makes an appearance. This is one of the most popular character meals in the park, so reserve far in advance. It's a great way to start your day in the Magic Kingdom.

Crystal Palace. Main Street, U.S.A. Magic Kingdom. Breakfast daily from park opening to 10:30am; lunch 11:30am–2:45pm; dinner 4pm to park closing.

Features Winnie the Pooh and friends. Menu changes weekly.

✪ Garden Grill. In The Land pavilion at Epcot. Daily 8:40–11:30am, 11:30am–4:20pm, and 4:40–8:10pm.

This is a revolving restaurant with seating in comfortable semicircular booths. As you dine, your table travels past desert, prairie, farmland, and rain-forest environments. There's a "momma's in the kitchen" theme here: You'll be given a straw hat upon entering, and the just-folks service staff speaks in country lingo. The hearty family-style meals are hosted by Mickey, Minnie, and Chip 'n' Dale. Extensive American breakfasts and lunches are offered; dinners include several entrees (roast chicken, farm-raised fish, and hickory-smoked steak), smashed potatoes, vegetables, squaw bread and biscuits, salad, beverage, and dessert.

✪ Liberty Tree Tavern. In Liberty Square in the Magic Kingdom. Daily 4pm to park closing.

This Williamsburg-like 18th-century pub offers character dinners hosted by Mickey, Goofy, Pluto, Chip 'n' Dale, and Tigger (some or all of them). Meals, served family style, consist of salad, roast chicken, marinated flank steak, trail sausages, homemade mashed potatoes, rice pilaf, vegetables, and a dessert of warm apple crisp with vanilla ice cream.

✪ Luau Cove. At Disney's Polynesian Resort, 1600 Seven Seas Dr. Daily 7:30–10:30am; dinner at 4:30pm.

Luau Cove, an exotic open-air facility, is the setting for an island-themed character show called Mickey's Tropical Luau. It's an abbreviated version of the Polynesian Luau Dinner Show described later in this chapter in section 15, featuring Polynesian dancers along with Mickey, Minnie, Pluto, and Goofy. Your set-price meal includes honey-roasted chicken, vegetables, glazed cinnamon bread, and an ice-cream sundae. Guests are presented with shell leis upon entering.

The Polynesian also hosts Minnie's Menehune Character Breakfast in the Polynesian-themed 'Ohana (described above). Traditional breakfast foods are prepared on an 18-foot fire pit and served family style. Minnie, Goofy, and Chip 'n' Dale appear, and there are children's parades with Polynesian musical instruments.

✪ 1900 Park Fare. At Disney's Grand Floridian Beach Resort, 4001 Grand Floridian Way. Daily 7:30–11:30am and 5:30–9pm.

This exquisitely elegant Disney resort hosts character meals in the festive exposition-themed 1900 Park Fare. Big Bertha—a French band organ that plays pipes, drums, bells, cymbals, castanets, and xylophone—provides music. Mary Poppins, Winnie the Pooh, Goofy, Pluto, Chip 'n' Dale, and Minnie Mouse appear at the elaborate buffet breakfasts. Mickey and Minnie appear at nightly buffets, which feature prime rib, stuffed pork loin, fresh fish, and more.

Restaurantsaurous. In Animal Kingdom. From park opening to 10am.

In this restaurant, located in what looks like a jumble of National park–style buildings, you can join Donald Duck and friends for an all-you-can-eat breakfast buffet.

Watercress Café. At the Buena Vista Palace, 1900 Buena Vista Dr. ☎ **407/827-2727.** Reservations not accepted. Sun 8–10:30am.

The plant-filled Watercress Café, with large windows overlooking Lake Buena Vista, is the setting for Sunday-morning character breakfasts featuring Minnie, Goofy, and Pluto. Both à la carte and buffet meals are offered. Since reservations are not accepted, arrive early to avoid a wait.

5 Tips for Visiting Walt Disney World Attractions

Walt Disney World encompasses the Magic Kingdom; the new Animal Kingdom; Epcot; Disney-MGM Studios; and Downtown Disney, which encompasses the Disney Village Marketplace, Disney's West Side, and Pleasure Island. There are also three water parks: Typhoon Lagoon, River Country, and Blizzard Beach. For the purposes of this chapter, I've limited the number of attractions to include only the Magic Kingdom, Epcot, Disney-MGM, and Animal Kingdom. Although I provide the most up-to-date information available, remember that the parks are a work in progress. While all the major attractions should be open and available, some of the minor attractions and shows or parades may change by the time of your visit.

TIPS FOR PLANNING YOUR TRIP

Rule #1: Planning is essential. Unless you're staying for considerably more than a week, you can't possibly experience all the rides, shows, and attractions here, not to mention the vast array of recreational facilities. You'll only wear yourself to a frazzle trying. It's better to follow a relaxed itinerary, including leisurely meals and recreational activities, than to make a demanding job out of trying to see everything.

Read the *Vacation Guide* and the detailed descriptions in this book. It's a good idea to make a daily itinerary, putting your activities in some kind of sensible geographical sequence so you're not zigzagging all over the place. Familiarize yourself in advance with the layout of each park. Schedule in sit-down shows, recreational activities (a boat ride or a swim late in the afternoon can be wonderfully refreshing), and at least one unhurried meal. Make sure to have an agreed-upon meeting place should the family get separated. My suggested itineraries are given below.

INFORMATION   Call or write the **Walt Disney World Co.,** P.O. Box 10000, Lake Buena Vista, FL 32830-1000 (☎ **407/934-7639**), for a copy of *Walt Disney World Vacations,* an invaluable planning aid. Once you've arrived in town, guest-services and concierge desks in all area hotels—especially the Disney properties and "official" hotels—have **up-to-the-minute information** about what's going on in the parks. If your hotel doesn't have this information, call ☎ **407/824-4321.**

There are also **information locations** in each park—at City Hall in the Magic Kingdom, at Innoventions East near the WorldKey terminals in Epcot, and at the Guest Services Building in Disney-MGM Studios.

BUY TICKETS IN ADVANCE   You can purchase 4- or 5-day passes (see details below) before your trip by calling **Ticket Mail Order** (☎ 407/824-6750). You can also order tickets online at **www.disneyworld.com**. Allow 21 days for processing your request, and include a $2 postage-and-handling charge. Of course, you can always purchase tickets at any of the parks, but why stand in an avoidable line? *Note:* One-day tickets can be purchased only at the park entrances.

ARRIVE EARLY   Always arrive at the parks a good 30 to 45 minutes before opening time, thus avoiding a traffic jam entering the park and a long line at the gate. Early arrival also lets you experience one or two major attractions before big lines form. In high season the parking lots sometimes fill up, and you may even have to wait to get in. The longest lines in all parks are between 11am and 4pm.

PARKING   Parking (free to guests at WDW resorts) costs $5 per day no matter how many parks you visit. *Be sure to note your parking location before leaving your car.* Write it down if necessary. There are special lots for travelers with disabilities at each park (call ☎ 407/824-4321 for details). Don't worry about parking far from the entrance gates; there is a constant tram service.

WHEN YOU ARRIVE IN THE PARKS   Upon entering any of the major Disney parks, you'll be given an **entertainment schedule** and a comprehensive park **guide map,** which contains a map of the park and lists all attractions, shops, shows, and restaurants. If you lose the map, ask at the cash register at one of the many shops. They usually have a few extra copies.

If you've formulated an itinerary before arrival, you already know the major shows (check show schedules for additional ideas) you'll want to see during the day and what arrangements you need to make. If you haven't done this, use your early arrival time, while waiting for the park to open, to figure out which shows to attend, and, where necessary, make reservations for them as soon as the gates swing open.

LEAVING THE PARKS   If you leave any of the parks and plan to return later in the day, be sure to get your hand stamped when exiting. You will also need your paper pass if you are park hopping.

BEST DAYS TO VISIT   The busiest days at the Magic Kingdom and Epcot are Monday through Wednesday; at Disney-MGM Studios, they're Thursday and Friday. Surprisingly, weekends are the least busy at all parks, including Animal Kingdom. Sunday is generally a slow day. In peak seasons, especially, arrange your visits accordingly.

OPERATING HOURS   Hours of operation vary somewhat throughout the year: The **Magic Kingdom** and **Disney-MGM Studios** are generally open from 9am to 7pm, with extended hours, sometimes as late as midnight, during major holidays and the summer months. Animal Kingdom opens from 8am to 6pm, sometimes as early as 7am. Since the wildlife is the main attraction at Animal Kingdom, plan on being there when the gates open, before the animals seek refuge during the heat of the day.

Epcot is generally open from 9am to 9pm, with Future World open from 9am to 9pm and World Showcase from 11am to 9pm—once again with extended holiday hours.

✪ **Typhoon Lagoon** and **Blizzard Beach** are open from 10am to 5pm most of the year (with extended hours during some holidays) and 9am to 8pm in summer.

River Country is open from 10am to 5pm most of the year (with extended hours during some holidays) and 10am to 7pm in summer.

Note: Epcot and MGM sometimes open 30 minutes or more before the posted time. Keep in mind, too, that Disney resort guests enjoy early admission to all the major parks, except Animal Kingdom, on designated days.

TICKETS   There are several ticket options, ranging from 1- to 7-day passes. Most people get the best value from 4- and 5-day passes. All passes offer unlimited use of the WDW transportation system.

The **4-Day Park Hopper Passes** provide unlimited admission to Magic Kingdom, Epcot, Animal Kingdom, and Disney-MGM. For a 4-day pass adults pay $167; children, $134. A **5-Day Park Hopper Plus Pass** also includes your choice of two admissions to either Typhoon Lagoon, River Country, Blizzard Beach, Pleasure Island, or Disney's Wide World of Sports. The 5-day pass costs adults $229; children, $183. Passes for 6 and 7 days are available, call ☎ **407/824-4321** for details.

Adult prices are paid by anyone over 10 years of age. **Children's rates** are for ages 3 to 9. **Children 2 and under** are admitted free.

A **1-day, one-park ticket for the Magic Kingdom, Epcot, Animal Kingdom, or Disney-MGM Studios** is $44 for adults, $36 for children.

A **1-day ticket to Typhoon Lagoon or Blizzard Beach** is $26.95 for adults, $21.50 for children.

A **1-day ticket to River Country** is $15.95 for adults, $12.50 for children.

A **1-day ticket to Pleasure Island** is $18.95. Since this is primarily an 18 and over entertainment complex, there is no special pricing for children.

If you're staying at any Walt Disney World resort or "official" hotel, you're also eligible for a money-saving **Unlimited Magic Pass,** which is priced according to length of your stay. It also offers special perks.

If you plan on visiting Walt Disney World more than one time during the year, inquire about a money-saving **annual pass** ($309 adults, $259 children).

Suggested Itineraries

You won't see all the attractions at any of the parks in a single day. Read through the descriptions, decide which are musts for you, and try to get to them. My favorite rides and attractions are starred. It's more fun to keep a relaxed pace than to race around like a maniac trying to do it all.

A Day in the Magic Kingdom

Get to the park well before opening time, tickets in hand. When the gates open, make a dash for Extra "TERROR"estrial Alien Encounter in Tomorrowland, which, as one of the newer major attractions, will have very long lines later in the day.

Then, hightail it to Frontierland and ride Splash Mountain—there's hardly any shade for those waiting in line at this attraction, so you don't want to do it in the afternoon. Afterward, it should still be early enough to beat the lines at one more major attraction—head over to Adventureland and do Pirates of the Caribbean.

Then, relax and take it slow. Complete whatever else interests you in Adventureland. Then, walk over to Frontierland and enjoy the attractions there until lunch. Have lunch while taking in the 12:15 or 1:30pm show at the Diamond Horseshoe Saloon Revue (they don't take reservations, so arrive early).

After lunch, continue visiting Frontierland attractions as you please, or proceed to the Hall of Presidents and the Haunted Mansion in Liberty Square. By 2:30pm (earlier in peak seasons), you should snag a seat on the curb in Liberty Square along the parade route. After the parade, continue around the park, taking in Fantasyland and Tomorrowland attractions. (If you really want to beat the lines, skip the parade and breeze through the minimal lines in the rest of the park.)

If you have little kids (age 8 and under) in your party, start your day instead by taking the WDW Railroad from Main Street to Mickey's Toontown Fair to meet the characters. Work your way through Fantasyland until lunch, once again at the Diamond Horseshoe. After lunch, visit the Country Bear Jamboree in Frontierland and proceed to Adventureland for the Jungle Cruise, Swiss Family Treehouse, and The Enchanted Tiki Room. If you have only 1 day, I'd skip the afternoon parade and take advantage of shorter lines at major attractions. That's a long enough day for most young children, and your best plan is to go back to your hotel for a nap or swim if you are staying on Disney property.

If, however, you wish to continue, return to Frontierland and/or Fantasyland for the rides you didn't complete earlier. Cap off your day with the Main Street Electrical Parade.

If You Can Spend Only 1 Day at Epcot

Epcot really requires at least 2 days, so this is a highlight tour. As above, arrive early, tickets in hand. If you haven't already made lunch reservations in advance by calling ☎ **407/WDW-DINE** (939-3463), make your first stop at the WorldKey terminals in Innoventions East. I suggest a 1pm lunch at the San Angel Inn Restaurant in Mexico. If you don't like Mexican food, move up one pavilion to Norway and reserve a table at the Akershus. You can make dinner reservations at the same time. Plan dinner for about 7pm, which will allow you time to eat and find a good viewing spot for Illumi-Nations (usually at 9pm, but check your schedule).

Spend no more than an hour exploring Innoventions. Then, move on to the Universe of Energy show. Continue to the Wonders of Life pavilion, where must-sees include Body Wars, Cranium Command, Test Track, and The Making of Me.

Head into World Showcase for lunch in Mexico. At lunch, check your show schedule and decide which shows to incorporate into your day.

Then, walk around the lagoon, visiting highlight attractions: Wonders of China, the American Adventure, Impressions de France, and O Canada!, allowing yourself some time for browsing and shopping. After dinner, stay on for IllumiNations.

A Word About Epcot Dining: Sit-down meals at World Showcase pavilions and the Living Seas are a pleasant but pricey part of the Epcot experience. There are plenty of less-expensive eateries throughout the park, including ethnic ones with cafe seating in many World Showcase pavilions. And since these don't require reservations, you're not tied down to specific mealtimes. See your *Epcot Guidemap* for details.

Factoid

A personal tour guide can be yours for $55 an hour for up to 4 hours. The guide, who can serve up to 10 people at a time, is described as a "walking, talking guide map" who will customize your visit to any of the parks. On the down side, there's still no cutting in line. Call ☎ 407/560-6233 for information, and book at least 72 hours in advance.

If You Can Spend 2 Days at Epcot

Ignore the 1-day itinerary above, but do begin your day by making all necessary restaurant reservations—once again for lunch in Mexico or Norway at about 1pm. Make reservations for your second day at the same time.

Skip Innoventions East for now and work your way thoroughly through the Universe of Energy, Wonders of Life, and Test Track pavilions, keeping your lunch reservation time in mind. After lunch, walk clockwise around the lagoon, visiting each foreign pavilion and taking in as many shows as you like (consult your show schedule and try to keep pace as well as possible). Leave IllumiNations for your second day's visit.

Begin your second day exploring Innoventions East, and proceed counterclockwise, taking in Spaceship Earth, Innoventions West, the Living Seas (its Coral Reef restaurant is a good choice for lunch), and all the other pavilions on the west side of the park. Cap your Epcot visit with IllumiNations.

A Day at Disney-MGM Studios Theme Park

Since show times change frequently here, it's impossible to really give you an absolutely firm itinerary, but here is a good outline. Upon entering the park, if you haven't already made dining arrangements, stop at the Hollywood Brown Derby and make lunch reservations. Or you may want to conserve touring time by having a light lunch at a casual eatery and saving the Derby for a relaxing dinner.

Make a beeline for the Twilight Zone Tower of Terror. While you're waiting in line, plan the rest of your schedule, being sure to include these not-to-be-missed attractions: Indiana Jones Epic Stunt Spectacular, Rock 'n' Roller Coaster, Star Tours, and Jim Henson's Muppet Vision 3-D. If you have kids 10 or under in your party, visit the back of the park, where there are exhibits and shows tied to whatever is the company's newest release. Get in line 30 minutes before at the Backlot Theater for these shows. Also be sure to be early for Indiana Jones; the shows often fill up. Kids love the parade; snag a good seat on the parade route 30 minutes ahead of time as well. Or, if parades aren't exactly your thing, take advantage of the shorter lines at the rides and shows.

Time for more? See the Beauty and the Beast Show and Voyage of the Little Mermaid. Ride the Great Movie Ride and Star Tours, and take time to take in ABC Sound Studio, Inside the Magic, and the Backstage Studio Tour. Don't forget to save some energy for Fantasmic, the multidimensional nighttime show that combines live action, special effects, and fireworks.

6 The Magic Kingdom

Centered around Cinderella Castle, the Magic Kingdom occupies about 100 acres, with 45 major attractions and numerous restaurants and shops through its seven

Find the Hidden Mickeys

Hiding Mickeys in designs began as an inside joke with early Walt Disney World "Imagineers" and became a park tradition. Today dozens of subtle hidden Mickeys (HMs)—the world-famous set of ears, profiles, and full figures—are concealed in attractions and resorts throughout Walt Disney World. No one knows their exact number. See how many you can locate during your visit. A few to look for include:

In the Magic Kingdom: In the Haunted Mansion banquet scene, check out the arrangement of plates and adjoining saucers on the table.

In the Africa scene of It's a Small World, note the purple flowers on a vine on the elephant's left side.

While riding Splash Mountain, look for Mickey lying on his back in the pink clouds to the right of the steamboat.

Hint: There are four HMs in the Timekeeper and five in the Carousel of Progress.

At Epcot: In Journey into Imagination, check out the little girl's dress in the lobby film of *Honey I Shrunk the Audience,* one of five HMs in this pavilion.

In The Land pavilion, don't miss the small stones in front of the Native American man on a horse and the baseball cap of the man driving a harvester in the *Circle of Life* film.

As your boat cruises through the Mexico pavilion on the El Rio del Tiempo attraction, notice the arrangement of three clay pots in the marketplace scene.

In Maelstrom, in the Norway pavilion, a Viking wears Mickey ears in the wall mural facing the loading dock.

There are four HMs in Spaceship Earth, one of them in the Renaissance scene, on the page of a book behind the sleeping monk. Try to find the other three.

At Disney-MGM Studios: On the Great Movie Ride, there's an HM on the window above the bank in the gangster scene, and four familiar characters are included in the hieroglyphics wall opposite Indiana Jones.

At Jim Henson's Muppet Vision 3-D, take a good look at the "Top five reasons for turning in your 3-D glasses" sign, and note the balloons in the film's final scene.

At the Monster Sound Show, check out Jimmy Macdonald's bolo tie and ring in the preshow video.

In The Twilight Zone Tower of Terror, note the bell for the elevator behind Rod Serling in the film. There are five other HMs in this attraction.

At Disney Resorts: There are also HMs at many Disney resorts. The best place to look for them is at Wilderness Lodge, which has more than a dozen that I know about.

"lands." From the parking lot, you'll have to take a short monorail or ferry ride to the Magic Kingdom entrance. During peak attendance times, arrive at the Magic Kingdom an hour prior to opening time to avoid long lines at these conveyances.

Upon entering the park, consult your *Magic Kingdom Guidemap* to get your bearings. It details every shop, restaurant, and attraction in every land. Also, consult your entertainment schedule to see what's on for the day.

If you have questions, most park employees are very knowledgeable, and City Hall, on your left as you enter, is both an information center and, along with Mickey's Toontown Fair, a likely place to meet up with costumed characters. There's a stroller-rental shop just after the turnstiles to your right, and the Kodak Camera Center, near Town Square, supplies all conceivable photographic needs, including camera and camcorder rentals and 2-hour film developing.

MAIN STREET, U.S.A.

Designed to replicate a typical turn-of-the-century American street (albeit one that culminates in a 13th-century castle), this is the gateway to the Kingdom. Don't dawdle on Main Street when you enter the park; leave it for the end of the day when you're heading back to your hotel.

WALT DISNEY WORLD RAILROAD & OTHER MAIN STREET VEHICLES

You can board an authentic 1928 steam-powered railroad here for a 15-minute journey clockwise around the perimeter of the park. There are stations in Frontierland and Mickey's Toontown Fair. There are also horse-drawn trolleys, horseless carriages, jitneys, omnibuses, and fire engines plying the short route along Main Street from Town Square to Cinderella Castle.

MAIN STREET CINEMA The Main Street Cinema is an air-conditioned hexagonal theater where vintage black-and-white Disney cartoons (including Steamboat Willie from 1928, in which Mickey and Minnie debuted) are aired continually on two screens. You'll have to watch these standing—there are no seats.

CINDERELLA'S CASTLE At the end of Main Street, in the center of the park, you'll come to a fairyland castle, 185 feet high and housing a restaurant (Cinderella's Royal Table) and shops. Cinderella herself, dressed for the ball, often makes appearances in the lobby area. Don't linger here; there's really not much to see.

ADVENTURELAND

Cross a bridge to your left and stroll into an exotic jungle of lush tropical foliage, thatch-roofed huts, and carved totems. Amid dense vines and stands of palm and bamboo, drums are beating and swashbuckling adventures are taking place.

SWISS FAMILY TREEHOUSE This attraction is based on Swiss Family Robinson, about a shipwrecked family who created an ingenious dwelling in the branches of a sprawling banyan tree. Using materials and furnishings salvaged from their downed ship, the Robinsons created bedrooms, a kitchen, a library, and a living room. Visitors ascend the 50-foot tree for a close-up look into these rooms. Note the Rube Goldberg rope-and-bucket device with bamboo chutes that dips water from a stream and carries it to treetop chambers. Older folks, people with disabilities, or those hauling children may want to be aware that this attraction involves a bit of climbing.

✪ JUNGLE CRUISE What a cruise! In the course of about 10 minutes your boat sails through an African veldt in the Congo, an Amazon rain forest, the Mekong River in Southeast Asia, and along the Nile. Lavish scenery, cascading waterfalls, and lush foliage (most of it real) include dozens of audio-animatronic birds and animals—elephants, zebras, lions, giraffes, crocodiles, tigers, and even fluttering butterflies. But the adventures aren't all on shore. Passengers are menaced by everything from water-spouting elephants to fierce warriors who attack with spears. Disney at its cheesy best.

PIRATES OF THE CARIBBEAN You'll proceed through a long grotto-like passage to board a boat into a pitch-black cave. There, amid fiery explosions and a

The Magic Kingdom

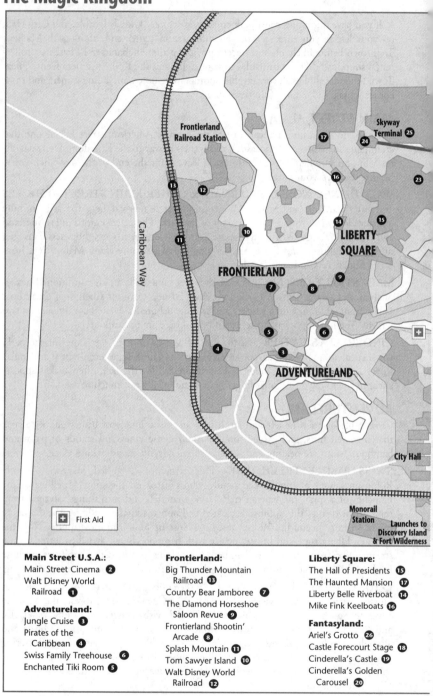

Main Street U.S.A.:
Main Street Cinema ❷
Walt Disney World
Railroad ❶

Adventureland:
Jungle Cruise ❸
Pirates of the
Caribbean ❹
Swiss Family Treehouse ❻
Enchanted Tiki Room ❺

Frontierland:
Big Thunder Mountain
Railroad ⓭
Country Bear Jamboree ❼
The Diamond Horseshoe
Saloon Revue ❾
Frontierland Shootin'
Arcade ❽
Splash Mountain ⓫
Tom Sawyer Island ❿
Walt Disney World
Railroad ⓬

Liberty Square:
The Hall of Presidents ⓯
The Haunted Mansion ⓱
Liberty Belle Riverboat ⓮
Mike Fink Keelboats ⓰

Fantasyland:
Ariel's Grotto ㉖
Castle Forecourt Stage ⓲
Cinderella's Castle ⓳
Cinderella's Golden
Carousel ⓴

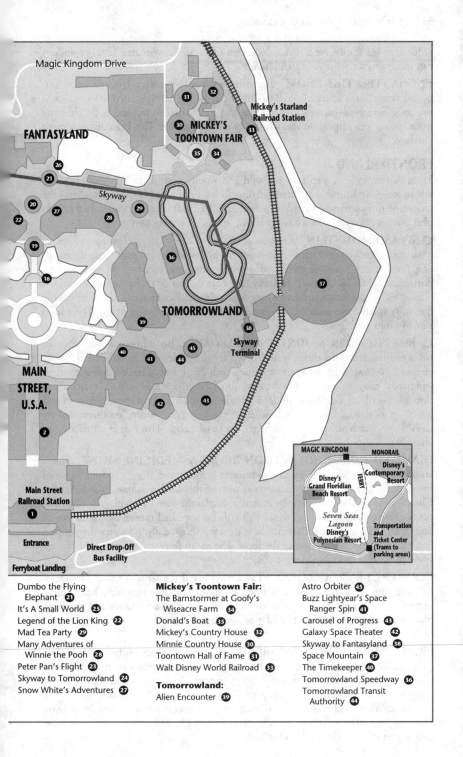

Magic Kingdom Drive

FANTASYLAND

Mickey's Starland
Railroad Station

MICKEY'S
TOONTOWN FAIR

Skyway

TOMORROWLAND

Skyway
Terminal

MAIN
STREET,
U.S.A.

Main Street
Railroad Station

Entrance

Direct Drop-Off
Bus Facility

Ferryboat Landing

MAGIC KINGDOM · MONORAIL

Disney's
Contemporary
Resort

Disney's
Grand Floridian
Beach Resort

FERRY

Seven Seas
Lagoon
Disney's
Polynesian Resort

Transportation
and
Ticket Center
(Trams to
parking areas)

Dumbo the Flying Elephant 21	**Mickey's Toontown Fair:**	**Astro Orbiter** 45
It's A Small World 25	**The Barnstormer at Goofy's Wiseacre Farm** 34	**Buzz Lightyear's Space Ranger Spin** 41
Legend of the Lion King 22	**Donald's Boat** 35	**Carousel of Progress** 43
Mad Tea Party 29	**Mickey's Country House** 32	**Galaxy Space Theater** 42
Many Adventures of Winnie the Pooh 28	**Minnie Country House** 30	**Skyway to Fantasyland** 38
Peter Pan's Flight 23	**Toontown Hall of Fame** 31	**Space Mountain** 37
Skyway to Tomorrowland 24	**Walt Disney World Railroad** 33	**The Timekeeper** 40
Snow White's Adventures 27		**Tomorrowland Speedway** 36
	Tomorrowland:	**Tomorrowland Transit Authority** 44
	Alien Encounter 39	

redundant sea shanty, are a ragtag collection of yo-ho-hoing mates. Loud explosions can make this scary for young children.

ENCHANTED TIKI ROOM   Recently renovated to reflect Disney's latest animated avians, such as Iago from Aladdin, the show has been updated but remains in the large hexagonal Polynesian-style dwelling, in which 250 tropical birds, chanting totem poles, and singing flowers whistle, tweet, and warble. This is a must for young children.

FRONTIERLAND

From Adventureland, step into the wild and woolly past of the American frontier, where rough-and-tumble architecture runs to log cabins and rustic saloons, and the landscape is Southwestern scrubby with mesquite, saguaro cactus, yucca, and prickly pear. Across the river is Tom Sawyer Island, reachable via log rafts.

✪ **SPLASH MOUNTAIN**   Themed after *Song of the South*, the first part of Splash Mountain takes you on a leisurely journey in a hollowed-out log craft along the canals of a flooded mountain. With its audio-animatronics and constant theme song, this portion of Splash Mountain is basically "It's a Small World" set in the backwoods. At 9 minutes, it's the longest of the Disney thrill rides. It all culminates in a breathtaking five-story splashdown from mountaintop to briar-filled pond at 40 m.p.h. There is no way to avoid getting wet.

✪ **BIG THUNDER MOUNTAIN RAILROAD**   This mining disaster–themed roller coaster derives its thrills from hairpin turns and descents in the dark. It's situated in a 200-foot-high red stone mountain with 2,780 feet of track winding through windswept canyons and bat-filled caves. You'll board a runaway train that careens through the ribs of a dinosaur, under a thundering waterfall, past spewing geysers and bubbling mud pots, and over a bottomless volcanic pool. Riders are threatened by flash floods, earthquakes, rickety bridges, and avalanches. This ride is especially fun after dark.

DIAMOND HORSESHOE SALOON REVUE & MEDICINE SHOW   Here's an opportunity to sit down in air-conditioned comfort and enjoy a rousing Western revue. The "theater" is a re-creation of a turn-of-the-century saloon. Marshall John Charles sings and banters with the audience, Jingles the Piano Man plays honky-tonk tunes, there's a magic act, and dance-hall girls do a spirited cancan—all with lots of humor and audience participation. There are seven shows daily; plan on going around lunchtime so you can eat during the show. The menu features deli or peanut-butter-and-jelly sandwiches served with chips.

COUNTRY BEAR JAMBOREE   I've always loved the Country Bear Jamboree, a 15-minute show featuring a troupe of fiddlin', banjo-strummin', harmonica-playin' audio-animatronic bears belting out rollicking country tunes and crooning plaintive love songs. A special holiday show plays throughout the Christmas season each year.

FRONTIERLAND SHOOTIN' ARCADE   Combining state-of-the-art electronics with a traditional shooting-gallery format, this vast arcade presents an array of 97 targets (slow-moving ore cars, buzzards, grave diggers) in a three-dimensional 1850s gold-mining–town scenario. To keep the Western ambience authentic, newfangled electronic firing mechanisms loaded with infrared bullets are concealed in genuine Hawkins 54-caliber buffalo rifles. When you hit a target, elaborate sound and motion gags are set off. You get 25 shots for 50¢.

LIBERTY SQUARE

Serving as a transitional area between Frontierland and Fantasyland, Liberty Square evokes 18th-century America with Georgian architecture and Colonial Williamsburg–type shops. You might encounter a fife-and-drum corps marching along Liberty Square's cobblestone streets.

THE HALL OF PRESIDENTS   In this redbrick colonial hall, all American presidents—from George Washington to Bill Clinton (who recorded the voice for his character)—are represented by audio-animatronic figures; if you look closely enough, you will see them fidget and whisper during the performance. They dramatize important events in the nation's history, from the signing of the Constitution through the space age. The show begins with a film, projected on a 180-degree screen, about the importance of the Constitution. Maya Angelou narrates.

✪ **THE HAUNTED MANSION**   Its eerie ambience enhanced by inky darkness, spooky music, and mysterious screams and rappings, this mansion is replete with bizarre scenes and objects: a ghostly banquet and ball, a graveyard band, a suit of armor that comes alive, luminous spiders, a talking head in a crystal ball, weird flying objects, and much more. At the end of the ride, a ghost joins you in your car. The experience is more amusing than terrifying, so you can take small children inside.

BOAT RIDES   A steam-powered sternwheeler called the *Liberty Belle* and two Mike Fink keel boats (the *Bertha Mae* and the *Gullywhumper*) depart (the latter during summers and holidays only) from Liberty Square for scenic cruises along the Rivers of America. Both ply the identical route and make a restful interlude for foot-weary parkgoers.

FANTASYLAND

The attractions in this happy "land"—based on such Disney film classics as *Snow White* and *Peter Pan*—are especially popular with young visitors. If your kids are 8 or under, you might want to make it your first stop in the Magic Kingdom.

LEGEND OF THE LION KING   This stage spectacular based on Disney's block-buster motion-picture musical combines animation, movie footage, sophisticated puppetry, and high-tech special effects.

SNOW WHITE'S ADVENTURES   Until recently, there was no Snow White at this attraction, which concentrated mostly on the cackling, toothless evil queen and left small children screaming in terror. It has been toned down now, with Snow White appearing in a number of pleasant scenes—at the castle-courtyard wishing well, in the dwarfs' cottage, receiving the prince's kiss that breaks the witch's spell, and riding off with the prince to live happily ever after. Even so, this could be scary for kids 6 and under.

MAD TEA PARTY   This is a traditional amusement park ride à la Disney with an *Alice in Wonderland* theme. Riders sit in oversized pink teacups on saucers that careen around a circular platform. Believe it or not, this can be a pretty wild ride or a tame one—it depends on how much you spin, a factor under your control via a wheel in the cup.

THE MANY ADVENTURES OF WINNIE THE POOH   This replaces Mr. Toad's Wild Ride, much to the chagrin of a small cadre of protesters who gathered to witness its demise. This ride, which is similar in concept to Pirates of the Caribbean, features the cute-and-cuddly fellow that Disney has helped make a resurgence. To take advantage of Pooh's best-selling status, second only to Mickey, the ride empties into a gift shop.

CINDERELLA'S GOLDEN CAROUSEL   It's a beauty, built by Italian wood-carvers in the Victorian tradition in 1917 and refurbished by Disney artists, who added scenes from the Cinderella story. The band organ plays such Disney classics as "When You Wish Upon a Star."

DUMBO, THE FLYING ELEPHANT   This is a very tame kiddie ride in which the cars—baby elephants (Dumbos)—go around and around in a circle, gently rising and dipping. But it's very exciting for wee ones.

IT'S A SMALL WORLD   You know the song—and if you don't, you will. It plays continually as you sail "around the world" through vast rooms designed to represent different countries. They're inhabited by appropriately costumed audio-animatronic dolls and animals, all singing in tiny voices. This cast of thousands includes Chinese acrobats, Russian dancers, Indian snake charmers, Arabs on magic carpets, African drummers, a Venetian gondolier, and Australian koalas. Cute. Very cute.

PETER PAN'S FLIGHT   Riding in Captain Hook's ship, passengers careen through dark passages while experiencing the story of *Peter Pan*. The adventure begins in the Darlings' nursery and includes a flight over nighttime London to Never-Never Land, where riders encounter mermaids, Indians, a ticking crocodile, the lost boys, Tinkerbell, Hook, Smee, and the rest. It's fun.

SKYWAY   Its entrance close to Peter Pan's Flight, the Skyway is an aerial tramway to Tomorrowland, which makes continuous round-trips throughout the day.

MICKEY'S TOONTOWN FAIR

Head off those cries of "where's Mickey?" by taking the kids to this 2-acre replacement for Mickey's Starland that was unveiled during the 25th anniversary celebration in 1996. Toontown Fair offers kids a chance to meet their favorite Disney characters, including Mickey, Minnie, Donald Duck, and Goofy. Set in a whimsical collection of candy-striped tents harking back to those turn-of-the-century county fairs, highlights include the Toontown Hall of Fame, animated shorts hosted by the stars, and both Mickey's and Minnie's country houses. Everything is brightly colored and kid-friendly in the best Disney tradition; there is even a kid-sized roller coaster. Toontown Fair has its own stop on the WDW Railroad.

TOMORROWLAND

In 1994, the Disney people decided that Tomorrowland (originally designed in the 1970s) was beginning to look like "Yesterdayland." It has now been revamped to reflect the future as a galactic, science fiction–inspired community inhabited by humans, aliens, and robots. A vast state-of-the-art video-game arcade has also been added.

✪ **EXTRA "TERROR"ESTRIAL ALIEN ENCOUNTER**   Director George Lucas contributed his space-age vision to this major new Tomorrowland attraction. The action begins at the Interplanetary Convention Center, where a mysterious corporation called X-S Tech, a company from a distant planet, is marketing an interplanetary "teletransporter" to Earthlings. In order to demonstrate it, X-S technicians try to teleport their sinister corporation head, Chairman Clench, to Earth. But the machine malfunctions, sending him to a distant planet instead and inadvertently teleporting a fearsome man-eating extraterrestrial to Earth. Dark and truly scary, it is not your

---

Money-Saving Tip

The hot thing for kids these days is getting autographs from all the Disney characters. You can purchase autograph books at the parks, but it may save you some money if you buy one before you leave home.

---

typical thrill ride. Lots of high-tech effects, from the alien's breath on your neck to a mist of alien slime. May not be suitable for young children.

THE TIMEKEEPER   This Jules Verne/H.G. Wells–inspired multimedia presentation combines CircleVision and IMAX footage with audio-animatronics. It's hosted by Timekeeper, a mad-scientist robot, and his assistant, 9-EYE, a flying female camera-headed droid and time-machine test pilot. In an unpredictable jet-speed escapade, the audience hears Mozart as a young prodigy playing his music to French royalty, visits medieval battlefields in Scotland, watches Leonardo at work, and floats in a hot-air balloon above Moscow's Red Square.

✪ SPACE MOUNTAIN   Space Mountain entertains visitors on its long lines with space-age music, exhibits, and meteorites, shooting stars, and space debris whizzing about overhead. These "illusioneering" effects, enhanced by appropriate audio, continue during the ride itself, which is a cosmic roller coaster in the inky starlit blackness of outer space. Your rocket climbs high into the universe before racing through a serpentine complex of aerial galaxies, making thrilling hairpin turns and rapid plunges. (Though it feels as though you're going at breakneck speed, your car actually never goes faster than 28 m.p.h.) Nab the front seat of the train for the best ride.

BUZZ LIGHTYEAR'S SPACE RANGER SPIN   Join Buzz as he tries to save the universe—you'll pilot your own cruiser with a joystick, and kids will enjoy using the laser cannons as you spin through a world filled with gigantic toys. One of the newer additions to Tomorrowland, it's one of the few that is truly interactive.

WALT DISNEY'S CAROUSEL OF PROGRESS   This 22-minute show in a revolving theater features an audio-animatronic family in various tableaux demonstrating a century of development (beginning in 1900) in electric gadgetry and contraptions from Victrolas to virtual reality.

SKYWAY   Its Tomorrowland entrance just west of Space Mountain, this aerial tramway to Fantasyland makes continuous round-trips throughout the day.

TOMORROWLAND TRANSIT AUTHORITY   A futuristic means of transportation, these small five-car trains have no engines. They work by electromagnets, emit no pollution, and use little power. Narrated by a computer guide named Horack I, TTA offers an overhead look at Tomorrowland, including a pretty good preview of Space Mountain. If you're in the Magic Kingdom for only a day, this can be skipped.

TOMORROWLAND SPEEDWAY   This is a great thrill for kids (including teens still waiting to get their driver's license), who get to put the pedal to the metal, steer, and vroom down a speedway in an actual gas-powered sports car. Maximum speed on the 4-minute drive around the track is about 7 m.p.h., and kids have to be 4 feet 4 inches tall to drive alone. Adults will find the ride's choppy steering irksome, and not worth the long wait time.

ASTRO ORBITER   This is a tame, typical amusement-park ride. The "rockets" are on arms attached to "the center of the galaxy," and they move up and down while orbiting spinning planets.

PARADES, FIREWORKS & MORE

You'll get an *Entertainment Show Schedule* when you enter the park, which lists all kinds of special goings-on for the day. These include concerts (everything from steel drums to barbershop quartets), encounters with Disney characters, holiday events, and the three major happenings listed below.

DISNEY'S MAGICAL MOMENTS With only six major floats, all showcasing Disney movies, your interest in this parade depends on how much time you are willing to take away from seeing other attractions. The parade, which includes dozens of dancers and extras, is entertaining, but with the masses camped out on the curb, this is a great chance to hit some of the most crowded rides. If you have the patience for only one parade, hit the Main Street Electrical Parade. Disney's Magical Moments is held at 3pm year-round, beginning on Main Street and meandering through Liberty Square and Frontierland. The route is outlined in your *Entertainment Show Schedule*.

Even during slow seasons, you have to snag a seat along the curb a good 30 minutes before it begins—earlier during peak travel times. (That's a long time to sit on a hard curb.)

✪ MAIN STREET ELECTRICAL PARADE This old Disney favorite, which ran for 20 years from 1971 until 1991, has been brought back. This parade includes the same floats and costumes once used at Disneyland. (The old Disney World show has been shipped to Disneyland Paris.) The Main Street Electrical Parade features a half million lights on floats depicting characters and scenes from Disney movies, such as Cinderella. If you can see only one parade, see this one.

✪ FIREWORKS Fantasy in the Sky Fireworks, immediately preceded by Tinker Bell's magical flight from Cinderella Castle, takes place nightly in summer, on selected nights during Christmas and Easter vacation times, and during other special celebrations. Consult your *Entertainment Show Schedule* for details. Suggested viewing areas are Liberty Square, Frontierland, and Mickey's Toontown Fair.

7 Epcot

Ever expanding, Epcot now occupies 260 acres so stunningly landscaped the park is worth visiting for its botanical beauty alone. There are two major sections, Future World and World Showcase.

Epcot is huge, and walking around it can be exhausting (some say Epcot's acronym stands for "Every Person Comes Out Tired")—so don't try to do it all in 1 day. Conserve energy by taking launches across the lagoon from the edge of Future World to Germany or Morocco. There are also double-decker buses circling the World Showcase Promenade and making stops at Norway, Italy, France, and Canada.

Unlike the Magic Kingdom, Epcot's parking lot is right at the gate. If you don't get an *Epcot Guidemap* and *Entertainment Schedule* in the parking lot or at the gate, stop by the Innoventions East information center when you come in to pick up a copy of each and, if you so desire, make reservations for lunch or dinner. Many Epcot restaurants are described in the "Dining" section, earlier in this chapter.

Strollers and wheelchairs can be rented to your left at the Future World entrance plaza and in World Showcase at the International Gateway between the United Kingdom and France.

FUTURE WORLD

The northern section of Epcot (where you enter the park) comprises Future World, centered on a giant geosphere known as Spaceship Earth. Future World's 10 themed areas, sponsored by major corporations, focus on discovery, scientific achievements, and tomorrow's technologies in areas running the gamut from energy to undersea exploration.

✪ **SPACESHIP EARTH**   This massive, silvery geosphere symbolizes Epcot, so it is a must-do. But you can avoid long lines by saving it until later in the day, when you can, more than likely, simply walk right in. Inside, a show takes visitors on a 15-minute journey through the history of communications. You're catapulted into outer space to see "Spaceship Earth" from a new perspective, returning for a finale that places the audience amid interactive global networks. High-tech special effects, animated sets, and laser beams make this quite an exciting experience.

At the end of this journey through time, AT&T invites guests to sample an interactive computer-video wonderland that includes a motion-simulator ride through the company's electronic network. This exhibit complements Innoventions, detailed below.

INNOVENTIONS   The pair of crescent-shaped buildings to your right and left just beyond Spaceship Earth house a constantly evolving 100,000-square-foot exhibit that showcases cutting-edge technologies and future products. Leading manufacturers sponsor ever-changing exhibit areas here. You'll get a chance to preview virtual reality, check out electric cars, experience interactive television, and try out more than 200 new computer programs and games. Kids will be thrilled to preview new Sega video games. It is a chance to feel, hear, and see the future, hands-on.

The **virtual reality offerings**—from swimming with sharks at the Vivid Group pod to a walking tour of St. Peter's Basilica by ENEL—are the latest high-tech wonders and a chance to experience what you have been reading about in science magazines.

There are several show areas: You can be interviewed by Jay Leno on TV; Sky Cyberguy takes you on a tour of the future of wireless communication; The Honeywell's Home Automation at the House of Innoventions Tour visits the computer-controlled abode of the future. The computer literate will find this a fascinating place to play, but the technologically challenged will find it less rewarding.

The two-story **Discovery Center,** located to the right of Innoventions, includes an information resource area where guests can get answers to all their questions about Epcot and Walt Disney World attractions. The Discovery Center also houses several shops, including Field Trips, which features educational products and software.

✪ **THE LIVING SEAS**   This pavilion contains the world's sixth "ocean," a 5.7-million-gallon saltwater aquarium (complete with a coral reef) inhabited by more than 4,000 sea creatures, including sharks, barracudas, parrot fish, rays, and dolphins among them. A 2½-minute multimedia preshow about today's ocean technology is followed by a 7-minute film demonstrating the formation of the earth and seas as a means to support life.

After the film, visitors enter hydrolators for a rapid descent to the ocean floor. Upon arrival, they board Seacabs that wind around a 400-foot-long tunnel to enjoy stunning close-up views of ocean denizens in a natural coral-reef habitat. The ride concludes in the Seabase Concourse, which is the visitor center of **Seabase Alpha,** a prototype ocean-research facility of the future. Here, informational modules focus on practical resources grown in controllable undersea environments, marine mammals, the study of oceanography from space, and life in a coral-reef community. You can step into a diver's JIM Suit and use controls to complete diving tasks, and expand your knowledge of oceanography via interactive computers.

Note: Via a program called **Epcot DiveQuest,** certified divers can participate in a program that includes a 30- to 40-minute scuba dive in the Living Seas aquarium; for details, call ☎ **407/WDW-TOUR.**

THE LAND This largest of Future World's pavilions highlights humankind's relation to food and nature.

Living with the Land: A 13-minute boat ride takes you through three ecological environments (a rain forest, an African desert, and windswept American plains), each populated by appropriate audio-animatronic denizens. New farming methods and experiments—ranging from hydroponics to plants growing in simulated Martian soil!—are showcased in real gardens. If you'd like a more serious overview, take a 45-minute guided walking tour of the growing areas, offered daily. Sign up at the Green Thumb Emporium shop near the entrance to Food Rocks. The cost is $5 for adults, $3 for children 3 to 9, free for children 2 and under. It's not, by the way, really geared to children.

Circle of Life: Combining spectacular live-action footage with animation, this 15-minute, 70mm motion picture based on *The Lion King* is a cautionary environmental tale.

Food Rocks: Audio-animatronic rock performers deliver an entertaining message about nutrition here.

✪ JOURNEY INTO IMAGINATION This terrific pavilion has been closed for most of 1999 and is scheduled to reopen in 2000, after adding more high-tech gadgets, and sprucing up some of the old favorites. At press time, the new rides were supposed to be associated with the *Honey I Shrunk the Audience* film (see below).

Honey I Shrunk the Audience is a 3-D attraction based on the Disney hit *Honey I Shrunk the Kids* films. The audience, after being menaced by hundreds of mice and a 3-D cat, is shrunk and given a good shaking by a gigantic 5-year-old. Dramatic 3-D action is enhanced by vibrating seats and creepy tactile effects. Finally, everyone returns to proper size—everyone but the family dog, which creates the final, not-altogether-pleasant special effect (I won't reveal it). *Note: This attraction will remain open while the rest of* Journey Into Imagination *is closed for renovation.*

TEST TRACK Called a mix of General Motors engineering and Disney imagineering, the newest Epcot attraction has guests in the driver's seat to experience the rigors of automobile testing. During a preshow (essentially a GM commercial), guests will learn how the company works to promote automotive safety, reliability, and performance. Then they'll board full-scale six-passenger test cars and travel on what appears to be an actual roadway, accelerating on long straightaways, hugging hairpin turns, climbing steep hills, and braking abruptly—often in less-than-perfect road conditions. The ride will culminate with a terrifying high-speed outdoor run along the track's steeply banked "speed loop" that extends far beyond the pavilion facility. Cars will go at a top speed of 65 m.p.h. This was formerly the World of Motion pavilion.

✪ WONDERS OF LIFE Housed in a vast geodesic dome fronted by a 75-foot replica of a DNA molecule, this pavilion offers some of Future World's most engaging shows and attractions, including the following:

The Making of Me: This captivating 15-minute motion picture starring Martin Short combines live action with animation and spectacular in utero photography to create the sweetest introduction imaginable to the facts of life. Don't miss it, but expect some questions from young children.

Body Wars: You're miniaturized to the size of a single cell for a medical rescue mission inside the immune system of a human body. Your mission: Save a miniaturized immunologist who has been accidentally swept into the bloodstream. This motion-simulator ride takes you on a wild journey through gale-force winds (in the lungs) and pounding heart chambers.

Epcot Center

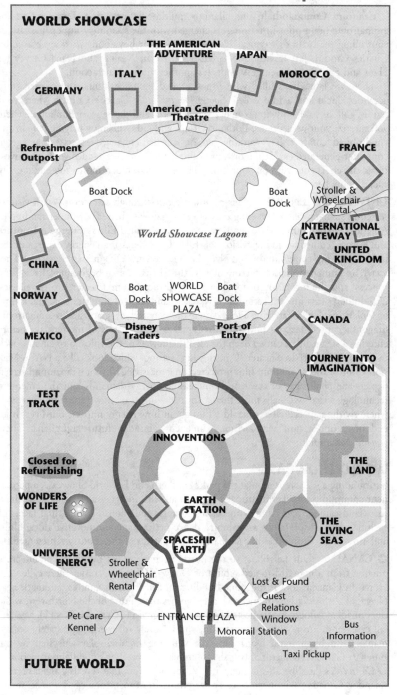

WORLD SHOWCASE

THE AMERICAN ADVENTURE

JAPAN

ITALY

MOROCCO

GERMANY

American Gardens Theatre

Refreshment Outpost

FRANCE

Boat Dock

Boat Dock

Stroller & Wheelchair Rental

World Showcase Lagoon

INTERNATIONAL GATEWAY

UNITED KINGDOM

CHINA

NORWAY

Boat Dock

WORLD SHOWCASE PLAZA

Boat Dock

CANADA

MEXICO

Disney Traders

Port of Entry

JOURNEY INTO IMAGINATION

TEST TRACK

INNOVENTIONS

THE LAND

Closed for Refurbishing

THE LIVING SEAS

WONDERS OF LIFE

EARTH STATION

UNIVERSE OF ENERGY

SPACESHIP EARTH

Stroller & Wheelchair Rental

Lost & Found

Guest Relations Window

Pet Care Kennel

ENTRANCE PLAZA

Bus Information

Monorail Station

Taxi Pickup

FUTURE WORLD

Cranium Command: In this hilarious multimedia attraction, Buzzy, an audio-animatronic brain-pilot-in-training, is charged with the seemingly impossible task of controlling the brain of a typical 12-year-old boy. The boy's body parts are played by Charles Grodin, Jon Lovitz, Bob Goldthwait, Kevin Nealon and Dana Carvey (as Hans and Franz), and George Wendt. It's another must-see attraction.

There are large areas filled with fitness-related shows, exhibits, and participatory activities, including a film called *Goofy About Health;* Coach's Corner, where your tennis, golf, or baseball swing is analyzed by experts; and the Sensory Funhouse, where you can test your perceptions. Both grown-ups and kids will enjoy playing here in air-conditioned comfort. Try working out on a video-enhanced exercise bike, get a computer-generated evaluation of your health habits, and take a video voyage to investigate the effects of drugs on your heart. There's much, much more. You could easily spend hours here.

UNIVERSE OF ENERGY   This 32-minute ride-through attraction—with visitors seated in solar-powered "traveling theater" cars—aims to better our understanding of America's energy problems. Recently refurbished, it's called **Ellen's Energy Adventure** and features comedian and television star Ellen DeGeneres as an energy expert tutored to be a *Jeopardy!* contestant by Bill Nye, the Science Guy. On a massive screen in Theater I, an animated motion picture depicts the earth's molten beginnings, its cooling process, and the formation of fossil fuels. You'll move from Theater I to travel back 275 million years into an eerie storm-wracked landscape of the Mesozoic era, a time of violent geological activity. Here, you'll be menaced by giant audio-animatronic dragonflies, pterodactyls, dinosaurs, earthquakes, and streams of molten lava before entering a steam-filled tunnel deep through the bowels of the volcano to emerge back in the 20th century in Theater II. In this new setting, which looks like a NASA Mission Control room, a 70mm film projected on a massive 210-foot wraparound screen depicts the challenges of the world's increasing energy demands and the emerging technologies that will help meet them. Your moving seats now return to Theater I, where swirling special effects herald a film about how energy impacts our lives. It all ends on an upbeat note, with a vision of an energy-abundant future and Ellen as a new *Jeopardy!* champion.

WORLD SHOWCASE

Surrounding a 40-acre lagoon at the park's southern end is World Showcase, a permanent community of 11 miniaturized nations, all with indigenous landmark architecture, landscaping, background music, restaurants, and shops. The cultural facets of each nation are explored in art exhibits, dance performances, innovative rides, films, and attractions. Employees in each pavilion are natives of the country represented.

✪ **CANADA**   Our neighbors to the north are represented by diverse architecture ranging from a mansard-roofed replica of Ottawa's Château Laurier (here called the Hôtel du Canada) to a rustic stone building modeled after a famous landmark near Niagara Falls. A Native American village signifies the culture of the Northwest, while the Canadian wilderness is reflected by a steep mountain (a Canadian Rocky), a waterfall cascading into a white-water stream, and a "forest" of evergreens, stately cedars, maples, and birch trees. Don't miss the stunning floral displays inspired by the Butchart Gardens in Victoria, British Columbia. The pavilion's highlight attraction is *O Canada!,* a dazzling 18-minute, CircleVision 360° film that reveals Canada's scenic splendor. Canada pavilion shops carry everything from soapstone carvings and snowshoes to rabbit-skin caps and heavy knitted sweaters—and, of course, maple syrup.

UNITED KINGDOM Centered on Brittania Square—a formal London-style park, complete with copper-roofed gazebo bandstand and a statue of the Bard—the U.K. pavilion evokes Merry Olde England. Four centuries of architecture are represented along quaint cobblestone streets, troubadours and minstrels entertain in front of a traditional British pub, and a formal garden replicates the landscaping of 16th- and 17th-century palaces. High Street and Tudor Lane shops display a broad sampling of British merchandise, including toy soldiers, Paddington bears, Scottish tartans, and shortbreads. A tea shop occupies a replica of Anne Hathaway's thatch-roofed 16th-century cottage in Stratford-upon-Avon. Don't miss the Old Globe Players who present delightfully wacky performances of Shakespeare in the square.

✪ **FRANCE** This pavilion is entered via a replica of the beautiful cast-iron Pot des Arts footbridge over the Seine. It leads to a park inspired by Seurat's painting *A Sunday Afternoon on the Island of La Grande Jatte*. A one-tenth replica of the Eiffel Tower looms above the *grands boulevards*. The highlight attraction is *Impressions de France*. Shown in a palatial (mercifully sit-down) theater à la Fontainebleau, this 18-minute film is a scenic journey through diverse French landscapes projected on a vast 200-degree wraparound screen and enhanced by the music of French composers. Emporia in the covered shopping arcade have interiors ranging from a turn-of-the-century bibliothèque to a French château. Merchandise includes French art prints, cookbooks, wines (there's a tasting counter), fancy French foodstuffs, Limoges boxes, Madeline and Babar books and dolls, perfumes, and original letters of famous Frenchmen ranging from Jean Cocteau to Napoléon. Another marketplace revives the defunct Les Halles, where Parisians used to sip onion soup in the wee hours. The heavenly aroma of a boulangerie penetrates the atmosphere, and mimes, jugglers, and strolling chanteurs entertain.

MOROCCO This exotic pavilion is heralded by a replica of the Koutoubia Minaret, the prayer tower of a 12th-century mosque in Marrakesh. The Medina (old city), entered via a replica of an arched gateway in Fez, leads to Fez House (a traditional Moroccan home) and the narrow winding streets of the *souk,* a bustling marketplace where all manner of authentic handcrafted merchandise—pottery, Berber and Rabat carpets, ornate silver boxes, straw baskets, and prayer rugs—is on display. There are weaving demonstrations in the souk throughout the day. The Medina's rectangular courtyard centers on a replica of the ornately tiled Najjarine Fountain in Fez, the setting for musical entertainment. The pavilion's Royal Gallery contains an ever-changing exhibit of Moroccan art, and the Center of Tourism offers a continuous three-screen slide show.

JAPAN Heralded by a flaming-red *torii* (gate of honor) on the banks of the lagoon, and the graceful blue-roofed Goju No To pagoda (inspired by a shrine built at Nara in A.D. 700), this pavilion focuses on Japan's ancient culture. In a traditional Japanese garden, trees and flowering shrubs frame a contemplative setting of pebbled footpaths, rustic bridges, waterfalls, exquisite rock landscaping, and a pond of golden koi. The **Yakitori House** is based on the renowned 16th-century Katsura Imperial Villa in Kyoto, considered by many to be the crowning achievement of Japanese architecture. Exhibits ranging from 18th-century Bunraki puppets to samurai armor take place in the moated White Heron Castle, a replica of the Shirasagi-Jo, a 17th-century fortress overlooking the city of Himeji. And the **Mitsukoshi Department Store** (Japan's answer to Macy's) is housed in a replica of the Shishinden (Hall of Ceremonies) of the Gosho Imperial Palace built in Kyoto in A.D. 794. It sells lacquerware, kimonos, kites, fans, dolls, samurai swords, bonsai trees, Japanese foods, and even modern electronics. In the courtyard, artisans demonstrate the ancient arts of *anesaiku* (shaping brown rice candy into dragons, unicorns, and dolphins), *sumi-e* (calligraphy), and origami (paper folding). Be sure to include a show of traditional Japanese music and dance at this pavilion in your schedule. It's one of the best in the World Showcase.

○ **AMERICAN ADVENTURE** Housed in a vast Georgian-style structure, the American Adventure is a 29-minute dramatization of U.S. history using a 72-foot rear-projection screen, rousing music, and a large cast of lifelike audio-animatronic figures, including narrators Mark Twain and Ben Franklin. The "adventure" begins with the voyage of the *Mayflower* and encompasses major historic events. You view Jefferson writing the Declaration of Independence, the expansion of the frontier, Mathew Brady photographing a family about to be divided by the Civil War, the stock market crash of 1929, the attack on Pearl Harbor, and the Eagle heading toward the moon. While waiting for the show to begin, you'll be entertained by the Voices of Liberty Singers performing American folk songs in the Main Hall. A shop called Heritage Manor Gifts sells signed presidential photographs, needlepoint samplers, quilts, Davy Crockett hats, books on American history, classic political campaign buttons, and vintage newspapers.

ITALY One of the prettiest World Showcase pavilions, Italy lures visitors over an arched stone footbridge to a replica of the Venetian Doge's Palace. Other architectural highlights include the 83-foot campanile (bell tower) of St. Mark's Square, Venetian bridges, and a central piazza enclosing a version of Bernini's Neptune Fountain. A garden wall suggests a backdrop of provincial countryside, and Mediterranean citrus, olive trees, cypress, and pine frame a formal garden. Gondolas are moored on the lagoon. Shops here carry Perugina chocolates, kitchenware, cameo and filigree jewelry, Murano and Venetian glass, alabaster figurines, and inlaid wooden music boxes. A troupe of street actors performs a contemporary version of 16th-century commedia del l'arte in the piazza.

GERMANY Enclosed by towered castle walls, this festive pavilion is centered on a cobblestone *platz* (plaza) with pots of colorful flowers girding a fountain statue of St. George and the Dragon. An adjacent clock tower is embellished with whimsical glockenspiel figures that herald each hour with quaint melodies. The pavilion's outdoor biergarten—where it's Oktoberfest all year long—was inspired by medieval Rothenberg. Shops here carry cuckoo clocks, cowbells, Alpine hats, German wines (there's a tasting counter), toys (including an extensive selection of beautiful German dolls and teddy bears), and books. An artisan demonstrates the molding and painting of Hummel figures; another paints exquisite detailed scenes on eggs.

○ **CHINA** Bounded by a serpentine wall that snakes around its outer perimeter, the China pavilion is entered via a vast ceremonial gate inspired by the Temple of Heaven in Beijing. Passing through the gate, you'll see a half-size replica of this ornate red-and-gold circular temple, built in 1420 during the Ming Dynasty. Gardens simulate those in Suzhou, with miniature waterfalls, fragrant lotus ponds, groves of bamboo, and weeping mulberry trees. The highlight attraction here is **Wonders of China,** a 20-minute, CircleVision 360° film that explores 6,000 years of dynastic and Communist rule and the breathtaking diversity of the Chinese landscape. Adjacent to the theater, an art gallery houses changing exhibits of Chinese art. A bustling marketplace offers an array of merchandise including silk robes, jade figures, cloisonné vases, dolls, fans, and wind chimes. Artisans here demonstrate calligraphy.

NORWAY Centered on a picturesque cobblestone courtyard, this pavilion evokes ancient Norway. A *stavekirke* (stave church), styled after the 13th-century Gol Church of Hallingdal, houses changing exhibits. A replica of Oslo's 14th-century Akershus

Castle, next to a cascading woodland waterfall, is the setting for the pavilion's featured restaurant. Other buildings simulate the red-roofed cottages of Bergen and the timber-sided farm buildings of the Nordic woodlands. There's a two-part attraction here. **Maelstrom,** a boat ride in a dragon-headed Viking vessel, traverses Norway's fjords and mythical forests to the music of *Peer Gynt*—an exciting journey during which you'll be menaced by polar bears prowling the shore and trolls that cast a spell on the boat. The watercraft crashes through a narrow gorge and spins into the North Sea, where a violent storm is in progress. But the storm abates, and passengers disembark safely in a 10th-century Viking village to view the 70mm film *Norway,* which documents a thousand years of history. Shops feature hand-knit wool hats and sweaters, toys (there's a Lego table where kids can play while you shop), wood carvings, Scandinavian foods, pewterware, and jewelry.

MEXICO   You'll hear the music of marimba and mariachi bands as you approach the festive showcase of Mexico, fronted by a towering Mayan pyramid modeled on the Aztec Temple of Quetzalcoatl (God of Life). Upon entering the pavilion, you'll find yourself in a museum of pre-Colombian art and artifacts. Down a ramp is a small lagoon, the setting for **El Rio del Tiempo,** where visitors board boats for 8-minute cruises through Mexico's past and present. *Note: At press time, it was likely that this ride would be shut down in 1999 for refurbishing, to reopen at some point in 2000.* Shops in and around the Plaza de Los Amigos (a "moonlit" Mexican *mercado*) display an array of leather goods, baskets, sombreros, piñatas, pottery, jewelry, serapes, colorful papier-mâché birds, and blown-glass objects (an artisan gives demonstrations). La Casa de Vacaciones, sponsored by the Mexican Tourist Office, provides travel information.

SHOWS & SPECTACULARS

As in the Magic Kingdom, check your show schedule upon entering the park, and plan ahead for one or more of the following performances.

WORLD SHOWCASE PAVILION SHOWS   These international entertainments make up an important part of the Epcot experience. There are Chinese lion dancers and acrobats, German oompah bands, Caledonian bagpipers, Italian "living statues" and stilt walkers, colonial fife-and-drum groups, Moroccan belly dancers, and much more. Don't miss the Voices of Liberty Singers at American Adventure and the traditional music and dance displays in Japan. The World Showcase will also host the **Walt Disney World Millennium Celebration** from October 1, 1999 to January 1, 2001. More than 35 nations will take part in the planned multi-cultural festivities. A new pavilion will feature countries from all over the world. Guests can journey through a Brazilian rainforest or experience firsthand the four seasons in Sweden.

✪ ILLUMINATIONS   A backdrop of classical music by international composers, high-tech lighting effects, darting laser beams, fireworks, and rainbow-lit dancing fountains combine to create this awesome 16½-minute Epcot spectacular, presented nightly. Each nation is highlighted in turn—colorful kites fly over Japan, the giant Rockies loom over Canada, a gingerbread house rises in Germany, and so on. The show is being revamped in 1999 for the millennium and will include even more lasers, fireworks, and special effects. Don't miss it! Find a seat around the lagoon about a half hour before show time.

RHYTHMS OF THE WORLD   Varied international cultural performances take place at the America Gardens Theater in World Showcase.

8 Disney-MGM Studios

Disney-MGM Studios offers exciting movie and TV-themed shows and behind-the-scenes "reel-life" adventures. Its main streets include Hollywood Boulevard and Sunset Boulevard, with art deco movie sets evocative of Hollywood's glamorous golden age. There's also a New York street lined with Gotham landmarks (the Empire State, Flat-iron, and Chrysler buildings) and typical New York characters, including peddlers hawking knock-off watches. More important, this is a working movie and TV studio, where shows are in production even as you tour the premises.

Arrive at the park early, tickets in hand. Unlike the Magic Kingdom and Epcot, MGM's 110 acres of attractions can pretty much be seen in 1 day. The parking lot is right at the gate, although trams do run. Pay attention to your parking location, which is not as distinctly marked as in the Magic Kingdom.

If you don't get a *Disney-MGM Studios Guidemap* and *Entertainment Show Schedule* when you enter the park, you can pick them up at **Guest Services** (MGM's information center). First thing to do is check show times and work out an entertainment schedule based on highlight attractions and geographical proximity. My favorite MGM restaurants are described in the "Dining" section of this chapter. **Strollers** can be rented at Oscar's Super Service inside the main entrance. Note the "Character Spotlight" on the back of the guide map. This will tell you the time and location that Disney characters will appear and be available for autographs.

✪ **THE TWILIGHT ZONE TOWER OF TERROR**   A thrilling journey to another dimension! Legend has it that during a violent storm on Halloween night 1939, lightning struck the Hollywood Tower Hotel, causing an entire wing—along with an elevator full of people—to disappear. Rod Serling is about to introduce you to those who disappeared as you become the star in a special episode of *The Twilight Zone*. After various spooky adventures, the ride ends in a dramatic climax: a terrifying 13-story, fitful, free-fall plunge into *The Twilight Zone!* The best thrill ride at Disney with a "preshow" so authentic that maintenance crews kept fixing leaking pipes designed to drip as part of the ambience.

THE MAGIC OF DISNEY ANIMATION   You'll see Disney characters come alive at the stroke of a brush or pencil as you tour actual glass-walled animation studios and watch artists at work. The tour also includes entertaining video talks by animators and a grand finale of magical moments from Disney classics. Try to visit this popular attraction early in the morning—long lines form later in the day.

DISNEY-MGM STUDIO BACKLOT TOUR   This 25-minute tram tour takes you behind the scenes for a close-up look at the vehicles, props, costumes, sets, and special effects used in your favorite movies and TV shows. You'll see real costumers stitching away in wardrobe, the house facade of television's *The Golden Girls,* and even carpenters building sets. Most of the sets are pretty dated or from short-lived shows you've probably never seen. Things pick up considerably once the tram ventures into **Catastrophe Canyon,** where an earthquake causes canyon walls to rumble and riders are threatened by a raging fire, massive explosions, torrents of rain, and flash floods! Then you're taken behind the scenes to see how filmmakers use special effects to create such disasters. After the tram tour, visit **Studio Showcase,** a changing walk-through display of sets and props from popular and classic movies.

✪ **BACKSTAGE PASS TO *101 DALMATIANS***   Have a "De Vil" of a good time spotting Cruella and the other stars of Disney's live-action remake of the animated classic. The stark, eerie sets from Cruella's movie are among the top attractions during this short tour. Wizzer, the most fluid of the canine actors, is featured in a film about the life of a four-pawed star. Taking a cue from Universal, where you Ride the Movies, the special-effects show allows one lucky—usually tall and male—spectator to ride in the movies by re-creating Jeff Daniels' runaway bike scene.

Note: The nearby "Making of" exhibit highlights the latest movie to come out. Check your park schedule.

❂ **VOYAGE OF *THE LITTLE MERMAID***   Hazy light, creating an underwater effect in the reef-walled theater, helps set the mood for this charming musical spectacular based on the Disney feature film. The show combines live performers with more than 100 puppets, movie clips, and innovative special effects. It all has a happy ending, as most of the young audience knows it will—they've seen the movie. A must for your little Ariel fan.

❂ **THEATER OF THE STARS**   This 1,500-seat covered amphitheater is currently presenting a live Broadway-style production of *Beauty and the Beast,* based on the Disney movie version. Sets and costumes are lavish, production numbers spectacular. Arrive early to get a good seat. Also catch the *Hunchback of Notre Dame* stage show at the nearby theater.

Note: Disney often changes shows to tie in with recent movies. Some other Disney release may be highlighted during this show by the time you visit.

❂ **JIM HENSON'S MUPPET VISION 3-D**   Disney has slightly revamped this longtime favorite. The film still stars Kermit and Miss Piggy and combines Jim Henson's puppets with Disney audio-animatronics and special-effects wizardry, 70mm film, and cutting-edge 3-D technology. The coming-at-you action includes flying Muppets, cream pies, cannonballs, fiber-optic fireworks, bubble showers, and even an actual spray of water. Statler and Waldorf critique the action (which includes numerous mishaps and disasters) from a mezzanine balcony. Kids in the first row interact with the characters. In the preshow area, guests view a hilarious Muppet video on overhead monitors and see an array of Muppet movie props.

STAR TOURS   Cutting edge when it first debuted, this galactic journey based on the original *Star Wars* trilogy (George Lucas collaborated on its conception) can't compete with the latest technology but is still plenty of fun. The movie was recently replaced to reflect on the new Star Wars "prequel" movie that hit the theaters in 1999. The preshow area—where R2-D2 and C-3PO are running an intergalactic travel agency—will be a hit with die-hard fans.

As with the old version, you'll board a 40-seat "spacecraft" for an other-worldly journey that includes sudden drops, violent crashes, and oncoming laser blasts. Check out the *Star Wars* merchandise shop at the end of the ride.

❂ **THE GREAT MOVIE RIDE**   Film footage and audio-animatronic replicas of movie stars take you on a nostalgic journey through some of the most famous scenes in movie history. The action is enhanced by dramatic special effects, and your tram is always hijacked en route by outlaws or gangsters. The setting for this attraction is a full-scale reproduction of Hollywood's famous Mann's Chinese Theatre, complete with hand- and footprints of the stars out front.

❂ **ABC SOUND STUDIO**   Scream. Wave your hands. Making a little noise is likely to help get you from the audience onto the stage, where you will then take part in creating the sound effects to go along with ABC Saturday morning television shows. The real stars are the tourists trying to make it all happen like the professionals. Volunteer. You're on vacation. You'll *probably* never see these people again. If you can't muster the gumption to go on stage, the postshow, Soundworks, provides the opportunity for a little joyful noise on interactive computers and away from the crowd.

✪ **INDIANA JONES EPIC STUNT SPECTACULAR** Visitors get an inside look at the world of movie stunts in this dramatic 30-minute show, which re-creates major scenes from the Indiana Jones series. The show opens on an elaborate Mayan temple backdrop. Indiana Jones crashes dramatically onto the set via a rope, and as he searches with a torch for the golden idol, he encounters booby traps, fire and steam, and spears popping up from the ground before being chased by a rolling boulder! The set is dismantled to reveal a colorful Cairo marketplace, where a sword fight ensues, and the action includes jumps from high places, virtuoso bullwhip maneuvers, lots of gunfire, and a truck bursting into flames. An explosive finale takes place in a desert scenario. Throughout, you'll get to see how elaborate stunts are pulled off and wonder how close the actors really do come to peril. (Here it is—another chance to be part of the fun. Arrive early and sit near the stage for your shot at short-lived stardom. Go ahead, you're running out of chances—*and this time you get to wear a turban.*)

ROCK 'N ROLLER COASTER In an attempt to go head to head with Universal's Islands of Adventure, this is Disney's first inverted roller coaster. The indoor coaster, similar to Space Mountain, is fast and furious and speeds through the darkness to the beat of rocking music. Speeding from zero to 60 and tearing through three buildings, this is a must for coaster fans, but not for the faint of heart. *Note:* Check for height restrictions.

DISNEY'S DOUG LIVE This show, one of the newest in MGM Studios, combines live performances and animation, and tells the story of a 12-year-old and his interaction with the popular television cartoon character. This is a must-see for fans of the show, no matter what their ages, but nonfans will find it less intriguing.

PARADES, SHOWS, FIREWORKS & MORE Disney uses its afternoon parade to plug its latest movie release. The parade takes place daily; check your entertainment schedule for route and times. Unless your child is a big fan of whatever title is featured at the time of your visit, I'd suggest taking advantage of shorter lines during the parade to hit some attractions.

'FANTASMIC! With more than 50 performers, more than 1 million gallons of water, a 32,000-pound dragon, a 59-foot-tall mountain, laser lights, and pyrotechnics, this is one of the best nighttime shows in Disney's World. The 25-minute show, which debuted late in 1998, has been shown at Disneyland since 1992, but Disney officials promise that those who have seen the California show are still in for some surprises. It mixes special effects with classic movie clips projected on huge water screens and features Sorcerer Mickey and a host of other Disney favorites, from the Little Mermaid to animal puppets from The Lion King. It is held in a 6,500-seat theater behind the Tower of Terror off Sunset Boulevard. There is also room for 2,500 standing guests, but try to arrive at least 30 minutes early to get a seat (earlier during peak seasons). The noise level may be intense for young children. *Tip:* Keep away from those splash zones if you don't want to get wet!

The **Visiting Celebrity** program features frequent appearances by stars such as Betty White, Burt Reynolds, Joan Collins, Leonard Nimoy, and Billy Dee Williams. They visit attractions, record their handprints in front of the Chinese Theater, and appear at question-and-answer sessions with park guests. Check your entertainment schedule to see if it's happening during your visit.

A movie-set replica serves as a playground in the *Honey, I Shrunk the Kids* **Movie Set Adventure.** Outside props include 30-foot blades of grass, giant Legos, and a sliding pond made from an immense film reel.

Centering on a gleaming 14½-foot bronze Emmy, the **Academy of Television Arts & Sciences Hall of Fame Plaza** honors TV legends. Bronze sculptures of Carol Burnett, Sid Caesar, Red Skelton, Milton Berle, and other television luminaries are displayed.

9 Animal Kingdom

Disney's fourth major park combines animals, elaborate landscapes, and a handful of rides to create yet another reason not to venture outside of the Disney World. The bulk of the park opened in 1998, the final "land" Asia, opened in 1999. Michael Eisner says it's the next best thing to going to Africa, but don't cancel that safari vacation yet. It is definitely a different theme park experience, filled with lush landscapes and exotic wildlife. There are also a few great shows—notably the Lion King. If the animals are cooperative, you can have an up close encounter that you aren't likely to find anywhere else.

This park does grow on you. I have enjoyed it a little more with each visit. However, if this is your first visit to Walt Disney World, and you have children, you'll probably want to target the parks with more thrill rides—Magic Kingdom and Disney MGM—before this one. Animal lovers, and those who like to photograph wildlife, may want to put it at the top of their lists.

Animal Kingdom is divided into five "regions": **Safari Village,** a shopping/entertainment area; **Africa,** the main animal-viewing area, which is dedicated to the wildlife in Africa today; **Dinoland,** focusing on issues of extinction; and **Camp Minnie-Mickey,** the Animal Kingdom equivalent of Mickey's Toontown in the Magic Kingdom. **Asia,** the final section to open, has a water roller coaster called **Kali River Rapids,** and features wildlife exhibits, including Bengal tigers, in the **Maharajah Jungle Trek.**

The park covers more than 500 acres—nearly twice the size of Epcot—and your feet will tell you that you have covered the territory at the end of the day.

THE OASIS

Basically the garden entrance to the park, the painstakingly designed landscape set with streams, grottoes, and waterfalls sets the tone for the rest of the park. Visit early in the day or late in the afternoon to get the best views of the animals.

SAFARI VILLAGE

Like Cinderella Castle in the Magic Kingdom and the silver golf-ball dome in Epcot, the 14-story Tree of Life located here is the park's central landmark. It is an intricately carved free-form representation of animals handcrafted by Disney artists. Teams of artists worked for months creating the various sculptures, and it is worth a leisurely stroll.

IT'S TOUGH TO BE A BUG!   If you loved the movie *A Bug's Life,* you'll feel right at home with the creepy (crawly) special effects at this 3-D attraction. There is a special surprise ending that will send a real shiver up your spine. In general, this is fun for the entire family. The arachnaphobic, however, and the very young will find it less enjoyable. Tots may be scared by the dark, cavelike atmosphere and the sometimes-scary bugs. Once the show starts it is difficult to leave. Located inside the Tree of Life in a 430-seat theater.

THE GARDEN PATH   Take a leisurely stroll (are you detecting a theme here?) through the root system of The Tree of Life. This soft landscape is filled with otters, flamingos, tamarinds, lemurs, tortoises, and colorful ducks, storks, cranes, and cockatoos. The cool, covered walkways—complete with piped-in sounds of nature—make for an enjoyable walk, and this is the place to get pictures of any number of birds and exotic animals, especially in the early morning or late afternoon.

RADIO DISNEY RIVER CRUISE   If you've already hit the major attractions, this round-trip cruise may be a nice break at the end of the day. Guests listen to a radio broadcast—supposedly emanating from the top of the Tree of Life—as they take a relaxing tour through the waterway snaking through the park. The "broadcast" consists of songs, special guests and trivia quizzes, and is hosted by "Just Plain" Mark and Zippy from the Radio Disney broadcast which airs across the nation.

DINOLAND U.S.A.

Enter by passing under "Olden Gate Bridge," a 40-foot-tall Brachiosaurus reassembled from excavated fossils, and you will find a world filled with a series of wooden cabins and national-park–like structures that give the land a nostalgic 1950s and 1960s look.

COUNTDOWN TO EXTINCTION   This ride is reminiscent of Snow White's Adventures in the Magic Kingdom. You hurl through the darkness in "time machines" past an array of snarling dinosaurs. This is far from a smooth ride, and children may find the dinosaurs and darkness frightening. As a thrill ride, well, it's not very thrilling. The snarling dinos are interesting, but you speed by them so quickly there's little time to appreciate them. In a weird glitch in Disney's usually faultless storytelling, the dinosaur that you are supposed to be retrieving by traveling back in time never appears at the end of the ride. *Note:* You must be 46 inches tall to ride.

CRETACEOUS TRAIL   Wander leisurely—there's that theme again—back in time as you stroll down a path filled with living plants and animal species that have survived since the age of the dinosaur. You'll encounter a Chinese alligator, a Florida soft-shelled turtle, and red-legged seriama. The animals are interesting, but skip the re-creation of the dig site.

THE BONEYARD   Kids love the chance to slip, slither, slide, and crawl through this giant playground and dig site. Discover the remains of triceratops, T-rex, and other vanished giants. You can even dig up the bones of a woolly mammoth in the dig site. This area is fun, but isn't nearly as inviting at the *Honey I Shrunk the Kids* play area in Disney–MGM Studios.

CONSERVATION STATION   This offers a behind-the-scenes look at how Disney cares for animals inside the park. It includes the **Affection Section,** where you can cuddle with some friendly animals, explore their private habitats, and learn how they are cared for and fed. Check out Eco Heroes, interactive videos that connect you to endangered-animal information and world-famous biologists and conservationists, and Song of the Rainforest, surrounding you with the sounds of the endangered wildlife of that deep jungle. But unless you are into doing a little research on your vacation, skip Eco Web, a computer link to conservation organizations worldwide.

CAMP MINNIE-MICKEY

Join your favorite Disney characters "on vacation" in Camp Minnie-Mickey, an entire land that re-creates a kid-friendly Adirondack resort.

GRANDMA WILLOW'S COVE   The hour-plus wait—and that was on a slow day—frankly wasn't worth this disappointing 15-minute show in a 350-seat theater. Pocahontas and Grandmother Willow, as well as some forest creatures from the forest, perform a heavy-handed skit about the importance of treating nature with respect. If you decide to go, arrive early to get a seat. They do allow standing-room crowds, but standing makes the slow-paced show even slower.

FESTIVAL OF *THE LION KING*   Arrive early for this popular attraction that regularly draws enough people to fill the 1,000-seat pavilion. Based loosely on the animated movie, this stage show combines the pageantry of a parade with a tribal celebration. In an interesting switch, the audience is seated in the center of the theater as the action moves around them. The show is fast-paced, the music is lively, and the acrobatic "monkeys" are a real treat to watch. This is definitely the best show in the park and a "must see" to make your visit complete.

CHARACTER-GREETING PAVILIONS   This is a must for people traveling with children. Various Disney characters greet you, from Winnie the Pooh to Timon and Baloo. Mickey, in recognition of his star status, can be found in his own pavilion. Even here the lines can be considerable as hundreds of kids line up to meet their favorite characters.

AFRICA

Enter through the town of Harambe, a realistic representation of an African coastal village poised on the edge of the 21st century. Whitewashed structures built of coral stone and thatched with reed by craftsmen brought over from Africa surround a central marketplace rich with local wares and colors.

PANGANI FOREST EXPLORATION TRAIL   There are no visible barriers between you and the animals as you watch a troop of African gorillas emerging from the reeds. Bathed in lush jungle foliage, this entire area is filled with exotic East African animals that range from toothy reptiles to brightly colored birds. Don't forget to visit the underwater hippo-viewing area and a savanna overlook. You have to pay close attention to see the animals as they move amid this realistic landscape, and small children may have a hard time seeing above the crowd.

KILIMANJARO SAFARIS   This is one of the few "rides" in Animal Kingdom. Essentially, you board a very big truck for a very bumpy ride through the faux African landscape. The vehicle is open, so open you can get thwacked in the face with foliage, and the animals sometimes wander in very close. But this is hit or miss, depending on how much wildlife you actually get to spot. Once you come within arms-length of a giraffe, however, you forget about all the vacant velt. A story line about chasing a poacher doesn't add much to the whole experience although you will really feel as if you are traveling over the back roads of a reserve. If you have small children, you will need to wrangle a seat on the end so they will be able to look out the sides of the car. The ride gets bumpy, so those with heart, back, and neck problems, as well as pregnant women, should skip it.

ASIA

Disney's Imagineers have outdone themselves in creating this mythical kingdom, **Anadapour.** The intricately painted artwork visible at the main attractions is something not to be missed—it also helps make the lines seem to move a little faster.

KALI RIVER RAPIDS   With churning water that mimics real-life rapids, and optical illusions that will have you wondering if you are about to go over the falls, this is a premiere water roller coaster. The ride begins with a peaceful tour of lush foliage, but soon you are dipping—and dripping—as your tiny ship is tossed. You will definitely get wet. The lines are long here, but keep your head up—literally—and enjoy some of the marvelous artwork painted overhead and on the beautiful murals. There is a 42-inch height requirement.

FLIGHTS OF WONDER   Mixing live-animal action with a traditional Disney character show, Flights of Wonder, which has undergone several transformations since the park opened, is a low-key break for the family, complete with a few laughs and some aviary feats that will ruffle your feathers.

MARAJAH JUNGLE TREK   The rain-forest environments of Nepal, India, Thailand, and Indonesia are all represented here, along with the species that call these tropical locales home. Bengal tigers seem just inches away as you peer through thick glass, watching the graceful cats in their grassy natural surroundings. Nothing but air divides you from the dozens of giant fruit bats hanging in what appears to be an abandoned courtyard, while cocooned in their leathery wings. (Fortunately for those with a bat-phobia, you can bypass the bat habitat.) Helpful guides are on-hand to answer questions, and you can also check a printed guide that lists the various animals you may spot; it's available on your right as you enter the exhibit. Small children may find the proximity to the animals, especially the bats, disturbing.

10 Other Walt Disney World Attractions

✪ TYPHOON LAGOON

Located off Lake Buena Vista Drive, halfway between Walt Disney World Village and Disney-MGM Studios, this is the ultimate in water theme parks. Its fantasy setting is a palm-fringed tropical-island village of ramshackle tin-roofed structures, strewn with wreckage left by a legendary "great typhoon." A storm-stranded fishing boat dangles precariously atop the 95-foot-high Mount Mayday, the steep setting for several major park attractions. Every half hour the boat's smokestack erupts, shooting a 50-foot geyser of water into the air.

In summer, arrive no later than 9am to avoid long lines; the park is often filled to capacity by 10am and closed to later arrivals. Beach towels and lockers can be obtained for a minimal fee, and all beach accessories can be purchased at Singapore Sal's. Light fare is available at two restaurants, and there are picnic tables. Guests are not permitted to bring their own floatation devices into the park.

The major attraction, of course, is **Typhoon Lagoon,** a large and lovely wave pool, the size of two football fields and surrounded by white sandy beach. It's the park's main swimming area; young children can wade in the lagoon's peaceful bay or cove.

Hop onto a raft or an inner tube and meander along the lazy 2,100-foot **Castaway Creek.** Circling the lagoon, Castaway Creek tumbles through a misty rain forest and past caves and secluded grottoes. There are exits along the route where you can leave the creek; if you do the whole thing, it takes about a half hour. There are also a variety of water slides, including the steep **Humunga Kowabunga,** and three white-water rides (Keelhaul Falls has the most winding spiral route, Mayday Falls the steepest drops and fastest water, while the slightly tamer Gangplank Falls uses large tubes so the whole family can ride together).

Guests are given free snorkel equipment (and instruction) for a 15-minute swim through **Shark Reef,** a 362,000-gallon simulated coral-reef tank populated by about 4,000 colorful denizens of the deep. If you don't want to get in the water, you can observe the fish via portholes in a walk-through area.

Many of the above-mentioned attractions require guests to be at least 4 feet tall. But the **Ketchakiddie Creek** section of the park is a kiddie area exclusively for those under 4 feet. An innovative water playground, it has bubbling fountains to frolic in, small water slides, a pint-sized white-water tubing adventure, spouting whales and squirting seals, rubbery crocodiles to climb on, grottoes to explore, and waterfalls to loll under.

✪ BLIZZARD BEACH

Blizzard Beach is Disney's newest, and zaniest, water park—a 66-acre "ski resort" in the midst of a tropical lagoon. The park centers on a 90-foot snowcapped mountain (Mt. Gushmore), which swimmers ascend via chair lifts, and the on-premises restaurant resembles a ski lodge.

It's located on World Drive, just north of the All-Star Sports and Music resorts. Arrive at or before park opening to avoid long lines and to be sure you get in. Beach towels and lockers are available for a small charge, and you can buy beach accessories at the Beach Haus.

Mt. Gushmore attractions include **Summit Plummet,** which starts 120 feet up and makes a 55-mile-per-hour plunge straight down to a splash landing at the base of the mountain, and the **Slush Gusher,** another Mt. Gushmore speed slide (a bit tamer than the other) that travels along a snowbanked mountain gully. **Teamboat Springs** is the world's longest white-water raft ride, with six-passenger rafts twisting down a 1,200-foot series of rushing waterfalls; and other water slides, flumes, an inner-tube run, and a chair lift complete the fun.

A nice-sized sandy beach below Mt. Gushmore offers **Tike's Peak,** a scaled-down kiddie version of Mt. Gushmore attractions; **Melt-Away-Bay,** a 1-acre free-form wave pool fed by melting-snow waterfalls; **Cross Country Creek,** where inner tubers can float in a lazy circle around the entire park; and **Ski Patrol Training Camp,** which is designed for preteens and features a rope swing, a T-bar drop over water, slides, and a challenging ice-floe walk along slippery floating icebergs.

RIVER COUNTRY

One of the many recreational facilities at the Fort Wilderness Resort campground, this miniature water park is themed after Tom Sawyer's swimming hole. Kids can scramble over artificial boulders that double as diving platforms over a 330,000-gallon clear-water pool. Two 16-foot water slides also provide access to the pool. Attractions on the adjacent Bay Lake, which is equipped with ropes and ships' booms for climbing, include a pair of flumes—one 260 feet long, the other 100 feet—that corkscrew through **Whoop-N-Holler Hollow; White Water Rapids,** which carries inner tubers along a winding 230-foot creek with a series of chutes and pools; and the **Ol' Wading Pool,** a smaller version of the swimming hole designed for young children. There are poolside and beachside areas for sunning and picnicking, plus a 350-yard boardwalk nature trail. Beach towels and lockers can be obtained for a minimal fee. Light fare is available at Pop's Place.

To get here, take a launch from the dock near the entrance to the Magic Kingdom or a bus from its Transportation and Ticket Center.

FANTASIA GARDENS

In an ever-growing effort to remove all reasons to leave Disney property, 1996 saw the addition of two 18-hole miniature golf courses based on the characters of the classic Disney animated film *Fantasia*. Hippos dance, broomsticks leap, and magic abounds, but it's still up to you to sink that hole in one. A second 36-hole course with a Winter Wonderland theme opened in 1999.

11 Universal Studios Escape

Universal Studios Escape has been busy expanding to better its position in the battle with Walt Disney World for tourist dollars. It now consists of the original Universal Studios Florida park; its new high-tech theme park, Islands of Adventure; the nighttime entertainment district, CityWalk (see "Dining," earlier in this chapter); and the Portofino Bay Hotel. Another four hotels will be added to the Universal empire over the next few years.

✪ UNIVERSAL STUDIOS FLORIDA

Universal Studios Florida, 1000 Universal Studios Plaza (☎ **407/363-8000;** www.usf.com), combines shorter lines and more thrill rides to make it my favorite park in town. (Sorry, Mickey.) And even with the fast-paced, grown-up rides such as Twister, Terminator, and Back to the Future, there is still plenty for the kids.

Universal bills itself as the "No. 1 Movie Studio and Theme Park in the World." It is a working motion-picture and television production studio, although most of the production goes on inside at the Nickelodeon sound stages. But remember cable's *The Swamp Thing* or the short-lived *SeaQuest*? Those television series were shot on the property. Occasionally, visitors will come upon an actual working shoot. But every day you will amble amid reel history in the form of some 40 actual sets displayed along "Hollywood Boulevard" and "Rodeo Drive." On hand to greet visitors are Hanna-Barbera characters (Yogi Bear, Scooby Doo, Fred Flintstone, and others) and a talented group of actors representing Universal stars from Harpo Marx to the Blues Brothers.

PRICES   A **1-day ticket** costs $44 for ages 10 and over, $36 for children 3 to 9; a **2-day pass** is $84.75 for ages 10 and over, $68.85 for children 3 to 9. The multiday tickets allow you to park hop between Universal Studios Florida and Islands of Adventure.

A **Flex Pass,** provides multiple-day admission to Universal Studios Florida, Islands of Adventure, Sea World, and Wet 'n' Wild. A 7-day pass costs $170 for ages 10 to adult or $135.65 for children under 10. A 10-day, five-park pass, which also includes **Busch Gardens** in Tampa sells for $209 for adults and $168 for children 3–9. (Children under 2 are free.) The Flex Pass can be ordered through Universal at ☎ **407/363-8000,** Sea World at ☎ **407/351-3600,** or Wet 'n' Wild at ☎ **800/ 992-WILD** or 407/351-WILD.

There is also a **VIP tour** available at Universal Studios Florida, which includes line-cutting privileges, for about $120 per person. This pass provides a 5-hour guided tour with quick entrance and preferred seating at seven Universal attractions.

If you are planning to visit Orlando more than once this year, consider an annual pass, which costs $191 for adults and $164.25 for children 3–9.

The park is open 365 days a year from 9am to 7pm; closing hours vary seasonally however, so call before you go. Universal is about half a mile north of I-4 exit 30B, Kirkman Road or Route 435. There may be construction in the area, so keep an eye out for the road signs directing you to Universal Studios. Be aware that it is a very long walk from the parking lot to the entrance gates, so strollers are a must for small children.

MAJOR ATTRACTIONS

Rides and attractions use cutting-edge technology, such as OMNIMAX 70mm film projected on seven-story screens, to create terrific special effects. While waiting in line, you'll be entertained by excellent preshows, better even than those at *that other theme park*. Universal, as a whole, takes itself less seriously than the Mouse That Roared, and the atmosphere is peppered by subtle reminders that in the competitive 1990s it is *not* a small world after all.

A DAY IN THE PARK WITH BARNEY Set in a parklike theater-in-the-round, this musical show, starring the popular purple one, Baby Bop, and BJ, uses song, dance, and interactive play to deliver an environmental message. For young children, this could be the highlight of the day. The adjacent play area has an enjoyable array of interactive activities—a good place to wait for the show to start.

TERMINATOR 2: 3-D BATTLE ACROSS TIME He's back, at least in Orlando. This is billed as "the quintessential sight and sound experience for the 21st century!" James Cameron, the director of T2 (and the more recent smash *Titanic*), has overseen this production. It features the Big Man, Ahrrnaald, himself, along with other original cast members, and combines 70mm 3-D film (using three 23-by-50-foot screens) with live stage action and thrilling technical effects.

JAWS You didn't *really* think it was safe to go back into the water, did you? As your boat heads out to the open seas, an ominous dorsal fin appears on the horizon. What follows is a series of terrifying attacks from a 3-ton, 32-foot-long great white shark that tries to sink its teeth into passengers. And there's more trouble ahead. The boat is surrounded by a 30-foot wall of flame from burning fuel that lets you truly feel the heat. I won't tell you how it ends, but let's just say, blackened shark, anyone? (The effects are more startling after dark.)

E.T. ADVENTURE You'll be given a passport to E.T.'s home, which needs his healing powers to rejuvenate it. You'll soar with E.T. on a mission to save his ailing planet, through the forest and into space, aboard a star-bound bicycle, all to the accompaniment of that familiar movie theme music. A cool wooded forest serves as one of the most pleasant waits for any ride in Central Florida, and the ride is worth the wait.

❂ BACK TO THE FUTURE You'll blast through the space-time continuum, plummet into volcanic tunnels ablaze with molten lava, collide with Ice Age glaciers, thunder through caves and canyons, and be swallowed by a dinosaur in this spectacular multisensory adventure. You twist, you turn, you dip and dive and feel like you are really flying. Stick to seats in the back of the car to avoid ruining the illusion by glimpsing your neighbors careening hydraulically in the next bay.

❂ KONGFRONTATION It's the last thing the Big Apple needs—King Kong is back! As you stand in line in a replica of a grungy, graffiti-scarred New York subway station, CBS newsman Roland Smith reports on Kong's terrifying rampage. Everyone must evacuate to Roosevelt Island, so it's all aboard the tram. Cars collide and hydrants explode below, police helicopters hover overhead putting you directly in the line of fire, the tram malfunctions, and, of course, you encounter Kong—32 feet tall and 13,000 pounds. He emits banana breath in your face and menaces passengers, dangling the tram over the East River. A great thrill, or just another day in New York.

❂ EARTHQUAKE, THE BIG ONE You board a BART train in San Francisco for a peaceful subway ride, but just as you pull into the Embarcadero station there's an earthquake—the big one, 8.3 on the Richter scale! As you sit helplessly trapped, vast slabs of concrete collapse around you, a propane truck bursts into flames, a runaway train comes hurtling at you, and the station floods (60,000 gallons of water cascade down the steps).

TWISTER . . . RIDE IT OUT Visitors from the twister-prone Midwest may find this re-creation a little too close to the real thing. An ominous funnel cloud, five stories

---
Factoid

Although most of the thrill rides have posted warnings for pregnant women and riders with heart, back, or neck problems, there are special areas set aside so even those folks can enjoy at least part of the thrill. Check your park map for specific instructions.

---

tall, is created by 2 million cubic feet of air per minute. And a sound like a freight train fills the theater, as cars, signs, and trucks fly about while the audience watches just 20 feet away. It's the windy version of Earthquake and it packs quite a wallop. Crowds have been known to applaud when it is all over.

NICKELODEON STUDIOS TOUR   You'll tour the soundstages where Nick shows are produced, view concept pilots, visit the kitchen where gak and green slime are made, play typical show games, and try out new Sega video games. There's lots of audience participation, and one volunteer will get slimed.

WILD, WILD, WILD WEST SHOW   Stunt people demonstrate falls from three-story balconies, gun and whip fights, dynamite explosions, and other oater staples. This is a well-performed, lively show that is especially popular with foreign visitors with celluloid visions of the American west. Kids, do not try this at home.

BEETLEJUICE GRAVEYARD REVUE   Dracula, Wolfman, the Phantom of the Opera, Frankenstein and his bride, and Beetlejuice put on a funky, and very funny, rock musical with pyrotechnic special effects and MTV-style choreography. Loud and lively enough to scare some small children.

THE FUNTASTIC WORLD OF HANNA-BARBERA   This motion-simulator ride takes guests careening through the universe in a spaceship piloted by Yogi Bear to rescue Elroy Jetson. Before this wild ride, you'll learn about how cartoons are created. After it, in an interactive area, you can experiment with animation sound effects—boing! plop! splash!—and color in your own cartoons. This is a great place for kids of all ages to take some time and play.

ADDITIONAL ATTRACTIONS

Other park attractions include the **Gory, Gruesome & Grotesque Horror Makeup Show** for a behind-the-scenes look at the transformation scenes from movies like *The Fly* and *The Exorcist;* **a tribute to Lucille Ball,** America's queen of comedy; **Fievel's Playland,** an innovative Western-themed playground based on the Spielberg movie *An American Tail;* **Woody Woodpecker's Kid Zone,** a wonderful children's play area that features a kid-sized roller coaster; **Hercules & Xena, Wizards of The Screen,** which puts you on the set with the buff gladiators as the audience battles to make the sound effects match the videos; and **Alfred Hitchcock's 3-D Theatre,** a tribute to the master of suspense in which Tony Perkins narrates a reenactment of the famous shower scene from *Psycho,* and *The Birds,* as if it weren't scary enough, becomes an in-your-face 3-D movie.

Descendants of Lassie, Benji, Mr. Ed, and other animal superstars perform their famous pet tricks in the **Animal Actors Show.** And **Dynamite Nights Stuntacular,** a nightly show, combines death-defying stunts with a breathtaking display of fireworks.

More than 25 shops in the park sell everything from Lucy collectibles to Bates Motel towels, and restaurants run the gamut from Mel's Drive-In (of *American Graffiti* fame) to Schwab's.

ISLANDS OF ADVENTURE

Universal's second park opened in 1999 with a vibrantly colored, cleverly themed collection of fast, fun rides aimed mostly at teenagers and adults. At 110-acres, it is the same size as the original park, but clever planning makes it seem packed with even more to do. Roller coasters roar above pedestrian walkways, water rides careen through the center of the park, and themed eateries are camouflaged to match their surroundings, adding to your overall immersion in the various "islands."

Islands of Adventure is divided into six areas, the **Port of Entry,** where you will find a collection of shops and eateries, and the themed sections **Seuss Landing, Toon Lagoon, Jurassic Park, Marvel Super Hero Island** and **The Lost Continent.** This park offers the biggest concentration of thrill rides and coasters of any park in the area, plus it has some play areas for the kids. The trade-off is fewer shows and stage productions.

PARKING   If you park in the multilevel garage, remember the theme and music on your floor to help you later identify your car. Or, do it the old-fashioned way: Write it down. Parking costs $6 for cars, $7 for RVs and trailers. Valet parking is available for $12. Be aware that it is a very long walk from the parking lot to the entrance gates, so strollers are a must for small children.

PLANNING YOUR VISIT   Get information before you leave by calling **Guest Relations** (☎ 407/363-8000). Request information about the new travel packages, as well as theme-park information. With the opening of Islands of Adventure and the Portofino Bay resort, there should continue to be good deals, especially for packages that include hotel stays.

You can also write Universal Studios Islands of Adventure, 1000 Universal Studios Plaza, Orlando, FL 32819-7610.

Information about Islands of Adventure can be found at **www.uescape.com**. Orlando's daily newspaper, the *Orlando Sentinel,* also produces *Orlando Sentinel Online* at **www.orlandosentinel.com**. Once there, click on Theme Park Central for a variety of information and for updates on what is going on at local attractions.

If you subscribe to AOL, type the keyword **Go2Orlando** to access a site with a lot of updated information about Universal and other theme parks.

TICKET PRICES   A **1-day ticket** costs $42 for ages 10 and over, $34 for children 3 to 9; a **2-day pass** is $79.95 for ages 10 and over, $64.95 for children 3 to 9; children 2 and under enter free. For more information on passes, see Universal Studios Florida above.

A **VIP TOUR** similar to the one offered at Universal Studios was being considered at press time. The Universal Escape Tour is a 5-hour guided tour providing line-cutting privileges, for about $120 per person. Call the main number (☎ 407/363-8000) for information.

HOURS   The park is open from 9am to 7pm, 365 days a year, and later during summer and holidays, when there are additional shows at night. Call before you go.

PORT OF ENTRY

Here you'll find six shops, four restaurants and the **Island Skipper Tours,** which ferry passengers between the front of the park and **Jurassic Park.** If you plan to save shopping for the end of the day, go to **Universal Studios Islands of Adventure Trading Company,** which offers a variety of merchandise linked to attractions throughout the park, everything from Jurassic T-shirts to stuffed Cat in the Hat dolls.

SEUSS LANDING

Here those wonderful Dr. Seuss characters come to life. Needless to say, the main attractions here are aimed at the younger set, though anyone who loved the good Doctor as a child will enjoy some nostalgic fun on these rides.

CAT IN THE HAT   Six-passenger couches travel through 18 show scenes past Thing 1 and Thing 2. The highlight is a revolving 24-foot tunnel that alters your perceptions and leaves your head spinning.

ONE FISH, TWO FISH, RED FISH, BLUE FISH   The point here is to avoid getting sprayed as you guide your fish through the ride, taking directions from a Seussian rhyme. Of course, if the kids are driving, bring a raincoat. Special adaptations are available for guests with disabilities to enjoy the fire from their chair. There are also special "squirt posts" which will spray unsuspecting riders who don't follow along with a special rhyme—so pay attention.

CARO-SEUSS-EL   Go in and out, up and down on one of seven characters from the world of Seuss, including the elephant-birds from *Horton Hatches an Egg.*

IF I RAN THE ZOO   An interactive playland for kids of all ages, this includes everything from flying water snakes to a chance to tickle the toes of a Seussian animal. A nice place to let the kids burn off some excited energy.

MARVEL SUPER-HERO ISLAND

Thrill junkies will love the twisting, turning, and stomach-churning rides, based on characters from Marvel comics, in this land filled with building-high murals of your favorite super heroes lining the street.

THE SPIDER-MAN ADVENTURE   Combines moving rides with 3-D action and special effects, taking guests on a tour of the *Daily Bugle,* where Peter Parker suddenly encounters evil villains and becomes Spider-Man. The high-tech ride, similar to Back to the Future, includes a simulated 400-foot drop that feels an awful lot like the real thing. This one's the best attraction in the park!

INCREDIBLE HULK COASTER   Blasting from zero to 40 m.p.h. in 2 seconds, you'll spin upside down 100 feet from the ground. Coaster lovers love this 2-minute, 15-second ride that includes seven roll-overs and two deep drops. As a nice touch, the metal roller coaster glows green at night.

DR. DOOM'S FEARFALL   You are in for a rush as you drop, with feet dangling, down one of two 200-foot steel towers. It's similar to Tower of Terror at Disney, but with the added thrill of hanging free.

TOON LAGOON

More than 150 life-sized sculpted cartoon images let you know you have entered this section dedicated to your favorites from the Sunday funnies.

DUDLEY DO-RIGHT'S RIPSAW FALLS   This water ride, touted as the first flume ride to send riders plummeting below the water's surface, takes you around a 400,000-gallon lagoon, culminating in a 75-foot drop at 50 m.p.h. Once again you will get wet. Very wet.

POPEYE & BLUTO'S BILGE RAT BARGES   Whirling 12-person rafts bump and churn their way through a white-water ride, encountering some scary creatures along the way, including the twirling octopus boat wash. *Note:* You will get very wet—or completely soaked.

ME SHIP, THE OLIVE   This three-story boat is a family-friendly playland with dozens of activities from bow to stern. Kids can toot whistles, clang bells, or play the organ.

COMIC STRIP LANE   Beetle Bailey, Hagar the Horrible, and Dagwood and Blondie are highlighted in this lively jaunt through some of the best-loved comic strips of all time.

JURASSIC PARK

Okay, stay with me here. This is the theme-park creation based on a movie featuring a theme-park creation that might become a movie. Yes, all the basics from Stephen Spielberg's wildly successful movies, and some of the high-tech wizardry, are incorporated in a lushly landscaped tropical locale.

JURASSIC PARK RIVER ADVENTURE   Come face-to-face with the living, breathing inhabitants of Jurassic Park. Five-story dinosaurs come within inches of the ride, where Tyrannosaurus Rex decides you look like a tasty morsel. To escape, you take an 85-foot plunge straight down the longest, fastest, steepest water descent ever built. Here's another chance to get waterlogged.

TRICERATOPS ENCOUNTER   Pet a "living" dinosaur and learn from the trainers about the care and feeding of the 24-foot-long, 10-foot-high triceratops. The creature's responses to touch include realistic blinks and muscle flinches.

DISCOVERY CENTER   Within the celebrated gates of Jurassic Park's Visitors Center, guests will find a variety of entertaining and educational opportunities. Mostly a good place to play in the air-conditioning, with a lot of stuff kids of all ages can touch and enjoy.

PTERANODON FLYERS   Get a bird's-eye view of the Jurassic Park compound while soaring on the backs of these gentle flying dinosaurs. It's a nice trip, but the long lines here aren't justified; skip it if it looks like you'll be waiting awhile.

CAMP JURASSIC   This interactive play area offers everything from lava pits with undiscovered dinosaur bones to a rain forest. Watch out for the dangerous spitters.

LOST CONTINENT

Although they've mixed their millennia here—ancient Greek gods with medieval forests—Universal has done a great job creating a foreboding mood in this section of the park.

POSEIDON'S FURY: ESCAPE FROM THE LOST CITY   Similar to the Earthquake attraction in the other Universal park, this ride exposes you to torrents of waters and blasts of heat and fire. The idea is that parkgoers are trapped in the midst of a battle between Poseidon and Zeus for divine supremacy. The highlight of the attraction is a 42-foot vortex of rushing water that guests must walk through. It's more interesting than frightening, but it still offers a thrill.

DUELING DRAGONS   This coaster ride holds you suspended with your legs dangling freely beneath you, like you're sitting on a jet-propelled swing. Be warned—it's not for the faint of heart. The intertwined tracks add an extra element of excitement as you zip through at 60 m.p.h. At times, riders of the dueling coasters are just 12 inches apart. I recommend the very first seat for a truly thrilling ride.

THE 8TH VOYAGE OF SINBAD   This stunt extravaganza explores the next voyage of the mythical traveler and relies heavily on pyrotechnics for its thrill factor.

It's a hot show—especially if you are in the first few rows. It may be too intense for younger children.

SHOPPING AT ISLANDS OF ADVENTURE

There are more than 20 shops within the park offering a variety of unusual themed merchandise. You may want to check out **Cats, Hats & Things** and **Dr. Seuss' All The Books You Can Read** for special Seussian material. The **Jurassic Outfitters Dinostore** offers an array of stuffed and plastic dinos plus safari-themed clothing. Super-hero fans should check out **The Marvel Alterniverse Store.**

12 Sea World

This popular 200-plus-acre marine-life park, at 7007 Sea World Dr. (☎ 407/351-3600; www.seaworld.com), explores the mysteries of the deep in a format that combines entertainment with wildlife-conservation awareness. Bell-bottoms and Marcia Brady prints may be the current rage in fashion, but Sea World of Florida certainly made the right decision in updating its dated 1970s look.

A 55-foot lighthouse topped with a rotating white light in the middle of a harbor decorated with a painting of Shamu anchors the nautically themed renovation. To get to the beacon, visitors will walk underneath a sea of blue and aquamarine "metal waves" and cross wooden bridges nestled amid a rocky shore complete with lapping water and splashing waves.

This is a beautifully landscaped park, centering on a 17-acre lagoon that includes flamingo and pelican ponds and a lush tropical rain forest. Shamu, a killer whale, is the star of the park, along with his expanding family, including several baby whales. The pace is much more laid-back than either Universal or Disney and is a good way to end a long week of trudging through the other parks. Be sure to budget some extra money to buy smelt to feed the animals—the close encounters offered at many wading and feeding pools are more than half the fun. Sea World can't compete with the high-tech wonders abounding elsewhere, but where else can you discover that a stingray feels like crushed velvet or learn the song of a seal?

TICKET PRICES A **1-day ticket** costs $44 for ages 10 and over, $35 for children 3 to 9. Sea World usually offers a second day free during the off season. See Universal Studios Florida above for details on getting a **Flex Pass.**

HOURS The park is open from 9am to 7pm, 365 days a year, and later during summer and holidays when there are additional shows at night. Call ☎ 800/351-3600 before you go.

MAJOR ATTRACTIONS

✪ **WILD ARCTIC** Enveloping guests in the beauty, exhilaration, and danger of a polar expedition, Wild Arctic combines a high-definition adventure film with flight-simulator technology to evoke breathtaking Arctic panoramas. After a hazardous flight over the frozen north, visitors emerge at a remote research base—home to four polar bears (including star residents and polar twins Klondike and Snow), seals, walruses, and white beluga whales.

✪ **JOURNEY TO ATLANTIS** This is the park's first true thrill ride. Taking a cue from Disney Imagineerers, Sea World has created a story line to go with the ride—something about Greek fishermen and ancient Sirens in a battle over good and evil. (A "media horde" is somehow involved.) But what really matters is the promise of "two of the steepest, wettest, fastest drops to be found in any theme park."

What's New with Shamu?

Discovery Cove, Sea World's second Orlando park, will open in the summer of 2000. About 1,000 guests will be admitted daily to this unique attraction—for a whopping price of $150 per person. The gate price will include an arrival tour, all activities, gear, towels, and a meal. Guests will swim with, snorkel with, and feed, Dolphins and other aquatic life. You can get more information by calling ☎ 877/434-7268 or 800/423-8368, or visit its Web site at **www.discoverycove.com**.

The bottom line is a wild ride down with 60-foot drops and the promise of luge-like curves. Journey to Atlantis breaks from Sea World's "edutainment" formula that seemed to stress equal measures of learning and fun. No hidden lessons here; it's just a splashy thrill.

TERRORS OF THE DEEP   This exhibit houses 220 specimens of venomous and otherwise scary sea creatures in a tropical-reef habitat. Immense acrylic tunnels provide close encounters with slithery eels, three dozen sharks, barracudas, lionfish, and poisonous pufferfish. A theatrical presentation focusing on sharks puts across the message that pollution and uncontrolled commercial fishing make humankind the ultimate "terror of the deep."

✪ MANATEES: THE LAST GENERATION?   Today the Florida manatee is in danger of extinction, with as few as 2,000 remaining. Underwater viewing stations, innovative cinema techniques, and interactive displays combine to create an exciting format for teaching visitors about the manatee and its fragile ecosystem. Also on display here are hundreds of other native fish, as well as alligators, turtles, and shorebirds.

✪ KEY WEST AT SEA WORLD   It's not quite the way Ernest Hemingway saw it, but this 5-acre paved paradise dotted with palms, hibiscus, and bougainvillea is set in a Caribbean village offering island cuisine, street vendors, and entertainers. The attraction comprises three naturalistic animal habitats: Stingray Lagoon, where visitors enjoy hands-on encounters with harmless southern diamond and cownose rays; Dolphin Cove, a massive habitat for bottlenose dolphins set up for visitor interaction; and Sea Turtle Point, home to threatened and endangered species such as green, loggerhead, and hawksbill sea turtles. Shortly after opening, dolphins showed their intelligence by realizing how easy humans are to tease. They'd routinely swim just out of arms' reach but discovered that there are advantages to coming in a little closer—namely, smelt. The underwater viewing area—where you can watch the dolphins swim and play—is a real treat.

KEY WEST DOLPHIN FEST   At the Whale and Dolphin Stadium, a partially covered stadium, whales and Atlantic bottlenose dolphins perform flips and high jumps, swim at high speeds, twirl, swim on their backs, and give rides to trainers—all to the accompaniment of calypso music. The tricks are impressive, but go before the show-stopping behemoth, Shamu, puts these little mammals to shame.

THE SHAMU ADVENTURE   Sea World trainers develop close relationships with killer whales, and in this partly covered open-air stadium, they direct performances that are extensions of natural cetacean behaviors—twirling, waving tails and fins, rotating while swimming, and splashing the audience. Splash zones are clearly marked; sit in the upper tiers if you don't want to get soaked. The evening show here, called "Shamu: Rocks America," uses rock music and special lighting effects. There is no reason to attend both shows, unless you really like whales. The tricks are much the same. I'd opt for the evening show, taking advantage of shorter lines as others flock to the stadium in the afternoon. If you do decide on the afternoon show, arrive at least 30 minutes early. The stadium does fill up.

Shamu: Close Up!, an adjoining exhibit, lets you get close up to killer whales and talk to trainers; don't miss the underwater viewing area here and a chance to see a mother whale with her offspring. Talk about a big baby!

✪ **PENGUIN ENCOUNTER** This display of hundreds of penguins and alcids (including adorable babies) native to the Antarctic and Arctic regions also serves as a living laboratory for protecting and preserving polar life. On a moving walkway, you'll view six different penguin species congregating on rocks, nesting, and swimming underwater. There's an additional area for puffins and murres (flying Arctic cousins of penguins).

CLYDE & SEAMORE TAKE PIRATE ISLAND Two sea lions, along with a cast of otters and walruses, appear in this fishy comedy with a conservation theme.

SWIM WITH THE DOLPHINS For a fee, you can also take a **DIP:** Dolphin Interactive Program.

Sea World has expanded this program that allows eight people a chance to frolic with some friends of Flipper. You pay $159 for roughly 20 minutes of hand-to-fin contact. The rest of the time is spent learning about how to interact with the dolphin and wrestling your body in and out of those tricky wet suits. (As you'll quickly learn, there is no graceful way.)

Make your reservations at least 6 weeks in advance. Children under 13 cannot participate but can observe for a fee if they accompany a paid participant (that rule applies to all observers). The cost of a DIP includes admission to the park (annual pass holders pay less). And, interestingly enough, you don't have to be able to swim. For information, call ☎ **407/363-1385.**

OTHER ATTRACTIONS

INTENSITY WATER SKI SHOW High-speed action and athletic grace are on display during this 30-minute waterski show in a covered theater overlooking a man-made lagoon.

CIRQUE DE LA MER This mix of acrobatics, physical comedy, and dance is an interesting, relaxing break during the day. You will marvel at the balance and flexibility of the acrobats and chuckle along with the Harpo-like ring leader of the performance, comic Cesar Aedo.

RED, WHITE & BLUE SPECTACULAR Sea World breaks out the firepower for this closing fireworks show that lights up the sky with pyrotechnic power and lasers—the most, they claim, of any theme-park show.

The park's other attractions include **Pacific Point Preserve,** a 2½-acre naturalistic setting that duplicates the rocky northern Pacific Coast home of California sea lions and harbor and fur seals; **Tropical Reef,** a tide pool of touchables, such as sea anemones, starfish, sea cucumbers, and sea urchins; a 160,000-gallon artificial **coral-reef aquarium,** home to 1,000 brightly hued tropical fish displayed in 17 vignettes of undersea life; and **Shamu's Happy Harbor,** an innovative 3-acre play area that has a four-story net tower with a 35-foot crow's-nest lookout, water cannons, remote-controlled vehicles, and a water maze, one of the most extensive play areas at any park. Bring extra clothes for the tots.

A **Hawaiian dance troupe** entertains in an outdoor facility at Hawaiian Village; if you care to join in, grass skirts and leis are available. You can ascend 400 feet to the top of the **Sea World Sky Tower** for a revolving 360-degree panorama of the park and beyond (there's an extra charge of $3 per person for this activity). And at the 5½-acre

Anheuser-Busch Hospitality Center, you can try free samples of Anheuser-Busch beers and snacks and stroll through the stables to watch the famous Budweiser Clydesdale horses being groomed (Anheuser-Busch owns Sea World). There is a gift shop, as well as special programs, perhaps a seminar on home brewing, offered periodically.

The **Aloha! Polynesian Luau Dinner and Show,** a musical revue featuring South Seas food, song, and fire dancing, takes place nightly at 6:30pm. Park admission is not required. The cost is $35.95 for adults, $25.95 for children 8 to 12, $15.95 for children 3 to 7, and free for children 2 and under. Reservations are required (☎ **800/ 227-8048** or 407/363-2559).

Visitors can take 90-minute behind-the-scenes **tours** of the park's breeding, research, and training facilities and/or attend a 45-minute presentation about Sea World's animal behavior and training techniques. The cost for either tour is $5.95 for ages 10 and over, $4.95 for children 3 to 9, and free for children 2 and under.

13 More Area Attractions

KISSIMMEE

Kissimmee's sights are about a 10- to 15-minute drive from the Walt Disney World area.

✪ **Gatorland.** 14501 S. Orange Blossom Trail (U.S. 441, between Osceola Pkwy. and Hunter's Creek Blvd.). ☎ **407/855-5496.** Admission $17.95 adults, $10.95 children 10–12, $7.95 children 3–9. Free for 1 child 3–9 with each paying adult. Daily 9am–6pm. Free parking.

Founded in 1949 with a handful of alligators living in huts and pens, Gatorland today features thousands of alligators and crocodiles on a 70-acre spread. Breeding pens, nurseries, and rearing ponds are situated throughout the park, which also displays monkeys, snakes, deer, goats, birds, sheep, Florida lake turtles, a Galápagos tortoise, and a bear. A 2,000-foot boardwalk winds through a cypress swamp and a 10-acre breeding marsh with an observation tower. Or you can take the free Gatorland Express Train around the park. Educational shows are scheduled throughout the day. An openair restaurant, a shop, and picnic facilities are on the premises. Plan to spend a couple of hours.

Splendid China. Formosa Gardens Blvd., off W. Irlo Bronson Memorial Hwy. (U.S. 192, between Entry Point Blvd./Sherbeth Rd. and Black Lake Rd.). ☎ **407/396-7111.** Admission $27 adults, $17 children 5–12, free for children 4 and under. Daily from 9:30am; closing hours vary seasonally (call ahead). Free parking.

This 76-acre outdoor attraction features more than 60 miniaturized replicas of China's most noted manufactured and natural wonders, spanning 5,000 years of history and culture. Park highlights include a ½-mile-long copy of the 4,200-mile Great Wall; the Forbidden City's 9,999-room Imperial Palace; Tibet's sacred Potala Palace; the massive Leshan Buddha, carved out of a mountainside between A.D. 713 and A.D. 803; the Stone Forest of Yunan; and the Mongolian mausoleum of Genghis Khan. Live shows (acrobats, martial-arts demonstrations, storytelling, dance, puppetry, and more) take place throughout the day; check your entertainment schedule. There's recorded commentary at each attraction.

INTERNATIONAL DRIVE

Like Kissimmee's attractions, these are about a 10- to 15-minute drive from the Disney area.

Ripley's Believe It or Not! Museum. 8201 International Dr. (1½ blocks south of Sand Lake Rd.). ☎ **407/351-0803.** Admission $10.95 adults, $7.95 children 4–12, free for children 3 and under. Daily 9am–midnight.

It's always fun to peruse a Ripley collection of oddities, curiosities, and fascinating artifacts from faraway places. Among the hundreds of items and mannequins on display here are a 1,069-pound man, a five-legged cow, a mosaic of the Mona Lisa created from 1,426 pieces of toast, torture devices from the Spanish Inquisition, a Tibetan flute made from human bones, a shrunken head, and Ubangi women with wooden plates in their lips. A baby boom among workers in 1995 was attributed to a fertility idol displayed at the museum, and it increased traffic from other women hoping for similar luck. Your visit shouldn't take more than an hour.

Wet 'n Wild. 6200 International Dr. (at Republic Dr.). ☎ **800/992-WILD** or 407/351-WILD. Admission $26.95 adults, $21.95 children 3–9, free for children 2 and under. Ages 55 and older, $13.50. Open daily; hours vary seasonally (call before you go). Parking, cars $5; RVs $7. Take I-4 east to Exit 30A and follow the signs.

When temperatures soar, head for this 25-acre water park and cool off by jumping waves, careening down steep flumes, and running rapids. Among the highlights: **Fuji Flyer** (a six-story toboggan ride along 450 feet of banked curves); **The Surge** (one of the longest, fastest multipassenger tube rides in the Southeast); **Bomb Bay** (enter a bomblike casing 76 feet in the air for a speedy vertical flight straight down to a target pool); **Black Hole** (step into a spaceship and board a two-person raft for a 30-second, 500-foot, twisting, turning reentry through total darkness, propelled by a 1,000-gallon-a-minute blast of water!); **Raging Rapids,** a simulated white-water tubing adventure with a waterfall plunge; and **Lazy River,** a leisurely float trip. There are additional flumes, a vast wave pool, a large and innovative children's water playground, a sunbathing area, and a picnic area. The newest attraction is the **Hydra Fighter,** which allows you to control—somewhat—your movement with a giant water hose.

Food concessions are located throughout the park, lockers and towels can be rented, and you can purchase beach accessories at the gift shop. It's easy to spend the whole day here, so remember your sunscreen.

ELSEWHERE IN ORLANDO

All the following Orlando attractions are in close proximity to one another, making for a pleasant day's excursion. Loch Haven Park is about 35 minutes by car from the Disney area. You can probably also incorporate some Winter Park sights into the same day.

✪ Orlando Science Center. 777 E. Princeton St. (between Orange and Mills aves.), in Loch Haven Park. ☎ **407/896-7151.** Basic admission $9.50 adults, $6.75 children 3–11, free for children 2 and under. Additional charges for CineDome movies and planetarium shows. Mon–Thurs 9am–5pm, Fri–Sat 9am–9pm, Sun noon–5pm. Closed Thanksgiving and Christmas. Take I-4 east to Exit 43 (Princeton St.). It is the building with the large, shiny silver dome.

A $44 million expansion completed in 1997 made the Orlando Science Center the largest center of its kind in the southeastern United States. The exhibits are state of the art and geared toward encouraging kids to have fun while learning. This is the kind of museum where kids are encouraged to touch. The CineDome projects images onto an eight-story domed screen with a powerful audio system generating more than 28,000 watts of sound. Families can easily spend half a day touring the 10 exhibit halls.

✪ Harry P. Leu Gardens. 1920 N. Forest Ave. (between Nebraska St. and Corrine Dr.). ☎ **407/246-2620.** Admission $4 adults, $1 children K–12, free for children 5 and under. Gardens daily 9am–5pm; Leu House tours daily 10am–3:30pm. Closed Christmas. Take I-4 east to Exit 43 (Princeton St.), follow Princeton St. east, make a right on Mills Ave., turn left on Virginia Dr., and look for the gardens on your left.

At this delightful 50-acre botanical garden on the shores of Lake Rowena, meandering paths lead through forests of giant camphors, moss-draped oaks, palms, cycads, and camellias. Exquisite formal rose gardens display 75 varieties. Free 20-minute tours of the Leu House, built in 1888, take place on the hour and half hour. The house is a veritable decorative-arts museum filled with Victorian, Empire, and Chippendale pieces. It takes about 2 hours to see the house and gardens.

Orlando Museum of Art. 2416 N. Mills Ave. (off U.S. 17/92), in Loch Haven Park. ☎ **407/896-4231.** www.omart.com. Admission $4 adults, $2 children 4–11, free for children 3 and under. Closed Monday. Museum Tues–Sat 9am–5pm, Sun noon–5pm; Closed New Year's Day, Memorial Day, July 4, Labor Day, Thanksgiving, and Christmas. Free parking. Take I-4 east to Exit 43 (Princeton St.) and follow the signs to Loch Haven Park.

Having undergone a multimillion-dollar expansion, the museum displays its permanent collection of 19th- and 20th-century American art, pre-Colombian art, and African art on a rotating basis. These holdings are augmented by long-term loans focusing on Mayan archaeology and arts of the African sub-Saharan region.

IN NEARBY WINTER HAVEN

✪ **Cypress Gardens.** On Fla. 540 at Cypress Gardens Blvd. (40 miles southwest of Walt Disney World), Winter Haven. ☎ **800/282-2123** or 941/324-2111. Admission $31.95 adults, $26.50 seniors, $14.95 children 6–17; free for children 6 and under. Daily 9:30am–5:30pm, with extended hours during peak seasons. Take I-4 West to U.S. 27 south, and proceed west to S.R. 540. Free parking.

Founded in 1936, Cypress Gardens came into being as a 16-acre public garden along the banks of Lake Eloise, with cypress-wood-block pathways and thousands of tropical and subtropical plants. Today it has grown to more than 200 acres, with ponds and lagoons, waterfalls, classic Italian fountains, topiary, bronze sculptures, manicured lawns, and ancient cypress trees shrouded in Spanish moss. All this forms a backdrop to ever-changing floral displays of 8,000 varieties of plants from more than 90 countries.

Strolling the grounds is, of course, the main attraction, but this being Central Florida, it's not the only one. Several shows are scheduled throughout the day (check your schedule upon entering the park). The world-famous **Greatest American Ski Team** performs on Lake Eloise in a show augmented by an awesome hang-gliding display. The breathtaking **ice-skating show** is the Russian answer to America's Ice Capades. **Variètè Internationale** features specialty acts from all over the world. An enchanting exhibit called **Wings of Wonder** surrounds visitors with more than 1,000 brightly colored free-flying butterflies in a 5,500-square-foot Victorian-style glass conservatory. **Electric boats** navigate a maze of lushly landscaped canals in the original botanical gardens area. You can ascend 153 feet to the **Island in the Sky** for a panoramic vista of the gardens and a beautiful chain of Central Florida lakes. **Carousel Cove,** with eight kiddie rides and arcade games, centers on an ornate turn-of-the-century-style carousel. It adjoins another kid pleaser, **Cypress Junction,** an elaborately landscaped model railroad that travels over 1,100 feet of track with up to 20 trains moving at one time. You'll find both restaurants and a picnic area on the premises.

✪ WINTER PARK

This lakeside town is a lovely place to spend an afternoon. Visit the Morse Museum, cruise the lakes, and browse in the posh boutiques that line Park Avenue.

To get to Winter Park from Orlando (about a 5-mi. drive), continue east on I-4 to Fairbanks Avenue (Exit 45), turn right, and proceed about a mile, making a left on Park Avenue.

○ **Charles Hosmer Morse Museum of American Art**. 445 Park Ave. (between Canton and Cole aves.). ☎ **407/645-5311.** Admission $3 adults, $1 students of any age. Tues–Sat 9:30am–4pm, Sun 1–4pm. Closed New Year's Day, Memorial Day, Labor Day, Thanksgiving, and Christmas.

This gem of a museum was founded by Hugh and Jeannette McKean in 1942 to display their art collection, which includes 40 magnificent, vibrant colored windows and 21 paintings by Louis Comfort Tiffany. In addition, there are non-Tiffany windows ranging from creations by Frank Lloyd Wright to 15th- and 16th-century German masters; leaded lamps by Tiffany and Emile Gallè; paintings by John Singer Sargent, Maxfield Parrish, and others; jewelry designed by Tiffany, Lalique, and Fabergé; photographic works by Tiffany and other 19th-century artists; and art nouveau furnishings.

Scenic Boat Tour. On the lake at the eastern end of Morse Blvd. ☎ **407/644-4056.** Admission $6 adults, $3 children 2–11, free for children under 2. Weather permitting, tours depart daily, every hour on the hour 10am–4pm. Closed Christmas.

For over half a century, tourists have been boarding pontoons at this location for leisurely hour-long cruises on Winter Park's beautiful chain of natural lakes. The ride traverses area lakes, winding through canals built by loggers at the turn of the century and tree-shaded fern gullies lined with bamboo and lush tropical foliage. You'll view magnificent lakeside mansions, pristine beaches, cypress swamps, and dozens of marsh birds—possibly even an American bald eagle. The captain regales passengers with local lore. It's a delightful, laid-back trip.

14 Outdoor Pursuits & Spectator Sports

OUTDOOR PURSUITS

The **Walt Disney World (WDW) recreational facilities** (☎ 407/939-7529) listed below are all open to the public, no matter where you're staying. Call for further information about WDW recreational facilities.

BICYCLING   Bike rentals (single- and multispeed bikes for adults, tandems, and children's bikes) are available from the **Bike Barn** (☎ 407/824-2742) at Fort Wilderness Resort and Campground. Rates are $5 per hour, $12 per day, $18 overnight. Both Fort Wilderness and Disney's Village Resort offer good bike trails.

BOATING   At the **Walt Disney World Village Marketplace Marina** (☎ 407/828-2204), you can rent Water Sprites, canopy boats, and 20-foot pontoon boats.

The **Bike Barn** at Fort Wilderness (☎ 407/824-2742) also rents canoes and paddleboats ($6 per half hour, $10 per hour). You can cruise the Seven Seas Lagoon on a 44-foot yacht, and you can even have a gourmet dinner and private butler. For information call ☎ 407/824-2439.

FISHING   Fishing excursions on Lake Buena Vista, mainly for largemouth bass, can be arranged up to 14 days in advance by calling ☎ 407/939-7529. No license is required. The fee is $137.50 for up to five people for 2 hours, and rates include gear and guide.

You can also rent cane poles and rods and reels at Disney's Dixie Landing Resort (☎ 407/934-5409) to fish in Fort Wilderness canals. No license is required since all fishing is catch and release.

○ **GOLF**   Like most of Florida, Orlando is a golfer's paradise, with 123 courses within a 45-minute drive of downtown. Courses are designed by Arnold Palmer, Jack Nicklaus, Tom Fazio, Pete Dye, Robert Trent Jones, and other major players.

Factoid _____

Since April of 1999, you must dial the area code and phone number for all numbers within the 407 area code covering Orlando. A rapidly growing population makes this 10-digit dialing necessary, even if you are calling somewhere just down the block.

Consider calling **Golfpac** (☎ **800/327-0878** or 407/260-2288), an organization that packages golf vacations (with accommodations and other features) and pre-arranges tee times at more than 40 Orlando-area courses. The further in advance you call (I'm talking months here), the better your options.

The most famous local courses include the legendary ✪ **Arnold Palmer's Bay Hill Club,** 9000 Bay Hill Blvd. (☎ **800/523-5999** or 407/876-2429), site of the Bay Hill Invitational. Its 18th hole, nicknamed the Devil's Bathtub, is supposed to be the toughest par-4 on the tour.

✪ **Walt Disney World Resorts** (☎ **407/939-4653**) offer 99 holes of golf; they operate five championship 18-hole, par-72 golf courses and one 9-hole, par-36 walking course. All are open to the general public and offer pro shops, equipment rentals, and instruction. For tee times and information, call up to 60 days in advance (up to 30 days for Disney resort and "official hotel" guests). The most famous hazard is a sand trap on the Magnolia Course's sixth hole in the shape of Mickey Mouse. Call ☎ **407/W-DISNEY** (934-7639) for information about golf packages.

Also notable are two beautifully landscaped facilities: the award-winning 45-hole, par-72 Jack Nicklaus–designed course at the **Villas of Grand Cypress** (☎ **800/835-7377** or 407/239-4700) and the 18-hole, par-71 Joe Lee–designed championship course at the **Marriott Orlando World Center** (☎ **800/621-0638** or 407/239-4200).

The **Falcon's Fire Golf Club,** 3200 Seralago Blvd., in Kissimmee (☎ **407/239-5445**), a challenging Ree Jones course, has 136 bunkers and water on 10 holes.

South of Kissimmee, in Haines City, is the **Grenelefe Golf & Tennis Resort** (☎ **800/237-9549** or 941/422-7511), with three championship courses. It's the home of the Wally Armstrong Golf School, and it annually hosts U.S. Seniors Open and U.S. Women's Open qualifiers.

HAYRIDES The hay wagon departs from Pioneer Hall at Fort Wilderness nightly at 7 and 9:30pm for hour-long old-fashioned hayrides with singing, jokes, and games. The cost is $6 for adults, $4 for children 3 to 10, free for children 2 and under; children under 12 must be accompanied by an adult. No reservations—it's first-come, first-served.

HORSEBACK RIDING Disney's Fort Wilderness Resort and Campground offers 45-minute scenic guided-tour **trail rides** (☎ **407/939-7529**) daily, with four to six rides per day. The cost is $17 per person. Children must be at least 9 years old and the maximum weight is 250 pounds. Call for information and reservations up to 5 days in advance.

TENNIS There are 23 clay courts and 9 hard courts all lit for night play. Clinics, and private and group lessons, are available. For information call ☎ **407/939-7529.**

SPECTATOR SPORTS

Disney's Wide World of Sports, at Walt Disney World (☎ **407/363-6600**), is a massive complex offering everything from basketball to gymnastics and soccer. It's also the spring-training site of the Atlanta Braves and the training site for the Harlem Globe-trotters. Ticket prices vary.

The Orlando Centroplex administers six public sports and entertainment facilities in the downtown area. These include three major sporting arenas: the Florida Citrus Bowl, the Orlando Arena, and Tinker Field.

The **Florida Citrus Bowl,** 1 Citrus Bowl Place, at West Church and Tampa streets (☎ 407/896-2442 for information, or 407/839-3900 to charge tickets), seats 70,000 people for major sporting events including the annual CompUSA Florida Citrus Bowl game, college football games, and NFL preseason games. Parking is $5. Take I-4 east to the East-West Expressway and head west to U.S. 441, make a left on Church Street, and follow the signs.

The **Orlando Magic** play at the **Orlando Arena,** 600 W. Amelia St., between I-4 and Parramore Avenue (☎ **407/849-2020** for information, or **407/839-3900** to charge tickets). Tickets to Magic games (about $13 to $50) usually have to be acquired far in advance. Generally about 1,000 tickets are available for sale before each game. Single tickets are often available when the Magic goes against low-profile NBA competition, such as the Timberwolves. Parking at the arena costs $5 (for up-to-the-minute parking information, tune your car radio to 1620 AM). Take I-4 east to Amelia Avenue, turn left at the traffic light at the bottom of the off-ramp, and follow the signs. Call to find out about other sporting events when you're in town. Orlando is also home to several other professional teams, including the **Predators,** an arena football team, and the **Solar Bears,** an ice-hockey team.

The **WNBA** team, the **Orlando Miracle,** began playing during the 1999 season. For ticket information call ☎ **407/916-9622.**

Spring training for the **Houston Astros** begins in late February, with exhibition games through March or early April at the **Osceola County Stadium,** 1000 Bill Beck Blvd., in Kissimmee (☎ **407/933-2520**). Tickets are $6, $8, and $10. Call for details and tickets.

Also, the **Atlanta Braves** have been holding Spring Training at Disney's Wide World of Sports Complex since 1998, and play is assured there through at least 2001. There are about 18 games during the 1-month season. Tickets are $10.50 and $15.50. Season tickets run about $250. The season's schedule generally is not announced until mid-December. For general information call ☎ **407/828-3267.** To purchase tickets call Ticketmaster at ☎ **407/839-3900.** You can also get information online at **www.majorleaguebaseball.com/springtraining/atl.sml.**

The Chicago Cubs farm team, the Orlando Rays, also plays at Walt Disney Wide World of Sports. Admission is $3 to $7. Season tickets, for all 70 or so games, range from $199 to $299. For general information call ☎ **407/828-3267.** To purchase tickets call TicketMaster ☎ **407/839-3900.**

The **Bay Hill Invitational,** hosted by Arnold Palmer and featuring some Orlando-based golfers like Tiger Woods, is a PGA Tour event held in mid-March at the Bay Hill Club, 9000 Bay Hill Blvd. Single-day admission on Tuesday and Wednesday is $28; weeklong tickets are $50 for grounds-only access; $70 for clubhouse access. Call ☎ **407/876-2888** for details.

Top PGA-tour players compete at WDW golf courses in October's major golf event, the **National Car Rental Golf Classic** at Walt Disney World Resort. Many tour professionals make Orlando home, so there is usually plenty of first-rate talent on display. Daily ticket prices range from $10 to $20. For the entire 3-day event tickets run about $35. You may also purchase tickets by writing to Walt Disney World Golf Sales, P.O. Box 10,000, Lake Buena Vista, FL 32830. For 1-day tickets call Ticket-master (☎ **407/839-3900**).

15 Walt Disney World & Orlando After Dark

My hat's off to those of you who, after a long day of traipsing around amusement parks, still have the energy to venture out at night in search of entertainment. That being said, you will find plenty to do. And this being kids' world, many evening shows inside the parks are geared to families. There is adult entertainment at Pleasure Island, at CityWalk, and in downtown Orlando at Church Street Station, as well as the many bars and restaurants that normally cater to locals.

Check the "Calendar" section of Friday's *Orlando Sentinel* for up-to-the-minute details on local clubs, visiting performers, concerts, and events. Also check out the *Orlando Sentinel Online* at **www.orlandosentinel.com**. It has hundreds of listings. The *Orlando Weekly* is a free magazine circulated through boxes in Central Florida and highlighting more offbeat and, often, up-to-date performers and performances. It is also online at **www.orlandoweekly.com**.

If you subscribe to AOL, type the keyword **GO2ORLANDO.** This site has regularly updated information about theme parks, accommodations, and special events. Another resource is **www.insidecentralflorida.com**.

Tickets to many performances are handled by **Ticketmaster** (☎ **407/839-3900** to charge tickets).

DINNER SHOWS
IN WALT DISNEY WORLD

Other nighttime park options include Main Street Electrical Parade, Fantasmic, fireworks, and IllumiNations (see sections 6 to 10 in this chapter for details).

Hoop-Dee-Doo Musical Revue. Disney's Fort Wilderness Resort and Campground, 3520 N. Fort Wilderness Trail. ☎ **407/WDW-DINE** (939-3463). Reservations required. Admission $38 adults, $19.50 children 3–11; taxes and gratuities extra. Show times daily at 5, 7:15, and 9:30pm. Free parking.

Fort Wilderness's rustic log-beamed Pioneer Hall is the setting for this 2-hour down-home musical revue. It's a high-energy show, with 1890s costumes, corny vaudeville jokes, rousing songs, and lots of good-natured audience participation. During the show, you'll chow down on an all-you-can-eat barbecue dinner, including a big slab of strawberry shortcake for dessert. Beverages are included. If you catch an early show, stick around for the Electrical Water Pageant at 9:45pm, which can be viewed from the Fort Wilderness Beach.

Polynesian Luau Dinner Show. At Disney's Polynesian Resort, 1600 Seven Seas Dr. ☎ **407/WDW-DINE** (939-3463). Reservations required. Admission $38 adults, $19.50 children 3–11, free for children 2 and under; taxes and gratuities extra. Show times daily at 6:45 and 9:30pm. Free valet and self-parking.

This delightful 2-hour dinner show features a colorfully costumed cast of entertainers from New Zealand, Tahiti, Hawaii, and Samoa performing authentic hula, warrior, ceremonial, love, and fire dances on a flower-bedecked stage. There's even a Hawaiian/Polynesian fashion show. It all takes place in a heated open-air theater (dress for the weather). The meal, served family style, includes a big platter of fresh island fruits, half a barbecued chicken, vegetables, cinnamon bread, beverages, and a tropical ice-cream sundae. There's also a 4:30pm version daily (see Luau Cove listing in "Dining with Disney Characters" in section 4 of this chapter).

IN KISSIMMEE

Medieval Times. 4510 W. Irlo Bronson Memorial Hwy. (between markers 14 and 15 or on U.S. Hwy. 192, 11 miles east of the main Disney entrance, next to Super Wal-Mart),

Kissimmee. ☎ **800/229-8300** or 407/239-0214. Reservations recommended. $37.95 adults, $22.95 children 3–12. AE, DISC, MC, V. Show daily 8pm. Free parking.

Jim Carrey fans know that the *Cable Guy* went to the California branch of Medieval Times to duel with his hapless friend. A long-time favorite for Orlando visitors, the Kissimmee-based show is billed as "dinner and tournament." It lives up to that billing, with jousting contests, armored clashes, and 80 Andalusian stallions that perform with military precision. It's all staged for the 1,000 "special guests" of the castle, who come to the dark, cavernous space to eat off of heavy pewter plates while watching the tournament contestants tumble about before them. The menu includes a wine cocktail, fresh vegetable soup, whole roasted chicken, spareribs, herb basted potato, and dessert. The price includes dinner, beverages, and the show. The castle is air-conditioned and accessible to travelers with disabilities. It's a popular spot, so reservations are suggested.

Wild Bill's Wild West Dinner Extravaganza. 5260 U.S. 192 (just east of I-4). ☎ **800/ 883-8181** or 407/351-5151. Reservations recommended. Admission $36.95 adults, $22.95 children 3–11, under 3 free. Nightly at 7pm, with 9:30pm shows on selected nights. Free parking.

Located at Fort Liberty, a 22-acre western-themed shopping/dining/entertainment complex, this rambunctious dinner show takes place in a big, barnlike wooden building. You'll be given a cardboard cowboy hat when you sit down, which identifies you as a shepherd or cowherd for audience-participation activities (there are a lot of these). The show includes rousing song-and-dance numbers ("Annie Get Your Gun," "Oklahoma," "Back in the Saddle Again"); rodeo roping, knife-throwing, and archery demonstrations; sing-alongs; a cancan; and Comanche ceremonial and war dances. All the children in the audience get to go up on the stage.

Dinner—served on pewterware—is a hearty four-course meal consisting of salad, soup, beef stew, fried chicken, barbecued pork ribs, biscuits with honey butter, corn, beans, a baked potato, and hot apple pie. Beer, wine, and soda are included.

ENTERTAINMENT COMPLEXES: DOWNTOWN DISNEY & CHURCH STREET STATION

Along with Universal Studio Escape's CityWalk (see "Dining" in the beginning of this chapter), Orlando's most popular entertainment districts are **Downtown Disney** (which consists of Pleasure Island, the Disney Village Marketplace, and Disney's West Side) and Church Street Station.

✪ **Pleasure Island.** In Walt Disney World, off Buena Vista Drive, adjacent to Disney Village Marketplace. ☎ **407/934-7781.** Free before 7pm, $19.05 after 7pm (admission included in Park Hopper Passes). Clubs daily 7pm–2am; shops daily 11am–2am. Valet parking $6; free self-parking.

This Walt Disney World nighttime entertainment district is a 6-acre complex of night-clubs, restaurants, and shops; for a single admission price, you can enjoy a night of club-hopping until the wee hours. To enter after 7pm, you must be 18 or older, unless accompanied by a parent or guardian. The complex is designed to suggest an abandoned waterfront industrial district with clubs in "converted" ramshackle lofts, factories, and warehouses, but the streets are festive with brightly colored lights and balloons. You'll be given a map and show schedule when you enter; take a look at it and plan your evening around shows that interest you.

The on-premises clubs come and go. At this writing they include the following: **Pleasure Island Jazz Company** is a big barnlike club featuring contemporary and traditional live jazz. **Mannequins Dance Palace** is a high-energy dance club with a large rotating dance floor and a deejay playing contemporary tunes at an ear-splitting decibel level (you must be 21 to get in).

The most unusual of Pleasure Island's clubs (and my personal favorite) is the **Adventurers Club,** chock-full of artifacts ranging from early aviation photos to shrunken heads. In the eerie Mask Room, more than 100 masks move their eyes, jeer, and make odd pronouncements. Improvisational comedy shows take place throughout the evening in the main salon, and there are diverse 20-minute cabaret shows in the library. You could easily hang out here all night sipping potent tropical drinks in the library and at the bar.

The **Comedy Warehouse,** another of my favorites, has a rustic interior with tiered seating. A very talented troupe performs improvisational comedy based on audience suggestions. There are five shows a night, and bar drinks are available. Arrive early.

Live bands play classic rock at the **Rock & Roll Beach Club.** There are bars on all three floors. The first level contains the dance floor; the second and third levels offer air hockey, pool tables, basketball machines, pinball, video games, darts, and a pizza and beer stand. There's also **8 Trax,** a 1970s-style club with about 50 TV monitors airing shows and videos over the dance floor. A deejay plays disco music, and guests can play Twister.

The **Wildhorse Saloon,** a massive country music club, opened in 1999 and regularly plays host to national acts. The **BET Soundstage** lets you dance to the best in Rhythm and Blues music.

In addition, live bands, including occasional big-name groups, play the **West End Plaza** outdoor stage and the **Hub Stage;** check your schedule for show times. There are carnival games, a video-game arcade, a Velcro wall, and an Orbitron (originally developed for NASA, it lets you experience weightlessness). And every night features a midnight **New Year's Eve celebration** with fireworks and confetti. **Shops and eateries** are found throughout the park (see "Dining," earlier in this chapter).

Disney Village Marketplace. In Walt Disney World, off Buena Vista Dr., adjacent to Pleasure Island. Free admission. Shops daily 9:30am–11pm. Valet parking $6; free self-parking.

At Disney Village Marketplace, you'll find a collection of specialty shops and galleries highlighted by the LEGO Imagination Center. (Check out the life-sized and bigger-than-life LEGO sculptures displayed out front.) There is also the largest Disney gift shop on Earth—**The World of Disney,** which carries everything from Mickey Mouse china to collectible dolls. A lushly tropical **RainForest Cafe** also calls Disney Village Marketplace home and is replete with indoor waterfalls, thunder, lightning, and tropical birds.

Disney's West Side. In Walt Disney World, off Buena Vista Dr., adjacent to Pleasure Island. Free admission. Shops and restaurants open daily 11am–2am. Valet parking $6; free self-parking.

A main attraction here is the 1,500-seat **House of Blues,** a three-story concert hall packed with folk art with an adjoining restaurant specializing in stick-to-your-ribs food. Diverse national acts regularly perform, everything from rappers to blues legends. In addition to a number of specialty shops offering everything from magnets to fine art with a Disney theme, there is a mammoth **Planet Hollywood.** There are also an expanded 24-screen movie complex; **Wolfgang Puck's Cafe,** serving his uniquely California cuisine; and **Bongo's,** a restaurant created by Miami's favorite homegirl, Gloria Estefan, featuring Latin American entertainment and delicious Cuban food.

This is also the home of **DisneyQuest** (see box).

You will also find ✪ **Cirque du Soleil** in Disney's West Side. The international theater company, known for combining acrobatics and avant-garde theatrics, has established its first permanent venue, a 1,671-seat arena, here in Downtown Disney. The troupe's stage production, "La Nouba," is a mixture of high-tech effects and old-fashioned showmanship. It features some 65 performers, mostly gymnasts from Russia, France, and other places around the world. Shows are 5:30 and 8:30pm Wednesday to Saturday, and 2:30 and 5:30pm Sunday. Ticket prices are $56.50 for adults and $45.20 for children 3 to 9. For information call ☎ **407/939-7600.** Although the cost of the Cirque is more than theme park admission, try to make room in your budget for this truly unique, invigorating experience.

✪ **Church Street Station.** 129 W. Church St. (off I-4 between Garland and Orange aves.), in downtown Orlando. ☎ **407/422-2434.** Free before 5pm, $16.95 after 5pm; always free to restaurants, the Exchange Shopping Emporium, and the Midway game area. Clubs daily until 2am; shops daily until 11pm. Valet parking $6 at Church St. and Garland Ave.; several parking lots are nearby (call for specifics). Take I-4 east to Exit 38 (Anderson St.), stay in the left lane, and follow the blue signs. Most hotels offer transportation to and from Church St.

Though not part of Walt Disney World, Church Street Station in downtown Orlando operates on a principle similar to that of Pleasure Island. Occupying a cobblestone city block lined with turn-of-the-century buildings, it too is a shopping/dining/nightclub complex offering an evening of diverse entertainment for a single admission price. There are 20 live shows nightly; consult your show schedule upon entering.

Stunning interiors are the rule here. It's worth coming by just to check out the magnificent woodwork, stained glass, and thousands of authentic antiques. The shopping is pretty good, also.

Highlights include **Rosie O'Grady's Good Time Emporium,** an 1890s antique-filled saloon, where Dixieland bands, banjo players, singing waiters, and cancan dancers entertain nightly. Light fare is available. Adjoining Rosie's, **Apple Annie's Courtyard** evokes a Victorian tropical garden. Patrons sip potent tropical drinks while listening to folk and bluegrass music.

The plush interior of **Lili Marlene's Aviator's Pub & Restaurant** is embellished with World War I memorabilia, stained-glass transoms, and accouterments from an 1850 Rothschild townhouse in Paris. The menu features premium aged steaks, prime rib, and fresh seafood. The whimsical **Phineas Phogg's Balloon Works,** with hot-air balloons and airplanes over the dance floor, is a high-energy club playing loud, pulsating music. Every Wednesday from 6:30 to 7:30pm, beers cost just 5¢ here. No one under 21 is admitted.

The stunning trilevel **Cheyenne Saloon and Opera House** is constructed of golden oak lumber from a century-old Ohio barn. Quality Western art is displayed throughout, including many oil paintings and 11 Remington sculptures. Balcony seating, in restored church pews, overlooks the stage, the setting for entertainment ranging from country bands to clogging exhibitions.

The **Orchid Garden Ballroom,** with ornate, white wrought-iron arches and Victorian lighting fixtures suspended from an elaborate oak-paneled ceiling, is the setting for an oldies dance club. A deejay plays rock-and-roll classics interspersed with live bands. As the evening progresses, so do the musical decades. Brick columns, oak paneling, and a gorgeous antique oak-and-mahogany bar characterize **Crackers Oyster Bar,** a cozy late-1800s–style dining room that features fresh Florida seafood and more than 50 imported beers.

In addition, the 87,000-square-foot Exchange houses the carnival-like **Commander Ragtime's Midway of Fun, Food and Games** (including an enormous

DisneyQuest

"It's like a miracle," said one awestruck, dark-haired tot, craning his neck to take in the wave-shaped blue building with the swirling lavender decorations.

The little tourist could only imagine that the impressive architecture at DisneyQuest was just the beginning. From the Cybrolator—an elevator, to the uninitiated—with an introductory video featuring Robin Williams as Genie to the human pinball machine to the virtual coaster CyberSpace Mountain, the 100,000-square-foot facility, located in Disney's West Side, is unlike anything you've experienced.

Inside you can create and ride your own virtual roller coaster, shoot the rapids without getting wet, or ride Aladdin's Magic Carpet. There is also skee ball, for those of us who remember it, and an Underground Arcade filled with the kind of shoot-'em-up games loved by boys of all ages. Older children may enjoy the Sports Arena Arcade, which has computerized games where you ski, drive a race car, or ride a motorcycle. Parents may enjoy a bit of nostalgia with "ancient" video games like Centipede and Space Invaders.

Although DisneyQuest is open from 10:30am until midnight, it's most crowded after dark as theme park crowds drift to Downtown Disney. Also inside is FoodQuest, on the fifth floor, and the Wonderland Cafe, on the fourth; both offer excellent food at traditional theme park prices. A meal and drink will run about $10 at FoodQuest; a piece of cheesecake and coffee at Wonderland Cafe, about $7. There is no specific children's menu, but the servings are plentiful and can easily be enough for two. Admission to DisneyQuest is $25 for adults, $20 for children 3 to 11. Children 10 and under are not admitted without an adult.

video-game arcade), a food court, and more than 50 specialty shops. You can rent a **horse-drawn carriage** out front for a drive around the downtown area and Lake Eola. And **hot-air balloon flights** can be arranged (☎ **407/841-8787**).

MAJOR CONCERT HALLS & AUDITORIUMS

Three large entertainment facilities, administered by the Orlando Centroplex, host most big-name performers playing the Orlando area.

The **Florida Citrus Bowl,** 1610 W. Church St., at Tampa Street (☎ **407/ 849-2020** for information, or 407/839-3900 to charge tickets), with 70,000 seats, is the largest. This is the setting for major rock concerts and headliners. To reach the Citrus Bowl, take I-4 east to the East-West Expressway, and head west to U.S. 441; make a left on Church Street, and follow the signs. Parking is $5.

The 17,500-seat **Orlando Arena** at 600 W. Amelia St., between I-4 and Parramore Avenue (☎ **407/849-2020** for information, or 407/839-3900 to charge tickets), also hosts major performers in addition to an array of family-oriented entertainment such as ice-skating and the circus every January. To reach the arena, take I-4 east to Amelia Avenue, turn left at the traffic light at the bottom of the off-ramp, and follow the signs. Parking is $5.

The area's major cultural venue is the **Bob Carr Performing Arts Centre,** 401 W. Livingston St., between I-4 and Parramore Avenue (☎ **407/849-2020** for information, or 407/839-3900 to charge tickets). Concert prices vary with performers; ballet tickets are $15 to $35; opera tickets, $12 to $45; the Broadway Series, $24.50 to $46.50. This 2,500-seat facility is home to the **Orlando Opera Company** and the

Southern Ballet Theater, both of which have October-to-May seasons. The **Orlando Broadway Series** (Sept to May) features original-cast Broadway shows. Also featured at the Bob Carr are concerts and comedy shows. To get here, take I-4 east to Amelia Avenue, turn left at the traffic light at the bottom of the off-ramp, and follow the signs. Parking is $5.

Northwest Florida: 13
The Panhandle

by Bill Goodwin

If you like beaches, you'll love Florida's northwestern Panhandle. Thanks to quartz washed down from the Appalachian Mountains, the beaches here along the Gulf of Mexico consist of dazzlingly white sand that is so talcum-like it actually squeaks when you walk across it. And walk across it you can, for some 100 miles of these incomparable sands are protected in state parks and the gorgeous Gulf Islands National Seashore.

Pensacola, Destin, Fort Walton Beach, and Panama City Beach have long been summertime beach meccas for families, couples, and singles from the adjoining states of Georgia and Alabama—a geographic proximity that lends this area the languid charm of the Deep South. Indeed, Southern specialties like turnip greens and cheese grits appear frequently on menus here.

But there's more here than beaches and Southern charm. Offshore, you'll find abundant marine life growing over the Gulf's natural sand-bar system, which makes for good snorkeling and scuba diving. Championship catches of grouper, amberjack, snapper, mackerel, cobia, sailfish, wahoo, tuna, and blue marlin have made Destin one of the world's fishing capitals. In the interior near Pensacola, the Blackwater, Shoal, and Yellow rivers teem with bass, bream, catfish, and largemouth bass, and also offer some of Florida's best canoeing and kayaking adventures.

The area also is steeped in history. Rivaling St. Augustine as Florida's oldest town, picturesque Pensacola carefully preserves a heritage derived from Spanish, French, English, and American conquest. Famous for its oysters, Apalachicola saw the invention of the air conditioner, a moment of great historical note in Florida. And Tallahassee, seat of state government since 1824, has a host of 19th-century buildings and homes, including the Old State Capitol.

EXPLORING NORTHWEST FLORIDA BY CAR

Both I-10 and U.S. 98 link Tallahassee and Pensacola, some 200 miles apart. The fastest route is I-10, but all you'll see is a huge pine forest divided by two strips of concrete. Plan to take U.S. 98, a scenic excursion in itself. Although it can be traffic-clogged in the beach towns during summer, U.S. 98 has some beautiful stretches out in the country, particularly as it literally skirts the bay east of Apalachicola and the Gulf west of Port St. Joe. It's also lovely along skinny Okaloosa Island and across the high-rise bridge between Fort Walton Beach and Destin. From the bridge you'll see the brilliant color of the Gulf and immediately understand why they call this the Emerald Coast.

1   Pensacola

191 miles W of Tallahassee, 354 miles W of Jacksonville

Native Americans left pottery shards and artifacts in the coastal dunes here centuries before Tristan de Luna arrived with a band of Spanish colonists in 1559. Although his settlement lasted only 2 years, modern Pensacolans claim that de Luna made their town the oldest in North America. Pensacola actually dates its permanence from a Spanish colony established here in 1698, however, so St. Augustine wins this friendly feud, having been permanently settled in 1565.

France, Great Britain, the United States, and the Confederacy subsequently captured (and in one case recaptured) this strategically important deep-water port. They left Pensacola with a charming blend of Old Spanish brickwork, colonial French balconies reminiscent of New Orleans, magnificent Victorian mansions built by British and American lumber barons, and its motto, "City of Five Flags."

West of town, the magnificent National Museum of Naval Aviation at the U.S. Naval Air Station celebrates the storied past of navy and marine-corps pilots who trained at Pensacola. Based here, the Blue Angels demonstrate the high-tech present with thrilling exhibitions of precision flying in the navy's fastest fighters.

Also on the Naval Station, historic Fort Barrancas looks across the bay to Perdido Key and Santa Rosa Island, which reach out like narrow pinchers to form the harbor. Out there, powdery white-sand beaches beckon sun-and-surf lovers to their spectacular gulf shores, which include Pensacola Beach, a small family-oriented resort, and most of Florida's share of Gulf Islands National Seashore, home of historic Fort Pickens.

ESSENTIALS

GETTING THERE   **Pensacola Regional Airport,** on 12th Avenue at Airport Road, is served by **Continental** (☎ 800/525-0280), **Delta Connection/ASA** (☎ 800/221-1212), **Northwest** (☎ 800/225-2525), and **US Airways** (☎ 800/428-4322).

Alamo (☎ 800/327-9633), **Avis** (☎ 800/331-1212), **Budget** (☎ 800/527-0700), **Enterprise** (☎ 800/325-8007), **Hertz** (☎ 800/654-3131), and **National** (☎ 800/CAR-RENT) have rental-car operations here.

Taxis wait outside the modern terminal. Fares are approximately $11 to downtown, $15 to Gulf Breeze, and $20 to Pensacola Beach.

The **Amtrak** transcontinental *Sunset Limited* stops in Pensacola at 980 E. Heinberg St. (☎ 800/USA-RAIL for information and reservations).

VISITOR INFORMATION   The **Pensacola Visitor Information Center,** 1401 E. Gregory St., Pensacola, FL 32501 (☎ **800/874-1234** or 850/434-1234; fax 850/432-8211; www.visitpensacola.com), gives away helpful information about the Greater Pensacola area, including maps of self-guided tours of the historic districts, and sells a detailed street map of the area. The office is at the mainland end of the Pensacola Bay Bridge and is open daily from 8am to 5pm (until 4pm Sat and Sun from Oct through Mar).

For information specific to the beach, contact the **Pensacola Beach Chamber of Commerce,** 735 Pensacola Beach Blvd. (P.O. Box 1174), Pensacola Beach, FL 32561 (☎ **800/635-4803** or 850/932-1500; fax 850/932-1551; www.pensacolabeach.com). The chamber's offices and visitor center are on the right-hand side as you drive onto Santa Rosa Island across the Bob Sikes Bridge. They're open daily from 9am to 5pm.

GETTING AROUND   To see the historic sights in town, park at the Pensacola visitor center (see above) and take the **Five Flags Trolley** (☎ **850/436-9383**). The

The Panhandle

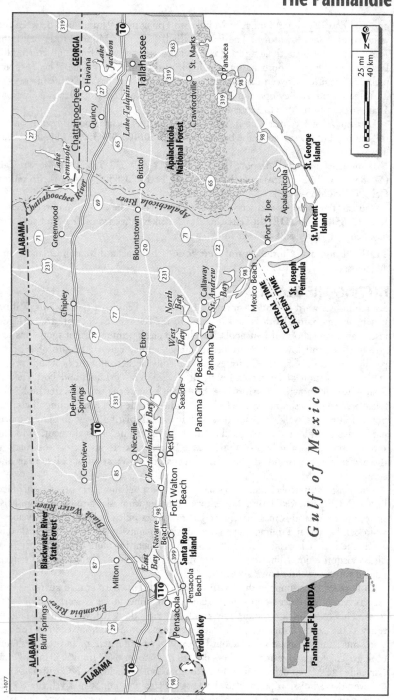

one-way East Bay (Blue) Line runs Monday to Friday from 9am to 4pm between the visitor center and downtown. The Palafox (Red) Line runs Monday to Friday from 7am to 6pm north-south along Palafox Street between the waterfront and North Hill Preservation District. Both pass through Historic Pensacola Village. The 25¢ fare includes a transfer between the two lines. The visitor center has free route maps.

A free **Island Trolley** operates along the full length of Pensacola Beach daily from 10am to 3am from May to September.

Escambia County Area Transit System (ECAT) runs **buses** around town Monday to Saturday but doesn't go to the beach. Call ☎ **850/463-9383,** ext. 611, for schedules.

If you need a cab, call **Airport Express Taxi** (☎ 850/572-5555), **Crosstown Cab** (☎ 850/456-TAXI), **Pensacola Red & Gold Taxi** (☎ 850/505-0025), or **Yellow Cab** (☎ 850/433-3333).

You can rent bicycles and scooters from **Floats-N-Spokes,** 500 Quietwater Beach Rd. (☎ **850/934-RIDE**), in Pensacola Beach. Bikes range from $5 a hour to $15 a day. Scooters go for $30 an hour to $90 a day.

TIME   Pensacola is in the **central time zone,** 1 hour behind Miami, Orlando, and Tallahassee.

HITTING THE BEACH

Stretching eastward 47 miles, from the entrance to Pensacola Bay to Fort Walton Beach, skinny **Santa Rosa Island** is home to the resorts, condominiums, cottages, restaurants, and shops of **Pensacola Beach,** the area's prime vacation spot. This relatively small and low-key resort began life a century ago as the site of a beach pavilion, or "casino" as such facilities were called back then, and the heart of town—at the intersection of Pensacola Beach Boulevard, Via de Luna, and Fort Pickens Road—is still known as **Casino Beach.** At the base of the town's water tank, this lively area sports restaurants, snack bars, a games arcade for kids, a minigolf course, public rest rooms, walk-up beach bars with live bands blaring away, an indoor sports bar, and an outdoor concert pavilion with summertime entertainment. And the shops, restaurants, and bars of **Quietwater Boardwalk** are just across the road on the bay side of the island. If you want an active beach vacation, it's all here in one compact zone.

One reason Pensacola Beach is so small is that most of Santa Rosa Island is included in the ✪ **Gulf Islands National Seashore.** Jumping from island to island from Mississippi to Florida, this magnificent preserve includes mile after mile of undeveloped white-sand beach and rolling dunes covered with sea grass and sea oats. Established in 1971, the national seashore is a protected environment for more than 280 species of birds. Visitors enjoy swimming, boating, fishing, scuba diving, camping, and ranger-guided fort tours and nature hikes.

✪ **Fort Pickens,** built in the 1830s to team with Fort Barrancas in guarding Pensacola's harbor entrance, stands silent guard in the dunes at the western end of Santa Rosa. This huge brick structure saw combat during the Civil War, but it's famous today as the prison home of Apache medicine man Geronimo from 1886 to 1888. A small museum features displays about Geronimo, coastal defenses, and the seashore's ecology. The fort and museum are open April to October daily from 9:30am to 5pm; November to March daily from 8:30am to 4pm. Both are closed on Christmas.

Seven-day admission permits to the Fort Pickens area are $6 per vehicle, $3 per pedestrian or bicyclist, free for holders of National Park Service passports. For more information, contact the **Gulf Islands National Seashore** at 1801 Gulf Breeze Pkwy., Gulf Breeze, FL 32561 (☎ **850/934-2600**).

Legend

North Hill Preservation District

Palafox Historic District

Seville Historic District

NATURE PRESERVES & ZOOS

A former federal tree plantation, the Gulf Islands National Seashore's 1,378-acre **Naval Live Oaks Area,** on U.S. 98 a mile east of Gulf Breeze (☎ 850/934-2600), is a place of primitive beauty. Nature trails lead through the oaks and pines to picnic areas and a beach; pick up a map at the headquarters building, which has a small museum and a gorgeous view through the pines to Santa Rosa Sound. Picnic areas and trails are open from 8am to sunset all year except Christmas. The visitor center is open April to October, daily from 8:30am to 5pm; November to March, daily from 8:30am to 4:30pm. Admission is free.

The Zoo, 5701 Gulf Breeze Pkwy. (U.S. 98), about 10 miles east of Gulf Breeze, 15 miles east of Pensacola (☎ 850/932-2229), has more than 700 exotic animals—including white tigers, rhinos, and gorillas—on 50 acres of landscaped habitats. Japanese gardens, a giraffe-feeding tower, and a petting farm make for a fun visit. A Safari Line train chugs through a 30-acre wildlife preserve with free-ranging herds, and youngsters also will love riding the wild animals instead of horses on a merry-go-round

($1.75 per ride covers both train and carrousel). Admission is $9.75 adults, $8.75 seniors, $5.75 children 3 to 11, free for children 2 and under. Open during summer daily from 9am to 4pm; off-season daily from 9am to 3pm. It's also open from 6 to 9pm from the day after Thanksgiving until January 4 for a holiday-lights festival, when proceeds go to charity. Closed Thanksgiving, Christmas Eve, and Christmas.

OUTDOOR PURSUITS

CANOEING & KAYAKING   Less than 20 miles northeast of Pensacola via U.S. 90, the little town of Milton is the official "Canoe Capital of Florida" (by an act of the state legislature, no less). It's a well-earned title, for the nearby Blackwater River, Coldwater River, Sweetwater Creek, and Juniper Creek are all perfect for canoeing, kayaking, tubing, rafting, and paddleboating.

The Blackwater is considered one of the world's purest sand-bottom rivers. It has remained a primordial, backwoods beauty, thanks in large part to Florida's largest state forest (183,000 acres of oak, pine, and juniper) and ✪ **Blackwater River State Park,** 7720 Deaton Bridge Rd., Holt, FL 32564 (☎ 850/983-5363), where you can closely observe plant life and wildlife along nature trails. The park has facilities for fishing, picnicking, and camping. Admission is $2 per day per vehicle with up to eight occupants. Campsites cost $8 per night ($10 with electricity), and weekly and monthly rates are available.

Adventures Unlimited, Route 6, Box 283, Milton, FL 32570 (☎ 800/239-6864 or 850/623-6197; fax 850/626-3124), is a year-round resort with canoeing, kayaking, and rafting expeditions. Special arrangements are made for novices. Canoe trips start at $13 per person, kayaking adventures from $17. Inner tubes rent for $9. Campsites cost $15 a night. The resort also has 14 cottages on the Coldwater River ($39 to $109 a night), and bed-and-breakfast accommodations at the Wolfe Creek School House Inn (eight rooms, all with bathrooms, $79 to $99 double).

Blackwater Canoe Rental, 10274 Pond Rd., Milton, FL 32570 (☎ 800/ 967-6789 or 850/623-0235), also rents canoes, kayaks, floats, tubes, and camping equipment. It has day trips by canoe, kayak, or inner tube ranging from $9 to $19 per person, and overnight excursions ranging from $19 to $28 per person. Tents, sleeping bags, and coolers are available for rent.

FISHING   Red snapper, grouper, mackerel, tuna, and billfish are abundant in these waters. Anglers congregate along both the **Pensacola Bay Bridge Fishing Pier** and the **Bob Sikes Bridge Fishing Pier** (both are on the old bridges).

Fishing charter services are offered by **Scuba Shack/Charter Boat** *Wet Dream,* 711 S. Palafox St., in Pensacola (☎ 850/433-4319); *Hooligan* **Charters** (☎ 850/ 968-1898) and *Rocky Top* **Charters** (☎ 850/432-7536), both at Pitt Slip Marina off East Main Street in Pensacola; and *Lo-Baby* **Charters,** 38 High-Point Dr., in Gulf Breeze (☎ 850/934-5285). At Pensacola Beach, choose from *Chulamar* (☎ 850/ 434-6977), *Lively One* (☎ 850/932-5071), *Boss Lady* (☎ 850/932-0305 or 850/477-4033), *Entertainer* (☎ 850/932-0305), *Exodus* (☎ 850/626-2545 or 850/932-0305), and *Lady Kady* (☎ 850/932-2065 or 850/932-0305). Expect to pay between $300 and $750 for one to four passengers, depending on length of trip. You may be able to save by driving to Destin, where party boats charge less per person (see "Outdoor Pursuits" in section 2, below). Sightseeing and evening cruises here go for about $50 per person.

GOLF   The Pensacola area has its share of Northwest Florida's numerous championship golf courses. Look for free copies of *Gulf Coast Tee Time,* an annual directory describing all of them, at the visitor information offices and in many hotel lobbies (see

"The Active Vacation Planner" in chapter 2 for information about ordering copies). Reasonably priced golf packages can be arranged through many local hotels and motels.

Among this region's best courses is **Marcus Pointe,** on Marcus Pointe Boulevard off North W Street (☎ **800/362-7287** or 850/484-9770), which has hosted the Nike Tour, the American Amateur Classic, and the Pensacola Open. *Golf Digest* magazine has described this wide-ranging, 18-hole course as a "great value," and it is: Greens fees with cart are about $40 to $49, depending on the season.

The Moors, on Avalon Boulevard north of I-10 (☎ **800/727-1010** or 850/ 995-4653), also has greeted the Nike Tour and is home to the Emerald Coast Classic, a PGA seniors event. Pot bunkers here make you think you're playing in Scotland. Greens fees here are about $30 without cart. The Moors also has a lodge with eight luxury rooms.

Others worth considering are **Scenic Hills,** on U.S. 90 northwest of town (☎ **850/ 476-9611**), whose rolling fairways are unique for this mostly flat area; the 36-hole **Tiger Point,** 1255 Country Club Rd., east of Gulf Breeze by Santa Rosa Sound (☎ **850/932-1330**), overlooking the water (the fifth-hole green of the East Course actually sits all by itself on an island); **Hidden Creek,** 3070 PGA Blvd., in Navarre between Gulf Breeze and Fort Walton Beach (☎ **850/939-4604**); **Creekside Golf Course,** 2355 W. Michigan Ave. (☎ **850/944-7969**); and **Osceola Municipal Golf Course,** 300 Tonawanda, off Mobile Highway (☎ **850/456-2761**).

In addition, the **Perdido Bay Golf Resort,** 1 Doug Ford Dr., near Perdido Key (☎ **800/874-5355** or 850/492-1223), has accommodations available for visiting golfers. It was home of the PGA Pensacola Open from 1978 to 1987.

WATER SPORTS   Visibility in the waters around Pensacola can range from 30 to 50 feet inshore to 100 feet 25 miles offshore. Although the bottom is sandy and it's too far north for coral, the battleship USS *Massachusetts,* submerged in 30 feet of water 3 miles offshore, is one of some 35 artificial reefs where you can spot loggerhead turtles and other creatures.

Scuba Shack, 711 S. Palafox St. (☎ **850/433-4319**), is Pensacola's oldest dive shop, offering sales, rentals, classes, and diving and fishing charters on the *Wet Dream,* moored behind the office. **Gulf Breeze Dive Pros,** 297B Gulf Breeze Pkwy. (U.S. 98), in Gulf Breeze (☎ **850/934-8845**), offers rentals, all levels of instruction, and diving excursions on the 30-foot *Easy Dive.* The *Chulamar,* at Pensacola Beach (☎ **850/ 434-6977**), and the *Lo-Baby,* in Gulf Breeze (☎ **850/934-5285**), both make arrangements for diving excursions.

Key Sailing Center, 500 Quietwater Beach Rd., on the Quietwater Beach Board-walk (☎ **850/932-5550**), and **Radical Rides,** 444 Pensacola Beach Blvd., near the Bob Sikes Bridge (☎ **850/934-9743**), rent Hobie Cats, pontoon boats, Wave Runners, jet skis, and windsurfing boards.

EXPLORING HISTORIC PENSACOLA

Civil War Soldiers Museum. 108 S. Palafox St. (south of Romana St.). ☎ **850/469-1900.** Admission $5 adults, $2 children 6–12, free for children 5 and under. Tues–Sat 10am–4:30pm. Closed New Year's Day, Thanksgiving, Christmas Eve, and Christmas.

Founded by Dr. Norman Haines Jr., a local physician who grew up discovering Civil War relics in Sharpsburg, Maryland, this storefront museum in the heart of the Palafox Street business district emphasizes how ordinary soldiers lived during that bloody conflict. The doctor's collection of military medical equipment and treatment methods is especially informative. A 23-minute video tells of Pensacola's role during the Civil War. The museum's bookstore carries more than 600 titles about the war.

✪ Historic Pensacola Village. 205 E. Zaragossa St. (east of Tarragona St.). ☎ **850/ 595-5985.** Admission $6 adults, $5 seniors, $2.50 children 4–16, free for children 3 and under. Tues–Sat 10am–4pm. Guided tours Mon–Sat 11am and 1pm. Closed state holidays.

Bounded by Government, Taragona, Adams, and Alcanz streets, this original part of Pensacola resembles a shady English colonial town—albeit with Spanish street names—complete with town green and **Christ Church,** built in 1823 and resembling Bruton Parrish in Williamsburg, Virginia. It has some of Florida's oldest homes (now owned and preserved by the state), along with charming boutiques and interesting restaurants. During summer, costumed characters go about their daily chores and demonstrate old crafts, and University of Florida archaeologists unearth the old Spanish commanding officer's compound at Zaragossa and Tarragona streets. Among the landmarks to visit are the **Museum of Industry,** the Museum of Commerce, the French Creole–style **Charles Lavalle House,** the elegant **Victorian Dorr House,** the French Colonial–Creole **Quina House,** and **St. Michael's Cemetery** (land was deeded by the king of Spain).

Another fascinating site is the **Julee Cottage Black History Museum,** 204 Zaragossa St. Built around 1790, this small house was owned by Julee Panton, a freed slave who ran her own business, invested in real estate, and loaned money to slaves so they could buy their freedom. Today the museum recalls her life and deeds, as well as the achievements of other African Americans with Pensacola associations.

Across Taragona Street, the **Pensacola City of Five Flags Exhibit,** in the **✪ Earle Bowden Building,** 120 E. Church St., traces the city's history from Spanish colonial times to the present. Of special interest is the archaeological section, where you can see one of the oldest coins ever found in North America, minted between 1471 and 1474.

Start your tour by buying tickets at **Tivoli House,** 205 E. Zaragossa St., just east of Tarragona Street, where you can get free maps and brochures and purchase audio driving tapes of the city's three historic districts for $5. Admission to the village includes the T. T. Wentworth Jr. Florida State Museum (see below), where you also can buy tickets.

Adjacent to the village, Pensacola's **Vietnam Memorial,** on Bayfront Parkway at 9th Avenue, is known as the "Wall South," since it is a three-quarters–size replica of the national Vietnam Veterans Memorial in Washington, D.C. Look for the "Huey" helicopter atop the wall.

✪ National Museum of Naval Aviation. Radford Blvd., U.S. Naval Air Station. ☎ **850/ 452-3604.** Free admission. IMAX movies $5 adults, $4.50 seniors and children under 13. Daily 9am–5pm; guided tours daily at 9:30am, 11am, 1pm, and 2:30pm; IMAX films on the hour daily 10am–4pm. Closed New Year's Day, Thanksgiving, and Christmas.

The U.S. Navy and Marine Corps have trained at the sprawling U.S. Naval Air Station since they began flying airplanes early in this century. Celebrating their heroics, this truly remarkable museum has more than 100 aircraft dating from the 1920s to the space age. There's even a torpedo bomber flown by former Pres. George Bush during World War II. Both children and adults can sit at the controls of a jet trainer. You can almost feel the tug of gravity while watching the Blue Angels and other naval aviators soaring about the skies in **The Magic of Flight,** a stunning IMAX film shown on a screen six times the size of the average cinema. All retired naval and marine-corps aviators, the guides bring a personal touch to the tours.

Fort Barrancas (☎ **850/934-2600**) also is definitely worth a visit while you're at the naval station. On Taylor Road near the museum, this imposing brick structure overlooks the deep-water pass into Pensacola Bay. The Spanish built the water battery in 1797. Linked to the battery by a tunnel, the incredibly intricate brickwork of the upper section was constructed by American troops between 1839 and 1844. Entry is by a drawbridge across a dry moat, and an interior scarp gallery goes all the way around the inside of the fort. Meticulously restored and operated by the National Park Service as part of Gulf Islands National Seashore, it's open from April to October, daily from 9:30am to 5pm; November through March, Wednesday to Sunday from 10:30am to 4pm. Guided-tour schedules change from season to season, so call for the latest information. Admission is free.

The **Pensacola Lighthouse,** opposite the museum entrance on Radford Boulevard, has guided ships to the harbor entrance since 1825. The lighthouse is not open to the public, but you can drive right up to it. The nearby **Lighthouse Point Restaurant** (☎ 850/452-3251) offers bountiful, all-you-can-eat luncheon buffets and magnificent bay views for about $6 per person; it's open Monday to Friday from 10:30am to 2pm, and reservations are not required.

The Naval Station is southwest of downtown Pensacola. Enter either at the Main Gate at the south end of Navy Boulevard (Fla. 295) or at the Back Gate on Blue Angel Parkway (Fla. 173). No passes are required.

Pensacola Museum of Art. 407 S. Jefferson St. (at Main Street). ☎ **850/432-6247.** Free admission on Tues; other days, $2 adults, $1 active-duty military and students, free for kids under 6. Tues–Fri 10am–5pm, Sat 10am–4pm.

Housed in what was the city jail from 1906 to 1954, this museum showcases permanent art and sculpture collections as well as art on loan, from tribal art to classic European pieces to avant-garde modern works.

T. T. Wentworth Jr. Florida State Museum. 330 S. Jefferson St. (at Church St.). ☎ **850/595-5989.** Admission $6 adults, $5 seniors and military, $2.50 children 4–16, children 3 and under free (includes Historic Pensacola Village). Tues–Sat 10am–4pm.

The classic yellow brick building houses exhibits of western Florida's history and has a special hands-on Discovery Museum for children on the third floor.

HISTORIC DISTRICTS

In addition to Historic Pensacola Village in the Seville Historic District (see above), the city has two other preservation areas worth a stroll. The Pensacola Visitor Information Center provides free walking-tour maps, and you can buy an audiotape driving tour for $5 at Tivoli House in Historic Pensacola Village (see above).

PALAFOX HISTORIC DISTRICT   Running up Palafox Street from the water to Wright Street, the Palafox Historic District is also the downtown business district. Beautiful Spanish Renaissance– and Mediterranean-style buildings stand from the early days, including the ornate Saenger Theatre. In 1821, Gen. Andrew Jackson formally accepted Florida into the United States during a ceremony in Plaza Ferdinand VII, now a National Historic Landmark. His statue commemorates the event.

The Palafox district is home to the **Pensacola Museum of Art,** in the old city jail, and the **T. T. Wentworth Jr. Florida State Museum** (see "Exploring Historic Pensacola," above).

NORTH HILL PRESERVATION DISTRICT   Another entry in the National Register of Historic Places, the North Hill Preservation District covers the 50 square blocks north of the Palafox Historic District bounded by Wright, Blount, Palafox, and Reus streets. Descendants of Spanish nobility, timber barons, British merchants, French Creoles, buccaneers, and Civil War soldiers still live in some of the more than 500 homes. They are not open to the public but are a bonanza for anyone interested in architecture. In 1863, Union troops erected a fort in Lee Square, at Palafox and

Gadsden streets. It later was dedicated to the Confederacy, complete with a 50-foot-high obelisk and sculpture based on John Elder's painting *After Appomattox.*

SHOPPING

Sightseeing and shopping can be combined in Pensacola's Palafox and Seville historic districts, where many shops are housed in renovated centuries-old buildings. The **Quayside Art Gallery,** on Plaza Ferdinand at the corner of Zaragossa and Jefferson streets (☎ 850/438-2363), is the largest cooperative gallery in the Southeast. More than 100 artists display their works here, and the friendly staff will direct you to other nearby galleries.

North T Street between West Cervantes Street and West Fairfield Drive has so many antique dealers and small flea markets that it's known as Antique Alley. Others have booths in the **Ninth Avenue Antique Mall,** 380 N. 9th Ave. between Gregory and Strong streets (☎ 850/438-3961). Get a complete list of local antique dealers from the Pensacola Visitor Information Center (see "Essentials" above).

Browsers will enjoy poking through the 400 dealer spaces covering 45 acres at the **Flea Market,** on U.S. 98, opposite the zoo about 10 miles east of Gulf Breeze (☎ 850/934-1971). It's open on Saturday and Sunday from 9am to 5pm. Admission is free.

WHERE TO STAY

Room rates at all Panhandle beaches are highest from mid-May to mid-August, and premiums are charged at Easter, Memorial Day, July 4, and Labor Day. Hotel or motel reservations are essential during these periods. There's another high-priced peak in March, when thousands of raucous college students invade during spring break. Economical times to visit are April (except Easter) and September—the weather's warm, most establishments are open, and room rates are significantly lower than during summer. The least expensive rates come during winter, but many attractions and some restaurants may be closed then.

The Pensacola Visitor Information Center (see "Essentials" above) publishes a complete list of rental condominiums and cottages. Among the leading rental agents are **Gulf Coast Accommodations,** 400 Quietwater Beach Rd., Box 12, Pensacola Beach, FL 32561 (☎ 800/239-4334 or 850/932-9788; fax 850/932-3449; www.innisfree.com/gca); **JME Management,** 22A Via de Luna, Pensacola Beach, FL 32562 (☎ 800/554-3695 or 850/932-0775; fax 850/932-0787); and **Tristan Realty,** P.O. Box 1611, Gulf Breeze, FL 32562 (☎ 800/445-9931 or 850/932-7363; fax 850/932-8361; www.pcola.com/tristan/).

For camping, the **Fort Pickens Area** of Gulf Islands National Seashore (☎ 800/365-2267 for reservations or 850/934-2621 for recorded information) has 200 sites (135 with electricity) in a pine forest about 7 miles west of Pensacola Beach on the bay side of Santa Rosa Island. Nature trails lead from the camp through Blackbird Marsh and to the beach. A small store sells provisions. Sites cost $15 a night without power, $20 a night with it, and you have to pay the admission fee to the Fort Pickens area (see "Hitting the Beach" above). Golden Age and Golden Access cardholders get a 50% discount. You can make reservations up to 5 months in advance.

Escambia County adds 11.5% to all hotel and campground bills.

The accommodations listed below are arranged by geographic area: downtown Pensacola and Pensacola Beach.

IN PENSACOLA

The University Mall complex at I-10 and Davis Highway, about 5 miles north of downtown, has a host of chain motels, including **Residence Inn by Marriott**

(☎ 800/331-3131 or 850/479-1000), in which all rooms and apartments have kitchens and fireplaces, and **Fairfield Inn by Marriott,** 7325 N. Davis Hwy. (☎ 800/331-3131 or 850/484-8001). The recently renovated **Motel 6-North** (☎ 800/466-8356 or 850/476-5386) is within walking distance on the north side of I-10. There's an ample supply of inexpensive restaurants on Plantation Road and in the adjacent mall.

A good bet here is the 1998-vintage **Hampton Inn Airport,** 2187 Airport Blvd. (☎ 800/HAMPTON or 850/478-1123; fax 850/478-8519). This area is not as congested as that around University Mall. The inn runs a free shuttle to nearby Cordova Mall and its adjacent chain restaurants.

New World Landing. 600 S. Palafox St. (at Pine St.), Pensacola, FL 32501. ☎ 850/ 432-4111. Fax 850/432-6836. 15 units. A/C TV TEL. $85 double; $130 suite. Rates include continental breakfast. AE, MC, V.

Near the scenic bay and in the historic district, this urban version of a comfortable country inn is enhanced by flower gardens and fountains. From the colonial-style lobby, a grand staircase leads to high-ceilinged and spacious rooms artistically decorated with antiques. The rooms depict aspects of Pensacola's rich history: Four flaunt Spanish decor, four are trés chic French style, four portray Early Americana, and four focus on Olde England.

The adjoining New World Landing Restaurant and pub recalls the city's colorful historic past, honoring Spain with a Barcelona Room, spotlighting French history in a Marseilles Room, and giving tribute to the city itself in the Pensacola Room. Fresh seafood in wine or butter sauce is a specialty, but the menu also features excellent steaks, prime rib of beef, veal, and more. Lunch is served Monday to Friday; dinner, Tuesday to Saturday.

Pensacola Grand Hotel. 200 E. Gregory St. (at Alcanz St.), Pensacola, FL 32501. ☎ 800/ 348-3336 or 850/433-3336. Fax 850/432-7572. 212 units. A/C TV TEL. $90–$100 double; $204–$408 suite. Weekend rates available. AE, DC, DISC, MC, V.

Opposite the Civic Center in the Seville Historic District near the southern end of I-110, this unique hotel has turned the historic L&N Railroad Depot into a grand lobby with a bar, restaurants, lounges, meeting rooms, and a cozy library. You'll see such turn-of-the-century accouterments as an ornate railroad clock, original oak stair rails, imported marble, ceramic mosaic tile floors, and old-fashioned carved furniture. The plush L&N Lobby Bar and the 1912 Restaurant capture this railroad ambience. A two-story glass Galleria links the depot to a modern 15-story tower, whose rooms and suites are popular with business travelers and groups. Facilities include a fitness center and an outdoor pool.

IN PENSACOLA BEACH
Moderate
Best Western Pensacola Beach. 16 Via de Luna Dr., Pensacola Beach, FL 32561. ☎ 800/ 934-3301 or 850/934-3300. Fax 850/934-4366. 122 units. A/C TV TEL. Summer $119–$179 double. Off-season $59–$109 double. Rates include continental breakfast. Golf packages available. AE, DC, DISC, MC, V.

On the Gulf front, this casual hotel is notable for bright, clean, and extra-spacious accommodations, complete with refrigerators, coffeemakers, microwaves, and wet bars. Outside corridors lead to all rooms. Although none has its own balcony or patio, units facing the beach have great views; the less-expensive "inland" rooms don't. Two swimming pools, the Cabana Bar, and a children's playground are on the beach. Chan's Market Cafe (see "Where to Dine," below) sits in the parking lot.

Clarion Suites Resort & Convention Center. 20 Via de Luna Dr., Pensacola Beach, FL 32561. ☎ **800/874-5303** or 850/932-4300. Fax 850/934-9112. 86 units. A/C TV TEL. Summer $115–$166 up to 4 persons. Off-season $72–$166 up to 4 persons. Rates include continental breakfast. AE, DC, DISC, MC, V.

Built to resemble a village of cottages, this tin-roofed, pastel-sided beachfront resort offers one-bedroom suites that can accommodate four people. The attractively deco-rated accommodations include a living room with a dining area, bathroom (39 bilevel loft suites have 1½ bathrooms), kitchen, and private entrance. The living rooms and bedrooms each have their own TVs and telephones. There's no restaurant; but com-plimentary continental breakfast is served daily in a lounge off the lobby, and eateries are within walking distance. Facilities include a swimming pool, a beach pavilion, a coin laundry, and conference rooms.

Comfort Inn Pensacola Beach. 40 Fort Pickens Rd., Pensacola Beach, FL 32561. ☎ **800/934-5470** or 850/934-5400. Fax 850/932-7210. 99 units. A/C TV TEL. Summer $109–$129. Off-season $59–$89. Rates include continental breakfast. AE, DC, DISC, MC, V.

On the bay side of Fort Pickens Road opposite Casino Beach and the Quietwater Boardwalk, this four-story motel has medium-size rooms with bright furniture, spreads, and drapes. They all open to external walkways, thereby eliminating balconies and reducing views and privacy. Armoires hide the televisions and provide closets. There are a pool and an exercise room here. Breakfast is served in a room off the lobby. You can save a few dollars here in the off-season, but note that summertime rates are about the same as at the beachfront properties.

The Dunes. 333 Fort Pickens Rd., Pensacola Beach, FL 32561. ☎ **800/83-DUNES** or 850/932-3536. Fax 850/932-7088. 76 units. A/C TV TEL. Summer $115–$145 double; $230–$275 suite. Off-season $70–$90 double; $195–$245 suite. Packages available. AE, DISC, MC, V.

This eight-story tower has spacious rooms, all with balconies with gorgeous gulf or bay vistas. They come equipped with coffeemakers and hair dryers, and the penthouse suites have their own Jacuzzis. The small but pleasant Gulf Front Cafe serves break-fast, lunch, and dinner. The kids can participate in the supervised children's program from May to Labor Day. The hotel will even take care of the kids so Mom and Dad can take Saturday night off. Facilities also include a heated swimming pool, jogging trail, bike path, and volleyball area. There's an undeveloped dune preserve next door.

Hampton Inn Pensacola Beach. 2 Via de Luna, Pensacola Beach, FL 32561. ☎ **800/320-8108** or 850/932-6800. Fax 850/932-6833. 181 units. A/C TV TEL. Summer $105–$165 double. Off-season $75–$125 double. Rates include continental breakfast. AE, DC, DISC, MC, V.

This pastel, four-story hotel sits right by the Gulf next to Casino Beach. The bright lobby opens to a wooden sundeck with beachside swimming pools on either side (one is heated). Half the oversize rooms have balconies overlooking the Gulf; these are more expensive than rooms on the bay side, which have nice views but no outside sitting areas. Each unit is equipped with a refrigerator, microwave oven, and wet bar. There's no restaurant on the premises, but Chan's Gulfside Cafe and Surfside Saloon is next door. Guests have their own coin laundry. Local calls are free to guests, and the TVs carry HBO.

Holiday Inn Pensacola Beach. 165 Fort Pickens Rd., Pensacola Beach, FL 32561. ☎ **800/465-4329** or 850/932-5361. Fax 850/932-7121. 150 units. A/C TV TEL. Summer $105–$130 double. Off-season $65–$110 double. Senior-citizen discounts. AE, DC, DISC, MC, V.

This nine-story establishment boasts terrific views from its brightly furnished upper-floor rooms and Penthouse Lounge. It's one of the oldest hotels in the area, which means the rooms aren't as large as at other new properties, such as the Hampton Inn; there's adequate space for a king-size bed, but rooms with two double beds are relatively cramped. They all have private balconies, however, with the most expensive rooms facing directly onto the Gulf. The Penthouse Lounge serves dinners and has summertime entertainment. Facilities include a lobby bar looking out to a beachside heated swimming pool.

Inexpensive

☼ **Five Flags Inn.** 299 Fort Pickens Rd., Pensacola Beach, FL 32561. ☎ **850/932-3586.** Fax 850/934-0257. 49 units. A/C TV TEL. Summer $85 double. Off-season $49–$69 double. Packages available. AE, DISC, MC, V.

This friendly motel between the Holiday Inn and The Dunes looks like a jail from the road, but don't be fooled. Big picture windows look out to the swimming pool (heated from Mar through Oct) and gorgeous white-sand beach, which comes right up to the property. Although the accommodations are small, the rates are a bargain for well-furnished gulf-front rooms.

WHERE TO DINE

If you're on a tight budget, this is a good place to meet **Barnhill's Country Buffet,** a popular gulf-coast chain of no-frills, all-you-can-eat, buffet-style restaurants. You pay when you enter, then graze tables filled with a cornucopia of fried chicken and fish, baked ham, roast beef, tasty pot roast, boiled cabbage and collard greens, old-fashioned 'Nilla Wafer banana pudding, and other Southern fare. Adults pay $5.70 a head for lunch, $7.10 for dinner, while kids 12 and under are charged 40¢ and 45¢ times their age, respectively. Pensacola has two branches, one on North Davis Highway and Olive Road north of I-10 (☎ 850/477-5465), and a second on Gulf Breeze Parkway (U.S. 98) at Oriole Beach Road, 3 miles east of Gulf Breeze (☎ 850/932-0403). Both are open Sunday to Thursday from 10:45am to 8pm, Friday and Saturday from 10:45am to 8:30pm (to 8:30 and 9pm, respectively, in summer). MasterCard and Visa are accepted.

IN PENSACOLA

☼ **Hopkins' Boarding House.** 900 N. Spring St. (at Strong St.). ☎ **850/438-3979.** Reservations not accepted. Breakfast $3.50; full meals $7. No credit cards. Tues–Sat 7–9:30am, 11am–2pm, and 5–7:30pm; Sun noon–2pm. SOUTHERN.

There's a delicious peek into the past when you dine at this Victorian boardinghouse in the heart of the North Hill Preservation District. Outside, ancient trees shade a wraparound porch with old-fashioned rocking chairs in which to await the next available place at the large dining tables inside. You could be seated next to the mayor or a mechanic, for everyone in town dines here, and everyone eats family style. Platters are piled high with seasonal Southern-style vegetables from nearby farms. Tuesday is famous as Fried Chicken Day, and you're likely to be served fried fish on Friday. Every Yankee should sample the piping-hot grits accompanying each bountiful breakfast. In true boardinghouse fashion, guests bus their own dishes and pay the one price when they're finished eating.

☼ **Jamie's Wine Bar & Restaurant.** 424 E. Zaragossa St. (between Alcanz and Florida Blanca). ☎ **850/434-2911.** Reservations recommended at both lunch and dinner. Main courses $18–$23. AE, DISC, MC, V. Mon 5:30–10pm, Tues–Fri 11:30am–2pm and 5:30–11pm, Sat 5:30–11pm. CAJUN/CARIBBEAN/ASIAN.

Occupying a restored Victorian home in Historic Pensacola Village, the town's classiest and most romantic restaurant enhances the dining experience with an art deco ambience enhanced by glowing fireplaces, soft candlelight, gleaming antiques, and subdued background music. With Cajun, Caribbean, and Asian influences, the varied menu changes regularly to include such creative dishes as veal Oscar with a Cajun-spiced hollandaise sauce, giving it a distinct Louisiana twist. The wine bar opens at 5pm for tasting from an extensive list.

Marina Oyster Barn. 505 Bayou Blvd. (on Bayou Texar). ☎ **850/433-0511.** Reservations not accepted. Sandwiches $2.50–$5.50; main courses $5.50–$12; lunch specials $3.75–$5.50. AE, DISC, MC, V. Tues–Sat 11am–9pm (lunch specials 11am–2pm). Go east on Cervantes St. (U.S. 90) across the Bayou Texar Bridge, then first left on Stanley Ave., and left again to the end of Strong St. SEAFOOD.

Exuding the ambience of the quickly vanishing Old Florida fish camps, this plain-but-clean restaurant at the Johnson-Rooks Marina has been a favorite with seafood lovers since 1969, for both its view and its down-home–style seafood. Served raw, steamed, fried, or Rockefeller, freshly shucked oysters are the main feature; but the seafood salad here is first-rate, and the fish, shrimp, and oysters are breaded with cornmeal in true Southern fashion. The daily luncheon specials give you a light meal at a bargain price. No smoking is allowed.

McGuire's Irish Pub & Brewery. 600 E. Gregory St. (between 11th and 12th aves.). ☎ **850/433-6789.** Reservations not accepted. Snacks, burgers, and sandwiches $7.50–$8; meals $13–$25. AE, DC, DISC, MC, V. Mon–Sat 11am–2am, Sun 11am–3pm (brunch) and 3pm–1am. AMERICAN/IRISH.

Every day is St. Patrick's Day here, with corned beef and cabbage, Irish stew, and such hybrids as *an scampi o'fettucini* (shrimp in Alfredo sauce). Super-size hamburgers, tender steak, grilled fish, beer-batter shrimp, barbecued and prime ribs, hearty bean soup, and salads are also on the menu. You can watch the house beer being brewed in copper kettles and dine in a cellar-like room with 8,000 bottles of wine on display. You can leave an autographed dollar bill; more than 125,000 of them line the bar's walls and ceilings (famous folks' bucks are framed near the entrance). Live music is offered most nights.

Skopelos on the Bay. 670 Scenic Hwy. (U.S. 90 east, at E. Cervantes St.). ☎ **850/432-6565.** Reservations recommended. Main courses $13–$19. AE, DISC, MC, V. Tues–Thurs and Sat 5–10:30pm, Fri 11:30am–2:30pm and 5–10:30pm. SEAFOOD/STEAKS/GREEK.

Perched on a bluff overlooking the bay, Skopelos has been famous hereabouts since 1959 for its great views and creative seafood dishes, such as the scampi Cervantes, a sautéed fillet of scampi topped with crabmeat. Other seafood selections range from broiled scallops to Mediterranean-style grouper prepared with a sauce of tomato and roasted eggplant. The menu also features charcoal-grilled steaks and chicken, and roast leg of lamb. Befitting the owner's Greek heritage, roast lamb is served with moussaka, dolmades, titopita, and spanakopita.

IN PENSACOLA BEACH

Chan's Gulfside Cafe & Surfside Saloon. 2½ Via de Luna (at Fort Pickens Rd.). ☎ **850/932-3525.** Reservations recommended upstairs, not accepted downstairs. Upstairs main courses $15–$26. Downstairs sandwiches and burgers $6.50–$9, main courses $11–$18. AE, DC, DISC, MC, V. Upstairs Sun–Thurs 5–10pm, Fri–Sat 5:30–11pm. Downstairs daily 11am–2am (to 11pm off-season). SEAFOOD.

Offering Pensacola Beach's only gulf-front dining, this modern complex on Casino Beach offers two lively dining choices. The upstairs Florida Room is more formal yet still relaxed, with blond wood and widely spaced tables enjoying terrific views of the beach and gulf. Cuisine here features mesquite-fired tuna, grouper, and shrimp, plus the likes of coconut shrimp, triggerfish with Rockefeller spinach, and grouper Lyonnaise. The downstairs pub is completely informal, with a long bar where fans can sample an extensive collection of beers from microbreweries while watching their favorite teams on several TVs. Although not of the same quality, many of the same wood-grilled items are offered down here, along with pub-style fare such as pastas, salads, burgers, sandwiches, pastas, and baskets full of fried seafood or chicken. The pub opens to a beachside patio, which has outdoor dining and live entertainment during summer.

✪ Chan's Market Cafe. 16 Via de Luna. ☎ **850/932-8454.** Breakfast/lunch/snacks $3–$7; meals $6–$10. AE, DISC, MC, V. Daily 7am–9pm. AMERICAN.

The aroma of cappuccino and pastries in the oven permeates this pleasant little cafe and bakery, which shares quarters with a liquor store in the parking lot of the Best Western Pensacola Beach. It's the best place on the beach for a breakfast of freshly baked croissants or bagels. Lunches and dinners feature economical specials such as meat loaf, barbecued chicken, pot roast, and grilled fish, all served with a choice of Southern-style veggies. Or you can order a heaping sandwich made with one of Chan's large flaky croissants.

Flounder's Chowder and Ale House. 800 Quietwater Beach Rd. (at Via de Luna and Fort Pickens Rd.). ☎ **850/932-2003.** Reservations not accepted. Main courses $15–$18; burgers and sandwiches $7–$8. AE, DC, DISC, MC, V. Mon–Sat 11am–2am (to 11pm in winter), Sun 11am–2pm (brunch) and 2pm–2am (to 11pm in winter). SEAFOOD.

From Cajun to Florentine, you can order flounder in many different preparations at this publike establishment, whose decor features stained-glass windows from an old New York convent and confessional-booth walls from a New Orleans church. Book-shelves give a cozy, studious feel to one dining room, but Flounder's lively atmosphere is more accurately captured by the glass walls of another dining area; these face a pop-ular beachside bar, where patrons boogie to live reggae bands during the summer season (see "Pensacola After Dark," below). Burgers, salads, and sandwiches are offered all day, and there's a children's menu. A glass of champagne accompanies a sumptuous bayside Sunday brunch.

Jubilee Restaurant & Entertainment Complex. 400 Quietwater Beach Rd. (Via de Luna at Fort Pickens Rd.), on Quietwater Beach Boardwalk. ☎ **850/934-3108.** Reservations not required. Topside main courses $16–$22. Beachside Cafe sandwiches and salads $6.50–$8, main courses $10–$17. AE, DC, DISC, MC, V. Beachside Cafe Mon–Sat 11am–11pm, Sun 10am–11pm; Topside daily 6–10pm (Sun brunch 9am–2pm). SEAFOOD/CAJUN/AMERICAN.

At this beachside restaurant complex, complete with Capt'n Fun's Beach Bar, most dining is very casual, even in the elegant Topside Restaurant. Up there, where you'll get a bird's-eye view of the sound, the chef prepares local fish and shellfish, especially with Louisiana flavors. There's a larger difference in quality than price downstairs in the pub-style Beachside Cafe, opening to a sound-side dock and offering a varied menu of fish, pastas, sandwiches, salads, and barbecue pork, shrimp, and oysters. The J-Sweet Coffee & Dessert Room has homemade sweets and gourmet coffees. On summer evenings there are live bands for dancing under the stars, and there's indoor entertainment year-round.

PENSACOLA AFTER DARK

THE CLUB & BAR SCENE   Pensacola's downtown entertainment center is at **✪ Seville Quarter,** 130 E. Government St., at Jefferson Street (☎ 850/434-6211), in the Seville Historic District. This restored antique brick complex with New Orleans–style wrought-iron balconies is actually a collection of pubs and restaurants whose names capture the ambience: Rosie O'Grady's Goodtime Emporium, Lili

Marlene's Aviator's Pub, Apple Annie's Courtyard, End o' the Alley Bar, Phineas Phogg's Balloon Works (a dance hall, not a balloon shop), and Fast Eddie's Billiard Parlor (which has electronic games for kids, too). The pubs all serve up libations, food, and live entertainment from Dixieland jazz to country and western. Get a monthly calendar at the information booth next to Rosie O'Grady's. Open daily from 11am to 2am.

Every night is party time at **McGuire's Irish Pub & Brewery,** 600 E. Gregory St. (☎ 850/433-6789), the city's popular Irish pub, brewery, and eatery (see "Where to Dine" above). Irish bands appear nightly during summer, on Saturday and Sunday the rest of the year.

Nightlife at the beach centers around **Quietwater Boardwalk,** Via de Luna at Fort Pickens Road (no phone), a shopping/dining complex on Santa Rosa Sound. With the lively Flounder's Beach and Reggae Bar just a few steps away, it's easy to barhop until you find a band and crowd to your liking. Across Via de Luna at Casino Beach, **The Dock** (☎ 850/934-3316) and **Chan's Gulfside Saloon** next door (☎ 850/932-3525) both have beachside live bands nightly during summer, on weekends off-season. You can catch all the games here at **Sidelines Sports Bar & Restaurant** (☎ 850/934-3660). See "Where to Dine," above, for details about Chan's and Flounder's.

Over on Perdido Key, about 15 miles west of downtown Pensacola, the ✪ **Flora-Bama Lounge,** on Fla. 292 at the Florida–Alabama line (☎ 850/492-0611), is almost a shrine to country music. This slapped-together gulfside pub is famous for its special jam sessions from noon until way past midnight on Saturday and Sunday. Flora-Bama is the prime sponsor and a key venue for the Frank Brown International Songwriters' Festival during the first week of November. If you've never attended an Interstate Mullet Toss, catch the fun here during the last weekend of April. The raw oyster bar is popular all the time. Take in the great gulf views from the Deck Bar. It's open daily from 8:30am to 2:30am.

THE PERFORMING ARTS Pensacola has a surprisingly sophisticated array of entertainment choices for such a relatively small city. For a schedule of upcoming events, get a copy of *Vision,* a bimonthly newsletter published by the Arts Council of Northwest Florida, P.O. Box 731, Pensacola, FL 32594 (☎ 850/432-9906). Also pick up *Sneak Preview,* a calendar of events at the Pensacola Civic Center and the Saenger Theater. Both publications are available at the Pensacola Visitor Information Center (see "Essentials" above). Tickets for all major performances can be purchased by phone from **Ticketmaster** (☎ 800/488-5252 or 850/433-6311).

The highlight venue here is the ornate **Saenger Theater,** 118 S. Palafox St., near Romano Street (☎ 850/444-7686), a painstakingly restored masterpiece of Spanish baroque architecture. The variety of presentations includes the local opera company and symphony orchestra, Broadway musicals, and touring performers. The 10,000-seat **Pensacola Civic Center,** 201 E. Gregory St., at Alcanz Street (☎ 850/433-6311), hosts a variety of entertainment. Call ahead for the current schedule.

2 Destin & Fort Walton Beach

40 miles E of Pensacola, 160 miles W of Tallahassee

At the outbreak of the Civil War in 1861, a small Confederate contingent set up camp on Santa Rosa Sound to guard the eastern approaches to Pensacola. The Rebels beat a hasty retreat when Yankee troops shelled their position from Okaloosa Island, but the name they gave their little outpost has remained to this day: Fort Walton.

Back then the only settlement in these parts was Destin, a tiny fishing village east of Fort Walton and separated from it by East Pass, which lets broad, beautiful Choctawhatchee Bay flow into the Gulf of Mexico. On a picturesque harbor, Destin today is neither tiny nor a sleepy village. World famous for its fishing, it's Northwest Florida's fastest growing vacation destination, with a multitude of high-rise condominiums, the huge Sandestin luxury resort, several excellent golf courses, and some of Northwest Florida's best restaurants and lively nightspots. By and large, it attracts a generally more affluent crowd than does Fort Walton Beach, its more down-to-earth neighbor.

Although it has its own gorgeous strip of white sand over on Okaloosa Island, Fort Walton Beach is a "real" city whose economy is supported less by tourism than by sprawling Eglin Air Force Base. Covering more than 700 square miles, Eglin is the world's largest air base and is home to U.S. Air Force's Armament Museum and the 33rd Tactical Fighter Wing, the "Top Guns" of Operation Desert Storm in 1991.

To the east of Destin, development is picking up steam along the beaches of southern Walton County. Still, this picturesque area has mostly cottages nestled among rolling sand dunes covered with sea oats. Here you'll find Grayton Beach State Recreation Area, which sports one of America's finest beaches, and the quaint village of Seaside, which served as the set for Jim Carey's movie *The Truman Show.* Seaside was built on a lovely stretch of beach in the 1980s—but with Victorian architecture that makes it look a century older. The village's gulfside honeymoon cottages make for one of Florida's most romantic retreats, and the village has interesting shops and art galleries, a stamp-size post office, and a resident population of artists, writers, and other creative folks, who permit only their own cars in their relatively expensive little enclave.

ESSENTIALS

GETTING THERE   Flights arriving at and departing from **Okaloosa County Air Terminal** actually use the enormous strips at Eglin Air Force Base. The terminal is on Fla. 85 north of Fort Walton Beach and is served by **AirTran** (☎ 800/AIR-TRAN), **Delta** (☎ 800/221-1212), **Northwest/KLM** (☎ 800/225-2525), and **US Airways Express** (☎ 800/428-4322).

Avis (☎ 800/331-1212), **Budget** (☎ 800/527-0700), **Hertz** (☎ 800/654-3131), and **National** (☎ 800/CAR-RENT) have rental cars at the airport, and **Enterprise** (☎ 800/325-8007) and **Rent-A-Wreck** (☎ 800/535-1391) are in town.

You can take a taxi or limousine that's waiting outside the modern terminal. Fares are based on a zone system: to Fort Walton Beach, $10 to $14; to Destin, $20 to $24; and to Sandestin, about $30.

The *Sunset Limited* transcontinental service on Amtrak (☎ **800/USA-RAIL**) stops at Crestview, 26 miles north of Fort Walton Beach.

VISITOR INFORMATION   For advance information about both Fort Walton Beach and Destin, contact the **Emerald Coast Convention and Visitors Bureau,** P.O. Box 609, Fort Walton Beach, FL 32549 (☎ **800/322-3319** or 850/651-7131; fax 850/651-7149; www.destin-fwb.com). The bureau shares quarters with the **Okaloosa County Visitors Welcome Center** in a tin-roofed, beachside building on Miracle Strip Parkway (U.S. 98) on Okaloosa Island at the eastern edge of Fort Walton Beach. Stop there for brochures, maps, and other information. The welcome center is open during summer daily from 8am to 5pm. Off-season hours are Monday to Friday from 8am to 5pm, Saturday and Sunday from 10am to 4pm.

The **Destin Area Chamber of Commerce,** P.O. Box 8, Destin, FL 32541 (☎ **850/837-6241;** fax 850/654-5612; www.destinfl.com/chamber), gives away brochures and sells maps of the area. The chamber resides in Regatta Commons Office Park, on U.S. 98 east of the Mid-Bay Bridge. Open Monday to Friday from 9am to 5pm all year.

For information about the beaches of South Walton, contact the **South Walton Tourist Development Council,** P.O. Box 1248, Santa Rosa Beach, FL 32459 (☎ **800/822-6877** or 850/267-1216; fax 850/267-3943; www.beachesofsouthwalton. com). Its **visitor center** is at the intersection of U.S. 98 and U.S. 331 in Santa Rosa Beach (☎ **850/267-3511**). Open daily 8:30am to 4:30pm during standard time, to 6pm during daylight saving time.

GETTING AROUND   For a cab in Fort Walton Beach, call **Charter Taxis** (☎ 850/863-5466), **Crosstown Taxi** (☎ 850/244-7303), **JC's Cab** (☎ 850/ 865-0578), **Veterans Cab Co.** (☎ 850/243-1403), **Yellow Cab** (☎ 850/244-3600), or **Checker Cab** (☎ 850/244-4491). In Destin, call **Destin Taxi** (☎ 850/ 654-5700). Fares are based on a zone system rather than meters, with a $3 minimum. Trips within Fort Walton Beach or Destin should range from $3 to $5.

FINDING A STREET ADDRESS   Don't worry if you're confused by the street addresses here, for even many local residents don't fully comprehend the post office's bizarre naming and numbering system along U.S. 98, the area's main east-west drag.

In Fort Walton Beach, U.S. 98 is known as the "Miracle Strip Parkway," with "southwest" and "southeast" addresses on the mainland and "east" addresses on Okaloosa Island.

In Destin, U.S. 98 is officially known as "Hwy. 98 East" between the Destin Bridge and Airport Road, and street numbers get progressively higher as you head east from the bridge. East of Airport Road, however, the post office calls U.S. 98 the "Emerald Coast Parkway"—although locals still say a place is on "98 East." The highway also is known as the Emerald Coast Parkway in Walton County, but the street-numbering system changes completely once you pass the county line.

Adding to the confusion in Destin, "Old Hwy. 98 East" is a short spur from Airport Road to the western side of Henderson Beach State Recreation Area, and "Scenic Hwy. 98 East" runs along the beach from the eastern side of Henderson Beach to Sandestin.

In other words, call and ask for directions if you're not sure how to find an establishment here.

TIME   The area is in the **central time zone,** an hour behind Miami, Orlando, and Tallahassee.

HITTING THE BEACH

DESTIN   The 208-acre ✪ **Henderson Beach State Recreation Area,** east of Destin Harbor on U.S. 98, allows easy access to swimming, sunning, surf fishing, picnicking, and seabird watching. There are rest rooms, outdoor showers, and surf chairs for persons with disabilities. The area is open daily from 8am to sunset. Admission is $2 per vehicle, $1 for pedestrians and cyclists. Several good restaurants are just outside the park's western boundary. Campsites will be opened here sometime in 1999. For more information, contact the area at 1700 Emerald Coast Pkwy., Destin, FL 32541 (☎ **850/837-7550**).

The **James W. Lee Park,** Destin and Sandestin on Scenic Hwy. 98, has a long white-sand beach overlooked by covered picnic tables, an ice-cream parlor, and **The Crab Trap Restaurant** (☎ **850/654-2822**), whose moderately priced snacks and seafood make it a fine spot for lunch with a view or dinner with a sunset.

FORT WALTON BEACH   Do your loafing on the white sands of **Okaloosa Island,** joined to the mainland by the high-rise Brooks Bridge over Santa Rosa Sound. Most resort hotels and amusement parks are grouped around the Gulfarium on U.S. 98 east of the bridge. Here you'll find **The Boardwalk,** a collection of tin-roofed beachside buildings between the Gulfarium and the Ramada Inn. It has an arcade for the kids, the Soggy Dollar Saloon for adults, covered picnic areas, a summertime snack bar, and another branch of the Crab Trap restaurant. Just to the east, you can use the free facilities at **Beasley Park,** home of the Okaloosa County Visitor Welcome Center.

Across U.S. 98, the **Okaloosa Area, Gulf Islands National Seashore** has picnic areas and sailboats for rent on Choctawhatchee Bay, plus access to the Gulf. Admission to this part of the national seashore is free.

SOUTHERN WALTON COUNTY   Sporting the finest stretch of white sand on the Gulf, ۞ **Grayton Beach State Recreation Area,** on County Road 30A, also has 356 acres of pine forests surrounding scenic Western Lake. There are a boat ramp and a campground with electric hookups on the lake (see "Where to Stay" below). Get a self-guided–tour leaflet for the nature trail at the main gate. It's open daily from 8am to sunset. Admission is $3.25 per vehicle with up to 8 occupants, $1 per pedestrian or bicyclist. For more information, contact the area at 357 Main Park Rd., Santa Rosa Beach, FL 32459 (☎ **850/231-4210**).

Seaside has free public parking along County Road 30A and is a good spot for a day at the beach, a stroll or bike ride around the quaint village, and a tasty meal at one of its restaurants.

OUTDOOR PURSUITS

BOATING & BOAT RENTALS   Pontoon boats are highly popular for use on the back bays and on Sunday-afternoon floating parties in East Pass. Several companies rent them, including **Best Boat Rentals** (☎ 850/664-7872) on Okaloosa Island in Fort Walton Beach, as well as **Adventure Pontoon Rentals** (☎ 850/837-3041), **B&J Boat Rentals** (☎ 850/243-4488), **East Pass Watersports** (☎ 850/654-4253), and **Premier Powerboat Rentals** (☎ 850/837-7755), all on Destin Harbor. Expect to pay about $70 for a half day, $120 for all day. Premier Powerboat Rentals also has speedboats for rent.

CRUISES   The *Emerald Magic* (☎ **888/654-1685** or 850/837-1293) and the *Southern Star* (☎ **850/837-7741**) have daily dolphin and sunset cruises from June through August, by arrangement the rest of the year. The *Emerald Magic* is operated by Moody's, on U.S. 98 at Destin Harbor (see "Fishing," below), while the *Southern Star* docks in Destin at the Harbor Walk Marina, behind the Lucky Snapper Restaurant. Expect to pay $15 for adults, $7.50 for kids 3 to 12.

Sailing South (☎ **850/837-7245**), on U.S. 98 at Destin Harbor, has half-day cruises aboard the 72-foot schooner *Daniel Webster Clements* for $25 per person. It also offers 3-day cruises at about $450 per person. You also can go out on the 54-foot schooners *Nathaniel Bowditch* (☎ **850/650-8787**), *Flying Eagle* (☎ **850/ 837-4986** or 850/837-3700), or *Blackbeard* (☎ **850/837-2793**), all of which have afternoon and sunset trips for about $25 per person.

On Okaloosa Island, **Leeside Bareboat Sailing,** at the Leeside Motel, 1352 U.S. 98 East (☎ **850/244-5454**), rents 25- and 30-foot Catalina sloops bareboat (you do the skippering) at prices ranging from $95 per half day to $450 for 3 days.

۞ **FISHING**   Billing itself as the "World's Luckiest Fishing Village," Destin has Florida's largest charter-boat fleet, with more than 140 vessels based at the marinas lining the north shore of Destin Harbor, on U.S. 98 east of the Destin Bridge.

Arranging a trip is as easy as walking along the Destin Harbor waterfront, where you will find the booking booths of several agents, such as **Pelican Charters** (☎ 850/837-2343), **Harbor Cove Charters** (☎ 850/837-2222), and **Fishermen's Charter Service** (☎ 850/654-4665). They all can arrange for you to fish to your heart's content. Rates for private charters range from about $400 to $900 per boat, depending on length of voyage.

A less-expensive way to try your luck is on a larger group-oriented party boat, such as those operated by **Moody's**, at 194 U.S. 98 East on Destin Harbor (☎ 888/654-1685 or 850/837-1293). Moody's charges $30 per person ($25 off-season) for its morning runs (the best fishing) and $25 for afternoon trips. Children 8 to 12 and nonfishing sightseers are charged half price. Other party boats are the *Destin Princess* (☎ 888/837-5088 or 850/5088), *Emmanuel* (☎ 850/837-6313), the *Lady Eventhia* (☎ 850/837-6212), and three craft operated by **Capt. Duke's Boat Service** (☎ 850/837-6152), all based at Destin Harbor.

You don't have to go to sea to fish from the catwalk of the 3,000-foot **Destin Bridge** over East Pass. The marinas and bait shops at Destin Harbor can provide gear, bait, information, and a fishing license.

GOLF　　The area takes great pride in having more than 250 holes of golf. For advance information on all area courses, contact the **Emerald Coast Golf Association,** P.O. Box 304, Destin, FL 32540 (☎ 850/654-7086). Also look for *Gulf Coast Tee Time,* the free annual directory published in Pensacola (see "Golf" under "Outdoor Pursuits" in section 1, above). And be sure to inquire whether your choice of accommodations here offers golf packages, which can represent significant savings.

On the mainland, nonresidents are welcome to play at the city-owned **Fort Walton Beach Golf Club,** on Lewis Turner Boulevard (County Road 189) north of town (☎ 850/862-3314 or 850/862-0933). The club has two 18-hole courses—**The Pines** (☎ 850/833-9529) and **The Oaks** (☎ 850/833-9530)—plus a pro shop. Greens fees at both courses are about $27 year-round, including a cart.

In Destin, scenic **Indian Bayou Golf and Country Club,** off Airport Road (☎ 850/837-6191), has three nine-hole courses with large greens and wide fairways. They look easy, but watch out for water hazards and strategically placed hidden bunkers! Greens fees, including a cart, are $58.

In southern Walton County, **The Resort at Sandestin,** on U.S. 98 East (☎ 850/267-8211 for tee times), is the largest facility here (see "Where to Stay" below). Its 63 holes are spread over three outstanding championship courses: Baytowne, Burnt Pine, and Links. The Baytowne and Links courses overlook Choctawhatchee Bay. Fees for 18 holes are about $66 for resort guests, $86 for nonguests.

Scenery is on display at **Emerald Bay Golf Club,** 2 miles east of the Mid-Bay Bridge on U.S. 98 (☎ 850/837-5197). Some of the 27 championship holes here run along Choctawhatchee Bay, so water adds both beauty and challenges to the otherwise wide and forgiving fairways. Greens fees are $75 with cart.

In southern Walton County, the semiprivate **Santa Rosa Golf & Beach Club,** off County Road 30A in Dune Allen Beach (☎ 850/267-2229 or 850/654-7888), offers a challenging 18-hole course through tall pines looking out to vistas of the Gulf. The club has a pro shop, a beachside restaurant, a lounge, and tennis courts. Fees are $44 in summer, $34 off-season. The **Seascape Resort & Conference Center,** 100 Seascape Dr. (☎ 850/837-9181), off County Road 30A, features a Joe Lee–designed 18-hole course winding through woods and around lakes, with a premium placed on accuracy rather than power. The center also has tennis courts, accommodations, restaurant, bar, and pro shop.

In Niceville, a 20-minute drive north via the Mid Bay Bridge, nonguests may play golf (four nine-hole courses) or tennis (21 courts) at the **Bluewater Bay Resort** (☎ 850/897-3613), which also has condos for rent.

Call ahead for reservations and current fees at all these clubs.

SCUBA DIVING & SNORKELING   At least a dozen dive shops are located along the beaches. Considered one of the best, **Scuba Tech Diving Charters** has two locations in Destin: at 301 U.S. 98 East in Destin (☎ 850/837-2822) and at 10004 U.S. 98 East (☎ 850/837-1933), about ½ mile west of the Sandestin Beach Resort. **Fantasea,** at the foot of the Destin Bridge, 1 U.S. 98 East (☎ 800/326-2732 or 850/ 837-6943), and the **Aquanaut Scuba Center,** 24 U.S. 98 East (☎ 850/837-0359), are other local operators.

The three diving operators and **Kokomo Snorkeling Adventures,** 500 U.S. 98 East in Destin (☎ 850/837-9029), all take snorkelers on excursions into the Gulf of Mexico and Choctawhatchee Bay for $25 per person, including gear.

TENNIS   **The Resort at Sandestin,** U.S. 98 East (☎ 850/837-2121), has 16 courts open to the public, including hard, clay, and grass. *Tennis* magazine rated it one of the nation's top-50 tennis resorts and the only ranked resort with natural grass courts.

WATER SPORTS   Hobie Cats, Wave Runners, jet boats, jet skis, and parasailing are available all along the beach. The largest selection of operators, including **Boogies** (☎ 850/654-4497), is at the marinas just east of the Destin Bridge, behind Hooter's and Fat Tuesday's pubs. **Paradise Water Sports** (☎ 850/664-7872) rents equipment and offers parasailing rides at seven locations along U.S. 98 in both Destin and Fort Walton Beach.

EXPLORING THE AREA

Gulfarium. 1010 Miracle Strip Pkwy. (U.S. 98) on Okaloosa Island. ☎ **850/244-5169.** Admission $15 adults, $13 seniors, $10.70 children 4–11, free for children 3 and under. Daily 9am through last show; shows daily at 10am, noon, 2pm, and 4pm; additional shows at 6 and 8pm in summer.

One of the nation's original marine parks features ongoing shows with dolphins, California sea lions, Peruvian penguins, loggerhead turtles, sharks, sting rays, moray eels, and alligators. There are fascinating exhibits, including the Living Sea, with special windows that provide viewing of undersea life. During one of the shows, a scuba diver explains the sea life while swimming among them. A gift shop offers an extensive collection of marine-oriented souvenirs.

Indian Temple Mound and Museum. 139 Miracle Strip Pkwy. SE, on the mainland. ☎ **850/833-9595.** Park free; museum $2 adults, $1 children 6–17, free for children 5 and under. Park daily dawn–dusk. Museum Sept–May Mon–Fri 11am–4pm, Sat 9am–4pm; June–Aug Mon–Sat 9am–4:30pm, Sun 12:30–4:30pm (summer hours may vary, so call ahead).

This ceremonial mound, one of the largest ever discovered, dates from A.D. 1200. The museum, located next to it, showcases ceramic artifacts from southeastern Native American tribes. The largest such collection, it contains more than 6,000 items. Exhibits depict the lifestyles of the four tribes that lived in the Choctawhatchee Bay region for 10,000 years.

✪ **U.S. Air Force Armament Museum.** At Eglin Air Force Base, Eglin Pkwy. (Fla. 85), 5 miles north of downtown. ☎ **850/882-4062.** Free admission. Daily 9:30am–4:30pm. Closed all federal holidays.

Located on the world's largest air-force base, this fascinating museum traces military developments from World War II through the Korean and Vietnam wars to Operation Desert Storm in the Persian Gulf. On display are reconnaissance, fighter, and bomber planes, including the SR-71 Blackbird spy plane. Also exhibited are war films, photographs, rockets, bombs, and missiles. The base itself is home to the world's largest environmental test chamber, in the McKinley Climatic Laboratory, and to the "Top Gun" 33rd Tactical Fighter Wing. World War II's historic Doolittle's Tokyo Raiders trained here.

Eden State Gardens. County Rd. 395, Point Washington. ☎ **850/231-4214.** Grounds and gardens $2 per vehicle; mansion tours $1.50 adults, 50¢ children 12 and under. Gardens and grounds daily 8am–5pm; mansion tours on the hour Thurs–Mon 9am–4pm.

Evoking images from *Gone With the Wind,* the magnificent 1895 Greek Revival–style Wesley Mansion has been lovingly restored and richly furnished. It stands overlooking scenic Choctawhatchee Bay and is surrounded by immense moss-draped oak trees and the Eden Gardens, resplendent with camellias, azaleas, and other typical Southern flowers. Picnicking is allowed on the plantation grounds. The gardens and mansion are north of Seagrove Beach in southern Walton County.

SHOPPING

The third-largest "designer" outlet mall in the United States, and still growing, ✪ **Silver Sands Factory Stores,** on U.S. 98 between Destin and Sandestin (☎ **800/ 510-6255** or 850/864-9780), has the upscale likes of Anne Klein, Donna Karan, J. Crew, Jones New York, Brooks Brothers, Hartman Luggage, Coach leathers, Bose electronics, and so many more you'll have to drive from one end to the other to spot your favorites. Shops are open Monday to Saturday from 10am to 9pm (to 7pm in Jan and Feb), Sunday from 10am to 6pm (noon to 6pm in Jan and Feb). The fine food court here, **Morgan's Market** (☎ **850/654-3320**), has counters serving pizzas and pastas, rotisserie chicken and country-style vegetables, burgers, salads, made-to-order deli sandwiches, and fresh breads, pastries, and desserts. There are electronic games for kids and a sports bar for adults.

Over at the Sandestin Beach Resort on U.S. 98, you can window-shop in **The Market at Sandestin,** where 28 shops purvey expensive clothing, gifts, and Godiva chocolates.

WHERE TO STAY

The area has a vast supply of condos and cottages for rent. One good-value example is Venus Condos, listed below. The tourist-information offices (see "Essentials" above) will provide lists of others for rent. The largest rental agent is **Abbott Realty Services,** 3500 Emerald Coast Pkwy., Destin, FL 32541 (☎ **800/336-4853** or 850/837-4853; fax 850/654-2937; www.abbott-resorts.com). It publishes a magazine-size annual brochure picturing and describing its many accommodations throughout the area.

For campers, **Grayton Beach State Recreation Area,** 357 Main Park Rd., Santa Rosa Beach (☎ **850/231-4210**), which actually is on County Road 30A, offers hookups for RVs as well as primitive sites in a beautiful 356-acre setting. Campfire interpretive programs are available to campers (call for the current schedule). Sites cost $14 ($16 with electricity) from March to September, $8 ($10 with electricity) from October to February. You can reserve sites up to 11 months in advance by contacting the park.

Camping on the Gulf Holiday Travel Park, 10005 W. Emerald Coast Pkwy. (U.S. 98), Destin, FL 32541 (☎ **877/226-7485** or 850/837-6334; fax 850/654-5048), just west of the Sandestin Beach Resort, is the area's largest and oldest campground and the only one with sites directly on the beach. During summer, campsites cost $51.50 on the beach, $30.50 inland; off-season, they go for $30 and $24, respectively. Reserve your summertime site well in advance.

State and local governments add 9% to all hotel and campground bills.

IN DESTIN

A former Comfort Inn, the local **Motel 6,** 405 U.S. 98 East (☎ **800/466-8356** or 850/837-0007; fax 850/837-5325), sitting across the highway from the harbor, has rooms which are generally larger than at many other members of this cut-rate chain. There's an outdoor swimming pool on premises. Room rates are $51 to $66 double in summer, $46 off-season.

Expensive

۞ Henderson Park Inn. 2700 Scenic Hwy. 98 E. (P.O. Box 30), Destin, FL 32541. ☎ **800/ 336-4853** or 850/837-4853. Fax 850/654-0405. 35 units. A/C TV TEL. Summer $180–$279 double. Off-season $114–$223 double. Rates include buffet breakfast. Packages and weekly rates available. AE, DISC, MC, V.

At the end of Old U.S. 98 on the undeveloped eastern edge of the Henderson Beach State Recreation Area, this shingle-sided, Cape Hatteras–style bed-and-breakfast is a romantic, get-away-from-it-all escape without screaming kids (no children are accepted). Individually decorated in a Victorian theme, the rooms have high ceilings, fireplaces, Queen Anne furniture, and gulf views from private balconies. Some have canopy beds. The main building (15 rooms are in a separate shingle-sided structure next door) sports a beachside veranda complete with old-fashioned rocking chairs to sit and admire the glorious sunsets.

Dining: All rates include daily Southern-style buffet breakfast and beer and wine at the nightly before-dinner social hour in The Veranda Restaurant, which opens to the wraparound porch of the main building. Reservations are recommended for The Veranda's gourmet-style dinners.

Amenities: Heated swimming pool, beachside sundeck, complimentary beach umbrellas and chairs, beach gazebo, nightly turndown.

Moderate

Best Western SummerPlace Inn. 14047 Emerald Coast Pkwy. (U.S. 98, at Airport Rd.), Destin, FL 32541. ☎ **888/BEACH-99** or 850/650-8003. Fax 850/650-8004. 72 units. A/C TV TEL. Summer $120–$170. Off-season $60–$100. Rates include continental breakfast and local telephone calls. AE, DC, DISC, MC, V.

Across U.S. 98 from the Hampton Inn Destin (see below), this four-story, Spanish-motif building opened in 1997, offering innlike rooms and suites decorated with wildlife prints. All units have refrigerators and coffeemakers, and a few suites have Jacuzzis in their living rooms. More expensive, the gulfside units have balconies (those facing the bay do not). Doors open from an indoor pool, a whirlpool, and exercise equipment to an outdoor pool. Amenities include a coin laundry, a small business center, and a video-games arcade. You'd have to negotiate your way across busy U.S. 98 to reach the Gulf. There are three restaurants next door, and those on Old Hwy. 98 East are a short walk away.

Hampton Inn Destin. 1625 Hwy. 98 E. (at Old Hwy. 98 and Airport Rd.), Destin, FL 32541. ☎ **800/HAMPTON** or 850/654-2677. Fax 850/654-0745. 104 units. A/C TV TEL. Summer $115–$135 double; $135–$175 suite. Off-season $59–$79 double; $85–$125 suite. Rates include continental breakfast. AE, DC, DISC, MC, V.

This pink two-story building sits at the junction of the new and old U.S. 98s, about 100 yards west of Henderson Beach State Recreation Area (see "Hitting the Beach" above) and near a covey of restaurants just outside the recreation area and another bunch of them across U.S. 98. There's beach access through a line of condos sitting across the old highway, which means you don't have to fight the traffic on U.S. 98 to reach the Gulf. External corridors lead to the standard motel-style rooms and suites with two rooms and kitchenettes. All units have coffeemakers and irons and boards. A gazebo-like sitting area offers shade next to a heated outdoor pool and whirlpool.

Holiday Inn of Destin. 1020 Hwy. 98 E. (P.O. Box 577), Destin, FL 32541. ☎ **800/ HOLIDAY** or 850/837-6181. Fax 850/837-1523. 233 units. A/C TV TEL. Summer $130–$195 double. Off-season $75–$125 double. Packages available. AE, DC, DISC, MC, V.

Most of the nicely furnished rooms in this gulf-front resort are in a round high-rise building. Get one facing south or east because a tall condo next door blocks southwest-facing units from enjoying the spectacular gulf views. The rooms in the older, four-story building are more spacious than those in the tower. Some of these older units open to an enclosed "Holidome," a fountained lobby sporting a comfortable mezzanine lounge with indoor pool, billiard, Ping-Pong, and Foosball tables. Whatever their age, all units have coffeemakers, hair dryers, and irons and boards. The tropically attired Destin Cafe in the lobby serves breakfast, lunch, and dinner. Children can play in their own pool or in a video-game arcade (there's a summertime activities program for them). Adults can use a whirlpool, a sauna, and an exercise room, or spend money at the gift shop.

IN FORT WALTON BEACH

Among the chain motels here, the moderately priced **Rodeway Inn,** 866 Santa Rosa Blvd. (☎ **800/458-8552** or 850/243-3114), and **Days Inn & Suites Gulfside Resort,** 573 Santa Rosa Blvd. (☎ **800/DAYS-INN** or 850/244-8686), are right on Okaloosa Island's beach.

Four Points Sheraton. 1325 E. Miracle Strip Pkwy. (U.S. 98), Fort Walton Beach, FL 32548. ☎ **800/874-8104** or 850/243-8116. Fax 850/244-3064. www.sheraton4pts.com. 229 units. A/C TV TEL. Summer $112–$185 double. Off-season $76–$155 double. Rates include full breakfast. AE, DC, DISC, MC, V.

This beachfront resort sports very spacious rooms decorated with vivid, tropical colors. The older, motel-style wings here surround a lush tropical courtyard with a whirlpool, heated swimming pool, and South Pacific–style bar. With their balconies overlooking the beach, the choice units are in a new seven-story gulfside building with a second swimming pool and bar to one side. All rooms have refrigerators, microwave ovens, and coffeemakers, and some also have kitchenettes. Dining is in the Plantation Grill dining room and in Dempsey's Grill and Bar, which, along with the beach bar, provides entertainment during summer. There are limited room service, newspaper delivery, valet laundry, coin laundry, exercise room, and summertime children's program.

Marina Motel. 1345 E. Miracle Strip Pkwy. (U.S. 98), Fort Walton Beach, FL 32548. ☎ **800/ 237-7021** or 850/244-1129. Fax 850/243-6063. 38 units. A/C TV TEL. Summer $60–$80 double; $95–$105 apt. Off-season $39–$58 double; $55–$75 apt. AE, DC, DISC, MC, V.

This family-operated, self-described "fisherman's motel" may be rather pedestrian-looking, but it makes up for a lack of charm with clean, comfortable rooms and a location directly across U.S. 98 from the magnificent public beach at Beasley Park. A low-slung, brick-fronted motel block holds most of the rooms. Other units are in two-story stucco structures near a marina whose 560-foot pier is home to charter-fishing boats. Two one-bedroom apartments at the end of the complex overlook the marina and bay. All units here have refrigerators and microwaves; 16 have full kitchens. If traffic is too busy to cross U.S. 98 to the beach, you can sun at the motel's little bayside beach or take a dip in its roadside pool. There's also a guest laundry.

Radisson Beach Resort. 1110 Santa Rosa Blvd. (at U.S. 98), Fort Walton Beach, FL 32548. ☎ **800/732-4853** or 850/243-9181. Fax 850/664-7652. 388 units. A/C TV TEL. Summer $109–$175 double. Off-season $65–$145 double. Packages available. AE, DC, DISC, MC, V.

A glass-enclosed elevator climbs up through a soaring, lean-to atrium lobby to rooms with spectacular gulf views from a six-story building at this resort (which until a recent upgrading was the Holiday Inn Fort Walton Beach). The least expensive units here are in the "Sand Dollar" wing, a two-story traditional motel-style building separated from the main complex by a parking lot. Next up are those flanking a lush courtyard surrounding a pool and open on one end to the beach. A lobby cafe serves breakfast, lunch, and dinner, and an atrium bar has nightly entertainment during summer. Facilities here include three outdoor pools, a children's playground, a beach bar and barbecue area, two lighted tennis courts, an exercise room, a gift shop, and a convention center.

✪ **Ramada Plaza Beach Resort.** 1500 E. Miracle Strip Pkwy. (U.S. 98), Fort Walton Beach, FL 32548. ☎ **800/874-8962** or 850/243-9161. Fax 850/243-2391. www.ramadafwb.com. 353 units. A/C TV TEL. Summer $110–$150 double; $235–$300 suite. Off-season $65–$85 double; $135–$160 suite. AE, DC, DISC, MC, V.

This big resort boasts one of the most beautiful ✪ **swimming pool/patio** areas anywhere, with waterfalls cascading over lofty rocks and a romantic grotto bar, all surrounded by thick tropical foliage. Unfortunately, all this is cut off from the beach by a six-story block of hotel rooms. The tastefully furnished rooms in this building have gulf or courtyard views, but the least-expensive units are next door in a two-story structure overlooking a parking lot. All units have refrigerators, coffeemakers, irons, and boards.

On-site dining options include the attractive Garden Cafe, the casual Pelican's Roost, and a barbecue shack near the pool. The family-oriented Lobster House serves moderately priced seafood in summer. The Boardwalk beach pavilion and restaurants are next door (see "Hitting the Beach" above). There's also a cozy lobby lounge with sports TVs. Facilities here include three swimming pools (one indoors), a children's pool, a health spa, three whirlpools, and a gift shop.

✪ **Venus Condos.** 885 Santa Rosa Blvd., Fort Walton Beach, FL 32548. ☎ **800/476-1885** or 850/243-0885. Fax 850/664-5221. 45 units. A/C TV TEL. Summer $105–$170 apt. Off-season $50–$125 apt. Weekly and monthly rates available. DISC, MC, V.

Offering considerably more space than a hotel would at these rates, this pleasant, three-story enclave on western Okaloosa Island is immaculately maintained. Each of the one-, two-, and three-bedroom units has a long living-dining-kitchen room, with a rear door leading to a balcony or patio. Facilities include a guest laundry (with 1970s prices) and a grassy courtyard with palm trees, swimming pool, lighted tennis court, shuffleboard, and large barbecue pit. The beach is a short walk across the dunes. Be sure to ask about special off-season deals here.

IN SOUTHERN WALTON COUNTY

If you want to stay near The Resort at Sandestin (see below) without paying its prices, there's a modern **Sleep Inn** a mile west at 5000 Emerald Coast Pkwy./U.S. 98 (☎ **800/627-5337** or 850/654-7022).

✪ **A Highlands House Bed & Breakfast.** 4193 W. County Rd. 30A (P.O. Box 1189), Santa Rosa Beach, FL 32459. ☎ **850/267-0110.** Fax 850/267-3602. E-mail: cxwq19a@prodigy.

com. 7 units (all with bathroom). A/C. $70–$150 double. Rates include full breakfast. DISC, MC, V.

Beautifully situated in Dune Allen Beach, this B&B was built by innkeepers Joan and Ray Robins in the style of luxurious 18th-century plantation homes in the South Carolina Low Country, where they once lived. Although the house isn't directly on the beach, a path leads along a streambed to the sands. The Robinses furnished their dream inn with four-poster rice beds, comfy wingback chairs, and antique accouterments. The most expensive rooms have French doors that open to an extra-wide porch with wicker furniture and a view of the Gulf. One unit has a fireplace; another, a whirlpool tub. The less-expensive models are in an old but modernized house to the rear of the main building. The delicious breakfasts often include brandy-battered French toast heaped with strawberries and cream.

The Resort at Sandestin. 9300 Hwy. 98 W., Destin, FL 32541. ☎ **800/277-0800** or 850/267-8000 in the U.S., or 800/933-7846 in Canada. Fax 850/267-8222. 175 rms, 500 condo apts. Summer $145–$215 double; $195–$676 condo apt. Off-season $75–$185 double; $90–$475 condo apt. Packages available. Rates include health-club, bicycle, boogie-board, canoe, and kayak use; 1 hour tennis daily; discounts on other amenities. AE, DC, DISC, MC, V.

One of Florida's best sports-oriented resorts, this luxurious real-estate development sprawls over 2,300 acres complete with a spectacular beach 5 miles west of Destin. An array of handsomely decorated accommodations overlooks the Gulf or Choctawhatchee Bay, the golf fairways, lagoons, or a nature preserve. The hotel rooms are in the Inn at Sandestin, on the bay. All the other accommodations—junior suites, condominium apartments, villas, and three-bedroom penthouses—are spread over the property and come complete with kitchen, living room, and patio or balcony. Most amenities are a short walk or bike or tram ride away, and a tunnel runs under U.S. 98 to connect Sandestin's gulf and bay areas.

Dining: The Sunset Bay Cafe offers breakfast, lunch, and dinner by the bay, but the dining delight here is the romantic **Elephant Walk** (☎ **850/267-4800**), located on the Gulf. There's a story here: In 1890 a tea planter in Ceylon named John Whiley tried to prevent damage to his trees by building a huge home across an elephant herd's path to the river. When the thirsty stampede reduced his house to ruins, Whiley vowed never to return. He roamed for 30 years, buying treasures in all four corners of the world. Then he discovered Northwest Florida and settled here. His eclectic purchases are displayed in this lovely building designed to evoke his Ceylon mansion. The candlelit dining room features entirely different, gourmet-quality choices for dinner each evening.

Amenities: Free shuttle tram around the resort; arrangements for deep-sea fishing and other outside activities; summer children's program for ages 3 to 13; rental bikes, boats, and water-sports equipment; fishing and charter boats based at Baytowne Marina; fully equipped sports spa and health center; nine swimming pools; three wading pools; children's playground; conference center; 63 holes of championship golf; Golf Learning Center with Tom Stickney; outstanding Bayside Tennis Center with clinic and hard, Rubico, and grass courts.

✪ **Sandestin Beach Hilton Golf & Tennis Resort.** 4000 Sandestin Blvd. S., Destin, FL 32541. ☎ **800/445-8667** or 850/267-9500. Fax 850/267-3076. 598 suites. A/C TV TEL. Summer $220–$335 suite. Off-season $110–$300 suite. Golf and tennis packages available. AE, DC, DISC, MC, V.

Consisting of adjacent 15- and 7-story towers, this all-suites beachside resort is the top full-service hotel here. It's nicely situated on the grounds of The Resort at Sandestin (see above) and shares its golf and tennis facilities. Units in the new wing are equipped primarily for business travelers and conventioneers, while the spacious suites in the old wing feature a special area for children's bunk beds, plus a dressing room with a second sink outside the bathroom. Hall rooms have plenty of closet space, wet bars, in-room refreshment centers, refrigerators, coffeemakers, small hot plates, irons and boards, and balconies looking out to splendid gulf views.

Dining/Diversions: On-premises dining includes Seagars for fine dining and the moderately priced Sandcastles Restaurant and Lounge in the lobby. The elegant Elephant Walk (see The Resort at Sandestin, above) is next door. In summer, the Barefoot's beach grill is enjoyably casual, and the Ice Cream Shop features sweet treats.

Amenities: Concierge, 24-hour room service, baby-sitting, summer programs for children and teenagers, two outdoor swimming pools (one heated), heated indoor pool with whirlpool and sauna, fitness center, guest laundry, gift shop, video rentals.

IN SEASIDE

If you decide to rent a home or romantic honeymoon cottage in this quaint village, contact the **Seaside Cottage Rental Agency,** P.O. Box 4730, Seaside, FL 32459 (☎ **850/231-1320** or 800/277-8696; fax 850/231-2293; www.seasidefl.com). It has some 275 cottages in its rental inventory, from one to six bedrooms, plus six rooms in a replica of a 1940s-style motel, starting at $145 double. The beachside ✪ **honeymoon cottages** are a favorite getaway for newlyweds or anyone else looking for a romantic escape.

✪ **Josephine's French Country Inn at Seaside.** County Rd. 30A (P.O. Box 4767), Seaside, FL 32459. ☎ **800/848-1840** or 850/231-1940. Fax 850/231-2446. www.josephinesfl.com. 9 units. A/C TV TEL. $130–$215 double. Rates include gourmet breakfast. Weekly rates available. AE, MC, V.

With its six large Tuscan columns reminiscent of a Virginia mansion, Josephine's is an elegant country inn, with mahogany four-poster beds, lace comforters, rich furnishings, and marble bathtubs. Most guest rooms also have fireplaces. Conveniences like wet bars, microwaves, coffeemakers, and small refrigerators are neatly incorporated into the design so they don't conflict with the nostalgic charm. Sumptuous breakfasts are served either in-room (beside the fireplace or on your private veranda) or in the gracious dining room. The Guest House offers four suites, two with gulf views. Each has a fireplace, kitchen, and full bath. No smoking or pets are allowed inside. Guests can use the house bicycles free.

With rich mahogany furniture and a wealth of period accoutrements, the dining room here is one of the region's finest places for a gourmet romantic dinner. Glowing with candlelight, this intimate room seats only 22 people (by reservation only). Josephine's Maryland-style crab cakes are consistently delicious.

WHERE TO DINE

Except for the strip on Okaloosa Island, a plethora of national fast-food and family chain restaurants line U.S. 98.

IN DESTIN

If you didn't catch a fish to be grilled at Fisherman's Wharf (see below), you buy one to brag about from **Sexton's Seafood,** 602 Hwy. 98 East opposite Destin Harbor (☎ 805/837-3040). It's the best market here.

A good budget choice here is **Morgan's Market** (☎ **850/654-3320**), the food court at Silver Sands Factory Outlets (see "Shopping" above).

Moderate

AJ's Seafood & Oyster Bar. 116 Hwy. 98 E., Destin Harbor. ☎ **850/837-1913.** Reservations not accepted. Main courses $12–$19; sandwiches and salads $6–$8. AE, DISC, MC, V. Summer daily 11am–midnight (bar until 4am). Off-season daily 11am–9:30pm. SEAFOOD.

Jimmy Buffet tunes set the tone at this fun, tiki-topped establishment on the picturesque Destin Harbor docks, where fishing boats unload their daily catches right into the kitchen. Obviously, the best items here are grilled or fried fish, but raw or steamed Apalachicola oysters also lead the bill of fare. You can sample a bit of everything with a "run of the kitchen" seafood patter. AJ's is most famous for its topside Club Bimimi, featuring reggae music and limbo contests every summer evening (you may want to have dinner elsewhere if you're not in the partying mood). At lunch, picnic tables on the covered dock make a fine venue with a view across the harbor to the Gulf.

✪ Back Porch. 1740 Old Hwy. 98 E. ☎ **850/837-2022.** Reservations not accepted. Main courses $11–$19; sandwiches, burgers, and pastas $6.50–$9. AE, DC, DISC, MC, V. Summer daily 11am–11pm. Off-season daily 11am–10pm. From U.S. 98, turn toward the beach at the Hampton Inn. SEAFOOD.

A cedar-shingled seafood shack whose long porch offers glorious beach and gulf views, this popular, casual restaurant originated charcoal-grilled amberjack, which you'll now see on menus throughout Florida. Other fish and seafood, as well as chicken and juicy hamburgers, also come from the coals. Monthly specials feature crab, lobster, and seasonal fish. Come early, order a rum-laden Key Lime Freeze, and enjoy the sunset. The Back Porch sits with a number of other restaurants near the western boundary of the Henderson Beach State Recreation Area.

Fisherman's Wharf. 210D Hwy. 98 E., Destin Harbor. ☎ **850/654-4766.** Reservations not accepted. Sandwiches and burgers $6–$9; main courses $10–18; cook-your-catch $6 lunch, $8 dinner. AE, DC, DISC, MC, V. Summer daily 11am–11pm (deck bar open later). Off-season daily 11am–9pm. SEAFOOD.

Have that fish you caught filleted, bring it here, and the chef will charcoal-grill it at this atmospheric restaurant next to a charter fleet marina (the restaurant hosts most of Destin's fishing competitions). If you had no luck, and didn't stop by Sexton's Seafood on the way here to buy a few fillets (see above), you can select from the restaurant's fresh-off-the-boat catch for grilling, broiling, frying, or blackening. Charcoal grilling is the house specialty—my triggerfish fillet was white and flaky but still moist. All main courses come with a trip to a central salad bar, and rice pilaf, baked potato, or roasted vegetables. Although this building dates from 1996, it evokes an Old Florida fish camp, with rough-hewed wood walls and double-hung windows looking out to a large harborside deck, a venue during the warmer months for two libation bars, an oyster bar, live music, and great sunsets.

Harbor Docks. 538 U.S. 98 E., Destin Harbor. ☎ **850/837-2506.** Reservations not accepted. Main courses $14–$20; burgers and sandwiches $8.50–$10. AE, DC, DISC, MC, V. Daily 5:30–10:30am and 11am–11pm. Closed for breakfast Nov–Jan. SEAFOOD/SUSHI.

The harbor views are spectacular from indoors or outdoors at this casual, somewhat-rustic establishment whose splendid hand-carved wood-and-marble bar dates from 1890. Specialties include a sautéed daily catch served with artichoke hearts. Appetizers on the dinner menu might feature smoked yellowfin tuna with mustard sauce. A Japanese-style hibachi table is open daily from 5:30 to 10pm. Hearty fishermen's breakfasts are cooked by the owners of the Silver Sands, a popular local haunt that burned down. The bar here is popular with charter boat skippers, and frequent live entertainment keeps the action going on the outdoor deck at night.

Harry T's Boat House. 320 U.S. 98 East, Destin Harbor. ☎ **850/654-4800.** Reservations not accepted. Main courses $10–$18; sandwiches and salads $8–$10. AE, MC, V. Summer Mon–Sat 11am–2am, Sun 10am–2am. Off-season Mon–Sat 11am–11pm, Sun 10am–11pm. Sun brunch year-round 10am–2pm. AMERICAN.

The family of trapeze artist "Flying Harry T" Baben opened this lively, fun restaurant on the ground floor of Destin Harbor's tallest building to honor his memory. Standing guard is a stuffed Stretch, Harry's beloved giraffe. Other decor features circus memorabilia and relics from the luxury cruise ship *Thracia*, which sank off the Emerald Coast in 1927; Harry T was presented with the ship's salvaged furnishings and fixtures for personally leading the heroic rescue of its 2,000 passengers.

The tabloid-style menu offers traditional seafood, steaks, chicken, and pasta dishes. Kids eat for 99¢ until 7pm and at Sunday brunch. Both the dining room and the downstairs lounge (with live entertainment Fri and Sat nights) enjoy harbor views.

✪ **Marina Cafe.** 404 Hwy. 98 E., Destin Harbor. ☎ **850/837-7960.** Reservations recommended. Main courses $16–$23; pizza and pasta $8–$17. AE, DC, DISC, MC, V. Daily 5–10pm. Closed Jan. ITALIAN/NEW AMERICAN.

Destin's finest restaurant provides a classy atmosphere with soft candlelight, subdued music, and formally attired waiters. The outdoor balconied deck overlooks Destin Harbor and is the setting for drinks and appetizers. Inside, window walls provide the same view. The creative chef prepares pizzas and pastas with a special flair, with an emphasis on light, spicy fare. Menu highlights include a fettuccine combined with andouille sausage, shrimp, crawfish tails, and a piquant tomato-cream sauce.

McGuire's Irish Pub & Brewery. 33 Hwy. 98 E., Destin Harbor (in Harborwalk Center near Destin Bridge). ☎ **850/650-0000.** Reservations not accepted. Snacks, burgers, and sandwiches $7.50–$8; meals $13–$25. AE, DC, DISC, MC, V. Mon–Sat 11am–2am, Sun 11am–1am (brunch 11am–3pm). AMERICAN/IRISH.

Like Pensacola's original McGuire's (see "Where to Dine" in section 1, above), this younger sibling sports thousands of dollar bills stuck on the ceilings and walls, plus Notre Dame University football schedules, a prominent logo of the Boston Celtics pro basketball team, and much other memorabilia recalling Irish American lore. This is Destin's most popular hangout, and many patrons congregate at the big oak bar in the center of the dining room, especially when live entertainment starts nightly at 9pm. If you're here to dine, you can opt for a table on either side of the bar or up on a rooftop deck. Dining here is almost secondary to the see-and-be-seen scene, but you can order corned beef and cabbage, Irish stew, *scampi o'fettucini* (shrimp in Alfredo sauce), big salads, super-size hamburgers, steaks, and various seafood offerings.

Inexpensive

✪ **Callahan's Island Restaurant & Deli.** 950 Gulf Shore Dr. (2 blocks south of U.S. 98). ☎ **850/837-6328.** Main courses $6–$15; sandwiches and burgers $3.50–$6. DISC, MC, V. Summer Mon–Thurs 10am–9pm, Fri 10am–10pm, Sat 8:30am–9pm. Off-season Mon–Fri 10am–9pm, Sat 8am–9pm. STEAKS/DELI.

The best place in the area for picnic fare, this family-operated deli offers burgers, excellent Rubens and other made-to-order sandwiches, pastas, and nightly specials such as charcoal-grilled chicken and grilled pork chops. A long refrigerator case across the rear holds a variety of top-grade cheeses, deli meats, steaks, and chops (choose your own cut, and the chef will charcoal-grill it to order). Tables and booths are set up garden fashion, adding an outdoorsy ambience to this pleasant storefront establishment. Locals like to do lunch here. Breakfast is served only on Saturday morning.

Donut Hole. 635 U.S. 98 E., Destin. ☎ **850/837-8824.** Reservations not accepted. Breakfast $4–$7.50; sandwiches, salads, burgers $4.50–$6.50. No credit cards. Mar–Oct daily 24 hours. Off-season daily 6am–10pm. Closed 2 weeks in Dec. SOUTHERN/AMERICAN.

Available around the clock during summer, breakfasts at this popular spot highlight eggs benedict, hot fluffy biscuits under sausage gravy, Belgian waffles, and freshly baked doughnuts and a variety of other pastries and breads, all displayed in a bakery case. Lunch sees fresh deli sandwiches, half-pound burgers, and big salads. The rough-hewn building has booths and counter seating. Be prepared to wait on the deck, especially on weekends.

There's a Donut Hole II Cafe and Bakery (☎ **850/267-3239**) on U.S. 98 East in southern Walton County 2½ miles east of the Sandestin Beach Resort. It's known more for its bakery than for meals. Open daily from 6:30am to 7pm (to 3pm Oct to Christmas).

IN FORT WALTON BEACH

The local **Barnhill's Country Buffet** is at 431 Mary Ester Cutoff, opposite Santa Rosa Mall (☎ **850/243-1103**). See "Where to Dine" in section 1 for details about these budget-priced, Southern-style restaurants. It has the same hours and prices as the Pensacola branches.

For a caffeine fix or an inexpensive breakfast or lunch, head to **Big City Coffeehouse and Cafe,** 201 Miracle Strip Pkwy. SE (U.S. 98) (☎ **850/664-0664**), on the mainland near the Brooks Bridge. In addition to gourmet coffees, it's known locally for salads such as herb roasted chicken with apples, walnuts, and tarragon dressing, and sandwiches served on homemade foccacia bread. Open Monday to Friday from 6am to 7pm, Saturday and Sunday from 8am to 7pm.

Moderate

✪ **Caffè Italia.** 189 Brooks St., on the mainland in the block west of Brooks Bridge. ☎ **850/664-0035.** Reservations recommended. Pizza and pasta $5.50–$13; main courses $13–$16. AE, DC, DISC, MC, V. Tues–Sun 11am–10pm. Closed Thanksgiving and Christmas. NORTHERN ITALIAN.

Nada Eckhardt is from Croatia, but she met her American husband, Jim, while working at a restaurant named Caffè Italia in northern Italy. The Eckhardts duplicated that establishment in this 1925 Sears & Roebuck mail-order house tucked away on the waterfront. You can dine on the patio with a view of the sound through sprawling live oak trees (one table is set romantically under its own gazebo), or inside, where Nada has installed floral tablecloths and photos from the old country. Her menu is limited to excellent pizzas; pasta dishes such as tortellini with tomatoes, chicken, and peas in Alfredo sauce; northern Italian risotto with either asparagus or smoked salmon; and meat and seafood dishes to fit the season. Don't expect to make a full meal by ordering only a pasta here, for meals are served in the authentic Italian fashion, with a small portion of pasta preceding the seafood or meat course. On the other hand, you can quickly fill up on the seasoned, pizza-dough breadsticks served with olive oil for dipping. The cappuccino here is absolutely first-rate, as are the genuine Italian desserts.

Pandora's Restaurant & Lounge. 1120B Santa Rosa Blvd. ☎ **850/244-8669.** Reservations recommended after 4pm. Main courses $11–$20. AE, DC, DISC, MC, V. Sun–Thurs 5–10pm, Fri–Sat 5–10:30pm. STEAKS/PRIME RIB/SEAFOOD.

The front part of this unusual restaurant is a beached yacht now housing the main-deck lounge. Below is a beamed-ceilinged dining room aglow with lights from copper chandeliers. Several varieties of freshly caught fish are among the seafood choices here, but steaks and prime rib keep the locals coming back for more. The tender beef is cut on the premises and grilled to perfection. The delicious breads and pies are home-made. Live entertainment and dancing are an added attraction in the lounge.

There's another Pandora's in Grayton Beach at the corner of Fla. 283 and County Road 30A (☎ 850/231-4102).

Staff's Seafood Restaurant. 24 SW Miracle Strip Pkwy. (U.S. 98), on the mainland. ☎ **850/243-3526.** Reservations accepted. Main courses $12–$27. AE, DISC, MC, V. Summer daily 5–11pm. Off-season Mon–Thurs 5–9:30pm, Fri–Sat 5–10pm. SEAFOOD/STEAKS.

Considered the first Emerald Coast restaurant, Staff's started as a hotel in 1913 and moved to this barnlike building in 1931. Among the display of memorabilia are an old-fashioned phonograph lamp and a 1914 cash register. All main courses are served with heaping baskets of hot, home-baked wheat bread from a secret 70-year-old recipe. One of the most popular main dishes is the "seafood skillet," sizzling with broiled grouper, shrimp, scallops, and crabmeat drenched in butter and sprinkled with cheese. Its tangy seafood gumbo also has gained fame for this casual, historic restaurant. In addition to the bread, main courses are accompanied by salad and dessert. A pianist plays at dinner year-round.

Inexpensive
○ **Magnolia Grill.** In Brooks Bridge 98 Center, 255 SE Miracle Strip Pkwy. (U.S. 98), on the mainland at the north end of Brooks Bridge. ☎ **850/302-0266.** Reservations accepted. Sandwiches and salads $3–$7. Main courses $8–$16. AE, MC, V. Mon–Sat 11am–9pm. SEAFOOD/CAJUN/ITALIAN.

Don't think this is just another shopping-center restaurant, for the Magnolia Grill is the province of Tom Rice, an accomplished local chef who honed his skills at several other establishments before opening his own here in 1996. Upon first impression, the decor resembles a diner with an old-fashioned ice-cream parlor, but look again. Tom and his wife, Peggy, scoured every attic in town for an amazing collection of 1940s to 1960s memorabilia. Every table has an old radio or portable typewriter, and the walls sport a collection of photos that show Fort Walton Beach a half century ago. You may not notice, but the divider down the center of the room actually is the art deco sign salvaged from Eloise Shop, once an elegant ladies' clothier here. Tom also has resurrected some favorite old local recipes, including a scintillating asparagus mold served under a horseradish sauce, and J.S.'s Famous Warm Cuban Sandwich. Otherwise, his seafood, Cajun, and Italian fare also shows the fine touch he has developed over the years.

IN SOUTHERN WALTON COUNTY
Buster's Oyster Bar and Seafood Restaurant. 125 Poinciana Blvd., in Delchamps Plaza, U.S. 98 at Scenic Hwy. 98. ☎ **850/837-4399.** Reservations not accepted. Main courses $11–$15; sandwiches and burgers $5.50–$7. AE, DC, DISC, MC, V. Apr–Oct daily 11am–11pm. Nov–Mar daily 11am–10pm. SEAFOOD.

Shingles, plants, and wood make this local favorite seem not at all like a shopping-center sports bar, 1 mile west of The Resort at Sandestin. Buster claims that more than five million oysters have been shucked here, and with good reason, since they go for $1.59 a dozen during his daily 5 to 6pm happy hour. Another winner here is Buster's spicy gumbo, which has won recent cook-off competitions. The colorful, tabloid-style menu also offers the likes of "a toasted sea spider sandwich" (soft-shell crab). Fried, broiled, steamed, or blackened fish and seafood dinners are prepared to order. Kids have their own menu.

○ **Cafe New Orleans.** 12273 Emerald Coast Pkwy. (U.S. 98), in Holiday Plaza, 3 miles east of Mid-Bay Bridge. ☎ **850/650-4545.** Reservations not accepted. Beignets and sandwiches

$2–$6; main courses $7–$10. AE, MC, V. Summer Mon–Fri 7am–9pm. Off-season Mon–Sat 7am–8pm. CAJUN.

Transplanted here from New Orleans, Ernie and Dawn Danjean bring a terrific taste of the Big Easy to their little fast-food–style restaurant, in a small shopping center about a mile west of the Silver Sands Factory Stores. Their breakfast beignets are made from dough blended back home by the same firm which supplies the French Quarter's famous Cafe du Monde. Or you can start your day with a po' boy of eggs, ham, and cheese. For lunch, their spicy gumbo comes in a whopping 18-ounce cup—that's large enough for a meal in itself. A platter of lightly breaded, highly seasoned fried seafood also will fill you up. They also offer a mouth-watering daily special, such as a lightly battered catfish under a spicy shrimp étoufée sauce. Order at the counter here.

✪ **Criolla's.** 170 E. Scenic Hwy. 30A, ¼ mile east of County Rd. 283, Grayton Beach. ☎ **850/267-1267.** Reservations recommended. Main courses $18–$28. DISC, MC, V. Jan–Feb and Oct–Dec Tues–Sat 5:30–10pm; Mar–Apr and Sept Mon–Sat 5:30–10pm; May–Aug daily 5:30–10pm. LOUISIANA CREOLE/CARIBBEAN.

One of Florida's finest restaurants, Johnny Earles's charming establishment derives its name from the archaic word *criollo*, signifying persons of pure Spanish descent born in the New World. The attractive decor, combining New Orleans with the Caribbean, features potted palms, whirling ceiling fans, and tropical-island paintings. Seasonal menus carry out the theme, always offering Creole and Caribbean selections. Many fish dishes carry the wonderful aroma of smoke from a wood-fired grill. It's worth asking in advance about special events featuring visiting chefs and spotlighting excellent vineyards (the wine cellar here has won awards).

Lake Place Restaurant. 5960 County Rd. 30A, Dune Allen Beach. ☎ **850/267-2871.** Reservations required in summer, recommended off-season. Main courses $17–$27. AE, DISC, MC, V. Tues–Sat 5:30–9pm. SEAFOOD.

Owners Richard and Evalee Grenamyer scour the markets each morning for fresh fish, which they serve at this rustic plank building on the shores of picturesque Lake Allen. You can order the daily catch crispy fried, sautéed with white wine and roasted garlic sauce, or herb crusted with jumbo crabmeat and butter sauce. There are steaks, lamb and pork chops, and free-range chicken for landlubbers. An excellent wine list changes daily to complement each evening's special dishes.

In Seaside

✪ **Bud and Alley's.** County Rd. 30A, in the beachside shops. ☎ **850/231-5900.** Reservations recommended. Lunch $7.50–$14; main courses $17.50–$24.50. MC, V. Sun–Thurs 11:30am–3pm and 6–9:30pm, Fri–Sat 11:30am–3pm and 6–10pm. Closed Jan. SEAFOOD/ STEAKS/MEDITERRANEAN.

Set among the gulfside dunes, Seaside's first restaurant is still number one to its steady patrons. The freshest of seafood can be selected from seasonal menus featuring an innovative selection of Basque, Italian, Louisianan, and Floridian dishes prepared by owners and accomplished chefs Scott Witcoski and Dave Raushkolb. You can dine indoors or outdoors, on the screened porch, or under an open-air gazebo where you hear the waves splashing against the white sands. Opening during the warm months at 3pm weekdays, 11am weekends, a roof deck offers a variety of appetizers and light meals. Jazz is usually in the spotlight on weekends. On New Year's Eve, everyone in town and from miles around celebrates at Bud and Alley's. Call ahead to see if a noted guest chef is cooking or a special wine-tasting dinner is scheduled (there's an extensive list here). No smoking.

Shades. Town Sq. and Markets. ☎ **850/231-1950.** Reservations not accepted. Main courses $14–$17; sandwiches and burgers $5–$9. AE, DISC, MC, V. Summer daily 8–10am and 11am–10pm. Off-season daily 8–10am and 11am–9pm. AMERICAN.

In another life this was a rustic house built in the early 1900s in the small town of Chattahoochee. It was moved to Seaside's Town Square some 70 years later and reborn as this quaint restaurant, which doubles as Seaside's community pub. Stacked-high sandwiches, hot wings, and hamburgers are popular for lunch. At dinner, the bountiful fried seafood platter is a big favorite. Dine inside or on the porch in warm weather.

DESTIN & FORT WALTON BEACH AFTER DARK

Most resorts spotlight live entertainment during the summer season, including the Radisson Beach Resort and the Ramada Beach Resort in Fort Walton Beach, and the Sandestin Hilton and The Resort at Sandestin in southern Walton County (see "Where to Stay" above). It's a good idea to inquire ahead to make sure what's scheduled, especially during the slow season from October through February.

DESTIN   Several Destin restaurants offer entertainment nightly during summer, on weekends off-season. The dockside **AJ's Club Bimini,** 116 U.S. 98 East (☎ 850/ 837-1913), has live reggae under a big thatch-roofed deck. A somewhat older, if not more sober, crowd gathers for entertainment at the big harborside deck at **Fisherman's Wharf,** on U.S. 98 East (☎ 850/654-4766); at **The Deck,** on U.S. 98 East at the Harbor Docks restaurant, overlooking the harbor (☎ 850/837-2506); at **Harry T's Boat House** (☎ 850/654-6555), also on the harbor; and for Irish tunes nightly year-round at **McGuire's Irish Pub & Brewery** (☎ 850/650-0000), in the Harborwalk Shops on U.S. 98 just east of the Destin Bridge. See "Where to Dine" above for details about the restaurants. The **Grande Isle Sky Bar,** above Grazti Italian Restaurant, 1771 Old Hwy. 98 (☎ 850/837-7475), draws the after-dinner crowd from the Back Porch and other adjacent restaurants.

Twenty-somethings are attracted to the dance club, rowdy saloon, Jimmy Buffet–style reggae bar, and sports TV and billiards parlor all under one roof at the acclaimed **Nightown,** 140 Palmetto St. (☎ 850/837-6448), near the harbor on the inland side of U.S. 98 East. One admission of $3 to $7 covers it all. Nearby, **Hogs Breath Destin,** 541 Hwy. 98 East (☎ 850/837-5991), is another lively pub with bands playing beach music.

Out toward Sandestin, **Fudrucker's Beachside Bar & Grill,** 20001 Hwy. 98 East (☎ 850/654-4200), opposite the Henderson Beach State Recreation Area, offers double the fun with two summertime stages, one on the bayside deck, the other in the Down Under Bar. There's another Fudrucker's at 108 Santa Rosa Blvd. on Okaloosa Island in Fort Walton Beach (☎ 850/243-3833).

FORT WALTON BEACH   Country music and dancing fans will find a home at the **Seagull,** on Miracle Strip Parkway (U.S. 98) opposite the Gulfarium (☎ 850/ 243-3413). The generations of air force pilots who have hung out here call it the "Dirty Gull." Its main rival for the country set is the **High Tide Oyster Bar,** at Okaloosa Island off the Brooks Bridge (☎ 850/244-2624). Over at the Boardwalk on U.S. 98 East, the **Soggy Dollar Saloon** (☎ 850/243-5500) has live music on weekends.

The young beach set is attracted to rock and reggae in Shanty Town, on the east side of Brooks Bridge, where **Hoser's,** 1225 Santa Rosa Blvd. (☎ 850/664-6113), is the liveliest pub (its name mirrors a fire-fighting motif).

3 Panama City Beach

100 miles E of Pensacola, 100 miles SW of Tallahassee

Panama City Beach has long been known as the "Redneck Riviera," since it's a summertime mecca for millions of low- and moderate-income vacationers from nearby southern states. It still has a seemingly unending strip of bars, amusement parks, and old-fashioned motels. But this lively and crowded destination now also has luxury resorts and condominiums to go along with its 20-plus miles of white-sand beach, golf courses, fishing, boating, and fresh seafood.

Panama City Beach is also the most seasonal resort in Northwest Florida, as many restaurants, attractions, and even some hotels close between October and spring break in March. Spring break is a big deal here; MTV even sets up shop in Panama City Beach for its annual beach-party broadcasts.

ESSENTIALS

GETTING THERE **Delta** (☎ 800/221-1212), **Northwest/KLM** (☎ 800/225-2525), and **US Airways** (☎ 800/428-4322) fly into **Panama City/Bay County International Airport,** on Airport Road, north of St. Andrews Boulevard, in Panama City.

Avis (☎ 800/331-1212), **Budget** (☎ 800/527-0700), **Hertz** (☎ 800/654-3131), and **National** (☎ 800/CAR-RENT) have rental-car booths at the airport.

Taxi fares to the beach range from about $12 to $25.

The *Sunset Limited* transcontinental service on **Amtrak** (☎ **800/USA-RAIL**) stops at Chipley, 45 miles north of Panama City.

VISITOR INFORMATION For advance information, contact the **Panama City Beach Convention & Visitors Bureau,** P.O. Box 9473, Panama City Beach, FL 32407 (☎ **800/PC-BEACH** or 850/233-6503; www.travelfile.com/get?pcbeach). It operates the **James I. Lark Sr. Visitors Information Center,** on the beach at 12015 Front Beach Rd. opposite the Miracle Strip Amusement Park. Open daily from 8am to 5pm.

You can buy detailed maps at **Alvin's Island Tropical Department Store,** across the street from the visitor center.

GETTING AROUND There is no public transportation at the beach. Call **AAA Taxi** (☎ 850/785-0533), **Yellow Cab** (☎ 850/763-4691), or **Deluxe Coach Service** (☎ **800/763-0211** or 850/763-0211). Fares are based on a zone system rather than on meters. Local fares in Panama City Beach will range from $5 to $9.

TIME The Panama City area is in the **central time zone,** 1 hour behind Miami, Orlando, and Tallahassee.

HITTING THE BEACH

A nearly unbroken strand of fine white sand fronts all the 22 miles of Panama City Beach, but the highlight for many here is ✪ **St. Andrews State Recreation Area,** 4607 State Park Lane, at the east end of the beach (☎ 850/233-5140). With more than 1,000 acres of dazzling white sand and dunes, this preserved wilderness demonstrates what the area looked like before motels and condominiums lined the beach. Lacy, golden sea oats sway in the refreshing gulf breezes, and fragrant rosemary grows wild. Picnic areas are on both the gulf beach and Grand Lagoon. Rest rooms and open-air showers are available for beachgoers. For anglers, there are jetties and a boat ramp. A nature trail reveals wading birds and perhaps an alligator or two. And drive carefully here, for the area is home to foxes, coyotes, and a herd of deer. Overnight camping is permitted (see "Where to Stay" below). On display is a historic turpentine still formerly used by lumbermen to make turpentine and rosin, both important for caulking the old wooden ships. Admission is $4 per car with two to eight occupants, $2 for single-occupant vehicles, and $1 for pedestrians and cyclists. The area is open daily from 8am to sunset.

A few hundred yards across an inlet from St. Andrews State Recreation Area sits pristine ✪ **Shell Island,** a 7½-mile-long, 1-mile-wide barrier island. This uninhabited natural preserve is great for shelling and also fun for swimming, suntanning, or just relaxing. Visitors can bring chairs, beach gear, coolers, food, and beverages. The island is accessible only by boat. **A ferry shuttle** (☎ **850/233-5140**) runs from April to October between St. Andrews State Recreation Area and the island every 30 minutes: daily from 9am to 5pm in summer, weekends from 10am to 3pm in spring and fall. Fares are $7.50 for adults, $5.50 for children 11 and under, plus admission fees to the state recreation area (see above). A special snorkel package costs $16.95, including shuttle ride and equipment, and a 3-hour "ecosnorkel" tour for $24.95 departs twice daily.

Several cruise boats go to Shell Island, including the glass-bottom *Capt. Anderson III,* which cruises there from Capt. Anderson's Marina, 5500 N. Lagoon Dr., at Thomas Drive (☎ **850/234-3435**). It charges $10 for anyone over age 12, $8 for kids. The *Glass Bottom Boat* (☎ **850/234-8944**) stops at Shell Island as part of its "sea school" trips from Treasure Island Marina, 3605 Thomas Dr. at Grand Lagoon (see "Cruises," under "Outdoor Pursuits," below).

OUTDOOR PURSUITS

BOATING   Various rental boats are available at the marinas near the Thomas Drive bridge over Grand Lagoon. These include the **Capt. Davis Queen Fleet,** based at Capt. Anderson's Marina, 5500 N. Lagoon Dr. (☎ 800/874-2415, or 850/234-3435 from nearby states); the **Panama City Boat Yard,** 5323 N. Lagoon Dr. (☎ 850/234-3386); the **Passport Marina,** 5325 N. Lagoon Dr. (☎ 850/234-5609); the **Port Lagoon Yacht Basin,** 5201 N. Lagoon Dr. (☎ 850/234-0142); the **Pirates Cove Marina,** 3901 Thomas Dr. (☎ 850/234-3839); and the **Treasure Island Marina,** 3605 Thomas Dr. (☎ 850/234-6533).

Many resorts and hotels provide beach toys for their guests' use. Wave Runners, jet boats, inflatables, and other equipment can be rented from **Panama City Beach Sports** (☎ 850/234-0067), **Raging Rentals** (☎ 850/234-6775), and **Lagoon Rentals** (☎ 850/234-7245).

CRUISES   You'll have your choice of numerous cruises here, from sailing to visiting the dolphins aboard noisy jet skis. The visitor information center (see "Essentials," above), has information about them all—and discount coupons for many.

One of the most comprehensive outings here is aboard the *Glass Bottom Boat,* based at Treasure Island Marina, 3605 Thomas Dr., at Grand Lagoon (☎ 850/234-8944). Its 3-hour, narrated "sea school" cruise includes underwater viewing, dolphin watching, bird feeding, and a 1-hour stop for swimming at Shell Island. Along the way, the crew picks up and rebaits a crab trap and explains the creatures brought up in a shrimp net. The boat has a snack bar and an air-conditioned cabin. The trips cost about $14 for adults and $8 for children. This same company operates a **Super Shelling Safari,** on which guests are taken to the eastern end of Shell Island to scavenge in the shallow water for shells (wear your bathing suit). Call for cruise times, exact prices, and reservations.

The venerable **Capt. Davis Queen Fleet,** based at Capt. Anderson's Marina, 5500 N. Lagoon Dr. (☎ **800/874-2415** from neighboring states, or 850/234-3435 in

Florida), has daily sightseeing trips, nature cruises, dolphin-watching and bird-feeding excursions, and dinner-dance cruises during the summer season.

FISHING   A relatively inexpensive way for novices to try their luck fishing is with **Capt. Anderson's Deep Sea Fishing,** at Capt. Anderson's Marina on Thomas Drive at Grand Lagoon (☎ **800/874-2415** or 850/234-5940). The captain's party-boat trips last from 5 to 12 hours, with prices ranging from about $30 to $50 per person, including bait and tackle. Observers can go along for half price.

More expensive are the charter-fishing boats that depart daily from March to November from the marinas mentioned in "Boating," above.

You can cast your line from the concrete **Dan Russell Municipal Pier.**

GOLF   Thirty-six holes of championship golf are offered at ✪ **Marriott's Bay Point Resort Village,** 4200 Marriott Dr., off Jan Cooley Road (☎ **850/234-3307**), where the Bruce Devlin–designed Lagoon Legends and the Club Meadows courses offer 36 holes of championship play—Lagoon Legends is rated as one of the country's most difficult. Both have clubhouses, putting greens, driving ranges, clinics, and private instruction. Greens fees with cart range from about $50 in summer to $80 in winter, depending on day of the week. See "Where to Stay" below.

The **Edgewater Beach Resort,** 11212 U.S. 98A (☎ **850/235-4044**), also has a nine-hole resort course.

O.J. Simpson made the rounds at **The Hombre,** 120 Coyote Pass, 3 miles west of the Hathaway Bridge off Panama City Beach Parkway/U.S. 98 (☎ **850/234-3573**). This par-72 championship course is home to the Nike Panama City Beach Classic. Fifteen of its 18 holes have water hazards (the unforgiving 7th hole sits on an island). Greens fees are about $65 in summer, $60 in winter, including cart.

The championship course at the semiprivate **Holiday Golf Club,** 100 Fairway Blvd. (☎ **850/234-1800**), sports lake-line fairways and elevated greens. Greens fees with cart are about $45 in summer, $35 in winter. You can play at night here on a lighted nine-hole, par-29 executive course.

The least expensive place to play here is the flat and forgiving **Signal Hill,** 9516 N. Thomas Dr. (☎ **850/234-3218**), where you'll pay about $20 to walk 18 holes in summer, $13 in winter. Add about $10 per person for a cart.

SCUBA DIVING & SNORKELING   Although the area is too far north for extensive coral formations, more than 50 artificial reefs and shipwrecks in the Gulf waters off Panama City attract a wide variety of sea life. Local operators include **Hydrospace Dive Shop,** 6422 W. Hwy. 98 (☎ **850/234-3036**); the **Panama City Dive Center,** 4823 Thomas Dr. (☎ **850/235-3390**); **Emerald Coast Divers,** 5121 Thomas Dr. (☎ **800/945-DIVE** or 850/233-3355); **West End Dive Center,** 17320 Panama City Beach Pkwy. (☎ **850/235-7873**); and **Pete's Scuba Center,** 9007 Front Beach Rd. (☎ **800/401-DIVE** or 850/230-8006). These companies lead dives, teach courses, and take snorkelers to the grass flats off Shell Island.

EXPLORING THE AREA

Gulf World Marine Park. 15412 Front Beach Rd. (at Hill Ave.), Panama City Beach. ☎ **850/234-5271.** Admission $17 adults, $10.50 children 5–12, free for children 4 and under. Summer daily 9am–7pm. Off-season daily 9am–3pm. Call for hours Oct–Nov.

This landscaped tropical garden and marine showcase features shows with talented dolphins, sea lions, penguins, and more. Not to be upstaged, parrots perform daily, too. Sea turtles, alligators, and other critters also call Gulf World home. Scuba demonstrations, shark feedings, and underwater shows keep the crowds entertained. Allow about 2½ hours to see it all.

Museum of Man in the Sea. 17314 Panama City Beach Pkwy. (at Heather Dr., west of Fla. 79), Panama City Beach. ☎ **850/235-4101.** Admission $5 adults, $2.50 children 6–16, free for children 5 and under. Daily 9am–5pm. Closed New Year's Day, Thanksgiving, and Christmas.

Owned by the Institute of Diving, this unusual museum exhibits relics from the first days of scuba diving, historical displays of the underwater world dating from 1500, and treasures recovered from sunken ships, including Spanish treasure galleons. Hands-on exhibits include experiments on water and air pressure, light refraction, and why diving bells work. Both kids and adults can climb through a submarine, see live sea animals in a pool, and look out of a diving helmet. Videos and aquariums explain the sea life found in St. Andrew Bay.

✪ **ZooWorld Zoological & Botanical Park.** 9008 Front Beach Rd. (near Moylan Dr.), Panama City Beach. ☎ **850/230-1243.** Admission $8.95 adults, $7.95 seniors, $6.50 children 3–11, free for children under 3. Daily 9am to 1 hour before sunset. Closed New Year's Day and Christmas.

The largest captive alligator in Florida ("Mr. Bubba") lives in a re-created pine forest habitat at this educational and entertaining zoo, an active participant in the Species Survival Plan, which helps protect endangered species with specific breeding and housing programs. Other guests here include rare and endangered animals as well as orangutans and other primates, big cats, more reptiles, and other creatures. Also included are a walk-through aviary, a bat exhibit, and a petting zoo.

AMUSEMENT PARKS

An exciting, 105-foot-high roller coaster is just one of the 30 rides at the **Miracle Strip Amusement Park,** 12000 Front Beach Rd., at Alf Coleman Road (☎ **850/234-5810**). Little ones will love the traditional carousel. The 9 acres of fun include nonstop live entertainment and tons of junk food. Hours and prices change from year to year, so call for the latest. It's closed from Labor Day to mid-March.

Adjoining the amusement park, the **Shipwreck Island Water Park** (☎ **850/234-0368**) offers a variety of water-related fun, including the 1,600-foot winding Lazy River for tubing and a daring 35 m.p.h. Speed Slide. The Tad Pole Hole is exclusively for young kids. Lounge chairs, umbrellas, and inner tubes are free, and lifeguards are on duty. Admission is less than $20. Open June to mid-August; call for hours.

SHOPPING

An attraction in itself is the main branch of **Alvin's Island Tropical Department Store,** 12010 Front Beach Rd. (☎ **850/234-3048**), opposite the James I. Lark Sr. Visitors Information Center. It not only sells a wide range of beach gear and apparel, but also has cages containing colorful parrots, tanks with small sharks, and an enclosure with alligators. The sharks are fed at 11am daily; the gators get theirs at 4pm (the older ones are too lethargic to eat during the cool winter months).

The **African Curio Shoppe,** 8730 Thomas Dr., at Joan Avenue (☎ **800/235-1351** or 850/235-1288), is another fascinating place to browse for stuffed animal heads and wood carvings, soapstone sculptures, leather bags, and other handcrafts from Africa. Open daily 9:30am to 9:30pm in summer, Wednesday to Saturday 9am to 6pm off-season.

WHERE TO STAY

There are literally scores of motels along the beach here, ranging from small mom-and-pop operations to sizable members of national chains. The annual guide distributed by the Panama City Beach Convention & Visitors Bureau has a complete list (see "Essentials" above). Among the beachside chain motels, you'll find the **Best Western Casa Loma** (☎ **800/528-1234** or 850/234-1100), the **Days Inn Beach** (☎ **800/ 329-7466** or 850/233-3333), and the **Ramada Inn Beach & Convention Center** (☎ **800/228-3344** or 850/234-1700). The somewhat–less-expensive **Best Western Del Coronado** (☎ **800/528-1234** or 850/234-1600) is open from March to September.

Panama City Beach also abounds with condominium complexes, such as the Edgewater Beach Resort listed below. Although it's not on the beach, the **Inn at St. Thomas Square,** 8730 Thomas Dr., Panama City Beach, FL 32408 (☎ **800/ 874-8600** or 850/234-0349; fax 850/235-8104), has charm and enjoys a quiet location. The complex consists of some units above the small St. Thomas Square shopping center, at Thomas Drive and Joan Avenue, but highly preferable are the Spanish-style, town-house–looking apartments set along the skinny upper arm of Grand Lagoon. There are a pool, a hot tub, and tennis court on the premises. Rates range from $85 for efficiencies to $175 for three-bedroom apartments in summer. Off-season they go for $55 to $99, respectively. The complex is operated by Basic Management Inc., which also has some beachfront units to rent.

Also among the many agencies offering condominium apartments are **St. Andrew Bay Resort Management,** 726 Thomas Dr., Panama City Beach, FL 32408 (☎ **800/ 621-2462** or 850/235-4075; fax 850/233-2833; www.sabre1.net); and **Condo World,** 8815A Thomas Dr. (P.O. Box 9456), Panama City Beach, FL 32408 (☎ **800/ 232-6636** or 850/234-5564; fax 850/233-6725; www.condoworld-pcb-fla.com).

This area has two of the Panhandle's finest campgrounds, both with sites right beside the water. ✪ **St. Andrews State Recreation Area,** 4607 State Park Lane, Panama City Beach (☎ **850/233-5140**), one of this area's major attractions (see "Hitting the Beach" above), has RV and tent sites beautifully situated in a pine forest right on the shores of Grand Lagoon. Rates from March to September are $19 to $21 for waterfront sites, $17 to $19 for others. They drop to $8 to $12 from October to February. Reservations are required, up to 11 months in advance. No pets are allowed.

You can bring your pet, but not your tent, to **Magnolia Beach RV Park,** 7800 Magnolia Beach Rd., Panama City Beach, FL 322408 (☎ **850/235-1581**), with great views of Panama City from an idyllic setting under magnolias and moss-draped oaks on the shores of St. Andrew Bay. Rates are $22 to $26 a night in summer, $18 to $21 off-season. The park is 2 miles from Marriott's Bay Point Resort Village. Take Magnolia Beach Road off Thomas Drive and go straight to the camp.

Bay County adds 3.5% tax to all hotel and campground bills, bringing the total add-on tax to 9.5%.

MODERATE

Beachcomber by the Sea. 17101 Front Beach Rd., Panama City Beach, FL 32413. ☎ **888/ 886-8916** or 850/233-3600. Fax 850/233-3622. www.beachcomberbythesea.com. 96 units. A/C TV TEL. Summer $99–$125. Off-season $39–$85. Rates include continental breakfast. Packages available. AE, DISC, MC, V.

Watercolors by local artist Paul Brent grace every unit in this eight-story all-suites resort, built and opened in 1998 at the junction of Front Beach Road and Fla. 79. They also have balconies overlooking a gulfside swimming pool and hot tub bordered by a concrete deck accented by areas of palm trees. The well-equipped suites come in two sizes. The larger editions have living rooms with sleeper sofas, bedrooms with either king-size or two full beds, plus their own phones and TVs. Bathrooms and kitchenettes separate the living rooms and bedrooms. The smaller units are more motel-like; they have microwaves, coffeemakers, and shower-only bathrooms. Two of the smaller units also have Jacuzzis. There's no restaurant here (several are nearby), but you will have a games room and guest laundry. Spring breakers are not welcome here.

Edgewater Beach Resort. 11212 Front Beach Rd. (P.O. Box 9850), Panama City Beach, FL 32407. ☎ **800/874-8686** or 850/235-4044. Fax 850/233-7599. 510 units. Summer $105–$358 condo. Off-season $57–$144 condo. Weekly rates and maid service available. AE, DC, DISC, MC, V.

One of the Panhandle's largest condominium resorts, this sports-oriented facility enjoys a beautiful beachfront location and 110 tropically landscaped acres. Units in five gulfside towers enjoy commanding views of the emerald Gulf and gorgeous sunsets from their private balconies. A pedestrian overpass leads across Front Beach Road to low-rise apartments and town homes fringing ponds and the fairways of the resort's own nine-hole golf course. A daytime shuttle runs around the resort to three swimming pools, whirlpools, 12 tennis courts (6 lighted), the resort's own nine-hole golf course, and the 18-hole Hombre Golf Club, a quarter mile north.

Food outlets here serve all three meals, and the Shoppes at Edgewater restaurants are across the road.

Holiday Inn SunSpree Resort. 11127 Front Beach Rd., Panama City Beach, FL 32407. ☎ **800/633-0266** or 850/234-1111. Fax 850/235-0888. 342 units. A/C TV TEL. Summer $149–$259 double. Off-season $59–$129 double. Weekly and monthly rates available. AE, DC, DISC, MC, V.

One building removed from the Edgewater Beach Resort and across the road from the Shoppes at Edgewater, this 15-story establishment is the top full-service gulf-front hotel here. It's designed in an arch, with all rooms having balconies looking directly down on the beach, where a foot-shaped swimming pool and wooden sundeck are separated from the beach by a row of palms and Polynesian torches, which are lighted at night. The hotel has won architectural awards for its dramatic lobby with a waterfall and the Fountain of Wishes (coins go to charity). The attractive, spacious guest rooms feature full-size ice-making refrigerators, microwave ovens, and two spacious vanity areas with their own lavatory sinks.

There's a poolside grill for lunches, while the lobby restaurant under a skylight dome features good breakfasts, lunches, and dinners at moderate prices. There's a Pizza Hut outlet for carryout pies. The lively Starlight Lounge serves drinks until late and usually offers entertainment during the peak summer season. The lobby bar has sports TVs, and there's poolside entertainment during summer evenings. Facilities include a swimming pool, a sundeck, a whirlpool, exercise and game rooms, a gift shop, and a children's playground.

✪ **Marriott's Bay Point Resort Village.** 4200 Marriott Dr., Panama City Beach, FL 32408. ☎ **800/874-7105** or 850/234-3307. Fax 850/233-1308. 355 units. A/C TV TEL. Summer $119–$169 double. Off-season $99–$129 double. Packages available. AE, DC, DISC, MC, V. From Thomas Dr., take Magnolia Beach Rd. and follow the signs for 3 miles.

Not only is this luxurious vacation miniworld ranked among the nation's top golf and tennis resorts, but it's an extraordinarily good value for Florida as well. Although guests pay extra for most activities, its room rates are among the top steals in the state. They would be higher if the property were beside the gulf; instead, it's the centerpiece of a real-estate development sprawling over 1,100 landscaped acres on a peninsula bordered by St. Andrew Bay and Grand Lagoon. Situated beside the lagoon, the luxurious, vivid-coral stucco hotel is surrounded by gardens, palm trees, oaks, and magnolias. From the glamorous three-story lobby, window walls look out to scenic water views and four swimming pools (one in its own glass-enclosed building). Furnished in dark woods, the Marriottesque rooms are spacious and luxurious.

You won't go hungry here, for the Bay View Restaurant in the hotel serves breakfast, lunch, and dinner featuring moderately price buffets. Outlets in the Lagoon Legends pro shop next door serve breakfast, snacks, and light meals at lunch. Snacks and libations also are proffered from March to October on the long pier in front of the hotel, where daylong beach parties go on during summer. Sports fans will find TVs going nonstop in the English-style bar off the lobby.

The highlights for duffers are the Lagoon Legends and the Club Meadows golf courses (see "Outdoor Pursuits," above). The Bay Point Tennis Center has 12 clay courts (4 lighted), a tennis shop, clinics, and lessons. Water sports here are at Grand Lagoon beach, reached by the hotel's long pier, where both guests and nonguests can rent Wave Runners and boats, and go waterskiing and parasailing during the season. The *Island Queen* paddle wheeler departs the pier for sunset cruises and excursions to Shell Island. Guests can burn off the calories at two health clubs, and excess money at the Bay Town Shops, which have a deli and dry cleaner. Over at the marina, the Bay Point Billfish Invitational in July is one of the world's richest. Rent a bike or scooter at the front desk to get around this widespread resort.

INEXPENSIVE

Flamingo Motel. 15525 Front Beach Rd., Panama City Beach, FL 32413. ☎ **800/ 828-0400** or 850/234-2232. Fax 850/234-8191. 118 units. A/C TV TEL. Summer $79–$129. Off-season $39–$89. AE, DISC, MC, V.

Evoking Key West, this well-maintained, family-owned motel takes great pride in its gorgeous tropical garden surrounding a heated swimming pool and a large sundeck overlooking the Gulf. The brightly decorated rooms have either full kitchens or refrigerators and microwave ovens. They can sleep two to six people, some in separate bedrooms. Kitchenette rooms in a two-story motel block across the road are less appealing but will accommodate six to eight. Budget-conscious families can opt for the low-priced rooms, accommodating two to four. Some units have shower-only baths. The Dan Russell fishing pier is only half a mile away, Gulf World is within walking distance, and Shuckums Oyster Pub & Seafood Grill is across the road (see "Exploring the Area" above, and "Where to Dine" below). Forget spending spring break here unless you're a family or a couple.

Next door, the seven-story **Flamingo Towers** contains 49 suites, all sporting living rooms with sofa beds and dining tables; bedrooms with ceiling fans, two full beds (a few have kings), and their own TVs; kitchens; combination tub/shower bathrooms; and balconies overlooking a gulfside swimming pool and hot tub.

Georgian Terrace. 14415 Front Beach Rd., Panama City Beach, FL 32413. ☎ and fax **888/882-2144** or 850/234-2144. www.georgianterrace.com. 28 units. A/C TV TEL. Summer $79–$94 double. Off-season $49–$69 double. AE, DISC, MC, V.

Right on the beach, Karen Grant's two-level motel offers clean, quiet, and cozy apartments. Opening to the beach, cheerfully decorated, and lined with knotty pine, they all have full kitchens separated by room dividers. The homey decor is extended to each unit's private enclosed sun porch. A greenhouse-enclosed heated pool area with lush tropical plantings and attractive lounge chairs makes this place a good pick off-season. There's a rare stretch of undeveloped beach almost next door.

Sunset Inn. 8109 Surf Dr., Panama City Beach, FL 32408. ☎ and fax **850/234-7370.** 62 units. A/C TV TEL. Summer $55–$155 double. Off-season $35–$110 double. Weekly and monthly rates available. AE, DISC, MC, V.

This very-well-maintained establishment, off Thomas Drive between Chicksaw and Snapper streets near the east end of the beach, is right on the Gulf but away from the crowds. The beachside units accommodate families in one- and two-bedroom apartments with kitchens, while across the street stand an older block of efficiencies and a new building with tropically furnished one- and two-bedroom condos (the most expensive units here). The inn sports a large unheated swimming pool and a spacious sundeck with steps leading down to the beach.

WHERE TO DINE

Except for fast-food joints, there aren't many national chain family restaurants in Panama City Beach (you'll find those along 15th and 23rd streets over in Panama City). There is one local chain worth a meal: the **Montego Bay Seafood Houses,** which offer a wide range of munchies, sandwiches, burgers, and seafood main courses, most in the inexpensive category. Branches are at the "curve" on Thomas Drive (☎ **850/234-8687**); at the intersection of Thomas Drive and Middle and Front Beach roads (☎ **850/236-3585**); and in the Shoppes at Edgewater, Front Beach Drive at Beckrich Road (☎ **850/233-6033**).

Pay attention to the restaurant hours here, for some places are closed during the winter months.

MODERATE

Boar's Head Restaurant. 17290 Front Beach Rd. (just west of Fla. 79). ☎ **850/234-6628.** Reservations accepted. Main courses $12–$20. AE, DC, DISC, MC, V. Summer daily 4:30–10pm. Off-season Sun–Thurs 4:30–9pm, Fri–Sat 4:30–10pm. STEAKS/SEAFOOD.

An institution here since 1978, this shingle-roofed establishment appears from the road to be a South Seas resort. Inside, its impressive beamed ceiling, stone walls, and fireplaces create a warm, almost-English tavern atmosphere suitable to the house specialties: tender, marbled prime rib of beef and perfectly cooked steaks. Beef eaters don't have the Boar's Head to themselves, however, for the coals are also used to give a charred flavor to shrimp and tuna. Other cooking styles are offered too, including a combination of lobster, shrimp, and scallops in a cream sauce over angel-hair pasta. And venison, quail, and other game find their way here during winter. An extensive wine list has won awards, and a cozy tavern to one side has live music, usually Wednesday to Saturday evenings.

✪ **Canopies.** 4423 W. Hwy. 98, Panama City (1 mile east of Hathaway Bridge on U.S. 98). ☎ **850/872-8444.** Reservations recommended. Main courses $14–$35. Early-bird specials $10. AE, DISC, MC, V. Daily 5–10pm. Early-bird specials daily 5–6pm. Closed Thanksgiving and Christmas. SEAFOOD/STEAKS.

This area's most elegant restaurant and purveyor of its finest cuisine occupies a 1910-vintage gray clapboard house with a magnificent view of St. Andrew Bay. Dining is on an enclosed veranda, but the dark, cozy bar in the old living room invites before- or after-dinner drinks. The menu changes every week or two, but consistent favorites are a creamy she-crab soup under a flaky croissant dome; grilled tuna, salmon, or grouper with a trio of sauces; sautéed grouper with lump crabmeat in a sherry-butter sauce; and sushi-quality yellowfin tuna in a sherry-soy sauce served over a haystack of leaks. Landlubbers can partake of award-winning beef, veal, lamb, pork, and game dishes. White chocolate mousse is among several gourmet dessert and coffee creations to top off these delicious meals.

Capt. Anderson's Restaurant. 5551 N. Lagoon Dr. (at Thomas Dr.). ☎ **850/234-2225.** Reservations not accepted. Main courses $11–$35. AE, DC, DISC, MC, V. Mon–Sat 4–10pm (or later, depending on crowds). Closed Nov–Jan. SEAFOOD.

Since 1953 this famous restaurant has been attracting early diners who come to watch the fishing fleet unload the catch of the day at the busy marina on Grand Lagoon. It's so popular, in fact, that you may have to wait 2 hours for a table during the peak summer months, either in the air-conditioned lounge or on the covered patio. The Captain's menu is noted for grilled local fish, crabmeat-stuffed jumbo shrimp, and a heaped-high seafood platter. If this is your first time at Panama City Beach, don't miss the local atmosphere at Capt. Anderson's.

Hamilton's Seafood Restaurant & Lounge. 5711 N. Lagoon Dr. (at Thomas Dr.). ☎ **850/234-1255.** Reservations not accepted. Main courses $13–$20. AE, DISC, MC, V. Sun–Thurs 4–10pm, Fri–Sat 4–11pm. Closed 2 days a week off-season (call ahead), Jan, first week of Dec. SEAFOOD.

Proprietor Steve Stevens continues in the tradition of his noted Biloxi, Mississippi, restaurateur father. The attractive blond-wood and knotty-pine restaurant lies on Grand Lagoon. The baked oysters Hamilton appetizer—a rich combination of oysters, shrimp, and crabmeat—almost left me too full for a main course. Several other dishes are unique to Hamilton's, such as spicy snapper étouffée and a Greek-accented shrimp Cristo. Mesquite-grilled fish and steaks are also house specialties, and vegetarians can order a coal-fired vegetable kebab served over angel-hair pasta. A Lagoon Saloon makes the wait for a table go by quickly, and you can choose from an extensive selection of well-chosen California and French wines.

INEXPENSIVE

Billy's Steamed Seafood Restaurant. 3000 Thomas Dr. (between Grand Lagoon and Magnolia Beach Rd.). ☎ **850/235-2349.** Reservations not accepted. Sandwiches $2.50–$5; seafood $4.50–$15. AE, DISC, MC, V. Feb–Oct Sun–Thurs 11am–9:30pm, Fri–Sat 11am–10pm. Nov–Jan Thurs–Sun 11am–9pm. SEAFOOD.

More a lively raw bar than a restaurant, Billy and Eloise Poole's casual spot is famous for serving the best crabs in town. These are hard-shell blue crabs prepared Maryland style: steamed with lots of spicy Old Bay Seasoning. Unlike the crab houses in Baltimore, however, Billy and Eloise remove the top shell, clean out the "mustard" (intestines), and cut the crabs in two for you; all you have to do is "pick" the meat. The staff will demonstrate how to do that. Other steamed morsels include shrimp (also with spicy seasoning), oysters, crabs, and lobster served with corn on the cob and garlic bread. Order anything from the briny deep here, but pass over other items. If you're in town during the off-season, check to see if the Pooles have an all-you-can-eat crab feast scheduled.

Cajun Inn. 817 Azalea Ave. (near Front Beach Rd./Middle Beach Rd. intersection). ☎ **850/ 233-0403.** Reservations not accepted. Main courses $8–$15; sandwiches $4–$6. AE, DC, DISC, MC, V. Daily 11am–10pm. LOUISIANA CAJUN.

This lively, family-owned restaurant with high-backed wooden booths brings the Big Easy to the Gulf. Offerings include jambalaya, seafood étouffée, peppered shrimp or crayfish, and Cajun-style blackened fish. Po-boys sandwiches stuffed with fried oysters or shrimp are a lunchtime specialty. You won't get gourmet New Orleans cuisine at these prices, but your tongue will have plenty of spice to savor. Dine inside or outside. There's live music on weekends.

✪ **Shuckums Oyster Pub & Seafood Grill.** 15614 Front Beach Rd. (at Powell Adams Dr.). ☎ **850/235-3214.** Reservations not accepted. Main courses $11–$17; burgers and sandwiches $6–$10. AE, DISC, MC, V. Summer daily 11am–2am. Off-season Sun–Thurs 11am–9pm, Sat–Sun 11am–midnight. SEAFOOD.

"We shuck 'em, you suck 'em" is the motto of this noisy, lively, and smoky pub, which became famous when comedian Martin Short tried unsuccessfully to shuck oysters here during the making of an MTV spring-break special. The original bar is virtually papered over with dollar bills signed by old and young patrons who have been flocking here since 1967. The obvious specialty is fresh Apalachicola oysters, served raw, steamed, or baked with a variety of toppings. Otherwise, the menu consists of pub fare and mediocre seafood main courses.

SPECIAL DINING EXPERIENCES

You've got to see the **Treasure Ship,** at Treasure Island Marina, 3605 S. Thomas Dr., at Grand Lagoon (☎ **850/234-8881**), to believe it. This amazing 2 acres of ship space claims to be the world's largest land-based Spanish galleon, a putative replica of the three-masted sailing ships that carried loot from the New World to Spain in the 16th and 17th centuries. You can get anything from an ice-cream cone to peel-it-yourself shrimp to a sophisticated dinner in the restaurant and bar here, which are open daily at 4:30pm; closed from October through December.

Lady Anderson **dinner-dance cruises** are a romantic evening escape; they're available from March through October. Boarding is at Capt. Anderson's Marina, 5550 N. Lagoon Dr. (☎ **850/234-5940**), at 6:30pm Monday to Saturday, with the cruises lasting from 7 to 10pm. Buffet dinners are featured, followed by live music for dancing Wednesday, Friday, and Saturday nights, and gospel music on Thursday. Dinner-dance tickets cost $32.50 for adults, $20 for children 11 and under (tips included), while the gospel cruises go for $27 and $18.50, respectively. This triple-decker fun boat is so popular that reservations must be made well in advance.

PANAMA CITY & PANAMA CITY BEACH AFTER DARK

THE CLUB & BAR SCENE   The **Breakers,** 12627 Front Beach Rd. (☎ **850/ 234-6060**), is the area's premier supper club, with unsurpassed gulf views and music for dining and dancing. Open daily at 4pm during summer, Monday to Saturday during the off-season. The beachfront **Harpoon Harry's Waterfront Cafe** is part of the same complex.

Romantic lounges with live entertainment are at the **Treasure Ship,** 3605 S. Thomas Dr. (☎ **850/234-8881**), where comedian-hypnotist Mike Harvey performs during summer in the top-floor Captain's Quarters, and the **Boar's Head,** 17290 Front Beach Rd. (☎ **850/234-6628**). See "Where to Dine" above for more information.

The 20-something crowd likes to boogie all night at beach clubs such as **Schooners,** 5121 Gulf Dr. (☎ **850/235-9074**), where every table has a gulf view; **Spinnaker's,** on the beach at 8795 Thomas Dr. (☎ **850/234-7882**); **Club La Vella,** one of Florida's largest nightclubs (it's a bikini-contest kind of place), also on the beach at 8813 Thomas Dr. (☎ **850/234-3866**); and **Sharkey's on the Gulf,** 15201 Front Beach Rd. (☎ **850/235-2420**). They often stay open until 4am in summer while their bands play on. **Pineapple Willie's Lounge,** beachside at 9900 S. Thomas Dr. (☎ **850/235-0928**), is open from 11am until 2am, serving ribs basted with Jack Daniels whisky and spotlighting live entertainment during summer, a host of sports TV all year.

THE PERFORMING ARTS   The Rader family and a cast of 20 perform year-round in the ✪ **Ocean Opry Show,** 8400 Front Beach Rd., Panama City Beach (☎ **850/234-5464**), the area's answer to the Grand Ole Opry. Popcorn, hot dogs, and soft drinks are sold at the theater. There's a show every night at 8pm during the summer, less frequently off-season. Admission is $18 for adults, $17 for seniors, and $9 for children ($20 to $30 when stars like Kitty Welles, B.J. Thomas, and the Wilkensons are in town, usually during winter). The box office opens at 9am Monday to Saturday, and reservations are recommended but not required.

4 Apalachicola

65 miles E of Panama City, 80 miles W of Tallahassee

Sometimes called Florida's Last Frontier, Apalachicola makes a fascinating day trip from Panama City Beach or Tallahassee for many visitors, as well as a destination in its own right. The long, gorgeous beaches here are among the nation's best, and the bays and estuaries—justifiably famous for Apalachichola oysters—are great for fishing and boating. And if you love nature, the area also is rich in wildlife preserves.

The charming little town of Apalachicola (pop. 2,600) was a major seaport during autumns from 1827 to 1861, when plantations in Alabama and Georgia shipped tons of cotton down the Apalachicola River to the Gulf. The town had a racetrack, an opera house, and a civic center that hosted balls, socials, and gambling. The population shrank during the mosquito-infested summer months, however, when yellow fever and malaria epidemics struck. It was during one of these outbreaks that Dr. John Gorrie of Apalachicola tried to develop a method of cooling his patients' rooms. In doing so, he invented the forerunner of the air conditioner, a device that made Florida tourism possible and life a whole lot more bearable for locals.

Apalachicola has traditionally made its living primarily from the Gulf and the lagoon-like bay that lies behind a chain of offshore barrier islands. Today Apalachicola produces the bulk of Florida's oyster crop, and shrimping and fishing are major industries. The town also has been discovered by a number of urban expatriates, who have moved here, restored old homes, and opened interesting antique and gift shops. (Do you know of any other town this size where you can buy Crabtree & Evelyn products?) They'll be glad to see you.

ESSENTIALS

GETTING THERE   The nearest airport is 65 miles to the west at Panama City Beach (see "Essentials" in section 3, above). From I-10, take Exit 21 at Marianna; then follow Fla. 71 south to Port St. Joe, and U.S. 98 East to Apalachicola.

VISITOR INFORMATION   The **Apalachicola Bay Chamber of Commerce,** 99 Market St., Apalachicola, FL 32320 (☎ **850/653-9419;** fax 850/653-8219; www.hometown.com/apalachicola; e-mail: chamber1@supernet.net), supplies information about the area from its office on Market Street (U.S. 98) between Avenue D and Avenue E. The chamber is open Monday to Friday from 9:30am to 4pm.

TIME   The town is in the **eastern time zone,** like Orlando, Miami, and Tallahassee (it's 1 hour ahead of Panama City Beach and the rest of the Panhandle). Many shops are closed on Wednesday afternoon, when Apalachicolans go fishing.

BEACHES, PARKS & WILDLIFE REFUGES

Countless terns, snowy plover, black skimmers, and other birds nest along the dunes and 9 miles of beaches (which some experts consider to be among America's best) at ✪ **St. George Island State Park,** on the island's eastern end (☎ **850/927-2111**). The wildlife can be viewed from a hiking trail and observation platform. The park has picnic areas, rest rooms, showers, a boat launch, and a campground with electric hookups. Entry to the park costs $2 for a vehicle with one occupant, $4 for vehicles with up to 8 occupants, and $1 for pedestrians and bicyclists.

The beaches are even longer at ✪ **St. Joseph Peninsula State Park,** at the end of County Road 30E, about 26 miles west of Apalachicola (☎ **850/227-1327**). The peninsula is populated by cottages and a few shops around Cape San Blas, but beyond the park entrance it's totally preserved. Facilities include picnic areas, a marina with a boat ramp, campgrounds with electricity, and eight remote cabins. Entry fees are $3.25 per vehicle with up to eight occupants, $1 for pedestrians and bicyclists.

Both state parks are open daily from 8am to sunset.

There are no facilities whatsoever at the **St. Vincent National Wildlife Refuge,** southwest of Apalachicola. This 12,358-acre barrier island has been left in its natural state by the U.S. Fish and Wildlife Service, but visitors are welcome to walk through its pine forests, marshlands, ponds, dunes, and beaches. In addition to native species like the bald eagle and alligators, the island is home to a small herd of sambar deer from Southeast Asia. Red wolves are bred here for reestablishment in other wildlife areas. Access is by boat only, usually from Indian Pass, 21 miles west of Apalachicola via U.S. 98 and County Roads 30A and 30B. The chamber of commerce (see "Essentials" above) has the names of boat captains who will take you over, and some cruise operators go there (see "Cruises" below). The refuge headquarters, at the north end of Market Street in town, has exhibits of wetland flora and fauna. It's open Monday to Friday from 8am to 4:30pm. Admission is free. The rangers conduct managed hunts for deer and wild hogs from November to January. For more information, contact the refuge at P.O Box 947, Apalachicola, FL 32329 (☎ **850/653-8808**).

The huge **Apalachicola National Forest** begins a few miles northeast of town. It has a host of facilities, including canoeing and mountain-bike trails. See section 5 of this chapter, on Tallahassee, for details.

OUTDOOR PURSUITS

CRUISES Jeanni McMillan of ✪ **Jeanni's Journeys** (☎ 850/927-3259) takes guests on narrated nature cruises to the barrier islands and on canoe and kayak trips in the creeks and streams of the Apalachicola River basin. She also has night hikes with blue crab netting, shelling excursions, and fishing and scalloping trips, plus excursions tailored exclusively for children. Prices range from $30 to $75 per person. Reservations are required, so call her to find out what she's offering when you'll be in town. Jeannie also rents canoes, kayaks, sailboats, and sailboards.

Other nature-cruise operators are **Capt. Tom's Adventures in Paradise** (☎ 850/653-8463), offering a variety of barrier island trip and backwater canoeing; and **Captain Tony Charters** (☎ 850/653-3560), which has sightseeing trips and excursions to St. Vincent Island. Contact them in advance for schedules and reservations.

The *Governor Stone,* an 1877-vintage Gulf Coast schooner, makes cruises on Apalachicola Bay each day during the summer months, less frequently off-season. This fine old craft has seen duty as a cargo freighter, an oyster buyer, a sponge boat, and a U.S. Merchant Marine training vessel. It departs from the Rainbow Inn dock on Water Street, but book in advance at the Maritime Museum at 268 Water St., north of Avenue F (☎ 850/653-8700 for schedule and reservations); reservations are recommended. The cruises cost $20 for adults, $10 for children 12 and under.

A scaled-down version of an 1890s stern-wheeler, Capt. Daniel Blake's *Jubilee!* (☎ 850/653-9502) makes 1½-hour voyages on the river, creeks, swamps, and marshes. This modern but old-looking vessel can accommodate up to 6 passengers. The trips usually depart the dock at 329 Water St., but reservations are required. Fare is $15 per person.

You can do it yourself on a houseboat rented from **Benigh Boatworks, Inc.,** 317 Water St. (☎ 850/653-8214; fax 850/653-3579; www.bnbcomp.net/benighnboat/). Rates range from $125 for a half day to $950 a week. The company is open Tuesday to Sunday from 8:30am to 5pm.

FISHING Fishing is excellent in these waters, where trout, redfish, flounder, tarpon, shark, drum, and others abound. The chamber of commerce (see "Essentials," above) can help arrange charters on the local boats, many of which dock at the Rainbow Inn on Water Street. For guides, contact **Professional Guide Service** (☎ 850/670-8834) or **Boss Guide Services** (☎ 850/653-8139).

EXPLORING THE TOWN

Start your visit by picking up a map and a self-guided tour brochure from the chamber of commerce (see "Essentials" above), and then stroll around Apalachicola's waterfront, business district, and Victorian-era homes.

Along Water Street, several tin warehouses evoke the town's seafaring days of the late 1800s, as does the 1840s-era **Sponge Exchange** at Commerce Street and Avenue E. A highlight of the residential area, centered around Gorrie Square at Avenue D and 6th Street, is the Greek Revival–style **Trinity Episcopal Church,** built in New York and shipped here in 1837. At the water end of 6th Street, Battery Park has a children's playground. A number of excellent art galleries and gift shops are grouped on Market Street, Avenue D, and Commerce Street.

The showpiece at the ✪ **John Gorrie State Museum,** Avenue D at 6th Street (☎ 850/653-9347), is a display replica of Doctor Gorrie's cooling machine, a prototype of today's air conditioner. Open Thursday to Monday from 9am to 5pm. Closed New Year's Day, Thanksgiving, and Christmas. Admission is $1, free for children 6 and under.

There's a small **Maritime Museum** at 268 Water St., north of Avenue F (☎ 850/653-8700). It's usually open Tuesday to Saturday from 1 to 4pm. Admission is free.

The **Raney House Museum,** on Market Street, at Avenue F (no phone), shows what life was like when Apalachicola was a booming cotton port. The stately house was built in 1838, and the Apalachicola Area Historical Society has furnished it with 19th-century pieces. It's open only Saturdays from 1 to 4pm, but check with the chamber of commerce (see "Essentials" above) to make sure. Admission is by $2 donation.

The **Estuarine Walk,** at the north end of Market Street on the grounds of the Apalachicola National Estuarine Research Reserve (☎ 850/653-8063), contains aquariums full of fish and turtles and displays of various other estuarine life. Open Monday to Friday from 8am to 5pm. Admission is free.

WHERE TO STAY

Built in 1997, the **Best Western Apalach Inn,** on U.S. 98 a mile west of downtown (☎ 800/528-1234 or 850/658-9131; fax 850/653-9136), is the only national chain hotel here. Rates range from $55 to $65 double.

Outside the state park, the dunes of St. George Island are virtually lined with beach cottages and a few condominiums. These are available on a weekly or monthly basis. Among the rental agents are **Anchor Realty & Mortgage Co.,** 212 Franklin Blvd., St. George Island, FL 32328 (☎ 800/824-0416 or 850/927-2625; www.fla-beach.com); **Gulf Coast Vacation Rentals,** 45 E. 1st St. (HCR Box 90), St. George Island, FL 32328 (☎ 800/367-1680 or 850/927-2596); and **Sun Coast Vacation Property Management,** HCR Box 2, St. George Island, FL 32328 (☎ 800/341-2021 or 850/927-2282).

At **St. George Island State Park,** summertime camping fees are $14.85 per night for a campsite with electricity, $12.70 without, including tax. Off-season they go for $10.60 and $8.50, respectively. Primitive camping (take everything with you, including water) costs $3 a night per adult, $2 for children. For more information, contact the park at 1900 E. Gulf Beach Dr., St. George Island, FL 32328 (☎ 850/927-2111).

Campsites at **St. Joseph Peninsula State Park** cost $15 a night from March 1 to October 31, $8 a night the rest of the year. Cabins rent for $70 a night during summer, $55 a night off-season, with minimum stays of 5 nights during summer, 2 nights off-season. You can contact the park at 8899 Cape San Blas Rd., Port St. Joe, FL 32456 (☎ **850/227-1327**).

○ **Coombs House Inn.** 80 6th St., Apalachicola, FL 32320. ☎ **850/653-9199.** Fax 850/653-2785. www.combshouseinn.com. 18 units. A/C TV TEL. $79–$139 double. Rates include continental breakfast. AE, MC, V.

This large house in the historic district was built in 1905 by a lumber baron, and it shows: Polished black cypress paneling lines the entire central hallway and grand parlor. Each of the 10 rooms in the main house is tastefully decorated, with lots of Victorian reproductions. Outstanding is the Coombs Suite, with bay windows, sofa, four-poster bed, and its own whirlpool. One room here is in the carriage house out back. Less grand but still impressive are eight rooms in another restored Victorian (the "Annex") half a block away. One of these rooms has a whirlpool tub and bidet. One room in each house is equipped for disabled guests. A major truck route, U.S. 98, runs along the north side of both houses; request a south room to escape the periodic road noise. Guests can use the house bikes free.

○ **Gibson Inn.** 51 Ave. C, Apalachicola, FL 32320. ☎ **850/653-2191.** Fax 850/653-3521. 30 units. A/C TV TEL. $70–$85 double; $85–$115 suite. AE, MC, V.

Built in 1907 as a seaman's hotel and gorgeously restored in 1985, this cupola-topped inn is such a brilliant example of Victorian architecture that it's listed on the National Register of Historic Inns. No two guest rooms are alike (some still have the original sinks in the sleeping area), but all are richly furnished with period reproductions. Nonguests are welcome to wander upstairs and peek into unoccupied rooms (whose doors are left open). Room and dining reservations are advised, especially on weekends, and rooms should be booked well in advance in summer—and as much as 5 years ahead for the seafood festival in November. Grab a drink from the bar and relax in one of the high-back rockers on the old-fashioned veranda. The dining room serves excellent seafood and is open to all comers, so don't expect this to be private like a bed-and-breakfast; instead, you'll find yourself in a reborn, absolutely charming turn-of-the-century hotel.

Magnolia Hall Guest House. 177 5th St., Apalachicola, FL 32320. ☎ **850/653-2431.** 2 units. A/C TV. $150 double first night, $100 double each additional night. Rates include full breakfast. MC, V.

Annegret and Douglas Gaidry have restored this two-story merchant's mansion to more than its 1838 splendor. It sits on a hill, giving the two huge upstairs guest rooms a view of the bay. The house has 12-foot ceilings and 11-foot windows, meaning that guests can step through their windows onto a wraparound porch, where the Gaidrys serve mint juleps while you rock away the late afternoon. Annegret also delivers morning coffee to the rooms and serves a full breakfast in the formal dining room. Many furnishings here are antiques, some dating from 1838 (one of the four-poster beds was in the house when the Gaidrys bought it). They have installed modern bathrooms, one of which has a spa tub, and walk-in closets stocked with robes. Guests can also swim in the pool and roam 4 acres of lovely Southern-style gardens.

Rainbow Inn. 123 Water St., Apalachicola, FL 32320. ☎ **850/653-8139.** Fax 850/653-2018. 23 units. A/C TV TEL. $70–$90 double, $130 suite. AE, DC, DISC, MC, V.

This two-story motel's rough-hewn exterior timbers make it look like one of the neighboring waterfront warehouses. And there's absolutely nothing fancy here, except views of Apalachicola Bay from the rooms. Those on the second floor have their own balconies with views. All are furnished with bright fabrics and have light paneled walls. The most expensive unit is a suite with kitchen and Jacuzzi. Caroline's Restaurant serves breakfast, lunch, and seafood dinners, and the Roseate Spoonbill Cocktail Lounge, over the restaurant, is a popular local watering hole with a grand view and music on an outdoor deck on weekends.

WHERE TO DINE

Townsfolk still plop down on the round stools at the marble-topped counter to order Coca-Colas and milk shakes at the **Old Time Soda Fountain & Luncheonette,** 93 Market St. (☎ 850/653-2006). This 1950s relic was once the town drugstore. It's open Monday to Saturday from 10am to 5pm.

Local sweet tooths also find satisfaction at **Delores Sweet Shoppe,** 29 Ave. E, at Commerce St. (☎ 850/653-9081), where Delores Roux's cookies, brownies, cakes, and key lime pies are famous hereabouts. She also serves sandwiches and chili for lunch. Open Monday to Friday from 9am to 5pm.

Apalachicola Seafood Grill & Steakhouse. 100 Market St. (at Ave. E/U.S. 98). ☎ **904/ 653-9510.** Reservations recommended in summer. Salads and sandwiches $6–$8; main courses $8–$15. AE, DISC, MC, V. Mon–Sat 11:30am–8pm. SEAFOOD/STEAKS.

With cafe curtains bedecking its storefront windows, this establishment from the outside looks like the typical small-town diner it once was, but this sophisticated restaurant offers Apalachicola-style gumbo and oyster stew; sautéed smoked oysters; meal-size salads and sandwiches; and charcoal-grilled grouper, yellowfin tuna, and salmon. The "basic meals" for $10 or less feature southern-style fried oysters, fish, scallops, and shrimp accompanied by potatoes and daily vegetable.

✪ **The Boss Oyster.** 125 Water St. ☎ **850/653-9364.** Reservations not accepted. Oysters $3–$12; sandwiches and baskets $7–$10; main courses $16–$21. AE, DC, DISC, MC, V. Sun–Thurs noon–9pm, Fri–Sat 2–10pm. SEAFOOD.

You've probably heard about the aphrodisiac properties of Apalachicola oysters. Well, you can see if it's true at this rustic dockside eatery, whose motto is "Shut up and shuck." The bivalves are served raw, steamed, or under a dozen toppings ranging from capers to crabmeat. They'll even steam three dozen of them and let you do the shucking. Steamed crabs and shrimp also are offered, as are delicious po-boy sandwiches. The cook here knows how to fry oysters and shrimp, too. My shrimp were perfect: lightly battered and fried just to the point of being done—in other words, still a bit crunchy and full of flavor. Dine inside or at picnic tables on a screened dockside porch. Everyone in town eats here, from bankers to watermen.

✪ **Chef Eddie's Magnolia Grill.** Ave. E (U.S. 98; at 11th St.). ☎ **850/653-8000.** Reservations advised. Main courses $12–$24. MC, V. Mon–Sat 6–9pm. Closed 2½ weeks starting weekend after Thanksgiving. SEAFOOD/LOUISIANA.

One of the top places to dine in Northwest Florida, Boston-bred owner/chef Eddie Cass's pleasant restaurant occupies a small bungalow built in the 1880s and still is in possession of the original black cypress paneling in its central hallway. Eddie has turned the old living room into the dining quarters, where he offers nightly specials emphasizing fresh local seafood and New Orleans–style sauces. His spicy seafood gumbo is a consistent hit at the Florida Seafood Festival (some 2,000 orders, with the profits going to charity), and you will long remember his mahimahi Pontchartrain, with cream and artichoke hearts. Eddie and his wife, Bettye, do not allow smoking inside the house.

5 Tallahassee

163 miles W of Jacksonville, 191 miles E of Pensacola, 250 miles NW of Orlando

Tallahassee was selected as Florida's capital in 1823 because it was halfway between St. Augustine and Pensacola, then the state's major cities. That location puts it almost in Georgia; in fact, Tallahassee has more in common with Macon than with Miami. There's as much Old South ambience here as anywhere else you're likely to visit in Florida. You'll find lovingly restored 19th-century homes and buildings, including the 1845 Old Capitol. They all sit among so many towering pines and sprawling live oaks that you'll think you're in an enormous forest. The trees form virtual tunnels along Tallahassee's five official Canopy Roads, which are lined with historic plantations, ancient Native American settlement sites and mounds, gorgeous gardens, quiet parks with picnic areas, and beautiful lakes and streams. And the nearby Apalachicola National Forest is a virtual gold mine of outdoor pursuits.

While tradition and history are important here, you'll also find the modern era, beginning with the New Capitol Building towering 22 stories over downtown. Usually sleepy Tallahassee takes on a very lively persona when the legislature is in session and when the powerful football teams of Florida State University and Florida A&M University take to the gridiron.

If you're inclined to give your credit cards a workout, the nearby town of Havana is Florida's antiquing capital.

ESSENTIALS

GETTING THERE   The Tallahassee Regional Airport, 10 miles southwest of downtown on Southeast Capital Circle, is served by **Continental** (☎ 800/525-0280), **Delta** (☎ 800/221-1212), **Gulf Stream International** (☎ 800/992-8532), and **US Airways** (☎ 800/428-4322).

Alamo (☎ 800/327-9633), **Avis** (☎ 800/331-1212), **Budget** (☎ 800/527-0700), **Dollar** (☎ 800/800-4000), **Hertz** (☎ 800/654-3131), **National** (☎ 800/CAR-RENT), and **Thrifty** (☎ 800/367-2277) have rental cars here.

You can take a taxi to downtown for about $10 to $15. There was no shuttle-bus service at press time.

The **Amtrak** transcontinental train *Sunset Limited* stops in Tallahassee at 918½ Railroad Ave. (☎ **800/USA-RAIL**).

VISITOR INFORMATION   For information in advance, contact the **Tallahassee Area Convention and Visitors Bureau,** 200 W. College Ave. (P.O. Box 1369), Tallahassee, FL 32302 (☎ **800/628-2866** or 850/413-9200; fax 850/487-4621; www.co.leon.fl.us/cvb).

Your first stop in town should be the **Tallahassee Area Visitor Information Center** (same phone numbers as the bureau), in the West Plaza foyer of the New Capitol Building, just inside the Duval Street entrance. The staff here dispenses free street and public-transportation maps, brochures, and pamphlets outlining tours of the historic districts and the Canopy Roads. The **Florida Welcome Center** in the same foyer has information about the entire state. Both are open Monday to Friday 8am to 5pm, weekends 9am to 3pm.

GETTING AROUND   Built like an old-time streetcar, the free **Old Town Trolley** (☎ 850/891-5200) is the best way to see the sights of historic downtown Tallahassee. You can get on or off at any point between Adams Street Commons, at the corner of Jefferson and Adams streets, and the Governor's Mansion. The trolley runs Monday to Friday every 10 minutes between 7am and 6pm.

TALTRAN provides city bus service from its downtown terminal at Tennessee and Adams streets (☎ **850/891-5200**). Both the ticket booth there and the Tallahassee Area Visitor Information Center in the New Capitol Building have route maps and schedules for the Old Town Trolley and TALTRAN buses.

For taxi service, call **Yellow Cab** (☎ **850/580-8080**) or **City Taxi** (☎ **850/ 562-4222**).

TIME   Tallahassee is in the **eastern time zone,** like Orlando, Miami, and Apalachicola. It's 1 hour ahead of the rest of the Panhandle.

EXPLORING THE CITY
THE CAPITOL COMPLEX

After stopping by the visitor information center on the first-floor foyer of the New Capitol, proceed to tour the rest of Florida's capitol complex, on South Monroe Street at Apalachee Parkway. It dominates the downtown area and should be the start of your sightseeing here.

The **New Capitol Building,** a $43 million skyscraper, was built in 1977 to replace the 1845-vintage Old Capitol. State legislators meet here from March to May. The chambers of the house and the senate have public viewing galleries. For a spectacular view, take the elevators to the 22nd-floor **observatory,** where on a clear day you can see all the way to the Gulf of Mexico. You can also view works by Florida artists while up here. The New Capitol is open Monday to Friday from 8am to 5pm (closed major holidays). Free **guided tours** (☎ **850/413-9200**) are scheduled on the hour, Monday to Friday from 9 to 11am and 1 to 3pm, and on Saturday, Sunday, and holidays from 9am to 3pm.

Directly in front of the skyscraper is the strikingly white ✪ **Old Capitol** (☎ **850/ 487-1902**). With its majestic dome, this "Pearl of Capitol Hill" has been restored to its original beauty. An eight-room exhibit portrays Florida's political history. Turn-of-the-century furnishings, cotton gins, and other artifacts are also of interest. The Old Capitol is open Monday to Friday from 9am to 4:30pm, Saturday from 10am to 4:30pm, and Sunday and holidays from noon to 4:30pm. Admission is free to both the old and the new capitols.

Facing the Old Capitol across Monroe Street are the twin granite towers of the **Vietnam Veterans Memorial,** honoring Florida's Vietnam vets.

The Old Town Trolley will take you to the lovely Georgian-style **Governor's Mansion,** north of the capitol at Adams and Brevard streets (☎ **850/488-4661**). Enhanced by a portico patterned after Andrew Jackson's columned antebellum home, the Hermitage, and surrounded by giant magnolia trees and landscaped lawns, the mansion is furnished with 18th- and 19th-century antiques and such collectibles as the hollowware from the battleship USS *Florida.* Tours are given when the legislature is in session from March to May. Call for a schedule and reservations.

Adjacent to the Governor's Mansion, **The Grove** was home to Ellen Call Long, known as "The Tallahassee Girl," the first child born after Tallahassee was settled.

HISTORIC DISTRICTS

While modern buildings have made inroads in downtown, Tallahassee makes an ongoing effort to preserve many of its historic homes and buildings. Many of them are concentrated in three historic districts within an easy walk north of the capitol complex. The information center in the New Capitol (see "Essentials" above) distributes free walking-tour brochures covering the three areas. Taken together, they're about 4 miles long and should take half a day. Most interesting is the Park Avenue District, 3 blocks north of the capitol, which you can see in about 1 hour.

Historic Tallahassee Tours, 734 E. Tennessee St. (☎ 850/222-4243), has 1½-hour walking tours of the capitol complex and nearby historic districts, departing from the plaza on the west side of the New Capitol at 10am, 1pm, and 3pm Monday to Saturday. These cost $6 adults, $4 seniors and students. They also will arrange driving tours of the area, and they offer horse-drawn carriage tours in spring and fall, for $15 per person. Call for reservations.

Tours With a Southern Accent, 209 E. Brevard St., at Monroe Street (☎ 850/513-1000), offers 2-hour walking tours, either guided ($20 adults, free for children under 5) or with tape cassettes ($6 per person). Van tours of the city ($20 adults, free for children under 5) usually depart Monday to Saturday at 10am and 2pm. Call ahead for reservations.

ADAMS STREET COMMONS   This 1-block winding brick and landscaped area along Adams Street begins on the north side of the capitol complex. It retains an old-fashioned town-square atmosphere. Restored buildings include the Governor's Club, a 1900s Masonic lodge, and Gallie's Hall, where Florida's first five African-American college students received their Florida A&M University diplomas in 1892. Restaurants, shops, and Gallie Alley are also here. Adams Street crosses Park Avenue 3 blocks north of the capitol. This is a good place for lunch at one of several cafes which cater to downtown office workers.

PARK AVENUE HISTORIC DISTRICT   The 7 blocks of Park Avenue between Martin Luther King Jr. Boulevard and North Meridien Street are a lovely promenade of beautiful trees, gardens, and outstanding old mansions. This broad avenue with a shady median strip lined with moss-bearded live oaks was originally named 200 Foot Street and then McCarty Street, but it was renamed Park Avenue to satisfy a snobbish Anglophile society matron who didn't want an Irish name imprinted on her son's wedding invitations.

Several Park Avenue historic homes are open to the public, including the **Knott House Museum,** at Calhoun Street (see "Museums & Art Galleries," below). **The Columns,** at Duval Street, was built in the 1830s and is the city's oldest surviving building (it's home of the Tallahassee Chamber of Commerce). **The First Presbyterian Church,** at Adams Street, built in 1838, is the city's oldest church and has been an important African-American historic site since slaves were welcome to worship here without their masters' consent. **The Walker Library,** between Monroe and Calhoun streets, was one of Florida's first libraries, dating from 1903 (it's home to Springtime Tallahassee, which sponsors the city's top special event). Just north of Park Avenue on Gadsden Street, the **Meginnis-Monroe House** contains the Lemoyne Art Gallery (see "Museums & Art Galleries," below).

At Martin Luther King Jr. Boulevard, the **adjacent Old City Cemetery** and **Episcopal Cemetery** contain the graves of Prince Achille Murat, Napoleon's nephew, and Princess Catherine Murat, his wife and George Washington's grand-niece. Also buried here are two governors and numerous Confederate and Union soldiers who died at the Battle of Natural Bridge during the Civil War. The cemeteries are important to African-American history since a number of slaves and the first black Florida A&M graduates are interred here. The visitor information center in the New Capitol has a cemetery walking-tour brochure.

CALHOUN STREET HISTORIC DISTRICT   Affectionately called "Gold Dust Street" in the old days, the 3 blocks of Calhoun Street between Tennessee and Georgia streets, and running east on Virginia Street to Leon High School, sport elaborate homes built by prominent citizens between 1830 and 1880. A highlight here is the

Brokaw-McDougall House, in front of Leon High School at the eastern end of Virginia Street, which was built in 1856.

MUSEUMS & ART GALLERIES

Black Archives Research Center and Museum. On the Florida A&M University campus, at Martin Luther King Jr. Blvd. and Gamble St. ☎ **850/599-3020.** Free admission. Mon–Fri 9am–4pm. Closed major holidays. Parking lot next to building.

Housed in the columned library built by Andrew Carnegie in 1908, this fascinating research center and museum displays one of the nation's most extensive collections of African-American artifacts, as well as such treasures as a 500-piece Ethiopian cross collection. The archives contain one of the world's largest collections on African-American history. Visitors here can listen to tapes of gospel music and of elderly people reminiscing about the past. Florida Agricultural and Mechanical University (FAMU) was founded in 1887, primarily as a black institution. Today it's acclaimed for its business, engineering, and pharmacy schools.

Florida State University Museum of Fine Arts. 250 Fine Arts Building, at Copeland and Call sts., on the FSU campus. ☎ **850/644-6836.** Free admission. Sept–Apr Mon–Fri 10am–4pm, Sat–Sun 1–4pm; May–July Mon–Fri 10am–4pm. Closed Aug.

A permanent art collection here features 16th-century Dutch paintings, 20th-century American paintings, Japanese prints, pre-Colombian artifacts, and much more. Touring exhibits are displayed every few weeks.

Foster Tanner Art Center. Florida A&M University, between Osceola and Gamble sts., off Martin Luther King Jr. Blvd. ☎ **850/599-3161.** Free admission. Mon–Sat 9am–6pm.

The focus in this gallery is on works by African-American artists, with a wide variety of paintings, sculptures, and more. Exhibits change five times between September and May with local, national, and international artists in the limelight.

Knott House Museum ("The House That Rhymes"). 301 E. Park Ave. (at Calhoun St.). ☎ **850/922-2459.** Free admission (donations encouraged). Wed–Fri 1–4pm, Sat 10am–4pm. Tours on the hour.

Adorned by a columned portico, this stately 1843 mansion is furnished with Victorian elegance and boasts the nation's largest collection of 19th-century gilt-framed mirrors. The most unusual feature is the eccentric rhymes written by Mrs. Knott and attached by satin ribbons to tables, chairs, and lamps. Her poems comment upon 19th-century women's issues, plus the social, economic, and political events of the era. The house is in the Park Avenue Historic District and is listed in the National Register of Historic Places. It's preserved as it looked in 1928, when the Knott family left it and all of its contents to the city. The museum gift shop carries Victorian greeting cards, paper dolls, tin toy replicas, reprints of historic newspapers, and other nostalgic items.

Lemoyne Art Gallery. 125 N. Gadsden St. (between Park Ave. and Call St.). ☎ **850/222-8800.** Admission $1, free for children 12 and under. Tues–Sat 10am–5pm, Sun 1–5pm. Closed New Year's Day, Easter, July 4, Thanksgiving, Christmas Day.

This restored 1852 antebellum home is listed on the National Register of Historic Places and is a lovely setting for fine art. Known as the **Meginnis-Monroe House,** the gallery itself is named in honor of Jacques LeMoyne, a member of a French expedition to Florida in 1564. Commissioned to depict the natives' dwellings and map the sea coast, LeMoyne was the first European artist known to have visited North America. Exhibits here include permanent displays by local artists, traveling exhibits, sculpture, pottery, and photography—everything from the traditional to the avant-garde. The gardens, with an old-fashioned gazebo, are spectacular during the Christmas holiday season. Programs of classical music are combined with visual arts during the year; check in advance for the current schedule.

Museum of Florida History. Lower level of R.A. Gray Building, 500 S. Bronough St. (at Pensacola St.). ☎ **850/488-1484.** Free admission (suggested donation $3 adults, $1 children). Mon–Fri 9am–4:30pm, Sat 10am–4:30pm, Sun and holidays noon–4:30pm. Closed Thanksgiving and Christmas.

An 11-foot-tall mastodon greets you at the official state history museum, which takes you back 12,000 years to the first Native Americans to live in Florida (mastodons were very much alive back then). Ancient artifacts from Native American tribes are exhibited, plus such relics from Florida's past as 16th- and 17th-century sunken Spanish galleon treasures and a reconstructed steamboat. Inquire about guided tours and special exhibits. There's an interesting museum gift shop. Visitor parking is available in the garage around the corner on St. Augustine Street between Bronough and Duvall streets.

ARCHAEOLOGICAL SITES

de Soto Historical Site. 1022 de Soto Park Dr. (off Lafayette St.). ☎ **850/922-6007.** Free admission. Grounds daily 8am–5pm (mansion closed to the public).

During the winter of 1539, Spanish conquistador Hernando de Soto, his troops, and friars set up an encampment here before continuing their ill-fated search for gold. It's believed the friars celebrated the first Christmas mass in North America. An archaeologist searching for Spanish-mission ruins discovered the de Soto encampment site in 1986. Rare copper coins, armor fragments, and a preserved pig's jaw have been unearthed. Former Gov. John Martin had no idea de Soto had camped here when he built his English hunting lodge–style mansion at the site in the 1930s. A colorful living-history time trail with exhibits and speakers is presented in January. Call for the date and program schedule.

Lake Jackson Mounds State Archaeological Site. 3600 Indian Mounds Rd. (off N. Monroe St., north of I-10). ☎ **850/922-6007.** Admission $2 per vehicle, $1 pedestrians and bicyclists. Daily 8am–sunset.

Artifacts discovered on this 18-acre excavation have revealed that native tribes settled on the shores of Lake Jackson (still one of the nation's best bass-fishing spots) centuries ago. A ceremonial complex flourished here around A.D. 1200, which includes six earth temple mounds and a burial mound. Part of the village and plaza area and two of the largest mounds are within the state site. The largest mound is 36 feet high with a base that measures 278 by 312 feet.

✪ Mission San Luís de Apalachee. 2020 Mission Rd. (between W. Tennessee and Tharpe sts.). ☎ **850/487-3711.** Free admission (suggested donation $3 adults, $1 children). Mon–Fri 9am–4:30pm, Sat 10am–4:30pm, Sun noon–4:30pm. Tours Sat 11am, Sun 2pm. Closed Thanksgiving and Christmas. From downtown, take Tennessee St. (U.S. 90) west, turn right on White Dr., then right on Mission Rd. to the entrance.

A Spanish Franciscan mission named San Luís was set up in 1656 on this hilltop, already a principal village of the Apalachee Indians. From then until 1704 it served as the capital of a chain of Spanish missions in Northwest Florida. The mission complex included a tribal council house, a Franciscan church, a Spanish fort, and residential areas. Based on extensive archaeological and historical research, the council house and the 10- by 50-foot thatch-roof church have been reconstructed. They are both open to the public. Work on the fort complex was scheduled to start by 2000. Interpretive markers are located across the 60-acre site, and self-guided–tour brochures are available at the visitor center. Rangers lead guided tours on weekends.

TRAVELING THE CANOPY ROADS

Graced by canopies of live oaks draped with Spanish moss, St. Augustine, Miccousukee, Meridian, Old Bainbridge, and Centerville roads are the five official Canopy Roads leading out of Tallahassee. Driving is slow on these winding, two-lane country roads (the locals only reluctantly are turning some limited sections of them into four-lane highways), some of them canopied for as much as 20 miles. Take along a picnic lunch, since there are few places to eat along these tranquil byways.

The visitor information center in the New Capitol provides a useful driving guide map of the Canopy Roads and Leon County's country lanes (see "Essentials," above).

If you have time for only one, take **Old Bainbridge Road,** which leads to the Lake Jackson Mounds State Archaeological Site in the northwest suburbs and on to Havana, Florida's antiquing capital 12 miles north of Tallahassee (see "Shopping" below).

PARKS & NATURE PRESERVES

In 1923 New York financier Alfred B. Maclay and his wife, Louise, began planting the floral wonderland of **Maclay State Gardens,** which surrounded their winter home on Lake Hall, 3540 Thomasville Rd. (U.S. 319), north of I-10 (☎ 850/487-4556). After her husband's death in 1944, Louise Maclay continued his dream of an ornamental garden to delight the public. In 1953 the land was bequeathed to the state of Florida. The more than 300 acres of flowers feature at least 200 varieties; 28 acres are devoted exclusively to azaleas and camellias. The beautifully restored home contains a camellia information center, and the surrounding park offers nature trails, canoe rentals, boating, picnicking, swimming, and fishing. The high blooming season is January to April, with the peak about mid-March. Admission to the park is $3.25 per vehicle with up to eight passengers, $1 for pedestrians and cyclists. Admission to the gardens during the blooming season from January to April is $3 for adults, $1.50 for children 11 and under; the gardens are free from May to December. The park and gardens are open daily from 8am to sunset. The Maclay House is open from January to April only, daily from 9am to 5pm.

Beyond the house and gardens, the state park also includes Lake Overstreet, around which wind 5½ miles of hiking, biking, and horseback-riding trails, making this a major venue for those outdoor activities.

SHOPPING

Antique hounds flock to the little village of ✪ **Havana,** 12 miles northwest of I-10 on U.S. 27. Havana used to make its living from shade tobacco, and when that industry went into decline in the 1960s, the town went with it. Things turned around 20 years later, however, when Havana began opening art galleries and antique, hand-craft, and collectible shops. Today these are housed in lovingly restored, turn-of-the-century brick buildings along Havana's commercial streets. Just drive into town on Main Street (U.S. 27), turn left on 7th Avenue, find a parking place, and start browsing. You'll have plenty of company on weekends. After shopping, stick around and have a humongous steak at the nearby Nicholson Farmhouse (see "Where to Dine," below).

Bradley's Country Store, about 8 miles north of I-10 on Centerville Road (☎ 850/893-1647), sells more than 80,000 pounds of homemade sausage per year, both over the counter and from mail orders. You can also buy coarse-ground grits, country-milled cornmeal, hogshead cheese, liver pudding, cracklings, and specially cured hams. On the National Register of Historic Places, the friendly store is also a sightseeing attraction with self-guided tours. Open Monday to Friday from 9am to 6pm, Saturday from 9am to 5pm.

OUTDOOR PURSUITS & SPECTATOR SPORTS

BICYCLING & IN-LINE SKATING   The 16-mile **Tallahassee–St. Marks Historic Railroad State Trail** is the city's most popular bike route. Constructed with the financial assistance of wealthy Panhandle cotton-plantation owners and merchants, this was Florida's oldest railroad, functioning from 1837 to 1984. Cotton and other products were transported to St. Marks (see "Side Trips from Tallahassee," below) for shipment to other cities. In recent years the tracks were removed, and 16 miles of the historic trail were improved for joggers, hikers, bicyclists, and horseback riders. A paved parking lot is at the north entrance, on Woodville Highway (Fla. 363) just south of Southeast Capital Circle.

Rental bikes and in-line skates are available at the north entrance from **About Bikes** (☎ 850/656-0001). Bike-rental rates are $9 for 2 hours, $16 for 4 hours, $35 for 24 hours, and various rates for families and groups. Guide maps and refreshments are also on hand. The shop is open April through October, Monday to Friday from 2 to 8pm, Saturday and Sunday from 9am to 5pm. Hours from November through March are Monday to Friday from noon to 6pm, Saturday and Sunday from 9am to 5pm.

The **Apalachicola National Forest** also has extensive biking trails (see "Side Trips from Tallahassee," below), and there are 5½ miles of trails at **Maclay State Gardens** (see "Parks & Nature Preserves," above).

GOLF   Play golf at outstanding Hilaman Park, 2737 Blair Stone Rd., where the ✪ **Hilaman Park Municipal Golf Course** features 18 holes (par-72), a driving range, racquetball, squash courts, and a swimming pool. Rental equipment is at the club, and there's a restaurant, too (☎ 850/891-3935 for information and fees). Compared to most courses in Florida, greens fees are a steal: $25 on weekdays, $30 on weekends, including cart (they're just $12.35 and $17.05, respectively, if you walk). The park also includes the **Jake Gaither Municipal Golf Course,** at Bragg and Pasco streets (☎ 850/891-3942), with a nine-hole, par-35 fairway and a pro shop. The Gaither course was recently renovated, so call for fees.

The leading golf course is at the **Killearn Country Club and Inn** (☎ 800/476-4101 or 850/893-2186), which once hosted the Sprint Classic. Moss-draped oaks enhance the beautiful 27-hole championship course, which is for members and hotel guests only (see "Where to Stay" below).

SPECTATOR SPORTS   Tallahassee succumbs to football frenzy whenever the perennially powerful Seminoles of **Florida State University** take to the gridiron. Hollywood star Burt Reynolds, who played defensive back for the 'Noles in 1957, can easily get tickets; the rest of us should call ☎ 850/644-1830 well in advance. Even when the Seminoles play on the road, everything except Tallahassee's many sport bars comes to a stop while fans watch the games on TV.

The **Florida A&M University** Rattlers are cheered on by the school's high-stepping, world-famous Marching 100 Band. Call ☎ 850/599-3230 for FAMU schedules and tickets.

Both FSU and FAMU have seasonal basketball, baseball, tennis, and track schedules. Call the numbers above for information.

WHERE TO STAY

There is no high or low season here, but every hotel and motel for miles around is completely booked during FSU and FAMU football weekends from September to November, and again at graduation in May. Reserve well in advance or you may have to stay 60 miles or more from the city. For the schedules, call FSU or FAMU (see "Spectator Sports," above).

Most hotels are concentrated in three areas: downtown Tallahassee, north of downtown along North Monroe Street at Exit 29 off I-10, and along Apalachee Parkway east of downtown.

North Monroe Street at I-10 has most of the national chain motels catering to the highway traffic. On Apalachee Parkway east of the Capitol, the choices are **Best Western Pride Inn & Suites** (☎ **800/827-7390** or 850/656-6312), **Days Inn** (☎ **800/235-2525** or 850/224-2181), **La Quinta Inn** (☎ **800/531-5900** or 850/878-5099), **Motel 6** (☎ **800/466-8356** or 850/87-6171), and **Ramada Inn** (☎ **800/721-9890** or 850/877-3171).

Tax on all hotel and campground bills is 10% in Leon County.

MODERATE

✪ **Courtyard by Marriott.** 1018 Apalachee Pkwy., Tallahassee, FL 32301. ☎ **800/ 321-2211** or 850/222-8822. Fax 850/561-0354. 154 units. A/C TV TEL. Sun–Thurs $104 double; Fri–Sat $69 double. AE, DC, DISC, MC, V.

Just a mile east of the Old Capitol, this comfortable member of the business traveler–oriented chain encloses a landscaped courtyard with a swimming pool and gazebo. About half the rooms face the courtyard; the others face parking lots. They are a bit cramped for families but ideal for singles and couples. All have sofas or easy chairs and rich mahogany writing tables and chests of drawers, plus features like two phones with modem ports, voice mail, and coffeemakers. Other facilities include an exercise room and indoor spa pool. The marble-floored lobby features a lounge with fireplace and a dining area open for a breakfast buffet only. An Olive Garden, Bennigan's, and several other restaurants are within walking distance or a short drive away. The Parkway Shopping Center is also across the road.

DoubleTree Hotel. 101 S. Adams St., Tallahassee, FL 32301. ☎ **800/222-TREE** or 850/224-5000. Fax 850/513-9516. 251 units. A/C TV TEL. $95–$150 double. AE, DC, DISC, MC, V.

This 16-story hotel is one of the tallest buildings in town. Just 2 blocks from the Capitol Building at Park Avenue, it's usually booked solid during legislative sessions from March through May. Politicians and lobbyists, who love the spacious guest rooms, have power lunches at Jacob's on the Plaza, the hotel's Southern-accented restaurant. Amenities include room service, an exercise room, golf privileges, same-day laundry service, and complimentary airport transportation. There are an outdoor swimming pool, a gift shop, a parking garage, and convention facilities.

✪ **Governors Inn.** 209 S. Adams St., Tallahassee, FL 32301. ☎ **800/342-7717** in Florida, or 850/681-6855. Fax 850/222-3105. 40 units. A/C TV TEL. $119–$129 double; $139–$219 suite. Rates include continental breakfast and evening cocktails. AE, DC, DISC, MC, V.

Just half a block from the Old Capitol, this elegant, richly furnished hotel was once a livery stable on historic Adams Commons. Part of the building's original architecture has been preserved, including the impressive beams. The guest rooms are distinctive, with four-poster beds, black-oak writing desks, rock-maple armoires, and antique accouterments. The suites, each one named for a Florida governor, are sumptuous, some with whirlpool bath or loft bedroom with wood-burning fireplace. Among the amenities are comfy robes.

Complimentary continental breakfast and afternoon cocktails are presented in the pine-paneled Florida Room. Services include valet parking, nightly turndown, newspapers delivered daily to rooms, same-day laundry service, shoe shine, room service, airport transportation, and health-club privileges.

✪ **Radisson Hotel.** 415 N. Monroe St. (at Virginia St.), Tallahassee, FL 32301. ☎ **800/ 333-3333** or 850/224-6000. Fax 850/222-0335. 116 units. A/C TV TEL. $111 double; $150–$197 suite. Weekend rates available. AE, DC, DISC, MC, V.

About half a mile north of the Capitol, this seven-story establishment is Tallahassee's second-most-elegant hotel (behind the Governor's Inn), with an innlike lobby with reproduction antiques and cheerfully decorated guest rooms. The master suites come equipped with canopy beds, whirlpool baths, wet bars, concierge, and turndown services. There's a fitness facility with a sauna, and the hotel provides business services and complimentary airport and capitol-complex transportation. The pleasant Plantation Dining Room is open daily for breakfast, lunch, and dinner, and the clubby Brass Oak Lounge provides libation.

INEXPENSIVE

Cabot Lodge North. 2735 N. Monroe St., Tallahassee, FL 32303. ☎ **800/223-1964** or 850/386-8880. Fax 850/386-4254. 160 units. A/C TV TEL. $72–$80 double. Rates include continental breakfast and evening reception. AE, DC, DISC, MC, V.

A clapboard plantation-style house with a tin roof and a partially screened wraparound porch provides Southern country charm to distinguish this friendly motel from its nearby competitors. Guests can sit and relax in straight-back rockers on the porch or on comfy sofas and easy chairs by a fireplace in the living room. Although the guest rooms in the two-story motel buildings out back don't hold up their end of the atmosphere factor, they're still quite satisfactory at these rates, and they give quick access to the outdoor swimming pool. Guests can graze at a continental breakfast buffet, drink coffee all day, and partake of free evening cocktails.

Killearn Country Club and Inn. 100 Tyron Circle, Tallahassee, FL 32308. ☎ **800/ 476-4101** or 850/893-2186. Fax 850/893-8267. 35 units. A/C TV TEL. $80 double. Golf packages available. AE, DISC, MC, V.

Located in upscale Killearn Estates between Thomasville and Centerville roads north of I-10, this country club is home to Tallahassee's leading 18-hole golf course, which house guests can play for $30 Monday to Friday, $40 on weekends, making this one of the region's best golf-resort bargains. The rooms and suites have sitting areas and dressing rooms; some have wet bars, and some open to central living rooms (which lobbyists turn into hospitality areas to influence legislators from Mar to May). Each unit is individually decorated and has a balcony overlooking the woodland-bordered golf course. The club also offers eight tennis courts. The swimming pool is Olympic size, and there are an exercise facility and miles of surrounding roads for jogging. Moderate prices prevail in the 19th Hole restaurant.

✪ **Quality Inn & Suites.** 2020 Apalachee Pkwy., Tallahassee, FL 32301. ☎ **800/228-5151** or 850/877-4437. Fax 850/878-9964. 100 units. A/C TV TEL. $65 double; $79 suite. Rates include continental breakfast. AE, DC, DISC, MC, V.

In contrast to most Quality Inns, there's real charm here. In fact, an almost English country inn atmosphere prevails in the classy, marble-lined lobby and spacious guest rooms, which are furnished with sofas, reclining wing chairs, two doubles or a king-size bed, desks, and coffeemakers. Complimentary continental breakfasts are served in a ground-level lounge with views of the inn's swimming pool. Guests can partake in a free wine bar Monday to Thursday evenings. There's a pool on the premises, and guests receive passes to the nearby YMCA. Several fast-food and family-style restaurants are within a short walk.

Riedel House Bed & Breakfast. 1412 Fairway Dr., Tallahassee, FL 32301. ☎ **850/ 222-8569.** www.supernet.net/~falcon/b&b. 3 units (all with bathroom). A/C. $75 double (higher on special weekends). Rates include breakfast. No credit cards.

Surrounded by majestic live oaks, pines, magnolias, and flowers, this white-brick, Federal-style, two-story home was built in 1937 for the Cary D. Landis family (he was a former Florida attorney general). The present owner and innkeeper is talented artist and art teacher Carolyn Riedel. A spiral staircase leads from the beautiful foyer to her art gallery and spacious guest rooms, each adorned with period furniture and antiques. Carolyn serves an extensive continental breakfast in the dining room overlooking terraced gardens. Located in the prestigious Capitol Country Club area, the Riedel House is within walking distance of public tennis courts and the club's golf course.

WHERE TO DINE

Numerous budget-priced fast-food and family chain restaurants lie along Apalachee Parkway and North Monroe Street. There's a branch of **Barnhill's Buffet** on Apalachee Parkway at Magnolia Drive (☎ **850/671-5008**), with a budget-priced cornucopia of Southern fare (see "Where to Dine" in section 1, above). For inexpensive seafood, the local **Shells** is at 2136 N. Monroe St., at Universal Drive (☎ **850/385-2774**). See "Where to Dine," in section 1 of chapter 11 for details about the Shells chain.

MODERATE

Anthony's. 1950 Thomasville Rd., at Bradford Rd. in the Betton Place Shops. ☎ **850/224-1447.** Reservations recommended. Main courses $12–$16. AE, DC, MC, V. Daily 5:30–9pm. ITALIAN.

Locals come to see and be seen at Dick Anthony's elegantly relaxed trattoria. Among his specialties are pesce Venezia, spinach fettuccine tossed in a cream sauce with scallops, crabmeat, and fish. Chicken piccata and chicken San Marino are also favorites, and Dick's thick, juicy steaks are always popular with beef eaters. A wall-size wine cupboard features choices from Italy and the United States by the bottle or glass. Espresso pie leads the dessert menu.

✪ **Chez Pierre.** 1215 Thomasville Rd. (at 6th Ave.) ☎ **850/222-0936.** Reservations recommended. Lunch $5.50–$11; main courses $12–$22. AE, DC, DISC, MC, V. Mon–Sat 11am–10pm, Sun brunch 10am–2:30pm. FRENCH.

You become an instant Francophile in Florida at this chic restaurant in a beautifully restored 1920s brick home a few blocks north of the intersection of North Monroe Street and Thomasville Road. French-born chef Eric Favier and his American wife and partner, Karen Cooley, offer traditional French cuisine either inside the house—the walls are adorned with changing works by local artists—or outside on a large deck nearly shaded by live oaks draped with Spanish moss. Opening to the deck, a bistro-style bar provides a light-fare menu between lunch and dinner. Eric offers daily specials to take advantage of fresh produce. Among his winners are chicken crepes, a version of provincial ratatouille, half a roasted chicken with a different sauce each day, Bretagne-style fresh mussels, and crab cakes with a luscious mustard sauce. French table wines are moderately priced, and California house wines are also served. Live music regularly accompanies dining. You can take a horse-drawn carriage ride Friday and Saturday evenings. No smoking except on the front porch, where stogies and brandy can be enjoyed while lounging in wicker chairs. Book as early as possible for Bastille Day (July 14), which sees a humongous party here.

Silver Slipper. 531 Scotty's Lane (off N. Monroe St., 1 block south of the Tallahassee Mall). ☎ **850/386-9366.** Reservations recommended. Main courses $11–$29. AE, DC, DISC, MC, V. Mon–Sat 5–11pm. STEAK/SEAFOOD.

Established in 1938, the oldest family-operated restaurant in Florida has served thick, tender, juicy Black Angus steaks to every president from Kennedy to Bush (they got a Christmas card from Clinton). From the award-winning menu, you can also select seafood dishes, lamb, and veal. Although steaks and tender prime rib draw the crowds, a dozen bacon-wrapped big shrimp or bits of Black Angus beef are the culinary stars here. Featuring live entertainment Tuesday to Saturday, the cocktail lounge is a favorite haunt of politicians and lobbyists. It's open until midnight Monday to Thursday, until 2am on Friday and Saturday. Private, curtained booths are available in the dining room.

INEXPENSIVE

✪ **Bahn Thai.** 1319 S. Monroe St. (near Oakland Ave.). ☎ **850/224-4765.** Reservations accepted. Main courses $5.75–$15. Lunch buffet $5.25. AE, DISC, MC, V. Mon–Thurs 11am–2:30pm and 5–10pm, Fri 11am–2:30pm and 5–10:30pm, Sat 5–10:30pm. THAI/CANTONESE.

Lamoi (Sue) Snyder and progeny have been serving the spicy cuisine of her native Thailand at this storefront since 1979. In deference to local Southerners, who may never have sampled anything spicier than cheese grits, much of her menu is devoted to mild Cantonese-style Chinese dishes. More adventurous diners flock here to order such authentic tongue-burners as *yon voon-sen,* a combination of shrimp, chicken, bean threads, onions, lemongrass, ground peanuts, and the obligatory chili peppers. Sue's specialty, however, is her deliciously sweet, ginger-hinted version of Penang curry. You can ask her to turn down the heat in her other Thai dishes. Come at lunch and sample it all from the all-you-can-eat buffet, a real bargain.

Barnacle Bill's Seafood Restaurant. 1830 N. Monroe St. (north of Tharpe St.). ☎ **850/385-8734.** Reservations not accepted. Main courses $8–$17 (most $9); sandwiches and salads $5–$8. AE, MC, V. Daily 11am–11pm (dance club to 2am). SEAFOOD.

There's always plenty of action at this noisy, very casual spot, with sports TVs over an enormous tile-topped raw bar in the middle of the room. Freshly shucked Apalachicola oysters are the feature at the bar, but the menu offers a mélange of seafood to please the palates of the singles, couples, and families who flock here. The cooking is simple (often done by FSU students working part-time jobs), but the ingredients are the freshest available. The young staff is accomplished at charcoal grilling mahimahi, tuna, amberjack, and grouper. Skillet dishes combine shrimp, oysters, or scallops with vegetables and kielbasa sausage, but order one only if you like the strong smoked flavor of kielbasa. For a smoked sensation you definitely will enjoy, try the mahimahi and amberjack cured on the premises. Carbohydrate lovers can order a half pound of their favorite seafood served with Alfredo or scampi sauce over linguine. During summer, guests can sit at outdoor tables under a lean-to tent. A dance club downstairs stays open until 2am.

Food Glorious Food. In Betton Place Shops, 1950 Thomasville Rd. at Bradford Rd. ☎ **850/224-9974.** Reservations not accepted. Sandwiches, salads, pastas $5–$9.50. AE, MC, V. Mon–Sat 11am–8pm (table service 11am–3pm). AMERICAN/INTERNATIONAL.

Very unusual and very healthy sandwiches, salads, and pastas make this deli/cafe one of the town's favorite lunch and early-dinner spots. Items displayed in a cold case change daily but always include gazpacho, a variety of gourmet salads, inventive sandwiches, a daily quiche, and plenty of tempting pastries and cookies. You can get it to go or dine at a few tables inside or, in good weather, on the outside courtyard.

Mom and Dad's Italian Restaurant. 4175 Apalachee Pkwy. (2 mi. east of Capital Circle). ☎ 850/877-4518. Reservations not accepted. Main courses $7.50–$16. AE, DC, DISC, MC, V. Tues–Thurs 5–10pm, Fri–Sat 5–11pm. ITALIAN.

Diane Violante and Gary McLean have been making their own pastas and baking Italian breads at this popular, aroma-filled trattoria since 1963. Diane is a native of

Abruzzo, Italy, so her specialty is "spaghetti à la Bruzzi"—a casserole of vermicelli, sautéed mushrooms, and tomato meat sauce topped with mozzarella and Parmesan cheeses. Diane, Gary, and their son, Gene, ensure that all plates are piled high, making the drive out here well worth the time.

NEARBY DINING

✪ **Nicholson Farmhouse.** Fla. 12, 3½ miles west of Havana. ☎ **850/539-5931.** Reservations recommended. Main courses $10–$25. AE, DISC, MC, V. Tues–Sat 4–10pm. STEAKS.

This quaint cottage was built in 1828 by Dr. Malcolm Nicholson and is now on the National Register of Historic Places. Longing for a place where he could order a 32-ounce steak, the doctor's great-great-grandson, Paul Nicholson, turned the old house into a restaurant in 1988. His casual, very informal operation has been so successful that he has added two turn-of-the-century farmhouses and made extra dining space of the smokehouse and other outbuildings. At least an inch thick and aged on the premises, Paul's tender steaks are charcoal-grilled to perfection. Grilled chicken breasts, boneless pork chops, shrimp, and fish are also offered. Each table gets a bowl of boiled peanuts as munchies. There's a children's menu. Nonalcoholic beverages are served, and you may bring your own wine or spirits. Guests can take mule-drawn wagon rides around the farm Thursday to Saturday. This is the most popular weekend dining spot in the area, so make reservations well in advance for FSU football and graduation weekends.

TALLAHASSEE AFTER DARK

Check the "Limelight" section of *Friday's Tallahassee Democrat* for what's playing.

As a college town, Tallahassee has numerous pubs and nightclubs with live dance music, not to mention a multitude of sports bars. A good place to pick up copies of the *Break* and other entertainment tabloids with news about what's going on is **Barnacle Bill's Seafood Emporium,** which is also one of several restaurants featuring entertainment. Others include **Chez Pierre** and the **Silver Slipper** (see "Where to Dine" above).

The major performing-arts venue is the **Tallahassee-Leon County Civic Center,** 505 W. Pensacola St. (☎ **800/322-3602** or 850/222-0400), which features a Broadway series, concerts, and sporting events including FSU collegiate basketball and Tiger Sharks pro hockey. Special concerts are presented by the **Tallahassee Symphony Orchestra** at FSU Ruby Diamond Auditorium, College Avenue and Copeland Street (☎ **850/224-0462**). **The FSU Mainstage/School of Theatre,** Fine Arts Building, Call and Copeland streets (☎ **850/644-6500**), presents excellent productions from classic dramas to comedies.

SIDE TRIPS FROM TALLAHASSEE

The following excursions generally are on the way to Apalachicola, so if you're headed that way, plan to make a detour or two.

WAKULLA SPRINGS

The world's largest and deepest freshwater spring is 15 miles south of Tallahassee in the 2,860-acre ✪ **Edward Ball Wakulla Springs State Park** (☎ **850/922-3632**). Edward Ball, a financier who administered the DuPont estate, turned the springs into a preservation area. Divers have mapped an underwater cave system extending more than 6,000 feet back from the spring's mouth. Wakulla has been known to dispense an amazing 14,325 gallons of water per second at certain times. Mastodon bones, including those of Herman, now in Tallahassee's Museum of Florida History, were found in the caves. The 1930s Tarzan movies starring Johnny Weissmuller were filmed here.

A free orientation movie is offered at the park's theater. You can hike or bike along the nature trails, and swimming is allowed, but only in designated areas. It's important to observe swimming rules since alligators are present. Glass-bottom–boat sightseeing and wildlife-observation tours are offered daily: from 9:45am to 5pm during daylight saving time, 9:15am to 4:30pm the rest of the year. They cost $4.50 for adults, half price for children.

Entrance fees to the park are $3.25 per vehicle with up to eight passengers, $1 for pedestrians and bicyclists. The park is open daily from 8am to dusk.

The park entrance is just east of the junction of Fla. 61 and Fla. 267. For more information, contact the park at 550 Wakulla Springs Dr., Wakulla Springs, FL 32305 (☎ **850/224-5950**; fax 850/561-7251).

Where to Stay & Dine

Wakulla Springs Lodge. 550 Wakulla Springs Dr., Wakulla Springs, FL 32305. ☎ **850/ 224-5950.** Fax 850/561-7251. 28 units. A/C TV TEL. $65–$90 double; from $250 suite. MC, V.

On the grounds of Edward Ball Wakulla Springs State Park, the lodge is distinctive for its magnificent Spanish architecture and ornate old-world furnishings, such as rare Spanish tiles, black-granite tables, marble floors, and ceiling beams painted with Florida scenes by a German artist (supposedly Kaiser Wilhelm's court painter). The high-ceilinged guest rooms are simple by today's standards but are beautifully furnished and have marble bathrooms.

You don't have to be a lodge guest to dine in the lovely Ball Room, enhanced by an immense fireplace and arched windows looking onto the springs. Very reasonably priced meals feature Southern cuisine. The coffee shop provides snacks and light meals (there's a 60-foot-long marble drugstore-style counter for old-fashioned ice-cream sodas).

THE ST. MARKS AREA

Rich history lives in the area around the little village of **St. Marks,** 18 miles south of the capital at the end of both Fla. 363 and the Tallahassee–St. Marks Historic Railroad State Trail (see "Outdoor Activities," above).

After marching overland from Tampa Bay in 1528, the Spanish conquistador Panfilo de Narvaez and 300 men arrived at this strategic point at the confluence of the St. Marks and Wakulla rivers near the Gulf of Mexico. Since their only avenue back to Spain was by sea, they built and launched the first ships made by Europeans in the New World. Some 11 years later, Hernando de Soto and his 600 men arrived here after following Narvaez's route from Tampa. They marked the harbor entrance by hanging banners in the trees, then moved inland. Two wooden forts were built here, one in 1679 and one in 1718, and a stone version was begun in 1739. The fort shifted among Spanish, British, and Native American hands until Gen. Andrew Jackson took it away from the Spanish in 1819.

Parts of the old Spanish bastion wall and Confederate earthworks built during the Civil War are in the **San Marcos de Apalache State Historic Site,** reached by turning right at the end of Fla. 363 in St. Marks and following the paved road. A museum built on the foundation of the old marine hospital holds exhibits and artifacts covering the area's history. The site is open Thursday to Monday from 9am to 5pm; closed New Year's Day, Thanksgiving, and Christmas. Admission to the site is free; admission to the museum costs $1, free for children 6 and under. For more information, contact the site at 1022 DeSoto Park Dr., Tallahassee, FL 32301 (☎ **850/925-6216** or 850/922-6007).

De Soto's men marked the harbor entrance in what is now the ✪ **St. Marks Light-house and National Wildlife Refuge,** P.O. Box 68, St. Marks, FL 32355 (☎ **850/925-6121**). Operated by the U.S. Fish and Wildlife Service, this 65,000-acre preserve occupies much of the coast from the Aucilla River east of St. Marks to the Ochlock-onee River west of Panacea, and it is home to more species of birds than anyplace else in Florida except the Everglades. The visitor center is off U.S. 98 about 2 miles east of St. Marks (turn south at Newport on Lighthouse Road [County Road 59]). Stop there for self-guided–tour maps of the roads and hiking trails through the preserve. Built of limestone blocks 4 feet thick at the base, the 80-foot-tall St. Marks Lighthouse has sig-naled the harbor entrance since 1842. The nearby beach is a popular crabbing spot.

Admission to the refuge is $4 per vehicle. The refuge is open daily from sunrise to sunset; the visitor center, Monday to Friday from 8am to 4:15pm and Saturday and Sunday from 10am to 5pm (closed all federal holidays). Contact the refuge for infor-mation about seasonal tours and hunting.

In 1865, during the final weeks of the Civil War, Federal troops landed at the lighthouse and launched a surprise attack on Tallahassee. The Confederates quickly assembled an impromptu army of wounded soldiers, old men, and boys as young as 14. This ragtag bunch fought the Federal regulars for 5 days at what is now the **Natural Bridge State Historic Site.** Surprisingly, the old men and boys won. As a result, Tallahassee remained the only Confederate state capital east of the Mississippi never to fall into Yankee hands. The historic site is on County Road 2192, 6 miles east of Woodville on the St. Marks River, halfway between Tallahassee and St. Marks. Follow the signs from Fla. 363 and go to the end of the pavement. It's open daily from 8am to sunset and admission is free. For more information, contact the San Marcos de Apalache State Historic Site (see above).

APALACHICOLA NATIONAL FOREST

The largest of Florida's three national forests, this huge preserve encompasses 600,000 acres stretching from Tallahassee's outskirts southward to the Gulf Coast and westward some 70 miles to the Apalachicola River. Included are a variety of woodlands, rivers, streams, lakes, and caves populated by a host of wildlife. There are picnic facilities with sheltered tables and grills, canoe and mountain-bike trails, campgrounds with tent and RV sites, and a number of other facilities, some of them especially designed for visi-tors with disabilities.

The **Leon Sinks Area** is closest to Tallahassee, 5½ miles south of Southeast Capital Circle on U.S. 319 near the Leon-Wakulla County line. Nature trails and boardwalks lead from one sinkhole (a lake formed when water erodes the underlying limestone) to another. The trails are open daily from 8am to 8pm.

A necessary stop before heading into this wilderness is the **Wakulla Area Ranger District,** 1773 Crawfordville Hwy., Crawfordville, FL 32327 (☎ **850/926-3561;** fax 850/926-1904), which provides information about the forest and its facilities and sells topographical and canoe trail maps. The station is on U.S. 319 about 20 miles south of Tallahassee and 5 miles north of Crawfordville. It's open Monday to Thursday from 8am to 5pm and Friday from 8am to 4pm.

14 Northeast Florida

by Bill Goodwin

Northeast Florida traces its history to 1513, when the Spaniard Juan Ponce de León, who later undertook a Quixotic quest for the Fountain of Youth, sighted this coast, landed somewhere between present-day Jacksonville and Cape Canaveral, and named it "La Florida." In 1565 the Spanish established a colony at St. Augustine, making it the country's oldest permanent settlement.

If they were to come back to life, those early colonists would feel right at home in St. Augustine, where the streets of the restored Old City look like they did in Spanish times. For us modern mortals, St. Augustine offers a rich look back to when the settlers struggled to establish a life in a new, unfamiliar, and often-hostile world.

But they would surely be astonished at what they would see elsewhere in Northeast Florida.

To the south, their eyes would pop open with disbelief at today's "Space Coast," where rockets blast off from the Kennedy Space Center at Cape Canaveral. Nearby in Cocoa Beach, they would see another of our peculiar curiosities: surfers. And in Daytona Beach, they would hear the deafening roar of the stock cars and motorbikes that make this beach town the "World Center of Racing."

Heading north along the coast, they would come to the rich folks' haven of Ponte Vedra Beach, where golf definitely takes precedence over manual labor. And they would marvel at sprawling Jacksonville, Florida's largest metropolis and a thriving example of today's New South.

Up on the Georgia border, they'd cross a bridge to Amelia Island, where exclusive resorts take full advantage of 13 miles of beautiful beaches. Amelia's Victorian-era town, Fernandina Beach, would seem modern to them; to us, it's a quaint and historic retreat.

1 Cocoa Beach, Cape Canaveral & the Kennedy Space Center

46 miles SE of Orlando, 186 miles N of Miami, 65 miles S of Daytona

The area around Cape Canaveral was once a sleepy place where city dwellers escaped the crowds from the exploding urban centers of Miami and Jacksonville. But then came the NASA space program. Today the region accommodates its own crowds, especially hordes of tourists who come to visit the Kennedy Space Center and enjoy 72 miles of beaches, plus fishing, surfing, golfing, and tennis.

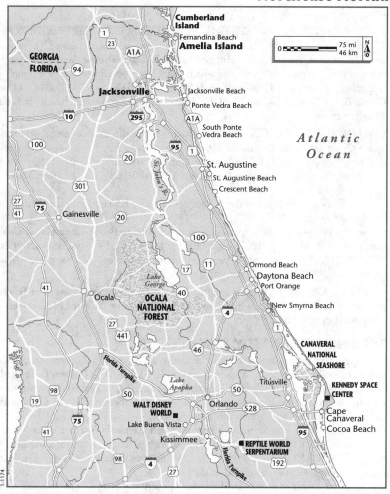

I Dream of Jeannie fans will recognize this as the home of television's most famous astronaut, Maj. Anthony Nelson, who lived with his bottle-dwelling Jeannie in Cocoa Beach. Many of the nation's first real spacemen did, too.

Thanks to NASA, this also is a prime destination for nature lovers. The space agency originally took over much more land than it has needed to launch rockets. Rather than sell off the unused portions, it turned them over to the Cape Canaveral National Seashore and the Merritt Island National Wildlife Refuge, which have preserved them in their pristine natural states.

A handful of the major Caribbean-bound cruise ships depart from the man-made Port Canaveral. The south side of the port is lined with seafood restaurants and marinas, which serve as home base for gambling ships and the area's deep-sea charter- and group fishing boats.

ESSENTIALS

GETTING THERE The nearest airport is **Melbourne International Airport,** 22 miles south of Cocoa Beach, which is served by **Continental** (☎ **800/525-0280**),

Delta (☎ **800/221-1212**), and **US Airways** (☎ **800/428-4322**). **Melbourne Airport Shuttle** (☎ **407/724-1600**) takes passengers to the Cocoa Beach hotels, about a 45-minute ride, for $20 for the first person, $10 for each additional person. The shuttle desk is located in the baggage-claim area. **Orlando International Airport,** about 35 miles to the southwest, is a larger hub with more flight options (see "Orientation" in chapter 12). From there, **Comfort Travel** (☎ **800/567-6139** or 407/799-0442) or the **Cocoa Beach Shuttle** (☎ **407/784-3831**) and will take you to the beach for about $15 per person.

VISITOR INFORMATION   For information about the area, contact the **Florida Space Coast Office of Tourism,** 8810 Astronaut Blvd., Suite 102, Cape Canaveral, FL 32920 (☎ **800/872-1969** or 407/868-1126; fax 407/868-1193; www. spacecoast.com). The office is on Fla. A1A at Central Boulevard and is open Monday to Friday from 8am to 5pm.

The office operates an information booth at the John F. Kennedy Space Center Visitor Center (see below).

You can also get specific information from the **Cocoa Beach Chamber of Commerce,** 400 Fortenberry Rd., Merritt Island, FL 32952 (☎ **407/459-2200;** fax 407/459-2232). The chamber is between Plumosa Street and Merritt Square Mall. Open Monday to Friday from 9am to 5pm.

GETTING AROUND   A car is essential in this area. The **Space Coast Area Transit** (☎ **407/633-1878**) operates buses, but routes tend to be circuitous and therefore extremely time-consuming.

TOURING THE KENNEDY SPACE CENTER

Whether you're a space buff or not, you're sure to appreciate the sheer grandeur of the facilities and the achievement of technology displayed at NASA's ✪ **John F. Kennedy Space Center.** Astronauts departed Earth at this site in 1969 en route to the most famous "small step" in history—man's first voyage to the moon—and today space shuttles regularly lift off on their missions in orbit.

All visitors must stop at the privately operated **Kennedy Space Center Visitor Center,** on NASA Parkway (Fla. 405), 6 miles east of Titusville and ½ mile west of Fla. 3 (☎ **407/452-2121;** www.kscvisitor.com). Other than Fla. 405 and Fla. 3, all roads in the space center are closed to the public.

The visitor center is open from 9am to dusk every day except Christmas and some launch days. Admission and parking are free, but you'll have to pay for bus tours and IMAX movies (see below). Arrive early and pick up a schedule of events, which change frequently, and a map to help plan your visit. You'll need at least a full day to see and do everything.

The visitor center has exhibits, rockets, IMAX movies, and several dining venues, but you will need to take the **Kennedy Space Center Tour** to see the facilities actually in use.

The tour's shuttle buses go to the massive Vehicle Assembly Building, where shuttles are prepared for launch; the Complex launch pads, where space shuttles blast off; the International Space Station Center, where scientists and engineers prepare additions to the space station now in orbit; and the impressive Apollo/Saturn V Center, which includes artifacts, photos, interactive exhibits, and the 363-foot-tall Saturn V, the most powerful rocket ever launched by the United States. The buses depart the visitor center every 10 minutes starting at 9:45am, with the last tour leaving at 3pm, later in summer. Don't start your tour after 3pm, since it will take at least 2 hours to see the highlights, up to 5 hours if you linger at the stops along the way. Buses run continuously, and you can reboard as you wish.

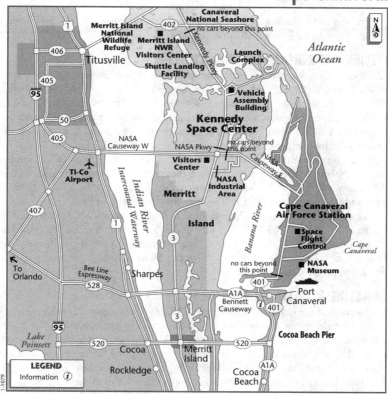

If you have time at the end of your day, the **Historic Cape Canaveral Tour** visits the Cape Canaveral Air Station, where America's first satellites and astronauts were launched into space. It passes the launch pads currently used for unmanned launches, the original site of Mission Control, and the Air Force Space Museum. The history tour runs only at 3:30pm daily and is subject to frequent cancellations.

Back at the visitor center, **IMAX movies** will both inform you and keep you entertained. Not to be missed, the 3-D IMAX movie *L-5: First City in Space* depicts future life among the stars. Two other IMAX films are also shown on the 5½-story-high screens every day: the 37-minute *Dream Is Alive*, giving an insider's view of the Space Shuttle program with in-flight footage shot by astronauts on various missions; and *Mission to Mir*, a tour of the aging Russian space station.

Either **bus tour** costs $14 for adults, $10 for children 3 to 11, free for children 2 and under.

The **IMAX films** cost $7.50 for adults, $5.50 for children 3 to 11, free for children under 3.

If you have a full day here, a **Mission Pass** is a better deal, offering a bus tour and any two IMAX movies at $26 for adults, $20 for children 3 to 11, free for children under 3. Or a **Crew Pass** includes a bus tour and one IMAX movie for $19 adults, $15 for kids 3 to 11, free for children under 3.

American Express, Discover, MasterCard, and Visa cards are accepted throughout the visitor center.

If you'd like to **see a launch,** call ☎ 407/867-4636 for a schedule of upcoming takeoffs and ☎ 407/452-2121 for ticket information. Launch tickets cost $10 per person, and you must buy them in person at the visitor center up to 5 days before a launch. They are sold on a first-come, first-served basis.

OTHER ASTRONAUT ATTRACTIONS

Children will enjoy a playful visit to the **Astronaut Hall of Fame,** 6225 Vectorspace Blvd., Titusville (☎ 407/269-6100), at the mainland end of NASA Causeway (Fla. 405). In addition to honoring our space voyagers, the hall has artifacts from the space program and several interactive exhibits. A flight simulator and a G Force Trainer will subject the kids (and you, too) to four times the pull of gravity. A moon walk uses swings to let them experience a degree of weightlessness. And a Mars mission ride will take them on a simulated trip to the red planet. That full-size replica of a space shuttle you see by the highway actually holds a theater with a multimedia presentation. Admission is $13.95 for adults, $9.95 for children 6 to 12, free for kids under 6. Or you can buy a family pass for $39.95. Open daily from 9am to 5pm.

The **Astronaut Memorial Planetarium and Observatory,** 1519 Clearlake Rd., Cocoa Beach (☎ 407/634-3732), south of Fla. 528, has its own International Hall of Space Explorers, but its big attractions are sound and light shows in the planetarium. Call for a schedule of events. Shows cost $4 for adults, $3 for seniors and students, and $2 for kids 12 and under.

BEACHES & WILDLIFE REFUGES

To the north of the Kennedy Space Center, ✪ **Canaveral National Seashore** is a protected 13-mile stretch of barrier-island beach backed by cabbage palms, sea grapes, palmettos, marshes, and Mosquito Lagoon. This is a great area for watching herons, egrets, ibis, willets, sanderlings, turnstones, terns, and other birds, and giant sea turtles nest here from May to August. You might also glimpse dolphins and manatees in Mosquito Lagoon. Canoeists can paddle along a marked trail through the marshes of Shipyard Island, and you can go backcountry camping here from November through April (permits required).

The southern access gate and ranger station are 8 miles east of Titusville on Fla. 402, just east of Fla. 3. A paved road leads from there to undeveloped ✪ **Playalinda Beach,** one of Florida's most beautiful. It's now officially illegal, but nude sunbathing has long been a tradition here (at least for those willing to walk a few miles to the more deserted areas). The main visitor center is at **Apollo Beach,** at the north end of the island, via Fla. A1A south from New Smyrna Beach. The seashore is open daily from 6am to 8pm during daylight saving time, daily 6am to 6pm during standard time. Admission fees are $5 per motor vehicle, $1 for pedestrians or bicyclists. For more information, contact the seashore at 308 Julia St., Titusville, FL 32796 (☎ 407/267-1110).

Its neighbor to the south and west is the 140,000-acre **Merritt Island National Wildlife Refuge,** home to hundreds of species of shorebirds, waterfowl, reptiles, alligators, and mammals, many of them endangered. Stop and pick up a map and other information at the visitor center, on Fla. 402 about 4 miles east of Titusville (it's on the way to Playalinda Beach). You can see some of nature's creatures from the 6-mile-long Black Point Wildlife Drive, or you can hike one of three nature trails through the hammocks and marshes. The visitor center is open Monday to Friday from 8:30am to 4:30pm, Saturday and Sunday from 9am to 5pm (closed Sun from Apr through Oct). Admission is free. For more information, contact the refuge at P.O. Box 6504, Titusville, FL 32782 (☎ 407/861-0667).

The beach at ✪ **Cocoa Beach Pier,** on Meade Avenue east of Fla. A1A (☎ 407/783-7549), is also a popular spot, especially for surfers. Appearing rustic and slapped-together, the pier was built in 1962 and shortly thereafter became the East Coast's surfing capital. It has 842 feet of fishing, shopping, and food and drinks overlooking a wide, sandy beach (see "Where to Dine" below).

Other beach areas here include **Jetty Park,** on Jetty Drive at the south entry to Port Canaveral. From here you can watch the big cruise ships as they enter and leave the port's narrow passage. It has lifeguards, fishing pier with bait shop, children's playground, volleyball court, horseshoe pitch, picnic tables, snack bar, grocery store, and campground (see "Where to Stay" below). The park is open daily from 7am to 10pm, 24 hours for fishing. Admission is $1 per car, $5 for RVs. No pets are allowed.

OUTDOOR PURSUITS

CRUISES You can go on day trips under sail on the 45-foot cutter *San John* with **Tradewinds Sail Charters,** on the south side of Port Canaveral (☎ **888/635-1898** or 407/635-1898; fax 407/456-5770; www.yourlink.net/tradewinds). Many cruises are offered, including a 2-hour port excursion ($70 per person), full-day excursions on the ocean or Intercoastal Waterway ($200 per person), and dinner cruises ($140 per person). The boat also is available for longer charters.

ECOTOURS **Funday Discovery Tours** (☎ **407/725-0796**) offers 16 day trips, including backcountry kayaking, airboat rides, horseback tours, and bird-watching expeditions. Prices range from $39 to $69 for adults, $19 to $49 for children 6 to 12. Call or pick up a copy of their list of trips from the visitor center (see "Essentials," above).

FISHING Whether you choose freshwater, shore, or deep-sea fishing, the Space Coast has endless opportunities to cast a line. **Mosquito Lagoon** and **Eddy Creek** to the north are where you'll find trout and redfish. The **Indian River** and **Banana River** also yield trout and redfish, as well as snook, ladyfish, and black drum. Bass fishers enjoy a region in the west called **Farm 13/Stick Marsh** with more than 20,000 acres of freshwater angling. For private outings, call **Dominics Guide Service** (☎ **800/BASS-909** or 407/242-892), one of the oldest licensed guides in the area.

Head to Port Canaveral for catches like snapper and grouper. **Jetty Park,** at the south entry to the port, has a fishing pier equipped with bait shop (see "Beaches & Wildlife Refuges," above). The south bank of the port is lined with charter boats, and you can go deep-sea fishing on two party vessels based here. The *Orlando Princess* (☎ **800/481-FISH** or 407/784-FISH) runs 6-hour trips, departing daily at 10:30am. These cost $38 for adults, $33 for children 11 to 17, and $28 for kids 6 to 10, including lunch, soft drinks, gear, and bait. The *Miss Cape Canaveral* (☎ **407/783-5274** or 407/648-2211 in Orlando) has 9-hour voyages departing daily at 8am, for $60 per person, including breakfast, lunch, soft drinks, gear, bait, and license.

GOLF You can read about Northeast Florida's best courses in the free *Golfer's Guide,* available at the tourist information offices and in many hotel lobbies. See "The Active Vacation Planner," in chapter 2, for information about ordering copies.

In Cocoa Beach, the municipal **Cocoa Beach Country Club,** 500 Tom Warringer Blvd. (☎ **407/868-3351**), has 27 holes of championship golf and 10 lighted tennis courts set on acres of natural woodland, rivers, and lakes. Greens fees are about $38 in winter, dropping to about $32 in summer, including cart.

On Merritt Island south of the Kennedy Space Center, **The Savannahs at Sykes Creek,** 3915 Savannahs Trail (☎ **407/455-1377**), has 18 holes over 6,636 yards bordered by hardwood forests, lakes, and savannahs inhabited by a host of wildlife. You'll have to hit over a lake to reach the seventh hole. Fees with cart are $35 in winter, less in summer.

The best nearby course is the Gary Player–designed **Baytree National Golf Club,** 8010 N. Wickham Rd., ½ mile east of I-95 in Melbourne (☎ **407/259-9060**).

Challenging marshy holes are flanked by towering palms. This par-72 course has 7,043 yards with a unique red-shale waste area. Fees are $85 in winter, dropping to about $50 in summer, including cart.

In Melbourne Beach, the expanded executive course at **Spessard Holland Golf Club,** 2374 Oak St. (☎ **407/952-4530**), lies between the Atlantic and the bays, making it one of the area's most scenic. The par-67 course covers 5,130 yards, with six holes of no more than 191 yards presenting opportunities for holes in one. Winter fees here are $32 with cart, less in summer.

KAYAKING   One way to venture into Mosquito Lagoon and other backwaters in Cape Canaveral National Seashore and Merritt Island National Wildlife Refuge (see "Beaches & Wildlife Refuges," above) is on a guided kayak trip with **Osprey Outfitters,** 132 S. Dixie Ave., Titusville (☎ **407/267-3535;** www.nbbd.com/osprey). Half-day trips cost $35 for one person, $20 for children under 13 or the second person in a kayak. Full-day trips cost $60 and $30, respectively. Kayaks, safety equipment, water, and snacks are included (plus lunch on the full-day trips). Reservations are required.

SPECTATOR SPORTS   The Boys of Spring here take the form of Miami's **Florida Marlins,** who play their spring-training baseball games from mid-February through March at the Space Coast Stadium, 5800 Stadium Pkwy., off I-95 Exit 73 in Melbourne (☎ **407/633-9200**). Tickets range from $5 to $12.

SURFING   Rip through some totally awesome waves at the **Cocoa Beach Pier** area or down south at **Sebastian Inlet.** Get outfitted at Ron Jon Surf Shop (see "Shopping" below). Or call **Cocoa Beach Surfing School,** 301 N. Atlantic Ave., at Desperados Restaurant (☎ **407/452-0854**). They offer equipment and lessons for beginners or pros at area beaches. Be sure to bring along a towel, flip-flops, sunscreen, and a lot of nerve.

SHOPPING

Hundreds of billboards will lure you to the **Ron Jon Surf Shop,** at 4151 N. Atlantic Ave. (☎ **407/799-8888**), a block from the beach. It's a Hollywood version of art deco gone wild with tropical colors, lights, and towering sand sculptures of famous sports heroes. The stock doesn't live up to the hype: It's mainly souvenirs of every description and equipment and clothing to make you look like a surfer, most at relatively high prices. The shop also rents beach bikes, boogie boards, surfboards, scuba-diving gear, and in-line skates by the hour, day, or week, and they teach scuba lessons. They even have a cafe (more like a fast-food burger joint).

The **Merritt Square Mall,** at 777 E. Merritt Island Causeway, has more than 100 stores, including Florida's own department store, Burdine's, and many specialty shops, as well as a 12-screen movie theater.

Bargain hunters can dig through the wares of hundreds of merchants at **Frontenac Flea Market,** open Friday through Sunday from 8am until 4pm. It's located at 5605 U.S. 1 midway between Cocoa and Titusville.

WHERE TO STAY

The hotels listed below are all in Cocoa Beach, the closest resort to the Kennedy Space Center, about a 30-minute drive to the north.

In addition to those below, Cocoa Beach has several other chain motels. **Days Inn Oceanfront,** 5600 N. Atlantic Ave. (☎ **800/962-0028** or 407/783-7621; fax 407/799-4576), is a good choice if you want to be on the beach and only a block from Cocoa Beach Pier and its action. It consists of an older motel and a newer six-story beachside tower. Even closer to the pier is the **Best Western Ocean Inn,** 5500 N. Atlantic Ave. (☎ **888/799-1631** or 407/784-2550; fax 407/868-7124), a modern, clean two-story motel. The **Comfort Inn & Suite Resort,** 3901 N. Atlantic Ave. (☎ **800/247-2221** or 407/783-2221; fax 407/783-0461), will put you a block from the congestion around Ron Jon Surf Shop (see "Shopping" above). Some of the older units here have cathedral ceilings, which lend an almost cottage-like ambience.

Closer to the space center and Port Canaveral, the **Radisson Resort at the Port,** 8701 Astronaut Blvd. (Fla. A1A) in Cape Canaveral (☎ **800/333-3333** or 407/ 784-0000; fax 407/784-3737), isn't on the beach, but you can relax in a lushly land-scaped courtyard with waterfall cascading over fake rocks into an outdoor heated pool. This comfortable, well-equipped hotel caters to business travelers and passengers waiting to board cruise ships departing Port Canaveral.

The area has a plethora of rental condominiums and cottages. **King Rentals Inc.,** 320 N. Atlantic Ave., Cocoa Beach, FL 32930 (☎ **888/295-0934** or 407/784-5046; www.kingrentals.com), has a wide selection in its inventory.

For camping, **Jetty Park,** 400 E. Jetty Rd., Cape Canaveral, FL 32910 (☎ **407/ 783-1111;** fax 407/783-5005), on the south side of Port Canaveral, has 82 sites, some of them shady, all with hookups. They cost from $14.85 to $20.35 a night. See "Beaches & Wildlife Refuges," above, for more information about Jetty Park.

Given the proximity of Orlando, the generally warm weather all year, and business travelers visiting the space complex, there is little if any seasonal fluctuation in room rates here. They are highest weekends, holidays, and during special events, such as space-shuttle launches.

You'll pay a 4% hotel tax on top of the Florida sales tax here.

Cocoa Beach Hilton. 1550 N. Atlantic Ave., Cocoa Beach, FL 32931. ☎ **800/526-2609** or 407/799-0003. Fax 407/799-0344. 298 units. A/C TV TEL. $129–$179 double. AE, DC, DISC, MC, V. Free parking.

Instead of balconies or patios from which you can enjoy the fresh air and view down the shore, the rooms at this seven-story Hilton have smallish, sealed-shut windows. That and other architectural features make it seem more like a downtown commercial hotel transplanted to a beachside location. Nevertheless, it's one of the few upscale properties here. No doubt you will run into a crew of name-tagged conventioneers, since it's especially popular with groups. Rooms are a decent size and all have cof-feemakers, irons and boards, and hair dryers. Club rooms also have a concierge and get complimentary breakfast and evening cocktails. A short boardwalk leads across the dunes from a modestly sized outdoor pool to the beach, where you can rent water and sports equipment. Other diversions include games and weight rooms. A restaurant-bar facing the ocean serves food and drinks, and limited room service is available. Laundry, dry cleaning, and complimentary weekday newspaper delivery are conve-nient features.

DoubleTree Oceanfront Hotel. 2080 N. Atlantic Ave., Cocoa Beach, FL 32931. ☎ **800/ 552-3224** or 407/783-9222. Fax 407/799-3234. 148 units. A/C TV TEL. $105–$150 double, $175–$275 suite. AE, DC, DISC, MC, V.

Formerly the Howard Johnson Plaza, this six-story hotel was extensively remodeled and upgraded in 1998 and is now the pick of the beachside properties here. All rooms have balconies with ocean views, and all sport bright writing desks and other furni-ture, coffeemakers, irons and boards, hair dryers, and at least one phone with dataport. Oceanfront units also have easy chairs, and 10 suites have living rooms with sleeper sofas, separate bedrooms with TVs and phones, and wet bars with microwaves. Plaza Club rooms on the top floor have their own concierge and complimentary continental breakfast and evening cocktails. Facing the beach, the charming Three Wishes restaurant serves Mediterranean fare and opens to a bilevel brick patio with water cascading between two heated swimming pools. Doubling as a gift shop, the Deli & Marketplace offers snacks. Amenities here include limited room service, exercise and games rooms, laundry service, and coin laundry. Conference facilities draw groups.

Econo Lodge of Cocoa Beach. 1275 N. Atlantic Ave. (Fla. A1A, at Holiday Lane), Cocoa Beach, FL 32931. ☎ **800/553-2666** or 407/783-2252. Fax 407/783-4485. 128 units. A/C TV TEL. $45–$125 double. AE, DC, DISC, MC, V. Pets accepted.

About half of the spacious rooms at this Econo Lodge—more charming than most members of this budget-priced chain—face a tropical courtyard with an L-shaped swimming pool whose bottom displays the names of the seven original astronauts, who once owned this establishment. A variety of comfortable and clean units here include standard motel rooms and suites with living rooms and kitchenettes. A poolside tiki hut and a sports bar serve libation and other refreshments, and there's a Chinese restaurant on the premises. The complex sits directly across the avenue from the Holiday Inn Cocoa Beach (see below).

Holiday Inn Cocoa Beach. 1300 N. Atlantic Ave. (Fla. A1A, at Holiday Lane), Cocoa Beach, FL 32931. ☎ **800/226-6587** or 407/783-2271. Fax 407/783-8878. 515 units. A/C TV TEL. $69–$199 double. AE, DC, DISC, MC, V.

Set on 30 beachside acres, this sprawling family-oriented complex offers a wide variety of spacious hotel rooms, efficiencies, and apartments. A few suites even come equipped with bunk beds and Nintendo games for the kids. Most are in 1960s-style motel buildings flanking a long central courtyard with tropical foliage and eight tennis courts. Only those rooms directly facing the beach or pool have patios or balconies; the rest are entered from exterior corridors. A large heated pool with adjacent bar sits to one side, and guests can use sports equipment at the beach. Dining outlets include Willard's Restaurant, specializing in buffets, and the Oceanside Cafe by the beach. There are a volleyball court, whirlpool, concierge desk, beauty salon, coin-op laundry, and gift shop. A convention center draws groups here.

WHERE TO DINE

On the **Cocoa Beach Pier,** at the beach end of Meade Avenue, you'll get a fine view down the coast to accompany the seafood offerings at **Atlantic Ocean Grill** (☎ 407/ 783-7549) and inexpensive pub fare at adjacent **Marlins Good Times Bar & Grill** (same phone). Even if you don't dine on the pier, the outdoor, tin-roofed **Boardwalk Bar** is a fine place to have a drink while watching the surfers or a sunset.

Cocoa Beach has fast-food outlets along Fla. A1A and Fla. 520, a profusion of bars serving bar snacks, Chinese restaurants, and barbecue joints. The best dining choices here, however, are on Fla. A1A about 3 miles south of the Fla. 520 causeway.

Bernard's Surf/Fischer's Seafood Bar & Grill. 2 South Atlantic Ave. (at Minuteman Causeway Rd.), Cocoa Beach. ☎ **407/783-2401.** Reservations recommended in Bernard's, not accepted in Fischer's. Bernard's main courses $13–$25; early-bird specials (4–6:30pm) $8–$11. Fischer's main courses $8–$13, sandwiches and salads $5–$9. AE, DC, DISC, MC, V. Bernard's Mon–Sat 11am–11pm, Sun 10am–2pm (brunch) and 5–10pm. Fischer's daily 11am–11pm (bar to 2am). Closed Christmas. SEAFOOD/STEAKS.

Photos on the walls testify that many astronauts—and Russian cosmonauts, too— come to these adjoining establishments to celebrate their landings. It all started as Bernard's Surf, which has been serving standard steak-and-seafood fare in a large and elegant setting since 1948. Bernard's offers house specials such as filet mignon served with sautéed mushrooms and béarnaise sauce, but your best bets are char-grilled fish supplied by the Fischer family's own boats. The fresh seafood also finds its way into Fischer's Seafood Bar & Grill, a friendly, *Cheers*-like lounge popular with the locals. Fischer's menu features fried combo platters, shrimp and crab claw meat sautéed in herb butter, and mussels with a wine sauce over pasta, to mention a few worthy selections. Fischer's also provides sandwiches, burgers, and other pub fare, and it has the same 25¢ happy-hour oysters and spicy wings as **Rusty's Seafood & Oyster Bar** (see below), also part of this complex.

✪ **The Mango Tree.** 118 N. Atlantic Ave. (Fla. A1A, between N. 1st and N. 2nd sts.), Cocoa Beach. ☎ **407/799-0513.** Reservations recommended. Main courses $13–$29. AE, MC, V. Tues–Sun 6–9pm. CONTINENTAL.

Gourmet seafood, pastas, and chicken are served in a plantation-home atmosphere with elegant furnishings in this stucco house, the finest dining venue here. Goldfish ponds inside and a waterfall splashing into a Japanese koi pond out in the lush tropical gardens provide pleasing backdrops. Start with finely seasoned Indian River crab cakes, then go on the chef's expert spin on fresh tuna fillets, roast Long Island duckling, tournedos with peppercorn mushroom sauce, and other excellent dishes drawing their inspiration from the continent.

Rusty's Seafood & Oyster Bar. 2 S. Atlantic Ave. (Fla. A1A, at Minuteman Causeway Rd.), Cocoa Beach. ☎ **407/783-2401.** Reservations not accepted. Sandwiches and salads $3–$8; main courses $7–$17.50. AE, DC, DISC, MC, V. Daily 11am–1am (bar to 2am). SEAFOOD/PUB FARE.

Part of the Bernard's Surf family (see above), this lively sports bar offers inexpensive chow ranging from very spicy seafood gumbo to a pot of seafood that will give two normal persons their fill of steamed oysters, clams, shrimp, crab legs, potatoes, and corn on the cob. There are indoor and outdoor seating. Daily happy hours from 3 to 6pm see tons of oysters (raw or steamed) and spicy Buffalo wings go for 25¢ each.

There's a waterfront **Rusty's** at 628 Glen Cheek Dr. in Port Canaveral (☎ **407/ 783-2033**), on the south side of the harbor. Like the original, it's a noisy sports bar, but the clientele tends to be somewhat older if not more reserved. Both have the same menu and hours.

THE SPACE COAST AFTER DARK

For a rundown of current performances and exhibits, call the **Brevard Cultural Alliance's Arts Line** (☎ 407/690-6819). For live music, walk out on the **Cocoa Beach Pier,** on Meade Avenue at the beach, where **Shuck's Seafood Bar & Grill** (☎ 407/783-7549) and **Marlins Good Times Bar & Grill** (☎ 407/783-7549) have bands on weekends, more often during the winter season, and the alfresco **Boardwalk Bar** is a great place to hang out over a cold beer.

2 Daytona Beach

54 miles NE of Orlando, 251 miles N of Miami, 78 miles S of Jacksonville

Daytona Beach is a town with many personalities. It is at once the "World's Most Famous Beach," the "World Center of Racing," and a mecca for spring break. It has been a destination for racing enthusiasts since the days when "horseless carriages" raced on the hard-packed sand beach. One thing is for sure: Daytonans still love their cars. Recent debate over the environmental impact of unrestricted driving on the beach caused an uproar from citizens who couldn't imagine it any other way. As it worked out, they can still drive on the sand, but not in areas where sea turtles are nesting.

Today, hundreds of thousands of race enthusiasts come to the home of the National Association for Stock Car Auto Racing (NASCAR) for the Daytona 500, the Pepsi 400, and other races throughout the year. The Speedway is home to Daytona USA, a state-of-the-art motor-sports entertainment attraction worth a visit even by nonracing fans.

Daytona Beach Shores even provides a drive-in church where a dedicated following flocks to hear Sunday-morning sermons from speakers hooked to their car windows.

But you don't have to be a car aficionado to enjoy Daytona. It has 23 miles of sandy beach, surprisingly good museums, and an active nightlife. Be sure to check the "Florida Calendar of Events" in chapter 2 to know when the town belongs to college students during spring break, hundreds of thousands of leather-clad motorcycle buffs during Bike Week, or racing enthusiasts for big competitions. Don't bother trying to find a hotel room, drive the highways, or enjoy a peaceful vacation at those times. You won't be able to.

ESSENTIALS

GETTING THERE **Continental** (☎ 800/525-0280) and **Delta** (☎ 800/221-1212) fly into Daytona Beach International Airport, 4 miles inland from the beach on International Speedway Boulevard.

Alamo (☎ 800/327-9633), **Avis** (☎ 800/331-1212), **Budget** (☎ 800/527-0700), **Dollar** (☎ 800/800-4000), **Hertz** (☎ 800/654-3131), and **National** (☎ 800/CAR-RENT) have booths at the airport.

But why not rent a Harley? This is Daytona, after all. Call **American Road Collection** (☎ 888-RENT-HD3 or 904/238-1999).

The ride from the airport to most beach hotels via **Yellow Cab Co.** (☎ 904/255-5555) costs between $10 and $15.

Daytona-Orlando Transit Service (DOTS) (☎ 800/231-1965 or 904/257-5411) provides van transportation to or from Orlando International Airport. The fare is $26 for adults one way, $46 round-trip; children 11 and under are charged half. The service brings passengers to the company's terminal at 1034 N. Nova Rd., between 3rd and 4th streets, or to beach hotels for an additional fee.

VISITOR INFORMATION The **Daytona Beach Area Convention & Visitors Bureau,** 126 E. Orange Ave. (P.O. Box 910), Daytona Beach, FL 32115 (☎ 800/854-1234 or 904/255-0415; fax 904/255-5478; www.daytonabeach.com), can help you with information on attractions, accommodations, dining, and events. The office is on the mainland just west of the Memorial Bridge. The information area of the lobby is open daily from 9am to 7pm; office hours are Monday to Friday from 9am to 5pm. The bureau also maintains a branch at Daytona USA, 1801 W. International Speedway Blvd., and a kiosk at the airport.

GETTING AROUND Although it's primarily a driver's town, VOTRAN, Volusia County's public transit system (☎ 904/761-7700), runs a **trolley** along Atlantic Avenue on the beach, Monday to Saturday from noon to midnight during summer. Fares are 75¢ for adults, 35¢ for seniors and children 6–17, free for kids under 6 riding with an adult. VOLTRAN also runs **buses** throughout downtown and the beaches.

For a taxi call **Yellow Cab** (☎ 904/255-5555) or **Komfort Cab** (☎ 904/252-2222).

Over at the beach, **Scooters Cycles,** 2020 S. Atlantic Ave. (Fla. A1A) (☎ 904/253-4131), rents both.

A VISIT TO THE WORLD CENTER OF RACING

Opened in 1959 with the first Daytona 500, the 480-acre ✪ **Daytona International Speedway complex,** at 1801 W. International Speedway Blvd. (U.S. 92 at Bill France

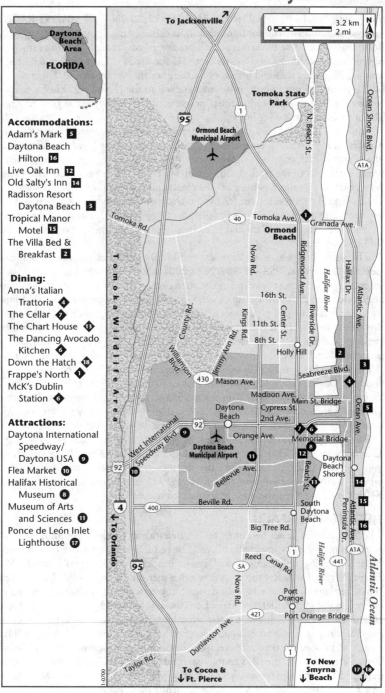

Daytona Beach

Daytona Beach Area
FLORIDA

0   3.2 km
     2 mi
N

To Jacksonville

Tomoka State Park

Ormond Beach Municipal Airport

Ormond Beach

Accommodations:
Adam's Mark **5**
Daytona Beach
  Hilton **16**
Live Oak Inn **12**
Old Salty's Inn **14**
Radisson Resort
  Daytona Beach **3**
Tropical Manor
  Motel **15**
The Villa Bed &
  Breakfast **2**

Dining:
Anna's Italian
  Trattoria **4**
The Cellar **7**
The Chart House **13**
The Dancing Avocado
  Kitchen **6**
Down the Hatch **18**
Frappe's North **1**
McK's Dublin
  Station **6**

Attractions:
Daytona International
  Speedway/
  Daytona USA **9**
Flea Market **10**
Halifax Historical
  Museum **8**
Museum of Arts
  and Sciences **11**
Ponce de León Inlet
  Lighthouse **17**

Tomoka Rd.

Tomoka Wildlife Area

Tomoka Ave.
Granada Ave.

N. Beach St.

Ocean Shore Blvd.

A1A

Nova Rd.

Ridgewood Ave.

Halifax River

Halifax Dr.

Atlantic Ave.

16th St.
Center St.
Riverside Dr.
11th St.
8th St.
Holly Hill

County Rd.

Jimmy Ann Rd.

Kings Rd.

Williamson Blvd.

Mason Ave.
Madison Ave.
Cypress St.
2nd Ave.

Daytona Beach

Seabreeze Blvd.
Main St. Bridge

Ocean Ave.

West International Speedway Blvd.

Daytona Beach Municipal Airport

Orange Ave.
Memorial Bridge

Bellevue Ave.

Beach St.

Daytona Beach Shores

Beville Rd.

South Daytona Beach

Big Tree Rd.

Reed Canal Rd.

Nova Rd.

Halifax River

Peninsula Dr.

Atlantic Ave.

A1A

Port Orange

Port Orange Bridge

Dunlawton Ave.

Taylor Rd.

To Orlando

To Cocoa &
Ft. Pierce

To New Smyrna Beach

Atlantic Ocean

11-0700

Boulevard; P.O. Box 2801), Daytona Beach, FL 32120-2801 (☎ **904/253-RACE** for tickets, or 904/254-2700 for information), is certainly the keynote of the city's fame. It presents about nine weekends of major racing events annually, featuring stock cars, sports cars, motorcycles, and Go-Karts, and is also used for automobile and motorbike testing. Its grandstands and infield can accommodate more than 120,000 fans.

Big events sell out months in advance (tickets to the Daytona 500 in February are gone as early as a year ahead of time), so get your tickets and reserve your accommodations well before leaving home.

You don't have to be a racing fan to enjoy the **World Center of Racing Visitors Center,** in the NASCAR office complex at the east end of the speedway. Admission to the center is free, and you can walk out to the track during nonrace days (there's a small admission to the track during qualifying races leading up to the main events). The center is also the departure site for entertaining 25-minute guided tram tours of the facility. The tram rides cost $6, free for children 6 and under. The center and track are open daily from 9am to 5pm (until 6pm during summer). The trams depart every 30 minutes between 9:30am and 4pm (until 6pm in summer), except during races and special events.

The visitor center houses a large souvenir shop, a snack bar, and the phenomenally popular ✪ **Daytona USA** (☎ **904/947-6800**), a 50,000-square-foot, state-of-the-art interactive motor-sports entertainment attraction. Here you can learn about the history, color, and excitement of stock car, Go-Kart, and motorcycle racing in Daytona. You can participate in a pit stop on a NASCAR Winston Cup stock car, see the actual winning Daytona 500 car still covered in track dust, talk via video with favorite competitors, and play radio or television announcer by calling the finish of a race. An action-packed IMAX film will put you in the winner's seat of a Daytona 500 race. Allow at least 3½ hours and bring your video camera: There are lots of colorful photo-ops here. Daytona USA is open daily except Christmas from 9am to 7pm (later during race events). Admission is $12 for adults, $10 seniors, $6 children 6 to 12, free for children 5 and under. Combination tickets including the speedway tram tour cost $16 adults, $14 seniors, $11 for children 6 to 12, free for kids under 6.

You can actually make three laps around the track in a real stock car from May to October with the **Richard Petty Driving Experience Ride-Along Program.** Neither you nor racing legend Petty does the driving—other professionals will be at the wheel—but you'll see just how fast an average 115 m.p.h. speed really is. Rides cost $105. Contact the speedway for schedules and reservations.

HITTING THE BEACH

The hard-packed beach here runs for 24 miles along a skinny peninsula separated from the mainland by the Halifax River. The bustling hub of activity is at the end of Main Street, near the Adam's Mark Daytona Beach Resort. Here you'll find the **Main Street Pier,** at 1,006 feet the longest wooden pier on the east coast. Out here you'll find a restaurant, a bar, a bait shop, beach-toy concessions, a chair lift running its entire length ($3 per ride), and views from the 180-foot-tall Space Needle ($2 round-trip on the elevator). Admission as far out as the restaurant and bar is free (at about a third of the way, this is far enough for a good view down the beach), but you'll have to pay $1 to walk out beyond there, more if you fish (see "Outdoor Pursuits" below). Beginning at the pier, the city's famous oceanside **Boardwalk** is lined with restaurants, bars, and T-shirt shops, as are the 4 blocks of Main Street nearest the beach. Adventure Landing is 2 blocks away (see "Amusement Parks," below).

There's another busy beach area at the end of **Seabreeze Boulevard,** which has a multitude of restaurants, bars, and shops.

Couples seeking greater privacy usually prefer the northern or southern extremities of the beach. Especially peaceful is **Ponce Inlet** at the very southern tip of the peninsula, where there is precious little commerce or traffic to disturb the silence.

You can drive and park directly on the sand along most of the beach, but watch for signs warning of sea turtles nesting. There's a $5 access fee, although in some areas like Ponce Inlet, the fee is waived in winter.

OUTDOOR PURSUITS

CRUISES   Take a leisurely cruise on the Halifax River aboard the 14-passenger, 25-foot *Fancy*, a replica of the old fantail launches used at the turn of the century. It's operated by **A tiny Cruise Line River Excursions,** 425 S. Beach St., at Halifax Harbor Marina (☎ **904/226-2343**). Captain Jim regales passengers with river lore and points out dolphins, manatees, herons, diving cormorants, pelicans, egrets, osprey, oyster beds, and other natural phenomena during the morning cruise. Cruises are $8.75 to $14 for adults, $5.50 to $7.50 for children 4 to 12, free for children 3 and under. Weather permitting, cruises depart year-round (with a brief hiatus during the holidays), Monday through Saturday at 11:30am. A 1-hour tour of riverfront homes is at 2pm and of historic downtown at 3:30pm; there are no Monday cruises in winter months. Call for reservations. Romantic sunset cruises are also available.

Water Wheels of Daytona (☎ **407/255-2400**) uses one vehicle for combined land-and-river tours: It's an amphibious "duck" that crawls into the river at the Riverfront Parking Lot, International Speedway Boulevard and Beach Street. Call for schedule and prices.

FISHING   The easiest and least expensive way to fish offshore for marlin, sailfish, king mackerel, grouper, red snapper, and more is with the **Critter Fleet,** 4950 S. Peninsula Dr., just past the lighthouse in Ponce Inlet (☎ **800/338-0850** or 904/767-7676), which operates two party boats. One goes on all-day trips ($50 adults, $30 kids under 12), while the other makes morning and afternoon voyages ($30 adults, $20 kids under 12). The fares include rod, reel, and bait.

Deep-sea charter fishing boats are available from the Critter Fleet and from **Sea Love Marina,** 4884 Front St., Ponce Inlet (☎ **904/767-3406**).

Save the cost of a boat and fish with the locals from the **Main Street Pier,** at the ocean end of Main Street near the Adam's Mark (☎ **904/253-1212**). Admission for fishers is $3.50 for adults, $1.50 for kids under 12. Bait and fishing gear are available, and no license is required.

GOLF   There are more than 25 courses within 30 minutes of the beach, and most hotels can arrange starting times for you. **Golf Daytona Beach,** 126 E. Orange Ave., Daytona Beach, FL 32114 (☎ **800/881-7065** or 904/239-7065; fax 904/239-0064; www.golf-daytona.com), publishes an annual brochure describing the major courses. It's available at the tourist information offices (see "Essentials" above).

Two of the nation's top-rated links for women golfers are at the ✪ **LPGA International,** 300 Championship Dr. (☎ **904/274-5742**): the Champions course designed by Rees Jones, and the Legends at LPGA course designed by Arthur Hills. Both boast 18 outstanding holes. LPGA International is a center for professional and amateur women golfers (workshops and teaching programs), and the pro shop carries a great selection of ladies' equipment and clothing. Greens fees with a cart are usually about $75, less in summer.

A Lloyd Clifton–designed course, the centrally located 18-hole, par-72 **Indigo Lakes Golf Course,** 2620 W. International Speedway Blvd. (☎ **904/254-3607**), has flat fairways and large bunkered Bermuda greens. Fees here are about $55 in winter, including a cart, less in summer.

The semiprivate South Course at **Pelican Bay Country Club,** 550 Sea Duck Dr. (☎ **904/788-6494**), is one of the area's favorites, with fast greens to test your putting skills. With-cart fees are $40 in winter, less in summer (no walking allowed). The North Course here is for members only.

The city's prime municipal course is the **Daytona Beach Country Club,** 600 Wilder Blvd. (☎ **904/258-3119**), which has 36 holes. Winter fees here are $18 to walk, $26.50 to share a cart. They drop $3 in summer.

HORSEBACK RIDING   Shenandoah Stables, 1759 Tomoka Farms Rd., off U.S. 92 (☎ **904/257-1444**), offers daily trail rides and lessons. Call for prices and schedules.

WATER SPORTS   Water-sports equipment, as well as bicycles, beach buggies, and mopeds, can be rented along the Boardwalk, at the ocean end of Main Street (see "Hitting the Beach" above), and in front of major beachfront hotels. For jet-ski rentals, contact **Daytona High Performance—MBI,** 925 Sickler Dr., at the Seabreeze Bridge (☎ **904/257-5276**).

AMUSEMENT PARKS

The first stage of Ocean Walk Village, a development which will include shops, entertainment, and resort facilities, **Adventure Landing,** 601 Earl St., west of Atlantic Avenue (☎ **904/258-0071**), offers an assortment of indoor and outdoor activities to keep you and especially the kids entertained—and thoroughly wet. You enter into a cacophony of deafening noise and music in a huge electronic games arcade. Doors at the back lead outside to the water park, with pools, slides, and waterfalls, plus Go-Kart rides and a 27-hole minigolf course. It cost nothing to enter the noisy arcade (vending machines dispense tokens for the games). Admission to the water park is $19.95 for anyone over 48 inches tall, $14.95 for anyone shorter, free for kids under 4. There's an $11.95 "night splasher" pass from 4 to 8pm. The facility is open during summer daily from 10am to midnight, with the water activities closing at 8pm. The water activities are closed off-season, but the arcade, Go-Kart, and minigolf are open Monday to Thursday 11am to 10pm, Friday 11am to midnight, Saturday 10am to midnight, Sunday 10am to 10pm.

MUSEUMS

Halifax Historical Museum. 252 S. Beach St. (just north of Orange Ave.). ☎ **904/255-6976.** Admission $3 adults, $1 children 11 and under; free for adults Thurs after noon; free for children Sat. Tues–Sat 10am–4pm.

Located on Beach Street, Daytona's original riverfront commercial district on the mainland side of the Halifax River (see "Shopping" below), this local history museum is worth seeing just for the 1912 neoclassical architectural details of its home, a former bank. A mural of Old Florida wildlife graces one wall, the stained-glass ceiling reflects the sunlight, and across the room an old gold metal teller's window still stands. Its eclectic collection includes Native American artifacts, more than 10,000 historic photographs, possessions of past residents (such as a ball gown worn at Lincoln's inauguration), and, of course, model cars.

Klassix Auto Attraction. 2909 W. International Speedway Blvd., at Tomoka Farms Rd., just west of I-95. ☎ **904/252-3800.** Admission $8.50 adults, $4.25 children 7–12, free for children under 7. Daily 9am–6pm.

True aficionados of the car will enjoy a visit to this attraction, which showcases Corvettes—a model from every year since 1953—and historic vehicles from every motor sport. The rest of us will head to the original "Batmobile" from the 1960s *Batman* TV series, the car from *The Flintstones* series, the "Dragula" owned by the Munsters, and the "Greased Lightening" from the movie *Grease*. A 1950s-style soda shop and gift shop are on the premises.

○ Museum of Arts and Sciences. 1040 Museum Blvd. (off Nova Rd./Fla. 5A between International Speedway Blvd. and Bellevue Ave.). ☎ **904/255-0285.** Museum $5 adults, $1 children and students with ID, free for children 5 and under; planetarium shows $3. Tues–Fri 9am–4pm, Sat–Sun noon–5pm. Take International Speedway Blvd. west, make a left on Nova Rd. (Fla. 5A), and look for a sign on your right.

An exceptional institution for a town Daytona's size, this museum is best known for its Cuban Museum, with paintings acquired in 1956, when Cuban dictator Fulgencio Batista donated his private collection to the city. Among them is a portrait of Eva ("Evita") Perón, said to be the only existing painting completed while she was alive (it hangs in the lobby, not in the Cuban Museum). The Dow Gallery displays Smithsonian-quality examples of American decorative arts, and the Bouchelle Study Center for the Decorative Arts contains both American and European masterpieces. Other rooms worth visiting include the Schulte Gallery of Chinese Art; Africa: Life and Ritual, with the largest collection of Ashante gold ornaments in the United States; and the Prehistory of Florida gallery, with the skeleton of a 13-foot-tall, 130,000-year-old giant ground sloth. Except for the skeleton, children are apt to be bored here.

Ponce de León Inlet Lighthouse & Museum. 4931 S. Peninsula Dr., Ponce Inlet. ☎ **904/761-1821.** Admission $4 adults, $1 children 11 and under. May–Aug daily 10am–8pm; Sept–Apr daily 10am–4pm. Follow Atlantic Ave. south, make a right on Beach St., and follow the signs.

If you are in the area, this 175-foot lighthouse—the second tallest in the United States—is worth a quick stop. Built in the 1880s, and restored in the 1970s, this brick-and-granite sentinel's beacon is visible for 16 nautical miles. The head lighthouse keeper's cottage now houses a museum of exhibits of maritime artifacts. The first-assistant keeper's house is furnished to reflect turn-of-the-century occupancy. A concise 12-minute video details the structure's history. Outside, you can walk around the tugboat *F. D. Russell,* now sitting high and dry in the sand. The museum shop here carries fascinating lighthouse-theme gifts.

SHOPPING

Daytona Beach's main riverside drag, Beach Street, is one of the few areas in town where people actually stroll. The street is wide and inviting, with palms down its median and decorative wrought-iron archways and fancy brickwork overlooking the Halifax River. Today, between Bay Street and Orange Avenue, Beach Street offers antique shops, art galleries, clothiers, a magic shop, an excellent historical museum (see "Museums," above) and several good cafes.

You "Hog" riders will find several shops to your liking along Beach Street north of International Speedway Boulevard, including the **Harley Davidson Store,** 290 Beach St., at Dr. Mary McLeod Bethune Boulevard (☎ **904/253-2453**), a 20,000-square-foot retail outlet and diner serving breakfast and lunch. It's one of the nation's largest dealerships. In addition to hundreds of gleaming new and used Hogs, you'll find as much fringy leather as you've ever seen in one place.

The **Daytona Flea Market,** on Tomoka Farms Road at the junction of I-95 and U.S. 92, a mile west of the Speedway (☎ **904/252-1999**), is huge, with 1,000 covered outdoor booths plus 100 antique vendors in an air-conditioned building. It's open year-round Friday through Sunday from 8am to 5pm. Admission and parking are free.

WHERE TO STAY

Room rates here are highest from the day after Christmas all the way to Labor Day, and they skyrocket during major events at the Speedway, during bikers' gatherings, and whenever college students are on break (see "Florida Calendar of Events," in chapter 2). Daytona Beach hotels fill to the bursting point during these periods, and even if you can find a room, there's often a minimum-stay requirement.

In addition to the listings below, there are dozens of hotels and motels along Atlantic Avenue, many of them family owned and operated. The Daytona Beach Area Convention & Visitors Bureau (see "Essentials" above) distributes a list of Superior Small Lodgings. None of these properties has more than 75 rooms, and all have been inspected for cleanliness, quality, comfort, privacy, and safety.

Among the other chain motels here, one of the better options is the **Days Inn,** 1909 S. Atlantic Ave., at Flamingo Ave. (☎ **800/224-5056** or 904/255-4492), a nine-story beachfront hotel with a swimming pool/kiddie pool and a sundeck overlooking the beach. There are three oceanfront **Howard Johnsons** to choose from (☎ **800/ 446-4656**).

In addition to the 6% state sales tax, Daytona levies a 4% tax on hotel bills.

AT THE BEACHES

Adam's Mark Daytona Beach Resort. 100 N. Atlantic Ave. (between Earl St. and Auditorium Blvd.), Daytona Beach, FL 32118. ☎ **800/872-9269** or 904/254-8200. Fax 904/253-0275. 413 units. A/C MINIBAR TV TEL. $99–$189 double; $159–$249 suite. AE, DC, DISC, MC, V. Valet parking $8.50; free self-parking in lot across the street.

Already Daytona's largest beachfront hotel, the Adams Mark at press time was planning to add another 350 units, bringing it to almost 800 rooms. With extensive on-site meeting facilities and the city's convention center virtually across the street, that means lots of big groups staying here. One of Daytona's most luxurious properties, it's designed so that every room has an ocean view. Although the lobby and common areas are more elegantly detailed, the existing guest rooms are not as spacious or well laid out as the less-expensive and quieter Hilton farther south (see below). It's centrally located right at the band shell, on the city's Boardwalk, and a block north of the Main Street pier (see "Hitting the Beach," above). Plenty of beach activities are out front: parasailing, bicycle rentals, motorized four-wheelers, surfboards, boogie boards, cabanas, and umbrellas.

Clock Towers Restaurant, with picture windows overlooking the beach and umbrella tables outside, serves all meals, and an adjacent lounge provides live music most evenings. Splash Bar and Grill has light fare, libation, and indoor-outdoor seating. There's also a small food court at the beach level.

Amenities here include concierge, room service, dry cleaning and laundry, self-service Laundromat, free newspapers in executive-level rooms, baby-sitting, secretarial services, express checkout, massage, indoor/outdoor heated swimming pool and kiddie pool, health club, two whirlpools, steam and sauna, bicycle rental, children's center, games arcade, business center, conference rooms, sundeck, water-sports equipment, sand volleyball court, playground, and gift shops.

Daytona Beach Hilton Oceanfront Resort. 2637 S. Atlantic Ave. (between Florida Shores Blvd. and Richard's Lane), Daytona Beach, FL 32118. ☎ **800/525-7350** or 904/767-7350. Fax 904/760-3651. 214 units. A/C TV TEL. $89–$198 double; from $250 suite. AE, DC, DISC, MC, V.

Far enough south to escape the maddening crowds at Main Street, the Hilton is among the best choices here. It welcomes you in an elegant terra-cotta–tiled lobby with comfortable seating areas, a fountain, and potted palms. The large guest rooms are grouped in pairs and can be joined to form a suite; one of each pair has a balcony, the other does not. All have ocean and/or river views and safes, coffeemakers, irons, full-size ironing boards, hair dryers, and small refrigerators. The hotel also has a small fitness room, unisex hair salon, and gift shop. Daily newspapers are complimentary. Kids appreciate the video-game room with pool table and the kiddie pool on the beautiful oceanfront sundeck, where you can often see seagulls drinking from the large heated pool. A surprisingly good lobby restaurant, one of Daytona's most beautiful, serves all meals; patio dining is an option. A comfy bar/lounge with game tables adjoins; it's the setting for nightly entertainment.

Old Salty's Inn. 1921 S. Atlantic Ave. (at Flamingo Ave.), Daytona Beach Shores, FL 32118. ☎ **800/417-1466** or 904/252-8090. Fax 904/441-5977. www.visitdaytona.com/oldsaltys. 19 units. A/C TV TEL. $45–$101. AE, DISC, MC, V.

The most unusual beachside property here, Old Salty's began life in 1954 as a simple mom-and-pop motel (there are scores of them still standing along this beach). Today it's a lush tropical enclave carrying out a *Gilligan's Island* theme, with old motors, rotting boats, life preservers, and a Jeep lying about, and the TV series' main characters depicted in big murals painted on the buildings. The two-story wings flank a courtyard festooned with palms and banana trees (you can pick one for breakfast). Facing this vista, the bright rooms have microwaves, refrigerators, and front-and-back windows to let in good ventilation. Efficiencies also have reclining chairs, dining tables, kitchens with coffeemakers, and ceiling fans over their beds. The choice units have picture windows overlooking the beach. There are gas grills and white rocking chairs under a gazebo out by a heated beachside swimming pool.

Radisson Resort Daytona Beach. 640 N. Atlantic Ave. (between Seabreeze and Glenview blvds.), Daytona Beach, FL 32118. ☎ **800/333-3333** or 904/239-9800. Fax 904/23-0735. 206 units. A/C TV TEL. $59–$169 double. AE, DC, DISC, MC, V. Valet parking $8 (weekends only); free self-parking.

An older hotel on this site, a half mile north of the Main Street Pier and around the corner from restaurants and bars on Seabreeze Boulevard, was gutted in 1998 and transformed into this 11-story, all-modern Radisson. The spacious rooms here are among the best on the beach, with bright furniture including easy chairs or sofas, writing desks or tables, two phones (one with dataport), ample lighting, coffeemakers, irons and boards, and angled balconies facing the beach. About a third have small additional rooms with wet bars with microwaves. Other than groups prowling around between meetings, the only drawback here is that your neighbor's air conditioner exhausts onto your balcony, which can create a bit of noise and heat when you're sitting out there. A sundeck surrounds an outdoor swimming pool with a kiddie pond. Off the lobby, Atlantic Jacks provides all meals and limited room service; the adjacent bar here looks out to the beach through huge windows. Other amenities include laundry service, coin laundry, gift and snack shop, and exercise and games rooms.

Tropical Manor Motel. 2237 S. Atlantic Ave. (at Bonner Ave.), Daytona Beach, FL. ☎ **800/253-4920** or 904/252-4920. 71 units. A/C TV TEL. Winter $33–$43 double; $34–$100 efficiency/suite; $95–$135 3-bedroom suite. High-season $52–$63 double; $54–$127 efficiency/suite; $165–$237 3-bedroom suite. AE, DC, DISC, MC, V.

This Caribbean-tinted beachfront motel wins points for its unique and colorful murals, pleasant staff/owners, and meticulous upkeep. Located square in the middle of Daytona's nicest beach, these funky accommodations also offer sundecks, umbrella-covered tables, lounge areas, a large heated pool, a water slide, a shuffleboard court, a cookout area, a heated kiddie pool, and two gazebos—all surrounded by lush tropical foliage. The rooms are not large or particularly fancy, but many come with cable TV, kitchens, and ocean views. Especially good for families are the two- and three-bedroom suites.

The Villa Bed & Breakfast. 801 N. Peninsula Dr. (at Riverview Blvd.), Daytona Beach, FL 32118. ☎ **904/248-2020.** Fax same as phone. 4 units (all with bathroom). A/C TV. $85–$190 double. Rates include continental breakfast. AE, MC, V.

You'll think you're in Iberia upon entering this Spanish mansion's great room with its fireplace, baby grand piano, terra-cotta floors, and walls hung with Mediterranean paintings. Also downstairs are a sun room equipped with a TV and VCR, a formal dining room, and a breakfast nook where guests gather at their leisure to start the day. The lush backyard surrounds a swimming pool and covered four-person Jacuzzi. Upstairs, the nautically themed Christopher Columbus room has a vaulted ceiling and a small balcony overlooking the pool. The largest quarters here are the King Carlos suite, the original master bedroom with a four-poster bed, an entertainment system, a refrigerator, a rooftop deck, a dressing area, and a bathroom equipped with a four-head shower. The Queen Isabella room has a portrait of the queen over a queen-size bed, and the Marco Polo room has Chinese black lacquer furniture and Oriental rugs evoking the great explorer's adventures. Owner Jim Camp's friendly black lab, Andy, keeps an eye on things, but he accepts neither your pets nor your children. The beach is 4 blocks away; the river, 1 block.

ON THE MAINLAND

Live Oak Inn. 444-448 S. Beach St. (at Loomis Ave.), Daytona Beach, FL 32114. ☎ **888/ 881-4667** or 904/252-4667. Fax 904/239-0068. 12 units (all with bathroom). A/C TV TEL. Spring and summer $100–$200 double. Off-season $75–$150 double. Rates include full breakfast. AE, MC, V. Free parking. No children 9 and under accepted.

Facing the river and occupying two adjoining Victorian-era houses with a front lawn enclosed by a white picket fence, this B&B in the city's historic district is surrounded by centuries-old live oaks. An inviting front porch with white wicker rocking chairs faces the street and a marina beyond. The guest rooms—seven with private sun porches or balconies—are delightfully decorated, with area rugs strewn on polished oak floors and wood-bladed fans whirring slowly overhead. Yours might be furnished with an Eastlake bed, or perhaps you'll get a Victorian sleigh bed with a patchwork quilt and a private plant-filled sun porch furnished with Adirondack chairs. The rooms look out on the Halifax Harbor Marina or a garden, and all are equipped with remote-control cable TVs, VCRs, and Victorian soaking tubs or Jacuzzis. Breakfast is served on an enclosed porch with lace-curtained windows. An independently operated restaurant in one of the houses is open Tuesday to Saturday for good, moderately priced lunches and dinners. No smoking is permitted in the house.

WHERE TO DINE

Don't come to Daytona Beach specifically for fine dining. The town has some interesting venues, but none is likely to leave an indelible memory. A profusion of fast-food joints line the major thoroughfares, especially along Atlantic Avenue on the beach and along International Speedway Boulevard near the racetrack. Restaurants come and go in the Beach Street district on the mainland, and along Main Street and Seabreeze Boulevard on the beach. A casual restaurant serves burgers and chicken wings and lots of suds out on the Main Street Pier.

The local **Shells** seafood restaurant is on the beach at 200 S. Atlantic Ave. (☎ **904/ 258-0007**), a block north of International Raceway Boulevard. See "Where to Dine" in section 1 of chapter 11 for details about this inexpensive chain.

AT THE BEACHES

✪ Anna's Italian Trattoria. 304 Seabreeze Blvd. (at Peninsula Dr.). ☎ **904/239-9624.** Reservations recommended. Main courses $9–$17. AE, DISC, MC, V. Daily 5–10pm. ITALIAN.

Originally from Sicily, the Triani family lends a warm, friendly air to this simple-yet-comfortable trattoria. Many of the pastas are homemade, but a star here is risotto alla Anna, an Italian version of Spanish paella. Portions are hearty; main courses come with soup or salad and a side dish of angel-hair pasta or a vegetable, and a bit of between-course sorbet will cleanse the palate. There's a good selection of Italian wines to complement your meal. Everything is cooked to order, so allow plenty of time. Free parking is available in a lot on Seabreeze Boulevard across Peninsula Drive.

Down the Hatch. 4894 Front St., Ponce Inlet. ☎ **904/761-4831.** Reservations not accepted; call ahead for priority seating. Breakfast $2–$5; main courses $8–$15; early-bird menu (served 11am–5pm) $5–$7. Kids' menu. AE, MC, V. Daily 7am–10pm. Take Atlantic Ave. south, make a right on Beach St., and follow the signs. SEAFOOD.

Occupying a half-century–old fish camp on the Halifax River, Down the Hatch serves up fresh fish and seafood (note its shrimp boat docked outside). You can start your day here with a bagel or a country-style breakfast while taking in the scenic views of boats and shorebirds through the big picture windows—you might even see dolphins frolicking. At night, arrive early to catch the sunset over the river, and also to beat the crowd at this very popular place. In summer, light fare is served outside on an awninged wooden deck. Portions are large.

ON THE MAINLAND

The Cellar. 220 Magnolia Ave. (between Palmetto and Ridgewood aves.). ☎ **904/258-0011.** Reservations accepted only for large parties. Soups, salads, sandwiches $6–$7. AE, DC, DISC, MC, V. Mon–Fri 11am–3pm. AMERICAN.

Another excellent place for lunch, this tea room occupies the basement of a Victorian home built in 1907 for Pres. Warren G. Harding and is now listed in the National Register of Historic Places. It couldn't be more charming, with low ceilings and fresh flowers on every table. In the warm months there's outdoor seating at umbrella tables on a covered garden patio. A small but varied menu includes soups, salads, sandwiches, fresh seafood, chicken, and pastas.

✪ The Chart House. 1100 Marina Point Dr. (off Beach St. south of business district). ☎ **904/255-9022.** Reservations recommended. Main courses $15–$36. AE, DC, DISC, MC, V. Sun–Thurs 5–9:30pm, Fri–Sat 5–10:30pm. SEAFOOD/STEAKS/PRIME RIB.

This member of the upscale chain offers some of the area's finest dining. The setting is stunning—under a soaring teepee roof and with big windows looking out to water views on three sides. The menu is led by gargantuan cuts of tender prime rib, but the daily fresh-catch dishes and perfectly grilled steaks also draw the locals for special-occasion dinners. Caviar stars on the bountiful salad bar.

The Dancing Avocado Kitchen. 110 S. Beach St. (between Magnolia St. and International Raceway Blvd.). ☎ **904/947-2022.** Reservations not accepted. Breakfast $2–$4.50; sandwiches, salads, pizzas $4–$5.50. MC, V. Mon–Sat 7:30am–3pm. DELI/VEGETARIAN.

A good place to start your day, or have lunch while touring downtown, this storefront establishment purveys a number of vegetarian omelettes, burritos, salads, personal-size pizzas, and hot and cold sandwiches such as an avocado Reuben. A few chicken and turkey items are on the menu, but the only red-meat selection is a hamburger. You can dine outside or inside the store with vegetable drawings on its brick walls and ceiling fans suspended from black rafters. Order at the counter and wait for your number to be called. When finished, take your waste to the recycling bins at the front door. No smoking.

New Smyrna Beach: Artists in a Jungle

Just 10 minutes south of Daytona via U.S. 1, the little town of New Smyrna Beach couldn't be more artsy-craftsy than its neighbor. Instead of being a mecca for racers and bikers, it attracts some of the world's most acclaimed artists.

New Smyrna Beach was founded in 1767 by a Scottish physician, Andrew Turnbull, who named it after his wife's Greek/Turkish hometown, Smyrna. It once brimmed with farms and mills, but about the most exciting thing that happens here these days is the perennial shuffleboard championships among the town's older occupants, who make up more than a third of its 17,500 or so residents.

The town's true calling, however, is as a retreat where artists come to work and escape from the world. The generic-sounding **Atlantic Center for the Arts,** 1414 Art Center Ave. (☎ 904/427-6975), sits on 69 acres of waterfront jungle, down a dirt road off U.S. 1 (turn west 1 mile north of the New Smyrna Beach Airport). Pulitzer Prize–winning director and playwright Edward Albee, choreographer Trisha Brown, and visual artist Robert Rauschenberg are among the noted celebrities who have come here to create. The administrative building holds a small gallery showing works by some of the artists-in-residence and a permanent exhibit of portraits of artists by noted photographer Jack Mitchell (free admission; open Mon–Fri 9am to 5pm, Sat 10am–2pm). Insect repellant is in order on the boardwalk nature trails linking the workshops here.

The center also operates the tiny, Cracker-style **Harris House,** in town at 214 S. Riverside Dr., at Douglas St. (☎ 904/423-1753), presenting exceptional exhibits of works by Florida artists. It's open Monday to Saturday from 10am to 4pm. Admission is free.

From U.S. 1, turn east on **Canal Street,** the town's charming, palm-lined main street. You can stop for information at the **Southeast Volusia Chamber of Commerce,** 115 Canal St., New Smyrna Beach, FL 32168 (☎ 800/541-9621 or 904/428-2449; fax 904/423-3512). The chamber's visitor center is open Monday to Friday from 9am to 5pm, to 3pm on Saturday.

At the foot of Canal Street, turn left on Riverside Drive. You'll pass Harris House (see above) and marinas with charter fishing boats. Follow the signs onto the North Causeway (Fla. 44) out to the beach. The causeway will dump you onto **Flagler Avenue,** which dead-ends at the Atlantic (you'll drive onto the hard-packed beach if you don't turn off Flagler Avenue). Near the sea, the avenue is lined with surf and gift shops, taverns, and restaurants, but five commercial art galleries 2 blocks inland are definitely worth a look. Find a parking space, have a lovely art-filled stroll, and then grab a bite at one of the restaurants.

A few motels and B&Bs host guests in this Old Florida town, and dozens of oceanfront condominiums offer very affordable rates for overnight visitors. The best are members of the Superior Small Lodging program operated by the **Daytona Beach Area Convention and Visitors Bureau** (see "Essentials" in section 2 of this chapter). You can also contact the Southeast Volusia Chamber of Commerce (see above).

○ **Frappe's North.** 123 W. Granada Blvd. (between Ridgeview Ave. and Washington St.), Ormand Beach. ☎ **904/615-4888.** Reservations recommended. Main courses $14–$24 ($4–$8 at lunch). AE, MC, V. Mon–Thurs 11:30am–2:30pm and 5–9pm, Fri 11:30am–2:30pm and 5–10pm, Sat 5–10pm. CREATIVE AMERICAN/FUSION/VEGETARIAN.

It's worth the 6-mile drive north from downtown Daytona to Ormand Beach and this sophisticated, hip establishment providing this area's best and most entertaining cuisine. It's in a storefront on the mainland stretch of Granada Boulevard, the town's main drag. Several chic dining rooms—one has beams extending like spokes from a central pole— set the stage for an inventive, ever-changing "Menu of the Moment" fusing a multitude of styles. Outstandingly presented with wonton strips and a multihued rice cake, my Southeast Asian–style pompano in a piquant peanut sauce was a dish to long remember. Frappe's always has at least two vegetarian main courses, plus a vegetable-broth soup. Lunch is a steal here, with dinner-size main courses at a fraction of the nighttime price.

McK's Dublin Station. 218 S. Beach St. (between Magnolia St. and Ivy Lane). ☎ **904/ 238-3321.** Reservations not accepted. Main courses $8–$14, salads and sandwiches $4–$7. AE, MC, V. Mon–Sat 11am–3am, Sun 11am–midnight. IRISH/AMERICAN.

Especially worth knowing about because it serves food until 3am, this upscale Irish tavern has a highly eclectic menu. The pub fare includes vegetarian burritos and a few main courses of steaks, chicken, and "Mumzy's" meat loaf. Club sandwiches and burgers round out the large and reasonably priced selection. The food is not exceptional, but it's perfectly acceptable, especially once you've had a few Bass ales. The service is sometimes rushed, but usually pleasant.

DAYTONA BEACH AFTER DARK

THE CLUB & BAR SCENE   In addition to the following, the sophisticated **Clock-tower Lounge** at the Adam's Mark (see "Where to Stay" above) is worth a visit.

   Main Street and **Seabreeze Boulevard** on the beach are happening areas where dozens of bars (and a few topless shows) cater to the black-leather set.

   A popular beachfront bar for more than 40 years, **Ocean Deck,** 127 S. Ocean Ave., next to the Mayan Inn (☎ **904/253-5224**), is packed with a mix of locals and tourists, young and old, who come for live music and cheap drinks. Often reggae or ska bands will play after 9:30pm. Park across Ocean Avenue at the beach and surf shop, Reggae Republic (under the same ownership).

THE PERFORMING ARTS   Check the Friday edition of the Daytona Beach *News-Journal* for weekly listings of upcoming events, or call the **Peabody Auditorium,** 600 Auditorium Blvd., between Noble Street and Wild Olive Avenue (☎ **904/ 255-1314**), the city's major venue for high-brow performances.

   Under the city auspices, the **Oceanfront Bandshell** (☎ **904/258-3169**), on the boardwalk next to the Adam's Mark Hotel, hosts a series of free big-band concerts at the band shell every Sunday night from early June to Labor Day. It's also the scene of raucous spring-break concerts.

   You can sample Polynesian food and dancing at **Teauila's Hawaiian Luau Feast,** atop the Daytona Beach Resort and Conference Center, 2700 N. Atlantic Ave. (☎ **800/654-6216** or 904/672-3770). Seating usually is at 6:30pm Wednesday through Sunday, with the show at 8pm. The schedule can vary, so call for reservations. Cost is $19.95 adults, $9.95 children 5 to 10, free for kids under 5.

3 St. Augustine: America's First City

105 miles NE of Orlando, 302 miles N of Miami, 39 miles S of Jacksonville

With its 17th-century fort, horse-drawn carriages clip-clopping along narrow streets, old city gates, and reconstructed 18th-century Spanish Quarter, St. Augustine seems more like a picturesque European village than a modern American city. This is an exceptionally charming town, complete with palm-lined ocean beaches, excellent restaurants, an active nightlife, and shopping bargains—but its primary lure is historic.

This is, after all, the oldest permanent European settlement in the United States (no, it wasn't Jamestown in 1607 or the Pilgrims at Plymouth Rock in 1620). A group of French Huguenots settled in 1562 near the mouth of the St. Johns River, in present-day Jacksonville. Three years later, a Spanish force under Pedro Menéndez de Avilés arrived on the scene, wiped out the Huguenot men (de Avilés spared their women and children), and established a settlement on the harbor he named St. Augustín.

The colony survived attacks by pirates, Indians, and the British over the next 2 centuries. The Treaty of Paris ending the French and Indian War ceded the town to Britain in 1763, but the British gave it back 20 years later. The United States took control when it acquired Florida from Spain in 1821.

Notwithstanding today's tourist attraction here, Ponce de León never did find his elusive Fountain of Youth.

ESSENTIALS

GETTING THERE   St. Augustine is about equidistant (a 1-hour drive) from airports in Jacksonville and Daytona Beach. See "Essentials" in sections 2 and 4 of this chapter for details.

VISITOR INFORMATION   Before you go, contact the **St. Johns County Visitors and Convention Bureau,** 88 Roberta St., Suite 400, St. Augustine, FL 32084 (☎ **800/OLD-CITY** or 904/829-1711; fax 904/829-6149; www.oldcity.com), and request the *Visitor's Guide,* detailing attractions, events, restaurants, accommodations, shopping, and more.

You Web browsers can also go to the advertiser-supported **www.staugustine.com.**

Upon arrival, stop first at the **St. Augustine Visitor Information Center,** 10 Castillo Dr., at San Marco Avenue opposite the Castillo de San Marcos National Monument (☎ **904/825-1000**). There are numerous ways to see the city, depending on your interest and time, and this is the best place to make your plans. And you can park for 2 days in the visitor center lots for $3. You can view a free visitor information video, pick up brochures, and obtain tickets for sightseeing trains and trolleys, which include discount admissions to the attractions (see "Getting Around" below). The center is open daily from 8:30am to 7:30pm from Memorial Day to Labor Day, until 6:30pm from April to Memorial Day and the day after Labor Day to the end of October, and until 5:30pm from November to March. It and most area attractions are closed on Christmas.

In the historic district, there's an **information desk** in Government House, King Street at St. George St. It's open daily from 9am to 6pm except Christmas.

Over on St. Augustine Beach, there's a walk-in visitor information center at the **St. Johns County Fishing Pier,** 350 A1A Beach Blvd., St. Augustine Beach, FL 32084 (☎ **904/471-1596**). It's open daily from 8:30am to 5pm.

GETTING AROUND   Your best bet is to park at the visitor information center ($3 for the first day, free second day) and to walk from there or take a trolley or train. On-street parking is non-existent in the historic district, and a number of metered parking lots there are difficult to find and often full.

Sightseeing **trolleys, trains, and horse-drawn carriages** are the easiest way to get around. The trolleys and trains follow 7-mile routes, stopping at the visitor center and at or near most attractions between 8:30am and 5pm daily. You can get off at any stop, visit the attractions, and step aboard the next vehicle that comes along. Several vehicles

St. Augustine

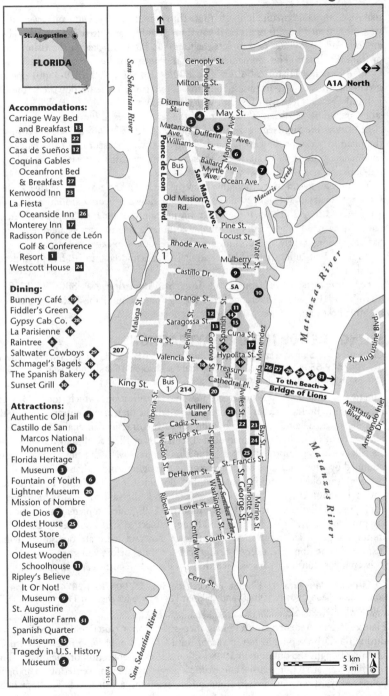

FLORIDA

St. Augustine

Accommodations:
Carriage Way Bed
  and Breakfast **13**
Casa de Solana **22**
Casa de Sueños **12**
Coquina Gables
  Oceanfront Bed
  & Breakfast **27**
Kenwood Inn **23**
La Fiesta
  Oceanside Inn **26**
Monterey Inn **17**
Radisson Ponce de León
  Golf & Conference
  Resort **1**
Westcott House **24**

Dining:
Bunnery Café **19**
Fiddler's Green **2**
Gypsy Cab Co. **28**
La Parisienne **16**
Raintree **8**
Saltwater Cowboys **29**
Schmagel's Bagels **18**
The Spanish Bakery **14**
Sunset Grill **30**

Attractions:
Authentic Old Jail **4**
Castillo de San
  Marcos National
  Monument **10**
Florida Heritage
  Museum **3**
Fountain of Youth **6**
Lightner Museum **20**
Mission of Nombre
  de Dios **7**
Oldest House **25**
Oldest Store
  Museum **21**
Oldest Wooden
  Schoolhouse **11**
Ripley's Believe
  It Or Not!
  Museum **9**
St. Augustine
  Alligator Farm **31**
Spanish Quarter
  Museum **15**
Tragedy in U.S. History
  Museum **5**

make a continuous circuit along the route throughout the day; you won't ever have to wait more than 15 or 20 minutes. If you don't get off at any attractions, it takes about an hour and 10 minutes to complete the tour. You can buy tickets at the visitor center or from the drivers. The companies also sell **discounted tickets** to some attractions.

St. Augustine Historical Tours (☎ 800/397-4071 or 904/829-3800) operates green-and-white, open-air buses. You can park your car at the headquarters (the Old Jail and Florida Heritage Museum, which are also stops on the tour). There are 25 stops, including Sebastian Winery, one of the few vintners in Florida.

St. Augustine Sightseeing Trains (☎ 800/226-6545 or 904/829-6545) covers all the main sites except the Old Jail and Florida Heritage Museum, but its vehicles are small enough to go down more of the narrow historic district streets. Its vehicles are red-and-blue open-air trains.

You may also want to see the sights from the back of a horse-drawn carriage. **Colee's Carriage Tours** (☎ 904/829-2818) has been showing people around town since 1877. The carriages line up at the bay front, just south of the fort. Slow-paced, entertainingly narrated 1-hour rides past major landmarks and attractions are offered from 8am to midnight. Private tours and hotel and restaurant pickups are available.

All three companies charge $12 for adults, $5 for children 6 to 12, free for children 5 and under.

For more personalized tours, call **Tour St. Augustine** (☎ 800/797-3778 or 904/471-9010), which offers guided walking tours around the historical area and nightly ghost tours ($6 per person).

SEEING THE TOP HISTORIC ATTRACTIONS

✪ **Castillo de San Marcos National Monument.** 1 E. Castillo Dr. (at San Marco Ave.). ☎ **904/829-6506.** Admission $4 adults, free for children 16 and under with adult. Daily 8:45am–4:45pm. Closed Christmas.

America's oldest and best-preserved masonry fortification, which took 23 years (1672–95) to build, is stellar in design, with a double drawbridge entrance over a 40-foot dry moat. Diamond-shaped bastions in each corner, which enabled cannons to set up a deadly crossfire, contained domed sentry towers. The seemingly indestructible Castillo was never captured in battle, and its coquina walls did not crumble when pounded by enemy artillery or violent storms throughout more than 300 years.

Today the old storerooms house exhibits documenting the history of the fort, a national monument since 1924. Also, you can tour the vaulted powder magazine, a dank prison cell, the chapel, and guard rooms. A self-guided–tour map and brochure are provided at the ticket booth. In addition, subject to staff availability, 20- to 30-minute ranger talks are given several times a day, and there are occasional living-history presentations and cannon firings (call for times before you go).

Even if you don't go in, it's well worth the walk up here just to take in the river view.

✪ **Lightner Museum.** 75 King St. (at Granada St.). ☎ **904/824-2874.** Admission $6 adults, $2 college students with ID and children 12–18, free for children 11 and under. Daily 9am–5pm (last tour 4pm).

Henry Flagler's opulent Spanish Renaissance–style Alcazar Hotel, built in 1889, closed during the Depression and stayed vacant until Chicago publishing magnate Otto C. Lightner bought the building in 1948 to house his vast collection of Victoriana. The building is an attraction in itself and makes a gorgeous museum, centering on an open palm courtyard with an arched stone bridge spanning a fish pond. The first floor houses a Victorian village, with shop fronts representing emporia selling period wares.

A Victorian Science and Industry Room displays shells, rocks, minerals, and Native American artifacts in beautiful turn-of-the-century cases. Other exhibits include stuffed birds, an Egyptian mummy, steam engine models, and amazing examples of Victorian glassblowing. And a room of automated musical instruments is best seen during the daily concerts of period music at 11am and 2pm. Guided tours take 1 hour.

The imposing building across King Street was Henry Flagler's opulent rival resort, the Ponce de Leon Hotel. It now houses **Flagler College.**

✪ **The Oldest House.** 14 St. Francis St. (at Charlotte St.). ☎ **904/824-2872.** Admission $5 adults, $4.50 seniors 55 and over, $3 students, free for children 6 and under; $12 families. Daily 9am–5pm; tours depart on the hour and half hour (last tour at 4:30pm).

Archaeological surveys indicate that a dwelling stood on this site as early as the beginning of the 17th century. What you see today, called the Gonzáles-Alvarez House (for two of its prominent owners), evolved from a two-room coquina dwelling built between 1702 and 1727. The rooms are furnished to evoke various historical eras.

Admission also entitles you to explore the adjacent **Manucy Museum of St. Augustine History,** where artifacts, maps, and photographs document the town's history from its origins through the Flagler era a century ago. Both are owned and operated by the St. Augustine Historical Society.

The Oldest Store Museum. 4 Artillery Lane (between St. George and Aviles sts. behind Trinity Episcopal Church). ☎ **904/829-9729.** Admission $5 adults, $1.50 children 6–12, free for children 5 and under. Mon–Sat 9am–5pm, Sun noon–5pm (in summer Sun 10am–5pm).

The C&F Hamblen General Store was St. Augustine's one-stop shopping center from 1835 to 1960, and the museum on its premises today replicates the emporium at the turn of the century. On display are more than 100,000 items sold here in that era, many of them gleaned from the store's attic. They include high-button shoes, butter churns, spinning wheels, 1890s bathing suits, barrels of dill pickles (you can purchase one), and medicines that were 90% alcohol. Some 19th-century brand-name products shown here are still available today, among them Hershey's chocolate, Coca-Cola, Ivory soap, and Campbell's soups. It all makes for fascinating browsing.

The Oldest Wooden Schoolhouse in the U.S.A. 14 St. George St. (between Orange and Cuna sts.). ☎ **800/428-0222** or 904/824-0192. Admission $2.50 adults, $2 for seniors 55 and over, $1.50 children 6–12, free for children 5 and under. Daily 9am–5pm (later during summer).

This red-cedar and cypress structure, held together by wooden pegs and handmade nails, is more than 2 centuries old, with hand-wrought beams still intact. The classroom is re-created today using animated pupils and teacher, complete with a dunce and a below-stairs "dungeon" for unruly children. The last class was held here in 1864.

✪ **Spanish Quarter Village.** Entrance at 33 St. George St. (between Cuna and Orange sts.). ☎ **904/825-6830.** Admission to all exhibit buildings $6 adults, $5 seniors, $3.75 students 6–18, free for children 5 and under; $12 per family. Daily 9am–6pm (tours Fri–Sat 6–9pm).

This 2-block area south of the City Gate is St. Augustine's most comprehensive historic section, where the city's colonial architecture and landscape have been re-created. Interpreters in 18th-century attire are on hand to help you envision the life of early inhabitants. Candlelight tours are offered at dusk on weekends during spring. About 90% of the buildings in the area are reconstructions, with houses named for prominent occupants. The Spanish Colonial–style **Florencia House** serves as the museum entrance and store.

MORE HISTORIC ATTRACTIONS

Authentic Old Jail. 167 San Marco Ave. (at Williams St.). ☎ **904/829-3800.** Admission $4.25 adults, $3.25 children 6–12, free for children 5 and under. Daily 8:30am–5pm.

You can do the tour of this compact Victorian prison, a mile north of the visitor center, in less than half an hour, but you'll learn lots while you're here. The brick structure was built in 1890, and it served the county until 1953. The sheriff and his wife raised their children upstairs and used the same kitchen facilities to prepare the inmates' meals and their own. Downstairs are a maximum-security cell where murderers and horse thieves were confined, a cell housing prisoners condemned to hang (they could see the gallows being constructed from their window), and a grim solitary-confinement cell—pitch-dark with no windows, bed, or mattress. There's a restaurant here serving inexpensive lunch fare.

Florida Heritage Museum at the Authentic Old Jail. 167 San Marco Ave. (at Williams St.). ☎ **904/829-3800.** Admission $4.25 adults, $3.25 children 6–12, free for children 5 and under. Daily 8:30am–5pm.

After you've seen the Authentic Old Jail, you can wander through this museum documenting 400 years of Florida's past, focusing on the colorful life of Henry Flagler, the Civil War, and the Seminole Wars. A replica of a Spanish galleon filled with weapons, pottery, and treasures complements display cases filled with actual gold, silver, and jewelry recovered by treasure hunters. A typical wattle-and-daub hut of a Timucuan in a forest setting illustrates the lifestyle of St. Augustine's first residents. There's also an extraordinary collection of toys and dolls, mostly from the 1870s to the 1920s.

Fountain of Youth Archaeological Park. 11 Magnolia Ave. (at Williams St.). ☎ **800/356-8222** or 904/829-3168. Admission $4.75 adults, $3.75 seniors, $1.75 children 6–12, free for children 5 and under. Daily 9am–5pm.

Never mind that Juan Ponce de León never did find the Fountain of Youth, this 25-acre archaeological park bills itself as North America's first historic site. It offers hokey 45-minute guided tours beginning with a planetarium show about 16th-century celestial navigation, during which the audience experiences a hurricane at sea. The spring claimed to be the fountain is located in the Springhouse, along with a coquina stone cross believed to date from Ponce de León's ostensible visit in 1513. Visitors get to sample the sulfurous and not very tasty spring water from a paper cup. Please let us know if it works!

Mission of Nombre de Dios. San Marco Ave. and Old Mission Rd. ☎ **904/824-2809.** Free admission; donations appreciated. Daily 7am–6pm.

This serene setting overlooking the Intracoastal Waterway is believed to be the site of the first permanent mission in the United States, founded in 1565. The mission is a popular destination of religious pilgrimages. Whatever your beliefs, it's a beautiful tree-shaded spot, ideal for quiet meditation.

The St. Augustine Lighthouse and Museum. 81 Lighthouse Ave. (off Fla. A1A east of the Bridge of Lions). ☎ **904/829-0745.** Admission $5 adults, $3.50 seniors, $2.50 children 7–11, free for kids under 7. Museum only $2.50 adults, $1.75 seniors, free for kids under 12. Daily 9am–6pm.

This 165-foot-tall structure was built in 1875 to replace the old Spanish lighthouse which had stood at the inlet since 1565. Sitting in a shady grove of live oaks, the light-keeper's Victorian cottage was destroyed by fire in 1970 but meticulously reconstructed by the local Junior League. It now houses a museum explaining the history of both the lighthouse and the area. You should be in reasonable physical condition to climb the 219 steps to the top of the lighthouse, where you can see 19 nautical miles on a clear day. Children must be 7 years old and at least 4 feet tall to make the ascent.

OTHER ENTERTAINING ATTRACTIONS

3-D World. 28 San Marco Ave. (at Castillo Dr.). ☎ **904/824-1220.** Admission $9 per person. Daily 10am–10pm.

Put on your Polaroid glasses and take a 3-D underwater plunge in the Bahamas at one of two movie theaters here. The second screen shows *Escape from Capt. Nemo,* an action adventure. One or the other of the 45-minute productions begins every 15 to 20 minutes. It's a good place to park the kids when they tire of walking through old buildings.

Ripley's Believe It or Not! Museum. 19 San Marco Ave. (at Castillo Dr.). ☎ **904/824-1606.** Admission $8.95 adults, $7.95 seniors, $4.95 children 5–12, free for children 4 and under. Mar–Oct daily 9am–10pm; Dec–Jan 9am–9pm. Free parking.

The original Ripley's museum is housed in a converted 1887 Moorish Revival residence—complete with battlements, massive chimneys, and rose windows. Like the Ripley's in a dozen other U.S. cities, the exhibits run a wide gamut, from a Haitian voodoo doll owned by Papa Doc Duvalier to letters carved on a pencil with a chain saw by Ray "Wild Mountain Man" Murphy. This retro freak show is augmented by videos, photos, and film, including footage of amazing people tricks, like the man who made a habit of banging nails into wood planks with his hands and pulling them out with his teeth. If you don't mind your kids being exposed to this kind of bizzaro, Ripley's is a good place to take them for all or part of an evening.

۞ St. Augustine Alligator Farm and Zoological Park. 999 Anastasia Blvd. (Fla. A1A), east of Bridge of Lions at Old Quarry Rd. ☎ **904/824-3337.** Admission $11.95 adults, $10.75 seniors 65 and over, $7.95 children 3–10, free for kids under 3. June–Labor Day daily 9am–6pm; Labor Day–May daily 9am–5pm. Free parking.

You can't leave Florida without seeing at least one real-live gator, and there are more than 1,000 of them on display at this century-old attraction. In fact, it houses the world's most complete collection of crocodilians, a category that includes alligators, crocodiles, caiman, and gavial. Other creatures living here include geckos, prehensile-tailed skinks, lizards, snakes, tortoises, spider monkeys, and exotic birds. There are ponds filled with a variety of ducks, geese, and swans, as well as a petting zoo with pygmy goats, potbellied pigs, miniature horses, mouflon sheep, and deer. Entertaining (and educational) 20-minute alligator and reptile shows take place hourly throughout the day, and spring through fall you can often see narrated feedings. If you're into this kind of thing, allow at least 2 hours to tour the extensive and well-maintained facilities.

World Golf Hall of Fame. 21 World Golf Place (5 miles north of St. Augustine at Exit 98B off I-95). ☎ **904/940-4123.** Admission $9 adults, $7 seniors and students, $4.50 children 5–12. IMAX movies $7 adults, $6 seniors and students, $4 children 5–12. Combination tickets $14 adults, $11 seniors and students, $7.50 children 5 to 12. Admission and movies free for children under 5. Daily 10am–6pm (IMAX movies to 8pm Fri–Sat).

Passionate golf fans can easily spend a day at this state-of-the-art museum, opened in 1998 to honor professional golf, its great players, and the sport's famous supporters (including comedian Bob Hope and singer Dinah Shore). It's part of **World Golf Village,** a new complex of hotels, shops, offices, and 18-hole golf courses (see "Fishing, Cruises & Other Outdoor Pursuits," below). A 10-minute film, *The Passion to Play,* will get you oriented. Portable tape players will then guide you through 18 "holes" of exhibits. The "Front Nine" explains golf's history, while the "Back Nine" concentrates on the modern game and its technology. In between, you can ascend the Shrine, a

190-foot tower with a fine view from its top. When done, you can watch the pros play on the big IMAX screen next door, buy high-quality golf souvenirs at the museum shop, and have an inexpensive bite at the cafeteria-style Cafe.

The Hall of Fame faces a round lake with a "challenge hole" 132 feet away out in the middle. You can hit two balls at it, or play a round on the nearby minigolf course, for $5 adults, $3 kids.

The Walkway of Champions (whose signatures appear in pavement stones) leads around the lake to a hotel (see "Where to Stay" below) and a shopping complex. The main tenant here is the two-story **Tour Stop** (☎ 904/940-0422), carrying a wide range of relatively expensive apparel and equipment sanctioned by the U.S. Professional Golfer's Association. You can try out the clubs indoors on a putting green and driving range (translated: a big net).

You can finish your day by watching "Inside Golf" and other TV shows being produced at the headquarters of **PGA Productions** (☎ 904/940-7000), also on the lake. It has free tours at 4pm Monday to Friday.

Plans call for World Golf Village to include a library and repository of all things written about golf, an academy offering instructions to all levels of players, and courses with a total of 54 holes. The complex is part of a real-estate development, so don't be surprised if you're hit with a timeshare sales pitch.

HITTING THE BEACH

There are several places to find sand and sea in **Vilano Beach** on the north side of St. Augustine Inlet, and in **St. Augustine Beach,** on the south side (the inlet dumps the Matanzas and North rivers into the Atlantic). Be aware, however, that erosion has almost swallowed the beach from the inlet as far south as Old Beach Road in St. Augustine Beach. The U.S. Army Corps of Engineers is slated to begin a reclamation project in 2000. In the meantime, hotels and homes there have rock seawalls instead of sand bordering the sea.

Erosion has made a less noticeable impact on **Anastasia State Recreation Area,** on Anastasia Boulevard (Fla. A1A) across the Bridge of Lions and just past the Alligator Farm, where the 4 miles of beach here are still backed by picturesque dunes. On its river side, the area faces a lagoon flanked by tidal marshes. Available here are shaded picnic areas with grills, rest rooms, windsurfing, sailing and canoeing (on a saltwater lagoon), a nature trail, and saltwater fishing (for bluefish, pompano, and whiting from the surf, as well as sea trout, redfish, and flounder—a license is required for out-of-state residents). In summer, you can rent chairs, beach umbrellas, and surfboards. There's good bird watching here too, especially in spring and fall; pick up a brochure at the entrance. Admission is $3.25 per vehicle and $1 for bicyclists and pedestrians. The day-use area is open daily from 8am to sunset. For more information, contact Anastasia State Recreation Area, 1340A A1A South, St. Augustine, FL 32084 (☎ 904/461-2033).

All St. Augustine beaches charge a fee of $3 per car at official access points from Memorial Day to Labor Day; the rest of the year you can park free, but there are no lifeguards on duty and no toilet facilities on the beach.

FISHING, CRUISES & OTHER OUTDOOR PURSUITS

For additional outdoor options, contact the St. Johns County Visitors and Convention Bureau (see "Essentials" above) and ask them to send you a copy of *Outdoor Recreation Guide.*

CRUISES The Usina family has been running **St. Augustine Scenic Cruises** (☎ 800/542-8316 or 904/824-1806) on Matanzas Bay since the turn of the century.

They offer 75-minute narrated tours aboard open-air sightseeing boats departing from the Municipal Marina just south of the Bridge of Lions. You can sometimes spot dolphins, brown pelicans, cormorants, and kingfishers. Snacks, soft drinks, beer, and wine are sold on board. Weather permitting, departures normally are at 11am and 1, 2:45, and 4:30pm daily except Christmas, with an additional tour at 6:15pm from April 1 to May 21 and Labor Day to October 15; May 22 to Labor Day there are two additional tours, at 6:45 and 8:30pm. Call ahead—schedules can change. Fares are $9.50 adults, $8 seniors, $6.50 juniors ages 13 to 18, $4.50 children 4 to 12, free for children under 4. If you're driving, allow extra time to find a parking space on the street.

FISHING   See **Anastasia State Recreation Area** under "Hitting the Beach" above for information about surf casting. You can also cast your line off **St. Johns County Fishing Pier,** on the north end of St. Augustine Beach (☎ 904/461-0119). The pier is open 24 hours daily and has a bait shop with rental equipment that is open from 6am to 10pm. Admission is $2 adults, $1 children for fishing, 50¢ per person for sightseeing.

For full-day, half-day, and overnight **deep-sea fishing** excursions (for snapper, grouper, porgy, amberjack, sea bass, and other species), contact the **Sea Love Marina,** 250 Vilano Rd. (Fla. A1A north), at the eastern end of the Vilano Beach Bridge (☎ 904/824-3328). Full-day trips on the party boat *Sea Love II* cost $45; half-day trips, $30. No license is required, and rod, reel, bait, and tackle are supplied. Bring your own food and drink.

GOLF   The area's best golf resorts are in Ponte Vedra Beach about a half-hour's drive north on Fla. A1A, closer to Jacksonville than St. Augustine (see "Where to Stay," in section 4, below, for details).

At World Golf Village, 5 miles north of St. Augustine at Exit 98B off I-95 (see the World Golf Hall of Fame listing under "Other Entertaining Attractions," above), **The Slammer and The Squire** (☎ 904/940-6100) offers 18 holes amid a wildlife preserve. Locals say it's not as challenging as its greens fees, $165 in summer, $90 in winter, including cart. By the way, the "Slammer" is in honor of Sam Sneed; the "Squire" is for Gene Sarazen.

There are only a few courses in St. Augustine, including a rather-flat 18 at the **Radisson Ponce de León Resort** (see "Where to Stay," below) and the **St. Augustine Shores Golf Club,** 707 Shores Blvd., off U.S. 1 (☎ 904/794-4653). The latter is a par-70 course featuring 18 holes, lots of water, a lighted driving range and putting green, and a restaurant and lounge. Greens fees are $25.50 to $29.50, including cart, less in the summer months.

SAILING   You can rent sailboats, go on a variety of cruises, or learn to sail with **St. Augustine Sailing,** 3076 Harbor Dr. (☎ 800/683-7245 or 904/829-0648). Call for details, prices, and reservations.

WATER SPORTS   Jet skis and surfing and windsurfing equipment can be rented at **Surf Station,** 1020 Anastasia Blvd. (Fla. A1A), a block south of the Alligator Farm (☎ 904/471-9463); **Raging Water Sports,** at the Conch House Marina Resort, 57 Comares Ave. (☎ 904/829-5001), which is off Anastasia Ave. (Fla. A1A) halfway between the Bridge of Lions and the Alligator Farm; and **Watersports of St. Augustine,** at Sea Love Marina, 250 Vilano Rd. (Fla. A1A north), at the eastern end of the Vilano Beach Bridge (☎ 904/823-8963).

SHOPPING

The winding streets of the historic district are home to dozens of **antique stores** and art galleries stocked full of original paintings, sculptures, bric-a-brac, fine furnishings, china, and other treasures. Brick-lined **Aviles Street,** 1 block from the river, has an especially good mix of shops for browsing, as does St. George Street south of the visitor center. The **Alcazar Court at the Lightner Museum** has a good selection of antique shops (see "Seeing the Top Historic Attractions," above). The visitor center has complete lists of art galleries and antique shops, the latter published by **The Antique Dealers Association of St. Augustine,** 60 Cuna St., St. Augustine, FL 32084 (no phone).

Chocoholics will find their version of heaven at **Whetstone Chocolates,** 2 Coke Rd. (Fla. 312), between U.S. 1 and the Mickler O'Connell Bridge (☎ **904/ 825-1700**). Free tours of the store and factory usually take place Monday to Saturday from 10am to 5:30pm, but call to make sure of the factory's schedule. Whetstone has a retail outlet at 42 St. George St. in the historic district.

The biggest shopping draw here is the **St. Augustine Outlet Mall,** on Fla. 16 just west of I-95 at Exit 95 (☎ **904/825-1555**), about a 10-minute drive from downtown. Among the 95-plus stores are outlets by Levi's, Adolfo II, Mikasa, Brooks Brothers, Coach, Jones New York, Ann Taylor, Maidenform, Calvin Klein, The Gap, Bose, OshKosh B'Gosh, and more than a dozen shoe manufacturers. They're open 9am to 9pm Monday to Saturday, 10am to 6pm on Sunday. A free trolley will take you along this ½-mile strip of stores.

Also be on the lookout for an even bigger outlet mall planned for the east side of I-95 here.

WHERE TO STAY

If you're going to be here for a week or longer, consider **Villas on the Bay,** 105 Marine St., between San Salvador and St. Francis streets (☎ **904/826-0575;** fax 904/ 826-1892; www.thevillas.com), whose nine one- and two-bedroom suites occupy a building that served as a Civil War military hospital. The spacious suites are furnished with antiques and Victoriana and have private balconies sporting spectacular bay views, rocking chairs, and/or hammocks. Most also have double Jacuzzi tubs. Rates range from $550 to $750 a week.

Out at the beach, the **Ocean Gallery,** 4600 Fla. A1A South, between Dondonville Road and Trade Winds Lane (☎ **800/940-6665** or 904/471-6663; fax 904/ 471-5994), has about 200 condo apartments in its rental inventory. The complex is set on 44 attractively landscaped acres with gardens, lakes, and lagoons. They range from $500 to $1,400 a week, depending on size, season, and view.

Almost all accommodations increase prices on weekends when the town is most crowded with visitors. St. Johns County charges a 9% tax on hotel bills.

The 139 wooded camp sites in the **Anastasia State Recreation Area** (see "Hitting the Beach," above) are in high demand all year. They have picnic tables, grills, and electricity and rent for $15.25 to $19.55 a night. Reservations are required: Make them up to 11 months in advance by writing or calling Anastasia State Recreation Area, 1340A A1A South, St. Augustine, FL 32084 (☎ **904/461-2033**).

IN ST. AUGUSTINE

St. Augustine has more than two dozen bed-and-breakfasts in restored historic homes. They all provide free parking, but most neither take young children nor allow smoking inside the house (check before booking). Those listed below are within walking distance of the historic district, or right in it. For more choices, write **Historic Inns of St. Augustine,** P.O. Box 5268, St. Augustine, FL 33085 (no phone), and ask for a brochure describing its member properties.

There are plenty of moderate and inexpensive motels and hotels here. Most convenient is the 40-room **Best Western Spanish Quarter Inn,** 6 Castillo Dr.

(☎ **800/ 528-1234** or 904/824-4457; fax 904/829-8330), directly across the street from the visitor center. It's completely surrounded by an asphalt parking lot but does have a swimming pool and hot tub.

Also close to the historic district, the two-story stucco **Comfort Inn,** 1111 Ponce de Leon Blvd., at Old Mission Road (☎ **800/575-5288** or 904/824-5554; fax 904/829-2948), has large suites with double-sink dressing rooms and parlor areas with extra TVs and pull-out sofas.

Among the budget-priced motels, the **Super 8,** 3552 N. Ponce de Leon Blvd., between Rambla and Fairbanks streets (☎ **800/800-8000** or 904/824-6399; fax 904/823-8687), has attractively landscaped grounds with a palm-fringed lawn surrounding a swimming pool. The upstairs units with peaked beamed ceilings are especially appealing.

Once one of the historic district's grand hotels, the 1888-vintage **Casa Monica** was being intricately restored and was due to come online in 1999. For details contact Grand Theme Hotels (☎ **888/GRAND-123;** www.grandthemehotels.com).

Carriage Way Bed and Breakfast. 70 Cuna St. (between Cordova and Spanish sts.), St. Augustine, FL 32084. ☎ **800/908-9832** or 904/829-2467. Fax 904/826-1461. 11 units. A/C TEL. $69–$175 double. Rates include full breakfast. AE, DISC, MC, V.

Primarily occupying an 1883 Victorian wood-frame house fronted by roses and hibiscus, the Carriage Way is like coming to an old friend's house. It is not fancy or formal, but it is comfortable and relaxed. Rooms are furnished with simple antique reproductions, including many four-poster beds. One room even retains its original fireplace. A console TV, books, magazines, and games are provided in a homey parlor. For more privacy, two more rooms are down the street in "The Cottage," a one-story clapboard house built in 1885. It has its own living room and kitchen, and Miranda's and Ashton's rooms both have clawfoot bathtubs. Miranda's also sports a two-person Jacuzzi, and Ashton's has its own small back porch. The energetic and hospitable owners/hosts Bill and Diane Johnson, who live in the main house, offer many extras: old one-speed bicycles, decanters of red wine and sherry on a buffet table in the hallway, and a refrigerator stocked with beer and soft drinks in both houses.

Casa de Solana. 21 Aviles St. (at Cadiz St.), St. Augustine, FL 32084. ☎ **904/824-3555.** Fax 904/824-3316. www.oldcity.com/solana. E-mail: solana@aug.com. 4 units. A/C TV. $125–$175 double. Rates include full breakfast. AE, DISC, MC, V.

Built circa 1763 on a narrow cobbled street, this charming colonial house is the seventh oldest in the city. In the mid-1800s, its coquina-stone exterior was covered over with the pale-pink stucco you see today. The house also sports a lovely walled garden with a Spanish-style fountain and planted with jasmine and trumpet vines. The rooms are nicely decorated with an eclectic mix of antique pieces. Yours might have a four-poster, brass, art deco, or mahogany bed. A welcoming decanter of sherry awaits your arrival in the room. Three suites have full living rooms (the fourth has a small parlor), and one has a balcony. Hostess Faye McMurry's homemade breakfasts always include delicious fresh-baked muffins. There's a baby grand in the dining room, scene of occasional impromptu nighttime sing-alongs.

Casa de Sueños. 20 Cordova St. (at Saragossa St.), St. Augustine, FL 32084. ☎ **800/ 824-0804** or 904/824-0887. Fax 800/735-7534 or 904/825-0074. www.casadesuenos.com. E-mail: suenos@aug.com. 6 units. A/C TV TEL. $95–$165 double; $145–$195 suite. Rates include full breakfast. DISC, MC, V.

Casa de Sueños offers small and thoughtfully decorated rooms in a turn-of-the-century house that was later transformed into the Mediterranean style you see today. When innkeepers Sandy and Ray Tool renovated the space in 1993, they updated with made-to-look-like antiques and many modern conveniences, including some whirlpools, dimmer switches on the lights, ceiling fans, hand-held shower attachments, and phones with modem jacks. In the downstairs parlor you'll find a CD/cassette/record player, a TV, a VCR, books, magazines, games, and a small refrigerator stocked with beer and soft drinks. A fax and copy machine are available, too. Breakfasts are superb here, and huge. When it is offered, the strawberry-covered French toast is especially delicious. You'll always appreciate fresh-baked breads, muffins, or biscuits. Services include nightly turndown with a chocolate and complimentary daily newspapers.

✪ **Kenwood Inn.** 38 Marine St. (at Bridge St.), St. Augustine, FL 32084. ☎ **904/824-2116.** Fax 904/824-1689. 14 units. A/C. $85–$135 double, bridal suite $175. Rates include continental breakfast. Extra person $10. DISC, MC, V.

Somewhere between a B&B and a cozy inn, Mark and Kerianne Constant's inn is one of Old Town's best accommodations. Everything from the carpeting to the linens to the china is first-class. Their Victorian wood-frame house with graceful verandas has served as a boardinghouse or inn since the late 19th century. Rooms are larger and more private than most other accommodations in converted single-family homes. It's unusual also because of its relatively large outdoor space, which includes an outdoor swimming pool, a lushly landscaped sundeck, and a secluded garden courtyard (complete with a fish pond and neat flower bed under a sprawling pecan tree). Complimentary sherry, tea, and coffee are offered throughout the day.

Monterey Inn. 16 Avenida Menendez (between Cuna and Hypolita sts.), St. Augustine, FL 32084. ☎ **904/824-4482.** Fax 904/829-8854. www.montereyinn.usrc.net. 59 units. A/C TV TEL. $39–$99 double. AE, DC, DISC, MC, V.

For the price, you can't find a better choice than this two-story, wrought iron–trimmed motel close to the attractions and nightlife of Old Town, and you couldn't ask for a more well-kept though modest place to spend the night. Three generations of the Six family have run this simple two-story motel overlooking the Matanzas Bay, and you'll find the 1960s building and grounds always clean and functional. Rooms are not especially spacious but they are comfortable. A small swimming pool, pleasant staff, and free coffee each morning are just some of the extras at this super-affordable and convenient spot.

Radisson Ponce de León Golf & Conference Resort. 4000 U.S. Hwy. 1 North, St. Augustine, FL 32095. ☎ **800/333-3333** or 904/824-2821. Fax 904/824-8254. 193 units. A/C TV TEL. $99–$179 double. Golf, family, and other packages available. AE, DC, DISC, MC, V. Free parking.

Located 2½ miles north of historic Old Town, this 400-acre complex is a good choice for golfers, who can get in a round on its Donald Ross–designed par-72 course before heading off to see the sights. Although it's been in business since Henry Flagler built a resort here in 1916, today's establishment is a modern motel. Rooms are in one- and two-story buildings spread out in a virtual forest of palms, magnolias, centuries-old live oaks, and clumps of sawgrass, with a large swimming pool in its center. Extensively renovated and upgraded in 1998, the units all are equipped with pine furniture, coffeemakers, hair dryers, irons and boards, and balconies or patios. Back by six lighted tennis courts, the minisuites are ideal for families, with trellises separating small sitting rooms from sleeping areas.

With its big window walls overlooking the golf course and the marshes beyond, Fairways Gill offers breakfast, lunch, and dinner. On weekend evenings you can join conferences unwinding in the lounge for live piano entertainment in a cozy bar overlooking the greens. Other amenities here are a putting green; volleyball, shuffleboard, croquet, boccie ball, and basketball courts; a horseshoe pitch; newspaper delivery; laundry service; and a guest laundry.

Westcott House. 146 Avenida Menendez (between Bridge and Francis sts.), St. Augustine, FL 32084. ☎ **904/824-4301.** Fax 904/824-4301. www.westcotthouse.com. E-mail: westcotth@aol.com. 9 units. A/C TV TEL. Sun–Thurs $95–$175 double; Fri–Sat $150–$175 double. Rates include continental breakfast. AE, DISC, MC, V. Parking is on the street or free in a nearby lot.

Overlooking Matanzas Bay on the edge of historic Old Town, this two-story, wood-frame house offers rare opportunities for an uncluttered view from a porch, a second-story veranda, and a shady courtyard. The rooms—some with bay windows and/or working fireplaces—are exquisitely furnished and immaculate; everything here just gleams! Yours might have authentic Victorian furnishings and a brass bed made up with a white quilt and lace dust ruffle, with extras like hair dryers and terry bathrobes. Complimentary fresh fruit and brandy are available all day in the parlor of one of the town's most well-kept inns.

AT THE BEACHES

St. Augustine Beach has its share of chain motels, all on A1A Beach Boulevard (Fla. A1A). Three are on the beach side of the highway: the **Hampton Inn St. Augustine Beach** (☎ 800/426-7866 or 904/471-4000; fax 904/471-4888), the **Holiday Inn Beachside** (☎ 800/626-7263 or 904/471-2555; fax 904/461-8450), and the **Howard Johnson Resort Hotel** (☎ 800/752-4037 or 904/471-2575; fax 904/471-1247). But note that erosion has removed the beach at the Hampton Inn and Howard Johnson (see "Hitting the Beach" above). On the western side of A1A are the **Best Western Ocean Inn** (☎ 800/528-1234 or 904/471-8010; fax 904/460-9124); **Comfort Inn** (☎ 800/228-5150 or 904/471-1474; fax 904/461-9659), **Days Inn Beach** (☎ 800/DAYS-INN or 904/461-4774; fax 904/471-4774), **Econo Lodge** (☎ 800/446-6900 or 904/471-2330), and **Ramada Limited** (☎ 800/2-RAMADA or 904/471-1440).

✪ **Coquina Gables Oceanfront Bed & Breakfast.** 1 F St., St. Augustine Beach, FL 32084. ☎ **904/461-8727.** Fax 904/461-4346. www.oldcity.com/coquinagables. E-mail: mg@aug.com. 5 units. A/C TV TEL. $129–$169. Rates include full breakfast. AE, DISC, MC, V.

The rather ordinary exterior of this 1920s peach-colored beachside home gives not a hint of the hand-hewn Honduran pine beams, ceilings, and floors in its great room, nor of the cypress paneling adorning its bedrooms. Flanking the great room and its fireplace, the three guest quarters in the main house all have a mix of antiques and quality reproductions, ceiling fans, huge walk-in closets with robes, fully tiled bathrooms, and at least partial views of the ocean from their curtained windows. On the front corner of the house, the master suite is the pick of the litter, with one window directly facing the beach, another looking south along the shore. A mosquito net hangs over its four-poster bed. More private are two suites in the cottage-like Garden House, across the backyard. These light and airy units have living rooms with sofa beds, small refrigerators, and coffeemakers. The rooms don't come equipped with TVs and phones, but you can request them. Innkeepers Michael and Melissa Giarratano, who live downstairs, serve gourmet breakfasts in a sun room facing the beach. Outside, you can relax beside the swimming pool or frolic in a screen-enshrouded, eight-person spa tub—robes are available, if you need them. You also get beach chairs, umbrellas, sandals, sunscreen, and bikes. The beach here has not eroded.

La Fiesta Oceanside Inn. 810 A1A Beach Blvd. (Fla. A1A; south of F St.), St. Augustine Beach, FL 32084. ☎ **800/852-6390** or 904/471-2220. Fax 904/471-0186. 44 units. A/C TV TEL. $59–$259 double. DISC, MC, V.

Far enough south to have a good beach, these two-story tan stucco buildings with Spanish-style terra-cotta roofs contain generic Formica and wood-outfitted motel-like rooms, but a new block contains six new suites with more charm and amenities, including Jacuzzis and kitchens. The location couldn't be better, since you are directly on the beach and close to dining and drinking spots. Some rooms have wet bars, small refrigerators, double-size tubs, and king-size beds. A cafe serves breakfast daily. Other facilities include coin-op laundry, a boardwalk over the dunes, a children's playground, a swimming pool, an 18-hole beachfront miniature golf course, and a picnic area with a barbecue grill.

AT WORLD GOLF VILLAGE

World Golf Village Resort Hotel. 500 S. Legacy Trail, St. Augustine, FL 32092. ☎ **888/ 446-5302** or 904/940-8000. Fax 904/940-8008. 302 units. A/C TV TEL. $129–$329 double. AE, DC, DISC, MC, V.

Built in 1997, this nine-story luxury hotel is among the centerpieces of World Golf Village (see the listing for World Golf Hall of Fame under "Other Entertaining Attractions," above), 5 miles north of St. Augustine. The tower's spacious rooms are traditionally decorated and have three TVs, wet bars, refrigerators, and two phones. All have views overlooking the complex and the adjoining golf course, some from balconies. Off a soaring atrium lobby with waterfalls, fountains, and palms, the Cypress Pointe restaurant serves all meals, at both indoor and outdoor seating, and a clubby lounge with a big horseshoe-shaped bar and billiard table provides libation and occasional entertainment. The dining venue opens to an outdoor swimming pool, hot tub, and sun deck. You can hone your game at a full-swing, 32-hole golf simulator, or have your swing checked by an analyzer. Other amenities include concierge, limited room service (including Pizza Hut pies), children's program, fitness center, massage, valet laundry, and 40,000-square-foot conference center (bringing lots of conventions and other groups).

WHERE TO DINE

In a town as heavily touristed as St. Augustine, there are, of course, a fair number of "tourist trap" restaurants. But on the whole, the food in St. Augustine, even at the popular eateries, is fairly priced and of good quality. For good burgers, sandwiches, or late-night bites, see **A1A Ale Works** and **Ann O'Malley's** under "St. Augustine After Dark," below.

The historic district has a branch of Tampa's famous **Columbia** restaurant, at 98 St. George St., at Hypolita Street (☎ **904/824-3341**). Like the original (see "Where to Dine" in section 1 of chapter 11), this one sports Spanish architecture, including intricate tile work and courtyards with fountains.

For more choices, pick up a copy of *Restaurant Times* at the visitor center.

IN ST. AUGUSTINE

Bunnery Café. 35 Hypolita St. (east of St. George St.). ☎ **904/829-6166.** Reservations not accepted. Everything under $4. No credit cards. Daily 9am–5:30pm. BAKERY.

Alluring aromas waft from the Bunnery, a bakery and cafe in the heart of the historic district. It's lovely to come here for breakfast. Or arrive weary from a day of sightseeing, plop yourself into a chair on the arcaded terra-cotta patio, and indulge in a fresh-baked cinnamon roll, pecan sticky bun, or strawberry and cream-cheese croissant accompanied by a big cup of cappuccino.

✪ **Gypsy Cab Co.** 828 Anastasia Blvd. (Fla. A1A, at Ingram St., east of Bridge of Lions). ☎ **904/824-8244.** Reservations not accepted. Main courses $9.50–$17; early-bird specials

$9. AE, DC, DISC, MC, V. Mon–Thurs 4:30–10pm; Fri 4:30–11pm, Sat 11am–11pm, Sun 10:30am–10pm. Early-bird specials daily 4:30–7pm. NEW AMERICAN.

Billing itself as a temple of "urban cuisine," this high-energy establishment, with gaudy purple neon strips outside and bright, art-filled dining rooms inside, offers the town's most interesting culinary experience. The creative menu changes daily, although a hearty black-bean soup is a constant winner. I ordered shrimp with artichokes sautéed with scallions, mushrooms, and julienne carrots and served with a sauce of white wine, butter, and enough pepper to leave a pleasant bite lingering at the back of my tongue. Expertly cooked, it presented a delightful combination of flavors. Grouper in a tomato basil sauce, strip steak under a peppercorn sauce, and Cayman Island–style pork were among the other offerings. The house salad dressing—red wine, vinegar, olive oil, garlic, tamarind, and nutritional yeast—is so good they sell it by the bottle. Also worshipped here during autumn: Beaujolais nouveau, by the glass or bottle. Park free behind the building, not in Trader Jack's lot next door.

La Parisienne. 60 Hypolita St. (between Spanish and Cordova sts.). ☎ 904/829-0055. Reservations recommended. Main courses $9–$24. AE, DISC, MC, V. Thurs–Tues 11am–3pm; Thurs–Sun 5–9pm. TRADITIONAL FRENCH.

La Parisienne will remind you of Paris. The lovely dining room has a rough-hewn beamed pine ceiling, lace-curtained windows, and ladder-back chairs. Begin with escargot in a garlic cream sauce, then go on to a classic steak au poivre and roast rack of lamb coated with Dijon mustard and fresh garlic. The lunch menu offers traditional bistro fare, such as quiche Lorraine, croque monsieur, and salad niçoise. At afternoon tea, you might enjoy oven-fresh chocolate eclairs, praline ganaches, or fruit tarts.

✪ Raintree. 102 San Marco Ave. (at Bernard St.). ☎ 904/824-7211. Reservations recommended. Main courses $12–$23; early dinner specials $9–$13; dessert bar $5.50. AE, MC, V. Sun–Fri 5–9:30pm, Sat 5–10pm. Early-bird specials 5–6pm except holidays and special events. Courtesy car provides transportation from/to downtown hotels. INTERNATIONAL.

Many a marriage has been proposed and accepted at this romantic 1879 Victorian house, about ½ mile north of the historic district. Bamboo furnishings and dozens of plants and ficus trees create an indoor-garden setting, and recessed lighting casts a soft glow. If there's a theme to the cuisine here, it's the use of fruit, starting with fruit salsa with the blue-crab cake appetizer and progressing to the likes of dried plums with duck in a Cognac sauce, or orange Muscat demiglace with cashew-encrusted veal chops. More traditional main courses include beef Wellington. It's all very good, though not as exciting as you'll find at Gypsy Cab Co. (see above). You don't have to dine here to visit the extensive dessert and coffee bar, tempting with a variety of hot crepes and an exemplary crème brûlée. The list of more than 300 vintages has won Wine Spectator awards.

Schmagel's Bagels. 69 Hypolita St. (at Cordova St.). ☎ 904/824-4444. Bagels and sandwiches $4–$5. No credit cards. Mon–Sat 7:30am–3pm, Sun 8:30am–2pm. BAGEL SANDWICHES.

Yes, bagels have made it to St. Augustine, and Schmagel's makes them almost like the real plump New York ones. They come in 12 varieties—everything from cinnamon-raisin to blueberry. Various toppings range from traditional cream cheese and lox to a BLT. For breakfast you can also get bacon and eggs, homemade soups, and fresh-baked fruit muffins.

The Spanish Bakery. 42½ St. George St. (between Cuna and Orange sts.). ☎ 904/471-3046. Reservations not accepted. Lunch specials $3; cookies and rolls 40¢–50¢ each. No credit cards. Daily 9:30am–3pm. Closed Thanksgiving and Christmas. COLONIAL.

Occupying a reconstructed 17th-century kitchen building, this little family-operated establishment bakes almond, lemon, and cinnamon cookies using recipes from the Spanish colonial period, when a lack of refrigeration limited the use of milk and eggs. A couple of these crunchy morsels, eaten at the picnic tables outside, make a fine snack while you're touring the historic district. Or you can have lunch here, choosing from daily specials such as spicy Spanish-style chili over rice served with soup, a small loaf of freshly baked bread, and a drink.

AT THE BEACHES

✪ Fiddler's Green. 2750 Anahma Dr. (at Ferrell Rd.), Vilano Beach. ☎ **904/824-8897.** Reservations recommended Sun–Fri, not accepted Sat. Main courses $9–$18. AE, CB, DC, DISC, MC, V. Jan–Sept daily 5–10pm; Oct–Dec Sun–Thurs 5–9pm, Fri–Sat 5–10pm. Take Fla. A1A north across the Vilano Bridge, turn right at first dead end, left at second. FLORIDIAN/SEAFOOD.

Situated right on the Atlantic, the shiplike Fiddler's Green is appropriately entered via a kind of gangplank. Inside, tropical elegance is achieved with a profusion of hanging plants and oversize rattan chairs at every table. Start your meal with crunchy-peppery conch fritters with a spicy pepper cocktail sauce or a platter of oysters "Rockefiddler" with oven-browned Cheddar topping. For a main course try fish Matanzas—fresh catch of the day (perhaps red snapper) pan-blackened with a mélange of spices and served with drawn butter. Oysters can be combined with a mixed grill of fish, shrimp, and scallops.

Salt Water Cowboy's. 299 Dondanville Rd. (off Fla. A1A), St. Augustine Beach. ☎ **904/471-2332.** Reservations not accepted, so arrive early to avoid a wait. Main courses $9–$15. AE, DC, DISC, MC, V. Jan–Oct daily 5–10pm. Nov–Dec Sun–Thurs 5–9pm, Fri–Sat 5–10pm. Follow A1A Beach Blvd. south; just past the restaurant's billboard make a right onto Dondanville Rd. at the traffic light. SEAFOOD/BARBECUE.

Arrive early for dinner at Salt Water Cowboy's—not only to beat the crowd but also to enjoy a spectacular view of the sun setting over a saltwater marsh. Designed to resemble a turn-of-the-century fish camp, this rambling restaurant has a rustic candlelit interior and a mix of dining areas ranging from intimate booths to an outdoor plant-filled deck shaded by live oaks and lit by tiki torches. Order up a half dozen oysters or perhaps some 'gator bits while you peruse the menu. For openers, there's a very rich and creamy chowder with big chunks of clam, potato, and celery. A main course of fork-tender baby back ribs or a skewer of shrimp from an open pit are great choices. Another winner: oysters, scallops, or shrimp fried in light cornmeal batter.

Sunset Grille. 421 A1A Beach Blvd. (Fla. A1A at 15th St.), St. Augustine Beach. ☎ **904/471-5555.** Reservations not accepted. Main courses $8–$13. DISC, MC, V. Mon–Fri 11am–10pm (limited late-night menu served until midnight), Sat–Sun 7am–10pm. Bar daily 11am–1am. AMERICAN.

This casual Key West–style sports bar is a kick-back kind of place with half a dozen TVs and a mixture of music blaring from loud speakers. You can escape the noise in a small dining room to one side, but what's the point? The action takes precedence over the food here. Sunday afternoon a live band plays oldies and the place is mobbed. At lunch or dinner you can dine on sandwiches, burritos, or burgers. A more substantial dinner might consist of grilled fresh fish or shrimp, with most main courses priced under $10. The windows latch up and have stools outside, so the beach crowd (the ocean is across the street) can eat and drink in bathing attire.

ST. AUGUSTINE AFTER DARK

Especially on weekends, the Old Town is full of strollers and partiers making the rounds to the dozens of active bars, clubs, and restaurants. For up-to-date details on what's happening in town, check the local daily, the *St. Augustine Record,* or the more irreverent *Folio Weekly.*

Ann O'Malley's, 23 Orange St., near the Old City Gate, (☎ **904/825-4040**), is the quintessential Irish pub open every day and night until 1am. Besides the selection of ales, stouts, and drafts, this is one of the only spots in town to grab a late-night bite. Granted, the deli-meat sandwiches and salads are nothing to write home about, but they're fresh and cheap.

The best-looking crowd in town can be found at the **A1A Ale Works,** 1 King St., at Avenida Menendez opposite the Bridge of Lions (☎ **904/829-2977**). Twenty-something hipsters and middle-age partiers mingle at this handsome, New Orleans–style microbrewery and restaurant. Thursday through Saturday nights downstairs, you'll find live music, often in the form of an acoustic guitarist and singer performing light rock and R & B tunes on a crowded windowfront stage.

Popular with locals, **Mill Top Tavern,** 19½ St. George St., at the Fort (☎ **904/ 829-2329**), is a warm and rustic tavern housed in a 19th-century mill building (the waterwheel is still outside). Weather permitting, it's an open-air space. There's music every day from 1pm until 1am.

One of St. Augustine's most famous nighttime hangouts is **Scarlett O'Hara's,** at 70 Hypolita St., at Cordova Street (☎ **904/824-6535**). A catacomb of cozy rooms with working fireplaces in a rambling 19th-century wood-frame house is the setting for live rock, jazz, and R & B bands nightly from 9:30pm. And though there's no dance floor, people get up and dance wherever. Sporting events are aired on a large-screen TV in a tropically themed oyster bar. Park in a lot across Cordova Street.

Out at St. Augustine Beach, a casual and happening beach club, **Cafe Iguana,** 321 A1A Beach Blvd. (☎ **904/471-7797**), hosts retro music, semifunny comedians, and a sloppy dance scene Tuesday through Saturday nights. Several nights will find local live music and various contests. Especially popular are Friday's Happy Hour from 4:30 to 8pm and Wednesday's ladies' night.

Also at the beach is **Panama Hattie's Saloon,** 361 A1A Beach Blvd. (☎ **904/ 471-2255**), a funky and very popular beach bar with a rustic interior housing bars and dance floors on two levels. The older crowd hangs downstairs, where on Friday and Saturday nights there are oldies bands, while upstairs on the beach deck a deejay plays Top 40 tunes.

4 Jacksonville

36 miles S of Georgia, 134 miles NE of Orlando, 340 miles N of Miami

Once infamous for its smelly paper mills, the sprawling metropolis of Jacksonville— residents call it "Jax," from its airport abbreviation—is now one of the South's insurance and banking capitals. Development is rampant throughout Duval County, with hotels, restaurants, attractions, and clubs rapidly springing up, especially in suburban areas near the interstate highways. Nevertheless, there are shady older neighborhoods to explore, 20 miles of Atlantic Ocean beaches upon which to sun and swim, many championship golf courses to play, and an abundance of beautiful and historic national and state parks to roam.

Spanning the broad, curving St. Johns River, downtown Jacksonville is a vibrant center of activity during weekdays and on weekend afternoon and evenings, when many locals return to the restaurants and bars of The Jacksonville Landing and Southbank Riverwalk, two dining and entertainment complexes facing each other across the river. Like Baltimore's Inner Harbor, the two centers have helped to revitalize downtown.

Although it claims to be the capital of Florida's historic "First Coast," Jacksonville dates its beginnings from an early 1800s settlement named Cowford, because cattle crossed the St. Johns River here. Cowford changed its name to Jacksonville in 1822 to honor Gen. Andrew Jackson, the provisional governor who forced Spain to cede Florida to the United States 2 years earlier.

ESSENTIALS

GETTING THERE   **Air South** (☎ 800/247-7688), **AirTran** (☎ 800/AIR-TRAN), **Air Transat** (☎ 800/470-1011), **American** (☎ 800/433-7300), **Continental** (☎ 800/525-0280), **Delta** (☎ 800/221-1212), **Northwest** (☎ 800/225-2525), **MetroJet** (☎ 800/428-4322), **Midway** (☎ 800/446-4392), **Southwest** (☎ 800/435-9792), **TWA** (☎ 800/221-2000), **United** (☎ 800/241-6522), and **US Airways** (☎ 800/428-4322) fly into **Jacksonville International Airport** on the city's north side, about 12 miles from downtown.

The **First Coast Information Booth,** on the lower level by the baggage area (☎ 904/741-4902), is open daily from 9am to 10pm.

Alamo (☎ 800/327-9633), **Avis** (☎ 800/331-1212), **Budget** (☎ 800/527-0700), **Dollar** (☎ 800/800-4000), **Enterprise** (☎ 800/325-8007), **Hertz** (☎ 800/654-3131), and **National** (☎ 800/CAR-RENT) have rental-car booths at the airport.

Gator City Taxi (☎ 904/741-0008) provides transportation to and from the airport. Fares are about $20 to downtown, $40 to $45 to beach hotels, $55 to $65 to the St. Augustine area.

There's an **Amtrak** station in Jacksonville at 3570 Clifford Lane, off U.S. 1, just north of 45th Street (☎ 800/USA-RAIL).

VISITOR INFORMATION   Contact the **Jacksonville and the Beaches Convention & Visitors Bureau,** 201 E. Adams St., Jacksonville, FL 32202 (☎ 800/733-2668 or 904/798-9111; fax 904/789-9103; www.jaxcvb.com), for maps, brochures, calendars, and advice. The bureau is open Monday to Friday from 8am to 5pm. There are information booths at the airport (see above) and in **Jacksonville Landing** (see "Exploring the Area," below). The latter is open Monday to Saturday from 10am to 8pm, Sunday 12:30 to 5:30pm.

GETTING AROUND   You're better off having a car if you want to explore this vast area. If you're only visiting downtown, you can cross the St. Johns River via **water taxis** which prowl the shoreline, looking for passengers standing at marked landings on the north and south banks (wave to hail them). The boats operate regularly from March to December, Monday to Thursday 11am to 9pm, Friday and Saturday 11am to midnight, Sunday 11am to 8pm. But be aware that they don't run in stormy or cold weather, and their schedules are strictly day-by-day during January and February. One-way fares are $2 adults, $1 seniors and children. **Bass Marine Service** (☎ 904/730-8685) operates the taxis. If a storm comes up and you get stranded, there's a pedestrian walkway across the Main Street Bridge.

You can hail a **taxi** downtown if you spot one, although it is usually best to call **Gator City Taxi** (☎ 904/355-8294) or **Yellow Cab** (☎ 904/260-1111) for a pickup. Fares are $1.25 when the meter drops, and 25¢ for each $1/5$ mile thereafter.

The Jacksonville Transportation Authority (☎ 904/630-3100) provides local bus service.

Out at the beaches, the **St. Johns River Ferry** (☎ 904/241-9969) shuttles vehicles across the river between Mayport, an Old Florida fishing village on the south side, and Fort George on the north shore. The boats depart Mayport on the hour and half hour Monday to Friday from 6am to 10pm, weekends from 6:20am to 10pm.

Jacksonville

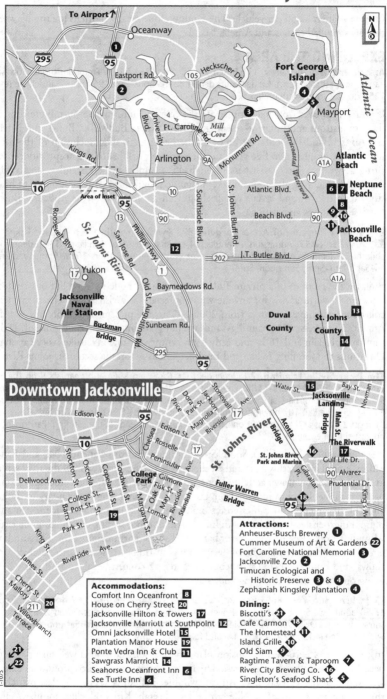

To Airport↑
Oceanway
1
295
95
Eastport Rd.
2
105 Heckscher Dr.
Fort George Island
4
5 Mayport
University Blvd.
Ft. Caroline Rd.
Mill Cove
3
Kings Rd.
Arlington
9A
Monument Rd.
Intracoastal Waterway
Atlantic Beach
A1A
10
Atlantic Ocean
10
Area of Inset
95
Atlantic Blvd.
6 **7** **Neptune Beach**
13
90
Southside Blvd.
St. Johns Bluff Rd.
Beach Blvd.
90
8
9 **10**
11 **Jacksonville Beach**
Roosevelt Blvd.
St. Johns River
San Jose Rd.
Phillips Hwy.
Old St. Augustine Rd.
1
90
12
202 J.T. Butler Blvd.
Yukon
17
Baymeadows Rd.
A1A
Jacksonville Naval Air Station
Buckman Bridge
Sunbeam Rd.
295
95
Duval County
St. Johns County
13
14

Downtown Jacksonville

Edison St.
95
10
Stockton St.
Dellwood Ave.
Osceola St.
Copeland St.
Goodwin St.
College Park
Gilmore
Fisk St.
Oak
May
Margaret St.
Lomax St.
Standish Pl.
Riverside
Price
Dora
Park Dr.
Jackson
Magnolia
Stonewall
Ave.
Riverside
17
Chelsea
Edison St.
Rosselle
17
Peninsular
Barrs
College St.
Post St.
Park St.
King St.
James St.
Riverside Ave.
Cherry St.
Mallory
Willowbranch Terrace
211
20
21
22
19
Water St.
15
Bay St.
Newman
Jackson
Jacksonville Landing
St. Johns River
Acosta Bridge
Main St. Bridge
The Riverwalk
17
Gulf Life Dr.
St. Johns River Park and Marina
16
Gibraltar Pl.
Fuller Warren Bridge
18
95
90 Alvarez
Prudential Dr.
King's Av.

Attractions:
Anheuser-Busch Brewery **1**
Cummer Museum of Art & Gardens **22**
Fort Caroline National Memorial **3**
Jacksonville Zoo **2**
Timucan Ecological and
  Historic Preserve **3** & **4**
Zephaniah Kingsley Plantation **4**

Accommodations:
Comfort Inn Oceanfront **8**
House on Cherry Street **20**
Jacksonville Hilton & Towers **17**
Jacksonville Marriott at Southpoint **12**
Omni Jacksonville Hotel **15**
Plantation Manor House **19**
Ponte Vedra Inn & Club **11**
Sawgrass Marrriott **14**
Seahorse Oceanfront Inn **6**
See Turtle Inn **6**

Dining:
Biscotti's **21**
Cafe Carmon **18**
The Homestead **11**
Island Grille **10**
Old Siam **9**
Ragtime Tavern & Taproom **7**
River City Brewing Co. **16**
Singleton's Seafood Shack **5**

1-1075

One-way fare is $2.50 per vehicle. The 5-minute ride greatly shortens the trip between the Jacksonville beaches and Amelia Island.

EXPLORING THE AREA

Anheuser-Busch Brewery. 111 Busch Dr. ☎ **904/751-8118.** Free admission. Mon–Sat 9am–4pm (last tour 3pm). Guided tours depart on the hour. Take I-95 north to Busch Dr. (exit 125), go east to brewery on left.

If you're into beer, you may appreciate the free and informative 30-minute tour of these monstrous and pungent-smelling facilities, where Budweiser, Bud Light, Michelob, Busch, and O'Doul's are brewed. The best part is the conclusion of the tour, when you can quaff two free glasses of beer (or soft drinks) in the hospitality center. Bring a sweater, since you'll pass through 45° chambers where stainless-steel vaults hold the fermenting ale. You can take the guided tour, show yourself around, or head straight to the bar and extensive gift shop. Call ahead to see if the Anheuser-Busch Clydesdale horses are visiting.

✪ Cummer Museum of Art & Gardens. 829 Riverside Ave. (between Post and Fisk sts.). ☎ **904/356-6857.** Admission $6 adults; $4 seniors over 65 and military; $3 students, $1 children under 5; free for everyone Tues after 4pm. Tues and Thurs 10am–9pm, Wed and Fri–Sat 10am–5pm, Sun noon–5pm.

Built on the grounds of a private Tudor mansion, this modestly sized but outstanding museum is worth a visit for anyone who appreciates the visual arts. The permanent collection encompasses works from 2000 B.C. to the present. It is especially rich in American impressionist paintings and includes an impressive collection of 18th-century porcelain and 18th- and early 19th-century Japanese Netsuke ivory carvings. Don't miss the stunning Italian and English gardens set on the scenic St. Johns River.

The Jacksonville Landing. 2 Independent Dr. (between Main and Pearl sts.), on the St. Johns River. ☎ **904/353-1188.** Free admission. Mon–Thurs 10am–8pm, Sat 10am–9pm, Sun noon–5:30pm; bars and restaurants open later. Parking $4.80 maximum daily charge. From I-95, take Exit 107 downtown to Main St., go over the Blue Bridge, turn left at Bay St., then go 2 blocks and make a left on Laura St., which dead-ends at the Landing. Parking lot is on east side of complex.

Resembling New York City's South Street Seaport, Boston's Faneuil Hall, and Baltimore's Inner Harbor, this glass-and-steel complex on the north bank of the river serves as the focus of downtown activity. There are more than 65 shops here, including some of the mall regulars, but judging from their turnover, shopping is secondary to dining and entertainment. You can choose from about half a dozen full-service restaurants plus an inexpensive food court with indoor and outdoor seating overlooking the river. Also on the premises are a couple of bars and a small maritime museum. The Landing is the scene of numerous special events, ranging from arts festivals to baseball-card shows, and outdoor rock, blues, country, and jazz concerts. Call to find out what's going on at the Landing during your stay.

✪ Jacksonville Zoo. 8605 Zoo Rd. ☎ **904/757-4462** or **904/757-4463.** Admission $6.50 adults, $4.50 seniors 65 and over, $4 children 3–12, free for children 2 and under; shows are free. Daily 9am–5pm (Memorial Day through Labor Day Fri–Sat until 8pm). Take I-95 north to Hecksher Dr. (Exit 124A) and follow the signs.

In the midst of a 10-year expansion plan, the Jacksonville Zoo is well on its way to becoming one of the country's best. The main exhibits are centered around an extensive and growing collection of African wildlife, including lions, impalas, ostriches, rhinos, elephants, antelopes, Nile crocodiles, cheetah, Kirk's dik-diks, monkeys, and South African crested porcupines. You'll enter the 73-acre park through the authentic thatched roof built in 1995 by 24 Zulu craftsmen. Whether you go on foot or by tram, allow at least 2 hours to tour this vast and lush zoo, just south of the airport. When you arrive, ask about current animal shows and special events. Strollers and wheelchairs are available for rent.

Southbank Riverwalk. On the south bank of the St. Johns River, flanking Main Street Bridge between San Marco Blvd. and Ferry St. ☎ **904/396-4900.** Take I-95 north to the Prudential Dr. exit, make a right, and follow the signs.

Bordering the St. Johns River directly opposite The Jacksonville Landing (see above), this 1.2-mile wooden zigzag boardwalk is usually filled with joggers, tourists, folks sitting on benches, and lovers walking hand in hand, all of them watching the riverboats, shorebirds, and downtown skyline reflected on the water. At 200 feet in diameter, the **Friendship Fountain** near the west end is the nation's largest self-contained fountain; it's especially beautiful at night when illuminated by 265 colored lights. Farther along, you'll pass military memorials, a small museum dedicated to the city's history, and the **Museum of Science & History of Jacksonville,** at Museum Circle and San Marco Boulevard (☎ **904/396-7062**). The latter is an interactive children's museum focusing on science and the history of northeast Florida. Admission is $6 adults, $4.50 seniors, $4 kids 3 to 12). Open Monday to Friday 10am to 5pm, Saturday 10am to 6pm, Sunday 1 to 6pm. The Riverwalk is the scene of seafood fests, parties, parades, and arts-and-crafts festivals. Hotels and restaurants line the route.

THE TIMUCUAN ECOLOGICAL & HISTORIC PRESERVE: A NEW BREED OF NATIONAL PARK

Named after the native people who inhabited Central and North Florida some 1,000 years before European settlers arrived, the **Timucuan Ecological and Historic Preserve** offers visitors an opportunity to explore untouched wilderness, historical buildings, and informative exhibits on the area's natural history. This 46,000-acre preserve is not your ordinary national park. Besides the enormous size, it's unusual in that it hasn't been hacked off from the rest of the community and drawn within arbitrary boundaries. The result is a vast, intriguing system of sites joined by rural roads alongside tumble-down fish camps, trailer parks, strip malls, condominiums, and stately old homes.

SOUTH OF THE RIVER

The prime attractions are on the south bank of the St. Johns River between downtown and the beaches. Your starting point here is the ✪ **Fort Caroline National Memorial,** on Ft. Caroline Road (☎ **904/641-7155**). This was the site of the 16th-century French Huguenot settlement that was wiped out by the Spanish who landed at St. Augustine. This two-thirds–size replica shows you what the original was like. You can see archaeological artifacts and two very well-produced half-hour videos highlighting the area. The fort and all other park facilities are open daily from 9am to 5pm except Christmas. Admission is free.

The fort sits at the northwestern edge of the 600-acre **Theodore Roosevelt Area,** a beautiful wood- and marshland rich in history and undisturbed since the Civil War. On a 2-mile hike along a centuries-old park trail, you'll see a wide variety of birds, wildflowers, and maritime hammock forest. Bring binoculars if you have them, since such birds as the endangered wood stork, great and snowy egrets, ospreys, hawks, and painted buntings make their home here in spring and summer. On the ground, you might catch sight of a gray fox or furry raccoon. You may also want to bring a blanket and picnic basket to spread out under the ancient oak trees that shade the banks of the St. Johns River, where recreational and commercial boats still ply the wide and winding waters. After the trail crosses Hammock Creek, you're in ancient Timucuan country, where their ancestors lived as far back as 500 B.C. Farther along is the site of a cabin in the wilderness that belonged to reclusive brothers Willie and Saxon Browne, who lived without the modern conveniences of indoor plumbing or electricity until the last brother's death in 1960. If you're here on a weekend, take the 1½-hour guided tours of the fort and Theodore Roosevelt Area, offered every Saturday and Sunday at 1pm (when weather and staffing permit); park rangers provide a wealth of fascinating information about history, flora, and fauna. Call the fort for details and schedules.

About ½ mile east of the fort is the **Ribault Monument** on St. Johns Bluff, erected in 1924 to commemorate the arrival in 1562 of French Huguenot Jean Ribault, who died defending Fort Caroline from the Spanish. It's worth a stop just for the dramatic view of the area.

To get here from downtown, take Atlantic Boulevard (Fla. 10) east, make a left on Monument Road, and turn right on Fort Caroline Road. The Theodore Roosevelt Area is entered from Mt. Pleasant Road, about 1 mile southeast of the fort; look for an inconspicuous sign on your left that says TRAILHEAD PARKING, and follow the narrow dirt road to the parking lot.

NORTH OF THE RIVER

On the north side of the river, history buffs also will appreciate the ✪ **Zephaniah Kingsley Plantation,** at 11676 Palmetto Ave. on Fort George Island (☎ **904/ 251-3537**). A winding 3-mile road runs under a canopy of trees with dense tropical foliage on either side to the remains of this 19th-century plantation owned by Zephaniah Kingsley, a white man who held some seemingly contradictory views on race. Although he owned more than 200 slaves, he believed that "the coloured race were superior to us, physically and morally." He married a Senegalese woman—one of his former slaves—and ultimately moved his family to Haiti in 1837 to escape what he called the "spirit of intolerant injustice" at home. The National Park Service maintains the well-preserved two-story residence, kitchen house, barn/carriage house, and remnants of 23 slave cabins built of "tabby mortar"—oyster shell and sand. A self-guided tour is the best way to see it all; clear and informative signs tell the history of this former citrus, cotton, and sugarcane farm, and of the workers who built it. Allot about an hour. A well-stocked book and gift shop will keep you even longer. Rangers sometimes offer interpretive programs.

To get here from I-95, take Heckscher Drive (Fla. 105) east and follow the signs. From Fort Caroline, take Fla. 9A north over the St. Johns River to Heckscher Drive east. The plantation is about 12 miles east of Fla. 9A, on the left. From the beaches, take Fla. A1A to the St. Johns River Ferry, and ride it from Mayport to Fort George; the road is ½ mile east of the ferry landing.

For more information, write to **The Timucuan Ecological & Historic Preserve,** 13165 Mt. Pleasant Rd., Jacksonville, FL 32225.

HITTING THE BEACH

You can fish, swim, snorkel, sail, sunbathe, or stroll on the sand dunes (at least from Mar to Nov, since winter can get downright chilly here). They're all just a 20- to 30-minute drive east of downtown at Jacksonville's four beach communities.

Atlantic Boulevard (Fla. 10) will take you to **Atlantic Beach** and **Neptune Beach.** The boulevard divides the two towns, and where it meets the ocean you'll come to **Town Center,** a quaint community with a number of shops, restaurants, pubs, the Sea Horse Oceanfront Inn, and the Sea Turtle Inn (see "Where to Stay" below). You won't need your car to hit the beach, shop, dine, or imbibe here.

Beach Boulevard (U.S. 90) dead-ends at **Jacksonville Beach,** where'll you find beach concessions, rental shops, and a fishing pier. This is also the most popular local surfing beach.

To the south, the freeway-grade ✪ **J. Turner Butler Boulevard** (Fla. 202) also leads to Jacksonville Beach, but a right turn there will take you to **Ponte Vedra Beach.** This ritzy enclave actually is in St. Johns County (St. Augustine), but it's so much closer to Jacksonville that I've included it in this chapter. Here you'll find the Sawgrass Marriott and the Ponte Vedra Inn & Club, both with outstanding golf courses (see "Where to Stay" below).

OUTDOOR PURSUITS & SPECTATOR SPORTS

BICYCLING, BALLOONS, BOATS & SKYDIVING   A one-stop outfitter for all kinds of outdoor fun is **Outdoor Adventures** (☎ 904/393-9030), offering kayaking and canoeing, ballooning, bicycle trips, and other outdoor adventures, both day trips and longer camping trips. Call for schedules, prices, and reservations. If you want to learn to skydive, **Blue Sky Adventures** (☎ 904/272-4864) offers parachute training.

FISHING   You can go **fishing** for whiting, mackerel, flounder, bluefish, catfish, and more off the **Jacksonville Beach Fishing Pier,** just south of Beach Boulevard at 6th Avenue South (☎ 904/246-6001). No license is required, and rods, reels, and bait can be rented on the premises. The pier is open daily: from 6am to 11pm Memorial Day to Labor Day, until 9pm the rest of the year. It costs $4 for adults to fish the pier, $2 for children 8 and under and seniors over 60. Sightseers pay 50¢.

Another option is to fish for red snapper, grouper, sea bass, small sharks, amberjack, and more, 15 to 30 miles offshore in the Atlantic Ocean aboard the *King Neptune,* a 65-foot air-conditioned deep-sea party boat. The 8am to 5pm trips depart at 8am daily from Monty's Marina, 4378 Ocean St. (Fla. A1A), ½ mile south of the Mayport Ferry landing (☎ 904/246-7575). The price is $40 for adults, $35 seniors, $30 for children 6 to 12, including all bait and tackle. You don't need a license, but reservations are required.

GOLF   Golfers will be glad to know that Jacksonville offers a great variety of public golf courses, many of which are ranked among the top in the country. Of course, the most famous course is the TPC at the Marriott Sawgrass, in Ponte Vedra, located in the next county and open only to resort guests (see "Where to Stay" below). Top courses open to the public include the semiprivate **Cimarrone,** at 2690 Cimarrone Blvd. (☎ 904/287-2000), a fast and watery course with affordable greens fees ranging from $30 to $50; and the public **Golf Club of Jacksonville,** at 10440 Tournament Lane (☎ 904/779-0800), which is managed by the PGA Tour. It's a great bargain, with rates ranging from $30 to $40.

On your way out to the beach, the semiprivate **Windsor Parke Golf Club,** at 4747 Hodges Blvd., at Turner Butler Boulevard (☎ 904/223-GOLF), is one of the most challenging and scenic courses in Jacksonville. Designed by Arthur Hill, the 6,740 yards of green are surrounded by towering pines and lots of water. After it opened in 1991, *Golf Digest* rated it the best new course in the Southeast. Fees are usually less than $45 and include a cart, even on the weekends. Nonmembers should call 4 or 5 days in advance for tee times.

For a review of other options in Northeast Florida, call ☎ 800/555-0807 to request a copy of *Florida Golf Vacations.* And be on the lookout for the free *Golfer's Guide* in the visitor centers and hotel lobbies (see "The Active Vacation Planner," in chapter 2, for information about ordering copies).

HORSEBACK RIDING   For a scenic ride along the sand and dunes, call **Sawgrass Stables,** 23900 Marsh Landing Pkwy., off Fla. A1A in Ponte Vedra Beach (☎ **904/ 285-3791**). Call for rates and reservations. Lessons are also available.

SPECTATOR SPORTS   The 73,000-seat **Alltel Municipal Stadium,** 1 Stadium Place, at East Duval and Haines streets (☎ **904/630-3901** for information, or 904/353-3309 to charge tickets), hosts the annual Florida-Georgia football game every October, other college football games September to December, motor-sports events, and the National Football League's **Jacksonville Jaguars** (☎ **800/618-8005** or 904/633-6000 for ticket information). One of the stadium's biggest draws is the **Toyota Gator Bowl,** usually on New Year's Day (see "Florida Calendar of Events," in chapter 2).

Adjacent to the stadium, and under the same auspices, is the 10,600-seat **Jacksonville Veterans Memorial Coliseum,** 1145 E. Adams St. (☎ **904/630-3900** for information, or 904/353-3309 to charge tickets). It's the home of the **Jacksonville Lizards** East Coast Hockey team, and a venue for NHL exhibition games, college basketball games, ice-skating exhibitions, wrestling matches, and various family shows.

Jax has yet to get a big-league baseball team, but you can see the **Jacksonville Suns,** a Detroit Tigers affiliate, play their Class AA minor-league games from April to early September at Wolfson Park, 1201 E. Duval St. (☎ **904/358-2842**). Tickets range from $4 to $7.

WATER & ENTERTAINMENT PARK   **Adventure Landing,** 1944 Beach Blvd., at 20th Street, Jacksonville Beach (☎ **904/246-4386**) is a pirate theme park with all kinds of fun activities for kids and adults. A giant water park, open March through September, is a great way to cool off. Or, you can try your hand in the huge arcade with video games, laser tag, virtual-reality machines, and carnival-style games. Outside, you can ride the Go-Karts or bumper boats, play miniature golf, and take some swings in the batting cages. Admission to the water park is about $16 for adults, $13 for children under 48 inches, free for children 3 and under. There are separate charges for activities.

SHOPPING & BROWSING

Jacksonville has shopping opportunities galore, including Jacksonville Landing (see "Exploring the Area," above); an upscale mall, **The Avenues Mall,** south of town at 10300 Southside Blvd.; and a number of flea markets, including the **Beach Boulevard Flea and Farmer's Market,** on Beach Boulevard (Fla. 90) (☎ **904/645-5961**). More than 600 vendors show up daily, from 9am to 5pm, to sell their wares in a partially covered facility.

The **San Marco Square** shopping district, at San Marco and Atlantic boulevards south of the river, is a quaint shopping district in the middle of a stunning residential area. Shops in meticulously refashioned Mediterranean revival buildings sell antiques and home furnishings, as well as clothing, books, and records.

Another worthwhile neighborhood to explore is the **Avondale/Riverside** historic district southwest of downtown on St. Johns Avenue between Talbot Avenue and Boone Park, on the north bank of the river. More than 60 boutiques, antique stores, art galleries, shoe stores, and cafes line the wide, tree-lined avenue.

Nearby, the younger set hangs out at **Five Points,** on Park Street, where used record stores, vintage clothiers, coffee shops, smoke shops, and funky art galleries stay open late.

Like St. Augustine, Jacksonville is a mecca for chocoholics, particularly **Peterbrooke Chocolatier Production Center,** 1470 San Marco Blvd., in the San Marco

Square neighborhood (☎ 904/398-4812). If you've never tried chocolate-covered popcorn or pretzels, this is the place. Open Monday to Friday from 10am to 5pm.

WHERE TO STAY

I've arranged the accommodations listed below geographically, in and around downtown first, followed by the beach scene. The suburbs have dozens more to choose from, especially along I-95. Many are clustered south of downtown in the **Southpoint** (Exit 101, Turner Butler Boulevard/Fla. 202) and **Baymeadows** (Exit 101, Baymeadows Road/Fla. 152) suburban areas. These locales have a multitude of chain restaurants, and you can hop on the highways and zoom to the beach or downtown— although you aren't really at either one if you stay out here. Tops is the **Jacksonville Marriott at Southpoint,** 4670 Salisbury Rd. (☎ 800/228-9290 or 904/296-2222), among the area's best all-around hotels. Also here are a comfortable and inexpensive **Baymont Inn & Suites,** 3199 Hartley Rd. (☎ 800/428-3488 or 904/268-9999); a recently enlarged and renovated **Embassy Suites** at 9300 Baymeadows Rd., east of I-95 (☎ 800/362-2779 or 904/731-3555); and a **Motel 6,** at 8285 Dix Ellis Trail (☎ 800/4-MOTEL-6 or 904/73l-8400).

For a complete list of lodgings, contact the Jacksonville and the Beaches Convention & Visitors Bureau (see "Essentials" above).

Note that rates in the downtown hotels are higher midweek when rooms are in demand by business travelers. Beach accommodations are somewhat less expensive in the cold months from December through March.

IN JACKSONVILLE

The House on Cherry Street. 1844 Cherry St. (on the St. Johns River), Jacksonville, FL 32205. ☎ 904/384-1999. Fax 904/384-5013. 4 units (all with bathroom). A/C TV. $79–$99 double. Rates include continental breakfast. AE, MC, V.

This colonial-style wood-frame house, nestled in a tree-shaded cul-de-sac on the St. Johns River, is ideal for a romantic B&B vacation (no small children are accepted). French doors open to a delightful screened-in back porch furnished with rocking chairs; it overlooks an expanse of tree-shaded lawn (where guests play croquet) leading to the river. You might select the Rose or Duck rooms, both with canopied four-poster beds and river views. Ducks are rather a theme here, with hundreds of antique decoys on display. All accommodations offer adjacent sitting rooms and ceiling fans and are supplied with fresh flowers, books, and magazines. Complimentary wine and hot and cold hors d'oeuvres are presented daily at 6pm on the patio or in the dining room. An upstairs refrigerator is stocked with free soft drinks and beer, and there are bicycles for guest use. Genial owners/hosts Carol and Merrill Anderson keep a gentle pet greyhound, formerly a racing dog, named Streak, but don't bring your own pet. No smoking is permitted.

Jacksonville Hilton & Towers. 1201 Riverplace Blvd. (at Main St. on Southbank Riverwalk), Jacksonville, FL 32207. ☎ 800/HILTONS or 904/393-8800. Fax 904/398-5570. 310 units. A/C TV TEL. $105–$180 double. AE, DC, DISC, MC, V. Valet parking $8; self-parking $6.

Designated as a Hilton in 1997 after extensive renovation, this 10-story tower features the Elvis Presley Suite, where "the King" purportedly stayed half a dozen times between 1955 and 1976, when this establishment was known as the Jacksonville Hotel. If you can afford its $300-a-night price tag, you'll see some of Elvis's million-seller gold records mounted on the walls, and watch some of his movies on the suite's two VCRs. It and the other units have dark wood furniture, two phones with dataports, irons and boards, hair dryers, coffeemakers, smallish marble-tiled baths, and balconies overlooking the river (those on the west end catch traffic noise from the Main Street Bridge below). A branch of Ruth's Chris Steakhouse offers expensive but extraordinarily tender beef, while a lobby cafe with open kitchen feeds the rest of us. There are an outdoor pool and an exercise room for keeping fit. Other amenities include concierge, limited room service, newspaper delivery, business center, and conference rooms.

Omni Jacksonville Hotel. 245 Water St. (between Pearl and Hogan sts.), Jacksonville, FL 32202. ☎ **800/THE-OMNI** or 904/355-OMNI. Fax 904/791-4809. 354 units. A/C MINIBAR TV TEL. $79–$169 double. AE, DC, DISC, MC, V. Valet parking $10 weekdays, $8 weekends; self-parking $6.

Directly across the street from the Florida Times Union Center for the Performing Arts (see "Jacksonville After Dark," below) and a block west of The Jacksonville Landing, downtown's best digs caters primarily to a corporate clientele who fill the meeting facilities during the week. The spacious guest rooms have blond-wood furnishings, plenty of lighting, and all the practical necessities you could ask for, including a minibar, a writing desk, two phones with voice mail and dataports, hair dryers, a fully prepped coffeemaker, large closets, and an iron and ironing board. Dining options include the reasonably priced Juliette's Restaurant & Bistro, providing a locally famous pasta bar as well as an extensive room-service menu until 12:45am. Sports-minded guests will appreciate the jogging and walking maps provided in each room, the outdoor swimming pool, and the well-equipped but closet-sized exercise room.

✪ Plantation Manor Inn. 1630 Copeland St. (between Oak and Park sts.), Jacksonville, FL 32204. ☎ **904/384-4630.** Fax 904/387-0960. 9 units. A/C TV TEL. $105–$160 double. Rates include full breakfast. AE, DC, MC, V.

The setting for many weddings and special events, this three-story plantation-style home in the historic Riverside district is just 10 minutes from downtown. Its homey interior, outfitted with a mix of thrift-store antiques, features glossy pine floors and gorgeous cypress paneling, wainscoting, and carved moldings. Breakfast, including fresh-baked muffins and breads, is served in a lovely dining room with a working fireplace. When the sun is shining, take the morning meal on an enclosed brick patio, a delightful setting with ivy-covered walls, flower beds, and garden furnishings under the shade of a massive oak tree. The patio also contains a lap pool and whirlpool spa. On the second floor you can enjoy a big wraparound porch with seating amid potted geraniums, hibiscus, and bougainvillea.

AT THE BEACHES

A dozen modest hotels line Jacksonville Beach's 1st Street, along the Atlantic Ocean, including **Holiday Inn Sunspree** (☎ **800/HOLIDAY** or 904/249-9071), where all rooms come with refrigerators, microwaves, and coffee pots; **Days Inn Oceanfront Resort** (☎ **800/321-2037** or 904/249-7924); and **Ramada Resort** (☎ **800/ 2-RAMADA** or 904/241-5333).

Worth checking out is the **Sea Turtle Inn,** 1 Ocean Blvd., Atlantic Beach, FL 32233 (☎ **800/874-6000** or 904/249-7402; fax 904/247-1517; www.seaturtle. com), an older property which was due to be gutted and considerably upgraded in 1999. This eight-story hotel enjoys an enviable location at the ocean end of Atlantic Avenue, in the quaint Town Center neighborhood. Although they have different city addresses, it's directly across the boulevard from the Sea Horse Oceanfront Inn (see below).

Comfort Inn Oceanfront. 1515 N. 1st St. (2 blocks east of Fla. A1A), Jacksonville Beach, FL 32250. ☎ **800/654-8776** or 904/241-2311. Fax 904/249-3830. E-mail: jabc1@aol.com. 180 units. A/C TV TEL. $89–$139 double; $140–$175 suite. Rates include continental breakfast. AE, DC, DISC, MC, V.

Completely renovated in 1998, this is one of the best-priced options on the beach-front, offering rooms with balconies or screened patios. Microwave and/or refrigerator units are available for an extra charge. An especially good deal here is a honeymoon suite with whirlpool tub and living-room area. Continental breakfast and light fare are served in a small poolside dining room. An oceanfront lounge features live music for dancing on weekend nights from April to Labor Day. There are a large pool with rock waterfalls and a palm-fringed sundeck, a secluded grotto whirlpool, a small fitness room, a gift/sundries shop, and a multicourt sand volleyball park.

Sea Horse Oceanfront Inn. 120 Atlantic Blvd. (at beach end of Atlantic Blvd.), Neptune Beach, FL 32266. ☎ **800/881-2330** or 904/246-2175. Fax 904/246-4256. www. seahorseresort.com. 38 units. A/C TV TEL. $69–$109 double; $175–$250 penthouse suite for up to 6. AE, DC, DISC, MC, V.

One of the anchors of quaint Town Center, this well-run beachfront property offers clean rooms with ocean views from balconies or patios. Families will appreciate the six units here with kitchenettes, not to mention a nice-size oceanfront pool, shuffleboard, picnic tables, and a barbecue grill. And young couples will enjoy proximity to some of Jacksonville's top nightspots. If you have a large family or group, consider the vast and lovely third-floor penthouse—it has a big living room and dining area, a full kitchen, a separate bedroom as well as sofa beds, and a huge balcony furnished with a dining table and chaise longues. A coffee shop adjoins the motel, and Town Center's restaurants and bars are across the street.

AT PONTE VEDRA BEACH

✪ **Ponte Vedra Inn & Club.** 200 Ponte Vedra Blvd. (off Fla. A1A), Ponte Vedra Beach, FL 32082. ☎ **800/234-7842** or 904/285-1111. Fax 904/285-2111. 202 units. A/C MINIBAR TV TEL. $150–$390 suite. Golf packages available. AE, DC, DISC, MC, V.

This luxurious 300-acre private country club and spa is the perfect place to pamper yourself. The Ponte Vedra Inn is ultra-elegant from the moment you drive up to its manicured front lawn, which doubles as a putting green. The property has a private sand beach and boardwalk. Inside, a charming lobby adjoins the lodgelike Great Lounge, with overstuffed sofas and armchairs and massive fireplaces at either end.

The spacious rooms, all with furnished patios or balconies, are individually decorated; some have four-poster or sleigh beds. In-room amenities include wet bars, coffeemakers, safes, and ceiling fans. You'll find a hair dryer, a scale, luxury bath products, and a plush terry robe in the bath, as well as a cosmetic mirror and a double sink in your large dressing room. Microwave ovens and small refrigerators are available on request.

A gorgeous on-premises spa offers oceanview massage rooms, hair-salon services, herbal and seaweed wraps, facials, hydrotherapy, fitness training, waxing, manicures, pedicures, nutrition consultations, and much more. Treat yourself to a "day of beauty."

Dining/Diversions: Breakfast is served in a formal dining room. Steak and seafood highlight the menu at the more casual dinner-only restaurant. A golf-club restaurant, with an adjoining bar, overlooks the greens and a lagoon. Another elegant dining room, with tiered oceanview seating, features American/continental lunches and dinners; a pianist entertains at dinner, and there's dancing on Friday and Saturday nights to a live trio in the adjoining lounge.

Amenities: Concierge, 24-hour room service, nightly turndown, shoe shine, complimentary newspaper each morning, dry-cleaning and laundry services, twice-daily maid service, baby-sitting, express checkout, valet parking, courtesy car or limo, 3 outdoor swimming pools (one Olympic size), kiddie pool, oceanfront whirlpool, 2 championship 36-hole golf courses, 15 tennis courts (7 lighted), golf/tennis pro shops and instruction, upscale shops, florist, water-sports equipment rental, bicycle rental, children's programs, steam, sauna, extensive 10,000-square-foot health club, sand volleyball court, business center, secretarial services, conference center, self-service Laundromat, library, beauty salon.

✪ **Sawgrass Marriott.** 1000 PGA Tour Blvd. (off Fla. A1A between U.S. 210 and J. Turner Butler Blvd.), Ponte Vedra Beach, FL 32082. ☎ **800/457-GOLF**, 800/228-9290, or 904/285-7777. Fax 904/285-0906. 508 units (including 160 condos). A/C MINIBAR TV TEL. $120–$309 double; $145–$600 suites and condos. Golf packages available. AE, DC, DISC, MC, V. Valet parking $9; free self-parking.

The nation's second-largest golf resort, this duffer's paradise is virtually surrounded by 99 holes, including the TPC-Stadium Course, home of the annual Players Championship every March. In fact, it has appeared on every critic's "best of" list since it was built by Pete Dye in 1980.

The guest rooms in the main building have two phones, hair dryers, irons and boards, and coffeemakers. Best for families are the one- and two-bedroom condo apartments on or ponte near a golf course. They offer fully equipped kitchens, living rooms, and large furnished patios or balconies. Especially luxurious are the one- to three-bedroom beachfront villas, which sport huge kitchens, living rooms with working fireplaces, full dining rooms, and large screened wooden decks.

Dining/Diversions: The resort's gourmet dining room serves steaks and seafood. The Cabana Club restaurant, a 10-minute drive from the resort, has simple beach food and light snacks downstairs and nouvelle cuisine upstairs; an outdoor patio and an adjoining lounge feature nightly music and dancing.

Amenities: Concierge, room service, dry-cleaning and laundry service, babysitting, secretarial services, express checkout, valet parking, complimentary shuttle to/from the beach and golf courses, newspaper delivery, nightly turndown on request, airport transfer available, rental VCRs, 2 swimming pools (one Olympic size), kiddie pool, use of 2½-mile private beach and pool at the nearby Cabana Club, 2 first-rate health clubs, whirlpool, sauna, bicycle rental, 5 championship golf courses, golf/tennis pro shop and teaching pros/clinics, 4 driving ranges, 6 putting greens, children's program offering daily activities for ages 3 to 12, recreation room, playground. There are also a teen program, business center, conference rooms, self-service Laundromat, 8 tennis courts, sports-equipment rentals (windsurfing boards, bicycles, fishing poles), lagoons stocked for fishing, nature and biking trails, horseback riding, an extensive complex of boutiques and specialty shops for sporting equipment, gifts, and resort wear.

WHERE TO DINE

Though Jacksonville was once a town where any dish other than Southern fried chicken or catfish was considered exotic, its dining scene is evolving into culinary diversity. The convention and visitors bureau's annual guide (see "Essentials" above) contains a complete list of restaurants, which now includes a handful of sushi bars, one or two authentic Mexican eateries, a few Jewish delis, and some Cuban diners. The area even has half a dozen Thai restaurants, such as Old Siam, listed below.

IN JACKSONVILLE

Don't forget that **The Jacksonville Landing** on the downtown riverfront has several full-service restaurants and an inexpensive food court with outdoor seating (see "Exploring the Area," above).

For more choices, check listings in the "Shorelines" and "Go" sections of Friday's *Florida-Times Union*, and in *FOLIOWEEKLY*, the free local alternative paper which is available at restaurants, hotels, and nightspots all over town.

○ Biscotti's. 3556 St. Johns Ave. (between Talbot and Ingleside aves. in the Avondale section). ☎ **904/387-2060.** Reservations not accepted. Sandwiches and salads $5–$7; pastas and pizzas $7–$10; nightly fish special from $12. AE, DC, DISC, MC, V. Tues–Thurs 7am–10pm, Fri 7am–midnight, Sat 8am–midnight, Sun 8am–3pm. CALIFORNIA/ECLECTIC.

This brick-walled little neighborhood gem might have come out of New York's East Village, San Francisco's downtown, or Washington's Georgetown. A young and hip wait staff is pleasant and well informed. Daily specials, like pan-seared salmon or pork loin, are always fresh and beautifully presented. The huge and inventive salads are especially good: Try the Oriental version with chicken breast, orange slices, roasted peppers, and creamy sesame dressing. Pizzas, too, are served with wonderfully exotic and delicious toppings—ever try guacamole and black beans on your slice? On warm days choose a seat outside for great people-watching.

○ Cafe Carmon. 1986 San Marco Blvd. (between Carlo St. and Naldo Ave.). ☎ **904/399-4488.** Reservations not accepted. Sandwiches $7–$8.50; main courses $7–$15. AE, DC, DISC, MC, V. Mon–Thurs 11am–11pm, Fri–Sat 11am–midnight, Sun 11am–9pm. FLORIDA CAFE.

A short drive from the Southbank Riverwalk, this comfy and casual restaurant is located in the heart of the San Marco Square shopping and dining district. In the daytime it's a mecca for shoppers and professionals; most nights the place is jammed with an after-theater crowd dropping in for cappuccinos and delectable desserts. The inside is sparsely decorated in black-and-white tile; the brick patio out front offers cafe seating. At lunch or dinner, you can order delicious salads, such as sautéed goat cheese with sun-dried tomatoes, toasted hazelnuts, cilantro, and mixed greens in a tangy vinaigrette. Generous-sized dinner options include a grilled, sautéed, or blackened fresh catch (often grouper) prepared Provençal, in beurre blanc sauce, or with pineapple salsa. Great lunch fare here, too.

River City Brewing Company. 835 Museum Circle (on Southbank Riverwalk). ☎ **904/398-2299.** Reservations only for parties of 8 or more. Main courses $16–$24; sandwiches and salads $6–$12; Sun brunch buffet $16 adults, $14 seniors, $8 children 3–12. AE, DC, DISC, MC, V. Dining room Mon–Thurs 11am–3pm and 5–10pm, Fri–Sat 11am–3pm and 5–11pm, Sun 10:30am–2:30pm and 5–10pm. Bar (light fare) Sun–Thurs 11am–midnight, Fri–Sat 11am–2am. CALIFORNIA/LOUISIANA.

Occupying a prime location on the Southbank Riverwalk, this gorgeous restaurant and microbrewery is an excellent choice for lunch or dinner. Its glass walls provide most tables with dramatic waterfront and skyline views. Or for an even better vantage point, sit outside on the enormous covered deck. Everyone raves about the super pastas, steaks, and seafood here. Appetizers are excellent, too, including crab cakes delicately sautéed and served with a mix of baby greens and a tangy mango salsa, and Asian pot stickers filled with morsels of shrimp and vegetables. For a main course, try the Cajun chicken linguine with mushrooms and ham in a spicy cream sauce, or snapper baked in paper with julienne vegetables and white wine sauce.

While you can easily drop a bundle in the main dining room, you can concoct an inexpensive meal in the Brew Haus, a large sports bar which opens to the big deck and riverbank. The menu out here features appetizers, soups, and salads from the dining room, plus a few sandwiches ranging from kosher hot dogs to fried, grilled, or blackened fish. Bands play on the deck weekend evenings and on Sundays when the Jaguars are playing.

Sunday brunch brings incredible buffets with fresh fruits and vegetables, bagels with smoked salmon and cream cheese, French toast, dozens of salads, and a carving station with honey-baked ham and prime rib. There is also a selection of decadent desserts.

AT THE BEACHES

In addition to the Ragtime Tavern (see below), you'll have several dining (and drinking) choices in the brick storefronts of Town Center, the old-time beach village at the end of Atlantic Boulevard.

○ **The Homestead.** 1712 Beach Blvd. (next to Adventure Landing, between 15th and 19th sts.), Jacksonville Beach. ☎ **904/249-5240.** Reservations only for large parties. Full dinners $7–$14. AE, DISC, MC, V. Mon–Sat 4:30pm–midnight, Sun noon–midnight. SOUTHERN.

This Jacksonville institution is usually packed with regulars waiting for a table in this log cabin–like restaurant that has been serving big eaters since 1947. There's a good reason for the greasy atmosphere, for the big draw here is Southern fried chicken served in a skillet with homemade buttermilk biscuits and fresh honey, coleslaw, black-eyed peas, rice and gravy, creamed peas, and a choice of daily vegetables. Other down-home favorites are meatloaf and chicken or beef pot pies, with all the fixings. The narrow 50-foot-long copper-topped bar is a popular hangout for local drinkers and the major nighttime haunt of celebrity golfers during Tournament Players Club championships.

○ **Island Grille.** 981 N. 1st St. (at 9th Ave.), Jacksonville Beach. ☎ **904/241-1881.** Reservations recommended. Main courses $10–$30; main-course salads $9–$12. AE, DC, DISC, MC, V. Mon–Tues 4:30–10pm, Wed–Thurs 11:30am–10pm, Fri–Sat 11:30am–11pm, Sun 11:30am–10pm. (Bar open to 1:30am.) FLORIBBEAN/CONTINENTAL.

On the beach but away from the crowds, this is one of the area's most popular dining venues, serving a varied menu with lots of innovative, always-fresh seafood, as well as basic offerings like shrimp scampi, New York strip steak, pasta primavera, and even burgers. The many salads, including one topped with sashimi-quality tuna, are delicious and large. The appetizers here are so good you might just graze; they range from Bahamian conch fritters served with spicy pink rémoulade to escargots served in mushroom caps. You can enjoy piano music Wednesday through Saturday evenings.

Old Siam. 1716 N. Third St. (Fla. A1A, in Holiday Plaza shopping center, between 16th and 17th aves. N.), Jacksonville Beach. ☎ **904/247-7763.** Reservations only for parties of 6 or more. Main courses $8–$16. AE, DISC, MC, V. Mon–Thurs 5–10pm, Fri–Sat 5–11pm, Sun 5–9:30pm. THAI.

The best of the area's Thai restaurants, Pam Souvannasoth's trendy little enclave serves fine cuisine from his homeland and a good selection of wines to match its spicy-yet-subtle flavors. Pam's signature dish is his seafood special: shrimp, sea scallops, mussels, squid, and crab claws in a red chile sauce accented with sweet basil. The chiles in his "number 3" spice level (out of six) touched my tongue but did not overwhelm the other seasonings. Standard favorites like Pad Thai are light and perfectly balanced with sweet and slightly sour fish sauce.

Ragtime Tavern & Taproom. 207 Atlantic Blvd. (at 1st Ave.), Atlantic Beach. ☎ **904/ 241-6406.** Reservations not accepted but call for preferred seating. Main courses $11–$22; sandwiches and salads $6–$8. AE, DC, DISC, MC, V. Sun–Thurs 11am–10:30pm, Fri–Sat 11am–11pm. SEAFOOD/PASTA.

In the heart of Town Center, this lively tavern offers six handcrafted brews, including a refreshing pilsner known as Dolphin's Breath. You can imbibe at one of the two British-style stand-up bars on either end of the building. In between, a rabbit's warren of dining rooms provides fine enough fare to keep it filled with local professional types right through the cool winter months. A variety of appetizers includes the usual conch fritters and spicy chicken wings, as well as more-entertaining items, such as wontons stuffed with crabmeat and served with a spicy mustard sauce. Likewise is the appetizer-or dinner-size curried spinach salad (go easy with the piquant dressing less it overwhelm the subtle curry flavor). For a main course, you can select from several treatments of fish, shrimp, chicken, and pastas, but save room for some New Orleans–style beignets for dessert. Also from the Big Easy, po-boy sandwiches are served at all hours. Good local bands make music here Thursday through Sunday evenings.

○ **Singleton's Seafood Shack.** 4728 Ocean St. (Fla. A1A, at St. Johns River Ferry landing), Mayport. ☎ **904/246-4442.** Full dinners $9–$16; sandwiches $3–$6. AE, DISC, MC, V. Sun–Thurs 10am–9pm, Fri–Sat 10am–10pm. SEAFOOD.

Capt. Ray Singleton has been serving fresh catches from his rustic fish camp since 1969. And rustic it is, constructed primarily of unpainted, well-weathered plywood nailed to two-by-fours. Unlike most other fish camps that tend to overbatter and overfry everything that comes into the kitchen, Singleton's offers a variety of preparations for every imaginable kind of seafood. A taste of any of the fresh catches like the blackened mahimahi or Cajun shrimp will confirm it. Of course, the fried standbys like conch fritters, shrimp, clam strips, and squid are available, too. Along with your entree, try the grouper or cobia with mushroom and wine sauce—your Styrofoam plate will come stacked with a choice of side items like black beans and rice, coleslaw, fries, and hush puppies. You can also choose from a selection of chicken. Just off the screened waterside deck, whose picnic tables overlook the marinas alongside the river, check out the captain's model boat "museum," a wood shop filled with his finely carved ships.

JACKSONVILLE AFTER DARK

In addition to the spots recommended below, check listings in the "Shorelines" and "Go" sections of Friday's *Florida-Times Union,* and *FOLIOWEEKLY,* the free local alternative paper, available at restaurants, hotels, and all over town.

THE PERFORMING ARTS   With the 73,000-seat **Alltell Stadium,** at East Duval and Haines streets (☎ **904/630-3900**), the 10,600-seat **Jacksonville Veterans Memorial Coliseum,** 1145 E. Adams St. (☎ **904/630-3900** for information or 904/353-3309 to charge tickets), and the 3,200-seat **Florida Times Union Center for the Performing Arts,** 300 Water St., between Hogan and Pearl streets (☎ **904/ 630-3900**), Jacksonville has plenty of seats for concerts, touring Broadway shows, dance companies, and big-name performers. Check the local papers mentioned above for current offerings, or call the *Times-Union's* automated information service for up-to-date schedules (☎ **904/355-1500,** ext. 7450).

THE BAR SCENE   You will find several libation options downtown at **Jacksonville Landing** (see "Exploring the Area," above), including a lively waterfront **Hooters** (☎ 904/356-5400), plus free outdoor rock, blues, country, and jazz concerts every Friday and Saturday night except during winter. The downtown post-teen crowd hangs at **Moto Lounge,** 214 W. Adams St. (☎ **904/355-6686**), where local and regional bands perform.

In the Avondale neighborhood, **Partners,** 3585 St. Johns Ave. at Ingleside Avenue (☎ 904/387-3585), has a mellow piano-bar ambience, innovative American food, and live jazz Wednesday to Saturday nights, making it a local favorite.

Out at Town Center, at the ocean end of Atlantic Boulevard, one of several popular spots is **Ragtime Tavern & Taproom** (see "Where to Dine" above), where local groups play live jazz and blues Wednesday to Sunday nights. Weekends, especially, the place is really jumping and the crowd is young; but it's lively rather than rowdy. Across the street is the **Sun Dog Diner,** at 207 Atlantic Blvd. (☎ **904/241-8221**), with nightly acoustic music and decent diner food. If these don't fit your mood, there are several more nightspots in Town Center.

The favorite pub in Jacksonville Beach, **Sloppy Joe's,** 200 N. 1st St. (☎ **904/ 270-1767**), is an offshoot of the Key West institution.

5 Amelia Island

32 miles NE of Jacksonville, 192 miles NE of Orlando, 372 miles N of Miami

With 13 beautiful miles of beach and a quaint Victorian town, Amelia Island is a charming getaway about a 45-minute drive northeast of downtown Jacksonville. Overall, this Manhattan-size barrier island has more in common with the Low Country of Georgia (across Cumberland Sound from here) and South Carolina than with its compatriots in Florida. It's more like St. Simons Island in Georgia or Hilton Head Island in South Carolina.

Amelia itself has three distinct personalities. Its southern third is occupied by Amelia Island Plantation, an exclusive real-estate development built in a forest of twisted, moss-laden live oaks. Here you will find world-class tennis and golfing at two of Florida's most luxurious resorts. The island's middle is a much more modest beach community, with a mix of affordable motels, cottages, condos, and a seaside inn. At its northern end, the bayside town of ✪ **Fernandina Beach** boasts a 50-block area of gorgeous Victorian and Queen Anne homes listed in the National Register of Historic Places.

The town's Victorian district dates from the late 19th century, when Amelia's timber, phosphate, and naval-stores industries boomed. Back then the town was an active seaport, with 14 foreign consuls in residence. Even earlier, a railroad went from here 155 miles across Florida to Cedar Key; it was part of a planned worldwide trade network cut short by the Civil War. You'll see (and occasionally smell) the paper mills which still stand near the small seaport here. The island experienced another economic explosion in the 1970s and 1980s, when real-estate developers built the condos, the cottages, and two big resorts. In recent years, Fernandina Beach has seen another big boom, this time in bed-and-breakfast establishments.

ESSENTIALS

GETTING THERE   The island is served by **Jacksonville International Airport** (see "Essentials," in section 4, above). Skirting the Atlantic in places, the scenic drive here from downtown Jacksonville is via Heckscher Drive (Fla. 105) and Fla. A1A. From the beaches, take Fla. A1A north and the St. John's River Ferry. The fast, four-lane way is via I-95 north and the Buccaneer Trail (Fla. A1A) east.

VISITOR INFORMATION   For advance information, contact the **Amelia Island–Fernandina Beach–Yulee Chamber of Commerce,** 102 Centre St. (P.O. Box 472), Fernandina Beach, FL 32035 (☎ **800/2-AMELIA** or 904/277-0717; fax 904/261-6997; www.ameliaisland.org). The chamber's visitor information center, in the old train station at the bay end of Centre Street, is open Monday to Friday from 9am to 5pm.

GETTING AROUND   There's no public transportation on this 13-mile-long island, so you'll need a vehicle. The **Old Towne Carriage Company** (☎ **904/ 277-1555**) offers narrated, horse-drawn carriage tours of Fernandina Beach's historic district, leaving from the waterfront on Centre Street. They close for 2 months during the winter when the horses are put out to pasture. Rides cost about $15 for adults, $7.50 for kids under 13.

HITTING THE BEACH

Thanks to a reclamation project, the widest beaches here are at the exclusive Amelia Island Plantation. North of the resort, the beach has public access points with free

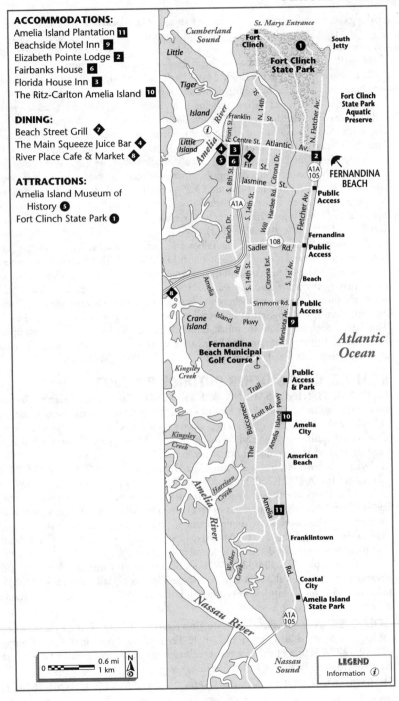

Amelia Island

ACCOMMODATIONS:
Amelia Island Plantation **11**
Beachside Motel Inn **9**
Elizabeth Pointe Lodge **2**
Fairbanks House **6**
Florida House Inn **3**
The Ritz-Carlton Amelia Island **10**

DINING:
Beach Street Grill **7**
The Main Squeeze Juice Bar **4**
River Place Cafe & Market **8**

ATTRACTIONS:
Amelia Island Museum of
   History **5**
Fort Clinch State Park **1**

St. Marys Entrance
Cumberland Sound
Little
Fort Clinch
South Jetty
Fort Clinch State Park
Little
Tiger
Island
Fort Clinch State Park Aquatic Preserve
Amelia River
Franklin St.
N. 14th St.
Front St.
Little Island
Centre St.
Atlantic Av.
N. Fletcher Av.
Fir St.
A1A 105
FERNANDINA BEACH
Jasmine St.
S. 8th St.
Will Hardee Rd.
Citrona Dr.
Fletcher Av.
Public Access
A1A
S. 14th St.
Clinch Dr.
Sadler Rd.
108
Citrona Ext.
S. 1st Av.
Fernandina Public Access
Beach
Amelia Island Pkwy
Simmons Rd.
Minnota Av.
Public Access
9
Atlantic Ocean
Crane Island
Kingsley Creek
Fernandina Beach Municipal Golf Course
The Buccaneer Trail
Scott Rd.
Amelia Island Pkwy
Public Access & Park
Kingsley Creek
10
Amelia City
American Beach
Amelia River
Harrison Creek
Amelia Island Rd.
11
Franklintown
Walker Creek
Coastal City
Amelia Island State Park
A1A 105
Nassau River
Nassau Sound

0 0.6 mi
0 1 km
N

LEGEND
Information ⓘ

parking every ¼ mile or so. The center of activity is **Main Beach,** at the end of Atlantic Avenue (Fla. A1A), with good swimming, rest rooms, picnic shelters, showers, a food concession, and a playground. There's lots of free parking, and this area is popular with families. Pets on leashes are allowed on all the island's public beaches.

The beach at ✪ **Fort Clinch State Park,** which wraps around the island's northern end, is backed by rolling dunes and is filled with shells and driftwood. The curving coast creates the feeling of being in a private cove. The park entrance is on Atlantic Avenue near the beach. Wooden boardwalks lead from the parking area to the sands. At the western end of the beach, a jetty and a pier jutting into Cumberland South are popular with anglers. You can also visit the remarkably well-preserved Fort Clinch, built in 1847 and abandoned after the Civil War except for a brief reactivation in 1898 during the Spanish-American War. The park is open from 8am to sunset. Entrance fees are $3.25 per vehicle with up to eight occupants, $1 for pedestrians and bicyclists. Admission to the fort costs $1, free for children under 5. For more information, contact the park at 2601 Atlantic Ave., Fernandina Beach, FL 32034 (☎ 904/277-7274).

Lying south of Amelia, both Big Talbot and Little Talbot barrier islands are preserved in their natural states. The highlight is **Little Talbot Island State Park,** whose entrance is on Fla. A1A, 8 miles south of Amelia Island Plantation. The 5 miles of beach here gently slope into the sea, making for good swimming. Boardwalks lead across the dunes from picnic shelters and bathhouses with cold-water showers. There are nature trails, a campground, and excellent fishing (bring your own gear and bait). The park is open from 8am to sunset. Entrance fees are $3.25 per vehicle with up to 8 occupants, $1 for pedestrians and bicyclists. For more information, contact the park at 12157 Heckscher Dr., Fort George, FL 32226 (☎ **904/251-2320**).

BOATING, GOLF & OTHER OUTDOOR PURSUITS

BOATING, FISHING, SAILING & KAYAKING The **Amelia Island Charter Boat Association,** at Tiger Point Marina on 14th Street north of the historic district (☎ **904/261-2870**), can help arrange deep-sea fishing charters, party-boat excursions, and dolphin-watching and sightseeing cruises. Other charter boats dock at Fernandina Harbor Marina, downtown at the foot of Centre Street.

Voyager Adventures, based at Fernandina Harbor Marina, 3977 1st Ave. (☎ **904/ 321-1244;** fax 904/321-2505), has several cruises aboard the *Voyager,* a 100-foot replica of a 19th-century gaff-rigged packet schooner. A prime destination is Cumberland Island, across the sound in Georgia (remember when John F. Kennedy Jr. was married over there without a single paparazzi present?). Also based at the marina, **Windward Sailing School** (☎ **904/261-9125**) will teach you to skipper your boat. Call these companies for details, prices, and reservations.

Kayak Amelia (☎ **904/321-0697;** www.kayakamelia.com) has learning and advanced-level trips on the back bays, creeks, and marshes. Half-day trips go for $50 per person, $85 for all day. Sunset paddles on Friday cost $25 per person. Reservations are required.

GOLF & TENNIS If you're not staying in a resort with golf and tennis facilities (see "Where to Stay" below), try the 27-hole **Fernandina Municipal Golf Course** (☎ **904/277-7370**) and the two tennis courts at the municipal park in Fernandina Beach at Atlantic Avenue and 11th Street.

HORSEBACK RIDING **Seahorse Stables,** 7500 Fla. A1A (☎ **904/261-4878**), is open daily and can arrange horseback riding on the beach at the south end of the island for $35. Reservations are required.

SCUBA DIVING **Aqua Explorers Dive Center,** 2856 Sadler Rd. (☎ 904/261-5989), open Monday to Saturday from 10am to 6pm, teaches certification courses, arranges charters, and sells and rents equipment.

AN OLD JAIL TURNED HISTORIC MUSEUM

Amelia Island Museum of History. 233 S. Third St. (between Beech and Cedar sts.). ☎ 904/261-7378. Admission by donation. Tours $3 adults, $1.50 students. Mon–Fri 10am–5pm, Sat 10am–4pm. Tours Mon–Sat 11am–2pm.

Housed in the Nassau County courthouse built of brick in 1878, this award-winning local museum explains Amelia Island's fascinating history, from Timucuan Indian times through its possession by France, Spain, Great Britain, the United States, and the Confederacy (the island changed flags 8 times). Only an upstairs photo gallery is open for casual inspection, so plan to take a 1 hour, 15 minute docent-led tour. The museum also offers history, architecture, Civil War, and cemetery walking tours; call at least a day in advance to arrange these.

SHOPPING

Stroll down **Centre Street** in downtown Fernandina Beach, with its vintage storefronts and charming boutiques. Quality antiques, consignment shops, and bookstores line the wide boulevard ending at the marina. Be sure to poke your head into the **Island Art Association Gallery,** 205 Centre St. (☎ 904/261-7020), a co-op exhibiting works by local artists.

On the south end of the island, **Palmetto Walk,** under a canopy of live oaks, and the **Village Shops,** at the entrance to Amelia Plantation, are other good shopping bets.

The chamber of commerce has complete lists and descriptions of the island's many upscale stores (see "Essentials," above).

WHERE TO STAY

More than two dozen of the town's charming Victorian and Queen Anne houses have been restored and turned into B&Bs, and apparently they all stay busy, at least on weekends. Industry veteran David Caples, who holds seminars nationwide for wannabe innkeepers, is based here at the Elizabeth Pointe Lodge (see below). For a complete list, contact the chamber of commerce (see "Essentials" above), or check out the Web site of the **Amelia Island Bed & Breakfast Association** at www.ameliaislandinns.com (the association does not have an address or a phone number). You can tour all of these B&Bs during an islandwide open house the first weekend in December.

A number of agencies will book vacation properties ranging from affordable cottages to magnificent mansions. Contact **Amelia Island Lodging Systems,** 584 S. Fletcher Ave., Fernandina Beach, FL 32034 (☎ 800/872-8531 or 904/261-4148; fax 904/261-9200), which even has a replica of a lighthouse for rent. Or try **Amelia Island Resort Rentals,** 5012 First Coast Hwy. (P.O. Box 6159), Amelia Island, FL 32035 (☎ 800/874-8679 or 904/261-9444; fax 904/261-9479; www.amelia.com).

A Hampton Inn & Suites is coming to downtown Fernandina Beach; meantime, the island has one chain motel, the **Hampton Inn** (☎ 800/HAMPTON or 904/321-1111) on Sadler Road a block from the beach.

Your best **camping** option here is **Fort Clinch State Park** (see "Hitting the Beach" above). The park has 62 campsites at $20.65 per night with electricity, $18.55 without. You can reserve a site up to 11 months in advance (a very good idea in summer) by contacting the park at 2601 Atlantic Ave., Fernandina Beach, FL 32034 (☎ 904/277-7274).

✪ **Amelia Island Plantation.** 3000 First Coast Hwy., Fernandina Beach, FL 32034. ☎ **800/874-6878** or 904/261-6161. Fax 904/277-5159. 249 rms, 430 condo apts. A/C TV TEL. $133–$200 double; $156–$650 condo. Packages available. AE, DISC, MC, V. Free valet and self-parking.

This huge real-estate development occupies 1,250 lush beachfront acres that encompass manicured emerald golf greens as well as a breathtaking coastal wilderness of marshes and lagoons. Twisted live oaks form a leafy canopy over the grounds, which are home to herons, egrets, sea turtles, deer, and other wildlife. The resort is so spread out that a free tram runs around the grounds every 15 minutes.

Along with the adjoining convention center, the six-story, Mediterranean-style **Amelia Inn** hotel serves as the resort's focal point here and holds its 249 spacious upscale rooms. Traditionally furnished with desks, easy chairs or sofas, and entertainment armoires, the rooms also boast patios or balconies facing the sea across a row of dunes, three phones with dataports, coffeemakers, hair dryers, and irons and boards. Fringed with palms, the hotel's big beachside play area has two adult pools, a children's pool, and a play area.

A majority of the accommodations here are one- to three-bedroom privately owned condo apartments (or "villas" in Florida-speak). All but a few have balconies or patios. Each is uniquely decorated with an eclectic mix of high-end furnishings. All offer fully equipped kitchens, living and dining areas, washer/dryers, hair dryers, and safes (VCRs can be rented).

Unless they're here to attend a convention, guests choose this rustically elegant resort for its natural beauty and its outstanding sports offerings. Most notable are the three consistently top-rated championship golf courses open to resort guests; they comprise 54 holes bordering the ocean, swamps, marshes, and woodlands. The Long Point course, a breathtakingly beautiful 18-holer, has two par-3s in a row bordering the ocean.

The plantation's 27 tennis courts (ranked among the nation's top 50 by *Tennis* magazine) are the setting for many professional tournaments, including the annual Bausch & Lomb Championships. The fitness center is state of the art, and there are 21 swimming pools dotting the complex.

Dining: The Amelia Inn's dining room, with stunning ocean views, offers exceptional and expensive new American cuisine. There are dancing and entertainment in an adjoining lounge. Next to the hotel's pool area, the Beach Club Grill provides pub-style fare during the day and more moderately priced main courses at night. Elsewhere, a grill overlooking woodlands specializes in fresh seafood. Other facilities include a golf-course snack shop and restaurant.

Amenities: Concierge, room service, tram transport around the property, shuttle to/from downtown Fernandina, nightly turndown on request, baby-sitting and kid's activities program, golf and tennis pro shops, resident tennis and golf pros/clinics, health and fitness center (including racquetball, indoor/outdoor lap pool, steam, sauna, whirlpool, massage, spa treatments, and more), unisex hair salon, 7 miles of bike and hiking trails, deep-sea and other fishing, bicycle rental, excellent year-round counselor-supervised youth program for children ages 3 through teens, horseback riding, sailing, basketball court, three children's playgrounds, boat and beach rentals in season, clothing boutiques, convenience store, snack shops, and gift store.

Beachside Motel Inn. 3172 S. Fletcher Ave. (Fla. A1A, south of Simmons Rd.), Fernandina Beach, FL 32034. ☎ **904/261-4236.** Fax 904/261-8336. 20 units. A/C TV TEL. $71–$118 double; $79–$165 efficiency. Rates include continental breakfast. Weekly discounts available. AE, MC, V.

The only motel beside the beach here, this family-run property is clean and well maintained. The white-and-blue two-story 1970s stucco building sits on a beautiful stretch of public but uncluttered beach. The rooms, many with ocean views, are spacious and furnished with standard motel furnishings. Many long-term visitors return each season to stay in the efficiencies with fully equipped kitchens. An outdoor pool is surrounded by lounge chairs and a spacious deck overlooking the ocean. The hotel is convenient to lots of sports activities and good restaurants (The Surf Restaurant and its outdoor pub are directly across the road). Room rates include free coffee each morning and a selection of store-bought breakfast rolls, doughnuts, and pastries.

Elizabeth Pointe Lodge. 98 S. Fletcher Ave. (just south of Atlantic Ave.), Fernandina Beach, FL 32034. ☎ **800/772-3359** or 904/277-4851. Fax 904/277-6500. www. elizabethpointelodge.com. 24 units, 1 cottage. A/C TV TEL. $140–$215 double; $235 cottage. Rates include buffet breakfast and evening social hour. Packages available. AE, DISC, MC, V.

Sitting right on the beach, this three-story, Nantucket-style shingle-sided building's Victorian appearance belies the fact that it was built in 1991 by B&B guru David Caples. Big-paned windows look out from the comfy lounge (with library and fireplace) and dining room to an expansive front porch and the surf beyond. Antiques and reproductions, handmade quilts, and other touches lend the 20 rooms in the main building a turn-of-the-century cottage ambience. They all have oversize bathtubs (some with Jacuzzi jets), robes, irons, and ironing boards. Four other rooms are in the Harris Lodge next door, and the two-bedroom, two-bathroom Miller Cottage is for rent. The main house's dining room provides breakfast, a light-fare lunch and dinner menu, and 24-hour room service.

Fairbanks House. 227 S. 7th St. (between Beech and Cedar sts.), Fernandina Beach, Amelia Island, FL 32034. ☎ **800/261-4838** or 904/277-0500. Fax 904/277-3103. www. fairbankshouse.com. 9 units, 3 detached cottages. A/C TV TEL. $150–$250 double; $200 cottage. Rates include full breakfast. AE, DISC, MC, V.

With all the amenities and almost as much privacy as a first-class hotel in a superbly refurbished 1885 Italianate home, the Fairbanks House is a top B&B choice for those looking to be pampered. All rooms have hair dryers, irons and boards, and refrigerators stocked with complimentary drinks. Many rooms and all the cottages offer private entrances for guests who prefer not to walk through the main house. Room no. 3, in the back of the house on the main floor, is one of the finest rooms, with a private entrance, a large sitting room, a plush king-size bed, period antiques, porcelain, oil paintings, and fresh flowers. Occupying the entire top floor, the two-bedroom Tower Suite has plenty of room to spread out, plus 360-degree views and its own Jacuzzi. Note that Fairbanks is the only B&B on the island with a pool. No smoking indoors.

Florida House Inn. 20 S. 3rd St (between Centre and Ash sts.), Fernandina Beach, FL 32034. ☎ **800/258-3301** or 904/261-3300. Fax 904/277-3831. www.floridahouse.com. 15 units. A/C TV TEL. $70–$145. Rates include full breakfast. AE, MC, V.

Built by a railroad in 1857, this clapboard Victorian building is Florida's oldest operating hotel. Ulysses S. Grant stayed here, as did Cuban revolutionary José Marti, and the Rockefellers and Carnegies broke bread at the boardinghouse-style dining room, still providing family-style, all-you-can-eat traditional Southern fare ($7 at lunch, $12 at dinner). You can rock away on the two gingerbread-trimmed front verandas (Grant made a speech from the upstairs porch) or on a back porch overlooking a brick courtyard shaded by a huge oak tree. All up to modern standards, the 11 rooms in the original building are loaded with antiques. Most have working fireplaces, and some have clawfoot tubs. Four rooms are in a wing added in 1998; one of these has log-cabin walls, while the other is done country style. Both have Jacuzzi tubs. The hotel has a cozy, ancient bar and an up-to-date guest laundry.

✪ **The Ritz-Carlton Amelia Island.** 4750 Amelia Island Pkwy., Fernandina Beach, FL 32034. ☎ **800/241-3333** or 904/277-1100. Fax 904/261-9064. 449 units. A/C MINIBAR TV TEL. $139–$269 double; $229–$299 suite. Golf and tennis packages available. AE, DC, DISC, MC, V. Valet parking $13; no self-parking.

Opened in 1991 on 13 acres of stunning beachfront, this member of the world-renowned chain offers glitzier and grander accommodations than its neighbor, the Amelia Island Plantation. Although not quite as plush as some Ritz-Carltons else-where, its public areas are nevertheless adorned with millions of dollars' worth of museum-quality art and furnishings. The lobby lounge has a working fireplace with floor-to-ceiling beachfront windows. The dining rooms proffer award-winning cui-sine, and the staff provides flawless Ritz-style service. Extensive recreational facilities include nine tennis courts and a beautiful and challenging 18-hole championship golf course.

The exquisite guest rooms—all oceanfront or ocean view, with balconies or patios—are furnished in handsome mahogany pieces. You'll find VCRs, safes, hair dryers, scales, cosmetic mirrors, and extra phones in the magnificent marble bath-rooms. Concierge-level guests enjoy a stunning lounge with a working fireplace.

Dining: The Ritz-Carlton offers four main dining venues. Overlooking the ocean, The Grill is one of the best restaurants in the state. Open seasonally, the Ocean Bar & Grill serves light fare and drinks by the pool. A cafe serves regional American fare at all meals and features healthful macrobiotic fare as well. Also, a gourmet take-out shop sells the oft-requested Ritz dressings, condiments, and sauces in addition to salads, sandwiches, and decadent desserts.

Amenities: Concierge, 24-hour room service, nightly turndown, dry-cleaning and laundry services, free daily newspaper, twice-daily maid service, baby-sitting/nannies, secretarial services, express checkout, outdoor pool on a palm-fringed island between the beach and beautiful manicured lawns, heated indoor pool, fitness center, personal trainers by advance reservation, whirlpool, sauna, spa treatments, bicycle rental, 18-hole golf course, resident golf and tennis pros, golf lessons and swing seminars, counselor-supervised program for children 3 to 17, children's playground, business center, conference rooms, nine night-lit tennis courts, golf and tennis pro shops, beauty salon, boutiques; jet-ski, sailboat, kayak, and beach rentals (umbrellas, cabanas, chaise longues) in summer.

WHERE TO DINE

You'll find several restaurants, pubs, and snack shops along Centre Street, between the bay and 8th Street (Fla. A1A), in Fernandina Beach's old town. And don't forget the boardinghouse-style dining room at the Florida House Inn (see "Where to Stay," above).

✪ **Beech Street Grill.** 801 Beech St. (at 8th St./Fla. A1A), Fernandina Beach. ☎ **904/277-3662.** Reservations strongly suggested. Main courses $19–$25; pastas $13–$19. AE, DC, DISC, MC, V. Daily 5:30–10pm. REGIONAL NEW AMERICAN.

Surpassed only by The Grill in the Ritz-Carlton as the island's premier restaurant, the Beech Street Grill pleases all palates with a menu of fish, chicken, and meat choices, including seasonal game like roasted venison loin in a black currant sauce with sweet potato and onion hash. Nightly fish specialties are always exceptional (some can be higher than printed menu options). A Parmesan-encrusted red snapper with a mus-tard basil sauce is superb. Seared tuna is always perfect, too. The dense and tasty crab cakes and the chewy steamed dumplings are great choices for starters, as is the huge mixed green salad with mustard-basil vinaigrette and toasted pecans and blue cheese. Housed in a century-old landmark home and a newer wing to one side, five dining rooms offer large tables in a lively atmosphere. Attentive and knowledgeable waiters serve the showy plates with efficiency and grace. Upstairs features a pianist.

The Main Squeeze Juice Bar. 105 S. 3rd St. (between Ash and Beech sts.). ☎ **904/277-3003.** Reservations not accepted. Breakfast $1.50–$5.50; sandwiches and salads $3.50–$5. MC, V (for purchases of $20 or more). Mon–Sat 7:30am–3pm. SANDWICHES/SNACKS.

This little outdoor juice bar, literally "squeezed" into a shady patio beside Courtyard Florist, is the town's most unusual spot for an alfresco breakfast or lunch. The cooking and juicing are done in a booth at the rear of the courtyard. Order there and grab a wrought-iron patio table. Breakfast is mostly of the pastry variety: bagels, cinnamon toast, waffles, fruit plates, coffee, cappuccino, latte, and the trademark squeezed-to-order orange, grapefruit, and carrot juice. Lunch features salads (the Fernandina is terrific), sandwiches (don't miss the crispy Cuban), and creative (as opposed to traditional Mexican) nachos, burritos, and quesadillas.

✪ River Place Cafe & Market. 4768 Wade Place (mainland end of Shave Bridge on Fla. A1A). ☎ **904/277-2336.** Reservations not accepted. Salads and sandwiches $3–$8; main courses $6–$17. AE, DC, DISC, MC, V. Daily 11am–9pm. SEAFOOD/DELI. Follow Fla. A1A across the Shave Bridge toward Jacksonville; take first left after bridge.

The same folks who own the outstanding Beech Street Grill (see above) operate this fascinating deli/market/restaurant on the western banks of the Amelia River. You enter through a deli-style market with cases full of today's catch, gourmet salads, and yummy pastries, all priced by the pound (it's a good place to stock up before heading to your condo). Place your restaurant orders at the cash register, then take a seat either inside the simple dining room with brown leatherette booths or out on a riverside deck. In a few minutes the wait staff will deliver this area's greatest food bargain. You can have the day's fish broiled, grilled, blackened, or fried, or select from specials such as teriyaki glazed wahoo or Caribbean-style snapper. In addition to salads, small pizzas, peel-and-eat steamed shrimp, and other fare, the regular menu features "shrimp and grits"—shrimp, scallions, and bacon expertly sautéed in a rich brown gravy and served atop a steaming bowl of grits. You Yankees who never thought you'd like grits will change your mind when you taste this creation. All meals include a trip to a gourmet salad bar stocked with field greens.

AMELIA ISLAND AFTER DARK

This romantic island goes to bed early. If you tire of the lounges in the island's resorts, check out the **Palace Saloon,** 117 Centre St., at 2nd St. (☎ **904/261-6320**). It claims to be Florida's oldest watering hole (open since 1878). Complete with a pressed-tin ceiling and a mahogany bar, it once hosted the Carnegies and the du Ponts; now, a lively bar and an adjacent pool bar and stage area are often packed. Some nights you'll find live local blues or rock.

Appendix:
Useful Toll-Free Numbers
& Web Sites

AIRLINES

Air Canada
☎ 800/776-3000
www.aircanada.ca

AirTran
☎ 800/AIR-TRAN
www.airtran.com

America West Airlines
☎ 800/235-9292
www.americawest.com

American Airlines
☎ 800/433-7300
www.americanair.com

British Airways
☎ 800/247-9297
☎ 0345/222-111 in Britain
www.british-airways.com

Canadian Airlines International
☎ 800/426-7000
www.cdnair.ca

Continental Airlines
☎ 800/525-0280
www.flycontinental.com

Delta Air Lines
☎ 800/221-1212
www.delta-air.com

Northwest Airlines
☎ 800/225-2525
www.nwa.com

Southwest Airlines
☎ 800/435-9792
www.iflyswa.com

Tower Air
☎ 800/34-TOWER
(800/348-6937)
www.towerair.com

Trans World Airlines (TWA)
☎ 800/221-2000
www.twa.com

United Airlines
☎ 800/241-6522
www.ual.com

US Airways
☎ 800/428-4322
www.usair.com

Virgin Atlantic Airways
☎ 800/862-8621 in
continental U.S.
☎ 0293/747-747 in Britain
www.fly.virgin.com

CAR-RENTAL AGENCIES

Advantage
☎ 800/777-5500
www.arac.com

Alamo
☎ 800/327-9633
www.goalamo.com

Avis
☎ 800/331-1212 in
continental U.S.
☎ 800/TRY-AVIS in Canada
www.avis.com

Budget
☎ 800/527-0700
www.budgetrentacar.com

Dollar
☎ 800/800-4000
www.dollarcar.com

Enterprise
☎ 800/325-8007
www.pickenterprise.com

Hertz
☎ 800/654-3131
www.hertz.com

National
☎ 800/CAR-RENT
www.nationalcar.com

Payless
☎ 800/PAYLESS
www.paylesscar.com

Rent-A-Wreck
☎ 800/535-1391
rent-a-wreck.com

Thrifty
☎ 800/367-2277
www.thrifty.com

Value
☎ 800/327-2501
www.go-value.com

MAJOR HOTEL & MOTEL CHAINS

Best Western International
☎ 800/528-1234
www.bestwestern.com

Clarion Hotels
☎ 800/CLARION
www.hotelchoice.com/
cgi-bin/res/webres?clarion.html

Comfort Inns
☎ 800/228-5150
www.hotelchoice.com/
cgi-bin/res/webres?comfort.html

Courtyard by Marriott
☎ 800/321-2211
www.courtyard.com

Days Inn
☎ 800/325-2525
www.daysinn.com

Doubletree Hotels
☎ 800/222-TREE
www.doubletreehotels.com

Econo Lodges
☎ 800/55-ECONO
www.hotelchoice.com/
cgi-bin/res/webres?econo.html

Fairfield Inn by Marriott
☎ 800/228-2800
www.fairfieldinn.com

Hampton Inn
☎ 800/HAMPTON
www.hampton-inn.com

Hilton Hotels
☎ 800/HILTONS
www.hilton.com

Holiday Inn
☎ 800/HOLIDAY
www.holiday-inn.com

Howard Johnson
☎ 800/654-2000
www.hojo.com/hojo.html

Hyatt Hotels & Resorts
☎ 800/228-9000
www.hyatt.com

ITT Sheraton
☎ 800/325-3535
www.sheraton.com

Marriott Hotels
☎ 800/228-9290
www.marriott.com

Motel 6
☎ 800/4-MOTEL6
(800/466-8536)

Quality Inns
☎ 800/228-5151
www.hotelchoice.com/
cgi-bin/res/webres?quality.html

Radisson Hotels International
☎ 800/333-3333
www.radisson.com

Ramada Inns
☎ 800/2-RAMADA
www.ramada.com

Red Roof Inns
☎ 800/843-7663
www.redroof.com

Residence Inn by Marriott
☎ 800/331-3131
www.residenceinn.com

Rodeway Inns
☎ 800/228-2000
www.hotelchoice.com/
cgi-bin/res/webres?rodeway.html

Super 8 Motels
☎ 800/800-8000
www.super8motels.com

Travelodge
☎ 800/255-3050

Wyndham Hotels and Resorts
☎ 800/822-4200 in continental
   U.S. and Canada
www.wyndham.com

Frommer's Online Directory

by Michael Shapiro

Michael Shapiro is the author of *Internet Travel 101: How to Plan Trips and Save Money Online* (The Globe Pequot Press).

Frommer's Online Directory is a new feature designed to help you take advantage of the Internet to better plan your trip. Section 1 lists some general Internet resources that can make any trip easier, such as sites for booking airline tickets. Please keep in mind that this is not a comprehensive list, but rather a discriminating selection of useful sites to get you started. In Section 2 you'll find some top online guides for Florida in general, as well as for cities or regions in particular.

1 The Top Travel-Planning Web Sites

Among the most popular travel sites are online travel agencies. The top agencies, including Expedia, Preview Travel, and Travelocity, offer an array of tools that are valuable even if you don't book online. You can check flight schedules, hotel availability, rental-car prices, or even get paged if your flight is delayed.

While online agencies have come a long way over the past few years, they don't always yield the best price. Unlike a travel agent, for example, they're unlikely to tell you that you can save money by flying a day earlier or a day later. On the other hand, if you're looking for a bargain fare, you might find something online that an agent wouldn't take the time to dig up. Because airline commissions have been cut, a travel agent may not find it worthwhile spending half an hour trying to find you the best deal. On the Net you can be your own agent and take all the time you want.

Online booking sites aren't the only places to book airline tickets—all major airlines have their own Web sites and often offer incentives, such as bonus frequent-flyer miles or Net-only discounts, for buying online. These incentives have helped airlines capture the majority of the online booking market. According to Jupiter Communications, online agencies such as Travelocity booked about 80 percent of tickets purchased online in 1996, but by 1999 airline sites (such as www.ual. com) were projected to own about 60 percent of the online market, with online agencies' share of the pie dwindling each year.

Note: See the appendix on pp. 676–678 for toll-free numbers and Web addresses for airlines, hotels, and rental-car companies.

WHEN SHOULD YOU BOOK ONLINE?

Online booking is not for everyone. If you prefer to let others handle your travel arrangements, one call to an experienced travel agent

Take a Look at Frommer's Site

We highly recommend Arthur Frommer's Budget Travel Online (**www. frommers.com**) as an excellent travel-planning resource. Of course, we're a little biased, but you will find indispensable travel tips, reviews, monthly vacation giveaways, and online booking.

Subscribe to Arthur Frommer's Daily Newsletter (**www.frommers.com/ newsletters**) to receive the latest travel bargains and inside travel secrets in your mailbox every day. You'll read daily headlines and articles from the dean of travel himself, highlighting last-minute deals on airfares, accommodations, cruises, and package vacations. You'll also find great travel advice by checking our Tip of the Day or Hot Spot of the Month.

Search our Destinations archive (**www.frommers.com/destinations**) of more than 200 domestic and international destinations for great places to stay, tips for traveling there, and what to do while you're there. Once you've researched your trip, you might try our online reservation system (**www.frommers.com/ booktravelnow**) to book your dream vacation at affordable prices.

should suffice. But if you want to know as much as possible about your options, the Net is a good place to start, especially for bargain hunters.

The most compelling reason to use online booking is to take advantage of last-minute specials, such as American Airlines's weekend deals or other Internet-only fares that must be purchased online. Another advantage is that you can cash in on incentives for booking online, such as rebates or bonus frequent-flyer miles. Online booking works best for trips within North America; for international tickets, it's usually cheaper and easier to use a travel agent or consolidator.

Online booking is certainly not for those with a complex international itinerary. If you require follow-up services, such as itinerary changes, use a travel agent. Though Expedia and some other online agencies employ travel agents available by phone, these sites are geared primarily for self-service.

LEADING BOOKING SITES

Below are listings for the top travel booking sites. The starred selections are the most-useful and best-designed sites.

Cheap Tickets. www.cheaptickets.com
Essentials: Discounted rates on domestic and international airline tickets and hotel rooms.

Sometimes discounters such as Cheap Tickets have exclusive deals that aren't available through more-mainstream channels. Registration at Cheap Tickets requires inputting a credit-card number before getting started, which is one reason many people elect to call the company's toll-free number rather than book online. Cheap Tickets actually regards this policy as a selling point, arguing that "lookers" who don't intend to buy will be scared off by its "credit card first" approach and won't bog down the site with their queries. Despite its misguided credit-card policy, Cheap Tickets is worth the effort because its fares can be substantially lower than those offered by its competitors.

✪ **Expedia. expedia.com**
Essentials: Domestic and international flight, hotel, and rental-car booking; late-breaking travel news, destination features, and commentary from travel experts; deals on cruises and vacation packages. Free registration is required for booking.

Factoid

Far more people look online than book online, partly due to fear of putting their credit cards through on the Net. Though secure encryption has made this fear less justified, there's no reason why you can't find a flight online and then book it by calling a toll-free number or contacting a travel agent. To be sure you're in secure mode when you book online, look for a little icon of a key (in Netscape) or a padlock (Internet Explorer) at the bottom of your Web browser.

Expedia makes it easy to handle flight, hotel, and car booking on one itinerary, so it's a good place for one-stop shopping. Expedia's hotel search offers crisp, zoomable maps to pinpoint most properties; click on the camera icon to see images of the rooms and facilities. But like many online databases, Expedia focuses on the major chains, such as Hilton and Hyatt, so don't expect to find too many one-of-a-kind resorts or B&Bs here.

Once you're registered (it's necessary to do this only once from each computer you use), you can start booking with the Roundtrip Fare Finder box on the home page, which expedites the process. After selecting a flight, you can hold it until midnight the following day or purchase online. If you think you might do better through a travel agent, you'll have time to try to get a lower price. And you may do better with a travel agent because Expedia's computer reservation system does not include all airlines. Most notably absent are some leading budget carriers, such as Southwest Airlines. (*Note:* At press time, Travelocity was the only major booking service that included Southwest.)

Expedia's World Guide, offering destination information, is a glaring weakness—it takes a lot of page views to get very little information. However, Expedia compensates by linking to other Microsoft Network services, such as its Sidewalk city guides, which offer entertainment and dining advice for many of the cities it covers.

Preview Travel. www.previewtravel.com
Essentials: Domestic and international flight, hotel, and rental-car booking; Travel Newswire lists fare sales; deals on cruises and vacation packages. Free (one-time) registration is required for booking. Preview offers express booking for members, but at press time this feature was buried below the fold on Preview's reservation page.

Preview features the most inviting interface for booking trips, though the wealth of graphics involved can make the site somewhat slow to load. Use Farefinder to quickly find the lowest current fares on flights to dozens of major cities. Carfinder offers a similar service for rental cars, but you can search only airport locations, not city pick-up sites. To see the lowest fare for your itinerary, input the dates and times for your route and see what Preview comes up with.

In recent years Preview and other leading booking services have added features such as Best Fare Finder, so after Preview searches for the best deal on your itinerary, it will check flights that are a bit later or earlier to see if it might be cheaper to fly at a different time. While these searches have become quite sophisticated, they still occasionally overlook deals that might be uncovered by a top-notch travel agent. If you have the time, see what you can find online, and then call an agent to see if you can get a better price.

With Preview's Fare Alert feature, you can set fares for up to three routes, and you'll receive e-mail notices when the fare drops below your target amount. For example, you could tell Preview to alert you when the fare from New York to Miami drops below $250. If it does, you'll get an e-mail telling you the current fare.

Minor quibbles: When you search for a fare, hotel, or car—at least when we went to press—Preview launched an annoying little "Please Wait" window which gets in the way of the main browser window, so when your results begin to appear, the small window obstructs what you want to see. The hotel search feature is intuitive, but the images and maps aren't as crisp as those at Expedia. Also, all sorts of other extraneous information (such as NYC public-school locations) is listed on maps, which is irrelevant to most travelers.

Note to AOL Users: You can book flights, hotels, rental cars, and cruises on AOL at keyword: Travel. The booking software is provided by Preview Travel and is similar to Preview on the Web. Use the AOL "Travelers Advantage" program to earn a 5% rebate on flights, hotel rooms, and car rentals.

Priceline.com. www.priceline.com

Even people who aren't familiar with too many Web sites have heard about Price-line.com. Launched in 1998 with a $10 million ad campaign featuring William Shatner, Priceline lets you "name your price" for domestic and international airline tickets. In other words, you select a route and dates, guarantee with a credit card, and make a bid for what you're willing to pay. If one of the airlines in Priceline's database has a fare that's lower than your bid, your credit card will automatically be charged for a ticket.

Furthermore, you can't say when you want to fly—you have to accept any flight leaving between 6am and 10pm—and you may have to make a stopover. No frequent-flyer miles are awarded, and tickets are nonrefundable and can't be exchanged for another flight. So if your plans change, you're out of luck. Priceline can be good for travelers who have to take off on short notice (and who are thus unable to qualify for advance-purchase discounts). But be sure to shop around first—if you overbid, you'll be required to purchase the ticket and Priceline will pocket the difference.

Travelocity. www.travelocity.com

Essentials: Domestic and international flight, hotel, and rental-car booking; deals on cruises and vacation packages. Travel Headlines spotlights latest bargain airfares. Free (one-time) registration is required for booking.

Travelocity almost got it right. Its Express Booking feature enables travelers to complete the booking process more quickly than they could at Expedia or Preview, but Travelocity gums up the works with a page called "Featured Airlines." Big placards of several featured airlines compete for your attention—if you want to see the fares for all available airlines, click the much smaller box at the bottom of the page labeled "Book a Flight."

Some have worried that Travelocity, which is owned by American Airlines's parent company AMR, directs bookings to American. This doesn't seem to be the case—I've booked there dozens of times and have always been directed to the cheapest listed flight, for example, on Tower or ATA. But this "Featured Airlines" page seems to be Travelocity's way of trying to cash in with ads and incentives for booking certain airlines. (*Note:* It's hard to blame these booking services for trying to generate some revenue—many airlines have slashed commissions to $10 per domestic booking for online transactions, so these virtual agencies are groping for revenue streams.) There are rewards for choosing one of the featured airlines. You'll get 1,500 bonus frequent-flyer miles if you book through United's site, for example, but the site doesn't tell you about other airlines that might be cheaper. If the United flight costs $150 more than the best deal on another airline, it's not worth spending the extra money for a relatively small number of bonus miles.

On the plus side, Travelocity has some leading-edge techie tools for modern travelers. Exhibit A is Fare Watcher Email, an "intelligent agent" that keeps you informed of the best fares offered for the city pairs (round-trips) of your choice. Whenever the fare changes by $25 or more, Fare Watcher will alert you by e-mail. Exhibit B is Flight Paging—if you own an alphanumeric pager with national access that can receive e-mail, Travelocity's paging system can alert you if your flight is delayed. Finally, though Travelocity doesn't include every budget airline, it does include Southwest, the leading U.S. budget carrier.

FINDING LODGINGS ONLINE

While the services above offer hotel booking, it can be best to use a site devoted primarily to lodging because you may find properties that aren't listed on more general online travel agencies. Some lodging sites specialize in a particular type of accommodations, such as bed-and-breakfast inns, which you won't find on the more mainstream booking services. Other services, such as TravelWeb, offer weekend deals on major chain properties, which cater to business travelers and have more empty rooms on weekends.

Note: See the appendix on pp. 676–678 for toll-free numbers and Web addresses for airlines, hotels, and rental-car companies.

All Hotels on the Web. www.all-hotels.com
Well, this site doesn't include all the hotels on the Web, but it does have tens of thousands of listings throughout the world. Bear in mind that each hotel listed has paid a small fee (of $25 and up) for placement, so it's not an objective list but more like a book of online brochures.

Hotel Reservations Network. www.180096hotel.com
Bargain room rates at hotels in more than two dozen U.S. regions, including Miami, Orlando, Tampa, and Fort Lauderdale. The cool thing is that HRN prebooks blocks of rooms, so sometimes it has rooms—at discount rates—at hotels that are "sold out." Select a city and input your dates, and you'll get a list of best prices for a selection of hotels. Descriptions include an image of the property and a locator map—to book online click the "Book Now" button. HRN is notable for some deep discounts, even in cities where hotel rooms are expensive. The toll-free number is printed all over this site; call it if you want more options than are listed online.

InnSite. www.innsite.com
B&B listings for inns in all 50 U.S. states and dozens of countries around the globe. Find an inn at your destination, have a look at images of the rooms, check prices and availability, and then send e-mail to the innkeeper if you have further questions. This is an extensive directory of bed-and-breakfast inns but includes listings only if the proprietor submitted one. (*Note:* It's free to get an inn listed.) The descriptions are written by the innkeepers, and many listings link to the inn's own Web sites, where you can find more information and images.

Places to Stay. www.placestostay.com
Mostly one-of-a-kind places in the U.S. and abroad that you might not find in other directories, with a focus on resort accommodations. Again, listing is selective—this isn't a comprehensive directory, but it can give you a sense of what's available at different destinations.

✪ TravelWeb. www.travelweb.com
TravelWeb lists more than 16,000 hotels worldwide, focusing on chains such as Hyatt and Hilton, and you can book almost 90 percent of these online. TravelWeb's Click-It Weekends, updated each Monday, offers weekend deals at many leading hotel chains. TravelWeb is the online home for Pegasus Systems, which provides transaction-processing systems for the hotel industry.

LAST-MINUTE DEALS & OTHER ONLINE BARGAINS

There's nothing airlines hate more than flying with lots of empty seats (well, maybe they hate competition more but that's another story). The Net has enabled airlines to offer last-minute bargains to entice travelers to fill those seats. Most of these are announced on Tuesday or Wednesday and are valid for travel the following weekend, but some can be booked weeks or months in advance. You can sign up for weekly e-mail alerts at airlines' sites (for airlines' Web site addresses, see the appendix on airlines, hotels and car-rental companies) or check sites such as WebFlyer (see below) that compile lists of these bargains. To make it easier, visit a site (see below) that will round up all the deals and send them in one convenient weekly e-mail. But last-minute deals aren't the only online bargains—other sites can help you find value even if you can't wait until the 11th hour.

✪ 1travel.com. www.1travel.com
Deals on domestic and international flights, cruises, hotels, and all-inclusive resorts such as Club Med. 1travel.com's Saving Alert compiles last-minute air deals so you don't have to scroll through multiple e-mail alerts. A feature called "Drive a little using low-fare airlines" helps map out strategies for using alternative airports to find lower fares. And Farebeater searches a database that includes published fares, consolidator bargains, and special deals exclusive to 1travel.com. *Note:* The travel agencies listed by 1travel.com have paid for placement.

BestFares. www.bestfares.com
Budget seeker Tom Parsons lists some great bargains on airfares, hotels, rental cars, and cruises, but the site is poorly organized. News Desk is a long list of hundreds of bargains, but because they're not broken down into cities or even countries, it's not easy trying to find what you're looking for. If you have time to wade through it, you might find a good deal. Some material is available only to paid subscribers.

Go4less.com. www.go4less.com
Specializing in last-minute cruise and package deals, Go4less has some eye-popping offers, such as off-peak Caribbean cruises for under $100 per day. The site has a clean design but the bargains aren't organized by destination. However, you avoid sifting through all this material by using the Search box and entering vacation type, destination, month, and price.

Moment's Notice. www.moments-notice.com
As the name suggests, Moment's Notice specializes in last-minute vacation and cruise deals. You can browse free, but if you want to purchase a trip, you have to join Moment's Notice, which costs $25.

Smarter Living. www.smarterliving.com
Best known for its e-mail dispatch of weekend deals on 20 airlines, Smarter Living also keeps you posted about last-minute bargains on everything from Windjammer Cruises to flights to Iceland.

✪ WebFlyer. www.webflyer.com
WebFlyer is the ultimate online resource for frequent flyers and also has an excellent listing of last-minute air deals. Click on Deal Watch for a roundup of weekend deals on flights, hotels, and rental cars from domestic and international suppliers.

TRAVELER'S TOOLKIT

Seasoned travelers always carry some essential items to make their trips easier. Following is a selection of online tools to smooth your journey.

ATM Locators: Visa. www.visa.com/pd/atm/.
MasterCard. www.mastercard.com/atm
Find ATMs in hundreds of cities in the U.S. and around the world. Both sites include maps for some locations, and both list airport ATM locations, some with maps. Remarkably, MasterCard lists ATMs on all seven continents (there's one at Antarctica's McMurdo Station). *Tip:* You'll usually get a better exchange rate using ATMs than exchanging traveler's checks at banks.

✪ CultureFinder. www.culturefinder.com
Up-to-date listings for plays, opera, classical music, dance, film, and other cultural events in more than 1,300 U.S. cities. Enter the dates you'll be in a city and get a list of events happening then—you can also purchase tickets online. Also see FestivalFinder (**www.festivalfinder.com**) for the latest on more than 1,500 rock, folk, reggae, blues, and bluegrass festivals throughout North America.

Intellicast. www.intellicast.com
Weather forecasts for all 50 states and cities around the world. Note that temperatures are in Celsius for many international destinations, so don't think you'll need that winter coat for your next trip to Athens.

✪ MapQuest. www.mapquest.com
Specializing in U.S. maps, MapQuest enables you to zoom in on a destination, calculate step-by-step driving directions between any two U.S. points, and locate restaurants, hotels, and other attractions on maps.

✪ Net Cafe Guide. www.netcafeguide.com
Locate Internet cafes at hundreds of locations around the globe. Catch up on your e-mail, log on to the Web, and stay in touch with the home front, usually for just a few dollars per hour.

The Travelite FAQ. www.travelite.org
Tips on packing light, choosing luggage, and selecting appropriate travel wear.

Trip.com. www.trip.com
A business travel site where you can find out when an airborne flight is scheduled to arrive. Click on Guides and Tools to peruse airport maps for more than 40 domestic cities.

2 The Top Web Sites for Florida

In the first section below are some general Web guides to the state as a whole. The next sections contain sites for the major metropolitan areas: Miami, Orlando, and Tampa–St. Petersburg. The last section covers Web sites for attractions beyond Florida's three major metro areas. The starred selections are choices for the most useful and best designed Web sites.

TOP GENERAL SITES FOR FLORIDA

Beach Directory. www.beachdirectory.com
A guide to beaches along Florida's Gulf Coast. The site includes a virtual tour, maps, recommendations from "Dr. Beach," and a guide to restaurants and lodgings along the coast.

Come to the Sun. www.goflorida.com
Though this site doesn't cover the entire state, it's a valuable guide to South Florida, including Miami, Fort Lauderdale, Palm Beach, Boca Raton, and the Florida Keys.

Listings include attractions, entertainment, dining, shopping, and lodging. The hotel and restaurant listings are very extensive and don't appear to be paid placements.

❂ FLA USA. www.flausa.com
A product of Florida's official tourism bureau, this extensive Web site includes information on attractions, beaches, golfing, and water sports, as well as airport information, weather, and maps. The beach guide is nicely organized by region, and there's advice on Florida's natural attractions in the Activities section. There's also a shopping guide, but at press time this was pretty thin and appeared to include only stores that had paid for placement.

Florida Association of Convention and Visitors Bureaus. www.facvb.org
Links to more than a dozen bureaus throughout the state. Most of the sites include information on attractions, dining, lodging, and shopping.

Florida Lighthouse Guide. www.erols.com/lthouse/home.htm
Featuring images, history, and tour information for more than 40 lighthouses, this is an ideal site to help you plan visits to some of the state's most historic landmarks.

Florida State Parks. www.dep.state.fl.us/parks
Though the home page is awkwardly designed (this is a government site after all), you can find parks by clicking on "Parks Map" or "Park Index." From there you can learn about camping at each park, including information on fees, nearby attractions, and facilities.

See Florida. www.see-florida.com
A nicely organized guide to theme parks, marine attractions, museums, boating, fishing, and much more. See Florida includes guides to dozens of Florida cities and has advice for first-time visitors to the Sunshine State.

TOP WEB SITES FOR MIAMI
ONLINE GUIDES, NEWSPAPERS & ENTERTAINMENT SITES

❂ CitySearch: Miami. miami.citysearch.com
Reviews and listings for Miami arts and entertainment, restaurants, shopping, and attractions. CitySearch is part of a national network of city guides, and it has editorial reviews as well as paid Web pages from restaurants and other business. CitySearch clearly labels its pages "editorial profile" and "advertiser's web site." Click on the calendar for events recommended by the editors. The extensive shopping listings range from clothing to specialty stores and include updates on sales. Along with Sidewalk, CitySearch is a leading directory for arts and dining in Miami.

For AOL Members: Digital City South Florida. Keyword: South Florida
Entertainment, dining, sports, and festivals produced in cooperation with the *Sun-Sentinel*. This site includes a lively forum, where you can read comments from others or post a question of your own. Digital City is also available on the Web at south-florida.digitalcity.com.

Just Go: South Florida. www.justgo.com/southflorida
This site includes listings and reviews for dining, music, theater, and movies. Just Go does a nice job in spotlighting upcoming concerts and makes it easy to find restaurants by cuisine and neighborhood.

Miami Herald. www.herald.com
Miami's leading news source can give you a sense of what's going on in the city, but don't expect extensive entertainment listings.

Check Your E-Mail at Internet Cafes While You're on the Road

Until a few years ago, most travelers who checked their e-mail while traveling carried a laptop, but this posed some problems. Not only are laptops expensive, but they also can be difficult to configure, incur expensive connection charges, and are attractive to thieves. Thankfully, Web-based free e-mail programs have made it much easier to check your mail.

Just open an account at a freemail provider, such as Hotmail (hotmail.com) or Yahoo! Mail (mail.yahoo.com), and all you'll need in order to check your mail is a Web connection, easily available at Net cafes and copy shops around the world. After logging on, just point the browser to **www.hotmail.com** and enter your username and password, and you'll have access to your mail.

Internet cafes have become ubiquitous, so for a few dollars an hour you'll be able to check your mail and send messages back to colleagues, friends, and family. If you already have a primary e-mail account, you can set it to forward mail to your freemail account while you're away. Freemail programs have become enormously popular (Hotmail claims more than 10 million members), because they enable everyone, even those who don't own a computer, to have an e-mail address they can check wherever they log on to the Web.

Miami New Times. www.miaminewtimes.com
Miami's leading alternative weekly includes features and listings for music, theater, film, and more. Click on Music and then Concerts This Week to see listings ranging from the Florida Philharmonic to the Blues Festival.

South Florida Sidewalk. southflorida.sidewalk.msn.com
Reviews and listings for entertainment, restaurants, shopping, and attractions. There are two types of Sidewalk sites—those with local city staffs and those that rely heavily on content from Sidewalk's national edition. At press time, South Florida Sidewalk had begun to add more local content and was hiring local staffers. Sidewalk also includes Yellow Pages for local businesses and features on what to do around town, such as HispanicFest. Like CitySearch, Sidewalk is geared for locals but is an excellent guide for travelers who want to do more than lie on a beach.

Sun-Sentinel: Showtime. www.sun-sentinel.com/showtime
A nice roundup of music, theater, sports, and dining choices for South Florida with coverage of local festivals and events. For hard news and weather, see **www.sun-sentinel.com**.

✪ Time Out: Miami. www.timeout.com/miami
This site features reviews and listings for attractions, entertainment, restaurants, hotels, and shopping throughout the city. It also includes categories for kids and gay/lesbian. Time Out is a lively guide with a youthful approach but has features for everyone, such as festival previews. Unlike some other city guides, Time Out Miami makes a concerted effort to cater to tourists as well as locals. The listings appear uninfluenced by ads, because no ads are visible. Plus, the site's clean design makes it a pleasure to navigate.

Tropicool Miami (Miami Convention & Visitors Bureau). www.miamiandbeaches.com
A nice site to get an overview of Miami and its beckoning beaches. Sure the content is boosterish, but it's still informative.

TOP MIAMI-AREA ATTRACTIONS

Fairchild Tropical Garden. www.ftg.org
Visitor information, events, and history for this lush botanical garden of rare tropical plants, flowering trees, and vines.

Historical Museum of Southern Florida. www.historical-museum.org
Tracing human history in South Florida back 10,000 years, the Historical Museum site lets you preview exhibitions online. Perhaps most interesting are the Historic Tours—by foot, bus, boat, metrorail, and bicycle. A schedule is available at the site.

Jungle Queen. www.junglequeen.com
Schedule, fares, and online reservations for this riverboat that cruises between Miami and Fort Lauderdale.

Miami Dolphins (Pro football). www.miamidolphins.com/home.html
Tickets, schedules, and news for the NFL team that spawned legends such as Bob Griese, Larry Csonka, and coach Don Shula.

Miami Film Festival. www.miamifilmfestival.com
If you'll be in Miami during the latter half of February, the film festival could be just the thing to wake up your mind. The site offers information about the films, events, and show times.

Miami Museum of Science. www.miamisci.org
Visitor information, exhibit previews, and a look inside the museum's Space Transit Planetarium, where you can lean back and search the night sky during the brightest Miami day.

Miami Seaquarium. miamiseaquarium.com
Featuring dolphins, whales, manatees, and alligators, Seaquarium is fascinating for the entire family. The site includes general park information (admission prices, hours, and so on), and a virtual tour of the attractions.

Parrot Jungle. www.parrotjungle.com
Homo sapiens isn't the only species that goes to Florida to retire—some colorful parrots and macaws spend their golden years at this south Miami park. The site includes park information, a $2 coupon, and audio samples of a park tour. *Note:* RealAudio software is required to hear this audio sample—the software is available free from **www.real.com**.

Venetian Pool. www.venetianpool.com
From its humble beginnings as a rock quarry, the 820,000-gallon Venetian Pool today features two waterfalls, coral caves, and grottoes. The site includes a tour, maps, photos, history, programs, and other visitor information.

TOP WEB SITES FOR WALT DISNEY WORLD & GREATER ORLANDO

ONLINE GUIDES, NEWSPAPERS & ENTERTAINMENT SITES

✪ Go2Orlando. **www.go2orlando.com**
Detailed practical information on attractions, dining, lodging, shopping, beaches, and recreation. Produced in conjunction with the *Orlando Sentinel,* Go2Orlando is a clean, well-organized place to browse. Planning tools include restaurant and hotel searches by area and price. The shopping guide lists malls, specialty shops, factory outlets, antique shops, and flea markets. The Beach Guide includes maps and tips for enjoying the coast, as well as safety information, fishing advice, and lodging options

in Daytona and Cocoa Beach. Clicking on Recreation leads to golfing, cruises, fishing, and even auto-racing schools. And there's extensive transportation information to help you get around if you don't rent a car.

For AOL Members: Digital City Orlando. Keyword: Orlando
Entertainment, dining, sports, and weather, produced in cooperation with the *Orlando Sentinel.* This site includes a lively forum, where you can read comments from others or post a question of your own. Digital City is also available on the Web at orlando.digitalcity.com.

InsideCentralFlorida. www.insidecentralflorida.com
This is clearly a site for locals, but it's also useful for visitors who want to check the weather, see what's on TV, or know where to find the best key lime pie. Click on Things to Do for upcoming music festivals, outdoor activities, and the latest additions to the big theme parks.

Orlando.com Vacation Guide. www.orlando.com/vacation
A well-organized roundup of attractions, events, and tips for planning your Orlando vacation. You'll also find dining, shopping, and lodging guides and can book a room through the site. Other sections cover nightlife, kids' activities, and outdoor recreation.

Orlando Sentinel. www.orlandosentinel.com
Everything you'd expect from a big-city newspaper—the online calendar, which includes listings for the arts, dining, attractions, and sports, is especially useful for visitors.

OrlandoTravel.com. www.orlandotravel.com
Theme park, lodging, and attractions information. Perhaps the biggest draw at the site is that you can sign up—online—for two free tickets to Disney World, Sea World, or Universal Studios if you're willing to sit through a 90-minute presentation on a con-dominium resort.

Orlando Weekly. www.orlandoweekly.com
Cutting-edge reviews and recommendations for arts, movies, music, and much more from Orlando's alternative weekly newspaper.

TOP ORLANDO-AREA ATTRACTIONS

SeaWorld. www.seaworld.com
Information on attractions, ticket prices, vacation packages, and special programs. At SeaWorld's site you can meet Shamu the killer whale and learn about attractions including Manatees: The Last Generation? and Journey to Atlantis. Click on Tickets for current prices, multiday passes, and online ordering—some passes include admission to SeaWorld, Universal Studios, Busch Gardens, and Wet 'n' Wild water park. The Park Information link includes hours (which vary by month) and directions to SeaWorld.

✪ Universal Studios Florida. www.usf.com
Information on tickets, vacation packages, attractions, and what's shooting. This Web site is more than just a way to get the facts—it has up-to-date schedules on what's going on at the park, as well as minimovies that give you a taste of the rides and attrac-tions. (*Note:* You'll need QuickTime to see and hear the movies—if you don't have it you can download it free at **www.apple.com/quicktime**.) The Studio Guide includes links to general information, directions, a park map, family services, and much more.

✪ Walt Disney World—Official Site. disney.go.com/disneyworld
Disney World's site on the Web is a vast virtual wonderland designed to help you take care of real-world tasks necessary to make your Disney fantasy come true. In the left

column of the home page, you'll find tools for planning and booking your vacation, as well as links to advice about the theme parks, resorts, entertainment, and dining options. The rest of the home page includes features on what's new at Disney World, such as the latest Cirque du Soleil extravaganza or the newest addition to Disney's Animal Kingdom. And don't miss the calendar link near the bottom of the home page to get a month-by-month update of what's going on.

TOP WEB SITES FOR TAMPA & ST. PETERSBURG
ONLINE GUIDES, NEWSPAPERS & ENTERTAINMENT SITES

City of St. Petersburg. www.stpete.org
A city roundup of what's going on in St. Pete. Though it's intended primarily for locals, the site has a nice calendar of events that's ideal for visitors looking for activities. To go straight to the calendar, visit **www.stpete.org/events.htm**.

St. Petersburg Times. www.sptimes.com
News, sports, and weather for Tampa's neighbor. Click on the A-Z Index, which lists arts, entertainment, and local activities, such as a guide to baseball spring training.

Tampa Bay CitySearch. www.tampabay.citysearch.com
Reviews and listings for arts and entertainment, restaurants, shopping, and attractions. Click on the calendar for events recommended by the editors. The extensive shopping listings range from clothing to specialty stores and include updates on sales. Not quite as good as its larger CitySearch cousins (thus no star ranking), but still a fine guide to Tampa/St. Pete.

Tampa Bay Online: Dining. tampabayonline.net/dining
Honest reviews from the *Tampa Bay Tribune* and suggestions for budget dining, defined as restaurants where two people can eat for under $20. There's also a search box that helps you find restaurants near your hotel.

Tampa Bay Online: Entertainment. tampabayonline.net/getalife
Peruse critics' picks for music, movies, and the arts. Search music listings based on type of club or type of music.

Tampa Tribune. www.tampatrib.com
Get up-to-date on happenings around town—entertainment links are at the bottom of the page.

TOP ATTRACTIONS FOR TAMPA & ST. PETERSBURG

Adventure Island. www.adventureisland.com
Park and ticket information, and a tour of the attractions, such as Caribbean Corkscrew, at this 36-acre Tampa Bay Water Park.

Busch Gardens. www.buschgardens.com
Check online to learn about the latest additions or see images of the zoo animals. Check "Tickets/Vacations" to find out about admission passes valid at several Florida theme parks.

Florida Aquarium. www2.sptimes.com/Aquarium
Ticket information, images of the sea creatures, and a sound clip round out this site, which is hosted by the *St. Petersburg Times*.

Florida International Museum. www.floridamuseum.org
See what's going on at this St. Petersburg museum, which has hosted blockbuster exhibitions since it opened in 1995. At press time, the museum offered a $2-off coupon that you could print from the Web site.

Museum of Science and Industry. www.mosi.org
An online guide to the almost 500 interactive exhibits. You'll also find a guide to MOSI's educational programs, planetarium, and IMAX theater.

The Pier. www.stpete-pier.com
Home to more than a dozen shops and boutiques, The Pier is a nice place to catch roving street theater, Dixieland bands, and other live music performance. Clowns and face painters entertain kids on weekends—check here for a calendar of events.

Salvador Dali Museum. www.webcoast.com/Dali
This is a clunky, slow-loading site with unnecessary bells and whistles, but it does offer a sense of the 94 Dali oils and hundreds of watercolors, drawings, holograms, and other Dali originals at this St. Petersburg museum.

Tampa Bay Buccaneers (Pro football). www.nfl.com/buccaneers/
This official NFL site includes statistics, features, and the team's schedule.

Tampa Bay Devil Rays (Pro baseball team). www.devilray.com
One of the newest additions to Major League Baseball, the Devil Rays play their home games in St. Petersburg. The site includes a schedule, ticket information and ordering, and a seat plan for Tropicana Field.

Tampa Bay Lightning (Pro hockey team). www.tampabaylightning.com
Another recent addition to the Florida sporting scene, the Lightning's site includes schedules and arena and ticket information.

TOP WEB SITES FOR SOME OTHER FLORIDA REGIONS
For regions not covered below, refer to the statewide guides listed above.

CAPE CANAVERAL

✪ Kennedy Space Center. www.kennedyspacecenter.com
If you visit the Kennedy Center's Web site before your trip, you'll probably make a point to visit the Space Center during your trip to Florida. The site includes lots of images and descriptions about the myriad attractions here, including the Rocket Garden, Space Shuttle Plaza, and Astronaut Memorial. Click on General Information for admission fees, hours, and the IMAX film schedule.

THE EVERGLADES REGION

Biscayne National Park. www.nps.gov/bisc
Just a hop, skip, and jump across Biscayne Bay, this park is a terrific place for recreation and is home to mangrove shorelines, a shallow bay, undeveloped islands, and living coral reefs. The site includes basic information on activities, attractions, and nearby lodgings.

The Everglades and 10,000 Islands. www.florida-everglades.com
Sponsored by the Everglades Area Chamber of Commerce, this site offers maps, fishing tips, and dining advice. You'll also find event listings, a wildlife photo gallery, and a guide to southwest Florida. Not the cleanest site ever designed, but it does have some valuable information.

✪ Everglades National Park. www.nps.gov/ever
This fairly comprehensive guide from the National Park Service includes everything you'd expect: information on attractions, activities, lodging, camping, fishing, and climate for this remarkable park. You'll also find superb features on the Everglades at GORP—visit **www.gorp.com** and search for "Everglades."

KEY WEST

Discover: Key West. key-west.com
A well-rounded guide to Key West, including an events calendar and extensive listings for attractions, sightseeing and eco tours, theater, and art galleries. You'll also find a dining guide, lodging options, and sections on dining, fishing, and shopping.

Gay Key West Travel Guide. www.gaykeywestfl.com
A guide to gay-friendly lodgings, restaurants, and clubs.

Index

Page numbers in *italics* refer to maps.

Index

Index

Index

Index

FROMMER'S® COMPLETE TRAVEL GUIDES

Frommer's® Dollar-a-Day Guides

Australia from $50 a Day
California from $60 a Day
Caribbean from $70 a Day
England from $70 a Day
Europe from $60 a Day
Florida from $60 a Day

Hawaii from $70 a Day
Ireland from $50 a Day
Israel from $45 a Day
Italy from $70 a Day
London from $85 a Day
New York from $80 a Day

New Zealand from $50 a Day
Paris from $85 a Day
San Francisco from $60 a Day
Washington, D.C.,
  from $60 a Day

Frommer's® Portable Guides

Acapulco, Ixtapa &
  Zihuatanejo
Alaska Cruises & Ports of Call
Bahamas
Baja & Los Cabos
Berlin
California Wine Country
Charleston & Savannah
Chicago

Dublin
Hawaii: The Big Island
Las Vegas
London
Maine Coast
Maui
New Orleans
New York City
Paris

Puerto Vallarta, Manzanillo
  & Guadalajara
San Diego
San Francisco
Sydney
Tampa & St. Petersburg
Venice
Washington, D.C.

Frommer's® National Park Guides

Family Vacations in the
  National Parks
Grand Canyon

National Parks of the
  American West
Rocky Mountain

Yellowstone & Grand Teton
Yosemite & Sequoia/
  Kings Canyon
Zion & Bryce Canyon

Frommer's® Great Outdoor Guides

New England
Northern California

Southern California & Baja
Washington & Oregon

Frommer's® Memorable Walks

Chicago
London

New York
Paris

San Francisco
Washington D.C.

Frommer's® Irreverent Guides

Amsterdam
Boston
Chicago
Las Vegas

London
Los Angeles
Manhattan

New Orleans
Paris
San Francisco

Seattle & Portland
Vancouver
Walt Disney World
Washington, D.C.

Frommer's® Best-Loved Driving Tours

America
Britain
California

Florida
France
Germany

Ireland
Italy
New England

Scotland
Spain
Western Europe

The Complete Idiot's Travel Guides

Boston
Chicago
Cruise Vacations
Planning Your Trip to Europe
Florida
Hawaii

Ireland
Las Vegas
London
Mexico's Beach Resorts
New Orleans
New York City

Paris
San Francisco
Spain
Walt Disney World
Washington, D.C.

THE UNOFFICIAL GUIDES®

Bed & Breakfast in New England
Bed & Breakfast in the Northwest
Beyond Disney
Branson, Missouri
California with Kids
Chicago

Cruises
Florida with Kids
The Great Smoky & Blue Ridge Mountains
Inside Disney
Las Vegas

London
Miami & the Keys
Mini Las Vegas
Mini-Mickey
New Orleans
New York City
Paris

San Francisco
Skiing in the West
Walt Disney World
Walt Disney World for Grown-ups
Walt Disney World for Kids
Washington, D.C.

SPECIAL-INTEREST TITLES

Born to Shop: France
Born to Shop: Hong Kong
Born to Shop: Italy
Born to Shop: New York
Born to Shop: Paris
Frommer's Britain's Best Bike Rides
The Civil War Trust's Official Guide to the Civil War Discovery Trail
Frommer's Caribbean Hideaways
Frommer's Europe's Greatest Driving Tours
Frommer's Food Lover's Companion to France
Frommer's Food Lover's Companion to Italy
Frommer's Gay & Lesbian Europe
Israel Past & Present
Monks' Guide to California

Monks' Guide to New York City
The Moon
New York City with Kids
Unforgettable Weekends
Outside Magazine's Guide to Family Vacations
Places Rated Almanac
Retirement Places Rated
Road Atlas Britain
Road Atlas Europe
Washington, D.C., with Kids
Wonderful Weekends from Boston
Wonderful Weekends from New York City
Wonderful Weekends from San Francisco
Wonderful Weekends from Los Angeles

WHEVER YOU TRAVEL, HELP IS NEVER FAR AWAY.

From planning your trip to providing travel assistance along the way, American Express® Travel Service Offices are always there to help you do more.

Florida

CORAL GABLES
American Express Travel Service
32 Miracle Mile
305/446-3381

FT. LAUDERDALE
American Express Travel Service
3312-14 N.E. 32nd St.
954/565-9481

JACKSONVILLE
American Express Travel Service
9908 Baymeadows Rd.
904/642-1701

MIAMI
American Express Travel Service
330 Biscayne Blvd.
305/358-7350

MIAMI BEACH
Zmax Travel & Tours
420 Lincoln Rd. Suite 239
305/532-0111

ORLANDO
American Express Travel Service
2 West Church St.
Sun Trust Bldg
407/843-0004

TALLAHASSEE
The Travel Center (R)
703 North Monroe St.
850/224-6464

TAMPA
American Express Travel Service
One Tampa City Center
813/273-0310

Travel

www.americanexpress.com/travel

American Express Travel Service Offices
are located throughout the United States.
For the office nearest you, call 1-800-AXP-3429.

Listings are valid as of August 1999. (R) = Representative Office.
Not all services available at all locations. © 1999 American Express.

METRIC CONVERSIONS FOR FOREIGN VISITORS

Liquid Volume

To convert	multiply by
U.S. gallons to liters	3.8
Liters to U.S. gallons	.26
U.S. gallons to imperial gallons	.83
Imperial gallons to U.S. gallons	1.20
Imperial gallons to liters	4.55
Liters to imperial gallons	.22
1 liter = .26 gal	1 gal = 3.8 liter

Distance

To convert	multiply by	
inches to centimeters	2.54	
centimeters to inches	.39	
feet to meters	.30	
meters to feet	3.28	
yards to meters	.91	
meters to yards	1.09	
miles to kilometers	1.61	
kilometers to miles	.62	
1 mi = 1.6 km	1 km = .62 mi	
1 ft = .30 m	1 m = 3.3 ft	

Weight

To convert	multiply by	
Ounces to grams	28.35	
Grams to ounces	.35	
Pounds to kilograms	.45	
Kilograms to pounds	2.20	
1 ounce = 28 gr	1gr = .04 ounce	
1 lb = .4555 kg	1 kg = 2.2 lb	

Temperature

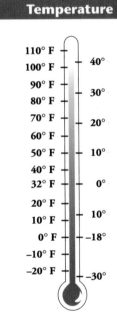

110° F	
100° F	40°
90° F	
80° F	30°
70° F	20°
60° F	
50° F	10°
40° F	
32° F	0°
20° F	
10° F	10°
0° F	−18°
−10° F	
−20° F	−30°

To convert F to C, subtract 32 and multiply by 5/9 (.555)

To convert C to F, multiply by 1.8 and add 32

32° F = 0° C

U.S. $18.95/CAN $28.95

Life is short. Vacations are shorter. Relax! Trust your trip to Frommer's.

Choose the *Only* Guide That Gives You:

♦ **Exact prices**, so you can plan the perfect trip no matter what your budget.

♦ The latest, most **reliable information** —completely updated every year!

♦ Dozens of easy-to-read **color maps**.

♦ The widest and best selection of hotels and restaurants in every price range, with **candid, in-depth reviews**.

♦ **All the pract___ ___ details** you need to make the most of your time and m___

♦ **One-of-a-k___** ___ gems, plus a new take on all ___

♦ **Outspoke___** ___time and what's not.

♦ **A fresh, ___** ___ fun and excitement back into travel!

It's a Whole New World with Frommer's.

A FROMMER BOOK   MACMILLAN ♦ USA

Cover design by Michael J. Freeland.   Front cover photo © M. Timothy O'Keefe.
Back cover photo © 1999 Universal Studios.

 Find us online at www.frommers.com

ISBN 0-02-863470-5

ISBN 0-02-863470-5

51895

9 780028 634708

0 21898 63470 2